Collins | COBUILD

PHRASAL
VERBS
DICTIONARY

T0312512

HarperCollins Publishers
Westerhill Road
Bishopbriggs
Glasgow
G64 2QT

HarperCollins Publishers
Macken House,
39/40 Mayor Street Upper,
Dublin 1, D01 C9W8, Ireland

Fourth Edition 2020

10 9 8 7 6

© HarperCollins Publishers 1989,
2002, 2011, 2012, 2020

ISBN 978-0-00-837546-1

Collins® and COBUILD® are registered
trademarks of HarperCollins Publishers
Limited

www.collinsdictionary.com
www.collins.co.uk/elt

A catalogue record for this book is
available from the British Library

Typeset by Davidson Publishing
Solutions, Glasgow

Printed and bound in the UK using
100% Renewable Electricity at
CPI Group (UK) Ltd

Acknowledgements
We would like to thank those authors
and publishers who kindly gave
permission for copyright material to be
used in the Collins Corpus. We would
also like to thank Times Newspapers
Ltd for providing valuable data.

All rights reserved. No part of this book
may be reproduced, stored in a retrieval
system, or transmitted in any form or
by any means, electronic, mechanical,
photocopying, recording or otherwise,
without the prior permission in writing
of the Publisher. This book is sold
subject to the conditions that it shall
not, by way of trade or otherwise, be
lent, re-sold, hired out or otherwise
circulated without the Publisher's prior
consent in any form of binding or cover
other than that in which it is published
and without a similar condition including
this condition being imposed on the
subsequent purchaser.

Entered words that we have reason
to believe constitute trademarks have
been designated as such. However,
neither the presence nor absence of
such designation should be regarded
as affecting the legal status of any
trademark.

HarperCollins does not warrant
that www.collinsdictionary.com,
www.collins.co.uk/elt or any other
website mentioned in this title will
be provided uninterrupted, that any
website will be error free, that defects
will be corrected, or that the website or
the server that makes it available are
free of viruses or bugs. For full terms
and conditions please refer to the site
terms provided on the website.

MIX
Paper | Supporting
responsible forestry
FSC™ C007454

This book is produced from independently certified FSC™
paper to ensure responsible forest management.
For more information visit: www.harpercollins.co.uk/green

Contents

Fourth Edition

Senior Editor
Penny Hands

Corpus Research
Julie Moore

For the Publishers
Maree Airlie
Lisa Todd
Sarah Woods

Third Edition

Managing Editor
Penny Hands

Senior Editors
Elizabeth Walter
Kate Woodford

Contributors
Rosalind Combley
Lucy Hollingworth

For the Publishers
Lucy Cooper
Kerry Ferguson
Elaine Higgleton
Mary O'Neill
Lisa Sutherland

Computing Support
Thomas Callan

Founding Editor-in-Chief
John Sinclair

We would like to thank the following people for their contributions
to previous editions of the text:

Maree Airlie, Henri Béjoint, Joanne Brown, Ela Bullon, Stephen Bullon,
Annette Capel, Ken Church, Michela Clari, Jeremy Clear, Alex Collier,
Sheila Dignen, Professor Malcolm Goodale, Bob Grossmith,
Patrick Hanks, Lorna Heaslip, Lorna Knight, Ramesh Krishnamurthy,
Tim Lane, Helen Liebeck, Alison Macaulay, Carol McCann, Duncan Marshall, Rosamund
Moon, Elaine Pollard, Elizabeth Potter, Maggie Seaton, Katy Shaw, Sue Smith, Mark Taylor,
Janet Whitcut, Douglas Williamson, Deborah Yuill

Introduction

The **Collins COBUILD Phrasal Verbs Dictionary** was created after much research among teachers and students of English. The information in this book has been presented in what we feel is the most helpful way – the layout of the entries is attractive and easy to follow; they convey grammatical and other information through carefully compiled explanations and examples that are easy to understand, with extra information separated into notes and boxes. The **Collins COBUILD Phrasal Verbs Dictionary** also offers useful supplementary information which helps with the meanings of particles and provides single-word equivalents for many phrasal verbs. New for this edition is a supplement that lists some of the latest phrasal verbs, arranged by common themes, such as business and social media. So, by means of clearly structured entries and thousands of concise examples of use, and without resorting to jargon, the dictionary gives learners confidence in one of the trickier aspects of the grammar and vocabulary of English: phrasal verbs.

What is a phrasal verb?

Phrasal verbs (sometimes known as 'multi-word verbs') are combinations of verbs with adverbial or prepositional particles. They are extremely common in English, and are often a particular problem for learners of English. One reason for this is that in many cases, even though students may be familiar with both the verb in the phrasal verb and the particle, they may not understand the meaning of the combination, since it can be very different from the meanings of the two words used independently. For example, *give, put, up,* and *off* are all very common words which students will encounter in their first weeks of learning English, and yet the combinations *give up* and *put off* are not transparent. The meanings are unrelated to the meanings of the individual words in the combinations. The fact that phrasal verbs often have a number of different meanings adds to their complexity.

Phrasal verbs in use

There are some particular grammatical problems associated with phrasal verbs. For example, some phrasal verbs can be only transitive (*ask after someone*), some can be only intransitive (*act up*), others can be both. In some phrasal verbs, the verb and the particle can be separated by an object (*back (something) up*), in others, they cannot be separated. The clear structure, explanations and examples in this dictionary make all these patterns apparent without showing a lot of distracting grammatical data.

There are other difficulties, such as the fact that there are frequently strong collocational associations between phrasal verbs and other words. In some cases a particular word or small set of words is the only one normally found as the subject or object of a particular verb. The explanations in the dictionary also give guidance on this, and feature boxes at many entries list the most common collocations of the phrasal verb, helping the learner to use phrasal verbs in a fluent and natural-sounding way.

It is often said that phrasal verbs tend to be rather 'informal' and more appropriate to spoken English than written, which is not generally true, but may be the case in more formal contexts such as business or academic English. Single-word equivalents are included in the text to highlight the kind of vocabulary that should be used in such contexts, and where these words are particularly formal, an additional note appears. On the other hand, single-word synonyms can seem out of place in many contexts. To help with this, we include synonyms and antonyms of phrasal verbs that are in themselves phrasal verbs, again with additional notes on those that offer more formal or informal alternatives. To make phrasal verbs even easier to find, and the distinction between phrasal verbs and single-word verbs even more clear, this edition contains an index of 200 single-word verbs and their phrasal-verb equivalents. Each single-word verb and phrasal verb is illustrated with an example that shows it in a typical context, which may be formal, informal or academic.

The set of English phrasal verbs is constantly growing and changing. New combinations appear and spread. The particular, fixed meanings of particles in phrasal verbs are used to create these new combinations. At the back of this dictionary there is an index focusing on the most productive and useful of these particles, showing the different meanings and listing the phrasal verbs containing those meanings. In this index, you can see clearly the relationship in meaning between, for example, *cool off*, *ease off*, and *wear off*, or between *hook up*, *join up*, and *link up*.

The examples in this edition are all up to date, authentic, and drawn from the Collins Corpus. Minor changes have been made to some examples to make them as simple as possible without affecting their authenticity or their meaning, so every example will give a clear understanding of the meaning and usage of each phrasal verb.

The scope of the dictionary

This edition of the **Collins COBUILD Phrasal Verbs Dictionary** lists over four thousand combinations of verbs with adverbs or prepositions, which includes numerous phrasal verbs and senses of phrasal verbs that are new to this dictionary. Furthermore, the key phrasal verbs in the dictionary are highlighted using the symbol ✪. We have based this information on the Collins Corpus, our vast database of 4.5 billion words of contemporary language.

Global internet communications mean that the boundaries between British and American English continue to blur. Many phrasal verbs still retain their British or American English labels, but we have removed others for this edition. When we have added new phrasal verbs, we have often not labelled them as they are frequent in both varieties.

What sort of item can you expect to find in this dictionary?

Different people have different definitions of 'phrasal verb', and different ideas about which particles can be used to form phrasal verbs. The following list contains all the particles which we use in this dictionary:

aback	among	before	for	on	to
about	apart	behind	forth	onto	together
above	around	below	forward	out	towards
across	as	beneath	from	over	under
after	aside	between	in	overboard	up
against	at	beyond	into	past	upon
ahead	away	by	of	round	with
along	back	down	off	through	without

In addition, there are cases of combinations with two particles, such as *talk out of* and *fall in with*.

There are four main types of combination in the dictionary:

1 combinations where the meaning of the whole cannot be understood by knowing the meanings of the individual verbs and particles. Examples are *go off* (= explode), *put off* (= postpone), and *turn down* (= reject).

2 combinations where the verb is always used with a particular preposition or adverb, and is not normally found without it. Examples are *refer to* and *rely on*. We also include similar cases where a verb is always used with a particular preposition or adverb in a particular meaning, such as *lead to* and *want for*.

3 combinations where the particle does not change the meaning of the verb, but is used to suggest that the action described by the verb is performed thoroughly, completely, or continuously. For example, in *slave away* and *slog away*, the particle *away* adds an idea of continuousness to the idea of hard work.

4 combinations where the verb and particle both have meanings which may be found in other combinations and uses, but where there is overwhelming evidence that they occur together. For example, in the combination *fight back*, the verb *fight* has the same meaning that it normally does in isolation, and *back* is used in a similar way in other combinations such as *phone back* and *strike back*. Yet *fight* and *back* frequently occur together in our data, and we have decided to treat this as a unit in the dictionary.

We also include in this dictionary fixed expressions with verbs and particles, for example, *go for it* and *keep up appearances*.

Exercises and downloadable worksheets

Teachers told us how important it is that a learner consolidates his or her knowledge of language through practice and use. With this in mind, in the centre of the dictionary there are 32 pages of self-study exercises that will help the learner really understand phrasal verbs and how to use them. Teachers will also want to download the ten activity worksheets to accompany the book that are available on the Collins Language website, ready to be printed off and taken straight to lessons. These cover topics such as 'computers' and 'transitive and intransitive', and reinforce students' knowledge of phrasal verbs through enjoyable exercises and crosswords. Go to **www.collins.co.uk/cobuild-resources**.

Finally...

The research we have carried out among teachers and students of English has proved invaluable, and we have benefited greatly from it in this dictionary. This new edition of the **Collins COBUILD Phrasal Verbs Dictionary** is now even more interesting and informative than ever before.

How to find a phrasal verb in the dictionary

Each of the phrasal verbs in the main dictionary text is listed below a bold single-verb headword, which is the verb in the phrasal verb. These verb headwords are arranged alphabetically. Thus, phrasal verbs containing the verb *go* are explained before phrasal verbs containing other verbs beginning with the letters *go–*, such as *goad* and *gouge*.

Phrasal-verb headwords appear in bold below the verb headword, making them easy to pick out. Phrasal verbs which contain the same verb but different particles are arranged in alphabetical order of the particle, for example **act out** is followed by **act up**.

Some phrasal verb combinations contain two particles. In the dictionary, combinations like this, where the second particle is compulsory, are listed as phrasal-verb headwords in their correct alphabetical place in the sequence, for example **get out**, **get out of**, **get over**, etc.

Other phrasal verbs are typically, but not always, used with a second particle. In these cases, the second particle does not appear in the phrasal-verb headword, but is shown in an example with the optional particle noted at the beginning of the example (for example [+ *with*]).

Onto is a special problem as it can be spelled both as one word and as two. We show both spellings as separate phrasal-verb headwords if each one is a phrasal verb in its own right, for example **come on to**, **come onto**. In other cases where *–to* is optional, it is given as a variation after the phrasal-verb headword. Phrasal verbs with *into* are treated separately from ones with *in*, even though there may be little difference in meaning.

Many phrasal verbs have more than one meaning. The different meanings are numbered and are usually arranged in order of frequency, so that the commonest ones come first.

Guide to the dictionary entries

Headwords are organized in alphabetical order. Phrasal verbs are listed under a headword

Typical patterns of the phrasal verb

→ **bring** /brɪŋ/ (**brings, bringing, brought**)

○ **bring 'down** ◄

1 If people or events **bring down** a government or ruler, they cause them to lose their power. = **topple** ◄

bring down someone/something
❏ *Unofficial strikes had brought down the regime.*

→ **bring someone/something down** ❏ *A national strike would bring the government down.*

2 To **bring down** the level of something means to reduce it.

bring down something or **bring something down** ❏ *The promised measures included steps to bring down prices.* ❏ *They want to bring population growth down further.* ◄

> **BRING DOWN + noun**
>
> bring down **inflation**
> bring down **the cost of** something
> bring down **the level of** something
> ❏ *Control of the money supply was necessary to bring down inflation.* ❏ *These new measures will bring down the level of violence in the area.*

Phrasal verb, with stress marks shown. A **star** highlights the most common phrasal verbs

Synonyms of the phrasal verb

Examples from the Collins Corpus show you how the phrasal verb is really used

Collocations boxes show the most common collocations

cast /kɑːst, kæst/ (**casts, casting**)

Information in boxes tells you more about the main verb

> The form **cast** is used in the present tense and is the past tense and past participle of the verb.

○ **cast 'down**

1 If someone **is cast down**, they lose their social status. ≠ **raise** [FORMAL]
be cast down ❏ *Men of high status were cast down.*

2 If someone **is cast down** by something, they are sad or worried because of it.
be cast down ❏ *She seemed cast down by the problems at work.* ● If you are **downcast** you are feeling sad and without hope.
= **depressed** ❏ *Cameron seemed unusually downcast and nervous.* ❏ *I looked anxiously at his downcast face.*

3 If you **cast** your eyes **down**, you look downwards. [FORMAL] ◄
cast something down ❏ *For a moment, Tiffany cast her eyes down to avoid my glance.*
NOTE **Lower** is a less formal word for **cast down**.

Antonyms of the phrasal verb

The **definition** tells you what the phrasal verb means and how to use it

Nouns or **adjectives** derived from the phrasal verb

Labels tell you more about the context in which the phrasal verb is used

Notes give more detail about equivalent verbs and phrasal verbs

About the dictionary entries

Verb forms

All the forms or inflections of a verb are given in bold letters and in brackets after the single-verb headword. They are listed in the order: third person form of the present tense (-*s* form), present participle (-*ing* form), past tense (-*ed* form), and past participle (-*n* form) if this is different from the past tense form. If there are alternative spellings for a form, both spellings are given.

climb /klaɪm/ (**climbs, climbing, climbed**)

leap /liːp/ (**leaps, leaping, leaped/leapt**)

Spelling

If a verb has two spellings, for example if it is spelled differently in British English and American English, this information appears in a box after the forms.

> **Plough** is also spelled **plow** in American English.

Pronunciation and stress

The pronunciation of every verb is shown in full after the headword. Variations in pronunciation are also shown where relevant.

duke /djuːk, AM duːk/

The stress pattern for each phrasal-verb headword is indicated by a stress mark, to show where the stress falls. A note is given in a box to point out any variations.

○ **roll 'in**

> In meaning 2, the stress is on **'roll**.

Definitions

The definitions of phrasal verbs in the **Collins COBUILD Phrasal Verbs Dictionary** are written in simple English. They do not just tell you about the meaning of the phrasal verb, but also show you how it is typically used.

For example, the definition will tell you if a phrasal verb is transitive (that is, it is used with an object) or intransitive (it is not used with an object). If it is transitive, the definition will tell you what kind of thing is usually mentioned as the object of the verb. For example:

> If you **pad out** a piece of writing or a speech with unnecessary words or pieces of information, you include them in order to make it longer.

This tells you that the phrasal verb is transitive, and that the object is usually a word which is similar in meaning to a piece of writing or speech. It also tells you that you typically use the phrasal verb with another particle, *with*.

If a phrasal verb can be used both transitively and intransitively, both possible structures are shown:

> **1** If you **sweep** something **up** or **sweep up**, you collect something such as dirt with a brush in order to get rid of it.

The definitions also tell you what sort of sentence structure a phrasal verb is used in. For example, the definition for the first meaning of **keep on** tells you that you often use the phrasal verb with the *-ing* form of a verb:

> **1** If you **keep on**, or **keep on** doing something, you continue doing something and do not stop.

The definition for the first meaning of **dream of** tells you that the phrasal verb is used in a negative construction:

> **1** If you say you **would not dream of** doing something, you mean that you would definitely not do it because it is wrong or stupid.

The definition for the third meaning of **sweep up** tells you that this sense of the phrasal verb is used in a passive construction:

> **3** If you **are swept up** in something, you become very involved in it, often without meaning to.

Typical patterns

The typical syntactical patterns of phrasal verbs are made more explicit in bold structures shown after the definition. These show you, for example, if a phrasal verb is transitive, and if the object is a person (*someone*) or a thing (*something*):

> **prey on something** ❑ *Short-eared owls prey on voles and small birds.*

If no bold structures are shown, it can be assumed that the phrasal verb is only used intransitively, that is, it does not take an object.

These bold structures also make it clear if a phrasal verb is 'separable', that is, an object can be, or should be, placed between the verb and the following particle. All possible structures are shown:

> **parcel something up** *or* **parcel up something**

This shows you that you can place the object either before or after the particle.

Along with the definition, these structures are used to demonstrate various grammatical features of phrasal verbs, for example:

That the phrasal verb is used with the present participle, or –*ing* form, of a verb:

> **end up doing something** ❑ *We ended up taking a taxi there.* ❑ *We always end up arguing.*

That the phrasal verb is used with a reflexive pronoun (*myself, yourself, himself, herself, itself, oneself, ourselves, yourselves,* or *themselves*):

> **throw yourself into something** ❑ *To take her mind off her troubles, she threw herself into her work.* ❑ *Everyone threw themselves energetically into clearing up.*

Fixed expressions with phrasal verbs

We include in this dictionary fixed expressions with phrasal verbs, for example, *go for it* and *keep up appearances*.

If a fixed expression is closely linked with one of the meanings given of the phrasal verb, it appears below it, and is introduced by the symbol ● :

> ◼ If you **call in**, you telephone the place where you work, usually to say that you are not able to go there. ❑ *He called in this morning to say he was ill.*
> ● If you **call in sick**, you telephone the place where you work to say that you are ill and cannot come to work. ❑ *She called in sick this morning.*

If there is not such a clear link to a meaning of the phrasal verb, it appears in a paragraph on its own:

> ◼ If something **comes in handy** or **comes in useful**, it is a helpful thing to have in a particular situation. ❑ *Savings may come in useful for holidays.* ❑ *A toothbrush would come in handy.*

Examples

The typical syntactical structures of each phrasal verb are further displayed in carefully chosen examples from the Collins Corpus. The examples show how speakers and writers of English actually use phrasal verbs.

If an example demonstrates a preposition that typically follows a phrasal verb, or the use of the infinitive verb form after a phrasal verb, this is noted in square brackets immediately before the example:

> **put something aside** ❑ [+ *to*-infinitive]
> *Many parents put money aside to help pay for their child's education.* ❑ [+ *for*] *I've been putting money aside for a car.*

Style and usage

Phrasal verbs are generally more common in spoken or informal English than in written or formal English. When phrasal verbs are only found in very informal contexts, we state this in the definition. Similarly, we tell you when a particular phrasal verb is found mainly in either British English or American English, or when it is used only in certain contexts, such as journalism or formal language. This information is shown in small capital letters and in square brackets. When it applies to all the meanings of a phrasal verb, it is shown after the phrasal-verb headword; if it applies to a single meaning, it is shown at the end of the definition. The labels we use are listed below.

AMERICAN	used mainly in the US
AUSTRALIAN	used mainly in Australia
BRITISH	used mainly in Britain
FORMAL	used mainly in official situations
INFORMAL	used mainly in informal situations, conversations, and personal letters
JOURNALISM	used mainly in newspapers, television, and radio
LITERARY	used mainly in novels, poetry, and other literature
OFFENSIVE	likely to offend people
OLD-FASHIONED	no longer in general common use
RUDE	used mainly to describe words which some people consider taboo
SPOKEN	used mainly in speech
TECHNICAL	used mainly about a specialist subject, such as business or science
VERY RUDE	used mainly to describe words which some people consider taboo

Synonyms and antonyms

Synonyms are words which mean almost the same as each other, and antonyms are words which mean the opposite. In this dictionary, we provide synonyms and antonyms for many phrasal verbs. Synonyms are introduced by the symbol **=** :

> **2** If something such as a building or bridge
> **falls down**, it breaks into pieces because it
> is old, weak, or damaged. **= collapse**

Antonyms are introduced by the symbol **≠** :

> **5** When schools or schoolchildren **go back**,
> they start a new term after the holidays.
> **≠ break up**

Where synonyms and antonyms require a little more explanation, for example if they are particularly formal or informal or a have a restricted geographical usage, they are presented in longer notes introduced by the symbol NOTE :

3 If you **fix up** something, you build it
quickly and roughly because you need it
immediately.
fix up something or **fix something up** ❑ *We
tried to fix up a shelter from the wind.* ❑ *I've fixed
up a sort of wire barrier.*
NOTE **Rig up** is a more informal expression
for **fix up**.

There are very few cases where two words or expressions mean exactly the same as each
other, but you should be able to substitute the synonyms which we give in most contexts,
without greatly changing the meaning. We often give another phrasal verb as a synonym,
and in most cases you can look up the other phrasal verb to find out about any differences
between them: there may be differences in grammar as well as slight differences in meaning.
Many phrasal verbs have synonyms which are single words, but these words are often more
formal. The antonyms which we give are usually other phrasal verbs, and in most cases these
pairs of antonyms describe opposite processes, such as *put on* and *take off*, or *come in* and *go out*.

Derived words

It is quite common in English for nouns and adjectives to be formed by combining verbs and
particles, and these are often very closely related to phrasal verbs. For example, if someone
makes a *getaway*, they *get away* from a place in a hurry, perhaps after committing a crime.
Sometimes the order of verb and particle is reversed: an *off-putting* person is someone who
puts you *off* or causes you to dislike them. Sometimes both orders are found: *break-out* and
outbreak are both linked to the phrasal verb **break out**. In the **Collins COBUILD Phrasal
Verbs Dictionary**, we give such nouns and adjectives in the entries, so that *getaway* is
explained in the entry for **get away**.

If they are closely linked with a meaning of the phrasal verb, derived words appear in
the same paragraph, after the examples and any synonym notes, and are introduced by
the symbol ● :

bank up something or **bank something up**
❑ *The storm had banked up the snow against the
front door.* ● Something solid which is
banked-up exists in a pile. ❑ *Nobody could
get through the banked-up snow.*

If there is not such a clear link to a meaning of the phrasal verb, they appear in a paragraph
on their own with a sense number:

2 If you describe someone as a **pushover**,
you mean that they are very easy to
persuade or influence.

Cross-references

Cross-references are given when a phrasal verb can be found at another place in the
dictionary. These are clearly indicated by an arrow, for example at **look upon**:

○ **'look upon** → see **look on**

Sometimes, verbs can be used with different particles, but the phrasal verb combinations may mean exactly the same as each other. For example, you can often substitute *about* or *around* for *round* without changing the meaning at all, although there is a difference between British and American usage in this case. In such cases, we treat the identical meanings together at the one form, and put a cross-reference at the other ones.

Collocations boxes

Often, phrasal verbs collocate strongly with a particular group of words. To make this information explicit, we have included feature boxes at many entries which list the most common collocations of the phrasal verb. These will help the learner to use the phrasal verbs in a fluent and natural-sounding way.

> **CALL OFF + noun**
> call off **a search**
> call off **a strike**
> call off **a protest**
> call off **a visit**
> call off **a meeting**
> call off **a wedding**
> ❑ *Union leaders have agreed to call off the strike.* ❑ *He has called off his visit to Texas.*

New phrasal verbs

We see new phrasal verbs in all sorts of areas, but especially in the worlds of technology, business, media and social media. They are formed in various ways: for example, people might use a new particle with an existing verb, or they might combine a noun with a particle to create a new phrasal verb. This section categorizes by topic some of the new phrasal verbs we have included in the **Collins COBUILD Phrasal Verbs Dictionary** and tells you about the trends and patterns we have found by analysing the Collins Corpus.

The particles index

At the end of the **Collins COBUILD Phrasal Verbs Dictionary** is an index of the most useful particles which occur in phrasal verbs. This index explains the common meanings that particles contribute to phrasal verb combinations, and lists the phrasal verbs in which those meanings appear. New phrasal verbs are continually being created, and you may hear or read a combination which is not in the dictionary. By using the index, you should be able to understand the meaning of many such new combinations.

Single-word equivalents

Also at the end of this dictionary is a section called **Single-word equivalents**, which is an index of 200 single-word verbs and their phrasal-verb equivalents. If you want to find a phrasal-verb equivalent to a single-word verb, then this index will help you. Each single-word verb and phrasal verb is illustrated with an example that shows it in a typical context, making the distinctions between the two forms even more clear.

PHRASAL VERBS
A–Z

Aa

abandon /əˈbændən/ (**abandons, abandoning, abandoned**)
○ **aˈbandon to**
If you **abandon** yourself **to** an emotion, you feel it so strongly that you cannot think about anything else.
abandon yourself to something ❑ *We are scared to abandon ourselves to our feelings in case we seem weak or out of control.*

abide /əˈbaɪd/ (**abides, abiding, abided**)
○ **aˈbide by** [FORMAL]
If you **abide by** a law, an agreement, or a decision, you accept it and do what it says.
= observe, respect; ≠ flout
abide by something ❑ *Germany and Russia agreed to abide by the agreement.* ❑ *Both parties must agree to abide by the court's decision.*

abound /əˈbaʊnd/ (**abounds, abounding, abounded**)
○ **aˈbound with** [FORMAL]
If a place or situation **abounds with** things or people, large numbers of them exist there.
abound with something/someone
❑ *Here the rivers and lakes abound with fish.*
❑ *The London jazz scene always used to abound with world-class players.*

absorb /əbˈzɔːb/ (**absorbs, absorbing, absorbed**)
○ **abˈsorb into**
If one group or organization **is absorbed into** a larger group or organization, it becomes part of it.
be absorbed into something ❑ *Scotland was absorbed into the Union with England in 1707.*

abstain /æbˈsteɪn/ (**abstains, abstaining, abstained**)
○ **abˈstain from** [FORMAL]
If you **abstain from** something, usually something you want to have or do, you deliberately do not have or do it.
abstain from something ❑ *He must abstain from eating fat of any kind.* ❑ *She was advised to abstain from alcohol.*

accede /ækˈsiːd/ (**accedes, acceding, acceded**)
○ **acˈcede to** [FORMAL]
1 If you **accede to** a request, you allow it or agree to it.
accede to something ❑ *He was upset by my refusal to accede to his request.*
2 If you **accede to** someone's opinion, you agree with it, usually rather unwillingly.
accede to something ❑ *To accede to such a view would be dangerous.*

acclimatize /əˈklaɪmətaɪz/ (**acclimatizes, acclimatizing, acclimatized**)
○ **acˈclimatize to** [FORMAL]
When you **acclimatize to** a new situation, place, or climate, or **acclimatize** yourself **to** it, you become used to it.
acclimatize to something ❑ *The athletes are acclimatizing to the heat by staying in Monte Carlo.*
acclimatize yourself to something ❑ *He trained on an exercise bike in a sauna to acclimatize himself to the extreme humidity.*
be acclimatized to something ❑ *They are acclimatized to the high altitude.*

accommodate /əˈkɒmədeɪt/ (**accommodates, accommodating, accommodated**)
○ **acˈcommodate to** [FORMAL]
If you **accommodate to** something new or **accommodate** yourself **to** it, you change your behaviour or ideas so that you are able to deal with it.
accommodate to something ❑ *Some animal and plant species cannot accommodate to the rapidly changing conditions.*
accommodate yourself to something
❑ *She walked slowly to accommodate herself to his pace.*

account /əˈkaʊnt/ (**accounts, accounting, accounted**)
✪ **acˈcount for**
1 If you **account for** something that has happened or that you have done, you explain how it happened or why you did it.
account for something ❑ *He was always*

prepared to account for his actions. ❑ The situation cannot be accounted for in such a simple way.

2 If something **accounts for** a particular fact or situation, it causes or explains it. = **explain**

account for something ❑ She was still angry with us. That accounts for her silence in the meeting.

3 If someone or something can **be accounted for**, people know where they are or what has happened to them.

be accounted for ❑ There was no way to make sure that all of the climbers were accounted for. ❑ A large sum of money could not be accounted for.

4 If something **accounts for** a particular part or proportion of something, it forms that part or proportion of it.

account for something ❑ Children's needs account for a good part of the family budget. ❑ Tea accounted for three fifths of Sri Lanka's exports. ❑ Fifty percent of manufacturing sales were accounted for by foreign-owned companies.

5 If a sum of money **is accounted for**, it has been included in a budget. = **budget for**

be accounted for ❑ Grants for each student must be accounted for by the authority. ❑ This equipment is not accounted for in existing defence budgets.

accrue /əˈkruː/ (accrues, accruing, accrued)

○ **acˈcrue to** [FORMAL]

If things such as profits or benefits **accrue to** a person or group, that person or group gets them.

accrue to someone/something ❑ Considerable benefit will accrue to the community as a result of this project.

accustom /əˈkʌstəm/ (accustoms, accustoming, accustomed)

○ **acˈcustom to** [FORMAL]

If you **accustom** yourself or another person **to** something, you make yourself or them become used to it.

accustom yourself to something ❑ The team has accustomed itself to the pace of first division rugby.

accustom someone to something

❑ Shakespeare has accustomed us to a mixture of humour and tragedy in the same play. ● If you are **accustomed to** something, you are used to it. ❑ He had grown accustomed to making his own decisions.

ache /eɪk/ (aches, aching, ached)

○ **ˈache for**

If you **ache for** something or your heart **aches for** something, you want it very much, and feel very unhappy because you cannot have it.

ache for something ❑ All the time my heart wa aching for my two babies.

acquaint /əˈkweɪnt/ (acquaints, acquainting, acquainted)

○ **acˈquaint with** [FORMAL]

1 If you **are acquainted with** something, you know about it and are familiar with it.

be acquainted with something ❑ Students became acquainted with all aspects of biology before choosing the course.

acquaint yourself with something ❑ She had acquainted herself with our technology.

2 If you **acquaint** someone **with** a subject, you give them information about it.

acquaint someone with something ❑ I will acquaint you with the facts.

acquaint yourself with something ❑ I want to acquaint myself with your strengths and weaknesses.

3 If you **are acquainted with** someone, you know them slightly but they are not a close friend.

be acquainted with someone ❑ Having a few close, supportive relationships is far better than being acquainted with hundreds of semi-strangers.

acquit /əˈkwɪt/ (acquits, acquitting, acquitted)

○ **acˈquit of**

If someone **is acquitted of** a crime in a court of law, it is formally stated that they did not commit the crime.

be acquitted of something ❑ Mr Ling was acquitted of disorderly behaviour by magistrates.

act /ækt/ (acts, acting, acted)

◑ **ˈact on** (or **act upon**)

If you **act on** advice or information, you do what has been suggested.

act on something ❑ Why didn't you act on my warning? ❑ The recommendations could not, for reasons of finance, be fully acted on. ❑ I was acting upon John's advice.

○ **act ˈout**

1 If someone **acts out** negative feelings, they express them in their behaviour.

act out something or **act something out**

❑ Children act out their frustration in temper tantrums. ❑ Either they repress their anger or they act it out all over the place.

2 If you **act out** an event which happened, you copy the actions which took place and make them into a play.

act out something or **act something out**

❑ The teacher gets the students to act out a historic event.

3 If a child **acts out**, they behave badly. [AMERICAN, INFORMAL] ❑ *One way of helping kids is to provide a significant male role model to boys who are showing signs of acting out.*

⊃ **act 'up**

1 If something **is acting up**, it is not working properly. = **play up** [INFORMAL] **be acting up** ❑ *Her washing machine was acting up again.*

2 If a child **acts up**, they behave badly. = **play up** [INFORMAL] ❑ *I'm sorry he had to act up like this.*

⊃ **'act upon** → see **act on**

adapt /əˈdæpt/ (**adapts, adapting, adapted**)

⊃ **a'dapt to**

If you **adapt to** a new situation or **adapt** yourself **to** it, you change your ideas or behaviour in order to deal with it successfully.

adapt to something ❑ *The world will be different, and we will have to be prepared to adapt to the change.*

adapt yourself to something ❑ *They have had to adapt themselves to social and economic changes.*

add /æd/ (**adds, adding, added**)

⊃ **add 'in**

If you **add** something **in**, you include it as a part of something else.

add in something ❑ *We had to add in a couple of extra scenes.* ❑ *If you add in his gains of last year, he'd made no less than £20,000.*

add something in ❑ *Add the meat in and then it'll just slowly simmer away.*

⊃ **add 'on**

If you **add** something **on**, you attach it to something else or include it as part of something else.

add on something ❑ *If the tip hasn't been added on, you will see the words 'service not included'.* ❑ *They add on about nine per cent for service.*

add something on ❑ [+ to] *You can either pay now or add it on to your bill.* ● An **add-on** is a piece of equipment or software that can be added to a computer so that it can do something extra. ❑ *The program will include word processing software and add-ons.*

⊃ **'add to**

1 If you **add** one thing **to** another, you put it in or on the other thing, to increase, complete, or improve it.

add something to something ❑ *Add the grated cheese to the sauce.* ❑ *Since 1908, chlorine has been added to drinking water.* ❑ *He wants to add a huge sports complex to Binfield Manor.*

2 If one thing **adds to** another, it makes the other thing greater in degree or amount. **add to something** ❑ *This latest incident will add to the pressure on the government.* ❑ *Smiles, nods, and cheerful faces added to the pleasant atmosphere.*

3 To **add** a particular quality **to** something means to cause it to have that quality. **add something to something** ❑ *The generous amount of garlic adds flavour to the sauce.*

○ **add to'gether**

1 If you **add together** several numbers or amounts, you calculate their total. = **add up add together something** or **add something together** ❑ *These amounts are added together to produce the total earnings.* ❑ *If you add these two numbers together, what do you get?* ❑ *If you add the periods together, it comes to 55 weeks.*

2 If you **add** several things **together**, you put them all in one place so that they are combined. = **mix**

add something together or **add together something** ❑ *Start by adding the eggs and butter together in a bowl.* ❑ *She added together the boiling water and the cold water in a tub.*

○ **add 'up**

1 If you **add up** several numbers, you calculate their total. = **add together add up something** ❑ *First, add up all your regular payments.*

add something up ❑ *We add all the marks up.* ❑ *Record your scores for each answer and add them up at the end of each section.*

2 If facts or statements do **not add up**, they do not seem correct because they cannot all be true.

not add up ❑ *Accident experts said that the official reports did not add up.*

3 If small amounts of something **add up**, they gradually form a large amount. ❑ *Even small savings, 50 cents here or a dollar there, can add up.* ❑ *It's the little minor problems that add up.*

○ **add 'up to**

1 If numbers or amounts **add up to** a particular total, they result in that total. = **amount to**

add up to something ❑ *This adds up to 75,000 miles of new streets.*

2 If things **add up to** a particular result, that is the effect of them.

add up to something ❑ *This adds up to an impressive list of qualifications.* ❑ *Most of the evidence adds up to the clear conclusion that human beings are able to control their feelings.* ❑ *The shapes, the glowing colours; they all seem to add up to a work of art.*

address /ə'dres, AM 'ædres/ (**addresses, addressing, addressed**)

○ **ad'dress to** [FORMAL]

1 If you **address** a remark **to** someone, you say something to them.
address something to someone ❑ *He addressed his remarks to Eleanor, ignoring Maria.*

2 If you **address** yourself **to** a problem or task, you try to understand it or deal with it.
address yourself to something ❑ *Throughout the book we have addressed ourselves to the problem of ethics.*

adhere /æd'hɪə/ (**adheres, adhering, adhered**)

○ **ad'here to** [FORMAL]

1 If you **adhere to** a rule or agreement, you act in the way that it says you should.
adhere to something ❑ *They did not adhere to the trainer's instructions.* ❑ *The fire regulations have been adhered to.*

2 If you **adhere to** an opinion or belief, you support or hold it.
adhere to something ❑ *Many people adhered to this view.* ❑ *They were idealists who adhered to the principles of peace.*

3 If something **adheres to** something else, it sticks firmly to it. [FORMAL]
adhere to something ❑ *Small pieces of dust adhere to the seed.*

adjust /ə'dʒʌst/ (**adjusts, adjusting, adjusted**)

○ **ad'just to**

When you **adjust to** a new situation or **adjust** yourself **to** it, you get used to it by changing your behaviour or your ideas.
adjust to something ❑ *I felt I had adjusted to the idea of being a mother very well.*
adjust yourself to something ❑ *We have been preparing our soldiers to adjust themselves to home life.*

admit /æd'mɪt/ (**admits, admitting, admitted**)

○ **ad'mit of** [FORMAL]

If an event or situation **admits of** something, it makes it possible for that thing to happen. = **allow**
admit of something ❑ *The relevant law admitted of one interpretation only.*

○ **ad'mit to**

1 If someone **is admitted to** hospital, they are taken into hospital for treatment.
be admitted to something ❑ *She was admitted to hospital with a very high temperature.*

2 If someone **is admitted to** an organization or group, they are allowed to join it.
be admitted to something ❑ *He was admitted to the Society of Authors.*

3 To **admit** someone **to** a place means to allow them to enter it. [FORMAL]
admit someone to something ❑ *A soldier checked his papers and admitted him to the hall.*
be admitted to something ❑ *Journalists are rarely admitted to the region.*

advise /æd'vaɪz/ (**advises, advising, advised**)

○ **ad'vise of** [FORMAL]

If you **advise** someone **of** a fact or situation, you tell them the fact or explain what the situation is.
advise someone of something ❑ *Police must advise suspects of their rights.*

affiliate /ə'fɪlieɪt/ (**affiliates, affiliating, affiliated**)

○ **af'filiate to** (or **affiliate with**) [FORMAL]

1 If an organization **affiliates to** another larger organization or **is affiliated to** it, it forms a close connection with the larger organization or becomes a member of it.
affiliate to something ❑ *All youth groups will have to affiliate to the National Youth Agency.*
be affiliated to something ❑ *He belonged to an organization affiliated to the Labour Party.*

2 If a professional person such as a lawyer or doctor **affiliates to** an organization or **is affiliated to** it, they become officially connected with that organization.
affiliate to something ❑ *He said he wanted to affiliate with a U.S. firm because he needed expert advice in legal affairs.*
be affiliated to something ❑ *We only employ electricians who are affiliated to a recognized professional organization.*

agonize /'ægənaɪz/ (**agonizes, agonizing, agonized**)

○ **'agonize over**

If you **agonize over** something, you feel very anxious about it and spend a long time thinking about it.
agonize over something ❑ *Perhaps he was agonizing over the moral issues involved.*

agree /ə'griː/ (**agrees, agreeing, agreed**)

❍ **a'gree on**

If people **agree on** something, they all decide to accept or do something.
agree on something ❑ *All parties agreed on a new peace plan.* ❑ *We need to agree on a date.*

○ **a'gree to**
If you **agree to** something, you accept it or say that you will do it.
agree to something ❏ Donna agreed to both requests.

○ **a'gree with**
1 If you **agree with** an action or suggestion, you approve of it.
agree with something ❏ You didn't ask anybody whether they agreed with what you were doing. ❏ In his heart he knew they would agree with his proposal.
2 If a particular food or drink **does not agree with** you, it makes you feel ill. **= upset**
not agree with someone ❏ Seafood doesn't agree with me.
3 If something **agrees with** you, it makes you feel healthy and contented. **= suit**
[OLD-FASHIONED]
agree with someone ❏ The sea air really agrees with her.
4 If one account of an event or one set of figures **agrees with** another, the two accounts or sets of figures are the same or are consistent with each other.
agree with something ❏ His second statement agrees with facts as stated by the other witnesses. ❏ You must make sure that the total figure agrees with the estimate.
5 In grammar, if a word **agrees with** a noun or pronoun, it has a form that is correct for the number or gender of the noun or pronoun.
agree with something ❏ In 'He hates it', the singular verb agrees with the singular pronoun 'he'.

aim /eɪm/ (**aims, aiming, aimed**)
✪ **'aim at**
1 If you **aim at** something, or if something that you do **is aimed at** having a particular effect, you hope to achieve it.
aim at something ❏ We should aim at paying them two-thirds of the average wage. ❏ They are aiming at a higher production level.
be aimed at something ❏ This package of public spending cuts is aimed at bringing down the government borrowing requirements.
2 If an action or activity **is aimed at** someone, it is intended to influence them or be of interest or help to them. **= be directed at**
be aimed at someone ❏ I knew that all this publicity was not really aimed at me as an individual. ❏ Many of the devices are aimed at people with hearing problems.

○ **'aim for**
If you **aim for** something, you hope to achieve it.

aim for something ❏ He is aiming for the 100 metres world record.

airbrush /'eəbrʌʃ/ (**airbrushes, airbrushing, airbrushed**)
○ **airbrush 'on**
If something **is airbrushed on** to an image, it is artificially added to it.
airbrush on something or **airbrush something on** ❏ His beard is so neat it looks as if it's been airbrushed on.

○ **airbrush 'out**
1 If something **is airbrushed out** of an image, it is removed from it because it is not attractive.
airbrush out someone/something ❏ Most of the models were happy for their wrinkles to be airbrushed out.
airbrush someone/something out ❏ I'm surprised they didn't airbrush him out of the photo.
2 If a person or an event **is airbrushed out** of history, they are removed from books and websites to make people think that they were not there or did not happen.
airbrush out someone/something or **airbrush someone/something out** ❏ The female contribution to science was airbrushed out of history for many years.

alert /ə'lɜːt/ (**alerts, alerting, alerted**)
○ **a'lert to**
If you **alert** someone **to** a situation, especially a dangerous or unpleasant situation, you tell them about it.
alert someone to something ❏ He wanted to alert people to the activities of the group.

alienate /'eɪliəneɪt/ (**alienates, alienating, alienated**)
○ **'alienate from**
To **alienate** a person **from** someone or something means to make them dislike them and not want to have anything to do with them.
alienate someone from someone/ something ❏ The disorder often alienates people from their families.

alight /ə'laɪt/ (**alights, alighting, alighted**)
○ **a'light on** [FORMAL]
1 If someone **alights on** something, they suddenly think of it or take an interest in it.
alight on something ❏ He would then suddenly alight on the tune he really wanted to play.
2 If someone's gaze or eyes **alight on** something, they suddenly see it.
alight on something ❏ Then her eyes alighted on a photograph that had been pushed back a little.

align /əˈlaɪn/ (aligns, aligning, aligned)
○ aˈlign with
If you **align** yourself or a group that you are part of **with** a particular person or group, you support them because you have the same political aim.
align yourself with someone/something
❏ There are signs that the prime minister is aligning himself with the liberals.
align something with someone/something
❏ He has attempted to align the Socialists with the environmental movement.

allot /əˈlɒt/ (allots, allotting, allotted)
○ alˈlot to
If something **is allotted to** someone, it is given to them as their share.
be allotted to someone ❏ The seats are allotted to the candidates who have won the most votes.

allow /əˈlaʊ/ (allows, allowing, allowed)
✪ alˈlow for
■ If you **allow for** something that might happen, you make sure that you can deal with it if it occurs.
allow for something ❏ If you are self-employed, allow for tax and national insurance. ❏ They were on fixed-price contracts which did not allow for rising costs.
■ If a person or their plan **allows for** something that does not yet exist or has not yet happened, they make sure that it will be possible.
allow for something ❏ We must make sure we allow for the possibility of delays. ❏ His original plans allowed for a playing field.

allude /əˈluːd/ (alludes, alluding, alluded)
○ alˈlude to [FORMAL]
If you **allude to** something, you mention it in an indirect way. **= refer to**
allude to something ❏ They very soon learned not to allude to the subject in the presence of their father.

ally /əˈlaɪ/ (allies, allying, allied)
○ alˈly with
If you **ally** yourself **with** someone or something, you support them, work with them or help them.
ally yourself with someone/something
❏ She allied herself with the most admired girl in the school.

alternate /ˈɔːltəneɪt/ (alternates, alternating, alternated)
○ ˈalternate with
When one thing **alternates with** another, the first regularly occurs after the other, and if you **alternate** one thing **with** another, you have, choose or present one first, then the other, and continue in this way.
alternate with something ❏ Her aggressive moods alternated with more gentle states.
alternate something with something
❏ The band alternated romantic love songs with bouncy dance numbers.

amount /əˈmaʊnt/ (amounts, amounting, amounted)
✪ aˈmount to
■ If something **amounts to** a particular sum or number, its total is that quantity.
= add up to, total
amount to something ❏ Their fees amount to £2,000 a year. ❏ She lost all her savings, which amounted to a large sum of money. ❏ This was a huge army which, with reserves, amounted to 200,000 men.
■ If one thing **amounts to** another, the two things are the same, or have the same effect.
amount to something ❏ His attitude towards her amounted to hatred. ❏ The message amounted to little more than personal regards.
■ If something **amounts to** little or does not **amount to** much, it is not important, large or successful.
amount to something ❏ The trouble had amounted to hardly anything. ❏ Her career had never amounted to much.

anchor /ˈæŋkə/ (anchors, anchoring, anchored)
○ ˈanchor in
If something **is anchored in** something, the second thing provides the basis for the first.
be anchored in something ❏ Politics should be anchored in ethical values.

angle /ˈæŋɡəl/ (angles, angling, angled)
○ ˈangle for
If you **are angling for** something, you are trying to make someone offer it to you without asking for it directly. **= fish for**
be angling for something ❏ He has been angling for an invitation to Washington. ❏ He was clearly angling for money.

answer /ˈɑːnsə, ˈæn-/ (answers, answering, answered)
○ answer ˈback
If someone, especially a child, **answers** you **back** or **answers back**, they speak rudely to you when you have spoken to them.
answer back ❏ What do you do with a child who answers back?

answer someone back ❏ *At first I couldn't resist the temptation to answer teachers back.*

○ **'answer for**

1 If you say that someone has something to **answer for**, you mean that they have done something bad and should be held responsible for it.
answer for something ❏ *More people should be sent to court to answer for their crimes.*

● If someone or something **has a lot to answer for**, they have caused a lot of trouble or problems ❏ *That Campbell man has a lot to answer for.*

2 If you can **answer for** a quality someone has, you are sure they have that quality. **= vouch for**
answer for something ❏ *I can answer for his loyalty.*

3 If you say that you **can't answer for** someone, you mean that you cannot say what they will do or what their opinion will be.
not answer for someone ❏ *I can't answer for my siblings, but I know my parents' miserable marriage made me more determined to make a better job of it.*

○ **'answer to**

1 If someone or something **answers to** a particular description, they have the characteristics described. **= fit**
answer to something ❏ *He knew of several boys who might answer to that description.*

2 If a person or animal **answers to** a particular name, that is the name they use and respond to.
answer to something ❏ *The woman who lived there answered to the name 'Madame Renard'.* ❏ *His name is Jonathan, but he answers to Jon.*

3 When someone **answers to** a person who has authority over them, they have to explain their actions to them and do what they tell them to. [FORMAL]
answer to someone ❏ *She had no boss, no board, no shareholders to answer to.* ❏ *You will answer to Brian and take your orders from him.*

ante /ˈænti/ (**antes, anted**)

○ **ante 'up** [AMERICAN, INFORMAL]
If you **ante up** an amount of money, you pay your share, sometimes unwillingly.
ante up something ❏ *Paul Reichmann offered to ante up $2 million.*

appeal /əˈpiːl/ (**appeals, appealing, appealed**)

○ **ap'peal against** [BRITISH]
If you **appeal against** an official decision, you ask someone in authority to change it.

appeal against something ❏ *He said they would appeal against the decision.*

○ **ap'peal to**

1 If you **appeal to** someone, you ask them in a strong way to do something or give you something.
appeal to someone ❏ [+ to-infinitive] *The Prime Minister appealed to young people to use their vote.* ❏ [+ for] *He will appeal to the government for more money.*

2 If something **appeals to** you, you find it attractive or interesting.
appeal to someone ❏ *The idea of working abroad appealed to him.* ❏ *Very spicy food doesn't really appeal to me.*

appear /əˈpɪə/ (**appears, appearing, appeared**)

○ **ap'pear before**
When someone **appears before** a court, a judge, or an official group, they go there to answer questions.
appear before something/someone ❏ *The American will appear before members of the disciplinary committee at Portman Square.*

○ **ap'pear in**
When an actor or performer **appears in** a play, a show, a movie or a television programme, they take part in it.
appear in something ❏ *She appeared in several of Osborne's plays.*

append /əˈpend/ (**appends, appending, appended**)

○ **ap'pend to** [FORMAL]
When you **append** something **to** something else, especially a piece of writing, you attach it or add it to the end of it.
append something to something ❏ *The '-gate' ending has been appended to every political scandal since Watergate.* ❏ *It was a relief that his real name hadn't been appended to the report.*

apply /əˈplaɪ/ (**applies, applying, applied**)

✪ **ap'ply for**
If you **apply for** a job or membership of an organization or for permission to do or have something, you write a letter or fill in a form in order to ask formally for it.
apply for something ❏ *I am continuing to apply for jobs.* ❏ *He had to apply for a new passport.*

✪ **ap'ply to**

1 If you **apply** yourself **to** something or **apply** your mind **to** something, you concentrate hard on doing it or on thinking about it.
apply yourself to something ❏ *Faulks has applied himself to this task with considerable energy.*

apply something to something ❏ *In spare moments he applied his mind to how he could make money.*

2 If something such as a rule or a remark **applies to** a person, thing or a situation, it is relevant to the person, thing or the situation.

apply to someone/something ❏ *The rule does not apply to us.* ❏ *His description only applied to the older animals.*

3 A name that **is applied to** someone or something is used to refer to them.

be applied to someone/something ❏ *Connell said a new medical term should be applied to Berg's actions.*

4 If you **apply** something **to** a surface, you put it on or rub it into the surface.

apply something to something ❏ *You should apply direct pressure to the wound.* ❏ *I applied cream to the affected area.*

apprise /əˈpraɪz/ (apprises, apprising, apprised)

○ **apˈprise of** [FORMAL]

If you **apprise** someone **of** something, you inform them about it.

apprise someone of something ❏ *I apprised him of the political situation in Washington.*

NOTE **Tell** is a more general word for **apprise of**.

approve /əˈpruːv/ (approves, approving, approved)

⊙ **apˈprove of**

If you **approve of** something or someone, you have a positive opinion of them.

approve of something/someone ❏ *My grandfather did not approve of my father's marriage.* ❏ *His return to the office was widely approved of.* ❏ *We all have the desire to be loved and approved of.*

approximate /əˈprɒksɪmeɪt/ (approximates, approximating, approximated)

○ **apˈproximate to**

If something **approximates to** something else, it is similar to it but is not exactly the same.

approximate to something ❏ *At least we achieved something approximating to a fair result.*

argue /ˈɑːgjuː/ (argues, arguing, argued)

○ **argue ˈdown** [AMERICAN]

If you **argue** someone **down**, you defeat them in an argument.

argue someone down ❏ *When we're discussing politics, I can always argue him down.*

○ **argue ˈout**

If you **argue out** an idea or plan, you discuss it in detail in order to reach a decision.

argue out something or **argue something out** ❏ *Our proposals were argued out in meetings that seemed never to end.* ❏ *We would discuss it and argue it out over a few drinks.*

NOTE **Thrash out** is a more informal expression for **argue out**.

○ **argue ˈout of**

If you **argue** someone **out of** doing something, you persuade them not to do it.

argue someone out of something ❏ *Bill tried to argue him out of leaving.*

NOTE **Talk out of** is a less formal expression for **argue out of**.

arrogate /ˈærəgeɪt/ (arrogates, arrogating, arrogated)

○ **arˈrogate to** [FORMAL]

If someone **arrogates** something such as a responsibility or privilege **to** themselves, they claim or take it even though they have no right to do so.

arrogate something to yourself or **arrogate to yourself something** ❏ *He arrogated the privilege to himself alone.* ❏ *The assembly arrogated to itself the right to make changes.*

arse /ɑːs/ (arses, arsing, arsed)

> **Arse** is a rude, offensive word used in spoken British English.

○ **arse aˈround** (or **arse about**) [BRITISH]

If someone **is arsing around**, they are behaving in a silly and irritating way and wasting time.

be arsing around ❏ *Let's stop arsing around and get on with the rehearsal.*

NOTE **Muck about** is an informal but less rude expression for **arse about**.

ascend /əˈsend/ (ascends, ascending, ascended)

○ **asˈcend to** [FORMAL]

1 If someone **ascends to** an important position, they achieve it or are appointed to it.

ascend to something ❏ *His son was born in the same year he ascended to power.* ❏ *Before ascending to the bench, she was a lawyer in a large New York firm.*

2 If something or someone **ascends to** a higher level, they reach a state that is better than the one they were in before.

ascend to something ❏ *The story ascends from a tragedy to a wonderful fairy-tale.*

ask /ɑːsk, æsk/ (asks, asking, asked)

○ **ˈask after**

If you **ask after** someone, you ask for

information about them, for example about their health or what they are doing.
= inquire after

○ **ask after someone** ☐ *She asked after my father.*

○ **ask a'round**

If you **ask around** or **ask around** a place, you ask several people for information or help.

ask around ☐ *She asked around but no-one seemed to know where the little boy had gone.*

ask around something ☐ *I asked around the village to see if any of the old men would like to come with me.*

✪ **'ask for**

1 If you **ask for** something, you say that you would like to have it.

ask for something ☐ *She asked for a drink of water.* ☐ *The publisher asked for time to think it over.* ☐ *Send the letter by recorded delivery and ask for a receipt.*

[NOTE] **Request** is a more formal word for **ask for.**

2 If you **ask for** someone when you are making a phone call, you say that you would like to speak to them.

ask for someone ☐ *Call the town hall and ask for the parks department.* ☐ *He rang the office and asked for Polly.*

3 If someone **is asking for** trouble or problems, they are behaving in a way that makes it likely that they will get these things.

be asking for something ☐ *To set off without a map was asking for trouble.* ☐ *It is not often the boss loses his rag but Mason was asking for it.*

○ **ask 'in**

If you **ask** someone **in**, you invite them to come into the room or building that you are in.

ask someone in ☐ *Gerald had gone out for a while. Mr Sutton asked me in.* ☐ *They were the kind of neighbours that ask you in for coffee every now and again.*

○ **ask 'into**

If you **ask** someone **into** a place, you invite them to come in.

ask someone into something ☐ *Mr Coles asked me into his office.*

✪ **ask 'out**

If you **ask** someone **out**, you invite them to go somewhere with you.

ask someone out or **ask out someone**
☐ *Every few weeks he and his wife would ask Brody and Ellen out to dinner.* ☐ *It had to be a cheap restaurant, since he was asking her out.* ☐ *He used to ask out complete strangers he met on trains.*

○ **ask 'over**

If you **ask** someone **over**, you invite them to come and visit you.

ask someone over ☐ [+ to] *He asked us over to his flat.* ☐ *What if he asks you over for the evening?*

○ **ask 'round** [BRITISH, INFORMAL]

If you **ask** someone **round**, you invite them to come and visit you.

ask someone round ☐ [+ to] *I hoped he'd ask me round to his pad.* ☐ *I'll ask Sylvia round for a drink.*

○ **'ask to**

If you **ask** someone **to** an event or place, you invite them to go there.

ask someone to something ☐ *Couldn't you ask Jon to the party?*

aspire /ə'spaɪə/ (aspires, aspiring, aspired)

○ **a'spire to**

If you **aspire to** something, you have a strong ambition to achieve it.

aspire to something ☐ *He has always aspired to leadership.* ☐ *She aspired to write a truly great novel.*

assent /ə'sent/ (assents, assenting, assented)

○ **as'sent to** [FORMAL]

If you **assent to** something, you agree to it or agree with it.

assent to something ☐ *I assented to the request of the American publishers to write this book.*

assign /ə'saɪn/ (assigns, assigning, assigned)

○ **as'sign to** [FORMAL]

1 If you **assign** a piece of work **to** someone, you give them the work to do.

assign something to someone ☐ *When I taught, I would assign a topic to children which they would write about.* ☐ *When teachers assign homework to the class, students usually feel they have to do it.*

2 If you **assign** something **to** someone, you say that it is for their use.

assign something to someone ☐ *Some of the money was assigned to us for equipment.*

3 If someone **is assigned to** a particular place, group, or person, they are sent there, usually in order to work at that place or for that person.

be assigned to something/someone ☐ *I was assigned to Troop A of the 10th Cavalry.* ☐ *I had a servant who was assigned to me on the first day.*

4 If you **assign** a particular function or value **to** someone or something, you say they have it.

assign something to someone/something ☐ *Under Mr. Harel's system, each business must assign a value to each job.*

associate /ə'səʊsieɪt/ (associates, associating, associated)

○ **as'sociate with**

1 If you **associate** someone or something

with another person or thing, the two are connected in your mind.

associate someone/something with someone/something ❑ *We tend to associate these colours with autumn.* ❑ *A young child may associate this type of music with relaxation.*

2 If you **are associated with** a particular organization, cause, or point of view, or if you **associate** yourself **with** it, you support it publicly.

be associated with something ❑ *I haven't been associated with the project over the last year.*

associate yourself with something ❑ *The company feels the need to associate itself with the green movement.*

atone /ə'təʊn/ (**atones, atoning, atoned**)

○ **a'tone for** [FORMAL]

If you **atone for** something that you have done, you do something to show that you are sorry you did it.

atone for something ❑ *He felt he had atoned for what he had done to his son.*

attend /ə'tend/ (**attends, attending, attended**)

○ **at'tend to**

1 If you **attend to** something, you deal with it. **= see to**

attend to something ❑ *I had two items of business to attend to before I could relax.* ❑ *Everyone has his own affairs to attend to.* ❑ *If we do not attend to the problem, it will certainly grow.*

2 If you **attend to** someone, you help them or deal with them.

attend to someone ❑ *Harry was attended to in a competent manner.* ❑ *I must go and attend to my guests.*

attribute /ə'trɪbjuːt/ (**attributes, attributing, attributed**)

○ **at'tribute to**

1 If you **attribute** something **to** an event or situation, you think that it was caused by that event or situation.

attribute something to something ❑ *They attributed their success to luck.*

2 If you **attribute** a particular quality or feature **to** someone or something, you

think that they have got it.

attribute something to someone/ something ❑ *People were beginning to attribute magical qualities to him.*

3 If a piece of writing, a work of art, or a remark **is attributed to** someone, people say that they wrote it, created it, or said it.

be attributed to someone ❑ *This, and the remaining paintings, are not attributed to Giotto.*

auction /'ɔːkʃən/ (**auctions, auctioning, auctioned**)

○ **auction 'off**

If you **auction off** furniture or property, you get rid of it by selling it at an auction.

auction off something or **auction something off** ❑ *The furniture was auctioned off.* ❑ *We auctioned off all my grandad's war memorabilia.* ❑ *They auctioned items off, including a poster signed by all the team members.*

average /'ævərɪdʒ/ (**averages, averaging, averaged**)

○ **average 'out**

If you **average out** a set of numbers, you work out the average figure.

average out something or **average something out** ❑ *We sort of averaged out the estimates.* ❑ *We find that, averaging it out, only 8,000 chairs could have been purchased.*

○ **average 'out at**

If a set of numbers **averages out at** a particular figure, that figure is the average for the set of numbers.

average out at something ❑ *'How many hours do you work?' – 'I suppose it averages out at about 40 a week.'*

awaken /ə'weɪkən/ (**awakens, awakening, awakened**)

○ **a'waken to**

When you **awaken to** a fact or when someone or something **awakens** you **to** it, you become aware of it.

awaken to something ❑ *At last she seems to have awakened to the truth.*

awaken someone to something ❑ *We are trying to awaken the public to the danger.*

Bb

back /bæk/ (**backs, backing, backed**)

back a'way

1 If you **back away**, you move slowly backwards away from someone, usually because you are nervous or frightened. ❑ *The waitress stood up and respectfully backed away.* ❑ *[+ from] She backed away from him.* [NOTE] **Retreat** is a more formal word for **back away**.

2 If you **back away**, you avoid supporting or stop supporting an opinion or plan. ❑ *The government refused to back away.* ❑ *[+ from] The Prime Minister appears to be backing away from the policy.*

back 'down

If you **back down**, you start to accept someone else's opinion or demand, even though you do not want to. **= give in** ❑ *The unions have refused to back down.* ❑ *[+ on] Eventually he backed down on the question of pay.*

back 'off

1 If you **back off**, you move backwards away from someone, usually because you are frightened. ❑ *Brody didn't want a fight and backed off.* ❑ *They backed off, handing him what money they had.* ❑ *Back off, or I shoot!* [NOTE] **Withdraw** is a more formal word for **back off**.

2 If you **back off**, you say that you no longer support a statement, demand, or plan that you made earlier. ❑ *When I challenged her, she backed off.* ❑ *[+ from] They appear to have backed off from plans to make an official complaint.* ❑ *Mr. Sylva's lawyers have, apparently, backed off from allegations of torture.*

back 'onto

If a building **backs onto** something, the back of it faces in that direction. **back onto something** ❑ *Their house backs onto the park.*

back 'out

1 If you **back out**, you decide not to do something you previously agreed to do. **= pull out** ❑ *You can't back out now. A deal's a deal.* ❑ *[+ of] We are worried that they will back out of the agreement.*

2 If you **back out** or **back** a vehicle **out**, you move the vehicle backwards out of a space such as a garage or a parking place. **back out** ❑ *Joe put the car in gear and backed out.* ❑ *[+ of] Harold backed out of the parking lot.* **back something out** ❑ *She backed the car out so fast, I thought she was going to hit something.*

○ back 'up

1 If you **back up** a statement, you give evidence to prove that it is true or reasonable. **= support** **back up something** ❑ *You need some statistics to back up your claim.* ❑ *He wouldn't publish anything unless it was backed up by absolute proof.* **back something up** ❑ *Supporters of this theory offer no evidence to back it up.* ❑ *Analysts have backed her view up.*

2 If you **back** someone **up**, you support them by telling other people that what they have said is true. **back someone up** ❑ *If there's any trouble, I'll certainly back you up.* ❑ *He had loyally backed James up in his statement.* **back up someone** ❑ *They know he will back up Goldwater in whatever he claims.* [NOTE] **Support** means almost the same as **back up**.

● **Back-up** is extra help or support from people or machines. ❑ *We need better computer back-up.* ❑ *We don't really need any back-up, do we? We solve our own problems.*

● If you have a second piece of equipment or set of plans as **back-up**, that equipment or those plans are available for use in case the first one does not work. **= stand-by** ❑ *Use a conventional heating system as back-up.* ❑ *We have a back-up crew of 25 actors.*

3 If you **back up** an idea or intention with action, you take action in order to support it or make sure it happens. **back up something** ❑ *It is time the Government backed up its advert campaigns with tougher measures.* **back something up** ❑ *You can't issue a threat if you don't have the military means to back it up.* ❑ *The Secretary General says the declaration must now be backed up by concrete and effective actions.*

4 If you **back up** or **back** a vehicle **up**, you move the vehicle backwards a short way.
= reverse
back up ❑ *I backed up three hundred yards to the entrance.*
back up something or **back something up**
❑ *You back up the car and I'll get the suitcases.*
❑ *I can't back it up – I can't get it into reverse gear.*
5 If you **back up**, you walk backwards a short way. ❑ *She backed up a few steps, then ran at the water.*
NOTE **Retreat** is a more formal word for **back up**.
6 If vehicles **back up** or **are backed up**, they form a line of traffic which has to wait before it can move on.
back up ❑ *Traffic is starting to back up in both directions.*
be backed up ❑ *Traffic into London on the M11 was backed up for several miles.*

backtrack /ˈbæktræk/ (**backtracks, backtracking, backtracked**)
○ **ˈbacktrack on**
If you **backtrack on** a statement or decision you have made, you do or say something that shows that you no longer agree with it or support it.
backtrack on something ❑ *The finance minister backtracked on his decision.*

bag /bæg/ (**bags, bagging, bagged**)
○ **bag ˈup**
If you **bag up** something, you put it into a bag or bags.
bag up something or **bag something up**
❑ *Bag up as many of the leaves as you can.*
❑ *We'll bag them up tonight and they can be delivered tomorrow.*

bail /beɪl/ (**bails, bailing, bailed**)

Bail is also spelled **bale** in meanings 2, 3 and 4.

○ **bail ˈout**
1 If you **bail** someone **out**, you pay money to a court so that the person can stay out of prison while they are waiting for their trial.
bail someone out ❑ *I went down to the Hall of Justice to bail my friend out.* ❑ *Look, can you come down here and bail me out?*
bail out someone ❑ *A high court judge had refused to bail out the teacher charged with this offence.*
2 If you **bail out** a person or organization, you help them out of a difficult situation, usually by providing money. **= rescue**
bail out someone ❑ *They assumed the*

government would always step in to bail out companies in difficulty. ❑ *A financial package was put together to bail out the corporation.*
bail someone out ❑ *We need government assistance to bail us out should things go wrong.*

> **BAIL OUT + noun**
> bail out **a bank**
> bail out **a company**
> bail out **an industry**
> bail out **investors**
> bail out **shareholders**
> ❑ *The government announced measures to bail out the banks.* ❑ *We should not use public money to bail out these companies.*

3 If you **bail out**, you jump out of an aircraft with a parachute because the aircraft is damaged and likely to crash.
❑ *He could have bailed out and saved his life.*
❑ *[+ of] Having bailed out of his aircraft in the dark, he landed near a cottage.*
4 If you **bail out** in a small boat, or if you **bail** water **out** of a boat, you remove water from the inside of it using a container.
bail out ❑ *We couldn't bail out fast enough and were forced to abandon it.*
bail something out or **bail out something**
❑ *Quickly! You bail the water out and I'll paddle.*
❑ *We were desperately bailing out the rain water from the bottom of the boat.*

balance /ˈbæləns/ (**balances, balancing, balanced**)
○ **ˈbalance against**
When you **balance** one thing **against** another, you decide how important the first thing is in relation to the second.
= set against
balance something against something
❑ *A company's interests must be balanced against its employees' well-being.*

○ **balance ˈout**
If two or more things **balance out**, they are equal in amount or value. **= even out**
❑ *If I am overdrawn one month, it should theoretically balance out in the following months.*
❑ *He does more of the cleaning while I do more of the gardening – it sort of balances out.*

○ **balance ˈup**
When things **balance up** or when you **balance** them **up**, they become equal in amount or value.
balance up ❑ *Five years ago, there were three men to one woman. Now it's two to one. Things are starting to balance up.*
balance something up or **balance up something** ❑ *You should add some positive arguments to your essay, just to balance things up*

a bit. ❑ *The Clearing House is the place where the banks balance up their claims on each other.*

bale /beɪl/ (**bales, baling, baled**) → see **bail**

balk /bɔːlk, AM bɔːk/ (**balks, balking, balked**)

> Balk is also spelled **baulk**.

○ **'balk at**

If you **balk at** something, you are very reluctant to do it or to let it happen. = **jib at**

balk at something ❑ *I balked at cleaning the lavatory.* ❑ *The administration does not baulk at such a prospect.*

ball /bɔːl/ (**balls, balling, balled**)

○ **ball 'up**

When you **ball** something **up**, you make it into a round shape.

ball something up or **ball up something** ❑ *She balled the letter up and threw it at his feet.*

balls /bɔːlz/ (**ballses, ballsing, ballsed**)

> Balls is a rude, offensive word used in spoken British English.

○ **balls 'up**

If you **balls** something **up**, you spoil it by making a lot of mistakes. = **cock up, mess up, botch**

balls something up or **balls up something** ❑ *Watton, you've ballsed it all up!* ● A **balls-up** is something that is done very badly with a lot of mistakes. = **cock-up** ❑ *I spend all my time sorting out other people's balls-ups.*

ban /bæn/ (**bans, banning, banned**)

◐ **'ban from**

If you **ban** someone **from** doing something, you officially prevent them from doing it.

ban someone from something ❑ *His visa banned him from work.* ❑ *He was banned from driving for three years.*

band /bænd/ (**bands, banding, banded**)

○ **band to'gether**

If people **band together**, they meet and act together as a group in order to achieve something. = **unite** ❑ [+ to-infinitive] *The smaller independent producers banded together to make a few good quality movies each year.*

bandage /ˈbændɪdʒ/ (**bandages, bandaging, bandaged**)

○ **bandage 'up**

If you **bandage up** a wound or part of someone's body, you wrap a bandage around it. = **bind up**

bandage someone/something up or **bandage up someone/something**

❑ *I bandaged his leg up with a rag.* ❑ *His mum bandaged him up and drove him to the nearest hospital.*

bandy /ˈbændi/ (**bandies, bandying, bandied**)

○ **bandy a'round** (or **bandy about** [mainly BRITISH])

1 When people **bandy** words **around**, they use them a lot, paying little attention to their meanings.

bandy around something or **bandy something around** ❑ *This is just another label for journalists to bandy around.* ❑ *Technical terms and jargon are bandied around by experts.*

❑ *We bandy about such phrases as 'the moral fabric' of society.*

2 If ideas **are bandied around**, a lot of people talk about them.

be bandied around ❑ *Various suggestions were bandied around by the younger members.*

bang /bæŋ/ (**bangs, banging, banged**)

○ **bang a'bout** (or **bang around**) [mainly BRITISH]

1 If you **bang** something **about**, you treat it roughly, knocking it against things. = **bash about** [INFORMAL]

bang something about ❑ *Don't bang your vacuum cleaner about – it's a delicate machine.* ❑ *I heard him banging things around in the garage.*

2 If you **bang about**, you move around doing things noisily. [INFORMAL] ❑ *She sang as she banged about in the kitchen.*

3 If a thing or things **bang about**, they move around and knock into nearby surfaces. ❑ *This strap stops the contents of the case banging around during the flight.* ❑ *I heard a tennis ball banging about.*

4 If a person **is banged about**, they are hit several times. = **bash about** [INFORMAL]

be banged about ❑ *LeClair practised with the team and was even banged about a bit.*

○ **bang a'way**

If you **bang away**, you hit something repeatedly and noisily. ❑ [+ at] *Tom was downstairs banging away at the piano.*

○ **bang 'down**

If you **bang** something **down**, you put it down violently so that it makes a loud noise. = **slam down**

bang something down or **bang down something** ❑ *She banged the plate down in front of him.* ❑ *He banged down the phone angrily.*

○ **bang 'into**

If you **bang into** someone or something, you bump against them accidentally.

bang into someone/something ❑ *You*

couldn't turn round without banging into her.
❑ She doesn't look where she's going so she's
always banging into things.

○ **bang 'on** [BRITISH, INFORMAL]
If you **bang on**, you talk or write about
something for a long time in a boring way.
❑ [+ about] Caroline was banging on about her gap
year in Germany.

○ **bang 'out**
 1 If you **bang out** a tune on a piano, you
play it loudly and rather badly. [INFORMAL]
bang out something or **bang something out**
❑ He was banging out 'Au Clair de la Lune' for all he
was worth.
 2 If you **bang out** a piece of writing on a
keyboard, you type it quickly and
sometimes carelessly or noisily. [INFORMAL]
bang out something or **bang something out**
❑ I managed to bang a few pages out last night.

○ **bang 'up** [BRITISH, INFORMAL]
If someone **is banged up**, they are in
prison.
be banged up ❑ He was banged up for fifteen
years for the crime.
 NOTE **Be imprisoned** is a more formal
expression for **be banged up**.

banish /'bænɪʃ/ (banishes, banishing,
banished)

○ **'banish from**
 1 If you **banish** someone **from** a place or
area of activity, you send them away from it
or say they cannot go there or do it.
banish someone from something ❑ The
queen banished them from court. ❑ They tried
to banish him from politics.
be banished from something ❑ He was
banished from England.
 2 If you **banish** thoughts or feelings **from**
your mind or heart, you stop yourself
thinking about them or feeling them.
banish something from something ❑ The
memory kept returning despite her efforts to banish
it from her mind.

bank /bæŋk/ (banks, banking, banked)
⊙ **'bank on**
If you **bank on** a situation or person,
you rely on them in order to achieve
something.
bank on something/someone ❑ The firm is
banking on better weather to improve results.
❑ I'm banking on Steve to get there early and set up
the equipment.
 • If you say to someone **Don't bank on it**,
you mean that something that they would
like will probably not happen. = **count on,
bet on** ❑ 'I'm sure they'll let me know,' he said

confidently. 'Don't bank on it,' warned Sarah.
 NOTE **Rely on** is a more formal expression
for **bank on**.

○ **bank 'up**
 1 To **bank up** something solid such as
earth or sand means to form it into a pile,
sometimes against a wall. = **build up**
bank up something or **bank something up**
❑ The storm had banked up the snow against the
front door. • Something solid which is
banked-up exists in a pile. ❑ Nobody could
get through the banked-up snow.
 2 If you **bank up** a fire, you put a lot of coal
onto it so that it will keep burning for a
long time.
bank up something or **bank something up**
❑ Mother nursed the fire with skill, banking it up
every night and blowing hard on the coals.

○ **'bank with**
If you **bank with** a particular bank, you
have an account with that bank.
bank with something ❑ My husband has
banked with the Co-op since before the war.

banter /'bæntə/ (banters, bantering,
bantered)

○ **'banter with**
If you **banter with** someone, you tease
them or joke with them in an amusing,
friendly way.
banter with someone ❑ The soldiers bantered
with him as though he was a kid brother.

bar /bɑː/ (bars, barring, barred)

○ **'bar from**
If something or someone **bars** you **from** a
place or an organization, or **bars** you **from**
doing something, they officially stop you
going there, belonging to it or doing that
thing.
bar someone from something ❑ He barred me
from the house. ❑ A court ruling barred him from
working for a rival firm.
be barred from something ❑ Aid workers have
been barred from the country.

bargain /'bɑːɡɪn/ (bargains, bargaining,
bargained)

○ **'bargain for** (or **bargain on**)
If you do not **bargain for** something, you do
not expect it to happen and so do not
prepare for it. = **reckon on**
not bargain for something ❑ The classes were
more difficult than I had bargained for. ❑ I hadn't
bargained on taking the kids as well.
 NOTE **Anticipate** is a more formal word for
bargain for.

○ **'bargain with**
When people **bargain with** each other,

they discuss what each of them will do, pay, or receive.

bargain with someone ❑ *They prefer to bargain with individual clients, for cash.*

arge /bɑːdʒ/ (**barges, barging, barged**)
▸ **barge 'in**

1 If you **barge in**, you suddenly enter a room or building without being invited, in a way that is rude. ❑ *He didn't knock or anything, he just barged straight in.*

2 If you **barge in**, you interrupt someone's conversation. ❑ *Sorry to barge in – can I have a quick word about these figures?*

▸ **barge 'into**

1 If you **barge into** a room or building, you suddenly enter it without being invited, in a way that is rude.

barge into something ❑ *Don't just barge into my bedroom without knocking!* ❑ *Two men had unexpectedly barged into his office eight days ago.*

2 If you **barge into** a conversation, you rudely interrupt the person who is speaking. **= butt in**

barge into something ❑ *She was always barging into our conversations.*

3 If you **barge into** someone or something, you bump against them rather roughly while you are walking. **= jostle**

barge into someone/something ❑ *I hate shopping in town – people are always barging into you.* ❑ *He barged into the table and knocked over a glass.*

▸ **'barge through**

If you **barge through** a crowd of people, you push past them rudely. **= push through**

barge through something ❑ *You can't just barge through a group of people like that.*

ark /bɑːk/ (**barks, barking, barked**)
▸ **'bark at**

If you **bark at** someone, you shout at them in a loud, angry voice.

bark at someone ❑ *I didn't mean to bark at you.*

▸ **'bark out**

If you **bark out** an order, you shout it out loudly and suddenly.

bark out something or **bark something out** ❑ *He stood on the bridge, barking out orders to the crowd.* ❑ *'Hurry up!' he barked out.*

ase /beɪs/ (**bases, basing, based**)
▸ **'base on** (or **base upon**)

If you **base** one thing **on** another thing, or if it **is based on** another thing, it takes its general form, subject or ideas from that other thing.

base something on something ❑ *I based my novel on my experiences as a nurse.*

be based on something ❑ *The new agreement is based on the original United Nations proposal.* ❑ *Many educational systems are based on this model.*

bash /bæʃ/ (**bashes, bashing, bashed**)
○ **bash a'bout** (or **bash around**) [INFORMAL]

If you **bash** something **about**, you treat it very roughly, knocking it against surfaces. **= bang about**

bash something about ❑ *This is my mobile phone – it's been bashed about a bit.*

○ **bash 'in**

1 If you **bash** something **in**, you break it or damage it by hitting it very hard. [INFORMAL]

bash something in or **bash in something** ❑ *The doors had been broken down and the windows bashed in.* ❑ *The police had to bash their door in.*

2 → see **bash up**

○ **bash 'on** [INFORMAL, OLD-FASHIONED]

If you **bash on**, you continue doing a task, often without enthusiasm. **= get on** ❑ [+ with] *I'd better bash on with this report.*

○ **bash 'out** [INFORMAL]

If someone **bashes out** something, they produce it quickly or in large quantities, but with little care or thought.

bash out something or **bash something out** ❑ *They'd bashed out three albums in five years.* ❑ *She can usually bash an article out in under an hour.*

○ **bash 'up** [BRITISH, INFORMAL]

If someone **bashes** a person or thing **up**, they attack them violently and hurt or damage them.

bash someone/something up or **bash up someone/something** ❑ *The other kids used to bash him up.* ❑ *Their car was bashed up overnight.*

bask /bɑːsk, bæsk/ (**basks, basking, basked**)
○ **'bask in**

1 If you **bask in** the sunshine, you lie somewhere sunny and enjoy the heat.

bask in something ❑ *All through the hot, still days of their holiday Amy basked in the sun.*

2 If you **bask in** someone's approval, favour, or admiration, you greatly enjoy their positive reaction towards you.

bask in something ❑ *Livy smiled and basked in Rachel's approval.*

bathe /beɪð/ (**bathes, bathing, bathed**)
○ **'bathe in**

If a place **is bathed in** light, it is covered with light, especially a gentle, pleasant light.

be bathed in something ❑ *The arena was bathed in warm sunshine.*

batten /ˈbætən/ (**battens, battening, battened**)

○ **batten 'down**

If you **batten** something **down**, you make it secure by fixing pieces of wood across it or by closing it firmly.
batten down something or **batten something down** ❑ *Terrified of being broken into, residents batten down their houses after dark.*

○ **'batten on** [LITERARY]

If someone **battens on** a particular person or thing, they use that person or thing to become successful, in a way that is not moral or fair.
batten on someone ❑ *These people batten on naive youngsters.* ❑ *Extremist parties batten on fears about mass immigration and unemployment.*

batter /ˈbætə/ (**batters, battering, battered**)

○ **batter 'down**

To **batter down** something such as a door means to hit it repeatedly and hard so that it breaks and falls down. = **break down**
batter down something or **batter something down** ❑ *The protesters got into the building by battering down the doors with metal bars.*

battle /ˈbætəl/ (**battles, battling, battled**)

○ **'battle with**

1 To **battle with** an opposing person or group means to take part in a fight or competition against them.
battle with someone ❑ *Thousands of people battled with police and several were reportedly wounded.*

2 If you **battle with** something unpleasant, you try to deal with it or end it.
battle with something ❑ *We spend our winter months battling with the cold.* ❑ *She has been battling with cancer.*

baulk /bɔːlk, AM bɔːk/ (**baulks, baulking, baulked**) → see **balk**

bawl /bɔːl/ (**bawls, bawling, bawled**)

○ **bawl 'out**

1 If someone **bawls** you **out**, they tell you off angrily. [INFORMAL]
bawl someone out or **bawl out someone** ❑ *Schultzy wasn't there to bawl him out.* ❑ *I got bawled out for being late.* ❑ *I saw him bawl out a junior clerk.*

2 If you **bawl out** a song or words, you shout or sing loudly in a harsh voice.
bawl out something or **bawl something out** ❑ *They gather round a piano and bawl out the old favourites.* ❑ *A heckler bawled out, 'What about pensions?'*

bay /beɪ/ (**bays, baying, bayed**)

○ **'bay for**

If people **are baying for** something, they are demanding something angrily, usually that someone should be punished.
be baying for something ❑ *The referee ignored voices baying for a penalty.* ❑ *Opposition politicians have been baying for his blood.*

bear /beə/ (**bears, bearing, bore, borne**)

○ **bear 'down on** (or **bear down upon**)

1 If something large **bears down on** someone or something, it moves quickly towards them in a threatening way.
bear down on someone/something ❑ *He saw the lights of the car bearing down on him and realized it was too late to brake.* ❑ *We struggled to turn the boat as the wave bore down on us.*

2 To **bear down on** someone or something means to push or press downwards with steady pressure.
bear down on someone/something ❑ *She felt a weight bearing down on her shoulders.*

○ **'bear on** (or **bear upon**) [FORMAL]

If a fact or situation **bears on** something, it is relevant to it or affects it.
bear on something ❑ *The delegates will be discussing a number of issues which bear on policy decisions.* ❑ *Government was only one of the forces bearing on the lives of the inhabitants.*

○ **bear 'out**

If someone or something **bears out** a statement, they support or prove what has been said.
bear out someone/something or **bear someone/something out** ❑ *Subsequent events certainly seemed to bear out the theory.* ❑ *Harris's assertion is hardly borne out by the facts.*

○ **'bear up**

1 If you **bear up** in a difficult or sad situation, you manage to be brave and cheerful in spite of your problems.
❑ *You have to bear up under the strain.*

2 If something **does not bear up**, it is not good enough or accurate enough when you examine it carefully. = **stand up**
not bear up ❑ *The results don't bear up at all.*

○ **'bear upon** → see **bear on**

○ **'bear with**

If you ask someone to **bear with** you, you are asking them to be patient.
bear with someone ❑ *If you'll bear with me, Frank, I'll do my best to explain.*

beat /biːt/ (**beats, beating, beaten**)

○ **beat 'back**

If someone or something **beats** someone

back, they force them to move backwards.
beat someone back or **beat back someone**
❑ Soldiers used heavy truncheons to beat the protestors back. ❑ Firefighters battled to save the man but they were beaten back by flames and thick smoke.

◯ **beat 'down**

▮ When the sun **beats down**, it is very hot and bright. ❑ [+ on] The sun beat down on her bare shoulders.

▮ When the rain **beats down**, it rains very hard. **= pour down** ❑ Outside, torrential rain beat down.

▮ When you **beat** someone **down**, you force them to accept a lower price for something that they are selling you. **= knock down**
beat someone down or **beat down someone**
❑ I beat him down from £500 to £400.

◯ **beat 'off**

▮ If you **beat off** someone who is opposing you, you prevent them from defeating you.
beat off someone or **beat someone off**
❑ The band beat off fierce opposition to win the award for best album.

▮ If you **beat off** a person or animal that is trying to attack you, you make them go away by hitting them with a stick or other weapon.
beat off someone/something or **beat someone/something off** ❑ The survivors formed a square and managed to beat off further attacks. ❑ The dog ran towards her but she beat it off with her walking stick.

◯ **'beat on** [AMERICAN]

If someone **beats on** you, they hit or kick you many times so that you are badly hurt.
beat on someone ❑ He set his dog on me and then he started beating on me.

◯ **beat 'out**

▮ If you **beat out** sounds on a drum, you make the sounds by hitting the drum.
beat out something or **beat something out**
❑ The drummers walked among them, beating out a rhythm to match their movements.

▮ If you **beat out** a fire, you stop it burning by hitting it repeatedly.
beat out something or **beat something out**
❑ She beat out the flames with her hands.
NOTE Extinguish is a more formal word for beat out.

▮ If you **beat out** a person, team or organization in a competition, you defeat them. [AMERICAN]
beat out something/someone or **beat something/someone out** ❑ Indianapolis has beat out nearly 100 other cities as the site for the

center. ❑ If we are certain a rival will beat us out, we become very jealous.

◯ **beat 'out of**

If someone **beats** another person **out of** something, they get that thing by deceiving the other person or behaving dishonestly.
beat someone out of something ❑ If he could beat his uncle out of a dollar he'd do it.

◉ **beat 'up**

▮ If someone **beats** you **up**, they hit or kick you many times so that you are badly hurt.
= bash up
beat someone up ❑ They beat her up in the street.
beat up someone ❑ I'd beat up anybody who was rude to you. ❑ He told us that he had been beaten up by the police. ● If someone gives you a **beating up**, they hit or kick you many times so that you are badly hurt.
❑ I can honestly tell you that I've never seen a beating-up here.

▮ Something that is **beat-up** or **beaten-up** is old and in bad condition. [INFORMAL]
❑ He was sitting in a beat-up old armchair.
❑ She drives an old, beaten-up yellow car.

▮ If you **beat** yourself **up**, you feel guilty about something, even though it may not be your fault.
beat yourself up ❑ [+ about] I let my friends down, and I'm beating myself up about it.

◯ **beat 'up on**

▮ If someone **beats up on** you, they hit or kick you many times so that you are badly hurt. [AMERICAN]
beat up on someone ❑ No one could beat up on a guy who looked that sick. ❑ You can't beat up on a little kid like that.

▮ If someone **beats up on** another person, they threaten them or treat them unkindly. [AMERICAN, INFORMAL]
beat up on someone ❑ She had to beat up on every customer just to get the bills paid.

beaver /'biːvə/ (**beavers, beavering, beavered**)

◯ **beaver a'way**

If someone **beavers away**, they work very hard at a job. **= slog away** ❑ They've been beavering away on the software for over a year now.

beckon /'bekən/ (**beckons, beckoning, beckoned**)

◯ **'beckon to**

If you **beckon to** someone, you signal to them to come to you.
beckon to someone ❑ He beckoned to the waiter.

become /bɪˈkʌm/ (**becomes, becoming, became**)

> The form **become** is used in the present tense and is the past participle of the verb.

○ be'**come of**

If you wonder what **has become of** someone or something, you wonder where they are and what has happened to them. If you wonder what will **become of** them, you wonder about their future.

become of someone/something ❏ He was a strange character – I wonder what became of him. ❏ Whatever became of that gold watch you used to have? ❏ She was on her own now. What would become of her?

bed /bed/ (**beds, bedding, bedded**)

○ bed '**down**

■ If you **bed** someone **down**, you put them to bed.
bed someone down ❏ There was so little time left at night after the kids were bedded down.
■ If you **bed down** in a place where you do not normally sleep, you sleep there. ❏ We ate and talked. At 9.30 we bedded down.
NOTE **Doss down** is a more informal expression for **bed down**.
■ When soil or another substance **beds down**, it becomes firm, so that further movement or use will not shake it loose. = **settle** ❏ We leave the pillows for a period of time, to allow the feathers to bed down.

○ bed '**out**

If you **bed out** young plants, you take them from the pot where they have been growing and plant them outside in the ground. = **plant out**
bed out something or **bed something out** ❏ Britons bed out plants by the tens of millions every spring.

beef /biːf/ (**beefs, beefing, beefed**)

○ '**beef about** [INFORMAL]

If someone **beefs about** something, they complain about it.
beef about something ❏ They spend all day beefing about their working conditions.

○ beef '**up** [INFORMAL]

If you **beef** something **up**, you add to it, making it bigger, stronger or more interesting.
beef up something or **beef something up** ❏ They had beefed up the early evening news programme. ❏ I read the report and told her she needed to beef it up a bit.

beg /beg/ (**begs, begging, begged**)

○ beg '**off**

If someone **begs off**, they say that they are unable to do something that they had agreed to do. = **cry off** ❏ They arranged another meeting but I begged off this time.

begin /bɪˈgɪn/ (**begins, beginning, began, begun**)

○ be'**gin by** → see **begin with**

○ be'**gin with**

■ If you **begin with** something, you deal with it or do it first.
begin with something ❏ The broadcast began with close-up film of babies crying. ❏ Let's begin with something familiar. ❏ We should perhaps begin with the issue of staffing.
■ If something that is printed or written **begins with** a particular letter, word, or sentence, this letter, word, or sentence is its first part.
begin with something ❏ Think of all the names beginning with D.

belch /beltʃ/ (**belches, belching, belched**)

○ belch '**out**

If smoke, gas or fire **belches out**, or if something such as a machine or chimney **belches** it **out**, large amounts appear from somewhere.
belch out something ❏ These power plants belch out tons of toxic gases and chemicals every day.
belch out ❏ [+ from] I was amazed by the quantity of smoke belching out from the chimney.

believe /bɪˈliːv/ (**believes, believing, believed**)

○ be'**lieve in**

■ If you **believe in** God or things such as fairies or miracles, you are sure that they really exist or happen.
believe in something ❏ Do you believe in ghosts? ❏ They believe in reincarnation. ❏ I don't believe in love at first sight.
■ If you **believe in** an idea or policy, you support it because you think it is right. = **support**; ≠ **oppose**
believe in something ❏ He's a conservative who believes in personal responsibility. ❏ She believes in capital punishment.
■ If you **believe in** someone, you have confidence in them and think that they will be successful. = **have confidence in**
believe in someone ❏ I won't give up on you, because I believe in you.

belly /ˈbeli/ (**bellies, bellying, bellied**)

○ belly '**out**

When a large piece of fabric such as the sail of a ship **bellies out**, it becomes rounded because the wind is filling it. **= billow** ❑ *The child pulled on a rope and the canvas bellied out.*

belong /bɪˈlɒŋ, AM -ˈlɔːŋ/ (**belongs, belonging, belonged**)

○ **beˈlong to**

1 If something **belongs to** someone, it is owned by them.
belong to someone ❑ *The jacket belongs to Emily.* ❑ *This coat doesn't belong to me.* ❑ *He had taken a watch belonging to another person.*
2 If someone **belongs to** a club or organization, they are a member of it.
belong to something ❑ *She belongs to the Labour Party.* ❑ *The majority of the nation did not belong to trade unions.*
3 If someone or something **belongs to** a particular type or category, they are of that type or in that category.
belong to something ❑ *There are several million bats, belonging to eight different species.* ❑ *Henry and I belong to very different generations.*
4 If someone or something **belongs to** a particular place or time, they come from that place or time.
belong to something ❑ *These works belong to an earlier period.*
5 If something **belongs to** a person or thing, they are the person or thing that will control or have responsibility for it.
belong to someone/something ❑ *The decision on the subject belongs to our managers.* ❑ *The future belonged to automation.*

○ **beˈlong together**

When people say that they **belong together**, they mean that they love each other and feel that they should be together. ❑ *I really think that we belong together.*

belt /belt/ (**belts, belting, belted**)

○ **belt ˈout** [INFORMAL]

If you **belt out** a song, you sing or play it very loudly.
belt out something or **belt something out** ❑ *She was belting out 'My Way' at the top of her voice.* ❑ *He's not a young man anymore but he can still belt them out.*

○ **belt ˈup**

1 If you tell someone to **belt up**, you tell them in a rude way to stop talking. **= shut up** [BRITISH, INFORMAL] ❑ *Belt up, will you?*
2 When you **belt up** while travelling in a car or a plane, you fasten yourself into the seat with a safety belt. ❑ *Could you belt up in the back there, kids?*

bend /bend/ (**bends, bending, bent**)

○ **bend ˈdown**

If you **bend down** when you are standing

up, you move the top part of your body downwards. ❑ *He bent down to stroke the dog.*

✪ **bend ˈover**

If you **bend over** or **bend over** something, you move the top part of your body downwards and forwards.
bend over ❑ *She had to bend over sharply because the roof was so low.*
bend over something ❑ *He watched them bend over the documents to sign them.*

○ **ˈbend to**

If someone **bends to** your wishes or if you **bend** them **to** your wishes, you persuade them or force them to do what you want them to.
bend to something ❑ *Congress has to bend to his will.*
bend someone to something ❑ *He was able to control people and bend them to his wishes.*

benefit /ˈbenɪfɪt/ (**benefits, benefiting, benefited**)

✪ **ˈbenefit from**

If you **benefit from** something, it helps you or improves your life.
benefit from something ❑ *Both sides have benefited from the talks.*

bequeath /bɪˈkwiːð/ (**bequeaths, bequeathing, bequeathed**)

○ **beˈqueath to** [FORMAL]

If you **bequeath** your money or property **to** someone, you legally state that they should have it when you die.
bequeath something to someone ❑ *He bequeathed all his silver to his children.*

bet /bet/ (**bets, betting**)

> The form **bet** is used in the present tense and is the past tense and past participle of the verb.

✪ **ˈbet on**

1 If you **bet on** the result of a horse race, football game, or other event, you give someone a sum of money which they give you back with extra money if the result is what you guessed, or which they keep if it is not.
bet on something ❑ *Jockeys are forbidden to bet on races.*
2 If you **bet on** something, you rely on it and expect it to help you.
bet on something ❑ *Investors were betting on a steady rise in house prices.* ❑ *I'm hoping for results next week but I'm not betting on it.*
● If you say to someone **Don't bet on it**, you mean that something that they would like may not happen. **= bank on, count on**

❑ 'I'm sure they'll lend us the money,' he said brightly. 'Don't bet on it,' warned Millie.

beware /bɪ'weə/
○ be'ware of

If you tell someone to **beware of** a person or thing, you are warning them that the person or thing may harm them or be dangerous.

beware of something/someone ❑ Motorists were warned to beware of ice on the roads. ❑ If you go there, beware of thieves.

bid /bɪd/ (bids, bidding)

> The form **bid** is used in the present tense and is the past tense and past participle of the verb.

○ 'bid for

▪ If you **bid for** something that is being sold, you offer to pay a particular amount of money for it.

bid for something ❑ She decided to bid for a large Victorian dining table.

▪ If a person or organization **bids for** a job or a contract, they formally try to get it.

bid for something ❑ The airline is bidding for a contract to run both airports.

○ bid 'up

If someone **bids up** the value of something, they increase it, for example by offering to buy it at a higher price than usual.

bid up something or **bid something up** ❑ Some sellers have been bidding up the price of their own items by making false offers.

big /bɪg/ (bigs, bigging, bigged)
○ big 'up

▪ If you **big** something **up**, you praise it a lot. [INFORMAL]

big up something or **big something up** ❑ Mr Kennedy does radio adverts bigging up his own airline. ❑ I found the series disappointing especially after they'd been bigging it up for weeks.

▪ If you **big it up**, you enjoy yourself a lot in a social situation, especially in a way that other people notice. [INFORMAL] ❑ He's been bigging it up in the clubs.

bilk /'bɪlk/ (bilks, bilking, bilked)
○ bilk 'out of [AMERICAN, INFORMAL]

To **bilk** someone **out of** something, especially money, means to cheat them out of it.

bilk someone out of something ❑ They are charged with bilking investors out of millions of dollars.

bill /bɪl/ (bills, billing, billed)
○ 'bill as

If you **bill** a person or event **as** a particular

thing, you advertise them in a way that makes people think they have particular qualities or abilities.

bill someone/something as something ❑ They bill it as Britain's most exciting museum. ❑ He was once billed as the funniest man in the world.

bind /baɪnd/ (binds, binding, bound)
○ bind 'over

If someone **is bound over** by a court or a judge, they have to do what the court or judge says for a particular period of time.

be bound over ❑ He was bound over to keep the peace for twelve months in May following a row with his wife.

○ bind to'gether

If something **binds** people **together**, it makes them feel as if they are all part of the same group.

bind someone together ❑ It is their memories that bind them together.

be bound together ❑ These people are bound together by shared language, culture, and beliefs.

○ bind 'up [OLD-FASHIONED]

If you **bind up** a wound, you wrap a bandage around it to stop it bleeding or to protect it.
= bandage up

bind up something or **bind something up** ❑ Let me bind up your knee.

○ bind 'up with

If one thing **is bound up with** another thing, the two things are related and influence each other.

be bound up with something ❑ Our sense of identity is very much bound up with our careers as well as our home life.

bitch /bɪtʃ/ (bitches, bitching, bitched)
○ 'bitch about [INFORMAL]

If someone **bitches about** a person, situation or thing, they complain about them or say cruel or unpleasant things about them.

bitch about someone/something ❑ They're forever bitching about their colleagues. ❑ The actors are all bitching about the costumes they have to wear

○ bitch 'up [VERY INFORMAL]

If you **bitch** something **up**, you spoil it.

bitch something up or **bitch up something** ❑ It seems like every damn message is bitched up o given to the wrong person.

bite /baɪt/ (bites, biting, bit, bitten)
○ bite 'back

▪ If you **bite back** a remark or feeling, you stop yourself from saying it or showing it.
= choke back

bite back something or **bite something back**
❏ He poured some more soda into his glass, biting back his anger.

NOTE **Suppress** is a more formal word for **bite back**.

2 If a person or a group of people who have been defeated or criticized **bite back**, they respond strongly or angrily. ❏ Houllier refused to bite back at criticism from the press.

NOTE **Retaliate** is a more formal word for **bite back**.

○ **bite 'into**
If an object **bites into** something firm, it cuts or presses into its surface.
bite into something ❏ His collar was biting into his neck.

blab /blæb/ (**blabs, blabbing, blabbed**)
○ **'blab about** [INFORMAL]
If someone **blabs about** something secret, they tell people about it.
blab about something ❏ Don't blab about your plans until you are ready to make a formal announcement.

black /blæk/ (**blacks, blacking, blacked**)
⊕ **black 'out**
1 If you **black out**, you become unconscious for a short time. = **pass out** ❏ Marianne told me you blacked out. ❏ Before blacking out, I noted that he had a gun. ● A **blackout** is a temporary loss of consciousness or memory. ❏ I started having blackouts – it was very frightening.
2 If a room or a building **is blacked out**, it is made completely dark by switching off all the lights and covering the windows.
be blacked out ❏ The room had been blacked out. ● A **blackout** is a period of time when the electricity supply to a place stops completely. = **power cut** ❏ The blackout was caused by the failure of the Northeast power station. ❏ We had a fifteen-hour power blackout.
● The **blackout** is a period of time during a war when buildings and streets are kept dark at night, so that enemy aircraft cannot see them and bomb them.
❏ They had to get home before the blackout.
3 If people **black out** a television or radio programme, they prevent it being broadcast, usually in protest against something.
black out something or **black something out**
❏ For Canadian viewers, the cable blacked out reports on the case by Seattle television stations.
● A **blackout** is the prevention of the broadcasting of a radio or television programme. ❏ The radio blackout would last only an hour. ● A news **blackout** is the

prevention of the reporting of news about a particular event. ❏ Talks had been held under a news blackout.
4 If you **black out** a piece of writing, you colour over it in black so that it cannot be seen.
black out something or **black something out**
❏ The government has even blacked out names of some officials. ❏ Certain sections were also blacked out due to secrecy restrictions.

blanch /blɑːntʃ, blæntʃ/ (**blanches, blanching, blanched**)
○ **'blanch at**
If someone **blanches at** something, they find it unpleasant or do not want to do it because they think it will be unpleasant.
blanch at something ❏ She blanched at the aggression in his voice. ❏ He must have blanched at the idea of talking to these people.

blare /bleə/ (**blares, blaring, blared**)
○ **blare 'out**
When noise or music **blares out** or a device such as a radio **blares it out**, loud noise or music is produced.
blare out something ❏ A radio was blaring out the news. ❏ Loud hailers blared out 'Keep in line! Keep in line!'.
blare out ❏ Indian music had been blaring out all evening.

blast /blɑːst, blæst/ (**blasts, blasting, blasted**)
○ **blast a'way**
1 If a gun **blasts away** or someone **blasts away** with a gun, the gun is fired continuously for a period. ❏ Thousands of men blasted away at each other. ❏ We could hear guns blasting away in the distance. ❏ [+ with] A man was blasting away with a shotgun in the main square.
2 If a person or object **is blasted away**, they are destroyed by a gun or a bomb.
be blasted away ❏ Half of his face had been blasted away in the fighting. ❏ The military headquarters were blasted away by mortar fire.
3 If music or a piece of equipment such as a radio **is blasting away**, music or another sound is being played very loudly. = **blare out**
be blasting away ❏ The music was blasting away – no one could have heard me if I yelled.

○ **blast 'off**
When a spacecraft **blasts off**, it leaves the ground at the start of a journey into space. ❏ A Japanese spacecraft has blasted off on a mission to bring the first asteroid samples back to Earth. ● **Blast-off** is the moment when a spacecraft leaves the ground and rises into

the air. = lift-off ❑ *The crew will climb into their seats about three hours before blast-off.*

○ **blast 'out**

When a device such as a radio **blasts out** noise or music or when noise or music **blasts out**, they are produced very loudly. = **blare out, blast away**

blast out ❑ *The awards' theme music suddenly blasted out over the sound system.*

blast out something ❑ *Radio speakers were blasting out military music and speeches on all the main street corners.*

blather /'blæðə/ (**blathers, blathering, blathered**)

○ **blather 'on** [INFORMAL]

If someone **blathers on**, they talk for a long time about something that you consider boring or unimportant. ❑ *The old men blather on and on.* ❑ [+ about] *She kept blathering on about her children.*

blaze /bleɪz/ (**blazes, blazing, blazed**)

○ **blaze a'way**

1 If a fire or flame **is blazing away**, it is burning very strongly and brightly.

be blazing away ❑ *The fire was blazing away now and the room was once again warm.*

2 If a light **blazes away**, it shines very brightly. ❑ *The signs outside the hotels and night clubs blaze away.*

3 If someone **blazes away** with a gun, they fire the gun rapidly and continuously for a period of time. = **blast away** ❑ [+ with] *The police burst into the building, blazing away with their guns.* ❑ *Up and down the line the other tanks began blazing away.*

4 If someone **blazes away**, they talk very loudly for a period of time and do not allow anyone else to interrupt them. = **sound off** [AMERICAN] ❑ *The room was empty, except for Miss Saunders who was blazing away.*

○ **blaze 'up**

If a fire **blazes up**, it suddenly begins to burn strongly and brightly. ❑ *Susie threw wood onto the fire and watched it blaze up.*

○ **'blaze with** [LITERARY]

If something **blazes with** light or colour, it is extremely bright.

blaze with something ❑ *The gardens blazed with colour.*

bleat /bli:t/ (**bleats, bleating, bleated**)

○ **'bleat about**

If someone **bleats about** something, they complain about it in a way which makes them sound weak and annoying.

bleat about something ❑ *They are always bleating about 'unfair' foreign competition.*

○ **bleat 'on about** [BRITISH]

If someone **bleats on about** something, they complain about something repeatedly, in a way that is annoying.

bleat on about something ❑ *Daytime TV is just full of people bleating on about stress.*

bleed /bli:d/ (**bleeds, bleeding, bled**)

○ **bleed 'into**

If one substance or colour **bleeds into** another, it spreads into it.

bleed into something ❑ *The reds and pinks of the roses bleed into the green of the trees.*

blend /blend/ (**blends, blending, blended**)

✪ **blend 'in**

If something **blends in**, it appears so similar to its surroundings that it becomes difficult to see it separately. ❑ *The spider's colour allows it to blend in.* ❑ [+ with] *I could not see them – they blended in so well with the landscape.*

○ **blend 'into**

If something **blends into** something in the background, it looks or sounds so similar to it that it is difficult to see or hear it separately. = **merge into**

blend into something ❑ *The clothes are deliberately chosen to blend into their surroundings.* ❑ *The driver's words blended into the roar of the engine.*

blind /blaɪnd/ (**blinds, blinding, blinded**)

○ **'blind to**

If something **blinds** you **to** the real situation, it prevents you from realizing that it exists or from understanding it properly.

blind someone to something ❑ *Her self-importance blinds her to the needs and rights of others.*

bliss /blɪs/ (**blisses, blissing, blissed**)

○ **bliss 'out** [AMERICAN, INFORMAL]

If something **blisses** you **out**, it makes you extremely happy.

bliss someone out ❑ *It was my chosen profession and I was good at it. It blissed me out, as Eddie used to say.* ● Someone who is **blissed-out** is extremely happy. [AMERICAN, INFORMAL] ❑ *The room was full of blissed-out babies and mothers.*

block /blɒk/ (**blocks, blocking, blocked**)

○ **block 'in**

1 If you **block** someone **in**, you park your car so close to their car that they cannot drive away.

block someone in or **block in someone** ❑ *Eric was late because I blocked him in by mistake.*

2 If you **block in** a drawing that is a simple outline, you add colour to the area inside the outline. **= shade in, colour in**

block in something *or* **block** something **in**
❑ Let me have another look at it after you've blocked in the buildings.

○ **block 'off**

When you **block off** a road or the entrance to a building, you put something across it and cover it completely so that nothing can pass through it. **= close off, seal off**

block off something *or* **block** something **off**
❑ Soldiers had blocked off the jail. ❑ The road was blocked off.

NOTE **Obstruct** is a more formal word for **block off**.

◐ **block 'out**

1 Something that **blocks out** light from a place prevents it from entering. **= shut out**

block out something *or* **block** something **out**
❑ Tall, dense bushes blocked out the light.

NOTE **Exclude** is a more formal word for **block out**.

2 If something **blocks out** something else, it is in front of it so that you cannot see it.

block out something *or* **block** something **out**
❑ The trees effectively block out the houses opposite.

NOTE **Obscure** is a more formal word for **block out**.

3 If someone **blocks out** something such as news or information, they prevent other people from hearing about it.

block out something *or* **block** something **out**
❑ Governments can try to block out unwelcome ideas from abroad.

NOTE **Suppress** is a more formal word for **block out**.

4 If you **block out** a feeling or an idea, you try not to think about it. **= shut out**

block something **out** *or* **block out** something
❑ In some situations the experience is so painful that the child blocks it out altogether ❑ In fact I barely remembered it: I had blocked it out.

NOTE **Suppress** is a more formal word for **block out**.

> **BLOCK OUT + noun**
>
> block out **pain**
> block out **a memory**
> block out **thoughts**
> ❑ She tried to block out the memory of his voice. ❑ He kept busy to block out the pain of her departure.

○ **block 'up**

1 If you **block up** something, you close it up completely so that nothing can get through it.

block up something *or* **block** something **up**
❑ Never block up ventilators. ❑ Drains must be left clear, so don't let leaves block them up.

NOTE **Obstruct** is a more formal word for **block up**.

2 If something **blocks up**, it becomes covered or filled and nothing can pass through it. ❑ The sink keeps blocking up.

blot /blɒt/ (**blots, blotting, blotted**)

○ **blot 'out**

1 If one thing **blots out** another thing, it hides it or stops it from being seen or heard.

blot out something *or* **blot** something **out**
❑ A cloud of dust blotted out the sun. ❑ The sound of running water can help to blot out other noises.

2 If you **blot out** a memory or thought, you try not to think of it. **= block out**

blot out something *or* **blot** something **out**
❑ He had made an effort to blot out all memories of this period.

○ **blot 'up**

If you **blot up** a small amount of liquid, you remove it by pressing something absorbent onto it. **= mop up**

blot up something *or* **blot** something **up** ❑ She blotted up the juice from the beans with her bread.

blow /bləʊ/ (**blows, blowing, blew, blown**)

○ **blow a'round** (or **blow about** [mainly BRITISH])

If things **blow around**, or if they **are blown around**, the wind moves them around in different directions.

blow around ❑ There was a lot of dust blowing around.

be blown around ❑ My papers had been blown around, and some were missing. ❑ Her hair had got blown about.

◐ **blow a'way**

1 If something **blows away** or if the wind **blows** it **away**, the wind moves it away from the place where it was.

blow away ❑ There was a massive storm one night and our tents blew away.

blow something **away** ❑ The wind blew his papers away.

blow away something ❑ Use the product near an open window in order to blow away fumes. ❑ My hat was blown away.

2 If you **blow** something **away**, you blow on it so that it moves away from the place where it was.

blow something **away** *or* **blow away** something ❑ I picked up the book and blew the dust away.

3 If a bomb or explosion **blows away** part of your body, it removes it or destroys it.

blow away something or **blow something away** ❏ *The other bullet had blown away the top of her shoulder.*

4 If something **blows** you **away**, it makes you feel very surprised and impressed. [INFORMAL]
blow someone away ❏ *She just totally blew me away with her singing.*
be blown away ❏ *I was blown away by the performance.*

5 If someone **blows** another person **away**, they kill them by shooting them. [INFORMAL]
blow someone away ❏ *They tied him up then blew him away with a shotgun.*

○ **blow 'back**
If something **blows back** or if the wind **blows** something **back**, the wind moves it back in the direction it came from.
blow back ❏ *The ashes from the dying fire blew back into Ralph's face.*
blow something back ❏ *The wind blew all the smoke back down the chimney.* ❏ *Fumes were frequently blown back into the cabin.*

○ **blow 'down**
If something **blows down** or **is blown down**, the wind makes it fall to the ground. = **blow over**
blow down ❏ *Our tents had blown down in the storm.*
be blown down ❏ *Several trees had been blown down.* ❏ *The tent was blown down during the gale.*

○ **blow 'off**
1 If something **blows off** or the wind **blows** something **off**, it is removed from a place by the force of the wind.
blow off ❏ *His hat blew off in the wind.*
blow something off ❏ *Whole roofs were blown off in the storm.*

2 If a gun or explosion **blows off** a part of your body, it removes it.
blow something off or **blow off something** ❏ *He blew his head off with a shotgun.* ❏ *The gun would have blown his hand off if he'd fired it.* ❏ *The explosion blew off his thumb and forefinger.*

3 If someone you are having a romantic relationship with **blows** you **off**, they end the relationship. = **dump** [AMERICAN, INFORMAL]
blow someone off ❏ *I was really in love with her and she blew me off.*

4 If you **blow** something **off**, you act as if it is not important. = **shrug off** [AMERICAN, INFORMAL]
blow something off ❏ *People criticize him, but he sort of blows it off.*

5 If you **blow off** something that you have planned to do, you do not do it. = **cancel** [AMERICAN, INFORMAL]

blow off something or **blow something off** ❏ *A true diva would have blown off the interview. Instead, Lopez apologized for the delay.*

○ **blow 'out**
1 When a person or the wind **blows out** a flame or fire, they stop it burning. = **put out**
blow out something ❏ *Rudolph blew out the candles.* ❏ *The wind almost blew out the flame.*
blow something out ❏ *He took down the lamp and blew it out.*
[NOTE] **Extinguish** is a more formal word for **blow out**.

2 If a storm **blows** itself **out**, it comes to an end.
blow itself out ❏ *This little dust storm will blow itself out soon enough.* ❏ *Eventually the storm blew itself out.*

3 A **blow-out** is a very big meal. = **binge** [INFORMAL] ❏ *Have a blow-out on your birthday.*

4 If the wind or an explosion **blows out** windows, or if windows **blow out**, they break violently and fall down.
blow out something or **blow something out** ❏ *Most of the glass in the windows had been blown out.* ❏ *The blasts blew out windows and scattered debris over hundreds of metres.*
blow out ❏ *The explosion was so forceful the windows blew out.*

5 If a tyre **blows out**, it bursts. ❏ *The car crashed after a tyre blew out.* ● A **blow-out** is a sudden loss of air from a tyre because the tyre has burst. = **puncture** ❏ *My car had a blow-out.* ❏ *A lorry travelling south had a tyre blow-out and crashed into a fence.*

6 If you **blow** someone **out**, you end a relationship with them. [INFORMAL]
blow someone out ❏ *She blew me out for another guy.*

7 If you **blow** someone **out**, you decide not to meet them or do something with them when you had made an arrangement to do so. [INFORMAL]
blow someone out or **blow out someone** ❏ *I was supposed to be meeting Bob for dinner, but I had to blow him out.*

8 If something **blows** you **out**, it impresses you very much. = **blow away** [INFORMAL]
blow someone out ❏ *When I first saw this picture, it really blew me out.*

9 A **blow-out** is a sudden uncontrolled rush of oil or gas from a well. ❏ *At worst, the gas can cause a catastrophic blow-out.*

○ **blow 'over**
1 If an argument or problem **blows over**, it ends and people forget about it. ❏ *The row has blown over.* ❏ *In time, the entire crisis blew over.*

2 When a storm **blows over**, it becomes less fierce and ends. **= die down** ❑ *The storm soon blew over.*

3 If something **blows over** or if the wind **blows** something **over**, the wind makes the thing fall to the ground. **= blow down**

blow over ❑ *A 20-metre spruce tree blew over in 60-kmh winds, landing on both men.*

blow something over ❑ *Wind had blown the tree over.*

blow over something ❑ *Heavy winds blew over an old tree at the Royal Botanical Gardens.* ❑ *All light structures were blown over.*

○ **blow 'up**

1 If you **blow** something **up** or if it **blows up**, it is destroyed by an explosion.

blow something up ❑ *He was going to blow the place up.* ❑ *He accidentally blew himself up in the process.* ❑ *The battleship had been blown up in the harbour.*

blow up something ❑ *The gunmen were threatening to blow up the embassy.*

blow up ❑ *One of the submarines blew up and sank.*

2 If you **blow up**, you lose your temper and become very angry. [INFORMAL] ❑ *He blew up at team-mate, Ian Howard, and a fight started.*

NOTE **Explode** is a more formal word for **blow up**.

3 If a difficult or dangerous situation **blows up**, it begins suddenly and unexpectedly. ❑ *The story blew up after it was revealed that the minister had lied.*

4 If a situation **blows up**, it suddenly becomes very difficult or dangerous. ❑ *The situation blew up in Miller's face when a demonstration turned into a riot.*

5 If you **blow up** something such as a balloon or a tyre, you fill it with air.

blow up something or **blow something up** ❑ *We spent the afternoon blowing up balloons for the party.*

NOTE **Inflate** is a more formal word for **blow up**.

6 If you **blow up** a photograph or picture, you make a larger copy of it.

blow something up or **blow up something** ❑ *Once the photos had been blown up, the gun in his hand was clearly visible.*

NOTE **Enlarge** is a more formal word for **blow up**.

• A **blow-up** is an enlargement of a photograph or picture.

7 If a storm **blows up**, it starts. **= get up**; ≠ **die down** ❑ *We were warned of a storm blowing up off the East coast.*

bludgeon /ˈblʌdʒən/ (**bludgeons, bludgeoning, bludgeoned**)

○ **bludgeon 'into**

If someone **bludgeons** you **into** doing something, they force you to do it.

bludgeon someone into something ❑ *Large supermarkets just bludgeon suppliers into accepting these deals.*

bluff /blʌf/ (**bluffs, bluffing, bluffed**)

○ **bluff 'into**

If you **bluff** someone **into** doing something, you persuade them to do it by telling them something that is not true.

bluff someone into something ❑ *They're just trying to bluff me into agreeing to it.*

blunder /ˈblʌndə/ (**blunders, blundering, blundered**)

○ **blunder a'round** (or **blunder about** [mainly BRITISH])

If you **blunder around**, you move about in a clumsy or uncertain way. ❑ *She didn't need me blundering around in the kitchen without my glasses.*

○ **blunder 'into**

If you **blunder into** a dangerous or difficult situation, you get involved in it by mistake.

blunder into something ❑ *People wanted to know how they had blundered into war, and how to avoid it in future.*

○ **blunder 'through**

If you **blunder through** an activity, you manage to finish it although you do not do it well. **= muddle through**

blunder through something ❑ *Somehow he blundered through the exercises.*

blurt /blɜːt/ (**blurts, blurting, blurted**)

○ **blurt 'out**

If you **blurt out** something, you say it suddenly, without thinking about it.

blurt out something or **blurt something out** ❑ *The astounded Reichert could only blurt out 'Where have you come from?'.* ❑ *I blurted out that I'd got a job.* ❑ *I hadn't intended to blurt it out like that.*

board /bɔːd/ (**boards, boarding, boarded**)

○ **board 'up**

If you **board up** a door or window, you fasten boards over it so that it is covered; if you **board up** a building, you do this to the doors and windows.

board up something or **board something up** ❑ *Shopkeepers were boarding up their windows in preparation.* ❑ *Everywhere you look, houses are boarded up, awaiting demolition.*

bob /bɒb/ (bobs, bobbing, bobbed)

○ **bob a'round** (or **bob about** [mainly BRITISH])

If something **bobs around**, it moves gently up and down, like something floating on water. ❑ *A float was bobbing about among the fishing boats.* ❑ *They bobbed around like corks.*

○ **bob 'up**

1 If something **bobs up**, it suddenly floats to the surface after it has been under water. ❑ *Suddenly an object bobbed up from below the surface.*

2 If someone **bobs up**, they appear or reappear suddenly. = **pop up** ❑ *Here and there at the cliff top, soldiers bobbed up.*

bog /bɒg/ (bogs, bogging, bogged)

○ **bog 'down**

If you **are bogged down**, you are not making progress with a task because you are spending too much time on unimportant issues.

be bogged down ❑ *From time to time, a creative team may get bogged down.* ❑ *[+ in] Try not to get bogged down in the details.*

○ **bog 'off** [BRITISH, INFORMAL]

If you tell someone to **bog off**, you are telling them rudely to go away. ❑ *Bog off, will you!*

boggle /'bɒgəl/ (boggles, boggling, boggled)

○ **'boggle at**

If you **boggle at** something, you find it surprising and difficult to believe.

boggle at something ❑ *We boggled at the brilliance of their acrobatic skills.*

boil /bɔɪl/ (boils, boiling, boiled)

○ **boil a'way**

When a liquid that is being heated **boils away**, it changes into steam or vapour. ❑ *This causes the engine to overheat and the water to boil away.* ❑ *Cook the rice until the water has boiled away.*

[NOTE] **Evaporate** is a more formal word for **boil away**.

○ **boil 'down**

1 When a liquid **boils down** or you **boil it down**, it boils until it decreases in amount, because some of it has changed into steam. **boil something down** or **boil down something** ❑ *Boil the sauce down until it is really thick.*

boil down ❑ *A panful of spinach boils down to virtually nothing.*

2 If you **boil down** some information, you keep only the most important parts. = **condense**; ≠ **pad out**

boil something down or **boil down something** ❑ *I'm just sorting through data and boiling it down.*

○ **boil 'down to**

If a situation or issue **boils down to** a particular thing, this is the most important aspect of it.

boil down to something ❑ *In the end, it all boils down to money. They simply don't have enough of it.* ❑ *The question boils down to one of social priorities.*

○ **boil 'over**

1 When a liquid that is being heated **boils over**, it rises and flows over the edge of its container. ❑ *The milk's boiling over.*

2 If a situation in which people are very angry **boils over**, the people become so angry that the situation gets out of control. ❑ *The simmering quarrel between the opposing parties had boiled over.* ❑ *His anger boiled over and he punched him.*

○ **boil 'up**

1 When you **boil up** a liquid, you heat it until it boils.

boil up something or **boil something up** ❑ *We boiled up some water in the pan.* ❑ *When the juice is boiled up with sugar it forms jelly.*

2 If anger **boils up** inside you, you feel suddenly very angry. ❑ *Resentment boiled up within him.*

○ **'boil with**

If you **are boiling with** anger, you are very angry.

be boiling with something ❑ *I used to be cheerful on the outside, but inside I would be boiling with rage.*

bolster /'bəʊlstə/ (bolsters, bolstering, bolstered)

○ **bolster 'up**

If you **bolster up** someone or something, you support them or help them.

bolster up someone/something or **bolster someone/something up** ❑ *To bolster up their case, they quoted a speech by Ray Gun.*

bolt /bəʊlt/ (bolts, bolting, bolted)

○ **bolt 'down** [INFORMAL]

If you **bolt down** food, you eat it very quickly.

bolt down something or **bolt something down** ❑ *He bolted down his lunch and rushed off to the airport.* ❑ *Try not to bolt your food down.*

○ **bolt 'on**

1 If you **bolt** something such as a system or piece of software **on**, you attach it to something else or include it with something else.

bolt something on or **bolt on something** ❑ *They have bolted on additional security features.*

● A **bolt-on** system or piece of software can be added to an existing piece of software, website, etc. ❑ *We used a bolt-on e-commerce solution.* ● A **bolt-on** is a system or piece of software that can be added to an existing piece of software, website, etc. ❑ *Cheap calls are now available with a new bolt-on.*

2 If you **bolt** something **on**, you add it, often without thinking about it much or preparing it properly.

bolt something on or **bolt on something** ❑ *There are basically three types of holiday on offer, with the opportunity to learn bolted on.*

● Something described as **bolt-on** is added without enough thought or planning. ❑ *Environmental policies are no longer a bolt-on activity for companies.* ● A **bolt-on** is something that has been added without enough thought or planning. ❑ *A conservatory should never be a bolt-on to your property.*

bomb /bɒm/ (**bombs, bombing, bombed**)

○ **bomb a'long** [INFORMAL]

If you **bomb along** or **bomb along** a place, you move or travel very quickly. ❑ *The wind surfers were bombing along in the wind.*

bomb along or **bomb along somewhere** ❑ *We went bombing along the motorway at 90 mph.*

○ **bomb 'out**

If a building **is bombed out** or if people in a building **are bombed out**, the building is completely destroyed by a bomb.

be bombed out ❑ *Their factories were bombed out.* ❑ *People who had been bombed out in the war were housed here.*

bombard /bɒmˈbɑːd/ (**bombards, bombarding, bombarded**)

○ **bom'bard with**

If you **bombard** someone **with** something, you direct a large amount of that thing at them in a forceful and continuous way.

bombard someone with something ❑ *The media bombards all of us with images of violence.*

bond /bɒnd/ (**bonds, bonding, bonded**)

○ **'bond with**

1 When people **bond with** each other, they form a strong relationship.

bond with someone ❑ *Belinda was having difficulty bonding with the baby.*

2 When one thing **bonds with** another, it sticks to it or becomes joined to it.

bond with something ❑ *Diamond may be strong, but it does not bond well with other materials.*

bone /bəʊn/ (**bones, boning, boned**)

○ **bone 'up on** [INFORMAL]

If you **bone up on** a subject, you revise it. = **swot up on**

bone up on something ❑ *He'd been boning up on French history.*

book /bʊk/ (**books, booking, booked**)

❍ **book 'in** [BRITISH]

1 When you **book in**, you announce that you have arrived at a hotel and sign your name in a book. = **check in**; ≠ **check out** ❑ [+ at] *He booked in at the Ritz Hotel.*

2 When you **book** someone **in**, you arrange for them to stay somewhere such as a hotel or you arrange for them to do something such as a course. [BRITISH]

book someone in ❑ *She had booked us in at a hotel in Torquay.* ❑ *I've booked you in for the residential course.*

❍ **book 'into** [BRITISH]

1 When you **book into** a hotel, you tell the receptionist that you have arrived and sign your name in a book. = **check into**; ≠ **check out of**

book into something ❑ *He had booked into the Warsaw Hotel.*

2 When you **book** someone **into** a hotel, you arrange for them to stay there.

book someone into something ❑ *He had been booked into the hotel by the travel agent.*

❍ **book 'up**

1 If you **book up** for a course, event, or other organized activity, you arrange to take part in it. ❑ [+ for] *We've still got time to book up for the French course.*

2 If something such as a hotel, concert or course **is booked up**, it has no rooms, seats, or tickets left.

be booked up ❑ *On the coast, hotels and campsites are all fully booked up for months in advance.* ❑ *Their highly popular study days get booked up well in advance.*

boom /buːm/ (**booms, booming, boomed**)

○ **boom 'out**

When someone **booms out** something or when their voice **booms out**, they speak in a very loud, deep voice.

boom out something ❑ *He boomed out: 'Good evening ladies and gentlemen!'.*

boom out ❑ *A great voice boomed out from the speakers.*

boot /buːt/ (**boots, booting, booted**)

○ **boot 'out** [INFORMAL]

If someone **boots** someone **out**, they force them to leave a job or place. = **kick out**

boot someone out ❑ *Simmons booted them out and took away their passes.*

be booted out ❑ [+ of] *All foreign journalists had been booted out of the country.*

NOTE Expel is a more formal word for **boot out**.

○ **boot 'up**

When you **boot up** a computer, you make it ready to be used, and when a computer **boots up**, it becomes ready to be used.
boot up something or **boot something up** ❑ I'm just booting up my laptop. ❑ Go over to your PC and boot it up.
boot up ❑ That's the sound of my computer booting up.

border /'bɔːdə/ (**borders, bordering, bordered**)

✪ **'border on**

◼ A country that **borders on** another country is next to that country and shares a border with it.
border on something ❑ The Republic of Moldova borders on Romania.
◼ When something **borders on** an extreme state or quality, it is almost that state or quality. = **verge on**
border on something ❑ I was in a state of excitement bordering on insanity. ❑ Their rough treatment of each other bordered on brutality.

bore /bɔː/ (**bores, boring, bored**)

○ **bore 'into**

If someone's eyes **bore into** you, they are staring hard at you.
bore into someone ❑ Vorster's eyes bored into me. He said 'We are at war. You cannot afford to refuse.'

boss /bɒs/ (**bosses, bossing, bossed**)

○ **boss a'round** (or **boss about** [mainly BRITISH])

If someone **bosses** you **around**, they keep telling you what to do in a way that is annoying. = **order around**
boss someone around ❑ He was never one to boss people about. ❑ He started bossing me around and I didn't like it.

botch /bɒtʃ/ (**botches, botching, botched**)

○ **botch 'up** [INFORMAL]

If you **botch up** a piece of work, you do it badly.
botch up something or **botch something up** ❑ He really botched up the last job he did for us. ❑ Our builder botched it up. ● If you make a **botch-up** of something that you are doing, you do it badly. [INFORMAL] ❑ Tourists were victims of a computer botch-up.

bottle /'bɒtəl/ (**bottles, bottling, bottled**)

○ **bottle 'out** [BRITISH, INFORMAL]

If you **bottle out** just before doing something difficult or frightening, you lose your courage at the last moment, and do not do it. = **chicken out** ❑ She'll bottle out

when she sees the other competitors. ❑ [+ of] He bottled out of the race at the last minute.

○ **bottle 'up**

◼ If you **bottle up** a feeling such as anger or sadness, you make an effort not to show it over a long period of time.
bottle up something or **bottle something up** ❑ He tends to bottle up his feelings but then, from time to time, he just explodes. ❑ All the rage that had been bottled up in him for so long flooded out in a torrent of abuse.
◼ If you **bottle up** a liquid, you transfer it from a large container into several smaller bottles.
bottle up something or **bottle something up** ❑ She's in the cellar, bottling up the home-made apple juice. ❑ All the ginger beer was bottled up and ready for the party.

bottom /'bɒtəm/ (**bottoms, bottoming, bottomed**)

○ **bottom 'out**

When something that is getting worse or decreasing **bottoms out**, it stops doing so and remains steady. = **level out** ❑ There are signs that the recession is starting to bottom out. ❑ Death rates from the disease have not bottomed out by any means.

noun + BOTTOM OUT
demand bottoms out
the economy bottoms out
a market bottoms out
a recession bottoms out
❑ Demand for the products has bottomed out recently. ❑ They are optimistic that the economy will bottom out soon.

bounce /baʊns/ (**bounces, bouncing, bounced**)

✪ **bounce 'back**

◼ If you **bounce back** after a bad experience, you return quickly to your normal activities or to your previous level of enthusiasm or success. ❑ He ran into some financial difficulties a while back but he's bounced back. ❑ He'll bounce back – he always does.
NOTE **Recover** is a more general word for **bounce back**.
◼ If an email **bounces back**, it is returned to you and not delivered to the person you sent it to. ❑ I sent him an email, but it bounced back.

○ **bounce 'off**

If you **bounce** ideas **off** someone, you tell them to that person, in order to find out what they think about them.
bounce something off someone ❑ It was good to bounce ideas off a few people.

bow /baʊ/ (**bows, bowing, bowed**)

○ **bow 'down**

1 If you **bow down**, you bend your body forwards very low in order to show great respect. ❑ *The servants were commanded to bow down.* ❑ [+ *to*] *They bowed down to the master.*

2 If you **bow down** to another person, you obey them and show them great respect. = **kow-tow** ❑ [+ *to*] *We shouldn't have to bow down to anyone.*

3 If you **are bowed down** by something, you are made unhappy and anxious by it, and have no hope. [LITERARY]
be bowed down by something ❑ *She was weary and bowed down by the weight of her problems.*

○ **bow 'out**

If you **bow out**, you stop doing something or taking part in something, often in order to allow someone else to take your place. = **step down** ❑ *Aged 73, he decided it was time to bow out.* ❑ [+ *of*] *I hear Annie has bowed out of the project.*

○ **'bow to**

If you **bow to** something or someone, you change your plans in order to do what someone else wants. = **yield to**
bow to something/someone ❑ *The Minister seems to be bowing to pressure from industry to ignore the recommendations.* ❑ *The government refused to bow to the nationalists.*

bowl /bəʊl/ (**bowls, bowling, bowled**)

○ **bowl a'long** [OLD-FASHIONED]

If you **bowl along** in a car or on a boat, you move along very quickly, especially when you are enjoying yourself. ❑ *Veronica looked at him, smiling, as they bowled along.*

○ **bowl 'out**

To **bowl out** a team in cricket means to get all their players out and end their innings (= the period in which a team tries to score points).
bowl out someone or **bowl someone out**
❑ [+ *for*] *We were bowled out for 220 runs.*
NOTE **Dismiss** is a more formal word for **bowl out**.

○ **bowl 'over**

1 If you **bowl** someone **over**, you knock them down by crashing into them when you are moving very quickly. = **knock over**
bowl someone over ❑ *They were nearly bowled over by three boys as they raced past.*

2 If you **are bowled over** by someone or something, you are very impressed or surprised because they are so beautiful or exciting.

be bowled over ❑ [+ *by*] *I was bowled over by the beauty of Malawi.* ❑ *He'd never met anyone like her and was completely bowled over.*
NOTE **Overwhelm** is a more formal word for **bowl over**.

box /bɒks/ (**boxes, boxing, boxed**)

○ **box 'in**

1 If someone **boxes** you **in**, they move too close to you or surround you, and you are unable to move. = **hem in**
box someone in or **box in someone** ❑ *Some fool parked his car too close to mine and boxed me in.* ❑ *Unless you go ahead early on in the race, there's a danger you'll get boxed in.*

2 If something **boxes** you **in**, it puts you in a situation where you have very little choice about what you can do.
box someone in ❑ *The government doesn't want to be boxed in by a time-frame imposed by others.* ❑ *Part of winning a mandate is having clear goals and not boxing yourself in.*

○ **box 'off**

To **box off** an area means to make a small enclosed area within a larger area by building walls around it.
box off something or **box something off**
❑ *You could box off the area under the stairs to make a cupboard.*

○ **box 'up**

If you **box** things **up**, you put them into boxes.
box up something or **box something up**
❑ *We've been boxing up medical supplies to send overseas.* ❑ *I've boxed all those books up.*

brace /breɪs/ (**braces, bracing, braced**)

○ **'brace against**

If you **brace** yourself **against** something, you press against something in order to avoid falling.
brace yourself against something ❑ *Elaine braced herself against the dresser and looked in the mirror.*

bracket /'brækɪt/ (**brackets, bracketing, bracketed**)

○ **bracket to'gether**

If you **bracket** two or more people or things **together**, you consider them to be similar or related in some way.
bracket someone/something together or **bracket together someone/something**
❑ *His book brackets together some of the greatest artists this country has produced.*
be bracketed together ❑ *The conditions are bracketed together under the heading of 'sleep problems'.*

branch /brɑːntʃ, bræntʃ/ (**branches, branching, branched**)

○ **branch 'off**

1 A road or path that **branches off** or **branches off** another, larger one, starts from the larger one and goes in a slightly different direction.
branch off ❑ *The road to Oxford branches off here.*
branch off something ❑ *A dirt path branched off the main road.*
2 If you **branch off** when you are speaking, you start talking about something slightly different. ❑ *Branching off a little, can I raise the related subject of fees?*

○ **branch 'out**

If you **branch out**, you do something different from your normal activities or work. ❑ [+ *into*] *Known until then for cheap horror films, the company branched out into crime films.*

brave /breɪv/ (**braves, braving, braved**)

○ **brave 'out**

If you **brave out** a dangerous or upsetting situation, you deal with it in a brave way.
brave out something or **brave something out** ❑ *We'll just have to brave out the return journey on our own.* ❑ *There was little clean water available for those who chose to brave it out in their own homes.*

brazen /'breɪzən/ (**brazens, brazening, brazened**)

○ **brazen 'out**

If you have done something wrong and you **brazen it out**, you behave confidently and show no shame or regret. ❑ *Of course he'll brazen it out; he's got no scruples at all.*

break /breɪk/ (**breaks, breaking, broke, broken**)

○ **break a'way**

1 When you **break away**, you stop being part of a group, usually because of a disagreement. = **split off** ❑ *Three United Party senators broke away to form the Federal Party.* ❑ [+ *from*] *Two regions have broken away from central government rule.* ● A **breakaway** group is one that has separated from a larger group. ❑ *So how well did Britain's new breakaway party do in the election?* ● A **breakaway** is the act of breaking away from a group. ❑ *The move towards a final breakaway began on 10 February.*
2 If you **break away**, you suddenly move away from someone who is holding you. ❑ *She made a half-hearted attempt to break away.*

❑ [+ *from*] *Florrie broke away from him and rushed upstairs.*
3 If a part of something **breaks away**, it separates and moves away. ❑ [+ *from*] *Australia had broken away from Antarctica and continued to drift.*
4 If you **break away** from a belief or a habit, you reject it. ❑ [+ *from*] *In his art, he very much wanted to break away from tradition.*

○ **break 'down**

1 When an arrangement, relationship or discussion **breaks down**, it fails because of a problem or disagreement. ❑ *The talks broke down over differences on doctrine.* ❑ *It is always very sad when a marriage breaks down, particularly when there are children affected.*
NOTE **Founder** is a formal word for **break down**.
● The **breakdown** of an arrangement, relationship or discussion is the failure and end of it. ❑ *There was a serious breakdown of communications.* ❑ *Politicians blame the police for the breakdown in community relations.*
2 When a machine or a vehicle **breaks down**, it stops working. ❑ *His car broke down on the motorway.* ❑ *The heating had broken down on the train and she was frozen.*
NOTE **Pack up** and **conk out** are more informal expressions for **break down**.
● If you have a **breakdown** when you are travelling in a car, the car stops working. ❑ *We had a breakdown on the motorway.*
● A **broken-down** vehicle or machine no longer works because it has something wrong with it. ❑ *The piles of rubbish and the broken-down cars had vanished.*
3 To **break down** information or a task means to separate it into smaller parts in order to understand it or deal with it more easily.
break down something or **break something down** ❑ *Learn to break down large tasks into manageable units.* ❑ *With a computer you can break the data down to suit particular requirements.* ● A **breakdown** of a set of figures is a simpler version of it arranged in separate sections. ❑ *I asked David for a breakdown of the sales figures.*
4 When a substance **breaks down** or when something **breaks** it **down**, it changes as a result of a chemical or biological process.
break down ❑ *The residue breaks down before reaching the sewer.*
break down something or **break something down** ❑ *Enzymes break down proteins by chemical action.* ❑ *This white powder then attacks*

the pollutants, breaking them down into harmless compounds.

5 If you **break down** a problem or obstacle, you weaken or remove it so that it no longer prevents you from doing something.
= overcome

break down something or **break something down** ❑ This would help break down the barriers between young and old. ●The **breakdown** of an idea or a tradition is the ending of it. ❑ These two decades saw a breakdown of the class system in England.

6 If someone **breaks down**, they start crying uncontrollably. ❑ He was terrified he was going to break down in public.

7 If someone **breaks down**, they become very depressed and cannot cope with their problems. **= crack up** ❑ She broke down completely and had to go into hospital. ❑ I was under enormous pressure for two years before I finally broke down. ●A **breakdown** is an illness involving severe mental depression. ❑ I'll have a nervous breakdown if I stay in this job.

8 To **break down** something such as a door or wall means to hit it hard so that it breaks and falls to the ground. **= smash down**

break down something or **break something down** ❑ Police broke down the door. ❑ Water had flooded their homes and broken down the walls. ❑ The troops knocked on the door of the intensive care unit, then broke it down.

NOTE Demolish is a more formal word for **break down**.

●A **broken-down** building is in very bad condition. ❑ We walked along a narrow street of broken-down shops.

break 'in

1 If someone **breaks in**, they get into a building illegally or by force. ❑ The police broke in and arrested all the brothers. ❑ They had broken in through a gardener's gate. ●A **break-in** is the act of getting into a building illegally or by force. ❑ The break-in and robbery had taken them only twenty minutes.

2 If you **break in** when someone is talking or doing something, you interrupt them.
= butt in, cut in ❑ 'Don't look at me,' Etta broke in brusquely. ❑ 'Crow...' began Spear excitedly, but his wife broke in.

3 If you **break** someone **in**, you get them used to a new job or situation.

break in someone or **break someone in**
❑ Chief Brody liked to break in his recruits slowly.
❑ He was breaking me in gently in situations I could handle.

4 When you **break in** a new pair of shoes, you wear them for short periods of time

until they become comfortable enough for normal use.

break in something or **break something in**
❑ It has been good weather recently for breaking in new boots.

5 If you **break in** a wild or young horse, you train it to obey you.

break in something or **break something in**
❑ It was her first chance to break in a pony.

break 'in on

If you **break in on** a person or a conversation, you interrupt them.

break in on someone/something ❑ Sorry to break in on you like this, Dr Marlowe. ❑ Could we just break in on that question?

break 'into

1 If someone **breaks into** a room or a building, they enter it illegally or by force.

break into something ❑ He broke into a shop one night and stole some food. ❑ Offices were broken into and files removed.

2 If you **break into** an action or activity, you suddenly start doing it. **= burst into**

break into something ❑ When Rudolph saw her, he broke into a run. ❑ Maria broke into noisy laughter. ❑ The boys broke into applause.

3 If you **break into** an activity or process, you interrupt it. **= disturb**

break into something ❑ He became so quiet that she did not like to break into his thought.

4 If you **break into** a new activity or business, you start to have success in it.
= get into, move into

break into something ❑ There are many women wanting to break into the labour market.

5 If you **break into** a sum of money that you have been saving, you start to spend it.
= dip into

break into something ❑ She was so desperate that she broke into her holiday money.

6 If you **break into** a container of food or drink, you open it and start to eat or drink the contents.

break into something ❑ Let's break into a bottle of champagne to celebrate.

7 If you **break** something **into** smaller parts, you divide it into smaller parts.

break something into something ❑ We tried breaking the words into syllables. ❑ You can break each period into several parts.

break 'off

1 If a part of something **breaks off** or if you **break** it **off**, it separates or is removed.

break off ❑ A little bit has broken off.

break off something ❑ Garroway broke off another piece of bread.

break something off ❑ *I broke a branch off and stabbed at the ground with it.*

2 If you **break off** when speaking, you suddenly stop. ❑ *He broke off, only to start speaking again almost immediately.* ❑ *'I thought...' he broke off, then smiled. 'Sorry, not my business.'*

3 If you **break off** something that you are doing, you stop doing it.

break off something or **break something off** ❑ *He would break off the rehearsal.* ❑ *They came over, breaking off their game reluctantly to say goodbye.*

4 If you **break off** a relationship or agreement, you end it.

break off something or **break something off** ❑ *Men seem to be more skilled at breaking off relationships than women.* ❑ *One day we may marry. Or we may break it off completely.*

NOTE **Terminate** is a more formal word for **break off**.

BREAK OFF + *noun*

break off **communication**
break off **contact**
break off **a dialogue**
break off **an engagement**
break off **ties**
break off **a relationship**

❑ *I broke off all contact with my family.* ❑ *We have broken off our ties with their organization.*

○ **break 'out**

1 If something unpleasant **breaks out**, it begins suddenly. ❑ *War broke out in Europe on 4 August.* ❑ *This row broke out on the eve of the Congress.* ❑ *A fire broke out on the third floor.*

● An **outbreak** of something unpleasant is a sudden occurrence of it. ❑ *There was a severe outbreak of food poisoning.* ❑ *Outbreaks of violence were reported.*

2 If a noise **breaks out**, it begins suddenly. ❑ *A clamour broke out at once.* ❑ *At this news, the smiles broaden, laughter breaks out.*

3 If someone **breaks out**, they escape from a place where they are a prisoner. = **escape** ❑ *He broke out one spring night in 1946 and travelled south.* ❑ [+ of] *It was hardly surprising that Neville decided to break out of jail.* ❑ [+ from] *They're going to break out from prison using guns.*

● A **break-out** is the act of escaping from a place. ❑ *We debated whether to make our break-out on Christmas Eve.*

4 If you **break out** of a routine, a habit, or a bad situation, you manage to change it and do something different. ❑ [+ of] *We've got to break out of this vicious circle.* ❑ *She has managed to break out of the mould and achieve something.*

5 If you **break out** in a rash or a sweat, or if it **breaks out** on your body, it suddenly

appears. ❑ [+ in] *She broke out in a rash.* ❑ *She felt the sweat break out on her forehead.*

● A **breakout** success or activity is one which suddenly makes someone very successful. ❑ *The series went on to become the breakout success of the new season.*

○ **break 'through**

1 If you **break through** a barrier, you force your way through it.

break through something ❑ *Some of the crowd attempted to break through police lines.* ❑ *A horse broke through the fence.*

2 If you **break through** a problem that prevents you from doing something, you find a way to deal with it or remove it.

break through something ❑ *She could not break through such a barrier of indifference.* ❑ *They gradually broke through her shyness.*

NOTE **Overcome** is a more formal word fo **break through**.

● A **breakthrough** is an important development or achievement. ❑ *Scientists are hovering on the brink of a major breakthrough.* ❑ *This is a breakthrough in government-industry relations.*

3 If a quality or aspect of something **break through**, it begins to appear or to be noticed. [LITERARY] ❑ *Sometimes the artistic impulses break through in your work.* ❑ *He is a young person, whose spirit is just breaking through*

4 If the sun **breaks through** or **breaks through** the clouds, it becomes visible afte being hidden by them.

break through ❑ *The ground will dry up quickly if the sun breaks through.*

break through something ❑ *As the sun broke through the clouds, I felt thoroughly happy.*

○ **break 'up**

1 When something **breaks up** or when yo **break** it **up**, it becomes divided into smalle parts.

break up ❑ *The great southern land-mass eventually began to break up.*

break up something ❑ *Most birds still need to break up their food.* ❑ *Here the paddy land is broken up like a jigsaw puzzle.*

break something up ❑ *I can break this bread u with my fingers.* ● The **break-up** of somethin is when it breaks or is broken into pieces. ❑ *He photographed the dramatic break-up of an oil tanker.*

2 If a group or organization **breaks up**, or i something **breaks** it **up**, the people in it separate from each other. = **split up**

break up ❑ [+ into] *His committee broke up into rival groups.*

break up something ❑ *There is nothing like*

sudden wealth for breaking up an ordinary family.
break something up ❑ *They are considering breaking the company up.* • When the **break-up** of a group, organization, or system occurs, it comes to an end. ❑ *We are on the brink of a break-up of the two-party system.*

3 If a relationship such as a marriage **breaks up** or if someone **breaks** it **up**, it ends. = **split up, finish**

break up ❑ *Their marriage is breaking up.*

break up something *or* **break something up** ❑ *Friends told me I was breaking up a happy marriage.* • If the **break-up** of a relationship occurs, it comes to an end. ❑ *All marriage break-ups are traumatic.*

4 If two people **break up**, their relationship ends. = **split up, finish** ❑ *Tim and I broke up.* ❑ [+ with] *Have you broken up with your boyfriend?*

5 If a gathering of people **breaks up** or if you **break** it **up**, it is brought to an end.

break up ❑ *The long drunken party had just broken up.* ❑ *The crowd broke up in panic.*

break something up *or* **break up something** ❑ *The rest of us were trying to break the fight up.* ❑ *Police tried to break up their meetings.*

6 If an event or activity **breaks up** your day, it helps to make your day less boring, because it is different from what you do the rest of the time.

break up something *or* **break something up** ❑ *Meals and drinks break up the hospital day.* ❑ *These games could be used to break up the monotony.*

7 If you **break up** something that is all one colour or pattern, you add new colours or patterns to make it more interesting.

break up something ❑ *Use lots of headings to break up the page and make it look attractive.*

8 When schools or schoolchildren **break up**, the school term ends and the children start their holidays. [BRITISH] ❑ *We're lucky, we break up quite early.*

9 If someone **is breaking up** when you speak to them on a mobile telephone, you can only hear parts of what they are saying because the signal is interrupted.

be breaking up ❑ *The line's gone; I think you're breaking up.*

○ **'break with**

1 If you **break with** a friend or an organization, you end your relationship with them because of a disagreement. [FORMAL]

break with someone/something ❑ *In 1929 he broke with the Liberal Party over Lloyd George's policies.*

2 If you **break with** a custom or tradition, you reject it and do something different. [FORMAL]

break with something ❑ *We have broken with the past completely.* ❑ *He broke with tradition by making his first speech on a controversial subject.*

breathe /briːð/ (**breathes, breathing, breathed**)

◉ **breathe 'in**

1 When you **breathe in**, you take air into your lungs through your nose or mouth. ❑ *Breathe in slowly.*

[NOTE] **Inhale** is a more formal word for **breathe in**.

2 If you **breathe in** air or another substance, you take it into your lungs through your nose or mouth.

breathe in something *or* **breathe something in** ❑ *We lifted our heads to breathe in the fresh air.* ❑ *If you use a spray, don't breathe it in.*

◉ **breathe 'out**

1 When you **breathe out**, you make the air in your lungs come out through your nose or mouth. ❑ *She breathed out through parted lips.*

2 If you **breathe out** air or another substance, you make it come out of your lungs through your nose or mouth.

breathe out something *or* **breathe something out** ❑ *They breathed out smoke.* ❑ *She breathed the smoke out slowly and spoke reasonably calmly.*

[NOTE] **Exhale** is a more formal word for **breathe out**.

breeze /briːz/ (**breezes, breezing, breezed**)

○ **breeze 'in**

If someone **breezes in**, they enter a place in a happy and relaxed way. ❑ *She just breezed in, as if nothing had happened.*

○ **breeze 'into**

If someone **breezes into** a place, they enter it in a happy and relaxed way.

breeze into something ❑ *He breezed into the office at eleven o'clock, without a word of apology for being late.*

○ **breeze 'out**

If someone **breezes out**, they leave a place in a happy and relaxed way. ❑ [+ of] *She breezed out of the bathroom, whistling loudly.*

brew /bruː/ (**brews, brewing, brewed**)

○ **brew 'up**

1 If you **brew up** or **brew up** something, you make a cup or pot of tea. [BRITISH, INFORMAL]

brew up ❑ *I'll be brewing up in a moment.*

brew up something ❑ *They were brewing up their morning cup of tea.*

2 If a difficult or unpleasant situation **is brewing up**, it is starting to develop.
be brewing up ❑ *There's another security scandal brewing up.*
3 If a storm **is brewing up**, it is starting to develop.
be brewing up ❑ *It was obvious that a big storm was brewing up.*

brick /brɪk/ (bricks, bricking, bricked)

○ **brick 'in**

If you **brick** something **in**, you build a wall of bricks to enclose it or to fill it.
brick something in or **brick in something**
❑ *They decided to brick the old fireplace in.*
❑ *Someone had bricked in the first-floor windows.*

○ **brick 'off**

If you **brick off** an area, you build a wall of bricks that separates this area from another.
brick off something or **brick something off**
❑ *The lift was long dead, and the shaft bricked off.*

○ **brick 'up**

If you **brick up** a hole or space, you build a wall of bricks to enclose it or to fill it.
brick something up or **brick up something**
❑ *To stop burglars you'd have to brick the windows up.* ❑ *Two of us bricked up the window.*

brighten /'braɪtən/ (brightens, brightening, brightened)

⊙ **brighten 'up**

1 If someone **brightens up**, they suddenly look or feel much happier. ❑ *She seemed to brighten up a bit at this news.*
NOTE **Perk up** is a more informal expression for **brighten up**.
2 If you **brighten** a place **up**, you make it more colourful and attractive.
brighten up something or **brighten something up** ❑ *These flowers will brighten up your garden.* ❑ *The apartment's a bit grim, but I can brighten it up.*
3 Someone or something that **brightens up** a situation makes it more pleasant and enjoyable. = **liven up**
brighten up something or **brighten something up** ❑ *She brightened up the rather gloomy atmosphere.* ❑ *The music brightened things up a little.*
4 If the weather **brightens up**, it becomes more sunny. ❑ *It should brighten up in the afternoon.*

brim /brɪm/ (brims, brimming, brimmed)

○ **brim 'over**

1 If a container or the liquid in it **brims over**, the liquid spills out. = **overflow**
❑ *He poured wine into Daniel's glass until it brimmed over onto the tablecloth.*

2 If someone **is brimming over** with a strong emotion, they are feeling it very strongly.
be brimming over ❑ [+ with] *His parents were brimming over with joy and pride.* ❑ *The team are enjoying their success and brimming over with excitement for the next match.*
3 If someone **is brimming over** with thoughts, ideas or questions, they have a lot of them and are excited about them.
be brimming over ❑ [+ with] *I was brimming over with questions.* ❑ *He's brimming over with ideas for new products.*

○ **'brim with**

1 If someone or something **is brimming with** a particular quality, they are full of that quality.
be brimming with something ❑ *England are brimming with confidence after two straight wins in the tournament.*
2 When your eyes **are brimming with** tears, they are full of fluid because you are upset, although you are not actually crying.
be brimming with something ❑ *Michael looked at him, eyes brimming with tears.*
3 If something **is brimming with** particular things, it is full of them.
be brimming with something ❑ *The flowerbeds were brimming with a mixture of lilies and roses.*

bring /brɪŋ/ (brings, bringing, brought)

⊙ **bring a'bout**

To **bring about** something means to cause it to happen.
bring about something ❑ *The Administration helped bring about a peaceful settlement.*
❑ *This damage to wildlife was brought about by intensive farming.*
bring something about ❑ *Naturally, one wonders what may have taken place to bring the separation about.*

BRING ABOUT + noun
bring about **a change**
bring about **an improvement**
bring about **peace**
bring about **reform**
❑ *New medication brought about a great improvement in her condition.* ❑ *Having children brings about huge changes for any couple.*

○ **'bring against**

If you **bring** a legal action **against** someone you start a legal case against them.
bring something against someone ❑ *He campaigned to bring charges of corruption against former members of the government.*

bring a'long

If you **bring** someone or something **along**, you bring them with you when you come to a place.

bring someone/something along ❏ *Bring your friends along.*

bring along someone/something ❏ *He brought along several examples of his work.*

bring 'back

1 If something **brings back** an event or memory from your past, it makes you think about it.

bring back something ❏ *The death of a friend can bring back memories of childhood loss.*

bring something back ❏ *These photos brings it all back.* ❏ *Seeing the place again would bring all the horrors back to me.*

2 When people **bring back** something that existed in an earlier time, they introduce it again.

bring back something or **bring something back** ❏ *He believes his old club needs more experience to bring back the good times.* ❏ *He promised he would bring honesty back to politics.*

NOTE **Revive** is a more formal word for **bring back**.

bring 'down

1 If people or events **bring down** a government or ruler, they cause them to lose their power. **= topple**

bring down someone/something
❏ *Unofficial strikes had brought down the regime.*

bring someone/something down ❏ *A national strike would bring the government down.*

2 To **bring down** the level of something means to reduce it.

bring down something or **bring something down** ❏ *The promised measures included steps to bring down prices.* ❏ *They want to bring population growth down further.*

> **BRING DOWN + noun**
>
> bring down **inflation**
> bring down **the cost of** something
> bring down **the level of** something
> ❏ *Control of the money supply was necessary to bring down inflation.* ❏ *These new measures will bring down the level of violence in the area.*

3 To **bring down** someone or something with a gun means to shoot them so that they fall to the ground.

bring down something/someone or **bring someone/something down** ❏ *A rifleman actually managed to bring down an enemy airplane.* ❏ *He was going to open fire from the ground and bring him down.*

4 If someone **brings** a person **down**, they make them fall, or pull them to the ground.

bring down someone or **bring someone down** ❏ *Clough scored a penalty when Sealy brought down Hodge.* ❏ *He brought the girl down rather heavily with a kind of rugby tackle.*

5 If someone or something **brings** you **down**, they make you feel unhappy or disappointed. **= get down**

bring someone down ❏ *A setback like this really brings you down with a thump.* ❏ *Whatever he said seemed to bring Sally down.*

bring 'forth [FORMAL]

To **bring forth** something means to cause it to exist or happen. **= result in**

bring forth something ❏ *His comment brought forth a gasp of horror.* ❏ *In time, this policy will bring forth new results.*

bring 'forward

1 If you **bring forward** a meeting or an event, you arrange for it to be at an earlier time or date than was planned. **≠ put back**

bring something forward ❏ *Ask him to bring the meeting forward to eight o'clock.*

bring forward something ❏ *The match would have to be brought forward.*

2 If you **bring forward** an argument or proposal, you state it so that people can consider it and discuss it. **= put forward**

bring forward something or **bring something forward** ❏ *He brought forward some very good arguments.* ❏ *The Government had invited us to bring forward proposals for the expansion of the airport.* ❏ *McGuinty said he intends to bring the idea forward for further discussion.*

3 In accounting, if a total financial value **is brought forward**, it is taken from the end of one financial period and put into the start of the next financial period. **= carry over** [TECHNICAL]

be brought forward ❏ *Profit was severely reduced owing to loss brought forward.*

bring 'in

1 When a government or other organization **brings in** a new law, rule, or system, they introduce it.

bring in something ❏ *We intend to bring in legislation to control their activities.* ❏ *The firm has just brought in a three-shift system.*

bring something in ❏ *Some people think that the government should bring laws in to restrict the sale of unhealthy food.* ❏ *Large companies will bring it in first.*

2 Someone or something that **brings in** money makes or earns it.

bring in something or **bring something in** ❏ *Tourism is a big industry, bringing in £7 billion a year.* ❏ *We will have to consider how we can bring funds in.*

3 If you **bring** someone **in**, you ask them to take part in an activity. = **call in**

bring someone in or **bring in someone** ❑ Why did they wait so long before bringing Patton in to defuse the situation? ❑ Police had to be brought in to protect him. ❑ It would be dangerous to bring in an outsider.

BRING IN + noun

bring in **a consultant**
bring in **expertise**
bring in **an outsider**
bring in **reinforcements**
❑ Police brought in heavy reinforcements and tried to move the protesters away. ❑ They have brought in a consultant to carry out an inspection.

---

4 If you **bring in** a particular point or subject, you include it or mention it.

bring in something or **bring something in** ❑ Try to bring in the moral points as well. ❑ The English always start bringing in Shakespeare! ❑ Why do you have to bring that in?

○ **bring 'into**

1 If you **bring** someone **into** an event or group, you ask them to take part in it or be part of it.

bring someone into something ❑ Greece has got to be brought into the talks. ❑ He planned to bring Northcliffe into the government.

2 If you **bring** a subject **into** a discussion or situation, you introduce it or start talking about it.

bring something into something ❑ A second major function of election campaigns is to bring issues into the political arena. ❑ They always bring money into it.

○ **bring 'off** [INFORMAL]

If someone **brings off** something difficult, they do it successfully. = **pull off**

bring off something or **bring something off** ❑ He's aiming for a peace deal. But can he bring it off?

○ **bring 'on**

1 Something that **brings on** an illness or pain causes it to occur.

bring on something or **bring something on** ❑ The cold weather will bring on his cough again. ❑ The hot weather had brought her headache on the day before.

2 To **bring on** someone means to improve their ability to do something.

bring on someone or **bring someone on** ❑ I want to learn to be a coach so that I can help to bring on young footballers. ❑ I think the run this weekend will bring her on no end.

3 If you **bring** a difficult or unpleasant situation **on** someone, you cause them to experience it.

bring something on someone ❑ It was a difficult situation, but he brought it all on himself. ❑ He had brought shame on the family.

○ **bring 'out**

1 When a person or company **brings out** a new product, they produce it and sell it.

bring out something ❑ I've just brought out a book on Dostoevski.

bring something out ❑ Colin Bradbury has now brought a second album out.

2 Something that **brings out** a particular kind of quality or feeling in someone causes them to show it although they do not normally have it or show it.

bring out something or **bring something out** ❑ [+ in] These dreadful circumstances bring out the worst in absolutely everybody. ❑ The situation seemed to bring his aggressive side out.

3 If someone **brings out** a quality or feature of something, they make people aware of it.

bring out something or **bring something out** ❑ The effect is to bring out all sorts of things in the poetry. ❑ Kotler brings this view out clearly in his lectures.

4 To **bring** someone **out** means to encourage them to be less shy or quiet.

bring someone out ❑ He talks to them and brings them out. ❑ Acting really brought him out, and it's done him the world of good.

5 If someone **brings out** some words, they say them with difficulty or with an effort.

bring out something ❑ They even brought out a few English words. ❑ 'It's so typical,' Etta at last brought out.

○ **bring 'out in**

If something **brings** you **out in** a rash or in spots, it causes you to have them on your skin.

bring someone out in something ❑ Spicy food brings me out in a rash.

○ **bring 'over**

If you **bring** someone or something **over**, you take them with you from one place, house, or country to another.

bring over something/someone ❑ She picked up a big white china mug which she brought over to us very carefully. ❑ They shot at aircraft bringing over military personnel.

bring something/someone over ❑ [+ from] She brought her children over from Pakistan.

○ **bring 'round**

1 If someone is unconscious and you **bring** them **round**, you make them conscious again. = **bring to**

bring someone round ❑ Nobody was making any attempt to bring her round.

2 If someone disagrees with you or is angry

with you and you **bring** them **round**, you cause them to agree with you or stop being angry with you. = **win over**

bring someone round ❑ *We suggested a fox hunt; nothing was so sure to bring Alethea round.* ❑ [+ to] *We tried to bring him round to our point of view.*

○ **bring 'to**

If someone is unconscious and you **bring** them **to**, you make them conscious again. = **bring round**

bring someone to ❑ *She was eventually brought to after several minutes of unconsciousness.*

○ **bring to'gether**

1 If you **bring** people or things **together**, you cause them to be in the same place.

bring together someone/something or **bring someone/something together** ❑ *The festival has also brought together artists from diverse parts of the country.* ❑ *These groups help to bring people together at similar stages of their development.* ❑ *It is probably the last time these works will be brought together, because travelling is not good for paintings.*

2 If you **bring together** people who have argued, you cause them to have contact with each other again.

bring together someone or **bring someone together** ❑ *My aim was to bring them together again.* ❑ *It is our duty to try to bring the two sides together.*

✪ **bring 'up**

1 If you **bring up** a child, you look after it until it is grown up and you try to give it particular beliefs and attitudes. = **raise**

bring up someone ❑ *I brought up two children alone.* ❑ *Tony was brought up strictly.*

bring someone up ❑ *His parents brought him up on socialist principles.* ● Your **upbringing** is the way your parents treat you and the things that they teach you to care about and believe in. ❑ *Tony never rebelled against his upbringing.* ❑ *She had a strict upbringing.*

2 If you **bring up** a particular subject, you start talking about it. = **raise**

bring something up ❑ *I advised her to bring the matter up at the next meeting.*

bring up something ❑ *I am sorry to bring up the subject of politics yet again.*

3 If you **bring** something **up** on a computer screen, you make it appear there.

bring up something or **bring something up** ❑ *Call centre staff can bring up your entire banking history.* ❑ [+ on] *When a customer comes in we can bring their account up on screen and deal with any queries.*

4 If you **bring up** food, you vomit. [INFORMAL]

bring up something or **bring something up** ❑ *I had some toast, but brought it up again soon after.*

NOTE **Throw up** is a more informal expression for **bring up**.

5 If a baby **brings up** wind, air is forced up from their stomach through their mouth.

bring up something or **bring something up** ❑ *It's hard for the baby to bring up wind.*

○ **bring 'up on**

1 If you **are brought up on** something, you have or experience a lot of it when you are a child.

be brought up on something ❑ *My wife was brought up on junk foods.*

2 If you **bring** a child **up on** a certain amount of money, you only have that amount of money to feed, clothe, and care for them.

bring someone up on something ❑ *We were poor and Mom had to bring us up on nothing.*

bristle /ˈbrɪsəl/ (**bristles, bristling, bristled**)

○ **'bristle at**

If you **bristle at** something, you are angry about it or offended by it.

bristle at something ❑ *Although he bristled at her tone, he did not refuse her request.*

○ **'bristle with**

1 Something that **bristles with** sharp, spiky things has a large number of them sticking out of it.

bristle with something ❑ *I saw a creature with a long nose, bristling with whiskers.* ❑ *The five command ships were bristling with radar and radio antennae.*

2 When a place or situation **bristles with** things, it seems to have a lot of them.

bristle with something ❑ *The hotel was bristling with police officers at every entrance.* ❑ *The pottery section bristled with exciting things.*

3 If you **bristle with** an emotion, you feel that emotion very strongly.

bristle with something ❑ *He was bristling with energy.*

broaden /ˈbrɔːdən/ (**broadens, broadening, broadened**)

○ **broaden 'out**

1 When a road or river **broadens out**, it becomes wider. ❑ *Aldgate High Street broadens out east to Whitechapel High Street.*

2 When something **broadens out** or when you **broaden** it **out**, it includes a larger number of things or people, or becomes more general.

broaden out ❑ *My knowledge was broadening out to include new ways of understanding the world.*

broaden out something or **broaden something out** ❑ I'd like to broaden the discussion out a bit.

brood /bruːd/ (**broods, brooding, brooded**)

○ **'brood on** (or **brood upon**)
If you **brood on** something that makes you feel sad or angry, you think about it a lot.
= **dwell on**
brood on something ❑ She had been brooding on the events of the past.

○ **'brood over**
If you **brood over** something that makes you feel sad or angry, you think about it a lot.
brood over something ❑ The more you sit and brood over your problems, the bigger they get.

○ **'brood upon** ➔ see **brood on**

brown /braʊn/ (**browns, browning, browned**)

○ **brown 'off** [BRITISH, INFORMAL, OLD-FASHIONED]
If you **are browned off**, you are bored or annoyed with something.
be browned off ❑ [+ with] He was a bit browned off with the job.

browse /braʊz/ (**browses, browsing, browsed**)

○ **'browse through**
If you **browse through** a book or magazine, you look through it without reading everything.
browse through something ❑ He was sitting on the sofa browsing through the TV pages of the paper.

brush /brʌʃ/ (**brushes, brushing, brushed**)

○ **'brush against**
If one person or thing **brushes against** another or if you **brush** one thing **against** another, the first thing or person touches the second thing or person lightly while passing it.
brush against something/someone ❑ Something brushed against her leg.
brush something against something ❑ She brushed her lips against his cheek and turned away to look at his office.

○ **brush a'side**
If you **brush aside** a remark or some information, you refuse to take any notice of it because it seems unimportant.
= **ignore, dismiss**
brush aside something or **brush something aside** ❑ Miss Crabbe continued, brushing aside my interruption. ❑ She brushed his protests aside, politely.

○ **brush a'way**
If you **brush** an idea or thought **away**, you ignore it because you do not want to think about it.
brush away something or **brush something away** ❑ She hurriedly brushed the thought away.
NOTE **Dismiss** is a more formal word for **brush away**.

○ **brush 'by**
If you **brush by** someone, you walk quickly past them, touching them slightly.
brush by someone ❑ I brushed by him, opened the door and stopped.

○ **brush 'down**
If you **brush down** something you are wearing, or if you **brush** yourself **down**, you remove dirt from your clothes with your hands.
brush down something or **brush something down** ❑ She crawled out and brushed down her skirt.
brush yourself down ❑ He was brushing himself down.

○ **brush 'off**
1 If you **brush** someone **off**, you avoid them or avoid speaking to them, because you want to end your relationship with them.
brush someone off ❑ He behaved as well as he could, buying her an expensive present, and then brushing her off in the nicest way possible.
❑ By brushing me off like this, she had probably done me a favour. ● If you give someone the **brushoff**, you show that you are not interested in them and do not want to spend time with them. [INFORMAL]
❑ She gave me the brushoff once too often.
2 If you **brush** someone **off**, you refuse to listen to them or answer them in a respectful way.
brush someone off ❑ He was not the sort of reporter to be brushed off like that.
NOTE **Rebuff** is a more formal word for **brush off**.
3 If you **brush off** a remark or some information, you refuse to take any notice of it because it seems unimportant.
= **brush aside**
brush off something or **brush something off** ❑ She brushed off Mike's concern about Tony's illness. ❑ He brushed the story off at a press conference.
NOTE **Dismiss** is a more formal word for **brush off**.

○ **brush 'off on**
If a quality or characteristic **brushes off on** someone, it influences the way they behave.
brush off on someone ❑ Some of their views had brushed off on me.

○ **brush 'out**

If you **brush out** your hair, or if you **brush out** the knots in it, you brush your hair very thoroughly to get rid of the knots.
brush out something *or* **brush something out** ❑ She was brushing out my tangled hair with sharp brush strokes. ❑ She spent ages brushing it out, washing it, drying it.

○ **brush 'past**

If you **brush past** someone, you walk quickly past them, touching them slightly.
brush past someone ❑ She laughed, and brushed past me out of the room.

○ **brush 'up**

If you **brush up** a subject you know or a skill you have, you improve your knowledge of it or ability in it.
brush up something *or* **brush something up** ❑ I would like to brush up my zoology. ❑ I need to brush my French up a bit.

○ **brush 'up on**

If you **brush up on** something, you improve it, or improve your knowledge of it.
brush up on something ❑ He was in New York, brushing up on his image as an expert in foreign affairs. ❑ The editor will have to brush up on baseball for the American edition.

bubble /ˈbʌbəl/ (**bubbles, bubbling, bubbled**)

○ **bubble 'over with**

If you **bubble over with** feelings or ideas, you are very excited about them and show it in your behaviour.
bubble over with something ❑ He was bubbling over with excitement. ❑ Mrs Finch was most enthusiastic and bubbled over with suggestions.

○ **bubble 'under**

If something **is bubbling under** or **bubbling under** a surface, it is continuing, but in a quiet way that not many people notice.
be bubbling under ❑ The confrontation has been bubbling under for nearly a year.
be bubbling under something ❑ I'm sure that talent is bubbling under the surface just waiting for a chance.

○ **bubble 'up**

If a liquid **bubbles up**, it rises up in the form of bubbles. ❑ Champagne bubbled up over the edge of the glass. ❑ The area has many thermal springs, bubbling up from the core of the earth.

buck /bʌk/ (**bucks, bucking, bucked**)

○ **'buck for** [AMERICAN, INFORMAL]

If you **are bucking for** something, you are working very hard to get it.
be bucking for something ❑ She is bucking for a promotion.

○ **buck 'up**

1 If someone **bucks up** or if you **buck** them **up**, they start to feel more cheerful. **= cheer up** [BRITISH, INFORMAL]
buck up ❑ She bucked up a bit once she started going out with Phillip. ❑ Come on, Charlie, buck up! It's not the end of the world, is it?
buck someone up *or* **buck up someone** ❑ J. B. Priestley bucked us all up in the war. ❑ The attempt to buck up Mrs. Halverston was hopeless.
2 If you tell someone to **buck up** or to **buck up** their ideas, you are telling them to start behaving in a more positive and efficient manner. **= pull your socks up** [INFORMAL]
buck up ❑ People are saying if we don't buck up we'll be in trouble.
buck up something *or* **buck something up** ❑ Buck up your ideas or you'll get more of the same treatment.
3 You tell someone to **buck up** when you want them to hurry. [INFORMAL, OLD-FASHIONED] ❑ Buck up, we haven't got all day!

bucket /ˈbʌkɪt/ (**buckets, bucketing, bucketed**)

○ **'bucket down** [BRITISH, INFORMAL]

If rain **is bucketing down**, it is falling very heavily. **= pelt down**
be bucketing down ❑ It really started bucketing down this afternoon.

buckle /ˈbʌkəl/ (**buckles, buckling, buckled**)

○ **buckle 'down**

If you **buckle down**, you start working seriously at something. **= knuckle down**
❑ [+ to] They buckled down to the task with relish. ❑ We buckled down and got on with our work.

○ **buckle 'in**

If you **buckle** someone **in**, you fasten them into a seat with a buckle (= metal fastener).
buckle someone in *or* **buckle in someone** ❑ You need a strap to buckle the baby in.

○ **buckle 'into**

If you **buckle** someone **into** a seat, you fasten them there with a buckle (= metal fastener). **= strap into**
buckle someone into something ❑ She was buckling herself into the seat of the plane.

○ **buckle 'on**

If you **buckle** something **on**, you attach it with buckles (= metal fasteners). **= put on**
buckle something on *or* **buckle on something** ❑ He buckled his seat belt on. ❑ He buckled on his revolver.

○ **buckle 'under**

If someone **buckles under**, they become defeated by a strong person or a difficult situation. ❑ [+ to] I admired their unwillingness to buckle under to authority. ❑ He said the army will not buckle under, whatever pressure.

○ **buckle 'up** [INFORMAL]
When you **buckle up** in a vehicle, you fasten your seat belt. ❑ A sign just ahead of me said, Buckle Up. It's the Law.

buddy /ˈbʌdi/ (buddies, buddying, buddied)
○ **buddy 'up** [INFORMAL]
If two people **buddy up**, they become friends. ❑ [+ with] Usually these people are the quickest ones to buddy up with new mates.

budge /bʌdʒ/ (budges, budging, budged)
○ **budge 'up** [INFORMAL]
If you **budge up**, you move along a seat in order to make space for someone else to sit down. ❑ Budge up, will you.

budget /ˈbʌdʒɪt/ (budgets, budgeting, budgeted)
○ **'budget for**
If you **budget for** something, you plan so that you will have enough money for it. ❑ The Chancellor budgeted for an unemployment rate of 8.5 per cent. ❑ These expenses can all be budgeted for.

buff /bʌf/ (buffs, buffing, buffed)
○ **buff 'up** [INFORMAL]
If you **buff up**, you do a lot of exercise so that your body becomes an attractive shape. ❑ The actor has buffed up very nicely after spending hours in the gym for his new role.

bug /bʌg/ (bugs, bugging, bugged)
○ **bug 'off** [AMERICAN, INFORMAL]
If you tell someone to **bug off**, you are telling them rudely to go away. ❑ He turned his back as a way of telling them to bug off.

○ **bug 'out**
■ If someone or something **bugs** you **out**, they annoy you. [AMERICAN, INFORMAL]
bug someone out ❑ I just couldn't find my stuff and it was bugging me out.
■ If someone **bugs out**, they leave a place quickly. [AMERICAN, INFORMAL] ❑ [+ of] It appears we're going to bug out of here and not leave anything. ● A **bug-out** is when someone leaves a place quickly. [AMERICAN, INFORMAL] ❑ The purpose of the demonstration was to force a unilateral bug-out of American troops.
■ If someone's eyes **bug out**, they suddenly open very wide, for example because the person is surprised, hurt, or interested. [INFORMAL] ❑ The trucker's eyes bugged out and he staggered backward. ❑ Their eyes just bug out when they see our website.

bugger /ˈbʌgə/ (buggers, buggering, buggered)

> **Bugger** is a rather rude word used in spoken British English.

○ **bugger a'round** (or **bugger about**) [INFORMAL]
■ If you **bugger around**, you waste time doing unnecessary things. ❑ What the hell do you mean by buggering about like this? ❑ It's no use buggering around with a calculator while you're solving a simultaneous equation.
■ If you **bugger** someone **around**, you treat them badly by not being honest with them, or by continually changing plans which affect them. = **mess around**
bugger someone around ❑ They are doing their best, despite being buggered around by management

○ **bugger 'off** [INFORMAL]
■ If someone **buggers off**, they go away quickly or suddenly. ❑ His wife just buggered off.
■ If you tell someone to **bugger off**, you are telling them rudely to go away. ❑ Oh, bugger off and leave me in peace.

○ **bugger 'up** [INFORMAL]
If you **bugger** something **up**, you spoil it or do it badly.
bugger up something or **bugger something up** ❑ If you bugger things up at this stage, I'll kill you. ❑ She'd been buggering up his life for years.

build /bɪld/ (builds, building, built)
⊕ **build 'in**
■ If you **build in** something, you deliberately make it part of a plan, system or total amount.
build in something ❑ This will enable the designers to build in a further piece of information. ❑ The government has built in a five per cent increase in tax.
[NOTE] **Incorporate** is a formal word for **build in**.
● An **inbuilt** quality is one that a person or thing has from the time they were born or produced. ❑ The child has got an inbuilt feeling of inferiority. ❑ This kind of thinking has inbuilt limitations.
■ If something **is built in**, it is made in such a way that it fits into a structure or is made as part of that structure.
be built in ❑ All the kitchen cupboards have been built in, of course. ● **Built-in** furniture is made in such a way that it is part of a wall and cannot be moved around. = **fitted** ❑ The room has a built-in wardrobe. ● **Built-in** devices or features are part of the structure of an object. ❑ These missiles are equipped with built-in homing devices.

○ build 'into

1 If you **build** something **into** a structure or object, you make it so that it fits in to it or becomes a part of it.

build something into something ❏ There was a cupboard built into the whitewashed wall.

2 If you **build** something **into** a plan, system or total amount, you make it a part of it. ❏ They tried to build authoritarian principles into the draft manifesto. ❏ There are many inequalities built into our system of financing.

❍ 'build on (or build upon)

1 If an activity, organization, system or belief **is built on** something, it is developed from that thing. **= base on**

be built on something ❏ Marriages are supposed to be built on trust. ❏ This is an outlook built on illusion rather than reality.

2 If you **build on** the success of something, you take advantage of it to make further progress.

build on something ❏ We must try to build on the success of these industries. ❏ They are building on existing skills and traditions.

❍ build 'up

1 If something **builds up** or if you **build** it **up**, it gradually increases in amount, size, or strength.

build up ❏ Mud builds up in the lake. ❏ Stress builds up until we feel like screaming.

build up something or **build something up** ❏ We helped to build up the wealth of this country. ❏ We're trying to build up a collection of herbs and spices.

NOTE **Accumulate** is a more formal word for **build up**.

● A **build-up** is a gradual increase in something. ❏ Over the island the build-up of clouds continued. ❏ That decade saw a massive build-up of nuclear weapons.

2 If people **build up** an organization, society, or system, they develop it or improve it.

build up something or **build something up** ❏ Japan successfully built up a modern capitalist economy. ❏ His organizational knowledge and personal reputation has built the business up.

3 If you **build up** someone's trust or confidence, you gradually make them more trusting or more confident.

build up something or **build something up** ❏ Being a cop means building up trust with the people on the streets.

4 If you **build up** someone or something, you tell people that they are very special or important.

build up someone/something or **build someone/something up** ❏ I've built up

Mr Reston's reputation. ❏ He does not need to build me up. ● A **build-up** is when you tell people that a person or thing is very special or important. ❏ She was getting a fair amount of publicity build-up.

5 If you **build** someone **up** after they have been ill, you help them put on weight and get stronger.

build someone up or **build up someone** ❏ The patient needs building up. ❏ We must build him up before he can go home.

6 When an area near a city or town **is built up**, a lot of houses are built there.

be built up ❏ It has been like this since the area was built up several years ago. ❏ The park and riverside are all now built up. ● A **built-up** area is a part of a city or town where there are many buildings. ❏ We visited the built-up area on the fringes of the city.

○ 'build upon → see build on

○ build 'up to

If you **build up to** something you want to do or say, you prepare for it gradually or prepare other people for it gradually.

build up to something ❏ Other actions we need to take may be more difficult, and we may have to build up to them gradually. ❏ The film is rather slow-paced, but it does build up to a shocking ending.

bulge /bʌldʒ/ (bulges, bulging, bulged)

○ 'bulge with

If you say that something **is bulging with** things, you are emphasizing that it is full of them.

be bulging with something ❏ They returned home with the car bulging with boxes.

bulk /bʌlk/ (bulks, bulking, bulked)

○ bulk 'up (or bulk out)

1 If someone **bulks up**, they put on weight, especially by developing large muscles. ❏ He bulked up for the part so he'd look convincing as a prison guard. ❏ I was on a weights programme to bulk out.

2 If you **bulk** something **up**, you make it bigger or heavier.

bulk up something or **bulk something up** ❏ They bulk the chicken up with water and other additives. ❏ His book shows signs of being a magazine article bulked out to book length at great speed.

bulldoze /ˈbʊldəʊz/ (bulldozes, bulldozing, bulldozed)

○ bulldoze 'into

If someone **bulldozes** you **into** doing something, they make you do it in an unpleasantly forceful way.

bulldoze someone into something ❑ *My parents tried to bulldoze me into going to college.*

○ **bulldoze 'through**
If someone **bulldozes** a plan **through**, they make sure it is agreed to in an unpleasantly forceful way.
bulldoze something through or **bulldoze through something** ❑ *Developers bulldoze their plans through despite opposition.* ❑ *The party in power planned to bulldoze through a full socialist programme.*

bully /'bʊli/ (**bullies, bullying, bullied**)
○ **bully 'into**
If someone **bullies** you **into** something, they make you do it by using force or threats.
bully someone into something ❑ *She used to bully me into doing my schoolwork.*

bum /bʌm/ (**bums, bumming, bummed**)
○ **bum a'round** (or **bum about, bum round** [mainly BRITISH]) [INFORMAL]
1 If you **bum around** a place, you travel there for pleasure and with very little money.
bum around somewhere ❑ *I just bummed around northern Europe for a few months.*
2 If you **bum around**, you live in a very lazy way, doing very little. ❑ *Are you going to bum around all summer?*

○ **bum 'out** [AMERICAN, INFORMAL]
If something **bums** you **out**, it makes you feel sad or angry.
bum someone out ❑ *He broke up with me over the phone, and it totally bummed me out.* ● If you are **bummed-out**, you feel sad or angry. [AMERICAN, INFORMAL] ❑ *He was probably pretty bummed-out by getting fired.*

○ **bum 'round** → see **bum around**

bumble /'bʌmbəl/ (**bumbles, bumbling, bumbled**)
○ **bumble a'round** (or **bumble about** [mainly BRITISH])
When someone **bumbles around**, they behave in a confused way, usually not achieving anything. ❑ *There were armies of tourists bumbling around.* ❑ *He spends most of his time bumbling about in the garden.*

bump /bʌmp/ (**bumps, bumping, bumped**)
⊙ **bump 'into**
If you **bump into** someone you know, you meet them by chance. = **run into**
bump into someone ❑ *I bumped into Mary an hour ago.* ❑ *I probably won't see him any more unless I bump into him on the street.*

○ **bump 'off** [INFORMAL]
To **bump** someone **off** means to kill them.
bump off someone or **bump someone off** ❑ *In his imagination, he bumps off his wife half a dozen times.*
NOTE **Murder** is a more formal word for **bump off**.

○ **'bump over**
If a vehicle **bumps over** a surface, it travels in a rough, bouncing way because the surface is very uneven.
bump over something ❑ *We left the road, and again bumped over the mountainside.*

○ **bump 'up** [INFORMAL]
To **bump** something **up** means to increase it suddenly by a large amount.
bump up something or **bump something up** ❑ *She was going to charge £140, but the extra work bumped up the price to £200.* ❑ *If my friends come, that might bump it up to £200 or more.*

○ **bump 'up against**
1 If you **bump up against** something, you experience something that causes difficulties for you.
bump up against something ❑ *Bumping up against a lack of support in your family can motivate you to build a stronger support system elsewhere.* ❑ *The demands of security often bump up against issues of personal liberty.*
2 If you **bump up against** someone, you meet them and get to know them by chance.
bump up against someone ❑ *He rarely bumped up against anyone who approved of what he was doing.* ❑ *We bumped up against some miners in a pub.*

bunch /bʌntʃ/ (**bunches, bunching, bunched**)
○ **'bunch around**
If clothing **bunches around** a part of your body, it becomes squashed together around it.
bunch around something ❑ *She clutched the sides of her skirt until it bunched around her waist.*

○ **bunch 'up**
If a piece of cloth **bunches up** or if it **is bunched up**, it is squashed into a tight bundle.
bunch up ❑ *The pocket linings are sewn into the seam so they won't bunch up and look bulky.*
be bunched up ❑ *His suit was bunched up over his shoulders.*

○ **bunch 'up** (or **bunch together**)
If people or things **bunch up**, or if you **bunch** them **up**, they move close to each other so that they form a small tight group.
bunch up ❑ *They were bunching up, almost treading upon each other's heels.*

bunch something up or **bunch up something**
❑ People were bunched up at all the exits. ❑ If they need to bunch aircraft more closely together to bring in one that is short of fuel, they will do so.

bundle /ˈbʌndəl/ (bundles, bundling, bundled)

○ **bundle 'off**
If you **bundle** someone **off** somewhere, you send them there in a hurry. = **pack off**
bundle someone off or **bundle off someone**
❑ [+ to] My father bundled me off to school. ❑ They made sure she was not bundled off too roughly.

○ **bundle to'gether**
1 If someone **bundles** people or things **together**, they think about them and treat them in the same way.
bundle someone/something together or **bundle together someone/something**
❑ It's hard to imagine what 18 to 49-year-olds have in common, yet they are bundled together by advertisers. ❑ Trade negotiations seem to work best when a range of issues can be bundled together.
2 If companies **bundle together** more than one product or service, they sell them together as one package.
bundle together something or **bundle something together** ❑ Competitive advantage will result from bundling together several services with the product.

○ **bundle 'up**
If you **bundle up** or **bundle** someone **up**, you dress yourself or that person in a lot of warm clothes. = **wrap up**
bundle up ❑ We bundled up warmly against the cold.
bundle someone up or **bundle up someone**
❑ She bundled them up and walked them down to the railway station. ❑ They were bundled up in woollen clothing.

○ **bundle 'up** (or **bundle together**)
If you **bundle** a mass of things **up**, you gather them together and tie or wrap them up.
bundle up something or **bundle something up** ❑ My mother bundled up all my comics and threw them out. ❑ All the parachute bags had been roughly bundled together into an untidy mass. ❑ Residents should bundle paper and cardboard up so it takes up the least room possible.

bung /bʌŋ/ (bungs, bunging, bunged)

○ **bung 'up** [INFORMAL]
If you **bung up** a hole, you fill it or block it.
bung something up or **bung up something**
❑ Don't put coffee grounds down the sink – they bung it up.
NOTE **Block up** is a more formal expression for **bung up**.

bunk /bʌŋk/ (bunks, bunking, bunked)

○ **bunk 'off** [BRITISH, INFORMAL]
If you **bunk off** or **bunk off** school or work, you leave without permission and do something else.
bunk off ❑ We could always bunk off early.
bunk off something ❑ We thought nothing of bunking off school and travelling 100 miles to find this or that record.
NOTE **Play truant** is a more formal expression for **bunk off**.

buoy /bɔɪ, AM ˈbuːi/ (buoys, buoying, buoyed)

○ **buoy 'up**
1 If you **buoy** someone **up**, you make them feel cheerful and excited.
buoy someone up or **buoy up someone**
❑ He did his best to buoy her up.
be buoyed up ❑ He was buoyed up by the prospect of coming home.
2 If you **buoy** something **up**, you stop it from sinking.
buoy up something or **buoy something up**
❑ The float needs to be fairly big so that it buoys up the 1/2 oz of lead necessary to sink the bait.
3 If something **buoys** something **up**, it supports it and helps it to survive.
buoy up something or **buoy something up**
❑ The newspapers are buoyed up with advertising. ❑ This may help to buoy up the family's motive for saving.

burden /ˈbɜːdən/ (burdens, burdening, burdened)

○ **'burden with**
If someone **burdens** you **with** something difficult or unpleasant, they cause you to have it, and if you **are burdened with** it, you have it.
burden someone with something ❑ We decided not to burden him with the news.
be burdened with something ❑ She was burdened with a deep sense of guilt. ❑ I soon found myself burdened with financial demands I could not afford.

burn /bɜːn/ (burns, burning, burned/burnt)

○ **burn a'way**
If something **burns away**, or if you **burn** it **away**, it burns until it disappears completely.
burn away ❑ My face was black and my eyebrows had burned away.
burn away something or **burn something away** ❑ We were trying to burn away the net.

○ **burn 'down**
If a building **burns down** or if someone **burns** it **down**, it is completely destroyed by fire.

burn down ❑ *The mansion burned down four years ago.*

burn down something ❑ *Lightning struck and burned down a wing of the cathedral.* ❑ *His school had been burned down in the riots.*

burn something down ❑ *He could have burned the place down.*

○ **burn 'off**

1 If someone **burns off** energy, they use it by doing physical activity.

burn off something or **burn something off** ❑ *This will improve your performance and help you burn off calories.*

2 If you **burn** something **off**, you remove it by burning it.

burn off something or **burn something off** ❑ *Prepare the surface by burning the flaking paint off beforehand.*

○ **burn 'out**

1 If a fire **burns out** or **burns** itself **out**, it stops burning because there is nothing left to burn.

burn out ❑ *We let the fire burn out.*

burn itself out ❑ *All the fires had now burned themselves out.* ● A **burnt-out** or **burned-out** vehicle or building has been very badly damaged by fire. = **gutted** ❑ *They barricaded the streets with burnt-out cars.*

2 If a piece of machinery **burns out** or if you **burn** it **out**, it stops working because it has been used too much or too roughly.

burn out ❑ *The bulbs in the light fittings had burnt out and never been replaced.*

burn out something or **burn something out** ❑ *He's going to burn out the pistons for sure.*

3 If you **burn** yourself **out** or **burn out**, you become exhausted or ill by working too hard. [INFORMAL]

burn out ❑ *She knew that if he continued to work at the same pace, he would burn out sooner rather than later.*

burn yourself out ❑ *I don't want you to burn yourself out.* ● Someone who is **burnt-out** or **burned-out** is unable to do things because they have no physical or mental energy left. [INFORMAL] ❑ *He was an old burnt-out actor.* ❑ *I was burnt-out emotionally.* ● **Burn-out** is the state of being exhausted or ill because of working too hard. ❑ *The burn-out rate in the job was high.*

○ **burn 'up**

1 If something **burns up** or if someone or something **burns** it **up**, it is completely destroyed by fire or strong heat.

burn up ❑ *The satellite had burned up on re-entering the atmosphere.*

burn up something or **burn something up** ❑ *Most of the material is burned up or falls as dust.*

2 If something **burns** you **up**, it makes you feel angry and upset. [AMERICAN, INFORMAL]

burn someone up or **burn up someone** ❑ *His attitude just burns me up.* ❑ *The girls seemed to be burned up about something.*

○ **'burn with**

If you **are burning with** an emotion, you feel that emotion very strongly.

be burning with something ❑ *The young boy was burning with a fierce ambition.*

burst /bɜːst/ (**bursts, bursting, burst**)

○ **burst 'in on**

If you **burst in on** someone, you suddenly enter the room that they are in.

burst in on someone ❑ *He suddenly burst in on me.*

⊙ **burst 'into**

1 If you **burst into** tears, laughter, or song, you suddenly begin to cry, laugh, or sing.

burst into something ❑ *I keep bursting into tears.* ❑ *Uncle Tony burst into song.* ❑ *The delegates burst into loud applause.*

2 If something **bursts into flames**, it suddenly starts to burn. ❑ *The plane burst into flames.*

3 If something **bursts into** a particular situation or state, it suddenly changes into that situation or state.

burst into something ❑ *This weekend's fighting is threatening to burst into full-scale war.* ❑ *The engine burst into life.*

4 If you **burst into** a place, you enter it suddenly with a lot of energy or force.

burst into something ❑ *Gunmen burst into his home and opened fire.*

⊙ **burst 'out**

1 If you **burst out** laughing or crying, you suddenly begin laughing or crying, usually loudly.

burst out something ❑ *Oliver felt a sudden desire to burst out crying.* ❑ *To my amazement, he burst out laughing.* ● An **outburst** is a sudden and strong expression of emotion, or a sudden period of activity. ❑ *I apologize for my outburst just now.* ❑ *There was an outburst of student protests.*

2 You use **burst out** when you are reporting what someone said, to indicate that they said it suddenly and loudly.

❑ *Then he burst out, 'Get into the car, Phil, can't you*

3 If a situation or problem **bursts out**, it suddenly appears. = **break out** ❑ *Malaria is bursting out again all over the world.* ❑ *Then war burst out.*

4 If you **burst out**, you leave a place suddenly with a lot of energy or force. ❑ *Rachel burst out as the door was flung open again.* ❑ [+ of] *They burst out of the room, singing and waving.*

○ **'burst with**
If you or your heart **bursts with** an emotion, you feel that emotion very strongly.
be bursting with something ❑ *I could tell that Richard was bursting with pride and excitement at the idea.*
burst with something ❑ *He almost burst with pride when his son John began to excel at football.* ❑ *He thought his heart would burst with grief.*

bury /'beri/ (buries, burying, buried)
○ **bury a'way**
If something or someone **is buried away** somewhere, they are in a place where it is difficult to find or reach them.
be buried away ❑ *I spent my childhood buried away in the countryside.*

○ **'bury in**
1 If you **bury** yourself **in** something, you concentrate hard on it and spend a lot of time doing it.
bury yourself in something ❑ *He buried himself in his departmental responsibilities.*
[NOTE] **Immerse** is a more formal word for **bury in**.
2 If you **bury** your face or head **in** something, you cover your face with that thing.
bury something in something ❑ *Nicole buried her face in her hands.* ❑ *Their faces were buried in their evening newspapers.*

bust /bʌst/ (busts, busting, busted)

> The form **bust** is used in the present tense and can also be used as the past tense and past participle of the verb.

○ **bust 'out of** [INFORMAL]
If you **bust out of** a place, you escape from it using force.
bust out of something ❑ *He bust out of jail.*

○ **bust 'up**
1 If you **bust up** an event or meeting, you stop it from continuing by causing a disturbance or fight. [INFORMAL]
bust something up or **bust something up** ❑ *They could come and bust up the meeting like they did yesterday.*
[NOTE] **Break up** is a less informal expression for **bust up**.
2 If you **bust** something **up**, you break it. [INFORMAL]
bust something up or **bust something up** ❑ *They bought a new chair to replace the one they'd bust up.*
3 If you **bust up** with your boyfriend or girlfriend, you end your relationship. [INFORMAL] ❑ *[+ with] She's been staying here since she bust up with Toby.* ❑ *They bust up last year.*

● A **bust-up** is a serious argument or a fight. [INFORMAL] ❑ *There was a bust-up down at the pub last night.*

bustle /'bʌsəl/ (bustles, bustling, bustled)
○ **bustle a'round** (or **bustle about** [mainly BRITISH])
If you **bustle around** or **bustle around** a place, you move about in a busy way.
bustle around ❑ *She bustled about, humming to herself.* ❑ *She was bustling around preparing a snack.*
bustle around something ❑ *She bustled around the kitchen.*

○ **'bustle with**
A place that **is bustling with** people or activity is full of people who are very busy or lively.
be bustling with someone/something ❑ *The sidewalks are bustling with people.*

butt /bʌt/ (butts, butting, butted)
○ **butt 'in**
If you **butt in**, you rudely interrupt a conversation or activity. ❑ *[+ on] You can't just butt in on someone else's discussion.* ❑ *I was always butting in and saying the wrong thing.*

○ **butt 'out** [INFORMAL]
If you tell someone to **butt out**, you are telling them angrily and rudely to stop interfering. ❑ *Butt out before I throw you out.* ❑ *[+ of] She gives courses to future mothers-in-law on how to butt out of their children's marriages.*

butter /'bʌtə/ (butters, buttering, buttered)
○ **butter 'up** [BRITISH, INFORMAL]
If you **butter** someone **up**, you praise them or try to please them, to try to make them do something you want.
butter someone up or **butter up someone** ❑ *I'm buttering him up for a pay rise.* ❑ *If you want to butter up your friends, invite them to a traditional afternoon tea.*

button /'bʌtən/ (buttons, buttoning, buttoned)
○ **button 'up**
If you **button up** a piece of clothing, you fasten it by pushing its buttons through buttonholes. = **do up**
button up something or **button something up** ❑ *He began to gather his papers and button up his coat.* ❑ *She put her coat on and buttoned it up.*

buy /baɪ/ (buys, buying, bought)
○ **buy 'in**
If you **buy in** something, you buy large amounts of it, often for a future occasion.

buy in something or **buy something in**
❑ We bought in a few loaves of bread.

○ **buy 'into**

1 If you **buy into** a business or organization, you buy part of it, for example in order to gain some control over it.
buy into something ❑ He's been trying for years to buy into the printing industry.

2 If you **buy into** an idea, a belief, or a way of behaving, you start to believe it or act in that way.
buy into something ❑ Many men don't want to buy into this heavily competitive work culture.

○ **buy 'off**

If you **buy** someone **off**, you pay them money so that they do not act against you.
buy off someone or **buy someone off**
❑ The workers were bought off by their employers.
❑ He thought he could buy them off.

○ **buy 'out**

If you **buy** someone **out**, you buy their share of a property or business that you previously owned together.
buy out someone or **buy someone out**
❑ He sold off the shops to buy out his partner.
❑ We bought him out. ● A **buyout** occurs when a group of people join together to buy the company that they previously worked for. ❑ Nobody has talked to us about a management buyout.

○ **buy 'up**

If someone **buys** something **up**, they buy large quantities of it, or all that is available.
buy up something ❑ They were trying to buy up every acre in sight.
buy something up ❑ My uncle Jack could buy this place up, no trouble.

buzz /bʌz/ (**buzzes, buzzing, buzzed**)

○ **buzz a'round** (or **buzz about, buzz round** [mainly BRITISH])

1 If something **buzzes around** or **buzzes around** something, it moves along making a buzzing sound.
buzz around ❑ It was one of those light planes

I had seen buzzing around all day.
buzz around something ❑ There was a wasp buzzing about her ear.

2 If someone **buzzes around** or **buzzes around** a place, they move around very quickly and busily.
buzz around ❑ The rickshaw drivers buzz around.
buzz around something ❑ He's always buzzing about the office.

3 If questions or ideas **are buzzing around** or **are buzzing around** your head, you are thinking about them, often in a confused way.
be buzzing around ❑ [+ in] Many more questions were buzzing around in my head.
be buzzing around something ❑ I couldn't find any answers to the dozen questions which were buzzing around my brain.

○ **buzz 'in**

1 If you **buzz** someone **in**, you push a button that makes a sound and lets someone into the building that you are in.
buzz someone in ❑ Unfortunately, security refused to buzz me in.

2 In a quiz, if someone **buzzes in**, they push a button that makes a sound to show that they want to answer a question.
buzz in ❑ A student buzzed in and gave the correct answer.

○ **buzz 'off** [BRITISH, INFORMAL]

If you tell someone to **buzz off**, you are telling them rudely to go away. ❑ 'Now buzz off,' shouted Mrs Coggs.

○ **buzz 'round** → see **buzz around**

○ **'buzz with**

If a place **is buzzing with** activity or conversation, there is a lot of activity or conversation there, especially because something important or exciting is happening.
be buzzing with something ❑ The rehearsal studio is buzzing with lunchtime activity.
❑ The capital is buzzing with rumours of possible demonstrations.

Cc

addie /'kædi/ (**caddies, caddying, caddied**)

'caddie for

If you **caddie for** a golfer, you carry their golf clubs and other equipment.
caddie for someone ❑ *Luckily, I have my dad to caddie for me.*

ajole /kə'dʒəʊl/ (**cajoles, cajoling, cajoled**)

cajole 'into

If you **cajole** someone **into** doing something, you gradually persuade them to do it, by being nice to them or by making promises.
cajole someone into doing something
❑ *It was Taylor who had cajoled Garland into doing the film.*

all /kɔːl/ (**calls, calling, called**)

'call after [BRITISH]

If you **call** someone or something **after** a person or thing, you give them the same name as that other person or thing.
= name after
call someone/something after someone/ something ❑ *Leonard was called after my grandfather.*

call a'way

If you **are called away**, you are asked to stop doing something in order to go somewhere else.
be called away ❑ *They were called away to another case.* ❑ *He's been called away on business.*

call 'back

1 If you **call back**, you go to see someone briefly for a second time. ❑ *I'll call back tomorrow and collect the shoes.* ❑ *Call back in half an hour.*

2 If you **call back**, you telephone someone for a second time. ❑ *I'll call back when you're not so busy.* ❑ *Pitts called back on Thursday, saying he hadn't been able to make the arrangements.*

3 If you **call** someone **back**, you telephone them again in return for a telephone call they have made to you. **= ring back**
call someone back ❑ *Can I call you back later?* ❑ *I'll make some enquiries and call you back.*

4 If you **call** someone **back** when they are walking away from you, you ask them to return.
call someone back ❑ *He started to walk off down the street, but Sylvia called him back.*

○ **call 'by**

1 If you **call by**, you visit a place for a short time, especially when you are going somewhere else afterwards. ❑ *I'll call by on my way to the bank.*

2 If you **call by** somewhere, you visit a place for a short time, especially when you are going somewhere else afterwards. [mainly AMERICAN]
call by somewhere ❑ *I'll call by the office on my way home.*

○ **call 'down on** [FORMAL]

If you **call** curses or vengeance (= bad wishes) **down on** someone, you pray that something unpleasant will happen to them.
call something down on someone ❑ *She called God's vengeance down on her husband.*

○ **'call for**

1 If you **call for** someone or something, you go to the building where they are to collect them.
call for someone/something ❑ *I'll call for you about eight.* ❑ *The parcel was kept at the Post Office until someone called for it.*

2 If you **call for** an action, you demand that it should be done.
call for something ❑ *Democrats are calling for a two-year tax cut.*

3 If something **calls for** a particular action or quality, it needs it in order to be successful. **= require**
call for something ❑ *This sort of work calls for very specific skills.* ❑ *Clearly, immediate action was called for.*

4 If something good that has happened **calls for** a celebration, it deserves it.
call for something ❑ *A wedding in the family! This calls for a celebration.*

5 You describe a remark or criticism as **uncalled-for** when you think that it was unkind or unfair. ❑ *That last remark was*

uncalled-for. ❑ *It was an uncalled-for outburst.*
6 If you **call** someone or something **for** a person or thing, you give them the same name as that other person or thing.
= **name for** [AMERICAN]
call someone/something for someone/something ❑ *I was called for my maternal grandmother.*

○ **call 'forth** [FORMAL]
If you **call forth** something, you make it exist. = **inspire**
call forth something or **call something forth** ❑ *He is not capable of calling forth much emotion in his readers.*

✪ **call 'in**
1 If you **call** someone **in**, you ask them to come somewhere to do something for you.
= **send for**
call in someone ❑ *Before you call in the engineer, check that the pipes are not frozen.* ❑ *The Army was called in to rescue 100 people from their cars.*
call someone in ❑ *They called me in for questioning.*
2 If you **call in**, you visit someone for a short time. ❑ *Lucy called in on her way home from school.* ❑ *I thought I'd call in for a chat as I was passing by.* ❑ [+ on] *I might call in on Karen and see how she's doing.*
3 If you **call in**, you telephone the place where you work, usually to say that you are not able to go there. ❑ *He called in this morning to say he was ill.*
• If you **call in sick**, you telephone the place where you work to say that you are ill and cannot come to work. ❑ *She called in sick this morning.*
4 If someone **calls in** something, they ask for it to be returned, for example because it might be dangerous or because it is needed.
call in something or **call something in**
❑ *This is the second time this year the company has had to call in some of its cars to check their brakes.* ❑ *The university called in all library books at the end of the year.*
NOTE **Recall** is a more formal word for **call in**.

✪ **call 'off**
1 If you **call off** an event or an arrangement that has been planned, you cancel it.
call something off ❑ *We planned the match for yesterday afternoon but had to call it off because of the weather.* ❑ *If you can't behave yourself, we might as well call the whole thing off.*
call off something ❑ *I can't call off the ceremony now.* ❑ *Classes will be called off on Thursday and Friday.*

CALL OFF + noun
call off **a search**
call off **a strike**
call off **a protest**
call off **a visit**
call off **a meeting**
call off **a wedding**
❑ *Union leaders have agreed to call off the strike.* ❑ *He has called off his visit to Texas.*

---

2 If you **call** a dog or a person **off**, you order them to stop attacking something or someone else.
call something/someone off or **call off something/someone** ❑ *He called his dog off when he saw that mine was frightened of it.*

✪ **'call on**
1 If you **call on** someone, you visit them for a short time.
call on someone ❑ *Shall we call on Charlotte since we're so near?*
2 If you **call on** someone to do something, you formally ask them to do it.
call on someone ❑ [+ to-infinitive] *The Opposition called on the Prime Minister to stop the arms deal.* ❑ *She was never called on to give evidence.*

○ **'call on** (or **call upon**) [FORMAL]
If you **call on** something, you use it in order to achieve something.
call on something ❑ *She had to call on all her strength to survive.* ❑ *She has plenty of experience to call upon.*

✪ **call 'out**
1 If you **call out** or **call out** something, you shout something.
call out ❑ *She called out in her sleep.* ❑ [+ to] *She turned into the yard, calling out to the porter that she'd arrived.*
call out something ❑ *One boy rushed forward, calling out his father's name.* ❑ *'Don't jump,' she called out.*
2 If you **call** someone **out**, you ask them to come to help, especially in an emergency.
call someone out ❑ *I called the coastguard out* ❑ *The ambulance had been called out.*
call out someone ❑ *At three in the morning I got so worried I called out the doctor.*
3 If you **call out** a group of workers, you order them to go on strike.
call out someone or **call someone out** ❑ *They were called out for half a day.*
4 If you **call** someone **out**, you criticize them, often publicly, by pointing out something that they have done wrong.
call out someone or **call someone out** ❑ *We'll be calling out celebrities who create fake love stories to make money.* ❑ [+ for] *They were quick to call him out for his racist comments.*

5 If you **call** something **out**, you say publicly that you think it is wrong.
call out something or **call something out**
❏ *People are more willing to call out bad behaviour now.*

○ **call 'out for**
If a situation **calls out for** something, it needs it very much.
call out for something ❏ *These terrible conditions call out for radical solutions.*

○ **call 'over**
1 If you **call** someone **over**, you ask them to come to you, usually in order to speak with them.
call someone over or **call over someone**
❏ *I called the waitress over and said, 'Bring us a bottle of red wine'.* ❏ *He called over the producer to speak to her.*
2 If you **call over**, you visit someone for a short time. = **call round** ❏ *We'll be calling over this afternoon anyway.*

○ **call 'round** [mainly BRITISH]
If you **call round**, you visit someone for a short time. = **call over** ❏ *Why don't you call round later and have a cup of coffee?* ❏ *[+ to] The next day I called round to her flat and there was no one there.*

○ **call 'up**
1 If you **call up** or **call** someone **up**, you telephone someone. = **phone up, ring up**
call someone up ❏ *People call me up to talk about what's on their minds.*
call up someone ❏ *She called up an old boyfriend to invite him out for dinner.*
call up ❏ *The radio station had an open line on which listeners could call up to discuss various issues.*
2 If someone **is called up**, they are ordered to join the army, navy, or air force. = **draft**
be called up ❏ *I was extremely lucky not to be called up at the time.* ● If a person gets their **call-up** papers, they receive an official order to join the army, navy, or air force. ● A **call-up** is when people are ordered to report for service in the armed forces.
3 If someone in authority in an activity or event **calls up** someone, they ask them to take part in that activity or event. = **call in, send for**
call up someone or **call someone up** ❏ *He has had plenty of time to call up replacements.* ❏ *The manager called him up for the World Cup qualifying match in Spain.*
4 If something **calls up** a memory or an idea of something, it makes you think about them. = **conjure up**
call up something ❏ *The museum called up memories of my childhood.*

NOTE **Evoke** is a more formal word for **call up**.
5 If you **call up** information on a computer, you obtain it.
call up something or **call something up**
❏ *He was able to call up the information he needed.* ❏ *This data can be called up at the press of a button.*

○ **'call upon** [FORMAL]
1 If you **are called upon** to do something or for something, you are formally asked to do it.
be called upon ❏ *[+ to-infinitive] Lord Shawcross was called upon to declare the hotel open.* ❏ *[+ for] This small band of highly trained fighters are only called upon for the biggest of jobs.*
2 → see **call on**

calm /kɑːm/ (**calms, calming, calmed**)
✪ **calm 'down**
1 If you **calm down** or if someone or something **calms** you **down**, you become less upset, excited, or angry.
calm down ❏ *'Please, Mrs Kinter,' said Brody. 'Calm down. Let me explain'.*
calm someone down ❏ *An officer tried to calm them down but had no success.* ❏ *One of the speakers tried to calm the crowd down.*
calm down someone ❏ *Staff came on board and tried to calm down the 300 passengers.*
calm yourself down ❏ *When she had calmed herself down, she started the engine.*
2 If a situation **calms down** or if you **calm** it **down**, the people involved in it become less upset, excited, or angry. = **settle down**
calm down ❏ *He told me that things appeared to be calming down a bit.*
calm something down ❏ *Dad managed to calm things down.*

camp /kæmp/ (**camps, camping, camped**)
○ **camp 'out**
If you **camp out**, you sleep outdoors in a tent. ❏ *Hundreds of fans camped out on Monday night to guarantee themselves entrance to the event.*

○ **camp 'up** [INFORMAL]
If you **camp it up**, you deliberately act in an exaggerated way that is not natural, usually to make people laugh. ❏ *The actors were really camping it up.*

campaign /kæmˈpeɪn/ (**campaigns, campaigning, campaigned**)
✪ **cam'paign for**
If someone **campaigns for** something, they try to achieve it by organizing activities with other people.
campaign for something ❏ *We are campaigning for law reform.* ❏ *At that time, women were campaigning for equal pay.*

cancel /'kænsəl/ (**cancels, cancelling, cancelled**)

> American English uses the spellings **canceling** and **canceled**.

○ **cancel 'out**

If one thing **cancels** another thing **out** or if two things **cancel** each other **out**, they have opposite effects, so that when they are combined no real effect is produced.

cancel out something or **cancel something out** ❑ The drug produces side effects, tending to cancel out the benefits. ❑ Increased productivity and generous staffing could be said to cancel each other out.

canvass /'kænvəs/ (**canvasses, canvassing, canvassed**)

○ **'canvass for**

If you **canvass for** a person or political party, you go around an area trying to persuade people to vote for that person or party.

canvass for someone/something ❑ They knocked on doors, canvassed for the party, and attended political meetings.

caper /'keɪpə/ (**capers, capering, capered**)

○ **caper a'bout**

If you **caper about**, you run and jump because you are happy or excited.

❑ Sometimes we're capering about, but we're very serious when we have to be.

capitalize /'kæpɪtəlaɪz/ (**capitalizes, capitalizing, capitalized**)

○ **'capitalize on**

If you **capitalize on** a situation, you make the most of it, usually in order to get an advantage for yourself.

capitalize on something ❑ The restaurant wants to capitalize on France's increasing enthusiasm for fast food.

care /keə/ (**cares, caring, cared**)

○ **'care about**

If you **care about** something, you think that it is important and are concerned about it.

care about something ❑ We are a company that cares about the environment. ❑ He didn't care about money.

○ **'care for**

1 If you **care for** someone or something, you look after them and keep them in a good state or condition.

care for something/someone ❑ She has to care for her elderly parents. ❑ Pets must be properly cared for. ● **Uncared-for** people or animals have not been looked after properly.

❑ Thousands of children were left uncared-for.

2 If you do **not care for** something, you do not like it. [OLD-FASHIONED]

not care for something ❑ He didn't drink – he didn't care for the taste of it. ❑ I didn't care for the play.

3 If you **care for** someone, you love them.

care for someone ❑ At last she had found a man that she cared for and who cared for her.

carry /'kæri/ (**carries, carrying, carried**)

○ **carry a'way**

If you **get carried away**, you are so enthusiastic and excited about something that you behave or speak in a way that is silly or not controlled. ❑ I got a bit carried away when I was singing and started inviting people up on the stage.

○ **carry 'back**

If something **carries** you **back**, it reminds you of something that happened in the past. = **take back**

carry someone back ❑ That marvellous smile carried me back nearly twenty-four years.

○ **carry 'forward**

1 When the sum of the figures on a page or in a column **is carried forward**, it is written at the top of the next page or column so that it can be added to the figures on that page or in that column. = **bring forward**

be carried forward ❑ The total is then carried forward for next month's accounts.

2 If you **carry forward** an amount of money that was intended for one period of time, you use it in a later period of time instead.

carry forward something or **carry something forward** ❑ Can we carry forward this marketing budget to next year?

○ **carry 'off**

1 If you **carry off** something that is difficult to do, you succeed in doing it. = **bring off**

carry something off or **carry off something** ❑ It's a very unusual dress but I think you could carry it off. ❑ He watched her to see how she was carrying off the lie.

2 If you **carry off** a prize or an award, you win it.

carry off something or **carry something off** ❑ Once again, Vita carried off all the prizes.

○ **carry 'on**

1 If you **carry on**, you continue doing an activity. ❑ [+ with] Are you telling me to carry on with my investigation? ❑ They just ignored her and carried on chatting.

2 If you **carry on** when you are in a difficult or unpleasant situation, you manage to continue with your normal, everyday activities. = **go on** ❑ Some people carry on as if nothing has happened. ❑ I could never have carried on without their support.

3 If you **carry on** a particular activity or conversation, you take part in it.
carry on something ❑ *She could not carry on a normal conversation.*
NOTE **Conduct** is a more formal word for **carry on**.
4 If someone **carries on**, they behave badly, in an uncontrolled way. [INFORMAL] ❑ *The child was screaming and carrying on.* ● A **carry-on** is an instance of bad behaviour. [BRITISH, INFORMAL, OLD-FASHIONED] ❑ *Well, what a carry-on!*
5 To **carry on** is to have a sexual relationship with someone that you should not be having a relationship with, usually in secret. [INFORMAL, OLD-FASHIONED] ❑ [+ with] *All this time, Helen was carrying on with Martin.*

○ **carry 'out**
1 If you **carry out** a task, you do it.
carry out something ❑ *They have to carry out a number of administrative duties.* ❑ *The first experiments were carried out by Dr Preston McLendon.*
carry something out ❑ *The magazine has just carried a survey out and its findings make interesting reading.*

> CARRY OUT + *noun*
>
> carry out **an examination**
> carry out **an experiment**
> carry out **an investigation**
> carry out **a search**
> carry out **a task**
> carry out **research**
> carry out **a check**
> ❑ *Experts are carrying out an investigation into the accident.* ❑ *Officers carried out a search of all the cells.*

2 If you **carry out** an idea, suggestion, or instruction, you put it into practice.
carry out something ❑ *He explained that he was simply carrying out instructions.*
carry something out ❑ *People at the top make the decisions and people at the bottom carry them out.*

○ **carry 'over**
1 If something **carries over** or you **carry** something **over** from one situation to another, an aspect of the first situation influences the second.
carry over ❑ [+ into] *Paolo's infectious enthusiasm and energy carries over into his music.*
carry something over or **carry over something** ❑ *Unfortunately, stresses at work can be carried over into one's home life.*
2 If a set of figures on a page **is carried over**, it is written at the top of the next page. = **be brought forward**

be carried over ❑ *The sum total to be carried over amounts to £76.*
3 If an amount of money **is carried over** from one period of time, it is used or recorded in a later period of time instead. = **be brought forward**
be carried over ❑ *Large deficits are usually carried over to next year's budget.*

○ **carry 'through**
1 If you **carry through** a plan, you succeed in putting it into practice.
carry through something or **carry something through** ❑ *The task of carrying through the necessary reforms will fall to them.* ❑ *We are united on these policies and determined to carry them through.*
2 If something **carries** you **through** or **carries** you **through** a period or experience, it makes it possible for you to deal with or survive something unpleasant or difficult.
carry someone through ❑ *They were against a more experienced side but their spirit and determination carried them through.*
carry someone through something ❑ *Her passion for music carries her through the endless hours of practice.*

cart /kɑːt/ (**carts, carting, carted**)
○ **cart 'off** [INFORMAL]
If you **cart** someone **off**, you take them somewhere using force. = **pack off**
cart someone off or **cart off someone** ❑ [+ to] *His father was carted off to jail.* ❑ *I was terrified they'd have me carted off to a police hospital.*

carve /kɑːv/ (**carves, carving, carved**)
○ **carve 'out**
1 If something or someone **carves out** a shape, they create it in a large area, often with difficulty.
carve out something or **carve something out** ❑ *The river sliced through the soft rock, carving out the gorge.* ❑ *It has taken the Colorado River a century to carve a canyon out of the red clay soil.*
2 If you **carve out** something useful or profitable, you create or obtain it for yourself, often with difficulty.
carve out something or **carve something out** ❑ *The company is carving out a huge slice of the electronics market.* ❑ *She's carved a role out for herself in the company.*

○ **carve 'up**
1 If you **carve up** an area, you divide it into smaller areas.
carve up something or **carve something up** ❑ *The former republic had been carved up into a number of small states.* ❑ *They prepared to carve up the British Empire.*

2 If someone **carves** a person **up**, they kill or injure them badly with a knife. = cut up [INFORMAL]

carve someone up or **carve up someone** ❑ He's carved up within ten minutes of the film's opening.

3 If someone **carves** you **up**, they go past your vehicle in their vehicle and move back in front of you too soon in a way that is dangerous. [BRITISH, INFORMAL]

carve someone up or **carve up someone** ❑ He carved me up at the turning to the college.

cascade /kæsˈkeɪd/ (**cascades, cascading, cascaded**)

○ **cascade 'down**

1 If a liquid such as water **cascades down**, it flows downwards very fast. ❑ Waterfalls cascade down the green walls of the valley.

2 If something **cascades down**, it falls down in large amounts. ❑ Her hair cascades down her back.

3 If information or knowledge **cascades down**, it is passed on from one generation to another, or from a higher level to a lower level. ❑ Monthly meetings ensure that information cascades down to everyone.

cash /kæʃ/ (**cashes, cashing, cashed**)

✪ **cash 'in**

1 If you **cash in** an investment such as shares, you exchange it for money.

cash in something ❑ She had to cash in her premium bonds to raise a bit of money.

cash something in ❑ I used to have a few shares, but I cashed them in last year.

2 If you **cash in**, you take advantage of a situation, usually to make money. ❑ [+ on] A range of branded products will be brought out to cash in on the show's popularity. ❑ The market is good, but if you want to cash in, you must act fast.

cast /kɑːst, kæst/ (**casts, casting**)

The form **cast** is used in the present tense and is the past tense and past participle of the verb.

○ **cast a'round** (or **cast about, cast round** [mainly BRITISH]) [FORMAL]

1 If you **cast around**, you look for something. ❑ [+ for] Casting around for something that might help, I found a large stick. ❑ Casting about for a hiding-place, she opened the kitchen door and noticed a cupboard.

2 If you **cast around**, you try to think of an idea. ❑ [+ for] I really didn't want to go and was desperately casting around for an excuse.

○ **'cast as**

1 To **cast** an actor **as** something in a play or film means to choose them to act that part.

cast someone as something ❑ Rosalind Russell was cast as George's mother.

2 To **cast** someone or something **as** a particular thing means to describe them in that way or suggest they are that thing.

cast someone/something as something ❑ He's casting his opponents as liars.

cast yourself as something ❑ He has cast himself as the victim.

○ **cast a'side** [FORMAL]

If you **cast** someone or something **aside**, you get rid of them because you no longer like them or want them.

cast aside something/someone or **cast something/someone aside** ❑ Casting aside my inhibitions, I walked straight up to him and introduced myself. ❑ At the age of 30 she was cast aside and replaced by a younger model.

○ **cast a'way**

1 If you **cast** something **away**, you get rid of it. [LITERARY]

cast away something or **cast something away** ❑ Why should he cast away something so valuable?

2 A **castaway** is a person who has managed to swim to an island where no one lives after their ship has sunk. ❑ It was a film about a bunch of castaways on a desert island.

○ **cast 'back**

If you **cast your mind back**, you try to remember something that happened in the past. ❑ He cast his mind back over the day. ❑ [+ to] Cast your mind back to your first day at school.

○ **cast 'down**

1 If someone **is cast down**, they lose their social status. ≠ raise [FORMAL]

be cast down ❑ Men of high status were cast down.

2 If someone **is cast down** by something, they are sad or worried because of it.

be cast down ❑ She seemed cast down by the problems at work. ● If you are **downcast** you are feeling sad and without hope. = depressed ❑ Cameron seemed unusually downcast and nervous. ❑ I looked anxiously at his downcast face.

3 If you **cast** your eyes **down**, you look downwards. [FORMAL]

cast something down ❑ For a moment, Tiffany cast her eyes down to avoid my glance.

NOTE **Lower** is a less formal word for **cast down**.

○ **cast 'off**

1 If you **cast** something **off**, you get rid of it because you no longer want it or because it is preventing you from making progress.

cast off something or **cast something off**
❑ *Organizations must cast off these bureaucratic practices.* ❑ *New year, of course, is traditionally a time for casting off the old and welcoming the new.* NOTE Discard is a more formal word for **cast off**.

● **Cast-off** clothes or **cast-offs** are clothes which you give to someone else, because you no longer want them. ❑ *He refuses to wear cast-off clothes.* ❑ *She was dressed head to foot in Polly's cast-offs.*

2 When you **cast off** or **cast off** a rope or line, you remove or untie the rope fastening a boat to the land so that the boat can move away.

cast off ❑ *She gave the order to cast off.*

cast off something or **cast something off**
❑ *Hendricks cast off the bow line and walked to the stern.*

3 In knitting, when you **cast off** or **cast off** stitches, you remove stitches from a needle after doing a special stitch, especially in order to finish a piece of knitting.

cast off ❑ *I'm just casting off here.*

cast off something or **cast something off**
❑ *The pattern says cast off fifty stitches.*

○ **cast 'on**
In knitting, when you **cast on** or **cast on** stitches, you make stitches on a needle in order to begin a piece of knitting.

cast on ❑ *I'm just about to cast on.*

cast on something ❑ *Using 4mm needles cast on 53 stitches.*

○ **cast 'out** [FORMAL]
If you **cast out** something or someone, you get rid of them or make them leave a place.

cast out someone/something or **cast someone/something out** ❑ *She had abandoned him; she had cast him out.* ❑ *What will such helpless creatures do when they are cast out into the open?* ● An **outcast** is someone who is not accepted by other people as part of their group. ❑ *He was regarded very much as a social outcast.*

○ **cast 'round** → see **cast around**

○ **cast 'up** [FORMAL]
If something **is cast up** on the shore or on a beach, it is left there by the sea. = **wash up**

be cast up ❑ *His body was cast up onto the shore.*

catch /kætʃ/ (catches, catching, caught)
✪ **catch 'on**

1 If someone **catches on**, they understand what is happening, especially after not understanding before. = **cotton on** ❑ *He'll catch on eventually.* ❑ [+ to] *They finally caught on to our game.*

2 If something **catches on**, it becomes popular. ❑ *The idea is catching on in business circles.* ❑ *When I first saw that hairstyle I thought it would never catch on.*

○ **catch 'out** [BRITISH]

1 If you **catch** someone **out**, you cause them to make a mistake, often by an unfair trick.

catch someone out ❑ *You were just trying to catch me out, I know you were, Anna.*

2 If you **are caught out** by something you were not prepared for, you find yourself in a bad situation because of it. [BRITISH]

be caught out ❑ *I was caught out by the rain yesterday so I made sure I packed my umbrella this morning.*

✪ **catch 'up**

1 If you **catch up** or **catch** someone **up**, you reach someone who is in front of you by walking faster than they are walking.

catch up ❑ [+ with] *Simon tried to catch up with the others.*

catch someone up ❑ *She stood still, allowing him to catch her up.*

catch up someone ❑ *He hurried to catch up the others.*

2 If a person or thing **catches up** or **catches** someone or something **up**, they reach the same standard or level.

catch up ❑ [+ with] *Most leaders were obsessed with catching up with the West.* ❑ *Once you become so behind with your studies, it's really hard to catch up.*

catch someone/something up ❑ *They did well early on, but other businesses are catching them up now.*

3 If you **catch up**, you talk to a friend that you have not seen for a while, finding out what has happened in his or her life since you last met. ❑ [+ on] *We spent a while catching up on each other's health and families.* ❑ [+ with] *She plans to return to Dublin to catch up with the relatives she hasn't seen since she married.* ❑ *It would be really nice to catch up over a cup of coffee sometime.*

✪ **catch 'up in**

1 If you **are caught up in** something, you are involved in it, usually without wanting to be.

be caught up in something ❑ *He was caught up in a gun battle and killed.* ❑ *The last thing he wanted was for Sam to get caught up in an affair that could only end badly.*

2 If you **are caught up in** something, you are prevented from moving by it.

be caught up in something ❑ *I got caught up in the traffic and was late.* ❑ *A bird had got caught up in the net.*

○ **catch 'up on**
When you **catch up on** something, you spend time doing something that you have

not had time to do properly until now.
catch up on something ❑ *I was just catching up on my sleep.* ❑ *I need to catch up on some work.*

○ **catch 'up with**

1 If the police or the authorities **catch up with** someone who has done something wrong, they succeed in finding them, especially in order to arrest or punish them.
catch up with someone ❑ *When Birmingham authorities finally caught up with her, she had spent all the money.*

2 If something **catches up with** you, it finally causes problems for you which you have managed to avoid for a long period of time.
catch up with someone ❑ *One day the truth will catch up with him and then he'll be sorry.*

cater /'keɪtə/ (**caters, catering, catered**)

○ **'cater for** [BRITISH]

To **cater for** a person or group means to provide all the things that they need in a particular situation.
cater for someone/something ❑ *We can cater for all age groups in our summer schools.* ❑ *Newspapers cater for a variety of tastes.*
NOTE In American English, **cater to** means almost the same as **cater for**.

○ **'cater to**

To **cater to** a need or taste means to provide things which satisfy it.
cater to something ❑ *These new writers catered to the public taste for new plays.*

cave /keɪv/ (**caves, caving, caved**)

○ **cave 'in**

1 When a roof, ceiling or other structure **caves in** or when something **caves** it **in**, it collapses inwards.
cave in ❑ *There was a loud bang as the ceiling caved in.*
cave in something or **cave something in** ❑ *The blow caved in his skull.* • A **cave-in** is the sudden collapse of a roof, ceiling or other structure into a building or room below it.

2 If you **cave in**, you agree to something that you opposed before after someone threatens you or tries to force you. ❑ *[+ to]* *Eventually they caved in to the agent's demands.* ❑ *Of course he keeps on at you because he knows you'll cave in and he'll get whatever he wants.*
NOTE **Capitulate** is a more formal word for **cave in**.

cavil /'kævəl/ (**cavils, cavilling, cavilled**)

American English uses the spellings **caviling** and **caviled**.

○ **'cavil at** [FORMAL]

If someone **cavils at** something, they complain about it or criticize it, in a way that seems silly or unnecessary to you.
cavil at something ❑ *He would be a fool to cavil at such a reasonable price.*

cede /siːd/ (**cedes, ceding, ceded**)

○ **'cede to** [FORMAL]

To **cede** land or power **to** someone else means to let them have it, often as a result of military or political pressure.
cede something to someone ❑ *The government has ceded all political control to the local tribal councils.* ❑ *After being colonized by Spain, Haiti was ceded to France in 1697.*

centre /'sentə/ (**centres, centring, centred**)

American English uses the spellings **center, centers, centering** and **centered**.

○ **'centre around** (or **centre round** [mainly BRITISH])

If one thing **centres around** another thing, the second thing is the main point or part of the first.
centre around something ❑ *The workers' demands centred around pay and conditions.* ❑ *Our holidays centred very much around horse-racing.*

○ **'centre on** (or **centre upon**)

If something **centres on** a person or thing or is **centred on** a person or thing, it concentrates on them.
centre on something ❑ *Much of this debate centres on different practices and systems.*
be centred on/upon something ❑ *Attention was for the moment centred on Striker.* ❑ *The struggle was now centred upon Pennsylvania.*

○ **'centre round** → see **centre around**

○ **'centre upon** → see **centre on**

certify /'sɜːtɪfaɪ/ (**certifies, certifying, certified**)

○ **'certify as**

1 To **certify** someone **as** something or **be certified as** something means to give them a certificate or have a certificate which shows that they have done a training course for a particular type of job.
be certified as something ❑ *He has recently been certified as a helicopter pilot.*
certify someone as something ❑ *In 2005, the college certified him as a specialist in gynaecology.*

2 To **certify** something **as** something means to officially state that something is true, especially after doing some tests.
certify something as something ❑ *The produce had been certified as organic.* ❑ *A coroner certified the death as due to natural causes.*

chafe /tʃeɪf/ (**chafes, chafing, chafed**)

○ **'chafe at** [FORMAL]

If you **chafe at** a restriction, problem, or unpleasant situation, you feel annoyed about it.

chafe at something ❑ *Powell chafed at the delay.*

chain /tʃeɪn/ (**chains, chaining, chained**)

○ **chain 'up**

If you **chain up** someone or something, you fasten them to something using a chain.

chain up something/someone or **chain something/someone up** ❑ *The rowing boats were chained up.*

chalk /tʃɔːk/ (**chalks, chalking, chalked**)

○ **chalk 'up**

If you **chalk up** a victory, a success, or a number of points in a game, you achieve it. = notch up

chalk up something or **chalk something up** ❑ *They chalked up several victories.* ❑ *She's chalked up four wins already this season.*

chance /tʃɑːns, tʃæns/ (**chances, chancing, chanced**)

○ **'chance on** (or **chance upon**)

If you **chance on** something or someone, you meet or discover them unexpectedly.

chance on something/someone ❑ *I chanced on an old friend in the street.* ❑ *He'd chanced upon an old book.*

change /tʃeɪndʒ/ (**changes, changing, changed**)

○ **change 'down** [BRITISH]

When you **change down**, you move the gear lever on a car or bicycle in order to use a lower gear. ❑ [+ into] *You'll have to change down into second to get round the corner.*

❂ **change 'over**

1 To **change over** from one thing to another means to stop doing, using, or having one thing and start doing, using, or having something else. ❑ [+ from] *Some schools have changed over from having a system of grouping by ability to having mixed ability classes.* ❑ [+ to] *They had been Liberal Democrat voters till several years ago; then they changed over to Conservative.* ● A **changeover** is a change from one activity, system, or way of working to another one. ❑ *The changeover took place at Easter.*

2 If two people **change over**, each of them starts to do what the other person was previously doing. ❑ *Let's change over – you paint the wall and I'll paint the door.*

○ **change 'up** [BRITISH]

When you **change up**, you move the gear lever on a car or bicycle in order to use a higher gear. ❑ [+ into] *She changed up into fourth.*

charge /tʃɑːdʒ/ (**charges, charging, charged**)

○ **charge 'up**

If a battery or piece of electrical equipment **charges up** or if you **charge** it **up**, electricity passes into it so that it can work.

charge up ❑ *My mobile is still charging up.*

charge up something or **charge something up** ❑ *You have to drive it every day to charge up the battery.*

chase /tʃeɪs/ (**chases, chasing, chased**)

○ **chase 'after**

1 If you **chase after** someone, you run after them or follow them quickly in order to catch them.

chase after someone ❑ *I chased after them but they were too quick for me.*

2 If you **chase after** something you want, you try very hard to obtain it.

chase after something ❑ *He spent his life chasing after money.*

3 If someone **chases after** someone, they try to persuade that person to have a sexual relationship with them.

chase after someone ❑ *His wife left him because he was always chasing after other women.*

○ **chase a'way**

To **chase away** worries, fears, or other bad feelings is to cause those feelings to end. = get rid of

chase away something ❑ *Will these latest figures chase away fears of a new recession?*

○ **chase 'down**

1 If you **chase** someone or something **down**, you run after them or follow them quickly and catch them. [AMERICAN]

chase someone/something down or **chase down someone/something** ❑ *Ness chased the thief down and held him until police arrived.* ❑ *He was determined to chase down the animal that had bitten him.*

2 If you **chase** someone or something **down**, you manage to find them after searching for them. = track down

chase someone/something down or **chase down someone/something** ❑ *I chased her down and asked her to be the singer in my band.* ❑ *Bank officials argued that it is not their job to chase down every bank debtor.*

○ **'chase from**

To **chase** someone **from** a job or position or **from** power means to force them to leave it.

chase someone from something ❑ *Mr Lambert was chased from his post as editor of the journal in 2008.*

○ chase 'off

To **chase** someone or something **off** is to run after them in order to frighten them or force them to go away.

chase something/something off or **chase off someone/something** ❑ *There was another snake but the dog chased it off.* ❑ *The adult male will chase off other males that enter its territory.*

○ chase 'up

1 If you **chase** someone **up**, you contact them to remind them to do something.

chase someone up or **chase up someone** ❑ [+ for] *I'll chase her up for those reports.* ❑ *The cash is generated largely by chasing up customers for prompt payment of bills.*

2 If you **chase** something **up**, you try to find it because it is needed. = **track down**

chase something up or **chase up something** ❑ *You'd better chase those addresses up tomorrow.* ❑ *Someone else is in charge of chasing up the missing books.*

chat /tʃæt/ (chats, chatting, chatted)

○ chat 'up [BRITISH, INFORMAL]

If you **chat** someone **up**, you talk to them in a friendly way because you are sexually attracted to them.

chat someone up ❑ *Was he chatting you up?*
chat up someone ❑ *Her idea of a good time was clubbing, dancing and chatting up lads.*

cheat /tʃiːt/ (cheats, cheating, cheated)

○ 'cheat on

1 If you **cheat on** your sexual partner, you secretly have a sexual experience or relationship with someone else. = **be unfaithful to**

cheat on someone ❑ *A private detective was assigned to find out whether she was cheating on her husband.*

2 To **cheat on** someone also means to lie to them or behave dishonestly towards them.

cheat on someone ❑ *He can cheat on us, but he's smart enough to say somebody else did it.*

3 If someone **cheats on** an agreement, rule, or law, they do not do what they should do under a set of rules. [AMERICAN]

cheat on something ❑ *Their job is to check that none of the countries is cheating on the agreement.*

○ cheat 'out of

If someone **cheats** you **out of** something that you have a right to have, they stop you from having it by doing something dishonest.

cheat someone out of something ❑ *The company engaged in a deliberate effort to cheat them out of their pensions.*

check /tʃek/ (checks, checking, checked)

◐ check 'in

1 When you **check in** or when someone **checks** you **in** at a hotel, you arrive at the hotel, collect the key to your room, and fill in any forms which are necessary.

check in ❑ *I checked in at the Gordon Hotel.*
check someone in ❑ *I'll just check you in, Madam.*
check in someone ❑ *He worked at the front desk checking in the guests when they arrived.*

2 When you **check in** at an airport or when someone **checks** you **in**, you show your ticket before getting on the plane.

check in ❑ *He checked in without baggage for a flight to Rome.*
check someone in ❑ *I'll need to check you in.*
check in someone ❑ *The remaining passengers were still being checked in.* ● A **check-in** is the place in an airport where you check in. ❑ *We were supposed to notice damaged bags at the check-in but rarely did.* ❑ *...a check-in counter.*

3 If you **check in** when you are using a mobile phone application that gives information about the area you are in, you key in information to say where you are. ❑ *The game asks users to check in when they visit real world places.* ● A **check-in** is an instance of checking in to a mobile phone application. ❑ *The database of music gigs is integrated with check-ins made on the service's mobile apps.*

○ check 'into

When you **check into** a hotel or if someone **checks** you **into** it, you arrive at the hotel, collect the key to your room, and fill in any forms which are necessary.

check into something ❑ *With no money, we couldn't even check into a motel.*
check someone into something ❑ *My colleague will check you into the hotel.*

○ check 'off

When you **check off** items on a list, you look again at each item to make sure you have everything you should have or have dealt with everything you should have.

check off something or **check something off** ❑ *We waited while Mr Wilde checked off the things on the list.* ❑ *I store the details in a file to check off when I'm ready to go.*

◐ check 'out

1 When you **check out**, you pay the bill at a hotel where you have been staying and leave. ❑ *The following morning he checked out.* ❑ [+ of] *She checked out of the hotel and took the train to Paris.*

2 If you **check** something **out**, you find out about it or examine it because you want to

make sure that everything is correct or safe.
check out something ❏ *An officer would be checking out the statement Mrs. Mossman just made.*
check something out ❏ *It might be difficult to transfer your money, so check it out with the manager.*
❸ If you **check out** a person, place or a thing that you have not seen before, you look at them in order to find out whether you like them. [INFORMAL]
check out something or **check something out** ❏ *We could check out the new club on Green Street.* ❏ *Hey, check out the guy in the green T-shirt!*
❹ If a fact **checks out**, it is proved to be correct. ❏ *He said he went as usual to visit his father in Liverpool and that all checked out.*
❺ If you **check** someone **out**, you obtain information about them secretly to find out if they are telling the truth.
check someone out or **check out someone** ❏ *They knew his habits, Luca thought; they must have been checking him out.* ❏ *Jenny was reserving judgement until she could check out the two men who had called her.*
❻ In a shop, if you **check out** the things you want to buy, you pay for them at a special counter. [AMERICAN]
check out something or **check something out** ❏ *Wait before you check those cards out, and I'll get some too.* ● In a supermarket, a **checkout** is a counter where you pay for the things you have bought. [BRITISH AND AMERICAN] ❏ *Only two checkouts were operating.* ❏ *I was waiting at the checkout.*

○ **check 'up**
❶ If you **check up** on someone or something, you make certain that the facts you have been told are true. ❏ [+ on] *If I tell my mum I'm staying at a friend's house I know she'll check up on me.* ❏ *They think there is a security leak and are trying to check up.*
❷ A **check-up** is an examination by a doctor to see that your health is all right. ❏ *See the doctor for a blood test and check-up.*

cheer /tʃɪə/ (**cheers, cheering, cheered**)
○ **cheer 'on**
If you **cheer** someone **on**, you shout things in order to encourage them, often in a race or other competition.
cheer someone on or **cheer on someone** ❏ *There was no one there to cheer him on or applaud.* ❏ *It was great to be cheered on and supported by a home crowd.*

○ **cheer 'up**
When you **cheer up** or when someone or something **cheers** you **up**, you stop feeling sad and become happier. = **buck up**
cheer up ❏ *He cheered up at the prospect of dinner.*

cheer someone up ❏ *Her friends tried to cheer her up, telling her she wasn't missing much.*
cheer up someone ❏ *I took some cake into work to try to cheer up my colleagues.*
cheer yourself up ❏ *She bought strawberries to cheer herself up.*

cheese /tʃiːz/ (**cheeses, cheesing, cheesed**)
○ **cheese 'off** [BRITISH, INFORMAL]
If you **are cheesed off** with something, you are annoyed or bored with it.
be cheesed off ❏ *I was really cheesed off when he didn't turn up.*

chew /tʃuː/ (**chews, chewing, chewed**)
○ **'chew on** [INFORMAL]
If you **chew on** an idea or a problem, you think about it carefully for a long time.
chew on something ❏ *He chewed on the idea that his brother had suggested.* ❏ *You've given me a lot to chew on.*
NOTE **Consider** is a more formal word for **chew on.**

○ **chew 'out** [AMERICAN, INFORMAL]
If you **chew** someone **out**, you speak angrily to them because they have done something wrong.
chew someone out or **chew out someone** ❏ *When Tom got back to Dallas, Perot called him over and chewed him out.* ❏ *He chewed out the player, who apologized immediately.*

○ **chew 'over**
If you **chew** something **over**, you think carefully about it or discuss the details of it. = **mull over**
chew something over or **chew over something** ❏ *I'll go home and chew it over.* ❏ *In discussion we chew over problems and work out possible solutions.*

○ **chew 'up**
❶ To **chew** something **up** is to chew it until it is crushed or destroyed.
chew something up or **chew up something** ❏ *Lally put it into her mouth and chewed it up happily.* ❏ *She doesn't want a dog in case it chews up the furniture.*
❷ To **chew** something **up** is to destroy or damage it in some way. [INFORMAL]
chew something up or **chew up something** ❏ *The ground was chewed up by the tanks.*

chicken /tʃɪkɪn/ (**chickens, chickening, chickened**)
○ **chicken 'out** [INFORMAL]
If you **chicken out**, you decide not to do something because you are afraid. ❏ *I thought of replying but chickened out.* ❏ [+ of] *In the end, he chickened out of tackling the problem.*

chill /tʃɪl/ (chills, chilling, chilled)

○ **chill 'out** [INFORMAL]

To **chill out** means to relax, especially after doing something tiring or stressful.
❏ *On Sunday we'll probably just chill out with the newspapers.*

chime /tʃaɪm/ (chimes, chiming, chimed)

○ **chime 'in**

If someone **chimes in**, they say something just after someone else has spoken.
❏ [+ with] *Other listeners began to chime in with their questions and opinions.* ❏ *'Yes,' he chimed in, 'we have exactly the same problem.'*

○ **'chime with**

If something that someone says **chimes with** another thing that is said, the two things are similar and contain the same ideas or opinions.
chime with something ❏ *Barbara's experience of the health service chimes with what you were saying about your treatment.*

chip /tʃɪp/ (chips, chipping, chipped)

○ **chip a'way at**

1 If you **chip away at** something, you gradually make it weaker or less likely to succeed by repeated efforts. = **erode**
chip away at something ❏ *The government have chipped away at our liberties in the name of protecting us.* ❏ *Over the years she had chipped away at his confidence with her negative remarks.*
2 If you **chip away at** a debt or an amount of money, you gradually reduce it.
chip away at something ❏ *The group had hoped to chip away at its debts by selling assets.*

○ **chip 'in**

1 If you **chip in** to pay for something, you contribute part of the cost so that you and several other people pay for it together.
= **club together** [INFORMAL] ❏ *They could all chip in and buy a present.*
2 If someone **chips in** during a conversation, they interrupt it by saying something. ❏ *'Do you know,' said Mrs Oliver, chipping in again, 'whether Celia was there or not?'.* ❏ *'What about me? I could do it' chipped in Olivia.*

○ **chip 'off**

If a layer of something **chips off** a surface, or if you **chip** it **off**, it gradually comes away from the surface in small pieces.
chip off ❏ *The car was only two years old, and already the paint had started to chip off.*
chip something off something ❏ *We watched the fishermen chipping ice off their trawlers.*
chip off something or **chip something off** ❏ *With extreme care, she began chipping off the white paint.*

choke /tʃəʊk/ (chokes, choking, choked)

○ **choke 'back**

1 If you **choke back** a strong emotion, you force yourself not to show it. = **suppress**
choke back something or **choke something back** ❏ *I choked back the sobs.* ❏ *She spoke with difficulty, choking back the tears.*
2 If you **choke back** something you are saying, you stop yourself from saying it.
choke back something or **choke something back** ❏ *'I'm...' she choked back the word.*
❏ *He turned to yell for Helen, but choked it back.*

○ **choke 'off**

To **choke off** financial growth means to limit the rate at which a country's economy can grow.
choke off something or **choke something off** ❏ *They warned the Chancellor that raising taxes in the Budget could choke off the recovery.*

○ **choke 'out**

If you **choke** words **out**, you only just manage to say them.
choke out something or **choke something out** ❏ *He finally choked out the word 'sorry'.*

○ **choke 'up**

1 If you **choke** something **up**, you produce it from your lungs by coughing.
choke up something or **choke something up** ❏ *She was pulled out of the sea, choking up salt water.*
2 If traffic or rubbish **chokes** a place **up**, it blocks it.
choke up something or **choke something up** ❏ *These trucks are choking up minor roads as they try to get their goods to market.*
3 If you **choke up**, or if something **chokes** you **up**, you find it difficult to speak because you are feeling a strong emotion.
choke up ❏ *Frank's eyes filled with tears and he began to choke up.*
choke someone up ❏ *The reaction I got from the fans really choked me up.*

chop /tʃɒp/ (chops, chopping, chopped)

○ **chop 'down**

If you **chop down** a tree, you cut through its trunk so that it falls to the ground.
chop down something or **chop something down** ❏ *They chopped down all the trees for fuel.* ❏ *I chopped the trees down every year, but they always grew back.*

○ **chop 'off**

If you **chop** something **off**, you cut it off with a sudden stroke, using a knife or other sharp instrument.
chop something off or **chop off something** ❏ *Don't bother peeling the carrots – just chop the*

ends off. ❑ *There were women in the fields, chopping off the long golden stalks of corn.*

○ **chop 'up**
If you **chop** something **up**, you cut it into many small pieces.
chop up something or **chop something up** ❑ *The crates are usually chopped up for firewood.* ❑ *I was chopping up carrots for the soup.*

chow /tʃaʊ/ (**chows, chowing, chowed**)
○ **chow 'down** [mainly AMERICAN, INFORMAL]
If you **chow down** you eat, especially in a restaurant. ❑ [+ on] *We chowed down on homemade quiche and scones.*

chuck /tʃʌk/ (**chucks, chucking, chucked**)
○ **chuck a'way** [INFORMAL]
If you **chuck** something **away**, you get rid of it, usually by putting it in a bin, because you do not want it any longer.
= chuck out
chuck something away or **chuck away something** ❑ *'What are you going to do with all those old clothes?' – 'Oh, just chuck them away I guess.'* ❑ *The heater had to be chucked away because it didn't work.*

○ **chuck 'in** [BRITISH, INFORMAL]
If you **chuck in** a job or a course, you stop doing it. **= jack in, pack in**
chuck something in or **chuck in something** ❑ *He got a new job but chucked it in after three months.* ❑ *She's talking about chucking in her course and travelling for a year.*

○ **chuck 'out**
1 If you **chuck** someone **out** of a place, you force them to leave. **= throw out** [INFORMAL]
chuck someone out or **chuck out someone** ❑ *He left home at fourteen – his mother chucked him out.* ❑ [+ of] *He was chucked out of school for bad behaviour.* • **Chucking-out** time is the time when pubs close. [BRITISH, INFORMAL] ❑ *Is it chucking-out time already?*
2 If you **chuck** something **out**, you get rid of it, usually by putting it in a bin, because you do not want it any longer. **= chuck away** [INFORMAL]
chuck something out or **chuck out something** ❑ *Chuck those old boots out, for goodness sake.* ❑ *She chucked out loads of books.*

○ **chuck 'up**
1 If you **chuck up** a job or a course, you stop doing it. **= chuck in** [BRITISH, INFORMAL]
chuck up something or **chuck something up** ❑ *She chucked up her job and left the country.*
2 If someone **chucks up**, they vomit.
= throw up [INFORMAL] ❑ *They get drunk and then they chuck up everywhere.*

churn /tʃɜːn/ (**churns, churning, churned**)
○ **churn 'out**
To **churn** things **out** means to produce them in large numbers very quickly.
= pump out
churn out something or **churn something out** ❑ *She writes two or three books a year – she churns them out.*

○ **churn 'up**
1 If something **churns up** mud or water, it moves it about violently.
churn up something or **churn something up** ❑ *The wind churned up the water into a swirling foam.* ❑ *The mud in the lakes has been churned up by motorboats.*
2 If something **churns** you **up**, it makes you feel strong emotions, especially of worry, sadness or anger.
churn someone up or **churn up someone** ❑ *The argument had churned her up inside.*

circle /'sɜːkəl/ (**circles, circling, circled**)
○ **'circle around**
1 If something **circles around** an object or a place, it forms a circle around it.
circle around something ❑ *We drove up the long curving driveway that circled around the vast lawn.*
2 To **circle around** or **circle around** someone or something means to move around in a circle or move around someone or something in a circle.
circle around ❑ *There were two helicopters circling around.*
circle around someone/something ❑ *He circled around the table and stood next to Naglek.*

clam /klæm/ (**clams, clamming, clammed**)
○ **clam 'up** [INFORMAL]
If someone **clams up**, they refuse to say anything about a subject. ❑ *If I even mention the subject, Guy just clams up.* ❑ *We had a row, and he clammed up and said nothing for a complete half-hour.*

clamour /'klæmə/ (**clamours, clamouring, clamoured**)

> American English uses the spellings **clamor, clamors, clamoring** and **clamored.**

○ **'clamour for**
If people **clamour for** something, they ask for it in a noisy way or in a way that makes people pay attention.
clamour for something ❑ *Competing parties are clamouring for the attention of voters.*

clamp /klæmp/ (**clamps, clamping, clamped**)

○ **clamp 'down**

To **clamp down** on people or activities means to take strong official action to stop or control them. = **crack down** ❏ [+ on] *The authorities have got to clamp down on these trouble-makers.* ● A **clampdown** is a sudden restriction on an activity by a government or other authority. ❏ *There has been a clampdown on wasteful spending.*

clap /klæp/ (**claps, clapping, clapped**)

○ **clap 'out**

1 If you **clap out** a tune, you produce it by hitting your hands together in a way which matches the rhythm of the tune.
clap out something or **clap something out** ❏ *A leader is selected, and he or she begins to clap out a rhythm which the others follow.*
2 Something such as a machine that is **clapped-out** is old and no longer working properly. = **beat-up** [BRITISH, INFORMAL] ❏ *They have a clapped-out old camper van.*

clash /klæʃ/ (**clashes, clashing, clashed**)

○ **'clash with**

1 If you **clash with** someone, you fight, argue, or disagree with them.
clash with someone ❏ *A group of 400 demonstrators clashed with police.*
2 If one idea, belief, or quality **clashes with** another, it is very different and therefore seems opposed.
clash with something ❏ *Don't make any policy decisions which clash with official company thinking.*
3 If one colour or style **clashes with** another, the colours or styles look bad together.
clash with something ❏ *This season's look is all about breaking rules: bright oranges clash with lime greens.*

class /klɑːs, klæs/ (**classes, classing, classed**)

○ **'class among**

If you **class** someone or something **among** a particular group, you consider them to be a member of that group.
class someone/something among something ❏ *It was classed among the top-rated restaurants which received nine out of ten for cooking.* ❏ *I would certainly class her among the top five female athletes today.*

claw /klɔː/ (**claws, clawing, clawed**)

○ **'claw at**

When people or animals **claw at** something, they try to get hold of it or damage it by using their nails or claws.
claw at something ❏ *He clawed desperately at the rock and then fell.*

○ **claw 'back** [BRITISH]

1 If someone **claws back** something that they no longer have, they get some of it back again.
claw back something or **claw something back** ❏ *Peterson managed to claw back three points for Glasgow.*
2 If an organization **claws back** money, it finds a way of getting money back which it has spent or lost earlier.
claw back something or **claw something back** ❏ *They will eventually be able to claw back all or most of the debt.* ● A **clawback** is a method of getting money back which was spent earlier. [BRITISH] ❏ *The report argued that there should have been some kind of clawback arrangement in the event of the companies being sold.*

clean /kliːn/ (**cleans, cleaning, cleaned**)

○ **clean 'down**

If you **clean down** a large surface, you clean it thoroughly.
clean down something or **clean something down** ❏ *Inside, a man was cleaning down the sides of a large steel milk tank.*

◉ **clean 'out**

1 If you **clean** something **out**, you clean it very thoroughly and remove anything that should not be there.
clean something out ❏ *I spent three days cleaning our flat out.* ❏ *I had to massage the wound and clean it out every day.*
clean out something ❏ *I was cleaning out my desk at the office on my last day there.* ● A **clean-out** is the activity of cleaning a place very thoroughly and throwing away things you do not want. ❏ *I was just having a clean-out in the kitchen.*
2 To **clean** a person **out** is to take or use all the money they have. [INFORMAL]
clean someone out or **clean out something** ❏ *We had to pay for all the building work and it cleaned us out.*
3 To **clean out** a place is to take everything of value that is in it. [INFORMAL]
clean out something or **clean something out** ❏ *Just for a moment, he considered cleaning out the cash register.*

◉ **clean 'up**

1 If you **clean up** something that is dirty or untidy, you get rid of it by wiping, sweeping, etc.
clean up something ❏ *Clean up food spills at once*

clean something up ❑ The kids had made a mess in the kitchen and we were asked to clean it up.

2 If you **clean up** or **clean up** a place or person, you clean them. = **clear up**

clean up something/someone ❑ They would stay behind to help me clean up the classroom.

clean something/someone up ❑ He cleaned the room up before leaving. ❑ He had a cut on his knee which was a bit dirty so I cleaned him up before taking him home.

clean up ❑ We were busy cleaning up after the party. ● A **clean-up** is a thorough clean. ❑ This room could do with a good clean-up.

3 If the police or the authorities **clean up** a place, they make it free from crime.

clean up something or **clean something up** ❑ Now they can begin to clean up the cities.

4 If people **clean up**, they make a large profit from a business deal. [INFORMAL] ❑ People who buy shares now will clean up when the price rises.

○ **clean 'up after**

If you **clean up after** a person or animal, you clean or tidy a place that they have made dirty or untidy.

clean up after someone/something ❑ I spend my life cleaning up after the kids. ❑ There are signs in the park telling you to clean up after your dog.

clear /klɪə/ (**clears, clearing, cleared**)

○ **clear a'way**

When you **clear away** or **clear away** things, you put the things that you have been using in the place where they belong. = **tidy away**

clear away ❑ After dinner, when we had cleared away and washed up, we went for a walk.

clear away something or **clear something away** ❑ Brody stood up and began to clear away the soup bowls. ❑ Clear the cutlery away.

○ **clear 'off** [BRITISH, INFORMAL]

If you say **clear off** to someone, you are telling them in a rude way to go away. = **buzz off** ❑ Now you clear off and leave me alone.

❂ **clear 'out**

1 If you **clear out**, you leave a place. = **get out** [INFORMAL] ❑ [+ of] I've got to clear out of my place by next week. ❑ I woke one night around midnight and decided to clear out.

2 If you **clear out** a cupboard or a place, or if you **clear** things **out**, you make somewhere tidy by getting rid of the things you no longer need.

clear out something ❑ It's about time I cleared out the kitchen cupboards.

clear something out ❑ We need to clear these drawers and cupboards out. ● A **clear-out** is the activity of collecting together all the things that you do not want and throwing them away. [BRITISH, INFORMAL] ❑ Every year I have a big clear-out and get rid of all the clothes I don't wear.

❂ **clear 'up**

1 When you **clear up** or **clear up** a place or things, you tidy things and put them where they belong.

clear up ❑ I was too tired to clear up.

clear up something ❑ Go and clear up your room.

clear something up ❑ I wonder who clears the mess up after everyone has left.

2 If you **clear up** a disagreement, misunderstanding or other problem between people, you explain it or deal with it so that the problem is ended. = **sort out**

clear up something or **clear something up** ❑ I am simply trying to clear up a messy situation. ❑ I went to clear the matter up with him.

3 If someone's illness **clears up**, they recover from it. ❑ I was very lucky, it was only a minor infection and it all cleared up in a week. ❑ The neck pains should clear up on their own.

4 When bad weather **clears up**, it stops raining or being cloudy. = **brighten up** ❑ If the weather clears up, we can go out.

click /klɪk/ (**clicks, clicking, clicked**)

❂ **'click on**

If you **click on** an area of a computer screen, you choose it by pressing a button on the mouse.

click on something ❑ You can request tickets by clicking on the link below. ❑ Click on the icon to open the program.

○ **click 'through**

If you **click through**, you follow an electronic link, for example to a website. ❑ [+ to] We want to encourage people to click through to our site. ● A **click-through** is an instance of someone following an electronic link. ❑ We can measure the number of **click-throughs** to the website.

○ **'click with** [INFORMAL]

If you **click with** someone, you like each other and become friendly as soon as you meet.

click with someone ❑ They had the apartment next to ours and we clicked with them from the start.

climb /klaɪm/ (**climbs, climbing, climbed**)

○ **climb 'down**

If you **climb down** in an argument, you

admit that you are wrong. = **back down**
❑ Even after these facts were published, he was unwilling to climb down. • A **climb-down** is the act of admitting that you are wrong and agreeing to accept what someone else wants. ❑ Many strikes end in a climb-down on the part of the management.

cling /klɪŋ/ (clings, clinging, clung)

✪ 'cling to (or cling onto)

1 If you **cling to** someone or something, you hold them tightly.
cling to someone/something ❑ Another man was rescued as he clung to the riverbank. ❑ Johnny flung himself at his father and clung to him.

2 If someone **clings to** a position or a possession they have, they do everything they can to keep it even though this may be very difficult.
cling to something ❑ He appears determined to cling to power. ❑ This photo of her children was all that she had to cling onto.

3 If you **cling to** a belief, hope, or way of behaving, you continue to believe in it or behave in a particular way, even though it may not be true or useful any longer.
cling to something ❑ The missing girl's parents are still clinging to the belief that she is alive. ❑ They're clinging to the past.

clip /klɪp/ (clips, clipping, clipped)

○ clip 'off

If you **clip** a small amount **off** the time taken to do something, you reduce it by that amount.
clip something off something ❑ Boardman finished in 1hr 43mins, clipping 49 seconds off his own course record.

clock /klɒk/ (clocks, clocking, clocked)

○ 'clock at

If you **clock** something or someone **at** a particular speed, you measure that they are travelling at that speed.
clock someone/something at something
❑ He was driving on the motorway when police clocked him at 125mph.

○ clock 'in (or clock on)

When workers **clock in** at a factory or office, they record the time that they arrive by putting a special card into a device. ❑ If they are late clocking in, they lose pay.

○ clock 'in at

1 If someone or something **clocks in at** a particular weight, they are shown to weigh that amount. = **weigh in**
clock in at something ❑ The van clocked in at 2,000 pounds.

2 If something such as a record or film **clocks in at** at a particular amount of time, it lasts for that amount of time.
clock in at something ❑ There are four more songs, each clocking in at around 12 minutes.

○ clock 'off → see clock out

○ clock 'on → see clock in

○ clock 'out (or clock off)

When workers **clock out** at a factory or office, they record the time that they leave by putting a special card into a device. ❑ I've already clocked out.

○ clock 'up

To **clock up** a large number or total means to reach that total. = **notch up**
clock up something ❑ He has clocked up more than 171,750 miles in a lifetime of running.

clog /klɒg/ (clogs, clogging, clogged)

○ clog 'up

If something **clogs up** or if something **clogs** it **up**, it becomes blocked and nothing in it can move.
clog up ❑ We have to call a mechanic every time the waste disposal unit clogs up.
clog up something or **clog something up**
❑ Too much animal fat will start to clog up the arteries. ❑ If the cooling unit is clogged up it can't do its job efficiently.

close /kləʊz/ (closes, closing, closed)

✪ close 'down

1 If someone **closes down** a factory or an organization, or if it **closes down**, all work or activity stops there, usually for ever.
= **shut down**
close down something ❑ They're closing down my old school. ❑ The mines had been closed down following a geological survey.
close something down ❑ There was a club but the police closed it down.
close down ❑ If the firms failed to make enough money, they would close down.

CLOSE DOWN + noun
close down **a branch**
close down **a factory**
close down **an operation**
close down **an office**
❑ They are closing down their Sydney branch.
❑ We had to close down our office in Edinburgh.

2 When a television or radio channel **closes down**, it stops broadcasting for the day. [BRITISH] ❑ Channel 4 closes down at midnight. • **Closedown** is the end of broadcasting for the day on the television or radio. [BRITISH] ❑ She liked to lie in bed late at night listening to the radio just before closedown.

close 'in

1 If a group of people **close in**, they come nearer and nearer to someone, gradually surrounding them. ❑ [+ on] *At least this way they would have a chance of avoiding the two forces that were closing in on them.* ❑ *Now the police were closing in.*

2 If something **closes in**, it starts to be present in a threatening way. ❑ *As night closed in, the invasion force continued to wait.* ❑ [+ on] *Blackness began to close in on me; panic and dread.*

3 When the days or nights **close in**, the days start to get dark earlier as winter gets nearer. ❑ *The leaves are falling from the trees and the nights are closing in.*

close 'off

To **close off** an area is to put a barrier in front of it so that nobody can get into it. **= seal off**

close off something or **close something off**
❑ *He hadn't been down that road since they closed it off.* ❑ *Some areas of the city had been closed off to the public.*

'close on

If you **close on** something or someone, you gradually get nearer and nearer to them, often in a threatening way. **= close in on**

close on someone/something ❑ *He was picking up his speed, raising his left hand as he closed on her.*

close 'out

If you **close out** light or sound, you stop it from being seen or heard.

close out something or **close something out**
❑ *To close out the bright light he finally had to shut his eyes completely.* ❑ *She shut the window, closing out the sound of the midday traffic.*

close 'up

1 If you **close up** or **close up** a building or a business, you close it for a period.

close up ❑ *We got to the shop just as they were closing up.*

close something up ❑ *They had closed the building up for winter.* ❑ *He used to have a hair salon, but he closed it up years ago.*

close up something ❑ *The big house was closed up for the holidays.*

2 If something **closes up** or if you **close** it **up**, it closes completely.

close up ❑ *One had a badly swollen face, and his left eye had closed up.*

close something up ❑ *He closed the luggage up and stored it by the door.* ❑ *He got out of the car and closed it up.*

close up something ❑ *The shutters of the house were closed up.*

3 If people **close up**, they move nearer to each other. ❑ *She told the children to close up to allow everyone into the hall.*

cloud /klaʊd/ (clouds, clouding, clouded)

○ cloud 'over

1 If it **clouds over** or if the sky **clouds over**, the sky becomes covered with clouds.
❑ *It was clouding over and we thought it was going to rain.* ❑ *The sky had clouded over completely.*

2 If your face **clouds over**, you suddenly look sad or angry. ❑ *Grace's face suddenly clouded over and she turned away.*

3 If your eyes **cloud over**, they seem to have a layer of something on them, often because you are about to cry. **= mist over**
❑ *Her eyes clouded over and she seemed about to cry.*

club /klʌb/ (clubs, clubbing, clubbed)

○ club to'gether [BRITISH]

If a group of people **club together**, they all give money so that they can buy something together. **= chip in** ❑ [+ to-infinitive] *We all clubbed together to buy her a present.*

cluck /klʌk/ (clucks, clucking, clucked)

○ 'cluck at

To **cluck at** someone or something means to make disapproving noises or say things in a disapproving way.

cluck at someone/something ❑ *The older women clucked at Melanie's short skirt.*

○ 'cluck over

To **cluck over** someone or something means to behave in a fussy or protective way towards them.

cluck over someone/something ❑ *All the time Carol clucked over him like a mother hen.*

clue /kluː/ (clues, clueing, clued)

○ clue 'up [BRITISH, INFORMAL]

If you **are clued up**, you know about something and understand it.

be clued up ❑ [+ on] *I'm not so clued up on the names of today's pop icons.* ❑ [+ about] *According to the report, young people are more clued up about the world than they were 20 years ago.*

cluster /'klʌstə/ (clusters, clustering, clustered)

○ cluster a'round (or cluster round [mainly BRITISH])

If people **cluster around** a thing or a person, they stand around them in a tight group. **= gather around**

cluster around something/someone
❑ *A small gathering clustered around the steps of the American Church.* ❑ *The children clustered round her.*

○ **cluster to'gether**
If people **cluster together**, they gather together in a small group. ❑ *The passengers clustered together in small groups.*

clutch /klʌtʃ/ (**clutches, clutching, clutched**)
○ **'clutch at**
If you **clutch at** something, you hold it tightly, usually because you are afraid or in pain.
clutch at something ❑ *He cried out in pain and fell to the ground, clutching at his leg.*

clutter /'klʌtə/ (**clutters, cluttering, cluttered**)
○ **clutter 'up**
If you **clutter up** a place, you fill it with a lot of unnecessary things in a way that is untidy.
clutter up somewhere or **clutter somewhere up** ❑ *Helen's bags were cluttering up the hall.* ❑ *I like the simplicity of the room – I don't want to clutter it up with loads of stuff.*

coax /kəʊks/ (**coaxes, coaxing, coaxed**)
○ **coax 'into**
If you **coax** someone **into** doing something, you persuade them to do it by speaking in a gentle and pleasant way to them.
coax someone into something ❑ *Teresa was trying to coax Amy into eating a few spoonfuls of cereal.*

cobble /'kɒbəl/ (**cobbles, cobbling, cobbled**)
○ **cobble to'gether**
cobble together something or **cobble something together**
If you **cobble** something **together**, you make or produce it roughly or quickly, by using things that are available to you. ❑ *Steve quickly cobbled together a list of equipment.* ❑ *The report isn't brilliant – I just cobbled it together from various bits of information.*

cock /kɒk/ (**cocks, cocking, cocked**)
○ **cock 'up** [BRITISH, INFORMAL, RUDE]
If you **cock** something **up**, you do it so badly that you spoil it.
cock something up or **cock up something** ❑ *If he's not careful he'll cock the whole thing up.* ❑ *Patrick cocked up the arrangements.* ●A **cock-up** is something that is done very badly. [BRITISH, INFORMAL, RUDE] ❑ *There has been a series of cock-ups.*

cocoon /kə'kuːn/ (**cocoons, cocooning, cocooned**)
○ **co'coon from**
If you **cocoon** someone **from** something, you protect them from it.
cocoon someone from something ❑ *Children cannot be cocooned from every danger in life.*

coerce /kəʊ'ɜːs/ (**coerces, coercing, coerced**)
○ **coerce 'into** [FORMAL]
If you **coerce** someone **into** doing something, you make them do it, although they do not want to.
coerce someone into something ❑ *He had been coerced into marriage by his parents.*

coexist /kəʊɪg'zɪst/ (**coexists, coexisting, coexisted**)
○ **coex'ist with**
If one thing **coexists with** another, they exist together at the same time or in the same place.
coexist with something ❑ *In the city, areas of affluence coexist with areas of poverty.*

coil /kɔɪl/ (**coils, coiling, coiled**)
○ **coil a'round** (or **coil round** [mainly BRITISH])
If something **coils around** something or you **coil** it **around** something, it forms loops or a ring around it.
coil around something ❑ *The snake coils around its prey and then slowly crushes it to death.*
coil something around something ❑ *She coiled her arms around his neck and held on tightly.*
○ **coil 'up**
If you **coil** something **up**, you wind it into a continuous series of loops.
coil up something or **coil something up** ❑ *He coiled up the garden hose.* ❑ *She plaited her hair and coiled it up in a bun.*

coincide /kəʊɪn'saɪd/ (**coincides, coinciding, coincided**)
✪ **coin'cide with**
If one event **coincides with** another, they happen at the same time.
coincide with something ❑ *The exhibition coincides with the 50th anniversary of his death.* ❑ *My visit coincided with the heaviest rain in Scotland for years.*

collaborate /kə'læbəreɪt/ (**collaborates, collaborating, collaborated**)
○ **col'laborate with**
1 When one person or group **collaborates with** another person or group, they work together, especially to write a book or do some research.
collaborate with someone/something ❑ [+ on] *He collaborated with his son Michael on the English translation of the text.*
2 If someone **collaborates with** an enemy,

they help them.

collaborate with someone/something
❏ *He was accused of having collaborated with the secret police.*

col·lect /kəˈlekt/ (collects, collecting, collected)

○ **col·lect for**
If you **collect for** a charity or **collect** something **for** a charity, you ask people to give you money for it.
collect for something ❏ *Someone knocked at the door, collecting for a children's charity.* ❏ *The bank is collecting for Unicef.*
collect something for something ❏ *They collected donations for a fund to help military families.*

○ **collect 'up**
If you **collect** things **up**, you gather them all together.
collect up something or **collect something up** ❏ *They collected up their gear.* ❏ *Just collect everything up in a bag and take it with you.*

col·lide /kəˈlaɪd/ (collides, colliding, collided)

○ **col·lide with**
1 If a moving person, vehicle or object **collides with** someone or something, they crash into them.
collide with someone/something ❏ *Racing up the stairs, he almost collided with Daisy.* ❏ *His car collided with a lorry on the A1 between Paris and Calais.*
2 If an aim, opinion, or interest **collides with** another, it is very different and is therefore opposed.
collide with something ❏ *The organization's aims have collided with economic reality.*

col·lo·cate /ˈkɒləkeɪt/ (collocates, collocating, collocated)

○ **'collocate with**
In linguistics, if one word **collocates with** another word, they often occur together.
collocate with something ❏ *'Detached' collocates with 'house'.*

col·lude /kəˈluːd/ (colludes, colluding, colluded)

○ **col·lude with**
If someone **colludes with** another person or organization, they work secretly with them to do something dishonest.
collude with someone ❏ *Several local officials are in jail on charges of colluding with the Mafia.*

col·our /ˈkʌlə/ (colours, colouring, coloured)

American English uses the spellings **color, colors, coloring** and **colored**.

○ **colour 'in**
If you **colour in** a shape or figure that is drawn on paper, you give it different colours using paints or crayons.
colour in something or **colour something in** ❏ *His little girl was busy colouring in her picture.*

○ **colour 'up**
When someone **colours up**, their face becomes red because they are angry or embarrassed. = **blush** ❏ *Christina coloured up at the mention of his name.*

comb /kəʊm/ (combs, combing, combed)

○ **comb 'out**
If you **comb out** your hair, or if you **comb** something **out** of it, you comb it very carefully in order to remove anything that should not be there, such as knots.
comb out something or **comb something out** ❏ *It took me an hour to comb out the tangles in her hair.* ❏ *Julia started combing out her long blonde hair.*

○ **'comb through**
If you **comb through** information or a place, you look at it very carefully in order to find something.
comb through something ❏ *Police spent two years combing through the evidence.* ❏ *Rescue workers have been combing through the wreckage looking for survivors.*

come /kʌm/ (comes, coming, came)

The form **come** is used in the present tense and is the past participle of the verb.

● **come a'bout**
When you say how something **comes about**, you explain how it happens.
❏ *The documentary tells how the discovery of the drug came about.* ❏ *So how did the invitation come about?*

● **come a'cross**
1 When someone **comes across** or **comes across** something, they cross an area towards the place where you are.
come across ❏ *She's coming across on the ferry.*
come across something ❏ *He came across the room and took her firmly by the shoulder.*
2 If you **come across** someone or something, you find or meet them by chance.
come across someone/something ❏ *In the years that followed, I came across him from time to time.* ❏ *He was cleaning out his attic one morning when he came across an old brass lamp.* ❏ *I've never come across anything like this.*

NOTE **Encounter** is a more formal word for **come across**.

3 If someone **comes across** as having a particular characteristic, they seem to have that characteristic by the things they say and do. ❏ [+ as] *From the tone of her letters, she comes across as a gentle, sensitive woman.* ❏ *I've gotten to know him and he's not how he comes across – he's actually quite shy.*

4 When an idea, quality or emotion **comes across**, especially in a film, book or something that someone says, it is communicated clearly. = **come over** ❏ *He's clearly a very angry man. That came across in the interview.*

○ **come 'after**

1 To **come after** a particular event, point in time or person is to happen or exist later than them. = **follow**
come after something/someone ❏ *Their words and actions inspired generations who came after them.* ❏ *These incidents came after the first world war.*

2 If someone **comes after** you, they chase you or hunt you.
come after someone ❏ *The faster I retreated, the faster they came after me.*

○ **come a'long**

1 When someone **comes along** or **comes along** a road or other area of ground, they move along somewhere towards you.
come along ❏ *They're coming along behind us, I think.*
come along something ❏ *The children came along the beach.*

2 If someone **comes along**, they go somewhere with you or go to the same place as you. ❏ [+ with] *We're going out for dinner. Why don't you come along with us?* ❏ [+ to] *You could come along to the fair with us this afternoon.*

3 When something or someone **comes along**, they start to happen or exist. ❏ *This was the greatest advance until X-rays came along in the 1890s.*

4 If something or someone **is coming along**, they are making progress or developing in the way you want. = **come on**
be coming along ❏ *The arrangements are coming along nicely.* ❏ *How is your Russian coming along?*

5 You say **come along** to someone when you want them to go somewhere more quickly. = **come on, hurry up** [OLD-FASHIONED] ❏ *Come along now, you two, off to bed!*

6 You say **come along** to someone when you think that they are saying something untrue or unreasonable. [OLD-FASHIONED] ❏ *Come along now, Marsha, that's not quite what he said!*

○ **come a'part**

If something **comes apart**, it breaks into pieces. ❏ *I've only had these boots three months and they're coming apart.*

❂ **come a'round** (or **come round** [mainly BRITISH])

1 When someone **comes around**, they call at your home to see you for a short time. = **come over** ❏ *I could come round this evening if you like.* ❏ *Come round and have a cup of coffee.*

2 When someone **comes around**, they go to see each person in a group, often to give something to them or take something from them. ❏ *The driver came around to collect fares.* ❏ [+ with] *Hazel will be coming round with drinks in a minute.*

3 When a letter or other message **comes around**, it is sent or given to all the members of a group of people. ❏ *A memo just came round to say that Lucas Sylva is leaving.*

4 If you **come around**, you start to like or agree to an idea or opinion, after not liking or agreeing to it at first. ❏ [+ to] *He'll come around to your way of thinking in the end.* ❏ *They may be against the idea now but they'll come round Parents always do.*

5 If something **comes around**, it happens as a regular event. ❏ *See how she feels when the new academic year comes around in the autumn.* ❏ *Don't wait for April to come round before planning your vegetable garden.*

○ **come at**

1 If someone **comes at** you, they move towards you in order to attack you.
come at someone ❏ *The minute I saw this one guy coming at me I knew I was really in trouble.*

2 If things such as questions, facts or ideas **come at** you, they are said to you, often all at the same time.
come at someone ❏ *She had to deal with a barrage of questions coming at her from all angles.*

❂ **come a'way**

1 If you **come away**, you leave a place, often feeling a particular emotion, or having a particular opinion. ❏ *I came away feeling sad about the whole situation.* ❏ [+ with] *He came away with the uncomfortable feeling that he had been deceived.*

2 When something **comes away**, it becomes separated from something else that it was attached to. ❏ [+ from] *She picked up the book. The cover had come away from the spine.*

3 If you **come away**, you move away from someone or something. ❑ [+ from] Come away from the river, Oliver.

come 'back

1 When someone or something **comes back**, they return. ❑ [+ from] He never came back from the war. ❑ I've just come back from the hairdresser's. ❑ [+ with] Lara left the room and came back with a bottle of water and two glasses.

2 When something **comes back**, it starts to happen again, after not happening for a while. ❑ My headache went away for a while and then came back. ❑ If the hot weather comes back, we'll go swimming in the lake.

3 When something **comes back**, it becomes fashionable again after not being popular for a while. ≠ **go out** ❑ Long dresses had come back into fashion. ● If something makes a **comeback**, it becomes fashionable again. ❑ Body painting made a brief comeback in the 1960s. ● If someone makes a **comeback**, they become successful again at something such as acting or singing that they were successful at before. ❑ He tried to make a comeback in the 1990s but failed.

4 If a message or answer **comes back**, it is given as a response to something you have said. ❑ The message which came back was that I could order the books online.

5 When someone **comes back**, they respond to something you have said ❑ [+ with] They came back with a very definite refusal.

6 If something that you had forgotten **comes back**, you remember it, often quite suddenly. ❑ [+ to] The scene of their encounter came back to him with a sense of embarrassment.

come 'back to

If you **come back to** a particular subject, you mention or start to discuss it again.
come back to something ❑ We always come back to the same point. ❑ We'll come back to that question a little later.

come be'fore

If a person, problem, or case **comes before** a judge, court of law, or other authority, they are brought or discussed there as part of an official process, so that a decision can be made.
come before someone/something ❑ His case came before a tribunal.

come be'tween

If a person or something that they disagree about **comes between** two people, it causes trouble between them and so spoils their relationship.
come between someone ❑ I know it's hard but I really don't want this to come between us.

come 'by

In meaning 2, the stress is on **'come**.

1 When someone **comes by** or **comes by** a place, they come to see you or come to a place for a short time.
come by ❑ Tom said he'd come by at around five.
come by somewhere ❑ She came by the office on the way to town.

2 If you **come by** something, especially something special or unusual, you get it.
come by something ❑ How did you come by this extraordinary picture?
● If something **is hard to come by**, it is difficult to get or find. ❑ At this time, jobs like this were hard to come by.

come 'down

1 When someone or something **comes down** or **comes down** something, they move from a higher position to a lower one.
come down ❑ She was sitting at the top of the climbing frame and wouldn't come down.
come down something ❑ We met them as they were coming down the hill. ❑ We came down the aircraft steps.

2 When someone in a building **comes down**, they move downstairs towards you. ❑ I showered, dressed and came down for breakfast.
NOTE **Descend** is a more formal word for **come down**.

3 If someone **comes down**, they come from a place that is further north than you to visit you. ❑ [+ from] They came down from Manchester last night. ❑ [+ to] When are you coming down to Devon?

4 If someone **comes down** to a place, they go there. ❑ [+ to] You should come down to the beach with us. ❑ Do you want to come down to the club tonight?

5 When a person or vehicle **comes down** a road, they move along the road.
come down something ❑ A taxi came down the street. ❑ I saw her coming down the road.

6 When something **comes down**, it collapses or falls to the ground. ❑ A huge tree came down in the storm.

7 If a plane **comes down**, it lands or crashes. ❑ The plane circled and came down in flames.

8 If the cost, level, or amount of something **comes down**, it becomes lower than it was before. ≠ **go up** ❑ Food prices are coming down all the time. ❑ Interest rates have come down again.
NOTE **Decrease** is a more formal word for **come down**.

noun + COME DOWN

the cost of something comes down
rates come down
prices come down
❏ *The cost of borrowing has come down.*
❏ *Oil prices have come down recently.*

9 If you **come down** when you are suggesting a price for something you are selling, you agree to accept a lower price. ❏ *The asking price is £600 but I suspect they'll come down a bit if you offer cash.*

10 Something that **comes down** stretches downwards. ❏ [+ to] *The window came down almost to the ground.* ❏ *His eyebrows came down over his nose.*

11 If something such as a tradition, belief, or land **comes down**, it is passed to the younger people in a society from the older people. = **be handed down** ❏ [+ to] *These are the religious doctrines that have come down to us.* ❏ *Folk tales traditionally come down from one generation to the next.*

12 If a message or order **comes down**, you get it from someone in authority. ❏ *Now word had come down that a group of activists were planning a protest.* ❏ *An instruction came down from Paris to investigate him.*

13 If rain, snow or fog **comes down**, it falls heavily. ❏ *Twenty centimetres of snow had fallen and more was coming down.* ❏ *Then the fog came down.*

14 If you **come down in favour of** something in an argument or discussion, you announce that you support it. ❏ *The subcommittees both came down in favour of the conservation programme.*

● If you **come down on the side of** something or someone in an argument or discussion, you announce that you support them. ❏ *They came down strongly on the side of Walker.*

15 A **come-down** is a situation which is very much less impressive or important than the one you were in before. ❏ *Aren't television soaps a bit of a come-down after Hollywood films?*

○ **come 'down on**
If you **come down on** someone, you criticize or punish them severely for something they have done.
come down on someone ❏ *I wouldn't come down on him too hard when you don't know his circumstances.*

● If you **come down on** someone **like a ton of bricks**, you punish them very severely for something they have done. ❏ *If you step out of line, he'll come down on you like a ton of bricks.*

○ **come 'down to**
If a problem, question, or situation **comes down to** a particular thing, that is the most important thing about it.
come down to something ❏ *Your final choice of kitchen may well come down to cost.* ❏ *It all comes down to what sort of education you received.*

○ **come 'down with**
If you **come down with** an illness or disease, you catch it or develop it.
come down with something ❏ *I don't feel so good – I think I'm coming down with something.*
NOTE **Contract** is a more formal word for **come down with**.

❍ **'come for**
1 When someone **comes for** a person or thing, they come to where you are in order to get them and take them away.
come for someone/something ❏ *I'll come for you at around 3:00.* ❏ *I'll come for the sandwiches later.*

2 If someone **is coming for** you, they are moving towards you in a threatening way, as if they might attack you.
be coming for someone ❏ *The taller guy was coming for me with a knife.*

○ **come 'forth**
1 If you **come forth**, you formally offer a suggestion or information. = **come forward** [FORMAL] ❏ [+ with] *The British came forth with a second proposal.* ❏ [+ to-infinitive] *A witness came forth to testify that the young man had indeed been present.* ● Someone who is **forthcoming** willingly gives information when you ask them about something. ❏ *He said little about the matter: nor was he forthcoming on the way in which he had risen to power.* ● If information is **forthcoming**, it is given or made available. [FORMAL] ❏ *No evidence of this was forthcoming.*

2 If something or someone **comes forth**, they appear from a place or move towards you. [LITERARY] ❏ *Great rockets of flame came forth.* ❏ *With fear in his eyes, he came forth bearing a lantern in his hand.*

3 A **forthcoming** event is planned to happen soon. ❏ *She spoke at length about her forthcoming marriage.*

❍ **come 'forward**
If someone **comes forward**, they give information or help or make an offer.
❏ [+ to-infinitive] *Two people later came forward to say they had seen the accident.*
❏ [+ with] *Others came forward with further suggestions.*

❍ **'come from**
1 If you **come from** a particular place, you

were born there or grew up there.

come from somewhere ❏ *Nuria comes from Madrid.* ❏ *I come from Oxford.* ❏ *'Where do you come from?' – 'India'.*

2 If you **come from** a particular type of family or a particular social class, that is the type of family or social class that you grew up in.

come from something ❏ *They all came from well-off families.* ❏ *Felicity came from a very theatrical background.*

3 If one thing **comes from** another thing, the second thing is its source or origin.

come from something ❏ *There was a smell of bread baking coming from the kitchen.* ❏ *Did you know the word 'idea' comes from Greek?*

4 If you say that you know where someone **is coming from**, you mean that you understand their opinion or attitude. [INFORMAL]

be coming from ❏ *I know where you're coming from.* ❏ *I just don't get where he's coming from, that guy.*

○ **come 'in**

1 When someone **comes in**, they enter the room or building where you are. ❏ *There was a knock on the door. 'Come in'.* ❏ *Jeremy came in looking worried.* ❏ *She usually comes in for a cup of coffee around this time.*

2 When someone **comes in**, they arrive at their place of work. ❏ *I came in early this morning.* ❏ *He called to say he's not coming in today.*

3 When someone such as a builder or cleaner **comes in**, they come to your house in order to work there. ❏ *We have a builder coming in tomorrow to fix the problem.*

4 When someone or something **comes in** from another place, they arrive at or approach the place where you are.
❏ [+ through] *Refugees are coming in through the border all the time.* ❏ *A great deal of produce comes in through these docks.*

5 When a plane, ship, train, or bus **comes in**, it arrives. ❏ *Her train should be coming in any minute now.* ❏ *She waited until the last bus came in.* • An **incoming** plane or passenger is travelling towards a place and about to arrive. ≠ **outward** ❏ *The notice only applies to incoming passengers.*

6 When light, sound, air, or rain **comes in**, it gets through a barrier or hole and reaches the place where you are. ❏ *Inside it was dark. No sunlight came in at all.* ❏ *Rain was coming in through a hole in the roof.*

7 If information or a report **comes in**, you receive it. = **arrive**; ≠ **go out** ❏ *New reports of*

fighting are coming in from the region. ❏ *A call had come in telling us that arrests had been made.*

• An **incoming** message, letter, or phone call has been sent to you or is received by you. ≠ **outgoing** ❏ *Isabel deals with all incoming mail.*

8 If money **comes in**, someone earns or receives it. ❏ *There is practically no money coming in to buy food.* • Your **income** is the amount of money that you earn from your work or business, or from other sources such as pension or investments. ❏ *My monthly income was just over three thousand pounds.*

9 When a type of clothes, make-up or hairstyle **comes in**, it becomes fashionable at a particular time. ≠ **go out** ❏ *Beards are coming in again.*

10 When something new such as a law or something that has just been discovered or invented **comes in**, it is introduced and begins to have an effect. ❏ *We used coal gas before natural gas came in.*

11 When something in a shop **comes in**, a supply of it reaches the shop and it becomes available. ❏ *The first copies of the novel had just come in that morning.* ❏ *We're waiting for the new brochures to come in.*

12 If someone **comes in** when people are discussing something, they join the discussion by starting to speak. ❏ [+ on] *Let me just come in on this, because Clive is not giving the whole story.* ❏ *Could I come in here?*

13 If someone **comes in** when there is a plan to do something, they join a group of other people and take part in what is being arranged. ❏ [+ on] *Tolley wants to come in on the deal.* ❏ [+ with] *He was sorry that he had asked Fred to come in with him.*

14 When a government **comes in**, it wins an election and starts governing the country.
❏ *That was when the last Labour government came in.* • An **incoming** official or government is one that has just been appointed or elected. ≠ **outgoing** ❏ *They gave their loyalty to the incoming government.*

15 You ask or say where someone **comes in** when you are talking about how they are involved in a situation. ❏ *We need someone to manage this project and that's where you come in.*

16 When the tide **comes in**, it rises, so that the water reaches higher up the shore. ≠ **go out** ❏ *The tide was coming in and all the muddy banks were being covered.* • An **incoming** tide or wave is coming towards the shore.

17 When a period of weather **comes in**, it begins. ❏ *At last, we have some warm weather coming in.*

18 If something **comes in handy** or **comes in useful**, it is a helpful thing to have in a particular situation. ❑ *Savings may come in useful for holidays.* ❑ *A toothbrush would come in handy.*

19 When someone or something **comes in** a particular position, they are in that position at the end of a competition.
come in something ❑ *David had begun the day well by coming in third in the junior riding class.*

20 When cricketers and baseball players **come in**, it is their turn to try to score points by hitting the ball with a bat.
❑ *He made a Test century only a week ago, coming in at number nine.*

○ **come 'in for**
If someone or something **comes in for** criticism, they are criticized.
come in for something ❑ *British industry comes in for a great deal of criticism in the report.*

❍ **come 'into**
1 If someone **comes into** a room, house, or other place, they enter it. ≠ **leave**
come into something ❑ *She came into the bookstore earlier this morning.*
NOTE **Enter** is a more formal word for **come into**.

2 If someone **comes into** their place of work, they arrive there.
come into something ❑ *I'll come into the office as normal next week.*

3 If something **comes into** force, effect, use, etc., it starts to exist or happen or starts to be used.
come into something ❑ *New legislation came into force in 1981.* ❑ *The law will come into effect from the start of next year.*

4 If someone or something **comes into** sight, you begin to be able to see it. ❑ *They turned the corner and a long harbour came into sight.*

5 If you say that something **doesn't come into** a situation or subject, you mean that it is not relevant to the situation or subject that you are talking about.
not come into something ❑ *I sell only what people want to buy. My own private tastes don't come into it.* ❑ *Privilege doesn't come into the argument.*

6 When a government **comes into** office or power, it wins an election and starts governing the country.
come into something ❑ *That happened before the Conservatives came into office.* ❑ *The Labour Government came into power in March 1974.*

7 If someone **comes into** money, property, or a title, they get it when

someone in their family dies.
come into something ❑ *She came into some money on her mother's death.*

○ **'come of**
1 If something **comes of** an event or situation, it happens because of it.
come of something ❑ *I'll let you know if anything comes of the meeting.* ❑ *It will be interesting to see what comes of the discussions.*

2 If a person **comes of** a particular family or group of people who lived long ago, they are related to them or part of that group.
[LITERARY]
come of something ❑ *He comes of a long line of actors.*

❍ **come 'off**
1 If someone or something **comes off** or **comes off** an area, place, or vehicle, they leave it.
come off ❑ *Their goalkeeper had to come off with an injury.*
come off something ❑ *She saw him come off the plane.*

2 When something **comes off**, it stops being attached or stuck to something.
❑ *All the wallpaper's coming off.* ❑ *He pulled the handle and it came off in his hand.*

3 If something **comes off**, it is successful.
❑ *It's an exciting plan – I just hope it comes off.*
❑ *I'm afraid the conference didn't come off quite as we had hoped.*

4 If you **come off** well or badly at the end of a process, you are in a good or bad position as a result of it. **= end up** ❑ *In a comparison between the two countries, England rarely came off well.* ❑ *Families in the wealthier classes come off comparatively better.*

5 When a play or film **comes off**, it stops being performed or shown in a particular theatre or cinema. ❑ *So few people came to see the show, it came off after three weeks.*

6 If mist, wind, or a smell **comes off** a particular place or thing, it starts in that place or thing.
come off something ❑ *There was mist coming off the water.*

7 If someone **comes off** a drug, medicine, or alcohol, they stop taking it.
come off something ❑ *With a lot of help from family and friends, she finally came off the drugs.*

8 If you say **Come off it!** to someone, you mean that you do not believe what they have just said, or think it is unreasonable.
[INFORMAL] ❑ *Come off it, Jim, that's not a letter.*

❍ **come 'on**

In meanings 5 and 6, the stress is on **'come**.

1 You say **come on** to someone when you want to encourage them. ❑ *Come on, honey, you can do it!*

2 You say **come on** to someone when you want them to come somewhere more quickly. = **come along** ❑ *Come on, Sophie, we're going to be late.*

3 If you tell someone to **come on** over/up/in, etc., you are asking them to come somewhere. ❑ *'Hello, there,' said Brody. 'Come on in.'* ❑ *Come on over – quick as you can.*

• **Oncoming** means moving towards you. ❑ *That sign means you have to give way to oncoming traffic.*

4 When a performer **comes on** or **comes on stage**, he or she appears on a stage or in a scene of a film.

come on ❑ *We waited so long for her that when she finally came on, it was a disappointment.*

come on something ❑ *Olivier dominated the play from the moment he came on the stage.*

5 If someone **comes on** or **comes on** the phone, they begin speaking to you.

come on something ❑ *One of the most powerful men in France came on the line.*

come on ❑ *There was a silence and then my mother came on.*

6 If you **come on** something or someone, you find them by chance. = **chance on**

come on something/someone ❑ *I came on the idea by pure chance.*

7 When a power supply or device **comes on**, it starts functioning. ≠ **go off** ❑ *At nine the street lights came on.* ❑ *The heating has just come on.*

8 When a programme or film **comes on**, it starts to be broadcast or shown. ❑ *At seven the news came on.*

9 When a season or part of the day **comes on**, it begins. ❑ *The night was coming on early outside.* ❑ *Winter was coming on again: the first snow had fallen.*

10 If a cold, headache, or other medical condition **comes on**, it starts. ❑ *I felt a cold coming on.* ❑ *My headache came on over dinner.*

11 If something or someone **is coming on**, they are making progress or developing in the way that you want. = **come along**

be coming on ❑ *The project is coming on quite well now.* ❑ *How's your research coming on?*

12 If someone **comes on** in a particular way, they behave in that way. [INFORMAL] ❑ *He was coming on fairly strong in the meeting. It was clear he was going to get what he wanted.*

○ **come 'on to** [INFORMAL, RUDE]

When a person **comes on to** someone, they make it obvious by what they say and do that they would like sex with them.

come on to someone ❑ *Did he come on to you?*

• A **come-on** is an openly sexual remark or action which is intended to attract someone. [INFORMAL] ❑ *These creepy come-ons are all too familiar for many women at work.*

○ **come 'onto**

If something **comes onto** the market, it becomes available to be sold.

come on to something ❑ *Very few houses of this size and quality come onto the market.*

◎ **come 'on to** (or **come onto**)

1 When someone **comes on to** a stage, court, or other area, they enter it.

come on to something ❑ *Whenever she came on to the stage everybody held their breath.*

2 If you **come on to** a particular topic or idea, you start discussing it. = **turn to**

come on to something ❑ *I want to come on to the question of cost in a minute.* ❑ *If we could come onto the matter of staffing for a moment.*

◎ **come 'out**

1 When someone **comes out** of their house or room, or a place where they were hidden, they leave it or appear from it. ❑ *I saw them go into the building and come out five minutes later.* ❑ *[+ of] We came out of the tunnel.*

2 If someone **comes out**, they go somewhere with someone socially. ❑ *Do you fancy coming out for a drink sometime?* ❑ *[+ with] Would you like to come out with us to the cinema?*

3 If someone **comes out**, they visit you in the country where you are. ❑ *[+ to] She came out to Egypt when we were there.* ❑ *Maybe one day I'll come out and visit you.*

4 If someone **comes out** of an organization or institution, they leave it. ≠ **go in** ❑ *[+ of] Her health got worse after coming out of hospital.* ❑ *He decided to come out of the army.*

5 If something **comes out** of a particular place or thing, it comes from there or is produced there. ❑ *[+ of] There's no sound coming out of this speaker.* ❑ *There were flames coming out of the engine.* ❑ *She opened her mouth to scream, but no sounds came out.*

NOTE **Emerge** is a more formal word for **come out**.

6 When something **comes out** from or onto a particular point, it joins something else at that point. ❑ *There are four big arteries coming out from the base of the heart.* ❑ *The road comes out onto a broad paved drive.*

NOTE **Emerge** is a more formal word for **come out**.

7 If something **comes out**, it becomes separated from the thing that it was

come

attached to. ❑ *I noticed that her hair was coming out in patches.* ❑ [+ of] *My shirt had come out of the top of my shorts.*

8 When information **comes out**, it becomes known. ❑ *All the facts came out after his death.* ❑ *It came out that she had been stealing from the company.*

9 When a gay person **comes out**, they let people know that they are gay. ❑ *John came out when he was at college.* ❑ [+ as] *I came out as a lesbian when I was still in my teens.*

10 If you **come out** for or against something, you announce that you do or do not support it. ❑ *He came out in support of the claim.* ❑ *Most Trade Union Group members came out against the proposal.*

11 When something such as a book or a film **comes out**, it is published or becomes available to be seen. **= appear** ❑ *When is your book coming out?* ❑ *She has a film coming out soon.*

12 If something or someone **comes out** in a particular position or in a particular way, they are in that position or condition at the end of a an event or process. ❑ *The press came out of the affair very badly.* ❑ *Who do you think will come out on top?* • The **outcome** of an action, event or process is its result. ❑ *No one dared to predict the outcome of the general election.*

13 If what you say **comes out** in a particular way, you say it in that way. ❑ *The words came out more harshly than she had intended.* ❑ *I didn't mean to say that – it just came out wrong.*

14 If workers **come out**, they go on strike. [BRITISH] ❑ *The whole workforce came out in protest when a driver got the sack.*

15 When the sun, moon, or a star **comes out**, it appears in the sky. ❑ *It's warm when the sun comes out.*

16 If colours or marks **come out** when you wash something, they disappear. ❑ *Wash these towels at a cool temperature or the colour will come out.* ❑ *I washed the shirt twice but the stains wouldn't come out.*

17 If a photograph or something that has been photographed **comes out** well, the photograph is good. ❑ *All the buildings came out well in the photos.*

18 When flowers, leaves, or plants **come out**, the flowers or leaves develop and open. ❑ *As soon as the leaves came out, the blossoms appeared.*

✪ come 'out in [BRITISH]

If you **come out in** spots, you become covered with them. **= break out in**

come out in something ❑ *She came out in a red rash after eating an egg.*

✪ come 'out of

If one thing **comes out of** something else, the first thing results from the second.

come out of something ❑ *If you only focus on the negative, nothing good can come out of it.*

○ come 'out with

If someone **comes out with** something, they say it, often unexpectedly.

come out with something ❑ *Children come out with the funniest things sometimes.*

✪ come 'over

1 When someone **comes over**, they move across a room or other place towards you. ❑ *He came over and stood beside me.* ❑ *Come over here and see this, Luca.*

2 When someone **comes over**, they come to the country which you are in, usually across the sea. ❑ *Janet and Jack are coming over in August.*

3 When someone **comes over**, they visit your house to see you for a short time. **= come around** ❑ *Come over and have lunch with us tomorrow.* ❑ *I've got some friends coming over.*

4 If someone **comes over** to a new group or organization, they leave their old group or organization and join an opposing one. ❑ [+ to] *They all came over to the new party.* ❑ [+ from] *Those were the five who came over from Labour.*

[NOTE] **Defect** is a more formal word for **come over**.

5 If a voice, sound, or message **comes over** a telephone or other piece of equipment, it is sent or broadcast through it.

come over something ❑ *A deep voice suddenly came over the loudspeakers.*

6 If a change or feeling **comes over** you or your face, it affects you or happens to you.

come over someone/something ❑ *A great change had come over him since the previous night.* ❑ *A look of contentment came over her face.*

7 If you **come over** a particular way, you start to feel or behave in that way. [INFORMAL] ❑ *She comes over all shy when she has to meet new people.*

8 When an idea, quality or emotion **comes over**, especially in a film, book or something that someone says, it is communicated clearly. **= come across** ❑ *A deep love of nature comes over in his later work.*

9 If someone **comes over** as having a particular characteristic, they seem to have that characteristic by the things they say and do. ❑ [+ as] *He comes over as honest, straightforward and decent.* ❑ *Nobody likes a* *boastful person, and that's how she comes over to me.*

NOTE **Come across** means almost the same as **come over**.

● come 'round

1 → see **come around**

2 When someone **comes round**, they become conscious again after not being conscious for a while. = **come to**; ≠ **pass out** ❑ *Later in the hospital he came round.*

● come 'through

1 When someone **comes through**, they move out of one room and enter another. ❑ *The doctor can see you now if you would like to come through.*

2 When something such as a document or some money **comes through**, it becomes available, often after official permission has been given. ❑ *Has my visa come through yet?* ❑ *She intended to look for a car as soon as the money came through.*

3 When a phone call or message **comes through**, you receive it. ❑ *A call came through on my mobile.*

4 When a quality, meaning or emotion **comes through**, especially in what someone says, it is communicated clearly. = **come across** ❑ *I think the teacher's own personality has got to come through.* ❑ *His charm really comes through in his letters.*

5 If you **come through** or **come through** a dangerous or difficult situation, you manage to survive it.
come through something ❑ *Most of the troops came through the fighting unharmed.*
come through ❑ *She'll come through – you'll see.*

6 When the sun or moon **comes through** or **comes through** the clouds, etc., it starts to appear. = **break through**
come through ❑ *The sun was struggling to come through.*
come through something ❑ *There was a wisp of sun coming through the mist.*

○ come 'through with

If someone or something **comes through with** something, they produce or provide what is expected.
come through with something ❑ *He finally came through with the documents.*

○ come 'to

In meaning 2, the stress is on **'come**.

1 If someone **comes to**, they become conscious again after being unconscious. = **come round**; ≠ **pass out** ❑ *That's about all I remember, until I came to in a lifeboat.*

2 If something **comes to** a particular number or amount, its total is that number or amount.
come to something ❑ *So, three times thirteen pounds – that comes to thirty-nine pounds, please.*

● 'come under

1 If someone or something **comes under** something difficult or unpleasant from other people, they experience it.
come under something ❑ *The department has come under fire for wasting public money.* ❑ *British produce came under pressure from foreign competition.*

COME UNDER + *noun*
come under **attack**
come under **criticism**
come under **pressure**
come under **strain**
❑ *Her policies have come under a lot of criticism.* ❑ *He came under a lot of pressure to resign.*

2 If something **comes under** a particular authority or control, it is controlled or owned by it.
come under something ❑ *Day nurseries come under the Department of Health and Social Security.*

3 If one thing **comes under** a particular title or category, it belongs to that group.
come under something ❑ *Cookery books come under 'leisure and hobbies'.*

● come 'up

1 When someone or something **comes up** or **comes up** something, they move from a lower position to a higher one, or move towards the place where you are.
come up something ❑ *I could hear him coming up the stairs.* ❑ *An enormous truck was coming up the hill.*
come up ❑ *As you come up, stretch your arms above your head.*

2 When someone in a building **comes up**, they move upstairs towards you. ❑ *I was about to come up and wake you.* ❑ *She came up and told us to keep the noise down.*

3 If someone **comes up**, they approach you until they are standing next to you. ❑ *[+ to] She came up to him and threw her arms around him.* ❑ *Loads of people came up and congratulated her after the speech.*

4 If someone **comes up**, they come from a place that is further south. ❑ *I'll come up to see you one of these days.* ❑ *A couple of months ago we sold the farm and came up north here.*

5 If someone **comes up** when they are underwater, they rise to the surface of the water. ❑ *I came up, and swam across a few metres.*

6 If something **comes up** in a conversation, it is mentioned or discussed. ❏ *His name came up over dinner last night.* ❏ *The subject didn't come up.*

7 If a job **comes up**, it becomes available. ❏ *An interesting post in Oxford has just come up.* ❏ *He was willing to take any job that came up.*

8 If something **is coming up**, it is going to happen soon.

be coming up ❏ *There's a royal wedding coming up.* ❏ *We have something coming up in the future where we might need your help.*

9 If something, especially a problem, **comes up**, it happens when you are not expecting it. **= crop up** ❏ *I'm afraid I can't see you tonight. Something's come up at work.* ❏ *If anything urgent comes up, you can always call me.*

10 In a court of law, if a case **comes up**, it is presented to the judge. ❏ *A case on Corporate fraud came up in the Chancery Courts recently.*

11 If something **comes up** as far as a particular point or level, it reaches that point or level. ❏ *Measure how far the water comes up.* ❏ [+ to] *The grass came up to my waist.*

12 When the sun or moon or a star **comes up**, it rises. **≠ go down** ❏ *The sun comes up in the East.* ❏ *The temperature dropped as the moon came up.*

13 When dawn **comes up** in the morning, it begins to get light. ❏ *We left the apartment just as dawn was coming up over the New Jersey skyline.*

14 If a wind or a sound **comes up**, it starts and gets stronger or louder. ❏ *By ten o'clock a breeze had come up – not strong, but fresh.* ❏ *A roar of applause came up as the spotlight hit me.*

15 If lights **come up** at the end of a performance, they get brighter. ❏ *The film had ended and the lights came up.*

16 When a seed or plant in the earth **comes up**, it grows and pushes through the soil. ❏ *The sunflowers we had planted were just coming up.*

17 If information **comes up**, it appears, for example on a computer screen, or on announcement boards in stations and airports. ❏ *We're still waiting for the flight time to come up.*

18 If someone **comes up** in society or in their profession, they achieve a more important position in it. **≠ go down** ❏ *Rosé wine has come up in the world, both in quality and variety.* ● Someone or something that is **up-and-coming** is likely to be very successful in the future. ❏ *They're very much an up-and-coming band.*

19 If someone **comes up** a particular way,

they appear that way at the end of a period of time or activity. ❏ *Jamie was one of those people – whatever happened to him, he always came up smiling.*

20 If something **comes up** looking a particular way, it appears that way at the end of a process, usually of cleaning, polishing, etc. ❏ *Most wooden surfaces come up beautifully after a bit of polishing.*

✪ come 'up against

If you **come up against** a problem, a problem happens and you have to deal with it.

come up against something ❏ *Everyone comes up against discrimination sooner or later.* ❏ *They came up against a lot of opposition.*

✪ come 'up for

1 When someone or something **comes up for** consideration or action of some kind, the time comes for them to be considered or dealt with.

come up for something ❏ *Their licence comes up for renewal later this year.* ❏ *A property that I'm interested in has just come up for sale.*

2 If someone **comes up for** election, they are officially suggested as a candidate in an election.

come up for something ❏ *A third of my colleagues will come up for election next May.*

✪ 'come upon [FORMAL]

1 If you **come upon** someone or something, you meet or find them by chance. **= come across**

come upon someone/something ❏ *They rounded a corner and came upon a family of lions.* ❏ *While she was tidying, she suddenly came upon a photo of Terry.*

2 If a feeling **comes upon** you, it suddenly develops, often when you do not expect it.

come upon someone ❏ *At the news, a great feeling of peace came upon her.*

✪ come 'up to

1 To **be coming up to** a time or state means to be getting near to it. **= approach**

be coming up to something ❏ *Some of them are coming up to retirement.* ❏ *It's just coming up to ten o'clock.*

2 If something **comes up to** a standard or hope, it is as good as it needs to be or people expect it to be.

come up to something ❏ *Only one of their later albums came up to the quality of their first.* ❏ *It must be said that the course never really came up to expectations.*

● If something or someone **comes up to scratch**, they are of a good enough standard or their work is good enough.

❏ *Ministers have given the school six months to come up to scratch.*

come 'up with

1 If you **come up with** a plan, idea, or solution, you think of it and suggest it.
come up with something ❏ *I hope to come up with some of the answers.* ❏ *It didn't take her long to come up with a very convincing example.*

> **COME UP WITH + noun**
> come up with **an answer**
> come up with **a suggestion**
> come up with **a plan**
> come up with **an excuse**
> come up with **an idea**
> come up with **a theory**
> ❏ *Every week he comes up with a new excuse for being late.* ❏ *She came up with a good theory about why these children are hard to teach.*

2 If you **come up with** a sum of money, you provide it when it is needed.
come up with something ❏ *You have no choice but to come up with the £120,000.*

comment /'kɒment/ (comments, commenting, commented)

❍ 'comment on

If you **comment on** something, you give your opinion about it or you give an explanation for it.
comment on something ❏ *So far, Mr Cook has not commented on these reports.* ❏ *Police refuse to comment on claims that he has been arrested.*

commit /kə'mɪt/ (commits, committing, committed)

❍ com'mit to

1 If you **commit** money or resources **to** something, you decide to use them for that purpose.
commit something to something ❏ *They called on Western nations to commit more money to the poorest nations.*
2 If you **commit to** something or **commit** yourself **to** something, you say that you will definitely do it.
commit to something ❏ *The city has committed to an ambitious building programme.*
commit yourself to something ❏ *Before I commit myself to doing this, I need some information.* ❏ *You are not just having a baby – you are committing yourself to at least eighteen years of motherhood.*
3 If you **commit to** or **commit** yourself **to** a person, you decide that you want to have a long-term relationship with them.
commit to someone ❏ *You are too afraid to*

commit to one man again for fear of being hurt or rejected.
commit yourself to someone ❏ *Think very carefully before committing yourself to a jealous partner.*

communicate /kə'mjuːnɪkeɪt/ (communicates, communicating, communicated)

❍ com'municate with

1 If you **communicate with** someone, you share or exchange information with them, for example by speaking, writing, or sending emails.
communicate with someone ❏ *Officials depend heavily on email to communicate with each other.*
2 If you **communicate with** someone else, you successfully tell them what you are thinking and feeling.
communicate with someone ❏ *Family therapy showed us how to communicate with each other.*

compensate /'kɒmpənseɪt/ (compensates, compensating, compensated)

❍ 'compensate for

1 To **compensate** someone **for** money or things that they have lost means to pay them money or give them something to replace that money or those things.
compensate someone for something ❏ *Farmers will be compensated for loss of earnings.* ❏ *The builders are obliged to compensate you for any damage.*
2 If you **compensate for** a lack of something or **for** something you have done wrong, you do something to make the situation better.
compensate for something ❏ *He's working this weekend to compensate for his time away.*
3 If you try to **compensate for** something that is wrong or missing in your life, you try to do something that removes or reduces the harmful effects.
compensate for something ❏ *No supportive words could ever compensate for the pain of being separated from her children for 10 years.*

compete /kəm'piːt/ (competes, competing, competed)

❍ com'pete with

1 When one firm or country **competes with** another, they try to be more successful than the other one by getting more people to buy their products.
compete with something ❏ *Small companies find it difficult to compete with large companies.*
2 To **compete with** a person or animal means

to try to get something for yourself and stop the other person or animal from getting it.
compete with someone ❏ *Emily was always competing with her older brother.* ❏ *[+ for] Schools should not be competing with each other for pupils.*

complain /kəm'pleɪn/ (complains, complaining, complained)

⊕ com'plain about
If you **complain about** something, you say that you are not satisfied with it.
complain about something ❏ *The neighbours complained about the noise.* ❏ *Fans have been complaining about the cost of tickets.*

comply /kəm'plaɪ/ (complies, complying, complied)

○ com'ply with
To **comply with** a law, rule or order means to do what the law, rule or order says you must do.
comply with something ❏ *If you do not comply with the requirements of this contract, we will terminate it.*

compress /kəm'pres/ (compresses, compressing, compressed)

○ com'press into
To **compress** an event or process **into** a short space of time means to make it continue for less time than usual.
compress something into something ❏ *The new primary schedule will compress the process into about four weeks.* ❏ *The four debates will be compressed into an eight-day period.*

compromise /'kɒmprəmaɪz/ (compromises, compromising, compromised)

○ 'compromise with
If you **compromise with** someone, you reach an agreement with them in which you both give up something that you originally wanted.
compromise with someone ❏ *[+ over] The government has compromised with its critics over monetary policies.*

concede /kən'siːd/ (concedes, conceding, conceded)

○ con'cede to
If you **concede** something **to** someone, you allow them to have it as a right or privilege.
concede something to someone ❏ *The latest draft concedes greater powers to UN envoys.*

conceive /kən'siːv/ (conceives, conceiving, conceived)

○ con'ceive as
If you **conceive** something **as** a particular

thing, you consider it to be that thing.
conceive something as something ❏ *Cancer was conceived as a disorder of the entire bodily system, not of any one part.*

○ con'ceive of
If you **cannot conceive of** something, you cannot imagine it or believe it. ❏ *I can't even conceive of that quantity of money.*

concentrate /'kɒnsəntreɪt/ (concentrates, concentrating, concentrated)

⊕ 'concentrate on
If you **concentrate on** something, or **concentrate** your mind or energy **on** it, you give all your attention to it.
concentrate on something ❏ *It had been difficult to concentrate on work with so much going on at home.* ❏ *Water companies should concentrate on reducing waste instead of building new reservoirs.*
concentrate something on something ❏ *From now on, I'm going to concentrate my efforts on passing these exams.*

concur /kən'kɜː/ (concurs, concurring, concurred)

○ con'cur with [FORMAL]
To **concur with** a person, belief, or opinion, etc. means to agree with them.
concur with someone/something ❏ *I cannot concur with this evaluation for several reasons.* ❏ *The findings concurred with Moyes' initial assessment.*

condemn /kən'dem/ (condemns, condemning, condemned)

○ con'demn to
1 If someone **is condemned to** a punishment or someone **condemns** them **to** a punishment, they are given this punishment.
be condemned to something ❏ *If found guilty he would be condemned to death.*
condemn someone to something ❏ *It is the judge who then condemns the criminal to death or imprisonment, after the jury decides on his guilt or innocence.*
2 If something **condemns** you **to** something unpleasant, it forces you to experience it.
condemn someone to something ❏ *Their lack of qualifications condemned them to a lifetime of boring, usually poorly-paid work.*
condemn yourself to something ❏ *I made the remark and then realized I had condemned myself to a sleepless night of worrying.*

condescend /ˌkɒndɪˈsend/ (**condescends, condescending, condescended**)

○ **conde'scend to**

If you say that someone **condescends to** other people, you are showing your disapproval because they behave as if they are better than other people.

condescend to someone ❑ *She always treated me like an equal and never condescended to me.* ❑ *We felt we were being condescended to by our U.S. colleagues.*

cone /kəʊn/ (**cones, coning, coned**)

○ **cone 'off** [BRITISH]

To **cone off** a road or an area of ground means to place a line of plastic cones there to prevent people driving on part of it.

cone off something or **cone something off** ❑ *The police were busy coning off the road where the accident had taken place.*

confer /kənˈfɜː/ (**confers, conferring, conferred**)

○ **con'fer on** [FORMAL]

If someone or something **confers** power or an honour **on** someone, they give it to them.

confer something on someone ❑ *The constitution also confers large powers on Brazil's 25 constituent states.* ❑ *An honorary doctorate of law was conferred on him by Newcastle University in 2009.*

○ **con'fer with**

When you **confer with** someone, you discuss something with them in order to make a decision.

confer with someone ❑ *He was conferring with his partner in the corner of the room.*

confide /kənˈfaɪd/ (**confides, confiding, confided**)

○ **con'fide in**

If you **confide in** someone, you tell them about a private problem or some other secret matter.

confide in someone ❑ *She used to confide in me when she had relationship problems.* ❑ *He doesn't have any close friends that he can confide in.*

confine /kənˈfaɪn/ (**confines, confining, confined**)

○ **con'fine to**

1 To **confine** something **to** a particular place or group means to prevent it from spreading beyond that place or group.

confine something to something ❑ *Firefighters managed to confine the fire to the basement of the house.* ❑ *They were hoping that the disease would be confined to patients and staff in hospitals.*

2 If you **confine** yourself or your activities **to** something, you do only that thing and are involved with nothing else.

confine yourself to something ❑ *I'd be glad if you'd confine yourself to answering my questions, Mrs Faraday.*

confine something to something ❑ *His genius was not confined to the decoration of buildings.*

3 If someone **is confined to** a place or something **confines** them **to** a place, they cannot leave it.

be confined to something ❑ *He has been confined to a wheelchair for the past two years, following an accident at work.* ❑ *The army had been confined to barracks.*

confine someone to something ❑ *The regime punished him by repeatedly confining him to psychiatric hospitals.*

conform /kənˈfɔːm/ (**conforms, conforming, conformed**)

○ **con'form to**

1 To **conform to** a rule or someone's wish means to obey it.

conform to something ❑ *The lamp conforms to new British Standard safety requirements.* ❑ *As individuals, they have to conform to the wishes of the leadership.*

2 If someone or something **conforms to** a pattern or type, they are exactly what people think they will be.

conform to something ❑ *She had tried to conform to his idea of what a good wife should be like.*

confront /kənˈfrʌnt/ (**confronts, confronting, confronted**)

○ **con'front with**

1 If you **are confronted with** a problem, task, or difficulty, you have to deal with it.

be confronted with something ❑ *She was confronted with severe money problems.* ❑ *The crew had been confronted with a sinking yacht.*

2 If you **confront** someone **with** something, you show them something or say something to them, especially as a way of accusing them of something.

confront someone with something ❑ *So I confronted her with the letter and she admitted it.* ❑ *You should be cautious about confronting her with the truth.*

conjure /ˈkʌndʒə, AM ˈkɑːn-/ (**conjures, conjuring, conjured**)

○ **conjure 'up**

If you **conjure up** a particular picture or

idea of something, or if your words **conjure**
it **up**, you make other people imagine that
idea or picture.

  conjure up something or **conjure something
  up** ❏ *The word 'western' conjures up images of
  John Wayne and characters wearing stetsons.*
  NOTE **Evoke** is a more formal word for
  conjure up.

conk /kɒŋk/ (conks, conking, conked)

○ **conk 'out** [BRITISH, INFORMAL]
  If a machine or vehicle **conks out**, it stops
  working or moving. ❏ *The washing machine
  has finally conked out.*

connect /kə'nekt/ (connects, connecting, connected)

○ **connect 'up**
  If you **connect up** a piece of equipment or a
  building to a source of power or water, you
  join it to that source so that it has power or
  water.

  connect up something or **connect
  something up** ❏ [+ to] *The shower unit still
  needs to be connected up to the hot and cold
  water supply.* ❏ *Is the house even connected up to
  the mains?*

○ **con'nect with**
  ◼ If one train, bus, etc. **connects with**
  another, it arrives at a time which allows
  passengers to change to the other one in
  order to continue their journey.

  connect with something ❏ *There is a train to
  Harwich which connects with the ferry.*
  ◼ If you **connect** a person or thing **with**
  something, you realize that there is a link
  or relationship between them.

  **connect someone/something with
  someone/something** ❏ *So far nobody had
  connected the crime with her father.*
  ◼ Something that **connects** a person or
  thing **with** something else shows or
  provides a link or relationship between
  them.

  **connect someone/something with
  something** ❏ *A search of Brady's house
  revealed nothing that could connect him with the
  robberies.*
  ◼ If you **connect with** someone, you like
  and understand them because you feel that
  you have similar ideas.

  connect with someone ❏ *He lost the election
  because voters found it hard to connect with him.*

connive /kə'naɪv/ (connives, conniving, connived)

○ **con'nive at** (or **connive in**)
  If you say that someone **connives at**
  something, you are critical of them because

they allow or help it to happen even though
they know that it is wrong.

  connive at something ❏ *He had already
  connived at the deaths of thousands of civilians.*
  ❏ *She suggested that the government had connived
  in the violence.*

consent /kən'sent/ (consents, consenting, consented)

○ **con'sent to** [FORMAL]
  If you **consent to** something, you agree to
  do it or to allow it to be done.

  consent to something ❏ *She had consented to
  the marriage.* ❏ *Before consenting to an operation
  you should speak to the surgeon about any
  possible risks.*

consign /kən'saɪn/ (consigns, consigning, consigned)

○ **con'sign to** [FORMAL]
  ◼ To **consign** someone or something **to** an
  unpleasant situation or place, means to
  make them be in that situation or place.

  consign someone/something to something
  ❏ *This policy is likely to consign thousands of
  families to poverty.* ❏ *I had been consigned to the
  back office.*
  ◼ To **consign** something **to** a place means
  to put it there, especially because you do
  not want it.

  consign something to something ❏ *It was
  time to consign his bat and glove to the cupboard.*
  ❏ *The papers had long ago been consigned to
  the bin.*

consult /kən'sʌlt/ (consults, consulting, consulted)

○ **con'sult with**
  ◼ If you **consult with** an expert or
  someone senior to you, you ask them for
  their opinion and advice about what you
  should do or for their permission to do
  something.

  consult with someone ❏ *He needed to consult
  with an attorney.*
  ◼ To **consult with** someone else means to
  talk to them and find out what they think
  before you make a decision.

  consult with someone ❏ *After consulting with
  her daughter and manager she decided to take on
  the part.*

contend /kən'tend/ (contends, contending, contended)

○ **con'tend with**
  ◼ If you have to **contend with** a problem or
  difficulty, you have to deal with it.

  contend with something ❏ *The ship's crew
  had to contend with strong wind and heavy rain.*

❑ *American businesses could soon have a new kind of lawsuit to contend with.* ❑ *You've got enough to contend with, without that sort of hassle.*

2 If you **contend with** someone or something, you compete with them to try to get something.

contend with someone or something

❑ *The companies are contending with rivals from Norway and Spain.* ❑ *[+ for] A year ago, Hudson was expected to contend with Homer Bush for the job.*

ontract /kən'trækt/ (**contracts, contracting, contracted**)

◗ **'contract in** [BRITISH, FORMAL]

If you **contract in** or **are contracted in**, you formally agree in writing to take part in a scheme or arrangement.

contract in ❑ *You have to contract in if you want to participate in the scheme.*

be contracted in ❑ *[+ to] Under the deal, members will be contracted in to the second state pension.*

◗ **'contract out**

1 If you **contract out**, you formally say in writing that you do not want to take part in a scheme or arrangement. [BRITISH, FORMAL] ❑ *You can apply to the Pensions Board to contract out.* ❑ *[+ of] She wants to contract out of the private health scheme.*

2 If a company **contracts out** work to another company, it employs that company to do it, rather than doing it itself.

contract out something or **contract something out** ❑ *We've now started contracting out some of these services.*

◗ **'contract out of** [FORMAL]

If you **contract out of** something that you are expected to do or take part in, you fail to do it.

contract out of something ❑ *Generally, the unions have contracted out of their responsibilities.*

◗ **con'tract with** [FORMAL]

If you **contract with** someone to do something, you formally agree in writing to do it.

contract with someone to do something ❑ *Scorsese contracted with Universal to produce one film a year.*

ontrast /kən'trɑːst, -'træst/ (**contrasts, contrasting, contrasted**)

◗ **con'trast with**

1 If you **contrast** one thing or person **with** another thing or person, you compare them and show how they are different.

contrast something/someone with

something/someone ❑ *The author contrasts the culture she was born in with the British culture she was educated in.* ❑ *They had contrasted him very unfavourably with his father.*

2 If one thing **contrasts with** another thing, it is very different from it.

contrast with something ❑ *Her general neatness contrasted with her sister's appearance which was always scruffy.*

contribute /kən'trɪbjuːt/ (**contributes, contributing, contributed**)

○ **con'tribute to**

1 If you **contribute to** something, you say or do things to help to make it successful.

contribute to something ❑ *The three sons also contribute to the family business.* ❑ *Everyone contributed to the discussion.*

2 To **contribute** money or resources **to** something means to give money or resources to help pay for something or to help achieve something.

contribute something to something

❑ *NATO officials agreed to contribute troops and equipment to the operation.*

3 If something **contributes to** an event or situation, it is one of the causes of it.

contribute to something ❑ *The infection may have contributed to her death.*

4 If you **contribute to** a magazine, newspaper, or book, you write things that are published in it.

contribute to something ❑ *He also contributed to newspapers and magazines such as 'The Guardian', 'City Limits' and 'Time Out'.*

converse /kən'vɜːs/ (**converses, conversing, conversed**)

○ **con'verse with** [FORMAL]

If you **converse with** someone, you talk to them.

converse with someone ❑ *Mark had returned, and was conversing with the other doctor.*

convert /kən'vɜːt/ (**converts, converting, converted**)

○ **convert 'into** (or **convert to**)

1 If one thing **is converted into** or **converts into** another, it is changed into a different form.

be converted into something ❑ *The signal will be converted into digital code.* ❑ *The stable had been converted to a garage.*

convert something into something ❑ *The body can convert these substances into vitamins.*

convert into something ❑ *The table converts to an ironing board.*

2 If you **convert** a quantity from one

system of measurement **into** another, you calculate what the quantity is in the second system.

convert something into something ❏ *Todd converted a hundred euros into sterling.* ❏ *Birth weight was recorded in pounds and ounces and converted to kilograms.*

✪ con'vert to

1 → see **convert into**

2 If someone **converts to** a different religion or someone **converts** them **to** it, they start to follow that religion.

convert to something ❏ *She converted to Islam.*

convert someone to something
❏ *Missionaries came and converted them to Christianity.*

3 If someone **converts** you **to** something, they make you very enthusiastic about it.

convert someone to something ❏ *His daughter Nancy had already converted him to vegetarianism.* ❏ *A trip to New York had converted her to the merits of neighbourhood policing.*

convict /kən'vɪkt/ (convicts, convicting, convicted)

○ con'vict of

To **convict** someone **of** a crime or be **convicted of** a crime, means that a judge or jury says they are guilty of that crime in a law court.

be convicted of something ❏ *He was convicted of murder and sentenced to life imprisonment.*

convict someone of something ❏ *The jury took 25 minutes to convict him of two charges of attempted robbery.*

convince /kən'vɪns/ (convinces, convincing, convinced)

○ con'vince of

If someone or something **convinces** you **of** something, they make you believe that it is true or that it exists.

convince someone of something ❏ *I tried to convince him of my innocence.*

cook /kʊk/ (cooks, cooking, cooked)

○ cook 'up

1 If someone **cooks up** a dishonest scheme, they plan it. [INFORMAL]

cook up something or **cook something up**
❏ *He claims it was all a conspiracy cooked up by his opponents.*

NOTE **Concoct** is a more formal word for **cook up**.

2 If someone **cooks up** an explanation or a story, they make it up. [INFORMAL]

cook up something or **cook something up**

❏ *She'll cook up a convincing explanation – she always does.*

3 If you **cook up** a meal, you make it, often quickly. = **rustle up**

cook up something or **cook something up**
❏ *He cooked up a delicious mushroom omelette.*

cool /kuːl/ (cools, cooling, cooled)

✪ cool 'down

1 If something or someone **cools down** or if you **cool** them **down**, they become cooler until they reach a satisfactory or comfortable temperature.

cool down ❏ *The machine takes half an hour to cool down.* ❏ *I'm just cooling down in the shade after my workout.*

cool something/someone down ❏ *Rinse the bowl in cold water to cool it down.*

2 If someone **cools down** or if you **cool** them **down**, they become less angry. = **calm down**

cool down ❏ *Tom had cooled down considerably since the meeting.*

cool someone down ❏ *I tried to cool him down with some calm words.*

○ cool 'off

1 If someone or something that is too hot **cools off**, they become cooler. ❏ *We went home and cooled off with a swim.* ❏ *These metal parts take a while to cool off.*

2 If you **cool off**, you become less excited or enthusiastic about something. ❏ *He seems to have cooled off on the negotiation idea.* ❏ *She was very keen on him at first but she seems to have cooled off a little recently.* ● A **cooling-off** period is an agreed period of time in which union and management try to solve the problem between them before taking any serious action. ❏ *Our union is opposed to any cooling-off period.* ● A **cooling-off** period is a period of time in which you can legally change your mind about an agreement you have signed. ❏ *Sign nothing during your first meeting with the salesperson, unless you are allowed a cooling-off period.*

coop /kuːp/ (coops, cooping, cooped)

○ coop 'up

If a person or animal **is cooped up**, they are kept in a place which is too small, with little freedom.

be cooped up ❏ *Imagine being a prisoner, cooped up in a cell.* ❏ *After being cooped up for so long, it was pleasant to be out driving.*

co-operate /kəʊ ˈɒpəreɪt/ (co-operates, co-operating, co-operated)

✪ co-'operate with

If you **co-operate with** someone, you work

with them or help them for a particular
purpose.

co-operate with someone ❑ *The U.N. had
been co-operating with the State Department on
the plan.*

:op /kɒp/ (**cops, copping, copped**)

○ **cop 'off with** [BRITISH, INFORMAL, RUDE]
If you **cop off with** someone, you meet
them and start a sexual or romantic
relationship with them. = **get off with**
cop off with someone ❑ *Did she cop off with
him?*

○ **cop 'out** [INFORMAL]
If you **cop out**, you decide not to do
something because you are afraid. = **duck
out** ❑ *He was going to tackle her about the
problem but then he copped out.* ● If you say that
something is a **cop-out**, you mean that
someone is not doing what they should do
because they are afraid or weak. [INFORMAL]
❑ *You can't say it's someone else's fault – that's just
a cop-out.*

:ope /kəʊp/ (**copes, coping, coped**)

○ **'cope with**
1 If you **cope with** a problem or task, you
deal with it successfully.
cope with something ❑ *Our ability to cope
with stress varies depending on our personalities.*
❑ *The president's staff was trying to cope with a
crisis in which they didn't have all the facts.*
2 If a machine or a system can **cope with**
something, it is large enough or efficient
enough to deal with it.
cope with something ❑ *The prison system is
unable to cope with the number of prisoners.*
❑ *A normal heart could cope with an almost
unlimited demand for oxygen.*

:opy /'kɒpi/ (**copies, copying, copied**)

○ **copy 'down**
If you **copy down** what someone has said or
written, you write it on a piece of paper.
copy down something or **copy something
down** ❑ *Can you copy down his address for me?*
❑ *I'm sure I have her name – I copied it down in my
little book.*

○ **copy 'in**
If you **copy** someone **in**, you send an email,
letter or other piece of written information
to them when you are sending it to another
person or other people as well.
copy someone in or **copy in someone**
❑ *I'll make sure you're copied in on all the emails.*
❑ *We've copied in all interested parties.*

○ **copy 'out**
If you **copy out** a piece of writing, you write
it down exactly as it was written before.

copy out something or **copy something out**
❑ *I remember copying out the whole play.* ❑ *Stuck
above his bed was a piece of paper with the words of
a pop song, neatly copied out.*

cordon /'kɔːdən/ (**cordons, cordoning,
cordoned**)

○ **cordon 'off**
If someone in authority **cordons off** an
area, they prevent people from entering or
leaving it by putting up a barrier. = **close off**
cordon off something or **cordon something
off** ❑ *The police had cordoned off an area near the
government offices.* ❑ *The city was split into areas,
cordoned off by barbed wire.*

cork /kɔːk/ (**corks, corking, corked**)

○ **cork 'up**
If you **cork up** a bottle, you close it by
putting a cork in it.
cork up something or **cork something up**
❑ *Get Catherine a glass of wine and then cork up
the bottle.*

correlate /'kɒrəleɪt, AM 'kɔːr-/ (**correlates,
correlating, correlated**)

○ **'correlate with** [FORMAL]
If one thing **correlates with** another, there
is a close connection between them, often
because one thing causes the other.
correlate with something ❑ *Obesity
correlates with increased risk of high blood
pressure.*

correspond /kɒrɪ'spɒnd, AM kɔːr-/
(**corresponds, corresponding,
corresponded**)

○ **corre'spond to**
If one thing **corresponds to** another, they
relate to each other or are similar to each
other.
correspond to something ❑ *All buttons and
switches were clearly numbered to correspond to
the chart on the wall.*

cost /kɒst, AM kɔːst/ (**costs, costing, costed**)

○ **cost 'out**
If you **cost out** a piece of work, you calculate
the exact amount of money you will need
for it in advance.
cost out something or **cost something out**
❑ *They train staff in how to draw up contracts and
cost out proposals.* ❑ *It is always worth having
any building work costed out.*

cosy /'kəʊzi/ (**cosies, cosying, cosied**)

○ **cosy 'up to**
If one person, country or organization
cosies up to another, they are very friendly
to them, especially in order to get an

advantage.

cosy up to someone ❏ *I hate the idea that the government has to cosy up to big business.*

cotton /'kɒtən/ (cottons, cottoning, cottoned)

○ **cotton 'on** [BRITISH, INFORMAL]

If you **cotton on**, you understand or realize something. = **catch on** ❏ [+ to] *At long last he has cottoned on to the fact that I'm not interested in him!* ❏ *The other man cottoned on and came running.*

○ **'cotton to** [AMERICAN, INFORMAL]

If you **cotton to** someone or something, you start to like them.

cotton to someone/something ❏ *He's very funny and that's why people cotton to him.* ❏ *She never really cottoned to the social scene here.*

couch /kaʊtʃ/ (couches, couching, couched)

○ **'couch in**

If something **is couched in** a particular type of language, it is expressed in that type of language.

be couched in something ❏ *The agreement was couched in legal jargon and she didn't understand it.*

cough /kɒf, AM kɔːf/ (coughs, coughing, coughed)

○ **cough 'up**

1 If you **cough up** or if you **cough up** an amount of money, you give someone money that they need or that you owe them. = **pay up** [INFORMAL]

cough up something ❏ *We're going to have to cough up another thousand pounds in legal fees.*

cough up ❏ *Come on, cough up!*

2 If you **cough up** a substance such as blood, you get rid of it from inside your throat by forcing it out of your mouth with a sudden, harsh noise.

cough up something or **cough something up** ❏ *By this time she was coughing up blood.*

count /kaʊnt/ (counts, counting, counted)

○ **count a'gainst**

count against someone

If a characteristic of someone or something they have done **counts against** them, it is a disadvantage and may cause them to fail or be punished. ❏ *His lack of experience might well count against him when applying for jobs.*

○ **count a'mong**

If you **count** someone or something **among** a particular group, you consider them to be a member of that group.

count someone/something among

something ❏ *I know William well and count him among my best friends.* ❏ *I would count it among the best films ever made.*

○ **'count as**

If something **counts as** or **is counted as** a particular thing, it is considered to be that thing, especially in particular circumstances or under particular rules.

count as something ❏ *No one agrees on what counts as a desert.* ❏ *What counts as 'polite' also varies from language to language.*

be counted as something ❏ *Any answer that's not legible will be counted as wrong.*

○ **count 'down**

If you **count down**, you count numbers aloud from the highest to the lowest until you reach zero, especially before something happens, such as a spacecraft being sent into space. ❏ *We have begun counting down to lift-off.* ● A **countdown** is the counting aloud of numbers from the highest to the lowest before something happens, especially before a spacecraft is sent into space. ❏ *Millions stand transfixed as the countdown begins.*

○ **'count for**

If you say that a particular thing **counts for** something, you mean that people value it and think it is important.

count for something ❏ *I have experience and I like to think that counts for something.* ❏ *I felt that all my years there counted for nothing.*

○ **count 'in** [INFORMAL]

If you **count** someone **in**, you include them in a particular activity. = **count out**

count someone in ❏ *You can count me in for the next outing.*

○ **'count on** (or **count upon**)

1 If you **count on** something, you expect it to happen and include it in your plans. = **rely on**

count on something ❏ *These workers can now count on a regular salary.* ❏ *The campaign can count on the public support of several MPs.*

2 If you **count on** someone, you rely on them to support you or help you. = **depend on**

count on someone ❏ *You can count on me.* ❏ [+ to-infinitive] *I'm counting on you to get me there on time.* ❏ *Unfortunately, he can't always be counted on.*

○ **count 'out**

1 If you **count out** coins or banknotes, you count them one by one.

count out something ❏ *She counted out the money.* ❏ *He took an envelope from his jacket and counted out five hundred dollars in hundred-*

dollar bills.

count something out ❏ *I know there was twenty pounds there because I counted it out myself.*

2 If someone **counts** you **out**, they do not include you in an activity. [INFORMAL]
count someone out ❏ *If you're going to gossip, you can count me out.*

3 When a referee **counts out** a boxer who has been knocked down, he or she counts to ten before the boxer can get up, and the boxer loses the match.
count someone out or **count out someone** ❏ *Etienne lay there as the referee counted him out only 49 seconds into the 10-round fight.*

○ 'count towards

If something **counts towards** a thing that you want, it is part of what you need in order to have that thing.
count towards something ❏ *Any contributions you have paid will count towards your pension.* ❏ *Dried fruit and frozen vegetables all count towards your recommended daily amount.*

○ count 'up

If you **count up** all the things in a group, you count them in order to find how many there are. = **add up**
count up something ❏ *Bored one evening, I counted up the times I had met the former Prime Minister.*
count something up ❏ *I took home the money that we'd earned and counted it up.*

○ 'count upon → see count on

:over /'kʌvə/ (**covers, covering, covered**)

○ cover 'over

To **cover** something **over** means to cover it completely with something else.
cover something over or **cover over something** ❏ *We planted the potatoes and covered them over with earth.* ❏ *The sky was covered over with cloud.*
NOTE **Obscure** is a more formal word for **cover over**.

○ cover 'up

1 If you **cover** something or someone **up**, you spread something over them in order to protect or hide them.
cover something/someone up ❏ *She has a small tattoo and she tries to cover it up with make-up.* ❏ *Cover him up with this blanket to keep him warm.*
cover up something ❏ *She took a blanket out of the car and covered up the windows.*

2 If you **cover up** or **cover up** something, you hide something that you do not want people to know about.
cover up ❏ [+ for] *She tried to cover up for*

her son.

cover something up ❏ *It is alleged that the minister knew about the scandal and tried to cover it up.*
cover up something ❏ *They tried to cover up what was really going on.*
NOTE **Conceal** is a more formal word for **cover up**.

• A **cover-up** is an attempt to hide the truth so that people do not realize that there has been a crime or mistake. ❏ *He denied being involved in a cover-up.*

crack /kræk/ (**cracks, cracking, cracked**)

○ crack 'down

To **crack down** is to start to be much stricter with people who are not obeying rules or laws, punishing them more severely.
= **clamp down** ❏ [+ on] *The police are cracking down on vandals and drug offenders.* ❏ *Her first reaction to the riots was to crack down hard.*

• A **crackdown** is strong official action taken to punish people who break laws or rules in order to stop this from happening. ❏ *The police are planning a crackdown on criminals.*

○ crack 'on [BRITISH, INFORMAL]

If you **crack on**, you continue doing a job or task quickly and with determination and energy. = **get on** ❏ *Anyway, I'll crack on because I've got to get this finished by tonight.* ❏ [+ with] *We've got a lot to do so let's crack on with it.*

○ crack 'up

1 If someone **cracks up**, they become mentally ill and cannot continue their life as normal. = **break down** [INFORMAL]
❏ *I'd crack up if there wasn't someone I could talk to.* • If someone has a **crack-up**, they become mentally ill and cannot continue their life as normal. = **breakdown** [INFORMAL] ❏ *People gossiped about his crack-up.*

2 If you **crack up** or if someone or something **cracks** you **up**, you start to laugh a lot. = **crease up** [INFORMAL]
crack up ❏ *We all just cracked up laughing.*
crack someone up ❏ *She told stories that cracked me up.*

cram /kræm/ (**crams, cramming, crammed**)

○ cram 'into

1 If you **cram** things or people **into** a container or place, you force them into it, even though there is not much space.
cram someone/something into something ❏ *While nobody was looking, she squashed her school hat and crammed it into a wastebasket.*

❏ *He was cramming food into his mouth.*

2 If people **cram into** a place or vehicle, so many of them enter it that it is completely full.

cram into somewhere ❏ *Twelve of us crammed into the tent.*

crank /kræŋk/ (cranks, cranking, cranked)

○ **crank 'out** [INFORMAL]

To **crank out** things means to produce them in large numbers very quickly.
= turn out

crank out something or **crank something out** ❏ *The movies were terrible, but they kept cranking them out.*

○ **crank 'up**

1 If you **crank up** a machine or a device, you make it function at a greater level. [BRITISH]

crank up something or **crank something up** ❏ *It's cold – can't we crank up the heating?*

2 If you **crank up** a machine or device, you start it. **= start up** [AMERICAN]

crank up something or **crank something up** ❏ *May's warm weather had many Americans cranking up their air conditioners.*

3 If you **crank up** the volume of something, you turn it up until it is very loud. **= turn up**

crank up something or **crank something up** ❏ *Someone cranked up the volume of the public address system.*

4 If you **crank up** a feeling or a quality, you increase the level of it or make it more intense. [BRITISH]

crank up something or **crank something up** ❏ *Just when you think the story can't get any more exciting, the author cranks it up a little more.*

crap /kræp/ (craps, crapping, crapped)

○ **'crap on** [INFORMAL, RUDE]

If someone **craps on**, they talk for a long time in a very boring way. ❏ *We spent the evening listening to him crapping on about immigration.*

crash /kræʃ/ (crashes, crashing, crashed)

○ **crash a'round** (or **crash about** [mainly BRITISH]) [INFORMAL]

To **crash around** means to move about and make a lot of loud noises. ❏ *What on earth is she doing, crashing around upstairs like that?* ❏ *Lucas was crashing about in the kitchen.*

○ **crash 'out**

1 If a noise **crashes out**, it starts and is very loud. **= ring out** ❏ *The opening chords crashed out.*

2 If you **crash out**, you suddenly fall asleep because you are extremely tired. **= flake out** [INFORMAL] ❏ *She'd crashed out on the floor.*

crate /kreɪt/ (crates, crating, crated)

○ **crate 'up**

To **crate** something **up** means to put it into a large wooden box so that it can be stored or taken somewhere.

crate up something or **crate something up** ❏ *By late summer two tons of files were crated up ready to be shipped to the office in London.*

cream /kriːm/ (creams, creaming, creamed)

○ **cream 'off**

1 To **cream off** people from a group means to take them away and treat them in a special way, because they are more clever or skilled than the rest of the group.

cream off someone or **cream someone off** ❏ *The best pupils would be creamed off and given a superior training.*

2 If a person or organization **creams off** a large amount of money, they take it and use it for themselves. [INFORMAL]

cream off something or **cream something off** ❏ *He creamed off vast sums given to the poor people in his country by governments and aid agencies.* ❏ *This means smaller banks can cream off big profits during lending booms.*

crease /kriːs/ (creases, creasing, creased)

○ **crease 'up** [BRITISH, INFORMAL]

If someone **creases up**, they start to laugh a lot and if someone or something **creases** you **up**, they make you start to laugh a lot.

crease up ❏ *He creased up with laughter when I told him.*

crease someone up ❏ *She creases me up with her stories.* ❏ *We were all creased up with laughter.*

credit /'kredɪt/ (credits, crediting, credited)

○ **'credit to**

When a bank **credits** an amount of money **to** an account, or an amount **is credited to** an account, the bank adds that amount of money to the account.

be credited to something ❏ *She noticed that only $80,000 had been credited to her account.*

credit something to something ❏ *The bank decided to change the way it credited payments to accounts.*

creep /kriːp/ (creeps, creeping, crept)

○ **creep 'in**

1 If things **creep in**, they gradually start to appear. **= slip in** ❏ *No matter how careful you are when you're writing a report, somehow errors always seem to creep in.*

2 If an attitude or a feeling **creeps in**, it begins to be expressed or felt. ❏ *A note of desperation crept in. 'Please, I need to talk to someone'.* ❏ *It was then that the doubts crept in.*

○ **creep 'into**

If an attitude or a feeling **creeps into** something, it begins to be expressed or felt.
creep into something ❏ *A note of impatience crept into her voice.*

○ **creep 'out** [INFORMAL]

If someone or something **creeps** you **out**, they make you feel afraid.
creep someone out or **creep out someone**
❏ *The way he was staring at me really creeped me out.*

○ **creep 'up**

If an amount, rate, number, etc. **creeps up**, it gradually increases. ❏ *He was concerned because the engine-cooling water temperature had started to creep up.* ❏ *Her weight had started to creep up.* ❏ [+ to] *This year the figure has crept up to £150,000.*

○ **creep 'up on**

1 If you **creep up on** someone, you move slowly closer to them without being seen by them.
creep up on someone ❏ *One child stands facing a wall while all the others creep up on him.* ❏ *He crept up on me from behind.*
2 If a feeling or state **creeps up on** you, you begin to experience it very slowly.
= **come over**
creep up on someone ❏ *The fear crept up on me.*

cringe /krɪndʒ/ (**cringes, cringing, cringed**)

○ **'cringe at**

If you **cringe at** something, you feel embarrassed or disgusted, and perhaps show this feeling in your expression or by making a slight movement.
cringe at something ❏ *Most writers probably cringe at the memory of their first novel.*

crop /krɒp/ (**crops, cropping, cropped**)

○ **crop 'up**

If something **crops up**, it happens or appears, sometimes unexpectedly. = **come up** ❏ *One name kept cropping up in each of the reports.* ❏ *I can come now, unless any other problems crop up.*

cross /krɒs, AM krɔːs/ (**crosses, crossing, crossed**)

✪ **cross 'off**

If you **cross off** one or more words on a list, you draw a line through them to show that they are no longer on the list. = **delete**
cross something off ❏ *With my red marker, I crossed each item off.* ❏ *Cross it off when you've completed the task.*
cross off something ❏ *Cross off the names as the children answer.*

cross something off something ❏ *I crossed my name off the list.*

✪ **cross 'out**

If you **cross out** one or more words on a page, you draw a line through them, usually because they are wrong. = **delete**
cross something out ❏ *Now and then he frowned, crossed something out and rewrote it.*
cross out something ❏ *I crossed out 'Unpublished' and wrote instead 'Works in preparation'.*

✪ **cross 'over**

1 When you **cross over** or **cross over** something, you go across to the other side of something, especially a road or border.
cross over ❏ *I crossed over to the grocery store.* ❏ *We crossed over into Tennessee.*
cross over something ❏ *I crossed over the road to avoid meeting him.*
2 If you **cross over**, you change to be in an opposing side. = **go over** ❏ [+ to] *If we ever crossed over to their side, war would be declared.*

crouch /kraʊtʃ/ (**crouches, crouching, crouched**)

○ **crouch 'down**

If you **crouch down**, you move to a position in which your legs are bent under you so that you are close to the ground and slightly leaning forward. ❏ *He crouched down and made a fuss of the dog.* ❏ *I crouched down, hoping she wouldn't see me.*

○ **'crouch over**

If you **crouch over** something or someone, you bend over them so that you are very close to them.
crouch over something/someone
❏ *A paramedic was crouching over one of the injured men.* ❏ *Turning on the ignition, she crouched over the wheel.*

crow /krəʊ/ (**crows, crowing, crowed**)

○ **'crow about** (or **crow over**) [INFORMAL]

If you say that someone **crows about** something they have achieved or are pleased about, you disapprove of them because they keep telling people proudly about it.
crow about something ❏ *The team crowed about its success.* ❏ *The president-elect was eager not to be seen to be crowing over his victory.*

crowd /kraʊd/ (**crowds, crowding, crowded**)

○ **crowd a'round** (or **crowd round** [mainly BRITISH])

If a group of people **crowd around** someone or something, they gather closely together around that person or thing.

crowd around someone/something
❑ *Reporters crowded around him, shouting questions from all sides.* ❑ *Children crowded round the ticket booth.*
crowd around/round ❑ *Lots of other kids crowded around, but Johnny stood at the back.*
NOTE **Surround** is a more formal word for **crowd around**.

○ **crowd 'in**
If a group of people or things **crowd in**, a lot of them try to get into a place at the same time. = **pile in** ❑ *They crowded in behind him and he shut the door.*

○ **crowd 'in on**
If a lot of things, especially problems or memories, **crowd in on** you, they cause you to be worried or upset.
crowd in on someone ❑ *Memories were crowding in on her and she could no longer bear it.*

○ **crowd 'into**
If a group of people or things **crowd into** a place, or if you **crowd** them **into** it, they are all pushed or squeezed into a small place.
crowd into something or **crowd someone/ something into something** ❑ *He helped his brother crowd the animals into a truck.* ❑ *Reporters and photographers were crowded into the lobby.*

○ **crowd 'out**
To **crowd** someone or something **out** means to deliberately take up so much space that they are forced to leave. = **push out, squeeze out**
crowd someone out or **crowd out someone** ❑ *I tried to keep my place in the queue, but they crowded me out.*

○ **crowd 'round** → see **crowd around**

crumble /'krʌmbəl/ (**crumbles, crumbling, crumbled**)

○ **crumble a'way**
◼ If an old building or piece of land **crumbles away**, parts of it break off until it is slowly destroyed. = **disintegrate** ❑ *Much of Britain's coastline is crumbling away.* ❑ *Parts of the church have crumbled away over the years.*
◼ If something such as a system, relationship, or hope **crumbles away**, it slowly ends. ❑ *Opposition more or less crumbled away.*

crumple /'krʌmpəl/ (**crumples, crumpling, crumpled**)

○ **crumple 'up**
If you **crumple up** a piece of paper, you squash it into a ball. = **screw up**
crumple something up or **crumple up something** ❑ *She looked at the scrap of paper, crumpled it up, and threw it into the wastebasket.*

cry /kraɪ/ (**cries, crying, cried**)

○ **cry 'off** [INFORMAL]
If you **cry off**, you decide not to do something that you had arranged to do. ❑ *We were going to go and visit him but she cried off at the last moment.*

✪ **cry 'out**
If you **cry out** or **cry out** something, you suddenly shout loudly because you are surprised or in pain.
cry out ❑ [+ in] *She cried out in terror.*
cry out something ❑ *Ralph cried out: 'Oh God, Oh God!'.*

○ **cry 'out against**
If you **cry out against** something, you complain about it strongly because you do not approve of it.
cry out against something ❑ *People are crying out against the new laws.* ● An **outcry** is a reaction of strong disapproval and anger shown by a lot of people about an action or decision. ❑ *There would be a public outcry if the law was introduced.*

○ **cry 'out for**
If one thing **is crying out for** another, it needs it very much.
be crying out for something ❑ *The garden was crying out for a bit of attention.*

cuddle /'kʌdəl/ (**cuddles, cuddling, cuddled**)

○ **cuddle 'up**
When two people **cuddle up**, they sit or lie very near to each other so they are touching. = **snuggle up** ❑ *They tried to cuddle up and get warm under the blanket.* ❑ *She cuddled up close to him.*

cue /kjuː/ (**cues, cueing, cued**)

○ **cue 'up**
If you **cue up** a record, you put it at the place where you want it to start playing, so that you can start it there immediately.
cue up something or **cue something up** ❑ *Millie handed out drinks while Stevie cued up the next track.*

cure /kjʊə/ (**cures, curing, cured**)

○ **'cure of**
If something **cures** someone **of** a habit, attitude or feeling, it makes them stop having it.
cure someone of something ❑ *The trip – which was fairly disastrous – had cured me of my love of adventure.*

curl /kɜːl/ (**curls, curling, curled**)

✪ **curl 'up**
◼ If you **curl up**, you lie down bringing your

arms, legs, and head in towards your stomach. ❑ *He likes to curl up in a chair with a good book.* ❑ *She could see the cat curled up asleep on the sofa.*

2 When something flat, such as a leaf or a piece of paper, **curls up**, its edges bend towards its centre. ❑ *The leaves curl up as they dry.*

curtain /ˈkɜːtən/ (**curtains, curtaining, curtained**)

○ **curtain 'off**

If you **curtain off** part of a room, you separate it from the rest of the room with a curtain.

curtain off something or **curtain something off** ❑ *The bedroom part of the trailer was curtained off from the rest.* ❑ *The rear of the passenger cabin was curtained off.*

cut /kʌt/ (**cuts, cutting**)

> The form **cut** is used in the present tense and is the past tense and past participle of the verb.

○ **cut a'cross**

1 If you **cut across** a place, you go across it because it is the quickest way of getting somewhere.

cut across something ❑ *I wanted to cut across country for the next hundred miles.*

2 If an issue or problem **cuts across** different groups of people, it is something that all those groups agree about or are interested in, even though they have very different opinions and interests generally.

cut across something ❑ *Stress is an issue that cuts across all classes and all types.*

3 If something **cuts across** a rule or law, it goes against or breaks it.

cut across something ❑ *For him, religion of any sort cut across basic scientific laws.*

○ **cut a'way**

If you **cut away** a part of something, you remove it by cutting it, using a knife or other sharp instrument.

cut away something or **cut something away** ❑ *All the rotten wood must be cut away and burned.* ❑ *Cut it away with a sharp knife.*

❍ **cut 'back**

If you **cut back** or **cut back** something, you reduce the amount of money that is spent on something or the number of people that are employed.

cut back something ❑ *Congress cut back the funds for NASA's space programme.* ❑ *The factory has cut back its workforce by 50%.*

cut back ❑ *We are all having to cut back.*

● A **cutback** is a reduction in something,

especially in the number of people that a firm or organization employs. ❑ [+ in] *We're now seeing a big cutback in public services.*

❍ **cut 'back on**

If you **cut back on** the money that you spend on something, you reduce it.

cut back on something ❑ *The government has had to cut back on public expenditure.*

❍ **cut 'down**

1 If you **cut** something **down** or **cut** something **down**, you reduce the amount of something you use or eat, or do something less often.

cut down something ❑ *He was told by his doctor to cut down his alcohol intake.*

cut something down ❑ *Save time for yourself by cutting your shopping down to twice a week.*

cut down ❑ *I used to eat chocolate every day but I've really cut down recently.*

> **CUT DOWN + noun**
>
> cut down **the amount of** something
> cut down **the numbers of** something
> cut down **expenditure**
> cut down **costs**
> ❑ *We need to cut down the amount of fat in our diets.* ❑ *The company has managed to cut down costs.*

2 If you **cut down** a piece of writing, you make it shorter.

cut down something or **cut something down** ❑ *The text was too long so we cut it down.*

3 If you **cut down** a tree, you cut through its trunk so that it falls to the ground.

= chop down

cut down something or **cut something down** ❑ *Globally, we're cutting down far too many trees.* ❑ *How much is it going to cost us to cut all these trees down?*

❍ **cut 'down on**

If you **cut down on** something, you try to reduce the amount of it that you use or eat, or do it less often.

cut down on something ❑ *I'm trying to cut down on the amount of fat in my diet.* ❑ *He wants to cut down on the number of business trips that he makes.*

○ **cut 'in**

1 If you **cut in**, you interrupt someone when they are speaking. **= break in**

cut in ❑ *Mrs Travers began a reply, but Mrs Patel cut in again.*

cut in something ❑ *'You have to employ a professional,' the Englishman cut in quietly.*

2 If you **cut** someone **in**, you give them part of the profits you have made on a business deal or sale.

cut someone in or **cut in someone** ❑ *We haven't got to cut Sam in have we? He didn't help* much. ❑ I think we should cut in all those who helped us organize the event.

○ **cut 'into**

If you **cut into** something, you push a knife or similar sharp tool into it.

cut into something ❑ When I cut into the meat I found it wasn't cooked properly.

◐ **cut 'off**

1 If you **cut** a part of something **off**, you remove it completely by cutting it, using a knife, scissors or other sharp instrument.

cut off something ❑ She'd cut off her hair.

cut something off ❑ Wash the carrots and cut the ends off. ● An **off-cut** is a piece of something that is left after the main part has been removed by cutting. ❑ They sell cheap off-cuts of carpets. ● **Cut-off** jeans or trousers have been made shorter by cutting off a large part of the legs. ❑ She was wearing cut-off jeans and a t-shirt.

2 If a person or place **is cut off**, they are separated from other people and places.

be cut off ❑ The town was cut off by the floods. ❑ Some mothers feel cut off during the day while everyone else is out working.

3 To **cut off** the supply of something means to stop it.

cut off something or **cut something off** ❑ People have been suggesting that we should cut off economic aid. ❑ Gas supplies had now been cut off. ● A **cut-off** or a **cut-off** point is the level or limit at which you decide that something should stop happening. ❑ Forty-five pounds is our cut-off, and we'll only go that high if we really have to. ❑ We thought it was already past the cut-off point.

4 If you **cut** someone **off** or **cut off** what they are saying, you stop them saying it.

cut someone off ❑ I waved my hand to cut him off.

cut off something ❑ 'Jenny, I'm sorry.' – 'Stop.' She cut off my apology.

NOTE **Silence** is a more formal word for **cut off**.

5 To **cut** someone **off** means to stop them being connected when they are having a telephone conversation.

cut someone off or **cut off someone** ❑ Sorry, I didn't mean to cut you off then. ❑ We just got cut off.

◐ **cut 'out**

1 If you **cut out** part of something, you remove it by cutting it.

cut out something ❑ She had cut out pictures of animals and stuck them on the wall. ❑ Badly decayed wood should be cut out and replaced.

cut something out ❑ [+ of] I cut an article out

of the paper and sent it to her. ● A **cut-out** is a shape that has been cut from card or cardboard. ❑ He had some cardboard cut-outs of his favourite characters in his bedroom.

2 If you **cut out** part of something that someone has written, you remove it from the text and do not print or broadcast it.

cut out something or **cut something out** ❑ He cut out all references to the prince being ugly. ❑ [+ of] Her publishers had cut several stories out of her memoirs.

3 If you **cut out** something that you are doing or saying, you stop doing or saying it.

cut out something or **cut something out** ❑ He ought to cut out the drinking.

● If you tell someone to **cut it out**, you are telling them angrily to stop doing or saying something. = **stop** ❑ Just cut it out, you two! I've had enough of your shouting.

4 To **cut out** something unnecessary or unwanted means to stop it existing or happening. = **eliminate**

cut out something or **cut something out** ❑ We will be trying harder to cut out waste. ❑ A guilty plea cuts out the need for a long trial.

5 If you **cut out** a particular kind of food or drink, you stop eating or drinking it. ❑ I eat everything else but I've cut out sugar completely.

6 If you **cut** someone **out**, you stop them from taking part in an activity or arrangement.

cut someone out ❑ [+ of] If you're not careful, he'll cut you out of the operation completely.

7 If an object **cuts out** light, it is between you and the light, so that you are in the dark or shade.

cut out something or **cut something out** ❑ Great trees soar above, cutting out most of the light.

8 If an engine **cuts out**, it suddenly stops working. ❑ The engine's cut out again.

● A **cut-out** is an automatic device that turns off a motor or engine, usually because there is something wrong with it. ❑ There's a cut-out to prevent the battery from overcharging.

○ **cut 'through**

1 To **cut** through something such as water means to move through it easily and smoothly.

cut through something ❑ A government patrol boat cuts through the water, making sure nobody tries to escape.

2 If a path **cuts through** an area of trees or plants, it goes through it.

cut through something ❑ We were making our way down a path that cut through the pine forest.

3 If you **cut through** a place, you go through it because it is the quickest way of getting somewhere.

cut through something ❑ *We cut through a field of cows.*

⊙ cut 'up

1 If you **cut** something **up**, you cut it into several pieces. **= slice up**

cut up something ❑ *You start the lesson by cutting up a worm.* ❑ *He has to have his food cut up for him.*

cut something up ❑ *First, cut the paper up with scissors.*

2 If you **are cut up**, you are upset or angry about something. [BRITISH, INFORMAL]

be cut up ❑ [+ *about*] *She heard the tragic news last night and she's really cut up about it.*

3 If one driver **cuts** another driver **up**, the first driver gets too close in front of the second one, usually after driving past them.

cut someone up ❑ *They were crossing from lane to lane, cutting everyone up.*

Dd

dab /dæb/ (dabs, dabbing, dabbed)

○ **'dab at**

If you **dab at** something, you touch it several times with quick, light movements.
dab at something ❑ *She wiped her nose and dabbed at her eyes.*

○ **dab 'on**

If you **dab** a substance **on** or **dab** it **on** a surface, you put it on with quick, light strokes.
dab something on something ❑ *Dab some antiseptic on the wound.*
dab something on ❑ *The liquid has to be dabbed on three times a day.*

dabble /'dæbəl/ (dabbles, dabbling, dabbled)

○ **'dabble in**

If you **dabble in** an activity or subject, you do it or study it for a short time or occasionally, but not seriously.
dabble in something ❑ *I knew he had dabbled in black magic.*

dally /'dæli/ (dallies, dallying, dallied)

○ **'dally with** [OLD-FASHIONED]

1 If you **dally with** an idea or plan, you think about it but not in a serious way.
= toy with
dally with something ❑ *I've been dallying with the idea of giving up my job.*
2 If you **dally with** someone, you have a brief romantic or sexual relationship with them.
dally with someone ❑ *He discovered that she had dallied with her co-star on the British set of the movie.*

dam /dæm/ (dams, damming, dammed)

○ **dam 'up**

1 If you **dam up** a river means to put a barrier across it to stop the water from flowing.
dam up something or **dam something up** ❑ *Rivers were dammed up and then flooded to carry logs downstream.*
2 If you **dam up** your feelings and emotions, you prevent yourself from expressing them. **= bottle up**

dam up something or **dam something up** ❑ *If we dam up our feelings, eventually they burst out uncontrollably.* ❑ *Talk about your feelings – don't try to dam them up.*

damp /dæmp/ (damps, damping, damped)

○ **damp 'down**

1 To **damp down** a situation in which there are a lot of arguments or strong emotions is to make it calmer. **= dampen down**
damp down something or **damp something down** ❑ *Now the government is trying to damp down the anger that this dispute has created.*
2 To **damp down** an activity of a particular type is to reduce the level of that activity.
damp down something or **damp something down** ❑ *The announcement was clearly intended to damp down press speculation that the marriage was in trouble.*
3 If you **damp down** a fire, you make it burn more slowly, often by reducing the amount of air around it.
damp down something or **damp something down** ❑ *My mother would damp down the fire with a layer of coal dust and water from the kettle.*
4 To **damp down** a surface is to spray a small amount of water over it. **= dampen down**
damp down something or **damp something down** ❑ *Damp down everything in the greenhouse each morning and again at midday.* ❑ *Rather than wash my hair, I usually just damp it down and comb through it.*

dampen /'dæmpən/ (dampens, dampening, dampened)

○ **dampen 'down**

1 To **dampen down** a situation in which there are a lot of arguments or strong emotions is to make it calmer. **= damp down**
dampen down something or **dampen something down** ❑ *His speech was clearly intended to dampen down a storm of criticism.*
2 To **dampen down** an activity of a

particular type is to reduce the level of that activity.

dampen down something or **dampen something down** ❑ *They introduced a scheme intended to dampen down consumer spending.*

■ To **dampen down** a surface is to spray a small amount of water over it. = **damp down**

dampen down something or **dampen something down** ❑ *Planes sprayed the area with water, which only served to dampen the fire down for a short period.*

dangle /'dæŋɡəl/ (**dangles, dangling, dangled**)

○ **'dangle before**

If you **dangle** something attractive **before** someone, you offer it to them in order to influence them in some way.

dangle something before someone ❑ *Holiday companies dangle temptation before us with pictures of white, sandy beaches.*

○ **'dangle from**

If something **dangles from** somewhere or if you **dangle** it **from** somewhere, it hangs or swings loosely.

dangle from something ❑ *A gold bracelet dangled from her left wrist.*

dangle something from something ❑ *Hanging baskets provide an opportunity to dangle trailing plants from the ceiling.*

dash /dæʃ/ (**dashes, dashing, dashed**)

○ **'dash against**

To **dash** something **against** a wall or other surface means to throw or push it violently against the surface.

dash something against something ❑ *Huge waves dashed the boat against the rocks.*

○ **dash 'off**

■ If you **dash off**, you leave somewhere quickly. ❑ [+ *to*] *She dashed off to an appointment.* ❑ *He had to dash off to give another interview.*

■ If you **dash off** a short piece of writing or a picture, you write or draw it quickly and without care. = **scribble**

dash off something or **dash something off** ❑ *She dashed off a note to Simon and left.* ❑ *Johnny spends hours doing a picture, whereas Maisie dashes them off in seconds.*

date /deɪt/ (**dates, dating, dated**)

○ **date 'back**

If something **dates back** a particular amount of time, it has existed since that time. ❑ [+ *to*] *The burial ground itself is thought to date back to the third century.* ❑ *Much of this debt dated back many years.*

○ **'date from**

If something **dates from** a particular time, it started or was made at that time.

date from something ❑ *The church in the village dates from about 1500.*

dawdle /'dɔːdəl/ (**dawdles, dawdling, dawdled**)

○ **'dawdle over**

If you **dawdle over** something, you spend more time than is necessary doing something.

dawdle over something ❑ *We were sitting in a cafe dawdling over a cup of coffee.*

dawn /dɔːn/ (**dawns, dawning, dawned**)

○ **'dawn on** (or **dawn upon**)

If a fact **dawns on** you, you begin to realize it. = **strike**

dawn on someone ❑ *The awful truth suddenly dawned upon him.* ❑ *It never dawned on her that her life was in danger.*

deal /diːl/ (**deals, dealing, dealt**)

✪ **'deal in**

■ If a company **deals in** a particular type of goods, it buys and sells those goods.

deal in something ❑ *He deals in spare parts for cars.*

■ Someone who **deals in** a particular activity or subject is involved in it or interested in it. = **deal with**

deal in something ❑ *I'm a lawyer – I deal in facts, not rumours.*

○ **deal 'out**

■ If you **deal out** a punishment to someone, you punish them.

deal out something or **deal something out** ❑ [+ *to*] *The same punishment would be dealt out to any boy who was ever late for his class.* ❑ *Beatings were routinely dealt out to those who refused to cooperate.*

NOTE **Mete out** and **administer** are more formal ways of saying **deal out**.

■ When you **deal out** playing cards, you give each player a number of cards.

deal out something or **deal something out** ❑ *He quickly dealt out the next hand.* ❑ *Helena sat back in her chair while I dealt the cards out.*

✪ **'deal with**

■ When you **deal with** something that needs attention, you do what is necessary in order to achieve the result that is wanted. = **handle**

deal with something ❑ *They learned to deal with any sort of emergency.* ❑ *The mail arriving at the house needed to be dealt with.*

DEAL WITH + noun

deal with **an issue**
deal with **a problem**
deal with **a situation**
deal with **a threat**
deal with **a complaint**
deal with **an emergency**
deal with **the consequences of**
something
deal with **an incident**
❑ *Police were called to deal with the incident.*
❑ *My job is to deal with complaints from customers.*

2 If something such as a book, film or discussion **deals with** a particular topic or idea, it discusses, explains or expresses it. **= cover**
deal with something ❑ *The film deals with the conflicts between two generations of a family.* ❑ *These questions will be dealt with in chapter 7.*
3 If you **deal with** a person or organization, you do business with them.
deal with someone/something ❑ *I planned to deal with this bank for many years.*
4 If you **deal with** a negative emotion or a situation that causes negative emotions, you manage to control your feelings and continue your normal life. **= cope with**
deal with something ❑ *Betty worried a lot, but she dealt with her worries by working.*

debar /dɪˈbɑː, ˈdiː-/ (**debars, debarring, debarred**)
○ **de'bar from** [FORMAL]
If a law **debars** you **from** doing something, it forbids you to do it.
debar someone from something ❑ *The law debars directors from speaking to the Press.*
❑ *Such a criminal offence would lead to a person being debarred from entering the teaching profession.*

decant /dɪˈkænt/ (**decants, decanting, decanted**)
○ **decant 'into** [FORMAL]
If you **decant** a liquid **into** another container, you put it into another container.
decant something into something ❑ *The perfume was decanted into bottles.*

decide /dɪˈsaɪd/ (**decides, deciding, decided**)
◉ **de'cide on** (or **decide upon**)
If you **decide on** something, you choose it after thinking carefully about the different options.

decide on something ❑ *Eventually, he decided on a career in the army.* ❑ *Have you decided on a date for the wedding?*

deck /dek/ (**decks, decking, decked**)
○ **deck 'out**
1 If you **are decked out** in something or **deck** yourself **out** in something, you wear very smart or unusual clothes for a special occasion. **= dress up**
be decked out ❑ [+ in] *He enjoyed being at his father's side, decked out in embroidered coats stiff with gold.*
deck yourself out ❑ *I decked myself out in a suit and tie, and set off.*
2 If you **deck** a place **out**, you decorate it for a special occasion.
deck something out or **deck out something** ❑ [+ in] *The apartment was decked out in balloons and coloured lights.* ❑ *They decked out the hall in flags and streamers.*

○ **'deck with**
If you **deck** a place **with** pretty things, or a place **is decked with** pretty things, you decorate it with them.
deck something with something ❑ *Villagers decked the streets with bunting.*
be decked with something ❑ *The house was decked with flowers.*

declare /dɪˈkleə/ (**declares, declaring, declared**)
○ **de'clare for** [FORMAL]
If you **declare for** someone or something, you publicly say that you support them.
declare for someone/something ❑ *Only a month earlier, Mr. Stenholm had declared for the tax cut.*

dedicate /ˈdedɪkeɪt/ (**dedicates, dedicating, dedicated**)
○ **'dedicate to**
1 If you say that someone **dedicates** themselves **to** something or **dedicates** their life **to** something, they give a lot of time and effort to it.
dedicate yourself to something ❑ *She became a nun and dedicated herself to prayer.* ❑ *Catherine selflessly dedicated herself to caring for the poor.*
dedicate something to something ❑ *He dedicated his life to working with children from poor areas.*
2 If someone **dedicates** something such as a book, play, or piece of music **to** you, they mention your name, for example in the front of a book or when a piece of music is performed, as a way of showing that they like or respect you.

dedicate something to someone ❑ *Trevor died during production, and the film is dedicated to him.*

3 If a church or other building **is dedicated to** someone, a formal ceremony is held to show that the building will always be associated with them.

be dedicated to someone ❑ *Peter was the most popular saint in the country, and many churches were dedicated to him.*

default (defaults, defaulting, defaulted)

○ **de'fault to**

If a computer system **defaults to** something, that is what it does or uses unless you instruct it to do or use something different.

default to something ❑ *The system will then default to its own settings.*

defer /dɪˈfɜː/ (defers, deferring, deferred)

○ **de'fer to** [FORMAL]

If you **defer to** someone or to their opinion, you accept their judgment or decision because you respect them.

defer to someone/something ❑ *He's a doctor and we'd be fools not to defer to him in medical matters.* ❑ *Of course, he would defer to the opinions of his superior.*

deflect /dɪˈflekt/ (deflects, deflecting, deflected)

○ **de'flect from** [FORMAL]

To **deflect** someone **from** something means to make them change their plan or decide not to continue with it.

deflect someone from something ❑ *Life was about to deflect me from my new goal.* ❑ *This setback did not deflect the party leaders from making grand plans for the future.*

delegate /ˈdelɪɡeɪt/ (delegates, delegating, delegated)

○ **'delegate to**

If you **delegate** duties, responsibilities, or power **to** someone, you give them those duties, those responsibilities, or that power so that they can do something for you.

delegate something to someone ❑ *He plans to delegate more authority to his deputies.*

delight /dɪˈlaɪt/ (delights, delighting, delighted)

○ **de'light in**

If you **delight in** something, you get a lot of pleasure from it.

delight in something ❑ *He seemed to delight in shocking people.* ❑ *Beware of friends who delight in breaking bad news.*

deliver /dɪˈlɪvə/ (delivers, delivering, delivered)

○ **de'liver of**

1 If you **deliver** yourself **of** an opinion, you express it in a confident way. [VERY FORMAL]

deliver yourself of something ❑ *Having delivered himself of this piece of wisdom, he sat back in his seat.*

2 If a woman **is delivered of** a baby, she gives birth to it. [OLD-FASHIONED]

be delivered of something ❑ *After twelve hours of labour she was delivered of a fine son.*

○ **deliver 'up** [FORMAL]

If you **deliver** something **up**, you give it to someone because you have been ordered to do so.

deliver up something or **deliver something up** ❑ *The court ordered him to deliver up the evidence.*

delve /delv/ (delves, delving, delved)

○ **'delve in** → see delve into

○ **delve in'side**

If you **delve inside** something such as bag or piece of clothing, you search inside it.

delve inside something ❑ *Mustafa delved inside his shirt and pulled out a key on a chain.*

○ **delve 'into** (or delve in)

If you **delve into** something, you search deep inside it.

delve into something ❑ *They delved into their desks for their pens.*

○ **delve 'into**

If you **delve into** something, you try in a determined way to discover more information about it.

delve into something ❑ *This is an excellent source for anyone interested in delving into the history of London.*

denude /dɪˈnjuːd, AM -ˈnuːd/ (denudes, denuding, denuded)

○ **de'nude of** [FORMAL]

To **denude** someone or something **of** a particular thing means to take it away from them.

denude someone/something of something ❑ *Military repression will denude the country of its resources.*

depart /dɪˈpɑːt/ (departs, departing, departed)

○ **de'part from**

1 If you **depart from** something, you do something differently from the usual or expected way.

depart from something ❑ *We saw no reason to depart from the original script.* ❑ *Departing from*

her usual repertoire, she sang a folk song.
2 To **depart from** a place means to leave it.
depart from somewhere ❑ *Our tour departs from Heathrow Airport on 31 March.*

depend /dɪˈpend/ (**depends, depending, depended**)

○ **deˈpend on** (or **depend upon**)
1 If you **depend on** someone or something, you need them in order to be able to exist, continue or do a particular thing. = **rely on**
depend on something/someone ❑ *Our lives and those of all other animals depend on oxygen.* ❑ [+ for] *I feel that he depends on me too much for a social life.* ❑ [+ to-infinitive] *I'm depending on you, Beth, to get the party started.*
2 If you can **depend on** someone or something, you know that you can trust them to do something. = **rely on**
depend on something/someone ❑ *I knew I could depend on you.* ❑ *Can he be depended upon to provide regular deliveries?*
3 If a result or situation **depends on** something else, it is affected by that thing.
depend on something ❑ *I might join you in the café after work – it all depends on what time I get out of the meeting this afternoon.* ❑ *The amount of money you make depends on the amount of effort you put in.*

deprive /dɪˈpraɪv/ (**deprives, depriving, deprived**)

○ **deˈprive of**
To **deprive** someone or something **of** something is to take it away from them or prevent them from having it.
deprive someone/something of something ❑ *Prison deprives the offender of their liberty.*
be deprived of something ❑ *He was kept in a small, dark room and deprived of light and company.*

deputize (**deputizes, deputizing, deputized**)

In British English, **deputise** is also used.

○ **ˈdeputize for**
If you **deputize for** someone, you do something on their behalf, for example attend a meeting.
deputize for someone ❑ *When poor health prevented him from attending the meeting, he asked Hannah to deputize for him.*

derive /dɪˈraɪv/ (**derives, deriving, derived**)

○ **deˈrive from**
1 If you **derive** pleasure or an advantage **from** something, you get pleasure or an advantage from it.
derive something from something ❑ *They*

derive enormous pleasure from their grandchildren.
2 If something **derives from** something else, it develops or comes from that thing. [FORMAL]
derive from something ❑ *This argument derives from a belief in the importance of education.*
3 If something **is derived from** something else, it is obtained from it.
be derived from something ❑ *The word 'detergent' is derived from the Latin word for 'cleaner'.* ❑ *In a balanced diet, all these vitamins are derived from the food that we eat.*

descend /dɪˈsend/ (**descends, descending, descended**)

○ **deˈscend on** (or **descend upon**)
1 If a lot of people **descend on** a place or person, they arrive there suddenly.
descend on someone/something ❑ *Visitors from London began to descend on her.* ❑ *A pack of reporters had descended on the village that afternoon.*
2 If a bad feeling or a silence **descends on** a group of people or a place, everyone suddenly starts to experience it.
descend on someone/something ❑ *A gloom descended on the group.* ❑ *An anxious silence had descended on the room.*

○ **deˈscend to**
If you **descend to** something, you start to do something that is bad.
descend to something ❑ *I'm certainly not going to descend to writing him anonymous letters.*

○ **deˈscend upon** → see **descend on**

desensitize /diːˈsensɪtaɪz/ (**desensitizes, desensitizing, desensitized**)

In British English, **desensitise** is also used.

○ **deˈsensitize to**
To **desensitize** someone **to** things such as pain or violence means to cause them to react less strongly to them.
desensitize someone to something ❑ *Research has shown that watching violence on television desensitizes children to real-life violence.*

designate /ˈdezɪgneɪt/ (**designates, designating, designated**)

○ **ˈdesignate as**
1 When you **designate** someone or something **as** a particular thing or they **are designated as** a particular thing, you formally give them that description or name.
designate someone/something as something ❑ *Queen Victoria designated Ottawa as the national capital in 1857.*

be **designated as something** ❑ *I live in Exmoor, which has been designated as a national park.*

◻ When you **designate** someone **as** something or they **are designated as** something, you formally choose them to do a particular job.

designate someone as something ❑ *You need to designate someone as the spokesperson.*

be **designated as something** ❑ *Seamus Mallon had been designated as deputy to Mr Trimble in the new executive.*

○ **'designate for**

If something **is designated for** a particular purpose or you **designate** something **for** a particular purpose, it is kept for that purpose.

be **designated for something** ❑ *The land had been designated for urban development.*

designate something for something ❑ *The organization has designated money for these programmes.*

desist /dɪˈzɪst/ (**desists, desisting, desisted**)

○ **de'sist from** [FORMAL]

If you **desist from** something, you stop doing it.

desist from something ❑ *They appealed to their community to desist from revenge attacks.*

despair /dɪˈspeə/ (**despairs, despairing, despaired**)

○ **des'pair of**

If you **despair of** something or someone, you stop feeling any hope that something will happen or that someone will do what you want them to.

despair of something/someone ❑ *At this point, we'd begun to despair of ever finding a place to stay.* ❑ *He takes so little interest in school that I sometimes despair of him.*

detach /dɪˈtætʃ/ (**detaches, detaching, detached**)

○ **de'tach from**

◻ If you **detach** one thing **from** another thing that it is fixed to, you remove it.

detach something from something ❑ *A young man was detaching the hose from the tap.*

◻ If one thing **detaches from** another thing, it becomes separated from it.

detach from something ❑ *Part of the spacecraft remains in orbit after detaching from the manned section.*

◻ If you **detach** yourself **from** something, you become less involved in it or less concerned about it than you used to be.

detach yourself from something ❑ *I've successfully detached myself from office politics.*

◻ If you **detach** yourself **from** a person or place, you leave them. [FORMAL]

detach yourself from someone/something ❑ *Alexis saw his father detach himself from the group and walk away by himself.*

deter /dɪˈtɜː/ (**deters, deterring, deterred**)

○ **de'ter from**

If someone or something **deters** you **from** doing something, they cause you not to do it.

deter someone from something ❑ *Rising house prices are deterring people from buying.*

NOTE **Put off** is a more informal expression for **deter from**.

detract /dɪˈtrækt/ (**detracts, detracting, detracted**)

○ **de'tract from** [FORMAL]

If something **detracts from** something else, it makes that thing seem less good or reduces its effect. = **diminish**

detract from something ❑ *I hope the rain didn't detract from your enjoyment of the occasion.*

deviate /ˈdiːvieɪt/ (**deviates, deviating, deviated**)

○ **'deviate from**

If someone or something **deviates from** what is usual or agreed, they behave differently or do something that is different. = **depart from**

deviate from something ❑ *These are people who deviate from society's ideas of what is normal.* ❑ *We haven't deviated from our original aims in any way.*

devolve /dɪˈvɒlv/ (**devolves, devolving, devolved**)

○ **de'volve to** (or **devolve on, devolve upon**) [FORMAL]

◻ If someone in authority **devolves** a job or responsibility **to** a less important person or group, they give it to them.

devolve something to someone ❑ *Throughout the system, more powers would be devolved to local hospital management.*

◻ If a job or responsibility **devolves to** a person or group, they are given it by someone in authority.

devolve to someone ❑ *Responsibility for each part of the company devolves to members of the team.*

devote /dɪˈvəʊt/ (**devotes, devoting, devoted**)

○ **de'vote to**

◻ If you **devote** yourself, your time, or your energy **to** something, you spend all or most of your time or energy on it.

devote something to something ❏ *Edith was a very good woman who had devoted her life to others.* ❏ *Now he could devote more time to looking after his mother.*

devote yourself to something ❏ *He gave up his job to devote himself entirely to his art.*

2 If you **devote** a particular amount of time or space **to** something, you use it for a particular purpose.

devote something to something ❏ *Several pages are devoted to the events leading to the Prime Minister's resignation.* ❏ *The afternoon had been devoted to planning the new project.*

diagnose /'daɪəgnəʊz, ᴀᴍ -nəʊs/ (diagnoses, diagnosing, diagnosed)

○ **'diagnose as**

1 If someone **is diagnosed as** something or **as** having a particular illness or problem, a doctor tells them what the illness or problem is, after examining them or doing tests.

be diagnosed as something ❏ *Her husband has just been diagnosed as having cancer.* ❏ *Anyone diagnosed as diabetic should be given help by a dietician.*

2 If an illness **is diagnosed as** something, a doctor says that is what it is, after examining you or doing tests.

be diagnosed as something ❏ *In 1894, her illness was diagnosed as cancer.*

○ **'diagnose with**

If you **are diagnosed with** a particular illness or condition, or a doctor **diagnoses** you **with** it, he or she says that you have it, after examining you or doing tests.

be diagnosed with something ❏ *Just over a year ago, I was diagnosed with leukaemia.*

diagnose someone with something
❏ *The doctor diagnosed me with pneumonia.*

dial /'daɪəl/ (dials, dialling, dialled)

○ **dial 'down**

If you **dial** something **down**, you make it less strong and so reduce its effect.

dial down something ❏ *All sides need to dial down the criticism of each other.*

dial something down ❏ *She's getting rather pushy and annoying. I think I'll have a word with her and ask her to dial it down a bit.*

○ **dial 'in**

1 If you **dial in**, you make a phone call or join a call online, for example.

dial in ❏ *We arranged a video chat, but she dialled in with his camera turned off.*

2 If you **dial in** your performance, you focus on it and try to do it very well.

dial in something ❏ *Once I dialled in my diet and*

exercise routine, the weight started to drop off me.
dial in ❏ *Her clear, bell-like voice dials in perfectl with classical solos.*

○ **dial 'up**

If you **dial** something **up**, you increase it and so make its effect stronger.

dial something up ❏ *It amazes me how my brother can just dial the charm up when he wishes.*

dial up something ❏ *This sort of talk just dials up the anger and division in the country.*

dictate /dɪk'teɪt, ᴀᴍ 'dɪkteɪt/ (dictates, dictating, dictated)

○ **dic'tate to**

If you **dictate to** someone, you tell them what they should do.

dictate to someone ❏ *He cannot dictate to me who I can see and who I cannot not see.*

be dictated to ❏ *I'm not prepared to be dictated to by my children.*

die /daɪ/ (dies, dying, died)

○ **die a'way**

If a sound or emotion **dies away**, it graduall becomes less loud or weaker and finally disappears. **= fade** ❏ *The buzz of chatter died away and everyone turned to look at her.*

○ **die 'back**

If a plant **dies back**, its leaves die but its roots remain alive. ❏ *Cut the leaves when the plant starts to die back after flowering.*

○ **die 'down**

If something **dies down**, it becomes quiete or weaker or disappears. ❏ *He decided to go away for a little while, until all the fuss had died down.* ❏ *The wind has died down now.*
[NOTE] **Subside** is a more formal word for **die down**.

○ **die 'off**

If a group **dies off**, all the people or animals in that group die, often over a short period of time. ❏ *Australia's big flightless birds all died off between 45,000 and 55,000 years ago.*

○ **die 'out**

If something **dies out**, it becomes less common and eventually disappears.
❏ *Traditional grocers' shops are fast dying out.*
❏ *The practice eventually died out.* ❏ *It was one o the many large mammals that died out during the Ice Age.*

differentiate /dɪfə'renʃieɪt/ (differentiates, differentiating, differentiated)

○ **diffe'rentiate between**

If you **differentiate between** things, you

recognize or show the difference between them.

differentiate between something ❏ *A child may not differentiate between his imagination and the real world.*

◗ **diffe'rentiate from**

■ A quality or feature that **differentiates** one thing **from** another makes the two things different.

differentiate something from something ❏ *So what differentiates this product from its competitors?*

■2 If you **differentiate** one thing **from** another, you recognize or show the difference between them.

differentiate something from something ❏ *At this age your baby can differentiate a happy expression from a sad one.*

dig /dɪg/ (**digs, digging, dug**)

◗ **dig a'round**

■ If you **dig around**, you search for something in a place or container.

= rummage around ❏ [+ *in*] *I went home to dig around in my closets for the letters.* ❏ [+ *for*] *I was just digging around for a pen.*

■2 If you **dig around**, you try to find information about someone or something. ❏ *And I suppose, if he digs around, he could find some evidence against you?*

◗ **dig 'in**

■ If you **dig** a substance **in**, you mix a substance into soil by digging.

dig something in *or* **dig in something** ❏ *Dig the compost in thoroughly and make sure you give it plenty of water.*

■2 If soldiers **dig in** or **dig** themselves **in**, they dig long holes in the ground where they hide and protect themselves against attack.

dig in ❏ *That night, they dug in for an attack expected the next day.*

dig yourself in ❏ *The enemy must be digging themselves in now ready for the attack.*

■3 If a person or side **digs in**, they prepare themselves for a period of arguments or fighting in a very determined way.

= entrench ❏ [+ *for*] *England was digging in for war.*

■4 If you tell someone to **dig in**, you are telling them to start eating. **= tuck in** [INFORMAL] ❏ *Dig in, everyone, before the food gets cold.*

◗ **dig 'into**

If you **dig into** something, you put your hand in it to search for something.

= delve into

dig into something ❏ *He dug into his pocket for his money.*

◯ **dig 'out**

■ If you **dig** someone or something **out**, you get them out of a place by digging.

= extract

dig someone/something out *or* **dig out someone/something** ❏ [+ *of*] *Rescue crews have been digging people out of collapsed buildings.* ❏ *We have always dug minerals out of the Earth.* ❏ *Farmers were struggling to dig out flocks of sheep buried beneath the snow.*

■2 If you **dig** something **out**, you find it and get it out after it has been hidden or stored for a long time. **= fish out**

dig something out *or* **dig out something** ❏ *I've had this shirt for years; I dug it out because it goes with this suit.* ❏ *We dug out our tour books and maps ready for the holiday.*

■3 If you **dig** yourself **out**, you succeed in getting out of a difficult or unpleasant situation, especially one which you caused yourself.

dig yourself out ❏ *Once I had said it, I had no choice but to try and dig myself out again.* ❏ [+ *of*] *He will need all his charm to dig himself out of the dreadful mess he's in.*

◯ **dig 'over**

If you **dig over** an area of earth, you break it into small pieces with a fork or spade so that plants can grow there.

dig over something *or* **dig something over** ❏ *Dad spent most of the afternoon digging over the old vegetable patch.* ❏ *Dig it over with a fork.*

✪ **dig 'up**

■ If you **dig up** something that has been buried or that is growing, you remove it from the ground.

dig up something ❏ *We've been digging up potatoes in the vegetable garden.* ❏ *The dog was playing with a bone that it had dug up.*

dig something up ❏ *The tree was diseased so we had to dig it up.*

■2 If you **dig up** an area of land, you dig holes in it.

dig up something *or* **dig something up** ❏ *Yesterday they continued the search of the house, digging up the back garden.* ❏ *They laid pipes under the road six months ago and now they're digging it up again.*

■3 If you **dig up** information that is not generally known, you discover it after searching. **= unearth**

dig up something *or* **dig something up** ❏ *Journalists had dug up some shocking facts about the company.* ❏ *I don't know where they found this information but they dug it up from somewhere.*

4 To **dig up** someone who is not generally known is to find them and arrange for them to do something for you. = **unearth** [INFORMAL]

dig up someone or **dig someone up** ❏ *When something like this happens, the news channels dig up an expert from someplace or other.* ❏ *She's completely crazy. Where did you dig her up?*

din /dɪn/ (**dins, dinning, dinned**)

O **din 'into** [OLD-FASHIONED]

If you **dins** something **into** you, they repeat it in a forceful way to make you remember it. = **drum into**

din something into someone ❏ *At school, it was dinned into us that we mustn't talk to strangers.*

dine /daɪn/ (**dines, dining, dined**)

O **'dine on** (or **dine off**) [FORMAL]

If you **dine on** a particular sort of food, especially an expensive or high-quality food, you eat it for dinner.

dine on something ❏ *The guests drank champagne and dined on caviar, pheasant and salmon.* ❏ *We had our apéritif and then dined off great steaks.*

O **dine 'out** [FORMAL]

If you **dine out**, you have dinner at a restaurant or at someone else's home. = **eat out** ❏ *We so rarely dine out these days.*

O **dine 'out on**

If you **dine out on** an experience, you enjoy telling people about it, especially during meals.

dine out on something ❏ *It would be a story to dine out on when they got back home.*

dip /dɪp/ (**dips, dipping, dipped**)

O **dip 'in**

If you **dip in**, you take a small amount of food from a larger amount, often as one of a group. = **dig in, tuck in** ❏ *If I put the bowl on the table, we can all dip in.*

O **dip 'into**

1 If you **dip into** a book, you look at it occasionally and briefly without reading or studying it seriously.

dip into something ❏ *I have a copy of his autobiography which I've dipped into now and then.*

2 If you **dip into** a sum of money or your pocket, you spend some money which you had intended to keep.

dip into something ❏ *Rita paid for the lawyer's fees by dipping into her savings.* ❏ *American diplomats are trying to get Congress to dip into its pocket.*

3 If you **dip into** a container with food in it you take a small amount of food from it.

dip into something ❏ *He had a large packet of popcorn on his lap that he kept dipping into.*

direct /daɪˈrekt, dɪ-/ (**directs, directing, directed**)

O **di'rect at**

1 If you **direct** something **at** a particular thing or person, you aim or point it at them.

direct something at something/someone ❏ *I directed the extinguisher at the fire without effect.* ❏ *He directed the tiny beam of light at the roof.*

2 If you **direct** your attention, emotions, or actions **at** a particular person or thing, you focus on that person or thing.

direct something at someone/something ❏ *Harper continued to direct attention at the problem.* ❏ *For now, he would direct his efforts at finding Tiffany's husband.*

3 If someone **directs** a remark or look **at** you, they say something to you or look at you.

direct something at someone ❏ *Arnold directed a meaningful look at Irma.* ❏ *The abuse was directed at the TV crews.* ❏ *His first question was directed at me.*

disabuse /dɪsəˈbjuːz/ (**disabuses, disabusing, disabused**)

O **disa'buse of** [FORMAL]

If you **disabuse** someone **of** something, you persuade them that what they believe is not true.

disabuse someone of something ❏ *She would always suggest that she was still in love with me – or at least never make any effort to disabuse me of the notion.*

disagree /dɪsəˈgriː/ (**disagrees, disagreeing, disagreed**)

O **disa'gree with**

1 If you **disagree with** something, you disapprove of it and believe that it is wrong

disagree with something ❏ *I disagreed with his politics and almost everything he stood for.* ❏ *If the farmer disagreed with the decision, he could take the case to court.*

2 If a particular food or drink **disagrees with** you, it makes you feel ill.

disagree with someone ❏ *Oranges and chocolate disagree with me – they give me migraines*

disapprove /dɪsəˈpruːv/ (**disapproves, disapproving, disapproved**)

O **disap'prove of**

If you **disapprove of** something or someone, you do not approve of them.

disapprove of something/someone
❑ *The other directors disapproved of his methods.*
❑ *No matter what kind of girl I bring home to meet my parents, my mother disapproves of her.*

disassociate /dɪsə'səʊʃɪeɪt/
(**disassociates, disassociating, disassociated**)

○ **disas'sociate from**
1 If you **disassociate** yourself **from** something or someone, you show that you are not connected with them, usually in order to avoid trouble or blame.
disassociate yourself from someone/ something ❑ *After the scandal broke, his agent had been keen to disassociate herself from him as quickly as possible.* ❑ *The party has disassociated itself from his views.*
2 If you **disassociate** one group or thing **from** another, you separate them.
disassociate something from something
❑ *This had been an attempt by the president to disassociate the military from politics.*

discharge /dɪs'tʃɑːdʒ/ (**discharges, discharging, discharged**)

○ **dis'charge from**
If you **are discharged from** hospital, prison or the army, navy etc., or someone **discharges** you **from** there, you are officially allowed or told to leave.
be discharged from something ❑ *She was discharged from hospital yesterday.* ❑ *He has been discharged from the army for medical reasons.*
discharge someone from something
❑ *They discharged him from hospital this afternoon.*
discharge yourself from something
❑ *The 55-year-old discharged himself from hospital on Christmas Eve.*

disconnect /dɪskə'nekt/ (**disconnects, disconnecting, disconnected**)

○ **discon'nect from**
If you **disconnect** something **from** something else, you separate the two things.
disconnect something from something
❑ *The equipment won't work if you disconnect it from the battery.*

discourse /dɪs'kɔːs/ (**discourses, discoursing, discoursed**)

○ **dis'course on** [FORMAL]
If someone **discourses on** a subject, they talk about it for a long time in a confident way.
discourse on something ❑ *Politicians discourse seriously on the greenhouse effect.*

discriminate /dɪs'krɪmɪneɪt/
(**discriminates, discriminating, discriminated**)

○ **dis'criminate against**
To **discriminate against** a group of people means to unfairly treat them worse than other groups.
discriminate against someone ❑ *They believe the law discriminates against women.*

○ **dis'criminate between**
If someone or something can **discriminate between** two things, they can recognize that they are different.
discriminate between something ❑ *He is incapable of discriminating between a good idea and a bad one.*

disengage /dɪsɪn'geɪdʒ/ (**disengages, disengaging, disengaged**)

○ **disen'gage from**
1 If an army **disengages from** an area, it leaves that area.
disengage from somewhere ❑ *The President has said troops will disengage from the region by next summer.*
2 If you **disengage from** something, you stop being interested or involved in it.
disengage from something ❑ *Surveys show that people are disengaging from politics.*

disentangle /dɪsɪn'tæŋgəl/
(**disentangles, disentangling, disentangled**)

○ **disen'tangle from**
If you **disentangle** someone or yourself **from** a complicated and unpleasant situation, you remove them or yourself from that situation.
disentangle someone from something
❑ *They are looking at ways to disentangle him from this major policy decision.*
disentangle yourself from something ❑ *He disentangled himself from a relationship that was making him unhappy.*
1 If you **disentangle** one part of confusing information or ideas **from** another part, you recognize each separate part.
disentangle something from something
❑ *It is important to disentangle fact from fiction.*
2 To **disentangle** someone or something **from** something means to separate them from something that is twisted around them.
disentangle yourself from something
❑ *Tammy disentangled herself from the bushes and hurried back to her car.*
disentangle something/someone from

something ❏ *He died after trying to disentangle a kite from a power cable.*

dish /dɪʃ/ (dishes, dishing, dished)

❍ dish 'out

1 If you **dish out** something, you give it to a lot of people. = **dole out** [INFORMAL]
dish out something ❏ *Who's dishing out the prizes tonight?*
dish something out ❏ *Doctors claim the pills are dangerous and criticize the clinics that dish them out.*

2 If you **dish out** something spoken, such as praise or advice, you say it to a lot of people, usually without thinking carefully. [INFORMAL]
dish out something or **dish something out**
❏ *My mother wasn't one for dishing out praise.*
❏ *People should take a closer look at the personal lives of those dishing out the advice.*

3 To **dish out** punishment or criticism means to punish or criticize someone. [INFORMAL]
dish out something or **dish something out**
❏ *As the children got older and their behaviour worse, it was Anne who dished out the discipline.*
❏ *I had to be able to withstand any punishments the prison officers could dish out.*

● If you say someone **can dish it out, but** they **can't take it**, you mean they often criticize other people but they are very upset when people criticize them. ❏ *See, you can dish it out, but you can't take it!*

4 When you **dish out** food, you serve it to people. = **dish up**
dish out something or **dish something out**
❏ *Could you dish out the stew for me?* ❏ *The food's ready. Shall I dish it out?*

❍ dish 'up

When you **dish up** or **dish up** food, you put food in dishes or on plates so that it is ready to eat.
dish up ❏ *If you're ready to eat, I'll dish up.*
dish up something or **dish something up**
❏ *Are you ready to dish up the main course?*
❏ *Until I've dished it up and we've eaten it, I won't be able to relax.*

NOTE **Serve** is a more formal word for **dish up**.

dispense /dɪsˈpens/ (dispenses, dispensing, dispensed)

❍ dis'pense with [FORMAL]

If you **dispense with** something, you stop using it or get rid of it because you no longer need it.
dispense with something ❏ *The weather had turned warm enough for her to dispense with her coat.*

dispose /dɪsˈpəʊz/ (disposes, disposing, disposed)

❍ dis'pose of

1 If you **dispose of** something, you get rid of it, for example, by throwing it away or selling it.
dispose of something ❏ *It may cost industry more to dispose of its waste in a safer manner.* ❏ *With Jones now dead, Miller had a body to dispose of.*

2 If you **dispose of** a problem or task, you deal with it so that it is finished. [FORMAL]
dispose of something ❏ *They soon got down to business, once the formalities were disposed of.*

3 To **dispose of** a person or an animal means to kill them. = **destroy** [FORMAL]
dispose of someone/something ❏ *Stein will have to be disposed of; you realize that, don't you?*

dissociate /dɪˈsəʊʃɪeɪt/ (dissociates, dissociating, dissociated)

❍ dis'sociate from [FORMAL]

If you **dissociate** yourself **from** something or someone, you show that you are not connected with them in order to avoid trouble or blame.
dissociate yourself from something/ someone ❏ *Bailey is keen to dissociate himself from the extremists in his party.*

dissolve /dɪˈzɒlv/ (dissolves, dissolving, dissolved)

❍ dis'solve into (or dissolve in)

If you **dissolve into** tears or laughter, you suddenly begin to cry or laugh.
dissolve into something ❏ *She dissolved into tears at the mention of Munya's name.*

dissuade /dɪˈsweɪd/ (dissuades, dissuading, dissuaded)

❍ dis'suade from

If you **dissuade** someone **from** something, you persuade them not to do it.
dissuade someone from something
❏ *Adeline tried to dissuade Amy from this latest idea.* ❏ *He thought about making the trip but was dissuaded from doing so by his wife.*

distance /ˈdɪstəns/ (distances, distancing, distanced)

❍ dis'tance from

If you **distance** yourself **from** a person or thing, you show that you are not involved with them, especially to avoid trouble or blame.
distance yourself from someone/ something ❏ *Guillotin tried to distance himself from the debate.* ❏ *As a civilian, the instructor liked to distance himself from the officers and their discipline regime.*

distil /dɪsˈtɪl/ (**distils, distilling, distilled**)

> American English uses the spelling **distill**.

○ **disˈtil from**

1 If an oil or liquid **is distilled from** a plant, it is removed from the plant by a process such as pressing or heating.
be distilled from something ❑ Clove oil is distilled from the flower buds of the clove tree.
2 To **distil** information **from** something means to get the most important ideas or facts from it.
distil something from something ❑ The department has its own guidelines which are distilled from the company's global policy.

distinguish /dɪˈstɪŋgwɪʃ/ (**distinguishes, distinguishing, distinguished**)

○ **disˈtinguish from**

1 If you can **distinguish** one thing **from** another thing, you can see or understand how they are different.
distinguish something from something ❑ Could he distinguish right from wrong? ❑ She is almost blind but is able to distinguish light from dark.
2 A feature or quality that **distinguishes** one thing **from** another thing, makes the two things different, because only the first thing has the feature or quality.
distinguish something from something ❑ There is something about music that distinguishes it from all other art forms.

distract /dɪˈstrækt/ (**distracts, distracting, distracted**)

○ **disˈtract from**

If something **distracts** you or your attention **from** something, it takes your attention away from it.
distract someone/something from something ❑ The noise continued to distract her from her work.
distract yourself from something ❑ Chronic pain sufferers can distract themselves from the pain by concentrating on activities which they find engaging.

distribute /dɪˈstrɪbjuːt/ (**distributes, distributing, distributed**)

○ **disˈtribute among**

If you **distribute** something **among** people in a group, you share it among those people.
distribute something among someone ❑ Immediately after his election, he began to distribute important jobs among his friends and supporters.

dive /daɪv/ (**dives, diving, dived**)

> American English uses the form **dove** as the past tense and past participle of the verb.

○ **dive ˈin**

If you **dive in**, you start doing something with great enthusiasm and often no preparation. = **rush in** ❑ It wasn't in his nature just to dive in. He approached every problem cautiously.

○ **dive ˈinto**

1 If you **dive into** something such as a bag, you put your hand into it quickly in order to get something out.
dive into something ❑ He suddenly dived into the chest and produced a wig.
2 If you **dive into** an activity, you start doing it with great enthusiasm and without any preparation. = **rush into**
dive into something ❑ Don't dive headlong into a task which you know you can't complete.

diverge /daɪˈvɜːdʒ, AM dɪ-/ (**diverges, diverging, diverged**)

○ **diˈverge from**

1 If one thing **diverges from** another similar thing, the first thing becomes different from the second or develops differently from it.
diverge from something ❑ His interests increasingly diverged from those of his colleagues.
2 If one opinion or idea **diverges from** another, it is very different from or the opposite of the other.
diverge from something ❑ The view of the government does not diverge that far from Lipman's thinking.
3 If one road, path, or route **diverges from** another, they go in different directions after starting from the same place.
diverge from something ❑ The two men parted at the point where the path to Gurneh diverged from the main road.

divest /daɪˈvest, AM dɪ-/ (**divests, divesting, divested**)

○ **diˈvest of** [FORMAL]

1 If you **divest** yourself **of** something, you get rid of it. = **rid of**
divest yourself of something ❑ Investors are beginning to divest themselves of unprofitable properties.
2 If you **divest** yourself **of** something that you are wearing or carrying, you take it off or put it down.
divest yourself of something ❑ They entered the room, divesting themselves of scarves and coats.

3 If you **divest** someone or something **of** their role or power, you cause them to lose it. = **strip of**
divest someone/something of something
❑ He was anxious to divest himself of governmental responsibilities.

divide /dɪ'vaɪd/ (**divides, dividing, divided**)

○ **di'vide among**
If you **divide** something **among** people or things, you separate it into several parts or quantities which you give to the people or things.
divide something among someone/ something ❑ Divide the sauce among 4 bowls.
❑ All work, including childcare, was divided equally among us.

⊙ **di'vide by**
If you **divide by** a number or **divide** a larger number **by** a smaller number, you calculate how many times a smaller number can fit into a larger number.
divide something by something ❑ Divide 35 by 7. ❑ 35 divided by 7 is 5. ❑ The total is then divided by 52 to arrive at your weekly payment.
divide by something ❑ Add 7 and 5, divide by 3 and add 2.

⊙ **di'vide into**
If you **divide** a smaller number **into** a larger number, you calculate how many times the smaller number can fit into the larger number.
divide something into something ❑ Divide 7 into 35.

○ **divide 'off**
If someone or something **divides off** an area, a barrier is put there to keep the area separate. = **separate off**
divide off something or **divide something off** ❑ Over in the far corner, a small office had been divided off with glass partitions.

⊙ **divide 'up**
1 If you **divide** something **up**, you separate it into completely separate groups or parts. = **split up**
divide something up ❑ Take a piece of paper and divide it up into two columns.
divide up something ❑ The house has been divided up and used as flats.
2 If you **divide up** a quantity of something, you share it out among a number of people or groups. = **parcel out**
divide up something ❑ We had divided up the little food we had left. ❑ [+ among] The proceeds had to be divided up among about four hundred people.
divide something up ❑ [+ between] Once we

know what profit we've made, we can work out how to divide it up between us.

divvy /'dɪvi/ (**divvies, divvying, divvied**)
○ **divvy 'up** [INFORMAL]
If you **divvy up**, or if you **divvy** something **up**, you share something, especially money, with other people.
divvy up ❑ We'll divvy up as soon as we get back to the club.
divvy up something or **divvy something up** ❑ Johnson was free to divvy up his share of the money as he chose.

do /duː/ (**does, doing, did, done**)
○ **'do about**
If you **do** something **about** a problem, you do something to try to solve it.
do something about something ❑ I decided that I definitely had to do something about my fear of flying. ❑ What are you going to do about it?

○ **'do as** → see **do for**

⊙ **do a'way with**
1 If you **do away with** something, you get rid of it.
do away with something ❑ The advent of radio and TV almost did away with this form of entertainment.
NOTE **Eliminate** is a more formal word for **do away with**.
2 To **do away with** someone means to kill them. = **do in** [INFORMAL]
do away with someone ❑ They were prepared to do away with Denton, and anyone else who stood in their way.

○ **do 'down** [BRITISH, INFORMAL]
If you **do** someone **down**, you criticize them and make them appear stupid or bad.
do someone down or **do down someone** ❑ Why was he trying to do her down like that? ❑ He seems convinced the world is trying to do him down.
do yourself down ❑ Don't do yourself down. You're very talented!

○ **'do for**
1 If something **does for** a person or thing, it causes them to die or be destroyed. [BRITISH, INFORMAL]
do for someone/something ❑ It was his love of fast cars that did for him in the end. ❑ All that walking on holiday has pretty much done for these boots. ● If a person or thing is **done for**, they have no chance of surviving or are destroyed. ❑ I realized there was no one there to help me and I thought I was done for. ❑ I think my bike is finally done for.
2 If someone **does for** another person, they

are employed by that person to clean their home. [INFORMAL, OLD-FASHIONED]

do for someone ❑ *Agnes did for us for thirteen years before retiring.*

○ **'do for** (or **do as**) [INFORMAL]

If you say that something will **do for** another thing, you mean that you can use it instead of the other thing. **= serve for**

do for something ❑ *That table will do as a desk for now.*

○ **do 'in**

1 To **do** someone **in** means to kill them. **= bump off** [INFORMAL]

do someone in ❑ *He even worried that they might do him in.*

do yourself in ❑ *You don't think she'd do herself in, do you?*

2 If something **does** you **in**, it makes you feel very tired. [INFORMAL]

do someone in ❑ *Walking up that hill just about did me in, I can tell you.* • If you are **done in**, you are extremely tired. ❑ *I need a rest. I feel done in.*

3 If something or someone **does** your **head in**, they make you very confused or upset. [VERY INFORMAL] ❑ *The past six weeks have been doing my head in and I'm desperate to get back out there playing again.*

○ **do 'out** [INFORMAL]

If you **do out** a cupboard or room, you clean and tidy it thoroughly.

do something out or **do out something** ❑ *I must do these cupboards out tomorrow.* ❑ *She offered to do out the kitchen for me.*

○ **do 'out in** [BRITISH]

If you **do** a room or building **out in** a particular colour or style, you decorate it in that way.

do something out in something ❑ *She had done the bedroom out in pale pink.* ❑ *I'm thinking of having the living room done out in yellow and blue.*

○ **do 'out of** [INFORMAL]

If you **do** someone **out of** something, you prevent them from getting it in a way that is not fair.

do someone out of something ❑ *I'm honestly not trying to do you out of a job.*

○ **do 'over**

1 If you **do** something **over**, you do it again from the beginning. **= do again** [AMERICAN]

do something over ❑ *Do we have to do this over?* ❑ *If the essay is no good, I'll have to do it over.*

NOTE **Redo** is a more formal word for **do over.**

2 If you **do over** a house or room, you decorate it and change its furniture. **= do up** [AMERICAN, INFORMAL]

do over something ❑ *Mrs Kennedy did over the White House.* ❑ *The hall looked as if it had been done over for a school prom.*

3 To **do over** a house or other building is to get into it by force and steal things from it. [BRITISH, INFORMAL]

do over something or **do something over** ❑ *That place has been done over a few times.* ❑ *Someone did it over at the weekend while the family were away.*

4 To **do** someone **over** means to hit and kick them in order to hurt them. **= beat up, duff up** [BRITISH, INFORMAL]

do someone over ❑ *He was done over by a gang of youths.*

○ **do 'up**

1 If you **do** something **up**, you fasten it. **= fasten**

do up something ❑ *He started to do up his boots, pulling fiercely at the laces.* ❑ *The trousers were so tight I could hardly get the zip done up.*

do something up ❑ *I can't do my top button up.*

2 If a piece of clothing **does up** in a particular place, it is fastened there. ❑ *The top does up at the back.*

3 If a woman **does** her hair **up**, she arranges it so that it is fastened close to her head rather than hanging loosely.

do something up or **do up something** ❑ *She did her hair up in a knot on top of her head.* ❑ *Her hair was done up in a neat bun at the back of her head.*

4 If you **do up** something that is old, you repair and decorate it so that it is good again. [BRITISH]

do up something or **do something up** ❑ *He does up old cars and sells them on.* ❑ *The theatre was horrible – they'd obviously done it up as cheaply as possible.*

NOTE **Renovate** is a more formal word for **do up.**

5 If something such as a present **is done up** in material or paper, it is wrapped in that material or paper to make it look attractive.

be done up ❑ [+ in] *I gave her a box, nicely done up in flowered paper.*

6 If you **do** someone **up**, you dress them in very smart or special clothes.

do someone up ❑ [+ as] *I'd done Isaac up as a pirate for the party.*

do yourself up ❑ [+ in] *She'd done herself up in a red dress and knee-high boots.*

be done up ❑ [+ to-infinitive] *Two of the children were done up to look like fairies.*

○ **'do with**

1 If someone **has something to do with** something else, they are involved in doing it or making it happen. ❏ *I suspect she had something to do with Kinnard's disappearance.*

2 If something **is nothing to do with** someone, that person has no reason to know about it or become involved with it. ❏ *Mind your own business; it's got nothing to do with you.* ❏ *What I do in my free time is nothing to do with him.*

3 If one thing **is to do with** or **has to do with** something else, the two things are related in some way. ❏ *So what was the discussion about? Was it to do with the new project?* ❏ *I don't know what he does exactly but it has to do with computers.*

4 If you ask someone **what** they **have done with** something, you are asking them where they have put that thing. ❏ *What have you done with the address book?* ❏ *James had my mobile this morning and I don't know what he's done with it.*

5 [INFORMAL] If you say you **could do with** something, you mean that you need it or would like it. ❏ *I think we could all do with a good night's sleep.* ❏ *I could do with a bit more money.*

✪ do with'out

1 If you **do without** or **do without** something or someone, you manage although you do not have a thing or person. = **go without**
do without something/someone ❏ *If you can do without me, I really have to leave now.*
do without ❏ *Anyway, we don't have any pillows so we'll have to do without.*

2 If you say that you **could do without** something, you mean that you would prefer not to have it, usually because it is causing problems. [INFORMAL] ❏ *I could do without that noise while I'm trying to work.* ❏ *I could do without Mila moaning all the time.*

dob /dɒb/ (**dobs, dobbing, dobbed**)

○ dob 'in [BRITISH, INFORMAL]
To **dob** someone **in** is to tell a person in authority that someone has done something bad.
dob someone in ❏ *If you dob me in, I'll get you. And I mean that.*

○ 'dob on [BRITISH, INFORMAL]
To **dob on** someone is to tell a person in authority that someone has done something bad.
dob on someone ❏ *Some Year 6 pupils decided to dob on us by claiming we were annoying them.*

dock /dɒk/ (**docks, docking, docked**)

○ 'dock with
When one spacecraft **docks with** or **is**

docked with another, the two crafts join together in space.
dock with something ❏ *The space shuttle Atlantis is scheduled to dock with Russia's Mir space station.*
be docked with something ❏ *The shuttle will spend five days docked with Mir.*

dole /dəʊl/ (**doles, doling, doled**)

○ dole 'out [INFORMAL]
If you **dole** something **out**, you give an amount of it to each person or animal in a group. = **dish out, hand out**
dole out something or **dole something out** ❏ *Women were doling out hot soup.* ❏ *On Tuesdays the accounts department doled out the weekly cash allowances.*

doll /dɒl/ (**dolls, dolling, dolled**)

○ doll 'up [INFORMAL]
If you **doll** yourself **up**, you put on very smart or fashionable clothes.
doll yourself up ❏ *She started dolling herself up to go out.* ● If you are **dolled up**, you are wearing very smart or fashionable clothes. = **dress up** ❏ *She was all dolled up in the latest gear.*

donate /dəʊ'neɪt/ (**donates, donating, donated**)

✪ do'nate to
If you **donate to** a charity or other organization or **donate** something **to** them, you give something to them.
donate something to something ❏ *He frequently donates large sums of money to charity.* ❏ *A new television had been donated to the orphanage by the mayor's office.*
donate to something ❏ *Perhaps people don't donate to the charity because they think it is funded by the government.*

doom /duːm/ (**dooms, dooming, doomed**)

○ 'doom to
If something or someone **is doomed to** something bad, or something **dooms** them **to** something bad, the bad thing will certainly happen.
be doomed to something ❏ *This latest ill-advised deal was doomed to failure.*
doom something/someone to something ❏ *One small error had doomed the project to disaster.*

dope /dəʊp/ (**dopes, doping, doped**)

○ dope 'up [INFORMAL]
If someone **dopes** a person **up**, they give them a drug, usually to reduce pain or to make them calmer. = **drugged**
dope someone up ❏ *Their attitude was dope them up and keep them quiet.*

be doped up ❑ *They were all so doped up they didn't know what was happening.*

dose /dəʊs/ (**doses, dosing, dosed**)

○ **dose 'up**

If you **dose** someone **up**, you give them the full amount of a medicine that can be given at one time.

dose someone up ❑ [+ with] *We'll dose her up with the medicine and see if she feels better.*

dose yourself up ❑ *I dosed myself up with flu remedy and set off for work.*

○ **'dose with**

If you **dose** a person or animal **with** medicine, you give them an amount of it.

dose someone with something ❑ *She had dosed him with painkilling drugs.*

dose yourself with something ❑ *Consult a doctor before dosing yourself with vitamins during pregnancy.*

doss /dɒs/ (**dosses, dossing, dossed**)

○ **doss 'down** [BRITISH, INFORMAL]

If you **doss down** or **doss down** somewhere, you sleep somewhere that is not a bed, usually for a short time. **= kip down**

doss down ❑ *Up to 3,000 men and women doss down for the night in doorways, subways and parks in central London.*

doss down somewhere ❑ *I can always doss down on friends' floors for a couple of weeks.*

dote /dəʊt/ (**dotes, doting, doted**)

○ **'dote on** (or **dote upon**)

If you **dote on** someone, you love them so much that you cannot see their faults.
= adore

dote on someone ❑ *This guy she's just met dotes on her.*

double /'dʌbəl/ (**doubles, doubling, doubled**)

○ **'double as**

If a person or thing **doubles as** someone or something else, they have a second job or purpose as well as their main one.

double as someone/something ❑ *During the war, Dr Harold Dicks doubled as pilot and engineer.* ❑ *The spare bedroom doubles as a study and computer room.*

○ **double 'back**

If you **double back**, you turn and go back in the direction that you came from. **= turn back** ❑ *When nobody was watching, they doubled back.*

○ **double 'back on**

When a line **doubles back on** itself, it bends in the middle, so that the second part is parallel to the first part.

double back on itself ❑ *The queue doubled back on itself.*

○ **double 'down**

If you **double down**, you commit more strongly to a position.

double down ❑ *Rather than admit his policies had failed, he simply doubled down.* ❑ [+ on] *In yesterday's interview, the Prime Minister doubled down on his pledge to increase security measures.*

○ **double 'over** (or **double up**)

If you **double over** or something **doubles** you **over**, you quickly bend your body forward, usually because you are laughing a lot or in pain.

double over ❑ *Stewart doubled over with laughter, holding his stomach.*

double someone over ❑ *The pain was so intense, it almost doubled me over.*

be doubled over ❑ *She was doubled over, her whole face distorted with pain.* ❑ *She was doubled up, she was laughing so much.*

○ **double 'up**

If two people **double up**, they both use the same thing because there is not enough for them to have one each. ❑ *There weren't enough offices for everyone, so we had to double up.* ❑ *Families who had previously doubled up in the same accommodation were housed in the new units.*

douse /daʊs/ (**douses, dousing, doused**)

○ **'douse with**

If you **douse** someone or something **with** a liquid, you throw a lot of that liquid over them.

douse someone/something with something ❑ *They began to douse the fire with water.*

douse yourself with something ❑ *He doused himself with water to cool down.*

dovetail /'dʌvteɪl/ (**dovetails, dovetailing, dovetailed**)

○ **'dovetail with**

If one thing **dovetails with** another thing or you **dovetail** one thing **with** another thing, the two things fit together well.

dovetail with something ❑ *His confession dovetailed with the evidence given by witnesses.*

dovetail something with something ❑ *The plan was to dovetail the meeting with a scheduled special general meeting.*

dowse /daʊs/ (**dowses, dowsing, dowsed**)

○ **'dowse for**

If someone **dowses for** underground water, minerals, or some other substance, they search for it using a special stick.

dowse for something ❑ *When she was a child, her grandfather had shown her how to dowse for water.*

doze /dəʊz/ (dozes, dozing, dozed)

○ **doze 'off** [INFORMAL]

If you **doze off**, you start to sleep, usually during the day. **= nod off** ❑ *I leant back against the sunny wall and dozed off.* ❑ *I nearly dozed off in today's meeting.*

draft /drɑːft, dræft/ (drafts, drafting, drafted)

○ **'draft into**

If people **are drafted into** a place or someone **drafts** them **into** a place, they are moved there to do a particular job.

be drafted into something ❑ *Extra police officers have been drafted into the city to deal with the protestors.*

draft someone into something ❑ *The manager drafted him into the team to face European champions, Denmark.*

drag /dræg/ (drags, dragging, dragged)

○ **drag 'down**

◼ If someone **drags** someone else **down**, they influence them badly, causing their behaviour to get worse or making them less important in society.

drag someone down ❑ *He was a drinker and an appalling man and he just dragged her down with him.*

◼ Something that **drags** you **down** makes you feel weak, ill or sad.

drag someone down ❑ *That bout of flu really dragged me down.*

○ **drag 'in**

To **drag in** a particular subject when you are talking is to mention that subject even though it does not relate to what you are saying.

drag something in or **drag in something** ❑ *Why do you have to drag in details about my previous relationships?*

○ **drag 'into**

To **drag** something or someone **into** a situation means to involve them in it when it is not necessary.

drag someone/something into something ❑ *It was the politicians who were dragging politics into sport, not the sportspeople.* ❑ *Don't drag me into your argument, thank you!*

○ **drag 'on**

If an event or process **drags on**, it takes longer than seems necessary. ❑ *Some legal cases have dragged on for eight years.* ❑ *The civil war dragged on.*

○ **drag 'out**

If you **drag** something **out**, you make it last for longer than is necessary. **= spin out**

drag something out or **drag out something** ❑ *It would have made a nice half-hour film but the makers dragged it out for an hour and spoilt it.* ❑ *They insisted on dragging out the talks for a further five days.*

NOTE **Prolong** is a more formal word for **drag out**.

○ **drag 'out of**

If you **drag** something **out of** someone, you force them to tell you something that they do not want to tell you.

drag something out of someone ❑ *He never talks about how he's feeling. It has to be dragged out of him.*

○ **drag 'up**

If someone **drags up** something unpleasant from the past, they mention it when someone does not want to be reminded of it.

drag up something or **drag something up** ❑ *I can't understand why everyone wants to drag up the past.* ❑ *I've apologized so many times for that – why are you dragging it up again?*

NOTE **Bring up** is a more general expression for **drag up**.

dragoon /drə'guːn/ (dragoons, dragooning, dragooned)

○ **dragoon 'into**

If someone **dragoons** you **into** something that you do not want to do, they persuade you to do it even though you try hard not to agree.

dragoon someone into something ❑ *Her husband had also been dragooned into the excursion.* ❑ *He'll be good at dragooning his friends into helping out.*

drain /dreɪn/ (drains, draining, drained)

○ **drain 'away**

◼ If a liquid **drains away** or you **drain** it **away**, it flows away from something.

drain away ❑ *All the water drained away overnight.*

drain something away or **drain away something** ❑ *If necessary, drain away any juices before transferring the meat to a serving dish.*

◼ If power or wealth **drains away**, it becomes less over time.

drain away ❑ *Slowly, his authority drained away.*

○ **drain 'off**

◼ If you **drain** a liquid **off**, or it **drains off**, you let it flow away from something.

drain off something *or* **drain something off**
❏ *Drain off the excess fat.* ❏ *If the sauce releases liquid, drain it off into a bowl.*

○ **drain 'out**

1 If you **drain** a liquid **out** or it **drains out** of something, you remove the liquid by causing it to flow somewhere else.
drain out ❏ *Make holes in the bottom so the water can drain out.*
drain something out ❏ *They drained the fluid out of her chest.*

2 If colour or strength **drains out** of something, it slowly becomes less.
drain out ❏ *The colour drained out of Amy's face.*

drape /dreɪp/ (**drapes, draping, draped**)

○ **'drape in**

If someone or something **is draped in** a piece of cloth or you **drape** yourself **in** a piece of cloth, they or you are loosely covered by it.
be draped in something ❏ *The coffin had been draped in a Union Jack.* ❏ *He was draped in a sheet.*
drape yourself in something ❏ *He draped himself in the Canadian flag and went round the track.*

draw /drɔː/ (**draws, drawing, drew, drawn**)

○ **draw 'back**

1 If you **draw back**, you move away from something or someone because you are surprised or because you do not like them. ❏ *He went to kiss her but she drew back.* ❏ [+ *from*] *She drew back from him.*
NOTE **Recoil** is a more formal word for **draw back**.

2 A **drawback** is a disadvantage. ❏ [+ *to*] *There are some drawbacks to this strategy.* ❏ *This machine has a major drawback from the technological point of view.*

○ **draw 'down** [FORMAL]

If you **draw down** anger or criticism, you do something which causes other people to be angry with you or to criticize you.
draw down something ❏ *In doing so, he drew down the wrath of the senior members of the party.*

○ **draw 'in**

1 When the days or evenings **draw in**, it gets dark at an earlier time each evening because autumn is coming. [BRITISH] ❏ *The evenings are drawing in and there's a smell of wood smoke in the air.*

2 When a train **draws in**, it comes into and stops at a station. = **pull in, come in** ❏ *She scanned the windows for his face as the train drew in.*

3 If you **draw in** breath, you breathe deeply. = **take in**

draw in something ❏ *He moved closer to her and drew in a deep breath.*

4 To **draw** someone **in** is to make them want to become involved with something or someone.
draw someone in ❏ *What was it about the theatre that first drew you in?* ❏ *There was just something about her manner that drew him in.*

○ **draw 'into**

If you **draw** someone **into** an activity or situation, you cause them to become involved in it.
draw someone into something ❏ *Peter drew her into the discussion.* ❏ *She got drawn into the relationship even though she knew it was wrong.*

○ **draw 'off**

If you **draw off** some liquid from a larger amount, you remove it, usually through a pipe or tube.
draw off something *or* **draw something off**
❏ *She drew off some of the beer, to see if it was ready to drink.*

○ **draw 'on**

In meaning 2, the stress is on **'draw**.

1 When a period of time **draws on**, it gradually gets nearer or passes. = **wear on**
❏ *As winter draws on, the leaves fall and the days get shorter.* ❏ *The evening drew on, and I started to feel tired.*

2 When someone **draws on** a cigarette, they breathe in, taking the smoke into their mouth.
draw on something ❏ *Sam looked at him long and hard, drawing on his cigarette.*

○ **'draw on** (*or* **draw upon**)

If you **draw on** something, you make use of it in order to do something.
draw on something ❏ *After twenty years in the profession, she has so much experience to draw on.* ❏ *They drew upon a variety of sources in developing their theory.*

○ **draw 'out**

1 When a train **draws out**, it moves out of a station. = **pull out** ❏ *She waved as the train drew out.*

2 If you **draw out** a sound or a word, you make it longer.
draw out something *or* **draw something out**
❏ *'It will be fine.' He said fine like 'faaaahn,' drawing it out into a much longer word.*

3 If you **draw** something **out**, you take longer to do it than is necessary.
draw something out *or* **draw out something** ❏ *It had been a tedious meeting and I had no desire to draw it out any longer.*

• Something that is **drawn-out** takes a

long time. ❏ *Matches tend to be long, drawn-out affairs.*

4 If someone or something **draws out** information or an emotion from you, they make you say or feel it. = **elicit**

draw out something or **draw something out**
❏ *Music has a way of drawing out our emotions.*
❏ *[+ of] It was impossible to draw the truth out of him.*

5 If you **draw** someone **out**, you make them feel less nervous and more willing to talk.

draw someone out ❏ *As an interviewer, you try to make people feel at ease so you can draw them out.*

6 When the days or evenings **draw out**, it gets dark later each evening because spring or summer is coming. [BRITISH] ❏ *The evenings are drawing out and you can really sense that spring is on its way.*

○ **draw 'up**

1 When you **draw up** a document, list, or plan, you prepare it and write it.
draw up something ❏ *We've drawn up a list of the candidates we would like to see again.*
❏ *A charter was drawn up, setting out their policies.*
draw something up ❏ *He certainly knows what's in the contract because he helped to draw it up.*

NOTE **Formulate** is a formal word for **draw up.**

DRAW UP + noun

draw up **a shortlist**
draw up **a plan**
draw up **guidelines**
draw up **a proposal**
draw up **a contract**
❏ *I have drawn up some guidelines for new managers.* ❏ *A contract was drawn up the following week.*

---

2 When a vehicle **draws up**, it comes to a particular place and stops. = **pull up** ❏ *Just before eleven a bus drew up.* ❏ *The taxi drew up in front of the house on Sixty-second Street.*

3 If you **draw up** a chair, you bring it nearer to a person or place, so that you can sit close to them. = **pull up**

draw up something or **draw something up**
❏ *Draw up a chair, and we'll go through these notes of yours.*

4 If you **draw** yourself **up**, you make your back very straight so that you look as tall as possible.

draw yourself up ❏ *Godfrey drew himself up to his full height and saluted.*

○ **'draw upon** → see **draw on**

○ **'draw with**

In a game or competition, if one person or team **draws with** another person or team, they have the same number of points or goals at the end of the game.

draw with someone/something ❏ *We drew with Ireland in the first game.* ❏ *Woods drew with Glen Johnson.*

dream /driːm/ (**dreams, dreaming, dreamed/dreamt**)

✪ **'dream of**

1 If you say you **would not dream of** doing something, you mean that you would definitely not do it because it is wrong or stupid. ❏ *I wouldn't dream of asking my mother to look after her.* ❏ *I wouldn't dream of asking them for money.*

2 If you say that you **dream of** something, you mean that you would like it to happen or you would like to have it, and you often think about it.

dream of something ❏ *He dreamed of one day winning an Olympic medal.* ❏ *For most of us, a brand new designer kitchen is something we can only dream of.*

3 Something that is **undreamed of** is much better or worse than people generally imagined or thought was possible. ❏ *People now have achieved a physical mobility previously undreamed of.*

○ **dream 'on** [BRITISH, INFORMAL]

If you tell someone to **dream on**, you are telling them that their hopes or wishes are not realistic. ❏ *'She won't be able to resist my charms.' – 'Dream on, mate.'*

✪ **dream 'up**

If you **dream up** a plan or idea, you create and develop it in your mind.
dream up something ❏ *He dreamed up wonderful, innovative and clever campaigns.*
❏ *She dreamed up the idea for the product after spending some time on the family farm.*
dream something up ❏ *It was a brilliant scheme – I could never have dreamed it up.*

dredge /dredʒ/ (**dredges, dredging, dredged**)

○ **dredge 'up**

If you **dredge up** something from the past, especially something bad or upsetting, you remember it or talk about it. = **dig up**
dredge up something or **dredge something up** ❏ *I didn't want to dredge up painful memories from this period.*

dress /dres/ (**dresses, dressing, dressed**)

○ **dress 'down**

1 If you **dress down**, you wear clothes that

are less formal or special than usual. ❏ *In public, she dresses down in dark glasses and baggy clothes to avoid being noticed.* ● **Dress-down day** is a day of the week, usually Friday, when employees are allowed to dress in clothes that are less formal or special than usual. ❏ *There is a theory that a 'dress-down day' actually makes people more productive.*

2 To **dress** someone **down** means to speak angrily to them about something bad or wrong that they have done. = **reprimand**

dress someone down or **dress down someone** ❏ *The Secretary of State dressed me down like a headmaster.* ❏ *The Foreign Minister was dressed down in public.*

NOTE **Tell off** is a more informal expression for **dress down**.

● If someone gives you a **dressing-down**, they speak angrily to you about something bad or wrong that you have done. = **reprimand, telling-off** ❏ *The Duke gave him a severe dressing-down for his lateness.*

○ **'dress for**

If you **dress for** something, you put on special clothes for it.

dress for something ❏ *We don't dress for dinner here.*

○ **dress 'up**

1 If you **dress up** or **dress** someone **up**, you put special, smart clothes on yourself or someone else, usually for a social occasion.

dress up ❏ *It's fun to dress up for a party.*

dress someone up ❏ [+ in] *I like having a little girl and being able to dress her up in pretty clothes.*

● If someone is **dressed up**, they are wearing special, smart clothes, usually for a social occasion. ❏ *She was all dressed up with her hair freshly done.* ❏ *Are you going to get dressed up for the party tonight?*

2 If you **dress up** or **dress** someone **up**, you put special costumes or unusual clothes on yourself or someone else, usually for fun, often at a party where everyone does this.

dress up ❏ [+ in] *Maisie loves to dress up in her Grandma's clothes.* ❏ [+ as] *He likes to dress up as characters from his favourite TV programme.*

dress someone up ❏ [+ as] *We dressed Alex up as Superman for Amelia's party.* ● If someone is **dressed up**, they are wearing special costumes or unusual clothes, usually for fun, at a party. ❏ [+ as] *Louis was dressed up as a pirate.* ● **Dressing-up** is the children's activity of putting on special costumes and pretending to be different people. ❏ *I used to love dressing up when I was a child.*

3 If you **dress** something **up**, you make it

seem more attractive, interesting, or acceptable than it really is.

dress something up or **dress up something** ❏ *However you dress it up, a bank only exists to lend money.* ❏ [+ as] *More and more papers are happy to publish rumours and gossip dressed up as news.*

NOTE **Tart up** is a more informal expression for **dress up**.

4 If you **dress** a piece of clothing **up**, you make it seem smarter or special by wearing something that is smarter or more special with it.

dress something up or **dress up something** ❏ *Keep the blouse simple for the daytime, or dress it up for the evening with accessories.*

drift /drɪft/ (**drifts, drifting, drifted**)

○ **drift a'bout** → see **drift around**

○ **drift a'long** → see **drift around**

○ **drift a'part**

If people who have had a close relationship **drift apart**, they become less close and the relationship gradually ends. ❏ *Friends sometimes drift apart as they get older and circumstances change.*

○ **drift a'round** (or **drift about** [mainly BRITISH], **drift along**)

If someone **drifts around**, they live their life with no clear plans or purpose, doing one thing and then another. ❏ *He drifted about from job to job for over a year.*

○ **drift 'into**

If someone **drifts into** a situation, they get into that situation without thinking about it or planning it.

drift into something ❏ *He left school and drifted into a life of crime.* ❏ *I just drifted into this job by accident.*

○ **drift 'off**

If you **drift off**, you gradually fall asleep. = **doze off** ❏ [+ to] *Finally, he gave up worrying and drifted off to sleep.* ❏ *I slept again, drifting off to the sound of the bells.*

drill /drɪl/ (**drills, drilling, drilled**)

○ **drill 'down**

If you **drill down**, you go to a more detailed layer of information. ❏ *You will need to drill down to find the exact figures you need.*

○ **'drill for**

When people **drill for** oil or water, they search for it by drilling deep holes in the ground or in the bottom of the sea.

drill for something ❏ *There have been proposals to drill for more oil.*

○ **drill 'into**

1 If you **drill** something **into** someone, you

teach it to them by saying it or making them repeat it many times. = **drum into**

drill something into someone ❑ *It was drilled into them that they must never drop the paddle.*
2 When you **drill into** something, you make a hole in it using a drill.

drill into something ❑ *He drilled into the wall.*

drink /drɪŋk/ (drinks, drinking, drank, drunk)

○ **drink 'down**

If you **drink down** a liquid in a glass or other container, you drink it all quickly, often without stopping.

drink something down or **drink down something** ❑ *I drank it down, then poured myself another one and drank that down as well.* ❑ *I drank down my double Scotch eagerly.*

○ **drink 'in**

If you **drink in** something that you see or hear, you give all your attention to it and enjoy it very much. = **take in**

drink in something or **drink something in** ❑ *He stood still, drinking in the beauty of the countryside.* ❑ *She sat listening attentively to the speaker, drinking it all in.*

○ **'drink to**

When you **drink to** someone or something, you raise your glass and say their name before drinking, to show that you hope they will be happy or successful.

drink to someone/something ❑ *Let's drink to the happy couple!* ❑ *They agreed on their plan and drank to it.*

○ **drink 'up**

When you **drink up** or **drink up** something, you finish what you are drinking.

drink up ❑ *Drink up, Alice. We have to go.*
drink up something or **drink something up** ❑ *Drink up your juice, darling.* ❑ *Drink your milk up and then you can go out to play.*

drive /draɪv/ (drives, driving, drove, driven)

○ **'drive at** [INFORMAL]

If you ask someone what they **are driving at**, you are asking them what they mean, usually because they have expressed an opinion in a way that is not direct. = **get at**

be driving at ❑ *What are you driving at, Amy? Are you suggesting I eat too much?* ❑ *I can see what you're driving at, but I'm still not convinced.*

○ **drive a'way**

To **drive** a person or animal **away** means to behave in a way that forces them to leave.

drive someone/something away or **drive away someone/something** ❑ *'Flies!' Etta cried and attempted to drive them away by waving her*

hand. ❑ *Scenes like this were starting to drive away her old friends.*

○ **drive 'down**

To **drive down** a price or cost means to force it to become lower.

drive down something or **drive something down** ❑ *Fierce competition has driven down prices.* ❑ *Some manufacturers manage to drive costs down by producing the products in Asia.*

○ **drive 'into**

1 If you **drive** something such as a nail into something else, you push it in or hammer it in using a lot of force.

drive something into something ❑ *I used a sledgehammer to drive the pegs into the ground.*
2 To **drive** someone **into** a particular state or situation means to force them into that state or situation.

drive someone into something ❑ *Unemployment had driven the family into debt.*

○ **drive 'off**

1 If you **drive off** someone or something that is attacking or threatening you, you force them to go away.

drive off someone/something or **drive someone/something off** ❑ *They had successfully driven off the enemy.* ❑ *The invaders were all killed or driven off.*
2 If a vehicle or the person driving it **drives off**, the vehicle starts to move and then moves away. ❑ *The van drove off at great speed.* ❑ *He drove off before I could speak to him.*

○ **drive 'out**

To **drive** someone or something **out** means to force them to leave or disappear.

drive someone/something out or **drive out someone/something** ❑ [+ of] *Employers' attitudes towards women have tended to drive them out of the workplace and back into the home.* ❑ *The magic man came to drive out evil spirits.*
NOTE **Expel** is a more formal word for **drive out**.

○ **'drive to**

If something or someone **drives** you **to** a feeling or action, they cause you to have that feeling or do that thing.

drive someone to something ❑ *Her voice sent a shiver down his spine, driving him to new desperation.*

drizzle /'drɪzəl/ (drizzles, drizzling, drizzled)

○ **drizzle over**

If you **drizzle** a liquid **over** food, you pour a small amount of the liquid all over the food.

drizzle something over something ❑ *Drizzle a little olive oil over the pasta to stop it sticking.*

rone /drəʊn/ (drones, droning, droned)

○ **drone 'on**

If someone **drones on**, they talk in a boring way for a long time. ❑ [+ about] I remember him droning on about how important it was to learn Latin. ❑ We all tried to stay awake as the priest droned on.

rool /druːl/ (drools, drooling, drooled)

○ **'drool over** [INFORMAL]

If someone **drools over** someone or something, they look at them with great interest or desire because they are very attractive.

drool over someone/something ❑ We drooled over the movie's beautifully filmed scenery even more than the main protagonist himself. ❑ Martin was drooling over all the beautiful cars on display.

rop /drɒp/ (drops, dropping, dropped)

○ **drop a'way**

1 If support or interest **drops away**, it becomes less strong. **= drop off** ❑ Public interest in the affair soon dropped away. ❑ Trade Union support dropped away during these years.

2 If land **drops away**, it slopes down so that it is at a lower level. ❑ To the south the hills dropped away to farmland.

○ **drop 'back**

If someone who is moving forward **drops back**, they go slower to allow other people to pass them. **= fall back** ❑ The two motorcycles dropped back to take up position at the rear of the convoy.

○ **drop 'by**

To **drop by** means to visit someone informally, usually without having arranged the visit. **= drop in, drop round** ❑ I could drop by some time on my way home.

○ **drop 'in**

To **drop in** means to visit someone informally, usually without having arranged the visit. **= drop by, drop round, pop in** ❑ I thought I'd just drop in and see how you were. ❑ [+ on] I dropped in on her on my way to Olivia's house. ● A **drop-in centre** is a building that people can visit to get help without having arranged an appointment first. ❑ I've been working at the drop-in centre for the last three months.

○ **drop 'off**

1 When you are driving, if you **drop off** a person or thing, you take them somewhere and leave them there, usually on your way to somewhere else.

drop someone/something off ❑ I can drop her off on my way home. ❑ Could you drop this parcel off at the post office for me, please?

drop off someone/something ❑ I need to drop off some books at the office.

2 If you **drop off**, you start to sleep. **= doze off** [INFORMAL] ❑ Eventually I dropped off to sleep. ❑ I went to bed at 10:00 but I didn't drop off till gone midnight.

3 If support or interest **drops off**, it becomes less strong. **= drop away** ❑ Public interest in the case soon dropped off.

○ **'drop onto**

If something **drops onto** something else or you **drop** it **onto** something else, it falls or you let it fall onto that thing.

drop onto something ❑ He felt tears dropping onto his fingers. ❑ Something dropped onto her head.

drop something onto something ❑ He dropped his keys onto the table.

○ **drop 'out**

1 If you **drop out**, you leave something that you are involved in before it is finished. ❑ [+ of] She had dropped out of college in the first term. ❑ He dropped out of school and went to work in the mine. ❑ Halfway through filming, the main actor had to drop out because of ill-health.

● A **dropout** is someone who leaves school or college before finishing their course. ❑ I was a dropout and my parents were ashamed of that.

2 If someone **drops out**, they stop living and working like most other people in society and live in a different way. ❑ She encourages people to keep their jobs rather than dropping out to live in a commune. ● A **dropout** is someone who has decided to stop living and working like most other people in society. ❑ He dismissed them as hippies and dropouts.

3 If your mobile phone **drops out**, it loses its signal. ❑ His cell phone kept dropping out on the trip from the airport to the hotel.

○ **drop 'out of**

If a word or expression **drops out of** the language, it stops being used.

drop out of something ❑ Today the word 'teeny-bopper' has virtually dropped out of use.

○ **drop 'round** [BRITISH]

1 To **drop round** means to visit someone informally, usually without having arranged the visit. **= drop in, drop by** ❑ I'll drop round when I've finished the shopping.

2 If you **drop** something **round**, you take it to a person's home for them.

drop something round or **drop round something** ❑ Bill can drop your books round on his way home. ❑ I'll drop round that article I told you about as I'm going past your house anyway.

drown /draʊn/ (**drowns, drowning, drowned**)

○ **'drown in** [INFORMAL]

If you say that a person or thing **is drowning in** something, you are emphasizing that they have a lot of it or too much of it.
be drowning in something ❑ He felt as if he was drowning in debt. ❑ According to a new study, we're drowning in hardware.

○ **drown 'out**

If one sound **drowns out** another sound, the first sound is so loud that you cannot hear the second sound.
drown out something or **drown something out** ❑ The noise from the plane drowned out the music.

drum /drʌm/ (**drums, drumming, drummed**)

○ **drum 'into**

If you **drum** something **into** someone, you say it to them a lot so that they remember it. = **din into**
drum something into someone ❑ I had the importance of tidiness drummed into me as a child.

○ **'drum on**

If something **drums on** a surface, or if you **drum** something **on** a surface, it hits it regularly, making a continuous beating sound.
drum on something ❑ Rain drummed on the roof of the car.
drum something on something ❑ He drummed his fingers on the desk.

○ **drum 'out** [OLD-FASHIONED]

To **drum** someone **out** is to make them leave an organization. = **kick out**
drum someone out ❑ [+ of] He had been drummed out of the club.
NOTE **Expel** is a more formal word for **drum out**.

○ **drum 'up**

If you **drum up** support for or interest in something, you do things to make people support it or feel interest in it. = **gather**
drum up something ❑ They're on a tour of world capitals to drum up support for the campaign. ❑ Bezos is in charge of drumming up new business.

dry /draɪ/ (**dries, drying, dried**)

○ **dry 'off**

If something or someone wet **dries off** or if you **dry** something or someone **off**, they become dry on the surface.
dry off ❑ I'll dry off in the sun.
dry something/someone off ❑ She took one of the big towels and dried him off. ❑ Do you have a towel I can dry myself off with?

○ **dry 'out**

1 If something that contains water **dries out** or if you **dry** something **out**, the water disappears and it becomes hard and completely dry.
dry out ❑ The soil gets as hard as brick when it dries out.
dry something out ❑ I put the wet towels on th line to dry them out.
dry out something ❑ Two days of high winds blew away the rain and dried out the playing-fields
2 If someone who is an alcoholic **dries out** they stop being an alcoholic. [INFORMAL]
❑ I told him to come back to me when he'd dried ou and not before.

○ **dry 'up**

1 If something **dries up** or if something **drie** it **up**, it loses all the water that was in it.
dry up ❑ My mouth always dries up under stress.
dry something up ❑ If the water is applied in th morning, the heat from the sun will quickly dry it up
dry up something ❑ Too much heat will dry up the ends of your hair.
2 If a river, lake, or well **dries up**, the water in it disappears. ❑ In the dry season these lakes will dry up completely. ● A **dried-up** river, lake or well has no water in it. ❑ All that is left are dried-up river-beds.
3 When you **dry up** or **dry up** dishes, knives, forks, etc. after they have been washed, you wipe water off dishes with a cloth. [BRITISH]
dry up ❑ Here, let me dry up for you.
dry up something or **dry something up** ❑ Could you dry up the dishes, Steve? ● **Drying-up** or **the drying-up** is the activity of drying dishes, knives, forks, etc. after they have been washed. ❑ Could you do the drying up?
4 If you **dry up** when you are speaking to a lot of people, you suddenly stop speaking because you cannot think what to say next ❑ Halfway through the speech she dried up completely.
5 If a supply of something **dries up**, it stop being available. ❑ The work dried up and suddenly there was no income. ❑ The market for luxury goods dried up during the recession.
6 If you tell someone to **dry up**, you are telling them in a rude way to stop talking. = **shut up, belt up** [BRITISH, INFORMAL, OLD-FASHIONED] ❑ Dry up, for goodness' sake!
7 Someone who is **dried-up** looks old, with skin that has many small lines on it. ❑ He was a sour, dried-up old man with gold-rimmed spectacles.
NOTE **Wizened** and **withered** are more formal words for **dried-up**.

dub /dʌb/ (**dubs, dubbing, dubbed**)

○ **dub 'in**

When film-makers **dub in** a voice, they use the recorded voice of one actor in place of the voice of the actor who appears on the film.

dub in something or **dub something in** ❑ *Later on, probably, a different voice will be dubbed in.*

○ **dub 'into**

To **dub** a film **into** another language is to replace the original recording with a different recording so that the actors appear to be speaking in a different language.

dub something into something ❑ *The series sells in forty-seven countries and is dubbed into seven languages.*

○ **dub 'over**

In a recording, when one sound **is dubbed over**, a different recording is used to replace the original one.

be dubbed over ❑ *McDowell's voice was dubbed over by actress Glenn Close because she couldn't shake her southern accent.*

duck /dʌk/ (**ducks, ducking, ducked**)

○ **duck 'out** [INFORMAL]

If you **duck out**, you leave somewhere quickly and secretly. ❑ *I'd just ducked out for a quick coffee.*

○ **duck 'out of** [INFORMAL]

If you **duck out of** something that you are supposed to do, you avoid doing it.

duck out of something ❑ *Look, you're coming with me to the party whether you like it or not. You're not ducking out of it this time!*

duff /dʌf/ (**duffs, duffing, duffed**)

○ **duff 'up** [BRITISH, INFORMAL]

To **duff** someone **up** means to hit and kick them in order to injure them. = **beat up, do over**

duff someone up or **duff up someone** ❑ *He put the boot in and duffed him up.* ❑ *He could have duffed up half the people in the club.*

duke /djuːk, AM duːk/ (**dukes, duking, duked**)

○ **duke 'out** [AMERICAN, INFORMAL]

If two people or groups **duke it out**, they fight or compete with one another. = **fight out** ❑ *The three candidates for the Liberal leadership duke it out in Quebec.*

dumb /dʌm/ (**dumbs, dumbing, dumbed**)

○ **dumb 'down**

1 To **dumb down** or **dumb down** something is to make something easier for people to understand, especially when this spoils it.

dumb down ❑ *We must resist the pressure to dumb down.*

dumb down something or **dumb something down** ❑ *He admits there has been a drift to dumb down content.*

2 If someone **dumbs down**, they try to appear less intelligent than they really are. ❑ *Clever kids are dumbing down at school to avoid being bullied.*

dummy /'dʌmi/ (**dummies, dummying, dummied**)

○ **dummy 'up** [AMERICAN, INFORMAL]

If someone **dummies up**, they stop speaking, sometimes pretending not to know about a subject. ❑ *Ask him too many questions and he'll just dummy up on you.*

dump /dʌmp/ (**dumps, dumping, dumped**)

○ **'dump on** [INFORMAL]

1 If you **dump on** someone, you treat them unfairly by giving them too much work or something unpleasant to do.

dump on someone ❑ *You let people dump on you.* ❑ *I hope you don't think I'm dumping on you.*

2 If you **dump on** someone or something, you criticize them too severely.

dump on someone/something ❑ *I can dump on my home town, but no outsider had better try.* ❑ *White House officials thought it best not to dump on him.*

dust /dʌst/ (**dusts, dusting, dusted**)

○ **dust 'down**

1 If you **dust** something **down**, you remove dust from it with a brush or dry cloth.

dust down something or **dust something down** ❑ *Dust down the walls and wipe paintwork thoroughly before starting.* ❑ *I dusted the shelves down and swept the floor.*

2 If someone **dusts down** an expression or a story, they use or say one that has been used or said many times before. = **dust off** [BRITISH]

dust down something or **dust something down** ❑ *Critics were busy dusting down the same superlatives they had applied to their first three films.*

3 If you **dust down** something that you have not used for a long time, you start to use it again.

dust down something or **dust something down** ❑ *The band dusted down a few old favourites from the eighties.*

4 If someone **dusts** himself or herself **down**, they manage to recover from a severe problem in their life. [BRITISH]

dust yourself down ❑ *She's taken her knocks,*

in a career sense, dusted herself down and got back up again.

○ **dust 'off**

1 If you **dust off** your clothes or your hands, you brush the dust from them.
dust off something or **dust something off**
❏ He climbed to his feet and dusted off his trousers.

2 If someone **dusts off** an expression or a story, they use or say one that has been used or said many times before. = **dust down**
dust off something or **dust something off**
❏ Journalists dust off the same old adjectives to describe the band.

3 If you **dust off** something that you have not used for a long time, you start to use it again.
dust off something or **dust something off**
❏ Dust off your dancing shoes and join in the fun at our free dance workshops. ❏ If you haven't used that racket in a while, maybe it's time to dust it off and get back on that court.

4 If someone **dusts** himself or herself **off**, they manage to recover from a severe problem in their life.
dust yourself off ❏ Eventually, after a bad experience, you just have to pick yourself up and dust yourself off.

○ **'dust with**

To **dust** something **with** a fine substance such as powder, means to cover it lightly with that substance.
dust something with something ❏ Dust the top of the cake with icing sugar. ❏ The hills were dusted with snow.

dwell /dwel/ (**dwells, dwelling, dwelled/ dwelt**)

○ **'dwell on** (or **dwell upon**)

If you **dwell on** something unpleasant, you think or speak about it a lot. ❏ It was a pretty unpleasant experience, but let's not dwell on it. ❏ People are reluctant to dwell on the subject of death.

Ee

earmark /ˈɪəmɑːk/ (**earmarks, earmarking, earmarked**)

○ **'earmark for**

1 If you **earmark** something **for** a particular purpose, you decide that it should be used for that purpose.

earmark something for something ❑ *This is the amount of money that the company needs to earmark for pensions.*

be earmarked for something ❑ *Two areas have been earmarked for industrial use.*

2 If something **is earmarked for** closure or disposal, for example, people have decided that it will be closed or got rid of.

be earmarked for something ❑ *The library is earmarked for closure despite protests from local people.*

earth /ɜːθ/ (**earths, earthing, earthed**)

○ **earth 'up**

If you **earth up** vegetables or plants, you put more soil around them in order to protect their roots or to encourage the roots to grow.

earth up something or **earth something up** ❑ *I went and earthed up my celery.* ❑ *I planted the leeks by dropping them straight onto muck, then earthing them up.*

ease /iːz/ (**eases, easing, eased**)

○ **ease 'off**

If you **ease off** clothes or something that is stuck to something else, you remove them carefully and gently.

ease off something or **ease something off** ❑ *She bent down and eased off her shoes.* ❑ *She took hold of the bandage and eased it off.*

○ **ease 'off** (or **ease up**)

1 If something **eases off**, it reduces its strength, force or speed. ❑ *The pace of our activity gradually eased off.* ❑ *Mum's headaches eased off.* ❑ *The rain had eased up.*

2 If you **ease off**, you stop putting so much energy or effort into what you are doing. ❑ *Hold your leg up for 10 seconds, then ease off and relax.* ❑ *You're working too hard – you need to ease up.*

○ **ease 'off on** (or **ease up on**) [INFORMAL]

1 If you **ease off on** someone, your behaviour or attitude towards them becomes less severe.

ease off on someone ❑ *Ease off on the kid a bit, Jack!* ❑ *The manager does not intend to ease up on his players for some time.*

2 If you **ease off on** something, you use less of it or use it with less force.

ease off on something ❑ *There's not much fuel left. We've got to ease off on the power.*

○ **ease 'out**

If you **ease** someone **out**, you make them leave a job in a way that is not very obvious.

ease someone out or **ease out someone** ❑ *The previous chair had been eased out by then.*

○ **ease 'up** → see **ease off**

○ **ease 'up on** → see **ease off on**

eat /iːt/ (**eats, eating, ate, eaten**)

○ **eat a'way**

1 If an animal **eats** something **away**, it destroys it by eating it.

eat something away or **eat away something** ❑ *He let rats eat away his walls without doing anything to stop them.*

2 If water, chemicals or other substances **eat** something **away**, they gradually destroy it.

eat something away or **eat away something** ❑ *As the rain fell, water rushed down, eating away the road.*

be eaten away ❑ *Most of the metal has been eaten away by rust.*

3 If a disease or a feeling **eats** someone **away**, it causes them physical or mental harm.

eat someone away ❑ *You have this cancer inside you eating you away.* ❑ *The loss of her daughter is eating her away.*

○ **eat a'way at**

1 If water, chemicals or other substances **eat away at** something physical, they gradually destroy it.

eat away at something ❑ *A small stream was*

eating away at the building's foundations.

2 If a negative emotion or an unpleasant situation or experience **eats away at** someone, it causes them to continue to be unhappy or worried.

eat away at someone ❑ *Disappointment had eaten away at him over the years.*

3 To **eat away at** something means to gradually destroy or weaken it.
= **undermine**

eat away at something ❑ *Constant criticism can eat away at your self esteem.*

○ **eat 'in**

When you **eat in**, you have a meal at home rather than going out to a restaurant.
≠ **eat out** ❑ *'We won't be eating in tonight,' Shoshana said.*

○ **eat 'into**

1 If something **eats into** a part of your body, it presses hard into it and hurts it or cuts it.

eat into something ❑ *The cord had eaten into his wrists and there was blood all over them.*

2 If a chemical or a chemical process **eats into** an object, it gradually destroys it.

eat into something ❑ *Iron pans are not suitable, as vinegar eats into them.*

3 If something **eats into** resources such as money, land, or time, it gradually uses more of them than was expected or intended. = **encroach on**

eat into something ❑ *Wages were rising faster than productivity and this was eating into profits.* ❑ *All this housework was eating into the time I had for studying.*

4 If a negative emotion or an unpleasant situation or experience **eats into** a person or their personality, it causes them to continue to be unhappy or worried.

eat into someone/something ❑ *Fear was a terrible thing. It ate into your soul.*

⊙ **eat 'out**

When you **eat out**, you have a meal at a restaurant instead of at home. ≠ **eat in** ❑ *Do you eat out a lot in London?* ❑ *Willie liked to eat out in restaurants and stay up late in bars.*

● **Eating out** is the activity of having a meal in a restaurant. ❑ *Eating out was beyond their means.*

⊙ **eat 'up**

1 If people or animals **eat up** food, they eat all the food that they have been given or all that is available.

eat up something ❑ *If you eat up all your dinner, you can have dessert.*

eat something up ❑ *She sat on my bed and made me eat it all up.*

NOTE **Polish off** is a more informal expression for **eat up**.

2 If you say **Eat up** to someone, you are encouraging them to eat as much as they can and to enjoy their food. ❑ *'Eat up, darling, that's it,' he would say.*

3 If water, chemicals or other substances **eat up** something, they gradually destroy it.

eat up something or **eat something up** ❑ *Nothing could stop the wind and the rain eating up the land.*

4 If a negative emotion or an unpleasant situation or experience **eats** you **up**, it makes you feel very upset for a long time.

eat someone up or **eat up someone** ❑ *Anger was eating her up.* ❑ *He wondered if it was guilt which was eating up Tarja.*

be eaten up ❑ *Many of the older country folk are eaten up with jealousy of the young.*

NOTE **Consume** is a more formal word for **eat up**.

5 If something **eats up** resources such as money, land, or time, it gradually uses the entire amount that is available.

eat up something ❑ *The children and work were eating up every minute of his time.* ❑ *Housing estates were eating up good agricultural land.*

eavesdrop /ˈiːvzdrɒp/ (**eavesdrops, eavesdropping, eavesdropped**)

○ **'eavesdrop on**

If you **eavesdrop on** someone or their conversation, you listen secretly to what they are saying.

eavesdrop on someone/something ❑ *He was eavesdropping on a conversation at the next table.* ❑ *She often eavesdropped on her neighbours as they sat in the garden.*

ebb /eb/ (**ebbs, ebbing, ebbed**)

○ **ebb a'way**

1 If a feeling or your strength **ebbs away**, it gradually becomes weaker until it disappears completely. ❑ *Their rage ebbed away, to be replaced by fear.* ❑ *Their confidence in him seems to be ebbing away.*

2 If something that someone wants to keep **ebbs away**, it gradually disappears. ❑ *Their chance of gaining power was ebbing away.*

3 If someone's life **ebbs away**, they slowly die. ❑ *He could see the man's life ebbing away.*

edge /edʒ/ (**edges, edging, edged**)

○ **edge 'out**

1 If you **edge out** a person, team or organization you are competing against, you just manage to beat them.

edge out someone/something or **edge someone/something out** ❑ [+ of] *McGregor's effort was enough to edge Johnson out of the top spot.*

2 If you **edge** someone or something **out**, you manage to get rid of them by replacing them with someone or something else.

edge out someone/something or **edge someone/something out** ❑ *Laughter and songs edged out thoughts of death.* ❑ [+ of] *Even though he edged Will out of his job, the two became lifelong friends.*

edit /ˈedɪt/ (**edits, editing, edited**)

○ **edit 'out**

If you **edit out** parts of a film or a piece of writing, you remove them before they are shown or printed.

edit something out or **edit out something** ❑ *They'll have to edit all the names out.* ❑ *They edited out the dull bits.*

egg /eg/ (**eggs, egging, egged**)

○ **egg 'on**

If you **egg** someone **on**, you encourage them to do something foolish, dangerous or wrong.

egg someone on or **egg on someone** ❑ *A crowd watched the fight, egging him on.* ❑ *Egged on by Iago, Othello makes up his mind to kill Desdemona.*

eject /ɪˈdʒekt/ (**ejects, ejecting, ejected**)

○ **e'ject from**

1 If you **eject** someone **from** a place or job, you force them to leave.

eject someone from something ❑ *He was ejected from the theatre for breaking the no-smoking rule.* ❑ *Eventually, the club staff ejected him from the building.*

2 When a pilot **ejects from** an aircraft, he or she leaves the aircraft quickly using a special seat, usually because the plane is going to crash.

eject from something ❑ *One of the crew managed to eject from the plane before it crashed.*

eke /iːk/ (**ekes, eking, eked**)

○ **eke 'out**

1 If you **eke** something **out**, you make it last as long as possible, by using it carefully.

eke something out or **eke out something** ❑ *Workers send home cash that helps eke out low village incomes.* ❑ *We tried to eke out the fuel.*

2 If you **eke out** a living or an existence, you manage with difficulty to get the food or money that you need in order to live.

eke out something ❑ *These people are trying to eke out a living from the land.*

elaborate /ɪˈlæbəreɪt/ (**elaborates, elaborating, elaborated**)

○ **e'laborate on** (or **elaborate upon**)

If you **elaborate on** something already mentioned, you give more details about it or explain it more clearly.

elaborate on something ❑ *Cook confirmed what Mr Cowie had said, and elaborated on it.*

elbow /ˈelbəʊ/ (**elbows, elbowing, elbowed**)

○ **elbow a'side**

To **elbow** someone or something **aside** means to get into a more successful position than them, especially by being determined or ruthless.

elbow aside someone/something or **elbow someone/something aside** ❑ *He elbowed aside his elder brother to take on the family business.* ❑ *Computer games have elbowed more traditional toys aside.*

elevate /ˈelɪveɪt/ (**elevates, elevating, elevated**)

○ **'elevate to** [FORMAL]

If someone **elevates** someone or something **to** a more important rank or status, they make them have it.

elevate someone/something to something ❑ *He was elevated to the post of prime minister.* ❑ *This designer elevates classic sportswear to new levels of sophistication.*

eliminate /ɪˈlɪmɪneɪt/ (**eliminates, eliminating, eliminated**)

○ **e'liminate from**

1 To **eliminate** an unnecessary or unwanted thing **from** something means to get rid of it.

eliminate something from something ❑ *Your kidneys and bladder work with your liver to eliminate waste from your body.*

2 When a person or team **is eliminated from** a competition or when a person or team **eliminates** them **from** a competition, they are defeated and cannot continue in the competition.

be eliminated from something ❑ *Canada was eliminated from the tournament after losing to New Zealand, Italy and Wales.*

eliminate someone/something from something ❑ *Marcelo Zalayeta's first-half goal eliminated Ajax from the competition.*

emanate /ˈeməneɪt/ (**emanates, emanating, emanated**)

○ **'emanate from** [FORMAL]

1 If something **emanates from** a place, it comes from that place.

emanate from somewhere ❑ *The smell*

seemed to emanate from the populated area to
the north.

2 If something **emanates from** a particular
person or thing, they start it or cause it.
emanate from someone/something ❑ *He
could feel the contempt emanating from the
prison officers.*

embark /ɪmˈbɑːk/ (**embarks, embarking,
embarked**)

○ **emˈbark on** (or **embark upon**)
If you **embark on** an activity, you start
doing it.
embark on something ❑ *Peru embarked on
a massive programme of reform.*
be embarked on something ❑ *We are already
embarked on a course which might have serious
consequences.*

embroider /ɪmˈbrɔɪdə/ (**embroiders,
embroidering, embroidered**)

○ **emˈbroider on** (or **embroider upon**)
If you **embroider on** a story or description,
you add details that are not true in order to
make it more interesting.
embroider on something ❑ *Other ancient
writers have embroidered on these early reports.*
NOTE **Embellish** is a more formal word
for **embroider on**.

embroil /ɪmˈbrɔɪl/ (**embroils, embroiling,
embroiled**)

○ **emˈbroil in**
To **embroil** someone **in** a fight, argument or
difficult situation means to make them
become involved in it.
embroil someone in something ❑ *The
university had become embroiled in a legal dispute.*

emerge /ɪˈmɜːdʒ/ (**emerges, emerging,
emerged**)

○ **eˈmerge as**
If someone or something **emerges as** a
particular thing, they become recognized
as that thing.
emerge as something ❑ *Hinduism was
emerging as the dominant religion of the country.*
❑ *Geraldine emerged as the undisputed winner.*

empathize /ˈempəθaɪz/ (**empathizes,
empathizing, empathized**)

○ **ˈempathize with**
If you **empathize with** a person or their
feelings or problems, you understand
them, especially because you have been in a
similar situation.
empathize with someone/something
❑ *Readers can empathize with characters who
have romantic problems.* ❑ *He had a strong need
for privacy. I can empathize with that.*

empty /ˈempti/ (**empties, emptying,
emptied**)

○ **empty ˈout**
1 If you **empty out** a container, or **empty**
something **out** of it, you remove the
contents from it.
empty out something or **empty something
out** ❑ *They emptied out their sacks.* ❑ [+ of]
You ought to empty the water out of those boots.
2 If a place **empties out**, people leave it.
❑ *An hour before closing time, the café emptied
out.*

encase /ɪnˈkeɪs/ (**encases, encasing,
encased**)

○ **enˈcase in**
If a person or an object **is encased in**
something or you **encase** them **in**
something, they are completely covered or
surrounded by it.
be encased in something ❑ *When nuclear fuel
is manufactured, it is encased in metal cans.*
encase something in something ❑ *The
original plan was to encase a small amount of
a radioactive substance in a protective steel
container.*

encroach /ɪnˈkrəʊtʃ/ (**encroaches,
encroaching, encroached**)

○ **enˈcroach on** (or **encroach upon**)
1 If something **encroaches on** something
that someone has, it gradually uses it or
takes it away. [FORMAL]
encroach on something ❑ *This new law
doesn't encroach on the rights of the citizen.*
2 If people or things **encroach on** an area
of land, they gradually cover or use more
and more of it, especially when they are not
wanted. [FORMAL]
encroach on something ❑ *The invading army
was encroaching on national territory.* ❑ *Fast-
growing towns and cities are encroaching on the
countryside.*
3 If someone **encroaches on** an area of
activity, they do that thing too, when
someone else does not want them to.
encroach on something ❑ *He gets furious if
anyone from another department tries to encroach
on his territory.*

end /end/ (**ends, ending, ended**)

○ **end ˈup**
1 If you **end up** in a particular place or
situation, you are in that place or situation
after a series of events, even though you did
not originally intend to be. = **wind up,
finish up** ❑ [+ in] *Two of my friends ended up in
prison for armed robbery.* ❑ [+ with] *Sylvia ended
up with no money, no husband and no house.*

2 If you **end up** doing something after a period of time, you do it even though you did not originally intend to. **= finish up**
end up doing something ❑ *We ended up taking a taxi there.* ❑ *We always end up arguing.*

○ **'end with**
If something such as a book, speech, or performance **ends with** a particular thing, or the writer or performer **ends** it **with** that thing, its final part consists of that thing.
end with something ❑ *His speech ended with a warning about the dangers of ignoring the environment.*
end something with something ❑ *They ended their performance with a piece by Mozart.*

endear /ɪnˈdɪə/ (**endears, endearing, endeared**)
○ **en'dear to**
If something **endears** you **to** someone, it makes you like them, and if you **endear** yourself **to** someone, you behave in a way that makes people like you.
endear someone to someone ❑ *She claimed she was the only one with any experience, which didn't endear her to the other team members.*
endear yourself to someone ❑ *Rachel endeared herself to fellow trainees by bringing in cakes for everyone.*

endow /ɪnˈdaʊ/ (**endows, endowing, endowed**)
○ **en'dow with** [FORMAL]
If someone or something **is endowed with** a particular quality, talent, or other valuable thing, they have it or are given it.
be endowed with something ❑ *He was a man endowed with great leadership talents.* ❑ *The area is richly endowed with minerals.*

engage /ɪnˈɡeɪdʒ/ (**engages, engaging, engaged**)
✪ **en'gage in**
1 If you **engage in** an activity, you take part in it.
engage in something ❑ *It was not considered appropriate for a former President to engage in business.*
be engaged in something ❑ *They were engaged in a life and death struggle.*
2 If you **engage** in conversation or **engage** someone **in** conversation, you talk to someone.
engage in something ❑ *Often he would engage in conversation with complete strangers.*
engage someone in something ❑ *I sometimes tried to engage him in conversation.*

○ **en'gage on** (or **engage upon**)
If you **are engaged on** an activity, you are doing it.
be engaged on something ❑ *Accountants engaged on this kind of work rarely have expense accounts.*

engrave /ɪnˈɡreɪv/ (**engraves, engraving, engraved**)
○ **en'grave on**
If you **engrave** a design or words **on** something, you cut the design or words into its surface.
engrave something on something ❑ *Their names had been engraved on a plaque.*

○ **en'grave with**
If you **engrave** something **with** a design or words, you cut the design or words into its surface.
engrave something with something ❑ *Your wedding ring can be engraved with a personal inscription.*

enlarge /ɪnˈlɑːdʒ/ (**enlarges, enlarging, enlarged**)
○ **en'large on** (or **enlarge upon**)
[FORMAL]
If you **enlarge on** a subject, you give more details about it. **= expand on**
enlarge on something ❑ *Would you care to enlarge on that?*

enquire /ɪnˈkwaɪə/ (**enquires, enquiring, enquired**) → see **inquire**

enshrine /ɪnˈʃraɪn/ (**enshrines, enshrining, enshrined**)
○ **en'shrine in** [FORMAL]
If an idea, a system, or a right **is enshrined in** something such as a constitution or law, or someone **enshrines** it **in** a constitution or law, it is protected by it.
be enshrined in something ❑ *Its banking monopoly had been enshrined in an Act of 1697.*
enshrine something in something ❑ *The apartheid system, which enshrined racism in law, still existed at this time.*

entangle /ɪnˈtæŋɡəl/ (**entangles, entangling, entangled**)
○ **en'tangle in**
1 If something **entangles** you **in** a difficult situation, it makes you become involved in it, and it is difficult to get out of it.
entangle someone in something ❑ *This decision had entangled the country in a very expensive war.*
2 → see **entangle with**
○ **en'tangle with** (or **entangle in**)
If one thing **entangles** itself **with** another

thing, the two things become caught together very tightly.

entangle itself with something ❑ *The blade of the oar had entangled itself with something in the water.* ❑ *The poor bird had entangled itself in some netting.*

enter /'entə/ (enters, entering, entered)

○ **'enter for**

If you **enter for** a competition, race, or examination, or if someone **enters** you **for** it, you take part in it.

enter for something ❑ *She fully intends to enter for the race.*

enter someone for something ❑ *She entered her mother for the 'Mum of the Year' award.*

◉ **enter 'into**

1 If you **enter into** an agreement or arrangement, you formally agree to it.

enter into something ❑ *They were asked to enter into a joint project with the company.*

> **ENTER INTO + noun**
>
> enter into **an agreement**
> enter into **a contract**
> enter into **an arrangement**
> enter into **a partnership**
> enter into **an alliance**
> ❑ *They entered into a long-term agreement to rent the property.* ❑ *His party entered into an alliance with the socialists.*

2 If you **enter into** an activity, you start it or become involved in it.

enter into something ❑ *The government refused to enter into negotiations.* ❑ *No correspondence will be entered into.*

> **ENTER INTO + noun**
>
> enter into **discussions**
> enter into **negotiations**
> enter into **correspondence**
> ❑ *They refused to enter into negotiations with the terrorists.* ❑ *We are unable to enter into correspondence with clients.*

3 If something **enters into** something else, it affects it and is an important factor in it.

enter into something ❑ *All sorts of emotional factors enter into a relationship.* ❑ *Whether you believe in him or not doesn't enter into it.*

4 If someone or something **enters into** a period of time, they start being in that period.

enter into something ❑ *The monarchy then entered into the most difficult period of its history.* ❑ *I was able to enter into a period of calm.*

○ **'enter upon** (or **enter on**) [FORMAL]

When you **enter upon** something, you start to do it or experience it. = **embark on**

enter upon something ❑ *I was entering upon one of the strangest episodes of my life.*

enthuse /ɪn'θjuːz, AM -'θuːz/ (enthuses, enthusing, enthused)

○ **en'thuse over** (or **enthuse about**)

If you **enthuse over** something, you talk about it in a way that shows that you are excited and pleased about it.

enthuse over something ❑ *They were enthusing over a weekend spent in the Lake District.* ❑ *Betty enthused about the wonderful views from her new house.*

entrust /ɪn'trʌst/ (entrusts, entrusting, entrusted)

○ **en'trust to**

If you **entrust** something important **to** someone, you make them responsible for looking after it or dealing with it.

entrust something to someone ❑ *She entrusted the ring to her father for safekeeping.* ❑ *Parents entrust the care of their children to the school.*

equate /ɪ'kweɪt/ (equates, equating, equated)

○ **e'quate with**

If you **equate** one thing **with** another thing, or if you say that one thing **equates with** another thing, you believe that they are strongly connected.

equate something with something ❑ *People often wrongly equate wealth with happiness.*

equate with something ❑ *Investment has become almost a bad word, because it equates with spending.*

equip /ɪ'kwɪp/ (equips, equipping, equipped)

◉ **e'quip with**

If you **equip** a person or thing **with** something, you give them the tools or equipment that they need.

equip someone/something with something ❑ *Their new kitchen will be equipped with a centre island and a breakfast bar.*

equip yourself with something ❑ *Martin equipped himself with a net and tried to catch the frog.*

erode /ɪ'rəʊd/ (erodes, eroding, eroded)

○ **erode a'way**

1 If something **erodes away** or if, wind, water, or the weather **erodes** it **away**, it gradually becomes damaged and disappears. = **wear away**

erode away ❑ *The central tower has eroded away to little more than a circular wall.*

erode something away or **erode away something** ❑ *River cliffs are formed by water eroding away the rock.*

be eroded away ❑ *The cliffs have been eroded away by waves.*

2 If something **erodes away** or if something **erodes** it **away**, it gradually becomes weaker, smaller, or less important.
erode away ❑ *You would think views of this kind would have eroded away.*
erode something away or **erode away something** ❑ *New cultural values are eroding away traditional family bonds.*
be eroded away ❑ *Our rights are being eroded away.*

escape /ɪˈskeɪp/ (**escapes, escaping, escaped**)
○ **es'cape from**
If a person or animal **escapes from** a place, they succeed in getting away from it.
escape from something ❑ *Two men escaped from prison.* ❑ *A monkey escaped from the local zoo.*

etch /etʃ/ (**etches, etching, etched**)
○ **etch 'into**
If a line or pattern **is etched into** a surface or you **etch** it **into** a surface, it is cut into the surface using acid or a sharp tool.
etch something into something ❑ *Use a small sharp knife to etch a pattern into the pastry.*
be etched into something ❑ *The words will be etched into the marble step of the Lincoln Memorial.*

even /ˈiːvən/ (**evens, evening, evened**)
○ **even 'out**
1 If you **even** something **out** or if it **evens out**, it becomes more equal.
even something out or **even out something** ❑ *Irrigation systems help to even out the supply of water over the growing season.*
even out ❑ *If I do some of the longer jobs, perhaps the work will even out.*
2 If you **even** something **out** or if it **evens out**, it improves or becomes less strange or extreme. **= balance out**
even something out or **even out something** ❑ *We have plenty of time to even out the problems.*
even out ❑ *After several weeks with us, her mood began to even out.*
○ **even 'up**
If you **even** something **up** or if it **evens up**, it becomes more equal.
even something up or **even up something** ❑ *Frank and I will change sides. That should even things up a bit.*
even up ❑ *At present, more men than women are losing their jobs, but things will even up in the coming months.*

evict /ɪˈvɪkt/ (**evicts, evicting, evicted**)
○ **e'vict from**
To **evict** someone **from** the place where they are living means to force them to leave, usually because they have broken a law or contract.
evict someone from somewhere ❑ *I was evicted from the house for not paying the rent.* ❑ *The landlord was threatening to evict him from the flat.*

excel /ɪkˈsel/ (**excels, excelling, excelled**)
○ **ex'cel in** (or **excel at**)
If someone **excels in** something, they are very good at it.
excel in something ❑ *Cathy excelled in everything she did.* ❑ *She had never excelled at exams.*

exclude /ɪksˈkluːd/ (**excludes, excluding, excluded**)
○ **ex'clude from**
If you **exclude** someone **from** a place or activity, you prevent them from entering it or taking part in it.
exclude someone from something ❑ *They had tried to exclude her from their conversation.*

excuse /ɪkˈskjuːz/ (**excuses, excusing, excused**)
○ **ex'cuse for**
If you **excuse** someone **for** something bad that they have done, you forgive them for it.
excuse someone for something ❑ *I hope he will excuse us for arriving so late.* ❑ *I'm not excusing him for what he did, but he has had a lot of problems recently.*
○ **ex'cuse from**
If someone **is excused from** a duty or responsibility, they are told that they do not have to do it.
be excused from something ❑ *She is usually excused from her duties during the school holidays.*

exempt /ɪgˈzempt/ (**exempts, exempting, exempted**)
○ **ex'empt from**
To **exempt** a person or thing **from** a particular rule, duty, or obligation means to say officially that they are not affected by it or that they do not have to do something.
exempt someone/something from something ❑ *In 1996 a law was introduced which exempted exports from sales taxes.* ❑ *Companies with fewer than 100 employees would be exempted from the requirements.*

exile /ˈeksaɪl, ˈegz-/ (**exiles, exiling, exiled**)
○ **'exile from**
1 To **exile** someone **from** a particular place

or situation means to send them away from it or remove them from it when they do not want this.

exile someone from something/somewhere ❏ Taking on this job would exile him from his beloved Yorkshire for too long.

be exiled from something/somewhere ❏ He has been exiled from the first team and forced to play in third team matches.

2 If someone **is exiled from** their own country, they are forced to leave and live in another country, usually for political reasons.

be exiled from somewhere ❏ Since being exiled from his native land he had become reasonably fluent in spoken Russian.

expand /ɪk'spænd/ (**expands, expanding, expanded**)

○ **ex'pand on** (or **expand upon**)

If you **expand on** a subject you have already mentioned, you give more information or details about it. **= enlarge on**

expand on something ❏ I went on to expand upon this theme.

expel /ɪk'spel/ (**expels, expelling, expelled**)

○ **ex'pel from**

1 If someone **is expelled from** a school or organization or someone **expels** them **from** it, they are officially told to leave because they have behaved badly.

be expelled from something ❏ He had been expelled from the army. ❏ I'd been expelled from school for fighting.

expel someone from something ❏ A headteacher has the authority to expel a child from school.

2 To **expel** someone **from** a place means to force them to leave it.

expel someone from somewhere ❏ An American academic was expelled from the country yesterday.

explain /ɪk'spleɪn/ (**explains, explaining, explained**)

○ **explain a'way**

If you **explain away** a mistake or unpleasant situation, you give reasons to show that it is not as bad or important as people think. **= excuse**

explain away something or **explain something away** ❏ All this can, of course, be explained away by other reasons.

extend /ɪk'stend/ (**extends, extending, extended**)

○ **ex'tend over**

If an event or activity **extends over** a period of time, it continues for that time.

extend over something ❏ The courses are based on a weekly two-hour class, extending over a period of 25 weeks.

○ **ex'tend to**

1 If something **extends to** a group of people, things, or activities, it includes or affects them.

extend to someone/something ❏ The service also extends to wrapping and delivering gifts. ❏ The talks will extend to human rights groups and other social organizations.

2 If you **extend** something **to** other people or things, you make it include or affect more people or things.

extend something to someone/something ❏ Could we extend the invitation to partners as well?

extort /ɪk'stɔːt/ (**extorts, extorting, extorted**)

○ **ex'tort from**

1 If someone **extorts** money **from** you, they get it from you using force, threats, or other ways that are unfair or illegal.

extort something from someone ❏ Corrupt government officials were extorting money from him.

2 If someone **extorts** something **from** you, they get it from you with difficulty or by doing something that is unfair.

extort something from someone ❏ Torture was used to extort confessions from suspects.

extract /ɪk'strækt/ (**extracts, extracting, extracted**)

❂ **ex'tract from**

1 If you **extract** something **from** a place, you take it out or pull it out.

extract something from something ❏ He extracted a small notebook from his pocket. ❏ She extracted the cork from the bottle with great ease.

2 If you **extract** information or a response **from** someone, you get it from them with difficulty, because they are unwilling to say or do what you want.

extract something from someone ❏ He was trying to extract further information from our director.

3 If part of a book or text **is extracted from** another book or text, it is taken from there.

be extracted from something ❏ This material has been extracted from 'Collins GoodWood Handbook'.

extricate /'ekstrɪkeɪt/ (**extricates, extricating, extricated**)

○ **'extricate from**

1 If you **extricate** yourself or another person **from** a difficult or serious situation, you free yourself or the other person from it.

extricate someone from something ❏ *The $50,000 would be sufficient to extricate him from his financial difficulties.*

extricate yourself from something ❏ *Anthony was quite confident of being able to extricate himself from the mess he had got into.*

2 If you **extricate** someone or something **from** a place where they are trapped or caught, you succeed in freeing them. [FORMAL]

extricate someone/something from something ❏ *He gently extricated his hand from Zabrina's hold.*

extricate yourself from something ❏ *'Let me get that,' she said, gently extricating herself from Carol's grasp.*

exult /ɪgˈzʌlt/ (exults, exulting, exulted)

○ **exˈult in** [FORMAL]

If you **exult in** something, you feel or show that you are very happy and pleased about it, especially about a success you have had.

exult in something ❏ *Leonard strolled about, exulting in his freedom.*

eye /aɪ/ (eyes, eyeing, eyed)

○ **eye ˈup** [BRITISH, INFORMAL]

1 If someone **eyes** you **up**, they look at you a lot because they find you sexually attractive. = **ogle**

eye someone up or **eye up someone** ❏ *I made tea while she sat there eyeing me up.* ❏ *I was eyeing up the girl in the corner.*

2 If someone **is eyeing** something **up**, they are looking at it or considering it in a way that shows that they want it.

be eyeing up something or **be eyeing something up** ❏ *Several companies were eyeing up the mobile phone market.* ❏ *I am not eyeing up something I can't afford.*

Ff

fabricate /'fæbrɪkeɪt/ (**fabricates, fabricating, fabricated**)

○ **fabricate from**

If an industrial product **is fabricated from** a material or substance, it is made from it.
be fabricated from something ❏ *All the tools are fabricated from high quality steel.*

face /feɪs/ (**faces, facing, faced**)

○ **face a'bout**

If you **face about**, you turn so that you are looking in the opposite direction. ❏ *She walked backwards a couple of steps, and then faced about, and walked toward me.*

○ **face 'down**

If you **face down** someone who is threatening you, criticizing you or arguing with you, you defeat them by acting confidently.
face someone down or **face down someone**
❏ *She was determined to face down her opponents.*

○ **face 'out** [BRITISH]

If you **face** a difficult situation **out**, you remain determined not to allow it to harm you or make you stop doing something.
= **see through**
face something out or **face out something**
❏ *We'll just have to face this crisis out.*

○ **face 'up to**

If you **face up to** a difficult situation, you accept it and deal with it.
face up to something ❏ *We have to face up to the fact that this relationship isn't going to work.*
❏ *His situation was desperate, but he faced up to it with courage.*

FACE UP TO + noun

face up to **the truth**
face up to **the fact that...**
face up to **reality**
face up to **a responsibility**
face up to **a problem**
face up to **the consequences of** something
face up to **a challenge**
❏ *I had to face up to the fact that I would never walk again.* ❏ *He decided to return home and face up to his responsibilities.*

---

factor /'fæktə/ (**factors, factoring, factored**)

○ **factor 'in**

1 If you **factor in** an amount or a cost, you include it in a calculation.
factor in something or **factor something in**
❏ *Factoring in inflation, spending has declined by 0.4 per cent.*

2 If you **factor in** a fact or a situation, you consider it when you are making a plan or a decision.
factor in something or **factor something in**
❏ *We hadn't factored in the possibility of winning.*
❏ *This is an important point that must be factored in*

○ **factor 'into**

If you **factor** something **into** an amount or a cost, you include it.
factor something into something ❏ *The disruption involved needs to be factored into the cost of moving to a new building.*

fade /feɪd/ (**fades, fading, faded**)

○ **fade a'way**

1 If something **fades away**, it slowly ends or disappears. ❏ *The sun's warmth began to fad away.* ❏ *My enthusiasm for running soon faded away.*

2 If a sound or sight **fades away**, it gradually becomes quieter or less easy to see and eventually disappears. ❏ *On the right were the hills fading away into the misty morning.* ❏ *The music and laughter gradually faded away as the procession moved off down the street.*

NOTE **Recede** is a more formal word for **fade away**.

3 If someone **fades away**, they become weaker and die. ❏ *He was fading quietly away day by day.*

○ **fade 'in** (or **fade up**) [TECHNICAL]

If someone **fades in** a picture or sound on a recording, they start it gradually and make it brighter or louder until people can see it or hear it properly.
fade in something or **fade something in**
❏ *They faded in some of her music at the end of the scene.*

fade 'out

1 If something **fades out**, it gradually ends or disappears. **= fizzle out** ❑ *The problems of last month will fade out gradually.*

2 When a sound or a radio signal **fades out**, it slowly becomes less loud or strong until you can no longer hear it or receive it. ❑ *The sound of the chopper had faded out.*

3 If someone **fades out** a picture or sound on a recording, they make them disappear gradually. [TECHNICAL]
fade something out or **fade out something** ❑ *By turning a little button, he could make the image fade out.*

fade 'up → see fade in

faff /fæf/ (faffs, faffing, faffed)

faff a'round (or faff about) [BRITISH, INFORMAL]

If someone **faffs around**, they spend a lot of time doing things in a way that is not efficient and does not achieve much.
❑ *We faffed around undoing the babies' seatbelts.* ❑ *I've been faffing about online, trying to find his email address.*

fag /fæg/ (fags, fagging, fagged)

fag 'out [BRITISH, INFORMAL, OLD-FASHIONED]

If something **fags** you **out**, it makes you feel tired.
fag someone out ❑ *That last game really fagged me out!*
⌐NOTE⌐ **Wear out** is a less informal expression for **fag out**.
• If you are **fagged out**, you feel very tired. [BRITISH, INFORMAL] ❑ *At times Essie looked fagged out.*

fall /fɔːl/ (falls, falling, fell, fallen)

fall a'bout [BRITISH, INFORMAL]

If you **fall about**, you laugh a lot. ❑ *When we complained, they fell about laughing.* ❑ *She admired her brother, and fell about at his jokes.*

fall a'part

1 If something **falls apart**, it breaks into pieces. ❑ *Cheap clothing lasts a little while and then falls apart.* ❑ *He lived in an old hut that was falling apart.*
⌐NOTE⌐ **Disintegrate** is a more formal word for **fall apart**.

2 If an organization, activity, system or relationship **falls apart**, it fails or ends. **= collapse** ❑ *The project fell apart when war broke out.* ❑ *Their marriage began to fall apart.*

3 If someone **falls apart**, they are unable to think or behave normally and calmly because they are in such a difficult or unpleasant situation. **= crack up** [INFORMAL] ❑ *His marriage ended eight months ago and he fell apart.*

fall a'way

1 If something **falls away**, it breaks off or comes away from the surface that it was attached to. **= fall off** ❑ *Patches of plaster had fallen away between the windows.* ❑ *The sheet fell away and we could see the objects beneath it.*

2 If land **falls away**, it slopes gently downwards. ❑ *We were in a long field that fell away from the house towards thick woods.*

3 If an unpleasant quality or a difficulty **falls away**, it disappears and no longer affects you. [LITERARY] ❑ *I thought of Charlotte, and for a second or two my anger fell away.*

4 If the degree, amount, or strength of something **falls away**, it becomes less or smaller. **= fall off** ❑ *During the general strike, the party's membership fell away.* ❑ *Student support fell away in this period.*

5 If a sound **falls away**, it gradually becomes quieter until you can no longer hear it. **= die away, fade away** ❑ *The sound of the aircraft's engine fell away again.* ❑ *His voice fell away and I couldn't catch his next few words.*

fall 'back

1 If an army **falls back** during a battle or war, it moves away from the enemy. ❑ *They fell back in confusion, surprised by the direction of attack.*

2 If you **fall back**, you suddenly move backwards away from someone or something because they have upset or frightened you. ❑ *I watched him fall back in horror.* ❑ *He fell back with a scream.*
⌐NOTE⌐ **Recoil** is a more formal word for **fall back**.

3 If you **fall back** when moving with a group of people, you move more slowly than them, so they get ahead of you.
❑ *He fell back to get a stone out of his shoe.*

4 If prices or values **fall back**, they become lower. ❑ *In London yesterday oil prices fell back.*

fall 'back on (or fall back upon)

If you **fall back on** something, you use it or do it when other things have failed.
= resort to
fall back on something ❑ *Although they live comfortably, they've nothing to fall back on if disaster strikes.* ❑ *This is the sort of dish you can fall back on when guests arrive unexpectedly.*
• A **fall-back** method, plan, or system, is one which you have in case the first method, plan, or system you use fails. **= back-up** ❑ *Natural caution had led me to have a fall-back position prepared.* • A **fall-back** is something you can use if your first method, plan, or system fails. ❑ *It is vital that more students see teaching as a great career option, not just as a fall-back if all else fails.*

✪ fall be'hind

1 If you **fall behind** or **fall behind** someone when moving with a group of people, you move more slowly than them, so they get ahead of you. **= lag behind**

fall behind ❑ *He fell so far behind that I decided to let him rest.*

fall behind someone ❑ *Don't fall behind the leaders or you'll never catch up.*

2 If someone or something **falls behind** or **falls behind** someone or something, they do not reach the standard or level of similar people or things.

fall behind ❑ [+ with] *These children often fall behind with their reading.*

fall behind someone/something ❑ *His salary has fallen behind those of many of his colleagues.*

3 If you **fall behind** with a task, or if the task **falls behind**, you gradually get later and later with it. ❑ *He had fallen behind with his book on British political history.* ❑ *The project had fallen so far behind that there was little chance of meeting the deadline.*

4 If you **fall behind** with a payment, you do not pay it at the time you should. ❑ [+ with] *Unfortunately, we have fallen behind with the payments.*

✪ fall 'down

1 If someone or something **falls down** when they have been in an upright position, they drop to the ground. ❑ *He tripped and fell down.* ❑ *The pile of books fell down and scattered all over the floor.*

2 If something such as a building or bridge **falls down**, it breaks into pieces because it is old, weak, or damaged. **= collapse** ❑ *That shelter might fall down if the rain comes back.*

3 If a building **is falling down**, it is in very bad condition and may collapse.

be falling down ❑ *The house was cheap because it was falling down.*

4 If an argument, idea, theory, or method **falls down**, it fails because it has a weakness or a mistake. ❑ *In one area only did the comparison fall down.* ❑ *The area of discipline is where a lot of teachers fall down.*

5 The **downfall** of a successful or powerful organization or person is their failure or ruin. ❑ *The argument led to the downfall of six government ministers.* ● Something that is the **downfall** of a particular person or thing is the thing that causes the person or thing to be ruined or to fail. ❑ *'She wasn't scared of anybody,' he said, 'and I guess that was her downfall.'*

✪ 'fall for

1 If you **fall for** someone or something, you start to love them or like them very much.

fall for someone/something ❑ *He fell for her the moment he set eyes on her.*

2 If you **fall for** a trick or a joke, you believe that it is true.

fall for something ❑ *It was a stupid trick and I fell for it.*

○ fall 'in

1 If a roof, ceiling, or wall **falls in**, it falls down to the ground. **= cave in** ❑ *The tunnel has fallen in.*

2 If you **fall in** with or beside someone, you start to walk with them. ❑ [+ beside] *He fell in beside Damian and they moved off again.* ❑ [+ with] *Burnell fell in with them, walking at the same pace.*

3 If soldiers or other people in a military organization **fall in**, they get into a line one behind the other. **≠ fall out** ❑ *Pick up your gear and fall in.*

✪ fall 'into

1 If something **falls into** a particular group or category, it belongs to that group or category.

fall into something ❑ *The army medical department fell into two categories, those who worked in hospitals, and those out with fighting soldiers.* ❑ *My work really falls into three parts.*

2 If something or someone **falls into** a particular bad state, they begin to be in that state.

fall into something ❑ *The practice had fallen into disuse and been forgotten.* ❑ *She fell into debt*

3 If you **fall into** an activity or way of behaving, you start to do it, often without intending to.

fall into something ❑ *She fell into the habit of sleeping for several hours in the afternoon.*

4 If you **fall into** conversation or a discussion with someone, you start having a conversation or discussion with them.

fall into something ❑ *I fell into conversation with the owner of a hardware shop.* ❑ *We fell into a discussion with the ticket seller about travel.*

5 If something or someone **falls into** someone's hands, the second person gets that thing or person, often when they should not.

fall into something ❑ *Why would he allow her to fall into the hands of his enemies?*

If something **falls into the wrong hands**, someone who should not have it gets it. ❑ *Of course we're concerned that the data shouldn't fall into the wrong hands.*

6 If someone **falls into a trap**, they are tricked by someone or something or they do something that causes trouble for them. ❑ *He fell into the trap of spending all his money on equipment.* ❑ *She promised that he would make money, and he fell into the trap.*

fall 'in with

1 If you **fall in with** an existing idea, plan or system, you accept it and do not try to change it. **= go along with**

fall in with something ❑ *I didn't know whether to fall in with this arrangement.*

2 If you **fall in with** someone, you meet them by chance and often become friends with them.

fall in with someone ❑ *He had the luck to fall in with the American humorist, Tom Lehrer.* ❑ *She fell in with a bunch of criminals.*

fall 'off

1 If something **falls off** or **falls off** something, it separates from the thing to which it was attached. **= drop off**

fall off ❑ *The back half of the boat had fallen off.*

fall off something ❑ *Some rotten apples fell off the tree.*

2 If the degree, amount, or standard of something **falls off**, it becomes less or lower. **= drop** ❑ *We knew that the numbers of overseas students would fall off drastically.* ❑ *Economic growth will fall off only slightly.*

● If there is a **falling-off** of something, there is a decrease in the degree, amount or standard of it. ❑ *There was a definite falling-off of active interest.* ❑ *A falling-off in business was expected.*

'fall on (or fall upon)

1 If a responsibility or duty **falls on** someone, it becomes their responsibility or duty. **= fall to**

fall on someone ❑ *Without a producer, the weight of responsibility fell upon me.* ❑ *When we landed at the airport, it fell on me to walk the chief executive to his waiting car.*

2 If someone **falls on** you, they hug you eagerly because they are very happy or excited.

fall on someone ❑ *People were falling on each other in delight and tears.* ❑ *They fell upon each other like old friends.*

3 If you **fall on** something when it arrives or appears, you eagerly seize it or welcome it.

fall on something ❑ *They fell on the sandwiches when they arrived.* ❑ *I saw the magazine and eagerly fell upon it.*

4 If someone **falls on** you, they attack you suddenly and violently. **= set upon**

fall on someone ❑ *Rebecca fell upon Richard, hitting his chest with both fists.*

5 If your eyes **fall on** someone or something, you see or notice them.

fall on something ❑ *His gaze fell on a small white bundle.* ❑ *As she passed the piano, her gaze fell upon a framed photograph of Tom.*

6 If a date **falls on** a certain day of the week, it occurs on that day.

fall on something ❑ *My birthday falls on a Thursday this year.*

✪ fall 'out

1 If something or someone **falls out** of a container or a place, they come out of it and drop towards the ground. ❑ *[+ of] I almost fell out of bed.* ❑ *He had to cling to Melanie to avoid falling out.*

2 If hair, a tooth, or a nail **falls out**, it becomes loose and separates from your body. ❑ *After about two weeks, your hair starts to fall out.* ❑ *Eventually your baby teeth get loose and then fall out.*

3 If people **fall out**, they have an argument and are no longer friendly. ❑ *[+ with] I've fallen out with certain members of the band.* ❑ *[+ over] How silly to fall out over something as trivial as that!* ❑ *Everybody will lose if the partners fall out.*

4 If soldiers or other people in a military organization **fall out**, they move out of the positions they were in. **≠ fall in** ❑ *He gave the order to fall out.*

5 **Fallout** is the radiation that is left in a place after a nuclear explosion. ❑ *Their job is to look at the effects of radioactive fallout.*

6 **Fallout** is the unpleasant effects of an event or activity. ❑ *We will all have to deal with fallout from her latest romantic disappointment.*

✪ fall 'over

1 If someone or something that is standing **falls over** or **falls over** something or someone, they become unbalanced and drop to the ground. **= topple over**

fall over ❑ *He pushed back his chair so hard that it fell over.* ❑ *'Look at me!' He pretended to fall over.*

fall over something/someone ❑ *He nearly fell over an old lady in a wheelchair.*

2 If people **fall over** themselves to do something, they are very eager to do it. [INFORMAL]

fall over yourself ❑ *[+ to-infinitive] Of course, they were all falling over themselves to serve us.* ❑ *Governments were falling over each other to win these valuable contracts.*

✪ fall 'through

If an arrangement or plan **falls through**, it fails to happen. ❑ *We arranged to book a villa but it fell through.* ❑ *Any number of things could lead to a sale falling through.*

○ 'fall to

1 If a responsibility or task **falls to** someone, they have to deal with it or do it. **= fall on**

fall to someone ❑ *That task of thanking the committee fell to Mrs Isabel Travers.*
❑ [+ to-infinitive] *It fell to Philip Crow to act the part of host.*

2 If someone **falls to** doing something, they start doing it. [LITERARY]
fall to something ❑ *I fell to wondering what she would do.*

○ **'fall under**

1 If something **falls under** a particular category or group, it belongs in that category or group.
fall under something ❑ *'Portrait of an Artist' falls under autobiography, not fiction.* ❑ *These studies fall under the 'sociology/psychology' heading.*

2 If someone **falls under** the influence or control of someone or something else, the second person or thing influences or controls the first.
fall under something ❑ *At school I fell under the influence of an inspiring history teacher.* ❑ *It seems that Marion was one of those who fell under his spell.*

○ **'fall upon**

1 If something unpleasant **falls upon** someone, it happens to them. = **befall** [LITERARY]
fall upon someone ❑ *She writes about the extreme suffering that falls upon some human beings.*

2 → see **fall on**

fan /fæn/ (**fans, fanning, fanned**)

○ **fan 'out**

1 If a group of people **fan out**, they move forwards together from the same point and gradually spread farther away from each other. ❑ *The five of us fanned out at intervals of not more than fifteen feet.*

2 If something **fans out**, or if it **is fanned out**, it forms a shape which is narrow at one end and wide at the other.
fan out ❑ *Her wide trousers fanned out in the wind.*
be fanned out ❑ *Her blonde hair was fanned out on the pillow.*

farm /fɑːm/ (**farms, farming, farmed**)

○ **farm 'out**

If you **farm out** something or someone that is your responsibility, you send them to other people for them to deal with or look after.
farm out something/someone or **farm something/someone out** ❑ *Many European businesses farmed out clerical jobs to London agencies.* ❑ *She farmed the child out for the day.*

fart /fɑːt/ (**farts, farting, farted**)

> **Fart** is a rude word used mainly in very informal British English.

○ **fart a'bout** (or **fart around**) [INFORMAL RUDE]

If someone **farts about**, they waste time doing silly or unimportant things.
❑ *He liked playing jazz and farting about in Paris.*
❑ *Mum was farting around putting stuff in a carrier bag.*
NOTE **Mess around** is a less rude expression for **fart about**.

fasten /'fɑːsən, 'fæs-/ (**fastens, fastening, fastened**)

○ **'fasten on** (or **fasten upon**)

1 If you or your mind **fasten on** something, or your attention or mind **are fastened on** something, you give all your attention to it.
= **latch on to**
fasten on something ❑ *They should not fasten on profit as the only aim of their work.* ❑ *His mind fastened upon it now: escape.*
be fastened on something ❑ *Too much attention was fastened on the fact that both victims were young white males.*

2 If your eyes **fasten on** or **are fastened on** something or someone, they start to look at them with interest.
fasten on something/someone ❑ *His eyes fastened on the briefcase.*
be fastened on something/someone ❑ *The girls had their eyes fastened on the priest.*

○ **fasten 'on to**

If someone **fastens on to** you, they keep following you or wanting to be with you.
fasten on to someone ❑ *The doctor had fastened on to an official of the Russian embassy.*

○ **'fasten to**

If you **fasten** one thing **to** another thing, you attach the first thing to the second thing.
fasten something to something ❑ *He fastened the rope to the back of the truck.*
❑ [+ with] *The photographs were fastened to the wall with sticky tape.*

○ **'fasten 'up**

If you **fasten** something **up**, you close it using buttons, straps, etc. = **do up**
fasten something up or **fasten up something** ❑ *Fasten your coat up.* ❑ *'The harm's been done,' the old man said, fastening up his jacket.*

○ **'fasten upon** → see **fasten on**

fathom /'fæðəm/ (**fathoms, fathoming, fathomed**)

○ **fathom 'out**

If you **fathom** something **out**, you eventuall*

understand it as a result of thinking carefully about it. = **work out**

fathom something out or **fathom out something** ❑ It was difficult to fathom things out. ❑ I can't fathom out why he did it.

fatten /ˈfætən/ (**fattens, fattening, fattened**)

○ **fatten 'up**

If you **fatten up** an animal or a person, or if an animal or person **fattens up**, they become heavier.

fatten up something/someone or **fatten something/someone up** ❑ My job was to fatten up the geese. ❑ You'd better come to us for a weekend and let Eileen fatten you up.

fatten up ❑ She is beginning to fatten up a little now, thank goodness!

fawn /fɔːn/ (**fawns, fawning, fawned**)

○ **fawn over**

If someone **fawns over** a powerful or rich person, they say nice things to that person so that they will like them, in a way that annoys other people.

fawn over someone ❑ People fawn over you when you're famous. ❑ He has been fawned over in the newspapers.

fear /fɪə/ (**fears, fearing, feared**)

○ **fear for**

If you **fear for** someone or something, you are very worried that they might be in danger.

fear for someone/something ❑ Morris began to fear for the safety of his aunt. ❑ She feared for her daughters.

feast /fiːst/ (**feasts, feasting, feasted**)

○ **feast on**

If you **feast on** a particular food, you eat a large amount of it with great enjoyment.

feast on something ❑ We feasted on fresh fish in a local restaurant.

feed /fiːd/ (**feeds, feeding, fed**)

○ **feed 'into**

1 If you **feed** something **into** a container or piece of equipment, you put it into it.

feed something into something ❑ She was feeding documents into a paper shredder.

2 To **feed** information **into** a computer means to put it into it.

feed something into something ❑ Graham handed her the card and she fed the name into a computer.

○ **feed on** (or **feed off**)

If an idea, feeling, system or process **feeds on** something, it continues to exist or grow because of that thing, often in a way that is unfair.

feed on something ❑ He's feeding off your creative energy. ❑ Creativity and curiosity are part of the same thing, they feed on each other.

○ **feed 'up** [BRITISH]

If you **feed up** an animal, child, or sick person, you give them plenty of food in order to make them strong and healthy. = **build up**

feed up someone/something or **feed someone/something up** ❑ Farmers feed up their sheep prior to mating.

feel /fiːl/ (**feels, feeling, felt**)

○ **'feel for**

If you **feel for** someone who has a problem or is upset, you have sympathy for them. = **sympathize with**

feel for someone ❑ Boy, I feel for you guys.

○ **feel 'out** [INFORMAL]

1 If you **feel** someone **out**, you carefully try to discover their opinions or attitudes. = **sound out**

feel someone out or **feel out someone** ❑ We felt him out, he wasn't willing to help.

2 If you **feel** something **out**, you start to find out what it is like.

feel something out or **feel out something** ❑ He was reading through the script, feeling out the part he would be playing.

○ **feel 'up** [INFORMAL, RUDE]

To **feel** someone **up** means to touch their body in order to gain sexual excitement. = **touch up**

feel someone up or **feel up someone** ❑ He had tried to feel her up in the car on the way home.

○ **feel 'up to**

If you **feel up to** doing something, you feel physically and mentally able to do it.

feel up to something ❑ 'I just hope I feel up to eating,' said Dr Cox. ❑ 'Look, I'll make the call if you don't feel up to it,' I offered desperately.

fence /fens/ (**fences, fencing, fenced**)

○ **fence 'in**

1 If an area **is fenced in**, it is surrounded by a fence.

be fenced in ❑ The playground is fenced in by iron railings.

2 If animals **are fenced in**, they are kept in an area with a fence.

be fenced in ❑ The antelope, fenced in on game ranches, had become sick.

3 If you **are fenced in**, something is limiting your freedom.

be fenced in ❑ These people hate being tied down or fenced in.

○ **fence 'off**

If an area **is fenced off**, it is separated from other areas by a fence.

be fenced off ❏ *A small field was fenced off for Susie's horse.*

fend /fend/ (fends, fending, fended)

○ **fend 'off**

1 If you **fend off** an attack or an attacker, you try to prevent them from hurting you.
= **ward off**
fend off someone/something or **fend someone/something off** ❏ *He raised his arms to fend off the blows.*

2 If you **fend off** questions, criticism, or things or people you do not want, you avoid dealing with them or refuse to accept them.
fend off something/someone or **fend something/someone off** ❏ *She asked Frank what had happened, but he fended off her questions.* ❏ *She had to fend off several unwanted admirers.*

ferret /'ferɪt/ (ferrets, ferreting, ferreted)

○ **ferret 'out** [INFORMAL]

If you **ferret** something or someone **out**, you find them by searching for them thoroughly and in a determined way.
= **unearth**
ferret out something/someone or **ferret someone/something out** ❏ *That's your job isn't it, to ferret out the truth?*

fess /fes/ (fesses, fessing, fessed)

○ **fess 'up** [mainly AMERICAN, INFORMAL]

If you **fess up**, you admit that you have done something wrong. = **confess** ❏ [+ *to*] *The government should fess up to the fact that almost half the price is tax.*

festoon /fe'stuːn/ (festoons, festooning, festooned)

○ **fe'stoon with**

If something **is festooned with** things or you **festoon** something **with** things, a lot of these things are hung from it or wrapped around it, especially in order to decorate it.
be festooned with something ❏ *The temple was festooned with lights.* ❏ *A storefront restaurant is festooned with American flags.*
festoon something with something ❏ *Sandra festooned the family home with her own paintings.*

fetch /fetʃ/ (fetches, fetching, fetched)

○ **fetch 'up** [INFORMAL]

If you **fetch up** somewhere, you arrive there, usually without intending to.
= **land up**
fetch up somewhere ❏ [+ *in*] *That first night we fetched up in the Hotel Tulip.*

feud /fjuːd/ (feuds, feuding, feuded)

○ **'feud with**

If one person or group **feuds with** another, they have an angry disagreement that continues for several months or years.
feud with someone ❏ *The wedding was awkward because one part of the family was feuding with another part.*

fiddle /'fɪdəl/ (fiddles, fiddling, fiddled)

○ **fiddle a'round** (or **fiddle about**)
[INFORMAL]

If you **fiddle around**, you waste time doing unimportant things. = **mess around**
❏ *Eddie and I were fiddling around making last-minute changes.*

○ **fiddle a'round with** (or **fiddle about with**) [INFORMAL]

1 If you **fiddle around with** something, you do things to try to improve it or make it work better, often in a way that is not effective. = **tinker**
fiddle around with something ❏ *Two of them got out to fiddle around with the engine.* ❏ *Right now in Congress, they're fiddling about with the budget.*

2 If you **fiddle around with** something, you continually touch it or move it. ❏ *Rolf stopped fiddling around with his glass and started to pay attention to what he was saying.*

fight /faɪt/ (fights, fighting, fought)

✪ **fight 'back**

1 If you **fight back** when someone or something attacks you or causes you problems, you defend yourself and try to beat them or stop them. ❏ *He had started the unpleasantness, but Mary had fought back.* ❏ [+ *against*] *He decided to fight back against the disease by educating others.*
NOTE **Retaliate** and **resist** are more formal words for **fight back**.

2 If you **fight back** a feeling or emotion, you try very hard not to let it affect you.
fight back something or **fight something back** ❏ *I waited, fighting back my fear.* ❏ *She fought back the tears.* ❏ *I felt panic rising, but I fought it back.*

○ **fight 'down**

If you **fight down** a feeling or emotion, you try very hard not to let it affect you.
= **suppress**
fight down something or **fight something down** ❏ *He had to fight down the impulse to sneak out.* ❏ *Fighting down panic and pain, she kicked at her attacker.*

✪ **fight 'off**

1 If you **fight off** an illness, an unpleasant

feeling, or something you do not want, you succeed in getting rid of it.

fight off something ❑ *Foods such as eggs, fish and whole grains may help fight off cancer.* ❑ *They fought off proposed taxes on imported steel.*

fight something off ❑ *He looked ill, but he kept saying he was going to fight it off.*

2 If you **fight off** something or someone that is competing with you, you defeat them.

fight off something/someone or **fight something/someone off** ❑ *You shouldn't have to fight off too much competition for the job.*

3 If you **fight off** an attack or someone who is attacking you, you make them stop or go away.

fight off something/someone ❑ *The woman fought off the attacker.* ❑ *They managed to fight off the invasion.*

fight something/someone off ❑ *Christopher says he surprised intruders in his flat and fought them off.*

○ **fight 'out**

When two people or groups **fight** something **out**, they fight or argue until one of them wins.

fight something out or **fight out something** ❑ *These decisions were fought out between contending groups.* ❑ *Group members have to fight out the issue amongst themselves.*

• When two people or groups **fight it out**, they fight or argue until one of them wins. ❑ *The European nations were fighting it out on the battlefields.*

figure /ˈfɪgə, AM -gjər/ (**figures, figuring, figured**)

○ **'figure in**

If a person or thing **figures in** something, they appear in or are included in it.

figure in something ❑ *A 40-acre sports park will also figure in the community plan.* ❑ *Golfers figured highly in the list of top earners.*

○ **'figure on** [INFORMAL]

If you **figure on** something, you think it will happen or plan for it to happen.

= **reckon on, count on**

figure on something ❑ *How soon are you figuring on getting married?* ❑ *I figured on going out tonight.*

○ **figure 'out** [INFORMAL]

1 If you **figure out** the solution to a problem, the answer to a question, or the reason for something, you work it out and understand it.

figure out something ❑ *I've figured out what the trouble is.* ❑ *We tried to figure out a way to get to Wimbledon.*

figure something out ❑ *Nancy for one couldn't figure it out.*

2 If you **figure** someone **out**, you understand them and why they behave in the way they do.

figure someone out ❑ *I just can't figure him out.*

○ **figure 'up** [AMERICAN]

If you **figure up** a cost or amount, you add numbers together to get the total.

= **calculate**

figure up something or **figure something up** ❑ *He figured up the balance in their checking account.*

file /faɪl/ (**files, filing, filed**)

○ **file a'way**

If you **file away** a fact or idea, you make an effort to remember it because you think it might be useful.

file away something or **file something away** ❑ *Dan carefully filed away this added reason for hating Joe Parker.* ❑ *Dominic filed this information away for future reference.*

fill /fɪl/ (**fills, filling, filled**)

◎ **fill 'in**

1 If you **fill in** a hole, you put a substance into it so that the surface becomes level.

fill in something ❑ *She bought a packet of cement mix and began to fill in some holes.*

fill something in ❑ *They used small stones to fill the holes in.*

2 If you **fill in** a document or the information on a document, you write all the information that is needed on it.

= **fill out** [BRITISH]

fill something in ❑ *Ask for a claim form, fill it in and send it to the social security office.* ❑ *We will fill the invoices in with all the necessary information.*

fill in something ❑ *We filled in all the customs forms.* ❑ *Fill in your name and address here.*

3 If you **fill in** a shape, you paint or draw all over the space inside the lines. = **colour in**

fill in something or **fill something in** ❑ *You could get the kids to fill in the various pieces in different colours.* ❑ *She drew a circle and filled it in.*

4 If you **fill** someone **in**, you give them information about something. [INFORMAL]

fill someone in or **fill in someone** ❑ [+ on] *I'll fill you in on the details now.* ❑ *Come back to the office and I'll fill you in.*

5 If you **fill in** a period of time, you find things to do during it.

fill in something or **fill something in** ❑ *He obviously said it to fill in an awkward pause.* ❑ *We encouraged them to fill the time in by doing some charity work.*

6 If you **fill in**, you do the work that someone else normally does because they are unable to do it. = **stand in** ❑ One of the other girls is sick, so I'm filling in. ❑ [+ for] We'll fill in for her until she gets back.

○ **fill 'out**

1 If you **fill out** a document or the information on a document, you write all the information that is needed on it. = **fill in**
fill out something ❑ Brody was filling out forms about the accident. ❑ You need to fill out your details to qualify for a free download.
fill something out ❑ They just tell you to fill a form out.

2 If a thin person **fills out**, they become fatter. ❑ He'd filled out a lot since I'd last seen him.

○ **fill 'up**

1 If you **fill up** a container, you put something into it, so that it becomes full.
fill something up ❑ Fill the tank up, please. ❑ Make sure you fill it up to the top.
fill up something ❑ [+ with] I filled up a bottle with the liquid.

2 If something **fills up** a space or area, it uses the whole amount of space there.
fill up something ❑ Early computers were massive, filling up a whole room.
fill something up ❑ An extra piece of furniture would have filled the room up better. ❑ The room was large, but the crowd of people filled it up.

3 If a place, area or container **fills up**, it becomes full. ❑ [+ with] His office began to fill up with people. ❑ Belfast hotels filled up with journalists from around the world.

4 If you **fill up** a period of time with a particular activity, you spend the time in this way. = **take up**
fill up something or **fill something up** ❑ [+ with] We fill our time up with useless activities.

5 If you **fill** yourself **up**, you eat as much as you can.
fill yourself up ❑ [+ with] No filling yourselves up with sandwiches and chips!. ❑ The boys and girls filled themselves up before they left.

6 A type of food that **fills** you **up** makes you feel that you have eaten a lot, even though you have only eaten a small amount.
fill someone up or **fill up someone** ❑ Potatoes fill us up without overloading us with calories. ❑ Too much juice may fill up the children and take the place of other foods.

○ **'fill with**

1 If something **fills** you **with** an emotion, you feel this emotion strongly.
fill someone with something ❑ The prospect of seeing her again filled him with joy. ❑ The

people were filled with hope and dreams for a brighter future.

2 If you **fill** yourself **with** food, you eat so much that you do not feel hungry.
fill yourself with something ❑ They drank coffee and filled themselves with chocolate cake.

film /fɪlm/ (**films, filming, filmed**)

○ **film 'over**

If something **films over**, it becomes covered with a very thin layer of a liquid. ❑ Her eyes became wide, then filmed over.

filter /'fɪltə/ (**filters, filtering, filtered**)

○ **filter 'into**

If light or sound **filters into** a place, it comes in weakly or slowly, either through a partly covered opening, or from a long distance away.
filter into something ❑ Sunlight filtered into the room through lace curtains. ❑ Music was filtering into the hallway.

○ **filter 'out**

1 If you **filter out** unwanted substances from a liquid or gas, you remove them by passing the liquid or gas through special equipment or through a barrier.
filter out something or **filter something out** ❑ Your lungs filter out most of the disease-causing particles in the air. ❑ All traces of the pesticide are filtered out in the laboratory.

2 If you **filter out** things or people that are not wanted, you remove them from a larger group.
filter out something/someone or **filter something/someone out** ❑ The technology can block websites by filtering out specific domain names. ❑ Alternative schemes had been filtered out at an earlier stage.

3 If news or information **filters out**, it gradually becomes known. ❑ Word of his resignation was filtering out. ❑ News of the contract filtered out a month later, via industry sources.

4 If people **filter out**, they leave a place in a line or in small groups. ❑ [+ of] As they filtered out of church, I could see Eleanor at the back of the queue.

find /faɪnd/ (**finds, finding, found**)

○ **'find against** [LEGAL]

When a judge **finds against** a person or organization in a court case, he or she says they have lost the case.
find against someone ❑ The court found against the museum's legal ownership of the works

○ **'find for** [LEGAL]

When a judge **finds for** a person or organization in a court case, he or she says they have won the case.

find for someone ❑ *The judge had found for the husband, describing him as a caring and responsible father.*

➋ find 'out

1 If you **find out** something, you learn something that you did not already know. **= discover**

find out something ❑ *I found out the train times.* ❑ *I'm only interested in finding out what the facts are.* ❑ *I've just found out that I won't have to start until Wednesday.*

find something out ❑ *I've been trying to find this out for weeks.* ❑ *I used the internet to find their names out.*

FIND OUT + noun

find out **the truth**
find out **an answer**
find out **information**
find out **the cause of** something
find out **the facts**
find out **a reason**

❑ *We eventually found out the truth about what happened.* ❑ *Where can I find out the information I need?*

---

2 If someone **finds** another person **out**, or if that person **is found out**, the second person is discovered to have done something wrong.

find someone out ❑ *The manager had found him out and was going to sack him.*

be found out ❑ *He tried to fool the investigators by removing some passages from the document, but he was found out and sent to prison.*

NOTE **Rumble** is an informal word for **find out.**

finish /ˈfɪnɪʃ/ (finishes, finishing, finished)
➋ finish 'off

1 When you **finish off** something that you are doing, you complete it.

finish off something ❑ *He had finished off his thesis.* ❑ *The farm workers were just finishing off the milking.*

finish something off ❑ *We had to work until midnight to finish them off.* ❑ *He finished the work off on Saturday.*

2 When you **finish off** by doing a particular thing, you do it as the last part of an event or series of actions. ❑ [+ with] *He used to play the piano on Saturday nights and always finished off with 'Spread A Little Happiness'.* ❑ [+ by] *Can I finish off by asking you one question?*

NOTE **Conclude** is a more formal word for **finish off.**

3 When you **finish off** food or drink, you eat or drink the last bit of it, so that there is none left.

finish off something ❑ *We decided to go back and finish off the cake.*

finish something off ❑ *He had cooked a chicken and they'd finished it off together in one afternoon.* ❑ *They finished the food off quickly.*

NOTE **Polish off** is an informal expression for **finish off.**

4 If something **is finished off** in a particular way, it is decorated or made to look neat in that way.

be finished off ❑ [+ with] *The shirt had a silver cross on the left breast and the neck was finished off with a frill.* ❑ *The front edges of the shelves are finished off with a 3 cm-wide strip of wood.*

5 To **finish off** a person or animal means to kill them.

finish someone/something off or **finish off someone/something** ❑ *Now was the time to go ahead and finish the intruders off.* ❑ *I'll never go there again as long as I live. It nearly finished me off.*

➋ finish 'up

1 If you **finish up** in a particular place or situation, you are in it at the end of an event or process. **= end up, wind up**

finish up somewhere/something ❑ [+ in] *She'll be going on tour, starting in Southampton and finishing up in London.* ❑ *After all that education, they finished up serving in a shop.*

2 When you **finish up** something that you have been eating or drinking, you eat or drink the last part of it.

finish up something or **finish something up** ❑ *They were just finishing up their lunch.* ❑ *Make sure you finish your dinner up.*

3 When you **finish up** something that you are doing, you complete it. **= finish off** [mainly AMERICAN]

finish up something ❑ *Hendricks was finishing up his paperwork when Brady walked in.* ❑ *I was just finishing up work on some Schubert manuscripts.*

○ finish 'up with

If you **finish up with** something, this is the result of your activity or efforts.

finish up with something ❑ *After working for years, he finished up with a very small pension.* ❑ *If you deleted that, you would finish up with a two sentence paragraph.*

➋ 'finish with

1 If you **finish with** someone or something, or **are finished with** them, you stop dealing with them or end your involvement with them.

finish with someone/something ❑ *I haven't finished with you yet.* ❑ *I thought I had finished with the play for ever.*

be finished with someone/something
❏ *He had decided several years before that he was finished with marriage.*
2 If you **finish with** someone, you end your romantic relationship with them. [BRITISH]
finish with someone ❏ *I went to his room and finished with him at about four o'clock this afternoon.*

fire /faɪə/ (**fires, firing, fired**)

○ **fire a'way** [INFORMAL]
You say **fire away** to someone to show that you are ready for them to begin speaking.
= shoot ❏ *'Can I have a word with you?' – 'Sure, Frank, fire away.'*

○ **fire 'off**
1 If you **fire off** a shot, you shoot with a gun or another weapon.
fire off something *or* **fire something off**
❏ *He pointed the pistol and fired off a shot.* ❏ *As they started to drive away, he fired several shots off in the direction of the car*
2 If you **fire off** questions, orders, or ideas, you say a lot of them quickly, one after the other.
fire off something *or* **fire something off**
❏ *Tony used to fire off suggestions faster than I could write them down.* ❏ *She was firing questions off left and right.*
3 If you **fire off** a letter, you write it quickly and often angrily.
fire off something *or* **fire something off**
❏ [+ *to*] *I fired off a letter to the most senior police officer I could think of.* ❏ *I fired several angry letters off to the head teacher.*

○ **fire 'up**
If you **fire** someone **up**, you make them feel very enthusiastic or angry about something.
fire someone up *or* **fire up someone** ❏ *I knew that Sam was trying to fire Costantino up. He kept saying 'You beat him, you beat him'.* ❏ *The band went out to fire up the crowd before the game.*
• If someone is **fired up**, they are enthusiastic or angry. ❏ [+ *about*] *Returning to the Moon is the only way to get the public all fired up about space again.*

○ **'fire with**
To **fire** someone **with** enthusiasm, determination, etc. means to make them feel very enthusiastic, determined etc.
fire someone with something ❏ *The incident fired him with a greater determination to succeed.* ❏ *Watching her lesson fired me with a passion to teach.*

firm /fɜːm/ (**firms, firming, firmed**)

○ **firm 'up**
1 If you **firm up** part of your body, you exercise to improve the condition of the muscles and reduce the amount of fat.
= tone up
firm up something *or* **firm something up**
❏ *This exercise will help to firm up those flabby thighs.* ❏ *I want to firm my tummy muscles up.*
2 If you **firm up** an idea or plan, you make it definite.
firm up something *or* **firm something up**
❏ *I think we're all agreed on the basic approach; we can firm up the details at next week's meeting.* ❏ *We'd like to firm the dates up as soon as possible.*
3 If an organization **firms up** the price or value of something, it takes action to keep its price or value at the same level.
firm up something *or* **firm something up**
❏ *These companies have agreed to freeze production slightly in order to firm up oil prices.*

fish /fɪʃ/ (**fishes, fishing, fished**)

○ **'fish for**
If you **fish for** information, praise, or an invitation, you try to get it from someone in an indirect way. **= angle for**
fish for something ❏ *I think he was just fishing for compliments.* ❏ *I was never invited, and I never fished for an invitation.*

○ **fish 'out**
1 If you **fish** something **out**, you pull it out or take it out of a liquid, substance, or container.
fish out something *or* **fish something out**
❏ [+ *of*] *A passer-by fished the boy out of the lake.* ❏ *One of her earrings dropped into her soup, and she fished it out and put it back in.*
2 If an area of water **is fished out**, most of the fish living in it have been caught.
be fished out ❏ *It is becoming clear that parts of the Pacific are in danger of being fished out.*

fit /fɪt/ (**fits, fitting, fitted**)

> **Fit** is sometimes used in American English as the past tense and past participle.

✪ **fit 'in**
1 If you manage to **fit in** a person or task, you manage to find time to deal with them. **= squeeze in**
fit someone/something in ❏ *They can't do the delivery today, so they will fit it in when they have a van in the area.* ❏ *I'm on holiday next week, but I can fit you in on the 9th.*
fit in something/someone ❏ *You seem to fit in an enormous amount every day.*

2 If you **fit in**, you are happy and accepted in a group of people because you are similar to the other people in it. ❑ *You can't bring outsiders into a place like this; they wouldn't fit in.* ❑ [+ with] *Maybe Art can fit in with my friends, I thought.*

3 If you understand how something or someone **fits in**, you understand how they form part of a particular situation or system. ❑ *It's difficult to know where these books fit in.* ❑ *I understand what the team does, but where does Jane fit in?*

✪ fit 'into

1 If you **fit into** a particular group, you are happy and accepted in it because you are similar to the other people in it.
fit into something ❑ *These children are unable to fit into ordinary society.* ❑ *I would have to make a great effort to fit into a mainly white world.*
2 If something or someone **fits into** a group, situation, or system, you can see that they belong to it or are part of it and understand why.
fit into something ❑ *There are some odd things on the list that don't fit into any category.* ❑ *Where does David fit into all this?*

✪ fit 'in with

1 If someone or something **fits in with** a person or a situation, they are suitable and convenient for it or make themselves suitable and convenient for it.
fit in with someone/something ❑ *She works part time to fit in with her family.* ❑ *He organized the house to fit in with the needs of his business.*
2 If a fact or a situation **fits in with** something that you have read or been told, it shows that the thing you have read or been told is probably true.
fit in with something ❑ *This story fits in with his explanation that he met them secretly.*

○ fit 'out

If you **fit** someone or something **out**, you provide them with equipment and other things that they need. **= kit out**
fit someone/something out *or* **fit out someone/something** ❑ *When the men arrive, they fit them out in uniforms and jungle boots.*

○ fit 'up

1 If you **fit** someone or something **up**, you provide them with equipment or other things that they need.
fit someone/something up *or* **fit up someone/something** ❑ [+ with] *Dr Bell was wanting to fit you up with a heart monitor.* ❑ *We fitted up a small shed to smoke fish.*
2 If someone **fits** you **up**, they provide false evidence so that other people think that

you are guilty of a crime although you are innocent. [BRITISH, INFORMAL]
fit someone up ❑ *I was left in no doubt that Cooper and Murphy had been fitted up.*
NOTE **Frame** is a more formal word for **fit up**.

fix /fɪks/ (fixes, fixing, fixed)

○ 'fix on

If you **fix on** a particular thing, you decide it or choose it. **= set**
fix on something ❑ *Have you fixed on a date for the party yet?* ❑ *We seem to have fixed on the same day for supermarket shopping.*

✪ fix 'up

1 If you **fix** someone **up**, you provide them with something they want or need. [INFORMAL]
fix someone up ❑ [+ with] *They told me that they could fix me up with tickets for the opera.* ❑ *'Can I stay at your place for a short time,' she said, 'till I get fixed up?'*
fix up someone ❑ [+ with] *He said he could fix up my mate with a job.*
2 If you **fix** something **up**, you arrange for it to happen or be obtained.
fix up something ❑ *Have you done anything about fixing up a meeting place?* ❑ *We'll fix up a nice meal for the three of us.*
fix something up ❑ *I'll talk to Sonny about fixing things up.*
NOTE **Arrange** is a more formal word for **fix up**.
3 If you **fix up** something, you build it quickly and roughly because you need it immediately.
fix up something *or* **fix something up** ❑ *We tried to fix up a shelter from the wind.* ❑ *I've fixed up a sort of wire barrier.*
NOTE **Rig up** is a more informal expression for **fix up**.
4 If you **fix up** something, you repair it. **= do up**
fix up something *or* **fix something up** ❑ *He was fixing up the flat, ready to move in.* ❑ *You promised us money to fix up the streets and alleys.*

○ 'fix with [LITERARY]

If you **fix** someone **with** a particular kind of expression, you look at them in that way.
fix someone with something ❑ *He took her hand and fixed her with a look of deep concern.* ❑ *He fixed me with a grin.*

fizzle /'fɪzəl/ (fizzles, fizzling, fizzled)

○ fizzle 'out

If something **fizzles out**, it ends in a weak or disappointing way, often after starting strongly. **= peter out** ❑ *The strike fizzled out after three days.* ❑ *It wasn't long before interest in the show fizzled out.*

flag /flæɡ/ (**flags, flagging, flagged**)
○ **flag 'down**
If you **flag down** a vehicle, you wave at it as a signal for the driver to stop.
flag down something or **flag something down** ❑ *We flagged down the tractor and climbed aboard.* ❑ *The police officer flagged the car down because it didn't have its headlights on.*

○ **'flag up**
If you **flag up** a fact or a problem, you make people aware of it.
flag up something or **flag something up** ❑ *The Chief Medical Officer flagged up obesity as one of the five major risks to the nation's health.* ❑ [+ with] *She told him about the claim, so he could flag it up with his colleagues.*

flail /fleɪl/ (**flails, flailing, flailed**)
○ **flail a'round** (or **flail about** [mainly BRITISH])
If you or your arms or legs **flail around**, or if you **flail** your arms or legs **around**, they wave around in an energetic but uncontrolled way.
flail around/about ❑ *He starting flailing around and hitting Vincent in the chest.*
flail something around ❑ *Ennis began to flail his arms around and struggle.*

flake /fleɪk/ (**flakes, flaking, flaked**)
○ **flake 'off**
If something **flakes off** or **flakes off** something, it separates from the surface it was attached to.
flake off ❑ *The nuts should be roasted until the skins flake off.*
flake off something ❑ *The paint was flaking off the walls of the shop.*

○ **flake 'out** [INFORMAL]
If you **flake out**, you collapse or fall asleep, usually because you are exhausted.
❑ *When I got to the top of the mountain I just flaked out.* ❑ *I flaked out on my bed.*

○ **flake 'out on** [AMERICAN, INFORMAL]
If you **flake out on** someone, you do not do something that you should do, or that you have said you will do.
flake out on someone ❑ *'How long have you been deputy project director?' – 'Eleven months, ever since Miriel flaked out on us.'*

flare /fleə/ (**flares, flaring, flared**)
○ **flare 'out**
Something that **flares out** spreads outwards at one end to form a wide shape.

= fan out ❑ *She spun around, making the skirt flare out.* ❑ *The long feathered tail flared out behind the bird.*

○ **flare 'up**
1 If a flame or something that is burning **flares up**, it suddenly burns very strongly and brightly. **= blaze** ❑ *The fire flared up high and showed up their little group clearly.* ❑ *He set fire to the wood, then stood watching it flare up.*
2 If violence, an argument, an emotion, or an illness **flares up**, it suddenly becomes very strong or serious. ❑ *The argument between the two groups flared up at the meeting.* ❑ *Panic flared up in her.*
[NOTE] **Erupt** is a more formal word for **flare up.**
● If there is a **flare-up** of violence, an emotion, or an illness, it suddenly becomes strong or serious again. ❑ *This incident produced a new flare-up of anxiety.* ❑ *The disease had shown occasional flare-ups.*
3 If someone **flares up**, they suddenly get very angry. ❑ [+ at] *He kept flaring up at her over quite reasonable requests.* ❑ *She would sometimes flare up at me as a way of relieving her own panic.*
● A **flare-up** is a sudden argument.
❑ *Ian found himself in another flare-up over umpiring.*

flash /flæʃ/ (**flashes, flashing, flashed**)
○ **flash 'back**
If your mind **flashes back** to an event in your past, you suddenly remember it.
❑ [+ to] *My mind flashed back to past demonstrations.* ❑ *His mind flashed back to what the sisters had said.* ● A **flashback** is an occasion, especially in a film or a play, when someone suddenly remembers an event in their past. ❑ *Then follows a brief flashback to the four earlier murders.* ● A **flashback** is a sudden, strong memory of something unpleasant that you experienced.
❑ *He suffers from flashbacks.*

○ **flash 'up**
If a picture or message **flashes up** or a computer **flashes up** a message, it is displayed on a screen briefly or suddenly, and often repeatedly.
flash up ❑ [+ on] *A strange message just flashed up on my screen.* ❑ *The figures flash up on the scoreboard.*
flash up something ❑ *The computer beeped, and flashed up a request for further information.* ❑ *There were plasma screens flashing up adverts.*

flatten /ˈflætən/ (**flattens, flattening, flattened**)
○ **flatten 'out**
1 If you **flatten** something **out** or if it

flattens out, it becomes flat or flatter.
flatten out ❑ *To the north of the ridge, the country flattened out.*

flatten out something or **flatten something out** ❑ *A bulldozer was flattening out the ruts in the road.* ❑ *Put the paper under something heavy to flatten the creases out.*

2 If something **flattens out** differences between things, it reduces the differences between them.
flatten out something or **flatten something out** ❑ *Comprehensive schools assisted in flattening out all regional accents.*

flee /fliː/ (**flees, fleeing, fled**)
○ **'flee from**
If you **flee from** something or someone, you escape from them.
flee from someone/something ❑ *These are refugees who have fled from wars, famine and persecution.* ❑ *He turned abruptly and fled from the room in tears.*

flesh /fleʃ/ (**fleshes, fleshing, fleshed**)
○ **flesh 'out**
If you **flesh** something **out**, you give more information about it or add details to make it complete.
flesh something out or **flesh out something** ❑ *We had several basic ideas for the scene and we are now seeing them fleshed out for the first time.* ❑ *This book fleshes out his original argument.*

flick /flɪk/ (**flicks, flicking, flicked**)
○ **flick 'over**
If you **flick over** pages, you turn them quickly.
flick over something or **flick something over** ❑ *He put his head down at once, flicking over the pages with a practised hand.*

○ **'flick through**
If you **flick through** pages or papers, you turn them over quickly and look at them quickly. = **leaf through**
flick through something ❑ *He flicked through the passport, not understanding a word.* ❑ *The interviewer started flicking through cards on her desk.*
flick through ❑ *She got out a book and began to flick through.*

flicker /'flɪkə/ (**flickers, flickering, flickered**)
○ **'flicker across**
If an expression **flickers across** your face or a feature on your face, it appears very briefly.
flicker across something ❑ *A smile flickered across Vincent's face.* ❑ *An expression of surprise flickered across the blue eyes.*

flinch /flɪntʃ/ (**flinches, flinching, flinched**)
○ **'flinch from**
If you **flinch from** something unpleasant, you do not want to do it or think about it, or you avoid doing it.
flinch from something ❑ *He has never flinched from difficult financial decisions.* ❑ *It was a painful question, and Tania flinched from answering.*

fling /flɪŋ/ (**flings, flinging, flung**)
○ **'fling into**
If you **fling** yourself **into** an activity, you begin to do it with a lot of enthusiasm, energy and effort. = **throw into**
fling yourself into something ❑ *They have flung themselves in the race to be first to reach Mars.* ❑ *She flung herself into her work.*

○ **fling 'off**
If you **fling off** your clothes, you take them off very quickly and carelessly. = **throw off**
fling off something ❑ *She ran into the bedroom, where she flung off her dress and took out a clean one.*

○ **fling 'out**
If you **fling out** a remark, you say it quickly and forcefully.
fling out something or **fling something out** ❑ *The Duke's men challenged them, flinging out insults and throwing one of them to the ground.* ❑ *'I told you,' she flung out, 'I won't hear anything more about Mr Edwards.'*

flip /flɪp/ (**flips, flipping, flipped**)
○ **'flip through**
If you **flip through** pages or papers, you turn them over quickly and look at them quickly. = **flick through**
flip through something ❑ *Renshaw flipped through the book.*
flip through ❑ *'Read it yourself,' he said, flipping through until he found the page.*

flirt /flɜːt/ (**flirts, flirting, flirted**)
○ **'flirt with**
1 If you **flirt with** someone, you behave towards them in a way that shows you are sexually attracted to them.
flirt with someone ❑ *Belinda was flirting shamelessly with another man.*
2 If you **flirt with** an idea, you consider it without making any definite plans. = **toy with, dally with**
flirt with something ❑ *Burlington has flirted with the idea of a wood-burning stove.* ❑ *Channon flirted with the idea of running for the Presidency.*

flit /flɪt/ (**flits, flitting, flitted**)
○ **'flit across**
If an expression **flits across** your face or an idea **flits across** your mind, it is there

for a short time and then goes again.

flit across something ❑ *A look of puzzlement flitted across his face.* ❑ *The thought of Carrie flitted across Ellen's mind.*

○ **'flit from to**

If someone **flits from** one person, thing or situation **to** another, they move or turn their attention from one to the other very quickly.

flit from someone/something to someone/ something ❑ *She flits from one dance partner to another.* ❑ *Marie spent her 20s flitting from job to job.*

float /fləʊt/ (floats, floating, floated)

○ **float a'round**

1 If an idea or a rumour **is floating around**, it is being discussed or thought about.

be floating around ❑ *There are a lot of strange ideas floating around.* ❑ *There are so many rumours floating around. We need to find out the truth.*

2 If something **is floating around**, you know it is in a place, but you do not know exactly where. [INFORMAL]

be floating around ❑ *There's a bag of sweets floating around somewhere. Would you like one?*

flock /flɒk/ (flocks, flocking, flocked)

○ **'flock to**

If people **flock to** a particular place or event, a lot of them go there because it is pleasant or interesting.

flock to something ❑ *The public have flocked to the show.* ❑ *As temperatures soared, people flocked to the coast.*

flood /flʌd/ (floods, flooding, flooded)

❂ **flood 'in**

If people or things **flood in**, they arrive somewhere in large numbers. ❑ *Cheap goods began to flood in from other countries.* ❑ *US troops were now flooding in.*

○ **flood 'into**

If people or things **flood into** a place, large numbers of them arrive in a short space of time. **= pour into**

flood into something ❑ *Nine million people a year were flooding into these cities.* ❑ *By now, messages were flooding into our offices.*

○ **flood 'out**

If people **are flooded out**, they have to leave their homes because river or sea water has come into the buildings.

be flooded out ❑ *If the rain continues, we'll be flooded out.*

○ **'flood with**

If you **flood** a place **with** a particular type of thing, the place becomes full of so many of

them that it cannot hold or deal with any more.

flood something with something ❑ *It was a policy aimed at flooding Europe with exports.* ❑ *Brokers expect the markets to be flooded with the shares.*

flop /flɒp/ (flops, flopping, flopped)

○ **flop 'down** [INFORMAL]

If you **flop down**, you let your body fall quickly downwards, usually because you are tired. ❑ *Jimmie flopped down in the chair.* ❑ *He flopped down next to her.*

flounder /'flaʊndə/ (flounders, floundering, floundered)

○ **flounder a'round** (or **flounder about** [mainly BRITISH])

1 If a person or animal **flounders around**, they move with difficulty, often because they are walking through something like mud or water. ❑ *Three men were floundering about in the water.* ❑ *We floundered around, trying to get out of the building.*

2 If a person or organization **flounders around**, they are confused and do not know what to say or do. ❑ *The party floundered around trying to agree on a set of policies.* ❑ *I think you have to have a plan – otherwise you just flounder about.*

flow /fləʊ/ (flows, flowing, flowed)

○ **'flow from**

If a situation, product, or quality **flows from** something, it occurs as a result of it. **= stem from**

flow from something ❑ *The consequences that flow from this event are endless.*

○ **flow 'over**

If a feeling **flows over** you, you suddenly feel it very strongly.

flow over someone ❑ *I felt a sense of peace flow over me, and I began to fall into a deep sleep.* ❑ *A wave of sympathy for Simmonds flowed over him.*

fluff /flʌf/ (fluffs, fluffing, fluffed)

○ **fluff 'out** (or **fluff up**)

If you **fluff** something **out**, you make it softer, looser, or lighter, for example by shaking or brushing it.

fluff something out or **fluff out something** ❑ *She fluffed her hair out in big waves.* ❑ *Put the mashed potato in a bowl, fluff it up with a fork and serve.*

flunk /flʌŋk/ (flunks, flunking, flunked)

○ **flunk 'out** [AMERICAN, INFORMAL]

If you **flunk out**, you are sent away from a school or college because your work is not good enough. ❏ *You're gonna flunk out if you just sit there watching TV!*

flush /flʌʃ/ (flushes, flushing, flushed)

○ **flush 'out**

1 If you **flush out** someone or something, you force them to come out of a place where they have been hiding.
flush someone/something out or **flush out someone/something** ❏ *They went into the area to flush out rebels who were sheltering there.* ❏ *She had many secrets which Cobb was trying to flush out.*

2 If you **flush** something **out**, you get rid of it with water or another liquid.
flush something out or **flush out something** ❏ *Waste products of the body must be flushed out by drinking plenty of liquids.*

3 If you **flush** something **out**, you clean it by forcing water or another liquid through it.
flush something out or **flush out something** ❏ *Let the cold water tap run for a few minutes to flush out the pipes.*

flutter /'flʌtə/ (flutters, fluttering, fluttered)

○ **flutter a'round** (or **flutter about** [mainly BRITISH])

If someone **flutters around**, or **flutters around** a person or place, they move about quickly and nervously without achieving much.
flutter around ❏ *Unable to sit down, she fluttered about from room to room.*
flutter around someone/something ❏ *They wasted half their time fluttering around the invalid.* ❏ *Servants fluttered around the house, trying to help.*

○ **flutter 'down**

If something light **flutters down**, it moves slowly and gently through the air towards the ground. ❏ *Pieces of paper fluttered down like large butterflies in the darkness.* ❏ *The first flakes of snow began to flutter down early in the afternoon.*

fly /flaɪ/ (flies, flying, flew, flown)

○ **'fly at**

If someone **flies at** you, they suddenly attack you. **= go for**
fly at someone ❏ *One day he flew at me in a temper.* ❏ *She looked at Tony as though she were about to fly at him.*

○ **fly 'in**

If someone **flies in**, or people or things **are flown in**, they arrive in a place by aeroplane.
fly in ❏ *[+ from] Howard had flown in from Atlanta at my request.*

be flown in ❏ *Medical equipment had been flown in.*

○ **fly 'into**

If someone **flies into** a temper, a rage, or a panic they suddenly become extremely angry or scared.
fly into something ❏ *She flies into a temper if I make a mistake.* ❏ *Something dropped onto his back and he flew into a panic.*

○ **fly 'out**

If someone **flies out**, or people or things **are flown out**, they go somewhere by aeroplane.
fly out ❏ *[+ to] I decided to fly out to Bombay in order to help.*
be flown out ❏ *The painting was flown out to Vienna for the start of its historic tour.*

fob /fɒb/ (fobs, fobbing, fobbed)

○ **fob 'off**

If you **fob** someone **off**, you tell them something that may not be true or useful in order to make them go away or stop asking you things.
fob someone off or **fob off someone** ❏ *[+ with] Any patient who complained about the treatment would be fobbed off with feeble excuses.* ❏ *Don't allow yourself to be fobbed off by his secretary.*

○ **fob 'off with**

If you **fob** someone **off with** something, you persuade them to accept it, although it is not what they want or need.
fob someone off with something ❏ *He may try to fob you off with a prescription for pills.* ❏ *Whatever you do, don't get fobbed off with second-rate products.*

focus /'fəʊkəs/ (focuses, focusing, focused)

⊙ **'focus on**

To **focus on** something or someone or to **focus** your attention or mind **on** them is to concentrate on them rather than other things or people.
focus on something/someone ❏ *Much of his research focuses on effective leadership.* ❏ *Petra ignored him and continued to focus on Carol.*
focus something on something ❏ *I leaned back in my chair and once more focused my mind on my work.*

fog /fɒg/ (fogs, fogging, fogged)

○ **fog 'up**

If something made of glass or a similar material **fogs up** or if something **fogs** it **up**, it becomes difficult to see through because it is covered with tiny drops of water.
= steam up
fog up ❏ *On cold mornings, the windows fog up.*

fog something up or **fog up something**
❑ Their breath fogged up the glass.

foist /fɔɪst/ (foists, foisting, foisted)

○ **'foist on** (or **foist upon**)

If you **foist** something **on** someone, you force them to have it or experience it.
foist something on someone ❑ They did not want to foist their ideas and views on other people. ❑ I still have all the books she foisted upon me.

fold /fəʊld/ (folds, folding, folded)

○ **fold 'in**

In cooking, if you **fold** something **in**, you mix it gently and carefully into a mixture, keeping as much air in the mixture as possible.
fold something in or **fold in something**
❑ When the mixture is ready, fold in the egg white with a metal spoon.

○ **fold 'into**

In cooking, if you **fold** one substance **into** another, you mix them gently and carefully, keeping as much air in the mixture as possible.
fold something into something ❑ Beat the egg whites until stiff and then fold them carefully into the sauce. ❑ Using a metal spoon, fold the dry ingredients into the cream.

○ **fold 'up**

1 If you **fold** something **up**, you make it into a smaller, neat shape by folding it several times. ≠ **unfold**
fold something up or **fold something up**
❑ She began to fold up the blanket. ❑ She folded the letter up and stuffed it down the side of the chair.

2 If the petals of a flower **fold up**, they close and come together in the centre of the flower. = **close up** ❑ The petals had folded up against the light.

3 If a business or organization **folds up** or if someone **folds** it **up**, it closes or comes to an end. = **pack up**
fold up ❑ She had known too many businesses fold up through bad management.
fold something up or **fold up something**
❑ They had no choice but to fold up their international operations.

follow /'fɒləʊ/ (follows, following, followed)

○ **follow 'out**

If you **follow out** instructions you do exactly what you have been told to do.
= **carry out**
follow out something or **follow something out** ❑ She knew she could trust him to follow out her instructions. ❑ Farmers can receive special

green payments for following out environmental improvements.

○ **follow 'through**

1 If you **follow through**, you do something as the next stage of an activity. ❑ Don't make threats unless you can follow through. ❑ [+ with] Graham stumbled backwards and Drago followed through with two vicious punches. • An action that continues something is called the **follow-through**. ❑ This wouldn't halt the attack but it would at least weaken the follow-through.

2 If you **follow** an idea or an activity **through**, you continue with it until it is finished.
follow something through or **follow through something** ❑ It wasn't a bad idea, but as Branagh tried to follow it through, he couldn't resist the temptation to exaggerate the story.

3 If you **follow through** in a sport, you complete the movement of hitting or kicking a ball. ❑ You're not following through after playing the stroke. • In sport, the **follow-through** is the completion of the movement you make after hitting or kicking a ball. ❑ The follow-through is part of the kick.

○ **follow 'through on**

If you **follow through on** an idea or an activity, you do what is needed to achieve it or continue with it.
follow through on something ❑ Although they become engaged to be married he made no effort to follow through on his promise. ❑ Shortly after, he followed through on Montini's offer.

○ **follow 'up**

1 If you **follow** something **up**, you try to find out more about it and perhaps do something about it.
follow something up ❑ When I heard the rumours, I tried to follow them up. ❑ It's an idea which has been followed up by the local council.
follow up something ❑ I followed up an advertisement for a second-hand Volkswagen.
NOTE **Investigate** is a more formal word for **follow up**.

2 If you **follow up** one action or thing with another, you do or have the second action or thing soon after the first.
follow something up ❑ [+ by] They must attend the course, and this is followed up by personal visits. ❑ [+ with] On their second date, they'd gone to the theatre and followed it up with a late-night pizza.
follow up something ❑ The President followed up the first round of voting by challenging his opponent to a public debate. • A **follow-up** or a **follow-up** activity is done as a continuation

or second part of something done previously. ❏ [+ to] *This conference is a follow-up to an earlier one in Gabon.* ❏ *He needed follow-up treatment from a specialist doctor.*

○ **'follow with**

If you **follow** one thing **with** another, you do or say the second thing after you have done or said the first thing.

follow something with something ❏ *'I quite agree,' Momma said and followed it with a laugh.* ❏ *The team followed this victory with another outstanding win.*

fool /fuːl/ (**fools, fooling, fooled**)

○ **fool a'bout** → see **fool around**

○ **fool a'round**

If someone who is in a serious relationship **fools around**, they have a sexual relationship with someone else. ❏ *She thinks he's been fooling around.* ❏ [+ with] *I'll bet you were fooling around with Miss Roach.*

○ **fool a'round** (or **fool about** [mainly BRITISH])

If you **fool around**, you behave in a silly and enjoyable way. = **mess around** ❏ *The boys passed them, laughing and fooling around and talking loudly.* ❏ *He was always fooling about.*

○ **fool a'round with** (or **fool about with** [mainly BRITISH])

If you **fool around with** something, you treat it in a careless or silly way.

fool around with something ❏ *Chemicals are very dangerous things to fool around with.* ❏ *At first, he thought someone was fooling around with a floodlight.*

force /fɔːs/ (**forces, forcing, forced**)

○ **force 'back**

If you **force back** an emotion or feeling, you make an effort to hide it or to prevent it from affecting your behaviour. = **fight back, suppress**

force back something or **force something back** ❏ *He forced back the strong urge to shout out.* ❏ *She took a deep breath and forced her tears back.*

◐ **force 'into**

If you **force** someone **into** doing something, you make them do it, although they do not want to.

force someone into something ❏ *They are trying to force their employers into increasing their wages.* ❏ *He felt that she was forcing him into the role of carer.* ❏ *'No one's forcing you into it,' Joyce said.*

○ **'force on** (or **force upon**)

1 If you **force** something **on** someone, you make them accept, use, or deal with it when they do not want to.

force something on someone ❏ *Did they try to force drinks on you?*

2 If someone **forces** themselves **on** another person, they make that person have sex with them. ❏ *Did he attack you, force himself on you?*

forewarn (**forewarns, forewarning, forewarned**)

○ **fore'warn about**

If you **forewarn** someone **about** something, you warn them that it is going to happen.

forewarn someone about something ❏ *The protesters had not forewarned the police about their protest.*

forge /fɔːdʒ/ (**forges, forging, forged**)

○ **forge a'head**

1 If you **forge ahead**, you make a lot of progress, or more progress than someone else. ❏ *The company has made use of the absence of competition to forge ahead.*

2 If you **forge ahead**, you move forwards quickly. ❏ *They could see the army forging ahead along the road.*

fork /fɔːk/ (**forks, forking, forked**)

○ **fork 'out** [INFORMAL]

If you **fork out** money or **fork out** for something, you pay for something.
= **cough up**

fork out something ❏ *She was prepared to fork out extra cash to install a large screen TV.*

fork out ❏ [+ for] *If it's your first apartment, you'll have to fork out for furniture.*

form /fɔːm/ (**forms, forming, formed**)

○ **form 'up**

When people **form up**, they move into a particular position, usually in lines. ❏ *Queues formed up in front of both banks and food stores.* ❏ *At about two in the afternoon we were ordered to form up for the final attack.*

forward /ˈfɔːwəd/ (**forwards, forwarding, forwarded**)

◉ **'forward to**

If you get a letter, message, email, etc. and you **forward** it **to** someone else, you send it to them.

forward something to someone ❏ *He forwarded the email to his friends.* ❏ *The calls will be forwarded to a staff of 15 nurses at a medical service near Minneapolis.*

foul /faʊl/ (**fouls, fouling, fouled**)

○ **foul 'up** [INFORMAL]

If someone **fouls up** or **fouls** something **up**, they do something very badly. = **mess up**

foul up something or **foul something up**

❑ So many good projects have been fouled up by mistakes in planning. ❑ The reason no-one employs them is that they foul up the simplest task.
foul up ❑ The team cannot afford to foul up like they have done in previous home games. ● A **foul-up** is a mistake that spoils something. [INFORMAL] ❑ There has been an administrative foul-up.

fraternize /ˈfrætənaɪz/ (fraternizes, fraternizing, fraternized)

○ **'fraternize with** [FORMAL]
If you **fraternize with** someone, you spend time with them as friends, especially when other people disapprove.
fraternize with someone ❑ At these conventions, executives fraternized with staff from other banks.

freak /friːk/ (freaks, freaking, freaked)

○ **freak 'out** [INFORMAL]
If someone **freaks out** or if something **freaks** them **out**, they suddenly become very scared, angry or excited.
freak out ❑ When I gave him an application form, he just freaked out completely.
freak someone out or **freak out someone** ❑ He was freaking the colonel out a little bit. ❑ I was freaked out by what we were seeing.

free /friː/ (frees, freeing, freed)

○ **free 'up**
■ To **free up** someone or something means to make them available to be used when they were not available before.
free up someone/something or **free someone/something up** ❑ This package can handle complex graphic jobs, freeing up your computer for other tasks. ❑ Building projects and improvements stopped, freeing up the men to fight.
■ To **free up** a market, economy, or system means to make it operate with fewer rules and controls.
free up something or **free something up** ❑ They introduced policies for freeing up markets and increasing competition.

freeze /friːz/ (freezes, freezing, froze, frozen)

○ **freeze 'out**
If you **freeze** someone **out** of an activity or situation, you prevent them from being involved in it by creating difficulties or being unfriendly. = **squeeze out**
freeze someone out or **freeze out someone** ❑ He did not trust them, and felt they were trying to freeze him out. ❑ [+ of] His younger colleague eventually froze him out of economic policy making.

○ **freeze 'over**
If an area of water **freezes over** or **is frozen over**, it becomes covered with a layer of ice. = **ice over, ice up**
freeze over ❑ Winter was mild and the lakes did not freeze over.
be frozen over ❑ Parts of the river Thames were frozen over as temperatures fell even more.

○ **freeze 'up**
■ If an area of water or a machine or piece of equipment **freezes up**, it becomes completely blocked or covered with ice. ❑ It was so cold last winter that even the river froze up. ❑ The lock has frozen up. ● A **freeze-up** is a period of extremely cold weather. = **ice up** ❑ Two overnight sleeper trains were halted by the freeze-up.
■ If a person **freezes up**, they suddenly become unable to speak or move in a normal way. ❑ I felt comfortable on stage with others, but I froze up completely if I had to go out there on my own. ❑ We freeze up when we are given too many choices.
■ If something that should move or operate **freezes up** or if something **freezes** it **up**, it is unable to move or operate.
freeze up ❑ My joints would freeze up in the mornings.
freeze something up or **freeze up something** ❑ High oil prices had begun to freeze up the world economy.

freshen /ˈfreʃən/ (freshens, freshening, freshened)

○ **freshen 'up**
■ If you **freshen up** or **freshen** yourself **up**, you wash and make yourself look neat and tidy.
freshen up ❑ Sarah and Barry returned to their hotel to freshen up.
freshen yourself up ❑ She'd used the opportunity to freshen herself up, put on new lipstick, etc.
■ If you **freshen** something **up**, you make it look cleaner, brighter and more attractive or fashionable.
freshen something up or **freshen up something** ❑ New wallpaper and curtains will freshen up the place. ❑ We must learn to use our existing wardrobes, freshening them up each season with just one or two new pieces.

frick /frɪk/ (fricks, fricking, fricked)

○ **frick 'off** [INFORMAL, RUDE]
If someone tells you to **frick off**, they are telling you in a very rude way to go away or to stop interfering. ❑ Frick off and don't come back until September.

rig /frɪg/ (frigs, frigging, frigged)
○ **frig a'bout** (or **frig around**) [BRITISH, INFORMAL, RUDE]

If someone **frigs about**, they waste time doing silly or unimportant things. ❏ *I don't want to spend a week frigging about in town.*
NOTE **Mess around** is a less informal expression for **frig about**.

righten /'fraɪtən/ (frightens, frightening, frightened)
○ **frighten a'way** (or **frighten off**)

1 If you **frighten** a person or animal **away**, you make them afraid so that they run away and do not harm you. = **scare off**
frighten someone/something away or **frighten away someone/something** ❏ *He waved his torch to frighten away some animal.* ❏ *We were waving our arms to frighten them off.*
2 If a person or event **frightens** someone **away**, they make them doubtful or nervous about something they were thinking of doing or becoming involved in. = **scare off**
frighten someone away or **frighten away someone** ❏ *Her show business lifestyle may frighten away potential boyfriends.* ❏ *He managed to attract the Communists without frightening off the more right-wing voters.*

○ **'frighten into**

If a person, situation, or event **frightens** you **into** something, they make you so frightened that you do it even if you do not want to.
frighten someone into something ❏ *'Don't you dare,' he said, frightening her into silence.* ❏ *Waste being dumped into rivers has frightened many people into using expensive bottled water.*

○ **frighten 'off** → see **frighten away**
○ **frighten 'out of**

If a person, situation, or event **frightens** you **out of** something, they make you so afraid that you do not do something that you had intended to do.
frighten someone out of something ❏ *She refused to be frightened out of going.*

·itter /'frɪtə/ (fritters, frittering, frittered)
○ **fritter a'way**

If you **fritter away** time or money, you waste it by spending it in a foolish way, a little bit at a time.
fritter something away or **fritter away something** ❏ *She was determined not to fritter away her vacation.* ❏ *The money just goes though, doesn't it; you just fritter it away.*
NOTE **Squander** is a more formal word for **fritter away**.

front /frʌnt/ (fronts, fronting, fronted)
○ **'front onto**

A building, window, or area of land that **fronts onto** a particular place is next to it and faces it.
front onto somewhere ❏ *They lived in a large house that fronted onto Leith Street.* ❏ *The windows fronted onto a verandah.*

frost /frɒst, ᴀᴍ frɔːst/ (frosts, frosting, frosted)
○ **frost 'over**

When something made of glass **frosts over** or **is frosted over**, it becomes covered with frost.
frost over ❏ *The windows had frosted over.*
be frosted over ❏ *It must have been cold last night – my windscreen's frosted over.*

○ **frost 'up**

If something **frosts up**, you cannot move it or use it because it is frozen. ❏ *The sliding windows tend to frost up in winter.*

○ **frost 'up** → see **frost over**

frown /fraʊn/ (frowns, frowning, frowned)
○ **'frown upon** (or **frown on**)

If something **is frowned upon**, people disapprove of it.
be frowned upon ❏ *They were brought up in a family where anger was generally frowned upon.* ❏ *These methods are frowned upon by traditional doctors.*

fry /fraɪ/ (fries, frying, fried)
○ **fry 'up** [BRITISH]

If you **fry up** food, you fry it to make a quick, informal meal.
fry up something or **fry something up**
❏ *Make yourself useful and fry up some bacon.*
● A **fry-up** is a quick, informal meal of fried food. [BRITISH, INFORMAL] ❏ *Breakfast is a couple of slices of toast or a fry-up if I've been working in the rain.*

fuck /fʌk/ (fucks, fucking, fucked)

> **Fuck** is an extremely rude word, which most people find very offensive.

○ **fuck a'round** (or **fuck about** [mainly BRITISH])

1 If someone **fucks around**, they behave in a way that is silly or annoying. ❏ *Cyril, for Christ's sake stop fucking around and get back on board.*
2 If someone **fucks** you **around**, they waste your time or cause problems for you.
fuck someone around ❏ *You know, I don't like people to fuck me around.*
NOTE **Mess around** is a more polite, informal expression for **fuck around**.

○ **fuck 'off**
1 If someone tells you to **fuck off**, they are telling you in a very rude way to go away or to stop interfering. ❑ *'I told her to fuck off,' said Napier.*
NOTE **Get lost** is a less offensive expression for **fuck off**.
2 If something **fucks** you **off**, it annoys you very much.
fuck someone off ❑ *People are so rude and it fucks me right off.*

○ **fuck 'over**
If someone **fucks** you **over**, they cheat you or behave very badly towards you.
fuck someone over ❑ *'They're just fucking us over!' he shouted.*

○ **fuck 'up**
1 If someone **fucks** something **up** or **fucks up**, they do something very badly or spoil something.
fuck something up or **fuck up something** ❑ *Even when you're shown exactly how to do it, you still fuck it up.*
fuck up ❑ *If anyone fucked up, it wasn't you.*
● A **fuck-up** is when someone does something completely wrong. ❑ *This was exactly the kind of fuck-up she'd wanted to avoid.*
2 If a person or an experience **fucks** someone **up**, it causes them to have emotional problems.
fuck someone up or **fuck up someone** ❑ *These parents fuck up their kids and then they send them to us to sort them out.*
NOTE **Mess up** is a more polite, informal expression for **fuck up**.

fulminate /ˈfʊlmɪneɪt, ˈfʌl-/ (**fulminates, fulminating, fulminated**)
○ **'fulminate against** [FORMAL]
If you **fulminate against** someone or something, you criticize them angrily.
fulminate against someone/something ❑ *Teachers fulminated against the new curriculum.*

fumble /ˈfʌmbəl/ (**fumbles, fumbling, fumbled**)
○ **'fumble for**
If you **fumble for** something, you try to find it in a clumsy way.
fumble for something ❑ *She was fumbling for the door handle in the dark.* ❑ *He reached the car and fumbled for his keys.*

○ **'fumble with**
If you **fumble with** something, you hold or move it in a clumsy way.
fumble with something ❑ *He was fumbling with the buckle on his belt.* ❑ *Taking out her cigarettes, she fumbled with her lighter.*

function /ˈfʌŋkʃən/ (**functions, functioning, functioned**)
○ **'function as**
If someone or something **functions as** a particular thing, they do the work or fulfil the purpose of that thing.
function as something ❑ *There was a wooden box, which also functioned as a table.* ❑ *During th public talks he has again functioned as chief negotiator.*

fur /fɜː/ (**furs, furring, furred**)
○ **fur 'up** [BRITISH]
1 If something such as a water pipe **furs up**, the inside of it becomes covered with a hard grey layer of calcium carbonate and other chemicals in the water. ❑ *Old brass taps fur up after years of use.*
2 If your veins or arteries **fur up** or if something **furs** them **up**, they become blocked, so that your blood cannot flow properly.
fur up ❑ *Three of my veins had furred up and I needed an operation.*
fur something up or **fur up something** ❑ *Cholesterol may be responsible for furring up the arteries.*

furnish /ˈfɜːnɪʃ/ (**furnishes, furnishing, furnished**)
○ **'furnish with** [FORMAL]
If you **furnish** someone **with** something, you provide or supply it.
furnish someone with something ❑ *My colleague here will be able to furnish you with the details.*

fuss /fʌs/ (**fusses, fussing, fussed**)
○ **'fuss over**
If you **fuss over** someone or something, yo pay too much attention to them because you like them very much or because you want them to be as good as possible.
fuss over someone/something ❑ *His mothe fussed over him a bit too much, I think.* ❑ *Flora we fussing over lunch.*

Gg

gad /gæd/ (**gads, gadding, gadded**)

○ **gad a'round** (or **gad about**) [mainly BRITISH, INFORMAL, OLD-FASHIONED]

If you **gad around** or **gad around** a place, you enjoy yourself by going to a lot of different places. = **gallivant**

gad around ❑ *I did all the work while Susannah was gadding about with her boyfriend.*

gad around somewhere ❑ *This is hardly the time to be gadding around town.* • A **gadabout** is someone who spends all their time going to different places, looking for ways to enjoy themselves. ❑ *New York one week, Vienna the next? Aren't you the gadabout these days?*

gag /gæg/ (**gags, gagging, gagged**)

○ **'gag for** [INFORMAL]

If you say that someone **is gagging for** something, you mean that they want to have it very much.

be gagging for something ❑ *Girls everywhere are gagging for a car like this.*

gain /geɪn/ (**gains, gaining, gained**)

○ **'gain from**

If you **gain from** an event or a situation, you get an advantage or benefit from it.

gain from something ❑ *It is sad that a major company should try to gain from other people's suffering.*

○ **'gain on**

If you **gain on** someone or something that you are chasing, you gradually get nearer to them.

gain on someone/something ❑ *You'll have to drive faster – they're gaining on us.* ❑ *We were gaining on him towards the end of the race.*

gallivant /'gælɪvænt/ (**gallivants, gallivanting, gallivanted**)

○ **gallivant a'round** [OLD-FASHIONED]

Someone who **is gallivanting around** or **gallivanting around** somewhere, is going to a lot of different places and not behaving in a serious way.

be gallivanting around ❑ *She should not be gallivanting around, filling her head with nonsense.*

gallivant around somewhere ❑ *She preferred*

staying at home with her baby to gallivanting around the West with the boys.

gamble /'gæmbəl/ (**gambles, gambling, gambled**)

○ **gamble a'way**

If you **gamble** money **away**, you lose it by betting on the result of a game or a competition.

gamble something away or **gamble away something** ❑ *He inherited a massive sum of money and within two years, he had gambled all of it away.* ❑ *She gambled away more than $60,000 during their six-month relationship.*

○ **'gamble on**

1 If you **gamble on** the result of a game or a competition, you bet money on that result.

gamble on something ❑ *He gambled heavily on the horses.* ❑ *He still gambled modestly on the football pools.*

2 If you **gamble on** something, you do something, such as spend money, that involves a risk, knowing that success depends on a situation developing in a particular way.

gamble on something ❑ *Speculators gambled on the market price of coffee rising.*

gang /gæŋ/ (**gangs, ganging, ganged**)

○ **gang 'up** [INFORMAL]

If a group of people **gang up**, they join together against someone else in a fight or argument. ❑ [+ on] *The other kids have started to gang up on her.* ❑ *I felt really ganged up on.*

gather /'gæðə/ (**gathers, gathering, gathered**)

○ **gather a'round** (or **gather round** [mainly BRITISH])

If people **gather around** or **gather around** someone or something, they come together in a group, sometimes surrounding a person or thing. = **cluster around**

gather around someone/something

❑ *A crowd had gathered around him to hear what he had to say.* ❑ *The boys gathered round the fire.*

gather around ❑ *Come on, everyone, gather around.*

○ **gather 'in** [LITERARY]

If you **gather in** crops, you collect them from the fields when they have finished growing and bring them together into one place.

gather in something or **gather something in** ❏ The men have three weeks to gather their harvest in. ❏ The main crops have to be gathered in and stored for the winter.

○ **gather 'round →** see **gather around**

○ **gather 'up**

1 If you **gather up** a number of things, you bring them together into a group. = **get together**

gather up something or **gather something up** ❏ He gathered up the papers and stuffed them into his briefcase. ❏ The letters were all over the floor so I gathered them up and put them in a pile on her desk.

NOTE **Assemble** is a more formal word for **gather up**.

2 If you **gather** someone **up**, you put your arms around them to hug them or carry them.

gather someone up ❏ I gathered her up and carried her to my room.

gawk (gawks, gawking, gawked)

○ **'gawk at** [INFORMAL]

To **gawk at** someone or something means to stare at them in a rude or stupid way.

gawk at someone/something ❏ The youth continued to gawk at her and did not answer.

gear /gɪə/ (gears, gearing, geared)

○ **'gear to** (or **gear towards**)

If you **gear** something **to** a particular purpose, you organize or design it to be suitable for that purpose.

gear something to something ❏ We need to gear our efforts to what the market really wants.

be geared to something ❏ Higher education is increasingly geared towards careers.

○ **gear 'up**

If someone or something **is geared up** to do something, or if they **gear** themselves **up** to do it, they are prepared and able to do it.

be geared up ❏ [+ to-infinitive] Many football teams are not geared up to attack.

gear yourself up ❏ [+ for] He's gearing himself up for his return to work. ❏ [+ to-infinitive] I'm just gearing myself up to call her.

gee /dʒiː/ (gees, geeing, geed)

○ **gee 'up** [BRITISH, INFORMAL, OLD-FASHIONED]

To **gee** someone **up** means to encourage them to perform well.

gee someone up or **gee up someone** ❏ She had a word with her team during the break to gee them up. ❏ He needs to do something to gee up the sales force.

NOTE **Encourage** is a more formal word for **gee up**.

geek /giːk/ (geeks, geeking, geeked)

○ **geek 'out** [INFORMAL]

If someone **geeks out** about something, they become very enthusiastic about something that they are very interested in but which seems boring to other people. ❏ [+ over] When they see these photos, they geek out over the construction of the buildings.

gen /dʒen/ (gens, genning, genned)

○ **gen 'up** [BRITISH]

If you **gen up**, you find out as much information about a subject as you can. = **swot up** ❏ [+ on] He's genning up on the legal position before he signs the contract. ❏ She genned up on the character before taking on the role.

● If you are **genned up**, you know a lot about a subject. ❏ [+ on] She's really genned up on all these old customs and traditions.

NOTE **Well-informed** is a more formal word for **genned up**.

get /get/ (gets, getting, got)

> **Gotten** is used in American English as the past participle.

○ **get a'bout** (or **get around**) [mainly BRITISH]

1 If you can **get about** after you have been ill or when you are old, you are able to move around without much difficulty. ❏ I can't get about as much as I used to. ❏ She can get around with a stick.

2 → see **get around**

○ **get a'bove**

If someone **gets above** themselves, they start to behave as if they are better or more important than everyone else.

get above yourself ❏ My parents rarely praised me. They didn't want me getting above myself.

◐ **get a'cross**

If an idea or argument **gets across**, or if you **get** it **across**, you succeed in making other people understand it. = **get over, put across**

get across ❏ The speaker needs to know that his words are getting across.

get something across ❏ We think we managed to get our message across.

get across something ❏ It was difficult to get across the basic idea.

○ **get 'after** [INFORMAL]

If you **get after** someone, you try to catch

them, especially after they have committed a crime.

get after someone ❑ *You have everything you need – now get after him!* ❑ *It is their job to get after the thieves as fast as possible.*

NOTE **Pursue** is a more formal word for **get after**.

○ **get a'head**

If you **get ahead**, you succeed in your career. **= get on** ❑ *The bright young graduate can get ahead quickly in industry.* ❑ *She was ambitious and determined to get ahead.*

◑ **get a'long**

1 If two people **get along**, they have a friendly relationship. **= get on** ❑ [+ with] *Dan likes her but I've never got along with her.* ❑ [+ together] *The brothers just can't get along together.* ❑ *We get along pretty well most of the time.*

2 If you **get along** in a situation, you cope with it or make progress in it, although it may be difficult. **= get on** ❑ *With his ninety dollars a week and her sixty they got along well enough.* ❑ [+ with] *How are you getting along with the German course?*

NOTE **Manage** is a more formal word for **get along**.

3 If you say that you must **be getting along**, you mean that you must leave, because you have to go somewhere else. [OLD-FASHIONED]

be getting along ❑ *Well, I'd better be getting along, the train's due.*

◑ **get a'round** (or **get about** [mainly BRITISH])

1 If you **get around**, you go to a lot of different places. ❑ *He was in New York last month and he goes to Italy next week – he gets around.*

2 If you say that someone **gets around**, you mean that they have a lot of sexual relationships. [INFORMAL, RUDE] ❑ *What do you mean, I get around?* ❑ *He has a bit of a reputation. He gets about, if you know what I mean.*

○ **get a'round** (or **get round** [mainly BRITISH])

1 If recent information **gets around** or **gets around** a place, a lot of people tell other people about it.

get around ❑ *The news got around that he was leaving.* ❑ *The word got round that Morris was going to England.*

get around somewhere ❑ *Gossip gets round the film industry much faster than in other places.*

2 To **get around** a problem or difficulty means to solve or avoid it. **= get over**

get around something ❑ *There are too few teachers and some schools are trying to get around the problem by recruiting teachers from abroad.* ❑ *To get round the law, their plays were staged in private houses.*

○ **get a'round to** (or **get round to** [mainly BRITISH])

If you **get around to** doing something, you finally do it after intending to do it for a long time.

get around to something ❑ *I meant to call her – I just didn't get around to it.* ❑ *It took her two years to get round to buying a car.*

◐ **'get at**

1 If you **get at** something, you manage to reach or obtain it.

get at something ❑ *Keep your tool box where you can get at it.* ❑ *You can't get at the public records until one hundred years has passed.*

2 If someone or something **gets at** facts or the truth, they succeed in discovering them. **= find out**

get at something ❑ *As a journalist, he had a determination to get at the facts.* ❑ *I am not confident that the enquiry will get at the truth.*

3 If you ask someone what they **are getting at**, you are asking them what they mean, usually because they have expressed an opinion in a way that is not direct. **= drive at** [INFORMAL]

be getting at ❑ *What are you getting at? Have I done something wrong here?* ❑ *I don't know what you're getting at.*

4 If someone **gets at** you, they keep criticizing you in an unkind way. **= pick on** [BRITISH, INFORMAL]

get at someone ❑ *You're always getting at me!* ❑ *I hope Andrew didn't feel I was getting at him last night.*

5 To **get at** someone is to persuade them to say something untrue or to act in an unfair way, usually by threatening them or offering them money.

get at someone ❑ *The trial wasn't fair because the chief witnesses had been got at.*

◐ **get a'way**

1 If you **get away**, you succeed in leaving a place or person. ❑ [+ from] *I couldn't wait to get away from home.* ❑ *If I'm lucky I might get away by midnight.*

2 If you **get away**, you go somewhere to have a holiday. ❑ *Is there any chance of you getting away this summer?* ❑ *It would be nice to get away for a couple of weeks.*

3 When someone or something **gets away**, they escape from a place. ❑ *The police followed the gang but they got away.* ❑ *I was* determined not to let him get away. ● If someone makes a **getaway**, they leave a place in a hurry, often after committing a crime. ❑ Duffield had already made his getaway down the stairs. ❑ He ran to the end of the road where a getaway car was waiting for him.

4 If someone says **Get away!** or **Get away with you!** they mean they do not believe what you have just said. = **go on** [INFORMAL, OLD-FASHIONED] ❑ Get away! You're never 50! ❑ 'I've been arrested,' I said—'Get away with you!' he laughed.

○ **get a'way from**
If you **get away from** an idea, habit or belief, you start thinking about things or doing things in a different way. = **break away from**
get away from something ❑ We've got to get away from the idea that the only thing that motivates people is money. ❑ He's trying to get away from his bad guy image.

○ **get a'way with**
1 If you **get away with** something that you should not have done, you are not criticized or punished for doing it.
get away with something ❑ I wasn't going to let Anne get away with an offensive remark like that. ❑ You mustn't let him get away with it when he's rude to you like that.
● If someone **gets away with murder**, they behave very badly and still do not get criticized or punished. [INFORMAL] ❑ Daniel gets away with murder at school because all the teachers are charmed by him.
2 If you **get away with** something, you do something slightly less well than you could, but still manage to succeed.
get away with something ❑ You're supposed to leave the fruit to soak for three hours but you could probably get away with two.

○ **get 'back**
1 If you **get back**, you return somewhere after being in another place. ❑ [+ to] I've got to get back to London. ❑ We didn't get back till midnight last night. ❑ [+ from] What time do you usually get back from work?
2 If you **get** something **back**, you get it again after losing it or giving it to someone else.
get something back ❑ Don't lend your clothes to Rosie – you'll never get them back! ❑ I'm going to return it to the shop and get my money back.
get back something ❑ Did she get back any of the jewellery she lost?
3 When you **get** your **breath back**, you pause after exercising in order to start breathing more slowly again. ❑ I had to

pause at the top of the steps to get my breath back.
4 If you tell someone to **get back**, you are telling them to move away from someone or something. = **stand back, back off** ❑ Get back or I'll shoot!
5 If you **get** someone **back**, you punish or hurt them in return for something unpleasant that they have done to you. = **pay back** [INFORMAL]
get someone back ❑ [+ for] I'll get him back for all the nasty things he said.

○ **get 'back at** [INFORMAL]
If you **get back at** someone, you punish or hurt them in return for something unpleasant that they have done or said to you.
get back at someone ❑ He just wanted to get back at Jamie because he took his girlfriend. ❑ [+ for] I wanted to get back at women for what my mother did to me.

○ **get back 'into**
If you **get back into** an activity that you were doing before, you start doing it or being involved in it again.
get back into something ❑ Maybe you could get back into journalism. ❑ Now her kids are grown up, she'd like to get back into research.

○ **get 'back to**
1 If you **get back to** what you were doing or talking about before, you start doing it or talking about it again. = **go back to**
get back to something ❑ I couldn't get back to sleep. ❑ Now I really must get back to work. ❑ To get back to what we were saying earlier, I agree we must start to save some money.
2 If you **get back to** someone, you contact them again after a short period of time.
get back to someone ❑ Leave a message and I'll get back to you. ❑ I'll get back to you when I know what the arrangements are. ❑ [+ on] I haven't got those figures to hand. I'll get back to you on that, Simon.

○ **get be'hind**
1 If you **get behind**, you make less progress than you should with a piece of work that you are doing. = **fall behind** ❑ [+ with] With so many days off, she's got behind with her schoolwork.
2 If you **get behind**, you stop making regular payments for something that you have promised to. ❑ [+ with] She's in trouble with her landlord because she's got behind with the rent.
3 If you **get behind** someone or something you support them and try to help them to succeed.
get behind someone/something ❑ Once they

see what she's like they'll get behind her. ❑ We need them to get behind the campaign.

○ get be'yond
If you **get beyond** a particular thing, you make progress so that you are no longer doing that thing. = **go beyond**
get beyond something ❑ I only met her once or twice and we never got beyond the small-talk stage. ❑ The article was so boring, I didn't get beyond the first paragraph.

○ get 'by
1 If you **get by**, you manage to pay for everything you need, but with difficulty.
❑ [+ on] How do people get by on such low wages? ❑ It's not easy but we get by.

2 If you **get by**, you manage to cope with a difficult situation, usually because you know just enough. ❑ [+ in] My French isn't great but I can just about get by in most situations. ❑ He hadn't prepared for the interview in any way but somehow he got by.

3 If someone or something that is moving **gets by**, they manage to get past something or someone that is in their way.
= **pass** ❑ The truck began hooting to get by. ❑ I moved away from the doorway to let her get by.

✪ get 'down
1 When someone or something **gets down** or **gets down** something, they move from a higher position or level to a lower one.
get down ❑ It was so cold up in the mountains. I was very pleased when we got down.
get down something ❑ When we eventually got down the mountain, he was rushed to hospital. ❑ Can your car get down this steep hill?

2 If you **get** someone or something **down**, or **get** them **down** a place, you move them or make them move from a higher position or level to a lower one.
get someone/something down ❑ Carlo is upstairs and refusing to come down. Could you get him down?
get down someone/something ❑ Could you get down some plates from the top cupboard, please?
get someone/something down something ❑ You'll never get the piano down the stairs.

3 If you **get down**, you move off an object that you are on and come down to the ground. ❑ [+ from] He got down from the step ladder. ❑ George has climbed up a tree, and now he can't get down.

4 If a child sitting at a table asks to **get down** at the end of a meal, they are asking permission to get down from their chair and leave the table. [OLD-FASHIONED] ❑ Can I get down now, Mum?

5 If you **get down**, you move your body so that you are near the ground in a sitting, kneeling or lying position. ❑ The soldiers shouted to us to get down. ❑ [+ on] I got down on my knees to get a better look. ❑ They got down on the ground.

6 If you **get down** to a place, you go there. [INFORMAL] ❑ Get down there and find out what they're planning. ❑ [+ to] I'd get down to the market, if I were you, and get yourself a leather bag.

7 If you **get** food **down**, you swallow it, especially with difficulty. [INFORMAL]
get something down or **get down something** ❑ I tried a mouthful of food but couldn't get it down. ❑ I needed some water to get down the medicine.

8 If you **get down** what someone is saying, you write it down. = **take down**
get something down or **get down something** ❑ I got the details down. ❑ Did you get that number down?

9 If something **gets** you **down**, it makes you unhappy.
get someone down ❑ I work all the time and it's really getting me down.
NOTE **Depress** is a slightly more formal word for **get down**.

○ get 'down to
When you **get down to** an activity, especially work, you start doing it seriously and with a lot of attention.
get down to something ❑ I was finally able to get down to work. ❑ Let's get down to business.

○ get down with
1 If you **get down with** something, you like it or enjoy it.
get down with something ❑ I just can't get down with their new album.

2 If you **get down with** young people, you try to understand the way they feel or think by behaving in the same way as them.
get down with someone ❑ Don't try and get down with the kids – you'll just make a fool of yourself.

✪ get 'in
1 If you **get in** or **get in** a place such as a car, house, or room, you go inside it.
get in ❑ I walked to the van, got in and drove away.
get in something ❑ Never get in a stranger's car. ❑ I wanted to get in the house as it was raining.

2 When a person or a vehicle **gets in**, they arrive at a place where people are expecting them to be. ❑ I'll tell him you called when he gets in. ❑ What time does the coach get in, do you know? ❑ Half the staff don't even get in on time.

3 If you **get in**, you succeed in entering a

building. ❑ *I need my pass to get in.* ❑ *We went to the seven o'clock movie but didn't get in.* ❑ *It cost three pounds to get in.*

4 If you **get in** or **get in** something, you succeed in becoming a member of a team or getting a place on a course, in an organization, etc.

get in ❑ *I wanted to go to Oxford, but I didn't get in.*

get in something ❑ *I think Stanton will get in the team.*

5 If you **get** something **in**, you bring something inside that is outside, to protect it from the weather.

get something in or **get in something** ❑ *It's raining. Could you get the washing in?*

6 To **get** crops **in** means to gather them from the land and take them to a particular place.

get something in or **get in something** ❑ *We didn't get the harvest in until Christmas, there was so much snow.*

7 If you **get in** food or other supplies that you need, you buy them and bring them back to your home.

get something in or **get in something** ❑ *We must remember to get some more coffee in.* ❑ *I must get in some food for the weekend.*

8 If you **get** someone **in**, you arrange for someone to come to your home to do a piece of work for you. = **call in**

get someone in or **get in someone** ❑ *Always get an expert in to deal with electrical wiring.* ❑ *You need to get in someone who knows about these things.*

9 When a political party or a politician **gets in**, they are elected. ❑ *What would Labour do if they got in?* ❑ *She got in by more than 5,000 votes.*

10 If you **get in** an activity, especially work or exercise, you find time to do it, even though you are busy doing other things. = **fit in**

get in something or **get something in** ❑ *We may even get in a little golf between sessions.* ❑ *Did you manage to get any work in?*

11 If you **get** a sentence or some words **in** when other people are talking, you manage to say something.

get in something or **get something in** ❑ *Phillip got a question in about the cost.* ❑ *As ever, Lucy had to get in the last word.* ❑ *'What I wanted to say,' I finally got in, 'is that I don't agree.'*

○ **get 'in on** [INFORMAL]
If someone **gets in on** an activity that someone else is already doing, they copy them and start doing it too.

get in on something ❑ *We were the first ones to provide the service but now everyone wants to get in on it.* ❑ *How did the four of you get in on the deal?*

● If someone **gets in on the act**, they start doing an activity that someone else is already doing. ❑ *People saw they could make a profit doing what we do and, naturally, they wanted to get in on the act.*

○ **get 'into**

1 If you **get into** a place such as a car, house, or room, you enter it.

get into something ❑ *How did they get into the building?* ❑ *They got into the bedroom through an open window.*

2 If a person or vehicle **gets into** a place, they reach it.

get into somewhere ❑ *We got into London at one o'clock.* ❑ *The train got into the station five minutes late.*

3 If you **get into** an activity, you start doing it or being involved in it.

get into something ❑ *I always get into arguments with people.* ❑ *He was determined to get into politics.* ❑ *He got into the campaign right at the start.*

4 If you **get into** a difficult situation, or if someone **gets** you **into** it, you start to be involved in it, often without intending to be.

get into something ❑ *Make sure you don't get into debt.* ❑ *She got into terrible trouble.*

get someone into something ❑ *'I'm in trouble,' said Carmen, 'and you got me into it.'* ❑ *He got himself into such a mess.*

5 If you **get into** a particular habit or way of behaving, you start to have that habit or behave in that way.

get into something ❑ *She'd got into the habit of watching TV when she came home from school.* ❑ *I really need to get into a routine.*

6 If you **get into** a subject, you start being interested in it. [INFORMAL]

get into something ❑ *She got into health foods and astrology.* ❑ *I got into comic books as a teenager.*

7 If you **get into** an organization such as a school, team, or club, you are accepted as a member of that organization.

get into something ❑ *There was no chance of her getting into university.* ❑ *If I don't get into the first team this year, I'm not playing at all.*

8 If you **get into** a piece of clothing, you put it on.

get into something ❑ *If you wait a moment, I'll just get into my swimsuit.* ❑ *I put on so much weight I couldn't get into any of my clothes.*

9 If you say **what has got into** someone, you mean that they are behaving in a strange or unreasonable way. [INFORMAL]
❑ *What's got into her these days?* ❑ *I don't know what's got into you, Emily!*

○ **get 'in with**

1 If you **get in with** someone, you make an effort to become friends with them, because you think that they can help you.
get in with someone ❑ *She's always very careful to get in with the people who matter.*

2 If you **get in with** a person or group, you start to spend time with them.
get in with someone ❑ *At school he got in with a bad crowd.*

✪ **get 'off**

1 If you **get off** something that you are on, you move your body from it, usually onto the ground.
get off something ❑ *He got off his bicycle.*
❑ *He got off the stool and came forward to greet me.*

2 If you **get off** or **get off** a bus, train, or plane, you leave a bus, train, or plane.
= get out
get off ❑ *When do we need to get off?* ❑ *Get off at Mayfield Church.*
get off something ❑ *I slipped as I was getting off the train.*

3 When you **get off**, you leave somewhere, often to start a journey. **= get away** ❑ *Did Myra get off all right?* ❑ *I plan to get off before the traffic gets bad.*

4 When you **get off** or **get off** work, you leave your place of work at the end of a day.
get off ❑ *I don't get off till six o'clock.*
get off something ❑ *What time do you get off work?*

5 If you **get** someone **off** to a place, you send them or take them there.
get someone off ❑ [+ to] *I've got to get the children off to school.* ❑ *What time do you normally get the kids off to bed?*

6 If you **get** a letter or parcel **off**, you send it.
get something off ❑ *I must get this letter off today.*

7 If you tell someone to **get off** a piece of land, you are telling them to leave a place where they should not be.
get off something ❑ *He told them to get off his property.*

8 If you **get off the phone**, you stop speaking on it. ❑ *By the time I'd got off the phone to Adrian it was almost midnight.* ❑ *I told him to get off the phone.*

9 If you tell someone to **get off** or to **get off** someone or something, you are telling them not to touch the person, or not to touch something.
get off ❑ *Colin kept trying to kiss me, so I told him to get off.*
get off someone/something ❑ *Get off me!* ❑ *Get off that cake, it's for tomorrow!*

10 If you **get** something **off** or **get** it **off** something, you remove it.
get something off ❑ *The top's stuck and I can't get it off.*
get something off something ❑ *Can you get the lid off this jar?*

11 If you **get** something **off** someone, you succeed in persuading them to give it to you. [INFORMAL]
get something off someone ❑ *I'll get some money off my dad.* ❑ *I managed to get the car off my mum for the weekend.*

12 If you **get** a period of time **off**, you do not have to go to work during that period.
get something off ❑ *Could you get two weeks off?* ❑ *She can't get time off to go to the clinic.*

13 If you **get off** when you have done something wrong, or if someone **gets** you **off**, you are not punished or receive only a small punishment for what you have done.
get off ❑ [+ with] *He got off with a £50 fine.*
❑ *She was sure that she would not get off so easily.*
get someone off ❑ *He hired a good lawyer who could get him off.*

14 If you **get off** a subject that you are talking about, you stop talking about it and start to talk about something else instead.
get off something ❑ *I think we'd better get off this subject.* ❑ *Somehow, we got off the subject, and I forgot to ask him about it.*

15 If you **get off the point** in a discussion, you start talking about things that are not connected with it. ❑ *Michael, I think you're getting off the point.*

16 If you **get off**, you start to sleep. [BRITISH]
❑ *I lay in bed for hours, but I couldn't get off.*

● If you **get off to sleep** or **get** a baby **off to sleep**, you start to sleep or make them start sleeping. ❑ *I didn't get off to sleep till three in the morning.* ❑ *I find that the music helps to get him off to sleep.*

○ **get 'off on** [INFORMAL]
If you **get off on** something, you become very excited by it.
get off on something ❑ *I saw you watching the fight and getting off on it.* ❑ *Rock-climbing is such a high – I really get off on it.*

○ **get 'off with** [BRITISH, INFORMAL]
If you **get off with** someone, you begin a romantic or sexual relationship with them.

get off with someone ❑ *He got off with her at Paolo's party.* ❑ *Mike thinks I'm trying to get off with his girlfriend.*

⚙ **get 'on**

1 If you **get on** an object, you move your body so that you are on it.

get on something ❑ *I was just getting on my bike when it started raining.* ❑ *Eventually, I managed to get on the horse.*

2 If you **get on** or **get on** a bus, train, or plane, you get into the bus, train or plane.

get on ❑ *Some new passengers were getting on.*

get on something ❑ *She got on the bus every morning.*

NOTE **Board** is a more formal word for **get on**.

3 If you **get on** the telephone to someone, or if you **get** them **on** it, you talk to them on the telephone.

get on something ❑ *He got on the phone to the President.*

get someone on something ❑ *Could you get him on the phone? I really want to speak to him.*

4 If you **get** a piece of clothing **on**, you dress yourself in it. **= put on**

get something on or **get on something** ❑ *Get your coat on.* ❑ *I put the pyjamas on the bed and told him to get them on.*

5 If you **get on**, you continue an activity. ❑ *[+ with] Anyway, I'll let you get on with your dinner.* ❑ *I'm going to have to leave now but you guys can get on.*

6 If you **get on**, you start an activity. ❑ *[+ with] We can get on with the meeting without Ava.* ❑ *Anyway, it's getting late so shall we get on?*

7 If you ask how someone **is getting on**, you are asking how much progress they are making with an activity or whether they are enjoying something. **= get along**

be getting on ❑ *How are you getting on?* ❑ *[+ with] How is Lena getting on with her studies?*

8 If you **get on**, you are successful in your career. **= get ahead** [BRITISH] ❑ *If you want to get on, you need to work hard.* ❑ *[+ in] You have to do these things to get on in the academic world.*

9 To **get on** means to manage to continue or succeed. ❑ *[+ without] To be honest, I think she'd get on better without him.* ❑ *We'll just have to get on as best we can.*

10 If two people **get on**, they have a friendly relationship. **= get along** [mainly BRITISH] ❑ *Mark and Jason don't get on.* ❑ *[+ with] You seem to be getting on well with the Chairman.* ❑ *[+ together] Our kids get on well together.*

11 If someone **gets on** a television or radio programme, or **gets** themselves **on** it, they are accepted to take part in it.

get on something ❑ *They were hoping to get on the evening show.*

get yourself on something ❑ *She's hoping to get herself on the panel for 'Any Questions'.*

12 If someone **is getting on**, they are old. [INFORMAL]

be getting on ❑ *Edward must be getting on now.* ❑ *Now I'm getting on, these stairs are a little difficult for me.*

13 If you say **it's getting on** or **time is getting on**, you mean that it is late. ❑ *It's getting on – we'd better go.* ❑ *We haven't got long before the flight. Time is getting on.*

○ **get 'on at** [INFORMAL]

If you **get on at** someone, you continually criticize them in an unkind way. **= keep on at**

get on at someone ❑ *[+ about] Mum's always getting on at me about my hair.* ❑ *It won't help if you keep getting on at him.*

○ **get 'on for**

If something **is getting on for** an amount or time, it is nearly that amount or time.

be getting on for something ❑ *The jacket alone was getting on for six hundred pounds.* ❑ *We'd better go – it's getting on for four o'clock now.*

○ **get 'on to** (or **get onto**)

1 If you **get on to** a particular topic, you start talking about it after you have been talking about something else.

get on to something ❑ *That's something we'll get on to in the future.* ❑ *I don't know how we got onto this.*

2 If you **get on to** someone, you contact them. [BRITISH]

get on to someone ❑ *I'll get on to her right away.* ❑ *Get straight on to the department chief about it.*

3 If someone in authority **gets on to** someone or something, they find out about something that someone has been trying to keep secret.

get on to someone/something ❑ *It wasn't long before the Ministry of Information got on to him.* ❑ *I don't imagine they will get on to this if we keep quiet.*

4 If you **get on to** something, you start doing it or dealing with it.

get on to something ❑ *'The heating system has broken.' – 'OK, I'll get on to it immediately.'*

⚙ **get 'out**

1 If you **get out**, you leave a place or a vehicle. ❑ *[+ of] We got out of the car.* ❑ *Brody got out of bed.* ❑ *I need to get out of New York for a while.* ❑ *She got out and slammed the door.*

2 If you tell someone to **get out**, you are telling them angrily to leave a room.

❏ *Get out, Donald – you make me sick!* ❏ [+ *of*] *Now get out of my sight!*

3 If you **get** someone **out**, you make them leave or help them to leave a place.

get someone out ❏ [+ *of*] *The only way to save his life was to get him out of the country.* ❏ *Get me out of here!*

4 If you **get** someone **out** of a difficult or dangerous situation, you help them to escape from it.

get someone out ❏ [+ *of*] *Who got you out of that mess in Omaha?* ❏ *I got you into this and now I must get you out.* ● A **getout** is something which helps you to avoid or prevent an unwanted situation. ❏ *What we need is a safe getout.* ❏ *Insurance companies always have a getout clause of some kind.*

5 If you **get out**, you go to places and meet people. = **go out** ❏ *You're young. Get out and enjoy yourself!* ❏ *You've got to get out and make friends.*

6 If you **get** something **out**, you take it out of the container that it is in.

get something out or **get out something**
❏ [+ *of*] *I got my glasses out of my bag.* ❏ *Where did I put my mobile? I just got it out a moment ago.* ❏ *He got out his book and started to read.*

7 If you **get** dirt or other substances **out**, you remove them from something.

get something out or **get out something**
❏ [+ *of*] *I couldn't get the stain out of your dress.* ❏ *How do you get out red wine marks?*

8 If you **get out** a product or a piece of work, you make it or produce it so that it is available to people. = **bring out**

get out something or **get something out**
❏ *The American Cancer Society got out its first report in 1954.* ❏ *We need to get the book out before Christmas.*

9 If you **get** something **out**, you manage to say it, with difficulty.

get something out or **get out something**
❏ *I can't get my words out today!* ❏ *He was sobbing so hard he couldn't get out the words.*

10 If news or information **gets out**, it becomes known. = **leak out, come out**
❏ *The news got out in the end.* ❏ *The word got out that Brown was leaving.*

11 If you **get out**, you leave an organization or club and stop being a member of it. = **pull out** ❏ *The sooner we get out the better.* ❏ [+ *of*] *The association does us no favours at all. We need to get out of it.*

12 In cricket, if you **get** a batsman **out**, you end their innings (= period in which they are trying to score), for example by hitting the wicket (= set of three sticks) with a ball, or catching the ball after they have hit it.

get someone out or **get out someone**
❏ *Within five minutes he'd got Taylor out.* ❏ *They have twenty minutes to get out the remaining batsmen.*

○ **get 'out of**

1 If you **get** something good, especially pleasure or satisfaction, **out of** something that you do or experience, you enjoy it or find it useful.

get something out of something ❏ *We get a lot of pleasure out of our grandchildren.* ❏ *I think she got more out of the course than I did.*

2 If you **get out of** doing something, you avoid doing it. = **wriggle out of**

get out of something ❏ *If there was work to be done around the house, Alec would always get out of it.* ❏ *He'll do anything to get out of going to his piano lesson.*

3 If you **get** something **out of** someone, you persuade them to give it to you or tell you it, even though they do not really want to.

get something out of someone ❏ *It was some charity on the phone, trying to get money out of me.* ❏ *Are you trying to get some kind of confession out of me?*

4 If you **get out of** a habit or an activity that you do regularly, you stop doing it.

get out of something ❏ *I used to go running every morning but I've recently got out of the habit.* ❏ *If I get out of my routine, I'm hopeless.*

○ **get 'over**

1 If you **get over** an illness or other unpleasant experience, you recover from it.

get over something ❏ *I'm glad to hear you've got over your cold.* ❏ *I don't think Rosa ever really got over his death.* ❏ *It's a bit of a shock but I'll get over it.*

GET OVER + *noun*
get over **a shock**   get over someone's **death**   get over **the disappointment of** something   get over **a surprise**   ❏ *He never got over the death of his wife.* ❏ *She didn't win, but she got over her disappointment fairly quickly.*

2 If you **get over** a problem or difficulty, you find a way of dealing with it.

get over something ❏ *We could get over the problem by hiring more staff.*

3 If you say that you **cannot get over** something, you mean that you are extremely surprised by it. [INFORMAL]
❏ *I just couldn't get over how much money Ian had spent on the boat!* ❏ *I still can't get over the fact that she's 66!*

4 If you **get** an idea or argument **over**, you succeed in making other people understand it. **= get across**

get something over or **get over something** ❑ *We have to find a better way of getting our message over.* ❑ *First, we have to get over the idea that this method is completely new.*

5 If you **get over** to a place, you go there or arrive there and if you **get** someone **over** to it, you arrange for them to come and visit you.

get over ❑ [+ *to*] *We could get over to your house by about six o'clock.*

get someone over ❑ *I thought I might get him over to dinner one evening.* ❑ *We should get her over some time.*

○ **get 'over with**
If you **get** something **over with**, you do and complete something unpleasant that you must do.

get something over with ❑ *I'll call him now and get it over with.* ❑ *Can we just get this interview over with?*

⊙ **get 'round**
  1 → see **get around**
  2 If you **get round** someone, you persuade them to let you do or have something, by being nice to them. **= win over**
get round someone ❑ *Chris isn't keen on the idea at the moment but I'll get round him.*
  3 If you **get round** or **get round** a course when you are in a race, you manage to finish the course.
get round ❑ *Schumacher got round in just over two hours and twenty minutes.*
get round something ❑ *I felt really tired, but I did get round the course.*

○ **get 'round to** → see **get around to**

⊙ **get 'through**
  1 If you **get through** a task, you succeed in finishing it.
get through something ❑ *I got through a lot of work this morning.* ❑ *How much of this editing do you think you can get through in an hour?*
  2 If you **get through** a difficult or unpleasant experience, or someone or something **gets** you **through** it, you survive it.
get through something ❑ *I just have to get through the next few months and then it'll be fine.* ❑ *She needs her coffee to get through the day.*
get someone through something ❑ *I think it was the counselling sessions that got me through this period of my life.*
get someone through ❑ *When things are difficult, it's your friendships that get you through.*
  3 If you **get through**, you succeed in

contacting someone on the telephone. ❑ *I telephoned Juliet in hospital and got through without difficulty.* ❑ [+ *to*] *I've been trying for a whole hour to get through to you.*

4 If something **gets through**, it succeeds in reaching a place. ❑ *I expect the letters just aren't getting through.* ❑ [+ *to*] *Urgent supplies are not getting through to the hospital.*

5 If you **get through** an examination, or if someone or something **gets** you **through** it, you pass it. [BRITISH]
get through something ❑ *He got through his exams all right.* ❑ *He'll qualify if he gets through his two subjects this year.*
get someone through something ❑ *He'll need a bit of help to get him through the written paper.* ❑ *I'm hoping the new instructor will get her through the driving test.*

6 If you **get through** in a competition, or if someone or something **gets** you **through**, you succeed in reaching a particular stage.
get through ❑ [+ *to*] *Davis has got through to the final again.*
get through something ❑ *It remains to be seen whether United will get through the 6th round of the Cup.*
get someone through ❑ [+ *to*] *It was only luck that got us through to the next round.*

7 If you **get through** an amount of something, you use it completely. **= run through** [BRITISH]
get through something ❑ *When he got through all his money he went back to Canada.* ❑ *We got through four jars of coffee in one morning.*

8 If a law or proposal **gets through**, or if someone **gets** it **through** a parliament or a committee, it is officially approved.
get through ❑ *If this new White Paper gets through, all this will change.*
get through something ❑ *The Bill got through all its stages and became law.*
get something through ❑ *The opposition got the amendment through with a majority of 117.*
get something through something ❑ *He felt there was a real possibility of getting it through Parliament.*

○ **get 'through to**
If a person or an idea **gets through to** you, you understand what they say or mean.
get through to someone ❑ *I'm always telling him he has to work harder but I don't seem to be able to get through to him.* ❑ *We need to find a way of getting through to them.*

⊙ **'get to**
  1 When you **get to** a place, you arrive there.
get to somewhere ❑ *It was midnight before we got to the village.*

2 If you **get to** doing something, you gradually begin to do it without intending to. [INFORMAL]

get to doing something ❑ *I got to thinking how lonely she must be.*

NOTE **Fall to** is a literary expression for **get to**.

3 If an experience **gets to** you, it upsets or annoys you. [INFORMAL]

get to someone ❑ *She can be quite rude sometimes but don't let it get to you.* ❑ *I think the stress is starting to get to him.*

get to'gether

1 When people **get together**, or when someone **gets** people **together**, two or more people meet in order to discuss something or to spend time with each other.

get together ❑ [+ to-infinitive] *Teams and team managers regularly get together to discuss issues that are affecting them.* ❑ *We should all get together and go out for a drink.*

get someone together ❑ *We plan to get childminders together in local self-help groups.*

get together someone ❑ *He got together a bunch of people who wanted to help out.*

• A **get-together** is an informal meeting or party. ❑ *We're having a little get-together to celebrate Helen's promotion.*

2 If you **get** several things **together**, you collect them and put them all in one place. = **gather up**

get something together ❑ *I got all my letters and papers together.*

get together something ❑ *I got together the rest of the notes and fastened them with rubber bands.*

NOTE **Assemble** is a more formal word for **get together**.

3 If you **get together** a plan, you succeed in writing or organizing it.

get together something ❑ *I'm hoping to get together a book proposal by the end of the month.*

get something together ❑ *Have you got that syllabus together yet?*

4 If you **get** money **together**, you succeed in getting all the money that you need in order to pay for something. = **scrape up**

get something together ❑ *We'd like to go away for a while if we could just get the money together.* ❑ *Somehow we have to get the fees together.*

get together something ❑ *We managed to get together enough money to pay for the course.*

NOTE **Raise** is a more formal word for **get together**.

5 If you **get** yourself **together**, you succeed in controlling your feelings so that you behave calmly and reasonably. = **pull together**

get yourself together ❑ *Eventually, she got herself together and called her lawyer.*

6 If two people **get together**, they start a romantic relationship. [INFORMAL] ❑ *Sam and Pete got together after meeting at Ann's party.*

7 If you **get it together**, you succeed in organizing your life so that you do things that you plan to do. [INFORMAL] ❑ *Patrick plans one day to open a small hotel but I doubt if he'll ever get it together.* ❑ [+ to-infinitive] *I didn't get it together to order the food.*

○ get 'up

1 When someone or something **gets up** or **gets up** something, they move from a lower position or level to a higher one.

get up ❑ *By the time we'd got up to the top of the hill, we were exhausted.*

get up something ❑ *I knew he would have difficulty getting up those steps.*

2 If you **get** someone or something **up**, or **get** them **up** a place, you move them or make them move from a lower position or level to a higher one.

get someone up ❑ *I thought, if he falls, I'll never get him up again.*

get someone up something ❑ *Jacob is so lazy – I'll never get him up that hill!*

3 If you **get up**, you rise to a standing position after you have been sitting or lying down. ❑ *She got up and strode across the room.* ❑ [+ off] *He got up off the floor.*

4 When you **get up**, or when someone **gets** you **up**, you get out of bed.

get up ❑ *She decided it was time to get up.*

get someone up ❑ *Don't get me up in the morning.* ❑ *We had to get the children up and dressed.* ❑ *We had until 7.15 to get ourselves up.*

5 If you **get up** to a place, you visit it, especially when the place is farther north than you or is in a big city. ❑ [+ to] *He'll have to get up to London for the day.* ❑ *I loved the Lake District and I really want to get up there again this summer.*

6 If you **get up** a public event or meeting, you arrange it or organize it, especially with very little preparation. = **fix up** [OLD-FASHIONED]

get up something or **get something up** ❑ *The women got up a march the next Saturday.* ❑ *A dance was got up in his honour.*

7 If someone **gets** themselves **up** in unusual clothes, or if they **are got up** in them, they are dressed in unusual clothes. = **rig out** [INFORMAL, OLD-FASHIONED]

get yourself up ❑ [+ in] *These were the days when band leaders got themselves up in smart jackets.*

be got up ❑ [+ as] *Several people were got up as soldiers.* • A **get-up** is an unusual set of clothes. ❏ *They arrived in full rock-star get-up, including the shades.*

8 If the wind or a storm **gets up**, it starts to blow very strongly. ❏ *A wind had got up and it had turned cold.*

○ **get 'up to**

1 If someone **gets up to** something, they do something, especially something that you do not approve of. [BRITISH, INFORMAL]
get up to something ❏ *What did you get up to while I was away?* ❏ *I don't really think he'd get up to anything behind my back.*

2 When you **get up to** a particular point in something, especially something that you are reading, writing or watching, you reach that point.
get up to something ❏ *I managed to get up to question six.* ❏ *I watched three episodes so I got up to the point where Tamara was leaving London.*

○ **get 'with** [INFORMAL, OLD-FASHIONED]
If you **get with it**, you become aware of the latest events, developments, or ideas.
❏ *Their teacher was trying to get with it by singing pop songs.*

ginger /'dʒɪndʒə/ (**gingers, gingering, gingered**)

○ **ginger 'up** [INFORMAL]
If you **ginger** something **up**, you make it more interesting and exciting. = **spice up**
ginger something up or **ginger up something** ❏ *With two or three new pieces of clothing, you can ginger up a wardrobe that's looking a bit stale.*

gird /gɜːd/ (**girds, girding, girded**)

○ **'gird for** [LITERARY]
If you **gird** yourself **for** a battle, contest, or difficult situation, you prepare yourself for it.
gird yourself for something ❏ *With audiences in the U.S. falling for the first time in years, Hollywood is girding itself for recession.*

give /gɪv/ (**gives, giving, gave, given**)

○ **give a'way**

1 If you **give** something **away**, you give it to someone without taking money in return.
give away something ❏ *She has given away jewellery worth millions of pounds.*
give something away ❏ *I couldn't decide whether to keep the money he left me or give it away.* ❏ *Her little boy was so upset when they gave the dog away.* ● A **give-away** is something which you are given free, for example a free gift that you get when you buy something else. ❏ *There was a give-away calendar on the wall.*

2 If you **give away** secret information, you let other people know about it, sometimes by mistake.
give away something ❏ *I wasn't going to give away more information than I had to.*
give something away ❏ *I haven't seen the film yet so don't give the ending away!* ❏ *He often wondered what Mary thought of him, but she gave nothing away.*
● If someone or something **gives the game away**, they let other people know secret information, sometimes by mistake. ❏ *The wigs stood slightly away from their heads at the back, just enough to give the game away.*
NOTE **Reveal** is a more formal word for **give away**.

3 If someone **gives away** an advantage, they accidentally cause their opponent or enemy to have that advantage. = **concede**
give away something or **give something away** ❏ *We gave away a silly goal.* ❏ *Military advantages should not be given away.*

4 If you **give** yourself **away** or if something that you do or say **gives** you **away**, your actions or words accidentally show something about you which you wanted to keep hidden.
give yourself away ❏ *I didn't dare speak – I was too afraid that I might give myself away by saying something stupid.*
give someone away ❏ *He claimed he was calm but his sweaty hands gave him away.*
NOTE **Betray** is a formal or literary word for **give away**.

5 When people get married in a church, the person who officially presents the bride to her husband during the ceremony **gives** her **away**.
give someone away ❏ *She asked her uncle to give her away.* ❏ *He was going to give his daughter away.*

○ **give 'back**

1 If you **give** something **back** or **give** someone something **back**, you return it to the person who gave it to you or who it belongs to.
give something back ❏ *I gave the book back.* ❏ *[+ to] He gave them back to her.*
give back something ❏ *I gave back his ring and his jacket.*
give someone back something ❏ *I gave her back her newspaper.*
give someone something back ❏ *Did you give me the keys back?*

2 If something **gives back** a quality, characteristic, or freedom that someone has lost, it allows them to have it again.

give back something ❑ [+ to] The new
Parliament at last gave back a voice to those who
had been silent for a generation.

give something back ❑ Now, at last, we can
give hope back to young people.

3 People **give** something **back** when they
do something for a group of people or for
society in return for everything they have
benefited from.

give something back ❑ I don't mind doing it at
all. I've had a great life and now I just want to give a
bit back.

give 'in

1 If you **give in**, you finally agree to do
what someone wants you to do after they
have used force or threats. **= surrender**
❑ He can say what he likes – I won't give in.
❑ [+ to] We mustn't give in to threats.

2 If you **give in**, you finally accept that
someone else has defeated you and you stop
competing. ❑ All right, I give in – what's the
answer?

3 If you **give in** a piece of work, you give it
to a teacher or to someone who will judge
it. **= hand in**

give in something ❑ You have to give in any
project-based work by the end of next week.

give something in ❑ Have you given your essay in?

give 'off

1 When objects or processes **give off** heat,
light, smoke, or sound, they release it into
the air. **= produce**

give off something ❑ I remember the
tremendous heat given off by the fire. ❑ The
brake-pads started to melt, giving off a smell like
burnt toast.

2 If a person **gives off** a particular quality,
you notice it in their appearance or actions.
= radiate

give off something ❑ He's quiet, thoughtful,
charming and gives off an air of vulnerability. ❑ He
gave off a tremendous intellectual aura.

give 'onto

If a door or window **gives onto** a particular
place, it leads straight there, or has a view
over it. **= open onto**

give onto something ❑ The narrow steps give
onto St. James's Park. ❑ The door gave onto a path
which led to the house.

give 'out

1 If you **give out** a large number of things,
you give them to a lot of people. **= hand out**

give out something ❑ They also give out
information about courses for teachers of English.
❑ Large sheets of paper were given out.

give something out ❑ Clare made the tea and
I gave it out.

2 If something **gives out**, it stops working,
because it is old, damaged, or used too
much. ❑ Both tyres had finally given out.
❑ I'd been shouting all afternoon and my voice was
about to give out.

NOTE **Pack up** is a more informal
expression for **give out**.

3 When a supply of something **gives out**,
there is no more left. **= run out** ❑ Turn all the
taps on until the water gives out. ❑ The oxygen
gave out.

4 When news or information **is given out**,
it is announced, sometimes unofficially.

be given out ❑ On the same day it was given out
that fresh documents had been discovered.

5 When something **gives out** light, heat,
or a gas, it produces it.

give out something ❑ Tail lights gave out red
reflections onto the wet road. ❑ The stove still gave
out a low heat.

6 If you **give out** a sound, especially a loud,
sudden sound, you make one. **= let out**
[LITERARY]

give out something ❑ He gave out a scream of
pain. ❑ She gave out a loud girlish laugh.

give 'over

1 If you **give over** an activity, you suddenly
stop doing it. [INFORMAL]

give over something ❑ I gave over my restless
tidying and sat by the window.

2 If you tell someone to **give over** or **give
over** doing something, you are asking
them to stop doing something that is
annoying you. **= leave off** [INFORMAL]

give over ❑ If you don't give over, I'll smack you.

give over doing something ❑ Give over
teasing him!

give 'over to

1 If something **is given over to** a particular
activity or purpose, it is used only for that
activity or purpose.

be given over to something ❑ The response
was so great that a whole page had to be given over
to readers' letters. ❑ The hills of the north and west
are given over mainly to sheep farming.

2 If you **give** yourself **over to** something,
you spend all your time and effort on it.
= give up to

give yourself over to something ❑ Once
embarked on a poem, she would give herself over to
the creative process.

3 If you **give** something **over to** someone,
you let them have it, so that they can look
after it or have responsibility for it.

give something over to someone ❑ I'm quite
thankful to be able to give the business over to the
girls now. ❑ The property was formally given over

to us three months ago.

✪ give 'up

1 If you **give up** or **give up** something, you stop doing an activity that you often used to do.

give up something ❑ *Philip has given up smoking.*

give something up ❑ *I used to jog but I gave it up because it was hurting my knees.*

give up ❑ *I used to smoke, but I gave up a couple of years ago.*

2 If you **give up** a plan or belief, you stop believing in it or supporting it.

give up something ❑ *She never completely gave up hope.* ❑ *By this time I'd given up the idea of becoming a writer.*

3 If you **give up** or **give up** something that you are trying to achieve, you stop doing something, often because it is too difficult.

give up something ❑ *Even Ruskin gave up the attempt in despair.* ❑ *She couldn't persuade him, although she never gave up trying.*

give something up ❑ *I tried various different approaches and then gave it up altogether.*

give up ❑ *Once you've set yourself a goal, the main thing is not to give up.*

4 If you **give** something **up**, you allow someone else to have it, because you no longer need it or they need it more than you do.

give something up or **give up something**
❑ [+ to] *They expect us to give our seats up to them in buses.* ❑ *He even gave up his bed so that Daniel could have a good night's sleep.*

NOTE **Relinquish** is a formal word for **give up**.

5 If you **give** yourself **up**, you allow yourself to be arrested or captured.
= **surrender**

give yourself up ❑ *He went straight to the local police station and gave himself up.* ❑ *Goodall again urged him to give himself up.*

6 To **give** someone **up** who is wanted by the police means to tell the police where that person is so that they can be arrested.
= **betray**

give someone up ❑ *They questioned her forcefully, but still she wouldn't give me up.*

7 If you **give up** someone that you are having a relationship with, you end the relationship.

give someone up or **give up someone** ❑ *Her father disapproved of her boyfriend but Taylor refused to give him up.* ❑ *He wanted me to give up all my other friends.*

NOTE **Throw over** is a more informal expression for **give up**.

8 If you **give up** your time, you spend time doing something for someone else.

give up something ❑ [+ to-infinitive] *These people give up their Saturday mornings to help us out.* ❑ *She gives up her time for the benefit of the local community.*

9 If you **give up** your job, you stop doing it.
= **quit**

give up something or **give something up** ❑ *She'd had to give up her job.* ❑ *I see that you gave up teaching to nurse your mother.* ❑ *The job wasn't suiting him so he gave it up, and found another.*

10 If you **give up**, you stop trying to guess the answer to a question or a joke. ❑ *I give up. Who did you meet this morning?*

11 If you say that you **give up**, you are saying that you are angry or disappointed about a situation and are not prepared to make any more effort to change it. [INFORMAL] ❑ *I give up, I really do. After everything we've done for her, you'd think she'd be a bit more grateful.*

12 If you ask an audience to **give it up for** a performer, you are asking the audience to clap them. [INFORMAL] ❑ *Ladies and gentlemen, please, give it up for Miss Tara Jones!*

○ give 'up on

If you **give up on** someone or something, you stop trying to do something that involves them, because you decide that you will never succeed. = **abandon**

give up on someone/something ❑ *Ever hopeful, McKellen never gave up on the cinema.* ❑ *I can do better, really I can. Don't give up on me.*

○ give 'up to [LITERARY]

If you **give** yourself **up to** a particular thing you give all your attention, time or energy to it. = **give over to**

give yourself up to something ❑ *She gave herself up to the sensation.* ❑ *In the years that followed, he gave himself up to his teaching.*

glance /glɑːns, glæns/ (glances, glancing, glanced)

○ 'glance at

If you **glance at** something or someone, you look at them very quickly and then look away again immediately.

glance at something/someone ❑ *He glanced at his watch.* ❑ *He quickly glanced at Moira to see her reaction.*

○ 'glance off

If something **glances off** an object, it hits the object at an angle and bounces away in another direction.

glance off something ❑ *The ball glanced off his foot into the net.* ❑ *Sun glanced off the window of the house opposite.*

lare /gleə/ (glares, glaring, glared)
'glare at
If you **glare at** someone or something, you look at them with an angry expression on your face.
glare at someone/something ❑ *The old woman glared at him.* ❑ *He glared at the map.*

laze /gleɪz/ (glazes, glazing, glazed)
glaze 'over
If your eyes **glaze over**, you show by your expression that you are bored and not paying attention. ❑ *I could see people's eyes start to glaze over at this point.* ❑ *His eyes glazed over as he looked at the list of technical terms.*

litch /glɪtʃ/ (glitches, glitching, glitched)
glitch 'out [INFORMAL]
If a machine or a system **glitches out**, it stops working because of an error. ❑ *Rather than suggest that I retry the stage, the game simply glitched out.*

lom /glɒm/ (gloms, glomming, glommed)
'glom onto [AMERICAN, INFORMAL]
If someone **gloms onto** something or someone, they become very interested in them or try to stay near them or be associated with them.
glom onto something/someone ❑ *This was simply an effort to glom onto the Hispanic vote.*

lory /'glɔːri/ (glories, glorying, gloried)
'glory in
If you **glory in** a situation or activity, you behave in a way which shows that you enjoy it very much. = **revel in**
glory in something ❑ *She gloried in the street markets, full of the fresh fruit and vegetables she hadn't seen at home.*

loss /glɒs, AM glɔːs/ (glosses, glossing, glossed)
gloss 'over
If you **gloss over** a problem or a mistake, you ignore it or deal with it quickly in order to make it seem unimportant.
gloss over something ❑ *I felt that they had glossed over the details.* ❑ *In an election campaign much of this could be glossed over.*

low /gləʊ/ (glows, glowing, glowed)
'glow with
1 If a place **glows with** a colour or a quality, it is bright, attractive, and colourful.
glow with something ❑ *Used together, these colours will make your rooms glow with warmth and vitality.*
2 If someone **glows with** an emotion such as pride or pleasure, the expression on their face shows how they feel.
glow with something ❑ *The new mothers that Amy had met positively glowed with pride.*

glower /glaʊə/ (glowers, glowering, glowered)
○ **'glower at**
If you **glower at** someone or something, you look at them angrily.
glower at someone/something ❑ *He glowered at me but said nothing.*

gnaw /nɔː/ (gnaws, gnawing, gnawed)
○ **'gnaw at**
1 If people or animals **gnaw at** something, they bite it repeatedly.
gnaw at something ❑ *Snails attack living plants and gnaw at the stems.*
2 If an unpleasant feeling or thought **gnaws at** you or your mind, it causes you to keep worrying.
gnaw at someone/something ❑ *The question that gnawed at her now was what Brunner intended to do.* ❑ *Suspicion began to gnaw at him.*

go /gəʊ/ (goes, going, went, gone)
✪ go a'bout
1 If you **go about** a task or problem in a particular way, that is the way you start to deal with it. = **tackle**
go about something ❑ *Clearly we've gone about this the wrong way.* ❑ *Is there any information on how to go about setting up a committee?*
2 When you **go about** a job or regular activity, you continue doing it in your usual way.
go about something ❑ *He wanted to be left alone to go about his business.* ❑ *All along the coast, people went about their usual daily chores.*
3 When you **go about** or **go about** a place, you move wherever you want to in a place.
go about something ❑ *I could go about the house as freely as I liked.* ❑ *It was quite possible to go about the streets without attracting attention.*
go about ❑ *He wanted to keep me at home, to stop me going about.*
4 If you **go about** doing something bad to other people, you often do it. = **go around** [BRITISH]
go about doing something ❑ *He has to learn that he can't go about hurting others like that.* ❑ *You can't just go about telling people how to lead their lives!*
5 If you **go about** or **go about** a place in a particular way, you usually dress or behave in that way. = **go around** [BRITISH]
go about ❑ [+ in] *Why couldn't he be like other*

men and go about in his shirt sleeves? ❑ He goes about in his jeans most of the time.

go about something ❑ He goes about the city in a long fur coat.

6 If two or more people **go about**, they regularly meet and go to different places together. ❑ [+ with] You used to go about with him a lot. ❑ [+ together] They rarely went about together.

7 If a story or piece of news **goes about** or **goes about** a place, a lot of people hear it or talk about it. = go around [BRITISH]

go about ❑ It was rumoured that he was going to leave. All sorts of stories were going about.

go about something ❑ There's a rumour going about the office.

NOTE **Circulate** is a more formal word for **go about**.

○ **go 'after**

1 If you **go after** someone, you follow them or chase them.

go after someone ❑ Don't you think you should go after Frederica? She seemed quite upset.

2 If you **go after** something, you try to get it.

go after something ❑ Go after a better deal. ❑ He needs a goal – something he can go after.

○ **go a'gainst**

1 If something **goes against** an idea, principle, or rule, it does not agree with it or is the opposite of it.

go against something ❑ I can't do it. It goes against everything I've ever believed in.

2 If you **go against** someone or their advice or wishes, you do something different from what they have advised you or want you to do.

go against someone/something ❑ One thing must be understood. I will never go against you. ❑ They want to assert themselves, even if it means going against their parents' wishes at times.

3 If a decision, judgment or vote **goes against** someone, it is not the final result that they wanted. ≠ favour

go against someone ❑ Decisions went against him at crucial moments in all three games. ❑ He threatened to resign if the vote went against him.

4 If something **goes against** you, it happens in a way that is bad for you.

go against someone ❑ At this point, the war was going against them. ❑ It seemed like everything was going against him.

5 If one group of soldiers **goes against** another, they attack them.

go against someone ❑ They had picked three hundred men to go against the British.

○ **go a'head**

1 When someone **goes ahead** with something which they planned or asked permission to do, they begin to do it, and when a plan **goes ahead**, it begins.

❑ [+ with] They are going ahead with the project. ❑ The election will go ahead immediately.

NOTE **Proceed** is a more formal word for **go ahead**.

● If you give the **go-ahead** for a plan, or give someone the **go-ahead**, you give permission to someone to start doing something. ❑ You have the go-ahead from the Prime Minister.

2 If you tell someone to **go ahead**, you are telling them they are allowed to do something. [INFORMAL] ❑ 'Would you like to hear it?' – 'Go ahead.' ❑ 'May I take this chair?' – 'Sure, go ahead.'

3 If someone **goes ahead**, they go in front of someone else who is going in the same direction or to the same place. ❑ You go ahead this time, we'll stay behind. ❑ [+ of] The minibus went ahead of us.

4 A **go-ahead** person or organization tries hard to succeed, often by using modern methods. = enterprising ❑ James is her go-ahead young assistant. ❑ The minister promised a 'dynamic and go-ahead Britain'.

○ **go a'long**

1 If you **go along** in a particular direction or manner, you move in that direction or manner. ❑ I went along to the recording room. ❑ We were going along at seventy miles an hour when it happened.

2 When you **go along**, you go to a place, often without planning it before. ❑ There was a leaving party for a colleague after work so I thought I'd go along and see who was there. ❑ I'm going along to keep Sara company.

3 If you do something **as** you **go along**, you do it while you are doing something else, sometimes without planning, rather than doing it as a separate task. ❑ Add everything up as you go along. ❑ I recited poems that I made up as I went along.

4 If you describe how something **is going along**, you describe how it is progressing. [INFORMAL]

be going along ❑ Both projects were going along nicely. ❑ I've got a cold but apart from that, everything is going along just fine.

○ **go a'long with**

1 If you **go along with** a person or idea, you agree with the person or idea, and accept that what they are saying is true. = support

go along with someone/something ❑ I tend

to go along with Adam on this one. ❑ I go along with the view that languages are essentially communication systems.

2 If you **go along with** a rule, decision, or plan, you accept it.

go along with something ❑ You agreed to go along with the decision. ❑ He is convinced that Rogers will go along with the deal.

NOTE **Abide by** is a more formal expression for **go along with**.

◗ **go a'round** (or **go round** [mainly BRITISH])

1 If you **go around** or **go around** a group of people or places, you visit or go to see people or places, one after the other.

go around ❑ Michelle, will you quickly go round and collect the books up? ❑ They want someone to go around collecting money.

go around something ❑ I want to go around the art galleries while I'm in London. ❑ I hate going around people's houses, asking for money.

2 If you **go around** or **go around** a country or other place, you travel in a country or other place and visit a lot of different things.

go around ❑ Interlaken was a very good centre for going around and seeing things.

go around something ❑ I'd like to go round Africa myself. ❑ He was going around the world during his gap year.

3 If you **go around** a room, building, or other area, you walk through every part of it.

go around something ❑ He went round the room and examined the windows. ❑ He took four hours to go round the golf course.

4 If you **go around** an area, you do a journey around the edge of it.

go around something ❑ Let's go around the block before we go in. ❑ When I run, I go around the park four times.

5 If a person or a vehicle **goes around** a bend, they move in a curving direction.

go around something ❑ The car went around the bend, and vanished from view.

6 If you **go around** or **go around** an object, you move in a circular direction so that you can get past something or get to the other side of it.

go around something ❑ He went around the table.

go around ❑ She went round to the back of the car again.

7 If you **go around** or **go around** a place in a particular way, you often dress or behave in that way. **= go about**

go around ❑ The kids just go around barefoot.

❑ [+ in] She goes round in jeans and trainers most of the time.

go around something ❑ Ann says Auntie Jo goes around the house with no clothes on in the mornings.

8 If you **go around** doing something bad, you often do it. **= go about**

go around doing something ❑ I don't go around deliberately hurting people's feelings. ❑ You mustn't go around telling people things that aren't true.

NOTE go about

9 If two or more people **go around**, they regularly meet and go to different places together. **= go about** ❑ [+ with] Don't go around with them. ❑ [+ together] Do you think it's wise for us to go round together like this?

10 If a story or piece of news **goes around** or **goes around** a place, a lot of people hear it or talk about it. **= go about**

go around ❑ A rumour went around that they were splitting up. ❑ A lot of strange stories began going around.

go around something ❑ These days there aren't so many jokes going around the office. ❑ There was a rumour going around the office that she was about to resign.

11 If an illness **goes around** or **goes around** a place, a lot of people get the illness.

go around ❑ 'There's a virus going around,' he said. 'My wife had it last week.'

go around something ❑ There are all sorts of bugs going around the school.

12 If there is enough of something to **go around**, there is enough of it to be shared among a group of people. ❑ There were never enough textbooks to go around. ❑ But the fact remains that there is plenty of food to go around.

○ **'go at** [INFORMAL]

If you **go at it**, you start doing something in a very energetic or enthusiastic way. ❑ The breakfast arrived and he went at it as if he hadn't eaten for a week. ❑ I had a lot to do today so I went at it flat-out.

◑ **go a'way**

1 If you **go away**, you leave somewhere. ❑ She went away to think about it. ❑ I want to be alone now. Just go away.

2 If you **go away**, you leave your home and spend time somewhere else, especially as a holiday. ❑ She had gone away for a few days. ❑ What did you do over the summer? Did you go away?

● A bride's **going-away** outfit is the set of clothes which she puts on after the wedding before leaving on honeymoon. [OLD-FASHIONED] ❑ I changed into my going-away outfit.

3 If something, especially a problem, **goes away**, it disappears. ≠ **come back**
❑ Sometimes the fever lasts for a day or two and then goes away. ❑ I have this feeling of dread about the whole thing that just won't go away.

⊕ **go 'back**

1 If you **go back**, you return to a place where you were before. ❑ [+ to] I have to go back to the US next week. ❑ I went back to the kitchen to continue cooking. ❑ It started to rain so I went back for my umbrella.

2 If something **goes back** to a particular time in the past, it has existed since that time. = **date back** ❑ [+ to] The shop goes back to 1707. ❑ These customs go back a long way.

3 If you **go back**, you consider things that happened at a time in the past. ❑ To trace its origins, we have to go back some thirty million years. ❑ [+ to] To understand this state of affairs, we have to go back to colonial days.

4 If you say that someone cannot **go back**, you mean that they can never again be in a situation that they were in before, because important things have changed.
not go back ❑ However much he wished it, he couldn't go back. ❑ He had left home and there was no going back.

5 When schools or schoolchildren **go back**, they start a new term after the holidays.
≠ **break up** ❑ The schools go back next week.

6 When people on strike **go back**, they end the strike and start working again. ≠ **come out** ❑ I say to those men, if you give in and go back now, many of you will lose your jobs.

7 When something which you have bought or borrowed **goes back**, you take it to the place where you got it, sometimes in order to change it. ❑ These shoes are too small – they'll have to go back. ❑ [+ to] The glasses have gone back to the wine shop.

8 When **the clocks go back** in Britain in the autumn, people change their clocks to be one hour earlier, to Greenwich Mean Time. ≠ **go forward**

9 If people **go back** a period of time, they have known each other for that amount of time.
go back something ❑ We go back more than twenty years.

● If people **go back a long way**, they have known each other for a long time. ❑ Roy and I go back a long way. We met at college, almost thirty years ago.

○ **go 'back on**

If you **go back on** a promise, agreement, or statement, you do not do what you promised or agreed, or you say something which is the opposite of what you said earlier.
go back on something ❑ It wouldn't be fair to go back on those promises. ❑ I can't go back on my word. ❑ Now you're going back on what you told me earlier.

○ **go 'back over**

If you **go back over** something, you consider or examine it again.
go back over something ❑ He went back over his calculations to check that they were right.

⊕ **go 'back to**

1 If you **go back to** something which you stopped doing or using, you start doing or using it again.
go back to something ❑ No, I'm all right, go back to sleep. ❑ Now go back to your work!
❑ She had gone back to staring out of the window.

2 If you **go back to** a point in a discussion or conversation, you start talking about it again.
go back to something ❑ To go back to Ian's point about the sales figures, we need to ask ourselves why this is happening. ❑ Going back to what you said earlier, we simply don't have the budget for this.

3 If a situation **goes back to** a state, it returns to the state it was in before something else happened.
go back to something ❑ We solved our problems and things soon went back to normal.
NOTE **Revert to** is a more formal expression for **go back to**.

4 If someone **goes back to** to a partner that they had previously left, they start living with them again or having a relationship with them again.
go back to someone ❑ After a while, she left him and went back to her husband.

○ **go be'fore**

In meaning 2, the stress is on **'go**.

1 You refer to what **has gone before** when you are referring to previous events, for example when you are comparing a situation with one in the past. ❑ The meeting was different from any that had gone before.
❑ Each stage depends on what has gone before.

2 If a person, problem, or case **goes before** a judge, court of law, or other authority, it is officially considered so that a decision or judgment can be made.
go before someone/something ❑ The matter has gone before a grand jury. ❑ The soldier went before a military judge last week.

○ **go be'low**

On a boat, if you **go below** or **go below** deck you go down the stairs into the living or sleeping area.

go below ❑ James went below and returned with two coils of rope.

go below something ❑ We even went below deck to check it out.

go be'yond

To **go beyond** a particular thing means to be better, bigger or more extreme than something else.

go beyond something ❑ In this series I have tried to go beyond the narrower meaning of the word 'civilised'. ❑ This was not just a hobby – it went beyond that. It was an obsession.

go 'by

> In meaning 4, the stress is on **'go**.

1 If a period of time **goes by**, it passes. ❑ Eight years went by. ❑ As time goes by more devices come on to the market. ❑ Sometimes hours go by without him saying a word. ● **Bygone** means happening or existing a very long time ago. ❑ This was a home built to the standards of a bygone age.

2 If someone or something **goes by**, they pass you without stopping. ❑ A car came along the street and I paused to let it go by. ❑ I saw her go by just now.

3 If someone **goes by** or **goes by** a place, they go somewhere for a short time in order to do or get something. = **drop by** [AMERICAN]

go by something ❑ Let's go by the store and get some food.

go by ❑ I could go by on my way home and pick them up.

4 If you **go by** a particular thing, you use the information that it gives you in order to do or understand something. = **go on**

go by something ❑ As for quantity, I usually go by the instructions on the packet.

5 If you let someone's remark or action **go by**, you ignore it and do not allow it to upset you. ❑ He made another irritating comment but I let it go by.

6 If you **go by** a rule, you obey that rule.

go by something ❑ You have to be consistent and go by the rules.

● If you **go by the book** you do everything according to the rules. ❑ Police say they had no choice but to go by the book when they arrested a 97-year-old woman for failing to stop at the lights.

go 'down

1 When someone or something **goes down** or **goes down** something, they move from a higher position to a lower one.

go down something ❑ Frank went down the hill as fast as he could. ❑ I tripped as I was going down the stairs.

go down ❑ [+ to] I felt like a diver going down to the bottom of the ocean. ❑ We went down in the lift.

2 When someone or something **goes down**, they collapse or fall over. = **fall down** ❑ He heard an explosion and saw Jefferson go down.

3 If you **go down** in a building, you move downstairs. ❑ Could you go down and see who's at the door? ❑ Together they went down to breakfast.

4 If you **go down**, you visit a place, especially a place that is farther south than you or is in the country. ❑ [+ to] I have to go down to Brighton this weekend. ❑ You ought to go down there some time.

5 If someone **goes down** a place such as a pub or a club, they go to that place to spend some time there. [BRITISH, INFORMAL, SPOKEN]

go down something ❑ Come on, Jim, let's go down the pub.

6 Something that **goes down** to a particular point or in a particular direction reaches that point or goes in that direction. ❑ [+ to] One road goes north, the other one goes down to Ullapool. ❑ The steps go down to the river. ❑ A steep slope went down towards open meadows.

7 If the cost, level or amount of something **goes down**, it becomes lower or less than it was before. ≠ **go up** ❑ We expect the price of food to go down. ❑ The Democratic vote actually went down by 1.6 per cent. ❑ The water level had gone down.

NOTE **Decrease** is a more formal word for **go down**.

8 If something **goes down**, its quality or standard becomes worse. ❑ It used to be a really nice hotel, but it's gone down since then. ❑ The neighbourhood has gone down a lot in recent years.

NOTE **Deteriorate** is a more formal word for **go down**.

9 If a tyre, balloon, or other object with air inside **goes down**, it becomes flatter or softer because air from it escapes. ❑ I pumped up that tyre but it's gone down again.

NOTE **Deflate** is a more formal word for **go down**.

10 To **go down** means to happen. = **happen** [INFORMAL] ❑ Hey, what's going down?

11 If a swelling on your body or skin **goes down**, it becomes less swollen or disappears completely. ❑ My ankle was really swollen at the weekend but it's gone down now.

12 When something **goes down** in a particular way, it causes a person or people to react in that way. ❑ [+ with] He told one or two funny stories which went down well with Jane and Rebecca. ❑ I told my boss I was taking the week off, which didn't go down too well. ❏ *This ruling would go down badly in Britain and Germany.*

13 If food or drink **goes down** well, people enjoy eating or drinking it. [INFORMAL] ❏ *A cup of tea would go down nicely.* ❏ *The chocolate cake went down well.*

14 When the sun or moon **goes down**, it moves down in the sky until you can no longer see it. ≠ **come up** ❏ *We watched the sun go down over the ocean.*

15 If a plane **goes down**, it falls to the ground. ❏ *His plane went down in the desert.*

16 If a ship **goes down**, it sinks. ❏ *The ship went down and all its 350 passengers died.*

17 If someone **goes down fighting**, they fight or argue in a determined way although they know they are being defeated. ❏ *She was determined to go down fighting.*

18 In sport, if a person or team **goes down**, they are defeated. = **lose** ❏ *Rafter went down by three sets to one.*

19 In sport, if a person or team **goes down**, they move to a lower position in an official list, or to a lower division in a league. ≠ **go up** [BRITISH] ❏ *Cambridge are almost certain to go down at the end of the season.*

20 If something **goes down** in writing, it is written down. ❏ *Whatever we said went down in her notes.*

21 If a computer **goes down**, it stops working for a time. ❏ *The whole system went down just after lunch.*

22 When university students **go down**, they leave university, especially at the end of their degree course, or at the end of term. ≠ **go up** [BRITISH, OLD-FASHIONED]

23 When someone having sex **goes down**, they start kissing or sucking their partner's genitals. [INFORMAL, RUDE] ❏ [+ on] *He asked her to go down on him.*

○ **go 'down as**
If someone or something **goes down as** a particular thing, they are remembered for being that thing.
go down as something ❏ *For this achievement alone, he will go down as one of the great leaders of the twentieth century.*

○ **go 'down on**
If you **go down on** your hands or knees, you lower your body until it is supported by your hands and knees. = **get down**
go down on something ❏ *I went down on one knee and asked her to marry me.* ❏ *He went down on his hands and knees and crawled forward slowly.*

○ **go 'down with**
If you **go down with** an illness such as a cold, you become ill with it.

go down with something ❏ *I was feeling tired and ill and finally went down with gastric flu.* ❏ *I hope I'm not going down with something.*

NOTE **Contract** is a more formal word for **go down with**.

⊙ **'go for**

1 If you **go for** a particular thing, you choose it or try to achieve it.
go for something ❏ *They urged the Chancellor to go for the first option.* ❏ *I think we might go for an even bigger project.*

● If you tell someone to **go for it**, you are encouraging them to choose a particular thing or to attempt to do something difficult. [INFORMAL] ❏ *You're going to train to do a marathon? Hey, go for it!*

2 If you **go for** someone or something, you like them very much. [INFORMAL]
go for someone/something ❏ *I don't really go for men with big muscles.*

3 To **go for** someone or something is to attack them.
go for someone/something ❏ *He went for me with the bread-knife.*

4 If you say that a statement you have made about one person or thing **goes for** another person or thing, you mean that the statement is also true of the second person or thing.
go for someone/something ❏ *You need to work harder, Rosa. The same goes for you, Tom.* ❏ *Life is like an experiment for him and that goes for his art as well.*

5 If something **goes for** a particular price, it is sold for that amount. = **fetch**
go for something ❏ *Some old machines go for as much as £35,000.* ❏ *That house over there went for £2m.*

6 If you **have** a particular thing **going for** you, that thing gives you an advantage in a situation. [INFORMAL] ❏ *I mean he's young – he's got that going for him.* ❏ *She has a lot going for her. She's intelligent, popular and pretty.*

○ **go 'forth** [LITERARY]
When someone **goes forth**, they leave the place where they are, usually in order to do a task. ❏ *They went forth into battle.*

○ **go 'forward**

1 If something **goes forward**, it makes progress and begins to happen.
❏ *Preparations were going forward for the annual Music Festival.*

● People use **going forward** to indicate that they are talking about plans for the future. ❏ *Going forward, how should we divide up the work.*

2 If someone's name **goes forward**, they are suggested as a candidate for a job or in an election. ❏ He has allowed his name to go forward.

3 ● When **the clocks go forward** in Britain in the spring, people set their clocks one hour later, to British Summer Time. ≠ **go back**

○ **go 'in**

1 When you **go in**, you enter a building. ❏ Let's go in and have some coffee. ❏ I pushed open the door of the office and went in.

2 When soldiers **go in**, they enter an area where there is fighting and try to deal with that situation. ≠ **pull out** ❏ They will be deciding if and when the troops should go in. ❏ The third American seaborne attack was going in.

3 When you **go in**, you go to a place of work or a hospital in order to work or receive treatment. ❏ He'll still be in hospital then. He's going in for a minor operation. ❏ She didn't go in yesterday. She wasn't well enough.

4 When someone **goes in** or **goes in** an organization, they join an organization. ≠ **come out**

go in ❏ With her qualifications, she should go in at a fairly high level.

go in something ❏ I thought you were going in the army.

5 If something **goes in** or **goes in** a container, object, or opening, it fits into it.

go in something ❏ The box is probably too big to go in the car. ❏ All those things could easily go in the dining-room cupboard.

go in ❏ The key wouldn't go in.

6 If a structure or piece of equipment **goes in**, it is built or put somewhere. ❏ The heaters will be the last things to go in. ❏ A new paved street went in.

7 If the sun **goes in**, it goes behind a cloud and can no longer be seen. ≠ **come out** [BRITISH] ❏ It's cold when the sun goes in.

8 If information **goes in** when you read or hear it, you understand and remember it. = **sink in** [INFORMAL] ❏ Nothing seemed to go in. ❏ I read this stuff over and over but it just doesn't go in.

○ **go 'in for**

1 If you **go in for** a particular type of thing, you like it and regularly do it or use it.

go in for something ❏ I don't really go in for team sports. ❏ I've never gone in for scarves – I don't know why.

2 If you **go in for** a particular type of work, you decide to do it as your career. = **go into, take up**

go in for something ❏ At one time I even thought of going in for teaching.

3 If you **go in for** a competition, you take part in it.

go in for something ❏ When they called her to tell her she'd won, she couldn't even remember going in for the competition.

NOTE Enter is a more formal word for **go in for**.

○ **go 'into**

1 When you **go into** a room, building, or area, you enter it.

go into something ❏ She went into the bedroom and shut the door. ❏ They went into the garden. ❏ Clem had to go into town on business.

2 When soldiers **go into** a place where there is fighting, they enter that place and try to deal with the situation.

go into something ❏ Ground troops went into the region last November.

3 When you **go into** a place of work or a hospital, you go there in order to work or receive treatment.

go into something ❏ He still goes into work most days. ❏ Her mother has to go into hospital for an operation next week.

4 If you **go into** a particular type of work, you decide to do it as your career. = **go in for, take up**

go into something ❏ Have you ever thought of going into journalism? ❏ I didn't want to go into politics.

5 If you **go into** an organization, you join it.

go into something ❏ More women are now choosing to go into the police force.

6 If you **go into** a particular subject, you describe it fully or in detail. = **discuss**

go into something ❏ He went into the matter in some detail. ❏ 'Did he say why he was leaving?' – 'No, he didn't go into it.'

7 If you **go into** a particular subject, you examine it in detail.

go into something ❏ I didn't have time to go into the subject in any depth.

8 If someone **goes into** a speech or sudden laughter, they start speaking or laughing. = **launch into**

go into something ❏ He went into a long monologue on the subject. ❏ At this, both girls went into screams of laughter.

9 When someone or something **goes into** a particular state or situation, they begin being in that state or situation.

go into something ❏ Hours passed and he went into a coma. ❏ Thompson, meanwhile, had gone into hiding. ❏ On the third lap, the Italian went into the lead.

10 If you **go into** an election, competition, or exam, you start taking part in it.

go into something ❏ They'll go into the next election with a significant lead. ❏ We're going into this competition with a very strong side.

11 If something such as money or effort **goes into** something, it is spent or used making or doing it.

go into something ❑ *So much of her energy goes into her work.* ❑ *He obviously has no idea how much effort goes into writing a novel.*

12 If something **goes into** something, it is one of the things that it is made of.

go into something ❑ *You may like to know just what goes into the tablets you are swallowing.* ❑ *So what type of information goes into these reports?*

13 If things **go into** a container, they fit in it or are put or kept in it.

go into something ❑ *These documents go into this folder here.* ❑ *She has so many clothes, they won't all go into the case.*

14 If someone or something **goes into** a particular way of moving, they suddenly start moving in that way.

go into something ❑ *The plane went into a nose dive.* ❑ *I went into a skid.*

15 If a vehicle or its driver **goes into** another vehicle or its driver, they hit that vehicle.
= crash into

go into something/someone ❑ *I went into the van in front.* ❑ *Three cars went into him.*

○ **go 'in with**

If you **go in with** someone, you form a business partnership or other close working relationship with them.

go in with someone ❑ *They invited Jarvis to go in with them but he declined.*

❂ **go 'off**

1 If you **go off**, you leave the place where you were, usually in order to do something.
= go away ❑ [+ to] *He'd gone off to work.* ❑ [+ to-infinitive] *She went off to look at the flowers.*

2 If a gun **goes off**, it is fired and if a bomb **goes off**, it explodes. ❑ *He could hear guns going off in the distance.* ❑ *A bomb went off in a busy marketplace, killing over a hundred people.*

3 If an alarm, or something else that makes a loud noise or a sudden light, **goes off**, it suddenly operates. ❑ *David's alarm went off at 6:30 this morning.* ❑ *A thousand flashbulbs went off as the singer got out of her car.*

4 If a light, heating system or electric device **goes off**, it stops operating. ≠ **come on** ❑ *The light only goes off at night.* ❑ *The heating's gone off and I'm freezing.*

5 If a broadcasting station or a show **goes off the air**, it stops broadcasting or being broadcast. ❑ *Both radio stations have since lost their funding and are now going off the air.* ❑ *It's been three years since this hugely popular programme went off the air.*

6 If an event or arrangement **goes off** well, it is successful or happens without any problems. ❑ *The meeting went off well.* ❑ *The ceremony went off exactly as planned.*

7 If a road **goes off**, it separates from another road and goes in a different direction. ❑ [+ to] *You need to take the road that goes off to the right.*

8 To **go off** on a different subject is to start discussing or covering a subject that is not related to what you were discussing or covering before. ❑ *I was going to ask him about his work, but he went off on a different subject.*

● If you **go off at a tangent**, you suddenly start talking about a subject that is not related to what you were talking about before. ❑ *He was telling us about his holiday when he suddenly went off at a tangent and started talking about the legal system.*

9 If you **go off** someone or something, you stop liking them. [BRITISH, INFORMAL]

go off someone/something ❑ *She was really into him but I think she's gone off him a bit recently.* ❑ *He was going to study chemistry but he's gone off the idea.* ❑ *I've gone off fish recently.*

10 If you **go off** a drug, you stop taking it.
= come off; ≠ go on

go off something ❑ *There's been such bad publicity about the drug lately that a lot of people are going off it.*

11 If you **go off**, you fall asleep. **= drop off** [INFORMAL] ❑ [+ to] *She went off to sleep at 10.00.* ❑ *I nearly went off in the middle of the film.*

12 If food or drink **goes off**, it stops being good to eat because it is too old. [BRITISH] ❑ *Drink it up within a week or so or it will go off.* ❑ *I think this fish has gone off.*

NOTE **Decay** is a more formal word for **go off**.

○ **go 'off on**

1 If someone **goes off on** you, they get very angry with you. [AMERICAN, INFORMAL]

go off on someone ❑ *He really went off on me.*

2 If someone **goes off on one**, they speak very angrily about something for a long time. [INFORMAL] ❑ *She went off on one in the meeting.*

○ **go 'off with**

1 If someone **goes off with** another person, they leave their husband, wife, or usual partner and have a relationship with that person. **= run off with**

go off with someone ❑ *My boyfriend went off with my best friend.* ❑ *His wife went off with a guy she met on a dating website.*

2 If someone **goes off with** something that belongs to someone else, they leave a place, taking that thing with them. **= make off with**

go off with something ❑ *Don't let him go off with your papers.* ❑ *Carol's gone off with my car key so I'm stuck here.*

✪ go 'on

> In meanings 12, 18, 20, and 22, the stress is on **'go**.

1 If you **go on** doing something, or **go on** with an activity, you continue to do it. **= carry on**

go on doing something ❑ *I went on writing.* ❑ *While she was pouring out their drinks, she went on talking.*

go on ❑ [+ with] *She stopped for a moment and then went on with what she was doing.*

2 If something **goes on** throughout a period of time, it continues to happen or exist. ❑ *The noise went on and on.* ❑ *The fighting had gone on all through the night.* ❑ *The strike went on for over a year before it was finally settled.*

• An **ongoing** situation continues to happen. ❑ *Nothing must be allowed to interfere with the ongoing investigation.* ❑ *The discussions are ongoing.*

3 To **go on** means to happen. **= happen** ❑ *Hey, what's going on?* ❑ *When I asked what was going on, she refused to say anything.* • **Goings-on** are activities that are strange, shocking or amusing. ❑ *Jane was telling me all about the goings-on at work.*

4 If you **go on** to do something, you do it after you have finished something else. ❑ [+ to-infinitive] *He later went on to form a successful band.* ❑ *She told us about Jeremy, and then went on to talk about his children.*

5 If you **go on**, you continue to the next part or stage of something. ❑ [+ to] *Once you have given the correct answer to the problem in step one you can go on to step two.* ❑ *I'm planning to go on and study for my masters degree next year.*

6 If you **go on** in a particular direction, you continue to travel or move in that direction. ❑ *I went on up the hill.* ❑ *Go on ahead of me and I'll catch up.*

7 If you **go on**, you go to another place, having visited a first place. ❑ [+ to] *We might go on to Italy after France.* ❑ *If you're not too tired we could go on somewhere else after.*

8 You say that land or a road **goes on** for a particular distance, when you are talking about how big or long it is. ❑ *The wide sand beach seems to go on forever.* ❑ *The road goes on for three hundred miles in that direction.*

9 If a period of time **goes on**, it passes. **= wear on** ❑ *As time went on, I got more and more depressed.* ❑ *The sun got hotter as the afternoon went on.*

10 If someone **goes on**, they continue talking. ❑ *'You know,' he went on, 'it's extraordinary.'.* ❑ *She knew he wasn't listening, but she went on all the same.* ❑ *He went on for 35 minutes without a pause.*

11 If someone **goes on**, they continue talking to you about the same thing, often in an annoying way. [INFORMAL] ❑ [+ at] *My dad keeps going on at me to have a smoke alarm fitted.* ❑ [+ about] *He's a nice enough guy but he does go on a bit.*

12 You say **Go on** to someone to encourage them to do something. **= come on** [INFORMAL] ❑ *Go on, have a biscuit.* ❑ *Go on, give her a call!*

13 You say **Go on** to someone to show that you do not believe what they have said. **= get away** [INFORMAL, OLD-FASHIONED] ❑ *Go on – you didn't say that!*

14 You say **Go on** to someone to agree to something they suggest. [INFORMAL] ❑ *'Would you like another biscuit?' 'Oh, go on then.'*

15 If you **go on** something that you have noticed or heard, you base an opinion or judgment on it.

go on something ❑ *I'm only going on what Rebecca told me.* ❑ *He had nothing to go on. There were no clues.*

16 If a light, machine, or other device **goes on**, it begins operating. **= go off** ❑ *The light goes on automatically.* ❑ *What time does the heating go on in the mornings?*

17 If an object **goes on**, it fits onto or around another object. **≠ come off** ❑ *He went back to the rifle. The silencer went on easily.* ❑ *He sat down to put on his shoes and socks. The shoes would hardly go on.*

18 If something, especially money, **goes on** something else, it is spent or used on that thing.

go on something ❑ *90 per cent of their income goes on basic living expenses.* ❑ *Most of her money goes on clothes and make-up.*

19 When an actor or actress **goes on**, they walk onto a stage. ❑ *I was just about to go on when I heard the news.*

20 If you **go on** a drug, you start taking it. **≠ come off**

go on something ❑ *She went on medication that seemed to make her better.*

21 If you say that someone **is going on** a particular age, you mean that they are nearly that age. [INFORMAL]

be going on something ❑ *Renata was going on fifty and divorced.* ❑ *I'm thirty-four now, going on thirty-five.*

22 If you **are gone on** someone, you are in love with them. [INFORMAL, OLD-FASHIONED]

be gone on someone ❑ *I was a bit flattered because he was so gone on me.*

○ **go 'on with** [INFORMAL]
If you say that you have enough of something **to be going on with**, you mean that you have enough for the present time. ❑ *You also have a report to write and two appraisals so that's enough to be going on with.*

♦ **go 'out**

1 When you **go out**, you leave a room, building, or other place. ≠ **come in** ❑ *He picked up his bag and went out, locking the door behind him.* ❑ *Why don't we go out into the garden?* ❑ *[+ of] She went out of the building and through the main gate.*

2 When you **go out**, you leave your house and go somewhere else. ≠ **stay in** ❑ *I'm just going out for a short while.* ❑ *[+ for] I thought we could go out somewhere for a picnic.* ❑ *Shall we go out tonight or would you prefer to stay in?* ❑ *I went out last night to a party.*

3 If two people **go out**, they have a romantic or sexual relationship with each other. = **date** ❑ *[+ with] My parents wouldn't let me go out with boys.* ❑ *She went out with him when she was a student.* ❑ *[+ together] Joe and Kate have been going out together for over a year.*

4 If you **go out**, you travel to a place, especially somewhere abroad or far away. ❑ *They want me to go out West and do a movie.* ❑ *They might find you a seat on some flight going out tonight.* ● **Outgoing** traffic or an **outgoing** plane or passenger is travelling away from the place where you are. ❑ *They searched all outgoing traffic.* ❑ *The sign said 'incoming and outgoing passengers'.*

5 If you say that someone **goes out and** does something, you mean that they actually do it and do not just talk or think about it. [INFORMAL] ❑ *Saying that we need something is very different from going out and fighting for it.* ❑ *Personally, I think he should go out and get a job.*

6 If news or a message **goes out**, it is announced or sent, often officially. ≠ **come in** ❑ *The news went out from Washington that he was dead.* ❑ *[+ to] Letters have already gone out to our members.* ● An **outgoing** message, letter, or phone call is one sent or made from the place where you are. ≠ **incoming** ❑ *They deal with outgoing mail.*

7 Money that **goes out** is spent on bills and regular expenses. ≠ **come in** ❑ *This helps you to keep a track of the money coming in and the money going out.* ● You use **outgoings** to refer to the money which you have to spend regularly, for example in order to pay your rent or bills. = **expenses** ❑ *We have a lot of outgoings.*

8 If a television or radio programme **goes out**, it is broadcast. [BRITISH] ❑ *The series goes out on Tuesday evenings on BBC 2.*

9 If a light **goes out**, it stops shining. ≠ **come on** ❑ *The lights suddenly went out in the big tent.*

10 If a fire or something that is burning **goes out**, it stops burning. ❑ *The fire had gone out, and we were both cold.*

11 If a person or team **goes out**, they are defeated in a game and therefore can no longer take part in a competition. ❑ *Cambridge went out in the first round.* ❑ *[+ of] Newcastle went out of the competition, losing 2-0.*

12 If something **goes out**, it stops being fashionable or used, and is replaced with something else. ≠ **come in** ❑ *[+ of] Styles can go out of fashion overnight.* ❑ *Frilly shirts for men went out years ago.* ❑ *Steam went out and diesel was introduced.*

13 If something **goes out**, someone gets rid of it because they no longer want or like it. ❑ *She suddenly decided she didn't like the sofa so that went out.*

14 When the tide **goes out**, it falls, so that the water does not reach so far up the beach. ≠ **come in** ❑ *The tide's going out now.*

15 An **outgoing** person is very friendly and confident with other people. = **extrovert** ❑ *She was a very outgoing and popular girl.*

16 You use **outgoing** to describe a person who has had an important job or position but who is now being replaced by someone else. ≠ **incoming** ❑ *Congress opened with an address by the outgoing president.*

○ **go 'out for** [AMERICAN]
To **go out for** something means to try to do it or be chosen for it.
go out for something ❑ *You should go out for Supreme Court Justice.* ❑ *In seventh grade Mark went out for all three sports.*

○ **go 'out of**
If a quality, especially a positive quality, **goes out of** someone or something, it leaves them.
go out of someone/something ❑ *All the vitality and originality seems to have gone out of him.* ❑ *Somehow, the vigour has gone out of the debate.*

♦ **go 'over**

1 When you **go over**, you move towards someone or something and reach them. ❑ *[+ to] I went over to her and had a few words.* ❑ *[+ to-infinitive] I went over to congratulate the parents.* ❑ *The phone on her desk rang.*

Eva went over and picked it up.

2 If you **go over**, you go to someone's house and visit them for a short time. **= go round**
❑ *There was a phone message from Jeremy, asking me to go over the next evening.* ❑ [+ to] *Can we go over to Ella's today?* ❑ *He had often invited me to go over and stay.*

3 If you **go over** to a place overseas, you travel there. ❑ [+ to] *My editor asked me to go over to England to cover a British general election.* ❑ *I've never been to Paris – I might go over there this summer.*

4 If you **go over** something, you examine or discuss each part of it, especially to make sure that someone understands it or that it is correct.
go over something ❑ *Could you go over the instructions with him and check that he understands them?* ❑ *I'll ask David to go over the figures before the meeting.* ● If you give something a **going-over**, you examine it carefully. [INFORMAL] ❑ *They had been giving our report a careful going-over.* ❑ *His room had received a thorough going-over.*

5 If you **go over** something that has happened or something that someone said, you think about it again.
go over something ❑ *I sat there, going over and over her words in my mind.* ❑ *I keep going over what happened, wondering if I could have done anything different.*

6 If someone gives you a **going-over**, they attack you violently, usually as a punishment or a warning. [INFORMAL]
❑ *Someone had given young Allen a very thorough going-over indeed. 'What happened this time?' I asked.*

7 If something **goes over** in a particular way, that is how people react to it. ❑ *I got him to sing 'Sonny Boy', but it didn't go over very well.* ❑ *I wondered how such a session would go over in America.*

○ **go 'overboard**
If someone **goes overboard**, they react more strongly or act more extremely than you think they should. ❑ *I'd be annoyed if I were you, but I think you're going a little bit overboard.* ❑ *They went overboard and said that it was the best film they'd ever seen.*

○ **go 'over to**
1 In a war, if someone **goes over to** the enemy, they join them and start fighting on their side.
go over to someone ❑ *At this point some troops mutinied and went over to the enemy.* ❑ *Some local chiefs have gone over to the opposition in the south.*
2 If someone or something **goes over to**

a different way of doing things, they change to it.
go over to something ❑ *They went over to the American system.* ❑ *We have recently gone over to the new method and it's proving a great success.*

○ **go 'round**
1 → see **go around**
2 If you **go round**, you go to someone's house and visit them for a short time. **= go over** [mainly BRITISH] ❑ *I'll go round and see Nell later.* ❑ *We went round to see him.* ❑ [+ to] *I went round to Clive's house.*
3 If a person or vehicle **goes round**, they move in a circular direction. ❑ *The speedboat driver has to stop or go round in circles.*
4 If something **goes round**, it turns continuously like a wheel. ❑ *The wheels of the bicycle were going round so fast that the spokes blurred into one.* ❑ *The blue light was going round and round on top of the police car.*
NOTE Revolve is a more formal word for **go round**.

○ **go 'through**

In meaning 3, the stress is on **'go**.

1 If you **go through** an event or period of time, especially an unpleasant one, you experience it. **= undergo**
go through something ❑ *Not all girls go through this stage.* ❑ *She went through hell trying to get her son back.*
2 If someone or something **goes through** an official procedure, they do all the things that are required.
go through something ❑ *She would have to go through all the legal formalities.* ❑ *Did you go through a passport check at the airport?*
3 If you **go through** a person or organization, you ask them to deal with a matter, and if a matter **goes through** a person or organization, it is dealt with by them.
go through someone/something ❑ *You have to go through the Head of Department.* ❑ *Both bills are currently going through parliament.*
4 If a law, agreement, or official decision **goes through**, it is agreed by the people who have the power or authority to do so.
❑ *Eventually, the adoption went through.* ❑ *We believed the deal would not be allowed to go through.*
5 If you **go through** or **go through** a room, you enter that room and cross it.
go through something ❑ *She went through the kitchen and out of the back door.* ❑ *We went through a large room into a smaller one.*
go through ❑ [+ to] *Eva went through to the galley.*
6 If you **go through** a town or country, you travel across it.

go through something ❑ *You must be going through Frankfurt anyway.* ❑ *Did you go through Italy?*

7 If you **go through** a lot of things such as papers or clothes, you examine them, usually in order to sort them into groups or to search for something. = **look through**

go through something ❑ *They went through her belongings.* ❑ *I began going through my pockets. Nothing was missing.*

8 If you **go through** a list, document or plan, you describe or discuss each part of it. = **run through**

go through something ❑ *You'd better go through the names, just to check they're all there.* ❑ *I'll just go through the instructions again.* ❑ *Secretary Cox went through the treaty, point by point.*

9 If someone **goes through** a series of actions or movements, they perform it.

go through something ❑ *They watched Molly going through some of the movements she had learned.* ❑ *The music started and we went through a series of warm-up exercises.*

10 If you **go through** a supply of something, you use it all. = **get through**

go through something ❑ *We've gone through three boxes of cereal in under a week.*

NOTE **Consume** is a more formal word for **go through**.

11 If something such as a piece of clothing **goes through**, a hole appears in it, because it has been used so much. = **wear through**

❑ *I noticed that his jacket had gone through at the elbows.*

12 In sport, if a person or team **goes through**, they win one stage of a competition and go on to the next stage. ❑ *Spain beat South Korea 3–1 and look set to go through.* ❑ [+ to] *West Germany go through to Sunday's final in Rome.*

○ **go 'through with**

If you **go through with** a decision or an action, you continue to do what is necessary in order to achieve it or complete it, although this may be difficult or unpleasant.

go through with something ❑ *Rather than go through with the marriage, she ran away.* ❑ *I thought about taking them to court but decided I just couldn't go through with it.*

○ **go to'gether**

1 If two things **go together**, they are often found with each other. ❑ *Power and money go together.* ❑ *Fear and hatred seem to go together.*

2 If two people **go together**, they have a romantic or sexual relationship with each other. = **go out** [AMERICAN] ❑ *We've been going together for two years.*

○ **'go towards**

1 If one thing **goes towards** another, it provides part of it.

go towards something ❑ *Most of the calories in our food go towards maintaining our body temperature.*

2 If an amount of money **goes towards** something, it is used as part of its cost.

go towards something ❑ *My bonus will go towards a deposit on the flat.* ❑ *Any money received from now on will go towards aid for future victims.*

○ **go 'under**

1 If something, especially a business, **goes under**, it fails. = **collapse** ❑ *Ten thousand small businesses have gone under.* ❑ *The smaller institutions could well go under during a recession.*

2 If someone or something in the water **goes under**, they sink below the surface of the water. ≠ **come up** ❑ *I bent my head back in an effort to keep my face above water but went under again.*

3 If land or trees **go under** something, such as the plough or the axe, they are destroyed or cut down.

go under something ❑ *The park had largely gone under the plough.* ❑ *Woods were going under the chain-saw right across the country.*

❍ **go 'up**

1 When someone or something **goes up** or **goes up** something, they move from a lower position to a higher one.

go up something ❑ *We saw a party of mountaineers going up the mountain.* ❑ *When I tried to go up the stairs he pushed me aside.*

go up ❑ [+ to] *Rockets went up to the moon.*

2 If you **go up** in a building, you move upstairs. ❑ [+ to] *She went up to her bedroom.* ❑ *We went up to the sixth floor.* ❑ *We can go up in the elevator.*

3 If you **go up**, you move towards someone or something until you are standing next to them. ❑ [+ to] *I went up to Clem where he sat smoking.* ❑ *Go up and introduce yourself.*

4 If you **go up**, you visit a place, especially when the place is farther north than you or is in a city. ❑ [+ to] *We went up to Manchester at the weekend.* ❑ *We'll go up to London early next week.*

5 Something that **goes up** to a particular point or in a particular direction, reaches that point or goes in that direction.

❑ [+ to] *An area of pine trees went up to a high ridge.* ❑ *A steep slope went up to a wood.* ❑ *One road goes up north to Inverness.*

6 If the cost, level or amount of something **goes up**, it becomes higher or more than it was before. **= rise; ≠ come down, go down** ❑ *The price of petrol and oil related products will go up steadily.* ❑ [+ to] *The budget is set to go up to $400 million.* ❑ *The crime rate has gone up alarmingly.*

noun + GO UP
tax goes up
bills go up
the price of something goes up
wages go up
the cost of something goes up
❑ *The cost of raw materials has gone up again.* ❑ *Tax on cigarettes has gone up.*

7 If you **go up** when you are making an offer or suggesting an amount, you increase the original offer or amount. ❑ *I'll go up as high as fifty pounds, but no further.*

8 If a building, wall, or other structure **goes up**, it is built or fixed in place. **≠ come down** ❑ *Small blocks of apartments are going up all over the city.* ❑ *Posters went up all over town.*

9 If a curtain **goes up**, it is raised. **≠ come down** ❑ *There was a burst of applause as the curtain went up.*

10 If something **goes up**, it explodes or suddenly starts to burn. ❑ *In seconds the whole structure had gone up in flames.* ❑ *With a huge explosion, another fuel-tank went up.*

11 If a cheer, shout, or other noise **goes up**, a lot of people cheer, shout, or make that sound at the same time. ❑ *A huge cheer went up as the players walked out onto the court.* ❑ *A kind of gasp went up from the tables.*

12 When university students **go up**, they begin a degree course or return to university at the start of term. **≠ go down** [BRITISH, OLD-FASHIONED] ❑ [+ to] *Before going up to Oxford, I started a diary.*

13 In sport, if a person or team **goes up**, they move to a higher position in a list, or to a higher division in a league. **≠ go down** [BRITISH] ❑ *I think Stoke will go up this season.*

○ **go 'up against**
If one person or organization **goes up against** another person or organization, they compete with them.
go up against someone/something ❑ *A number of retailers in America have gone up against Wal-Mart and survived.*

○ **'go with**
1 If one thing **goes with** another, they suit each other or are pleasant or attractive together.
go with something ❑ *The sofa doesn't really*

go with the carpet. ❑ *Do you think that mushrooms go with salmon?*

2 If one thing **goes with** another, the two things often exist or are found together.
go with something ❑ *He enjoyed his wealth and all the privileges that went with it.* ❑ *She describes really well the fatigue that goes with having a small baby.*

NOTE **Attend** is a formal word for **go with**.

3 If one thing **goes with** another, the second thing is provided with the first.
go with something ❑ *Do you remember the house that went with his old job?* ❑ *I didn't want the thirty acres of land that went with the place.*

4 If you **go with** a plan, idea, or the people who are suggesting it, you decide to support them and try to make them succeed.
go with something/someone ❑ *I think we should go with Pete's earlier suggestion.*

5 If someone **goes with** another person, they have a sexual or romantic relationship with them. [INFORMAL, RUDE]
go with someone ❑ *He certainly never went with other women.*

○ **go with'out**
If you **go without** or **go without** something, you do not have something that you usually have or would like. **= do without**
go without something ❑ *The family went without food all day.* ❑ *How long could you go without sleep?*
go without ❑ *If they couldn't get coal, they had to go without.*

goad /ɡəʊd/ (**goads, goading, goaded**)
○ **goad 'into**
If you **goad** someone **into** doing something they did not want to do, you make them angry so that they do it.
goad someone into something ❑ *You were practically goading him into a fight.* ❑ *He was goaded into losing his temper.*

○ **goad 'on**
If someone **goads** you **on**, they try to make you do something, especially something bad, often by making you angry. **= spur on**
goad someone on or **goad on someone** ❑ *The crowd goaded him on with insults and abuse.*

gobble /'ɡɒbəl/ (**gobbles, gobbling, gobbled**)
○ **gobble 'down** (or **gobble up**) [INFORMAL]
If you **gobble down** food, you very quickly eat all of it. **= wolf down**
gobble down something or **gobble something down** ❑ *He gobbled down the two remaining eggs.* ❑ *Daisy loved her lunch – she gobbled it up.*

○ **gobble 'up**

1 If an organization **gobbles up** a smaller organization, it takes control of it or destroys it.
gobble up something or **gobble something up** ❑ They have built an empire in the mid-west by gobbling up smaller banks.

2 If something **gobbles up** money or resources, it uses or takes a lot of them.
gobble up something or **gobble something up** ❑ Research and development now gobble up a sizeable chunk of the military budget. ❑ British agriculture gobbled up more energy than it produced. ❑ Graduates are having a tough time finding jobs, as the Internet companies which gobbled them up in the nineties, are no longer able to do so.

3 → see **gobble down**

goggle /ˈɡɒɡəl/ (**goggles, goggling, goggled**)

○ **'goggle at**

If you **goggle at** something or someone, you stare at them with your eyes wide open, usually because you are surprised by them.
goggle at something/someone ❑ I goggled at her clothes, a casual jacket in dazzling colours worn over a blue T-shirt and black ski-pants. ❑ She goggled at me.

goof /ɡuːf/ (**goofs, goofing, goofed**)

○ **goof a'round** [mainly AMERICAN, INFORMAL]

If someone **goofs around**, they spend their time doing silly things. = **mess around**
❑ There was nothing to do but goof around all day long. ❑ She was goofing around in front of the camera.

○ **goof 'off** [AMERICAN, INFORMAL]

If you **goof off**, you spend your time doing silly things, often when you should be doing something more important. ❑ God help you if I catch you goofing off at the mall. ❑ We love hanging out and goofing off.

NOTE In British English, **skive off** is an informal expression for **goof off**.

○ **goof 'up** [AMERICAN, INFORMAL]

If you **goof up**, you make a mistake or do something very badly. ❑ The burglars goofed up by turning up when there were people in the house.

gouge /ɡaʊdʒ/ (**gouges, gouging, gouged**)

○ **gouge 'out**

If you **gouge** something **out**, you cut, pull or dig it with great force from the place where it is, using your fingers, a tool, or a machine.

gouge out something or **gouge something out** ❑ We watched a bulldozer gouging out a huge hole in the rock.

grab /ɡræb/ (**grabs, grabbing, grabbed**)

○ **'grab at**

1 If you **grab at** an object or person, you suddenly try to take hold of them.
grab at something/someone ❑ She grabbed at my shoulder for support. ❑ One of the men grabbed at my bag.

2 If you **grab at** a chance to do something, you accept it eagerly.
grab at something ❑ Why didn't you grab at the chance to go to New York?

graduate /ˈɡrædʒʊeɪt/ (**graduates, graduating, graduated**)

○ **'graduate from**

If you **graduate from** something, you go from a less important job or position to a more important one.
graduate from something ❑ He has graduated from TV commercials and is now making movies.

○ **'graduate to**

If you **graduate to** something, you go from a less important job or position to a more important one.
graduate to something ❑ Bruce graduated to chef at the Bear Hotel. ❑ From commercials she quickly graduated to television shows.

graft /ɡrɑːft, ɡræft/ (**grafts, grafting, grafted**)

○ **graft 'onto**

1 If a piece of healthy skin or bone or a healthy organ **is grafted onto** a damaged part of your body, it is attached to that part of your body by a medical operation.
be grafted onto something ❑ The top layer of skin has to be grafted onto the burns.

2 If you **graft** one idea or system **onto** another, you try to join one to the other.
graft something onto something ❑ The new managers tried to graft their own methods onto this different structure.

grapple /ˈɡræpəl/ (**grapples, grappling, grappled**)

○ **'grapple with**

1 If you **grapple with** a problem or difficult task, you try many different methods to solve it, do it or understand it.
grapple with something ❑ I grappled with this moral dilemma. ❑ He was one of the few scientists who had seriously grappled with these problems.

2 If you **grapple with** a person or animal, you take hold of them and struggle with them, as part of a fight. = **wrestle with**

grapple with someone/something ❏ *He was grappling with an alligator in a lake.*

grasp /grɑːsp, græsp/ (**grasps, grasping, grasped**)

○ **'grasp at**

1 If you **grasp at** an object, you suddenly try to take hold of it. = **grab at**
grasp at something ❏ *She grasped at my arm as she fell.*

2 If you **grasp at** an opportunity, you try to take advantage of it, even though you know you are not likely to succeed.
grasp at something ❏ *Such is the severity of the situation that these people will grasp at any chance to escape it.*

3 If you **grasp at straws**, you try anything that you think might possibly help you because you are desperate. = **clutch at**
❏ *I didn't really think it was the answer to our problems – I was just grasping at straws.*

grass /grɑːs, græs/ (**grasses, grassing, grassed**)

○ **'grass on** [BRITISH, INFORMAL]
If one person **grasses on** another, the first person tells the police or other authorities about something criminal or wrong which the second person has done.
grass on someone ❏ *The men were caught only when other inmates grassed on them.*
NOTE **Inform on** is a more formal expression for **grass on**.

○ **grass 'over**
To **grass over** an area of ground means to plant or lay grass all over it.
grass over something or **grass something over** ❏ *You've grassed over the back garden, I see.* ❏ *If you don't want to plant up that area, you could just grass it over.*

○ **grass 'up** [BRITISH, INFORMAL]
If one person **grasses up** another, the first person tells the police or other authorities about something criminal or wrong which the second person has done.
grass up someone or **grass someone up** ❏ *[+ to] How many of them are going to grass up their own kids to the police?*

gravitate /'græviteit/ (**gravitates, gravitating, gravitated**)

○ **'gravitate towards**
If you **gravitate towards** a particular place, thing, or activity, you are attracted by it and go to it or get involved in it.
gravitate towards something ❏ *Traditionally young Asians in Britain have gravitated towards medicine, law and engineering.* ❏ *In the supermarket, I always gravitate towards the meat.*

green (**greens, greening, greened**)

○ **green 'up**

1 If a person or company **greens** something **up**, they try to make it be or seem more environmentally friendly.
green something up or **green up something** ❏ *He is trying to encourage people to green up their own lifestyle.* ❏ *The president is trying to green up his image.*

2 If grass or plants **green up**, they become greener and healthier. ❏ *Don't worry, the lawn will soon green up again after some decent rainfall.*

grey /greɪ/ (**greys, greying, greyed**)

○ **grey 'out**
If text on a computer screen **is greyed out**, it appears in grey to indicate that it is not active and you cannot click or tap on it.
be greyed out ❏ *The 'Delete' button is greyed out for me.*

grieve /griːv/ (**grieves, grieving, grieved**)

○ **'grieve over**
If you **grieve over** someone who has died or something sad, especially someone's death, you feel very sad about it.
grieve over someone/something ❏ *He's grieving over his dead wife and son.*

grill /grɪl/ (**grills, grilling, grilled**)

○ **'grill about** [INFORMAL]
If you **grill** someone **about** something or someone, you ask them a lot of questions about them in a forceful way.
grill someone about something/someone ❏ *I apologize for grilling you about your friends.* ❏ *She grilled me about what we were doing last night.*

grind /graɪnd/ (**grinds, grinding, ground**)

○ **grind a'way** [INFORMAL]
To **grind away** means to work very hard for a long period, usually doing a boring task. = **plug away** ❏ *[+ at] Millions of children today are forced to spend precious hours of their lives grinding away at pointless tasks.* ❏ *I keep grinding away and one day, I might even finish the job.*

○ **grind 'down**

1 If someone or something unpleasant **grinds** you **down** over a long period, they gradually cause you to feel depressed and without hope. = **wear down**
grind someone down or **grind down someone** ❏ *The poverty was grinding her down.* ❏ *The kids were so horrible day in, day out and eventually, it just ground me down.* ❏ *Ground down after years of mistreatment, they gave in to all his demands.*

2 To **grind** something hard **down** is to rub it against another hard surface or machine until it becomes smooth or worn.
grind something down or **grind down something** ❏ *The stone is then ground down to the desired shape.* ❏ *The hardest rock in the world will be ground down in time.*

○ **grind 'into**
If you **grind** something **into** a surface, you press and rub it hard into the surface using small circular or sideways movements.
grind something into something ❏ *'Well,' I said, grinding my cigarette nervously into the ground.*

○ **grind 'on**
When something **grinds on**, it continues in a boring way for a long time. ❏ *Slowly the meeting ground on.* ❏ *I wished I could stop his voice grinding on and on.*

○ **grind 'out**
1 If a person or machine **grinds out** information or work, they produce a lot of similar information or work, often in a way that is boring. **= churn out** [INFORMAL]
grind out something or **grind something out** ❏ *Most US film directors spend their careers grinding out movies that will make money.* ❏ *For years, the press would grind these books out, and no one ever read them.*
2 If you **grind out** a lighted cigarette, you press it down with your hand or foot in order to stop it burning. **= stub out**
grind out something or **grind something out** ❏ *She finished her cigarette and ground it out with the heel of her shoe.* ❏ *Cigarette ends had clearly been ground out on the carpet.*

○ **grind 'up**
If you **grind** something **up**, you completely crush it until it becomes a fine powder.
grind up something or **grind something up** ❏ *The seeds are ground up to make a paste.* ❏ *It is not easy to grind it up in a coffee grinder.*

groan /grəʊn/ (**groans, groaning, groaned**)
○ **'groan about**
If you **groan about** something, you complain about it.
groan about something ❏ *His parents were beginning to groan about the price of college tuition.*

○ **'groan under**
If you say that something such as a table **groans under** the weight of food, you are emphasizing that there is a lot of food on it.
groan under something ❏ *The bar counter groans under the weight of huge plates of the freshest fish.*

groom /gruːm/ (**grooms, grooming, groomed**)
○ **'groom for**
If you **are groomed for** a special job, someone prepares you for it by teaching you the skills you will need.
be groomed for something ❏ *George was already being groomed for the top job.*

grope /grəʊp/ (**gropes, groping, groped**)
○ **'grope for**
1 If you **grope for** something that you cannot see, you try to find it by moving your hands around in order to feel it.
grope for something ❏ *With his left hand he groped for the knob.*
2 If you **grope for** a word or a solution to a problem, you try to think of it, when you have no real idea what it could be.
grope for something ❏ *They were groping for a new strategy.* ❏ *She groped for a simple word to express a simple idea.*

gross /grəʊs/ (**grosses, grossing, grossed**)
○ **gross 'out** [mainly AMERICAN, INFORMAL]
If something **grosses** you **out**, it makes you feel disgusted.
gross someone out or **gross out someone** ❏ *The thought of kissing him grossed me out.* ❏ *My daughter was so grossed out by the state of the washrooms, she refused to use them.*
NOTE **Disgust** is a more formal word for **gross out**.
● If you describe something such as comedy or humour as **gross-out**, it makes you feel disgusted. [AMERICAN, INFORMAL] ❏ *There's something about their gross-out humour that is hilarious.* ● A **gross-out** is something which makes you feel disgusted. [AMERICAN, INFORMAL] ❏ *The film ends in a series of gross-outs.*

grow /grəʊ/ (**grows, growing, grew, grown**)
○ **grow a'part**
If people who have a close relationship **grow apart**, they gradually start to have different opinions and interests from each other, and their relationship starts to fail. **= drift apart** ❏ *We met when we were still at school, and we have simply grown apart over the years.*

○ **grow a'way from**
If you **grow away from** someone, you develop different opinions and interests from them so that you gradually feel less close to them.
grow away from someone ❏ *In truth, also, she had grown away from her friends.*

grow 'into

1 If you **grow into** a job or situation, you gradually learn how to do it or deal with it well.

grow into something ❏ *He's really grown into the role in the six months that he's been here.*

2 If a child **grows into** an item of clothing, he or she becomes taller or bigger so that the clothing fits properly.

grow into something ❏ *It's a bit big, but she'll soon grow into it.*

grow on

If someone or something **grows on** you, you start to like them, although you did not like them at first.

grow on someone ❏ *I wasn't so sure about her at first, but she's grown on me.* ❏ *The landscape has a simple beauty which grows on you.*

grow 'out

If you **grow out** a hairstyle or let it **grow out**, you let your hair grow so that the style changes or so that you can cut off the part that you do not want.

grow out something or **grow something out** ❏ *I let my hair go darker and grew out my fringe.* ❏ *If you don't like the colour, you can always grow it out.*

grow out ❏ *The red rinse had grown out completely.*

grow 'out of

1 If a child **grows out of** an interest or way of behaving, they stop being interested in something or behaving in a particular way because they have grown older. **= outgrow**

grow out of something ❏ *I've rather grown out of my taste for ice cream.* ❏ *It's just a phase – he'll grow out of it.*

2 If a child **grows out of** an item of clothing, he or she becomes so tall or big that the clothing no longer fits them properly.

grow out of something ❏ *The coat cost a small fortune and she grew out of it in three months.* ❏ *She keeps growing out of all her clothes.*

3 If a child **grows out of** an illness, they stop suffering from it as they grow into an adult.

grow out of something ❏ *There are some allergies that children simply grow out of.*

4 If one idea or plan **grows out of** another, it develops from it.

grow out of something ❏ *She'd had an idea for a story that grew out of a dream.* ● An **outgrowth** of something is a natural development from it or result of it. ❏ *This theory was an outgrowth of Einstein's 'unified field theory'.*

grow 'up

1 When a child **grows up**, they gradually change into being an adult. ❏ *I grew up in New York.* ❏ *She grew up on a farm outside Albany.* ❏ *Children seem to grow up so fast these days.*

● A **grown-up** is an adult. [INFORMAL] ❏ *There are ten children coming to the party and five grown-ups.* ● **Grown-up** children are someone's children who are now adults. ❏ *They had grown-up children of their own.*

● If you say that a child is being **grown-up**, you mean that he or she is behaving in a mature way. ❏ *Your brother's very grown-up for his age.*

2 If you tell an adult to **grow up**, you are telling them in an angry way to stop behaving in a silly or childish way. [INFORMAL] ❏ *You're upset because she's giving the baby more attention than you? Grow up, Gene!*

3 When a place, organization, or idea **grows up**, it starts to exist and becomes larger or more important. **= develop** ❏ *Cities grew up as markets, centres of religion or trade.* ❏ *The idea has grown up that science cannot be wrong.*

grow 'up on

If you **grow up on** something, it is an important part of your childhood and has had a strong influence on you.

grow up on something ❏ *Tony grew up on tales of London politics.* ❏ *My parents loved country music so I grew up on it.*

grub /grʌb/ (**grubs, grubbing, grubbed**)

grub a'round (or grub about [mainly BRITISH])

If you **grub around**, you search for something by moving things or by digging. **= root about** ❏ [+ in] *She was grubbing around in the mud as if she'd dropped her keys or something.* ❏ *I spend my life grubbing about in these drawers, looking for a pen that works.*

grub 'up (or grub out)

If you **grub up** a tree or plant, you dig it out of the ground.

grub up something or **grub something up** ❏ *They grubbed up roots and gathered berries.*

guard /gɑːd/ (**guards, guarding, guarded**)

'guard against

If you **guard against** something bad, you do what is necessary to make sure that it does not happen or does not affect you.

guard against something ❏ *He wore a hard hat to guard against head injury.* ❏ *Jealousy is something to be particularly guarded against.*

guess /ges/ (**guesses, guessing, guessed**)

'guess at

If you **guess at** something, you imagine it because you do not know the real facts about it or you have no experience of it.

guess at something ❑ *We can only guess at the number of deaths it has caused.* ❑ *I can only guess at his state of mind at the time.*

gulp /gʌlp/ (gulps, gulping, gulped)

○ **gulp 'down**

If you **gulp down** food or drink, you eat or drink it all very quickly by swallowing large quantities of it at a time.

gulp down something or **gulp something down** ❑ *After gulping down his breakfast, he hurried to the station.* ❑ *I made a quick coffee, gulped it down and left the house.*

gum /gʌm/ (gums, gumming, gummed)

○ **gum 'up**

1 If your eyes **are gummed up**, they are blocked by a sticky substance so that it is difficult to open them.

be gummed up ❑ *When he woke in the morning his eyes were all gummed up.*

2 To **gum up** a system means to stop it working properly or efficiently. [INFORMAL]

gum something up or **gum up something** ❑ *The federal government is often criticized for being gummed up with inefficient processes.*

gun /gʌn/ (guns, gunning, gunned)

○ **gun 'down**

To **gun** someone **down** means to shoot them when they are not in a position to defend themselves.

gun down someone or **gun someone down** ❑ *Nobody has ever gunned down a New York police captain and gotten away with it.* ❑ *They gunned him down in broad daylight.*

○ **'gun for** [INFORMAL]

If someone **is gunning for** you, they are trying in a very determined way to harm you or cause you trouble.

be gunning for someone ❑ *I certainly don't want to have half the school gunning for me.*

gussy /'gʌsi/ (gussies, gussying, gussied)

○ **gussy 'up** [AMERICAN, INFORMAL]

If you **gussy up** someone or something, you make them smarter, more attractive or more interesting.

gussy up someone/something ❑ *I was here 2000 when the monument was in disrepair, but it" since been gussied up.* ❑ *Gussy up canned soup by adding sliced mushrooms or sauteed onions.*

gut /gʌt/ (guts, gutting, gutted)

○ **gut 'out** [AMERICAN]

If you **gut it out**, you continue doing something in a determined way even though it is difficult and you are not succeeding. ❑ *It wasn't our best game but we gutted it out.*

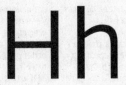

Hh

hack /hæk/ (**hacks, hacking, hacked**)

○ **hack a'bout** (or **hack around**)
If you **hack** something **about**, you make changes to it and cut parts out.
hack something about or **hack about something** ❏ My book's been hacked about terribly by the editor. ❏ You are free to use the software, and hack it about in any way you like.

○ **'hack at**
If you **hack at** something, you try to cut it by hitting it with a sharp tool such as an axe or knife.
hack at something ❏ They hacked at the bushes with an axe.

○ **hack a'way at**
If you **hack away at** something, you cut it by hitting it many times with a sharp tool such as an axe or knife.
hack away at something ❏ He started to hack away at the tree trunk.

○ **hack 'down**
If you **hack** something **down**, you cut it down roughly.
hack down something or **hack something down** ❏ They have to stop hacking down the rain forests. ❏ There were wild shrubs growing everywhere so I hacked them down.

○ **hack 'off**
1 If you **hack** something **off**, you remove it by cutting it roughly. = **chop off**
hack something off or **hack off something**
❏ She had hacked her hair off without caring what it looked like. ❏ He hacked off a branch with an axe.
2 If someone or something **hacks** you **off**, they make you angry. [BRITISH, INFORMAL]
hack someone off or **hack off someone**
❏ All that money being wasted really hacks me off. ❏ His actions hacked off the people who should have supported him. ● If someone is **hacked off**, they are angry about something. ❏ She was jealous and hacked off. ❏ I'm really hacked off with you people!

○ **hack 'through**
If you **hack through** trees or plants growing close together, you move forward by cutting them down roughly.
hack through something ❏ The undergrowth became so thick we had to hack through it.

hail /heɪl/ (**hails, hailing, hailed**)

○ **'hail as**
If someone or something **is hailed as** something or if people **hail** them **as** something, people say publicly that they are very important, successful, or good.
be hailed as something ❏ They were hailed as heroes by the entire country.
hail someone/something as something
❏ He hailed insulin as 'the greatest discovery of modern medicine'.

○ **'hail from** [FORMAL]
If you **hail from** a place, you were born there or live there.
hail from somewhere ❏ I hail from America.

ham /hæm/ (**hams, hamming, hammed**)

○ **ham 'up** [INFORMAL]
If someone **hams** it **up**, they act or perform in a very exaggerated way, often deliberately in order to amuse people. ❏ She was obviously hamming it up for the audience.

hammer /'hæmə/ (**hammers, hammering, hammered**)

○ **hammer a'way at**
1 If you **hammer away at** something, you work on it for some time in a very determined way.
hammer away at something ❏ They hammered away at the problem all morning until they found a solution.
2 If you **hammer away at** someone or something, you keep arguing with them, criticizing them, or attacking them in a very determined way.
hammer away at someone/something
❏ We have to keep hammering away at the government until they admit they're wrong.

○ **hammer 'in**
If you **hammer** something **in**, you force it into place using a hammer.
hammer something in or **hammer in something** ❏ Position the posts in the ground

then hammer them in very firmly. ❑ He hit his thumb while he was hammering in a nail.

○ **hammer 'into**

If you **hammer** something such as an idea or a rule **into** someone, you keep repeating it so that it will have an effect on them.
hammer something into someone ❑ Discipline is hammered into soldiers by the drill sergeant.

○ **hammer 'out**

If you **hammer out** an agreement, you achieve it after a long or difficult discussion.
hammer out something or **hammer something out** ❑ We need to sit down together and hammer out an agreement for the future. ❑ A deal was eventually hammered out.

hand /hænd/ (**hands, handing, handed**)

○ **hand a'round** (or **hand round** [mainly BRITISH])

If you **hand around** things, you pass them to several people in a group.
hand around something or **hand something around** ❑ She handed round the pencils. ❑ He took the tray in and handed the glasses around.

○ **hand 'back**

◼ If you **hand** something **back** or **hand** someone back **something**, you give it to someone after you have borrowed or taken it from them. = **give back**
hand back something ❑ She handed back our passports and waved us through. ❑ [+ to] He handed back his room key to the receptionist.
hand something back ❑ I examined the book, then handed it back. ❑ [+ to] She handed the photo back to the police officer.
hand someone back something ❑ The girl handed him back his card.
◼ If a television or radio reporter **hands back** to someone or something or **hands** the people watching or listening **back**, the programme returns to another studio, place, or reporter.
hand someone back ❑ [+ to] We are now handing you back to our reporter at the scene of the accident.
hand back ❑ [+ to] She delivered her report, then handed back to the studio.

○ **hand 'down**

◼ If something **is handed down** or if someone **hands** it **down**, it is given to by someone to their children or to a younger generation. = **pass on**
be handed down ❑ Is it possible for genius to be handed down? ❑ [+ from] A house or a plot of land can be handed down from generation to generation.
hand something down or **hand down something** ❑ [+ to] He wanted to keep the coins

and hand them down to his kids. ❑ These stories were created to hand down traditions to younger generations. ● **Hand-me-downs** are things, especially clothes, which have been used by other people and then given to you. ❑ I had to wear my elder sister's hand-me-downs.
◼ If an official decision or judgment **is handed down** or if someone **hands** it **down** it is given publicly.
be handed down ❑ The next day the decision was handed down by the jury.
hand down something or **hand something down** ❑ A judge would be likely to hand down a heavy sentence for this kind of crime.

☻ **hand 'in**

◼ If you **hand in** a piece of work, you give it to someone so that they can read it or deal with it.
hand something in ❑ At half-past eleven they handed their exam papers in. ❑ You have to fill out an application form and hand it in.
hand in something ❑ Don't forget to hand in your homework. ❑ [+ to] He handed in the finished version of the novel to the publishers.
◼ If you **hand** something **in**, you give it to someone in authority.
hand something in ❑ She handed the money in, thinking it was probably stolen. ❑ If you find any lost property, please hand it in.
hand in something ❑ He took off his uniform, handed in his badge, and left the building. ❑ All keys have to be handed in before you go.
◼ If you **hand in** your **resignation** or your **notice**, you officially announce that you are going to leave your job. ❑ The Director has handed in her resignation. ❑ I handed in my notice and left.
◼ If you **hand** yourself **in**, you go to the police and tell them that you have committed a crime.
hand yourself in ❑ He walked into a police station and handed himself in.

○ **hand 'on**

If you **hand** something **on**, you give it to your children or to people that live after you. = **pass on**
hand something on or **hand on something** ❑ [+ to] They handed on their knowledge to their children.
be handed on ❑ [+ from] Property is handed on from generation to generation.

☻ **hand 'out**

◼ If you **hand** things **out**, you give them to people in a group so that each person has one or some.
hand out something ❑ There were helpers to guide visitors and hand out leaflets. ❑ [+ to] They

handed out questionnaires to the audience.

hand something out ❏ _The teacher asked me to hand the books out._ ❏ [+ to] _She took sweets and handed them out to the crowd._ • A **handout** is something such as money, clothing, or food that is given free to help someone who needs it. ❏ _He doesn't like relying on handouts._
• A **handout** is a document that is given to people to give them information about something. ❏ _All the books I mention in my talk are listed in the handout._

2 If you **hand out** advice, you tell people what you think they should do.

hand out something or **hand something out** ❏ _If you watch the show they actually hand out some very useful tips._ ❏ _We are happy to take advice as well as hand it out._

3 If a judge or court **hands out** a punishment, they say officially how someone should be punished.

hand out something or **hand something out** ❏ _The court should hand out a really tough sentence in this case._

be handed out ❏ _There is concern that the penalties being handed out do not fit the crime._

hand 'over

1 If you **hand** something **over**, you give it to someone so that they have or own it.

hand something over ❏ _She saw the package, and demanded that he hand it over._ ❏ [+ to] _He had to hand the keys to his car over to the police._

hand over something ❏ _People have handed over large sums of money for work that was never done._ ❏ [+ to] _She refused to hand over the tape to her boss._

2 If you **hand over** to someone or **hand** something **over**, you give another person responsibility for dealing with something.

hand over ❏ [+ to] _The head teacher handed over to his deputy._

hand something over ❏ _I will willingly retire from this investigation and hand it over._ ❏ [+ to] _He recently handed control of the company over to his son._

hand over something ❏ _The detective was forced to hand over the case._ • A **handover** is the process of officially giving responsibility or power to another person or organization. ❏ _The leader refused to agree to a handover of power._

HAND OVER + _noun_

hand over **responsibility**
hand over **control**
hand over **power**
❏ _I am handing over responsibility for the firm to my sister._ ❏ _He is refusing to hand over control of the organization._

3 If someone **hands over** another person, they give the control and responsibility for that person to someone else.

hand over someone ❏ _They refused to hand over the prisoners._ ❏ [+ to] _The children were handed over to their grandparents for the weekend._

hand someone over ❏ [+ to] _We handed the men over to the police._

○ **hand 'over to**

If you **hand over to** someone, you invite or allow them to start talking during a discussion, meeting, or programme.

hand over to someone ❏ _Now let's hand over to our reporter at the scene._

○ **hand 'round** → see **hand around**

○ **'hand to** [INFORMAL]

If you say **you have to hand it to** someone, you mean that you admire them for something and think they deserve praise for it. ❏ _You have to hand it to them, they're wonderful singers._

hang /hæŋ/ (**hangs, hanging, hung**)

✪ **hang a'bout**

1 → see **hang around**

2 If you tell someone to **hang about**, you are asking them to wait or stop what they are doing or saying. [BRITISH, INFORMAL]
❏ _Now hang about, I'm not going to let you get away with a statement like that._

✪ **hang a'round** (or **hang about, hang round** [mainly BRITISH])

1 If you **hang around**, you stay in the same place doing nothing, usually because you are waiting.

hang around ❏ _There didn't seem much point in hanging around any longer._ ❏ _I hung round outside the classroom waiting for her to come out._

2 If you **hang around** a place, you spend time there doing nothing or waiting.

hang around somewhere ❏ _The kids hang around street corners._ ❏ _Taxis hang around the station hoping to pick up tourists._

3 If you **hang around** someone or **hang around** with them, you spend a lot of time with them. [INFORMAL]

hang around ❏ [+ with] _I don't like the people he hangs around with._ ❏ [+ together] _Jo and I used to hang around together at school._

hang around someone ❏ _He was always hanging around his older brother._

○ **hang 'back**

1 If you **hang back**, you stay in a place after everyone else has left. = **stay behind**
❏ _Often I hung back after classes to ask more questions._

2 If someone **hangs back**, they hesitate before doing something, especially because they are afraid or do not want to do it. ❑ *He stepped forward to stroke the horse but the rest of the children hung back.*

3 If you **hang back**, you wait before doing or deciding something. ❑ *Both candidates seem to be hanging back, waiting to see what the other will do.*

○ **hang 'in** [INFORMAL]

If you say to someone **Hang in there!**, you are asking them to wait or remain in a difficult situation, because you believe it will get better. ❑ *Tell him to hang in there and we'll be with him as soon as we can.*

○ **hang 'on**

> In meanings 2 and 5, the stress is on **'hang**.

1 If you **hang on**, you wait for a short time. = **hold on** [INFORMAL] ❑ *I can hang on a bit longer until dinner's ready.* ❑ *Hang on a minute, I'm not ready.*

2 Something that **hangs on** something else depends on it in order to be successful. **hang on something** ❑ *His whole political future hung on this election.*
[NOTE] hinge on

3 If you **hang on**, you hold something very tightly so that you do not fall. = **hold on** ❑ *Hang on tight, everybody! The bus is about to start.*

4 If you **hang on**, you manage to continue in a difficult situation until it gets better. ❑ *Manchester United hung on and eventually won the Cup.*

5 If you **hang on** someone's **words** or **hang on** someone's **every word**, you listen to everything they say in an admiring and interested way. ❑ *She has many admirers who hang on her every word.*

○ **hang 'on in** [INFORMAL]

If someone **hangs on in there**, they manage to remain in a difficult situation until it gets better. ❑ *If you hang on in there, your children will eventually be more able to take care of themselves.*

○ **hang 'onto** (or **hang on to**)

1 If you **hang onto** something, you hold it very tightly in your hands.
hang onto something ❑ *We were both hanging onto the side of the boat.*

2 If you **hang onto** something, you keep it although it may not be useful or valuable.
hang onto something ❑ *Shall I throw these old magazines out, or do you want to hang onto them?*

3 If you **hang onto** power or a position, you manage to keep it when you are in great danger of losing it.
hang onto something ❑ *He is desperately hanging on to his job.*

4 If someone **hangs onto life**, they stay alive when they are in great danger of dying. ❑ *Some of these patients manage to hang onto life for three to four months.*

5 ➔ see **hang on**

❂ **hang 'out**

1 If you **hang out** washing, you hang up clothes that have been washed so that they dry. = **peg out**
hang out something or **hang something out** ❑ *She was hanging out her washing in the garden.* ❑ *If those socks are wet, hang them out on the line.*

2 If you **hang out** somewhere or **hang out**, you spend a lot of time in a place, often not doing very much. [INFORMAL]
hang out somewhere ❑ *I don't hang out at the park any more.*
hang out ❑ *Shall we go to town and just hang out?* • A **hangout** is a place where you like spending time relaxing with other people. ❑ *This café is one of my favourite hangouts.*

○ **hang 'out with** [INFORMAL]

If you **hang out with** someone, you spend time with that person in a social situation.
hang out with someone ❑ *He spends a lot of time hanging out with friends.*

○ **hang 'over**

1 If a problem **hangs over** you, it worries you a lot.
hang over someone ❑ *I had my exams hanging over me.*

2 A **hangover** is an idea or attitude that existed in the past but is no longer important or relevant now. ❑ *That sort of thinking is a hangover from the past.*

3 If someone has a **hangover**, they feel tired and ill because they have drunk too much alcohol. • Someone who is **hungover** feels tired and ill because they have drunk too much alcohol. ❑ *He felt really hungover the morning after the party.*

○ **hang 'round** ➔ see **hang around**

○ **hang to'gether**

If ideas or parts of something **hang together**, they seem to fit well together to form a whole. ❑ *The different elements of the film's plot don't really hang together.*

❂ **hang 'up**

1 If you **hang** something **up**, you attach it in a high place so that it does not touch the ground.
hang something up ❑ *The children hung their coats up.* ❑ *Don't drop your towel on the floor – hang it up.*
hang up something ❑ *They hung up lanterns all around the garden.* ❑ [+ on] *Howard hung up his scarf on a hook behind the door.*

2 Something that **is hanging up** in a high place is attached there so that it does not touch the ground.

be hanging up ❑ *There are some tools hanging up in the shed.*

3 If you **hang up** or you **hang up** the phone, you end a phone call.

hang up ❑ *'Thank you. Goodbye.' He hung up.*
hang up something ❑ *When she heard my voice, she hung up the phone.*

4 If you **hang up** something that you use for a particular activity, you stop using it because you stop doing the activity.

hang up something or **hang something up**
❑ *He used to play a lot of tennis, but now he has hung up his racket.*

5 Someone who is **hung up** worries or thinks about something too much, so that they cannot behave normally. [INFORMAL]
❑ *He was too hung up to relax.* ❑ [+ about] *You're hung up about your father.* ❑ [+ on] *Some people are so hung up on the way they look.* ● A **hang-up** is a feeling of being worried or embarrassed about something that makes it difficult for you to behave normally. ❑ *He's got a hang-up about flying.*

○ **hang 'up on**
If you **hang up on** someone, you suddenly end a phone call to them.

hang up on someone ❑ *He didn't answer. He just hung up on me.*

○ **'hang with** [AMERICAN, INFORMAL]
If you **hang with** people, you spend a lot of time with them.

hang with someone ❑ *She mainly hangs with kids from her school.*

hanker /'hæŋkə/ (**hankers, hankering, hankered**)

○ **'hanker for** (or **hanker after**)
If you **hanker for** something, you want it very much.

hanker for something ❑ *He hankered for a successful diplomatic career.* ❑ *We always hankered after a house of our own.*

NOTE **Crave** is a more formal word for **hanker after**.

happen /'hæpən/ (**happens, happening, happened**)

○ **happen a'long** (or **happen by**)
[OLD-FASHIONED]
If someone or something **happens along**, they arrive or appear by chance. ❑ *She stood at the bus stop and chatted to whoever happened along.* ❑ *You're very lucky I happened by.*

○ **'happen on** (or **happen upon**)
[LITERARY, OLD-FASHIONED]

If you **happen on** someone or something, you find them or meet them by chance.

happen on someone/something ❑ *We happened on them in the street.* ❑ *He happened upon this rare example of Art Nouveau in the home of a colleague.*

NOTE **Come across** is a more common expression for **happen on**.

hare /heə/ (**hares, haring, hared**)

○ **hare 'off** [BRITISH]
If you **hare off**, you run or move quickly away from a place. ❑ *The children hared off down the street.*

hark /hɑːk/ (**harks, harking, harked**)

○ **hark 'back to** [LITERARY]
1 If something **harks back to** another thing in the past, it is similar to it and makes you think of it.

hark back to something ❑ *The pictures harked back to nineteenth-century religious paintings.*
2 If you **hark back to** something, you remember it or remind someone about it.

hark back to something ❑ *Arthur constantly harked back to the theme of money.*

harp /hɑːp/ (**harps, harping, harped**)

○ **harp 'on**
If you **harp on** or **harp on** a subject, you keep on talking about a subject in a way that is annoying.

harp on ❑ [+ about] *Why do you keep harping on about him?*
harp on something ❑ *I'm sorry to harp on this, but we do have to be careful.*

hash /hæʃ/ (**hashes, hashing, hashed**)

○ **hash 'out**
If people **hash** something **out**, they discuss and agree the details of it.

hash out something or **hash something out**
❑ *The Senate will soon have to hash out details of a new tax bill.* ❑ *We'll let them hash it out between them.*

○ **hash 'over** [AMERICAN]
If people **hash over** a subject, they discuss it in great detail.

hash over something ❑ *Let's not waste time hashing over the past.*

hatch /hætʃ/ (**hatches, hatching, hatched**)

○ **hatch 'out**
If an egg or a baby bird or other animal **hatches out** or if a person, bird or animal **hatches** them **out**, the baby bird or animal comes out of the egg by breaking the shell.

hatch out ❑ *If any chicks have hatched out you will hear them cheeping.* ❑ [+ into] *Some of the eggs hatched out into caterpillars.*

hatch something out or **hatch out something**
❑ We left the hens in the shed to hatch out their chicks.

hate /heɪt/ (**hates, hating, hated**)

○ **'hate on**

To **hate on** someone is to express hate for them publicly, for example, on social media.

hate on someone ❑ When people hate on you, it's because you've got something they want.

haul /hɔːl/ (**hauls, hauling, hauled**)

○ **'haul before**

If someone **is hauled before** a court or someone in authority, they are forced to go to court or talk to that person about something they may have done wrong.

be hauled before someone ❑ He was hauled before the managing director and fired.

○ **haul 'in**

1 If the police or someone in authority **hauls** someone **in**, they force that person to go somewhere, usually to answer questions or to be punished.

haul someone in or **haul in someone** ❑ His manager hauled him in for a telling-off.

be hauled in ❑ He was hauled in for questioning about the theft.

2 If you **haul** something **in**, you pull it, often towards you or towards the land.

haul something in or **haul in something**
❑ They were hauled in one by one and unceremoniously dumped on deck.

○ **haul 'off**

If someone **is hauled off**, they are taken by force to a place. = **cart off**

be hauled off ❑ [+ to] Some of the protesters were hauled off to jail.

○ **haul 'up**

If someone **is hauled up**, they have to answer questions from people in authority about something they may have done wrong.

be hauled up ❑ [+ before] He was arrested for assault and hauled up before a judge. ❑ [+ for] A police officer was hauled up for speeding.

● If someone **is hauled up in court**, they have to appear in court accused of a crime.
❑ He got hauled up in court accused of criminal damage.

have /hæv, hæf/ (**has, having, had**)

Have got is often used in informal English in some meanings to mean the same as **have**.

○ **have a'gainst**

If you **have** something **against** someone or something, you do not like them or are angry with them for a particular reason.

have something against someone/ something ❑ My new boss seems to have something against me.

● If you **have nothing against** someone or something, you do not dislike them and are not angry with them. ❑ I have nothing against television, but I think we watch too much.

○ **have a'way** ➜ see **have off**

○ **have 'in**

1 If you **have** someone **in**, you have them doing some work for you in your home or workplace for a period of time.

have someone in ❑ It's not very convenient for you to stay, as we have the painters in.

2 If a shop **has** something **in**, they have it available for people to buy.

have something in ❑ We did have some bread in this morning, but it's all sold out.

○ **have 'off** [BRITISH, INFORMAL, RUDE]

If people **have it off**, they have sex.
❑ [+ with] He's been having it off with his boss.

⊕ **have 'on**

1 If you **have** clothing **on**, you are wearing it.

have something on ❑ He had nothing on so he grabbed a towel. ❑ I can't wait to take these shoes off – I've had them on all day.

have on something ❑ She had on an old bathrobe.

2 If you **have** something **on**, it is switched on and working.

have something on ❑ They have the heating on all night in winter. ❑ I like listening to the radio, and I often have it on when I'm working.

3 If you **have** something **on**, you have arranged to do something.

have something on ❑ I have a lot on this week, so I might not be able to come. ❑ [+ for] Do you have anything on for tomorrow night?

4 If you **have** something **on** you, you are carrying it with you.

have something on you ❑ Do you have any cash on you? ❑ You should have ID on you at all times.

5 If you **are having** someone **on**, you are teasing them by pretending that something is true when it is not true.

be having someone on ❑ Was he having me on when he said he was a doctor?

6 If you **have** something **on** someone, you know some information about them that shows they have done something wrong or illegal.

have something on someone ❑ She was confident that they had nothing on her.

○ **have 'out**

1 If you **have** something **out**, you have a tooth or organ removed from your body by a dentist or doctor.

have something out ❑ *The dentist told him he had to have a tooth out.*

2 If you **have it out with** someone, you have a discussion or argument about something that has been causing problems between you. ❑ *He felt like picking up the telephone and having it out with him.*

○ **have 'over** (or **have round** [BRITISH])

If you **have** someone **over**, you invite them to your house to eat or drink something with you.

have someone over ❑ *I can't come out – I have some people over.* ❑ *[+ for] We're having friends over for dinner tonight.*

○ **have 'up for**

If someone **is had up for** something or if someone **has** them **up for** something, they are officially accused of a crime.

be had up for something ❑ *He knocked someone down and was had up for assault.*

have someone up for something ❑ *They could have you up for libel.*

hawk /hɔːk/ (**hawks, hawking, hawked**)

○ **hawk a'round** (or **hawk about** [BRITISH])

If someone **hawks** something **around** or **hawks** it **around** a place, they take it to several places to try to sell it.

hawk something around ❑ *After the writer's death, his wife hawked his manuscript around.*

hawk something around somewhere ❑ *Pictures of her are being hawked around women's magazines.*

○ **hawk 'round** → see hawk around

head /hed/ (**heads, heading, headed**)

✪ **head 'back**

If you **head back** or **head back** somewhere, you start to return to the place where you came from. ❑ *It's getting late, so we should head back.*

head back somewhere ❑ *We wanted to turn around and head back to L.A.*

✪ **'head for**

1 If you **head for** a place, you start moving towards it. = **make for**

head for something ❑ *We had decided to head for Miami.* ❑ *I headed for the door.*

2 If you **are heading for** or **are headed for** a situation, that situation is likely to happen.

be heading for something ❑ *Mr Reagan was heading for a personal triumph.*

be headed for something ❑ *If you don't change, you are headed for disaster.*

○ **head 'into**

1 If you **head into** a place, you go to that place.

head into something ❑ *I think I'll head into town and get something to eat.*

2 If you **are heading into** a situation or **are headed into** a situation, especially a bad one, you are likely to experience it.

be heading into something ❑ *Their marriage seemed to be heading into a difficult time.*

be headed into something ❑ *The figures suggest that the country may be headed into a recession.*

✪ **head 'off**

1 If you **head off** or **head off** somewhere, you leave a place in order to go somewhere.

head off ❑ *He said goodbye and headed off at a brisk pace.* ❑ *It's late – we should be heading off.*

head off somewhere ❑ *She headed off back down the mountain.*

2 If you **head** someone or something **off**, you try to stop them moving in a particular direction by blocking their way.

head someone/something off ❑ *Police were instructed to head the protesters off.* ❑ *I tried to head him off before he reached the headteacher's office.*

head off someone/something ❑ *After heading off the convoy, the army escorted it to a safe location.*

3 If you **head off** something unpleasant, you prevent it from happening.

head off something or **head something off** ❑ *The company's management was doing its best to head off the crisis.* ❑ *They knew there would be a lot of public anger, but they did nothing to head it off.*

✪ **'head towards**

1 If you **head towards** a place, you move in the direction of that place.

head towards something ❑ *The boat was heading towards shore when the accident happened.*

2 If you **are heading towards** or **are headed towards** a situation or event, that situation or event is likely to happen.

be heading towards something ❑ *We were heading towards disaster.*

be headed towards something ❑ *He said the company is headed towards profitability.*

○ **head 'up**

If you **head up** a group or team, you are in charge of it.

head up something or **head something up** ❑ *Sara will be heading up the sales team.* ❑ *When we opened a new agency, he was the obvious choice to head it up.*

heal /hi:l/ (**heals, healing, healed**)

○ **heal 'over**

When a wound **heals over**, the wounded part becomes healthy and normal again. ❏ *The cut may take a few days to heal over.*

○ **heal 'up**

When an injury **heals up**, the injured part becomes healthy and normal again. ❏ *After his leg had healed up, Tom worked harder than ever.*

heap /hi:p/ (**heaps, heaping, heaped**)

○ **'heap on** (or **heap upon**)

If you **heap** praise or criticism **on** someone or something, you praise or criticize them a lot.

heap something on someone ❏ *The captain heaped praise on his team.* ❏ *The crowd heaped abuse on them.*

○ **heap 'up**

If you **heap** things **up**, you put them on top of each other in a large pile. **= pile up**

heap up something or **heap something up** ❏ *She heaped up pillows around me to make me comfortable.* ❏ *I swept the leaves and heaped them up in the yard.* ● **Heaped-up** things are on top of each other in a large pile. ❏ *There were several heaped-up piles of clothes on the floor.*

○ **'heap upon** → see **heap on**

hear /hɪə/ (**hears, hearing, heard**)

❂ **'hear about**

If you **hear about** something or someone or **hear** something **about** them, you get news or information about them.

hear about something ❏ *They heard about a new restaurant that was opening in town.* ❏ [+ from] *I heard about the accident from Andy.*

hear something about something/someone ❏ *I've heard lots of good things about him.*

❂ **'hear from**

1 If you **hear from** someone or **hear** something **from** them, you receive a phone call, email, or other message from them.

hear from someone ❏ *I don't hear from my sister very often.*

hear something from someone ❏ *Have you heard anything from Oliver since he went to university?*

2 If you **hear from** someone or **hear** something **from** them, you listen to their opinions in a discussion.

hear from someone ❏ *Now it's time to hear from our audience.*

hear something from someone ❏ *I would have liked to hear more from the patient.*

❂ **'hear of**

1 If you **hear of** something, you find out something about it or find out that it exists for the first time.

hear of something ❏ *How did you first hear of his work?*

2 If you **have heard of** someone or something, you are aware that they exist.

have heard of someone/something ❏ *Have you heard of Justin Bieber?* ❏ *I had never heard of the writer they were talking about.* ● An event or situation that is **unheard of** happens so rarely that it is very surprising or shocking. ❏ *In those days it was quite unheard of for anyone to get divorced.*

3 If you **will not hear of** something, you will not accept or allow it.

not hear of something ❏ *I offered to pay, but he wouldn't hear of it.*

○ **hear 'out**

If you **hear** someone **out**, you listen without interrupting until they have finished speaking.

hear someone out ❏ *They dismissed the boys' story without even hearing them out.* ❏ *I know it sounds crazy, but hear me out.*

heat /hi:t/ (**heats, heating, heated**)

❂ **heat 'up**

1 When something **heats up** or something else **heats** it **up**, it gradually becomes hotter.

heat up ❏ *The iron only takes a few seconds to heat up.* ❏ *The climate seems to be heating up.*

heat something up ❏ *The sun slowly heats the ground up.*

heat up something ❏ *This process makes the Earth warmer and heats up the atmosphere.*

2 If you **heat up** cold food, you make it hot. **= warm up**

heat up something ❏ *I heated up a frozen pizza.*

heat something up ❏ *The soup's delicious cold, or you can heat it up.*

3 If a situation or an activity **heats up**, it becomes more exciting, extreme or dangerous. ❏ *Arguments about the war are heating up again in Parliament.*

heave /hi:v/ (**heaves, heaving, hove**)

○ **heave 'to**

If you **heave to** or if a ship **heaves to**, the ship stops. ❏ *The warship hove to and lowered a small boat.*

○ **heave 'up** [INFORMAL]

If you **heave up** or **heave up** food, you vomit. **= throw up**

heave up ❏ *I could hear someone heaving up.*

heave up something or **heave something up** ❏ *He had heaved up his dinner.*

hedge /hedʒ/ (**hedges, hedging, hedged**)

○ **hedge a'bout with** → see **hedge around with**

○ **'hedge against**
If you **hedge against** something bad, you try and prevent it from affecting you.
hedge against something ❏ *This savings account helps you hedge against changes in interest rates.*

○ **hedge a'round with** (or **hedge about with, hedge round with**) [mainly BRITISH])
If something **is hedged around with** problems or restrictions, they make it very difficult or complicated.
be hedged around with something ❏ *The system is hedged around with a lot of bureaucratic restrictions.*

○ **hedge 'in**
If someone or something **is hedged in**, they are limited in what they can do by problems or restrictions.
be hedged in ❏ [+ by] *His power is hedged in by laws and restrictions.* ❏ [+ with] *Medicine has to be hedged in with ethical rules.*

○ **hedge 'round with** → see **hedge around with**

heel /hiːl/ (**heels, heeling, heeled**)
○ **heel 'over**
If a boat **heels over**, it leans over to one side. ❏ *The boat heeled over so far she seemed about to capsize.*

help /help/ (**helps, helping, helped**)
○ **help a'long**
To **help** something **along** means to make it happen more quickly or easily.
help something along ❏ *Putting the plants on a sunny window sill can help the process along.*

○ **help 'off with**
If you **help** someone **off with** a piece of clothing, you help them to remove it.
help someone off with something ❏ *Let me help you off with your coat.*

○ **help 'on with**
If you **help** someone **on with** a piece of clothing, you help them to dress.
help someone on with something ❏ *I helped the children on with their gloves and scarves.*

◆ **help 'out**
If you **help out** or **help** someone **out**, you do something to help someone.
help out ❏ *Thanks for coming and helping out.* ❏ [+ with] *My sister helps out with the kids a lot.*
help someone out ❏ *I was asked to come in for a few days to help them out.* ❏ [+ with] *You should help your parents out with the housework.*
help out someone ❏ *He's helping out some friends who are moving house this weekend.*

○ **'help to**
If you **help** someone **to** food or drink, you serve it to them.
help someone to something ❏ *I helped him to some more cake.*
help yourself to something ❏ *She was in the kitchen, helping herself to biscuits.*

○ **help 'up**
If you **help** someone **up**, you help them to get into a standing position.
help someone up ❏ *She took his hand and helped him up.* ❏ [+ from] *Howard helped his father up from the bench.*

hem /hem/ (**hems, hemming, hemmed**)
○ **hem 'in**
1 If a place **is hemmed in** by things, it has them on all sides.
be hemmed in ❏ *The playing field was small and hemmed in by buildings.*
2 If people **are hemmed in**, something prevents them from being free to do what they want.
be hemmed in ❏ *Their lives are hemmed in by petty rules and regulations.*

herd /hɜːd/ (**herds, herding, herded**)
○ **herd to'gether**
If you **herd** animals or people **together**, you make them form a group.
herd something/someone together or **herd together something/someone** ❏ *The dogs rushed about trying to herd the sheep together.*

○ **herd 'up**
If you **herd** people or animals **up**, you make them move together to form a group.
= **round up**
herd something/someone up or **herd up something/someone** ❏ *We herded up the children and got them back on the bus.*

hew /hjuː/ (**hews, hewing, hewed, hewn**)

> The past participle is either **hewed** or **hewn**.

○ **hew 'down** [LITERARY]
If you **hew** something **down**, you cut it with something such as an axe so that it falls down. = **chop down**
hew down something or **hew something down** ❏ *They had to hew down trees and make a raft.*

○ **hew 'out** (or **hew from**) [LITERARY]
If an object **is hewn out** of a substance, it has been made from a large solid piece of the substance by cutting. = **carve out**
be hewn out of something ❏ *The church was hewn out of solid rock.*

hide /haɪd/ (**hides, hiding, hid, hidden**)

⊕ **hide a'way**

◼ If you **hide** something **away** or **hide** it **away** somewhere, you put it in a place where nobody else can find it. = **stash away**
hide something away ❑ *He hid his drawings away so no-one could see them.* ❑ *He told me to take the money and hide it away.*
hide away something ❑ *She has hidden away all the biscuits.*
hide something away somewhere ❑ *I've hidden the key away in a secret place.*
◼ If you **hide away**, you go to a place where people cannot find you. ❑ *I need a place where I can hide away and get on with my novel.* ● A **hideaway** is a place you can go where people cannot find you. ❑ *The star spent the weekend at her hideaway in the mountains.*
◼ If someone or something **is hidden away**, they are far from places where people usually go.
be hidden away ❑ *These little mountain villages are hidden away and get very few tourists.* ❑ *Her office is hidden away at the top of the house.*

○ **'hide behind**

◼ If you **hide behind** something, you use it as a reason not to say or do something that you do not want to say or do.
hide behind something ❑ *Politicians must not hide behind parliamentary privilege to avoid telling the truth.*
◼ If you **hide** your feelings or character **behind** something, you use it as a way to avoid showing them.
hide something behind something ❑ *He hid his feelings for her behind a rough manner.* ❑ *He hides a kind heart behind his stern behaviour.*

⊕ **'hide from**

◼ If you **hide from** someone, you go somewhere where they cannot see you.
hide from someone ❑ *They hid from him among the trees.*
◼ If you **hide from** something, you try to pretend that you do not know it.
hide from something ❑ *It's time to stop hiding from the truth.*
◼ If you **hide** something **from** someone, you try to prevent them from seeing it or noticing it.
hide something from someone ❑ *The teacher could see he was trying to hide something from her under the desk.* ❑ *She tried to hide herself from photographers as she left court.*
◼ If you **hide** information or facts **from** someone, you try to prevent them from finding out about it.

hide something from someone ❑ *I can tell you're trying to hide something from me.*

○ **hide 'out**

If you **hide out**, you go somewhere where people cannot find you. ❑ *He decided to hide out until the scandal blew over.* ● A **hideout** is a place you can go where people cannot find you. ❑ *Perhaps the gang used this house as a hide-out?*

○ **hide 'up**

If you **hide up**, you go somewhere where people cannot find you. ❑ *She is safe and well, hiding up at her mother's house.*

hike /haɪk/ (**hikes, hiking, hiked**)

○ **hike 'up**

◼ If you **hike up** something that you are wearing, you pull it up quickly. = **hitch up**
hike up something or **hike something up**
❑ *He hiked up his trouser leg to show her his scar.*
◼ If someone **hikes up** a price, they increase it suddenly by a large amount. = **push up**
hike up something or **hike something up**
❑ *They tend to hike up their prices in the summer when the tourists arrive.*

hinge /hɪndʒ/ (**hinges, hinging, hinged**)

○ **'hinge on** (or **hinge upon**)

◼ If one thing **hinges on** another, it depends completely on the other thing. = **hang on**
hinge on something ❑ *Everything hinges on what happens to the US economy.*
◼ If a story **hinges on** a subject, that is the most important subject in it.
hinge on something ❑ *The film hinges on two relationships, both of which are spoiled by greed.*

hint /hɪnt/ (**hints, hinting, hinted**)

○ **'hint at**

If you **hint at** something, you suggest in an indirect way that it may be true. = **imply**
hint at something ❑ *She hinted at the possibility of their marriage breaking up.*

hire /haɪə/ (**hires, hiring, hired**)

○ **hire 'out**

If you **hire out** something, you allow it to be used in exchange for payment. = **rent out**
hire out something or **hire something out**
❑ *They hire out sun beds and beach umbrellas.*
❑ *If you don't have a baby seat, some companies hire them out.*

hiss /hɪs/ (**hisses, hissing, hissed**)

○ **'hiss at**

If people **hiss at** someone such as a performer or a person making a speech, they show their disapproval or dislike of that person by making long, loud 's' sounds.

hiss at someone ❏ *Some of the audience whistled and hissed at him as he walked onto stage.*

hit /hɪt/ (**hits, hitting**)

> Hit is used in the present tense and is the past tense and past participle of the verb.

○ **'hit at**

1 If you **hit at** someone or something, you try to hit them with your hands or with an object.

hit at someone/something ❏ *She hit at my legs as I ran away.* ❏ *The children were hitting at the branches with sticks.*

2 If you **hit at** something, you try to harm or destroy it.

hit at something ❏ *Their aim was to hit at the enemy's morale.*

○ **hit 'back**

1 If you **hit back** or **hit** someone **back**, you hit them after they have hit you.

hit back ❏ *If a child hits you, it's best not to hit back.*

hit someone back ❏ *He hit me, so I hit him back.*

2 If you **hit back**, you criticize or harm someone after they have criticized or harmed you. ❏ *After being criticized in the local press, the mayor has hit back.* ❏ [+ at] *He wanted to hit back at those who had done him wrong.*

○ **hit 'off**

If people **hit it off**, they like each other and become friends as soon as they meet. ❏ *The new team members hit it off straight away.* ❏ [+ with] *She did not hit it off with her mother-in-law at first.*

○ **'hit on** (or **hit upon**)

1 If you **hit on** an idea, you think of it. = **stumble on**

hit on something ❏ *He hit on the idea of using songs as teaching aids.*

2 If someone **hits on** you, they behave in a way that shows they are sexually attracted to you. [INFORMAL, RUDE]

hit on someone ❏ *She was hitting on me and I was surprised and flattered.*

○ **hit 'out**

1 If you **hit out**, you try to hit people or things in all directions around you. = **lash out** [BRITISH] ❏ *He hit out wildly as they tried to arrest him.* ❏ [+ at] *An autistic child who hits out at another child in school may not be aggressive; they may simply feel threatened.*

2 If you **hit out**, you attack or criticize someone strongly. = **lash out** ❏ [+ at] *The*

Prime Minister hit out at his critics, accusing them of dishonesty.

○ **hit 'up** [INFORMAL]

If you **hit** someone **up**, you contact them, especially through social media.

hit someone up ❏ *He's really cool and often hits me up on social media to ask me how I'm doing.*

○ **hit 'up for**

If you **are hit up for** an amount of money, or if someone **hits** you **up for** it, you are made to pay it. [AMERICAN, INFORMAL]

be hit up for something ❏ *We were immediately hit up for a $5 per head cover charge.*

hit someone up for something ❏ *They hit him up for $90,000 in taxes.*

○ **'hit upon** → see **hit on**

hitch /hɪtʃ/ (**hitches, hitching, hitched**)

○ **'hitch to**

If you **hitch** something **to** something else, you fasten it to that thing using a rope, chain, etc.

hitch something to something ❏ *He was hitching the trailer to the back of his car.* ❏ *The horse had been hitched to the cart.*

○ **hitch 'up**

If you **hitch up** a piece of clothing, you pull up higher on your body.

hitch up something or **hitch something up** ❏ *Stein hitched up his trousers and tucked in his shirt.*

hive /haɪv/ (**hives, hiving, hived**)

○ **hive 'off** [BRITISH]

If you **hive off** part of a business, you sell it as a separate business. = **sell off**

hive off something or **hive something off** ❏ *The agency hived off its media department.*

hoard /hɔːd/ (**hoards, hoarding, hoarded**)

○ **hoard a'way**

If you **hoard** something **away**, you keep it in a secret place to use later.

hoard something away or **hoard away something** ❏ *We used to hoard chocolate away in our lockers at school.*

○ **hoard 'up**

If you **hoard up** something, you keep a lot of it in a secret place to use later.

hoard up something or **hoard something up** ❏ *There's no point in hoarding up stuff you won't use.*

hobnob /'hɒbnɒb/ (**hobnobs, hobnobbing, hobnobbed**)

○ **'hobnob with** [INFORMAL]

If someone **hobnobs with** rich or famous people, they spend time with them.

hobnob with someone ❏ *They hobnob with the rich and take their holidays in the Seychelles.*

hoke /həʊk/ (**hokes, hoking, hoked**)

○ **hoke 'up** [AMERICAN, INFORMAL]

If you **hoke** something **up**, you try to make it seem better or more important than it really is.

hoke something up or **hoke up something** ❏ It's just pop music hoked up with a folk background.

hold /həʊld/ (**holds, holding, held**)

○ **hold a'gainst**

If you **hold** something **against** someone, you are angry with them or have a low opinion of them because of it.

hold something against someone ❏ You can't hold one small mistake against him. ❏ Nobody would hold it against you if you left now.

◎ **hold 'back**

1 If you **hold back**, or if something **holds** you **back**, you do not do or say something that you want to do or say.

hold back ❏ She always says exactly what she thinks, without holding back. ❏ [+ from] Police have held back from going into a holy place to arrest him.

hold someone back ❏ She wanted to ask his name, but something held her back.

2 If you **hold** someone **back**, you prevent them from going somewhere.

hold someone back ❏ He started to run towards them, but Judy held him back.

hold back someone ❏ Police held back the crowd.

3 If someone or something **holds** someone **back**, they prevent them from achieving things.

hold someone back ❏ If she is ambitious, don't try to hold her back. ❏ His shyness holds him back.

hold back someone ❏ Poor literacy is holding back too many young people.

4 If you **hold back** something, you prevent it from happening or make it happen more slowly.

hold back something ❏ Concern about the environment has held back economic development.

hold something back ❏ Technological problems have been holding progress back. ❏ We resisted the changes, but in the end we could not hold them back.

5 If you **hold back** information, you do not reveal it.

hold back something ❏ He is concerned that politicians may be holding back some key facts.

hold something back ❏ I could see she was holding something back. ❏ He's known the truth all along, but he's been holding it back.

NOTE **Suppress** is a more formal word for **hold back**.

6 If you **hold back** part of something, you keep it to use later.

hold back something or **hold something back** ❏ We will hold back 10% of the funding for new projects. ❏ We bought him so many presents we decided to hold some back for his next birthday.

7 If you **hold back** tears or laughter, you prevent yourself from crying or laughing. = **keep back**

hold back something ❏ Holding back the tears Charles said goodbye and left.

NOTE **Contain** is a more formal word for **hold back**.

○ **hold 'back on**

If you **hold back on** something, you do not do it immediately.

hold back on something ❏ He held back on signing the contract.

◎ **hold 'down**

1 If you **hold** someone or something **down**, you use force to keep them in place.

hold someone/something down ❏ They had to hold him down to give him the injection. ❏ Push the button and hold it down for a few seconds.

hold down someone/something ❏ I was trying to hold down the lid of the box with one hand.

2 If you **hold down** prices or other amounts, you prevent them from increasing. = **keep down**

hold down something ❏ The Chancellor's policy was intended to hold down inflation.

hold something down ❏ It is vital for the business to hold costs down.

3 If something **holds** someone **down**, it prevents them from achieving things or making progress.

hold someone down ❏ We want to get these boys away from the street gangs that are holding them down. ❏ Poverty and disadvantage can hold people down.

hold down someone ❏ Nothing can hold down someone as talented as she is.

4 If you **hold down** a job, you manage to keep it.

hold down something ❏ Some of these people have never held down a steady job. ❏ I'm not sure he's capable of holding a job down.

5 If you **hold down** an emotion, you do not allow yourself to show it.

hold something down or **hold down something** ❏ I could no longer hold down my anger. ❏ She felt panic, but held it down.

6 If you cannot **hold down** food, you are unable to eat it without vomiting. = **keep down**

hold something down or **hold down something** ❏ I was really sick and couldn't hold *anything down.* ❏ *He can only hold down liquids at the moment.*

7 If someone **holds** people **down**, they do not allow them to have freedom or rights. = **keep down**

hold someone down or **hold down someone** ❏ *I'm a free man and nobody can hold me down.*

○ hold 'forth

If you **hold forth**, you talk about something for a long time in a boring way. ❏ *I could hear him holding forth in the bar.* ❏ *[+ on] He was holding forth on the pleasures of travel.*

○ hold 'in

If you **hold in** an emotion, you do not allow yourself to express it.

hold in something or **hold something in** ❏ *She struggled to hold in her anger.* ❏ *I couldn't hold it in any longer, and started to cry.*

○ hold 'off

1 If you **hold** someone or something **off**, you manage to stop them from successfully attacking or competing with you. = **fight off**

hold someone/something off ❏ *Chelsea held Liverpool off until the 70th minute, when Downing scored.* ❏ *A handful of troops held them off until the rest of the army arrived.*

hold off someone/something ❏ *The company's global expansion is helping it hold off competition from its rivals.*

2 If you **hold off** or **hold off** doing something, you delay doing something.

hold off ❏ *Let's hold off for a while before we make a decision.* ❏ *[+ on] Small firms have been holding off on investments due to economic uncertainty.*

hold off doing something ❏ *Everyone holds off buying if they think prices are going to fall.*

3 If rain or snow **holds off**, it does not fall although you expected it. ❏ *Thank goodness the rain held off for the picnic.*

○ hold 'on

1 If you **hold on**, you hold something firmly, especially to stop yourself from falling. ❏ *I grabbed the railing and held on.* ❏ *[+ to] Someone should hold on to the ladder.*

2 If you **hold on**, you manage to continue in a difficult situation. ≠ **give up** ❏ *If you hold on, things will get better eventually.*

3 If you **hold on**, you wait or stop what you are doing for a short time. = **hang on** ❏ *Let's just hold on a minute until we find out what's happened.* ❏ *Hold on! I can't hear you if you all talk at once!*

4 If you ask someone you are speaking to on the phone to **hold on**, you want them to wait for a short time. ❏ *Hold on a moment,*

please, I'll put you through. ❏ *Do you mind holding on while I get a pen?*

○ hold 'on to (or hold onto)

1 If you **hold on to** something that is in your hand, you grip it tightly so that it cannot fall or cannot be taken away from you.

hold on to something ❏ *She walked slowly down the steps, holding on to the hand-rail.*

2 If you **hold on to** someone, you keep your arms around them.

hold on to someone ❏ *Suddenly they stopped, holding on to each other and laughing.*

3 If you **hold on to** something, you keep it for yourself.

hold on to something ❏ *Some politicians want to hold on to power at all costs.*

4 If you **hold on to** something, you keep it rather than throwing it away.

hold on to something ❏ *I'll hold on to this box – it might be useful.* ❏ *People hold onto letters for years.*

5 If you **hold on to** a belief or feeling, you continue to have it.

hold on to something ❏ *I had always held on to my dream of becoming a writer.*

6 If you **hold on to** someone, you prevent them from leaving you.

hold on to someone ❏ *His mother tried to hold on to him even after he was married.* ❏ *He's our best player and we have to hold onto him.*

○ hold 'out

1 If you **hold** something **out**, you hold it in front of you, so that someone can take it or see it.

hold out something ❏ *He held out his plate for a second portion.*

hold something out ❏ *He held his arm out, saying 'Look.'* ❏ *[+ to] He took off his glasses and held them out to Ralph.*

2 If you **hold out your hand** or **hold your hand out**, you stretch it out in front of you. ❏ *Dan held out his hand for the briefcase.* ❏ *She held a hand out and he shook it.*

3 If you **hold out**, you manage to continue or survive despite an attack or very difficult situation. ≠ **give in** ❏ *They could either surrender or hold out.* ❏ *[+ against] He could not hold out against the pressures that were building up.* ● A **holdout** is someone who refuses to agree or give in to something, even when most others have done so. ❏ *A few holdouts still refused to sell their land.*

4 If you **hold out hope** you believe something could happen or succeed. ❏ *You can try asking her, but I don't hold out much hope.* ❏ *[+ of] She held out little hope of being offered a job.*

5 If something or someone **holds out** a possibility or opportunity, they make a good thing seem possible.

hold out something ❏ *The minister held out the possibility of further tax cuts.*

6 If something **holds out**, there is enough of it to last for a certain period of time.

= last out ❏ *I decided to stay as long as the water held out.* ❏ *My money was holding out better than I had expected.*

○ **hold 'out for**

If you **hold out for** something that you want, you refuse to agree or do something until you get it.

hold out for something ❏ *His ex-wife was holding out for a bigger divorce payment.*

○ **hold 'out on**

If you **hold out on** someone, you refuse to tell or give them something.

hold out on someone ❏ *I know you're holding out on me – tell me the truth.*

○ **hold 'over**

1 If you **hold** something **over** someone, you use it in order to threaten them or make them do what you want.

hold something over someone ❏ *He knew what she'd done, and tried to hold it over her.*

2 If you **hold** something **over**, you delay it until a future date.

hold something over or **hold over something** ❏ [+ until] *The newspaper agreed to hold over publication until after the election.* ❏ [+ for] *Could we hold the show over for a couple of weeks?*

be held over ❏ [+ until] *If no one wins the prize, it will be held over until next month.*

NOTE **Defer** is a more formal word for **hold over**.

3 A **holdover** is something from the past that continues to exist or be used. ❏ *This custom is a holdover from the past.*

○ **'hold to**

1 When you **hold** something **to** part of your body, you put it close to your body and keep it there.

hold something to something ❏ *What should you do if someone holds a knife to your throat.* ❏ *He took the phone and held it to his ear.*

2 If you **hold** someone or something **to** you, you put your arms around them and press them against your body.

hold something/someone to you ❏ *She picked up the child and held him to her.*

3 If you **hold to** an opinion or belief, you will not change it. **= stick to**

hold to something ❏ *Some still hold to the belief that these illnesses are psychological.* ❏ *They argued, but he held to his decision.*

4 If you **hold** someone **to** something, you expect them to do what they have said or promised.

hold someone to something ❏ *They should hold the Prime Minister to his word.* ❏ *'I'll take you there one day.' – 'I'll hold you to that!'*

5 If you **hold** someone **to** a particular standard, you expect them to achieve it.

hold someone to something ❏ *The mayor promised to hold all the city's schools to a high standard.*

● If you **hold** someone **to account**, you expect them to explain or take responsibility for something. ❏ *If serious mistakes are made, then someone must be held to account for them.*

○ **hold to'gether**

1 When you **hold** people **together** or when they **hold together**, they manage to live or work together.

hold someone/something together or **hold together someone/something** ❏ *The parents managed to hold the family together in spite of all their problems.*

hold together ❏ *At times of national crisis it's important for the country to hold together.*

2 If something **holds together** or **is held together**, it stays in one piece without breaking or falling apart.

hold together ❏ *The problem seemed to be whether the car would hold together.*

be held together ❏ [+ with] *Her books seemed to be held together with sticky tape and rubber bands.*

3 If you **hold it together**, you manage in a difficult situation without becoming so upset or worried that you cannot continue. [INFORMAL] ❏ *He only just managed to hold it together during their conversation.*

○ **hold 'up**

1 If you **hold** something **up**, you hold it in a high position so that someone can see or reach it.

hold something up ❏ *She held the bowl up so I could fill it.* ❏ *'Who do these shoes belong to?' I asked, holding them up.*

hold up something ❏ *The children all held up their drawings.*

NOTE **Raise** is a more formal word for **hold up**.

2 If you **hold up** your hand or **hold your hand up**, you raise it above your shoulder, usually in order to get someone's attention. ❏ *If you know the answer, hold up your hand.*

NOTE **Raise** is a more formal word for **hold up**.

3 If one thing **holds up** another, it supports it or prevents it from falling. = **prop up**
hold up something ❏ They make steel girders to hold up buildings.
hold something up ❏ These posts hold the fence up. ❏ How does the tent stay like that, with nothing holding it up?

4 If something or someone **holds** something **up**, they make it late or make it happen more slowly.
hold up something or **hold something up** ❏ Bad weather held up our flight. ❏ They threatened to hold negotiations up even longer.
● A **hold-up** is a delay or something which causes a delay. ❏ I nearly missed my flight because of a traffic hold-up.

5 If something or someone **holds** you **up** or you **are held up**, you are delayed so that you are late for something.
hold someone up or **hold up someone**
❏ I don't want to hold you up, but can I just ask one more quick question?
be held up ❏ Ms Thomas has been held up, so we will start the meeting without her.

6 To **hold** someone or something **up** means to rob them by threatening them with a weapon. = **rob**
hold something/someone up or **hold something/someone up** ❏ They held up a bank with sawn-off shotguns. ❏ He held me up at gun point. ● A **holdup** is a robbery in which weapons are used. ❏ Seven people were wounded in a bank hold-up.

7 If something **holds up**, it remains in good condition after rough use. ❏ How did your old car hold up on the journey? ❏ I intend to walk all the way, if my boots hold up.

8 If a person **holds up**, they manage to deal with a very difficult situation without becoming too upset to continue. ❏ He's holding up fairly well since he lost his job.

9 If something such a business **holds up**, it remains fairly successful in difficult conditions. ❏ Children's clothes is one area that is holding up well in the recession.

10 If an idea or argument **holds up**, it can be proved to be correct or true. = **stand up**
❏ Your argument doesn't really hold up. ❏ None of his stories held up when you looked at them logically.

○ **hold 'up as**
If you **hold** someone or something **up as** something, you use them as an example of what you are talking about, or as an example of something particularly good or bad.
hold someone/something up as something
❏ We hold these three things up as desirable goals.

❏ I wasn't the sort of child anyone would ever hold up as an example to others.
be held up as something ❏ This comment was held up as another example of his rudeness.
hold yourself up as something ❏ I don't hold myself up as a perfect parent.

○ **hold 'up to**
If you **hold** someone or something **up to** ridicule or contempt, you invite other people to laugh at them in an unkind way.
hold someone/something up to something
❏ The article held her up to ridicule, depicting her as eccentric and unreliable.

○ **'hold with** [OLD-FASHIONED]
If you do not **hold with** something, you do not approve of it. = **agree with**
not hold with something ❏ You know I don't hold with children staying up so late.

hole /həʊl/ (**holes, holing, holed**)
○ **hole 'out**
In golf, if you **hole out**, you finish one of the holes or the course. ❏ He holed out from 116 yards.

○ **hole 'up** [INFORMAL]
If you **hole up** or **are holed up** somewhere, you hide there.
hole up ❏ I decided to hole up at my mother's house for a while.
be holed up ❏ The men were holed up on the top floor of the hotel.

hollow /'hɒləʊ/ (**hollows, hollowing, hollowed**)
○ **hollow 'out**
1 If you **hollow out** something solid, you make a space in it by removing the inside part.
hollow out something or **hollow something out** ❏ They hollowed out pumpkins to make lanterns. ❏ You make a large mound of snow, then hollow it out. ● Something that is **hollowed-out** has had the inside part of it removed. ❏ Its nest was in a hollowed-out tree-stump.
2 If someone **hollows out** a company or a department, they reduce the number of people who work there.
hollow out something or **hollow something out** ❏ There has been a trend to hollow out in-house IT departments.

home /həʊm/ (**homes, homing, homed**)
○ **home 'in on**
1 If something **homes in on** on something else, it moves directly and very quickly towards it.
home in on something ❏ The missile can home in on the target with great accuracy.

2 If someone **homes in on** someone or something, they move towards them quickly.

home in on someone/something ❑ She homed in on the pool, where she discovered Bella and Lorri swimming.

3 If you **home in on** a subject, you pay more attention to it.

home in on something ❑ She quickly homed in on the things that worried me most.

hook /hʊk/ (hooks, hooking, hooked)

○ **hook 'into**

If something **hooks into** a computer, network, or electronic device, it connects to it.

hook into something ❑ The driving control pad hooks into your games console.

○ **'hook to** (or **hook onto**)

If you **hook** one thing **to** another thing, you attach it using a hook.

hook something to something ❑ She hooked the hanger onto the wardrobe door. ❑ Several paintings were hooked to the walls.

⊙ **hook 'up**

1 If you **hook up** a computer or electronic device, you connect it to something.
= **link up**

hook something up ❑ [+ to] You can load music onto the device by hooking it up to a computer. ❑ Can you hook the printer up for me?

hook up something ❑ Nicola hooked up her headphones and listened to some music.

● A **hook-up** is an electronic or radio connection. ❑ Is there a hook-up for the electricity supply?

2 If you **hook** something **up**, you hang or fix it somewhere using a hook.

hook something up or **hook up something** ❑ [+ to] He hooked the trailer up to the back of his car.

3 If people **hook up**, they meet and start having a relationship or working together. [INFORMAL] ❑ Seeing as we got on so well together, it just seemed natural that we should hook up. ❑ [+ with] They moved to LA where they hooked up with drummer Ginger Baker.

○ **hook 'up to**

If you **are hooked up to** a machine, you are connected to it by wires or tubes.

be hooked up to something ❑ She was lying in the hospital bed hooked up to a heart monitor.

hoot /huːt/ (hoots, hooting, hooted)

○ **hoot 'down**

If someone **is hooted down**, their audience prevents them from speaking by shouting.
= **shout down, boo**

be hooted down ❑ Scientists who tried to spea at the recent meeting were hooted down.

hoover /'huːvə/ (hoovers, hoovering, hoovered)

○ **hoover 'up**

1 If you **hoover up** or **hoover** something **up**, you clean dirt from a surface using a vacuum cleaner. [BRITISH]

hoover up ❑ After everyone had gone, I hoovere up, then went to bed.

hoover something up or **hoover up somethin** ❑ Will you hoover those crumbs up off the rug, pleas

2 To **hoover** something **up** means to take for yourself in an unfair or greedy way.

hoover something up or **hoover up something** ❑ The guests hoovered up the free food and drink.

hop /hɒp/ (hops, hopping, hopped)

○ **hop 'off** [INFORMAL; OLD-FASHIONED]

If you tell someone to **hop off**, you are telling them rather rudely to go away.
= **buzz off** ❑ Hop off, I'm busy.

hope /həʊp/ (hopes, hoping, hoped)

⊙ **'hope for**

If you **hope for** something, you want it an expect to have it.

hope for something ❑ The team is hoping for a big win today. ❑ He paused, hoping for the answer 'yes'.

horn /hɔːn/ (horns, horning, horned)

○ **horn 'in** [AMERICAN, INFORMAL]

If you **horn in**, you get involved with something when other people do not wan you to. ❑ Letting him horn in was a mistake. ❑ [+ on] What gives you the right to horn in on someone else's conversation?

horse /hɔːs/ (horses, horsing, horsed)

○ **horse a'round** (or **horse about** [mainl BRITISH]) [INFORMAL]

If you **horse around**, you play roughly.
= **fool around** ❑ They're out in the yard, horsing around.

hose /həʊz/ (hoses, hosing, hosed)

○ **hose 'down**

If you **hose** something **down**, you clean it using water from a hose. = **wash down**

hose something down or **hose down something** ❑ Joseph was hosing down the tracto

○ **hose 'out**

When you **hose** something **out**, you clean the inside of it using water from a hose.
= **wash out**

hose something out or **hose out something** ❑ Would you mind hosing the bins out?

hot /hɒt/ (hots, hotting, hotted)

○ **hot 'up** [BRITISH]

If a situation or activity **hots up**, it becomes more active or exciting. ❑ *The election campaign was hotting up.*

hound /haʊnd/ (hounds, hounding, hounded)

○ **hound 'out**

If someone **is hounded out** of a place or if someone **hounds** them **out**, they are forced to leave.

be hounded out ❑ [+ of] *We should not allow an innocent minister to be hounded out of office.*

hound someone out or **hound out someone** ❑ *Extremists in their own community have hounded them out.*

howl /haʊl/ (howls, howling, howled)

○ **howl 'down** [BRITISH]

If someone **is howled down**, they are prevented from speaking by people shouting at them angrily. = **shout down**

be howled down ❑ *He was howled down by supporters of the king.*

○ **'howl with**

If you **howl with laughter** or **delight**, you laugh very loudly. ❑ *Booker howled with delight.* ❑ *They howled with laughter at this.*

huddle /ˈhʌdəl/ (huddles, huddling, huddled)

○ **huddle a'round** (or **huddle about**, **huddle round** [mainly BRITISH])

If people **huddle around** something or someone or **are huddled around** them, they stand or sit close to them in a group. = **cluster around**

huddle around something/someone ❑ *They huddled around the fire.*

huddle around ❑ *We huddled around to listen.*

be huddled around something/someone ❑ *The actors were all huddled round the director.*

○ **huddle 'down**

If you **huddle down**, you move into a low or curled position with your legs bent. ❑ *She huddled down under the bedclothes.*

○ **huddle 'round** → see huddle around

○ **huddle to'gether**

❶ If people **huddle together** or **are huddled together**, they stand, sit, or lie close to each other.

huddle together ❑ *We had to huddle together for warmth.*

be huddled together ❑ *Refugees were huddled together on the railway platform.*

❷ If a group of buildings **are huddled together**, they are very close each other.

be huddled together ❑ *The village consisted of a few houses huddled together.*

○ **huddle 'up**

If people **huddle up** or **are huddled up**, they stay close together or under blankets or clothes because it is cold.

huddle up ❑ *All I wanted to do was huddle up in bed.*

be huddled up ❑ *Rose was huddled up, her coat pulled tight around her.*

hunger /ˈhʌŋgə/ (hungers, hungering, hungered)

○ **'hunger for** (or **hunger after**)

If you **hunger for** something, you want it very much. = **hanker for**

hunger for something ❑ *Why do people hunger for power?*

hunker /ˈhʌŋkə/ (hunkers, hunkering, hunkered)

○ **hunker 'down**

❶ If you **hunker down**, you move close to the ground so that you are on your feet with your legs bent. = **crouch down** ❑ *He hunkered down behind the counter so they couldn't see him.*

❷ If someone **hunkers down**, they wait for a difficult or dangerous situation to end. = **lie low** ❑ *Their strategy is to hunker down until the scandal dies down.*

hunt /hʌnt/ (hunts, hunting, hunted)

○ **hunt 'down**

If you **hunt** someone or something **down**, you succeed in finding them, usually in order to punish or harm them. = **track down**

hunt someone/something down or **hunt down someone/something** ❑ *The hero goes to hunt the bad guys down.*

be hunted down ❑ *Many of the escaped prisoners were hunted down and shot.*

○ **'hunt for**

If you **hunt for** something, you try to find it.

hunt for something ❑ *Police were hunting for clues.* ❑ *Pete is still hunting for a job.*

○ **hunt 'out**

If you **hunt out** something, you succeed in finding it. = **dig out**

hunt out something or **hunt something out** ❑ *We've been hunting out bargains in the shops.* ❑ *Mum hunted some old photographs out for me.*

○ **hunt 'up**

If you **hunt up** something, you manage to find it. = **chase up**

hunt up something or **hunt something up** ❑ *The staff are very good at hunting up information for you.*

hurl /hɜːl/ (**hurls, hurling, hurled**)

○ **hurl a'round** (or **hurl about, hurl round** [mainly BRITISH])

If you **hurl** things **around**, you throw them in many different directions with great force.

hurl something around or **hurl around something** ❑ We were being hurled around in the back of the car.

○ **'hurl at**

If you **hurl** abuse, insults, or accusations at someone, you shout rude things or accusations at them in a very angry way.

hurl something at someone ❑ Rival football fans chanted and hurled insults at each other.

○ **hurl 'round** → see **hurl around**

hurry /'hʌri, AM 'hɜːri/ (**hurries, hurrying, hurried**)

○ **hurry 'on**

1 If you **hurry on**, you continue walking quickly or running. ❑ The man hurried on with a worried look on his face. ❑ [+ to] She was hurrying on to her next appointment.

2 If you **hurry on**, you quickly continue speaking. ❑ [+ to] He did not wait for a reply but hurried on to his next point. ❑ 'But,' she hurried on, 'this was not intentional.'

♦ **hurry 'up**

1 If you tell someone to **hurry up**, you are telling them to do something more quickly. = **buck up** ❑ Hurry up, Bill, we're going to be late. ❑ She yelled at me to hurry up.

2 If you **hurry** someone **up**, you make them do something more quickly than they would have done.

hurry someone up ❑ The nurse stood outside the washrooms to hurry us up. ❑ We need to hurry the children up or they'll be late for school.

3 If you **hurry** something **up**, you make it happen faster or sooner than it would have done. = **speed up**

hurry something up ❑ Can't you hurry things up a bit? ❑ If you're making a baked potato, you can hurry it up by cooking it in the microwave first.

hurry up something ❑ You can't hurry up the process of grieving.

hush /hʌʃ/ (**hushes, hushing, hushed**)

○ **hush 'up**

If people in authority **hush** something **up** or if it **is hushed up**, they prevent the public from knowing about it. = **cover up**

hush something up or **hush up something** ❑ The government tried to hush the matter up.

be hushed up ❑ His association with these men had been hushed up.

NOTE **Suppress** is a more formal word for **hush up**.

hype /haɪp/ (**hypes, hyping, hyped**)

○ **hype 'up**

1 If people **hype** something **up** or if it is **hyped up**, people try to create a lot of interest in it.

hype something up or **hype up something** ❑ The actress has been on TV hyping up her new film. ❑ There's a lot of pressure to win the game because the media have hyped it up so much.

be hyped up ❑ Their bad reputation has been hyped up out of all proportion.

2 If something or someone **hypes** someone **up**, they are excited.

hype someone up or **hype up someone** ❑ I realized the job was not to hype up the team, but to calm them down. ● If someone is **hyped up**, they are excited and full of energy. = **psych up** ❑ The children were so hyped up they could not concentrate.

I i

ice /aɪs/ (ices, icing, iced)

○ **ice 'over**

When something **ices over**, it becomes covered with a layer of ice. **= freeze over** ❑ *The lake began to ice over.* ❑ *The road had iced over in the night.*

○ **ice 'up**

When something **ices up**, it becomes so cold that ice forms on it and stops it from working properly. **= freeze up** ❑ *It was so cold that the lock had iced up.*

identify /aɪˈdentɪfaɪ/ (identifies, identifying, identified)

○ **i'dentify with**

1 If someone or something **is identified with** something, they are very closely involved or connected with it.

be identified with something ❑ *In many cultures, beauty is identified with youthfulness.*

2 If you **identify with** someone or their feelings, you feel that you understand them because they are similar to you or they have similar feelings.

identify with someone/something ❑ *A daughter is more likely to identify with her mother than her father.* ❑ *He couldn't identify with other people's troubles.*

idle /ˈaɪdəl/ (idles, idling, idled)

○ **idle a'round** (or **idle about** [mainly BRITISH])

If you **idle around** or **idle around** a place, you spend your time in a place, relaxing or doing nothing.

idle around ❑ *It annoys me the way he idles around all day.*

idle around somewhere ❑ *I can't have you idling around the house all afternoon.*

○ **idle a'way**

If you **idle away** a period of time, you relax by sitting or lying somewhere and doing nothing. **= while away**

idle away something or **idle something away** ❑ *Three old men were idling away the summer afternoon under the trees.* ❑ *They idled the time away in a local café.*

impact /ɪmˈpækt/ (impacts, impacting, impacted)

○ **im'pact on**

1 To **impact on** a situation, process, or person means to affect them.

impact on someone/something ❑ *They are carrying out research into how the Internet impacts on our lives.* ❑ *Relationship problems between parents can impact on children.*

2 If one object **impacts on** another object, it hits it with great force. [FORMAL]

impact on something ❑ *As the car hit the wall, there was the sound of metal impacting on stone.*

impart /ɪmˈpɑːt/ (imparts, imparting, imparted)

○ **im'part to** [FORMAL]

1 If you **impart** information **to** someone, you tell it to them.

impart something to someone

❑ *Unfortunately, he failed to impart this information to me.*

2 To **impart** a particular quality **to** something means to give it that quality.

impart something to something ❑ *The oil imparts a wonderful shine to the hair.* ❑ *The herbs impart a delicate flavour to the fish.*

impinge /ɪmˈpɪndʒ/ (impinges, impinging, impinged)

○ **im'pinge on** (or **impinge upon**) [FORMAL]

If something **impinges on** someone or something, it affects them, especially in a way that is bad.

impinge on someone/something ❑ *Make sure your behaviour does not impinge on other people's enjoyment of the campsite.*

NOTE **Affect** is a less formal word for **impinge on**.

implant /ɪmˈplɑːnt, -ˈplænt/ (implants, implanting, implanted)

○ **im'plant in**

1 When an egg or embryo **implants in** the womb, it becomes established there and can then develop.

implant in something ❑ *Non-identical twins*

are the result of two fertilised eggs implanting in the uterus at the same time.

2 To **implant** something **in** a person's body means to put it there, usually in a medical operation.

implant something in something ❑ *Surgeons implanted electrodes in his brain.*

3 To **implant** an idea or attitude **in** a person or their mind means to make them start to accept or believe it.

implant something in someone/something ❑ *False memories can be implanted in a person's mind through repeated suggestions by someone they trust.*

impose /ɪm'pəʊz/ (**imposes, imposing, imposed**)

✪ im'pose on (or **impose upon**)

1 If you **impose** something **on** people, you use your authority to force them to accept it.

impose something on someone/something ❑ *She was a harsh mother and imposed severe discipline on her children.*

be imposed on someone/something ❑ *The rule was imposed on small businesses.*

2 If someone **imposes on** you, they unreasonably expect you to do something for them or to spend time with them when you do not want to.

impose on someone ❑ *I don't want to impose on you, but if you'd like to come, you are very welcome.*

3 If you **impose** your opinions or beliefs **on** someone else, you try to make them have the same opinions or beliefs as you.

impose something on someone ❑ *Parents should beware of imposing their own tastes on their children.* ❑ *I believe it is wrong to impose your religious beliefs on others.*

4 To **impose** something bad **on** someone or something means to make them suffer it.

impose something on someone/something ❑ *Financial problems can impose stress on any relationship.*

5 If someone **imposes** themselves **on** you, they try to spend time with you although you may not want them to.

impose yourself on someone ❑ *I didn't want to impose myself on my married friends.* ❑ *I hoped I wasn't imposing myself on them.*

○ im'pose upon → see **impose on**

impregnate /'ɪmpregneɪt, AM ɪm'preg-/ (**impregnates, impregnating, impregnated**)

○ 'impregnate with [FORMAL]

To **impregnate** something **with** a

substance means to make the substance spread through it.

impregnate something with something ❑ *The scented candles have been impregnated with essential oils.*

impress /ɪm'pres/ (**impresses, impressing, impressed**)

○ im'press as [FORMAL]

If someone or something **impresses** you **as** something, you think they are that type of person or thing.

impress someone as something ❑ *Byrne had impressed him as being an honest man.* ❑ *It didn't impress me as a good place to live in.*

○ im'press on (or **impress upon**)

1 If you **impress** something **on** someone, you try to make them understand that it is very important.

impress something on someone or **impress on someone something** ❑ *She impressed the importance of honesty on us.* ❑ *The teacher had impressed on the children not to go near the water.*

2 If something **impresses** itself **on** on you, you notice and remember it. [FORMAL]

impress itself on someone ❑ *He has a childlike curiosity which impresses itself on everyone who meets him.*

3 If you **impress** something **on** something else, you cause the image or memory of it to remain on the other thing.

impress something on something ❑ *I repeated the last verse several times, hoping to impress it on my memory.*

○ im'press upon → see **impress on**

imprint /ɪm'prɪnt/ (**imprints, imprinting, imprinted**)

○ im'print on

When something **is imprinted on** someone or their mind or memory, or you **imprint** it **on** your mind or memory, it is firmly fixed in your memory so that you will not forget it.

be imprinted on something ❑ *Even today, the view is imprinted on my memory.*

imprint something on something/someone ❑ *Amy looked at him, trying to imprint every line of his face on her memory.*

○ im'print with

If a surface **is imprinted with** a mark or design, that mark or design is printed on the surface or pressed into it.

be imprinted with something ❑ *Stationery can be imprinted with your name and address.*

improve /ɪm'pruːv/ (**improves, improving, improved**)

✪ im'prove on (or **improve upon**)

To **improve on** something means to make it

better than it was before, or do something better than you did before. = **better**

improve on something ❑ *The team hopes to improve on last week's poor performance.*

be improved on ❑ *For social justice, this system could hardly be improved upon.*

impute /ɪmˈpjuːt/ (imputes, imputing, imputed)

○ **imˈpute to** [FORMAL]

If you **impute** something **to** someone or something, you say that they are responsible for something or that they have a particular characteristic, especially something bad. = **attribute**

impute something to someone/something ❑ *They imputed no blame to the doctor involved.*

be imputed to someone ❑ *He suddenly shows a little of the ruthlessness that is often imputed to him.*

include /ɪnˈkluːd/ (includes, including, included)

✪ **inˈclude in**

■ If you **include** someone **in** a particular plan or activity, you allow them to take part in it.

include someone in something ❑ *The school plans to include all students in this project.* ❑ *He wanted to include her in the discussion.*

■ If you **include** one thing **in** another thing, you make it a part of that other thing.

include something in something ❑ *Few novelists would have dared include it in a work of fiction.* ❑ *Nothing should be included in the curriculum unless it is relevant.*

NOTE **Incorporate** is a more formal word for **include in**.

○ **include ˈout** [INFORMAL]

If you say to someone **Include me out**, you are saying in a humorous way that you do not want to do a particular activity with them. ❑ *If you're going to leave at 4 a.m., you can include me out!*

incorporate /ɪnˈkɔːpəreɪt/ (incorporates, incorporating, incorporated)

○ **inˈcorporate into** [FORMAL]

To **incorporate** someone or something **into** something means to make them become a part of it.

incorporate someone/something into something ❑ *The party promised to incorporate environmental considerations into all its policies.* ❑ *The agreement would allow the rebels to be incorporated into a new national police force.*

inculcate /ˈɪnkʌlkeɪt, AM ɪnˈkʌl-/ (inculcates, inculcating, inculcated)

○ **ˈinculcate in** [FORMAL]

If you **inculcate** an idea or opinion **in**

someone, you teach it to them by repeating it until it is fixed in their mind.

inculcate something in someone ❑ *These are the values that we must inculcate in our children.* ❑ *The company aims to inculcate a sense of pride in its employees.*

index /ˈɪndeks/ (indexes, indexing, indexed)

○ **ˈindex to**

If something such as a payment or pension **is indexed to** something else, or if you **index** it **to** something else, you link them so that when one increases or decreases the other one does too.

be indexed to something ❑ *Minimum pensions and wages were indexed to inflation.*

index something to something ❑ *The Government indexed pensions to 25 per cent of average weekly earnings.*

indict /ɪnˈdaɪt/ (indicts, indicting, indicted)

○ **inˈdict for** [mainly AMERICAN]

If someone **is indicted for** a crime or someone **indicts** them **for** it, they are officially charged with it.

be indicted for something ❑ *He was indicted for murder.*

indict someone for something ❑ *A tribunal indicted him for his role in the violence.*

induct /ɪnˈdʌkt/ (inducts, inducting, inducted)

○ **induct ˈinto**

■ To **induct** someone **into** a job or group or to **be inducted into** it means to give them the job or accept them into the group in a special ceremony. [FORMAL]

be inducted into something ❑ *Six new members have been inducted into the Provincial Cabinet.*

induct someone into something ❑ *She inducted Nina into the cult.*

■ If someone **is inducted into** the army, they are officially made to join the army. [AMERICAN]

be inducted into something ❑ *In December he was inducted into the army.*

indulge /ɪnˈdʌldʒ/ (indulges, indulging, indulged)

○ **inˈdulge in** [FORMAL]

If you **indulge in** something, you do or have it because it is something you really enjoy.

indulge in something ❑ *He travelled to Scotland to indulge in his favourite pastime of fishing.* ❑ *Sweet foods should not be indulged in too often.*

infiltrate /'ɪnfɪltreɪt/ (**infiltrates, infiltrating, infiltrated**)

○ **infiltrate 'into**

◼ If someone **infiltrates into** a place or organization, they enter it secretly in order to get secret information about it or harm it.

infiltrate into something ❑ *A reporter tried to infiltrate into the prison.*

◾ To **infiltrate** someone **into** a place or organization means to get them into it secretly so that they can find out secret information or harm it.

infiltrate someone into something ❑ *The question remains, how did they manage to infiltrate him into the service of their enemies?*

inflict /ɪn'flɪkt/ (**inflicts, inflicting, inflicted**)

○ **in'flict on** (or **inflict upon**)

To **inflict** something bad **on** someone or something means to make them suffer it.

inflict something on someone/something ❑ *The scandal inflicted serious damage on the Conservative party.* ❑ *He had inflicted more then fifty injuries on his victim.*

inform /ɪn'fɔːm/ (**informs, informing, informed**)

○ **in'form of**

If you **inform** someone **of** something, you officially tell them about it.

inform someone of something ❑ *I asked them to inform me of any progress they had made.* ❑ *Commissioner Hassett had been informed of the arrest.*

○ **in'form on**

If you **inform on** someone, you give information about them to the police or other authority because you think they have done something wrong. = **betray**

inform on someone ❑ *A neighbour suspected he had stolen the car, and informed on him.*

infringe /ɪn'frɪndʒ/ (**infringes, infringing, infringed**)

○ **in'fringe on** (or **infringe upon**)

If something **infringes on** an activity or right, it limits it. = **encroach on, restrict**

infringe on someone/something ❑ *Employees complain that longer workdays infringe on their evening activities.* ❑ *Our legal rights are being infringed upon.*

infuse /ɪn'fjuːz/ (**infuses, infusing, infused**)

○ **infuse 'into** [FORMAL]

To **infuse** a quality **into** someone or something means to fill them with it.

infuse something into something/someone ❑ *She had tried to infuse some humour into her art.* ❑ *He managed to infuse his great energy and enthusiasm into his students.*

○ **in'fuse with** [FORMAL]

To **infuse** someone or something **with** a quality means to fill them with it.

infuse someone/something with something ❑ *The beauty of the landscape infused me with a sense of deep peace.*

be infused with something ❑ *His writing is infused with warmth and humour.*

ingratiate /ɪn'greɪʃieɪt/ (**ingratiates, ingratiating, ingratiated**)

○ **in'gratiate with**

If someone tries to **ingratiate** themselves **with** another person, they say and do things to try to make that person like them, often in an annoying way.

ingratiate yourself with someone ❑ *Byers was always trying to ingratiate himself with his boss.* ❑ *Politicians are trying to ingratiate themselves with voters in the run-up to the election.*

inhibit /ɪn'hɪbɪt/ (**inhibits, inhibiting, inhibited**)

○ **in'hibit from**

To **inhibit** someone **from** doing something means to prevent them from doing it, although they want to do it or should be able to do it.

inhibit someone from doing something ❑ *Uncertainty about jobs is inhibiting shoppers from spending money.*

initiate /ɪ'nɪʃieɪt/ (**initiates, initiating, initiated**)

○ **initiate 'into**

◼ If you **initiate** someone **into** something, you tell them about something, or you teach them how to do it.

initiate someone into something ❑ *Clarke has initiated many young people into jazz music.* ❑ *Jameson was initiated into the sport two years ago when his father joined a golf club.*

◾ If someone **is initiated into** a religion, secret society, or social group or if someone **initiates** them **into** it, they become a member of it by taking part in a special ceremony.

be initiated into something ❑ *This is where the Maori holy men came to be initiated into the priesthood.*

initiate someone into something ❑ *That night they gathered to initiate three new members into their tribe.*

nject /ɪnˈdʒekt/ (**injects, injecting, injected**)
○ **inject 'into**

1 To **inject** a new, exciting, or interesting quality **into** something means to add it.
inject something into something ❑ *His arrival will inject new life into the team.* ❑ *She wanted to inject some fun into their relationship.*
2 To **inject** money **into** an organization, service, or economy means to provide more money for it.
inject something into something ❑ *More than £5.6 billion has been injected into the health service.*

ink /ɪŋk/ (**inks, inking, inked**)
○ **ink 'in**

1 If you **ink** something **in**, you write it in ink to show that it is now definite or final, after you have written it in pencil before.
≠ **pencil in**
ink something in or **ink in something** ❑ *The revisions can now be inked in.* ❑ *Then I go over the sketches later and ink them in.*
2 If you **ink** someone or something **in**, you decide that they will definitely be used after you have discussed other possibilities. [INFORMAL]
ink someone/something in or **ink in someone/something** ❑ *Gooch was the opener we had inked in after his tour of West Indies.*
be inked in ❑ *Both players are inked in for the tour of Japan.*

inquire /ɪnˈkwaɪə/ (**inquires, inquiring, inquired**)

(**Inquire** is also spelled **enquire.**)

○ **in'quire after** [FORMAL]
If you **inquire after** someone, you ask how they are or what they are doing. = **ask after**
inquire after someone ❑ *She inquired after my parents.* ❑ *I inquired after Mrs. Merry's health.*
○ **inquire 'into**
To **inquire into** a matter is to officially try to find out all the facts about it.
inquire into something ❑ *Police are inquiring into the background of Mr Kiley.*

insert /ɪnˈsɜːt/ (**inserts, inserting, inserted**)
○ **insert 'into**
If you **insert** an object **into** something, you put the object inside it.
insert something into something ❑ *He took a key from his pocket and inserted it into the lock.* ❑ *She inserted the card into the slot to open the door.*

insinuate /ɪnˈsɪnjueɪt/ (**insinuates, insinuating, insinuated**)
○ **insinuate 'into** [FORMAL]
If someone **insinuates** themselves **into** a particular situation or position, they get into it by being clever but slightly dishonest.
insinuate yourself into something ❑ *The Internet is insinuating itself into all aspects of our lives.*

insist /ɪnˈsɪst/ (**insists, insisting, insisted**)
⊙ **in'sist on** (or **insist upon**)
If you **insist on** something, you ask for it firmly and refuse to accept anything else.
insist on something ❑ *Most universities used to insist on an interview before accepting a student.* ❑ *He insisted on paying for the meal.*

install /ɪnˈstɔːl/ (**installs, installing, installed**)
○ **in'stall in** [FORMAL]
If you **install** yourself **in** a particular place, you go there and make yourself comfortable.
install yourself in something ❑ *Tony installed himself in an armchair looking out over the square.* ❑ *Within a week she had installed herself in his apartment.*

instruct /ɪnˈstrʌkt/ (**instructs, instructing, instructed**)
○ **in'struct in** [FORMAL]
Someone who **instructs** people **in** a subject or skill teaches it to them.
instruct someone in something ❑ *She also instructed them in the art of French cooking.* ❑ *The young princes were instructed in literature, history, and geography.*

insulate /ˈɪnsjuleɪt, AM -sə-/ (**insulates, insulating, insulated**)
○ **'insulate from**
To **insulate** someone or something **from** something means to protect them from it.
insulate someone/something from something ❑ *His immense wealth had insulated him from ordinary people.*
insulate yourself from something ❑ *To insulate himself from the pressures of fame, he regularly returns to his home town.*

insure /ɪnˈʃʊə/ (**insures, insuring, insured**)
○ **in'sure against**
1 If you **insure against** something unpleasant, you do something to prevent it happening or affecting you.
insure against something ❑ *During years of good rainfall they expand their stocks to insure against drought.* ❑ *Attempts were made to insure against that possibility.*
2 To **be insured against** a particular bad thing happening is to have paid money to a company who will then give you money if that bad thing happens.

be insured against something ❏ *Is your bicycle insured against theft?* ❏ *I'm insured against loss.*

integrate /ˈɪntɪɡreɪt/ (integrates, integrating, integrated)

○ **'integrate with**

If you **integrate** one thing **with** another thing, or one thing **integrates with** another thing, the two things become closely linked or form part of a whole idea or system.

integrate something with something ❏ *The software allows firms to integrate their operations with outside organisations.*

integrate with something ❏ *Acupuncture treatment integrates well with other forms of therapy.*

interact /ɪntəˈrækt/ (interacts, interacting, interacted)

○ **inte'ract with**

◼ When people **interact with** each other, they communicate while they work or spend time together.

interact with someone ❏ *The rhymes and songs help parents interact with their babies.*

◾ When people **interact with** computers, or when computers **interact with** other machines, information is sent between them.

interact with something ❏ *Some older people need simplified ways of interacting with a computer.* ❏ *This software tells your computer how to interact with a piece of hardware.*

◾ When one thing **interacts with** another thing, the two things affect each other.

interact with something ❏ *Grapefruit interacts with some drugs and makes them more potent and potentially dangerous.*

interchange /ɪntəˈtʃeɪndʒ/ (interchanges, interchanging, interchanged)

○ **inter'change with**

If you **interchange** one thing **with** another thing or if one thing **interchanges with** another, each thing takes the place of the other or is exchanged for the other.

interchange something with something ❏ *The fuel can be interchanged with today's conventional fuels.*

interchange with something ❏ *Some operators now arrange for taxis to interchange with night buses.*

interface /ˈɪntəfeɪs/ (interfaces, interfacing, interfaced)

○ **'interface with** [FORMAL]

If one thing **interfaces with** another thing, or if you **interface** one thing **with** another

thing, you connect the two things.

interface something with something ❏ *He had interfaced all this machinery with a computer hidden under the stage.*

interface with something ❏ *This affects the way we interface with the environment.*

interfere /ɪntəˈfɪə/ (interferes, interfering, interfered)

○ **inter'fere in**

If you **interfere in** a situation, you become involved in it and start changing it when you should not because the situation involves other people and not you.

= **meddle in**

interfere in something ❏ *Well next time, don't interfere in things that don't concern you.* ❏ *It makes him furious to have anyone interfere in his work.*

○ **inter'fere with**

◼ If something or someone **interferes with** a process or situation, they prevent the process or situation from continuing efficiently or successfully.

interfere with something ❏ *Personal and family stresses will inevitably interfere with work at times.* ❏ *His father-in-law had interfered with his marriage right from the very beginning.*

◾ If something **interferes with** an electronic signal, sound waves etc. it stops it so that it cannot be heard or received easily.

interfere with something ❏ *Tall buildings can interfere with the signal.*

◾ Someone who **interferes with** a child touches the child in a sexual way. = **molest**

interfere with someone ❏ *He was arrested for interfering with children.*

◳ Someone who **interferes with** a witness tries to persuade them to give information that is not true in a court of law.

interfere with someone ❏ *There are strong penalties for people who interfere with witnesses.*

◱ If someone **interferes with** something, they touch or change it without permission, and damage it.

interfere with something ❏ *He noticed that someone had interfered with the seal on the box.*

interpose /ɪntəˈpəʊz/ (interposes, interposing, interposed)

○ **inter'pose between** [FORMAL]

If you **interpose** something or yourself **between** two people or things, you put it or yourself between them.

interpose something between something ❏ *He interposed his arm between the two men.*

interpose yourself between something

❏ Police forces had to interpose themselves between the two rival groups.

intervene /ˌɪntəˈviːn/ (intervenes, intervening, intervened)

○ inter'vene in

To **intervene in** a situation means to become involved in it and try to change it or stop it.
intervene in something ❏ The government decided to intervene in the crisis. ❏ The United States has intervened in the dispute between the two countries.

introduce /ˌɪntrəˈdjuːs, AM -ˈduːs/ (introduces, introducing, introduced)

✪ intro'duce to

1 If you **introduce** one person **to** another person, you tell them each other's names, so that they can get to know each other.
introduce someone to someone ❏ Tim, may I introduce you to my colleague Ahmed Thamer?
2 If you **introduce** yourself **to** someone, you tell them your name.
introduce yourself to someone ❏ I went up on stage and introduced myself to him.
3 If you **introduce** someone **to** something, you tell them about it or let them experience it for the first time.
introduce someone to something ❏ He introduced us to the delights of Indian food. ❏ It was Jane who introduced me to this restaurant.

intrude /ɪnˈtruːd/ (intrudes, intruding, intruded)

○ intrude 'into

1 To **intrude into** a situation means to become involved when you are not wanted.
intrude into something ❏ The Press intrude into people's personal lives in a wholly unacceptable way.
2 If someone **intrudes into** a place, they go there even though they are not allowed to be there.
intrude into somewhere ❏ An enemy aircraft had intruded into the country's airspace.

○ in'trude on (or intrude upon)

1 If someone **intrudes on** a situation that involves another person, they upset the other person by being present or becoming involved.
intrude on something ❏ We left her alone, not wishing to intrude on her grief. ❏ These photographers regularly intrude on the privacy of famous people.
2 If something **intrudes on** a good thing that someone experiences, it spoils it.
intrude on something ❏ Doubts began to intrude on his happiness.

inure /ɪnˈjʊə/ (inures, inuring, inured)

○ in'ure to [FORMAL]

If you **are inured to** something unpleasant, you are used to it and do not notice it or suffer because of it.
be inured to something ❏ Having seen so much violence over the years, he had become inured to pain and suffering. ❏ By now we were inured to the cold.

inveigh /ɪnˈveɪ/ (inveighs, inveighing, inveighed)

○ in'veigh against [FORMAL]

If you **inveigh against** something, you strongly criticize it.
inveigh against something ❏ He inveighed against the government.
NOTE **Rail against** is a less formal expression for **inveigh against**.

invest /ɪnˈvest/ (invests, investing, invested)

✪ in'vest in

1 If you **invest in** something, or if you **invest** money **in** something, you use your money in a way that you hope will increase its value, for example by buying shares or property.
invest in something ❏ They have invested in an oil field in Russia.
invest something in something ❏ He invested all our profits in gold shares. ❏ The money was invested in shares.
2 When a government or organization **invests in** something or **invests** money **in** it, it spends money on it in order to improve it or make it more successful.
invest in something ❏ We recognize the importance of investing in education and training.
invest something in something ❏ The government needs to invest more money in the transport network.
3 If you **invest** time or energy **in** something, you spend a lot of time or energy on it.
invest something in something ❏ I wish I had invested more time and effort in our relationship. ❏ She invested all her energies in raising her children.
4 If you **invest in** something, you buy it because it will be useful.
invest in something ❏ It is worth investing in some good quality walking boots.

invite /ɪnˈvaɪt/ (invites, inviting, invited)

○ invite a'round (or invite round [mainly BRITISH])

If you **invite** someone **around**, you ask them to come and visit you in your home.

invite someone around or **invite around someone** ❑ *He hoped Jane would invite him round, but she didn't.* ❑ [+ for] *She invited a few friends around for drinks.*

⊙ **invite 'in**

If you **invite** someone **in**, you ask them to come into your house, usually when they have knocked on the door or rung the bell.

invite someone in ❑ *Aren't you even going to invite me in?* ❑ [+ for] *I invited Adam in for coffee.*

○ **invite 'out**

If you **invite** someone **out**, you ask them to go with you to something like a restaurant, party, or play.

invite someone out ❑ *Some friends have invited me out.* ❑ [+ for] *To cheer her up, Morris invited her out for a meal.*

NOTE **Ask out** is a more informal expression for **invite out**.

○ **invite 'over**

If you **invite** someone **over**, you ask them

to come and visit you in your home.

invite someone over ❑ *Why don't you invite Juan over?* ❑ [+ for] *The neighbours invited us over for a party.* ❑ *I've invited them over on Thursday for the barbecue.*

○ **invite 'round** ➔ see **invite around**

iron /aɪən/ (**irons, ironing, ironed**)

○ **iron 'out**

If you **iron out** small problems or difficulties, you find a way to solve them.

iron something out or **iron out something** ❑ *We need to iron out these problems now before they become worse.*

itch /ɪtʃ/ (**itches, itching, itched**)

○ **'itch for** [INFORMAL]

If you **are itching for** something, you want it very much.

be itching for something ❑ *Dean was restless and itching for change.*

Jj

jab /dʒæb/ (jabs, jabbing, jabbed)
○ **'jab at**
If you **jab at** something or someone, or you **jab** something **at** them, you push them hard several times with something long and thin. = **poke at**
jab at something/someone ❑ *She could hear him jabbing viciously at the keyboard.* ❑ [+ with] *Bella got very angry and jabbed at him with her pen.*
jab something at someone ❑ *He raised his voice and jabbed his finger at me.*

jabber /'dʒæbə/ (jabbers, jabbering, jabbered)
○ **jabber a'way**
If someone **jabbers away**, they talk so quickly that it is difficult to understand what they say. ❑ *The train was full of people jabbering away on their phones.*

jack /dʒæk/ (jacks, jacking, jacked)
○ **jack a'round** [AMERICAN, INFORMAL]
If someone **jacks** you **around**, they cause problems for you especially by wasting your time.
jack someone around ❑ *I know you're just jacking me around.*
○ **jack 'in** [BRITISH, INFORMAL]
If you **jack in** a job, course, or other regular activity, you stop doing it. = **pack in**
jack something in *or* **jack in something**
❑ *One of these days I'm going to jack this job in and sail round the world.* ❑ *He used to play golf but he jacked it in.*
○ **jack 'off** [AMERICAN, INFORMAL, RUDE]
If someone **jacks off**, they touch their own sexual organs to get sexual pleasure. = **jerk off, toss off**
○ **jack 'up**
1 If you **jack up** a car or heavy object, you lift it off the ground using a jack or other lifting tool.
jack up something *or* **jack something up**
❑ *John jacked up the car and changed the tyre.*
2 To **jack up** a price, amount etc. means to increase it by a large amount. [INFORMAL]

jack up something *or* **jack something up**
❑ [+ by] *Her car insurance had been jacked up by more than $400.* ❑ *Some universities have jacked up fees by 40%.* ❑ *Oil companies are jacking the price of gas up.*
NOTE **Inflate** is a more formal word for **jack up**.
3 If someone **jacks up**, they take a drug such as heroin or cocaine by injecting it. [INFORMAL] ❑ *There is blue lighting in the public toilets to stop people jacking up in there.*
4 If you **jack up** something, you improve it and make it more successful. [INFORMAL]
jack up something *or* **jack something up**
❑ *He tried to jack his career up by ruining mine.*
❑ *The actor Johnny Depp was there to jack up the acting department.*
5 If someone **jacks up**, they refuse to do something. [AUSTRALIAN, INFORMAL]
❑ *Clem stood up and announced that he was jacking up.*

jam /dʒæm/ (jams, jamming, jammed)
○ **jam 'into**
If a lot of people **jam into** a place, there are so many of them that it is difficult to move.
jam into somewhere ❑ *More than 10,000 fans jammed into the arena to watch the game.*
○ **jam 'on** [INFORMAL]
If you **jam on the brakes** while you are driving, you push the brake hard and stop very suddenly. ❑ *She jammed on the brakes when a child ran into the road.* ❑ *Marty jammed the brakes on but couldn't avoid hitting the car.*
○ **jam 'up**
1 If people or things **are jammed up** against an object, they are very close to the object and cannot move.
be jammed up ❑ [+ against] *The train was full and I was jammed up against other passengers.*
2 If people or vehicles **jam up** a place or if a place **jams up**, people or vehicles block it so that it is difficult to move.
jam up something *or* **jam something up**
❑ *Groups of tourists jam up the narrow streets of*

the town. ❑ *The traffic caused by the national holiday can jam the roads up.*

jam up ❑ *The bridge jams up every morning with traffic.* ● If there is a **jam-up**, people or vehicles block a place so that it is difficult to move. ❑ *Several runners tripped in a jam-up at the start of the race.*

3 If a machine or piece of equipment **jams up** or something **jams** it **up**, it does not work because a part of it cannot move properly.
jam up ❑ *Once again, the camera jammed up.*
jam something up or **jam up something** ❑ *The paper had jammed up the printer.*

jar /dʒɑː/ (jars, jarring, jarred)

○ **jar 'off** [INFORMAL]
If something or someone **jars** you **off**, they make you angry.
jar someone off or **jar off someone** ❑ *It really jars me off when these people tell us what to do.*
● If someone is **jarred-off**, they are angry.
❑ *He's really jarred-off with his job.*

○ **'jar on**
If something **jars on** you, you think it is slightly unpleasant or shocking.
jar on someone ❑ *I know the remark jarred on some people.* ❑ *Something about her manner jarred on him.*

jazz /dʒæz/ (jazzes, jazzing, jazzed)

○ **jazz 'up** [INFORMAL]
If you **jazz** something **up**, you make it more interesting or exciting. = **liven up**
jazz something up or **jazz up something** ❑ *They've certainly jazzed this place up since the last time I was here.* ❑ *Wear a pretty scarf to jazz up a plain sweater.* ● Music that is **jazzed-up** has been changed in order to sound more like popular music or jazz. ❑ *The music was a jazzed-up version of one of the Brandenburg Concertos.* ● Something that is **jazzed-up** has been changed to make it more interesting or exciting. ❑ *Some parents give their children old names with jazzed-up spellings.*

jeer /dʒɪə/ (jeers, jeering, jeered)

○ **'jeer at**
If someone **jeers at** a person, they laugh at them or shout rude things to them to show that they do not like them.
jeer at someone ❑ *Kids followed her down the street, jeering at her.* ❑ *The speaker was whistled and jeered at by the crowd.*

jerk /dʒɜːk/ (jerks, jerking, jerked)

○ **jerk a'round** [INFORMAL]
If someone **jerks** you **around**, they are not honest with you about something.

jerk someone around ❑ *Don't jerk me around, Mr Crook.*

○ **jerk 'off** [INFORMAL, RUDE]
If someone **jerks off**, or **jerks** someone else **off** they touch their sexual organs to get or give sexual pleasure. = **jack off, toss off**

○ **jerk 'out**
If you **jerk out** a remark, you say it very suddenly.
jerk something out or **jerk out something** ❑ *'What have you done with my money?' jerked out Mr. Roberts angrily.*

jib /dʒɪb/ (jibs, jibbing, jibbed)

○ **'jib at** [OLD-FASHIONED]
If you **jib at** something, you do not want to accept or do it.
jib at something ❑ *Many banks had jibbed at handing out such big loans.*

jockey /'dʒɒki/ (jockeys, jockeying, jockeyed)

○ **'jockey for**
If someone **jockeys for** position or status, they compete against other people to get more power.
jockey for something ❑ *Several members of the party were jockeying for the job of party leader.*

jog /dʒɒg/ (jogs, jogging, jogged)

○ **jog a'long**
If you **jog along**, you continue in a situation, without trying to change it. ❑ *James and I had always jogged along comfortably without any arguments.*

○ **jog 'on** [BRITISH, VERY INFORMAL]
If you tell someone to **jog on**, you mean that you do not like their opinions or actions and you would like them to go away.
jog on ❑ *He asked me to lend him £10 the other day and I told him to jog on.*

join /dʒɔɪn/ (joins, joining, joined)

○ **join 'in**
If you **join in** or **join in** an activity, you start to do something with other people who are already doing it.
join in something ❑ *He took his coat off and joined in the work.* ❑ *Several people joined in the applause.*
join in ❑ *Is this a private conversation or can anyone join in?* ❑ [+ with] *We joined in with the celebrations.*
[NOTE] **Participate** is a more formal word for **join in**.

○ **join 'up**
1 If one person **joins up** with another

person, or if two people **join up**, they decide
to go somewhere together. **= get together**
❏ *The two families joined up for the rest of the
holiday.* ❏ [+ with] *We joined up with some other
tourists to visit Pompeii.*
2 If someone **joins up**, they become a
member of the army, the navy, or the air
force. **= enlist** ❏ *He didn't join up until 1940.*
3 If you **join up** two things or if they **join
up**, they become connected. **= link up**
join up something ❏ *I used to join up all the
paper clips in a long chain.*
join something up ❏ *Join the dots up using a
pencil.*
join up ❏ *This takes place when two cells join up
and exchange genes.* ❏ [+ with] *The road joins up
with Museum Street.*

olly /'dʒɒli/ (**jollies, jollying, jollied**)
○ **jolly a'long** [BRITISH, INFORMAL]
If you **jolly** someone **along**, you keep them
in a good mood, so that they will do
something or continue to work.
jolly someone along ❏ *I was tired of her
attempts to jolly me along.*

ot /dʒɒt/ (**jots, jotting, jotted**)
○ **jot 'down**
If you **jot** something **down**, you write it
down quickly in the form of a short note.
= note down
jot something down or **jot down something**
❏ *Renshaw jotted down the phone number in his
notebook.* ❏ *He jotted some notes down on a pad.*
❏ *She noted the exact time of the call and jotted it
down.*

uggle /'dʒʌgəl/ (**juggles, juggling,
juggled**)
○ **'juggle with**
1 If you **juggle with** things such as
numbers or ideas, you keep changing them
slightly until they seem right.
juggle with something ❏ *He was juggling with
the statistics.*
2 If you **juggle with** several objects, you try
to hold onto all of them or control all of
them, but with difficulty.
juggle with something ❏ *He juggled with the
controls.*

umble /'dʒʌmbəl/ (**jumbles, jumbling,
jumbled**)
○ **jumble 'up**
If someone **jumbles** things **up** they mix
them together in a way that is untidy or
confusing. **= mix up**
jumble something up or **jumble up
something** ❏ *We've jumbled up the letters and*

you have to try and guess the word. ❏ *You can
encode information by jumbling it up.* ● If things
are **jumbled up**, they are all mixed together
in a way that is untidy or confusing. ❏ *The
bags were jumbled up and it was difficult to see
which was which.* ❏ *The ideas were all jumbled up
in my head.*

jump /dʒʌmp/ (**jumps, jumping, jumped**)
○ **'jump at**
If you **jump at** an opportunity or offer, you
accept it immediately. **= leap at**
jump at something ❏ *He had jumped at the
chance to go to Japan.* ❏ *Private companies have
not exactly jumped at the opportunity.*
○ **jump 'in**
1 If you **jump in**, you do something
immediately, often without thinking
much about what you are doing. ❏ *If an
opportunity presents itself, you have to jump in
before someone else does.*
2 During a conversation or discussion
with someone, if you **jump in**, you
interrupt them or say something that they
do not want you to say. **= butt in** ❏ [+ with]
*Try not to jump in with advice and instant
solutions.* ❏ *'But they sent that letter,' Josephine
jumped in.*
○ **'jump on**
1 If you **jump on** someone or something,
you criticize them immediately.
[INFORMAL]
jump on someone/something ❏ *Leaders of
the opposition parties quickly jumped on Mr
Howard's comments.* ❏ [+ for] *We are so quick to
jump on people for their beliefs.*
2 If someone **jumps on** you, they attack you
suddenly.
jump on someone ❏ *He was jumped on from
behind, and beaten over the head.*
○ **jump 'out at**
If something **jumps out at** you, it is so
obvious that you notice it immediately.
jump out at someone ❏ *The quality of the
writing jumps out at you from the start of chapter
one.*
○ **jump 'up**
If someone who is sitting down **jumps up**,
they suddenly stand up. ❏ *He slumped back
into his chair and then jumped up again.*
❏ [+ from] *'Mabel!' he cried, jumping up from
his chair.*

jut /dʒʌt/ (**juts, jutting, jutted**)
○ **jut 'out**
1 If an area of land or an object **juts out**, it
sticks out so that it is more obvious than
the surrounding parts. ❏ [+ from] *A concrete*

pipe jutted out from the brick wall. ❏ [+ into] *The rocks jut out into the ocean.*

NOTE **Protrude** is a more formal word for **jut out**.

2 If you **jut out** your chin, jaw or lip, or it juts out, you move it forwards, often to show your determination to do something. = stick out

jut something out *or* **jut out something**
❏ *'What?', she demanded, jutting out her chin.*
❏ *He jutted his jaw out to look heroic.*
jut out ❏ *Her bottom lip started to jut out in anger.*

Kk

eel /ki:l/ (keels, keeling, keeled)

keel 'over

1 If someone **keels over**, they fall over sideways, especially because they suddenly become ill. ❑ *One of the athletes keeled over and was rushed to hospital.* ❑ [+ with] *Newman keeled over with a heart attack.*

2 If a boat **keels over**, it turns upside down. ❑ *At the height of the storm, the ship began keeling over.*

eep /ki:p/ (keeps, keeping, kept)

keep 'at

If you **keep at it**, or **keep** someone **at it**, you continue, or make them continue, doing something, even if it is difficult or unpleasant. = **stick at, stick to** ❑ *It is hard, but you've just got to keep at it.* ❑ *I kept at it for another hour.*

NOTE **Persevere** is a more formal word for **keep at**.

keep a'way

1 If you **keep away**, you avoid something or someone or do not go near them. = **stay away** ❑ *The police are keeping away – they believe their presence could make the situation worse.* ❑ [+ from] *Keep away from the cliff edge.* ❑ *You should keep away from anyone who is unwell.*

2 If someone or something **keeps** someone **away**, they stop them from going somewhere or doing something.
keep someone away ❑ *The singer employed bodyguards to keep photographers away.* ❑ [+ from] *You should keep young children away from fire.* ❑ *Keep him away from me! I don't want to talk to him.*
keep away someone ❑ *The bad weather kept away most visitors.*

3 If something **keeps** something unpleasant or unwanted **away**, it stops it from affecting and harming you.
keep away something ❑ *They hang this stone in the room to keep away evil spirits.*
keep something away ❑ *Eating plenty of fruit and vegetables may keep the disease away.*

keep 'back

1 If you **keep back**, you do not go near something. ❑ *The dog probably won't bite, but it's better to keep back just in case.* ❑ *'Keep back!' snapped Louis.* ❑ [+ from] *Keep back from the edge of the platform.*

2 If a person or object **keeps** something or someone **back**, it stops them from going somewhere.
keep someone/something back ❑ *If the barrier is broken, it's hard to keep the water back.*
keep back someone/something ❑ *Police were there to keep back the crowd of reporters.* ❑ [+ from] *Her hair was kept back from her forehead by a red velvet band.*

3 If you **keep** part of something **back**, you do not use or give away all of it, so that you still have some to use later.
keep back something ❑ *Remember to keep back enough cream to put on the top of the cake.*
keep something back ❑ *She did keep some things back for when Pam came.*

NOTE **Reserve** is a more formal word for **keep back**.

4 If you **keep** some information **back**, you do not tell someone everything.
keep something back ❑ *You can't write an autobiography without keeping something back.* ❑ [+ from] *You aren't keeping anything back from me, are you?*
keep back something ❑ *Ministers have been keeping back information which is clearly in the public interest.*

NOTE **Withhold** is a more formal word for **keep back**.

5 If you **keep back** your emotions, feelings, or ideas, you try to hide them from other people. = **hold back**
keep back something ❑ *He tried very hard to keep back the tears.* ❑ *Michael couldn't keep back the excitement he felt.*
keep something back ❑ *She said she was happy, but I could tell she was keeping something back.*

6 If something or someone **keeps** you **back**, they stop you from being as successful as you could be.
keep someone back ❑ *It is only one small problem that is keeping you back.*

7 If you **keep** someone **back**, you delay them by talking to them.

keep someone back ❑ *Ann was probably keeping him back and that was why he was late.* ❑ *[+ from] I won't keep you back from your work any longer.*

8 If you **keep** some money **back**, you do not pay someone all the money that you owe them.

keep something back ❑ *[+ from] Steve told his wife to keep some money back from his lawyer.*

keep back something ❑ *Keep back some of the builder's payment until a surveyor has checked the work.*

○ **keep 'down**

1 If someone or something **keeps** the number, size, or amount of something **down**, they stop it increasing and keep it at a low level.

keep something down ❑ *They employ fewer staff to keep costs down.* ❑ *I don't want any more cake, I'm trying to keep my weight down.*

keep down something ❑ *We need to keep down production costs.* ❑ *[+ to] Costs should be kept down to a reasonable level.*

2 If you **keep** noise or your voice **down**, you try to be quieter.

keep something down ❑ *'Keep your voice down!' Caroline whispered.* ❑ *We kept the noise down to avoid disturbing Peggy.*

keep down something ❑ *The band were forced to keep down the volume during their practice sessions.*

If you tell someone to **keep it down**, you are telling them to make less noise. [INFORMAL] ❑ *Keep it down, will you. I'm trying to read.*

3 If you **keep down** or if you **keep** your head **down**, you stay in a lying or low position in order to avoid being seen or attacked.

keep down ❑ *Keep down!*

keep something down ❑ *They kept their heads down.*

4 If you **keep** your **head down**, you try not do anything that makes people notice you. ❑ *If you keep your head down and work hard, you'll be fine here.*

5 If someone or something **keeps** a person, group or country **down**, they stop them from being powerful or successful.

keep someone/something down ❑ *By moving to places where workers are not protected, companies are keeping poor countries down.* ❑ *It will take more than illness to keep her down.*

keep down someone/something ❑ *The government wanted to keep down the trade unions.*

NOTE **Oppress** is a more formal word for **keep down**.

6 If you **keep** food or drink **down**, you are able to keep it in your stomach and not

vomit after you have eaten or drunk something. = **hold down**

keep something down or **keep down something** ❑ *I can't keep anything down, not even water.* ❑ *He was so ill he couldn't even keep down a cup of tea.*

○ **'keep from**

1 To **keep** someone **from** doing something or **keep** something **from** happening mean to stop them doing it or stop something from happening.

keep someone/something from something ❑ *Dad tried to keep me from going.* ❑ *We tied rope round the bundles to keep them from falling off.*

2 If you **keep from** doing something, you manage to stop yourself doing it, but it is difficult. [FORMAL]

keep from doing something ❑ *He had managed to keep from telling the secret.*

NOTE **Resist** is a more formal word for **keep from**.

3 If you **keep** information **from** someone, you do not tell them about it.

keep something from someone ❑ *I felt that he was keeping something from me.*

○ **keep 'in**

1 If a parent or teacher **keeps** children **in**, they make them stay indoors or they make them stay late at school, usually as a punishment.

keep someone in or **keep in someone** ❑ *John was kept in at school one day last week.*

2 If you **keep in** when you are walking, cycling, or driving along a road or path, you stay near the edge of the road or path. ❑ *Keep in! There's some cars coming.*

3 If a hospital **keeps** you **in**, doctors say you must stay because you are not well enough to leave.

keep someone in ❑ *They kept me in overnight for tests.*

4 If you **keep** a feeling or opinion **in**, you stop yourself from showing it or saying what you think.

keep something in or **keep in something** ❑ *I stayed cool and kept my anger in.* ❑ *He was very open and never kept in his feelings.*

○ **keep 'in with** [BRITISH]

If you **keep in with** someone, you stay friendly with them because you want something from them.

keep in with someone ❑ *Try to keep in with him – he might be able to help you with your career.*

○ **keep 'off**

1 To **keep off** an area or **keep** someone or something **off** an area means to not go in a particular area or to stop a person or animal from going there.

keep someone/something off something
❑ These kids need something to keep them off the streets. ❑ Could you keep your dog off my property?

keep off something ❑ There was a sign saying 'Keep off the grass'. ❑ Keep off the main roads and you'll be all right.

keep off ❑ Christopher was warned to keep off.

2 If a person or thing **keeps** something **off** or **keeps** something **off** someone, they prevent it from touching, harming, or attacking someone.

keep something off ❑ They sat in a shelter to keep the rain off.

keep off something ❑ She covered the food to keep off the flies.

keep something off someone/something
❑ She wore a hat to keep the sun off her face.
❑ Keep those dogs off me!

3 If you **keep off** a particular food or drink or **keep** someone **off** it, you avoid eating or drinking it or stop someone else from eating or drinking it, because it would cause problems.

keep off something ❑ She can drink skimmed milk, but she has to keep off the butter.

keep someone off something ❑ Their son has an allergy and they have to keep him off all dairy products.

4 If you **keep off** a particular subject, you deliberately do not talk about it. **= avoid**

keep off something ❑ He kept off the question of whose fault it was. ❑ She carefully kept off the subject of money.

5 If rain or snow **keeps off**, it does not start. **= hold off** [BRITISH] ❑ Luckily the rain kept off.

6 If a parent **keeps** a child **off**, or **keeps** a child **off** school, they do not let the child go to school, especially because they are ill.

keep someone off ❑ If your child has been sick, you should keep him or her off for at least 48 hours.

keep someone off something ❑ She had a high temperature so I kept her off school.

○ **keep 'on**

1 If you **keep on**, or **keep on** doing something, you continue doing something and do not stop. **= carry on**

keep on ❑ My hands were shaking but I kept on.

keep on doing something ❑ Keep on rinsing until the water is clear. ❑ He kept on staring at me.

2 If something **keeps on**, it continues.
❑ If the rain keeps on, the game will be cancelled.
❑ The screams kept on but no one answered.

3 If you **keep** someone **on**, you continue to employ them.

keep someone on ❑ Only half the workforce will be kept on after this order has been completed.

keep on someone. ❑ Few companies will keep on an employee with a criminal record.

4 If you **keep on**, you continue to talk about something in a boring or annoying way. **= go on, harp on** [BRITISH, INFORMAL]
❑ [+ about] She kept on about the stupid car.
❑ Jamie, don't keep on, please!

○ **keep 'on at** [BRITISH, INFORMAL]

If you **keep on at** someone, you ask or tell them something several times in a way that annoys them.

keep on at someone ❑ I made no reply, but he kept on at me. ❑ [+ about] While I was training, people kept on at me about how bad the pay was.
❑ [+ to-infinitive] She kept on at me to go to the doctor about the pain I was getting.

● **keep 'out**

1 To **keep** someone or something **out** means to stop them from entering a place or being there.

keep out someone/something ❑ There is a guard dog to keep out intruders. ❑ They built a dam to keep out the water.

keep someone/something out ❑ The net keeps mosquitoes and other insects out. ❑ [+ of] He lifted his hand to keep the sun out of his eyes.

2 If a sign says **Keep Out**, it is warning you not to go onto that piece of land. ❑ 'Private property. Keep out.'

● **keep 'out of**

1 To **keep** someone or something **out of** a situation means to stop them from becoming involved in it.

keep someone/something out of something ❑ Getting a job will keep him out of trouble. ❑ I believe we should keep religion out of politics. ❑ Children need to learn how to keep themselves out of danger.

2 If you **keep out of** a situation, you avoid becoming involved in it. **= stay out of**

keep out of something ❑ You keep out of this. It's got nothing to do with you. ❑ I kept out of trouble as best I could. ❑ We kept out of her way and never spoke to her again.

● **'keep to**

1 If you **keep to** a rule, agreement or method, you do exactly what you are expected or supposed to do. **= stick to**

keep to something ❑ He drove calmly and kept to the speed limit. ❑ Try to keep to a routine.

2 If you **keep to** a particular subject, you talk only about that subject, and do not talk about anything else.

keep to something ❑ Let's keep to the subject, or we'll all get confused. ❑ Over lunch, they kept to safe topics and avoided talking about their relationship.

• If you **keep to the point**, you only mention important facts and do not mention things that are not connected. = **stick to**; ≠ **get off** ❑ *Keep to the point – don't be tempted to bring in other issues and past experiences.*

3 If you **keep** something **to** a particular number or amount or **keep to** a particular number or amount, you limit it to that number or amount.

keep something to something ❑ *Try to keep costs to a minimum.*

keep to something ❑ *Control your alcohol intake, keeping to two or three units a week, maximum.*

4 If you **keep to** something such as a path, you do not move away from it as you go somewhere. = **stick to**

keep to something ❑ *Please keep to the paths.* ❑ *When driving in Britain, you should keep to the left.*

5 If you **keep to** a place such as your bed or a room in your home, you stay there for a period of time, for example if you are ill or if the weather is bad. = **stay in** [FORMAL]

keep to something ❑ *He kept to his bed when he had flu.*

6 If you **keep** something **to** yourself, you do not tell anyone about it.

keep something to yourself ❑ *Keep it to yourself, won't you? I don't think she wants people to know yet.*

7 If you **keep to** yourself, or **keep** yourself **to** yourself, you do not talk to other people very much or form friendships with them.

keep to yourself ❑ *He kept to himself, eating alone, wary of forming friendships.*

keep yourself to yourself ❑ *She made it clear that she wanted to keep herself to herself.*

○ **keep 'under**

If a doctor **keeps** you **under**, they keep you in a state in which you are unconscious by giving you drugs.

keep someone under ❑ *She was kept under with a mixture of morphine and chloroform.*

✪ **keep 'up**

1 If you **keep up** an activity, you continue to do it and do not let it stop or end.

keep up something ❑ *I tried to keep up the conversation.* ❑ *He was unable to keep up the payments.*

keep something up ❑ *He kept a commentary up throughout the game.* ❑ *I can run fast over a short distance but I can't keep it up.*

[NOTE] **Maintain** is a more formal word for **keep up**.

2 If you **keep** something **up**, you continue to pretend that it is true.

keep up something ❑ *He kept up this story even*

when he was interviewed by the police.

keep something up ❑ *He tried to appear happy but he couldn't keep it up.*

3 If something **keeps up**, it continues. ❑ *If this trend keeps up, even more students will be in debt.* ❑ *If this keeps up, Aunt Lydia and the vineyard will be ruined.*

4 If you **keep up**, you manage to deal with a situation that is changing quickly. ❑ *Technology changes and it can be difficult to keep up as you get older.* ❑ [+ with] *Changes are being made to the system all the time and it's hard to keep up with them.*

5 If you **keep up**, you work at the necessary speed so that you do as well as other people or so that you get all your work done at the right time. = **fall behind** ❑ *I'll be taking work home every night just to keep up.* ❑ [+ with] *He can't keep up with the rest of the class.*

6 If you **keep it up**, you continue to work hard or to achieve the high standard that you have in the past. ❑ *This is very good work, Oliver. Keep it up!* ❑ *I was working very hard, but with a young baby, I couldn't keep it up.*

7 If you **keep up**, you move at the same speed as someone else. ❑ *Howard had to hurry to keep up.* ❑ [+ with] *The children had to run to keep up with her.*

8 If you **keep** something **up**, you stop it from becoming less or worse.

keep something up ❑ *I can't see how we can keep this pace up for more than a day or two.* ❑ *You've got to eat to keep your strength up.*

keep up something ❑ *Morris could keep up the pace no longer.* ❑ *It's important to keep up the standard.*

KEEP UP + noun
keep up **the pressure on** someone
keep up **the momentum**
keep up **the pace**
keep up **morale**
❑ *We have to keep up pressure on the government.* ❑ *We are doing well, and need to keep up the momentum.*

9 If you **keep up** a subject or skill that you learned a long time ago, you continue to study, practise, or use it.

keep up something ❑ *I do try to keep up my physics.*

keep something up ❑ *He's managed to keep his Spanish up quite well.*

10 If one process **keeps up** with another, it increases at the same speed and in the same way as the other is increasing. ❑ [+ with] *Supply can't keep up with demand.* ❑ *Pensions were increased to keep up with the rise in prices.*

11 If you **keep up** with a situation or subject, you learn all the most recent facts about it. ❑ [+ with] *Even in Zurich he kept up with the football scores back home in England.* ❑ *If you work in IT, you need to keep up with all the latest developments.*

12 If you **keep** someone **up**, you delay them going to bed.

keep someone up ❑ *I shouldn't have kept you up so late.* ❑ *I am sorry. I won't keep you up a minute longer.*

13 If you **keep up** a building or area of land, you look after it and make sure that it stays in good condition. **= maintain**

keep up something or **keep something up** ❑ *They provided the income for him to keep up this magnificent estate.* ❑ *You know what this place costs to keep up.* ●The **upkeep** of a building is the continual process of keeping it in good condition. **= maintenance** ❑ *We have to pay for the upkeep of the chapel.*

14 If you **keep up appearances**, you pretend that a situation is good, for example your financial situation or marriage, but you are really having problems. ❑ *Amy tried to keep up appearances even though her home life was a disaster.*

○ **keep 'up with**

If you **keep up with** a friend, you stay in contact with them by writing, telephoning, or seeing them regularly.

keep up with someone ❑ *We've kept up with each other ever since we left school.* ❑ *I didn't know that you'd kept up with Toby.*

key /kiː/ (**keys, keying, keyed**)

○ **key 'in**

When you **key** something **in**, you give information to a computer or phone by pushing buttons on a keyboard. **= type in, enter**

key something in or **key in something** ❑ *He keyed in the number Kramer had given him and waited to be connected.* ❑ *Key in the appropriate words.* ❑ *Your height and weight need to be keyed in before standing on the scales.*

NOTE **Input** is a more technical word for **key in**.

○ **key 'into**

When you **key** information **into** a computer, phone etc. you type it on the keyboard. **= type into, enter**

key something into something ❑ *He keyed her number into his mobile and waited.* ❑ *Employees confirm their identity by keying a PIN into a keypad.*

NOTE **Input** is a more technical word for **key into**.

○ **'key to**

1 If something **is keyed to** a particular person or situation, it is changed or designed so that it is suitable for that person or situation.

be keyed to something/someone ❑ *We offer lifestyle advice that is keyed to an individual's needs.*

2 If the price, value, or level of something **is keyed to** another price, value etc., it is related to it and changes when the other one does.

be keyed to something ❑ *Depressed car sales are a danger signal because so much of the economy is keyed to the car industry.*

kick /kɪk/ (**kicks, kicking, kicked**)

○ **kick a'bout** → see kick around

○ **kick a'gainst** [BRITISH]

If you **kick against** a situation you cannot control, you show by your behaviour that you do not like it. **= kick out against**

kick against something ❑ *Some young people want to kick against authority.*

○ **kick a'round** (or **kick about, kick round** [mainly BRITISH])

If you say that something **is kicking around** or **kicking around** somewhere, you mean that it is there and unwanted or forgotten. **= lie around**

be kicking around ❑ *It is a question which has been kicking about for thousands of years: is our universe infinite?* ❑ *There's a lot of difference between fresh fish and fish which has been kicking around in a freezer for months.*

be kicking around somewhere ❑ *I'm sure I've seen that book kicking around the office.*

○ **kick a'round** (or **kick about**)

1 When people **kick around** ideas or suggestions, they discuss them informally.

kick something around or **kick around something** ❑ *The first step was to call in some writers and kick around ideas.* ❑ *My boss called me in to kick some ideas round.*

2 If someone **kicks** you **around**, they treat you very badly, roughly, or unfairly. **= push around** [INFORMAL]

kick someone around ❑ *He didn't like being kicked around.* ❑ *I don't feel that anyone can kick me around any more.*

3 If someone **kicks around** or **kicks around** a place, they stay there, but without any plans about what they will do. [INFORMAL]

kick around ❑ *Guapo was going back to New York to kick around for a while with some people he'd met there.*

kick around somewhere ❑ *After kicking around Tampa Bay for four years, he decided to get a job.*

○ **kick 'back**

1 If someone **kicks back** an amount of money, they illegally give some money back to a person who is buying something in order to encourage them to buy it. [AMERICAN]

kick back something ❑ *The doctors kicked back a percentage of the fee.* ● A **kickback** is money that is paid to a government official or company to encourage them to buy something or help. ❑ *He's often takes kickbacks from the hiring agencies he works through.*

2 If someone **kicks back**, they relax. [INFORMAL] ❑ *He kicked back and read the newspaper.* ❑ *The actor can now afford to kick back.*

NOTE **Relax** is a more formal word for **kick back.**

● Someone or something that is **kicked-back** is relaxed. ❑ *Her house has a kicked-back stylishness.*

○ **kick 'down**

If you **kick down** a door or other structure, you kick it violently with your foot so that it falls. = **break down, smash down**

kick down something or **kick something down** ❑ *Burglars kicked down the front door.* ❑ *Some children had tried to kick the fence down.*

⊕ **kick 'in**

1 If you **kick in** something such as a door or window, you kick it violently with your foot so that it breaks into pieces. = **smash in**

kick in something ❑ *Firefighters kicked in one of the windows.* ❑ *Doors and windows were smashed and televisions were kicked in.*

kick something in ❑ *Police had to kick the door in to gain access.*

2 If something **kicks in**, it begins to have an effect. [INFORMAL] ❑ *The painkillers are starting to kick in.* ❑ *By then the shock had kicked in and she was shaking violently.*

3 If someone **kicks in** some money, they provide money to help pay for something. = **contribute** [AMERICAN, INFORMAL]

kick in something ❑ *Kansas City churches kicked in $35,000 to support the event.*

⊕ **kick 'off**

1 When you **kick off** your shoes, you shake your feet so that your shoes come off.

kick something off ❑ *She kicked her shoes off and lay down on the bed.*

kick off something ❑ *Dan sat on the sofa and kicked off his boots.*

2 When you **kick off** an event or discussion, you start it.

kick off something ❑ *The singer kicked off the tour last week.* ❑ *President Obama himself kicked off the latest debate.*

kick something off ❑ [+ with] *They kicked the party off with a fireworks display.*

3 When an event **kicks off**, it starts. [INFORMAL] ❑ *The competition kicks off next weekend.* ❑ *The Christmas party always kicked off between half eight and nine.* ❑ [+ with] *The day kicks off with coffee and a tour of building.*

4 When football players **kick off**, they start the game by kicking the ball from the centre of the pitch. ❑ *The first goal was scored within twenty seconds of kicking off.* ● The **kick-off** is the kick that officially starts a game of football, or the time that the game starts. ❑ *The kick-off's at 3 o'clock.*

5 To **kick** someone **off** something means to force them to leave it. [INFORMAL]

kick someone off something ❑ *The manager kicked him off the team.* ❑ *He was kicked off his accountancy course for failing his exams.*

6 If someone **kicks off**, they suddenly become angry and start shouting. [INFORMAL] ❑ *If we were late home, Mum used to kick off.*

○ **kick 'on** [AUSTRALIAN, INFORMAL]

If someone or something **kicks on**, they continue. ❑ *Hopefully we can kick on and get ourselves out of trouble.* ❑ *The duo kicked on until 5am.*

⊕ **kick 'out**

If you **kick** someone **out**, you force them to leave a place or organization. = **throw out**

kick someone out ❑ *She kicked him out when she discovered he was stealing from her.* ❑ *He started off at university but he got kicked out.* ❑ [+ of] *He helped me after I'd been kicked out of ar school.* ❑ *They kicked her out of her house.*

○ **kick 'out against**

If you **kick out against** a situation that you cannot control, you show that you do not like it by reacting in an extreme or violent way. = **kick against**

kick out against something ❑ *She got herself into trouble by kicking out too violently against life's injustices.*

○ **kick 'over**

1 If someone **kicks** something **over**, they kick it so that it falls to the ground. = **knock over**

kick over something or **kick something over** ❑ *John was so furious he kicked over the table.* ❑ I panic, she started to run and kicked the chair over.*

2 If an engine **kicks over**, or someone **kicks it over**, it starts to work. [AMERICAN, INFORMAL]

kick over ❑ *The motor wouldn't kick over.*

kick over something or **kick something over** ❑ *They kicked over the engines and began to sail up the river.*

○ **kick 'round** → see **kick around**

○ **kick 'up**

1 If someone **kicks up a fuss/stink/row**, they get very annoyed or upset about something, especially when this seems unnecessary. [INFORMAL] ❏ *He kicked up a great fuss and swore our friendship was at an end.* ❏ *She's kicking up a stink over the £500 cleaning bill.*

2 If you **kick up** dust or dirt, you create a cloud of dust or dirt as you move. = **raise**
kick up something or **kick something up**
❏ *They struggled amid the dust clouds that their feet kicked up.* ❏ *Mud was being kicked up by the horse's hoofs as it ran.*

3 If something **kicks up**, it increases and if you **kick** something **up**, you increase it. [AMERICAN, INFORMAL]
kick up ❏ *The humidity really kicks up in September.* ❏ [+ to] *Temperatures will kick up to 100 degrees by the end of the week.*
kick something up or **kick up something**
❏ *Companies have kicked up hiring as spending has grown.* ❏ [+ to] *They kicked the price up to $100*

kill /kɪl/ (**kills, killing, killed**)

✪ **kill 'off**

1 To **kill** people or living things **off** means to make a lot of them die. = **wipe out**
kill off something/someone ❏ *The virus is now killing off some of our best-loved garden birds.* ❏ *The bacteria are killed off by the drug.*
kill something/someone off ❏ *Cornflowers were common until a few years ago, when the modern pesticides killed them off.*
NOTE **Eradicate** is a more formal word for **kill off**.

2 If someone or something **kills** something **off**, they stop it from existing any more. = **wipe out**
kill something off ❏ *It was Douglas Holmes who killed that idea off.*
kill off something ❏ *Out of town shopping centres have killed off many local shops.*
NOTE **Eradicate** is a more formal word for **kill off**.

3 If a writer **kills off** a character in a book or television series, they make that character die.
kill off someone or **kill someone off** ❏ *When the actor died, the two writers had no choice but to kill off Brambell's character.* ❏ *There were rumours that the author JK Rowling would kill Harry Potter off.*

kip /kɪp/ (**kips, kipping, kipped**)

○ **kip 'down** [BRITISH, INFORMAL]
If you **kip down** at someone's house, you sleep there for the night instead of going home. = **doss down** ❏ *Why don't you take one of these mattresses and kip down here?*

kiss /kɪs/ (**kisses, kissing, kissed**)

○ **kiss a'way**
If you **kiss** someone's tears or an unpleasant feeling **away**, you make that person feel better by kissing them.
kiss away something or **kiss something away** ❏ *He held her close and kissed away her tears.* ❏ *She kissed his worries away.*

○ **kiss 'off** [AMERICAN, INFORMAL]

1 If someone tells you to **kiss off**, they are telling you rudely to go away. ❏ *I can remember her telling Derek to kiss off.* ● A **kiss-off** is when you tell someone that you do not want them any more. ❏ *Employees at the radio station got the big kiss-off yesterday.*

2 If you **kiss** someone or something **off**, you get rid of them quickly.
kiss off something/someone or **kiss someone/something off** ❏ *Buchanan kissed off the issue with two short sentences.* ❏ *We see him kissing off the caller in a few rude comments.* ❏ *I thought she'd kissed you off and moved back to Milwaukee.*

○ **kiss 'up to** [AMERICAN, INFORMAL]
If you **kiss up to** someone powerful or important, you are too nice to them because you want something from them. = **suck up to**
kiss up to someone ❏ *Some contestants try very hard to kiss up to the judges.*

kit /kɪt/ (**kits, kitting, kitted**)

○ **kit 'out** (or **kit up**) [BRITISH, INFORMAL]
If someone or something **is kitted out** or you **kit** them **out**, they are provided with everything they need for a particular situation, for example with clothing, equipment, or furniture. = **fit out**
be kitted out ❏ *Before you climb any mountain, you have to be properly kitted out.* ❏ [+ with] *The restaurant had been kitted out with new tables and chairs.*
kit someone/something out or **kit out someone/something** ❏ *Lizzie had kitted us out safely for climbing.* ❏ *He bought and kitted out his own van.*
kit yourself out ❏ *Kitting yourself out with all the trendy ski gear can be expensive.*
NOTE **Equip** is a more formal word for **kit out**.

kneel /niːl/ (**kneels, kneeling, kneeled/knelt**)

○ **kneel 'down**
When you **kneel down**, you sit with your legs bent underneath you and your weight on your knees. ❏ *He knelt down beside the girl.*

❏ He kneeled down and prayed. ❏ My sister was kneeling down, looking at something on the floor.

knit /nɪt/ (knits, knitting, knitted)

> The form **knit** is used in the present tense, and can also be used as the past tense and past participle of the verb.

○ **knit to'gether**

When two things **knit together**, or you **knit** them **together**, they join together to form a whole. **= fuse**

knit together ❏ Billy's eyebrows knitted together in a little frown. ❏ The new and old bones should eventually knit together to make a continuous join.

knit something together or **knit together something** ❏ Their aim was to knit together both sides of the community.

knock /nɒk/ (knocks, knocking, knocked)

○ **knock a'bout** → see knock around

○ **knock a'bout with** → see knock around with

○ **knock a'round** (or **knock about** [BRITISH, INFORMAL])

1 If a person **knocks** someone else **around** they hit or kick them several times.

knock someone around ❏ He used to knock her around a bit. ❏ He was always being knocked about by the other boys.

2 If you **knock** an idea or plan **around**, you discuss it with other people so that they can suggest ways of improving it.

knock something around or **knock around something** ❏ We'll get together tonight and knock some ideas around.

3 If someone **knocks around**, or **knocks around** a place, they get experience in a lot of different situations, especially by travelling to different places and meeting people.

knock around ❏ I knocked around for a few years after university.

knock around somewhere ❏ I knocked about Europe for a couple of years.

4 If someone or something **is knocking around** or **is knocking around** somewhere, they are present there, usually not doing anything in particular. **= hang around**

be knocking around ❏ If you have a spare £50 knocking around, you might want to spend it on this. ❏ There are some odd people knocking about.

be knocking around somewhere ❏ My brothers should be knocking around somewhere.

5 If people **knock** a ball **around**, they kick or hit it to each other in an informal way and not as part of a game.

knock something around or **knock around something** ❏ We were knocking a football around

and our ball hit a car. ❏ Matt and the other students went to knock about a ball. ● A **knockabout** is when people kick or hit a ball to each other in an informal way and not as part of a game. ❏ The player was injured during a pre-match knockabout.

○ **knock a'round with** (or **knock about with** [mainly BRITISH, INFORMAL])

If you **knock around with** someone, you spend time with them, either because you are one of their friends or because you are their boyfriend or girlfriend.

knock around with someone ❏ She's been knocking around with a guy I used to know. ❏ He's knocking about with a gang from the next village.

NOTE **Consort with** is a more formal expression for **knock around with**.

❍ **knock 'back**

1 If you **knock back** an alcoholic drink, you drink it quickly. [INFORMAL]

knock back something ❏ Lola knocked back the gin in one go.

knock something back ❏ She knocked the first glass of wine back.

● If you say that someone **knocks** it **back**, you mean that they drink a lot of alcohol. **= swig**

2 If something **knocks** you **back** a particular amount of money, it costs you that amount of money. **= set back** [INFORMAL]

knock someone back something ❏ How much did that car knock you back? A few thousand?

3 If someone **knocks back** an offer, suggestion or person, they say they do not want them. [BRITISH, INFORMAL]

knock back someone/something or **knock someone/something back** ❏ I have applied for numerous jobs over the years and I've been knocked back repeatedly.

NOTE **Reject** is a more formal word for **knock back**.

● A **knockback** is a refusal or rejection. ❏ Despite the knockback, McGrail refused to give up on his dream of owning the club.

4 If something **knocks** someone or something **back**, it stops them from being successful. [BRITISH]

knock someone/something back ❏ It seemed that whenever she started to win games another injury would knock her back. ❏ Then he was knocked back again by his personal problems. ● A **knockback** is something that delays progress or stops something or someone from being successful. ❏ The schedule has suffered a knockback.

5 If you **knock** dough **back**, for example

when making bread, you press and push it very hard to get rid of air before you cook it.

knock something back or **knock back something** ❑ *By now the dough has swollen and needs to be knocked back by kneading.*

⊙ **knock ˈdown**

1 If you **knock** someone **down**, you hit them or push them, deliberately or accidentally, so that they fall to the ground. = **knock over**

knock someone down ❑ *The group turned so suddenly that they nearly knocked the man down.*

knock down someone ❑ *I bumped into and nearly knocked down a person at the bus stop.*

2 If a car or other vehicle **knocks** someone **down**, it hits them so that they fall to the ground. = **knock over**

knock someone down ❑ *She had been crossing the road, and a car pulled out suddenly, knocking her down.*

knock down someone ❑ *Police are hunting a driver who sped away after knocking down two pedestrians.*

be knocked down ❑ *He was knocked down by a car and killed instantly.*

3 To **knock down** a building or part of a building means to destroy it, often deliberately. = **pull down**

knock something down ❑ *I'd knock the wall down between the front room and dining room.*

knock down something ❑ *The earthquake knocked down several buildings.*

4 If you **knock down** an idea or opinion, you argue successfully against it. = **demolish**

knock down something ❑ *Jane systematically knocked down each one of our suggestions.*

knock something down ❑ *I put forward an argument and Ella knocks it down.* ● A **knockdown** argument is very powerful and difficult to argue against. ❑ *Opponents of expansion believe they have a knockdown argument.*

5 If you **knock** someone **down** or if you **knock** a price **down** when someone is selling you something, you persuade the seller to reduce the price. [INFORMAL]

knock someone/something down or **knock down someone/something** ❑ *I tried to knock him down a few pounds but he wouldn't have it.* ❑ *We managed to knock the price down quite a lot because it was torn.* ● A **knockdown** price is one that is a lot lower than it would be normally. ❑ *I got it for a knockdown price.*

NOTE **Reduced** is a less informal word for **knockdown**.

6 To **knock down** a price, rate or value means to reduce it. [INFORMAL]

knock something down ❑ *The bigger stores can afford to knock the prices down.*

knock down something ❑ *The Federal Reserve Board have been knocking down interest rates.*

⊙ **knock ˈoff**

1 If you **knock** something **off** a surface, you hit it so that it falls to the ground.

knock something off ❑ *There was a photo on the shelf and I accidentally knocked it off as I walked past.*

knock something off something ❑ *Gareth sat up so abruptly he almost knocked the drink off the arm of his chair.*

2 To **knock off** an amount means to reduce something by that amount.

knock something off or **knock off something** ❑ *She offered to knock £15 off because there was a hole in the sleeve.*

knock something off something ❑ *He said he'd knock £50 off the price.* ❑ *Using the motorway will knock at least twenty minutes off your journey time.*

3 When you **knock off**, you finish work at the end of the day or before a break. [INFORMAL] ❑ *We knock off at five o'clock.*

4 If you **knock** something **off** a list or document, you remove it.

knock something/someone off something ❑ *Hopefully I'll be able to knock a few more things off my list of tasks to do.*

5 To **knock** someone **off** means to murder them. = **bump off** [INFORMAL]

knock someone off or **knock off someone** ❑ *You can't go around knocking people off for their money.*

6 If you **knock off** a piece of work, you finish it very quickly and easily. [INFORMAL]

knock something off or **knock off something** ❑ *I can usually knock off an essay in a couple of hours.* ❑ *He knocked off an email to the editor of the newspaper.*

7 If you **knock off** some food or drink, you finish eating or drinking it very quickly. [INFORMAL]

knock off something or **knock something off** ❑ *They knocked off the remains of the bottle of coke.*

8 If someone **knocks** something **off**, they steal it. = **nick** [BRITISH, INFORMAL]

knock off something or **knock something off** ❑ *He had knocked off a lorryload of cigarettes.* ● **Knock-off** goods are things which have been stolen. ❑ *He was selling knock-off gear in a pub.*

9 If someone **knocks off** a bank or a shop, they steal things or money from it. [BRITISH, INFORMAL]

knock off something or **knock something off** ❑ *He'd knocked off three banks before police caught up with him.*

10 If someone **knocks off** a product, they make illegal copies of it and sell them at a cheap price. [INFORMAL]

knock something off or **knock off something** ❑ Expensive watches are being knocked off and sold to unsuspecting tourists. ● A **knockoff** or a **knockoff** product is a cheap and illegal copy of something. ❑ Her bag was a Chanel knockoff. ❑ He was wearing a pair of knockoff Nike trainers.

11 To **knock** someone **off** means to have sex with them. [BRITISH, INFORMAL, RUDE]

12 If you say **Knock it off!** to someone, you are telling them to stop doing something which is annoying you. [INFORMAL] ❑ Hey, knock it off, will you?

○ **'knock on**

If you **knock on** something such as a door or window, you hit it, usually several times, to get someone's attention.

knock on something ❑ She went to Simon's apartment and knocked on the door. ❑ I knocked on the car window to wake him up.

❍ **knock 'out**

1 To **knock** someone **out** means to cause them to become unconscious or to fall asleep. ≠ bring round

knock someone out ❑ The man hit him so hard that he knocked him out. ❑ The tablet had knocked her out for four solid hours.

knock out someone ❑ The explosion hurt no one, except that it knocked out Colonel Lacour.

knock yourself out ❑ He must have fallen and knocked himself out. ● A **knockout** dose of medicine or injection makes you become unconscious or fall asleep. ❑ The doctor gave me a knockout pill. ● In boxing or wrestling, a **knockout** is a punch or throw that makes your opponent fall to the ground and unable to stand up before the referee has counted to ten. ❑ Davies won by a knockout.

2 If you knock a person or team **out**, you defeat them so they cannot take part in a competition any more.

knock someone out ❑ Germany's win knocked Portugal out.

knock out someone ❑ Federer knocked out Murray in the semi-finals. ❑ Williams just avoided being knocked out in the second round. ❑ [+ of] France has been knocked out of the World Cup football finals.

NOTE **Eliminate** is a more formal word for **knock out**.

● A **knockout** competition is one in which the winner of each game goes on to the next round but the loser drops out, until one person or team is the winner. ❑ The World Cup is a knockout competition.

3 If something **knocks** you **out**, it makes you feel very tired, and if you **knock** yourself **out**, you do something which makes you very tired. [INFORMAL]

knock someone out ❑ The walk really knocked me out.

knock yourself out ❑ In the past I knocked myself out trying to make my business successful.

4 To **knock** something **out** means to destroy or damage it and stop it from working properly.

knock something out or **knock out something** ❑ A huge storm had knocked all the power out. ❑ Radars were knocked out, aircraft were shot down. ● A **knockout** blow is one that causes a lot of damage to something. ❑ The poor weather delivered a knockout blow to the region's tourist industry.

5 If you **knock out** a piece of work, you do it very quickly.

knock out something or **knock something out** ❑ He can knock out a short story in less than a day. ❑ I knocked a few more pages out later.

6 If an event or piece of news **knocks** you **out**, it shocks you so much that you cannot think clearly or react immediately. = stun [INFORMAL]

knock someone out ❑ The news absolutely knocked me out.

7 If something **knocks** you **out**, you are surprised because it is so good. [INFORMAL]

knock someone out ❑ Her performance completely knocked me out.

NOTE **Astound** and **stun** are more formal words for **knock out**.

● If you say that someone is a **knockout**, you mean that they are extremely attractive. ❑ Sandra looked a knockout in her new dress.

● A **knockout** person is extremely attractive. ❑ He has a knockout wife and two cute little daughters.

○ **knock 'out of**

If a characteristic **is knocked out** of someone, or someone or something **knocks** it **out** of them, they lose it because of the experiences they have had.

knock something out of someone ❑ That experience knocked the confidence out of me.

be knocked out of someone ❑ His creativity was in danger of being knocked out of him. ❑ He had all the fight knocked out of him.

❍ **knock 'over**

1 To **knock** someone or something **over** means to push them or hit them so that they fall or turn on their side.

knock something over ❑ Careful you don't knock the paint over.

knock over something ❑ *I almost knocked over my coffee cup in my rush to pick up the phone.*
2 If someone **is knocked over**, a car or other vehicle hits them and they fall to the ground.
be knocked over ❑ *I was knocked over by a car when I was six.*

○ **knock to'gether**
1 If someone **knocks** two rooms or buildings **together**, they make them form one room or building by removing a wall.
knock something together or **knock together something** ❑ *The spacious kitchen was achieved by knocking together three small rooms.* ❑ *The hotel was two large houses that had been knocked together.*
2 → see **knock up**

○ **knock 'up** (or **knock together**) [BRITISH, INFORMAL]
If you **knock** something **up**, you make it or build it very quickly, using whatever materials are available.
knock up something or **knock something up** ❑ *Do you want me to knock up a meal for you?* ❑ *I could knock some shelves together in an afternoon.*

○ **knock 'up**
1 If you **knock** someone **up**, you knock on the door of their bedroom or of their house to wake them. [BRITISH, INFORMAL]
knock someone up ❑ *He asked me to knock him up at 6 a.m.*
NOTE **Rouse** is a formal word for **knock up**.
2 If a man **knocks** a woman **up**, he makes her pregnant. [INFORMAL, RUDE]
knock someone up or **knock up someone**
3 In a game such as tennis, squash, or badminton, when the players **knock up**, they practise hitting the ball or shuttlecock to each other before they begin a game.
❑ *The players were knocking up before the game.*
• A **knock-up** is a period of time in which the players practise hitting the ball, etc. to each other before beginning a game of tennis, squash, or badminton. ❑ *Let's have a knock-up before we start.*

know /nəʊ/ (**knows, knowing, knew, known**)

✪ **'know about**
If you **know about** a subject, you have studied it and understand part or all of it.
know about something ❑ *You ought to ask John, he knows about photography.*
know something about something ❑ *She knew a lot about acoustics.* ❑ *What do you know about the film industry?* ❑ *I don't know much about geography.*

○ **'know as**
1 If someone or something **is known as** a particular name, they are called by that name.
be known as something ❑ *Lev Davidovitch Bronstein was otherwise known as Leon Trotsky.*
2 If you **know** someone or something **as** a particular type of person or thing, you think of them in that way.
know someone/something as someone/ something ❑ *Lots of people know her as a very kind woman.* ❑ *People began to know it as the restaurant with the best garlic soup in town.*
3 If you **know** someone **as** a person with a particular job or role, you know them in that job or role, rather than in any other.
know someone as something ❑ *I knew him as a colleague rather than a friend.*

○ **'know of**
If you **know of** something or someone, you have heard of them but you may not have a lot of information about them.
know of something/someone ❑ *I know of one girl who was fined because of it.* ❑ *Many people did not even know of her existence.*

knuckle /'nʌkəl/ (**knuckles, knuckling, knuckled**)

○ **knuckle 'down**
If someone **knuckles down**, they begin to work or study very hard, especially after a time when they have not done much.
= **buckle down** ❑ *He's got to knuckle down and start working.* ❑ [+ to] *It's time you knuckled down to some hard study.* ❑ *The thought of knuckling down to a mundane routine was quite frightening.*

○ **knuckle 'under**
If you **knuckle under**, you do what someone else tells you to do or what a situation forces you to do, because you realize that you have no choice. = **buckle under**
❑ *He refused to knuckle under, and was asked to leave.* ❑ [+ to] *You're wrong to knuckle under to their pressure.*

kowtow /kaʊ'taʊ/ (**kowtows, kowtowing, kowtowed**)

○ **kow'tow to** [INFORMAL]
If someone **kowtows to** a powerful person, a powerful group, or their demands, they are too eager to obey them or to be polite to them.
kowtow to someone/something ❑ *She had money so people kowtowed to her.* ❑ *We need to find alternative sources of energy rather than kowtowing to the oil industry.*

Ll

label /'leɪbəl/ (labels, labelling, labelled)

> American English uses the spellings **labeling** and **labeled**.

○ **'label as**
If you **label** someone or something **as** something, you use a word or phrase to describe them which is unfair or wrong.
label someone/something as something ❏ *His teachers quickly labelled him as a failure.*
be labelled as something ❏ *Many young people are being unfairly labelled as criminals.*

labour /'leɪbə/ (labours, laboured, labouring)

> American English uses the spelling **labor**.

○ **'labour under**
1 If you **labour under** an illusion or belief, you believe something that is not true or correct.
labour under something ❏ *He seemed to labour under the illusion that I knew what I was doing.*
2 If you **labour under** something, you have a particular problem that makes things more difficult for you.
labour under something ❏ *As a shy young man with no money or connections, he laboured under many disadvantages.*

lace /leɪs/ (laces, lacing, laced)

○ **lace 'up**
If you **lace up** something, you fasten it by pulling strings on it tight and tying them together.
lace up something or **lace something up**
❏ *He bent and laced up his shoes.*
NOTE **Do up** is a more informal, general expression for **lace up**.
● **Lace-ups** are shoes which fasten with strings. ❏ *She wears black lace-ups for school.*

ladle /'leɪdəl/ (ladles, ladling, ladled)

○ **ladle 'out**
1 If you **ladle out** food such as soup or stew, you serve it using a large spoon.
ladle out something or **ladle something out**

❏ *She was ladling out the soup.* ❏ [+ *into*] *Ladle it out into jars.*
2 To **ladle** something **out** means to give a lot of it to people. = **dish out, dole out** [INFORMAL]
ladle out something or **ladle something out**
❏ *He ladled out money to voters in the hope of winning their favour.*

lag /læg/ (lags, lagging, lagged)

○ **lag be'hind**
1 If someone **lags behind** other people or if they **lag behind**, they move more slowly than other people. = **fall behind**
lag behind ❏ *He set off at a brisk walk, Kate lagging behind.*
lag behind someone ❏ *They lagged behind the rest of the group, talking.*
2 If someone or something **lags behind** another person or thing or if they **lag behind**, they do not achieve as much or progress as quickly. = **fall behind**
lag behind someone/something ❏ *Britain's economic development lagged behind that of many other European countries.*
lag behind ❏ *At school, he lagged behind.*

lam /læm/ (lams, lamming, lammed)

○ **lam 'into** [BRITISH, INFORMAL]
To **lam into** someone means to attack them violently. = **lay into**
lam into someone ❏ *The men lammed into him, kicking and punching.*

land /lænd/ (lands, landing, landed)

○ **'land in** [INFORMAL]
If someone or something **lands** you **in** a difficult situation or if you **land in** it, you find yourself in a difficult situation. = **get into**
land someone in something ❏ *This Government has landed us in a terrible situation.*
land in something ❏ *They said if I didn't tell the truth I would land in a lot of trouble.*
land yourself in something ❏ *I wouldn't be surprised if he'd landed himself in prison.*

○ **land 'up** [BRITISH, INFORMAL]
If you **land up** in a place or situation, you

arrive there without having intended to.
= **end up, wind up**
land up somewhere ❏ *He landed up in hospital.*
land up doing something ❏ *We somehow landed up driving through the outskirts of Glasgow.*

○ **'land with** [BRITISH, INFORMAL]
If you **are landed with** something or someone, or if someone **lands** you **with** them, you have to have them or deal with them although you do not want to. = **saddle with, lumber with**
be landed with something/someone ❏ *I was landed with all the washing up.*
land someone with something/someone ❏ *You landed us with that awful man at dinner.*

lap /læp/ (**laps, lapping, lapped**)
○ **lap 'up**
1 When an animal **laps up** a drink, it drinks it.
lap up something or **lap something up** ❏ *The cat lapped up the milk as if it had not been fed for days.*
2 If someone **laps up** praise, attention or information, they accept it eagerly.
lap up something or **lap something up** ❏ *He was smiling, lapping up the attention.* ❏ *She told her story and the audience lapped it up.*

lapse /læps/ (**lapses, lapsing, lapsed**)
○ **lapse 'into**
1 If you **lapse into silence**, you stop talking and become silent. ❏ *They ran out of things to say, and lapsed into silence.*
2 If you **lapse into** sleep or unconsciousness, you enter that state.
= **sink into**
lapse into something ❏ *At last she lapsed into a troubled sleep.* ❏ *He lapsed into a coma from which he never recovered.*
3 If you **lapse into** a particular kind of behaviour, you start doing something without realizing it, because you cannot prevent yourself.
lapse into something ❏ *She would lapse into German when trying to explain something complicated.*

lard (**lards, larding, larded**)
○ **'lard with**
1 If you **lard** your writing or speech **with** something or if it **is larded with** something, you include a lot of something in it.
be larded with something ❏ *His speech was larded with jokes and stories.*
lard something with something ❏ *He larded his conversation with respectful references to his colleagues.*

2 If something **is larded with** a substance, it is covered with it.
be larded with something ❏ *His coat was torn and his boots were larded with mud.*

large /lɑːdʒ/ (**larges, larging, larged**)
○ **large 'up** [INFORMAL]
If someone **larges it up**, they have a lot of fun, often in a way that involves spending a lot of money. = **live it up** ❏ *On this holiday island, you can large it up 24 hours a day.*

lark /lɑːk/ (**larks, larking, larked**)
○ **lark a'bout** (or **lark around**) [mainly BRITISH, INFORMAL]
If you **lark about**, you enjoy yourself doing silly things. = **fool around, mess around** ❏ *We had a lovely holiday, sunbathing and larking about.*

lash /læʃ/ (**lashes, lashing, lashed**)
○ **lash 'down**
1 If you **lash** something **down**, you fasten it firmly in position using ropes.
lash something down or **lash down something** ❏ *They loaded the equipment onto the ship and lashed it down.*
2 If rain **lashes down**, it falls very heavily. ❏ *The rain lashed down so fiercely that we could hardly see.*

○ **lash 'into**
If you **lash into** someone, you criticize them very angrily. = **lay into**
lash into someone ❏ *I opened my mouth to lash into him.*

○ **lash 'out**
1 If a person or animal **lashes out**, they suddenly try to hit someone with their arms or legs or with a weapon. = **hit out** ❏ *When cornered, the horse may lash out.* ❏ [+ at] *She lashed out at the men trying to arrest her.*
2 If you **lash out** at someone, you criticize them very angrily. ❏ [+ at] *I lashed out at him, calling him names.* ❏ [+ against] *Harris used the speech to lash out against his former employer.*
3 If you **lash out** or **lash out** an amount of money, you spend a lot of money to buy something. = **splash out** [INFORMAL]
lash out ❏ [+ on] *He was tempted to lash out on the car of his dreams.*
lash out something ❏ *He's just lashed out almost a thousand pounds on a new computer.*

last /lɑːst, læst/ (**lasts, lasting, lasted**)
○ **last 'out**
1 If something or someone **lasts out** or **lasts out** a period of time, they manage to stay alive or continue to function.
❏ *I don't think I can last out without a cup of tea.*

❏ [+ until] *Do you think the car will last out until the end of the year?*

last out something ❏ *She is very sick and may not last out the winter.*

2 If a supply of something **lasts out** or **lasts out** a period of time, there is enough of it for a particular period of time.
= hold out

last out ❏ *Will our fuel supplies last out?*

last out something ❏ *There is enough water in the wells to last out the dry months.*

latch /lætʃ/ (latches, latching, latched)

○ **latch 'on to** (or **latch onto**)

1 If someone **latches on to** you, they want your attention and want to spend time with you.

latch on to someone ❏ *These kids latch on to any adults who are willing to play with them.*

2 If someone **latches on to** something, they realize it.

latch on to something ❏ *They never once latched on to the fact that he was using a code.*

3 If something **latches on to** something else, it attaches itself firmly to that thing.

latch on to something ❏ *The grubs latch on to plant stems where they feed.*

laugh /lɑːf, læf/ (laughs, laughing, laughed)

✪ **'laugh at**

If you **laugh at** someone or something, you make jokes about them.

laugh at someone/something ❏ *People used to laugh at his ideas.* ❏ [+ for] *I'm sick of being laughed at for the way I talk.* ❏ *One of his most charming qualities was the ability to laugh at himself.*

NOTE Ridicule is a more formal word for **laugh at**.

○ **laugh 'off**

If you **laugh** something **off**, you try to make people think that it is amusing and unimportant.

laugh off something or **laugh something off** ❏ *Despite being in serious trouble, he tried to laugh it off.*

launch /lɔːntʃ/ (launches, launching, launched)

○ **launch 'into**

If you **launch into** something, you start it with enthusiasm.

launch into something ❏ *She launched into a long speech about duty and patriotism.*

launch yourself into something ❏ *It might be time to launch yourself into a new career.*

○ **launch 'out**

If you **launch out**, you start to do something

new. ❏ [+ into] *I decided to take a chance and launch out into marriage.* ❏ [+ on] *He launched out on one new project after another.*

lavish /ˈlævɪʃ/ (lavishes, lavishing, lavished)

○ **'lavish on** (or **lavish upon**)

If you **lavish** something such as money, time or affection **on** someone or something, you give them a lot of it.
= heap on

lavish something on someone/something ❏ *Why do the media lavish so much attention on people like her?*

lawyer (lawyers, lawyering, lawyered)

○ **lawyer 'up**

If someone **lawyers up**, they get a lawyer to represent them. ❏ *He'll more than likely lawyer up, get out on bail, and disappear.*

lay /leɪ/ (lays, laying, laid)

Lay is also the past tense of the verb **lie**.

○ **lay a'bout**

1 If someone **lays about** another person, they a hit them repeatedly.

lay about someone ❏ [+ with] *They began to lay about the boys with sticks.*

2 A **layabout** is a very lazy person who does little or no work. ❏ *She dedicated the song to her layabout brother Alfie.*

○ **lay a'side**

1 If you **lay** something **aside**, you put it down or leave it for a while. **= put aside**

lay something aside or **lay aside something** ❏ *He laid the newspaper aside and turned his attention to breakfast.* ❏ *She took her gloves off and laid them aside.*

2 If you **lay** something **aside**, you save it to use later. **= put aside**

lay something aside or **lay aside something** ❏ *They never laid any money aside.* ❏ [+ for] *Something needs to be laid aside for the children's future.*

3 If you **lay** something **aside**, you stop being affected by a feeling or belief.
= set aside

lay something aside or **lay aside something** ❏ *All rivalry between them was laid aside as they worked together.*

○ **'lay before**

If you **lay** something **before** someone, you present it in detail for them to consider.
= put before

lay something before someone ❏ *If you have any proof, I advise you to lay it before the police.* ❏ *Their policies have been laid before the electors and rejected.*

lay 'by

1 If you **lay** something **by**, you save it to use later. **= put by**

lay something by or **lay by something**
❑ His pay was not sufficient for him to lay any money by. ❑ [+ for] I've got some savings laid by for my old age.

2 A **lay-by** is a short strip of road by the side of a main road, where cars can stop for a while. ❑ Pull into the next lay-by.

lay 'down

1 If you **lay** something **down**, you put it down on a surface.

lay something down ❑ Albert laid his glasses down carefully on the table beside him. ❑ I took a fifty dollar bill and laid it down on the counter.

lay down something ❑ She laid down her pen and pushed the sheet of paper away from her.

2 If you **lay** yourself **down**, you lie flat on a surface, usually to rest.

lay yourself down ❑ She laid herself down on a bench. ❑ Why don't you lay yourself down and go to sleep for a while?

3 To **lay down** what people should do means to officially state what they must do.

lay down something ❑ There are laws which lay down what employers have to do. ❑ The rules of the game were laid down a long time ago.

lay something down ❑ We are going to define the requirements of the job and lay them down.

NOTE **Stipulate** is a more formal word for **lay down**.

4 If something such as food **is laid down** or if you **lay** it **down**, it is stored for future use.

be laid down ❑ Carbohydrate not used up during the day will get laid down by the body as fat.

lay something down or **lay down something** ❑ To enjoy wine, you need a cellar or somewhere similar to lay it down.

5 To **lay down** something new means to establish or create it.

lay down something or **lay something down** ❑ Habits that are laid down in adolescence can last for a lifetime.

6 If something **is laid down** or if someone **lays** it **down**, it is constructed over an area of ground.

be laid down ❑ A 600-metre tarmac airstrip was laid down.

lay something down or **lay down something** ❑ His father laid the golf course down in 1962.

7 When layers of sand or rock **are laid down**, they form into a solid mass over a long period of time.

be laid down ❑ Most of this stone has been laid down in layers under water and therefore splits easily.

8 If you **lay down** a position of power or responsibility, you decide to stop having it. **= lay aside** [FORMAL]

lay down something or **lay something down** ❑ Ageing can be an opportunity to lay down some of our responsibilities.

9 If someone **lays down the law**, they say very firmly and exactly what they want to be done or what is allowed. ❑ Helping young people to make independent decisions is better than just laying down the law.

10 If people **lay down** weapons, they stop fighting. [LITERARY]

lay down something ❑ It is time for both sides to lay down their arms.

11 If someone **lays down** their **life**, they are killed because they believe in or support a particular cause. **= give** [LITERARY] ❑ [+ for] Not many people today are willing to lay down their lives for their country.

lay 'in

If you **lay in** something, you buy it and store it to be used later. **= buy in**

lay in something or **lay something in** ❑ They have laid in food stocks for the winter.

lay 'into [INFORMAL]

1 If someone **lays into** another person, they start to hit or kick them violently.

lay into someone ❑ The gang laid into them, forcing them to run into a near-by park.

2 If someone **lays into** you, they start to criticize you angrily. **= lash into**

lay into someone ❑ Bob really laid into us: 'You're useless, you're not even trying!'

3 If you **lay into** food or drink, you eat or drink a lot of it very eagerly. **= tuck into**

lay into something ❑ I watched him laying into his breakfast as if he hadn't eaten in days.

lay 'off

1 If workers **are laid off** or if their employer **lays** them **off**, they are told that they have to leave their jobs for a period of time or permanently, because there is no work for them to do.

be laid off ❑ City workers are being laid off at the rate of a hundred a week.

lay someone off ❑ If demand falls, the company lays people off. ❑ Her employer laid her off eight months later.

lay off someone ❑ Factories are warning that they may have to lay off workers. ● If there is a **layoff**, workers are told by their employer to leave their jobs. ❑ Textile companies announced 2,000 layoffs last week. ● A **layoff** is a period of time in which someone does not work or play sport, often because they are resting or are injured. ❑ He was playing badly after his long layoff.

LAY OFF + *noun*

lay off **employees**
lay off **staff**
lay off **workers**
❑ *We were forced to lay off staff.* ❑ *The factory has laid off half its workers.*

2 If you tell someone to **lay off** or to **lay off** someone or something, you are telling them to leave someone alone or to stop doing something that is annoying you. [INFORMAL]

lay off ❑ *They warned him to lay off, but he kept interrupting.*

lay off someone/something ❑ *Lay off me – I'm doing the best I can.* ❑ *Lay off the stupid jokes, would you?* ❑ *He wished she would lay off telling him what to do.*

3 If you **lay off** something, you stop using it, eating it or doing it. [INFORMAL]

lay off something ❑ *Lay off the chips and cookies and you'll soon lose weight.* ❑ *He decided to lay off exercising for a while.*

○ **lay 'on** [BRITISH]
If you **lay on** something, you provide or supply it.

lay on something or **lay something on** ❑ *The organisers had laid on buses to transport people from the city.* ❑ *[+ for] A welcome party was laid on for them when they arrived.*

○ **'lay on** (or **lay upon**)
1 If you **lay** blame or responsibility **on** someone, you state that they are responsible for something.

lay something on someone ❑ *Admit your mistakes, without laying the blame on other people.*

2 To **lay** stress or emphasis **on** something means to stress or emphasize it. = **put on**

lay something on something ❑ *Less stress is laid on competition, and more on co-operation.*

3 If you **lay it on** or **lay it on thick**, you deliberately exaggerate something in order to impress or persuade someone. [INFORMAL] ❑ *She really laid it on, telling him how great I was.* ❑ *I called in sick to work, coughing and gasping, laying it on thick.*

4 If you **lay** an unpleasant task **on** someone, you give them that task to do. [INFORMAL]

lay something on someone ❑ *I'm sorry to lay this on you, but your mom really needs you to be there with her.*

5 If you **lay** unpleasant information **on** someone, you tell them that information. [mainly AMERICAN, INFORMAL]

lay something on someone ❑ *I hate to lay this on you, Bill, but she's dangerous and you need to know the truth about her.*

6 If you **lay hands on** something or **lay** your **hands on** something, you get or take it. ❑ *People stole pictures, clocks, furniture – everything they could lay their hands on.*

7 If you **lay hands on** someone or **lay a hand on** them, you hit or hurt them physically. ❑ *At least they don't seem to have laid hands on him, which is a good thing.* ❑ *He said he would kill any man who laid a hand on her.*

8 If you **lay a finger on** something or someone, you touch them, especially in order to hurt or damage them. ❑ *He would never lay a finger on any of his kids.*

9 If you **lay eyes on** something or someone, you see them for the first time. ❑ *I fell in love with her the moment I laid eyes on her.* ❑ *It was the most beautiful room I'd ever laid eyes on.*

○ **lay 'out**
1 If you **lay** things **out**, you put them down carefully in a particular place or arrangement. = **put out**

lay out something ❑ *Lily was setting the table, laying out the plates and cups.*

lay something out ❑ *He laid the papers out on the table in the conference room.* ❑ *Shuffle the cards, then lay them out in a fan shape.*

2 To **lay out** an idea or information means to express or present it in detail. = **set out**

lay out something ❑ *The manual lays out exactly what is expected of company employees.* ❑ *The situation is laid out very clearly in the report.*

lay something out ❑ *[+ for] They didn't understand, so I laid it out for them as well as I could.*

3 If something such as a document or town **is laid out** in a particular way, or if someone **lays** it **out**, it is designed or arranged in a particular way.

be laid out ❑ *The website is beautifully laid out so that information is easy to find.* ❑ *[+ in] The streets are laid out in a grid pattern.*

lay something out or **lay out something** ❑ *They planned how to lay out their new garden.*

• The **layout** of something is the way in which the parts of it are arranged. ❑ *He wanted to change the general layout of the farm.* ❑ *The report was difficult to read due to its poor layout.*

4 To **lay out** a dead person means to clean and dress their body for the funeral.

lay someone out or **lay out someone** ❑ *After her death, her daughters came to lay her out.* ❑ *One of their duties was to lay out the dead.*

5 To **lay** someone **out** means to knock them unconscious by hitting them hard. = **knock out** [INFORMAL]

lay someone out or **lay out someone**

❏ Someone crept up behind him and laid him out with a heavy object.

6 If you **lay out** money, you spend a large amount of it. **= shell out, fork out** [INFORMAL]

lay out something ❏ Some people might not be able to lay out large sums in the middle of the month. ❏ [+ on] I had to lay out £150 on textbooks.

lay 'up

1 If an illness **lays** you **up**, or if you **are laid up** with it, it causes you to stay in bed. [INFORMAL]

lay someone up ❏ The baby was just beginning to walk when an illness laid her up.

be laid up ❏ [+ with] He had been laid up for five days with a bad cold.

2 If a vehicle or ship **is laid up**, it is not being used for a period of time.

be laid up ❏ From this week, the boat will be laid up for the winter.

3 If you **lay up** something, you gradually save quantities of it for future use. [OLD-FASHIONED]

lay up something or **lay something up** ❏ They lay up supplies of grain for the winter.

4 If a person or animal **lays up**, they go to a place where they are difficult to find. ❏ I decided to lay up for a few days.

'lay upon → see lay on

aze /leɪz/ **(lazes, lazing, lazed)**

laze a'round (or **laze about** [mainly BRITISH])

If you **laze around**, you relax and do not do any work or anything that requires effort. **= lounge around** ❏ At the weekend he likes to laze around listening to music.

ead /liːd/ **(leads, leading, led)**

lead 'in

If you **lead in** with a particular subject or statement, you start speaking or writing by mentioning it. ❏ [+ with] She led in with a few remarks about her predecessor. ● A **lead-in** is a short speech, activity, piece of music, etc. that happens at the beginning of an activity. ❏ Several people missed the lead-in.

lead 'into

1 If a door or path **leads into** a place, you reach that place by going through the door or following the path.

lead into something ❏ The door on the left led into the main dining room. ❏ He noticed a gate, and a track leading into a wood.

2 If something **leads into** a discussion, it results in a discussion starting.

lead into something ❏ His comments led into a discussion about lateness at work.

○ **lead 'off**

1 If something such as a path or room **leads off** a place or **leads off** from it, it is connected to it or joins it to another place.

lead off something ❏ She has a dressing room leading off her bedroom. ❏ Two doors led off the hallway.

lead off ❏ [+ from] Four corridors lead off from the lobby. ❏ There is a lane leading off beside the restaurant.

2 If someone **leads off**, they start an event or performance. ❏ [+ with] The chair led off with a financial statement. ❏ He asked us to sing with him, then he led off in the wrong key.

3 In baseball, the player who **leads off** is the first player to bat for their team in a game. ❏ [+ for] Terry Puhl led off for the Houston Astros. ● The **lead-off** player is the first to play for their team in a game or inning. ❏ Otis Nixon was the lead-off batter.

○ **lead 'on**

1 If someone **leads** you **on**, they deliberately make you believe something false, especially that they like you or intend to do something nice for you.

lead someone on or **lead on someone** ❏ I really cared about you, but you led me on – you didn't care about me at all. ❏ She claims he led her on with false promises.

2 If someone **leads** you **on**, they encourage you to do something bad.

lead someone on ❏ He blames Catherine, saying she led him on and encouraged him to steal.

○ **lead 'on to**

1 If one event or action **leads on to** another, it causes it or makes it possible. [BRITISH]

lead on to something ❏ If you do this job well, it could lead on to other things. ❏ This discovery led on to further research.

2 If something such as a door or gate **leads on to** a place, the place is on the other side of it.

lead on to something ❏ There were glass doors leading on to a balcony.

○ **'lead to**

1 If something **leads to** a situation or event, usually an unpleasant one, it causes it.

lead to something ❏ Unhappiness at home may lead to problems at school. ❏ He warned yesterday that pay increases would lead to job losses.

2 If something **leads** you **to** a feeling, idea, or experience, it causes you to have it.

lead someone to something ❏ These thoughts led him to other memories of childhood. ❏ So many failures almost led me to desperation.

○ lead 'up to

1 If events or times **lead up to** a situation, they happen before it.
lead up to something ❏ *Witnesses described the events leading up to Gregory's death.* ❏ *During the days that led up to the conference, we did a lot of preparation.*
2 If someone **leads up to** a subject, they try to move the conversation gradually to that subject.
lead up to something ❏ *Ever since you came in you've been leading up to a question.*

○ 'lead with

1 If you **lead with** something, you mention it or deal with it first or as the most important thing.
lead with something ❏ *The newspapers all led with the story of his disappearance.*
2 If you **lead with** a part of your body, you move that part forward first.
lead with something ❏ *Leading with your head, begin bending slowly forwards.* ❏ *The batsman leads with his elbow when he hits the ball.*

leaf /liːf/ (leafs, leafing, leafed)

○ leaf 'through

If you **leaf through** a book or magazine, you turn the pages quickly without reading them carefully. **= thumb through**
leaf through something ❏ *While he waited he leafed through a magazine.* ❏ *She took a book from the shelf and began leafing through the pages.*

leak /liːk/ (leaks, leaking, leaked)

○ leak 'out

If secret information **leaks out**, it becomes known. **= get out** ❏ *News of their engagement leaked out.* ❏ *Terrible stories were leaking out about the war.*

lean /liːn/ (leans, leaning, leaned/leant)

○ 'lean on (or lean against)

1 If you **lean on** someone or something, you rest against them.
lean on someone/something ❏ *She was feeling tired and was glad to lean on him.* ❏ *Some leant on walking sticks.*
2 If you **lean** something **on** something, you put it against something so part of its weight is supported.
lean something on something ❏ *She leaned her head against the window.* ❏ *I leant the ladder against the wall.*

○ 'lean on

1 If someone **leans on** you, they try to influence you using pressure or threats.
lean on someone ❏ *Powerful bankers leaned on the government to change its mind.*

NOTE **Pressurize** is a more formal word for **lean on**.
2 If you **lean on** someone, you depend on them for support. **= rely on**
lean on someone ❏ *He leans on his assistant a lot.* ❏ *Sometimes we all need a friend we can lean on.*

○ lean 'out

If you **lean out**, you put your head and shoulders through a window or opening so that you are looking outside. ❏ *[+ of] She leaned out of the window and waved at him.* ❏ *Please don't lean out while the train is moving.*

○ lean 'over

If someone or something **leans over**, they bend in a particular direction, and if they **lean over** something or someone, they bend so that they are above them.
lean over ❏ *You'll have to lean over to see it.*
lean over someone/something ❏ *He was leaning over me trying to see if I was OK.*

○ 'lean towards (or lean toward)

If you **lean towards** a particular idea or belief, you usually think or act in a particular way.
lean towards something ❏ *Politically, I lean towards the right.* ❏ *Most scientists would probably lean toward this view.*

leap /liːp/ (leaps, leaping, leaped/leapt)

○ 'leap at

If you **leap at** a chance or opportunity, you accept it eagerly. **= jump at**
leap at something ❏ *When he asked her to go with him, she leaped at the chance.* ❏ *Most people would leap at the opportunity to work with us.*

○ 'leap on (or leap upon)

1 If someone **leaps on** you, they suddenly jump on top of you or take hold of you.
leap on someone ❏ *The dog leapt on Sam, snarling and biting his leg.*
2 If you **leap on** an idea or suggestion, you show a lot of interest in it or enthusiasm about it. **= seize on**
leap on something ❏ *We should leap on this opportunity to get involved.*
3 If you **leap on** something that happens or something that someone says or does, you quickly use it as a reason to criticize them. **= seize on**
leap on something ❏ *His opponents leapt on the comments.*

○ leap 'out

If someone or something **leaps out**, they suddenly appear from a place where they have been hiding. ❏ *They opened the gate, and I leapt out.* ❏ *[+ on] Someone could leap out on you from behind a bush.*

⟩ leap 'out at
If something **leaps out at** you, it is very obvious or easy to notice.
leap out at someone ❑ Her name leapt out at me from the list of applicants. ❑ He scanned the pictures for clues, but nothing leapt out at him.

⟩ 'leap to
To **leap to** a particular position or amount means to improve or increase suddenly to that position or amount.
leap to something ❑ Profits leaped to $103.3 million. ❑ The Sonics leapt to a 22-point lead over Utah.

⟩ 'leap upon → see leap on

earn /lɜːn/ (**learns, learning, learned, learnt**)

> American English uses the form **learned** as the past tense and past participle. British English uses either **learned** or **learnt**.

⟩ 'learn from
If you **learn from** an unpleasant experience or **learn** something **from** it, you change the way you behave so that the bad thing does not happen again or so that, if it happens again, you can deal with it better.
learn from something ❑ I am convinced that he has learned from his mistakes.
learn something from something ❑ Have we learned nothing from the past?

eave /liːv/ (**leaves, leaving, left**)

⟩ leave a'side
If you **leave** something **aside**, you do not think or talk about it now.
leave something aside or **leave aside something** ❑ Let's leave that aside for a moment and get back to practical matters. ❑ Leaving aside the question of his guilt or innocence, there was not enough evidence to send him to prison.

⟩ leave be'hind
1 If you **leave** someone or something **behind**, you do not take them with you when you go somewhere.
leave someone/something behind ❑ The box wouldn't fit in the car, so we had to leave it behind. ❑ I couldn't leave Hilary behind to cope on her own.
leave behind someone/something ❑ She had to go and find work in the city, leaving behind four children. ❑ He read a newspaper that had been left behind on the train.
2 If you **leave** an object or situation **behind**, or if you **leave** it **behind** you, it remains after you leave.

leave behind something ❑ The water retreated, leaving behind a layer of mud that covered the road. ❑ He worried about the debts he would leave behind if he died.
leave something behind ❑ I want to leave some sort of legacy behind. ❑ Doctors removed the lump, leaving a scar behind.
leave something behind you ❑ She has gone, but she left many wonderful memories behind her. ❑ The truck left a trail of debris behind it.
3 If you **leave** something **behind**, you stop having a past feeling or experience and progress to something new.
leave something behind ❑ This is your chance to leave the past behind and make a new start.
leave behind something ❑ It can be hard to leave behind these bad experiences.
4 To **leave** someone or something **behind** means to move forward more quickly than them so that they are behind you.
leave someone/something behind ❑ She soon left all the other runners behind. ❑ The other men were fitter and left me behind on the steeper slopes.
leave behind someone/something ❑ They walked on, leaving behind a few stragglers at the back.
5 If someone or something **is left behind**, or if someone **leaves** them **behind**, they do not progress or develop as successfully as others.
be left behind ❑ If you don't understand technology, you're going to be left behind.
leave someone/something behind ❑ She was a quick learner, and soon left the other children behind.
leave behind someone/something ❑ The company has left behind most of its rivals.

✪ leave 'off
1 If you **leave** someone or something **off** something, you do not include them in it.
leave someone/something off something ❑ He was furious that they had left him off the guest list. ❑ The coach threatened to leave him off the team.
2 If you **leave off** a piece of clothing, you do not wear it on a particular occasion.
leave something off or **leave off something** ❑ It's so warm, we can leave our jackets off. ❑ He was wearing his uniform but had left off the tie.
3 If something or someone **leaves off** something or **leaves off**, they stop or finish.
leave off ❑ He sat down at the piano again and started playing from where he left off. ❑ The next book picks up the story where the first one leaves off.

leave off something ❏ *He left off his preparations and went to the window.*

4 If someone **leaves off** or **leaves off** doing something, they stop doing something, especially something annoying. = **lay off** [INFORMAL]

leave off ❏ *Just leave off, will you!*

leave off doing something ❏ *If you'd all leave off shouting, then you could hear me.*

○ **leave 'out**

1 If you **leave** someone or something **out**, you do not include them in something.

leave out someone/something ❏ *You've left out my name.* ❏ *[+ of] One or two scenes in the play were left out of the film.*

leave someone/something out ❏ *I invited the whole class because I didn't want to leave anyone out.* ❏ *If you don't like carrots, you can leave them out.*

2 If you tell someone to **leave it out**, you are telling them to stop doing something or stop saying something that isn't true. [BRITISH, INFORMAL] ❏ *Leave it out, Charlie, this bloke's alright.*

○ **leave 'over**

1 If something **is left over**, it remains when the rest has been taken away or used.

be left over ❏ *'How much money is left over?' – 'About forty-five pounds.'* ❏ *Anything that is left over is fed to the animals.* ● **Leftovers** are the food that remains after a meal. ❏ *We can make a pie with the leftovers.* ● **Leftover** is used to describe an amount of something that remains after you have finished using it. ❏ *She gave me some of the leftover cake from her birthday.*

2 If something **is left over** from the past, it still exists although it belongs to a past period.

be left over ❏ *[+ from] She had a few dolls left over from her childhood.* ❏ *Winter had ended, though some patches of ice were still left over.* ● A **leftover** is something that belongs to the past but still exists. ❏ *Perhaps this instinct is a leftover from our hunting past.*

○ **'leave to**

1 If you **leave** something **to** someone, you let them do it or deal with it.

leave something to someone ❏ *You can leave all the arrangements to us.* ❏ *[+ to-infinitive] We should leave it to the police to sort the problem out.* ● If someone says **Leave it to me**, they mean that they will do everything necessary to deal with something. ❏ *I promise everything will be OK. Leave it to me.*

2 If you **leave** someone **to** something, you go away or stop talking so that they can continue doing it.

leave someone to something ❏ *Well, I'll go now and leave you to your dinner.* ● If you **leave** someone **to it**, you let them continue doing something without trying to help or interfere. ❏ *Sometimes children lear best if you just leave them to it.*

3 If you **leave** something **to** someone, you arrange for it to be given to them after you have died.

leave something to someone ❏ *He died two and a half years later, leaving everything to his wife*

○ **leave 'up to**

If you **leave** something **up to** someone, you let them decide what to do.

leave something up to someone ❏ *I will give you some advice, but leave the final choice up to you.* ❏ *[+ to-infinitive] She always left it up to me to suggest what to do.*

○ **'leave with**

To **leave** someone **with** something unpleasant or difficult to deal with means to make them have it or make them responsible for it.

leave someone with something ❏ *The car crash left Dan with a broken leg.* ❏ *The death of a partner often leaves the survivor with feelings of guilt.*

lecture /'lektʃə/ (lectures, lecturing, lectured)

○ **'lecture on**

If you **lecture on** a particular subject or you **lecture** a group of people **on** a subject, you talk about it in order to teach people something.

lecture on something ❏ *She then invited him to Atlanta to lecture on the history of art.*

lecture someone on something ❏ *Wendy Rigby was recently invited to lecture a group of doctors on the benefits of aromatherapy.* ❏ *Some months earlier, Faulds had lectured his medical students on each of the five senses.*

○ **'lecture on** (or **lecture about**)

If you **lecture** someone **on** something, you talk to them in order to criticize them or tell them how to behave, in a way which they find annoying.

lecture someone on something ❏ *He lecture Randolph on the importance of being cheerful.* ❏ *Mum was lecturing me about how I needed to ea more healthily.*

lend /lend/ (lends, lending, lent)

○ **lend 'out**

If you **lend** something **out**, you allow someone to borrow it for a particular perio of time.

lend out something or **lend something out**

❏ She had lent out her camera and had never got it back. ❏ Sorry, that book's been lent out.

et /let/ (lets, letting)

> The form **let** is used in the present tense and is the past tense and past participle of the verb.

let 'down

1 If someone or something **lets** you **down**, they fail to do something that you expected or wanted them to do.
let someone down ❏ He would never let a friend down. ❏ I trust her to do a good job, and she's never let me down.
let down someone ❏ She didn't feel like having the party but she could not let down all her guests.
● If something is a **letdown**, it is disappointing. ❏ For the visitor expecting something special, it is a bit of a letdown.
2 If you **let** yourself **down**, you do something that you are ashamed of.
let yourself down ❏ I feel I've let myself down by losing my temper like that.
3 If something **lets** someone or something **down**, it stops them from being as successful as they could be.
let someone/something down ❏ Many believe it was his shyness that let him down. ❏ His poor performance let the rest of the team down.
let down someone/something ❏ What lets down the film is its ending.
4 If you **let** something **down**, you make it move to a lower position.
let something down or **let down something** ❏ I unfastened the blind and let it down. ❏ They let down a rope so he could climb up to them.
5 If you **let** something **down**, you allow air to escape from it. [BRITISH]
let down something or **let something down** ❏ When he got back to his car, someone had let the tyres down.
NOTE **Deflate** is a more formal word for **let down**.
6 If you **let down** a piece of clothing, you make it longer using the hem (= piece of material that is turned up) at the bottom.
= lengthen
let down something or **let something down** ❏ His mother had to let down his school trousers.

let 'in

1 If you **let** someone **in**, you allow them to come into a place, usually by opening a door.
let someone in ❏ We rang the doorbell and someone came and let us in. ❏ Don't let any strangers in.
let in someone ❏ He locked himself away in his study and refused to let in anyone but his wife. ❏ Evidently she had let herself in with a key.
NOTE **Admit** is a more formal word for **let in**.
2 If you **let** someone **in**, you allow them to enter an area or join a group.
let someone in ❏ They won't let you in without a visa. ❏ The club is not letting any new members in at the moment.
let in someone ❏ He claimed the university was letting in too many students with poor grades.
3 To **let in** something such as water or light means to allow it to enter a place.
let in something ❏ My old boots had been letting in water.
let something in ❏ Make a hole to let air in. ❏ I could see the sun was shining, and opened the curtains to let it in.
4 An **inlet** is a narrow strip of water going from a sea or lake into the land. ❏ We weren't in the main part of the lake, but in a narrow inlet thirty yards across.

let 'in for [INFORMAL]
If you **let** yourself **in for** something, you get involved in something that is more difficult or unpleasant than you expected.
let yourself in for something ❏ New parents don't always realize what they're letting themselves in for.

let 'in on
If you **let** someone **in on** something, you tell them about it or allow them to become involved.
let someone in on something ❏ Are you going to let us all in on your little secret? ❏ They decided to let him in on the plan.

let 'into

1 If you **let** someone **into** a place, you allow them to go into it, especially by opening a door.
let someone into something ❏ Mr Thomas let him into the building with the spare key. ❏ The cleaner let herself into his apartment.
2 If you **let** someone **into** a group, an organization, or a country, you allow them to join it or enter it.
let someone into something ❏ They won't let you into the country without a passport. ❏ Some of the older members were reluctant to let women into the club.
3 If you **let** someone **into** a secret, you allow them to know about it. = let in on
let someone into something ❏ If I let you into a secret, do you promise not to tell anyone?
4 If something **is let into** a surface or you **let** something **into** a surface, it is fixed into a space or hole there. = set into

be let into something ❑ *At the back of the house a wooden tub was let into the earth.*

let something into something ❑ *Couldn't you let a window into the door?*

○ **let 'off**

1 If you **let** someone **off** something or **let** them **off**, you say that they do not have to do something they would normally have to do. [BRITISH]

let someone off something ❑ *She let them off homework, since they had been so good.*

let someone off *or* **let off someone** ❑ *We were supposed to have a test, but the teacher let us off.*

2 If you **let** someone **off**, you give them a less serious punishment than was expected or no punishment at all.

let someone off ❑ *They just tell you to be more careful next time and let you off.* ❑ *[+ with] The owner of the car was let off with a warning.*

let off someone ❑ *He claimed that the system encouraged police to let off criminals.*

3 If you **let off** something such as a gun or a bomb, you fire it or make it explode.

let off something *or* **let something off** ❑ *Everyone let off fireworks and waved banners.* ❑ *The youths had rockets and they were letting them off late at night.*

4 To **let off** sound, light or energy means to produce it.

let off something *or* **let something off** ❑ *The kettle let off a shrill whistle.* ❑ *A lamp with a paper shade lets off a really nice light.*

5 If someone **lets off** energy, they do something to release and use their energy.

let off something *or* **let something off** ❑ *He jumped up and down on the bed, letting off the final ounce or two of energy.*

● If you **let off steam**, you do something to release energy or anger, in order to help you relax. ❑ *Physical play is an important way for children to let off steam.*

6 If someone **lets off**, they release gas from their bowels. [OLD-FASHIONED, RUDE]

7 To **let** someone **off** means to stop to allow them to get out of a vehicle.

let someone off *or* **let off someone** ❑ *He stopped in front of my house to let me off.* ❑ *The bus stopped to let off passengers.*

○ **let 'on** [INFORMAL]

If you **let on**, you tell someone about something that was intended to be secret. ❑ *If she was upset, she didn't let on.* ❑ *He didn't let on that he knew the whole story.*

○ **let 'out**

1 If you **let** people or animals **out**, you allow them to leave a place, especially by opening a door.

let someone/something out ❑ *After a week in the hospital I was begging the doctors to let me out.* ❑ *[+ of] The prisoners were let out of their cells for an hour a day.*

let out someone/something ❑ *We let out the dogs so that they could get some exercise.*

2 If you **let** yourself **out**, you go to the door and leave a building by yourself in a situation where someone might be expected to come with you.

let yourself out ❑ *Don't worry, I can let myself out.*

3 To **let** something **out** means to allow it to flow out freely.

let something out ❑ *He let the water out and refilled the bath.* ❑ *Take a deep breath, then let it out through your nose.* ❑ *[+ of] Someone had let all the air out of the tyres.*

let out something ❑ *Pete let out his breath slowly.* ● An **outlet** is a hole or pipe through which something can flow out. ❑ *The sink outlet is blocked.*

4 If you **let out** a particular sound, you make that sound. [LITERARY]

let out something *or* **let something out** ❑ *The dogs let out excited yelps.* ❑ *Martin let out a low whistle.*

NOTE **Emit** is a more formal word for **let out**.

5 If you **let** something **out**, you say something that you should have kept secret.

let something out *or* **let out something** ❑ *As soon as I said this I cursed myself for letting it out.* ❑ *Everyone was terrified of letting out the secret.*

● An **outlet** is a way of expressing feelings or ideas. ❑ *Young people need outlets for creative expression.*

6 If you **let** something **out**, you make a house or room available for people to rent.
= **rent out**

let something out *or* **let out something** ❑ *We could let the spare room out to a student.* ❑ *[+ to] My father owned two houses which he let out to his friends.*

7 If you **let** a garment **out**, you make it larger using the extra cloth in the seams.
= **take in**

let something out *or* **let out something** ❑ *I put on weight before the wedding and had to let my trousers out.*

8 If something **lets** you **out**, it prevents you from having to do something. [INFORMAL]

let someone out *or* **let out someone** ❑ *'Who's going to drive?' – 'Well, my car's being repaired, so that lets me out.'* ● A **let-out** is something that allows you to avoid doing something. ❑ *He had to work that day, which gave him a let-out.*

9 An **outlet** is a shop or organization which sells goods made by a particular manufacturer. ❑ *Their clothes are sold in outlets across Canada and North America.*

○ **let 'through**

1 If you **let** someone or something **through** or **let** them **through** something, you allow them to pass a point or move through a place.
let someone/something through or **let through someone/something** ❑ *The crowd parted to let the ambulance through.* ❑ *Police at the entrance refused to let me through.*
let someone/something through something ❑ *Visitors are given a magnetic card that lets them through the security gate.*

2 To **let** something **through** means to allow something such as water to enter a place.
let something through or **let through something** ❑ *The cover lets water through but keeps dirt out.* ❑ *The windows in my classroom let through the rain.*

○ **'let to** [mainly BRITISH]

If you **let** your house or land **to** someone, you allow them to use it in exchange for money that they pay you regularly.
let something to someone ❑ *She is thinking of letting her house to students.*

○ **let 'up**

1 If something unpleasant **lets up**, it stops or becomes less. **= ease off** ❑ *We thought that the rain would let up after a while.* ● If there is a **let-up**, something unpleasant stops or becomes less. ❑ *The bombing lasted for three days and nights without any let-up.*

2 If someone **lets up**, they stop doing something or do it with less determination. ❑ *He worked seven days a week and he never let up.* ❑ *I wouldn't let up until she told me the truth.*

○ **let 'up on**

1 If you **let up on** someone, you stop being so strict with them.
let up on someone ❑ *Though the kids complained bitterly, Mama would not let up on them.*

2 If you **let up on** an activity, you stop doing it or do it with less determination.
let up on something ❑ *We will not let up on the search until she is found.*

level /ˈlevəl/ (**levels, levelling, levelled**)

> American English uses the spellings **leveling** and **leveled**.

○ **'level at** (or **level against**)

If a criticism or accusation is **levelled at** someone, or if you **level** a criticism or accusation **at** them, they are criticized or accused of something.
be levelled at someone ❑ *Criticism was leveled at her for being 'anti-American'.*
level something at someone ❑ *She levelled some serious allegations against him.*

○ **level 'off** (or **level out**)

1 If something **levels off**, it stays at a particular point and stops changing or developing. **= stabilize** ❑ *After initial quick results, weight loss often levels off.* ❑ *This growth in demand levelled out in 2018.*

2 If you **level** a surface **off**, you make it flat.
level something off or **level off something** ❑ *Fill the spoon with the powder and level it off with a knife.* ❑ *A scraper can be used for levelling out small lumps of earth.*

3 If something **levels off**, it becomes flat or horizontal after sloping or travelling upwards or downwards. ❑ *After a steep downward slope, the tunnel levelled off* ❑ *[+ at] The planes levelled out at 20,000 feet and headed north.*

○ **level 'out** → see **level off**

○ **level 'up**

To **level** something **up** means to make it more equal. **= even up**
level something up or **level up something** ❑ *It was 2–1 at half-time, then Rooney levelled up the score in the second half.* ❑ *She let me go first to level things up.*

○ **'level with** [INFORMAL]

If you **level with** someone, you tell them the truth.
level with someone ❑ *Why won't you level with me?* ❑ *I'll level with you – I'm not really interested.*

liaise /liˈeɪz/ (**liaises, liaising, liaised**)

○ **li'aise with**

When one person or organization **liaises with** another, they work together and tell each other about what is happening.
liaise with someone ❑ *Detectives are liaising with Dutch police.* ❑ *The three groups will all liaise with each other to complete the project.*

liberate /ˈlɪbəreɪt/ (**liberates, liberating, liberated**)

○ **'liberate from**

To **liberate** someone **from** an unpleasant situation or feeling means to help them escape from it or stop having it.
liberate someone from something ❑ *Internet shopping has helped liberate us from crowded stores and busy supermarkets.*
liberate yourself from something ❑ *The people had liberated themselves from the fear which dominated their lives just a few years ago.*

lick /lɪk/ (**licks, licking, licked**)

○ **lick 'up**

If you **lick** something **up**, you remove it from a surface using your tongue.

lick up something or **lick something up** ❑ I could lick up the sauce while no-one was watching. ❑ She spilled milk on the floor, and the cat immediately licked it up.

lie /laɪ/ (**lies, lying, lay, lain**)

○ **lie a'bout** → see **lie around**

○ **lie a'head**

If an event or situation **lies ahead**, it will happen in the future. ❑ None of us knows what lies ahead. ❑ The task that lies ahead looks extremely difficult.

✪ **lie a'round** (or **lie about** [mainly BRITISH])

1 If someone **lies around** or **lies around** a place, they spend their time relaxing and not doing anything. = **lounge around** [INFORMAL]

lie around ❑ We lay around on the living room floor, chatting.

lie around something ❑ How can you just lie around the house all day doing nothing?

2 If things **are lying around** or **are lying around** a place, they are left somewhere, especially in an untidy way. = **kick around**

be lying around ❑ Papers lay around on his desk in random piles. ❑ The kids always leave their shoes lying about.

be lying around something ❑ I don't like to leave money lying around the house.

○ **lie 'back**

If you **lie back**, you move into a horizontal position with your back and head resting on something. ❑ Now lie back and relax.

○ **lie be'fore** [FORMAL]

If something **lies before** you, you will have to do it or experience it in the future.

lie before someone ❑ She thought about the task that lay before her.

○ **lie be'hind**

The thing that **lies behind** a situation or event is the reason or explanation for it. = **underlie**

lie behind something ❑ We are interested in the causes that lie behind the rise in crime. ❑ I recognized the genuine concern that lay behind Bill's words.

✪ **lie 'down**

When you **lie down**, you move into a horizontal position, usually in order to rest or sleep. ❑ I'm tired. I need to lie down. ❑ We lay down side by side. ❑ [+ on] Go and lie down on your bed. ● If you have a **lie-down**, you lie down on a bed and have a short rest. [INFORMAL] ❑ I think I'll go and have a lie-down.

○ **lie 'in**

1 If you **lie in**, you intentionally stay in bed later than usual in the morning. [BRITISH, INFORMAL] ❑ Late nights were no problem for him, as he could lie in till midday. ● If you have a **lie-in**, you stay in bed later than usual in the morning. [BRITISH, INFORMAL] ❑ The meeting's not until ten o'clock, so I can have a lie-in.

2 If one thing **lies in** another, the second thing is the reason for or the cause of the first. ❑ The origin of the story lies in a belief in animal spirits.

○ **lie 'round** → see **lie around**

○ **lie 'up** [BRITISH]

If you **lie up** somewhere, you go there to hide or rest for a while. ❑ Small groups of soldiers were still lying up in the hills.

○ **'lie with**

1 If a responsibility, fault or choice **lies with** someone, they caused it or are responsible for it. [FORMAL]

lie with someone ❑ The fault generally lies with the management. ❑ The decision lay with the doctor, not the patient.

2 If one person **lies with** another person, they have sex with each other. [OLD-FASHIONED, RUDE]

lie with someone ❑ Did she lie with him?

lift /lɪft/ (**lifts, lifting, lifted**)

○ **lift 'off**

When an aircraft or space craft **lifts off**, it leaves the ground and rises into the air. = **take off** ❑ The plane lifted off and climbed steeply into the night sky. ❑ Crowds watched as the balloon lifted off. ● **Lift-off** is the time when a space craft leaves the ground to travel into space. ❑ The countdown to lift-off had begun.

✪ **lift 'up**

1 If you **lift** something **up**, you hold it and move it upwards. = **lift**

lift up something ❑ I lifted up a corner of the sheet. ❑ The man lifted up his walking stick and pointed.

lift something up ❑ She lifted the baby up and kissed him. ❑ There was a big rock and I lifted it up to see what was underneath.

2 If you **lift up** part of your body, you raise it. = **raise**

lift up something ❑ She lifted up her head to smile at him. ❑ They lifted up their arms in prayer.

3 If you **lift up** your **voice**, you speak or sing loudly. [FORMAL, LITERARY] ❑ Lift up your voice and sing.

4 If something **lifts** you **up**, it makes you feel happier or more hopeful.

lift someone up or **lift up someone** ❑ Their positive outlook and enthusiasm can lift you up.

• **Uplift** is something that makes people feel happier or more hopeful. ❑ *It gave us an incredible uplift to know they were still alive.*

5 Uplift is an increase in the rate or amount of something. ❑ *There may be a short-term uplift in sales.*

light /laɪt/ (lights, lighting, lighted/lit)

○ **'light on** (or **light upon**)

1 If you **light on** something, you suddenly notice or discover it. **= hit upon**
light on something ❑ *Her eyes lit upon the piece of paper in the corner.*

2 If a bird or insect **lights on** something, it lands on it. [LITERARY]
light on something ❑ *The bird lit on a rock.*

○ **light 'out** [AMERICAN, INFORMAL]
If you **light out**, you leave a place in a hurry. ❑ *The cats lit out and found safety on the roof.*

○ **light 'up**

1 To **light** something **up** means to shine light on or in it, so that it is bright and easy to see.
light up something ❑ *The fire was still blazing, lighting up the sky.* ❑ *The match lit up her face.*
light something up ❑ *The lamp is so bright it lights the whole room up.* ❑ *The red leaves look amazing when the sun lights them up.*
NOTE **Illuminate** is a more formal word for **light up**.

2 If something **lights up**, a bulb inside it is turned on, making it shine. ❑ *A warning sign lights up to tell the driver more fuel is needed.* ❑ *When you press a key it lights up.* • **Lighting-up** time is the time when drivers in the UK are required by law to switch on their vehicle lights on.

3 If your face or your eyes **light up**, you suddenly look very happy or excited. ❑ *His face lit up at the sight of Cynthia.* ❑ *I saw his face light up as he heard the news.*

4 If you **light** something **up**, you make it start burning, especially using a match.
light something up or **light up something** ❑ *George lit up his pipe.* ❑ *I switched on the gas and lit it up.*

5 If you **light up**, you light something such as a cigarette and start smoking it. [INFORMAL] ❑ *There was a 'No Smoking' sign, but he lit up anyway.*

○ **'light upon → see light on**

lighten /'laɪtən/ (lightens, lightening, lightened)

○ **lighten 'up**

1 If someone tells you to **lighten up**, they think you should be less serious and more

relaxed. [INFORMAL] ❑ *Come on, this is a party. Lighten up!*

2 If you **lighten** something **up**, you make it less serious and more fun.
lighten something up or **lighten up something** ❑ *That was a joke. I just wanted to lighten things up.* ❑ *A few pictures can lighten up a dull lecture.*

liken /'laɪkən/ (likens, likening, likened)

○ **'liken to**
If one thing or person **is likened to another**, or if you **liken** one thing or person **to** another, you say that they are similar.
be likened to someone/something ❑ *Its taste has often been likened to chicken.*
liken someone/something to someone/something ❑ *They praised his achievements and likened him to Mozart.*

limber /'lɪmbə/ (limbers, limbering, limbered)

○ **limber 'up**

1 If you **limber up**, you prepare your body for a sport or activity by doing exercises. **= loosen up** ❑ *The players were on the pitch limbering up.*

2 If you **limber up** for an event or an activity, you prepare for it. ❑ [+ for] *He certainly looks as if he is limbering up for a run at the presidency.* ❑ *Both sides were limbering up for an argument.*

limit /'lɪmɪt/ (limits, limiting, limited)

○ **'limit to**
If something **is limited to** a particular place or group of people, it exists only in that place, or is had or done only by that group.
be limited to something ❑ *Entry to this competition is limited to U.K. residents.* ❑ *The protests were not limited to New York.*

limp /lɪmp/ (limps, limping, limped)

○ **limp a'long**
If something such as an organization, process, or vehicle **limps along**, it moves slowly or continues in a way that is not very successful. ❑ *The economy is still limping along after two decades of civil war.* ❑ *The truck limped along with its exhaust pipe hanging off.*

line /laɪn/ (lines, lining, lined)

○ **line 'up**

1 If people or things **line up** or if you **line** them **up**, they form a row or line.
line up ❑ *The children line up outside the classroom door.*
be lined up ❑ *Cars were lined up along the road.* ❑ *By 8.30 people were already lined up outside the stadium.*
line someone/something up ❑ *They lined us up and marched us off.* ❑ *He lined the three designs up and asked me which I preferred.*

line up someone/something ❑ *We lined up all the empty bottles.*

2 A **line-up** is a line of people waiting for something. [AMERICAN] ❑ *He was unhappy about the length of the line-up ahead of him.*

3 A **line-up** is a row of people, one of whom is a suspected criminal, for a victim or witness to try to identify. [BRITISH] ❑ *Witnesses failed to pick him out of a line-up, and he was released without charge.*

4 If something **lines up** or if you **line** it **up**, it is straight or in its correct position in relation to something else.

line up ❑ *Make sure that all the columns of your text line up.*

be lined up ❑ *Adjust the controls so that the two arrows are exactly lined up.*

line up something ❑ *He lines up the scene in the viewfinder and focuses the camera.*

line something up ❑ *She arranged all her books alphabetically and lined them up exactly on the shelf.* ❑ [+ with] *Line the edge of the fabric up with the pattern.*

5 If you **line** something or someone **up** in preparation for an event or activity, you arrange for them to be ready and available. = **fix up**

line something/someone up or **line up something/someone** ❑ *I've lined up a little treat for his birthday.* ❑ *A buyer was already lined up for the house.* ❑ *I had plenty of questions lined up for him.*

6 A **line-up** is a team of people who will play in a particular game. ❑ *The England line-up for the match against Poland was announced this morning.*

7 A **line-up** is a series of events or people that are planned to appear in a programme or performance. ❑ *We've got a great line-up of entertainment for you on tonight's show.*

8 If you **line up** with or behind someone, you support them. If you **line up** against them, you oppose them. ❑ [+ with] *At that time Mussolini had lined up with Britain and France and not with Germany.* ❑ [+ behind] *Most business leaders have lined up behind the plan.* ❑ [+ against] *What can we do, with all those people lined up against us?*

9 If people **line up** to do something, many of them are eager to do it. ❑ [+ to-infinitive] *Companies were lining up to sponsor us.* ❑ *People didn't exactly line up to offer help.*

linger /ˈlɪŋgə/ (**lingers, lingering, lingered**)
○ **linger 'on**

1 If something **lingers on**, it remains or continues to exist after something else has

stopped. ❑ *She has gone, but her memory lingers on.*

2 If someone **lingers on**, they stay alive although they are very ill and close to death. ❑ *After the accident, he lingered on for two days in hospital before he died.*

link /lɪŋk/ (**links, linking, linked**)
○ **link 'up**

1 If you **link up** two things or places, you connect them to each other. = **join up**

link up something/someone ❑ *He planned a network of bike paths linking up all the parts of the city.*

link something/someone up ❑ *It's possible to link the games consoles up so you can play against your friends.* ❑ [+ to] *They linked her up to a machine to measure her brain waves.* ● A **linkup** is a connection between systems or machines. ❑ *The debate will be shown on TV via an international satellite linkup.*

2 If you **link up** with someone, you meet them somewhere. = **meet up** ❑ [+ with] *He's away for the weekend, linking up with some old college friends.* ❑ *Hopefully we can link up soon.*

3 If you **link up** with another person or organization or if two people or organizations **link up**, you join together in order to do something. ❑ [+ with] *Should we be linking up with other movements in the UK?* ❑ *Colleges in the city have linked up to put on a jobs fair.*

liquor /ˈlɪkə/ (**liquors, liquoring, liquored**)
○ **liquor 'up** [AMERICAN, INFORMAL]

If someone **is liquored up**, they have drunk too much alcohol.

be liquored up ❑ *On Friday night some of the men go out and get liquored up.*

listen /ˈlɪsən/ (**listens, listening, listened**)
○ **'listen for** → see **listen out for**
○ **listen 'in**

If you **listen in**, you listen to something, especially using radio or telephone equipment. ❑ *He turned up the speaker on the phone so they could listen in.* ❑ [+ on] *'You listened in on our conversation,' she said angrily.* ❑ [+ to] *They were able to listen in to the enemy's radio broadcasts.*

○ **listen 'out for** (or **listen for**)

If you **listen out for** something, you stay ready to hear something that you are expecting to hear.

listen out for something ❑ *Will you listen out for the car arriving? They should be here soon.* ❑ *Listen out for the signal.* ❑ *She listened for their voices but could hear nothing.*

○ 'listen to

1 When you **listen to** someone or something, you give your attention to a sound or to what someone says.

listen to someone/something ❑ You need to sit quietly and listen to the teacher. ❑ She's in her room listening to music.

2 If you **listen to** someone or to what someone says, you pay attention to them and let them influence you.

listen to someone/something ❑ He never listened to his mother. ❑ I wish I'd listened to his advice.

○ listen 'up [mainly AMERICAN, INFORMAL]

If you tell someone to **listen up**, you want them to listen to what you are going to tell them. ❑ Listen up, everyone! The show is about to start.

live /lɪv/ (lives, living, lived)

○ 'live by

1 If you **live by** something, you always behave according to a particular rule or belief. = **abide by**

live by something ❑ She lived by her own rules and didn't care what others thought.

2 If you **live by** something, you get money that you need to live in a particular way.

live by something ❑ Her dream was to be able to live by her writing.

○ live 'down

If you are unable to **live** something **down**, you are unable to make people forget something wrong or foolish that you did.

live something down or **live down something** ❑ If I make a mess of this, I'll never live it down. ❑ This is the story of a young girl who finds it impossible to live down her past.

○ 'live for

If you **live for** something or someone, they are the most important thing in your life and you consider them your reason for living.

live for something/someone ❑ She really lives for her work. ❑ She lives for her family and wants to protect her son.

○ live 'in

1 If someone **lives in**, they live in the place where they work or study. ❑ We are looking for a nanny who would be prepared to live in. ❑ I lived in during my first year at college. ● **Live-in** workers live in the place where they work. ❑ Martha was the live-in maid. ● A **live-in** boyfriend or girlfriend is one that someone lives with. ❑ She has a demanding job and a live-in boyfriend.

2 If a building or room looks **lived-in**, it looks comfortable and a little untidy

because it is used often. ❑ His bedroom had a lived-in look.

○ 'live off

1 If you **live off** something or someone, you get the money that you need to live from them.

live off someone/something ❑ They lived off the rents from their farms. ❑ All his life he had lived off his father.

● If you **live off the land**, you grow your own food or find the food and other things you need to live in the area around you. ❑ They live off the land, growing their own crops.

2 If you **live off** something, it is the only kind of food you eat. = **live on**

live off something ❑ These kids seem to live off junk food. ❑ They lived off berries and roots they found in the forest.

○ 'live on

In meaning 3, the stress is on 'on.

1 If you **live on** an amount of money, you have that amount of money to buy things.

live on something ❑ How do you expect me to live on £150 a month? ❑ I don't have enough to live on.

2 If you **live on** something, it is the only kind of food you eat. = **live off**

live on something ❑ She lived on berries and wild herbs. ❑ A lot of office workers live on sandwiches.

3 If something **lives on**, it continues to exist. ❑ She is dead, but her legend lives on. ❑ The tradition lives on, handed down from generation to generation.

○ live 'out

1 If you **live out** something, you do something that you have thought about or planned, or that was planned for you. [FORMAL]

live out something ❑ Each of us lives out our destiny. ❑ She was able to live out her fantasy of being a film star.

NOTE **Fulfil** is a more formal word for **live out**.

2 If you **live out** your life, you spend the rest of your life in a particular place or situation.

live out something ❑ Some people live out their lives in ignorance. ❑ This was the perfect place for them to live out their retirement years.

3 If someone **lives out**, they do not live at the place where they work or study. ❑ Most postgraduate students live out, rather than living in halls of residence.

○ live 'through

If you **live through** something difficult, you experience it and survive it.

live through something ❏ *You've got to have courage to live through something like that.* ❏ *We can help children to live through family breakup.*

NOTE **Endure** is a more formal word for **live through**.

○ **'live to**

If someone **lives to** a particular age, they stay alive until they are that age.

live to something ❏ *My mother lived to 95.* ❏ *I never believed I would live to this age.*

❍ **'live together**

◼ If two people **live together**, they share the same house and have a sexual relationship but are not married to one another. ❏ *Many people choose to live together rather than to marry.*

NOTE **Cohabit** is a formal word for **live together**.

◻ If people **live together**, they live in the same house. ❏ *They were friends who had lived together as students.*

○ **live 'up**

If you **live it up**, you have a lot of fun, usually in a way that involves spending a lot of money. ❏ *We spent a week living it up in the luxury of the Intercontinental Hotel.*

❍ **live 'up to**

If someone or something **lives up to** what is expected, they are as good as they were expected to be. = **match up to**

live up to something ❏ *The film didn't live up to my expectations.* ❏ *She succeeded in living up to her extraordinary reputation.*

❍ **'live with**

◼ If you **live with** someone, you live in the same house as them.

live with someone ❏ *He lived with his mother until he was thirty-seven.*

◻ If you **live with** someone, you share a house with them and have a sexual relationship with them but are not married to them.

live with someone ❏ *She's living with her boyfriend now.*

▣ If you have to **live with** something unpleasant, you have to accept it and carry on with your life or work.

live with something ❏ *They have to live with the consequences of their decision.* ❏ *The job involved a lot of stress, but you learnt to live with it.*

NOTE **Put up with** is a more informal expression for **live with**.

▤ If you can **live with** yourself, you can accept something that you have done and think that it was right or that you could not have acted in a different way.

live with yourself ❏ *He'd never be able to live with himself if he let anything bad happen to her.* ❏ *How can these people live with themselves?*

liven /ˈlaɪvən/ (**livens, livening, livened**)

○ **liven 'up**

◼ If something **livens up** a place or event, or if a place or event **livens up**, it becomes more interesting and exciting.

liven up something or **live something up** ❏ *She tried to liven things up by suggesting a game.*

liven up ❏ *The party livened up a bit when Sara arrived.*

◻ If something **livens** you **up**, or if you **liven up**, you become more cheerful and energetic. = **perk up**

liven someone up or **liven up someone** ❏ *Do a bit of exercise to liven you up.*

liven up ❏ *Jane livened up when I asked her about her job.*

load /ləʊd/ (**loads, loading, loaded**)

○ **load 'down**

◼ If you **load** someone or something **down** with things or if they **are loaded down** with things, they have a large number of things to carry or hold.

load someone/something down or **load down someone/something** ❏ [+ *with*] *Their grandparents would load them down with presents before sending them home.*

be loaded down ❏ [+ *with*] *We saw a line of trucks loaded down with personal belongings.*

◻ If you **are loaded down** with something, you have a lot of work or responsibility to deal with. = **snowed under**

be loaded down ❏ [+ *with*] *I'm loaded down with work at the moment.*

○ **load 'up**

If you **load** something **up** or if you **load up**, you put things into a vehicle or container.

load up something or **load something up** ❏ [+ *with*] *They helped us load up the wagons with fresh fruit and vegetables.* ❏ *I loaded the dishwasher up.*

load up ❏ *Dad took the luggage out to the car and started loading up.*

loaf /ləʊf/ (**loafs, loafing, loafed**)

○ **loaf a'round** (or **loaf about** [mainly BRITISH])

If you **loaf around** or **loaf around** a place, you spend time being lazy and not doing any work. = **laze around**

loaf around ❏ *She went to college and just loafed around for three years.*

loaf around something ❏ *We loafed around the house all morning.*

oan /ləʊn/ (loans, loaning, loaned)

◌ **loan 'out**

If you **loan** something **out**, you allow someone to borrow it for a particular period of time.

loan out something or **loan something out** ❑ We loan out classroom materials and educational films. ❑ [+ to] She has an apartment in the city which she loans out to friends.

ock /lɒk/ (locks, locking, locked)

◌ **lock a'way**

▪ If you **lock** something **away**, you put it in a place which you lock.

lock something away ❑ He took the papers and locked them away in the bottom drawer of his desk. ❑ Make sure you lock medicines away, out of the reach of young children.

lock away something ❑ He locked away the food whenever he left the house.

be locked away ❑ Everything of value must be locked away.

▪ To **lock** someone **away** means to put them in prison or a place where they cannot get out. = **lock up**

lock someone away ❑ It would be better to help these young people than to lock them away. ❑ An open government does not lock political opponents away.

lock away someone ❑ Our society is locking away more people than ever. ❑ People like that should be locked away for life.

▪ If you **are locked away** or you **lock** yourself **away**, you remain in a particular place alone and do not want to be disturbed. = **shut away**

be locked away ❑ I was locked away all summer, finishing my thesis.

lock yourself away ❑ She locked herself away in her room and wouldn't come out.

▪ If someone **locks** something **away**, they prevent it from becoming known.

lock something away or **lock away something** ❑ They have arrogantly locked away facts that we are entitled to know. ❑ The government would have preferred to lock this report away.

NOTE **Suppress** is a more formal word for **lock away**.

◌ **lock 'down**

If the police **lock down** an area, they stop people from entering or leaving it because of a dangerous event.

lock down something or **lock something down** ❑ Police were searching for an armed gunman and the town was locked down for several hours. ❑ Secret service agents locked the area down and cornered him. ● A place that is in

lockdown has been closed by police because of a dangerous event.

❑ The school was in lockdown yesterday after gunshots were heard from the sports ground.

◌ **lock 'in**

▪ If you **lock** someone **in** or **lock** them **in** a place, you put them somewhere and lock the door so that they cannot get out.

lock someone in ❑ They lock the patients in at night. ❑ She pushed me into a room and locked me in. ❑ I ran into the bathroom and locked myself in.

lock in someone ❑ They locked in the prisoners for the night.

lock someone in something ❑ The prisoners were locked in their cells for 23 hours a day. ❑ She locked herself in her bedroom and wouldn't come out.

▪ If someone **is locked in** something, they are in a bad situation from which they cannot escape.

be locked in something ❑ She is locked in a cycle of hope and despair. ❑ He found himself locked in conflict with his teenage daughter.

▪ If you **lock in** something, you prevent it from being lost.

lock in something or **lock something in** ❑ The cream helps to lock in the skin's natural moisture.

◌ **lock 'out**

▪ If you **lock** someone **out**, you prevent them from entering a place by locking the doors.

lock someone out ❑ [+ of] One night he locked her out of the house. ❑ She shut the door of the hotel room, accidentally locking her husband out.

lock out someone ❑ They bolted the doors to lock out anyone who came to cause trouble. ❑ They were locked out of the room where the meeting was taking place.

▪ If you **lock** yourself **out** of a place or **are locked out**, you cannot get in because you do not have your keys.

lock yourself out ❑ I went out to empty the bins and found that I'd locked myself out. ❑ [+ of] I've locked myself out of the car again!

be locked out ❑ A friend was locked out so I invited her round for coffee until her husband got home.

▪ If managers of a company **lock out** the workers, they prevent them from coming into a factory or office until they accept the company's conditions.

lock someone out or **lock out someone** ❑ The miners refused; the owners then locked them out. ❑ Workers were locked out in industrial disputes. ● A **lockout** is a situation in which the managers of a company prevent workers from coming into a workplace until they accept the company's conditions. ❑ *The Court can stop a strike or lockout.*

✪ lock 'up

1 To **lock** someone **up** means to put them in prison or a place where they cannot escape. = **lock away**

lock someone up ❑ *If they found out what he'd done, they'd lock him up.* ❑ [+ in] *You can't just lock people up in jail without trial.*

lock up someone ❑ *She argues that we lock up too many mentally ill people.* ❑ *They should be locked up.* ● A **lockup** is a jail or a cell in a police station. [AMERICAN, INFORMAL] ❑ *They dragged him off and put him in the lockup.*

2 If you **lock** something **up**, you put it in a place or container that you lock with a key.

lock something up ❑ *You need a garage where you can lock your car up.* ❑ *If you leave valuables in your room, it's best to lock them up.*

lock up something ❑ *I usually lock up my bike in the bike shed.* ❑ *The original of the document is locked up in the safe.*

3 When you **lock up** or **lock** something **up**, you close and lock the door or doors.

lock up ❑ *I was about to lock up when a customer came in.*

lock something up ❑ *He locked the house up for the winter and went travelling.* ❑ *She parked her car, locked it up and walked away.*

lock up something ❑ *He locked up the workshop before going to bed.* ● A **lock-up** garage is one that is available for rent. [BRITISH] ❑ *At the end of the street was a row of lock-up garages.* ● A **lock-up** is a lock-up garage. [BRITISH] ❑ *He kept all his fishing equipment in a lock-up.*

4 If something **is locked up** in something or if something **locks** it **up**, it is in a state from which it cannot easily be made available.

be locked up ❑ [+ in] *A huge amount of water is locked up in the polar ice.* ❑ *The money they need is locked up in various investments.*

lock something up or **lock up something** ❑ *The problem with these bonds is they lock your money up for some time.*

5 If you **lock** something **up**, you do something to make sure that you definitely succeed or win. [INFORMAL]

lock something up or **lock up something** ❑ *They are close to winning the cup, and a victory today would lock it up.*

lodge /lɒdʒ/ (lodges, lodging, lodged)

○ 'lodge in

If something **lodges in** your mind or

memory or **lodges** itself **in** your mind or memory, you remember it for a long time o you cannot stop thinking about it.

lodge in something ❑ *Two scenes from that da lodged in his head.* ❑ *The names had not lodged in my memory.*

lodge itself in something ❑ *Once the thought had lodged itself in my brain, I could think of little else.*

log /lɒg, AM lɔːg/ (logs, logging, logged)

✪ log 'in (or log on)

1 When someone **logs in**, they enter a computer system, network, or website, usually by typing a particular name or word. ≠ **log out** ❑ *When I logged in this mornin, I had over 50 emails waiting for me.* ❑ [+ to] *You need a password to log on to the network.* ❑ [+ as] *Someone logged in as me and read my private messages.*

2 If you **are logged in**, you are currently using a computer system under a particular name.

be logged in ❑ *She went off to lunch while she was still logged in.* ❑ [+ to] *He's been logged on to social networking sites all morning.*

○ log 'into (or log onto)

When someone **logs into** a computer system, they enter it, usually using a particular name or word.

log into something ❑ *I can't log into my email for some reason.*

○ log 'off → see log out

✪ log 'on → see log in

○ log 'onto → see log into

○ log 'out (or log off)

1 When someone **logs out**, they leave a computer system, network, or website. ≠ **log in** ❑ *Don't forget to log off at the end of you session.* ❑ [+ of] *If you're having problems, try logging out of the system and logging back on again.*

2 If you **are logged out**, or if a computer system **logs** you **out**, you are not able to use a computer system.

log someone out or **log out someone** ❑ *If you don't press any key for ten minutes, the system logs you out.*

be logged out ❑ [+ of] *Users were frustrated because they kept being logged out of the system.*

loll /lɒl/ (lolls, lolling, lolled)

○ loll a'round (or loll about [mainly BRITISH])

If you **loll around** a place or **loll around**, you spend time somewhere in a lazy way, not doing anything. = **loaf around**

loll around ❏ *He should be at home and not lolling about in the sun.*

loll around somewhere ❏ *Teenagers love to loll around the house.*

ong /lɒŋ, AM lɔːŋ/ (**longs, longing, longed**)

○ **'long for**

If you **long for** something, you want it very much.

long for something ❏ *I longed for a change.* ❏ *This was the moment she had longed for.*

• A **longed-for** thing or event is one that someone wants very much. ❏ *At last the longed-for drinks arrived.*

ook /lʊk/ (**looks, looking, looked**)

○ **look 'after**

1 If you **look after** someone or something, you take care of them and make sure they have what they need.

look after someone/something ❏ *My mother looks after the baby during the week.* ❏ *Will you look after my garden while I'm away?* ❏ *The patients were being well looked after.*

2 If you **look after** something, you are responsible for it and deal with it.

look after something ❏ *We need someone to look after the paperwork.* ❏ *The organization is supposed to look after the interests of ordinary investors.*

NOTE **Attend to** is a more formal expression for **look after**.

3 If you **look after** something that belongs to someone else, you keep it for them so that it does not get lost or damaged.

look after something ❏ [+ for] *Will you look after my watch for me while I go swimming?*

4 If you **look after** yourself, you make sure that you stay healthy or avoid being harmed.

look after yourself ❏ *He has clearly looked after himself, and is in very good shape for his age.* ❏ *Don't worry about me. I can look after myself.*

○ **look a'head**

If you **look ahead**, you think about what is going to happen in the future. ❏ *In business, it's important to look ahead.* ❏ [+ to] *I'm always looking ahead to the next task.* ❏ *Looking ahead four or five years, what do you see yourself doing?*

○ **look a'round** (or **look round** [mainly BRITISH])

1 If you **look around**, you turn to look behind you. ❏ *He heard a noise and looked round, but there was no-one there.* ❏ *She walked away without once looking around.*

2 If you **look around** or **look around** you, you look in various directions to find something, or to see what is there.

look around ❏ *If you look around, you will see*

many different styles of building. ❏ [+ for] *He looked around for a chair and, since there wasn't one, sat on the floor.* ❏ [+ at] *'What's going on?' He looked round at the group.*

look around you ❏ *She looked around her, admiring the view.*

3 If you **look around**, you try to find something that you want by considering different things. ❏ *I need a new car, but I'm going to look around for a while before I decide.* ❏ [+ for] *Sarah is looking around for a new job.* ❏ *I've heard they might be looking around for a babysitter.*

4 If you **look around** a place or **look around**, you walk around a place and look at different parts of it. = **go round**

look around something ❏ *Shall we look round the Cathedral this afternoon?*

look around ❏ *I was in town on business, and I had no time to look around.*

○ **'look at**

1 If you **look at** something or someone, you turn your eyes towards them.

look at something/someone ❏ *Everyone turned to look at the painting.* ❏ *She looked at her face in the mirror.* ❏ *Why are you looking at me like that?*

2 If you **look at** something, you quickly read it or read parts of it. = **look through**

look at something ❏ *I've looked at your essay and I think it's very good.* ❏ *She just had time to look at the front page of the newspaper before going to work.*

3 If an expert **looks at** something, they examine it.

look at something ❏ *Your leg's a bit swollen. I think you should get a doctor to look at it.* ❏ *I took my car into the garage to be looked at.*

4 If you **look at** a subject, problem, or situation, you consider or study it.

look at something ❏ *His research looked at the way language is acquired.* ❏ *When they have looked at all the results, they will make a diagnosis.*

5 If you tell someone to **look at** someone or something, you are asking them to consider someone or something as a good example of what you are saying.

look at someone/something ❏ *Look at me. I manage perfectly well without a car.* ❏ *If you look at the case of Europe, you'll see she's right.*

6 If you **look at** a situation in a particular way, you judge it or consider it in that way. = **see**

look at something ❏ [+ in] *I tend to look at things in a very different way to my parents.* ❏ [+ as] *She looks at life as a series of challenges.* ❏ *Was he to blame? It all depends how you look at it.*

○ **look a'way**

If you **look away**, you turn your eyes away from something or someone. ❑ *Their eyes met and Ida blushed and looked away.* ❑ *He glanced at the picture, then quickly looked away.*

✪ **look 'back**

1 If you **look back**, you turn to see what is behind you. ❑ *I looked back and saw my car moving slowly down the hill.* ❑ [+ at] *Jack turned and looked back at me.*

2 If you **look back**, you think about something that happened in the past. ❑ *It all seems very silly when I look back, but it was awful at the time.* ❑ [+ on] *The past always seems better when you look back on it.*

3 If you say that someone **never looked back**, you mean that they continued to progress or succeed from a particular point. ❑ *She taught him to play, and he never looked back.*

✪ **look 'down**

If you **look down**, you lower your eyes to see what is below. ❑ *He paused on the narrow ledge and looked down.* ❑ [+ at] *She looked down at the floor, embarrassed.*

○ **look 'down on**

If you **look down on** someone or something, you think they are less important than you or not good enough for you. = **despise**

look down on someone/something ❑ *They are arrogant people who look down on everyone else.* ❑ *Foreign food used to be looked down on.*

✪ **'look for**

1 If you **look for** something or someone, you try to find them.

look for something/someone ❑ *Someone came to the office looking for you.* ❑ *The boys went into the garden to look for their ball.* ❑ *He found the book he was looking for.*

2 If you **look for** something, you try to achieve it or get it.

look for something ❑ *We must look for a peaceful solution.* ❑ *Millions of people are now looking for work.* ❑ *I think he was really looking for forgiveness.*

NOTE **Seek** is a more formal word for **look for.**

● **Unlooked-for** is used to describe something which you did not expect or want to happen. ❑ *There was an unlooked-for change in the weather.*

✪ **look 'forward to**

1 If you **look forward to** something, you are happy it is going to happen because you expect to enjoy it.

look forward to something ❑ *I was not looking forward to my meeting with the manager.* ❑ *It's*

important to have something to look forward to.

2 If you say that someone **is looking forward to** something, you mean they expect something good to happen.

be looking forward to something ❑ *Motor traders are looking forward to a further increase in sales.*

○ **look 'in**

1 If you **look in**, you visit a person or place for a short time, especially to check on them. = **drop in, call in** ❑ *You stay in bed, and I'll look in later in case you need anything.* ❑ [+ on] *I think I'll look in on my parents on the way home from work.* ❑ [+ at] *He decided to look in at the lab to see how the work was going.*

2 If you do not get a **look-in**, you are unable to take part in something because other people are more successful or forceful than you. ❑ *James talks so much that the others barely get a look-in.*

✪ **look 'into**

If you **look into** something, you find out and examine the facts about a problem or situation.

look into something ❑ *I complained to the manager, and he promised to look into it.*
NOTE **Investigate** is a more formal word for **look into.**

✪ **look 'on**

If you **look on**, you watch something happen without taking part yourself. ❑ *His parents looked on proudly as he collected his prize.* ● **Onlookers** are the people watching an event take place, without taking part. ❑ *Reporters and onlookers lined the fence beside the airfield.*

○ **'look on** (or **look upon**)

If you **look on** something or someone in a particular way, you think of them in that way.

look on something/someone ❑ [+ as] *If she went out with Mark, John would look on it as a great insult.* ❑ *I look on her as a friend.* ❑ *Local people would not look kindly upon such a development.*

✪ **look 'out**

1 You say **look out** to warn someone about something that you have noticed, especially danger. = **watch out** ❑ *'Look out,' I said. 'There's someone coming.'* ● If someone keeps a **lookout**, they keep watching to try and notice something, especially something dangerous. ❑ *Keep a lookout for any small boats.* ● A **lookout** is someone who is watching for something, especially danger. ❑ *Two of the burglars were tipped off by a lookout and escaped.* ● A **lookout** is a place from which someone can watch the area around them for any danger.

2 If you **look** something **out**, you find and take out something that is stored away. **= dig out**

look out something or **look something out** ❑ She offered to look out some old baby clothes for me. ❑ I think I've got some books on that – I'll look them out.

look 'out for

1 If you **look out for** something, you try to find or notice it. **= watch out for**

look out for something ❑ I was looking out for stories that I could use in the magazine. ❑ Look out for anything that seems suspicious.

2 If you **look out for** someone or **look out for** their interests, you try to protect them from harm and make sure they have what they need.

look out for someone/something ❑ We all look out for each other in the family. ❑ Everyone looks out for people in their own team.

look out for yourself ❑ You're grown-up now and have to start looking out for yourself.

look 'out over

If a room **looks out over** something, you can see that thing outside and below you from the room.

look out over something ❑ Her hotel bedroom looked out over the bay.

look 'over

If you **look** something or someone **over**, you examine them in order to get a general idea of what they are like.

look over something/someone or **look something/someone over** ❑ Would you look over what I've written and give me some feedback? ❑ If you're worried about your pet, get the vet to look it over.

look 'round → see look around

look 'through

1 If you **look through** something, you look in its direction to see what is on the other side of it.

look through something ❑ Michael looked through the window into the street. ❑ The captain looked through his binoculars at the long column of ships.

2 If you **look through** things or you **look through** a place, you examine all the things in a place in order to find something. **= go through**

look through something ❑ They'll look through the applications and pick out the best ones. ❑ Did you look through all your drawers and cupboards?

3 If you **look through** something that has been written or printed, you read it, usually fairly quickly and briefly.

look through something ❑ You may find it helpful to look through your notes on the morning of the examination.

4 If you **look through** someone, you look at them without showing that you have seen or recognized them.

look through someone ❑ I called her name, but she looked straight through me.

○ 'look to

1 If you **look to** someone or something for a particular thing, you expect them to provide it. **= turn to**

look to someone/something ❑ [+ for] They are looking to us for leadership. ❑ [+ to-infinitive] People look to education to solve social problems.

2 If you **look to** something, you make sure that it is in a good state. **= attend to** [FORMAL]

look to something ❑ They must look to their defences. ❑ He should look to his own family before criticizing others.

3 If you **look to** the future, you think about it.

look to something ❑ Some look to the future with a certain anxiety.

○ look 'up

1 If you **look up**, you raise your eyes. ❑ I looked up and saw a big bird overhead. ❑ [+ from] She did not even look up from her work when he came in.

2 If you **look** something **up**, you find a piece of information by looking at something such as a book or website.

look up something ❑ He fetched his dictionary to look up the word 'apotheosis'. ❑ [+ in] I looked up his contact details on the university's website.

look something up ❑ I don't know – look it up online. ❑ If you don't know where it is, look it up on Google Maps.

3 If you **look** someone **up**, you visit them after not having seen them for some time.

look someone up or **look up someone** ❑ Look me up when you're next in the area. ❑ While she was in London, she decided to look up some old friends.

4 If a situation **is looking up**, it is improving. [INFORMAL]

be looking up ❑ Things started looking up at last when he met Debbie. ❑ [+ for] With the local economy on the upturn, things are looking up for the region.

○ 'look upon → see look on

○ look 'up to

If you **look up to** someone, you respect and admire them.

look up to someone ❑ She looks up to her father. ❑ The students look up to you and admire you.

loom /luːm/ (looms, looming, loomed)

○ loom a'head

If something bad **looms ahead**, it is likely to happen quite soon. ❑ They were not aware of the disaster that loomed ahead. ❑ She saw various problems looming ahead.

○ 'loom over

1 If something or someone **looms over** someone or something, they appear as a large or unclear shape, often in a frightening way.

loom over someone/something ❑ The vast Yarnarrow Castle loomed over the city. ❑ He woke up to find a man looming over him.

2 If something bad **looms over** you, it is likely to happen and affect you quite soon.

loom over someone ❑ The prospect of factory closure is looming over the workforce. ❑ The court case was looming over us.

○ loom 'up

If something **looms up**, it appears as a large, unclear shape in front of you, often in a way that seems threatening. ❑ The huge Victorian building loomed up against the skyline. ❑ Cliffs loomed up out of the fog.

loop /luːp/ (loops, looping, looped)

○ loop 'in

If you **loop** someone **in**, you keep them informed, for example, by including them in email correspondence.

loop someone in ❑ You could loop your boss in so that she's aware of the situation. ❑ Could someone loop me in on this?

loose /luːs/ (looses, loosing, loosed)

○ loose 'off [BRITISH]

If you **loose off** something, you make it explode by setting light to it or firing it.

loose off something or **loose something off** ❑ The enemy loosed a few grenades off.

○ 'loose upon [FORMAL, LITERARY]

If something unpleasant **is loosed upon** a place or person, it is allowed to affect them.

be loosed upon someone/something ❑ Then anarchy will be loosed upon the world.

loosen /'luːsən/ (loosens, loosening, loosened)

○ loosen 'up

1 When you **loosen up** or **loosen up** part of your body, you make your body more flexible and relaxed.

loosen up ❑ The dancers loosen up with a few exercises.

loosen something up or **loosen up something** ❑ If the muscles are painful, a massa_ can help loosen them up. ❑ Stretch every mornin_ to loosen up the joints.

2 If someone **loosens up** or if something c someone **loosens** them **up**, they become more relaxed.

loosen up ❑ As the day wore on, he loosened up and became more talkative.

loosen someone up or **loosen up someone** ❑ She smiled and joked, trying her best to loosen him up.

lop /lɒp/ (lops, lopping, lopped)

○ lop 'off

1 If you **lop** something **off**, you cut it away from something with a quick, strong stroke. = **chop off**

lop off something or **lop something off** ❑ If the tree gets too big, you could always lop off a few branches. ❑ She took some scissors and lopped her hair off.

2 To **lop** an amount **off** or **lop** it **off** something means to reduce a total by that amount. = **knock off** [INFORMAL]

lop something off or **lop off something** ❑ They took the current figure and lopped off a litt_ to allow for energy conservation.

lop something off something ❑ They lopped nearly $2 million off the asking price. ❑ He lopped_ six seconds off the previous world record.

lord /lɔːd/ (lords, lording, lorded)

○ 'lord over

If someone **lords it over** you, they act as if they are better or more important than you. = **queen over** ❑ He seemed to enjoy lordir_ it over his junior colleagues.

lose /luːz/ (loses, losing, lost)

◎ 'lose in

If you **lose** yourself **in** something, you give lot of attention to it and do not think abou anything else.

lose yourself in something ❑ Jett ignored the problem and tried to lose himself in his music.

○ lose 'out

If you **lose out**, you do not get something that others have or that you should have. = **miss out** ❑ She was quiet and shy at work, an_ this meant she lost out when it came to work get-togethers. ❑ [+ on] Children who spend a lot _ time in hospital lose out on their education.

○ lose 'out to

If you **lose out to** someone else, they are more successful than you.

lose out to someone ❑ British companies are losing out to overseas competition.

ounge /laʊndʒ/ (lounges, lounging, lounged)

○ **lounge a'round** (or **lounge about, lounge 'round** [mainly BRITISH])
If you **lounge around** or **lounge around** a place, you spend time in a relaxed and lazy way, not doing any work. = **loaf around**
lounge around ❏ *People were lounging about, apparently with nothing to do.*
lounge around something ❏ *We lounged around the pool all day.*

○ **lounge 'round** → see **lounge around**

ouse /laʊs/ (louses, lousing, loused)

○ **louse 'up** [INFORMAL]
To **louse** something **up** means to spoil it or do it extremely badly. = **foul up**
louse something up or **louse up something** ❏ *This is an important job. Don't louse it up.* ❏ *They've managed to completely louse up the economy.*

uck /lʌk/ (lucks, lucking, lucked)

○ **luck 'into** [AMERICAN, INFORMAL]
If you **luck into** something good, you get it by chance.
luck into something ❏ *They are four working class boys who have lucked into the best possible jobs.*

○ **luck 'out** [AMERICAN, INFORMAL]
If you **luck out**, you are very lucky. ❏ *You really lucked out when you met Teddy.*

ull /lʌl/ (lulls, lulling, lulled)

○ **lull 'into**
To **lull** someone **into** feeling safe or confident means to make them feel safe or confident with the result that they are shocked when something bad happens.
lull someone into something ❏ *A cool wind had lulled sunbathers into a false sense of security.* ❏ *I had been lulled into thinking this would be a trivial matter.*

umber /'lʌmbə/ (lumbers, lumbering, lumbered)

○ **lumber with** [BRITISH, INFORMAL]
If you **are lumbered with** something or someone, or if someone **lumbers** you **with** them, you have to have them or deal with

them when you do not want to. = **saddle with**
be lumbered with something/someone
❏ *Now we are lumbered with a house that we can't sell.* ❏ *I can see I'm going to get lumbered with the washing-up.*
lumber someone with something/someone
❏ *Joe went out, lumbering her with all the children.*

lump /lʌmp/ (lumps, lumping, lumped)

○ **lump to'gether**
If you **lump together** different things or people, you consider them in the same way or as one group.
lump together something/someone or **lump someone/something together** ❏ *She believes it is a mistake to lump all these issues together.* ❏ *Why are older people all lumped together regardless of their different needs?*

lurch /lɜːtʃ/ (lurches, lurching, lurched)

○ **'lurch from to**
If a person or organization **lurches from** one thing **to** another, they are affected by a lot of changing feelings or events that they do not seem to have any control over.
lurch from something to something ❏ *We lurched from hope to despair all the time Helen was in hospital.* ❏ *I seemed to lurch from one crisis to another.*

lust /lʌst/ (lusts, lusting, lusted)

○ **'lust after** (or **lust for**)
1 If you **lust after** something, you want to have it very much. = **crave**
lust after something ❏ *They lusted after money and power.*
2 If you **lust after** someone, you feel strong sexual desire for them.
lust after someone ❏ *She had lusted after other men.*

○ **'lust for** → see **lust after**

luxuriate /lʌg'ʒʊərieɪt/ (luxuriates, luxuriating, luxuriated)

○ **lux'uriate in**
If you **luxuriate in** something, you enjoy it very much.
luxuriate in something ❏ *He was luxuriating in the first real holiday he'd had for years.* ❏ *We lay there and luxuriated in the warmth of the sun.*

Mm

magic /ˈmædʒɪk/ (magics, magicking, magicked)

○ **magic a'way**

If you **magic** something **away**, you make it disappear very quickly or unexpectedly.
magic something away or **magic away something** ❑ *It was a serious problem; he could not magic it away.* ❑ *There are no simple solutions that can magic away the economic crisis.*

mail /meɪl/ (mails, mailing, mailed)

○ **mail 'out** [mainly AMERICAN]

If someone **mails** something **out**, they send a large number of copies of something in the mail. = **send out**
mail out something or **mail something out** ❑ *This week, the company mailed out its annual report.* ❑ [+ to] *We mailed out the conference schedule to all participants.*

maintain /meɪnˈteɪn/ (maintains, maintaining, maintained)

○ **main'tain at**

To **maintain** something **at** a particular rate or level means to keep it at that rate or level.
maintain something at something ❑ *The government was right to maintain interest rates at a high level.*

major /ˈmeɪdʒə/ (majors, majoring, majored)

○ **'major in** [mainly AMERICAN]

If you **major in** a subject, you study it as your main subject at university.
major in something ❑ *White had majored in Chinese history at Harvard.*

make /meɪk/ (makes, making, made)

○ **make 'after**

If you **make after** someone or something, you chase them.
make after someone/something ❑ *They made after him in the car.*

○ **make a'way with** [INFORMAL]

If you **make away with** something, you steal it and take it away. = **make off with**
make away with something ❑ *They tied him up and made away with his wallet.*

○ **'make for**

1 If you **make for** a place, you move towards it in a quick or determined way.
= **head for**
make for something ❑ *The best thing would be to make for high ground.* ❑ *I made straight for the kitchen to get something to eat.*

2 To **make for** something means to have it as a result.
make for something ❑ *I had to tell him things he did not want to hear, which did not make for an easy conversation.* ❑ *What are the values that make for happy family life?*

NOTE **Produce** is a more formal word for **make for**.

○ **make 'into**

1 If you **make** one thing **into** something else, you change it so that it becomes that other thing. = **turn into**
make something into something ❑ *I was planning to make the fabric into cushion covers.* ❑ *They cut down the forest to make it into farmland.* ❑ *Her novel is being made into a Hollywood film.*

2 If someone or something **makes** you into a particular type of person, they help or make you become that thing. = **turn into**
make someone into something ❑ *They are trying to make these men into soldiers.* ❑ *He thought he could make her into a star.*

○ **'make of**

If you ask someone what they **make of** someone or something, you are asking what they think of them or how they understand them.
make of something/someone ❑ *What did you make of today's events?* ❑ *He was an unusual person – people didn't know quite what to make of him.*

○ **make 'off**

If you **make off**, you leave somewhere as quickly as possible, often in order to escape ❑ *The vehicle made off at once.* ❑ *She let go of the child and he made off.*

○ **make 'off with**

If you **make off with** something, you steal it and take it away. = **make away with**

make off with something ❑ *The thieves made off with money and jewellery.* ❑ *The dog tried to make off with one of his sausages.*

◗ **make 'out**

1 If you **make** something **out**, you manage to see or hear it.

make out something ❑ *He could just make out the number plate of the car.* ❑ *It was hard to make out what he was doing in the photograph.*

make something out ❑ *She was mumbling something but I couldn't make it out.* ❑ *I stared at them, trying to make their faces out.*

2 If you **make** something **out**, you manage to understand it. **= work out**

make out something or **make something out** ❑ *I just couldn't make out his motives for leaving.* ❑ *The essay was full of complex ideas and we struggled to make them out.*

3 If you **make out** that something is true, you try to make people believe it. **= imply**

make out something ❑ *He made out that he was a close friend of the family.* ❑ *It really is not as easy as they make out.*

4 If you **make** someone **out** to be something, you give the impression that they are that sort of person.

make someone out ❑ [+ *to*-infinitive] *She makes me out to be some sort of monster.*

make yourself out ❑ [+ *to*-infinitive] *They aren't as important as they make themselves out to be.*

5 If you **make out a case for** something, you argue that it is right or correct. ❑ [+ *for*] *You could certainly make out a case for this point of view.* ❑ *Alice continued making out her case.*

6 When you **make out** a document such as a cheque, you write on it all the necessary information. **= write out**

make out something or **make something out** ❑ *I made out a cheque for £250.* ❑ [+ *to*] *I'll just make a receipt out for you.*

7 If you **make out**, you manage to do something or to live fairly well. **= get by, cope** [INFORMAL] ❑ *How am I going to make out alone?* ❑ *I think we're going to make out fine.*

8 If two people **make out**, they kiss or touch in a sexual way or they have sex. [AMERICAN, INFORMAL] ❑ *They printed pictures of the couple making out on the beach.*

◗ **make 'over**

1 If you **make** something **over**, you legally change the ownership of it from one person to another.

make over something or **make something over** ❑ [+ *to*] *He made over his family home to a trust, and moved into a small cottage.* ❑ *I was willing to make over every penny I had.*

2 If you **make over** something or someone, you change them to make them look more attractive.

make over something/someone or **make something/someone over** ❑ *If you watch the show, you can learn how to make over your house and garden.* ● A **makeover** is the process of changing someone or something to make them look more attractive. ❑ *She's had a complete wardrobe makeover.*

✪ **make 'up**

1 If people or things **make up** something, they form it.

make up something ❑ *Women now make up two-fifths of the work force.*

make something up ❑ *The EU's budget has to be agreed by the member states that make it up.*

be made up of something ❑ *All substances are made up of molecules.* ❑ *Nearly half the Congress is made up of lawyers.*

[NOTE] **Comprise** is a more formal word for **make up**.

● The **make-up** of something is the parts that it consists of. ❑ *We want to change the make-up of the committee so that it reflects the general population.* ● Someone's **make-up** is their character. ❑ *It's not part of his make-up to be jealous.*

MAKE UP + *noun*
make up **the bulk of** something
make up **the majority of** something
make up **the rest of** something
make up **a proportion of** something
❑ *Household waste makes up a small proportion of the total.* ❑ *Family law makes up the bulk of my work.*

2 If you **make up** something, you invent it.

make up something ❑ *He used to make up stories for his children.* ❑ *He was accused of making up some of the stories in his autobiography.*

make something up ❑ *She continued to talk, making it up as she went along.* ● A **made-up** story or excuse has been invented and is not true. ❑ *It's all a made-up story and you know it.* ❑ *Some of these titles are completely made-up.*

3 If you **make** something **up**, you prepare it so that it is ready for someone to use or have.

make up something ❑ *She was making up a packed lunch for her daughter.* ❑ *Her mother made up a bed in her old room.*

make something up ❑ *Do you mind waiting in the hotel lounge while we make your room up?* ❑ *She took her prescription to a pharmacist and got him to make it up.* ● Something that is **made-up** has already been prepared so that you do not have to make it yourself.

❏ *We just used a ready made-up sauce for the chicken.*

4 When you **make up** your **mind**, you decide which of a number of possible things you will have or will do. ❏ *He has a hard time making up his mind.* ❏ *I can't decide; help me make my mind up.* ❏ *If you don't make your mind up soon, I'll make it up for you.*

5 If you **make up** an amount, you add something to it so that it is as large as it should be.
make up something or **make something up**
❏ *We need another £50 to make up the balance.* ❏ *It's going to be fifteen cents short, but Mr Harper will make it up.* ❏ *[+ to] Make the cooking liquid up to 250 ml with water.*

> **MAKE UP + *noun***
> make up **a shortfall**
> make up **a deficit**
> make up **the difference**
> ❏ *I paid £350 and my parents made up the difference.* ❏ *And extra £3million will make up the shortfall in funding.*

6 If you **make up** time, you work extra hours because you have previously taken time off work.
make up something or **make something up**
❏ *They'll have to make up time lost during the strike.* ❏ *Can I leave early today? I'll work on Saturday to make it up.*

7 If you **make** someone **up**, you put substances such as lipstick and powder on their face.
make someone up or **make up someone**
❏ *He sits in a chair whistling to himself as they make him up.* ❏ *She spent two hours making herself up.* ● **Make-up** is substances such as lipstick, powder, and eye-shadow, which people use to make themselves look more attractive, or which actors use when they are acting. ❏ *She never wears eye make-up.* ❏ *She quickly brushed her hair and put on some make-up.*
NOTE **Cosmetics** is a more formal word for make-up.
● If you or your face, lips, or eyes are **made-up**, you are wearing make-up. ❏ *Kate reappeared with freshly made-up lips.* ❏ *Their eyes were heavily made-up.*

8 If two people **make up**, or **make** it **up**, they become friends again after they have had a quarrel.
make up ❏ *They'd kissed and made up.* ❏ *[+ with] I want you to make up with her.*
make something up ❏ *They had a quarrel but Marsha wanted to make it up.* ❏ *We row all the time, but we always make things up.*

○ **make 'up for**
1 To **make up for** something means to replace something that has been lost or damaged or to provide something instead of it.
make up for something ❏ *She hurried on to make up for the minutes she had lost.*
● If you **make up for lost time**, you do something a lot because you have not had the opportunity to do it before. ❏ *Her parent had never allowed her to go to parties or see friends so she was making up for lost time.*
2 If you **make up for** something, you do something to show that you are sorry or to make someone less unhappy.
make up for something ❏ *She tried to make up for her rudeness earlier by being extra nice to me.* ❏ *I know it's disappointing, but let me buy you dinner to make up for it.*

○ **make 'up to**
1 If you **make up to** someone, you are very friendly towards them because they have something you want. [OLD-FASHIONED]
make up to someone ❏ *I hate the way politicians make up to rich businesspeople.*
2 If you **make it/things up to** someone, you do something to show them you are sorry for something bad you have done, or to thank them for something good they have done. ❏ *I'm really sorry. I'll make it up to you, I promise.* ❏ *Somehow, some day, he'd make things up to his father.*

○ **'make with** [AMERICAN, INFORMAL]
If you tell someone to **make with** something you want them to get it or give it to you.
make with something ❏ *I need some money. So make with the cash.*

man /mæn/ (**mans, manning, manned**)
○ **man 'up**
If someone **mans up**, they behave in a way thought to be typical of men, especially by showing courage. ❏ *Why not man up and admit you were wrong?*

manage /'mænɪdʒ/ (**manages, managing, managed**)
○ **manage 'up**
You **manage up** when you form good relationships with the people who are above you in a company's structure.
manage up ❏ *Some middle managers are good at managing up, but terrible when it comes to supervising their own team.*

map /mæp/ (**maps, mapping, mapped**)
○ **map 'out**
If you **map** something **out**, you work out in detail what you will do.

map out something or **map something out**
❑ We began to map out plans for our journey.
❑ His parents seemed to have his life all mapped out for him.

> **MAP OUT + noun**
> map out **a strategy**
> map out **a plan**
> map out **a future**
> ❑ The two leaders met to map out a strategy for peace. ❑ He already felt that his future was mapped out.

mark /mɑːk/ (**marks, marking, marked**)

○ **'mark as**
Someone or something that **marks** someone **as** a particular type of person shows that they are that type of person. = **mark down as, label**
mark someone as something ❑ He worried that his shabby clothes marked him as inferior.

✪ **mark 'down**
1 If you **mark** something **down**, you write it down. = **jot down**
mark something down ❑ [+ on] I marked the number down on a scrap of paper. ❑ Every time they score a point, mark it down.
mark down something ❑ If you witness an accident, mark down the licence number of the car.
2 If you **mark down** a price, you reduce it. = **reduce**; ≠ **mark up**
mark something down ❑ If the fish doesn't sell, we have to mark it down.
mark down something ❑ Dealers marked down the company's share price.
be marked down ❑ [+ from] Trousers are marked down from £39.95 to £20.00. ● A **mark-down** is a reduction in the price of something. ❑ We bought too much stock and had to sell it at a mark-down.
3 If a teacher **marks** a student **down**, the student's work gets a lower grade. ≠ **mark up**
mark someone down or **mark down someone** ❑ If you miss out a comma, they mark you down. ❑ [+ for] You could be marked down for getting a date wrong.

○ **mark 'down as**
If you **mark** someone **down as** a particular type of person, you consider that they are that type of person, often unfairly. = **mark as**
mark someone down as something ❑ They had marked her down already as a bad mother.

○ **mark 'off**
1 If you **mark off** a piece of something, you show that it is separate from everything around it.
mark off something or **mark something off** ❑ He marked off the area with lengths of string.

❑ We now mark off certain forests to protect them.
2 If something **marks** one person or thing **off** from another, it makes them very different from one another.
mark something/someone off ❑ [+ from] There are certain personality differences that mark her off from her brother. ❑ His accent and his way of dressing marked him off.
NOTE **Distinguish** is a more formal word for **mark off**.
3 If you **mark off** something on a list, you put a mark near it to show that it has been dealt with. = **cross off, tick off**
mark off something or **mark something off** ❑ He marked off the places he had seen on his map. ❑ She called out names and marked them off.

✪ **mark 'out**
1 To **mark out** an area means to show its shape by making marks on a surface.
mark out something ❑ They marked out a football pitch on the playing field. ❑ A landing strip was marked out for the pilots of incoming aircraft.
mark something out ❑ He surveyed the site and marked it out with white stones.
2 If something **marks** someone or something **out**, it makes them different from other people or things. = **distinguish**
mark someone/something out ❑ There was a stillness about Ralph that marked him out.
mark out someone/something ❑ In music, it can be hard to identify what marks out a hit.
3 If someone **is marked out** to achieve something, they seem likely to achieve it. = **be destined**
be marked out ❑ [+ to-infinitive] Ian was always marked out to become a musician. ❑ He thought of himself as a great man, marked out by destiny for his task.

○ **mark 'out as**
If something **marks** someone or something **out as** a particular type of person or thing, it shows that they are that type of person or thing.
mark someone/something out as something ❑ Their clothes and cars mark them out as important. ❑ There were no obvious signs which marked it out as a restaurant.

○ **mark 'up**
1 To **mark up** goods means to increase their price. = **put up**; ≠ **mark down**
mark up something or **mark something up** ❑ They buy them cheaply, mark them up, and sell them on. ● A **mark-up** is an amount added to the price of something when it is sold. ❑ They sell cold drinks at a large mark-up.
2 If you **mark up** a number or score, you count it or record it by writing it on a

surface such as a wall or board so that other people can see it.

mark something up or **mark up something**
❑ [+ on] *Mark the score up on the whiteboard.*
❑ *Every time a plane flew overhead, he marked it up.*
3 If you **mark** text **up**, you write marks on it in order to correct mistakes or make it ready for a particular process.

mark something up or **mark up something**
❑ *She read all the scripts, marking them up in blue pencil.* ❑ *I'll mark up the artwork and fax it to you.*
4 If a teacher **marks** a student **up**, they put a higher grade on the student's work.
≠ **mark down**

mark someone up or **mark up someone**
❑ *You must treat candidates equally and not mark them up or down on the basis of age.*

marry /'mæri/ (**marries, marrying, married**)

○ **marry a'bove** [OLD-FASHIONED]
If someone **marries above** themselves, they marry someone richer or with higher social status.
marry above yourself ❑ *Her mother was a servant girl who married above herself.*

○ **marry be'neath** [OLD-FASHIONED]
If someone **marries beneath** themselves, they marry someone poorer or with lower social status.
marry beneath yourself ❑ *People felt that the Duke married beneath himself.*

○ **marry 'into**
If you **marry into** a family, especially a wealthy family, you become part of it by marrying someone in it.
marry into something ❑ *He had visions of marrying into the family and starting an empire.*
❑ *She had married into money.*

○ **marry 'off**
If you **marry** someone **off**, you find a suitable person for them to marry.
marry off someone or **marry someone off**
❑ *He hoped to marry off all his daughters.* ❑ *They wanted to marry her off to the Prince, but she refused.*

○ **marry 'out** [OLD-FASHIONED]
If someone **marries out**, they marry someone who is not of the same religion as they are. ❑ *Her father disowned her when she told him she was marrying out.*

○ **marry 'up**
If things **marry up** or if you **marry** them **up**, they are the same or go well together.
marry up ❑ [+ with] *We have to make sure that the information the application form marries up with what the candidate says at interview.* ❑ *The music and the images marry up beautifully.*
marry something up or **marry up something**
❑ [+ with] *Like many business people, he is trying*

to marry up the need for profits with the social role of a business. ❑ *There is a need for jobs and a need for manpower – why can't we marry them up?*

marvel /'mɑːvəl/ (**marvels, marvelling, marvelled**)

> American English uses the spellings **marveling** and **marveled**.

○ **'marvel at**
If you **marvel at** something, you are filled with surprise and admiration by it.
marvel at something ❑ *Early travellers marvelled at the riches of Mali.*

mash /mæʃ/ (**mashes, mashing, mashed**)

○ **mash 'up**
1 If you **mash up** food, you crush it until it is soft and smooth in texture.
mash up something or **mash something up**
❑ *Mash up the strawberries and strain the pips out.*
❑ *When you serve vegetables to a baby, mash them up with a fork.*
2 If you **mash up** things such as pieces of music, film or software, you mix them to create something new.
mash something up or **mash up something**
❑ *This is what happened when we mashed up Bob Dylan and Dr Seuss.* ● A **mash-up** is a mixture of things such as pieces of music, film or software. ❑ *Users will be able to post video playlists and create mash-ups.*

mask /mɑːsk, mæsk/ (**masks, masking, masked**)

○ **mask 'out**
If part of a picture or text **is masked out** or someone **masks** it **out**, it is hidden.
be masked out ❑ *He asked for the names of his clients to be masked out.*
mask something out or **mask out something**
❑ *He masked out the man's hair with a piece of card.*

masquerade /mæskə'reɪd/ (**masquerades, masquerading, masqueraded**)

○ **masque'rade as**
To **masquerade as** something means to pretend to be that thing.
masquerade as something ❑ *He tried to masquerade as a police officer.* ❑ *She gave a short speech masquerading as a question.*

match /mætʃ/ (**matches, matching, matched**)

○ **'match against**
1 If you **match** one thing **against** another, you compare the two things to see whether they are similar.
match something against something
❑ *Police took samples of his blood and hair and*

matched them against traces found at the scene.
2 If you **match** one thing or person **against** another, you make them compete to see which one is better.

match something/someone against something/someone ❑ *Their army matched its advanced technology against the vast numbers commanded by the enemy.*

match yourself against someone/ something ❑ *Many amateurs were matching themselves against the professionals.*

○ **match 'up**

1 If two things **match up**, they are the same or similar. ❑ *They examine the fingerprints and see if they match up.* ❑ [+ with] *What he told me did not match up with what I saw myself.*

2 If two things or people **match up** or if you **match** them **up**, they fit together or form the right combination.

match up ❑ *Make sure that the lines on each side of the page match up.*

match up something ❑ [+ with] *She was always trying to match up her friends with boyfriends.*

match something up ❑ *The aim of the game is to match the cards up.* ❑ [+ with] *We can match you up with the right college course for you.*

○ **match 'up to**

If something **matches up to** something or someone else, it is good enough for it or as good as it. = **measure up to**

match up to something/someone ❑ *The product did not match up to expectations.* ❑ *I could never match up to him physically so I had to use my brain.*

maul /mɔːl/ (**mauls, mauling, mauled**)

○ **maul a'round** (or **maul about**) [INFORMAL]

If you **maul** something or someone **around**, you handle them roughly.

maul someone/something around or **maul around someone/something** ❑ *I don't want doctors mauling her around unnecessarily.*

max /mæks/ (**maxes, maxing, maxed**)

○ **max 'out** [INFORMAL]

If you **max out** a credit card or **are maxed out** on it, you use all of your available money or credit.

max out something or **max something out** ❑ *The thieves maxed out my credit card and withdrew everything from my savings account.*

be maxed out ❑ *I'm maxed out on all my cards.*

measure /'meʒə/ (**measures, measuring, measured**)

○ **'measure against**

If you **measure** someone or something **against** another person or thing, you judge

them by comparing them with the other person or thing.

measure something/someone against something/someone ❑ *If you measure his achievements against those of his contemporaries, they are very impressive.*

○ **measure 'out**

If you **measure** something **out**, you take the particular amount that is needed.

measure out something or **measure something out** ❑ *She carefully measured out 250 grams of flour.* ❑ *The shopkeeper measured the fabric out for her.*

○ **measure 'up**

1 If someone or something **measures up**, they are good enough or as good as someone or something else. ❑ *When I realized what was expected of me, I was afraid I couldn't measure up.* ❑ [+ to] *His father wanted him to measure up to almost impossible standards.* ❑ [+ to] *It will be hard for her to measure up to her predecessor.*

2 When you **measure up**, you measure a place in order to fit or build something there. ❑ [+ for] *We are measuring up for new carpets.* ❑ *The carpenter came round to look at the kitchen and measure up.*

meddle /'medəl/ (**meddles, meddling, meddled**)

○ **'meddle in**

If you **meddle in** something, you interfere in it.

meddle in something ❑ *He never wanted me to meddle in his affairs.*

○ **'meddle with**

If you **meddle with** something, you interfere with it or try to change it.

meddle with something ❑ *I don't like anyone meddling with my arrangements.*

mediate /'miːdieɪt/ (**mediates, mediating, mediated**)

○ **'mediate between**

If someone **mediates between** two people or groups, or **mediates** an agreement **between** them, they try to settle an argument between them by talking to both groups and trying to find things that they can both agree to.

mediate between someone ❑ *I tried to mediate between Zelda and her mom.* ❑ *He offered to mediate between the two sides.*

mediate something between someone ❑ *The therapist offered to mediate a meeting between mother and son.* ❑ *United Nations officials have mediated a series of peace meetings between the two sides.*

meet /miːt/ (meets, meeting, met)

⊘ **meet 'up**

1 If people **meet up**, they meet each other, either by chance or because they have arranged to. ❑ [+ with] *We planned to meet up with them later in town.* ❑ *Let's meet up after the show.* ❑ *We met up by chance when we were out shopping.*

2 If two or more things **meet up**, they join or come together. ❑ *The two wires will meet up here.* ❑ [+ with] *This track should meet up with the main road.*

⊘ **'meet with**

1 If you **meet with** a particular experience or event, you experience it or it happens to you.
meet with something ❑ *Troops met with strong resistance as they entered the city.* ❑ *Their plans met with little success.*

2 If something **meets with** a particular reaction or if you **meet** something **with** a particular reaction, that is the reaction it gets.
meet with something ❑ *His comments met with great public approval.*
meet something with something ❑ *She met his refusal with indifference.* ❑ *They are determined to meet any attack with retaliation.*
be met with something ❑ *I told him where I was and was met with silence.*

3 To **meet with** someone means to meet them after arranging to do this.
meet with someone ❑ *We can meet with the professor Monday night.*

mellow /'meləʊ/ (mellows, mellowing, mellowed)

○ **mellow 'out**

If someone **mellows out**, or if someone or something **mellows** them **out**, they become calm and relaxed.
mellow out ❑ *Chris has really mellowed out.*
mellow someone out or **mellow out someone** ❑ *Has marriage mellowed you out?*

melt /melt/ (melts, melting, melted)

○ **melt a'way**

1 When something **melts away**, it gradually disappears. = **fade away** ❑ *His great fortune melted away.* ❑ *My fears soon melted away.*

2 If people **melt away**, they move so that you can no longer see them. [FORMAL] ❑ *The crowd seemed to melt away into the night.*

3 If something **melts away** or if heat **melts** it **away**, it melts completely until it has disappeared.
melt away ❑ *She let the chocolate melt away on her tongue.*
melt something away or **melt away something** ❑ *The sun came out, melting away the last remaining snow.*

○ **melt 'down**

If you **melt down** an object, you heat it until it melts, so that you can use the material to make something else.
melt down something or **melt something down** ❑ [+ for] *Railings were melted down for weapons.* ❑ *It is now economically viable to melt down old glass.* • A **meltdown** in a nuclear reactor is an incident in which the fuel rods melt and radioactivity is released because of a fault in the cooling system. ❑ *A wrong command nearly led to a meltdown of one of the ship's two nuclear reactors.*

○ **melt 'into**

1 If someone **melts into** something, they become hidden by it.
melt into something ❑ *I searched for him, but he had melted into the crowd.*

2 If one thing **melts into** another, it is hard to see where one thing ends and the other starts.
melt into something ❑ *The river seemed to melt into the golden sunset.* ❑ *We could see the edge of the hills, where they melt into the plain.*

3 If one feeling or expression **melts into** another, it changes into something more gentle.
melt into something ❑ *He felt his aggression melt into tender care.*

mention /'menʃən/ (mentions, mentioning, mentioned)

○ **'mention as**

If someone **is mentioned as** a candidate for a job or position, or someone **mentions** them **as** a candidate for it, it is suggested that they might do that job.
be mentioned as something ❑ *Her name has been mentioned as a potential leadership candidate.*
mention someone as something
❑ *Administration sources have mentioned her as a possibility to head the FBI.*

merge /mɜːdʒ/ (merges, merging, merged)

○ **merge 'in**

If something **merges in**, it is difficult to see because it is similar to its surroundings.
= **blend in** ❑ [+ with] *The fence has been cleverly designed to merge in with the surrounding trees.*

⊘ **merge 'into**

1 If one thing **merges into** another, it becomes difficult to see because it is similar to the other thing. = **blend into**
merge into something ❑ *The houses were painted so that they would merge into the landscape.* ❑ *After a few days all these meetings seem to merge into one.*

2 If you **merge** two or more things **into** one, you make them become one thing.

merge something into something ❑ *We've decided to merge the two departments into a general sales department.*

○ **'merge with**
If one thing **merges with** another thing, or you **merge** it **with** another thing, they join together to make one thing.
merge with something ❑ *Bank of America merged with a rival bank.* ❑ *The old road continued for some miles before it merged with the A50.*
merge with something ❑ *The school will be merged with another high school.*

mess /mes/ (**messes, messing, messed**)
⊙ **mess a'bout** → see **mess around**
⊙ **mess a'bout with** → see **mess around with**
⊙ **mess a'round** (or **mess about** [mainly BRITISH])
❚ If you **mess around**, you do unimportant or silly things rather than what you should be doing. ❑ *Some of the lads had been messing around when they should have been working.*
= **muck about**
• If you say that someone **doesn't mess around**, you mean that they are very determined and do not hesitate before doing something. ❑ *These people do not mess around. They could have you sent to jail.*
❚ If you **mess** someone **around**, you cause problems for them by changing plans or not being honest with them. [BRITISH]
mess someone around ❑ *I'm really sorry to mess you around, but I need to change the time of the meeting again.* ❑ *Her boyfriend had been messing her around.*

⊙ **mess a'round with** (or **mess about with** [mainly BRITISH])
If you **mess around with** something, you touch it or interfere with it when you are not supposed to. = **tamper with**
mess around with something ❑ *I don't want the kids coming into my office and messing around with things.*

⊙ **mess 'up**
❚ If you **mess** something **up**, you spoil it or do it badly.
mess up something ❑ *One mistake will mess up the whole project.* ❑ *She messed up her exams and didn't get into university.*
mess something up ❑ *She gave me an opportunity and I messed it up.* • A **mess-up** is a mistake or an occasion when something has been done badly. [INFORMAL] ❑ *There was some mess-up over the dates.*
❷ If you **mess** something **up**, you make it untidy or dirty.
mess up something ❑ *When he cooks, he really*

messes up the kitchen.
mess something up ❑ *You can go in my bedroom, but please don't mess it up.* ❑ *The wind has messed my hair up.* • If something is **messed up**, it is untidy or dirty. ❑ *He came downstairs in his pyjamas with his hair all messed up.*
❸ If something **messes** someone **up**, it causes them emotional or psychological problems. [INFORMAL]
mess someone up or **mess up someone** ❑ *An experience like that can really mess you up.*
• If someone is **messed up**, they have emotional or psychological problems. [INFORMAL] ❑ *That man is really messed up.*
❹ If you **mess up**, you do something very badly. [INFORMAL] ❑ *This is important, so don't mess up.*

○ **'mess with** [INFORMAL]
❚ If you **mess with** something or someone dangerous, you become involved with them.
mess with something/someone ❑ *He would never mess with drugs or alcohol.* ❑ *You shouldn't mess with those people – they're criminals.*
❷ If you **mess with** something, you touch or interfere with it when you should not.
mess with something ❑ *Who's been messing with the things on my desk?*

mete /miːt/ (**metes, meting, meted**)
○ **mete 'out** [FORMAL]
If a punishment **is meted out** or if someone **metes** it **out**, it is given. = **deal out**
be meted out ❑ [+ to] *Severe punishments will be meted out to anyone who does not obey.*
mete out something or **mete something out** ❑ *The courts meted out fines of as much as £1,000.*

mike /maɪk/ (**mikes, miking, miked**)
○ **mike up**
You **mike** someone **up** when you attach a small microphone to them.
mike someone up or **mike up someone** ❑ *Even when the actors were miked up, we could hardly hear what they were saying.* ❑ *They brought me to the studio, miked me up and put me in front of the camera.*

militate /'mɪlɪteɪt/ (**militates, militating, militated**)
○ **'militate against** [FORMAL]
If something **militates against** something else, it makes it less likely to happen or succeed. = **discourage**
militate against something ❑ *Family problems can militate against learning.*

mill /mɪl/ (**mills, milling, milled**)
○ **mill a'round** (or **mill about** [mainly BRITISH])
If people **mill around** or if they **mill around** a

place, they all move around within a place.

mill around ❑ *There were hundreds of guests milling around on the lawn.*

mill around something ❑ *Students milled about the corridors looking for their classrooms.*

○ **mill 'round** → see **mill around**

mind /maɪnd/ (**minds, minding, minded**)

○ **mind 'out** [BRITISH]

If you tell someone to **mind out**, you are telling them to be careful. = **look out, watch out** ❑ *Mind out! There's a car coming!*

mingle /'mɪŋgəl/ (**mingles, mingling, mingled**)

○ **'mingle with**

1 If you **mingle with** people at a party or other event, you move around and talk to them.

mingle with someone ❑ *The performers then left the stage and mingled with the audience.* ❑ *The prince spent an hour mingling with guests at the party.*

2 If something such as a sound, smell or feeling **mingles with** another one, they become mixed together but are usually still recognizable.

mingle with something ❑ *The smell of cigarettes mingled with her perfume.*

minister /'mɪnɪstə/ (**ministers, ministering, ministered**)

○ **'minister to** [FORMAL]

If you **minister to** people or their needs, you make sure that they have everything they need or want.

minister to someone/something ❑ *She was a nurse who ministered to troops during the Crimean War.* ❑ *His parents ministered to his every need.*

minor /'maɪnə/ (**minors, minoring, minored**)

○ **'minor in** [mainly AMERICAN]

If you **minor in** a subject, you study it at university but it is not your main subject.

minor in something ❑ *I'm minoring in computer science.*

miss /mɪs/ (**misses, missing, missed**)

○ **miss 'out**

1 If you **miss out** something or someone, you fail to include them in something. = **leave out** [BRITISH]

miss out something/someone ❑ *I gave her a list of people to invite, but I missed out Tom.* ❑ *The brochure had missed out the fact that the hotel was right by a busy road.*

miss something/someone out ❑ *There's an 'L' in his name – you've missed it out.* ❑ [+ of] *He missed some important details out of his report.*

NOTE **Omit** is a more formal word for **miss out**.

2 If you **miss out**, you do not do or get something which would have been of interest or benefit to you. ❑ *This was his chance to shine and he didn't want to miss out.* ❑ *If you've never seen any of his films, you're missing out.* ❑ [+ on] *They are worried they will miss out on promotion.*

mist /mɪst/ (**mists, misting, misted**)

○ **mist 'over**

1 If a piece of glass **mists over** or **is misted over**, it becomes covered with tiny drops of moisture. = **steam up, mist up**

mist over ❑ *When he came in from the cold his glasses misted over.*

be misted over ❑ *The car windows were misted over.*

2 If your eyes **mist over**, tears come into your eyes. ❑ *I saw his eyes mist over when her name was mentioned.*

○ **mist 'up**

If a piece of glass **mists up** or **is misted up**, it becomes covered with tiny drops of moisture. = **mist over, steam up**

mist up ❑ *Could you pass that cloth, the windscreen has misted up again.*

be misted up ❑ *My glasses are all misted up.*

mix /mɪks/ (**mixes, mixing, mixed**)

○ **mix 'in**

1 If you **mix** a substance **in**, you put it with another substance and combine them. = **add in**

mix in something ❑ *I think he must have mixed in too much sand.*

mix something in ❑ *Add the flour gradually, mixing it in.* ❑ *You can mix a bit of water in if it's too dry.*

2 If you **mix in**, you join in an activity and talk in a friendly way to the other people there. ❑ *He didn't feel like mixing in.*

○ **mix 'into**

If you **mix** one substance **into** another, you put it with the other substance and combine them.

mix something into something ❑ *Mix a pinch of mustard into the flour.*

○ **mix 'up**

1 If you **mix** things or people **up**, you are confused about which one is which.

mix up something/someone ❑ *I have somehow mixed up two events.* ❑ [+ with] *I think you're mixing up the American Civil War with the English Civil War.*

mix something/someone up ❑ *People even mix us up and call us by each other's names.*

• If you **get** people or things **mixed up**, you think that one of them is the other one. = **muddle up** ❑ *I'm sorry, I've got the dates mixed up.* ❑ [+ with] *I always get her mixed up with her sister.*

2 If something or someone **mixes** someone up, they make them confused.

mix someone up or **mix up someone** ❏ *You're mixing me up with all these conflicting messages.* ● If you are **mixed-up**, you are confused or have emotional problems. ❏ *If you're feeling mixed-up, it's good to talk to someone.* ❏ *Tim was in a strange mixed-up frame of mind.* ● A **mix-up** is a mistake. **= muddle** ❏ *Due to an administrative mix-up the letters had not been sent out.*

3 If you **mix** things **up**, you put a number of different things together.

mix up something or **mix something up** ❏ *He mixed up all the ingredients and stirred them around.* ❏ *Try mixing different vegetables up to make delicious combinations.* ❏ *[+ with] He takes elements of reggae and mixes them up with other styles.*

4 If you **mix up** something, you make it by mixing things together.

mix up something or **mix something up** ❏ *You can buy the paint ready made or you can mix up your own colours.* ❏ *She makes her own curry powder, mixing it up from freshly ground spices.*

○ **mix 'up in**
If you **are mixed up in** something, you are involved in something bad.

be mixed up in something ❏ *I hope you're not mixed up in anything illegal.* ❏ *It's a shame his family had to get mixed up in it.*

○ **mix 'up with**
If you are **mixed up with** someone, you spend a lot of time with someone, usually someone bad.

be mixed up with someone ❏ *She was mixed up with the son of a gang leader.*

○ **'mix with**

1 If two substances **mix with** each other, or if you **mix** one substance **with** another, you combine them, so that they become one substance.

mix with something ❏ *The powder mixes easily with cold water to make a tasty drink.*
mix something with something ❏ *Mix the cinnamon with the rest of the sugar.*

2 To **mix** one activity or quality **with** another means to combine them.

mix something with something ❏ *Tom managed to mix business with pleasure.*

3 If you **mix with** other people, you spend time with them and talk to them.

mix with someone ❏ *My parents don't like the people I mix with.* ❏ *He just didn't seem to want to mix with anybody at all.*

4 [INFORMAL] If someone **mixes it with** someone else, they fight them. ❏ *Don't try mixing it with him, Ted.*

mock (mocks, mocking, mocked)

○ **mock 'up**

1 If you **mock** something **up**, you make a model or picture of it to show people what it looks like or will look like.

mock something up or **mock up something** ❏ *We've mocked up a picture to show how the couple might look in twenty years' time.* ● A **mock-up** is a model or picture of something, made to show people what the real thing looks like. ❏ *He looked with interest at a mock-up of Tenochtitlan city, the Aztec capital.*
2 If you **mock** something **up**, you create something that looks like it.

mock something up or **mock up something** ❏ *The video was shot in an underground car park mocked up as a shed.* ❏ *They mocked up a letter from the police, threatening residents with action.*

model /'mɒdəl/ (models, modelling, modelled)

> American English uses the spellings **modeling** and **modeled**.

○ **'model on**

1 If something **is modelled on** something else, or if someone **models** it **on** something else, it is deliberately made to be similar to that other thing. **= base on**

be modelled on something ❏ *The schools were modelled on traditional English boarding schools.*
model something on something ❏ *Australia's founding fathers modelled their Senate on the US Senate.*
2 If you **model** yourself **on** someone, you copy them because you admire them.

model yourself on someone ❏ *She modelled herself on her mother.*

molder /'məʊldə/ (molders, moldering, moldered) → see moulder

monkey /'mʌŋki/ (monkeys, monkeying, monkeyed)

○ **monkey a'bout** → see monkey around
○ **monkey a'bout with** → see monkey around with

○ **monkey a'round** (or **monkey about** [mainly BRITISH]) [INFORMAL]
If someone **monkeys around**, they behave in a silly way. ❏ *The actors were monkeying around on the set before filming started.*

○ **monkey a'round with** (or **monkey about with**) [INFORMAL]
If someone **monkeys around with** something, they touch it or interfere with it when they are not supposed to.

monkey around with something ❏ *Have you been monkeying about with my computer again?*

mooch /muːtʃ/ (**mooches, mooching, mooched**)

○ **mooch a'round** (or **mooch about** [mainly BRITISH])

If you **mooch around** or **mooch around** a place, you wander around a place with no particular purpose.

mooch around ❑ I had no money, so I just went to town and mooched around.

mooch around something ❑ He mooched about the house in his pyjamas.

moon /muːn/ (**moons, mooning, mooned**)

○ **moon a'round** (or **moon about** [mainly BRITISH])

If you **moon around** or **moon around** a place, you spend time doing nothing because you are feeling unhappy.

moon around ❑ It's no good mooning about by yourself.

moon around something ❑ Since the break-up she just moons around the house.

○ **'moon over**

If you **moon over** someone, you think about them a lot, especially in a sad way, because you are in love with them.

moon over someone ❑ She told me I was wasting my time mooning over Andrew.

mop /mɒp/ (**mops, mopping, mopped**)

✪ **mop 'up**

1 If you **mop up**, or if you **mop** something **up**, you clean liquid from a surface using a cloth or mop

mop up something ❑ A waiter came to mop up the mess.

mop something up ❑ He fetched a napkin to mop the drink up. ❑ First mop it up, then try to remove the stain with cold water.

mop up ❑ Use this old cloth to mop up.

2 To **mop** something **up** means to use or take all of it that exists or is available.

mop up something or **mop something up** ❑ He believes that government spending could generate enough jobs to mop up unemployment.

3 When an army **mops up** resistance, it defeats anyone who is still fighting against it after a war or battle has been mostly won. = **eliminate**

mop up something or **mop something up** ❑ Infantry divisions succeeded in mopping up local resistance. ● In a **mop-up** operation, soldiers go to defeat anyone in an area who is still fighting against them. ❑ He was involved in mop-up operations after the main battle.

mope /məʊp/ (**mopes, moping, moped**)

○ **mope a'round** (or **mope about** [mainly BRITISH])

If you **mope around** a place, or if you **mope around**, you spend time in a place doing nothing and feeling unhappy.

mope around something ❑ I moped around the house for a few days after he left.

mope around ❑ It won't do any good to mope around.

morph /mɔːf/ (**morphs, morphing, morphed**)

○ **morph 'into** [INFORMAL]

If one thing **morphs into** another thing, the first thing changes into the second.

morph into something ❑ In the film, the love she has for him eventually morphs into hatred and revenge.

moulder /'məʊldə/ (**moulders, mouldering, mouldered**)

> **Moulder** is spelled **molder** in American English.

○ **moulder a'way**

1 Something that **is mouldering away** is decaying slowly. = **rot away**

be mouldering away ❑ Millions of pounds of tea leaves were mouldering away in storehouses.

2 If someone **is mouldering away** in a place, they remain there without their situation improving.

be mouldering away ❑ In twenty years you might be mouldering away in some old folks' home.

mount /maʊnt/ (**mounts, mounting, mounted**)

○ **'mount on**

If you **mount** an object **on** something, you fix it there firmly.

mount something on something ❑ She mounted the photo on card. ❑ A CCTV camera was mounted on the wall beside the gate.

○ **mount 'up**

If something **mounts up**, it increases as more and more is added to it. = **build up**

❑ The soil becomes more and more acidic as pollution mounts up. ❑ If you put a little money away each week, you'll be surprised how quickly it mounts up.

mourn /mɔːn/ (**mourns, mourning, mourned**)

○ **'mourn for**

1 If you **mourn for** someone, you show that you are very sad because they have died.

mourn for someone ❑ He continued to mourn for his son.

2 If you **mourn for** something, you feel very sad about something that no longer exists or has been lost.

mourn for something ❑ I found myself mourning for what might have been.

mouse /maʊs/ (mouses, mousing, moused)

○ **'mouse over**

If you **mouse over** text or an image on a computer screen, you move the mouse so that the cursor is on it, usually to get more information.

mouse over something ❑ *You can mouse over any word to see its definition.*

mouth /maʊð/ (mouths, mouthing, mouthed)

○ **mouth 'off** [INFORMAL]

If someone **mouths off**, they say a lot of rude or annoying things or give their opinion about things in a forceful way. ❑ *He got into trouble for mouthing off in class.* ❑ *[+ to] He needs to stop mouthing off to the media all the time.*

move /muːv/ (moves, moving, moved)

○ **move a'bout** → see **move around**

○ **move a'long**

1 If someone or something **moves along** a place or **moves along**, they go forwards along a place.

move along something ❑ *We moved along the bus so more people could get on.* ❑ *She could see a light moving along the road.*

move along ❑ *The boat moved along at a brisk pace.*

2 To **move** something **along** a place or **move** them **along** means to make them go forwards along it.

move something along ❑ *Air pressure keeps the plane in the air; engines just move it along.*

move something along something ❑ *He moves his toy car along the edge of the table.* ❑ *The containers are moved along a conveyor belt.*

3 If someone tells you to **move along** or if they **move** you **along**, they tell you to leave and not stand or wait somewhere.

move along ❑ *'What happened?' I asked. 'I don't know,' the guard said. 'Now move along.'* ❑ *A police officer told us to move along.*

move someone along or **move along someone** ❑ *Cops arrived to move us along.*

● If you say to someone **move it along**, you are telling them not to stand or wait somewhere. ❑ *The show's over. Now move it along.*

4 If a task or process **moves along** or if someone **moves** it **along**, it continues and progresses.

move along ❑ *Things were moving along on the campaign.* ❑ *The work moved along smoothly.*

move something along ❑ *It's important to keep moving the plot along to retain the viewer's interest.* ❑ *There's a lot of work and we're trying to move it along as fast as we can.*

○ **move a'round** (or **move about, move round** [mainly BRITISH])

1 When you **move around** a place or **move around**, you keep going from one part of a place to another.

move around something ❑ *She moved around the office, checking everyone was working.*

move around ❑ *It's probably best if you sit here and don't move around for a while.*

2 When you **move** something **around** or **move** it **around** a place, you move it from one position or place to another.

move something around ❑ *The cleaners have moved all the furniture around.* ❑ *Stretch your limbs, or move them around gently.*

move around something ❑ *What's the best way to move around the equipment?*

move something around something ❑ *You can move plants around the garden until you find the spot where they're happiest.*

3 If you **move around**, you keep changing your job or keep changing the place where you live. ❑ *I went to several different schools because my parents moved around a lot.* ❑ *The workers move about freely, getting the best wages they can.* ❑ *[+ from/to] They moved round from one market town to another selling their wares.*

4 If you **move** someone **around**, you make them move to a different job or live in a different place.

move someone around ❑ *I think my kids' education suffered because I moved them around with me.* ❑ *[+ from/to] Promising young executives are moved around from one branch to another.*

5 If you **move** something **around**, you change an arrangement or the way that something is organized.

move something around ❑ *This year we've moved the timetable around so that students finish early on Fridays.* ❑ *I'm flexible about the date – we can move things around to suit you.*

6 If you **move around** an obstacle, you move so that you can get past it.

move around something ❑ *I moved round the desk.* ❑ *He was lying on the sidewalk, people moving around him as if he were not there.*

○ **move a'way**

1 If you **move away**, you go and live in a different town or area. ❑ *They had decided to retire from farming and move away.* ❑ *[+ from] We had some very dear friends that moved away from this area.*

2 If someone or something **moves away**, or if you **move** them **away**, they move in a direction further away from a place.

move away ❑ *The boat was quickly moving away.* ❑ [+ *from*] *She moved away from me a little.*
move something/someone away ❑ *He moved his hand away.* ❑ [+ *from*] *Please move the children away from the fire.*

○ **move a'way from**
If you **move away from** something, you start believing or supporting something new.
move away from something ❑ *We have moved away from the idea that the government should pay for everything.* ❑ *Fashion has moved away from short skirts this season.*

✪ **move 'down**
1 If someone or something **moves down** or **moves down** something, they move to a position further away from the top or front of something. **= move up**
move down ❑ *If everyone moves down, other passengers will be able to get on the bus.* ❑ [+ *to*] *His pen moved down to the next item on the list.*
move down something ❑ *We moved down the side of the mountain.* ❑ *Move down the aisle, please.*
2 If you **move** something or someone **down** or **move** them **down** something, you move them to a position further away from the top or front of something.
move something down ❑ *I've moved your things down so you can reach them more easily.* ❑ [+ *to*] *If the car is in the way I'll move it down to the end of the drive.*
move something down something ❑ *She moved her finger down the column of figures.*
3 If you **move down** to an area or if someone **moves** you **down**, you go to live there, especially when the place is farther south.
move down ❑ [+ *from*] *They're moving down from New Jersey.* ❑ *I moved down here on security work.*
move someone down ❑ *My parents are old and need support so we decided to move them down here.*
4 If something or someone **moves down**, or if someone **moves** them **down**, they go to a lower level or a lower position on a list.
move down ❑ *The university has moved down this year in the international league tables.* ❑ [+ *to*] *The bottom three teams have to move down to the next division.*
move someone/something down ❑ *The teacher is moving some pupils down into a lower set.* ❑ *They lost two games, moving them down from second to fifth.*
move down something ❑ *If they fail their exams, they move down a year.*

move someone/something down something ❑ *I might have to move you down a group.*
5 If a rate, level, or amount **moves down**, it decreases. **= go down, fall; ≠ move up**
❑ *Do you really think the unemployment figures are moving down?*

✪ **move 'in**
1 When you **move in**, you begin to live in a house or place. **≠ move out** ❑ *I've got the keys and I'm moving in on Saturday.* ❑ *This house didn't even have a proper kitchen when we moved in.*
2 If someone **moves in**, they come to live with you. **≠ move out** ❑ *His mother is moving in for a while to help out.* ❑ [+ *with*] *I had decided to move in with Margaret.*
3 If someone **moves in** on a place or person they go towards them in order to attack them or do something to them. **= close in** ❑ [+ *on*] *He was moving in on me, his fists clenched.* ❑ *Police moved in to arrest the protesters.*
4 If someone **moves in**, they try to take control of an activity or something that gives an advantage or profit, often in an unfair way. ❑ [+ *on*] *Rivals moved in on his business while he was in prison.* ❑ *Governments will move in to exploit the Arctic's resources.*

✪ **move 'into**
1 When you **move into** a place, you start to live there.
move into something ❑ *She moved into an apartment in the city.* ❑ *We had recently moved into the area and didn't know anyone.*
2 When you **move** something or someone **into** a place, you take them there or make them go there.
move something/someone into something ❑ *I could move my things into that room.* ❑ *I moved the plant into a sunnier spot.*
3 If people **move into** a particular activity or area of business, they start to be involved in it.
move into something ❑ *More and more companies are moving into electronics.* ❑ *Could the firm diversify, move into new markets?* ❑ *She later moved into the field of education.*
4 If a group **moves into** an area, they go there in order to do a particular thing.
move into something ❑ *An occupying army moved into the city.* ❑ *Criminal gangs were moving into the area.*

✪ **move 'off**
If vehicles or people **move off**, they leave a place. **= set off** ❑ *The fleet of cars prepared to move off.* ❑ *They mounted their horses and moved off.*

move 'on

1 If someone **moves on**, they continue a journey after stopping for a short time. = **carry on** ❑ They moved on as soon as the fog lifted. ❑ [+ to] After three weeks in Hong Kong, we moved on to Japan.

2 If you **move on**, you stop doing or talking about one thing and start doing or talking about something else. = **go on, carry on** ❑ Let's leave that point for now, and move on. ❑ [+ to-infinitive] The men moved on to talk about something else. ❑ [+ to] Get the actors to move on to the next scene. ·

3 If you **move on**, you leave your job to start a better job. ❑ [+ from/to] John wanted to move on from the Post to a bigger paper. ❑ This training will be an advantage when you want to move on.
NOTE Progress is a more formal word for **move on.**

4 If someone **moves** you **on**, they order you to leave a place.
move someone on or **move on someone**
❑ They sat on park benches until the cops came and moved them on. ❑ An angry motorist was moved on by police.

5 If things **move on**, they change and progress. ❑ [+ from] The world is moving on from the era where knowledge came in books. ❑ Public opinion had moved on.

6 If time **moves on**, it passes. = **wear on**
❑ As the months moved on, my understanding increased. ❑ Time moved on, and the new building was nearly complete.

7 If you **move on** after a bad experience, you recover from it enough to be able to continue with other things in your life.
❑ It's time to let go of the past and move on.

move 'on to (or move onto)

If you **move on to** a topic, you start talking about it after talking about something else. = **turn to, come on to**
move on to something ❑ Let's now move on to voting behaviour. ❑ By the time I returned, the conversation had moved onto other matters.

move 'out

1 If you **move out**, you stop living in a particular house or place and go to live somewhere else. = **move in** ❑ The man that used to share the apartment moved out. ❑ Her father moved out when she was only two. ❑ [+ of] I want to move out of the city.

2 If you **move** someone **out** of a place, you arrange for them to leave that place.
move someone out or **move out someone**
❑ [+ of] We decided to move her out of her apartment and into a nursing home. ❑ He moved his family out to a house in the country.

3 If people **move out** of a particular activity or area of business, research, etc., they stop being involved in it. ❑ [+ of] People are moving out of the public sector and into private enterprise. ❑ They entered the market just when the big companies were all moving out.

4 If soldiers **move out**, they leave a place in order to go and fight somewhere. ❑ Almost a thousand men were awaiting the order to move out.

◐ move 'over

1 If you **move over**, you move to one side to make more room for another person.
❑ Move over a bit, will you? I'm squashed. ❑ Anna moved over so I could sit down. ❑ [+ to] The tractor moved over to the side to let the cars pass.

2 If something **moves over** a surface, it travels across it.
move over something ❑ His tongue moved over his lips nervously. ❑ Clouds moved over the sun.

3 If you **move over**, you start doing something different or using a different system. ❑ [+ to] More and more people are moving over to solar power. ❑ [+ into] She had moved over into French so that Georges could understand.

4 If you **move over**, you stop doing something in order to allow someone else to do it. = **step aside** ❑ It's time for you to move over and let someone else have a turn.

◐ move 'round → see move around

○ 'move to

If you **move to** a new subject in a conversation, you start talking about something different.
move to something ❑ Let's move to another subject, Dan.

○ 'move towards

To **move towards** something means to develop in a way that will make it likely to happen.
move towards something ❑ We seem to be moving towards a system of free education.

◐ move 'up

1 If someone or something **moves up** or **moves up** a place, they go from a lower position to a higher one. ≠ **move down**
move up ❑ The sun had moved up in the sky. ❑ [+ to] The cold began in his feet and quickly moved up to his waist.
move up something ❑ We moved up the hill a few feet. ❑ I saw something moving up the tree trunk.

2 If you **move** something or someone **up** or **move** them **up** something, you move them to a higher position.
move something/someone up ❑ She moved her feet up and down. ❑ [+ to] I'll move these old clothes up to the attic.

move something/someone up something
❑ He moved his hands up the ladder to hold it more firmly. ❑ In summer the farmer moves his cows up the mountain.

3 If someone or something **moves up**, or if someone **moves** them **up**, they go to a higher level or rank.

move up ❑ New recruits can move up quickly if they work hard. ❑ He has moved up in the financial world since I last met him. ❑ [+ to] You'll need new books when you move up to secondary school.

move someone/something up ❑ Their win today moves them up into second place. ❑ [+ to] She got moved up to the top group.

move up something ❑ They moved up the league rapidly and ended the season as champions.

move someone up something ❑ The teacher thought he was bored, and moved him up a class.

4 If you **move up**, you move closer to the side or front of something, especially to make more room. = **move over** ❑ Move up, John, I've got no space. ❑ Everyone moved up so that he could sit on the end.

5 If soldiers **move up** or if they **are moved up**, they go to a particular position so that they are ready to act.

move up ❑ It would be some time before their tanks could move up.

be moved up ❑ Two army groups had been moved up.

6 If a rate, level, or amount **moves up**, it increases. = **go up, rise**; ≠ **go down** ❑ When interest rates are moving up fast, a fixed rate loan is an attractive option. ❑ [+ to] Unemployment moved up to 6% in March.

mow /məʊ/ (**mows, mowing, mowed, mown**)

> The past participle is either **mowed** or **mown**.

○ **mow 'down**
If people **are mowed down** or if someone **mows** them **down**, they are killed violently and suddenly, usually by being shot or driven over.

be mowed/mown down ❑ Unarmed citizens were mown down by tanks.

mow someone down or **mow down someone** ❑ Six prisoners tried to run away, but guards mowed them down.

muck /mʌk/ (**mucks, mucking, mucked**)

> **Muck** is an informal word used mainly in British English.

○ **muck a'bout** (or **muck around**)
1 If you **muck about**, you behave in a silly way and waste time. = **mess around** ❑ The

boys were mucking around at the back of the class. ❑ [+ with] Stop mucking about with that phone and listen to me.

2 If you **muck** someone **about**, you cause problems for them by changing plans or not being honest with them. = **mess aroun**

muck someone about ❑ The staff really mucked us about. ❑ Look, stop mucking me around. I need a definite answer.

○ **muck a'bout with** (or **muck around with**)
If you **muck about with** something, you change it or interfere with it when it woul be better not to.

muck about with something ❑ They've mucked around with the timetable so much that nobody knows where they're supposed to be.

○ **muck a'round** → see **muck about**

○ **muck a'round with** → see **muck about with**

○ **muck 'in**
If you **muck in**, you join in or help with a task. ❑ Management worked the same hours as the men and mucked in whenever necessary. ❑ [+ with] Everyone mucks in with the chores.

○ **muck 'out**
If you **muck out** animals or a place where they live, or if you **muck out**, you clean the place where animals live.

muck out something or **muck something out** ❑ I mucked out the pigsty and generally helpe with the heavy work. ❑ Don't forget to muck the horses out.

muck out ❑ She went over to the stables to muck out.

○ **muck 'up**
1 If you **muck** something **up**, you do it badly so that you do not achieve what you wanted to. [INFORMAL]

muck something up or **muck up something** ❑ I think I mucked the interview up. ❑ I've taken my driving test twice, and both times I've mucked it up.

2 If you **muck** something **up**, you make it dirty.

muck something up or **muck up something** ❑ Don't muck up that clean dress now.

muddle /'mʌdəl/ (**muddles, muddling, muddled**)

○ **muddle a'long**
If you **muddle along**, you manage to continue or deal with things reasonably well, although you have not planned or understood them very clearly. ❑ Until we ge a new manager we will just have to muddle along as best we can.

muddle 'through

If you **muddle through** or **muddle through**
something, you manage to deal with
something even though you have not
planned or understood it very well.
= get by
muddle through ❑ *The children are left to
muddle through without any help.*
muddle through something ❑ *Relaxed and
confident, I muddled through life and did okay
for myself.*

muddle 'up

◼ If you **muddle** things **up**, you cause them
to become mixed up or in the wrong order,
and if they **are muddled up**, they are mixed
up or in the wrong order. **= mix up**
muddle something up or **muddle up
something** ❑ *I'm afraid I've muddled your
directions up.* ❑ [+ with] *They have muddled up
your names with those of your cousins.*
be muddled up ❑ *The words are all muddled up
on the page.* ❑ [+ with] *Put them away so that
they do not get muddled up with other things.*
❑ *You've got the dates all muddled up.*
◻ If you **muddle** someone **up**, you confuse
them.
muddle someone up ❑ *Don't keep interfering,
you'll muddle me up.*

muffle /'mʌfəl/ (muffles, muffling, muffled)

muffle 'up

If you **are muffled up** or if you **muffle**
yourself **up**, you are wearing a lot of heavy
clothes. **= wrap up**
be muffled up ❑ *A boy muffled up in a blue scarf
was waiting outside.*
muffle yourself up ❑ *Why muffle yourself up like
that on such a warm day?*

mug /mʌg/ (mugs, mugging, mugged)

mug 'off

If you **mug** someone **off**, you cheat them,
especially by charging them too much
money for something.
mug someone off or **mug off someone** ❑ *I felt
mugged off, but it was too late to do anything
about it.* ❑ *She mugged me off and she'll probably
mug you off too.*

mug 'up [BRITISH, INFORMAL]

If you **mug up**, or if you **mug up** a subject,
you study it quickly in order to make sure
you know the main facts. **= swot up**
mug up ❑ *I wish I'd mugged up a bit before the
interview.* ❑ [+ on] *If he doesn't know that,
he needs to mug up on his history.*

mug up something or **mug something up**
❑ *I must mug up my French before the exam.*

mull /mʌl/ (mulls, mulling, mulled)

mull 'over

If you **mull** something **over**, you think
about it for a long time. **= chew over**
mull something over or **mull over something**
❑ *I mulled that question over for a while.* ❑ *She
began to mull over the possible meaning of what
he had said.*

multiply /'mʌltɪplaɪ/ (multiplies, multiplying, multiplied)

multiply 'out

If you **multiply out** numbers, you multiply
them.
multiply out something or **multiply
something out** ❑ *You solve the equation by
multiplying out the two terms.*

muscle /'mʌsəl/ (muscles, muscling, muscled)

muscle 'in

If you **muscle in**, you force your way into a
situation or an activity where you are not
welcome. **= push in** ❑ [+ on] *Rival companies
are muscling in on their territory.* ❑ *They felt this
was their business and resented her muscling in.*

muscle 'out

If someone **is muscled out** or someone else
muscles them **out**, they are unfairly forced
out of a situation or position.
be muscled out ❑ *Small grocery shops are being
muscled out by supermarkets.*
muscle someone out or **muscle out someone**
❑ [+ of] *They muscled everyone else out of the game.*

muss /mʌs/ (musses, mussing, mussed)

muss 'up [AMERICAN]

If something or someone **musses up** your
hair, or if it **is mussed up**, it looks untidy.
muss up something or **muss something up**
❑ *The wind had mussed up her hair.*
be mussed up ❑ *She looked sleepy and her hair
was mussed up.*

muster /'mʌstə/ (musters, mustering, mustered)

muster 'up

If you **muster up** your strength, energy, or
courage, you make a great effort in order to
do something. **= summon up**
muster up something or **muster something
up** ❑ [+ to-infinitive] *I mustered up enough
courage to ask for a pay rise.* ❑ *I mustered up all my
strength and pushed.*

Nn

naff /næf/ (**naffs, naffing, naffed**)

O **naff 'off** [BRITISH, INFORMAL]

If you tell someone to **naff off**, you are telling them rudely or angrily to go away.

nag /næg/ (**nags, nagging, nagged**)

O **'nag at**

If a doubt, thought or question **nags at** you, you cannot stop thinking or worrying about it.

nag at someone ❑ *What if he'd been wrong about her? The thought nagged at him.* ❑ *The suspicion had been nagging at me for some time.*

nail /neɪl/ (**nails, nailing, nailed**)

O **nail 'down**

1 If something **is nailed down** or if someone has **nailed** it **down**, it is fastened firmly in place with nails.

be nailed down ❑ *The lid of the box was nailed down.*

nail something down or **nail down something** ❑ *If it won't stay there we'll have to nail it down.*

2 If you **nail** someone **down**, you force them to state something clearly or exactly. **= pin down**

nail someone down or **nail down someone** ❑ [+ to] *It's difficult to nail him down to any kind of commitment.*

3 If you **nail** something **down**, you manage to describe or identify something. **= pin down**

nail down something or **nail something down** ❑ *We need to nail down exactly what is wrong with you.*

4 If you **nail down** something, especially money, you succeed in getting it or achieving it. [AMERICAN]

nail down something or **nail something down** ❑ *The next big task is to nail down the funding for the next part of the project.*

O **nail 'up**

1 If you **nail** something **up**, you fix it to a wall with nails.

nail something up or **nail up something** ❑ *He nailed up a warning notice on the fence.*

❑ *She passed a house with a brass plate nailed up outside.*

2 If something **is nailed up**, it is fastened shut with nails.

be nailed up ❑ *The windows and doors were all nailed up.*

name /neɪm/ (**names, naming, named**)

✪ **'name after** [BRITISH]

If you **name** someone or something **after** a person or thing, you give them the same name as that person or thing.

name someone/something after someone/something ❑ *He built a city and named it after his son.* ❑ *She is named after her great-grandmother.*

O **'name for** [AMERICAN]

If you **name** someone or something **for** a person or thing, you give them the same name as that person or thing.

name someone/something for someone/something ❑ *They named their son for the President.* ❑ *Hayman Creek was named for Charles Hayman.*

narrow /'nærəʊ/ (**narrows, narrowing, narrowed**)

✪ **narrow 'down**

If you **narrow** something **down**, you make a list or a group of choices smaller so that you do not have so many things to think about.

narrow something down ❑ [+ to] *They narrowed the choice down to about a dozen sites.* ❑ *We know the teacher was a woman, which narrows it down a bit.*

narrow down something ❑ [+ to] *We finally narrowed down the list of candidates to three.*

NARROW DOWN + noun
narrow down **the list of** something
narrow down **the possibilities**
narrow down **a choice**
narrow down **the options**
narrow down **the range of** something
❑ *We have narrowed down the list of possible schools to three.* ❑ *They have had to narrow down the range of courses they can offer.*

negotiate /nɪˈgəʊʃieɪt/ (**negotiates, negotiating, negotiated**)

○ **neˈgotiate with**

If you **negotiate with** someone or **negotiate** something **with** them, you talk to them in order to reach an agreement, especially in politics or business.

negotiate with someone ❑ *It is not clear whether the president is willing to negotiate with the democrats.*

negotiating something with someone ❑ *He's negotiating a deal with American publishers for his memoirs.* ❑ *Contracts had to be negotiated with suppliers.*

nestle /ˈnesəl/ (**nestles, nestling, nestled**)

○ **nestle ˈup**

If you **nestle up**, you press your body against someone in a comfortable way. ❑ [+ to] *The child nestled up to me and went to sleep.*

nibble /ˈnɪbəl/ (**nibbles, nibbling, nibbled**)

○ **ˈnibble at**

1 When a small animal **nibbles at** something, it takes many small quick bites out of it.

nibble at something ❑ *I saw squirrels nibbling at the red berries.*

2 If you **nibble at** your food, you eat it slowly, taking small bites.

nibble at something ❑ *She didn't feel like eating, but nibbled at a biscuit.*

○ **ˈnibble at** (or **nibble away at**)

To **nibble at** something means to gradually affect, harm, or destroy it.

nibble at something ❑ *Military tanks nibbled at the edges of the city before retreating.* ❑ *Competitors have nibbled away at the company's market share in PCs.*

nod /nɒd/ (**nods, nodding, nodded**)

○ **nod ˈoff** [INFORMAL]

If you **nod off**, you fall asleep, usually unintentionally, while you are sitting down. = **doze off** ❑ *Grandad had nodded off in front of the television.* ❑ *I must have nodded off for a minute because I missed the end of his speech.*

nose /nəʊz/ (**noses, nosing, nosed**)

○ **nose aˈround** (or **nose about, nose round** [mainly BRITISH]) [INFORMAL]

If you **nose around** or **nose around** a place, you try to find interesting things or information in a place that belongs to someone else. = **poke around**

nose around ❑ *Someone has been here nosing around, asking questions about you.*

nose around something ❑ *I couldn't resist nosing around his room while he was out.*

○ **nose ˈout**

1 If you **nose out** information, you discover it by searching thoroughly or asking a lot of questions.

nose out something or **nose something out** ❑ *He will nose the truth out eventually.*

NOTE **Uncover** is a more formal word for **nose out**.

2 If someone **noses** you **out** or you **are nosed out**, someone manages to beat you by a small amount in a competition or race.

be nosed out ❑ *Federer was nosed out by the younger man this year.*

nose someone out or **nose out someone** ❑ *I think he will nose Smith out for the award.*

○ **nose ˈround** → see **nose around**

notch /nɒtʃ/ (**notches, notching, notched**)

○ **notch ˈup**

If you **notch up** something, you achieve it. = **chalk up**

notch up something or **notch something up** ❑ *The other candidate had notched up eleven hundred more votes than Mr Jones.* ❑ *She notched up another victory.*

note /nəʊt/ (**notes, noting, noted**)

○ **note ˈdown**

If you **note down** something, you write it down so you can remember it later.

note down something ❑ *He noted down his observations as he made them.*

note something down ❑ *I told her my name, and she noted it down.* ❑ *I've noted a few ideas down which we can discuss tomorrow.*

number /ˈnʌmbə/ (**numbers, numbering, numbered**)

○ **ˈnumber among**

If someone or something **numbers among** or **is numbered among** a particular group, or if the group **numbers** them **among** it, they are a member of it.

number among something ❑ *The inventor James Watt numbered among his students.*

be numbered among something ❑ *They can be numbered among the truly great champions.*

number something/someone among something or **number among something someone/something** ❑ *He numbered among his clients several large corporate firms.*

Oo

object /əb'dʒekt/ (**objects, objecting, objected**)

○ **ob'ject to**
If you **object to** something, you do not like it or approve of it.
object to something ❑ *The other tenants objected to him playing the piano at three in the morning.* ❑ *Local resident have objected to the plan.*

obsess /əb'ses/ (**obsesses, obsessing, obsessed**)

○ **ob'sess about** [INFORMAL]
If you **obsess about** something, you keep thinking and worrying about it.
obsess about something ❑ *She began obsessing about her weight.* ❑ *I don't obsess about every little mark on my skin.*

occur /ə'kɜː/ (**occurs, occurring, occurred**)

○ **oc'cur to**
If something **occurs to** you, you think of it or realize it.
occur to someone ❑ *As soon as that thought occurred to him, he felt worse.* ❑ [+ to-infinitive] *It never occurred to me to ask.* ❑ *It had never occurred to her that he might come too.*

offend /ə'fend/ (**offends, offending, offended**)

○ **of'fend against** [FORMAL]
If something or someone **offends against** a law, rule, or principle, they break it.
offend against something ❑ *These people repeatedly offend against society's rules.*

offer /'ɒfə, AM 'ɔːfər/ (**offers, offering, offered**)

○ **offer 'up**
1 To **offer up** something such as a prayer means to give it to God.
offer up something *or* **offer something up** ❑ *We offered up a prayer of thanks.* ❑ [+ as] *They slaughtered animals, offering them up as a sacrifice to the gods.*
2 If you **offer** something **up**, you give it or make it available to someone.
offer up something *or* **offer something up** ❑ *Eventually, she offered up an explanation.*

officiate /ə'fɪʃieɪt/ (**officiates, officiating, officiated**)

○ **of'ficiate at**
1 When someone **officiates at** a ceremony or formal occasion, they are in charge and perform the official part of it.
officiate at something ❑ *Bishop Silvester officiated at the funeral.* ❑ *Priests are authorized to officiate at weddings and funerals.*
2 When someone **officiates at** a sports game or competition, they are in charge and make sure the players do not break the rules.
officiate at something ❑ *Mr Ellis was selected to officiate at a cup game between Grimsby and Rotherham.*

ooze /uːz/ (**oozes, oozing, oozed**)

○ **ooze 'out**
If a gas or liquid **oozes out**, it slowly appear or leaks out. ❑ *There was a crack in the pipe, and something sticky was oozing out.* ❑ [+ from] *Tears oozed slowly out from between her eyelids.*

open /'əʊpən/ (**opens, opening, opened**)

○ **open 'into**
If a street, corridor, etc. **opens into** a place, you can go straight from one to the other.
open into something ❑ *The corridor opened into a large room.* ❑ *The street opened into the marketplace.*

○ **open 'off**
If a room or area **opens off** a place, it connects directly with it.
open off something ❑ *Four bedrooms open off the first floor landing.* ❑ *A small study opened off the living room.*

○ **open 'onto**
If a building or room **opens onto** another place, you can go straight from one to the other. **= give onto**
open onto something ❑ *There are small houses, opening directly onto the street.* ❑ *The French windows open onto a beautiful patio.*

○ **open 'out**
1 If something **opens out**, or if you **open** it **out**, it becomes separated or open after

being in one piece or tightly closed.

open out ❏ *The flower only opens out in full sun.*

open something out ❏ *Slit the fish down one side and open them out.*

open out something ❏ *She opened out her arms in greeting.*

2 If you **open** something **out**, or if it **opens out**, you unfold it so that you can see or use it.

open out ❏ [+ *into*] *The sofa opens out into a bed.*

open out something ❏ *He opened out the paper and began to read.*

open something out ❏ *He picked the letter up and opened it out.* ❏ *We opened the map out on the table.*

3 If a place **opens out**, it gradually becomes wider so that you can see further around you. ❏ [+ *into*] *At this point the valley opens out into a plain.* ❏ *Around the corner, the view opened out.*

4 If someone **opens out**, they become more relaxed and start to talk more. = **open up** ❏ *Chatting with Laura he was able to relax and open out.*

5 If something **opens out**, or if you **open** it **out**, it starts to include more different things or people than before.

open out ❏ *When she left home and went to university her life opened out.*

open out something or **open something out** ❏ *We need to open out the discussion to involve people of all political views.* ❏ *This question concerns everyone, so let's open it out for general debate.*

○ open 'up

1 If you **open up** something such as a door or container, you open it.

open up something ❏ *I opened up the sunroof as I drove along.* ❏ *He went into the study and opened up a drawer in the desk.*

open something up ❏ *We had to open our suitcases up so they could be searched.* ❏ *She fetched another bottle and opened it up.*

2 If you **open up** a building or **open up**, you unlock and open the door so that people can get in.

open up ❏ *Open up! It's snowing out here.* ❏ *The caretaker came and opened up for me.*

open up something ❏ *Paul opened up the café as usual.*

open something up ❏ *He gets to the office early every day and opens it up.* ❏ *We are opening the school up in the holidays for summer courses.*

3 If a new shop or business **opens up** or if someone **opens** it **up**, it starts to do business.

open up ❏ *A new supermarket is opening up.*

open up something ❏ *There were plans to open up a new factory.*

open something up ❏ *A restaurant chain is opening a branch up in the High Street.* ❏ *The business failed, but he plans to open it up again in a new location.*

4 To **open up** a place means to make it easier to reach, to build on, or to do business in.

open up something ❏ [+ *to/for*] *The change of government has opened up the country to tourism.* ❏ *He talked about the old days when settlers first opened up the region.*

open something up ❏ *New federal highways will open these remote areas up and encourage development.*

5 To **open up** a market means to make it possible or easier to sell goods or services to a particular group of people.

open up something or **open something up** ❏ [+ *to*] *The EU has opened up its markets to sugar producers in the developing world.* ❏ *His skill lies in identifying and opening up new markets.*

6 When an opportunity **opens up**, or when something **opens** it **up**, that opportunity becomes available.

open up ❏ *All sorts of possibilities began to open up.*

open up something or **open something up** ❏ *The Internet opened up a new era of instant communication.* ❏ *His wife had opened up a whole new world for him.*

7 If a hole or space **opens up**, or if someone or something **opens** it **up**, it appears or is made.

open up ❏ *A hole had opened up in the body of the aircraft.* ❏ *Cracks opened up in the ground beneath their feet.*

open up something or **open something up** ❏ *A mud slide had opened up a huge gap in the side of the mountain.*

8 If a difference between people or groups **opens up**, or if someone or something **opens** it **up**, it is created.

open up ❏ [+ *between*] *A gulf of mistrust opened up between the two nations.*

open up something or **open something up** ❏ *We risk opening up a digital divide in developing countries – between those who have access to high-speed Internet and those who don't.*

9 If someone **opens up** a lead or if it **opens up**, one person or side in a race or competition starts to lead, usually by a large amount.

open up something or **open something up** ❏ *The Chinese runner had opened up a lead of more than two minutes.* ❏ [+ *on*] *He has opened up a 10-point gap on his nearest rival.*

open up ❏ [+ to] *Her lead opened up to 300 metres.*
10 If someone **opens up**, they start to relax and talk about personal things. = **open out** ❏ *It can be hard to get teenagers to open up and talk to their parents.* ❏ [+ about] *After we had met a few times he began to open up about his life.*
11 If a doctor **opens** someone or something **up**, they cut into a person's or animal's body.
open someone/something up or **open up someone/something** ❏ *They opened him up and removed the tumour.* ❏ *When they opened up the alligator's stomach they found human remains.*
12 If someone **opens up**, they start shooting. ❏ *They opened up as the convoy came level with them.*
13 If a game **opens up**, it becomes more exciting because both sides are trying harder to win, rather than just trying to prevent the other team from winning.
open up ❏ *The game finally opened up and Scotland were able to score some good tries.*

○ **'open with**
If an event such as a meeting or discussion **opens with** something or you **open** it **with** something, that thing is the first thing that happens.
open with something ❏ *The service opened with a hymn.*
open something with something ❏ *They opened the meeting with a moment of silence in memory of those who had died.*

operate /'ɒpəreɪt/ (**operates, operating, operated**)

◐ **'operate on**
If doctors **operate on** someone or part of their body, they cut into their body to remove, repair, or replace something.
operate on someone/something ❏ *We can't operate on the leg until the patient is stronger.* ❏ *They operated on her at once.*

oppose /ə'pəʊz/ (**opposes, opposing, opposed**)

◐ **op'pose to**
1 If you **are opposed to** something, you disagree with it or disapprove of it.
be opposed to something ❏ *I am opposed to capital punishment.* ❏ *It was the principles that we were opposed to.*
2 If you say that you are referring to one thing **as opposed to** another, you are making it clear which thing you mean, or making a contrast between them. ❏ *What are the advantages of showers as opposed to bathtubs?*

opt /ɒpt/ (**opts, opting, opted**)

◐ **'opt for**
If you **opt for** a particular thing, you decide to do or have that thing.
opt for something ❏ *Unsure what to study at university, she eventually opted for Law.* ❏ *Tom went sightseeing, while I opted for a day by the pool.*

○ **opt 'in**
If you **opt in**, you choose to take part in a particular arrangement or activity.
❏ [+ to] *If you opt in to our mailing list we can let you know about new products and offers.*
❏ *The management buyout will go ahead only if 75% of the staff opt in.*

◐ **opt 'out**
If you **opt out**, you choose to be no longer involved in something. ❏ *Rather than pursue a stressful career, some people opt out.* ❏ [+ of] *Member countries want the right to opt out of some aspects of the treaty.*

order /'ɔːdə/ (**orders, ordering, ordered**)

○ **order a'round** (or **order about** [mainly BRITISH])
If you **order** someone **around**, you tell them what to do in an unpleasant way. = **push around**
order someone around or **order around someone** ❏ *They think because they've got money they can order you around.* ❏ *I'm fed up with being ordered around.*

○ **order 'in**
If you **order in** food, you order it from a restaurant and they bring it to your house.
order in something or **order something in** ❏ *We just ordered in some pizzas for lunch.*

orient /'ɔːrient/ (**orients, orienting, oriented**)

○ **'orient to** [FORMAL]
When you **orient** yourself **to** a new situation, you learn about it and prepare to deal with it.
orient yourself to something ❏ *When you move to a new country, it can take time to orient yourself to your new way of life.*

oscillate /'ɒsɪleɪt/ (**oscillates, oscillating, oscillated**)

○ **'oscillate between** [FORMAL]
1 If the level or value of something **oscillates between** one amount and another, it keeps going up and down between the two amounts.
oscillate between something ❏ *Our sailing speed has been oscillating between 28 and 35 knots.*

2 If you **oscillate between** two moods, attitudes, or types of behaviour, you keep changing from one to the other.
oscillate between something ❑ I oscillated between hope and despair.

overdose /ˈəʊvədəʊs/ (**overdoses, overdosing, overdosed**)
○ **'overdose on**
1 If someone **overdoses on** a drug, they take too much of it.
overdose on something ❑ Overdosing on drugs can be fatal.
2 You can say that someone **overdoses on** something if they have or do too much of it. [INFORMAL]
overdose on something ❑ Many of us overdose on rich foods during the holiday season. ❑ I overdosed on television while I was off work.

overflow /əʊvəˈfləʊ/ (**overflows, overflowing, overflowed**)
○ **over'flow with**
1 If a place or container **overflows with** people or things, it is too full of them.
overflow with someone/something ❑ The hall was overflowing with people. ❑ The bins are overflowing with rubbish.
2 If someone **overflows with** a feeling, they feel it very strongly and other people can see it.
overflow with something ❑ I arrived at the party, overflowing with confidence. ❑ He was overflowing with enthusiasm for the project.

overlay /əʊvəˈleɪ/ (**overlays, overlaying, overlaid**)
○ **over'lay with**
1 If something **is overlaid with** something else or you **overlay** it **with** something, it is covered by something.
be overlaid with something ❑ The floor was overlaid with rugs.
overlay something with something

❑ We put in the underfloor heating and then we overlaid it with beautiful oak flooring.
2 If something **is overlaid with** a feeling or quality, that feeling or quality is the most noticeable one, but there may be other ones involved. [LITERARY]
be overlaid with something ❑ But anger was overlaid with embarrassment.

overreact /əʊvəriˈækt/ (**overreacts, overreacting, overreacted**)
○ **overre'act to**
If someone **overreacts to** something, they are more angry or upset than they should be in a situation, or they take action that is too extreme.
overreact to something ❑ I'd overreacted to Cheryl's comments.

owe /əʊ/ (**owes, owing, owed**)
○ **'owe to**
1 If you **owe** money **to** someone, they have lent it to you and you have not yet paid it back.
owe something to someone ❑ The company owes money to more than 60 banks.
2 If someone or something **owes** a particular quality or their success **to** a thing or person, they only have it because of that thing or person.
owe something to something/someone
❑ She owed her first job to her friendship with Roger. ❑ He owed his survival to his strength as a swimmer.

own /əʊn/ (**owns, owning, owned**)
○ **own 'up**
If you **own up**, you admit that you have done something wrong. ❑ Come on, own up! Who broke this? ❑ [+ to] No-one owned up to taking the money.
NOTE **Confess** is a more formal word for **own up**.

Pp

pace /peɪs/ (**paces, pacing, paced**)

○ **pace 'out** (or **pace off**)

If you **pace out** a distance, you measure that distance by counting the number of steps you have to take.

pace out something or **pace something out**
❑ *Placing the gun beside a tree he paced out a hundred and fifty paces.* ❑ *They paced off distances to measure the length of the pier.*

pack /pæk/ (**packs, packing, packed**)

○ **pack a'way**

1 If you **pack** something **away**, you put it in the bag, suitcase or box where it is usually kept.

pack something away or **pack away something** ❑ *Rosie was packing her books away.* ❑ *I packed away the clothes that I had worn the previous day.*

2 If someone **packs** food **away**, they eat a lot of it. [INFORMAL]

pack something away or **pack away something** ❑ *She packs her food away and can still fit into her skinny jeans.* ❑ *Teenagers can pack away an enormous quantity of food.*

⊙ **pack 'in**

1 If someone **packs in** activities or experiences, they do a lot of them in a period of time. **= cram in**

pack in something ❑ *I like to pack in as much as I can in my leisure time.*

pack something in ❑ *You'll get tired if you try to pack too much in.*

2 To **pack in** people means to fit a lot of them in a limited space. **= cram in**

pack in someone ❑ *The town tries to pack in as many tourists as possible.*

pack someone in ❑ *Train companies want to pack passengers in to make more money.*

3 If you **pack in** a job or activity, you stop doing it. **= jack in** [BRITISH, INFORMAL]

pack something in ❑ *It's a good job. I don't think he'd pack it in.* ❑ *He packed school in at the age of fourteen and went to work on his father's farm.*

pack in something ❑ *I've often thought about*

packing in my job and travelling around the world.

4 If you **pack** someone **in**, you stop having a romantic or sexual relationship with them. [INFORMAL]

pack someone in ❑ *She's just packed her boyfriend in.*

5 If an event or performer **packs** people **in**, they attract a lot of people. [INFORMAL]

pack in someone ❑ *Obama packed in the crowds during his election campaign.*

pack someone in ❑ *The event usually packs around 30,000 people in.*

● If you say that an event or performer **is packing them in**, you mean that they are attracting a lot of people. **= pull in** ❑ *The film is packing them in at cinemas around the country.*

6 If a machine, engine or part of someone's body **packs in**, it stops working because there is something wrong with it. [BRITISH, INFORMAL] ❑ *The boat's engines have packed in.* ❑ *His kidneys have packed in so he is having dialysis.*

7 If you tell someone to **pack it in**, you are telling them to stop doing something because it is annoying you. [BRITISH, INFORMAL] ❑ *Pack it in or someone will get hurt!*

○ **pack 'into**

1 If someone **packs** a lot of something **into** a limited space or time, they fit a lot into it. **= cram into**

pack something into something ❑ *She has packed a lot into her life already.* ❑ *Don't try to pack too many ideas into one sentence.*

2 If people or things **are packed into** a place, or someone **packs** them **into** a place, a lot of them are put there and the place becomes very full. **= be crammed into**

be packed into something ❑ *The prisoners were packed into three small railway carriages.*

pack someone into something ❑ *We need to avoid packing more people into already overcrowded prisons.*

○ **pack 'off** [INFORMAL]

If you **pack** someone **off** somewhere, you send them there to stay for a period of time, even though they may not want to go there

pack someone off ❑ *He was packed off to stay with one of his mother's relatives.* ❑ [+ to] *I packed her off to bed.*

○ **pack 'out**

1 If people **pack out** a place, there are so many of them that the place is full.
pack out something or **pack something out**
❑ *Clubbers continue to pack out this nightclub every weekend.* ❑ *People pack the stadium out when the team are playing.* ● *If a place is* **packed out**, *it is full of people.* ❑ *The bar was packed out that evening.*
2 If a performer or form of entertainment **packs** a place **out**, they attract so many people that the place is full. [INFORMAL]
pack out something or **pack something out**
❑ *This Cuban band packs out the club every weekend.*

❂ **pack 'up**

1 If you **pack up** or **pack up** your belongings, you put all your belongings in a case or bag, often because you are leaving one place and going to another.
pack up something ❑ *I was sad when we had to pack up our things and leave.*
pack something up ❑ *She began to pack all her books and clothes up.*
pack up ❑ *She packed up and left the next day.*
2 If you **pack up** or **pack up** a job or activity, you stop doing the job or activity. [INFORMAL]
pack up ❑ *I started playing cricket when I was eleven and only packed up five years ago.*
pack up something or **pack something up**
❑ *She says she's packing up work.* ❑ *If the job doesn't improve he'll probably pack it up.*
3 If a machine **packs up**, it stops working because there is something wrong with it.
= **break down** [BRITISH, INFORMAL] ❑ *The heating in the hall has packed up.*
4 If a part of someone's body **packs up**, it stops working. [BRITISH, INFORMAL] ❑ *In the end, it was his stomach and lungs that packed up.*

pad /pæd/ (**pads, padding, padded**)
○ **pad 'out**

If you **pad out** a piece of writing or a speech with unnecessary words or pieces of information, you include them in order to make it longer.
pad out something or **pad something out**
❑ [+ with] *She pads out her essays with a lot of long quotes.*

page /peɪdʒ/ (**pages, paging, paged**)
○ **page 'down**

If you **page down**, you press a key on a computer to make the next page of a document appear. ❑ *Page down until you get to the section on health.*

○ **page 'up**

If you **page up**, you press a key on a computer to make the previous page of a document appear. ❑ *I paged up to the previous section.*

paint /peɪnt/ (**paints, painting, painted**)
○ **paint 'out**

If you **paint** something **out**, you cover or hide it with paint.
paint out something or **paint something out**
❑ *He painted the previous owner's name out.*
❑ *The sign had been painted out, and could no longer be read.*

○ **paint 'over**

If you **paint over** something, you cover it with paint so that it is hidden.
paint over something or **paint something over** ❑ *I didn't like the wallpaper so I just painted over it.*

○ **paint 'up**

If you **paint** something **up**, you decorate it with paint to make it look attractive.
paint something up or **paint up something** ❑ *They repaired the house and painted it up.*

pair /peə/ (**pairs, pairing, paired**)
○ **pair 'off**

1 When two people **pair off**, they start a romantic relationship. ❑ *At the end of the evening everyone was pairing off.* ❑ [+ with] *Kate had paired off with model Alex.*
2 If you **pair** two people **off**, you bring them together because you want them to start a romantic relationship.
pair someone off or **pair off someone**
❑ *I'm really not trying to pair people off.* ❑ [+ with] *My friends are always attempting to pair me off with people.*
3 If two people, organizations, groups, etc. **pair off**, or you **pair** them **off**, they come together or you make them come together to do something.
pair off ❑ *After the hunt, we paired off and introduced each other to the rest of the group.*
pair someone off or **pair off someone**
❑ [+ with] *Firstly, pair off everyone with a partner.*
❑ *After the break, the novices were paired off with an experienced person.*

○ **pair 'up**

If two people or groups **pair up**, or you **pair** them **up**, they come together or you make them come together to do something.
= **team up**
pair up ❑ *The actors previously paired up in the 1991 film "Dutch".* ❑ *The two men paired up to play doubles in a tennis tournament.*

pair someone up *or* **pair up someone**
❏ [+ with] *He was paired up with a younger contestant.*

pal /pæl/ (**pals, palling, palled**)

○ **pal 'around with**
If you **pal around with** someone, you spend time with them as friends, often in order to get some benefit for yourself.
pal around with someone ❏ *She can often be seen palling around with various celebrities.*

○ **pal 'up with**
If you **pal up with** someone, you become friendly with them.
pal up with someone ❏ *I palled up with a fellow Scot on my first day and we've been friends ever since.*

palm /pɑːm/ (**palms, palming, palmed**)

○ **palm 'off**
☐ If someone **palms** something **off**, they give or sell it to someone in order to get rid of it.
palm off something *or* **palm something off**
❏ *New security measures mean it will be harder to palm off fake notes.* ❏ [+ on] *She's always palming her children off on somebody else.*
☐ If someone **palms** you **off**, they tell you something that is not true in order to stop you asking questions or causing trouble for them. [BRITISH]
palm someone off ❏ *Don't let them palm you off.* ❏ [+ with] *There's no point in asking her where she's been, because she'll only palm you off with excuses.*

○ **palm 'off as**
To **palm** something or someone **off as** something else is to pretend they are something, in order to deceive people.
palm something/someone off as something ❏ *They were palming the grape juice off as wine.* ❏ *The film had British actors trying to palm themselves off as Americans.*

pan /pæn/ (**pans, panning, panned**)

○ **'pan for**
If someone **pans for gold**, they use a shallow metal container to try to find small pieces of gold in a river. ❏ *People came westward in the 1800s to pan for gold.*

○ **pan 'out** [INFORMAL]
☐ If a situation **pans out** in a particular way, it develops in that way. = **work out**
❏ *Things didn't pan out too well.* ❏ *We'll have to see how things pan out.*
☐ If something **pans out**, it develops in a successful way. = **work out** ❏ *I'll look for a new job if my current one doesn't pan out.* ❏ *If current drug research pans out, there could soon be a pill to make us all slim.*

pander /'pændə/ (**panders, pandering, pandered**)

○ **'pander to**
If you **pander to** someone or to their wishes or beliefs, you try to please them by doing or saying what they want, often in a way that seems unreasonable.
pander to someone/something ❏ *Many companies pander to teenagers because they've got the money and the time to spend it.* ❏ *Parents who spoil their children and pander to their every desire are storing up trouble for the future.*

paper /'peɪpə/ (**papers, papering, papered**)

○ **paper 'over**
If someone **papers over** a problem or mistake, they try to hide it and pretend that it does not exist.
paper over something ❏ *In those remarks, McClelland papered over the fact that his relationship with Farley was not good.*
• If someone **papers over the cracks**, they try to hide disagreements or problems.
❏ *His acting is poor but the rest of the cast do a good job of papering over the cracks.*

parachute /'pærəʃuːt/ (**parachutes, parachuting, parachuted**)

○ **parachute 'into**
If a person **parachutes into** an organization or if they **are parachuted into** it, they are brought in to help it.
parachute into something ❏ *As a consultant, she parachutes into corporations and helps provide strategic thinking.*
be parachuted into something ❏ *He was parachuted into the company to try to rescue its failing clothing business.*

parcel /'pɑːsəl/ (**parcels, parcelling, parcelled**)

American English uses the spellings **parceling** and **parceled**.

○ **parcel 'out**
When you **parcel** something **out**, you divide it into several parts or amounts and give them to different people.
parcel something out *or* **parcel out something** ❏ *They reached an agreement on how to parcel out the money.* ❏ [+ among] *The responsibility for it had been parcelled out among them.*

○ **parcel 'up**
☐ When you **parcel** something **up**, you wrap it in paper and fasten it with string or tape. = **wrap up**
parcel something up *or* **parcel up something** ❏ *We spent all of last night parcelling Christmas*

presents up. ❏ *I parcelled up two copies of my book to send to Maggie.*

2 When something **is parcelled up** or you **parcel** it **up**, it is divided into separate sections.

parcel something up or **parcel up something** ❏ *They parcelled the company up and sold most of it.*
be parcelled up ❏ *[+ into] The land had been parcelled up into fields.*

pare /peə/ (**pares, paring, pared**)

○ **pare a'way** → see **pare off**

○ **pare 'down**
When you **pare** something **down**, you reduce it or make it more simple by removing something.

pare something down or **pare down something** ❏ *The manuscript has been pared down, but it is still 773 pages long.* ❏ *I had pared my possessions down to a minimum.* ● If something is **pared-down**, it is smaller r more simple because parts have been removed. ❏ *This is a pared-down version of the software.*

○ **pare 'off**
If you **pare** an amount **off** something, you reduce it by that amount.

pare something off something ❏ *People who tried this weight-loss treatment pared an average of 9cm off their waist-size.*

○ **pare 'off** (or **pare away**)
When you **pare off** the skin or outer layer of something, you cut it off using a knife or other sharp tool.

pare something off or **pare off something** ❏ *He gently pared off the rind of the cheese and took a bite.* ❏ *Part of the horse's hoof had to be pared away.*

part /pɑːt/ (**parts, parting, parted**)

○ **'part from**
1 When two people **part from** each other, they leave each other. [FORMAL]
part from someone ❏ *I was sick with worry at the thought of parting from my parents.*
2 When two people **part from** each other, they end their relationship. [FORMAL]
part from someone ❏ *He has since parted from his second wife.*
3 If you **are parted from** someone or something, you are made to leave them or be in a place where they are not.
be parted from someone ❏ *It's perfectly natural that a mother should not wish to be parted from her children.*

○ **'part with**
If you **part with** something, you give it or sell it to someone else. ≠ **hold on to**

part with something ❏ *I took the book, thanked her, and told her I would never part with it.* ❏ *She didn't want to part with the money.*

partake /pɑːˈteɪk/ (**partakes, partaking, partook, partaken**)

○ **par'take in** [FORMAL, OLD-FASHIONED]
If you **partake in** an activity, you do it.
partake in something ❏ *I was made to partake in a good deal of menial work.*

○ **par'take of** [FORMAL, OLD-FASHIONED]
1 If you **partake of** food or drink, you eat or drink it.
partake of something ❏ *He did not partake of either meal.* ❏ *He was invited to partake of refreshment.*
2 If something **partakes of** a particular quality, it has that quality.
partake of something ❏ *Education is at its most effective when it partakes of the nature of discovery.*

participate /pɑːˈtɪsɪpeɪt/ (**participates, participating, participated**)

○ **par'ticipate in**
If you **participate in** an activity, you take part in it.
participate in something ❏ *Over half the population of this country participate in sport.* ❏ *Students are encouraged to participate in the discussion.*

partition /pɑːˈtɪʃən/ (**partitions, partitioning, partitioned**)

○ **partition 'off**
If you **partition off** part of a room, you separate that part from the rest by putting something between the two parts.
partition something off or **partition off something** ❏ *He had partitioned part of the kitchen off.* ❏ *[+ from] The bar was partitioned off from the restaurant by thick glass.*

pass /pɑːs, pæs/ (**passes, passing, passed**)

○ **pass a'long** (or **pass down**)
If a person or vehicle **passes along** a path or place, they move along there.
pass along something ❏ *Almost no traffic passes along the road.* ❏ *Thousands of people must have passed down the street.*

○ **pass a'long** [FORMAL]
If you **pass** information or a message **along**, you send it or give it to someone else.
pass something along or **pass along something** ❏ *I'll pass that news along to Martin.* ❏ *She had been passing along information that turned out to be false.*

◐ **pass a'round** (or **pass round** [mainly BRITISH])
If you **pass** things **around**, you give them

from one person to another in a group.

pass around something ❑ *Her mother passed around a plate of cakes.*

pass something around ❑ *She opened the chocolates and passed them round.*

○ **'pass as** (or **pass for**)

To **pass as** something or someone means to seem to be that thing or that type of person.

pass as someone/something ❑ *He's only fourteen but he looks older and could easily pass for eighteen.*

○ **pass a'way**

1 When something **passes away**, it slowly disappears. ❑ *All hopes of compromise had now passed away.*

2 You can say that someone **passes away** to mean that they die, especially if you want to avoid saying the word 'die'. **= pass on** ❑ *Your husband sent the letter to us shortly before he passed away.* ❑ *I've seen both my parents pass away from cancer.*

3 If you **pass** time **away** in a particular place, you are there for that time.

pass something away or **pass away something** ❑ *The café is a pleasant place to pass away an hour or two.* ❑ *He wanted to pass the days away in a remote place.*

○ **pass be'tween**

1 If remarks, letters or looks **pass between** two people, those people say or write something to each other, or look at each other.

pass between someone ❑ *No word had passed between them during the entire journey.*

2 To **pass between** two people or things or **pass** something **between** two people or things means to move through them so there is one on either side or to cause something to do this.

pass between something/someone ❑ *She passed between the two men.* ❑ *The nail passed between two of the bones in his foot.*

pass something between something ❑ *They then pass the grain between rollers to crush it.*

○ **pass 'by**

1 To **pass by** or **pass by** something or someone means to go past something or someone without stopping.

pass by ❑ *He sat and watched all the people passing by.* ❑ *A police car happened to be passing by at the time.*

pass by something/someone ❑ *Jo called out to me as I passed by her office.* ❑ *She passed by James without looking at him.*

pass someone by ❑ *Helen flinched as the armed police officers passed her by.* ● A **passer-by** is a person who is walking past something or

someone. ❑ *Passers-by dived in to the sea to rescue them.* ● A **bypass** is a main road which is built to take traffic round the edge of a town rather than through the middle. ❑ *The construction of a new bypass around the ancient town should reduce traffic in the town centre.*

2 If something **passes** you **by**, it happens or exists but you do not notice it or take advantage of it.

pass someone by ❑ *Don't let this opportunity pass you by.* ❑ *She felt that life was passing her by.*

○ **pass 'down**

1 If things such as stories, traditions, or characteristics **are passed down**, or you pass them down, they are told, taught, or given to younger people and the people who live after them. **= hand down**

be passed down ❑ *Characteristics such as eye colour and height are passed down in the genes.* ❑ *[+ from] This diamond ring has been passed down to me from my grandmother.*

pass something down ❑ *[+ to] His grandfather had passed these stories down to him.*

pass down something ❑ *The generations before us passed down these customs.*

2 → see **pass along**

○ **'pass for** → see **pass as**

○ **'pass from to**

If something **passes** or **is passed from** one person **to** another, the first person gives it to the second person or the second person has it instead of the first person.

pass from someone to someone ❑ *Power passes from the ruling party to the Communist party.*

be passed from someone to someone ❑ *It is a genetic trait, which can be passed from parent to child.* ❑ *In crowded places, infections are easily passed from one person to another.*

○ **pass 'off**

1 If an event **passes off** in a particular way especially in a good way, it happens and ends in that way. ❑ *The conference passed off reasonably well.*

2 If you **pass** someone else's unpleasant remarks **off**, you say or pretend that they were not really important or serious.

= shrug off

pass something off or **pass off something** ❑ *Marc had smiled and passed her comments off lightly.* ❑ *She passed off his criticisms contemptuously, considering his opinion of little value.*

3 If a feeling or condition **passes off**, it gradually disappears. **= wear off** ❑ *Fortunately, the effects of the gas passed off relatively quickly.*

pass 'off as

If you **pass** something or someone **off as** something or someone else, you make people think that they are that thing or person.

pass off something/someone as something or **pass something/someone off as something** ❏ He had tried to pass somebody else's work off as his own. ❏ She tried to pass him off as her son.

pass yourself off as something ❏ The man passed himself off as a doctor to gain access to medical records.

pass 'on

1 If you **pass** something **on**, you give or tell it to someone else.

pass something on ❏ I'll pass it on when I've finished reading it. ❏ If you hear any tips, do pass them on.

pass on something ❏ I could pass on a message if you like. ❏ [+ to] I'll pass on the news to Ahmed.

> **PASS ON + noun**
>
> pass on **a message**
> pass on **a tip**
> pass on **information**
> pass on **knowledge**
> pass on **advice**
> ❏ David passed on your message to me.
> ❏ We passed on all the information we had to the police.

2 If things such as stories, traditions, or money **are passed on**, or you **pass** them **on**, they are taught or given to someone who belongs to a younger generation. = **hand down**

be passed on ❏ Skills such as this should be passed on.

pass something on ❏ He had passed the tradition on.

pass on something ❏ They pass on their tradition through storytelling. ❏ [+ to] She assumed that her father would wish to pass on to her most of his money. ❏ I have nothing that I can pass on to you.

3 When parents **pass on** a characteristic or disease to their children, the children develop it or have it because of the genes that they inherit from their parents.

pass on something ❏ Parents can pass on a gene that makes their child more likely to develop the disease.

pass something on ❏ [+ to] Adults can be tested to see whether they might pass the disease on to their own children.

NOTE **Transmit** is a more formal word for **pass on**.

4 If you **pass** someone **on** to someone else,

you tell them to speak to that person because you think that person might be able to help.

pass someone on or **pass on someone** ❏ [+ to] I was passed on to another doctor.

5 If a company **passes on** costs or savings, they increase or lower the prices that customers pay because of changes in the cost of making or doing something.

pass on something or **pass something on** ❏ Governments have tried to prevent firms from passing on cost increases. ❏ [+ to] Any saving will automatically be passed on to all clients.

6 If you **pass on**, you begin to talk or write about a new subject. = **move on** ❏ I think we should pass on now if no one has any questions. ❏ [+ to] They passed on to other matters.

7 If you **pass on**, you continue, and move to a different place or stage. ❏ The man lowered his eyes and quickly passed on. ❏ [+ to] We passed on to a small hall and entered the living room.

8 You can say that someone **passes on** to mean that they die, especially if you want to avoid using the word 'die'. = **pass away** ❏ My husband passed on last year.

9 If someone makes you an offer or asks you a question and you say **I'll pass on that**, you mean that you do not want to accept or answer it now. ❏ 'We're going out for a curry if you want to come?' – 'I'll pass on that, thanks.'

✪ pass 'out

1 If you **pass out**, you become unconscious for a short time. = **black out** ❏ It was so hot I thought I was going to pass out. ❏ He hit his head on a rock and passed out.

2 If you **pass** something **out**, you give it to each person in a group. = **hand out**

pass out something ❏ We all sat on the grass, and I passed out the lemonade. ❏ She passed out a copy of the document to each of us.

pass something out ❏ He began passing the plates out. ❏ [+ to] I had business cards printed and passed them out to as many people as I could.

3 If someone **passes out**, they successfully finish a training course at a police or military college. [BRITISH] ❏ He was killed in Belfast only two weeks after passing out from Sandhurst. ● A **passing-out** ceremony or parade is a special event when people have successfully finished a training course at a police or military college. ❏ The army cadets were due to hold their passing-out parade.

✪ pass 'over

1 If you **are passed over** for a job that you are trying to get, it is given to someone who has less experience or fewer qualifications than you. = **be rejected**

be passed over ❏ *Neither of us got the job. We were both passed over.* ❏ *[+ for] He resigned after being passed over for promotion.*

2 If you **pass over** a particular subject, you deliberately do not mention it. **= ignore**
pass over something or **pass something over** ❏ *He passed over the events of that week.* ❏ *He didn't give a reason and Robertson passed it over in silence.*

3 When something **passes over** or **passes over** something, it moves above someone or something without stopping.
pass over ❏ *A helicopter had passed over a few moments before.*
pass over something ❏ *The first shot passed over our heads.* • An **overpass** is a road which is built like a bridge so that it is above another road. **= flyover** ❏ *They're building a new overpass.*

○ **pass 'round** → see **pass around**

○ **pass 'through**
To **pass through** an experience means to have that experience and survive it.
pass through something ❏ *As children, we pass through a number of stages.*

○ **'pass to**
1 If you **pass** something **to** someone, you take it in your hand and give it to them.
pass something to someone ❏ *She passed the books to Ahmed.* ❏ *Bergstein filled the glass and passed it to her.*

2 If you **pass to** someone or **pass** a ball **to** someone in your team in a game such as football, hockey, or rugby, you kick, hit, or throw the ball to them.
pass to someone ❏ *In the third minute Pettigrew passed to Barton, who in turn passed to Jones.*
pass something to someone ❏ *He then passed the ball to Berger, who scored.*

3 When something **passes to** someone, it becomes their property or responsibility. [FORMAL]
pass to someone ❏ *The land will pass to her son when she dies.*

○ **'pass under**
When someone or something **passes under** another thing, they go underneath it.
pass under something ❏ *After four miles the stream passes under the road.* • An **underpass** is a road or path that goes under another road or a railway. ❏ *Princess Diana died in a car crash in a Paris underpass.*

○ **pass 'up**
If you **pass up** an opportunity, you do not take advantage of it.
pass up something or **pass something up**

❏ *She never passed up a chance to eat in a restaurant.* ❏ *You'd be a fool to pass this opportunity up.*

paste /peɪst/ (**pastes, pasting, pasted**)
○ **paste 'up**
If you **paste** something **up**, you stick it to a wall or door, using glue.
paste something up or **paste up something**
❏ *Posters had been pasted up advertising the event.* ❏ *[+ on] He cut out pictures and pasted them up on the wall.*

pat /pæt/ (**pats, patting, patted**)
○ **pat 'down** [INFORMAL]
If a police officer or guard pats someone down or someone **is patted down**, a police officer or guard touches a person's body all over to see if they are carrying a weapon or anything illegal. **= frisk**
be patted down ❏ *Leona was patted down and her luggage searched.*
pat someone down or **pat down someone**
❏ *An official at the airport asked him to raise his arms, so she could pat him down.*

patch /pætʃ/ (**patches, patching, patched**)
○ **patch to'gether**
If you **patch** something **together**, you make it quickly or carelessly from several parts or ideas. **= cobble together**
patch something together or **patch together something** ❏ *The President's first task will be to patch together a compromise.* ❏ *The book was clearly patched together from a few old essays.*

○ **patch 'up**
1 If you **patch up** something which is damaged or broken, you mend it quickly and often not very well. **= fix up**
patch up something ❏ *They have to patch up the mud walls that the rains have battered.*
patch something up ❏ *They had used plastic to patch the roof up.* ❏ *[+ with] The original wooden hut had been patched up with tin sheets.*

2 To **patch** someone **up** or **patch up** their injuries means to give them basic medical treatment after they have been injured. **= treat** [INFORMAL]
patch someone/something up ❏ *The doctor who patched me up said I was lucky that my injuries were not more serious.*
patch up someone/something ❏ *A nurse patched up the cuts on my face.*

3 If you **patch up** an argument or a relationship, you become friends again with someone after arguing.
patch up something ❏ *She seemed to want to make peace and patch up our quarrel.*

patch something up ❑ *Many years later they patched their relationship up.*

● If you **patch it up** or **patch things up**, you become friends with someone again after arguing. ❑ *Is there any chance of patching things up with your friend?*

◤4◢ If people or countries **patch up** an agreement, they agree on it after difficult discussions.

patch up something or **patch something up** ❑ *Trade ministers patched up a compromise.* ❑ *Both governments are frantically trying to patch the deal up before the elections.*

attern /'pætən/ (**patterns, patterning, patterned**)

'pattern on

If you **pattern** something new **on** something else that already exists, you try to make it like that thing.

pattern something on something ❑ *The city patterned the program on one started three years ago in Westland.* ❑ *The show was patterned on one from the 1970s.*

ave /peɪv/ (**paves, paving, paved**)

pave 'over

If you **pave over** an area of ground, you cover it with blocks of stone, bricks, or concrete.

pave over something or **pave something over** ❑ *Flooding has been caused by large areas of farmland being paved over.* ❑ *Even a garden that has been paved over can be made more interesting with pots of flowers.*

aw /pɔː/ (**paws, pawing, pawed**)

'paw at

When an animal **paws at** something, it tries to touch it several times with its paw or hoof.

paw at something ❑ *The dog pawed at the door again and again.*

ay /peɪ/ (**pays, paying, paid**)

pay 'back

◤1◢ If you **pay** money **back** to someone or **pay** them **back**, you give them money that you borrowed from them. = **repay**

pay someone/something back ❑ *Loan me a hundred dollars, I'll pay you back on Monday when I go to the bank.* ❑ *Cheetham had paid all the money back.* ❑ [+ to] *I'm going to pay every penny of it back to him.*

pay back something ❑ *I knew business was going well enough to pay back the loan on time.* ❑ *I've already paid back $17.50 of it.*

◤2◢ If you **pay** someone **back**, you do something bad to them because they did something bad to you.

pay someone back ❑ [+ for] *I'm going to pay her back for all the trouble she's caused me.* ❑ *Sinclair did not pay him back as he had threatened to.*

○ **pay 'down** [mainly AMERICAN]

If you **pay down** a debt, you pay some money to reduce it.

pay down something or **pay something down** ❑ *Now we can start to pay down the debt.*

◎ **'pay for**

◤1◢ If you **pay for** something, you give someone money for it.

pay for something ❑ *Who paid for the drinks?* ❑ *The ticket was reserved but not paid for.*

◤2◢ If something that you buy **pays for** itself, it saves you as much money as you spent on it.

pay for itself ❑ *New condensing boilers are more efficient and will pay for themselves within five years.* ❑ *Install a smart meter. It soon pays for itself by reducing your heating bills.*

◤3◢ If someone **pays for** something bad that they have done, they suffer or are punished because of it.

pay for something ❑ *The team paid for mistakes made earlier in the game and lost 4-0.* ❑ *He made me look stupid, and I'm determined he's going to pay for it.*

◎ **pay 'in**

When you **pay** money **in**, you put it into a bank account.

pay something in ❑ *Roberto called in at the bank to pay his cheque in.*

pay in something ❑ *I paid in £150 this morning.*

◎ **pay 'into**

When you **pay** money **into** a bank account, you put it into the account. = **deposit**

pay something into something ❑ *I've already paid the cheque into my bank account.*

◎ **pay 'off**

◤1◢ If you **pay off** a debt or bill, you pay all the money that you owe. = **repay**

pay off something ❑ *The most common reason for borrowing is to pay off existing loans.*

pay something off ❑ *She paid her debts off by selling her house.*

PAY OFF + noun
pay off **money**
pay off **a debt**
pay off **a loan**
pay off **a mortgage**
❑ *We used the money to pay off our debts.*
❑ *We soon paid off the loan.*

◤2◢ If you **pay** someone **off**, you stop them threatening you or causing you trouble by giving them money. = **buy off**

pay someone off or **pay off someone** ❑ *He pays off most of the guards so they don't tell anyone.*

• A **payoff** is a payment that you make to someone so that they do not cause trouble for you. ❑ *It was usually possible to make a payoff to a high police official to keep quiet.*

3 If you **pay off** someone, you pay them for the work they have done for you, then tell them to leave.

pay off someone ❑ *Tweed paid off the driver and the cab departed.*

pay someone off ❑ *The football club does not have the money to pay him off.*

4 If something that you do **pays off**, it is successful and has benefits for you. ❑ *It was a risk but it paid off.* ❑ *The athletes have been training very hard, and the effort has paid off for them today.*

> **noun +PAY OFF**
>
> **a gamble** pays off
> **a risk** pays off
> **persistence** pays off
> **hard work** pays off
> ❑ *We took a gamble, and it paid off.* ❑ *All our hard work has paid off at last.*

• A **payoff** is the benefit to you of something that you do. ❑ *Compared to the possible payoff, the risk seemed small.*

○ **pay 'out**

1 If you **pay out** or **pay out** money, you spend a lot of money on a particular thing.

pay out something ❑ *She had paid out a lot of money to send Julie to school.* ❑ *[+ for] We paid out £200 each for these tickets.* ❑ *[+ in] They pay out half of their income in rent.*

pay something out ❑ *Fans paid a lot of money out to see the team play in this game.*

pay out ❑ *They have to pay out for the maintenance of the building even though they don't live there.*

2 When an insurance policy or financial investment that you have **pays out**, you get money from it. ❑ *Many policies pay out only after a period of weeks or months.* • A **payout** is a payment that is made to someone from an insurance policy or financial investment. ❑ *The investment guarantees a payout after ten years.*

3 When you **pay out** a rope or cable, you unwind it slowly and carefully.

pay out something *or* **pay something out** ❑ *The man paid out the rope a metre at a time.*

○ **'pay to**

When you **pay** an amount of money **to** someone, you give it to them because you are buying something from them or because you owe it to them.

pay something to someone ❑ *The company paid $75,000 to shareholders.* ❑ *A sum of money would be paid to him when the job was finished.*

○ **pay 'up**

When you **pay up** or **pay up** something, you give someone the money that you owe them, although you do not want to.

pay up ❑ *Come on, pay up.* ❑ *She said if I didn't pay up she'd take me to court.*

pay up something ❑ *Allen told them to meet him at a hotel where he'd pay up his debt.*

peal /piːl/ (peals, pealing, pealed)

○ **peal 'out**

When bells, laughter or voices **peal out**, they make a loud sound. = **resound**
❑ *The bells would peal out across the town.*
❑ *Joey's laughter pealed out.*

peck /pek/ (pecks, pecking, pecked)

○ **'peck at** [INFORMAL]

If you **peck at** your food, you eat only small amounts of it.

peck at something ❑ *He could do no more than peck at his food, constantly watching the clock.*

peel /piːl/ (peels, peeling, peeled)

○ **peel 'off**

1 If you **peel** the outer layer **off** something or if it **peels off**, you remove it or it separates easily.

peel something off something ❑ *I peeled some moss off the wood.*

peel something off ❑ *She peeled the wrapping paper off.*

peel off ❑ *On the statues, the gold leaf was beginning to peel off.*

2 If you **peel off** some money from a pile of banknotes, you take some of the notes from the top of the pile one at a time.

peel off something *or* **peel something off** ❑ *He took a wad of bills out of his pocket and peeled off five tens.*

3 If you **peel off** a tight or wet piece of clothing, you remove it by pulling it slowly. = **strip off**

peel off something *or* **peel something off** ❑ *She peeled off her wet trousers.* ❑ *She peeled her sweater off.*

4 If some of a group of moving vehicles or people **peel off**, they leave the group and start moving in a different direction.
❑ *As the cars arrived, the police motorcycle escort peeled off and circled round the courtyard.*

peer /pɪə/ (peers, peering, peered)

○ **'peer at**

If you **peer at** something or someone, you look at them very hard, usually because it is difficult to see clearly.

peer at something/someone ❑ *I peered at*

each house through the rain, trying to see the number. ❑ *Marcus peered at me in the faint light.*

peg /peg/ (**pegs, pegging, pegged**)

○ **'peg at**

If a price or amount **is pegged at** a particular level or if someone **pegs** it **at** that level, it is fixed at that level.

be pegged at something ❑ *The tax has been pegged at last year's level.*

peg something at something ❑ *It says its goal is to peg the value at no more than 80 percent of the likely sales price.*

○ **peg a'way** [INFORMAL]

If you **peg away**, you continue to do something in a very determined way, even though it is difficult or unpleasant. **= plug away** ❑ *We must just keep pegging away and hope our luck will change.* ❑ [+ at] *This project has always been our top priority so we'll just keep pegging away at it.*

○ **peg 'down**

If you **peg** something **down**, you fix it to the ground with pegs.

peg down something or **peg something down** ❑ *Peg the plastic sheet down so it can't blow away in the wind.*

○ **peg 'out**

◼ If someone **pegs out**, they die. [BRITISH, INFORMAL] ❑ *With his bad heart, he could peg out at any time.*

◼ If someone **pegs out**, they stop doing something because they are too tired to continue. **= flake out** [BRITISH, INFORMAL] ❑ *She just pegged out halfway round the course.*

◼ If you **peg out** wet clothes or sheets that you have washed, you fasten them to a washing line with pegs. **= hang out**

peg out something or **peg something out** ❑ *She went into the garden and began to peg out the clothes on the line.* ❑ *Mrs Poulter began to peg her washing out.*

◼ If you **peg** something **out**, you spread it on the ground and fasten it there with pegs.

peg something out or **peg out something** ❑ *We pegged the tent out with considerable difficulty.*

pelt /pelt/ (**pelts, pelting, pelted**)

○ **'pelt down** [INFORMAL]

If it **pelts down** or rain **pelts down**, it rains very hard. **= pour down** ❑ *It pelted down all day yesterday.* ❑ *The rain was still pelting down.*

pen /pen/ (**pens, penning, penned**)

○ **pen 'in** (or **pen up**)

If animals or people **are penned in** or you

pen animals or people **in**, you make them move into an enclosed area.

be penned in ❑ *Thousands of protestors were penned in by riot police.*

pen in something/someone or **pen something/someone in** ❑ *The dog was trying to pen in some reluctant sheep.*

pencil /'pensəl/ (**pencils, pencilling, pencilled**)

> American English uses the spellings **penciled** and **penciling**.

○ **pencil 'in**

If you **pencil** something or someone **in**, you arrange for something to happen or for someone to do something, knowing that you may change this later.

pencil in something/someone or **pencil something/someone in** ❑ *We've pencilled in a date for the meeting.* ❑ [+ for] *The band were pencilled in for six UK concerts.*

pension /'penʃən/ (**pensions, pensioning, pensioned**)

○ **pension 'off**

◼ If an organization **pensions** someone **off**, it makes them leave their job when they are old or sick, and gives them some money.

pension someone off or **pension off someone** ❑ *Older police officers were pensioned off to make way for younger recruits.*

◼ If you **pension off** something that you have used for a long time, you stop using it. [INFORMAL]

pension something off or **pension off something** ❑ *I bought a new jacket, pensioning off the old denim one I'd worn for years.*

pep /pep/ (**peps, pepping, pepped**)

○ **pep 'up**

◼ If you **pep** something **up**, you make it more lively or interesting. **= liven up**

pep something up or **pep up something** ❑ *The store has pepped up its range of clothing.* ❑ [+ with] *How about pepping plain tiles up with transfers?*

◼ If something **peps** you **up**, it gives you more energy. **= perk up**

pep someone up or **pep up someone** ❑ *Morell gave him a cup of coffee to pep him up.* ❑ *Drinks were served to pep up the tired travellers.*

pepper /'pepə/ (**peppers, peppering, peppered**)

○ **'pepper with**

◼ To **pepper** something or someone **with** bullets means to hit them several times with bullets.

pepper something/someone with something ❏ *He peppered the target with a hail of bullets from his pocket pistol.*

2 If something **is peppered with** things, there are a lot of the things on it or in it.

be peppered with something ❏ *The area is peppered with lovely villages.*

3 If you **pepper** your speech or writing **with** a particular type of language, you use a lot of that type of language.

pepper something with something ❏ *Jamie peppered his conversation with insults.* ❏ *Lee's speech was peppered with musical references.*

4 If you **pepper** someone **with** questions, requests, etc., you ask a lot of questions, make a lot of requests, etc. [AMERICAN]

pepper someone with something ❏ *Reporters peppered the minister with questions about the budget.*

perch /pɜːtʃ/ (perches, perching, perched)

○ **'perch on**

1 If you **perch on** something or **are perched on** something, you sit on the edge of something.

perch on something ❏ *He perched on the corner of the desk.*

be perched on something ❏ *She was perched on the edge of the sofa.*

2 When a bird **perches on** something such as a branch or a wall, it lands on it and stands there.

perch on something ❏ *A noisy bird perched on a branch just above us.*

perk /pɜːk/ (perks, perking, perked)

○ **perk 'up**

1 If someone **perks up**, or if someone or something **perks** them **up**, they suddenly become more cheerful, interested or energetic. = **liven up**

perk up ❏ *Joe seemed to perk up after a little food.* ❏ [+ at] *Tom perked up at the idea.*

perk someone up or **perk up someone** ❏ *Todd drank some coffee, which perked him up.*

perk yourself up ❏ *We offer tips on how to perk yourself up when you're feeling low.*

2 If something **perks up** or you **perk** something **up**, it becomes more interesting or exciting or you make it more interesting or exciting.

perk something up or **perk up something** ❏ *A little vinegar can perk soups and casseroles up.* ❏ *Some exciting scenes perk up the story line.*

perk up ❏ *Her love life perked up when she met a German actor.*

3 If sales, prices, or economies **perk up**, or if something **perks** them **up**, they begin to increase or improve. [JOURNALISM]

perk up ❏ *House prices could perk up during the autumn.*

perk something up or **perk up something** ❏ *This would save the company some money and perk up its cash flow.*

4 If you **perk up** coffee, you make some coffee to drink, using a machine called a percolator. [AMERICAN]

perk something up or **perk up something** ❏ *Let me get you a coffee – I was going to perk some up anyway.*

permit /pəˈmɪt/ (permits, permitting, permitted)

○ **per'mit of** [FORMAL]

If something **permits of** a particular thing, it makes it possible.

permit of something ❏ *The military and police arrangements were too thorough to permit of any protest in the streets.*

persevere /pɜːsɪˈvɪə/ (perseveres, persevering, persevered)

○ **perse'vere with**

If you **persevere with** something, you keep trying to do it, even though it is difficult.

persevere with something ❏ *The longer children persevere with their music training, the greater the benefits.* ❏ *The marriage was unhappy but they persevered with it for the sake of the children.*

pertain /pəˈteɪn/ (pertains, pertaining, pertained)

○ **per'tain to** [FORMAL]

If one thing **pertains to** another thing, it relates to that other thing.

pertain to something ❏ *We were asked to examine all evidence pertaining to the case.*

peter /ˈpiːtə/ (peters, petering, petered)

○ **peter 'out**

If something **peters out**, it gradually stops completely. ❏ *The track petered out a mile or two later.* ❏ *His rage gradually petered out.*

phase /feɪz/ (phases, phasing, phased)

○ **phase 'in**

To **phase in** a new product, method, or law means to gradually start using it.

phase in something or **phase something in** ❏ *The company planned to phase in the computer system over a period of two to three months.* ❏ *All parties agree that any change should be phased in to allow households time to adjust.*

● The **phasing-in** of a new product, method, or law is when you start to use it gradually.

❑ *The next six months will see the gradual phasing-in of the new policy.*

○ **phase 'into**
To **phase** a new product, method, or law **into** something means to gradually start using it in that place or situation.
phase something into something ❑ *More advanced airbags are being phased into new vehicles.*

● **phase 'out**
To **phase out** a product, method, or law means to gradually stop using it.
phase out something ❑ *The government will begin phasing out nuclear power.* ❑ *Some power plants will be phased out in the next four years.*
phase something out ❑ *Environmentalists believe stores should phase plastic bags out altogether.* ● The **phasing out** of a product, method, or law is when you gradually stop using it. ❑ *His most important reform was the phasing out of tax reliefs for business.*

phone /fəʊn/ (**phones, phoning, phoned**)
● **phone a'round → see phone round**
○ **phone 'back**
If you **phone back** or **phone** someone **back**, you phone them for a second time or after they have phoned you. = **call back, ring back**
phone back ❑ *She phoned back later.* ❑ *She phoned back to say that she couldn't come.*
phone someone back ❑ *I said I'd phone them back this morning.* ❑ *I've got to phone my dad back.*

○ **phone 'down**
If you are in a building and you **phone down**, you phone someone on one of the floors below you, usually to ask them to do something for you. ❑ *Just wait while I phone down.* ❑ *[+ to] Nicole phoned down to the hotel switchboard and asked for a wake-up call.*

○ **'phone for**
If you **phone for** something, you phone someone to ask them to provide it for you.
phone for something ❑ *When we've had breakfast you can phone for a taxi.* ❑ *He phoned for an ambulance.*

● **phone 'in**
1 If you **phone in**, you phone a radio or television station because you want to talk on a programme that is being broadcast at the time. ❑ *[+ to] She phoned in to the Charles Boon show.* ● A **phone-in** or **phone-in** programme is a radio or TV programme in which people can phone and give their opinions or ask questions while the programme is being broadcast. ❑ *There's a*

phone-in about it. ❑ *We were listening to a late-night phone-in programme.*
2 If you **phone in**, you phone an organization that helps people because you need their help. ❑ *If you're feeling depressed, you can phone in and speak to one of our counsellors.*
3 If you work for an organization such as a newspaper, the armed forces, or the police and you **phone in** or **phone in** information, you phone them to tell them something.
phone in ❑ *He phoned in to tell them where he was.*
phone in something or **phone something in** ❑ *Reporters phoned in another news story.* ❑ *Lewis phoned the details in.*
4 If you **phone in**, you phone your employer, usually to tell them that you are ill and cannot work that day. ❑ *Judy phoned in to say she had food poisoning.* ❑ *She had phoned in and said she was sick.*
● If you **phone in sick**, you phone your employer to say that you are ill and cannot come to work that day. ❑ *Rob phoned in sick this morning.*
5 If a performer **phones in a performance**, they perform in a way that shows little effort or thought. [mainly AMERICAN, INFORMAL] ❑ *He clearly cares about his art – you never see him phone in a performance.*

○ **phone 'round** (or **phone around**)
[BRITISH]
If you **phone round** or **phone round** a group of people, you phone several people, often to ask them something.
phone round ❑ *I phoned round and eventually my friend Polly agreed to look after our dog.*
phone round someone ❑ *Sally phoned round all Jodie's friends to see if she was with them.*

○ **phone 'through**
If you **phone through**, you make a phone call, usually to get or give information or make some arrangements. ❑ *At the end of the week he phoned through with the news of a possible job.*

❍ **phone 'up**
When you **phone up** or **phone** someone **up**, you telephone someone. = **ring up, call up**
phone someone up ❑ *I'll phone her up tonight.* ❑ *I phoned Joe up, and told him I had to see him.*
phone up someone ❑ *He phoned up everyone he could think of and told them the good news.*
phone up ❑ *Greg phoned up to get the results of his test.* ❑ *She phoned up and apologized.*

pick /pɪk/ (**picks, picking, picked**)
○ **'pick at**
1 If you **pick at** food, you eat very small amounts of it because you are not hungry. = **nibble at**

pick at something ❏ *She picked at her food with obvious lack of interest.*

2 If you **pick at** something, you keep pulling it or scratching it with your fingers.

pick at something ❏ *She sat at her desk, nervously picking at her nail polish.*

3 If you **pick at** a person or their work, you criticize small details.

pick at something/someone ❏ *Let me run through it first, Michael, before you start picking at it.*

○ **pick 'off**

1 If someone **picks off** animals or enemy soldiers, aircraft, or weapons, they shoot at them one at a time and kill or destroy them.

pick off someone/something or **pick someone/something off** ❏ *He circled the soldiers, and began picking them off one by one.*

2 If you **pick off** something, you remove it by pulling it or scratching it with your fingers or a tool.

pick off something or **pick something off** ❏ *She noticed some fluff on the sleeve of her sweater and began picking it off.*

○ **'pick on**

1 If you **pick on** someone, you treat them badly or in an unfair way, often repeatedly. **= get at**

pick on someone ❏ *Maria had complained that the teacher was picking on her.*

2 If you **pick on** one particular person or thing, you choose that one. [BRITISH]

pick on someone/something ❏ *Of all the girls in town, why did you pick on her?* ❏ *Why did you pick on London as a place to study?*

○ **pick 'out**

1 If you can **pick out** someone or something, you can see them but not very clearly. **= make out**

pick out someone/something ❏ *In the mist, I could just pick out two men walking across the field.*

pick someone/something out ❏ *She pointed to a building in the distance and I could just about pick it out.*

NOTE **Discern** is a more formal word for **pick out**.

2 If you **pick out** one thing, you choose it from a group. **= select**

pick out something ❏ *They'll look through the applications and pick out the ones they like.*

pick something out ❏ *She picked a skirt out that she thought Ellie would like.*

3 If you **pick** someone or something **out**, you recognize them in a group of people or things.

pick someone out ❏ *I looked around intently, trying to pick Maggie out in the crowd.*

pick out someone ❏ *Rachel could not pick out Mahina among the crowd.*

4 If part of a painting or design **is picked out**, it is in a different material or colour so that it is very noticeable.

be picked out ❏ [+ *in*] *The letters had been picked out in silver.*

5 If a light **picks out** someone or something, it shines only on them, so you can see them very clearly.

pick out someone/something or **pick someone/something out** ❏ *The headlights picked out an approaching bend.* ❏ *The moonlight picked them out very clearly.*

6 If you **pick out** a tune on a musical instrument, you play it slowly or with difficulty.

pick out something or **pick something out** ❏ [+ *on*] *He picked out a tune on the piano.*

○ **pick 'over**

1 If you **pick over** a group of things, you look at them carefully and choose the ones that you want.

pick over something or **pick something over** ❏ *I saw one old lady picking over a pile of old coats in a corner.* ❏ *By the time I got to the sale, the clothes had been picked over and there was nothing much left.*

2 If someone **picks over** something, they discuss or think about all the details of something unpleasant or embarrassing that has happened.

pick over something ❏ *Journalists picked over the President's alleged affair.*

○ **'pick through**

If you **pick through** things, you look at them carefully to see what you want or if there is anything interesting.

pick through something ❏ *Pick through the pieces and see if you can find one you like.*

○ **pick 'up**

1 If you **pick** something or someone **up**, you lift them up from a surface. **= lift up**

pick up something/someone ❏ *He stooped down to pick up a small child.* ❏ *I bent over to pick up a coin that was on the pavement.*

pick something/someone up ❏ *Dean picked the bags up and walked out of the room.* ❏ *The telephone rang and Judy picked it up.* ❏ *The baby was crying so I picked her up.*

2 If you **pick up**, you answer your phone. [INFORMAL] ❏ *I've called her a few times, but she not picking up.*

3 When you **pick up** someone or something that is waiting to be collected, you go to the place where they are and take them away, often in a car.

pick up someone/something ❑ *We drove to the airport the next morning to pick up Susan.* ❑ *She was going to her parents' house to pick up some clean clothes.*

pick someone/something up ❑ *I picked her up at Covent Garden to take her to lunch.* ● A **pick-up** point, area or place is the place where you go to collect someone or something. ❑ *We track the shipments from the pick-up point to their destinations.* ● A **pick-up** is the act of going to collect someone or something and taking them somewhere. ❑ *I'll leave a message for Kenny to make the pick-up first thing in the morning.*

4 When you **pick** yourself **up** after you have fallen, you stand up again.

pick yourself up ❑ *I picked myself up and brushed the dirt off my trousers.*

5 When you **pick** yourself **up** after a bad experience, you start to do normal things again, and you do not let the bad experience affect you.

pick yourself up ❑ *These things happen and you just have to pick yourself up and move on.*

6 If the police **pick** someone **up**, they arrest the person and take them somewhere to ask them questions. **= take in**

pick up someone or **pick someone up** ❑ *Police had picked up three men in the neighbourhood carrying guns.* ❑ [+ for] *He was picked up for speeding.*

7 If you **pick up** a skill, habit, or attitude, you learn it or start having it after watching and listening to other people.

pick up something or **pick something up** ❑ *Did you pick up any Swedish while you were in Stockholm?* ❑ *I chew gum but I don't want my children to pick up the habit.*

8 If you **pick** something **up**, you buy it.

pick up something or **pick something up** ❑ *I picked up a bargain in the market today.* ❑ *If you're after a camera, you can probably pick one up cheaply here.*

9 If you **pick up** an interesting or useful idea, piece of information, etc., you get it from somewhere.

pick up something or **pick something up** ❑ *I may pick up a couple of useful ideas for my book.* ❑ [+ from] *You can pick up some useful tips from the experts.* ❑ *I picked this recipe up from my mother.*

10 If you **pick up** an illness, you get it from somewhere or something. **= catch**

pick up something or **pick something up** ❑ *She picked up a really nasty infection on her travels.* ❑ [+ from] *I don't know where he got this*

bug from – probably picked it up from school.

11 If you **pick up** a prize, a reputation, or something else that improves your situation, you get it or win it.

pick up something ❑ *Timberlake picked up an award for best album at the MTV Music Awards.* ❑ *He was picking up a lot of support because the public admired his policies.*

12 If someone **picks up the bill/cheque/tab**, they pay for something. [INFORMAL] ❑ [+ for] *Who's picking up the tab for the research?* ❑ *Let me pick up the check this time.*

13 If someone **picks up** a particular amount of money for the work they do, they earn that amount. [INFORMAL]

pick up something ❑ *A nurse picks up around 500 pounds a week.*

14 If you **pick up** someone you do not know, you start talking to them and being friendly towards them because you want to have a sexual relationship with them. [INFORMAL]

pick up someone or **pick someone up** ❑ *I doubt whether Tony ever picked up a woman in his life.* ❑ *Then she went into the bar and nobody tried to pick her up.* ● A **pick-up** is a situation in which someone is trying to start a sexual relationship with someone they have just met. ❑ *I clearly know a pick-up when I see one.*

15 If you **pick up** a room or house, you make it tidy. [AMERICAN, INFORMAL]

pick up something ❑ *When the kids have left home, there'll be no arguing over picking up the family room.*

16 If a person or animal **picks up** a faint smell or a quiet sound, they notice it.

pick up something or **pick something up** ❑ *He sniffed the air, trying to pick up their scent.* ❑ *His ears picked up a strange, muted sound.*

NOTE **Detect** is a more formal word for **pick up**.

17 If a piece of equipment such as a radio or microphone **picks up** a signal or sound, it receives or discovers it.

pick up something or **pick something up** ❑ *These bugging devices were capable of picking up both telephone and room conversations.*

18 If you **pick up** a mistake or problem, you notice it.

pick something up or **pick up something** ❑ *If there are any mistakes in the report, I'll pick them up when I read it.* ❑ *Parents often pick up early problems that health professionals fail to notice.*

19 If you **pick up** a point or subject that someone mentioned before, you mention it again and say something relating to it.

pick up something ❑ *I'd like to pick up the point David made.* ❑ *The President picked up the theme.*

20 If you **pick up** something that you had stopped doing, you start doing it again from the point where you had stopped.
pick up something or **pick something up** ❑ *I have to go now – we can pick up this conversation later.* ❑ *Angelo picked the story up.*

• If you **pick up where you left off**, you start something again from the place where you had stopped. ❑ *I settled down at my desk and picked up where I'd left off on Friday.*

NOTE **Resume** is a more formal word for **pick up**.

21 If trade, business, or the economy of a country **picks up**, it increases or improves after an unsuccessful period. ❑ *The economy is finally picking up.* ❑ *Sales have picked up in recent months.* • A **pick-up** in trade, business, or the economy of a country is an increase or improvement in it. ❑ *Small traders are now reporting a significant pick-up in business.*

22 If someone **picks up**, or their health **picks up**, they get better. ❑ *She's been quite ill but she's starting to pick up now.* ❑ *His health has picked up recently.* • A **pick-me-up** is a drink that you have in order to make you feel healthier and more energetic. = **tonic** [INFORMAL]

23 If the wind **picks up**, it becomes stronger. ❑ *The air was colder and a northwest wind had picked up.*

24 When a vehicle **picks up speed**, or its **speed picks up**, it begins to move more quickly. ❑ *With the wind in the right direction, their speed picked up.* ❑ *We picked up speed going downhill.*

25 When you **pick up the pieces** after something bad has happened, you try to get the situation back to normal again. ❑ *She was left to pick up the pieces of a failed marriage.*

○ **pick 'up after** [INFORMAL]
If you **pick up after** someone, you tidy things that they have left untidy.
pick up after someone ❑ *I'm always cleaning and picking up after everyone.*
pick up after yourself ❑ *We all learned to pick up after ourselves.*

○ **pick 'up on**
1 If you **pick up on** something, you notice it even though other people do not notice it.
pick up on something ❑ *Children are highly sensitive and they will probably pick up on the change in atmosphere in the house.*

2 If you **pick up on** something, you talk more about something that was mentioned before.

pick up on something ❑ *The interviewer picked up on something I'd written in my application.*
❑ *If I can just pick up on something you said earlier.*
3 If you **pick** someone **up on** something that they have said or done, you tell them that you think it is wrong. = **take up on** [BRITISH]
pick someone up on something ❑ *He picked Jane up on the way she'd dealt with the problem.*
❑ *He made one or two mistakes, but no-one picked him up on them.*

○ **pick 'up with** [OLD-FASHIONED]
If you **pick up with** someone, you start meeting them regularly and doing things together.
pick up with someone ❑ *Janice would pick up with anyone who happened to speak to her.*

piece /piːs/ (**pieces, piecing, pieced**)
○ **piece 'out**
If you **piece out** the truth or facts about something, you gradually discover them.
= **work out, suss out**
piece out something or **piece something out** ❑ *We'll see if we can piece out the full story about your ancestors.*

◉ **piece to'gether**
1 If you **piece together** the truth about something, you gradually discover it.
= **work out**
piece together something ❑ *I tried to piece together exactly what had happened.* ❑ [+ from] *In the past, historians would piece together the evidence from diaries.*
piece something together ❑ *Using manuscript sources, it has been possible to piece the whole story together.*
NOTE **Deduce** is a more formal word for **piece together**.
2 If you **piece** something **together**, you make it by joining several things together.
piece together something ❑ *This is a nation struggling to piece together a new identity.*
piece something together ❑ *He took the torn letter from the waste basket and carefully pieced it together.*

pig /pɪɡ/ (**pigs, pigging, pigged**)
○ **pig 'out** [INFORMAL]
If someone **pigs out**, they eat a lot of food at one time. = **gorge** ❑ *He'd pigged out in a fast-food place beforehand.* ❑ [+ on] *I pigged out on burgers, popcorn and pizza.* • A **pig-out** is when someone eats a lot of food. ❑ *To many people these days, the winter holiday period is little more than a week-long pig-out.*

pile /paɪl/ (**piles, piling, piled**)
○ **pile 'in**
If a group of people **pile in**, they all quickly

get into a place or vehicle at the same time.
= crowd in ❑ *The engine started and we all piled in.*

○ **pile 'into**
If a group of people **pile into** a place or vehicle, they all quickly get into it at the same time. **= crowd into**
pile into something ❑ *We quickly packed up and piled into the bus.*

○ **pile 'on**
1 If people **pile on**, they all try to get on something, especially a vehicle, at the same time. ❑ *The bus came and we all piled on.* ❑ *[+ to] A crowd of schoolkids were piling on to the train, trying to get the best seats.*
2 If you **pile on** something, or **pile** it **on** someone, you give more and more of it to other people to deal with.
pile on something or **pile something on**
❑ *They really pile the work on, don't they?* ❑ *Schools pile on the pressure to make sure that their pupils reach exam targets.*
pile something on someone ❑ *They pile the work on you as if you were three secretaries instead of just one.*
3 If you **pile on weight** or **pile on the pounds**, you become much fatter and heavier. ❑ *Now a month old, Claudia is at home and piling on weight.* [INFORMAL] ❑ *Carly started to pile on the pounds when she was 18.*

○ **pile 'out**
If a group of people **pile out** they all get out of a place or vehicle quickly, at the same time. ❑ *[+ of] Everyone piled out of the car.* ❑ *They all piled out with their cameras.*

○ **pile 'up**
1 If things **pile up** or if you **pile** them **up**, they form a pile or you make them form a pile. **= heap up**
pile up ❑ *Garbage is piling up on the sidewalks.*
pile up something ❑ *He piled up the plates.* ❑ *Her hair had been piled up on top of her head.*
pile something up ❑ *Joanne piled the dishes up next to the sink.* ❑ *He told his men to gather some rocks and pile them up.*
2 If several vehicles **pile up**, they crash into each other. [AMERICAN] ❑ *Cars piled up on the icy roads.* ● A **pile-up** is a road accident in which several vehicles crash into each other. ❑ *There had been a twenty-car pile-up on the motorway.*
3 If things, especially bad things **pile up**, or you **pile** them **up**, you get more and more of them. **= mount up**
pile up ❑ *Bills were piling up and she didn't know how she was going to pay them.* ❑ *Problems were piling up at work.*

pile up something or **pile something up**
❑ *Last year alone, the company piled up losses totalling £4 billion.*

pimp /pɪmp/ (**pimps, pimping, pimped**)
○ **pimp 'up**
You **pimp** something such as a car **up** when you add extra decoration to make it different from other things of its type, often in a way that people consider to be extreme or in bad taste.
pimp up something or **pimp something up**
❑ *They are famous for pimping up Range Rovers with colourful leather seats and screens for the children in the back.* ❑ *He buys secondhand cars and pimps them up.*

pin /pɪn/ (**pins, pinning, pinned**)
○ **pin 'down**
1 If you try to **pin down** something, you try to say exactly what it is or what it is like.
= nail down
pin down something or **pin something down**
❑ *Police have managed to pin down when and where he was last seen.* ❑ *The project failed for reasons that were hard to pin down.*
NOTE **Specify** is a more formal word for **pin down**.
2 If you **pin** someone **down**, you make them give you exact details or a definite decision about something, which they have tried to avoid doing. **= nail down**
pin someone down ❑ *[+ to] Try to pin him down to a date.* ❑ *[+ on] Barnier refused to be pinned down on a deadline for completing the talks.*
3 If someone or something **pins** you **down**, they hold you on the ground or other surface and stop you from moving.
= hold down
pin someone down or **pin down someone**
❑ *The strong arms were around me, pinning me down so that I couldn't move.* ❑ *They pinned down the guards.*

○ **'pin on** (or **pin to**)
If you **pin** something **on** something, especially a surface, you attach it to that thing with a pin.
pin something on something ❑ *Two photos had been pinned on the noticeboard.* ❑ *She pinned the badge on the little boy's coat.*

○ **'pin on** (or **pin upon**)
1 If you **pin** a crime or the blame for something **on** someone, you say that they did it, especially when this is not true.
pin something on someone ❑ *We didn't steal the car. You can't pin that on us.* ❑ *Pinning the responsibility on one individual is just unfair.*

2 If you **pin your faith/hopes on** something or someone, you hope very much that a thing will happen or that a person will help you. ❑ *Many cancer sufferers are pinning their hopes on this new drug.*

○ **'pin to → see pin on**

○ **pin 'up**

1 If you **pin up** a notice, a picture, etc., you fix it to a wall using a pin. **= put up**
pin something up or **pin up something**
❑ *She printed the notice and pinned it up.* ❑ *You might like to pin up a large calendar.* ❑ [+ on] *The map was pinned up on the wall.* ● A **pin-up** is a picture of an attractive or famous person that someone puts on a wall. ❑ *The bathroom wall was plastered with pin-ups of film stars.*

2 If you **pin up** part of a piece of clothing or material, you use pins to fasten the bottom of it to a part of it that is higher up.
pin up something or **pin something up**
❑ *She was bending down, pinning up the hem of her sister's dress.* ❑ *He watched in the mirror as the tailor pinned his trousers up.*

3 If a woman **pins** her hair **up**, she fixes it to the top of her head with hairpins.
pin something up or **pin up something**
❑ *Julia was pinning up her freshly-washed hair.*

○ **'pin upon → see pin on**

pinch-hit (pinch-hits, pinch-hitting, pinch-hit)

○ **'pinch-hit for** [AMERICAN]
If you **pinch-hit for** someone, you do something for them because they are suddenly unable to do it.
pinch-hit for someone ❑ *The staff here can pinch-hit for each other when the hotel is busy.*

pine /paɪn/ (pines, pining, pined)

○ **pine a'way**
If someone **pines away**, they stop eating and enjoying life, usually because they are sad that they are not with someone they love. **= waste away** ❑ *I believe she actually pined away – lost her will to live.* ❑ *I've been pining away without you.*

pip /pɪp/ (pips, pipping, pipped)

○ **'pip to**
If someone **is pipped to** something such as a prize or an award, or someone **pips** them **to** it, they are defeated by only a small amount.
be pipped to something ❑ *Lazio were pipped to the title by Milan.*
pip someone to something ❑ *She pipped actress Meryl Streep to the part.*

pipe /paɪp/ (pipes, piping, piped)

○ **pipe 'down** [INFORMAL]
If someone **pipes down**, they stop talking so loudly or they stop complaining. ❑ *Pipe down at the back there!* ❑ *Officials suggested she should pipe down on the issue.*

○ **pipe 'up**
If someone who has been silent, **pipes up**, they suddenly say something.
pipe up something ❑ *A man shouted at them, and after a pause a small voice piped up, 'Can we have our ball back?'*
pipe up ❑ *'She may know,' Ted piped up, struggling to be helpful.*

piss /pɪs/ (pisses, pissing, pissed)

> **Piss** is a very rude, informal word.

○ **piss a'bout** (or **piss around**) [BRITISH]
1 If someone **pisses about**, they waste a lot of time and annoy other people by behaving in a silly or childish way. ❑ *We spent a lot of time just pissing about.* ❑ *For me, 30 was the age to stop pissing around.*
2 To **piss** someone **about** means to treat someone badly by not doing what you have said you will do, or by changing your mind a lot.
piss someone about ❑ *Don't start pissing me about, Billy.* ❑ *I've been pissed around by too many people already.*

○ **piss a'way**
If you **piss** something **away**, you waste it in a silly way.
piss something away or **piss away something**
❑ *He earns a lot of money but just pisses it away.* ❑ *I'm not going to piss away this opportunity.*
NOTE **Squander** is a more formal word for **piss away**.

○ **'piss down** [BRITISH]
If it **pisses down**, it rains very hard. ❑ *It's really pissing down out there.*

❂ **piss 'off**
1 If a person tells someone else to **piss off**, they are telling them in a rude way to go away. [BRITISH] ❑ *Now, piss off, and take your friend with you!*
2 If someone **pisses off**, they leave. [BRITISH] ❑ *Jules pissed off after ten minutes.* ❑ *Maybe I should just piss off home?*
3 If someone or something **pisses** you **off**, they annoy you.
piss someone off ❑ *The guy was beginning to piss me off.*
piss off someone ❑ *She left, having pissed off everyone in the room.* ● If you are **pissed off**, you are annoyed. ❑ *She sounded pissed off.* ❑ [+ with] *I'm pretty pissed off with the lot of them*

○ **'piss with** [BRITISH]
If it **pisses with rain**, it rains very hard.
❏ *It pissed with rain all day.*

pit /pɪt/ (**pits, pitting, pitted**)
○ **'pit against**
To **pit** one person or thing **against** another person or thing means to make them compete or fight against each other.
pit someone/something against someone/something ❏ *He was pitted against a really first-class player.*
● To **pit your wits against** something or someone means to compete against them using all your knowledge, skill or intelligence. ❏ *I'll be pitting my wits against some of the finest minds in the business.*

pitch /pɪtʃ/ (**pitches, pitching, pitched**)
○ **'pitch at**
1 If you **pitch** something **at** a particular level or something **is pitched at** a particular level, you set it at that level.
be pitched at something ❏ *I think the material is pitched at too high a level for our purposes.*
pitch something at something ❏ *The government has pitched High Street interest rates at a new level.*
2 If a product or service **is pitched at** a particular group of people or a company **pitches** it **at** them, the product or service is mainly intended for that group.
be pitched at someone ❏ *The magazine is pitched at teenagers.*
pitch something at someone ❏ *The company is also pitching this software at image-editing enthusiasts.*

○ **'pitch for**
If someone **pitches for** something such as a business deal or people's votes, they try to persuade people to give them to them.
pitch for something ❏ *Most architects have to pitch for jobs.* ❏ *It was middle-class votes they were pitching for.*

○ **'pitch 'in** [INFORMAL]
1 If you **pitch in**, you help other people with a job that needs to be done. **= muck in**
❏ *The farm was small and we all had to pitch in.*
❏ [+ *to*-infinitive] *Richard's family have all pitched in to help with the move.*
2 If someone **pitches in** or **pitches in** an amount of money, they pay part of the cost of something, and other people pay the rest.
pitch in ❏ [+ *to*-infinitive] *The club's members have pitched in to pay his legal fees.*
pitch in something ❏ *He pitched in about $25,000.*

○ **pitch 'into**
1 If you **pitch into** something, you start doing it with a lot of energy. **= dive into**
pitch into something ❏ *Be careful not to pitch into your exercises before warming up.*
2 If someone **pitches into** you, they attack you, either by hitting you, or by criticizing you. **= lay into** [INFORMAL]
pitch into someone ❏ *The boss really pitched into me and told me I wasn't working hard enough.*

pivot /'pɪvət/ (**pivots, pivoting, pivoted**)
○ **'pivot on** (or **pivot upon**)
If something **pivots on** something else, it depends on that thing or is based on that thing. **= hang on**
pivot on something ❏ *Success or failure pivoted on a single exam.* ❏ *November's election will pivot on two issues – foreign policy and security.*

plague /pleɪg/ (**plagues, plaguing, plagued**)
○ **'plague with**
1 If someone or something **is plagued with** something bad, it causes a lot of problems or suffering for them for a long time.
be plagued with something ❏ *The development of this technology has been plagued with problems.* ❏ *He has been plagued with injuries this season.*
2 To **plague** someone **with** something such as questions or requests means to annoy them by asking a lot of questions or repeatedly requesting something.
plague someone with something ❏ *He plagued her with questions.* ❏ *A stalker who plagued his ex-girlfriend with offensive phone calls has been jailed.*

plan /plæn/ (**plans, planning, planned**)
○ **plan a'head**
If you **plan ahead**, you make decisions and arrangements about something that will or might happen in the future. ❏ *I admire people who plan ahead.* ❏ *Sometimes, however much you plan ahead, things change.*

❍ **'plan for**
If you **plan for** a particular thing or event, you consider it when you are making your arrangements.
plan for something ❏ *Why hadn't I planned for this possibility?* ❏ *The fact is that staff leave and, as a business, you have to plan for this.*

❍ **'plan on**
1 If you **plan on** doing something, you intend to do it.
plan on doing something ❏ *Are you planning on staying in London?* ❏ *He was planning on visiting his parents the next day.*

2 If you do **not plan on** a particular thing, you do not realize that it might happen and so do not consider it when making arrangements.

not plan on something ❑ *I hadn't planned on the bad weather.* ❑ *I didn't plan on so many people coming.*

NOTE **Expect** is a more general word for **plan on**.

○ **plan 'out**

If you **plan** something **out**, you decide exactly what you will do and how you will do it.

plan out something or **plan something out** ❑ *Bob poured himself a drink and planned out the rest of his day.* ❑ *I'm going to ask her for a date – I've planned it all out in my head.*

plane /pleɪn/ (**planes, planing, planed**)

○ **plane 'down**

If you **plane down** a piece of wood, you make it smaller or smoother using a piece of equipment called a plane.

plane down something or **plane something down** ❑ *I planed down the four corners.* ❑ *He planed the panel down.*

plant /plɑːnt, plænt/ (**plants, planting, planted**)

○ **plant 'out**

When you **plant out** young plants, you take them out of a container and put them in the ground where you want them to grow.

plant out something or **plant something out** ❑ *Don't plant out the herbs until after the last frost.* ❑ *Start the bean plants off indoors and then plant them out in May.*

○ **'plant with**

When someone **plants** land **with** a particular type of plant or crop, they put that plant or crop into the land to grow there.

plant something with something ❑ *They plan to plant the area with grass and trees.*

plaster /'plɑːstə, 'plæs-/ (**plasters, plastering, plastered**)

○ **'plaster with**

If something **is plastered with** pictures, notices etc., or if you **plaster** something **with** pictures, notices, etc., you stick a lot of them all over it.

be plastered with something ❑ *His room is plastered with pictures of cars.*

plaster something with something ❑ *They had plastered the streets with posters advertising the event.*

plate /pleɪt/ (**plates, plating, plated**)

○ **plate 'up**

You **plate up** food when you put it on a plate ready to be served, especially in a restaurant.

plate up something or **plate something up** ❑ *Grill the fish and plate it up with some green sauce.* ❑ *I suggest you plate up the starter before your guests arrive.*

play /pleɪ/ (**plays, playing, played**)

✪ **play a'bout** → see **play around**

○ **play a'bout with** → see **play around with**

○ **play a'long**

1 If you **play along**, you pretend to agree with someone or do what they want for a short time because you do not want to make them angry or because you want something from them. ❑ *You could fight back, or you might play along and wait to escape.* ❑ [+ with] *He had realized I wouldn't play along with his plan.*

2 If you **play** someone **along**, you tell them something that is not true.

play someone along ❑ *'Is it true that you used to play football for Liverpool?' I decided to play him along and said it was.*

✪ **play a'round** (or **play about** [mainly BRITISH])

1 When children **play around** or **play around** somewhere, they play in a place.

play around ❑ *Teresa would be doing the housework while the kids played around.* ❑ *The children were playing about in the sand.*

play around somewhere ❑ *Didn't I tell you to play around the yard?*

2 If someone **plays around**, they behave in a silly way. ❑ *Stop playing around, and eat your dinner!* ❑ *At school, I just played about and didn't care about doing any work.*

3 If someone **plays around**, they have sex with someone who is not their husband, wife or partner. [RUDE] ❑ *Adrian was a happily married man who didn't play around.* ❑ [+ with] *She's been playing around with another man.*

○ **play a'round with** (or **play about with** [mainly BRITISH])

1 If you **play around with** something, you keep moving it from one place or position to another.

play around with something ❑ *We spent the whole afternoon playing around with bits of string.*

2 If someone **plays around with** something, they change it in a way that is bad. = **mess around with, tamper with**

play around with something ❑ *It's frightening*

that scientists are playing around with the hormone content of plants.

3 If you **play around with** things, you think of several ideas or try several things before deciding which is best.

play around with something ❑ *Don't be afraid to play around with the colours and shades – you might find some exciting new styles!*

4 If someone **plays around with** another person, they have a sexual relationship with them although they do not love them.

play around with someone ❑ *You've just been playing around with me.*

○ **'play at**

1 If someone **plays at** something, they do it but not in a serious way.

play at something ❑ *You can't play at being a farmer. It's a hard job.* ❑ *She felt hurt when people said she was just playing at politics.*

2 If a child, **plays at** being a particular type of person, they pretend to be that person when they are playing.

play at something ❑ *Small children often play at being grown-ups.* ❑ *The children were playing at doctors and nurses.*

3 If you do not know what someone **is playing at**, you do not understand what they are trying to achieve. [INFORMAL]

be playing at ❑ *She began to wonder what he was playing at.*

● If you ask **What are you playing at**, you are asking someone angrily what they are doing. ❑ *What are you playing at? Bring my keys back right now!*

○ **play 'back**

When you **play back** a tape or film on which you have recorded sound or pictures, you listen to it or watch it.

play back something ❑ *I played back a taped interview with Dr. Sanger.*

play something back ❑ *Let's play the tape back and hear the conversation again.* ❑ *He recorded the conversation and then played it back.*

● **Playback** is when you listen to or watch a tape onto which you have recorded something. ❑ *On playback he found that he had a very clear recording of the telephone call.* ❑ *Then all you have to do is tap on the playback button.*

○ **play 'down**

If you **play** something **down**, you try to make people think that it is less important than it really is. ≠ **play up, exaggerate**

play down something ❑ *The Minister tried to play down the seriousness of the problem.*

play something down ❑ *Mr Wang was determined to play the crisis down and pretend that*

all was normal. ❑ *I tried to play it down so my parents wouldn't be worried.*

○ **play 'off**

When two people or teams who have the same number of points in a sports competition **play off**, they play a game to decide which one is the winner. ❑ *Liverpool and Everton will play off for third place.* ● A **play-off** game is a game between two people or teams who have the same number of points, to decide which one is the winner. ❑ *Andrews lost to Daly in the play-off.*

○ **play 'off against**

If you **play** one person or group **off against** another, you try to make them compete or argue because you think it will help you.

play someone off against someone ❑ *Children sometimes play one parent off against the other.*

○ **play 'on**

1 If you **play on**, you continue playing a musical instrument. ❑ *She forced herself to play on.*

2 If the referee tells players to **play on** during a game of football or rugby, he or she is telling them to continue playing even though someone has broken the rules of the game. ❑ *The referee told them to play on.*

○ **'play on** (or **play upon**)

1 If you **play on** people's feelings, attitudes, or weaknesses, you deliberately use them in order to achieve what you want. = **exploit**

play on something ❑ *He used to play on their prejudices and their fears.* ❑ *A ruthless con man, he had played upon her loneliness.*

2 If a writer or speaker **plays on** a particular idea or word, they use it in a clever way.

play on something ❑ *An older child will really appreciate the sense of humour in books that play on words.*

○ **play 'out**

1 If people **play out** roles or events, they perform them or are involved in them without controlling them. = **enact**

play out something or **play something out** ❑ *Parents play out the roles assigned to them.* ❑ *The final drama was played out on June 17th.*

2 When actors **play out** a scene, they act it.

play out something ❑ *He was playing out scenes for his next movie.*

3 If someone **plays out** a feeling or situation that they have imagined, they express it in their actions.

play out something ❑ *Children frequently play out their fantasies, whether this means being a pirate or a princess.*

4 If you **play out** a sports game, you play it until the end.

play out something or **play something out** ❏ He once broke his jaw twenty minutes in, but still played out the game. ❏ He showed courage in playing the game out.

5 If something **plays out** or **plays** itself **out**, it happens over a period of time.

play out ❏ We'll just have to see how the situation plays out.

play itself out ❏ By the time the drama had played itself out, the defence minister had quit.

○ **play 'through**

If you **play** a piece of music **through**, you play it from beginning to end.

play something through ❏ She opened a book of Bach preludes and played one through.

✿ **play 'up**

1 If you **play up** a fact or feature, you emphasize it and try to make people think that it is more important than it really is. **= exaggerate**; **≠ play down**

play up something ❏ The temptation for a journalist is to play up the sensational aspects of the story.

play something up ❏ In England, the media would play it up.

2 If a machine **is playing up**, it is not working properly. [BRITISH, INFORMAL]

be playing up ❏ My phone is playing up again.

3 If a part of your body **is playing up** or **is playing** you **up**, it is not working properly or is hurting. [BRITISH, INFORMAL]

be playing up ❏ Is your arm playing up? ❏ His leg was playing up, causing him to limp slightly.

be playing someone up ❏ My leg's been playing me up again.

4 If a child **plays up** or **plays** you **up**, they behave badly and are difficult to control. [BRITISH, INFORMAL]

play up ❏ Louis was playing up and refusing to eat.

play someone up ❏ If she starts playing you up, let me know.

○ **'play upon** → see **play on**

○ **play 'up to**

1 If you **play up to** someone, you try to please them because you want them to like you or do something for you.

play up to someone ❏ He says and does exactly what he likes – no one could accuse him of playing up to journalists.

2 To **play up to** an impression that people generally have about someone or something is to deliberately do things to make that impression continue.

play up to something ❏ He's keen to play up to his image as the wild man of rock.

✿ **'play with**

1 When children **play with** a toy, they use it to amuse themselves, often in an imaginative way.

play with something ❏ She was playing with a doll. ❏ He didn't have any toys to play with.

2 If you **play with** something, you keep moving it from one position to another without thinking about what you are doing, for example because you are bored or nervous.

play with something ❏ She sat there playing with a bottle of suntan lotion. ❏ I told her off for playing with her food.

3 If you **play with the idea of** doing something, you consider doing it, although you will probably not do it. **= toy with** ❏ She had played with the idea of moving to an apartment of her own.

4 If a writer or speaker **plays with** words or ideas, he or she uses them in a clever and unusual way for a special effect.

play with something ❏ The movie plays with the idea that a seemingly trivial decision can affect your whole life. ❏ Comedians make their living by playing with words.

5 When a child **plays with** another child, the two children play together.

play with someone ❏ You'll enjoy having other boys to play with. ❏ Go upstairs and play with your friends. ❏ Babies needs to be played with.

6 If someone **is playing with** someone else they are treating them unfairly because they are not telling them their real feelings.

be playing with someone ❏ 'Al,' she suddenly said, 'Stop playing with me like this.'

7 If someone **plays with** himself or herself they touch their own sexual organs in order to get sexual pleasure. [INFORMAL, RUDE]

play with yourself

plead /pliːd/ (pleads, pleading, pleaded)

✿ **'plead for**

1 If you **plead for** something, you ask for it in a very determined and emotional way.

plead for something ❏ Daniel held up one finger, pleading for a little more time. ❏ The more he pleaded for mercy, the more they beat him.

2 When a lawyer **pleads for** someone, they speak for them and try to defend them in court.

plead for someone ❏ She faced the difficult task of pleading for a defendant who was obviously guilty.

✿ **'plead with**

If you **plead with** someone, you ask them for something in a very determined and emotional way.

plead with someone ❑ [+ to-infinitive]
I pleaded with him to tell me. ❑ *I pleaded with her, but she didn't want to go.*

plod /plɒd/ (plods, plodding, plodded)

○ **plod a'way** [INFORMAL]
If you **plod away**, you continue doing something without much enthusiasm.
❑ *Keep plodding away and it'll get done.* ❑ [+ at] *I plodded away at the hard subjects, like English and Maths.*

○ **plod 'on**
If you **plod on**, you continue walking or doing something slowly or without much enthusiasm. ❑ *The horse plodded on, exhausted.* ❑ [+ with] *She plodded on with her work, feeling tired and bored.*

plonk /plɒŋk/ (plonks, plonking, plonked)

○ **plonk 'down** [BRITISH, INFORMAL]
① If you **plonk** something **down**, you put it down quickly and carelessly.
plonk something down or **plonk down something** ❑ *The waitress plonked down the tray of food.* ❑ *He plonked the bags down on the table.*
② If you **plonk down** or **plonk** yourself **down**, you sit down quickly and heavily.
plonk down ❑ *She plonked down in the armchair and closed her eyes.*
plonk yourself down ❑ *He plonked himself down on the sofa next to Mary.*

plop /plɒp/ (plops, plopping, plopped)

○ **plop 'down** [INFORMAL]
If you **plop down** or **plop** yourself **down** somewhere, you sit down quickly. = **sit down**
plop down ❑ *I plopped down on one of the dark red sofas.*
plop yourself down ❑ *He plopped himself down on the grass.*

plot /plɒt/ (plots, plotting, plotted)

○ **'plot against**
If people **plot against** someone, they plan secretly to kill them or remove them from an important and powerful job.
plot against someone ❑ *He had been accused of plotting against the President.*

○ **plot 'out**
If you **plot out** a plan or course of events, you decide what you will do. = **plan out**
plot something out or **plot out something**
❑ *I had already plotted out the scenario in my mind.* ❑ *I was 27 and already had my future plotted out.*

plough /plaʊ/ (ploughs, ploughing, ploughed)

Plough is also spelled **plow** in American English.

○ **plough a'head**
If a person or organization **ploughs ahead**, they continue to do something in spite of problems or disagreement. = **forge ahead**
❑ *He didn't wait for my reply, he simply ploughed ahead.* ❑ [+ with] *The government ploughed ahead with expansion plans despite the opposition.*

○ **plough 'back**
If you **plough** profits **back**, you spend them on improving the business so that you can make more money.
plough something back or **plough back something** ❑ *He intended to plough some of that money back.* ❑ [+ into] *Profits are ploughed back into the business in order to expand or create more jobs.*

○ **plough 'in**
If someone **ploughs in** a crop, they dig plants into the ground to make the soil better for growing crops.
plough something in or **plough in something**
❑ *The stalks are left to be ploughed in for the next planting.*

❂ **plough 'into**
① If something **ploughs into** something else, it hits it with a lot of force.
plough into something ❑ *The car skidded before ploughing into the bank.* ❑ *He ploughed into the back of the van.*
② If you **plough** money **into** something or money **is ploughed into** something, you spend a lot of money on it.
plough something into something ❑ *The company has ploughed more than 400 million pounds into the new factory.*
be ploughed into something ❑ *Nearly half a million pounds has been ploughed into the new venture.*
③ If someone **ploughs** a crop **into** the land, they dig the plants into the ground to make the soil better for growing crops.
plough something into something ❑ *The crop can be grown as green manure to be ploughed into the land.*

○ **plough 'on**
If you **plough on**, you continue walking or doing something even though it is difficult. ❑ *James hesitated for a moment and then ploughed on.* ❑ [+ with] *He is ploughing on with the tour despite being advised not to walk on his injured foot.*

○ **'plough through**
① If you **plough through** a meal or piece of work, you eat it all or do it all, although there is a lot of it.
plough through something ❑ *He ploughed through a large plate of spaghetti.* ❑ *I haven't had time to plough through all these files yet.*

2 To **plough through** something means to move through it with difficulty.
plough through something ❑ They ploughed slowly through the snow.

3 If a vehicle or a missile **ploughs through** something, it goes through it with a lot of speed and force.
plough through something ❑ The car ploughed through three gardens and flattened a tree.

○ **plough 'up**
If you **plough up** an area of land, you turn the soil over using a plough, usually to prepare it for growing crops.
plough up something or **plough something up** ❑ The farmer was keen to buy the field, plough it up and turn in to arable land.

plow /plaʊ/ (plows, plowing, plowed) → see **plough**

pluck /plʌk/ (plucks, plucking, plucked)
○ **'pluck at**
If you **pluck at** something, you pull it quickly several times, especially because you are nervous or because you want to get someone's attention. = **pull at**
pluck at something ❑ Lucas plucked at my jacket and asked if he could come too. ❑ He sat there plucking at the grass.

○ **'pluck from** [LITERARY]
1 If you **pluck** something **from** somewhere, you pull it quickly from where it is.
pluck something from something ❑ I plucked a lemon from the tree. ❑ She plucked the note from Adam's hand.

2 To **pluck** someone **from** a state or position in which they are not known means to make them suddenly famous.
pluck someone from something ❑ The agency plucked Naomi from obscurity and turned her into one of the world's top models.

3 To **pluck** someone **from** a dangerous place or situation means to rescue them from it.
pluck someone from something
❑ Helicopters plucked survivors from the sinking ship.

○ **pluck 'out of**
You **pluck** something such as a figure **out of** the air when you state it without doing any research, often getting it wrong.
pluck something out of something ❑ The minister seems to have just plucked this figure out of the air.

plug /plʌg/ (plugs, plugging, plugged)
○ **plug a'way** [INFORMAL]
If you **plug away**, you keep working hard at something even though it is difficult or

boring. ❑ Just keep plugging away. ❑ [+ at] She plugged away at her maths.

○ **plug 'in**
If you **plug in** a piece of electrical equipment, you connect it to an electricity supply by pushing its plug into an electric socket. ≠ **unplug**
plug in something ❑ I plugged in the kettle.
❑ He picked up his MP3 player and plugged in the earphones. ❑ You shouldn't leave electrical equipment plugged in while you're away.
plug something in ❑ Plug the television in and then switch it on.

○ **plug 'into**
1 If you **plug** a piece of electrical equipment **into** something, you connect it to the thing, for example by using a plug.
plug something into something ❑ She plugged one end of the cable into the back of the monitor. ❑ Plug it into the mains.

2 If a piece of electrical equipment **plugs into** a source of electricity or another piece of equipment, it is designed to be powered by electricity or to be connected to the other piece of equipment.
plug into something ❑ This USB stick plugs into the back of any TV or radio. ❑ The charger plugs into an ordinary mains socket.

3 If you **plug** something **into** a hole, you fit it into the hole.
plug something into something ❑ He plugged some cotton wool into his ear.

4 If you **plug into** a computer system, you are able to use it or see the information stored on it.
plug into something ❑ It is possible to plug into remote databases to pick up information.

5 If you **plug into** a group of people or their ideas, you find out about them and try to understand them. [AMERICAN, INFORMAL]
plug into something ❑ It is difficult to get business leaders to plug into social and community causes.

○ **plug 'up**
If you **plug up** a hole, you put something in it so that it is blocked. = **block up, bung up**
plug up something or **plug something up**
❑ She suggested plugging up the hole. ❑ He had tried to plug the leaks up.

plumb /plʌm/ (plumbs, plumbing, plumbed)
○ **plumb 'in** [BRITISH]
If you **plumb in** a bath, toilet, or washing machine, you connect it to the water pipes in a building.
plumb in something or **plumb something in**
❑ She knew how to plumb in a bath. ❑ We've

bought the washing machine, but it needs to be plumbed in. ❑ *Someone's coming to plumb the washing machine in.*

plumb 'into [BRITISH]

If you **plumb** something **into** the heating, water, or drainage system in a building, you connect it to that system.

plumb something into something ❑ *The shower can be plumbed into the existing central heating system.*

lump /plʌmp/ (**plumps, plumping, plumped**)

plump 'down [INFORMAL]

1 If you **plump down** or **plump** yourself **down**, you sit down quickly and heavily. **= plonk down**

plump down ❑ *She plumped down next to me.*
plump yourself down ❑ *Clara plumped herself down on the bed.*

2 If you **plump** something **down**, you put it down quickly and carelessly. **= plonk down**
plump something down or **plump down something** ❑ *She picked up the bags and plumped them down on the table.* ❑ *He plumped down three pairs of shoes on the counter.*

'plump for [INFORMAL]

If you **plump for** someone or something, you choose them, especially after you have thought carefully. **= opt for**
plump for something/someone ❑ *In the end, they plumped for the purple sofa.*

plump 'out [OLD-FASHIONED]

If someone **plumps out**, they become fatter. **= fill out** ❑ *Her face had plumped out.*

plump 'up

If you **plump up** something soft, you shake it in order to make it more round in shape.

plump up something or **plump something up** ❑ *She was making the bed and plumping up the pillows.* ❑ *Jackie plumped the cushions up and switched on the table lamps.*

lunge /plʌndʒ/ (**plunges, plunging, plunged**)

plunge 'in

If you **plunge in**, you suddenly start doing or saying something, without thinking carefully or preparing for it. ❑ *Hardly stopping to think, I plunged in and told him the problem.* ❑ *I plunged in hastily with another question.*

plunge 'into

1 If you **plunge** an object **into** something, you push it quickly or violently into it.
plunge something into something ❑ *She plunged her face into a bowl of cold water.*

2 If you **plunge into** an activity, you suddenly start doing it with great energy. **= dive into**
plunge into something ❑ *Marx immediately plunged into political work.*

3 To **plunge into** or **be plunged into** a bad state is to suddenly start to be in that state.
plunge into something ❑ *We must stop these countries from plunging into economic chaos.*
be plunged into something ❑ *You got the feeling that at any moment, he could be plunged into depression.*

ply /plaɪ/ (**plies, plying, plied**)

○ **'ply with**

1 If you **ply** someone **with** food or drink, you keep on giving them more of it.
ply someone with something ❑ *Dolly plied me with marshmallows and potato chips.* ❑ *Martha was plying me with drinks all evening.*

2 If you **ply** someone **with questions**, you keep asking them questions. ❑ *I plied him with questions about his novel.*

poach /pəʊtʃ/ (**poaches, poaching, poached**)

○ **'poach from**

If an organization **poaches** a member or customer **from** another organization, they secretly or dishonestly persuade them to join them or become their customers.
poach someone from something ❑ *The new editor was poached from a rival newspaper.* ❑ *The company continued to poach customers from its competitors.*

point /pɔɪnt/ (**points, pointing, pointed**)

✪ **point 'out**

1 If you **point out** an object or person, you tell someone that they are there or use your hand to show them.
point something/someone out ❑ *Dino had pointed her out at the party.* ❑ [+ to] *The taxi driver pointed the cathedral out to us.* ❑ *Point her out to me if you see her.*
point out something/someone ❑ *They walked up the street, and she pointed out the café.*

2 If you **point** something **out**, you give people an important piece of information that they did not know.
point out something ❑ *Critics were quick to point out the weaknesses in these arguments.* ❑ *She pointed out that he was wrong.*
point something out ❑ [+ to] *When I pointed this out to Graham, he got angry.*

✪ **'point to**

1 If you **point to** a fact or event, you mention it to prove what you are saying in an argument or discussion.

point to something ❏ *Supporters of the scheme point to a number of recent success stories.*
2 If one fact or event **points to** another, it shows that the other one is likely to be true or to happen.
point to something ❏ *Any one of these symptoms point to a severe infection.*

○ **point 'up** [FORMAL]
To **point up** something is to emphasize it.
point up something ❏ *The research points up the differences between men and women.*

poke /pəʊk/ (pokes, poking, poked)

○ **poke a'round** (or **poke about, poke round** [mainly BRITISH])
1 If you **poke around**, you move a lot of things in a place in order to look for something. ❏ *I don't want him poking around in my drawers.* ❏ [+ in] *I poked around in the kitchen, checking out the fridge and the cupboards.* ● If you have a **poke around**, you move a lot of things because you are looking for something. ❏ *She had a poke around in his office.*
2 If you **poke around** a place such as a shop or town, you go there and look at what is there.
poke around something ❏ *I spent one morning poking around a music shop specializing in 1980s music.*

○ **'poke at**
If you **poke at** something, you push something sharp towards it and touch it with it several times. **= prod at**
poke at something ❏ *Dan was poking at the food on his plate.* ❏ [+ with] *He started poking at the fire with a stick.*

○ **poke 'out**
1 If a small part of something **pokes out**, that part can be seen while the larger part of it is covered. **= stick out** ❏ *The blanket was too small and my feet were poking out.* ❏ [+ of] *An umbrella was poking out of her bag.*
[NOTE] **Protrude** is a more formal word for **poke out.**
2 If you **poke** something **out**, you move it so that it suddenly appears from a place where before it was covered. **= stick out**
poke something out or **poke out something** ❏ *She poked her tongue out at me.* ❏ [+ of] *I poked my head out of the tent to see what the noise was.*

○ **poke 'round** → see **poke around**

○ **poke 'through**
1 If something **pokes through** or **pokes through** something, a small part of it starts to appear, although the rest is still covered.
poke through ❏ *The spring flowers are starting to poke through.*

poke through something ❏ *The chair had a rusty spring poking through the fabric.*
2 If you **poke** something **through** something, you push it through a hole or gap in something.
poke something through something ❏ *He poked a finger through the bars of the cage.*

○ **poke 'up**
1 If something **pokes up**, a small part of it appears over the top of something else. ❏ *He could see the church tower poking up from the valley.*
2 If you **poke up** a fire, you use a sharp tool to make the fire burn more strongly.
[OLD-FASHIONED]
poke up something or **poke something up** ❏ *I poked up the fire and warmed my hands by it.*

polish /'pɒlɪʃ/ (polishes, polishing, polished)

○ **polish 'off**
1 If you **polish off** food or a drink, you eat or drink all of it. **= eat up** [INFORMAL]
polish off something or **polish something off** ❏ *Ian polished off the pizza.* ❏ *Peter polished his drink off and got up to leave.*
2 If you **polish off** some work, you finish it completely and quickly.
polish off something or **polish something off** ❏ *He's just polished off another novel.*
3 If you **polish off** an opponent, especially in sports, you beat them easily. [INFORMAL]
polish off someone/something or **polish someone/something off** ❏ *He polished off his opponents 21-2, 21-8 and 21-8.* ❏ *Williams polished her off in the third set.*

○ **polish 'up**
1 If you **polish up** a skill or a piece of work you have done, you improve it by spending more time or effort on it. **= brush up**
polish up something ❏ *Anne went to classes to polish up her French.* ❏ *He's currently polishing up the script for his latest movie.*
2 If you **polish up** an object, you rub it with a cloth to make it shine.
polish up something or **polish something up** ❏ *I polished up the sword until it shone.* ❏ *My sister had the spoons and was polishing them up with a yellow duster.*

ponce /pɒns/ (ponces, poncing, ponced)

○ **ponce a'bout** (or **ponce around**)
[BRITISH, INFORMAL]
If you say that someone **is poncing about**, you mean that they are wasting time doing silly things. **= muck about, lark about**
be poncing about ❏ *He needs to stop poncing*

about and get on with the job. ❑ *While he's poncing around taking photos, I'm working in an office all day.*

◖ontificate /pɒnˈtɪfɪkeɪt/ (**pontificates, pontificating, pontificated**)
▷ **pon'tificate about** (or **pontificate on**) [FORMAL]
If someone **pontificates about** something, they give their opinion in a way that shows they are certain they are right.
pontificate about something ❑ *They shouldn't be pontificating about a subject they know so little about.* ❑ *Most people who pontificate on crime, law and order have no idea what they are talking about.*

◖ony /ˈpəʊni/ (**ponies, ponying, ponied**)
▷ **pony 'up** [AMERICAN, INFORMAL]
If you **pony up** or **pony up** an amount of money, you pay money for something, often when you do not want to. = **stump up**
pony up something ❑ *The IMF is not prepared to pony up $4 billion.*
pony up ❑ [+ for] *People can't even afford to pony up for movie tickets.*

◖ootle /ˈpuːtəl/ (**pootles, pootling, pootled**)
▷ **pootle a'long**
If you **pootle along**, you travel in a slow, relaxed way.
pootle along ❑ *We're perfectly happy to pootle along at 50 miles per hour.*
▷ **pootle a'round** (or **pootle about**)
If you **pootle around**, you spend time doing things in a slow, relaxed way.
pootle around ❑ *Today is your chance to pootle around the town on a bike.*

◖op /pɒp/ (**pops, popping, popped**)
▷ **pop 'back**
If you **pop** something **back** in a place, you quickly return it to the place where it is usually kept.
pop something back ❑ *Top it with grated cheese and pop it back in the oven for five minutes.*
▷ **pop 'in** [BRITISH, INFORMAL]
If you **pop in**, you go to a friend's house or a shop for a short time. ❑ *They sometimes pop in for a coffee and a chat.* ❑ *I'll pop in on my way back from work.*
▷ **pop 'off**
◼ If you **pop off**, you leave the place that you are in for a short time. [BRITISH, INFORMAL] ❑ *Is it okay if I pop off for a moment?* ❑ *I'll pop off to the shops after lunch.*
◼ When someone **pops off**, they die. [BRITISH, INFORMAL] ❑ *They'll inherit a lot of*

money when he pops off.
◼ If someone **pops off**, they talk or write in an emotional and angry way about a subject. [AMERICAN, INFORMAL] ❑ *Before you start popping off, think about what you're saying.* ❑ [+ about] *He got into trouble after popping off about his manager's leadership style.*
◼ If something that is attached **pops off**, or if you **pop** it **off**, it comes off suddenly or you remove it.
pop off ❑ *If a button popped off, we would sew it back on.*
pop something off or **pop off something** ❑ *When I finally managed to pop the lid off, the soup sprayed everywhere.*
○ **pop 'on** [BRITISH, INFORMAL]
If you **pop on** a piece of clothing, you put it on quickly.
pop something on or **pop on something** ❑ *Ella popped her shoes on and went into the garden.* ❑ *Pop on your sunglasses and get down to the beach.*
❂ **pop 'out**
◼ If someone or something that you could not see **pops out**, they suddenly appear. ❑ *She suddenly popped out from behind a bush.* ❑ *A station wagon popped out of the leafy shade of the avenue.*
◼ If you **pop out**, you go out of a building for a short time. [BRITISH, INFORMAL] ❑ *Sorry he's not here – he's just popped out.* ❑ [+ for] *I popped out for a drink.* ❑ [+ to-infinitive] *She just popped out to buy some milk.*
○ **pop 'up**
◼ If someone or something **pops up**, they suddenly appear in a place or situation when you are not expecting them. ❑ *Glazunov had popped up out of nowhere.* ❑ *A message just popped up on my screen.*
NOTE **Surface** is a more formal word for **pop up**.
◼ If the pictures in a children's book **pop up**, they stand up from the pages as you open it. ❑ *Johnny likes books with pictures that pop up.* ● **Pop-up** describes pictures that stand up from the pages of a book or the books that have these pictures. ❑ *Some books are toys in disguise, like those with pop-up pictures.*
◼ If a business **pops up**, it opens in a particular place for a short time. ❑ *These so-called 'festaurants' will be popping up at music events across the country this year.* ● A **pop-up** shop or restaurant opens in a particular place for a short time. ❑ *They're opening an Abba-themed pop-up restaurant during the festival.*

pore /pɔː/ (pores, poring, pored)

○ **'pore over**

If you **pore over** something, you read or look at it very carefully for a long time.

pore over something ❑ He spent his evenings poring over his collection of maps. ❑ I left her poring over a document.

portion /'pɔːʃən/ (portions, portioning, portioned)

○ **portion 'out**

If you **portion** something **out**, you give a part of it to each person in a group. **= share out**

portion something out or **portion out something** ❑ She took a piece of the pie that Tim was carefully portioning out. ❑ We've portioned the work out between the team.

post /pəʊst/ (posts, posting, posted)

○ **post 'up**

If you **post up** a notice, you fix it to a wall or other surface so that people can see it.

post up something or **post something up** ❑ They posted up a set of rules for the house. ❑ The list was posted up in a prominent place.

potter /'pɒtə/ (potters, pottering, pottered)

○ **potter a'bout** (or **potter around**) [mainly BRITISH]

If you **potter about** or **potter about** a place, you spend time in a relaxed and pleasant way, doing things that are not important.

potter about ❑ He loved to potter around in the garden. ❑ At the weekend we potter about and go to the beach.

potter about something ❑ Pottering around the house and garden always makes me feel better.

pounce /paʊns/ (pounces, pouncing, pounced)

○ **'pounce on** (or **pounce upon**)

◼ If someone **pounces on** you, they jump on you and hold you in a violent way.

pounce on someone ❑ Three men wearing masks pounced on him. ❑ He was pounced upon by a gang of youths.

◼ When an animal or bird **pounces on** something, it jumps on it and holds it, in order to kill it.

pounce on something ❑ The cat was waiting to pounce on the mouse.

◼ If you **pounce on** something that someone says or does, you eagerly draw attention to it, especially in order to criticize them. **= seize on**

pounce on something ❑ His colleagues were watching, ready to pounce on any mistake he made.

pour /pɔː/ (pours, pouring, poured)

○ **pour a'way**

If you **pour** a liquid **away**, you pour it out of a container because you no longer need it or cannot use it any more.

pour something away or **pour away something** ❑ I had to pour my drink away after a wasp landed in it. ❑ She poured away the milk.

NOTE **Throw away** is a more general expression for **pour away**.

○ **'pour down**

When it **pours down** or rain **pours down**, it rains very heavily. **= pelt down** ❑ It was pouring down as we set off home. ❑ The rain was pouring down. ● A **downpour** is a time when it rains very heavily. ❑ We sat in the car waiting for the downpour to pass.

○ **pour 'forth** [FORMAL]

When things **pour forth** or something **pours** them **forth**, they suddenly come from somewhere in large amounts.

pour forth ❑ Suggestions continued to pour forth. ❑ [+ from] Steam poured forth from both cars.

pour forth something ❑ The volcano poured forth lava and ash.

✪ **pour 'in**

When a lot of people or things **pour in**, they arrive somewhere at the same time. **= flood in** ❑ Messages of encouragement poured in.

❑ [+ from] Refugees poured in from across the border. ❑ Food donations have poured in from all over the country.

✪ **pour 'into**

◼ When a lot of people or things **pour into** a place, they arrive there at the same time. **= flood into**

pour into something ❑ Visitors pour into the city for this festival. ❑ Donations poured into our office.

◼ If a company, government, etc. **pours** money **into** something, they spend a lot of money on it because they want it to be successful.

pour something into something ❑ Billions of dollars have been poured into the industry.

○ **pour 'off**

When you **pour off** some liquid from a container, you pour some of the liquid out and leave the rest in the container.

pour off something or **pour something off** ❑ Pour off a little of the cream and keep it for the sauce.

○ **'pour on**

If someone **pours scorn on** someone or

something, they talk about them in a way that shows they do not think they are good. ❏ *He poured scorn on all my suggestions.*

○ **pour 'out**

1 If you **pour out** a drink, you fill a cup or glass with the drink. = **serve**

pour out something ❏ *She poured out two glasses of orange juice.*

pour something out ❏ *Waiters were pouring tea out from silver tea pots.*

2 If you **pour out** your thoughts, feelings or experiences or if they **pour out**, you tell someone about them because you are so sad, worried, excited, etc.

pour out something or **pour something out** ❏ *I poured out all my troubles while he listened, patiently.* ❏ *I poured it all out to him – the arguments, fights, the hatred.*

pour out ❏ *Feelings of anger and resentment suddenly poured out in response to her criticisms.*

• If you **pour out your heart**, you tell someone honestly what you are feeling, especially when you are very sad or worried. ❏ *She poured out her heart, saying how worried she was about her mother.* • An **outpouring** is a strong expression of emotion. ❏ *There was a massive outpouring of grief when the princess died.*

• An **outpouring** is a long and emotional speech or piece of writing which shows that someone is very angry or upset. ❏ *She didn't want to listen to the hysterical outpourings of fanatics.*

3 When a lot of things or people **pour out** or you **pour** them **out**, they come out of somewhere quickly.

pour out ❏ *The school bell went, and children started to pour out.* ❏ [+ of] *Black smoke was pouring out of the chimney.* ❏ *Water was pouring out of the tap.*

pour out something ❏ *Factories poured out new plastic products.* • An **outpouring** is a large quantity of something coming from somewhere very quickly. ❏ *The pipe burst and there was an outpouring of scalding water.*

○ **'pour upon** → see pour on

power /ˈpaʊə/ (**powers, powering, powered**)

○ **power 'down**

If you **power down** a machine or device or if it **powers down**, you switch it off completely.

power something down ❏ *Users were asked to power down their phones and return them to the shop.* ❏ *This machine is the server. Do not power it down.*

power down ❏ *Halfway through the day, the battery suddenly powered down.*

○ **power 'through**

If you **power through** something or **power through**, you keep doing something when you are in a difficult situation.

power through something ❏ *Life is hard: you have to try to power through it.*

power through ❏ *For a few weeks you will be tired, but you will power through on adrenaline.*

○ **power 'up**

When an engine or computer **powers up** or someone **powers** it **up**, it is switched on and starts working.

power up ❏ *The computer takes a little while to power up.*

power something up or **power up something** ❏ *It allows administrators to remotely power equipment up from the comfort of their desk.* ❏ *Power up your phone and key in your passcode.*

prang /præŋ/ (**prangs, pranging, pranged**)

○ **prang 'out** [mainly AMERICAN, VERY INFORMAL]

If someone **prangs out**, they take drugs and become unaware of what is going on around them. ❏ *We spent the whole summer pranging out.*

prattle /ˈprætəl/ (**prattles, prattling, prattled**)

○ **prattle 'on** [INFORMAL]

If someone **prattles on**, they talk a lot about things that are not important. ❏ *As Barney prattled on, I put the phone against my shoulder.* ❏ [+ about] *Clearly nervous, he prattled on about the weather.*

preclude /prɪˈkluːd/ (**precludes, precluding, precluded**)

○ **pre'clude from** [FORMAL]

If something **precludes** you **from** doing something, it stops you from doing it.

preclude someone from doing something ❏ *Injury precluded him from continuing his career.*

predispose /priːdɪˈspəʊz/ (**predisposes, predisposing, predisposed**)

○ **predis'pose to** (or **predispose towards**) [FORMAL]

If something **predisposes** you **to** a particular action, belief, or illness, it makes you more likely to behave or think in that way or to suffer from a particular illness.

predispose someone to something ❏ *The environment we live in can predispose us to cancer.* ❏ *A high-fat diet appears to predispose men towards heart disease.*

preface /'prefɪs/ (prefaces, prefacing, prefaced)

○ **'preface with** [FORMAL]

If you **preface** an action or speech **with** something else, you do or say this other thing first.

preface something with something ❏ He prefaced the request with a joke. ❏ The show is prefaced with a warning that it is not suitable for children.

prepare /prɪ'peə/ (prepares, preparing, prepared)

○ **pre'pare for**

If you **prepare for** an event or action that will happen soon, or **prepare** yourself **for** it, you do things so that you will be ready for it.

prepare for something ❏ The team is busy preparing for next week's game.

prepare yourself for something ❏ To prepare myself for the interview, I read as much as I could about the company's work.

present /prɪ'zent/ (presents, presenting, presented)

✪ **pre'sent with**

◼ If you **present** someone **with** something, you give it to them formally or officially.

present someone with something ❏ He was presented with a medal for bravery. ❏ That afternoon he presented her with a diamond engagement ring.

◼ To **present** someone **with** a difficulty, challenge, or opportunity means to cause them to have it.

present someone with something ❏ The changes in regulations presented us with a new set of problems.

preside /prɪ'zaɪd/ (presides, presiding, presided)

○ **pre'side over**

◼ If you **preside over** an official occasion or event, you are in charge of it and have official responsibility for it. [FORMAL]

preside over something ❏ The Pope was invited to preside over the funeral.

◼ To **preside over** an important change or event means to be in charge at a time when it is happening.

preside over something ❏ The Prime Minister is presiding over the worst economic crisis in the country's history.

◼ If an object **presides over** a place, it is much larger or taller than anything else there. [FORMAL]

preside over something ❏ His statue presides over the garden next to the museum.

press /pres/ (presses, pressing, pressed)

○ **press a'head**

If you **press ahead**, you start or continue doing something in a determined way, although you know that it may take a long time or be difficult. = **go ahead** ❏ He is determined to press ahead despite opposition from his parents. ❏ [+ with] The government has pressed ahead with its road building programme.

○ **'press for**

If you **press for** something or **press** someone **for** something, you try to get or achieve it by persuading people that it is important.

press for something ❏ He continued to press for a peaceful solution. ❏ Workers formed a union to press for higher wages.

press someone for something ❏ When I pressed him for an explanation, he refused to speak.

○ **press 'into**

If you **press** someone **into** something, you force them to do it.

press someone into something ❏ She felt that her family were pressing her into marriage. ❏ His parents had pressed him into staying on at school.

✪ **press 'on**

◼ If you **press on**, you continue doing something in a determined way. = **carry on**; ≠ **give up** ❏ Undeterred by these problems, he pressed on. ❏ [+ with] The President has vowed to press on with tax reforms.

◼ If you **press on**, you continue a journey, even though it is becoming more difficult or dangerous. = **carry on**; ≠ **turn back** ❏ I wanted to press on, in spite of the weather.

○ **'press on** (or **press upon**)

If you **press** something **on** someone, you make them accept it, even if they do not want it. = **thrust upon**

press something on someone ❏ She pressed biscuits and lemonade on them. ❏ They were embarrassed by the gifts that were pressed upon them.

pretty /'prɪti/ (pretties, prettying, prettied)

○ **pretty 'up**

If you **pretty** something **up**, you try to make it seem more attractive or acceptable.

pretty something up or **pretty up something** ❏ The house had been prettied up to impress the visitors. ❏ There is no way to sanitize war or pretty it up.

prevail /prɪ'veɪl/ (prevails, prevailing, prevailed)

○ **pre'vail on** (or **prevail upon**) [FORMAL]

If you **prevail on** someone to do something

you persuade them to do something that they did not want to do.

prevail on someone to do something ❏ *Some of his colleagues prevailed on him to address the meeting.* ❏ *Ted had been prevailed upon to bring his flute.*

prey /preɪ/ (preys, preying, preyed)

○ **'prey on** (or **prey upon**)

1 An animal or bird that **preys on** other creatures lives by catching and eating them.

prey on something ❏ *Short-eared owls prey on voles and small birds.*

2 Someone who **preys on** a particular type of person looks for that type of person in order to harm them.

prey on someone ❏ *The judge described him as a ruthless conman who preyed on vulnerable old people.*

3 If something **preys on your mind**, it worries you a lot and you cannot stop thinking about it. ❏ *Barton reluctantly agreed, but the decision preyed on his mind.*

prick /prɪk/ (pricks, pricking, pricked)

○ **prick 'out**

If you **prick out** young plants, you plant them in small holes which you make in the soil using a thin stick.

prick out something or **prick something out** ❏ *Prick out the seedlings in fine soil.* ❏ *Prick the young plants out and continue feeding them each week.*

○ **prick 'up**

If someone **pricks up** their **ears** or if their **ears prick up**, they suddenly start to listen after hearing an interesting sound or piece of information. ❏ *I pricked up my ears at the mention of Guy.* ❏ *My ears pricked up at this news.*

print /prɪnt/ (prints, printing, printed)

○ **print 'off**

To **print off** a computer document means to make a copy of it using a machine attached to the computer.

print off something or **print something off** ❏ *When making any booking online, print off confirmation of your reservation.* ❏ *He printed the letter off, and sent it.*

○ **print 'out**

1 To **print out** a computer document means to make a copy of it using a machine attached to the computer.

print out something ❏ *You need to print out your combined ticket and boarding pass.*
print something out ❏ *I printed a few pictures out.* • A **printout** is a paper copy of a computer document. ❏ *Visitors using the*

system can make printouts of selected images.
2 If a machine **prints out** information, it produces it on paper.

print out something or **print something out** ❏ *These transmitters will actually display or print out the information.*

○ **print 'up**

If someone **prints up** something, they produce a lot of copies of it using a printer.

print up something or **print something up** ❏ *We printed up some leaflets advertising the event.* ❏ *He had some business cards printed up.*

prise /praɪz/ (prises, prising, prised)

> **Prise** is sometimes spelled **prize**.

○ **prise 'out** [BRITISH]

If you **prise** something such as money or information **out**, you make someone give it to you when they do not want to.

prise something out or **prise out something** ❏ *It took a long time to prise out the truth.* ❏ *[+ of] He really didn't want to tell me – I had to prise it out of him.*

NOTE In American English, **pry out** means almost the same as **prise out**.

prize /praɪz/ (prizes, prizing, prized) → see prise

probe /prəʊb/ (probes, probing, probed)

○ **probe 'into**

If you **probe into** a subject that concerns other people, you ask questions or try to discover facts about it.

probe into something ❏ *I didn't want people to probe into my life.*

proceed /prə'siːd/ (proceeds, proceeding, proceeded)

○ **pro'ceed against** [FORMAL]

To **proceed against** a person or organization means to start a legal action against them. = **prosecute**

proceed against someone ❏ *There is insufficient evidence to proceed against Mr McLean.*

○ **pro'ceed from** [FORMAL]

If something **proceeds from** a particular idea, belief or situation, it starts and develops from there.

proceed from something ❏ *His directness proceeded from an absolute honesty, and a determination to achieve results.*

prod /prɒd/ (prods, prodding, prodded)

○ **'prod at**

If you **prod at** something, you push it several times with your finger or with a long instrument such as a stick. = **poke at**

prod at something ❏ *She prodded at the*

contents of the pan. ❑ She didn't like the dentist prodding at her teeth and gums.

profit /'prɒfɪt/ (profits, profiting, profited)

○ **'profit from**

■ If you **profit from** something, you earn money from it.

profit from something ❑ He profited from the sale of the club.

■ If you **profit from** a situation or activity, you get something good from it. [FORMAL]

profit from something ❑ Employees will profit from this type of training. ❑ I think we've all profited from the experience.

project /prə'dʒekt/ (projects, projecting, projected)

○ **pro'ject onto**

■ If you **project** a feeling or idea **onto** another person, you imagine that they have the same idea or feeling as you.

project something onto someone ❑ Aren't you projecting your own thoughts onto her? ❑ She was projecting her own fears onto me.

■ If you **project** a film or picture **onto** a screen or wall, you use a machine to make it appear there.

project something onto something ❑ The team tried projecting the maps onto the same screen.

pronounce /prə'naʊns/ (pronounces, pronouncing, pronounced)

○ **pro'nounce on** (or **pronounce upon**) [FORMAL]

If you **pronounce on** something, you give an opinion or judgment about it.

pronounce on something ❑ It is far too early to be pronouncing on the success or failure of this project.

prop /prɒp/ (props, propping, propped)

✪ **prop 'up**

■ If you **prop** a thing or a part of your body **up**, you support it in a particular position by putting something underneath it or by leaning it against something.

prop something up ❑ Timbers are sometimes used to prop a building up during alterations. ❑ [+ on] He propped his feet up on a stool.

prop up something ❑ There was a pile of books propping up the kitchen table. ❑ [+ with] Anne lay in bed, propped up with pillows.

prop yourself up ❑ [+ on] He propped himself up on an elbow and watched her.

■ If a government or group of people **props up** an organization or country, it gives them money and help so that they can continue to exist.

prop up something or **prop something up** ❑ The Government does not intend to prop up declining industries.

propel /prə'pel/ (propels, propelling, propelled)

○ **propel 'into**

If something **propels** you **into** a particular activity or situation, it causes you to do it or be in it.

propel someone into something ❑ His undoubted talent had propelled him into the post of chief executive. ❑ He was propelled into the newspaper headlines when he was arrested.

protect /prə'tekt/ (protects, protecting, protected)

✪ **pro'tect against**

■ To **protect against** something bad or harmful or to **protect** someone or something **against** it means to prevent it from happening, or from having a harmful effect. = **protect from**

protect against something ❑ Eating plenty of fruit and vegetables may help protect against cancer.

protect someone/something against something ❑ This product will help condition your hair and protect it against sun.

protect yourself against something ❑ So how do you protect yourself against burglary?

■ If an insurance policy **protects against** or **protects** you **against** events such as death, injury, or theft, you get money if that event happens. = **insure against**

protect against something ❑ Card-protection policies protect against fraud if credit cards are stolen.

protect someone against something ❑ Critical illness policies protect people against illnesses that could prevent them from working.

✪ **pro'tect from**

To **protect** someone or something **from** something bad or harmful means to prevent it from happening or having a harmful effect. = **protect against**

protect someone/something from something ❑ His hat was pulled down over his face to protect it from the sun. ❑ The soldiers were there to protect their country from invasion.

protect yourself from something ❑ Any animal will struggle to protect itself from a threat of death.

protest /prə'test/ (protests, protesting, protested)

✪ **pro'test against** (or **protest about**)

If people **protest against** something, they say or show publicly that they do not like it.

protest against something ❑ *Students are protesting against the increase in university fees.* ❑ *People marched through the streets to protest about wage cuts.*

protrude /prə'truːd, AM prəʊ-/ (protrudes, protruding, protruded)
○ **pro'trude from** [FORMAL]
If something **protrudes from** somewhere, some of it can be seen and some of it is covered.
protrude from somewhere ❑ *A rock was protruding from the water.* ❑ *A handkerchief protruded from his pocket.*

provide /prə'vaɪd/ (provides, providing, provided)
○ **pro'vide against** [FORMAL]
To **provide against** a bad event or situation means to make plans to prevent it or deal with it if it happens.
provide against something ❑ *Banks must provide against bad loans.* ❑ *It is not possible to ensure that all risks are provided against.*

○ **pro'vide for**
1 If you **provide for** someone, you give them the things they need such as money, food, or clothes.
provide for someone ❑ *Our nursery provides for all the needs of very young children.* ❑ *Is he provided for financially?*
2 To **provide for** something that may happen in the future means to make plans to deal with it. **= allow for** [FORMAL]
provide for something ❑ *The school had provided for just such an emergency and was ready to deal with it.*
3 If a law or decision **provides for** something, it allows it to happen. [FORMAL]
provide for something ❑ *The Act provided for financial penalties to be imposed on all offenders.*

○ **pro'vide with**
To **provide** someone **with** something means to give it to them or make it available to them when they need it.
provide someone with something ❑ *They provided us with accommodation and meals.* ❑ *She provided police with a detailed description of her attacker.* ❑ *We were provided with wetsuits, and told to go and collect a surfboard.*

prowl /praʊl/ (prowls, prowling, prowled)
○ **prowl a'round**
If someone **prowls around** or **prowls around** a place, they move around quietly, for example when they are looking for something or are going to steal something.
prowl around ❑ *The caretaker had reported seeing someone prowling around the previous week.*

prowl around something ❑ *The police officer took notes and prowled around the room.*

prune /pruːn/ (prunes, pruning, pruned)
○ **prune 'back**
1 When you **prune back** a tree or bush, you cut off some of the branches so that it will grow better the next year.
prune something back or **prune back something** ❑ *He was pruning back some bushes by the side of the road.* ❑ *Apples, pears and cherries can be pruned back when they've lost their leaves.*
2 If you **prune back** something, you get rid of all the parts that you do not need.
prune back something or **prune something back** ❑ [+ by] *The company has pruned back its workforce by 20,000 since 2000.* ❑ [+ to] *There used to be eight games per season but this has been pruned back to six.*

pry /praɪ/ (pries, prying, pried)
○ **pry 'out** [AMERICAN]
If you **pry** money or information **out**, you persuade someone to give it to you even though they do not want to.
pry something out or **pry out something** ❑ *Judy was determined to pry out the truth.* ❑ [+ of] *He didn't volunteer the information – I had to pry it out of him.*
NOTE In British English, **prise out** means almost the same as **pry out**.

psych /saɪk/ (psychs, psyching, psyched)

> **Psych** and **psychs** are also spelled **psyche** and **psyches**.

○ **psych 'out** [INFORMAL]
If you **psych out** your opponent in a game or competition, you try to make them feel less confident by behaving in a very confident or aggressive way.
psych someone out or **psych out someone** ❑ *I took my position at the baseline and tried to psych her out with a stare.* ❑ *I was trying to psych out my opponent.*

○ **psych 'up** [INFORMAL]
If you **psych** yourself **up** before a game, competition or a difficult task, you prepare yourself for it mentally so that you feel confident.
psych yourself up ❑ *As usual, they spent an hour before the kick-off psyching themselves up.* ❑ *She paused, psyching herself up for what she was going to say.* ● If someone is **psyched up**, they are mentally prepared to do something difficult. ❑ *I know the crew and team are really psyched up now.*

psyche /'saɪk/ (psyches, psyching, psyched) → see **psych**

puff /pʌf/ (puffs, puffing, puffed)

○ **'puff at** (or **puff on**)

If someone **puffs at** a cigarette or a pipe, they keep sucking smoke into their mouth and blowing it out again.
puff at something ❑ Mike was puffing at a cigarette. ❑ Her father puffed on his pipe for a moment.

○ **puff a'way**

If someone **puffs away** when they are smoking a cigarette or a pipe, they keep sucking smoke into their mouth and blowing it out again. ❑ George would light up and puff away for a while. ❑ [+ on] Richie nodded and puffed away on his pipe.

○ **'puff on** ➜ see **puff at**

○ **puff 'out**

1 If part of your body **puffs out**, or if you **puff** it **out**, it becomes larger and rounder as if it is filled with air.
puff out ❑ Craig's cheeks puffed out like a hamster's.
puff out something or **puff something out** ❑ He sat back and puffed out his cheeks. ❑ 'We can do that easily,' said Bobby, puffing his chest out.

2 If exercise **puffs** you **out**, it makes you tired and unable to breathe easily.
[INFORMAL]
puff someone out ❑ It was climbing all those stairs that had puffed him out. • If you are **puffed out**, you are tired and unable to breathe easily because you have just exercised. ❑ I felt puffed out at the end of my jog.

○ **puff 'up**

If part of your body **puffs up** it becomes swollen because of an injury or allergy.
= **swell up** ❑ I twisted my ankle and it started to puff up.

pull /pʊl/ (pulls, pulling, pulled)

○ **pull a'bout** ➜ see **pull around**

○ **pull a'head**

1 To **pull ahead** means to move in front of a vehicle or person that was in front of you or was moving at the same speed as you. ≠ **fall behind** ❑ The cars got faster and faster, each trying to pull ahead. ❑ [+ of] I raced towards the foot of the hill and pulled ahead of Robin.

2 To **pull ahead** means to start to become more successful than other people, groups, or organizations. = **get ahead**; ≠ **fall behind** ❑ [+ of] The opinion polls show that the party is beginning to pull ahead of its rivals.

○ **pull a'part**

1 When you **pull** something **apart** or when it **pulls apart**, it separates into two or more pieces.

pull something apart or **pull apart something** ❑ Cameron pulled the soft dough apart. ❑ The baby was busy pulling apart a stuffed toy.
pull apart ❑ The plates of rock eventually pull apart, and molten rock flows through.

2 If you **pull** people or animals **apart** when they are fighting, you separate them.
pull someone/something apart or **pull apart someone/something** ❑ I rushed in and tried to pull the dogs apart. ❑ William got hurt trying to pull them apart.

3 If someone **pulls apart** something that you have written or said, they criticize it. = **take apart**
pull something apart or **pull apart something** ❑ The critics just pulled his last novel apart. ❑ She pulled my argument apart in about five minutes.

4 To **pull** someone **apart** means to upset them a lot. = **tear apart**
pull someone apart ❑ All this trouble with his son must be pulling him apart.

○ **pull a'round** (or **pull about, pull round** [mainly BRITISH])

If you **pull** someone or something **around**, you move or handle them in a rough, violent way.
pull someone/something around ❑ Stop pulling me about, would you!

○ **pull a'round** (or **pull round** [mainly BRITISH])

If something or someone **pulls around** or you **pull** them **around**, they turn so that they are facing in the opposite direction.
pull someone/something around ❑ He caught her hand, and pulled her around to face him.
pull around ❑ The helicopter pulled round in a tight circle.

○ **pull a'side**

If you **pull** someone **aside**, you take them away to a different part of a room in order to have a private conversation with them. = **take aside**
pull someone aside ❑ At the airport, two immigration officers pulled me aside.

○ **'pull at**

1 If you **pull at** something, you pull something quickly several times.
pull at something ❑ 'Come home now, Jim,' she said, pulling at his sleeve. ❑ He frowned and pulled at his moustache.

2 If you **pull at** a cigarette or pipe, you take a long, deep breath of smoke from it when it is in your mouth.
pull at something ❑ 'Oh, I'm not complaining,' David said, pulling at his cigarette.

✪ pull a'way

1 When a vehicle **pulls away**, it starts moving forward. **= pull off** ❑ *The bus pulled away.* ❑ [+ *from*] *He watched the taxi pull away from the kerb.*

2 If you **pull away**, you suddenly move away from someone who is holding you. **= pull back** ❑ *She bent and kissed the top of his head, but he pulled away.* ❑ [+ *from*] *He burst into tears and pulled away from me.*

3 If you **pull** someone or something **away**, you take hold of them and move them away. **pull something/someone away** ❑ *Hendricks bent down to pull some of the weeds away.* ❑ *He pulled me away before I could examine the letter too closely.* ❑ [+ *from*] *Felix managed to pull him away from me.*

pull away something/someone ❑ *I pulled away her hands which covered her face.*

4 If something **pulls away**, it becomes separated from something else. **= come away** ❑ [+ *from*] *The sole had pulled away from the shoe.*

5 If you **pull away**, you deliberately start to be less friendly with someone who you used to have a close relationship with. ❑ [+ *from*] *During adolescence, children tend to pull away from their parents.*

✪ pull 'back

1 If you **pull back**, you suddenly move away from someone or something. **= draw back** ❑ *He tried to kiss her but she pulled back.* ❑ [+ *from*] *She pulled back from the window so he wouldn't see her.*

2 When you **pull** someone or something **back**, you take hold of them and move them backwards.

pull something/someone back ❑ *He pulled his chair back.* ❑ *The women pulled their children back in fear.* ❑ [+ *from*] *She carefully pulled her hair back from her face.*

pull back something ❑ *He walked over to the bed and pulled back the covers.*

3 When an army **pulls back** or someone **pulls** it **back**, it moves away from the place where it is fighting. **= withdraw**

pull back ❑ *The soldiers pulled back after about six hours.* ❑ [+ *from*] *Troops began pulling back from the town of Ramallah.*

pull back something ❑ *They tried to persuade both countries to pull back troops.*

pull something back ❑ *He urged the country to pull its troops back.* ● A **pullback** is when soldiers move away or are moved away from the place where they are fighting. ❑ *There are reports of a pullback from the town.*

4 If you **pull back**, you decide not to do something that you were going to do. **= back out, draw back** ❑ *I thought it might be dangerous, and decided to pull back.* ❑ [+ *from*] *It is hard to believe they will pull back from this deal.*

✪ pull 'down

1 If you **pull** something **down**, you move it from a higher position to a lower one. **≠ pull up**

pull something down ❑ *She pulled his head down to kiss him.*

pull down something ❑ *She pulled down the blinds to shut out the light.* ❑ *His baseball cap was pulled down over his eyes.*

2 To **pull down** a building or other structure means to destroy it because it is not wanted any more. **≠ put up**

pull something down ❑ *They pulled the church down and built apartments on the site.*

pull down something ❑ *She could remember the day when they started to pull down the Berlin Wall.* ❑ *The council said the building was dangerous and should be pulled down.*

NOTE **Demolish** is a more formal word for **pull down**.

3 If someone or something **pulls** you **down**, they make you feel unhappy. **= drag down** [INFORMAL]

pull someone down ❑ *Negative people just pull you down.* ❑ *Homesickness was starting to pull me down.*

4 The amount of money someone **pulls down** is the amount of money they earn regularly from their job. [AMERICAN, INFORMAL]

pull down something ❑ *Daniel was pulling down a weekly income of six hundred dollars.*

◯ 'pull for [INFORMAL]

If you **pull for** someone, you help or support them. **= root for**

pull for someone ❑ *There's no jealousy on the team – we're all here pulling for each other.* ❑ *This is a team effort, where everyone pulls for everyone else.*

✪ pull 'in

1 If a driver or vehicle **pulls in**, they drive to the side of the road or to another place where they can stop. **= pull up** ❑ *They decided to pull in at a roadside restaurant.* ❑ *We saw a petrol station and pulled in.* ● A **pull-in** is a cafe on a main road where you can get cheap meals. [BRITISH, INFORMAL] ❑ *We stopped at a pull-in on the way.*

2 When a train **pulls in**, it arrives at a station and stops. **≠ pull out** ❑ *As the 4.30 to Newcastle pulled in, everyone rushed to get on.*

3 If an event or place **pulls** people **in** it attracts a lot of people.

pull in someone or **pull someone in** ❑ *The*

city's clubs and restaurants pull in *about 50,000 people every Saturday.* ❑ *The football matches pulled in big crowds.*

4 When the police pull someone in, they go to find them and arrest them. [INFORMAL]

pull someone in or **pull in someone** ❑ *The police decided to pull the suspects in.* ❑ *Police pulled in the elusive Jonathan Logan.*

5 If you pull in money, you earn a lot of it. = **rake in** [INFORMAL]

pull in something or **pull something in** ❑ *They were pulling in £5000 a week.* ❑ *She's a popular writer and can still pull the money in.*

○ **pull 'into**

1 When a car, train, or other vehicle pulls into a place, it arrives there and stops.

pull into something ❑ *He pulled into the small parking lot.* ❑ *The London train pulled into the station.*

2 To pull someone or something into a particular situation or activity means to make them become involved in it.

pull someone/something into something ❑ *We have been pulled into an arrangement against our will.*

○ **pull 'off**

1 When you pull a piece of clothing off or pull a piece of clothing off someone else, you take it off quickly.

pull something off ❑ *I managed to pull my boots off.*

pull off something ❑ *Anna had already kicked off her shoes and was pulling off her socks.*

pull something off something/someone ❑ *I was busy pulling Tom's boots off his feet.*

2 If you pull something off, you succeed in doing something difficult. = **carry off**

pull off something ❑ *The team pulled off a surprise victory against Liverpool.* ❑ *They pulled off a deal with an Australian firm.*

pull something off ❑ *She had succeeded, triumphantly: she had pulled it off.*

3 When a driver or vehicle pulls off or pulls off the road, they drive off it so that they can stop or so that they can drive on a smaller road.

pull off ❑ *We were looking for a place where we could pull off and have a picnic.*

pull off something ❑ *I pulled off the motorway and took one of the country roads.*

4 When a driver or vehicle pulls off, they start moving forward. = **pull away** ❑ *She got to the bus stop just as the bus was pulling off.* ❑ *You should always check the mirrors before you pull off.*

5 If you pull off a person or animal that is attacking someone, you take hold of them

and move them away, using force.

pull someone/something off ❑ *I got into a fight with him and my dad had to pull me off.*

pull someone/something off someone ❑ *A neighbour managed to pull the dog off him.*

○ **pull 'on**

In meanings 2 and 3, the stress is on **'pull.**

1 When you pull on your clothes, you put them on quickly.

pull on something ❑ *He started to pull on his shorts.*

pull something on ❑ *Still sitting, he pulled his shirt on.* ❑ *I grabbed my dress and pulled it on.*

2 If you pull on something, you take hold of it and move it towards you.

pull on something ❑ *He began to pull on the rope.* ❑ *He noticed an electrical cord, and pulled on it.*

3 If you pull on a cigarette or pipe, you take a long, deep breath of smoke from it when it is in your mouth.

pull on something ❑ *The vicar sat back in his chair and pulled on his pipe.*

4 If someone pulls a gun/knife on someone, they take a gun or knife from a pocket and threaten to attack them with it. ❑ *He was arrested after pulling a gun on another driver.*

5 [INFORMAL] If you pull a trick/stunt on someone, you do something in order to trick them. ❑ *The twins often pull stunts on their teachers by pretending to be each other.*

○ **pull 'out**

1 When a vehicle or driver pulls out, they drive out of a place and into the road. ❑ *The car pulled out suddenly and knocked her down.* ❑ [+ of] *Ellen waited at the door until the car had pulled out of the driveway.*

2 When a vehicle or driver pulls out they drive from one traffic lane into another. ❑ *I pulled out to overtake a bus.* ❑ *The car in the next lane suddenly pulled out in front of me.*

3 When a train pulls out, it leaves a station. = **draw out** ❑ *He waved at her as the train pulled out.* ❑ [+ of] *As the train pulled out of Marseille station, Nancy started to cry.*

4 If you pull out or pull someone out, you decide not to continue with an activity or agreement. = **back out**

pull out ❑ *We've invested too much money to pull out now.* ❑ [+ of] *Murray had to pull out of the competition because of injury.*

pull someone/something out of something ❑ *She pulled her son out of the school because she wasn't happy with the standard of teaching.*

5 If soldiers or an army pull out or if

someone **pulls** them **out**, they leave a place. **= withdraw**

pull out ❑ [+ of] *Troops had begun to pull out of the area.*

pull someone/something out ❑ *The Prime Minister has said he intends to pull all 10,000 soldiers out by the end of June.* ❑ [+ of] *They ordered me to pull my men out of Fort Esther immediately.*

pull out someone/something ❑ *Khartoum has pulled out the Sudanese army.* ● When there is a **pull-out**, soldiers leave a place. ❑ *United Nations officers supervising the pull-out said they expected 3,000 to be out by the weekend.*

6 When you **pull** something or someone **out**, you take them out of a thing or place.

pull out something ❑ *He would pull out his notebook and begin writing.*

pull something/someone out ❑ *She pulled an umbrella out and put it up.* ❑ [+ of] *Pull the baby's arms out of the sleeves first.* ❑ *I pulled him out of the chair.*

pull yourself out ❑ [+ of] *O'Brien managed to cling on to the rock and pull herself out of the water.* ● A **pull-out** section in a magazine is a separate part in the middle that you can remove easily. ❑ *A full pull-out programme of festival events will be available in the Edinburgh Evening News.*

7 To **pull out** information means to find it in a lot of other information, so that you can use it. **= take out**

pull out something or **pull something out** ❑ *The computer does a search and pulls out all the relevant information.* ❑ *You need to read through the text and pull the relevant facts out.*

NOTE **Extract** is a more formal word for **pull out**.

○ **pull 'out of**

To **pull** yourself **out of** a bad situation or to **pull** someone or something else **out of** it, is to succeed in getting out of it or getting someone or something else out of it.

pull yourself out of something ❑ *Somehow you've got to pull yourself out of this mess.*

pull someone/something out of something ❑ *We must pull the country out of this economic recession.*

○ **pull 'over**

1 When a vehicle or driver **pulls over**, they move closer to the side of the road, and stop. ❑ *I started to feel unwell and had to pull over.* ❑ *Police signalled to the driver to pull over.*

2 If the police **pull** a car or driver **over**, they signal to the driver to drive the car to the side of the road and stop.

pull over someone/something ❑ *We saw a police car pulling over a lorry.*

pull someone/something over ❑ *A police car pulled them over.* ❑ [+ for] *He'd been pulled over for going through a red light.*

○ **pull 'round** [mainly BRITISH]

1 If you **pull round** after you have been ill or unconscious, you start to recover. ❑ *He'll pull round, don't worry.*

2 → see **pull around**

○ **pull 'through**

1 When someone who is very ill **pulls through** or when doctors or nurses **pull** them **through**, they do not die. ❑ *The doctors think he'll pull through.*

pull someone through ❑ *I can't thank the doctors enough for pulling her through.*

2 If you **pull through** a difficult situation or if something **pulls** you **through** it, you succeed in dealing with it.

pull through ❑ *It was a terrible time but I pulled through.*

pull through something ❑ *I know we can pull through this together.*

pull someone through ❑ *When my daughter died, it was my faith that pulled me through.*

pull someone through something ❑ *He got a loan to pull him through a bad patch.*

○ **pull 'to**

When you **pull** a door, gate or window **to**, you pull it so that it is closed or very nearly closed. **= shut**

pull something to ❑ *Could you pull the door to, please? I want to talk to you.*

○ **pull to'gether**

1 When you **pull** yourself **together**, you start to control your feelings and behave calmly after you have been upset or angry.

pull yourself together ❑ *Come on, now, pull yourself together!* ❑ *He had taken some minutes alone in his room to pull himself together.*

2 If people **pull together**, they all work together to achieve something, and ignore the things they disagree about. **= band together** ❑ *We all pulled together during the war.* ❑ *We have to pull together for the sake of the company.*

3 If you **pull together** different pieces of information, you find out about them and consider them altogether.

pull together something or **pull something together** ❑ *This chapter pulls together some of the key arguments presented earlier.* ❑ *To understand this illness, we must pull facts together from such fields as psychology and neurology.*

4 If you **pull** a piece or work, event or meeting **together**, you organize it. **= set up**

pull something together or **pull together something** ❏ We decided to have a party for him, and had only a few days to pull it all together. ❏ We managed to pull the exhibition together in four months.

○ **pull 'under**

If someone or something **pulls** you **under** when you are in water, they pull you down so that the water completely covers you.
pull someone under ❏ The rope tightened around his legs and pulled him under.
pull someone under something ❏ Dan grabbed my legs and pulled me under the water.

○ **pull 'up**

■ When a vehicle or driver **pulls up**, they slow down and stop. ❏ The ambulance was just pulling up. ❏ [+ to] The rain stopped as we pulled up to the hotel.

② If you **pull up** a chair, you move it so that you can sit close to something. = **draw up**
pull up something ❏ I pulled up a chair and sat back to watch the news.
pull something up ❏ [+ to] Maria pulled her stool up to the table.

③ When you **pull** something or someone **up**, you move them from a lower position to a higher one.
pull something/someone up ❏ She pulled the blanket up. ❏ John took hold of my hand and pulled me up.
pull up something ❏ He had to pull up his pants which had started slipping.
pull yourself up ❏ He took hold of the branch to pull himself up.

④ If you **pull up** something which is fixed to the ground or the floor, you remove it by pulling hard.
pull up something ❏ They started pulling up the floorboards.
pull something up ❏ Don't pull the plants up. ❏ Either dig the weeds out, or pull them up.

⑤ If someone **pulls** you **up**, they criticize you for something that you have done. [INFORMAL]
pull someone up ❏ [+ on] If they don't like what you're doing, they'll soon pull you up on it. ❏ When I asked about the photographs, the young man pulled me up quite sharply.

⑥ If someone or something **pulls** you **up**, they do or say something that suddenly makes you stop moving or talking.
pull someone up ❏ Mr Wright pulled me up as soon as I left the classroom.
pull yourself up ❏ Kate pulled herself up short and shouted: 'Don't start that again.'

⑦ If you **pull up**, you improve at something you are doing, and reach the same standard as other people. = **catch up** ❏ She's been working hard and has pulled up quite a bit over the last few months.

pump /pʌmp/ (pumps, pumping, pumped)

○ **'pump about** [INFORMAL]

If you **pump** someone **about** something or someone, you keep asking them questions in order to get information.
pump someone about something/someone ❏ He was obviously trying to pump Eve about her new boyfriend.

○ **pump a'way**

■ To **pump away** means to move quickly and continuously in and out or up and down. ❏ His heart was pumping away. ❏ This machine is pumping away all the time.

② To **pump** a liquid or gas **away** means to remove it by forcing it to flow in a particular direction, using a pump.
pump something away or **pump away something** ❏ We had pumped most of the water away by the afternoon. ❏ It's used to pump away water in an emergency.

○ **'pump for** [INFORMAL]

If you **pump** someone **for** information or details, you keep asking them questions to get information.
pump someone for something ❏ Reporters were pumping him for stories about the singer.

○ **pump 'in** [INFORMAL]

If a government or organization **pumps** money **in**, they give a lot of money to something.
pump in something or **pump something in** ❏ It's not simply a question of pumping in money. ❏ They have pumped a lot of money in over the years.
NOTE **Inject** is a more formal word for **pump in**.

○ **pump 'into** [INFORMAL]

If a government or organization **pumps** money **into** something, they give a lot of money to it.
pump something into something ❏ The government should pump funds into rural development. ❏ Investors pumped £5 billion into the Stock Exchange last year.

○ **pump 'out**

■ To **pump** a liquid or gas **out** means to remove it from a place by forcing it to flow in a particular direction, using a pump.
pump something out or **pump out something** ❏ [+ of] Miners used the device to pump water out of the mines. ❏ We seal one of the tubes and pump out all the air.

② To **pump out** someone's stomach means to remove the contents of their stomach using a pump, because they have swallowed something that is poisonous or taken too much of a drug.

pump out something or **pump something out** ❏ Rob was rushed to hospital to have his stomach pumped out.

◾ To **pump** something **out** means to produce a lot of it continuously. = **churn out** [INFORMAL]

pump out something or **pump something out** ❏ A radio was pumping out pop music. ❏ Factories are ready to pump these drugs out by the billions.

◾ If pop music **pumps out**, it plays very loudly. ❏ Dance music pumped out at every station. ❏ [+ of] Rock music was pumping out of huge speakers.

○ **pump 'out of**
If you **pump** information **out of** someone, you make them tell you something that they want to keep secret.

pump something out of someone ❏ They tried to pump every bit of information out of me. ❏ I tried to pump it out of him, but he wouldn't say a word.

○ **pump 'up**
◾ If you **pump up** something such as a tyre, you fill it with air, using a pump. = **blow up**

pump up something ❏ I have to pump up the airbeds. ❏ Do your tyres need pumping up?

pump something up ❏ Ben started to pump the mattress up.

NOTE **Inflate** is a more formal word for **pump up**.

◾ To **pump** liquid **up** from a place underground means to force it out of that place to the surface, using a pump.

pump up something or **pump something up** ❏ [+ from] Oil has to be pumped up from deep boreholes. ❏ You could use a windmill to pump up water from the well.

◾ If you **pump** someone or yourself **up** you make them or yourself feel excited, confident and ready to do something. = **psych up** [AMERICAN, INFORMAL]

pump up someone or **pump someone up** ❏ He always knew how to pump up the troops.

pump yourself up ❏ [+ for] The guys are pumping themselves up for the next game.
If someone is **pumped up**, they are excited, confident and ready to do something. ❏ Richard was one of those pumped-up salesman types. ❏ [+ for] I'm pretty pumped up for the game.

◾ To **pump** something **up** means to increase it. [INFORMAL]

pump something up or **pump up something** ❏ They plan to reduce taxes and pump up

investment. ❏ Greedy stores have pumped prices up.

punch /pʌntʃ/ (**punches, punching, punched**)

○ **punch 'in**
◾ If you **punch in** numbers or information, you push buttons to put them in a telephone, computer or machine.

punch in something or **punch something in** ❏ I punched in the code and opened the door. ❏ Insert your credit card and then punch your PIN in.

◾ When workers **punch in** at a factory or office, they record the time that they arrive by putting a special card into a machine. = **clock in**; ≠ **punch out** [AMERICAN] ❏ We get into trouble if we don't punch in.

○ **punch 'into**
If you **punch** numbers or information **into** a telephone, computer or machine, you push buttons to give that information to the telephone, computer, etc.

punch something into something ❏ He punched some numbers into the key pad.

○ **punch 'out**
◾ When you **punch** something **out** you make it out of a substance such as wood, metal, or paper, by making a hole or other shape in it using a special machine or tool.

punch out something or **punch something out** ❏ They use an old-fashioned machine that punches out coins.

◾ If you **punch out** numbers or information, you push buttons to put them in a telephone, computer, or machine. [AMERICAN]

punch out something or **punch something out** ❏ 'So, where's the fire?' he asked, punching out the name on his computer.

◾ When workers **punch out** at a factory or office, they record the time that they leave by putting a special card into a machine. = **clock out**; ≠ **punch in** [AMERICAN] ❏ At the end of the day, they punch out and wish each other a good evening.

◾ To **punch** someone **out** means to hit them so hard that they fall over. [AMERICAN, INFORMAL]

punch someone out ❏ Glenn punched the guy out. ❏ Wesley got punched out by some guy in a bar.

◾ [INFORMAL] To **punch** someone's **lights out** means to hit them hard in the face. ❏ He said, 'You're lucky I didn't punch your lights out.'

○ **punch 'up** [AMERICAN]
◾ If you **punch** something **up**, you make it appear on a screen by pressing buttons.

punch up something or **punch something up**
❑ 'This card hasn't been used for a long time,' the clerk said, punching up the account on her computer.

2 To **punch** something **up** means to make it more interesting or exciting. [INFORMAL]

punch up something or **punch something up**
❑ There's nothing like bright colours to punch up your wardrobe.

purge /pɜːdʒ/ (purges, purging, purged)

○ **'purge of** [FORMAL]

1 To **purge** an organization **of** people that are not wanted means to force them to leave.

purge something of someone ❑ The government began purging the army of officers accused of human rights abuse.

2 If you **purge** something or yourself **of** things or feelings that you do not want, you get rid of them.

purge something of something ❑ He closed his eyes and lay still, trying to purge his mind of anxiety.

purge yourself of something ❑ The country's police promised to purge themselves of racism.

push /pʊʃ/ (pushes, pushing, pushed)

○ **push a'bout** ➔ see push around

○ **push a'head**

1 When you **push ahead**, you continue doing something, with a lot of energy or enthusiasm. = **push on, press on** ❑ Now was the time to push ahead and finish the job. ❑ By the time dinner was finished, he was clearly in a mood to push ahead.

2 If you **push ahead**, you continue with a plan, arrangement, or event, often when there are problems, or when other people want you to stop. ❑ The Prime Minister pushed ahead despite opposition from other parties. ❑ [+ with] The Government was anxious to push ahead with a fresh round of negotiations.

○ **push a'long** [INFORMAL, OLD-FASHIONED]
If you say that you must **push along**, you mean that you must leave a place.
= **push off** ❑ I must be pushing along now, it's getting late.

○ **push a'round** (or **push about, push round** [mainly BRITISH])
When you **push** something **around** or **push** it **around** something, you move it from one position to another without lifting it away from the surface that it is on.

push something around ❑ She stared at the cups and pushed them around.

push something around something ❑ She was pushing her salad around her plate. ❑ Noah

was playing with his pens, pushing them slowly round the table.

○ **push a'round** (or **push about**)
If someone **pushes** you **around**, they keep telling you what to do in a rude and annoying way.

push someone around ❑ Don't let him push you around. ❑ I'm sick and tired of being pushed about.

○ **push a'side**

1 When you **push** something or someone **aside**, you move them to a position where they are not in your way.

push something/someone aside or **push aside something/someone** ❑ I handed him a toy but he pushed it aside. ❑ He leaned forward and pushed aside his notes.

2 If you **push** something **aside**, you try to forget about it and think about or do something else instead. = **brush aside**

push something aside or **push aside something** ❑ If she does ever worry about him, she soon pushes it aside. ❑ These issues tend to get pushed aside and forgotten.

○ **push 'back**

1 To **push back** a group of people such as a crowd or an army means to make them move backwards.

push back someone ❑ The Allied forces were pushed back.

push someone back ❑ People protested but the police pushed them back.

2 When you **push** something or someone **back**, you move them backwards, using your hand.

push something/someone back ❑ She had pushed her sunglasses back, so they rested on her hair. ❑ Oliver took a step forward, but Charlie pushed him back.

push back something/someone ❑ He pushed back his chair so hard that it fell over.

3 To **push back** means to resist a change or plan.

push back ❑ Florida was the first state to push back, refusing to allow drilling in its waters. ❑ [+ against] It's normal for children to push back against homework.

4 If you **push back** an arrangement, you postpone it to a later date.

push back something or **push something back** ❑ We're concerned that the delivery date could be pushed back again.

○ **push 'by**
If someone **pushes by** or **pushes by** someone, they rudely push someone so that they can move past them.
= **push past**

push by ❑ *Say 'excuse me' – don't just push by!*
push by someone ❑ *She just pushed by us without so much as an 'excuse me'.*

'push for

If you **push for** something, you try to persuade other people to help you achieve it. **= press for**

push for something ❑ *Unions were pushing for higher wages.*

push 'forward

1 If you **push forward** your ideas, opinions, or plans, you try very hard to get other people to pay attention to them.

push forward something or **push something forward** ❑ *His job was to push forward the Party's principles.* ❑ *If he had any views of his own, he should have pushed them forward.*

NOTE **Promote** is a more formal word for **push forward**.

2 If someone **pushes** themselves **forward**, they try to make other people notice them.

push yourself forward ❑ *Ted's not the sort to push himself forward.*

3 If you **push forward**, you continue doing something. ❑ *We need to push forward and get this done.* ❑ *[+ with] Both sides are said to be pushing forward with the peace plan.*

push 'in

1 When someone **pushes in**, they come into a queue in front of other people who have been waiting longer. ❑ *Annette got cross with someone for pushing in.* ❑ *No-one was allowed to push in.*

2 When someone **pushes in**, they annoy other people by getting involved in a situation or activity which does not concern them. ❑ *I didn't mean to push in. I just thought I might be able to help.* ❑ *You can't just push in and tell her what to do!*

push 'into

1 If you **push** someone **into** doing something, you try to persuade or force them to do it.

push someone into doing something
❑ *Research groups were trying to push the government into giving money for scientific research.* ❑ *Don't let yourself be pushed into making a decision.*

2 If a person or situation **pushes** you **into** a difficult or unpleasant situation, they force you into it.

push someone into something ❑ *Her parents had pushed her into marriage.* ❑ *Unavoidable circumstances could push the country into war.*

push 'off

1 When you **push off**, you leave the person or place that you are visiting. [INFORMAL]

❑ *I'll push off now and leave you to get on with your work.* ❑ *He must have pushed off when he heard us.*

2 If someone tells you to **push off**, they are telling you in a rude way to go away. ❑ *'I've got something to show you.' – 'You push off,' I said.* ❑ *I told him to push off, and he did.*

3 When a boat **pushes off**, or when you **push** it **off**, it starts to move away from the edge of the water

push off ❑ *As the launch pushed off, the sea turned from smooth to choppy.*

push something off ❑ *The boats were pushed off and drifted down the river.*

○ push 'on

1 When you **push on**, you continue travelling somewhere. ❑ *If we want to get there before dark, we'll have to push on.* ❑ *We pushed on towards the coast for a while.*

2 When you **push on**, you continue doing something. **= carry on** ❑ *I think we'll just push on and get as much finished as we can.* ❑ *[+ with] The government is pushing on with reform.*

○ 'push on (or push onto, push upon)

If someone **pushes** something **on** you, they try to make you buy or accept it when you do not really want it.

push something on someone ❑ *I didn't like the way he tried to push his religious beliefs on me.*

✪ push 'out

1 When you **push** someone or something **out**, you use your hands to move them out of a place.

push someone/something out ❑ *He pushed Minnie out and slammed the door.* ❑ *[+ of] I was pushed out of the door before I could put on my shoes.* ❑ *She pushed her dark hair out of her face.*

2 If people **push** you **out**, they force you to leave an organization or stop doing an activity.

push someone out or **push out someone**
❑ *I've shown I won't be pushed out by their bullying.* ❑ *[+ of] The chief marketing officer has been pushed out of the job after less than a year.*

3 To **push out** something means to produce a lot of it and send it out somewhere. **= churn out** [INFORMAL]

push out something ❑ *The software company has pushed out five major releases of this operating system.* ❑ *The engines had been tweaked to push out more power than normal.*

✪ push 'over

1 If you **push** someone or something **over**, you push them so that they fall onto the ground. **= knock over**

push someone/something over ❑ *Someone had pushed her over in the playground and she'd hurt her knee.*

push over someone/something ❑ *Vandals*

had pushed over gravestones in the cemetery.

2 If you describe someone as a **pushover**, you mean that they are very easy to persuade or influence. ❏ *Lester's mother was no pushover, either physically or emotionally.*

○ **push 'past**

If someone **pushes past** or **pushes past** someone, they push someone as they go past them. = **push by**

push past ❏ *She pushed past without saying 'excuse me'.*

push past someone ❏ *Frank pushed past him and jumped into the cab.*

○ **push 'round** → see push around

⊙ **push 'through**

1 If you **push** a law or plan **through**, you succeed in getting it accepted, especially quickly.

push something through ❏ *The Government was determined to push the legislation through.*

push through something ❏ *The economic crisis is hampering the government's ability to push through necessary reforms.*

push something through something ❏ *The administration pushed four measures through Congress.*

2 If you **push through** or **push through** people or things that are blocking your path, you push them so that you can move past them.

push through someone/something ❏ *A fair-haired woman pushed through the crowd and ran to him.* ❏ *They pushed through the doors and went out across the pavement.*

push through ❏ *Tasha pushed through to the front of the crowd.*

3 If you **push** someone **through** an examination or course, you help and encourage them to pass or finish it. = **get through**

push someone through something ❏ *There was constant pressure to push everyone through the exam.*

push yourself through something ❏ *It takes determination and courage to push yourself through a hard running schedule.*

○ **push 'to**

When you **push** a door, gate, or window **to**, you push it so that it is closed or nearly closed.

push something to ❏ *Push that gate to before the dog gets out.* ❏ *Don't shut it, just push it to.*

○ **'push towards**

If you **push towards** a particular aim, you try very hard to achieve something or to get other people to accept it.

push towards something ❏ *We need to keep pushing towards that target of $4 million.* ❏ *They*

will need more sales staff as they push towards their goal.

○ **push 'up**

To **push up** the price, rate, or amount of something means to increase it.

push something up or **push up something** ❏ *Growing demand for property has pushed house prices up.* ❏ *The party had pushed up its share of the vote.*

○ **'push upon** → see push on

pussyfoot /'pʊsifʊt/ (**pussyfoots, pussyfooting, pussyfooted**)

○ **pussyfoot a'round** [INFORMAL]

If someone **pussyfoots around**, they do not say or do anything definite because they are worried about what will happen if they do. ❏ *Why don't they stop pussyfooting around and say what they really mean?*

put /pʊt/ (**puts, putting**)

> The form **put** is used in the present tense and is the past tense and past participle of the verb.

○ **put a'bout** [BRITISH]

1 If someone **puts about** false information or false information **is put about**, someone tells it to a lot of people.

be put about ❏ *It was put about that they were having an affair.*

put about something or **put something about** ❏ *He put about rumours that she was leaving.* ❏ *Clark had put it about that she was looking for another job.*

2 If you **put** one thing **about** another, you put it so that it surrounds the other thing.

put something about someone/something ❏ *She knelt beside him and put her arms about him.* ❏ *He put a blanket about her shoulders.*

3 When a ship **puts about**, it turns and begins to sail in the opposite direction. ❏ *Three hours out of Southampton we had to put about and go back.*

○ **'put above**

If you **put** one thing **above** another thing, you think the first thing is more important than the second thing. = **put before**

put something above something ❏ *Companies must put safety above profits.* ❏ *Mothers usually put their children's needs above their own.*

⊙ **put a'cross**

1 If you **put across** information, ideas, or opinions, you succeed in telling them or explaining them to other people.

put across something ❏ *I was finally given the chance to put across my point of view.*

put something across ❏ [+ to] *The government needs to put its message across more clearly to voters.*
NOTE **Convey** is a more formal word for **put across**.

2 If you **put** one thing **across** another, you put it on top of the other thing or against it, so that it reaches from one side to the other.
put something across something ❏ *We put some boards across the stream so that we could walk across it.*

�〉 **put a'round** (or **put round** [mainly BRITISH])

1 If you **put** something **around** another thing or a person, you put it so that it surrounds the other thing or person.
put something around something/someone ❏ *I put an arm around her shoulders.* ❏ *She put her arms round me.*

2 If someone **puts around** false information or false information **is put around**, someone tells it to a lot of people.
be put around ❏ *It's just a rumour put round by students.*
put around something or **put something around** ❏ *Somebody put around a rumour that I was getting divorced.* ❏ *People started putting it around that he was seriously ill.*

◇ **put a'side**

1 If you **put aside** an activity, a problem, or a feeling, you stop doing it, thinking about it, or showing it. = **set aside**
put aside something ❏ *Let's put aside the issue of money for a moment.*
put something aside ❏ *I put the idea aside, and for a year thought no more of it.* ❏ *I tried to put my doubts aside and get on with the task.*

2 If you **put aside** an object you were using, you put it somewhere next to you because you do not need it. = **lay aside**
put aside something ❏ *Jimmie put aside his papers.*
put something aside ❏ *The old man put his books aside and spoke to us.*

3 If you **put aside** money, food, clothes, etc., you save them for a particular purpose or until you need them. = **put by**
put something aside ❏ [+ to-infinitive] *Many parents put money aside to help pay for their child's education.* ❏ [+ for] *I've been putting money aside for a car.*
put aside something ❏ *Luckily, he'd put aside some savings.*

4 If you **put aside** time, you keep it free for a particular purpose.
put aside something or **put something aside** ❏ [+ for] *Many women find it hard to put aside time for themselves.* ❏ [+ to-infinitive]

I try to put aside a couple of hours every week to read. ❏ *Couples should put time aside to go out together.*

○ **'put at**

If someone **puts** the cost, age, value, etc. of something **at** a particular amount or it **is put at** that amount, they guess that it is that amount.
put something at something ❏ *I put her age at somewhere between forty and fifty.* ❏ *The United Nations has put the figure at about seventy thousand.*
be put at something ❏ *The cost of the pipeline is now put at 2.7 billion pounds.*

◎ **put a'way**

1 If you **put** something **away**, you put it in the place where you usually keep it.
put something away ❏ *She put her shopping away in the kitchen.* ❏ *Al folded the newspaper neatly and put it away.*
put away something ❏ *She closed her notebook and put away her pen.*

2 If you **put away** food or drink, you eat or drink a lot of it. [INFORMAL]
put away something ❏ *He put away two plates of spaghetti and was still hungry.*

3 If you **put** money **away**, you save it. = **put by**
put something away or **put away something** ❏ *I try to put some money away each month.* ❏ *Most people are not putting away sufficient money to provide for a comfortable old age.* ❏ [+ for] *This was money that he had put away for a holiday.*

4 If a judge or other official **puts** someone **away** or they are **put away**, they are sent to prison. = **lock away** [INFORMAL]
put someone away ❏ *We've now got enough evidence to put him away for life.*
be put away ❏ *You assume that the killer will be put away for a long time.*

5 To **put** someone **away** means to kill them. [INFORMAL]
put someone away or **put away someone** ❏ *He was put away by a single bullet to the head.*

◎ **put 'back**

1 If you **put** something **back** somewhere, you put it in the place it was in before it was moved.
put something back ❏ *She put the telephone back.* ❏ *Shall I put it back in the box for you?*
put back something ❏ *'OK,' said Stein, putting back the clothes.*
NOTE **Replace** is a more formal word for **put back**.

2 If you **put your head back**, you move it so that your face is pointing upwards. ❏ *He put* his head back and closed his eyes. ❑ He put back his head and laughed.

3 To **put** someone or something **back** means to change them so that they are in the state they were in before.

put something/someone back ❑ He put the car back in gear and drove on. ❑ They gave her enough medication to put her back to sleep. ❑ It's an issue that must be put back on the agenda.

4 To **put back** an event or appointment means to make it happen later than planned. ≠ **bring forward** [BRITISH]

put back something or **put something back** ❑ Illness prompted the singer to put back several concerts. ❑ [+ to] Race organizers had planned an 11am start, but this has now been put back to 12.30. ❑ We had to put the meeting back.

NOTE **Defer** is a more formal word for **put back**.

5 To **put back** the progress of something means to make it happen more slowly. = **set back**

put something back or **put back something** ❑ Injury put my training back a week or two. ❑ The collapse of the company will almost certainly put back the project by several months.

6 If you **put** a clock or watch **back**, you change it so that it shows an earlier time, for example when you travel from one time zone to another. ≠ **put forward**

put something back or **put back something** ❑ I put my watch back an hour before we landed at Kennedy Airport.

7 If you **put back** alcoholic drink, you drink a large amount of it in a short time. = **knock back** [INFORMAL]

put back something or **put something back** ❑ He'd put back rather too much wine the night before.

○ **put 'back into**

If you **put** money **back into** a business or a country's economy, you use some of the profits or taxes to pay for new development.

put something back into something ❑ They put all their earnings back into the company. ❑ Only a small percentage of this revenue is being put back into maintaining roads.

○ **put back 'on**

If you **put** a piece of clothing **back on**, you wear it again after taking it off.

put something back on ❑ If we're going out again, I'll put my coat back on. ❑ Ben took off his glasses, wiped them, and put them back on.

○ **put be'fore**

1 If you **put** one thing **before** another thing, you think the first thing is more important than the second thing.

put something before something ❑ Louise complains that I put my work before my family. ❑ She had always put the needs of others before her own.

2 If you **put** food **before** someone, you put it in front of them so that they can eat it. [FORMAL]

put something before someone ❑ I eat what's put before me.

3 If you **put** facts or ideas **before** someone in authority, you officially explain or tell them to them.

put something before someone ❑ Grant did not put any of this evidence before the jury. ❑ They would put the joint plan before the security council on Friday.

○ **put be'hind**

1 If you **put** a bad experience **behind** you, you try to forget it and not allow it to affect you.

put something behind you ❑ We need to move forward, put the past behind us. ❑ I've tried to put it behind me, but I cannot help remembering.

2 If you **put** money, knowledge, etc. **behind** a project or person, you use it to support that project or person.

put something behind something/someone ❑ Be sure to investigate any such schemes before putting your money behind them.

○ **put 'by** [BRITISH]

If you **put by** a sum of money or a supply of something, you save it so that you can use it later. = **put aside**

put by something or **put something by** ❑ I put by a few pounds every week for such things as holidays. ❑ He had prudently put it by for future use.

○ **put 'down**

1 If you **put down** someone or something that you are holding or carrying, you put them on the floor or on a table, bed, etc. = **set down**; ≠ **pick up**

put someone/something down ❑ He put the basket down and looked inside it. ❑ She put the baby down for a moment. ❑ [+ on] Greene put his drink down on the table.

put down someone/something ❑ She put down her case and kissed him.

2 If you **put the phone down**, you end your call. ❑ He put the phone down without saying goodbye. ❑ Tweed put down the phone and sighed with relief.

3 If you **put down** a lawn, a carpet, or other covering, you cover a ground, floor or other flat surface with it.

put something down or **put down something** ❑ We put carpets down to make the *house more cosy.* ❏ *Don't be in too big a hurry to put down a lawn; prepare the ground thoroughly beforehand.*

4 If someone **puts down** poison, they spread it on the ground to kill animals.

put down something or **put something down** ❏ *How do they get rid of these rats and mice? Do they put down poison?*

5 If you **put down** a part of your body, you move it to a lower position.

put something down or **put down something** ❏ *OK, you can put your hands down now, children.*

NOTE **Lower** is a more formal word for **put down**.

6 If you **put down** money when you are buying something, you pay a part of the money that you owe.

put down something or **put something down** ❏ *We've put down a deposit of five thousand pounds on each plot.* ❏ *Do you want me to put a deposit down to secure the offer?*

7 When you **put down** something, you write it somewhere.

put down something or **put something down** ❏ *All you have to do is put down exactly what we've just said.* ❏ *You haven't put Professor Mangel's name down on the list.*

8 If someone in a meeting **puts down** a suggestion, they officially ask for it to be discussed and voted on. [TECHNICAL]

put down something ❏ *The Tribune Group had put down a motion condemning the government's policy.*

NOTE **Table** is a more formal word for **put down**.

9 If people in authority **put down** a protest, they use force to stop people from protesting.

put down something or **put something down** ❏ *The government had successfully put down a series of revolts.* ❏ *The President ordered the military to put the rebellion down.*

NOTE **Suppress** is a more formal word for **put down**.

10 If you **put** someone **down**, you criticize them and make them feel stupid.

put someone down or **put down someone** ❏ *Another thing that upsets me is the way Alex tries to put me down in public.* ❏ *I hate the way she puts down people in meetings.*

put yourself down ❏ *Stop putting yourself down.*

NOTE **Slag off** is a very informal expression for **put down**.

• A **put-down** is a statement that is intended to criticize someone and make them feel stupid. ❏ *The word 'ambitious' is often used as a put-down, as in 'I like her, but she's so ambitious'.*

11 When someone **puts** a baby **down**, they put him or her in a bed or cot so they can sleep.

put someone down ❏ *I fed Isabel and put her down for her nap.* ❏ *She had just put the baby down for a rest.*

12 If you **put** someone or their name **down**, you put their name on a list or document as a way of arranging for them to do or have something.

put someone/something down or **put down someone/something** ❏ *I'm looking for some parents to help at the school fair. Can I put your name down?* ❏ [+ for] *We've put her down for a school in the next village.*

13 If you **put down** or **put** yourself **down** for something, you formally apply to have it or do it.

put down ❏ [+ for] *There were morning sessions for women. My wife put down for Tuesdays and Thursdays.*

put yourself down ❏ [+ for] *He claims the CEO has put himself down for a 75 per cent raise.*

14 If a vet **puts down** an animal, he or she kills it, because it is ill, old, or dangerous. = **destroy** [BRITISH]

put something down or **put down something** ❏ *The cat had to be put down after it was found with serious injuries.* ❏ *They put the dog down because it had bitten a child.*

15 When the driver of a vehicle **puts down** a passenger, he or she stops in order to let them get out. ≠ **pick up**

put someone down or **put down someone** ❏ *The taxi put me down outside the museum.* ❏ *The cab had stopped suddenly to put down a passenger.* • A **put-down** point is a place where a bus or coach stops in order to let people get off. ❏ *The bus had used the shop as its pick-up and put-down point.*.

16 When an aeroplane **puts down** somewhere, it lands there for a short time. ❏ *We should put down at Aumont some time between five thirty and six.* ❏ *They will put down in Rome to refuel.*

○ **put 'down as**

If you **put** someone or something **down as** a particular type of person or thing, you think they are that type, especially when this is wrong.

put someone/something down as something ❏ *I knew he'd been in trouble but I would never have put him down as a car thief.* ❏ *Their deaths had been put down as a tragic accident.*

○ **put 'down to**

If you **put** one thing **down to** another

thing, you think that the first thing is caused by the second thing.

put something down to something ❏ *She put her stomach pain down to some seafood she had eaten the night before.* ❏ *He sounded a bit depressed, which I put down to Jane's departure.*

○ **put 'forth** [FORMAL]

If you **put forth** an idea or theory, you state it or publish it so that people can consider it and discuss it. = **set forth**

put forth something ❏ *Psychologists have put forth several theories to explain this phenomenon.*

✪ **put 'forward**

1 If you **put forward** an idea or plan, you state it or publish it so that people can consider it and discuss it. = **set out**

put forward something ❏ *The government put forward a plan for economic recovery.* ❏ *The theory was first put forward by scientists in the U.S.*

put something forward ❏ *She planned to put her suggestions forward at the next meeting.*

PUT FORWARD + noun
put forward **an idea**
put forward **a proposal**
put forward **an argument**
put forward **a suggestion**
put forward **a theory**

❏ *They put forward a proposal to build a new bridge.* ❏ *She put forward the argument that torture is wrong in any circumstance.*

2 If you **put forward** a person or their name, you suggest that they should be considered for a particular job or position.

put forward someone/something ❏ [+ for] *The organization put forward eight candidates for the role.*

put someone/something forward ❏ [+ for] *I asked him to put my name forward for the vacancy in Zurich.* ❏ [+ as] *No one put me forward as a possible alternative to Jefferson.*

put yourself forward ❏ [+ as] *He put himself forward as a candidate for the election.* ❏ [+ for] *I put myself forward for the job.*

NOTE **Nominate** is a more formal word for **put forward**.

3 If you **put forward** an event, you arrange for it to happen earlier than planned. = **bring forward**

put forward something or **put something forward** ❏ *It was decided to put forward the dance display.* ❏ [+ to] *The meeting was put forward to the eleventh of March.*

4 If you **put** a clock or watch **forward**, you change it so that it shows a later time, for example when you travel from one time zone to another. ≠ **put back**

put something forward or **put forward something** ❏ *I forgot to put my watch forward while I was on the plane.*

○ **put 'in**

1 If you **put** something **in** or **put** one thing **in** another, you put one thing inside another thing.

put something in ❏ *I need to put a new battery in.*

put in something ❏ *He put in a ten-dollar bill.*

put something in something ❏ *She put a spoonful of sugar in her tea.* ❏ *I folded my apron and put it in the drawer.*

2 If you **put in** plants or crops, you plant them in the ground.

put in something or **put something in** ❏ *Brazilian farmers put in a few hundred more coffee bushes.* ❏ *I'll put the cabbages in.*

3 If you **put in** a piece of new equipment or a new part, you fix it in the correct place in a building or a machine.

put in something or **put something in** ❏ *They've put in a more powerful engine.* ❏ *I had new windows put in.* ❏ *Jim put that door in himself.*

NOTE **Install** is a more formal word for **put in**.

4 If you **put** money **in** a bank or an account you give the money to the bank, which will look after it for you. = **pay in**

put in something or **put something in** ❏ *His father put the money in for him.* ❏ *You can put in and draw out cash at any branch of the bank.*

put something in something ❏ *You may prefer to put the money in a savings account.*

NOTE **Deposit** is a more formal word for **put in**.

5 If you **put** money **in** a business, a project, or a country, you provide money that it needs.

put in something or **put something in** ❏ *The European Union is expected to put in 14.4 million euros.* ❏ *If we're putting more money in, we want to see some improvements.*

put something in something ❏ *He has put a lot of money in shows, including 'Evita'.*

NOTE **Invest** is a more formal word for **put in**.

6 If you **put in** time or effort doing something, you spend time or work hard doing it.

put in something or **put something in** ❏ *Half of them were putting in forty-five hours a week or more.* ❏ *I was certainly pleased by the level of effort everyone put in today.* ● The **input** in an activity is the time or effort spent on it. ❏ *Input from the workers is vital.*

7 If you **put in** a remark, you say it when

someone else is speaking. **= chip in**
put in something ❏ 'We're not talking about that,' Alison put in smartly. ❏ 'But didn't you hear what I said?' put in Sally.

NOTE **Interject** is a more formal word for **put in**.

8 If you **put** something **in** a piece of writing, speech, or a drawing, you include it.

put in something or **put something in** ❏ She read my story and suggested I put in a description of the girl. ❏ Why don't you put a few more jokes in?
put something in something ❏ I think you need to put some more details in your drawing. ❏ I'm glad you made that point and I'll put it in my report. ● Someone's **input** is all the things that they say in a conversation or discussion. ❏ Both groups provided an important input into the discussion.

9 If you **put in** an order, a bill, or a request, you officially ask for something.

put in something or **put something in** ❏ She put in a request for some time off work. ❏ The Americans put in an order for five of the new planes.

10 To **put** someone or something **in** a particular state or situation means to cause them to be in that state or situation.

put someone in something ❏ This puts me in a rather difficult position. ❏ The events of the morning had put me in a bad mood.
put yourself in something ❏ Firefighters put themselves in danger every day.

11 If you **put** someone or something **in** a particular group of people or things, you consider that they belong in that group.

put someone/something in something ❏ Many people wouldn't put him in the same class as Verdi.

12 When people **put in** a person or group, they officially choose that person or group to do a particular job. **= bring in**

put someone in or **put in someone** ❏ [+ as] They're putting me in as editor. ❏ They preferred a system of direct rule, putting in their own governors.

13 To **put** someone **in** something such as a prison or hospital means to make them go and stay there.

put someone in something ❏ Should he put his elderly father in a nursing home? ❏ He was put in prison for nine years.

14 If you **put** someone **in** a particular room in a building, you arrange for them to be there or sleep there.

put someone in something ❏ They put us in two single rooms. ❏ We were put in a room on the first floor.

15 If you **put** someone **in** particular clothes, you make them wear them.

put someone in something ❏ Put children in shorts and a T-shirt if the weather's warm. ❏ The inspectors were put in uniform and given truncheons.

16 If you **put** faith, trust, or hope **in** someone or something, you feel confident or hopeful that they will do or be what you want.

put something in someone/something ❏ The family put all their hopes in their son. ❏ They did not put much faith in banks and preferred to keep their money at home.

17 When a ship **puts in**, it stops at a place for a short time. ❏ The ship had to put in here during the storm. ❏ [+ at] We were refused permission to put in at Corfu.

○ **put 'in for**
If you **put in for** something, you officially ask for it.

put in for something ❏ She'd put in for a transfer to the company's office in San Diego. ❏ The club has put in for planning permission to build a new stadium.

✪ **put 'into**

1 If you **put** one thing **into** another, you put it inside the other thing.

put something into something ❏ He put his hands into his pockets.

2 If you **put** money **into** a bank or an account, you give the money to the bank, which will look after it for you. **= pay into; ≠ take out**

put something into something ❏ I put three hundred pounds into Joe's account. ❏ Put the money into the bank as quickly as possible.

3 If you **put** money **into** a business or a project, you provide money that it needs.

put something into something ❏ The government has put an extra £21 billion into the health service. ❏ A lot of funding has been put into this research.

4 If you **put** time, effort, or other resources **into** an activity, you use it for doing that activity.

put something into something ❏ They'd obviously put a lot of time and effort into preparing the meal. ❏ She put all her energy into the business.

5 If you **put** something **into** a piece of writing, a speech, or a drawing, you include it. **= insert**

put something into something ❏ He tried to put some jokes into his speech. ❏ You need to put more detail into your essay.

6 To **put** a feeling or attitude **into** someone or something means to make them feel it or have it.

put something into someone/something
❑ He needs to put a bit more expression into his voice when he's giving a speech.

7 To **put** someone or something **into** a state, form, or situation means to make them be in it.

put someone/something into something
❑ Reading this put me into a state of total panic. ❑ He found it difficult to put his feelings into words.

put yourself into something ❑ By putting yourself into a positive frame of mind, you will feel better.

8 To **put** someone or something **into** a particular group or type means to think that they belong to that group or type.

put someone/something into something
❑ She had definitely put Kate into the troublemaker category.

9 To **put** someone **into** a job or position means to officially choose them for it.

put someone into something ❑ It was part of the plan to put Eisenhower into the job of Supreme Commander.

10 To **put** someone **into** a place such as prison or a home for old people means to make them go and stay there.

put someone into something ❑ We had to put my mother into a nursing home. ❑ She was arrested and put into prison.

11 If someone **is put into** a particular room in a building or someone **puts** them **into** it, they are told or allowed to be there or stay there.

be put into something ❑ When Josie arrived, she was put into a room on the ground floor.

put someone into something ❑ The police put me into a separate room and told me they were arresting me too.

12 If someone **is put into** particular clothes, they are made to dress in those clothes.

be put into something ❑ Even tiny girls were put into black dresses.

13 If a ship **puts into** a port, it stops there for a short time.

put into something ❑ We might have to put into Hammerfest for shelter.

○ put 'off

1 If you **put off** something, you delay it or arrange to do it at a later time than planned.

put off something ❑ She used tiredness as an excuse to put off unpleasant tasks. ❑ Women are putting off having children until their thirties or forties.

put something off ❑ I know I've got to call him but I keep putting it off. ❑ [+ until] Don't put it off

until tomorrow. ❑ [+ for] As for the meeting, could we put it off for a few days?

2 If you **put** a person **off**, you delay seeing them or doing what they want you to do.

put someone off ❑ He's asked me to meet him twice now and I've put him off both times.

3 To **put** someone **off** something or someone means to make them not want to do something or not like something or someone.

put someone off ❑ It put me off when he started talking about how much money he earned.
❑ Don't be put off because something doesn't have instant results.

put off someone ❑ The country's high prices have put off many tourists.

put someone off something/someone
❑ The disgusting smell put me off my breakfast.
● If someone or something is **off-putting**, it makes you dislike them or not want to do something. ❑ The restaurant was painted in a rather off-putting scarlet colour. ❑ I found her manner rather off-putting. ● A **put-off** is something that makes you dislike someone or something or not want to do something. [AMERICAN] ❑ The weather was a put-off. ❑ High prices could be a put-off for many consumers.

4 If something or someone **puts** you **off** what you are doing, they cause you to stop concentrating.

put someone off ❑ Stop laughing – you're putting me off!

5 If you **put** a light **off**, you move a switch so that it no longer shines. = **switch off, put out**

put something off or **put off something**
❑ I put the light off again. ❑ She lay down again and put off the light.

6 When a ship or vehicle **puts** someone **off**, it stops somewhere so they can get off.

put someone off or **put off someone**
❑ He was put off at Singapore.

○ 'put on

> In meanings 3–11, 19 and 20, the stress is on **'on**.

1 If you **put** something **on** something, you put it above that thing and touching it.

put something on something ❑ I put the book on his desk. ❑ He put a hand on my shoulder.
❑ She put the drinks on a tray.

2 If you **put** one thing **on** another, you attach or fix it to the other thing.

put something on something ❑ We put a new lock on the bathroom door. ❑ He put some pictures on the wall.

3 When you **put on** a piece of clothing, you

put it over a part of your body and wear it, or you put it over a part of someone else's body so they are wearing it. ≠ **take off**

put something on ❏ She put her coat on.

put on something ❏ I put on my warmest jacket.

put something on someone ❏ I put that new sweater on him.

4 When you **put on** make-up, a cream, or perfume, you spread or spray it on your skin.

put something on or **put on something** ❏ She put lipstick on before every class. ❏ He puts on too much aftershave.

put something on something ❏ I put some cream on the cut.

5 To **put on** a play, concert, or other entertainment means to organize it or to perform in it.

put on something or **put something on** ❏ The school is putting on a show for parents. ❏ More than 100 people have been involved in putting this concert on.

NOTE **Stage** is a more formal word for **put on**.

6 When a person or organization **puts on** a service, they provide it. = **lay on**; ≠ **take off**

put on something or **put something on** ❏ They're putting on a special train service. ❏ The airline plans to put extra flights on to cope with the demand. ❏ Free IT courses are put on for people who are unemployed.

7 If someone **puts on** weight, they become heavier. = **gain**; ≠ **lose**

put on something or **put something on** ❏ I put on over ten kilograms. ❏ I put weight on very quickly.

8 If you **put on** an electrical or gas device, you make it work by pressing or turning a switch. = **turn on, switch on**

put on something or **put something on** ❏ He put on the light. ❏ Shall I put the oven on? ❏ I'll put the kettle on.

9 If you are driving a vehicle and **put on** the brake, you use it to make the vehicle stop.

put on something or **put something on** ❏ She had to put on her brake rather suddenly. ❏ Put the brake on and leave the car in gear.

NOTE **Apply** is a more formal word for **put on**.

10 If you **put on** a DVD or CD, you put it in a machine so that you can hear it or see it.

put something on or **put on something** ❏ We put a movie on for the kids to watch. ❏ She put on a track from her favourite band.

11 If you **put on** food or a meal, you start to cook it.

put something on or **put on something** ❏ I must put the dinner on. ❏ He went into the kitchen and put on some potatoes to boil.

12 If you **put** money **on** a race, a competition, or one of the competitors, you guess who will win so that you will win money if you are right.

put something on something/someone ❏ He was so convinced she was going to win, he put fifty pounds on it.

put something on ❏ I put ten pounds on for you.

13 If you say that you would **put money on** something, you mean that you are confident or sure that it is true, will happen, or will be successful. ❏ He'll be back. I'd put money on it. ❏ He might succeed but I wouldn't put money on it.

14 To **put** an amount **on** the cost or value of something means to add it to the cost or value. ≠ **knock off**

put something on something ❏ That decision will put another 2p a litre on petrol. ❏ An improvement like this might put an extra twenty thousand on the value of your home.

15 To **put** a limit or a ban **on** something means to make a law which stops people from doing it or makes them do it less.

put something on something ❏ The President put an immediate ban on all television coverage. ❏ Last month, the government put new restrictions on pesticide use.

16 If you **put** emphasis or reliance **on** something, you consider it to be very important.

put something on something ❏ Society puts too great an emphasis on women's appearances. ❏ Too much reliance was put on the use of cars.

17 If you **put the blame on** someone, you say that they are responsible for doing something bad. ❏ It just isn't right to put all the blame on him. ❏ He had tried to put the blame on his brother.

18 To **put** extra work, responsibility, or pressure **on** someone means to make them do it or have it.

put something on someone ❏ It puts a tremendous responsibility on us. ❏ They put pressure on her to get the work done.

19 If you **put on** a way of speaking or behaving, you speak or behave in a way that is not your normal voice or way of behaving or does not show what you really feel or think.

put something on or **put on something** ❏ I don't understand why she puts on this phoney English accent. ❏ Like a lot of people, she puts on a special voice for the phone.

• If you say that someone **is putting it on**,

you mean that they are pretending to feel something or to be something, or that they are pretending to be more upset, ill etc. than they really are. ❏ *I knew she was ill and not putting it on.*

20 If someone **puts** you **on**, they try to make you believe something that is not true, as a joke. **= have on, kid** [AMERICAN, INFORMAL]

put someone on ❏ *He didn't say that! You're putting me on.* ❏ *He's fifty? Are you putting me on?*

• A **put-on** is an action or way of behaving that is intended to make someone believe something that is not true. [INFORMAL] ❏ *I bet the whole thing was a put-on.*

21 If you **put** someone **on** a bus, plane, train, or ship, you take them to it and make sure they get onto it.

put someone on something ❏ *My mother put me on the train at Victoria station.* ❏ *We put him on a plane to California this morning.*

22 If you **put** someone **on** a committee or a particular job, you officially give them that position or that work.

put someone on something ❏ *Some companies put trade union representatives on their boards.* ❏ *They put me on security work again at the weekends.*

23 If you **put** someone **on**, or **put** them **on** the phone, you give the phone to them so that they can speak to someone.

put someone on or **put on someone** ❏ *Just put on Nell for one moment, will you?* ❏ *Can you put Carlos on? I need to ask him something.*

put someone on something ❏ *I asked him to put Lloyd on the phone.* ❏ *Can you put her on the phone?*

24 If a doctor, nurse, etc. **puts** someone **on** a particular type of food or medical treatment, they say that person should have it.

put someone on something ❏ *They had to put him on oxygen.* ❏ *My doctor put me on antibiotics.* ❏ *Laura's been put on a low-fat diet.*

○ **put 'on to, put 'onto**

1 If you **put** one thing **onto** another, you put it on top of the other thing or attach it to the other thing.

put something onto something ❏ *Maria put her hand gently onto the other woman's arm.* ❏ *She put a piece of wood onto the fire.*

2 If you **put** someone **onto** a bus, plane, train, or plane, you take them to it and make sure they get on it.

put someone onto something ❏ *They were put onto buses and sent back over the border.*

3 If you **put** someone **onto** someone or something, you tell them about someone

or something good that they will like or that could help them.

put someone onto someone/something ❏ *It was my sister-in-law who put me onto this hotel.* ❏ *Annette put me onto a really good doctor.*

○ **put 'out**

1 To **put out** information means to officially tell it to many people. **= issue**

put out something ❏ *The company put out a statement saying that the chief executive had resigned.* ❏ *Police put out a warning not to approach the man.*

put something out ❏ *He's put the story out himself.*

2 To put out a message or programme is to send or broadcast it on radio or television.

put out something or **put something out** ❏ *The pilot put out a radio message giving the exact position.* ❏ [+ on] *A general call was put out on the police radio.*

NOTE **Broadcast** is a more formal word for **put out**.

3 If you **put out** something that is burning, you cause it to stop burning.

put something out ❏ *He put the fire out.* ❏ *Ava lit another cigarette, but immediately put it out.*

put out something ❏ *We remembered to put out the candles.* ❏ *The fire was put out very quickly.*

NOTE **Extinguish** is a more formal word for **put out**.

4 If you **put out** a light, you cause it to stop shining by pressing or turning a switch. **= switch off, turn off**

put out something or **put something out** ❏ *Castle got into bed and put out the light.* ❏ *He put his torch out.*

5 If you **put** something **out**, you take it out of your home and leave it for someone else to collect. **≠ bring in**

put out something or **put something out** ❏ *I asked John to put out the rubbish.* ❏ *You must not put your bin out before 7.30 a.m.*

6 If you **put out** a baby or an animal, you put them outside a building for a while.

put someone/something out or **put out someone/something** ❏ *They put their horses out to graze.* ❏ *We put out the cat at night.*

7 If you **put** something **out**, you put it somewhere where someone will notice and use it. **= lay out; ≠ collect up**

put something out or **put out something** ❏ *I put clean clothes out for you on the bed.* ❏ *She changed the sheets and put out fresh towels.*

8 If you **put out** a hand, an arm, or a foot, you move it forward and away from your body. **= hold out**

put out something or **put something out**
❑ I slipped and put out my arm to save myself.
❑ Denise put her hand out to restrain him.

9 If someone **puts** their **tongue out**, they put their tongue through their lips so that other people can see it, usually to be rude.
= **stick out** ❑ A small boy ran up and put his tongue out. ❑ 'Put out your tongue,' she said, and I obeyed. ❑ [+ at] She put her tongue out at me.

10 If you **put** your back or a joint in your body **out**, you hurt it by causing a bone to move from its normal position.
put something out ❑ I'd put my back out and was in agony. ❑ Careful or you'll put your shoulder out again.
NOTE **Dislocate** is a more formal word for **put out**.

11 If you **are put out**, someone or something has upset or annoyed you.
be put out ❑ Julian was understandably put out by Jim's refusal to listen to him.
NOTE **Be disconcerted** is a more formal expression for **be put out**.
● Someone's **put-out** expression indicates that they have been upset or annoyed.
❑ 'He'll be right back,' she said in a slightly put-out tone. ● If you are **put out**, you are upset or annoyed. ❑ Lally looked a bit put out.
NOTE **Be disconcerted** is a more formal expression for **be put out**.

12 If you **put** yourself **out**, you make an effort to do something for someone, even though it is inconvenient.
put yourself out ❑ [+ to-infinitive] He was putting himself out to please her. ❑ She didn't exactly put herself out to help us.

13 If you **put** someone **out**, you cause problems for them or make extra work for them.
put someone out ❑ I'll come, as long as it doesn't put you out in any way.

14 If you **put** someone **out**, you make them leave a place, vehicle or job, sometimes by force.
put someone out ❑ [+ of] We put him out of the house. ❑ You can be put out at the end of the month if you don't make the target.

15 In a sports competition, to **put out** a player or team means to defeat them so that they are no longer in the competition.
= **knock out**
put out someone/something or **put someone/something out** ❑ Spaniard Emilio Sanchez put out Jens Woehrmann in three sets. ❑ [+ of] This was the team that put England out of the competition last year.

16 When a boat or ship **puts out**, it leaves and sails into the sea. ❑ We could see the boats putting out.

17 If someone **puts out**, they agree to have sex. [INFORMAL]

18 To **put** someone **out** means to cause them to become unconscious.
put someone out ❑ The doctor agreed to put her out altogether during the birth.

19 When a plant or tree **puts out** buds, leaves or flowers, the buds, leaves or flowers appear.
put out something ❑ When it starts putting out leaves, you know that summer is near.

20 If a company **puts out** products, it makes or sells them. = **produce**
put out something or **put something out**
❑ Several companies are putting out similar software. ❑ No company would put a product out without testing the market first. ● The **output** of someone or something is the amount of something that they produce, or the thing that they produce. ❑ There was a 3 per cent fall in industrial output.

○ put 'out of
To **put** someone or something **out of** a state or condition means to stop them being in it.
put someone/something out of something ❑ Always put poisons out of reach. ❑ Technological developments may put them completely out of business. ❑ Come on, put me out of my misery. Did you pass the test or not?

○ put 'over
1 If you **put** one thing **over** another, you cover the second thing with the first.
put something over something ❑ She put a hand over his. ❑ He took off his coat and put it over the back of the chair.

2 If you **put** one thing **over** another on a vertical surface or on a piece of paper, you put or write it above the other thing.
put something over something ❑ Alan put a sign over the door. ❑ She put dots over each letter.

3 When you **put** an idea **over**, you succeed in describing or explaining it to someone.
= **put across, get across**
put over something or **put something over** ❑ Hockney has a great talent for putting over complicated ideas. ❑ I think she has to be careful about how she puts her opinions over.

○ put 'past
If you say that you **wouldn't put it past** someone to do something bad, you mean that you think they might do it. ❑ It could have been Anita that took the books. I wouldn't put it past her. ❑ I wouldn't have put it past him to have listened in to our conversation.

○ put 'round → see **put around**

○ put 'through

1 If you **put** something **through** a solid object, you pass it from one side to the other either by pushing it through a hole, or by making a hole through it by force.
put something through something ❑ *She simply put her hand through the letter-box and opened the door from the inside.* ❑ *He put his foot through the plaster.*

2 If you **put** your arm **through** someone else's arm, you put your arm in the space between their body and their arm and bend your arm around their arm, either to show affection or to control the direction they are moving in.
put something through something
❑ *Gertrude put her arm through Tim's and led him away.*

3 If you **put** an object or substance **through** a machine or a process, you use this machine or process to change or affect it.
put something through something ❑ *Put cooked vegetables and fruit through the blender.* ❑ *The plasma is saved and then put through a process which removes the virus.* ● The **throughput** of a machine or factory is the amount of material that it deals with or the speed at which it deals with it. [TECHNICAL] ❑ *These machines can handle a rapid throughput of raw materials.*

4 If you **put** a plan or problem **through** an official system, organization or person, you give them information about it in order to get approval or advice.
put something through something ❑ *No need to put it through my department at all. I'll handle it personally.*

5 If people in authority **put through** a proposal or plan, they formally agree to it.
put through something or **put something through** ❑ *The team was set up to put through a series of radical proposals.* ❑ *They had at last succeeded in putting the reform through.*

6 If you **put** a message **through**, you succeed in sending it to someone.
put through something or **put something through** ❑ [+ to] *I've put a request through to Washington.*

7 If you **put through** a phone call or the person making the call, you connect them with the person they want to speak to.
put someone/something through ❑ *Please don't put any calls through until this class is over.* ❑ *Who? Martha? Okay. Yes, put her through.* ❑ [+ to] *I called and was put through to the customer services department.*

8 If you **put** someone **through** school or college, you pay for them to be there.
put someone through something ❑ *His grandparents offered to put him through dental school.*
put yourself through something ❑ *He took two jobs in order to put himself through medical school.*

9 If you **put** someone or something **through** an event or experience, you make them do it or suffer it.
put someone/something through something ❑ *I'm sorry to put you through this again.* ❑ *Candidates were put through a rigorous selection process.*

○ 'put to

1 If you **put** one thing **to** another, you move it so that it touches the other thing.
put something to something ❑ *He put a finger to his lips in a gesture of silence.* ❑ *They put a gun to his head.*

2 If you **put** a name, figure, date, or face **to** something or someone, you are able to say who, what, or how much they are.
put something to something/someone
❑ *He recognised the face, but he couldn't put a name to it.* ❑ *It's difficult to put a figure to the real cost.*

3 If you **put** something **to** someone, you say it to them in order to find out how they react to it.
put something to someone ❑ *These are the sort of questions that I'll be putting to the politicians.* ❑ *This suggestion will be put to the next party conference.* ❑ *Police put it to him that he had been driving the car.*

4 If someone **puts** you **to** a lot of trouble or expense, they make you spend a lot of your time or money doing something.
put someone to something ❑ *I'm only sorry that I put you to so much trouble.*

○ put to'gether

1 If you **put together** an object or its parts, you join its parts to each other so that it can be used. ≠ **take apart**
put together something ❑ *It's very interesting to see how they put together these huge structures.*
put something together ❑ *I have all the parts here – I just need to put them together.* ❑ *He helped me to put my new bed together.*

NOTE **Assemble** is a more formal word for **put together**.

2 If you **put together** similar things, you put them near or touching each other, or in the same container.
put something together ❑ *We put the tables together so we could all have dinner.* ❑ *They put the substances together in a test-tube.*

put together something ❑ *She put together a fresh fruit salad.*

3 If you **put together** a team, group, etc. you form it by choosing people for it.

put together something ❑ *They put together a baseball team.* ❑ *The lawyers had put together an impressive assembly of witnesses.*

put something together ❑ *So many players were injured that the manager was struggling to put a team together.*

4 If you **put together** a project or a piece of work, you organize it or arrange it.

put together something or **put something together** ❑ *The U.S. Congress has put together a 33-volume report on what happened.* ❑ *He agreed to give them more time to put a proposal together.* ❑ *The whole production was somewhat hastily put together.*

5 If you **put together** facts, you consider a number of facts at the same time and think about the way that they are connected.

put something together or **put together something** ❑ *Officers have spent six months putting together the evidence.*

6 If you say that one person or thing is better, bigger, etc. than a group of other people or things **put together** or has achieved more than a group of other people or things **put together**, you mean they are much better, bigger, etc. or have achieved far more. ❑ *This museum brings in more visitors than all the other museums put together.* ❑ *She was more intelligent than the other two put together.*

) **put to'wards**

If you **put** an amount of money **towards** something, you use that money as part of the payment for something.

put something towards something ❑ *If I do win, I'll put the money towards a new car.* ❑ *She gave me fifty dollars, which I'm going to put towards a new jacket.*

▶ **put 'up**

1 If you **put** something **up**, you move it to a higher position.

put up something ❑ *He put up the collar of his jacket.*

put something up ❑ *Anna put her feet up on the desk.* ❑ *Put your hands up if you know this answer.*

2 If you **put** one thing **up** another, you lift it so that it is inside the other thing.

put something up something ❑ *She put her hand up her sleeve and pulled out the glove that was stuck there.*

3 If you **put up** a building, wall or other structure, you build it. ≠ **pull down**

put up something ❑ *We'll have to put up a*

fence. ❑ *They're going to put up a whole block of apartments.* ❑ *In Stirling, they've put up a statue of William Wallace.*

put something up ❑ *It would ruin the square to put a building up in the middle of it.*

NOTE **Erect** and **construct** are more formal words for **put up**.

4 If you **put up** a shelf, you fix it to a wall.

put up something or **put something up** ❑ *He was busy putting up some shelves.* ❑ *New shelves! When did you put those up?*

5 If you **put up** something that is folded, such as an umbrella, tent, or hood, you open it or spread it out so that it can be used.

put something up or **put up something** ❑ *Put your umbrella up.* ❑ *Why doesn't she put the hood up?* ❑ *I put up a tent in the garden.*

6 If you **put up** a notice or poster, you fasten it to a wall, board, door, etc. = **stick up, post up**; ≠ **take down**

put up something. or **put something up** ❑ *She put up a large sign outside her house.* ❑ *They put posters up to advertise the event.*

7 If you **put up** opposition or a fight, you argue against something or fight someone.

put up something ❑ *Tim realized he couldn't win, so he put up little resistance.* ❑ *I may not win this battle but I'm certainly going to put up a fight.*

8 If you **put up** an idea or suggestion, you tell it to people so that they can consider and discuss it. = **put forward, put forth**

put something up or **put up something** ❑ *He would always get people to put ideas up, but he never used any of them.* ❑ *We put up a proposal which is under discussion at the moment.*

9 If you **put up** money for something, you provide the money to pay for it.

put up something or **put something up** ❑ *The United States is putting up $450 million to start the program.* ❑ *The National Arts Council put up half the cost.*

10 To **put up** a price or rate means to increase it. = **raise**; ≠ **bring down**

put something up or **put up something** ❑ *Travel companies usually put their prices up in summer.* ❑ *The bank is hinting that it might put up interest rates.*

11 If someone **puts** you **up**, they let you stay with them for a short time.

put someone up or **put up someone** ❑ [+ for] *The Murrays had put him up for the night.* ❑ *We can't put him up here.* ❑ *He offered to put up Tony for the night.*

12 If you **put** someone **up** in a hotel, you pay for them to stay there.

put someone up ❑ *When our flight was delayed, the travel company put us up in a hotel.* ❑ *She was* *put up at the Grand Hotel.*

13 If you **put up** somewhere, you stay there for a short time. [BRITISH, OLD-FASHIONED]
❑ *The car broke down, and we had to put up in a hotel for the night.*

14 If you **put** something or someone **up** for something, you make them available for that thing.

put something/someone up or **put up something/someone** ❑ [+ for] *The old flower market has been put up for sale.* ❑ *She put up her daughter for adoption in 1967.*

15 If you **put up** or someone **puts** you **up** in an election or competition, you suggest yourself or they suggest you as a suitable person to be chosen.

put up someone or **put someone up** ❑ *They put up several candidates in Cornwall.*
put up ❑ *He put up as an independent candidate.*

○ **'put upon**

1 If you **put** one object **upon** another, you put it on top of the other thing. = **put on** [LITERARY, OLD-FASHIONED]
put something upon something ❑ *He put his hand gently upon her cheek.* ❑ *A red cloth had been put upon the table.*

2 If you **put** a particular value or explanation **upon** something, you think it has that value or meaning. [FORMAL]
put something upon something ❑ *What value would they put upon her work?*

3 To **put** pressure, demands, or restrictions **upon** someone means to cause them to suffer by what you ask them to do or not to do. [FORMAL]
put something upon something ❑ *His parents put demands upon him that he resented.* ❑ *Doctors describe the pressures put upon them to prescribe more drugs.*

4 If you **are put upon** or someone **puts upon** you, someone asks or expects you to do too much. = **impose on** [OLD-FASHIONED]
be put upon ❑ *We are not prepared to be put upon.*
put upon someone ❑ *Thank you, Ibrahim. I really am sorry to put upon you.* ● A **put-upon** person has been unfairly asked to do too much. Their **put-upon** expression shows this. [INFORMAL] ❑ *In the film, she plays his*

tolerant and put-upon wife. ❑ *Amy felt put-upon and unappreciated.*

○ **put 'up to**

If you **put** someone **up to** something, you ask and encourage them to do something wrong or silly.
put someone up to something ❑ *Someone put Sid up to this.* ❑ *Did Charlie put you up to that*

◉ **put 'up with**

If you **put up with** something or someone, you accept them, even though you do not like them.
put up with something/someone ❑ *Don't put up with any nonsense from Howard.* ❑ *He disliked the idea of surgery and decided instead to put up with the pain.* ❑ *I don't know how you put up with him.*
NOTE **Endure** is a more formal word for **put up with**.

putter /ˈpʌtə/ (**putters, puttering, puttered**)

○ **putter a'round** [AMERICAN]

If you **putter around** or **putter around** a place, you spend time in a relaxed and pleasant way, doing things that are not important.
putter around ❑ *He heard her puttering around*
putter around something ❑ *Mary was puttering around her house.*

puzzle /ˈpʌzəl/ (**puzzles, puzzling, puzzled**)

○ **puzzle 'out**

If you **puzzle** a problem **out**, you find the answer by thinking carefully.
puzzle something out or **puzzle out something** ❑ *I leave them to puzzle it out.*
❑ *It's interesting to see how a child puzzles things out.* ❑ *I stared at the letters and lines, trying to puzzle out their meaning.*
NOTE **Solve** is a more formal word for **puzzle out**.

○ **'puzzle over**

If you **puzzle over** something, you think hard about it in order to try to understand i
puzzle over something or **puzzle something over** ❑ *Lola had been puzzling over this question all day.* ❑ *He frowned and puzzled the matter over*
NOTE **Ponder** is a more formal word for **puzzle over**.

Qq

qualify /'kwɒlɪfaɪ/ (**qualifies, qualifying, qualified**)

○ **'qualify as**
To **qualify as** something means to have all the features that are needed to be that thing, and to **qualify** someone or something **as** something means to make someone or something have all the features that are needed to be that thing.
qualify as something ❑ *13 percent of American households qualify as poor.* ❑ *A bit of spilled water hardly qualifies as a disaster.*
qualify someone as something ❑ *They seem to think that reading a few books qualifies them as experts.*

quarrel /'kwɒrəl, AM 'kwɔːr-/ (**quarrels, quarrelling, quarrelled**)

> American English uses the spellings **quarreling** and **quarreled**.

○ **'quarrel with**
■ If you **quarrel with** someone, you argue with them.
quarrel with someone ❑ *'I don't want to quarrel with her,' she said. 'She's my oldest friend.'* ❑ *[+ over] She quarrelled with Christopher over the lease.*
■ If you **quarrel with** an idea, opinion, decision, etc. you think it is wrong.
quarrel with something ❑ *Nobody could quarrel with his reasons for leaving.*

queen /kwiːn/ (**queens, queening, queened**)

○ **'queen over**
If someone **queens it over** you, they act in a way that shows that they think they are better than you, for example by telling you what to do. **= lord over** ❑ *Don't you try to queen it over me!*

quest /kwest/ (**quests, questing, quested**)

○ **'quest for** [FORMAL]
If you **quest for** something, you search for it.
quest for something ❑ *All his life, he felt he had been questing for the truth.*

queue /kjuː/ (**queues, queueing/queuing, queued**)

○ **queue 'up** [BRITISH]
■ If you **queue up**, you stand in a line of people and wait for something. ❑ *[+ for] People were queueing up for his autograph.* ❑ *He had to queue up at the factory every morning to see if there was any work.*
■ If people **are queueing up to** do something, a lot of them are keen to do it.
be queueing up to do something ❑ *People were queueing up to join the police.*

quibble /'kwɪbəl/ (**quibbles, quibbling, quibbled**)

○ **'quibble over** (or **quibble about**)
When people **quibble over** something, they argue about it even though it is not important.
quibble over something ❑ *Morgan earns a six-figure salary but still quibbles over the cost of a can of lemonade.* ❑ *We could quibble about what you mean by "severe" weather.*

quicken /'kwɪkən/ (**quickens, quickening, quickened**)

○ **quicken 'up**
If you **quicken** something **up**, or if it **quickens up**, its speed increases. **= speed up**
quicken something up or **quicken up something** ❑ *Start these movements slowly and then quicken them up.* ❑ *We're quickening up the process to deal with these claims.*
quicken up ❑ *Then the pace began to quicken up.*

quiet /kwaɪət/ (**quiets, quieting, quieted**)

○ **quiet 'down** [mainly AMERICAN]
If someone or something **quiets down**, or if you **quiet** them **down**, they become less noisy or active, or more calm. **= calm down**
quiet down ❑ *When he quieted down, I began to tell him the simple truth.* ❑ *Meanwhile, things quieted down in Los Angeles.*
quiet someone/something down or **quiet down someone/something** ❑ *Try gradually to quiet them down as bedtime approaches.* ❑ *He was soon able to quiet down the animals.*

quieten /ˈkwaɪətən/ (quietens, quietening, quietened)

○ **quieten 'down** [BRITISH]

If something or someone **quietens down**, or if you **quieten** them **down**, they become less noisy or active, or more calm. = **calm down**

quieten down ❑ He had matured and quietened down considerably.

quieten someone/something down or **quieten down someone/something** ❑ The promises were intended to quieten down the protestors. ❑ I was given another injection and that quietened me down.

quiver /ˈkwɪvə/ (quivers, quivering, quivered)

○ **'quiver with**

If someone or their voice **quivers with** an emotion such as anger or excitement, they shake slightly because of it, or their voice sounds slightly weak.

quiver with something ❑ He was quivering with rage. ❑ 'This has been a difficult time for me,' he began, his voice quivering with emotion.

Rr

rabbit /'ræbɪt/ (rabbits, rabbiting, rabbited)

rabbit 'on [BRITISH, INFORMAL]

If someone **rabbits on**, they talk about something for a long time in a rather boring way. ❑ [+ about] They started rabbiting on about classical music.

rack /ræk/ (racks, racking, racked)

rack 'up

If you **rack up** things such as profits, losses, or points in a competition, you get a large amount or a large number of them.

rack up something ❑ The company has racked up more than 50 major awards for its work.

NOTE **Accumulate** is a more formal word for **rack up**.

radiate /'reɪdieɪt/ (radiates, radiating, radiated)

'radiate from (or **radiate out from**)

If things **radiate from** a place, they form a pattern that is like lines drawn from the centre of a circle to places on its edge.

radiate from something ❑ The village consists of just four streets radiating from a roundabout.

'radiate from

If an emotion or quality **radiates from** you, people can see it very clearly in your face and in your behaviour.

radiate from someone/something

❑ Pleasure radiated from her face while she talked about her trip.

rage /reɪdʒ/ (rages, raging, raged)

'rage against [LITERARY]

If you **rage against** a person or situation, you express great anger about them.

rage against something/someone

❑ She continually raged against everything and everyone.

rail /reɪl/ (rails, railing, railed)

'rail against [LITERARY]

If you **rail against** a person or situation, you express great anger about them.

rail against something/someone ❑ He still railed against the politicians back home.

railroad /'reɪlrəʊd/ (railroads, railroading, railroaded)

○ **railroad 'into**

If you **railroad** someone **into** something, you make them do it although they do not want to.

railroad someone into something ❑ Many staff were either made redundant or railroaded into early retirement.

rain /reɪn/ (rains, raining, rained)

○ **rain 'down** [LITERARY]

If a lot of things **rain down** on a person or place, they fall rapidly on them. ❑ Millions of tons of volcanic ash rained down over a huge area. ❑ Blows rained down on his head.

○ **rain 'off** [BRITISH]

If a sports match **is rained off**, it has to stop, or it is not able to start, because of rain.

be rained off ❑ Today's match between Yorkshire and Kent has been rained off.

○ **rain 'out** [AMERICAN]

If a sports game **is rained out**, it has to stop, or it is not able to start, because of rain.

be rained out ❑ Saturday's game was rained out.

NOTE **Rained off** means the same as **rained out** in British English.

rake /reɪk/ (rakes, raking, raked)

○ **rake 'in** [INFORMAL]

If someone **rakes in** money, they earn a lot of money fairly easily.

rake in something or **rake something in**

❑ Western countries raked in 78 per cent of the income.

● If someone **is raking it in**, they are earning a lot of money. ❑ They've got so many shops, they must be raking it in!

○ **rake 'over**

If someone **rakes over** an unpleasant event in the past, they keep talking about it even though it would be better to forget it.

rake over something or **rake something over**

❑ Why travel back into the past to rake over old worries? ❑ I can't stop thinking about it, raking it all over.

○ **rake 'up** [INFORMAL]

1 If someone **rakes up** something unpleasant or embarrassing that happened to you in the past, they find out about it and tell other people in order to cause trouble.
rake up something or **rake something up**
❑ I hoped I'd left the past behind. I truly don't want it all raked up again. ❑ I didn't see much point in raking up the past.

2 If you **rake up** people or things, you find them and bring them together for a particular purpose.
rake up someone/something or **rake someone/something up** ❑ I'll see if I can rake up a few people to help you.

○ **'rake with**

To **rake** an area **with** gunfire or light means to cover the area with it by moving the gun or the light across the whole area.
rake something with something ❑ The caravan was raked with bullets.

rally /'ræli/ (**rallies, rallying, rallied**)

○ **rally a'round** (or **rally round** [mainly BRITISH])

1 If people **rally around** or **rally around** someone, they work together to support someone at a difficult time.
rally around ❑ The girls have rallied round and coped magnificently.
rally around someone ❑ Her recovery was helped by the stream of visitors and family that rallied around her.

2 If you **rally around** an aim or action or someone who is trying to achieve an aim, you support them.
rally around someone/something
❑ Americans of both parties rallied around the President's decision.

○ **'rally to**

When people **rally to** something or someone, they work together to support them.
rally to something/someone ❑ His supporters have rallied to his defence. ❑ Politicians on the left of the party have rallied to her.

ram /ræm/ (**rams, ramming, rammed**)

○ **ram 'down**

1 If you **ram** an object **down**, you push it hard and suddenly towards the ground.
ram something down or **ram down something** ❑ He rammed his foot down. ❑ He slammed the door and rammed down the locks.

2 If you **ram** a fact or idea **down** someone's throat, especially when they know it already or do not want to know it, you tell them about it forcefully and repeatedly.

ram something down something ❑ There's no point ramming it down his throat when he's no interested.
be rammed down something ❑ The symbolis is never rammed down the reader's throat.

○ **ram 'in**

If you **ram** an object **in** or **ram** it **in** something, you push it very hard and suddenly into a container.
ram something in or **ram in something**
❑ He took out his pipe, rammed in some tobacco and lit up.
ram something in something ❑ The old man rammed the key in the lock with trembling fingers

○ **ram 'into**

1 If a person or object **rams into** somethir or someone, they hit them very hard whil moving towards them very quickly.
ram into something/someone ❑ He lost control of the car and rammed into a tree. ❑ He pushed the desk away from him with such force that it rammed into the chair and knocked it over.

2 If you **ram** one object **into** another, you move it quickly so that it hits the other object very hard.
ram something into something ❑ He rammed his fist into Hooper's throat.

3 If you **ram** ideas or facts **into** someone, you force that person to learn them or remember them.
ram something into someone ❑ It's important to ram these rules into their minds.

ramble /'ræmbəl/ (**rambles, rambling, rambled**)

○ **ramble 'on**

If someone **rambles on**, they talk or write for a long time in a confused way. ❑ We sat listening to Miriam as she rambled on. ❑ [+ abou Brian listened while his uncle rambled on and on about Gloria.

ramp /ræmp/ (**ramps, ramping, ramped**)

○ **ramp 'up**

To **ramp up** something means to increase i
ramp up something or **ramp something up**
❑ Producers were ramping up production to meet demand. ❑ They wasted no time in ramping up security.

range /reɪndʒ/ (**ranges, ranging, ranged**)

○ **'range against**

If people or things **are ranged against** someone, or if people **range** themselves **against** someone, they are opposed to ther or trying to stop them doing something.
be ranged against someone/something
❑ The whole of Catholic Europe was ranged against her.

**range yourself against someone/
something** ❑ *He hadn't even noticed his enemies
ranging themselves against him.*

'range between (or **range from**)
If things **range between** two amounts,
they include those amounts and others in
between.
range between something ❑ *Temperatures
range between 5°C and 20°C.* ❑ *They range in price
from $3 to $15.*

ank /ræŋk/ (**ranks, ranking, ranked**)

'rank among
If a person or thing **ranks among** a particular
type or group or **is ranked among** that type
or group, they have the qualities of that
type or group.
rank among something ❑ *Academically, Tony
never ranked among the scholars.* ❑ *This county
ranks among the wealthiest in the country.*
be ranked among something ❑ *These frogs are
ranked among the world's most poisonous animals.*

ap /ræp/ (**raps, rapping, rapped**)

'rap for (or **rap over**)
To **rap** a person or organization **for**
something bad means to criticize or blame
them for it.
rap someone/something for something
❑ *The report raps government departments for
inadequate monitoring of the project.* ❑ *Car
makers were rapped for charging higher prices in
Britain than in the rest of Europe.*

rap 'out
If you **rap out** something, especially an
order or a question, you say it quickly
and forcefully.
rap out something or **rap something out**
❑ *'Is that the truth?' he suddenly rapped out.*
❑ *She rapped out the orders urgently.*

'rap over → see **rap for**

'rap with [AMERICAN, INFORMAL]
If you **rap with** someone, you talk to them
in a relaxed and informal way.
rap with someone ❑ *Performers rapped with
the audience, "How are you Denver?"*

at /ræt/ (**rats, ratting, ratted**)

'rat on [INFORMAL]
If someone **rats on** you, they tell someone
in authority about something wrong you
have done.
rat on someone ❑ *So you ratted on Jamie?*
❑ *I just hope they don't rat on us.*

rat 'out [AMERICAN, INFORMAL]
If someone **rats** you **out**, they tell
someone in authority about something
wrong you have done.

rat someone out ❑ *A lot of kids think that if they
go to the counselors, people are going to rat them out.*

ratchet /'rætʃɪt/ (**ratchets, ratcheting,
ratcheted**)

○ **ratchet 'down**
If you **ratchet** something **down** or it
ratchets down, it decreases by a fixed
amount or degree, and seems unlikely to
increase again. ≠ **ratchet up**
ratched something down or **ratchet down
something** ❑ *We're trying to ratchet down
the administrative costs.* ❑ *The board of the
company needed to ratchet pay levels down to
reasonable levels.*
ratchet down ❑ *By the end of the year, that ratio
ratchets down to 4 to 1.*

○ **ratchet 'up**
If you **ratchet** something **up** or it **ratchets
up**, it increases by a fixed amount or
degree, and seems unlikely to decrease
again. ≠ **ratchet down**
ratchet something up or **ratchet up
something** ❑ *Audiences' expectations are
ratcheted up as they are exposed to high-budget
productions.* ❑ *They are attempting to ratchet up
pressure on the government.*
ratchet up ❑ *He fears inflation will ratchet up as
the year ends.*
NOTE **Escalate** is a more formal word for
ratchet up.

ration /'ræʃən/ (**rations, rationing, rationed**)

○ **ration 'out**
If you **ration out** something that you have
very little of, you give it in small amounts
to each person in a group.
ration out something or **ration something
out** ❑ *I rationed out the last of the food.* ❑ *The
limited funds available have to be rationed out
among local groups.*

rattle /'rætəl/ (**rattles, rattling, rattled**)

○ **rattle a'round**
If you say that someone **rattles around** in a
room or other space, you mean that the
space is too large for them. ❑ *There are
only two of us now, rattling around in this big
family house.*

○ **rattle 'off**
To **rattle** something **off** means to say or do
it quickly and without effort. = **reel off**
rattle something off or **rattle off something**
❑ *She rattled off a list of names.* ❑ *Rhoda,
surprisingly, rattled off the Mozart sonata with ease.*

○ **rattle 'on**
If someone **rattles on**, they speak quickly
about something for a long time, often in

an annoying way. = **rabbit on** ❏ [+ *about*]
She rattled on excitedly about Mrs Moffat. ❏ *The announcer had been rattling on in the background.*

○ **rattle 'through** [BRITISH]
If you **rattle through** something, you say it or deal with it very quickly in order to finish it.
rattle through something ❏ *They rattled through the rest of the meeting.* ❏ *He rattled through a list of incidents that had occurred.*

rave /reɪv/ (**raves, raving, raved**)
○ **'rave about** (or **rave on about**)
If someone **raves about** something, they speak or write about it very enthusiastically.
rave about something ❏ *He was raving about a new writer he had discovered.*

○ **rave 'up** [BRITISH, OLD-FASHIONED]
If you **rave it up**, you enjoy yourself by drinking and dancing and behaving in a noisy and uncontrolled way. ❏ *There was a huge audience raving it up under the stars.*
● A **rave-up** is an event at which people drink, dance, and behave in a noisy and uncontrolled way. [OLD-FASHIONED] ❏ *I was looking forward to a real rave-up.*

reach /riːtʃ/ (**reaches, reaching, reached**)
○ **reach 'down**
If you **reach down**, you bend your body towards the ground and stretch your arms in order to touch or hold something.
❏ *I reached down and removed the cover.* ❏ *David reached down and grabbed her wrists.*

○ **reach 'down to**
If something **reaches down to** a particular level, it goes downwards as far as that level.
reach down to something ❏ *A long bank of dark cloud reached down to sea level a mile ahead.* ❏ *She wore a long blue skirt reaching down to the ground.*

❍ **reach 'out**
❶ If you **reach out**, or **reach out** a hand, you stretch your arm, and sometimes your body, in order to get or touch something slightly far away from you.
reach out ❏ [+ *for*] *Otto reached out for the bottle of wine.*
reach out something ❏ *He reached out a hand and touched the man's arm.*
❷ People **reach out** when they try to get other people to be interested in their ideas.
reach out ❏ *She has always refused to reach out across party lines.* ❏ [+ *to*] *This is a great way to reach out to a larger audience.*
❸ If someone **reaches out** to you, they contact you to offer something or to ask you for advice or information.
reach out ❏ [+ *to*] *I'm reaching out to you to see if*

you're available to work on our next project.

○ **reach 'out for**
If people **reach out for** better things, they make great efforts to get or achieve them.
reach out for something ❏ *We are reaching ou for new standards.* ❏ *It was a society reaching out for a better quality of life.*

○ **reach 'out to**
❶ If you **reach out to** people, you give them help, advice, or comfort.
reach out to someone ❏ *He has a wonderful ability to reach out to people.* ● **Outreach** workers are employed by local government to find people who need help and persuade them to apply for it, so that social problem can be dealt with before they become sever ❏ *There are several vacancies for outreach workers*
❷ If you **reach out to** people, you ask them for help, advice, or comfort.
reach out to someone ❏ *They may reach out to another person for reassurance.*

❍ **reach 'up**
If you **reach up**, you stretch your body and arms upwards in order to touch or hold something. ❏ *He reached up and opened the top lock.* ❏ *He reached up and took from the shelf above him, a leather-cased file.*

○ **reach 'up to**
If something **reaches up to** a particular level, it goes upwards as far as that level.
reach up to something ❏ *Huge mountains reached up to a thin layer of cloud.*

react /riˈækt/ (**reacts, reacting, reacted**)
❍ **re'act to**
❶ When you **react to** something that has happened, you behave in a particular way because of it.
react to something ❏ *How did Karlov react to your phone call?* ❏ *They reacted angrily to the news*
❷ If you **react to** a drug or something you have eaten or touched, it has a bad effect on you or makes you ill.
react to something ❏ *Someone who is allergic to milk is likely to react to cheese too.*

○ **re'act with**
❶ When one chemical substance **reacts with** another, they both change because they have been mixed together.
react with something ❏ *Calcium reacts with water.*
❷ If you **react with** a particular feeling, that is the feeling you have and show because of something that has happened.
react with something ❏ *She had reacted with delight when she heard he was coming to stay.* ❏ *Ministers reacted with fury.*

ead /riːd/ (**reads, reading**)

> The form **read** is used in the present tense and is the past tense and past participle of the verb.

read 'back

If you **read** a piece of writing **back**, you read it again after writing it, in order to check that it is correct or acceptable.

read something back or **read back something** ❑ I read back what I'd written, just to check that it was clear.

'read for [OLD-FASHIONED]

If you **read for** a university degree, you study for it.

read for something ❑ Two students reading for the same degree may study very different material.

read 'into

If you **read** a meaning or importance **into** something, you think it has that meaning or importance.

read something into something ❑ The authors warn us about reading too much into the figures.

read 'off

If you **read off** a measurement on a machine or other device, you look at the measurement that it shows.

read off something or **read something off** ❑ You read off the number at the top of the bar.

read 'out

◼ If you **read out** a piece of writing, you say the words aloud as you read it.

read out something ❑ John Tyme read out a statement on behalf of 600 objectors.

read something out ❑ People who read their speeches out are so boring. ❑ One of the students wrote a paper and read it out to the rest of us.

◼ The **read-out** from a computer or similar machine is the printed information that it produces. ❑ These machines give an extremely fast, efficient read-out and are low in cost.

read 'over

If you **read over** a piece of writing, you read it in order to check it or comment on it before it is used or published.

read over something or **read something over** ❑ When my director read over what I had written, he was puzzled. ❑ The manuscript is taken back to the authors, read over, and discussed.

read 'through

If you **read through** a piece of writing, you read it from beginning to end.

read through something ❑ I've still got to read through all the reports Jacques wrote up on the case.

read something through ❑ I read her note through again. ❑ Ask the student to read it through first.

read 'up

If you **read up**, you read a lot about a subject because you want to learn about it. ❑ [+ about] I got out the encyclopaedia and read up about iron production. ❑ [+ on] Lucas had read up on economic theory just in case he was asked.

readjust /riːəˈdʒʌst/ (**readjusts, readjusting, readjusted**)

read'just to

If someone or something **readjusts to** a situation that they have not been in for a long time, they change in order to be suitable for the new situation.

readjust to something ❑ For many ex-soldiers it can be difficult to readjust to life outside the army. ❑ I found it difficult to readjust to being single again after my divorce.

rear /rɪə/ (**rears, rearing, reared**)

rear 'up

When an animal such as a horse **rears up**, it suddenly lifts its front legs in the air and stands on its back legs. ❑ The horse was rearing up on its hind legs and striking out.

reason /ˈriːzən/ (**reasons, reasoning, reasoned**)

reason 'out

If you **reason out** a problem or puzzle, you solve it by thinking about it carefully.
= **work out, figure out**

reason something out or **reason out something** ❑ She was able to reason out many of the passages and their meanings. ❑ Leave it to me. I can reason it out later.

'reason with

If you **reason with** someone, you use sensible arguments in order to persuade them to agree with you or to do something.

reason with someone ❑ I've tried to reason with him but it's no use. ❑ Have you tried reasoning with her?

rebound /rɪˈbaʊnd/ (**rebounds, rebounding, rebounded**)

re'bound on (or **rebound upon**)

If someone's action or attitude **rebounds on** them or on someone else, it affects them or someone else in the future.

rebound on someone ❑ It is not true that every anxiety a parent has rebounds on their child. ❑ I was determined to make their trick rebound on them.

recall /rɪˈkɔːl/ (**recalls, recalling, recalled**)

re'call to

◼ If you **are recalled to** your home, country, or the place where you work, or someone **recalls** you **to** it, you are ordered to return there.

be recalled to somewhere ❑ *War was getting closer, and von Keller knew that he would soon be recalled to his regiment.*

recall someone to somewhere ❑ *Dr Riekert recalled me to Cape Town before the situation got worse.*

2 In sport, if a player **is recalled to** a team or someone **recalls** them **to** the team, he or she is included in that team again, after a time when they have not been in the team.

be recalled to something ❑ *Dean Richards was recalled to the England team for the match with Wales.*

recall someone to something ❑ *Kyrastas was the coach who recalled him to the first team last year.*

reckon /'rekən/ (reckons, reckoning, reckoned)

○ **reckon 'in**

If you are calculating something and **reckon** an item **in**, you include it.

reckon something in or **reckon in something** ❑ *When all the benefits are reckoned in, they are not so badly paid.* ❑ *Don't forget to reckon in the service charge.*

○ **'reckon on**

If you **reckon on** something, you feel certain that it will happen or you will get it, and include it in your plans. **= bank on**

reckon on something ❑ *The amount was far beyond the four figure sum she had reckoned on.* ❑ *They had not reckoned on such a fight.*

○ **reckon 'up**

If you **reckon up** a set of figures, you add them together to find the total. **= tot up**

reckon up something or **reckon something up** ❑ *On holiday, it was their custom to reckon up the various amounts each had spent.* ❑ *I'll need a calculator to reckon it all up.*

NOTE **Calculate** is a more formal word for **reckon up**.

○ **'reckon with**

1 If you had **not reckoned with** an event, you had not expected it and so were not prepared for it. **= bargain for**

not reckon with something ❑ *She had not reckoned with a surprise of this sort.*

2 If you have to **reckon with** something or someone, you have to be aware of them and able to deal with them.

reckon with something/someone ❑ *This is another factor to be reckoned with.* ❑ *If he hurts her, he'll have me to reckon with.*

● If you say that someone or something is **to be reckoned with**, you mean that they are strong or important. ❑ *The union had become a force to be reckoned with.* ❑ *Mary was*

a Northfleet, a family to be reckoned with.

○ **'reckon without**

If you **reckon without** something or someone, you do not expect it or expect them to do something, and are not prepared for them.

reckon without something/someone ❑ *They thought they would get away with the crime. But they had reckoned without Inspector Barker.*

recline /rɪ'klaɪn/ (reclines, reclining, reclined)

○ **re'cline on**

If you **recline on** something, you sit or lie in a relaxed way with your back supported by something.

recline on something ❑ *Maggie was reclining on the sofa in the sitting room.*

recoil /rɪ'kɔɪl/ (recoils, recoiling, recoiled)

○ **re'coil from** (or **recoil at**)

If you **recoil from** something, you refuse to do it or accept it because you dislike it so much.

recoil from something ❑ *People used to recoil from the idea of getting into debt.*

recompense /'rekəmpens/ (recompenses, recompensing, recompensed)

○ **'recompense for** [FORMAL]

If you **recompense** someone **for** something they have done or for a loss, you give them something, usually money, as a payment or reward.

recompense someone for something ❑ *The increase in pay will recompense teachers for the additional responsibility.* ❑ *He wanted to recompense Beth for letting him use her car.*

reconcile /'rekənsaɪl/ (reconciles, reconciling, reconciled)

○ **'reconcile with**

1 If you **are reconciled with** someone, you become friendly with them again after a disagreement.

be reconciled with someone ❑ *He was an old man, who wanted to be reconciled with his daughter.*

2 If you **reconcile** someone **with** another person, you try to make them become friends again after a disagreement.

reconcile someone with someone ❑ *My attempt to reconcile him with Toby had failed.*

3 If you **reconcile** a belief, fact, or demand **with** another one that seems completely different, you find a way in which they can both exist together.

reconcile something with something
❏ He had problems in reconciling his ideals with real life. ❏ He was involved in work that could not easily be reconciled with his Christian faith.

recover /rɪˈkʌvə/ (**recovers, recovering, recovered**)

○ **reˈcover from**

1 When you **recover from** an illness or an injury, you become well again.
recover from something ❏ He is recovering from a knee injury. ❏ It can take several weeks to fully recover from flu.

2 If you **recover from** an unhappy or unpleasant experience, you stop being upset by it.
recover from something ❏ She never fully recovered from the death of her son. ❏ It took me several minutes to recover from the shock.

3 If something **recovers from** a period of weakness or difficulty, it improves or gets stronger again.
recover from something ❏ The team recovered from a poor start and won the game 5-2. ❏ The economy recovered strongly from its slump of 2017–18.

reduce /rɪˈdjuːs, ᴀᴍ -ˈduːs/ (**reduces, reducing, reduced**)

○ **reˈduce to**

1 If you **reduce** an amount **to** a lower amount, you decrease it to the lower amount.
reduce something to something ❏ My father's wages had been reduced to 10 shillings a week. ❏ This drug reduces the number of cancer tumours to less than half.

2 If someone **is reduced to** tears or silence or if someone or something **reduces** them **to** tears or silence, something makes them cry or shocks or frightens them so much that they cannot speak.
be reduced to something ❏ A tough reporter was reduced to tears at the sight.
reduce someone to something ❏ A single question was all it took to reduce the poor girl to tears. ❏ The scale of the damage reduced him to silence.

3 If something, especially a building or a city, **is reduced to** a state where it is broken or destroyed or if someone **reduces** it **to** this state, someone or something breaks or destroys it.
be reduced to something ❏ Every building in the town was reduced to rubble.
reduce something to something ❏ William dealt with his fish expertly, while Anne reduced hers to a messy pile of bones.

4 If someone **is reduced to** doing something that they would not usually do, usually something that they are ashamed of, they have to do it.
be reduced to something ❏ He had been reduced to working as a truck driver since the failure of his business.

reek /riːk/ (**reeks, reeking, reeked**)

○ **ˈreek of**

1 If someone or something **reeks of** a substance, they smell very strongly of it, usually in a way that is bad.
reek of something ❏ His breath reeked of gin. ❏ We walked past warehouses reeking of rotten bananas.

2 If something **reeks of** an unpleasant quality, it has that quality.
reek of something ❏ He had an air about him that reeked of arrogance. ❏ The whole place reeked of neglect and decay.

reel /riːl/ (**reels, reeling, reeled**)

○ **reel ˈback**

If you **reel back**, you move backwards suddenly, in a way that you cannot control. ❏ Daisy reeled back against the wooden partition. ❏ She pushed against her attackers, who reeled back in surprise.

○ **ˈreel from**

To **reel from** a shock or bad experience means to feel extremely shocked or upset because of it.
reel from something ❏ My wife left me three weeks ago and I'm still reeling from the shock. ❏ Most of Britain was reeling from the devastating effect of floods.

○ **reel ˈin**

1 If you **reel in** a fish or a fishing line, you pull it towards you by turning the handle of the reel to shorten the line.
reel something in or **reel in something**
❏ A small blue shark took the line and Brody reeled it in. ❏ He reeled in his line.

2 If you **reel** someone **in**, you do something to attract them in order to make them do something you want them to do.
reel someone in or **reel in someone** ❏ I talk to possible customers, then when they're in a good mood, George takes over to reel them in.

○ **reel ˈoff**

If you **reel off** a speech or some information, you say it quickly without having to think about it. = **rattle off**
reel off something or **reel something off**
❏ He could reel off the names of all the capitals of Europe. ❏ I have to memorize all this information so I can reel it off to people I meet.

refer /rɪˈfɜː/ (**refers, referring, referred**)

○ **reˈfer to**

1 If you **refer to** a particular subject or person, you talk about them or mention them.

refer to something/someone ❑ *In his letters to Vita he rarely referred to political events.* ❑ *I am not allowed to describe the officers or refer to them by name.*

2 If you **refer to** something or someone as a particular thing, this is the name or expression you use to describe them or talk about them.

refer to someone/something ❑ [+ *as*] *This kind of art is often referred to as 'minimal art'.*

3 If a word or code **refers to** something, it relates to it or describes it in some way.

refer to something ❑ *The serial number refers to the country of origin.* ❑ *Until the end of the 18th Century, 'antique' referred specifically to Greek and Roman objects.*

4 If you **refer to** a source of information such as a reference book, you look at it in order to find something out. = **consult**

refer to something ❑ *She could make a new dish without referring to any cookery books.* ❑ *The website has information which can be referred to on future occasions.*

5 If you **refer** someone **to** a source of information, you suggest that they look there because it contains useful information.

refer someone to something ❑ *I refer you to a paper by Sutherland.* ❑ *On two occasions at least Gray refers us to Chekhov.*

6 If someone **refers** a person or problem **to** another person or organization, they ask that person or organization to deal with them.

refer someone/something to someone/ something ❑ *She referred the matter to the European Court of Justice.* ❑ *She was referred by her doctor to a consultant.*

reflect /rɪˈflekt/ (**reflects, reflecting, reflected**)

○ **reˈflect on** (or **reflect upon**)

1 If you **reflect on** something, you spend a lot of time thinking about it.

reflect on something ❑ *He reflected on how different things might have been.* ❑ *As she flew back to London, Katrina reflected on her visit to Paloma Blanca.*

2 If something **reflects on** someone or something, it makes people have a particular opinion of them.

reflect on someone/something ❑ *As my staff, your actions reflect on me.* ❑ *The incident has caused a great many problems, and reflects very badly on me.*

refrain /rɪˈfreɪn/ (**refrains, refraining, refrained**)

○ **reˈfrain from**

If you **refrain from** doing something, you do not do it, although you may want to.

refrain from something ❑ *He had to refrain from speaking when adults were speaking.* ❑ *We refrain from violence in any situation.*

regard /rɪˈɡɑːd/ (**regards, regarding, regarded**)

○ **reˈgard as**

If you **regard** someone, something, or yourself **as** being a particular thing or **as** having a particular quality, you think that they or you are that thing or have that quality.

regard someone/something as something ❑ *We live in a society which regards hard work and achievement as virtues.* ❑ *At school Louis was regarded as an average student.*

regard yourself as something ❑ *Dan was with a woman who clearly regarded herself as his girlfriend.*

○ **reˈgard with**

If you **regard** someone or something **with** a particular feeling, you have that feeling about them.

regard someone/something with something ❑ *He regarded Ryan with some suspicion.* ❑ *His remarks should be regarded with caution.*

register /ˈredʒɪstə/ (**registers, registering, registered**)

○ **ˈregister on**

1 When something **registers on** a scale or measuring instrument, or **registers** a particular amount **on** it, it shows on the scale or instrument.

register on something ❑ *The fracture will only register on sophisticated X-ray equipment.*

register something on something ❑ *The earthquake registered 5.3 points on the Richter scale.*

2 If a feeling **registers on** someone's face, their expression shows clearly that they have that feeling.

register on something ❑ *Astonishment registered on every face.* ❑ *A look of shock and pain registered for a second on Ted's face.*

reimburse /riːɪmˈbɜːs/ (**reimburses, reimbursing, reimbursed**)

○ **reimˈburse for** [FORMAL]

If you **reimburse** someone **for** something, you pay them back the money that they have spent or lost because of it.

reimburse someone for something ❑ *I'll be happy to reimburse you for any expenses you might have incurred.* ❑ *The banks are reimbursing their customers for these losses.*

rein /reɪn/ (**reins, reining, reined**)

○ **rein 'back**

1 If you **rein** something **back** you control it and stop it from continuing or growing. = **check**

rein back something or **rein something back** ❑ *The government are trying to rein back inflation.*

2 If you **rein back**, you do not do something you were going to do, or stop doing something you were doing as fast or with as much force. ❑ *He was about to shout at them, but suddenly he reined back.*

○ **rein 'in**

1 If you are riding and you **rein in** your horse, you make it stop or go more slowly by pulling its reins.

rein in something or **rein something in** ❑ *He reined in his horse to a walk.*

2 If you **rein** someone or something **in**, you control them so that they do not cause problems. [FORMAL]

rein someone/something in or **rein in someone/something** ❑ *The committee wanted to rein in Callum's activities.* ❑ *She could never manage to rein in her curiosity.*

rein yourself in ❑ *Something told him he had lost control, that he should rein himself in, but the excitement was too great.*

relate /rɪˈleɪt/ (**relates, relating, related**)

○ **re'late to**

1 If something **relates to** a particular subject, it is about that subject or is connected with it.

relate to something ❑ *I wanted to ask you a question that relates to electricity.* ❑ *They want changes in the law relating to pet ownership.*

2 If you can **relate to** other people, you can understand how they feel and communicate with them easily.

relate to someone ❑ *Children need to learn to relate to other children.* ❑ *All these factors affect the way we relate to one another.*

3 If you **relate to** something, you understand it because you have had a similar experience or emotion or have a similar opinion.

relate to something ❑ *These people have a way of looking at the world that most of us find hard to relate to.* ❑ *I could really relate to the things she was saying about loneliness.*

release /rɪˈliːs/ (**releases, releasing, released**)

○ **re'lease from**

1 If a person or animal **is released from** a place where they have been kept, or someone **releases** them **from** there, they are set free or allowed to go.

be released from somewhere ❑ *He was released from prison in 2019.* ❑ *Fifty-five foxes were released from a fur farm by animal rights activists.*

release someone from somewhere ❑ *They're releasing her from hospital tomorrow.*

2 If someone or something **releases** you **from** a duty, task, or feeling, they free you from it.

release someone from something ❑ *Divorce releases both the husband and wife from all marital obligations to each other.* ❑ *The club have since released him from his contract.*

relegate /ˈrelɪɡeɪt/ (**relegates, relegating, relegated**)

○ **'relegate to**

If you **relegate** someone or something **to** a less important position, you give them this position.

relegate someone/something to something ❑ *He was relegated to a minor role in the company.* ❑ *Other newspapers relegated the story to the middle pages.*

relieve /rɪˈliːv/ (**relieves, relieving, relieved**)

○ **re'lieve of** [FORMAL]

If you **relieve** someone **of** something, you take it away from them.

relieve someone of something ❑ *He relieved her of the plates she was holding.* ❑ *He wished to relieve her of any financial worries.*

rely /rɪˈlaɪ/ (**relies, relying, relied**)

○ **re'ly on** (or **rely upon**)

1 To **rely on** something or someone means to need them in order to survive or be successful. = **depend on**

rely on something/someone ❑ *She is forced to rely on her mother's money.* ❑ *This country's success relies heavily on foreign businesses.*

2 If you can **rely on** someone or something to work or behave in a particular way, you trust them to do this.

rely on someone/something

❑ [+ *to*-infinitive] *You could always rely on him to be polite and do the right thing.* ❑ *They cannot be relied upon to offer much support or advice.*

NOTE **Count on** is a more informal expression for **rely on**.

remark /rɪˈmɑːk/ (**remarks, remarking, remarked**)

○ **re'mark on** (or **remark upon**)

If you **remark on** something, you say or write something that shows you have noticed it.

remark on something ❑ *Friends remarked on her weight loss.* ❑ *He remarked upon how lovely Rose looked.*

remember /rɪ'membə/ (remembers, remembering, remembered)

○ **re'member to**

If you ask someone to **remember** you **to** another person, you are asking them to pass your greetings to that person.
remember someone to someone ❑ *Don't forget to remember me to your father.*

remind /rɪ'maɪnd/ (reminds, reminding, reminded)

✪ **re'mind of**

1 If you **remind** someone **of** something, you tell them about it so that they remember it.
remind someone of something ❑ *Howard came to the door to remind him of their appointment.* ❑ *May I remind you of something you said earlier?*
2 If one person or thing **reminds** you **of** another, they make you think of the other person or thing, because they are similar in some way.
remind someone of someone/something ❑ *You remind me of my friend Baxter.* ❑ *I like this place – it reminds me of home.*

remonstrate /'remənstreɪt, AM rɪ'mɒnstreɪt/ (remonstrates, remonstrating, remonstrated)

○ **'remonstrate with** [FORMAL]

If you **remonstrate with** someone, you complain to them about something they have done.
remonstrate with someone ❑ *He remonstrated with the referee.* ❑ *When I remonstrated with him, he told me to mind my own business.*

render /'rendə/ (renders, rendering, rendered)

○ **render 'down**

If you **render** something **down**, you make it change into liquid, usually by heating it.
render something down or **render down something** ❑ *The fat was rendered down to make soap.*

rendezvous /'rɒndeɪvuː/ (rendezvous, rendezvousing, rendezvoused)

○ **'rendezvous with** [FORMAL]

If you **rendezvous with** someone, you meet them at a time and place that you have arranged.
rendezvous with someone ❑ *The plan was to rendezvous with him on Sunday afternoon.*

renege /rɪ'niːg, AM -'nɪg/ (reneges, reneging, reneged)

○ **re'nege on**

If someone **reneges on** a promise or an agreement, they do not do what they have promised or agreed to do.
renege on something ❑ *Pakistan's government is unlikely to renege on the deal.* ❑ *That pledge has now been reneged on by the government.*

rent /rent/ (rents, renting, rented)

✪ **rent 'out**

If someone **rents out** something such as a room or a piece of land, they allow it to be used for a period of time in return for payment. = **let out**
rent out something ❑ *They had to rent out the upstairs room for years.*
rent something out ❑ [+ to] *She rented the house out to an American couple.* ❑ *Councils have sold a large number of new homes instead of renting them out.*

replace /rɪ'pleɪs/ (replaces, replacing, replaced)

✪ **re'place with**

If you **replace** one thing or person **with** another, you put something or someone else in their place.
replace someone/something with someone/something ❑ *She crossed out the word 'wonderful' and replaced it with the word 'terrible'.* ❑ *The bandage was removed and replaced with a fresh one.*

report /rɪ'pɔːt/ (reports, reporting, reported)

✪ **report 'back**

If you **report back**, you tell someone something that you were asked to find out about. ❑ [+ to] *These problems made him late reporting back to the Governor.* ❑ [+ on] *I used to attend the meetings and report back on their activities.*

○ **re'port on**

If you **report on** someone or something, you tell people about them, because it is your job or duty to do so.
report on something/someone ❑ *Many journalists enter the country to report on political affairs.*

○ **re'port to**

1 If you **report** someone or something **to** the police or another authority, you tell the police, etc. about something wrong that someone has done or about something that has happened.

report someone/something to someone
❏ *His ex-wife reported him to police a few days later.* ❏ *Andrea reported the theft to the police.*
2 If you **report to** a person or place, you go to that person or place and say that you are ready to start work or say that you are there.
report to someone/something ❏ *All visitors must report to the reception desk.* ❏ *He has to report to the police every five days.*
3 If you **report to** someone in your job, they tell you what to do and are in charge of you. [FORMAL]
report to someone ❏ *They both report directly to the chief operating officer.*

repose /rɪ'pəʊz/ (**reposes, reposing, reposed**)
○ **re'pose in**
1 If you say someone **reposes in** a place, you mean they are buried there. [LITERARY]
repose in something ❏ *All his uncles were now reposing in the local churchyard.*
2 If you **repose** your trust **in** someone, you trust them. [FORMAL]
repose something in someone ❏ *He was aware of the trust reposed in him by Crewe.*

represent /reprɪ'zent/ (**represents, representing, represented**)
○ **repre'sent as**
If you **represent** a person or thing **as** a particular thing, you describe or show them as being that thing.
represent someone/something as something ❏ *The media represented him as a hero.* ❏ *In this painting, heaven is represented as a garden.*
represent yourself as something ❏ *He was put in prison for falsely representing himself as a US citizen.*

reserve /rɪ'zɜːv/ (**reserves, reserving, reserved**)
○ **re'serve for**
To **reserve** something **for** a particular person or purpose means to keep it for that person or purpose.
reserve something for someone/something ❏ *The top shelf was reserved for his collection of trophies.* ❏ *Reserve some of the cream for decoration.* ❏ *This lane is reserved for cyclists.*

reside /rɪ'zaɪd/ (**resides, residing, resided**)
○ **re'side in** [FORMAL]
If a quality **resides in** something, it exists or is present in that thing.
reside in something ❏ *Her real value resides in her ability to get information out of people.*

resign /rɪ'zaɪn/ (**resigns, resigning, resigned**)
○ **re'sign to**
If you **resign** yourself **to** an unpleasant situation or fact, you accept it because you realize that you cannot change it.
resign yourself to something ❏ *I'd already resigned myself to the fact that I would never see her again.* ❏ *She has resigned herself to being alone for the rest of her life.*

resort /rɪ'zɔːt/ (**resorts, resorting, resorted**)
○ **re'sort to**
If you **resort to** doing something that you do not think is right or acceptable, you do it because you cannot see any other way of achieving what you want.
resort to something ❏ *Eventually the police resorted to plastic bullets to control the crowd.* ❏ *He had resorted to stealing to feed his children.*

resound /rɪ'zaʊnd/ (**resounds, resounding, resounded**)
○ **re'sound with** (or **resound to**) [LITERARY]
If a place **resounds with** a loud sound, it is filled with it.
resound with something ❏ *The whole place resounded with music.* ❏ *The city resounded to gunfire.*

respond /rɪ'spɒnd/ (**responds, responding, responded**)
○ **re'spond to**
1 When you **respond to** something that is done or said, you react to it by doing or saying something yourself.
respond to something ❏ *They are likely to respond positively to the President's request for aid.* ❏ *Less than an hour had passed before he responded to her message.*
2 When you **respond to** a need or challenge, you do what is necessary or suitable.
respond to something ❏ *Small class sizes allow our teachers to respond to the needs of each student.* ❏ *He never responded to a challenge unless he was sure of succeeding.*
3 If a patient or their injury or illness **responds to** a treatment, the treatment works and they get better.
respond to something ❏ *Flu will not respond to antibiotic drugs.* ❏ *Paul has responded well to treatment and is now a lot better.*

rest /rest/ (**rests, resting, rested**)
○ **'rest on**
1 If something **rests on** a particular thing, it depends on that thing or is based on it.

rest on something ❏ *He felt as if his entire future rested on this meeting.*

② If your eyes **rest on** a particular person or thing, you look at them for a period of time.
rest on something/someone ❏ *Her eyes rested on her husband.* ❏ *Finally he looked up, his eyes resting on Pamela.*

○ **'rest with** [FORMAL]
If a duty or decision **rests with** a person, that person is responsible for it.
rest with someone ❏ *Responsibility for spending rests with the Committee.* ❏ *The decision rested with his boss.*

restore /rɪˈstɔː/ (**restores, restoring, restored**)

○ **re'store to**

■ To **restore** someone or something **to** a condition that they were in before means to cause them to be in that condition again.
restore someone/something to something ❏ *He hoped that more sleep and some healthy food would restore him to health.* ❏ *The President was restored to power five years later.*

② To **restore** something that was lost or stolen **to** its owner means to give it back to them. [FORMAL]
restore something to someone ❏ *Security marking makes it easier for police to restore stolen property to its rightful owner.*

restrict /rɪˈstrɪkt/ (**restricts, restricting, restricted**)

○ **re'strict to**
To **restrict** someone or something **to** someone or something means to limit them to that thing or group.
restrict someone/something to someone/something ❏ *Each person will be restricted to one ticket.* ❏ *Police restricted their efforts to dealing with serious crimes.*
restrict yourself to something ❏ *When using the sauna, you should restrict yourself to a session of no more than fifteen minutes.*

result /rɪˈzʌlt/ (**results, resulting, resulted**)

✪ **re'sult from**
If a situation **results from** an event or action, it is caused by that event or action.
result from something ❏ *Most of the damage resulted from bombing.*

✪ **re'sult in**
If something **results in** a particular situation or event, it causes that situation or event to happen.
result in something ❏ *A warming of the earth's surface might result in the melting of the polar ice caps.* ❏ *Such behaviour may result in the staff member being asked to leave.*

retail /ˈriːteɪl/ (**retails, retailing, retailed**)

○ **'retail at** (or **retail for**)
If a product **retails at** a particular price, that is the price shops sell it at.
retail at something ❏ *The series contains seven volumes and normally retails at £125.* ❏ *This neat little camera retails for around £149.99, and is available now.*

retire /rɪˈtaɪə/ (**retires, retiring, retired**)

✪ **re'tire from**
When a sports player **retires from** a sport, race, or game, they stop competing in it.
retire from something ❏ *I have decided to retire from Formula One racing at the end of the season.* ❏ *Radcliffe was forced to retire from the race with a leg injury.*

○ **re'tire to** [FORMAL]
If you **retire to** another room or place, you go there.
retire to somewhere ❏ *After dinner, they retired to the lounge for coffee.* ❏ *After the marriage service, everyone retired to a local hotel for a meal.*

retreat /rɪˈtriːt/ (**retreats, retreating, retreated**)

○ **re'treat from**
If you **retreat from** a plan or statement, you change your mind about it because of criticism or problems.
retreat from something ❏ *This week, the White House retreated from a claim that 2.6m new jobs would be created this year.* ❏ *They are threatening to retreat from the deal.*

return /rɪˈtɜːn/ (**returns, returning, returned**)

✪ **re'turn to**

■ When you **return to** a place, you go back there after you have been away.
return to something ❏ *I returned to my hotel.*
② If you **return** something **to** someone, you give it back to them after having it for a time.
return something to someone ❏ *Could you return the book to Annie when you've read it?*
③ If you **return** something **to** a place, you put it back there after removing it for a time.
return something to something ❏ *He returned the jar to the shelf.*
④ If you **return to** a previous topic when talking or writing, you mention it or discuss it again.
return to something ❏ *Now let me return to the question of inflation.* ❏ *We shall return to this theme in Chapter 7.*
⑤ If you **return to** a previous activity or

state, you start doing it again or being in it again after a break.

return to something ❑ *After lunch, Edward returned to his gardening.* ❑ *The Labour Party seems poised to return to power.*

rev /rev/ (revs, revving, revved)

◯ rev 'up

If you **rev up** or **rev up** a vehicle, you increase the speed of the vehicle's engine by pressing the accelerator.

rev up ❑ *Moses revved up and the car shot forward.*

rev something up or **rev up something** ❑ *I told you not to rev it up like that.* ❑ *Victor revved up his motorbike.*

revel /'revəl/ (revels, revelling, revelled)

> American English uses the spellings **reveling** and **reveled**.

◯ 'revel in

If you **revel in** a situation or experience, you enjoy it very much. = **glory in**

revel in something ❑ *She seemed to revel in her success.* ❑ *Happy schoolchildren were revelling in the bright sunshine.*

revert /rɪ'vɜːt/ (reverts, reverting, reverted)

◯ re'vert to

◼ If people or things **revert to** a previous state, condition, or way of behaving, often a worse or less developed one, they start being in that state or condition or behaving in that way again. = **return to, go back to**

revert to something ❑ *Fields that once yielded good crops are reverting to desert.* ❑ *Once in Vienna, Sophia reverted to her old ways.*

◼ If you **revert to** something you used before, you start to use it again.

revert to something ❑ *She has reverted to her maiden name.* ❑ *He spoke a few words of English before reverting to Russian.*

◼ If you **revert to** something that was mentioned earlier, you begin talking about it again. [FORMAL]

revert to something ❑ *At this point in the discussion I reverted to money matters.* ❑ *Can I revert to one other point before you continue?*

◼ When money or property **reverts to** someone, it becomes their property because they owned it before or because they are a descendant of the previous owner. [FORMAL]

revert to someone ❑ *On his death, ownership of the land reverts to his cousin.*

revise /rɪ'vaɪz/ (revises, revising, revised)

◯ re'vise for

When you **revise for** an exam, you read your

work again in order to be prepared for it.

revise for something ❑ *I have to revise for my maths exam.*

revolt /rɪ'vəʊlt/ (revolts, revolting, revolted)

◯ re'volt against

If people **revolt against** someone or something, they refuse to accept the authority of that person or refuse to accept that thing.

revolt against someone/something ❑ *He had revolted against his strict parents.* ❑ *Last year investors revolted against the two-year contract.*

revolve /rɪ'vɒlv/ (revolves, revolving, revolved)

◯ re'volve around (or revolve round [mainly BRITISH])

◼ If a discussion **revolves around** a particular subject, it is mainly about that subject.

revolve around something ❑ *The discussion revolved round three topics.*

◼ If something **revolves around** a person or thing, they are the most important person or thing in it. = **centre around**

revolve around someone/something ❑ *Their whole lives revolve around their children.* ❑ *He seems to think that the universe revolves around him.*

rhyme /raɪm/ (rhymes, rhyming, rhymed)

◯ 'rhyme with

If one word **rhymes with** another word, they have a very similar sound.

rhyme with something ❑ *'Cold' rhymes with 'bold'.*

rib /rɪb/ (ribs, ribbing, ribbed)

◯ 'rib about [INFORMAL]

If you **rib** someone **about** something, you tease them about it in a friendly way.

rib someone about something ❑ *He's always ribbing me about my taste in books.* ❑ *The actor has often been ribbed about his appearance.*

rid /rɪd/ (rids, ridding)

> The form **rid** is used in the present tense and is the past tense and past participle of the verb.

◯ 'rid of [FORMAL]

If you **rid** a place, thing, or person **of** something or someone unpleasant or unwanted, you remove them completely.

rid someone/something of something/someone ❑ *It is difficult to rid clothes of cooking smells.* ❑ *Occupiers must rid their premises of rats and mice.*

ride /raɪd/ (rides, riding, rode, ridden)

○ ride 'out

If you **ride out** a period of difficulty or danger, you manage to survive it without suffering serious harm. = **weather**
ride out something or **ride something out**
❑ The company can ride out the recession and do well again. ❑ You could ride the scandal out if you just refuse to say anything about it.

○ ride 'up

If a piece of clothing **rides up**, it moves upwards so that it is not in the correct position. ❑ This skirt is really annoying me – it keeps riding up.

riffle /'rɪfəl/ (riffles, riffling, riffled)

○ 'riffle through

1 If you **riffle through** sheets of paper or the pages of a book, you look at them briefly, turning the pages quickly. [mainly AMERICAN]
riffle through something ❑ I riffled through four or five newspapers, trying to find the article.
2 If you **riffle through** someone's belongings, you examine them quickly because you are trying to find something. [mainly AMERICAN]
riffle through something ❑ Tom passed the handbag to me. I riffled quickly through it.

rifle /'raɪfəl/ (rifles, rifling, rifled)

○ 'rifle through

1 If you **rifle through** sheets of paper or the pages of a book, you look at them briefly, turning the pages quickly. = **leaf through**
rifle through something ❑ She had picked up Amy's book and was rifling through it.
2 If you **rifle through** someone's belongings, you examine them quickly because you are trying to find something.
rifle through something ❑ Jean rifled through his desk.

rig /rɪg/ (rigs, rigging, rigged)

○ rig 'out [INFORMAL]

If you **rig** yourself **out** or **are rigged out** in special or unusual clothes, you are wearing that particular kind of clothing. = **get up**
be rigged out ❑ They were rigged out in black hats and stiff white collars.
rig yourself out ❑ He had rigged himself out as a cowboy. ● A **rig-out** is a set of clothes that someone is wearing, especially unusual or very fashionable clothes. [INFORMAL] ❑ Of course, she'd got herself a whole new rig-out for the trip. ❑ What an amazing rig-out!

○ rig 'up

If you **rig up** a device or piece of equipment,

you make it or fix it in place using whateve you have available.
rig up something or **rig something up** ❑ He had rigged up a listening device. ❑ Some of the me had rigged up tents with their coats.

ring /rɪŋ/ (rings, ringing, rang, rung)

○ ring a'round → see ring round

❂ ring 'back [BRITISH]

If you **ring back** or **ring** someone **back**, you telephone them for a second time or after they have telephoned you. = **call back, phone back**
ring back ❑ Tell her to ring back later.
ring someone back ❑ He asked if you'd ring him back when you got in. ❑ By the time I rang Sally back, she'd left the office.
ring back someone ❑ I need to ring back the accountant.

○ 'ring for

If you **ring for** someone or something, you ring a bell to call someone or to call someone to bring something to you.
ring for someone/something ❑ She rang for her maid. ❑ Shall I ring for another pot of tea?

○ ring 'in [BRITISH]

If you **ring in**, you telephone someone at your place of work. ❑ I rang in to say I was ill.
● If you **ring in sick**, you telephone someone at your place of work to tell them you are too ill to work. = **phone in** ❑ On Friday, England play Argentina and 700,000 workers are expected to ring in sick.

○ ring 'off [BRITISH]

When you **ring off** at the end of a telephone conversation, you end the conversation by putting down the part of the telephone you speak into or by pressing a button. = **hang up** ❑ The girl laughed and rang off.

○ ring 'out

If a sound **rings out**, it is heard loudly and clearly. ❑ His voice rang out into the night. ❑ Three shots rang out.

○ ring 'round (or ring around) [BRITISH]

If you **ring round** or **ring round** people, you telephone several people to discuss or ask about a particular thing. = **phone round**
ring round ❑ I got out the telephone book and began ringing round to heating contractors for estimates. ❑ I'll ring around and see what I can get.
ring round someone ❑ I'll ring round some more people and see if anyone can help out.

❂ ring 'up

1 If you **ring up** or **ring** someone **up**, you telephone someone. = **phone up** [BRITISH]
ring someone up ❑ I rang her up to thank her.
❑ He rang his mother up and asked her to fetch him

ring up someone ❏ *She rang up Emily and told her all about it.*

ring up ❏ *It's a good idea to ring up first to make an appointment.*

2 When a sales assistant in a shop **rings up** an amount on the till (= machine where money is kept), he or she records the amount of money that is being paid into the till by pressing the buttons.

ring up something or **ring something up** ❏ *She rang up £10.47 and gave me the receipt.*

3 If someone **rings up** an amount of something, they get it or achieve it. [AMERICAN]

ring up something ❏ *The company is on its way to ringing up more than $5 million in sales this year.*

inse /rɪns/ (rinses, rinsing, rinsed)

○ **rinse 'out**

1 When you **rinse out** something that you have washed in soap, you get rid of the soap by washing the thing in clean water. = **rinse**

rinse something out or **rinse out something** ❏ *She left the socks in soapy water overnight, then rinsed them out the next morning.*

2 If you **rinse** the inside of something **out**, you wash it quickly with water, often without using soap. = **wash out**

rinse something out or **rinse out something** ❏ *She rinsed out the glasses.*

3 If you **rinse** your mouth **out**, you wash it by holding a mouthful of liquid in it, for example to get rid of an unpleasant taste. = **wash out**

rinse something out or **rinse out something** ❏ *Encourage him to rinse his mouth out with fresh water after eating.* ❏ *I rinsed out my mouth and splashed cold water on to my face.*

ip /rɪp/ (rips, ripping, ripped)

○ **rip a'part**

1 If something **rips** people **apart**, it causes them to argue or fight so seriously that they can no longer be friends. = **tear apart**

rip someone apart ❏ *I didn't want to risk ripping the family apart.* ❏ *Money worries are ripping them apart.*

rip apart someone ❏ *This issue is ripping apart our town.*

2 If you **rip** a person or their opinions **apart**, you criticize them and say that they are wrong, in a very forceful way. = **tear apart**

rip someone/something apart ❏ *The presenters and audience ripped her apart, enjoying a laugh at her expense.*

rip apart someone/something ❏ *He started by ripping apart the president's policy.*

○ **rip 'into** [INFORMAL]

If someone **rips into** you or your opinions, they criticize you strongly. = **lay into**

rip into someone/something ❏ *If they disputed his claim, Paul would rip into them with frightening force.* ❏ *We listened to him rip into organised religion.*

○ **rip 'off**

1 If someone **rips** you **off**, they cheat you by charging you too much money for something. = **fleece** [INFORMAL]

rip off someone ❏ *The local shopkeepers were all trying to rip off the tourists.*

rip someone off ❏ *The court wastes my time and the lawyers rip me off!* • If you say that something that you bought was a **rip-off**, you mean that you were cheated into paying too much for it. [INFORMAL] ❏ *They knew it was a rip-off.*

2 To **rip** something **off** means to steal it. [INFORMAL]

rip something off or **rip off something** ❏ *Rob told us that the men had ripped off some clothes from him.*

NOTE **Nick** is an informal word for **rip off**.

3 If someone **rips off** something such as an idea or a product, they copy it in a way that is not fair. [INFORMAL]

rip off something or **rip something off** ❏ *I discovered that he had ripped off some of my work on this topic.* ❏ *I checked and found they had ripped off whole pages of my website.*

○ **rip through**

If something **rips through** a place, it moves through it very quickly and violently.

rip through something ❏ *A roaring explosion ripped through the house.* ❏ *A speedboat ripped through the water.*

○ **rip 'up**

1 If you **rip up** a piece of paper or cloth, you tear it into small pieces. = **tear up**

rip up something ❏ *I wanted to rip up my schedule and fill out a new one.*

rip something up ❏ *He took the bill from me and ripped it up.*

2 If you **rip** something **up**, you remove it from the ground or a surface with force.

rip something up or **rip up something** ❏ *I longed to rip up the brown carpet in the hall.*

rise /raɪz/ (rises, rising, rose, risen)

○ **rise a'bove**

If you **rise above** a difficulty or problem, you manage to deal with it without letting it affect you.

rise above something ❏ *Anyone who can rise above such disadvantages is clearly exceptional.* ❏ *Great thinkers have always been mocked by lesser minds. All you can do is rise above it.*

○ 'rise from

If a sound **rises from** a group of people or a place, it comes from them.

rise from someone/somewhere ❑ *There were low, muffled voices rising from the hallway.* ❑ *Laughter rose from the crowd.*

✿ rise 'up

1 If something **rises up**, it moves upwards. = **rise** ❑ *He could see the smoke from his bonfire rising up in a white column.* ❑ *A whole flock of blackbirds rose up suddenly when we went by.*
2 You can say that something **rises up** when it appears as a large, tall shape. ❑ *The hills rose up in the distance.* ❑ *Steep mountainsides rise up on either shore.*
3 If a thought, image, or feeling **rises up**, you suddenly think about it or feel it. ❑ *All of a sudden, an image of Maria rose up in his mind.* ❑ *Old terrors rose up within him.*
4 If people **rise up**, they start to fight against people in authority. ❑ *They will rise up and overthrow your imperialist government.* ❑ *Women, she predicted, would rise up and demand their rights.* ● An **uprising** is an occasion when many people start to fight against people in authority. ❑ *They had to deal with an armed uprising.*

rob /rɒb/ (**robs, robbing, robbed**)

○ 'rob of

To **rob** someone **of** something good means to take it away from them or to stop them from having it.

rob someone of something ❑ *The illness had robbed her of her independence.* ❑ *Worrying can rob you of sleep.* ❑ *The team were robbed of victory by the referee's decision to disallow the goal.*

rock /rɒk/ (**rocks, rocking, rocked**)

○ rock 'up [INFORMAL]

If someone **rocks up** somewhere, they arrive there. ❑ *If people want us to rock up and just do food, great, but we're more than that.*

roll /rəʊl/ (**rolls, rolling, rolled**)

○ roll a'round (or **roll about** [mainly BRITISH])

If you **roll around** or **roll around** somewhere, you move in a lying position by turning your body over and over in different directions.

roll around ❑ *Two smallish children were rolling around fighting.*
roll around something ❑ *Next moment they were rolling about the floor.*

○ roll 'back

1 If you **roll back** something that has been increasing in amount or importance, you cause it to start decreasing.

roll back something ❑ *They began by rolling back the power of the trade unions.* ❑ *The gains of last year are in danger of being rolled back.*
2 To **roll back** prices, taxes, or benefits means to reduce them. [AMERICAN]
roll back something ❑ *One provision of the law was to roll back taxes to the 1975 level.*

○ roll 'down

If you **roll down** a piece of clothing or material that has been folded over and over, you unfold the edge of it, in order to make it longer.

roll down something or **roll something down** ❑ *He began rolling down his sleeves.*

○ roll 'in

> In meaning 2, the stress is on **'roll**.

1 If something such as money **rolls in**, you receive it in large quantities. [INFORMAL] ❑ *We've got to attract the visitors and keep the money rolling in.* ❑ *Soon orders began to roll in.*
2 If you **are rolling in** something, especially money, you have a lot of it.
be rolling in something ❑ *If you'd bought shares in the company, you'd be rolling in gold now.* ● If you say that someone **is rolling in it**, you mean that they are rich. [INFORMAL] ❑ *He's not exactly rolling in it, but who is these days?*
3 If tanks or troops **roll in**, they move into a place in order to take control. ❑ *When the tanks rolled in, nearly 100 civilians were killed.*
4 If someone **rolls in**, they arrive somewhere in a very casual way. [BRITISH, INFORMAL] ❑ *He rolled in early Friday afternoon, played poker until midnight, then slept on the couch overnight.* ❑ *He rolled in at 1 a.m., asking what all the fuss was about.*
5 If bad weather or a storm **rolls in**, it arrives. ❑ *Thunder rumbled louder as another storm rolled in.* ❑ *We watched the fog roll in.*

○ roll 'into

1 If you **roll** a piece of a substance or material **into** a round shape, you fold it so that it is in that shape.
roll something into something ❑ *She rolled the socks into a ball.*
2 When tanks or troops **roll into** a place, they move into that place in order to take control.
roll into something ❑ *A convoy of United Nations trucks rolled into the city.*
3 If someone **rolls into** a place, they arrive there in a casual way. [BRITISH, INFORMAL]
roll into something ❑ *They rolled into the bar at a quarter to seven.*

○ roll 'on

1 If an activity or process **rolls on**, it

continues to happen in a rather unexciting way. ❑ *The jokes and laughter rolled on.* ❑ *Life rolled on with all its routine pleasures.*

2 If you say **roll on** something, you mean that you want it to happen soon. [BRITISH, INFORMAL]

roll on something ❑ *'Roll on half-term!' Daniel said.* ❑ *Roll on four o'clock!*

3 Roll-on deodorant (= substance used under the arms to prevent smells) is sold in a container with a round ball in the top.

4 Roll-on roll-off ferries (= boats that carry people and vehicles) have a sloping part so that vehicles can be driven onto them and off them.

roll 'out

1 If a company **rolls out** a new product or service or if that product or service **rolls out**, it is produced and made available to the public.

roll something out or **roll out something** ❑ *The company is now able to roll the service out to all its construction partners.* ❑ *Facebook just rolled out their new user interface.*

roll out ❑ *With a year left before the new model rolls out, the 6 Series still looks as modern as it did back in 2003.*

2 If an organization **rolls out** a new system or way of working, it gradually introduces it to more parts of the organization.

roll something out or **roll out something** ❑ *NASA's intention is to roll out the system across its nationwide operations.*

3 If you **roll out** a food such as pastry, you make it flat by rolling an object shaped like a tube over it.

roll out something or **roll something out** ❑ *I had taken my rings off because I was rolling out cookies.*

roll 'over

1 If you are lying down and you **roll over**, you turn your body so that a different part of you is facing upwards. **= turn over** ❑ *I rolled over onto my stomach.*

2 If someone or something **rolls** someone or something **over**, they turn them so that a different part is facing upwards.

roll something/someone over or **roll over something/someone** ❑ *I reached around and rolled her over.* ❑ *An enormous wave covered the yacht and rolled it over.*

3 If you **roll over**, you accept a bad situation without fighting against it. [INFORMAL] ❑ *I'm not going to just roll over and let them do what they want.*

4 If you **roll over** text or images on a computer screen, you move your cursor

onto them, usually to get more information.

roll over something ❑ *When you need more information about a setting, roll over the text to the left.*

5 If prize money for a regular competition **rolls over**, it is added to the prize money for the following competition because no one has won it. ❑ *If the winner fails to collect their prize, the money rolls over.* ● A **rollover** is a situation in which prize money is added to the prize for the next competition. ● A **rollover** is also the total prize money itself. ❑ *Nobody had Saturday's winning numbers, thus creating a huge rollover.*

○ roll 'up

1 If you **roll up** something such as a piece of paper or material, you wrap it several times around itself in the shape of a tube or a ball.

roll up something ❑ *You sort out the tent while I roll up the sleeping bags.*

roll something up ❑ *She took off her jumper and rolled it up to use as a pillow.* ● A **rolled-up** piece of paper or material has been folded or wrapped into a tube or ball shape. ❑ *He lunged at the wasp with a rolled-up newspaper.*

● **Roll-up** describes things which can be folded or rolled into a cylindrical shape. ❑ *They have a roll-up garage door.* ❑ *We took a roll-up map.* ● A **roll-up** is a cigarette that you make yourself with tobacco and paper. ❑ *She gave me one of her roll-ups.*

2 If a person or animal **rolls up** or **rolls** themselves **up**, they curl their bodies into a round shape.

roll up ❑ *The dog rolled up and fell asleep on the sofa.*

roll yourself up ❑ *I rolled myself up into a ball with my arms around my head.*

3 If you **roll up** your sleeves or trouser legs, you fold the edges over several times to make them shorter.

roll up something or **roll something up** ❑ *Just roll your trousers up and have a paddle.* ❑ *His father had his sleeves rolled up.*

4 If people **roll up** somewhere, they arrive in large numbers. [INFORMAL] ❑ *I was desperate for a quiet weekend, but all these visitors kept rolling up.*

5 If someone shouts **Roll up!**, they are encouraging people to come and look at something or watch a performance. [BRITISH] ❑ *Roll up! Roll up! Come and see the Elephant Man!*

romp /rɒmp/ (romps, romping, romped)

○ 'romp through

If you **romp through** something, you do it quickly and easily.

romp through something ❏ *This is easy stuff, you'll romp through it.* ❏ *She romped through the last 10 games against Sharapova on Tuesday.*

room /ruːm, rʊm/ (rooms, rooming, roomed)

○ **'room with** [AMERICAN]

If you **room with** someone, you share a room, apartment, or house with them, for example when you are a student.
room with someone ❏ *I roomed with him when we were both at Yale Law School.*

root /ruːt/ (roots, rooting, rooted)

○ **root a'round** (or **root about** [mainly BRITISH])

If you **root around** or **root around** something, you move things around in order to search for something.
root around ❏ [+ in] *She was rooting around in the cupboard, looking for something to eat.*
root around something ❏ *They were nervous of having the bears rooting around their dustbins.*

○ **'root for** [INFORMAL]

If you **are rooting for** someone, you are supporting them or hoping they will be successful.
be rooting for someone ❏ *Editorial friends on the newspapers were rooting for us.* ❏ *Good luck in the interview – I'll be rooting for you.*

○ **root 'out**

1 If you **root out** someone or something that you do not want or that is causing problems, you find them and remove them in a determined way from a place or organization.
root out someone/something or **root someone/something out** ❏ *He was determined to root out corruption in his department.* ❏ *We use all sorts of methods to root out cheats.*
2 If you **root out** someone or something that you want, you find them.
root out someone/something or **root someone/something out** ❏ *He's in the library somewhere. Let's go and root him out.* ❏ *His job is to root out the facts.*

○ **'root through**

If you **root through** something, you search for something by moving other things around.
root through something ❏ *Tania was rooting through her bag to find her purse.*

○ **root 'up**

If you **root up** a plant, you dig it up from the ground. = uproot
root up something or **root something up** ❏ *I had to root up all the plants and burn them.*

rope /rəʊp/ (ropes, roping, roped)

○ **rope 'in** [BRITISH, INFORMAL]

If you **rope** someone **in**, you persuade them to help you to do something.
rope someone in or **rope in someone** ❏ [+ to-infinitive] *Some amazing people were rop in to work on these books.* ❏ *Parents, teachers ar other adults could be roped in as support figures.*

○ **rope 'into** [BRITISH, INFORMAL]

If you **rope** someone **into** something, you persuade them to do it or take part in it.
rope someone into something ❏ *Soon everyone was being roped into the search parties.* ❏ *Percy roped me into helping out on the farm.*

○ **rope 'off**

If an area **is roped off**, it is separated from another area by a rope.
be roped off ❏ [+ from] *The track was roped off from the rest of the field.* ❏ *The shop is roped off because they are doing major alterations.*

rot /rɒt/ (rots, rotting, rotted)

○ **rot a'way**

When something **rots away**, it gradually decays until it falls to pieces or disappears completely. ❏ *Their bodies were now rotting away in the earth.* ❏ *Eventually the old hut simp rotted away.*

rough /rʌf/ (roughs, roughing, roughed)

○ **rough 'out**

1 If you **rough out** a drawing or idea, you draw or list the main features of it before you do it in detail.
rough out something ❏ *I've roughed out a scene for my new play.* ❏ *She roughed out a sketc of the harbour.*
2 If you **rough it out**, you survive in very uncomfortable conditions. ❏ *Judd will roug it out in the Australian Outback with Melissa Rivers and others.* ❏ *These are tough times for a man roughing it out on the street.*

○ **rough 'up** [INFORMAL]

If someone **roughs** you **up**, they attack you by hitting or beating you.
rough someone up or **rough up someone** ❏ *They roughed me up a bit.* ❏ *She accused the police of roughing up her son.*

round /raʊnd/ (rounds, rounding, rounde

○ **round 'down**

If you **round down** a figure or total, you change it by lowering it to the nearest whole number, the nearest 10, or the nearest 100, for example.
round something down or **round down something** ❏ [+ to] *We round down any tax you owe to the nearest pound.*

round 'off

1 If you **round** something **off** or **round off**, you do something to complete something in a satisfactory way. **= finish off**

round off something ❑ I think you ought to work abroad – round off your education a bit.

round something off ❑ We'll round the session off with some observations on Indian history.

round off ❑ [+ with] At the end of a lunch, we round off with a brandy or a liqueur.

2 If a point or shape **is rounded off**, it has been made into a smooth, curved shape.

be rounded off ❑ The front of the boat is rounded off to cut through the water. ❑ The southern end of the mountain is rounded off by a huge lake.

'round on

If you **round on** someone, you suddenly criticize or attack them.

round on someone ❑ In Denver, he rounded on his critics. ❑ The girl rounded on me furiously. 'Do you think I'm ashamed?'

round 'up

1 If the police or army **round up** a number of people, they arrest or capture them.

round up someone ❑ The police rounded up a number of suspects. ❑ The rebels were rounded up in prison camps.

round someone up ❑ They rounded everybody up and forced us into police vans. ● A **round-up** is an occasion when many people are arrested or captured. ❑ In a massive round-up they arrested several hundred prominent leaders.

2 If you **round up** animals or things, you gather them together.

round up something ❑ He looked for work as a cowboy, rounding up cattle. ❑ We've rounded up a selection of products.

round something up ❑ Jess was rounding the sheep up for me.

3 If you **round up** a figure or total, you change it by increasing it to the nearest whole number, the nearest 10, or the nearest 100, and so on.

round something up or **round up something** ❑ [+ to] Round up any odd half unit to the next whole number. ❑ We round the monthly total up to the nearest ten pounds.

4 A **round-up** on radio or television, or in a newspaper, is a brief summary of the news. ❑ The eleven o'clock news is followed by the sports round-up. ❑ We have a round-up of world news at midday.

out /raʊt/ (routs, routing, routed)

rout 'out

1 If you **rout** someone or something **out**, you make them come out from where they are.

rout someone/something out or **rout out someone/something** ❑ Sometimes, the boys would rout out little squirrels and chase them. ❑ [+ of] Rafferty appeared to have been routed out of bed.

2 If you **rout** someone or something **out**, you find them and get rid of them.

rout someone/something out or **rout out someone/something** ❑ He accused the West of going beyond its stated objective of routing out terrorism.

row /rəʊ/ (rows, rowing, rowed)

○ row 'back [JOURNALISM]

If someone **rows back**, they change their mind about a decision or plan that they have made. **= backtrack** ❑ [+ from] The administration has been rowing back from its early opposition to the visit. ❑ [+ on] The government was forced to row back on a plan that would have involved wage cuts.

rub /rʌb/ (rubs, rubbing, rubbed)

○ 'rub against

If you **rub against** a surface or **rub** a part of your body **against** a surface, you move a part of your body backwards and forwards along the surface.

rub against something ❑ A cat was rubbing against my leg.

rub something against something ❑ 'Daddy,' she said, rubbing her cheek against his.

○ rub a'long [BRITISH, INFORMAL]

If people **rub along**, they are able to live or work together in a reasonably friendly way. **= get on** ❑ I share a flat with three other women, and we rub along pretty well.

○ rub 'down

1 If you **rub down** a surface, you prepare it by rubbing it with something rough such as sandpaper.

rub down something or **rub something down** ❑ The boards have been rubbed down several times to get that perfect finish. ❑ Eliminate bad marks by rubbing down the area gently with wire wool.

2 If you **rub** a person or animal **down**, you rub them hard with a towel or a cloth, usually to dry them.

rub someone/something down or **rub down someone/something** ❑ I began by rubbing the horse down and brushing his mane and tail. ❑ She rubbed me down with a towel.

○ rub 'in

1 If you **rub** a substance **in**, you press it into a surface or into another substance by rubbing it on it or together with it.

rub in something ❑ When hair is dry, rub in a

little oil to make it smooth and glossy. ❑ *Sift together the flour, salt and mustard, and rub in the margarine.*

rub something in ❑ *Now rub the fat in.*

2 If someone **rubs it in**, they remind you about something that makes you feel upset, guilty, or embarrassed, often deliberately in order to make you feel worse. ❑ *When a child fails, never rub it in.* ❑ *'How old are you, Mr Sharpe?'—'All right, no need to rub it in.'*

○ **rub 'into**

If you **rub** a substance **into** a surface or another substance, you rub it on it or together with it.

rub something into something ❑ *Rub the fat into the flour.* ❑ *She rubbed the cream into my skin.*

○ **rub 'off**

1 If you **rub** something **off** a surface, you remove it by rubbing the surface with something, and if it **rubs off**, it is removed by something rubbing it.

rub something off or **rub off something** ❑ *She rubbed off the dirt with her hand.* ❑ *Use a soft pencil, because you can rub it off afterwards.*

rub something off something ❑ *She was trying without success to rub the stain off her skirt.*

rub off ❑ *The dye in the ink stays on the paper and does not rub off.*

2 If someone else's quality or mood **rubs off**, it affects you and you start to have it or feel it. ❑ *Anna felt proud to be the friend of someone so glamorous. Some of it must rub off, she thought.* ❑ [+ on] *The more you associate with these people, the greater the likelihood that their own characteristics will rub off on you!*

○ **rub 'out**

1 If you **rub out** something that you have written in pencil or chalk, you remove it by rubbing it with a rubber or a cloth.

rub out something or **rub something out** ❑ *I drew faint lines in pencil and rubbed them out when I had finished.*

[NOTE] **Erase** is a more formal word for **rub out**.

2 To **rub** someone **out** means to kill them. [INFORMAL]

rub someone out or **rub out someone** ❑ *He decided to destroy the documents, and rub out anyone who knew about them.*

○ **rub to'gether**

If you **rub** two things **together** or if they **rub together**, they move backwards and forwards, pressing against each other.

rub something together ❑ *He rubbed his hands together to try and warm them up.* ❑ *He managed to light a fire by rubbing two sticks together.*

rub together ❑ *When two materials rub together, small areas of their surfaces become incredibly hot.*

ruck /rʌk/ (**rucks, rucking, rucked**)

○ **ruck 'up** [BRITISH]

If cloth or a person's clothing **rucks up** or if someone or something **rucks** it **up**, it moves upwards, out of its correct position.
= **bunch up**

ruck up ❑ *The shirt rucked up under his braces.* ❑ *There she was, with her jumper rucking up at the back.*

ruck something up or **ruck up something** ❑ *The toe of his shoe had rucked up one corner of the rug.*

rule /ruːl/ (**rules, ruling, ruled**)

○ **rule 'in** [BRITISH]

If you **rule** something **in**, you decide that you will definitely do something.

rule something in or **rule in something** ❑ *At the moment, he is ruling nothing in or out.* ❑ *We must take care not to rule in or rule out any one solution.*

○ **rule 'off**

If you **rule off** a section on a piece of paper, you draw a straight line below it on the paper to divide it from the next section.

rule off something or **rule something off** ❑ *He ruled off sections of the notebook to record th fish he caught.*

❍ **rule 'out**

1 If you **rule out** something or someone, you decide that they are impossible or unsuitable or that they are not responsible for something. = **dismiss**

rule out something/someone ❑ *The government has not ruled out military action.* ❑ *They can't rule out the possibility that he was kidnapped.*

rule something/someone out ❑ *You have to be under thirty, so that rules me out.*

2 If one thing **rules out** another, it prevents it from happening or being possible.

rule out something ❑ *A search had ruled out the possibility of further bombs.* ❑ *The radio was on, effectively ruling out conversation.*

[NOTE] **Preclude** is a formal word for **rule out**.

○ **rule 'out of**

1 If someone **rules** you **out of** a contest or activity, they say that you cannot be involved in it.

rule someone out of something ❑ *Organiser ruled him out of the game because he failed a fitness test.*

2 If something **rules** you **out of** a contest or activity, it prevents you from being involved in it.

rule someone out of something ❏ *A damaged muscle has ruled him out of tomorrow's final.*

umble /'rʌmbəl/ (**rumbles, rumbling, rumbled**)

▷ **rumble 'on** [BRITISH]

If process or situation **rumbles on**, it continues for a long time. ❏ *The row rumbled on in the newspapers.*

uminate /'ruːmɪneɪt/ (**ruminates, ruminating, ruminated**)

▷ **'ruminate on** [FORMAL]

If you **ruminate on** something, you think about it very carefully.

ruminate on something ❏ *She sits in her backyard, ruminating on her problems.* ❏ *He ruminated on this as he walked along the shore.*

ummage /'rʌmɪdʒ/ (**rummages, rummaging, rummaged**)

▷ **'rummage through**

If you **rummage through** something, you search for something by moving a lot of things around quickly.

rummage through something ❏ *She rummaged through a drawer in her desk and pulled out a folder.* ❏ *He rummaged through his papers until he found the sheet he wanted.*

un /rʌn/ (**runs, running, ran**)

> The form **run** is used in the present tense and is also the past participle of the verb.

● **run a'bout**

1 → see **run around**

2 A **runabout** is a small car that you use mainly for short journeys. [BRITISH, INFORMAL] ❏ *It makes an ideal shopping runabout.*

3 A **runabout** is a car with an open top. [AMERICAN, INFORMAL] ❏ *She bought a runabout.*

● **run a'cross**

1 If you **run across** a place or area, you run from one side of it to the other.

run across something ❏ *Then they all ran across the street to the church.* ❏ *A small toy car ran across the floor.*

2 If you **run across** someone, you meet them unexpectedly. = **come across, bump into, run into**

run across someone ❏ *She had not seen him for two days when she ran across him in the street.* ❏ *It is very unusual to run across Americans in this part of the world.*

○ **run 'after**

1 If you **run after** someone or something that is moving, you chase them in order to catch them or stop them.

run after someone/something ❏ *Thomas ran after him, yelling to him to stop.*

2 If you **run after** something you want, you keep trying very hard to obtain it or to achieve it.

run after something ❏ *She has spent her life running after fame.* ❏ *We seem to be running after a goal which always escapes us.*

[NOTE] **Pursue** is a formal word for **run after**.

3 If you **run after** someone, you try hard to persuade them to have a romantic or sexual relationship with you. [INFORMAL]

run after someone ❏ *He was a useless husband, drinking and running after other women.* ❏ *Beautiful women run after me and I can't resist them.*

○ **run a'long** [OLD-FASHIONED]

If you tell a child to **run along**, you are telling him or her to go away. ❏ *Run along and play.* ❏ *Run along up to bed now, Sam.*

○ **run a'round** (or **run about** [mainly BRITISH])

1 If you **run around** or **run around** a place, you run in different directions within a particular area.

run around ❏ *We needed a large garden where the kids could run around freely.* ❏ *A dog was running around in the yard.*

run around something ❏ *She let them run about the place just as they pleased.*

2 If you **run around** doing something, you go to several places or do many different things in order to achieve something. ❏ *He was running around taking photos all night.* ❏ *You can't expect her to run around sorting out all your problems.*

3 If someone **gives** you **the runaround**, they deliberately behave in an unhelpful way. [INFORMAL] ❏ *Everybody I ask for advice gives me the runaround.*

○ **run a'round with** [INFORMAL]

If you **run around with** a person or group of people, you spend a lot of time with them socially. = **go about**

run around with someone ❏ *In the 1980s he used to run around a lot with Prince Andrew.* ❏ *What's his name – that guy you run around with?*

○ **run a'way**

1 If you **run away**, you leave a place or person by running. ❏ *The children run away if you approach them.* ❏ *She ran away laughing up the road.*

2 If you **run away**, you secretly leave a place because you are unhappy. ❑ *She ran away one night, leaving these pictures.* ❑ [+ to] *Some of these boys ran away to Canada.* ❑ [+ from] *He had run away from home.* ● A **runaway** is a person who leaves a place secretly. ❑ *They failed to find any trace of the runaways.*

3 If two people **run away**, they secretly leave their homes in order to live together or marry each other. ❑ *They ran away and got married.* ❑ [+ with] *She left him and ran away with another man.* ❑ [+ together] *He and Belinda were planning to run away together.*

4 A **runaway** animal or vehicle is moving but is no longer under the control of its rider or driver. ❑ *She attempted to stop the runaway horse.* ❑ *He was hit by a runaway tractor.*

5 A **runaway** situation happens very quickly or forcefully and cannot be controlled. ❑ *They were amazed at the runaway success of the play.* ❑ *Their savings were destroyed by runaway inflation after the war.*

○ **run a'way from**

If you **run away from** something difficult or unpleasant, you try to avoid dealing with it.

run away from something ❑ *We cannot run away from technology.* ❑ *I knew I had to face the truth that I had been running away from.*

○ **run a'way with**

1 If your feelings **run away with** you, you cannot control them, and they affect you so strongly that you cannot think or behave sensibly.

run away with someone ❑ *They let their emotions run away with them.* ❑ *They did not allow their enthusiasm to run away with them.*

2 If you **run away with** a prize or competition, you win it very easily. = **walk off with**

run away with something ❑ *Her sister ran away with every prize at school.*

3 If someone **runs away with the idea that** something is true, they think it is true when it probably is not. ❑ *Do not run away with the idea that all actors can handle comedy.*

○ **run 'by**

1 If you **run** something **by** someone, you tell them about it to see if they think it is a good idea. = **run past**

run something by someone ❑ *I'm definitely interested, but I'll have to run it by my partner first.*

2 If you **run** information **by** someone again, you repeat it to make sure they have understood it.

run something by someone ❑ *Can you run those figures by me again?*

○ **run 'down**

1 To **run down** somewhere means to run to a lower level or away from a place.

run down ❑ [+ to] *Marian, could you run down t the post box with this letter, please?*

run down something ❑ *She ran down the steps.*

2 If a liquid **runs down** something, it moves from the top to the bottom of it.

run down something ❑ *The old man had tears running down his face.* ❑ *There was blood running down his leg.*

3 If you **run down** someone or something, you criticize them strongly.

run down someone/something ❑ *She was not used to people running down their own families*

run someone/something down ❑ *Anne has professional duty not to run her colleagues down in public.* ❑ *Of course they'll run their competitors down and say how bad they are.*

4 If someone **runs down** an industry, organization, or service, they deliberately reduce its size, importance, or level of activity. [BRITISH]

run down something ❑ *This Government will go on running down the railways.*

run something down or **be run down**
❑ *Hospitals were being run down because of the spending cuts.* ● If something is **run down**, it has been made smaller, less important or less active. ❑ *Our forces are so run down they don't deter anybody any more.* ● The **run-down** of an industry or organization is the deliberate reduction of its size, importance or level of activity. [BRITISH] ❑ *Union leaders fought against the run-down of the coal industry.*

5 If someone **runs down** their stock or supply of something, they reduce the amount of it. [BRITISH]

run down something or **run something down** ❑ *Start to run down any freezer supplies as soon as possible.*

6 If a machine or device **runs down** or if something **runs** it **down**, it gradually loses power or works more slowly.

run down ❑ *The batteries in your radio are running down.*

run down something or **run something down** ❑ *Turn the light off – you're running down the batteries.*

7 If a vehicle or its driver **runs** someone **down**, the vehicle hits and injures that person. = **knock down, run over**

run someone down or **run down someone**
❑ *A coach nearly ran us down in front of Trinity Church.* ❑ *The car ran down and killed a French soldier.*

8 If you **run down** someone or something

you have been searching for, you find them after a lot of effort. **= track down, trace** [INFORMAL]

run down someone/something or **run someone/something down** ❑ *He went to the library to run down a reference.*

9 If you **run down** a list of items, you read or mention them briefly and quickly. **= run through**

run down something ❑ *We listened as Woodward ran down what details the reporters had given him.* ● If you give someone a **rundown** on a situation or subject, you describe briefly the important facts. ❑ *We've had a rundown on everyone connected with Olympus.* ❑ *I can give you a quick run-down.*

10 If someone is **run down**, they are very tired and ill after working too hard or not having enough sleep for a while. ❑ *'You're probably run down,' Clarissa said. 'You need a holiday.'*

11 A building or area that is **run-down** is in poor condition, because it has not been looked after. ❑ *They rented two small rooms in a run-down building.* ❑ *We lived in a run-down urban area.*

ᗡ 'run for

If someone **runs for** an official position, they try to be elected for it.

run for something ❑ *In February he announced he would run for president.* ❑ *Two or three years later, she ran for Congress, and almost won.*

ᗡ run 'in

1 If someone **runs in** from outside a room or building, they enter it, moving fast. ❑ *He ran in through the open glass doors of the sitting-room.* ❑ *I'll run in and get them.*

2 If the police **run** someone **in**, they find them and arrest them. [INFORMAL]

run someone in or **run in someone** ❑ *I could run you in for that.*

be run in ❑ *Shortly after the incident, Michael was run in.*

3 If you have a **run-in** with someone, you have an argument with them. [INFORMAL] ❑ *He's probably had a run-in at work with Ted.*

4 The **run-in** to an event is the period of preparation just before it takes place. ❑ *We did it for two weeks in Birmingham as a run-in for the main season.* ❑ *We have a lot to do in the run-in to the next general election.*

ᗡ run 'into

1 To **run into** a place means to enter it running.

run into something ❑ *I remember running into the playroom in tears.* ❑ *They had run into the nearest apartment and asked for help.*

2 If you **run into** problems or difficulties, you unexpectedly begin to experience them.

run into something ❑ *He ran into trouble with his economic policies.* ❑ *Once he revealed these proposals, he ran into considerable opposition.*

3 If you **run into** someone, you meet them unexpectedly. **= bump into, run across, come across**

run into someone ❑ *You might run into him one of these days.* ❑ *I first ran into him at the theatre.*

4 If something **runs into** a large number or amount, it reaches that number or amount.

run into something ❑ *If you include fuel, the cost runs into the thousands.* ❑ *The bibliography runs into more than fifteen thousand books.*

5 If a vehicle or its driver **runs into** something or someone, the vehicle accidentally hits them.

run into something/someone ❑ *The bus ran into a car in St. Andrew's Square.* ❑ *He ran into the back of a van at a zebra crossing.*

6 If one thing **runs into** another, it is difficult to see or hear where one thing ends and another begins. **= merge into**

run into something ❑ *The painting has a streak of red running into purple.* ❑ *The words run into each other.*

ᗧ run 'off

> In meaning 8, the stress is on **'run**.

1 If you **run off**, you run away from a place or person. ❑ *She gave a brief wave and ran off across the lawn.* ❑ *He dumped the stones he was carrying and ran off to look for more.*

2 If you **run off**, you leave a place secretly. **= run away** ❑ [+ from] *She had run off from home as a child.* ❑ *All the servants have run off and they have taken our horses.*

3 If two people **run off**, they secretly go away together to marry each other or live together. ❑ [+ with] *His wife ran off with another man.* ❑ [+ to] *She ran off to Paris with a guy ten years her junior.*

4 If a path, track, or corridor **runs off** from a place, it starts at that place and goes away from it. **= lead off** ❑ *We followed a narrow track running off into the forest.* ❑ *Another tunnel ran off on one side.*

5 If you **run off** copies of a document, you produce them using a machine such as a photocopier or a printer.

run off something or **run something off** ❑ *Could you run off five copies of this article for me, please?*

6 If you tell a child to **run off**, you are telling him or her to go away. ❑ *Run off and play with the others.*

7 If a liquid **runs off** the ground or a surface, or if it **runs off**, it flows over it.

run off ❏ *The rainwater may run off in sudden sheets, which can do tremendous damage.*

run off something ❏ *These streams are caused by water running off the mountains.*

8 If a machine or piece of equipment **runs off** a particular supply of power, it uses that power in order to make it work.

run off something ❏ *These vehicles can run off fuel made from cooking oil.*

○ **run 'off with**

If someone **runs off with** something, they steal it.

run off with something ❏ *Someone ran off with the proceeds from the sale.*

○ **run 'on**

In meaning 5, the stress is on **'run**.

1 If you **run on**, you continue to run in the same direction. ❏ *You run on and I'll catch up with you.* ❏ *I ran on ahead.*

2 If a road or track **runs on** to a particular place, it continues in that direction. ❏ [+ to] *From here, the railway line runs on to Gloucester.* ❏ [+ towards] *The main dusty track ran on towards Lesotho.*

3 If someone **runs on**, they continue talking for a long time. ❏ *Sometimes she let him run on for what seemed hours.*

4 If something **runs on**, it continues for longer than expected. ❏ *The list of British troops in the region ran on and on.* ❏ *He let the discussion run on until nine o'clock.*

5 If a machine or piece of equipment **runs on** a particular type of power, it uses it in order to work.

run on something ❏ *The heating system runs on half-price electricity.* ❏ *The van runs on diesel.*

○ **run 'out**

1 If you **run out** of a room or building, you leave it, running. ❏ *I ran out and slammed the door.* ❏ [+ of] *He ran out of the room and down the stairs.* ❏ *Mrs Todd came running out into the garden.*

2 If a substance **runs out** from somewhere, it flows from there. ❏ *The filter lets the milk run out, but collects the cream.*

3 If you **run out** of something, you have no more of it left. ❏ [+ of] *We were rapidly running out of money.* ❏ *I need some flour, but we've run out.*

4 If something **runs out**, it becomes used up so that there is no more left. ❏ *Time is running out fast.* ❏ *My luck seemed to have run out.* ❏ *Their money ran out.*

5 If a legal document or contract **runs out**, it is no longer valid. ❏ *My passport's run out.*

❏ *The agreement runs out in 2025.*

NOTE **Expire** is a more formal word for **run out**.

6 In cricket, if you are batting and someone **runs** you **out**, you are out, because the other team manage to get the ball to the wicket before you reach it.

run someone out *or* **run out someone** ❏ *Flintoff ran out Ponting in the 40th over.*

be run out ❏ *Howarth was unluckily run out.*

run yourself out ❏ *He ran himself out in the last Test against Pakistan.*

7 If you **run out** something such as a length of rope, you unwind some of it and let it pass away from you; if something such as a length of rope **runs out**, it unwinds.

run out something *or* **run something out** ❏ *It was magnificent climbing. I ran out 130 feet of rope to bring Richard up.* ❏ *I ran the line out behind the boat.*

run out ❏ *The line is allowed to run out until it bumps the bottom.*

○ **run 'out of**

If someone **runs** another person **out of** a place, they use force to make that person leave.

run someone out of something ❏ *My father will run your family out of town.* ❏ *He grabbed the shotgun, and ran them out of the house.*

○ **run 'out on**

If someone **runs out on** someone they are having a relationship with, they suddenly leave them.

run out on someone ❏ *You know I wouldn't run out on you.*

○ **run 'over**

1 If you **run over**, you move quickly to someone or something. ❏ *She ran over and clutched her mother's hand.* ❏ [+ to] *Ellen ran over to the bed and threw herself across it.*

2 If a vehicle or its driver **runs over** someone or something, the vehicle hits them or drives over them, causing injury or damage. = **run down, knock down**

run over someone/something ❏ *We almost ran over a fox that was crossing the road.*

run someone/something over ❏ *I'm sure he would have run us over if we hadnÖt jumped away.*

3 If a container of liquid **runs over**, it is too full and the liquid flows down its sides. ❏ *Turn the tap off – the sink's running over.*

NOTE **Overflow** is a more formal word for **run over**.

4 If you **run over** something, you explain it or read it quickly, in order to practise it, check it or make sure that people understand it. = **go over, run through**

run over something ❑ *He ran over his notes.*
❑ *I would just like to run over the arrangements again with you.*

5 If a meeting or event **runs over** or **runs over** time, it lasts longer than it should.
run over ❑ *The meeting ran over so that he was late for lunch.*

run over something ❑ *Each of you will be allocated fifteen minutes. Please try not to run over time.*

◖ **run 'past**

If you **run** something **past** someone, you tell them about it or mention it, to see if they think it is a good idea, or can understand it. = **run by**
run something past someone ❑ *Before agreeing, he ran the idea past Johnson.*

◖ **run 'through**

1 If an idea, piece of news, or emotion **runs through** a place or a group of people, it spreads through the place or group quickly.
run through someone/something ❑ *A kind of shock-wave ran through the room.* ❑ *A tremor of excitement ran through the ship as Bill announced that they had sighted land.*

2 If a quality or feeling **runs through** something, it affects every part of it or is present everywhere within it.
run through something ❑ *There is a prejudice that runs through our society.*

NOTE **Pervade** is a formal word for **run through**.

3 If you **run through** something, you explain it or read it quickly, in order to practise it, check it or make sure that people understand it. = **go through, run over**
run through something ❑ *Some of you won't know this so I'll just briefly run through it.*
❑ *Dawlish ran through the notes that he had prepared.* ● A **run-through** for an event or performance is a rehearsal or practice for it.
❑ *He agreed to come to a run-through.*

4 If you **run through** a large amount of money, you spend it quickly.
run through something ❑ *How he managed to run through £100,000 so quickly I will never know.*

5 If someone **runs** a person **through** with a sharp weapon, they push it violently all the way through the person's body. [LITERARY]
run someone through ❑ *As he turned I ran him through with my sword.*

◖ **'run to**

1 If you **run to** someone, you go to them for help, advice or protection.
run to someone ❑ *I didn't think he'd run to you with the story.* ❑ *We must learn to trust our own judgment, and not always run to the experts.*

2 If something **runs to** a particular amount or size, it is that amount or size.
run to something ❑ *A parent's work can run to ten or twelve hours a day if he or she has small children.* ❑ *The transcript runs to 1,200 pages.*

3 If you **cannot run to** a particular item, you cannot afford to buy it or pay for it. [BRITISH]
not run to something ❑ *I developed a taste for expensive clothes, but my allowance didn't run to that sort of thing.*

4 If someone's taste **runs to** a particular kind of thing, that is what they like.
run to something ❑ *His taste for the arts also ran to poetry.*

❍ **run 'up**

1 To **run up** or **run up** something means to move quickly from a lower position to a higher one.
run up ❑ *People from downstairs ran up to see what was happening.*
run up something ❑ *These small tropical lizards can run up walls.* ❑ *I heard her running up the stairs.*

2 If someone **runs up**, they come quickly to where you are. ❑ *They ran up and started to attack me.* ❑ [+ to] *I ran up to him and asked, 'Did you see two ladies come by?'* ● In sport, a **run-up** is the running approach by an athlete or player to gather speed before jumping, throwing something, or kicking a ball.
❑ *He had no rhythm or speed in his run-up.*

3 If a set of steps or a road **runs up** to a place, or **runs up** an area of land, it leads in that direction.
run up ❑ [+ to] *Wooden steps ran up to an open front door.*
run up something ❑ *At first the road ran up a wide flat valley.*

4 If someone **runs up** bills or debts, they start to owe a lot of money because they fail to pay their bills.
run up something ❑ *She ran up a phone bill of five hundred pounds.*

5 If you **run up** a piece of clothing, you make it quickly.
run up something or **run something up** ❑ *He had a jacket run up for him.*
run someone up something ❑ *I wonder if Mrs Moffat could run me up a clown costume.*

6 If a flag **is run up**, it is raised to the top of a flag pole or mast.
be run up ❑ *The flag was run up and the National Anthem was sung.*

7 The **run-up** to an event is the period of time and the things that happen just before it. ❑ [+ to] *The run-up to the election has been a busy time for us.*

○ **run 'up against**

If you **run up against** problems or difficulties, you suddenly and unexpectedly begin to experience them. **= run into, come up against**
run up against something ❑ *Their plans ran up against opposition from within the party.* ❑ *Economic growth would sooner or later run up against problems.*

rush /rʌʃ/ (**rushes, rushing, rushed**)

○ **rush 'in**

If you **rush in**, you do or decide something too quickly, without thinking about it carefully enough. ❑ *I'm not going to rush in and change everything.*

○ **rush 'into**

If you **rush into** something, you do it or decide about it too quickly, without thinking about it carefully enough.
rush into something ❑ *Don't rush into marriage.* ❑ *It's not safe to rush into hasty judgements.*

○ **rush 'out**

If a company **rushes out** a product, it produces the product quickly in a very short period of time.
rush out something or **rush something out** ❑ *Three biographies were rushed out within a couple of weeks of his death.*

○ **rush 'through**

If you **rush** something **through**, you deal with it quickly so that it is ready in a shorter time than usual. **= push through**
rush something through or **rush through something** ❑ *The government rushed the legislation through before the summer recess.* ❑ *Could you rush this application through?*

rust /rʌst/ (**rusts, rusting, rusted**)

○ **rust a'way**

When a metal object **rusts away**, it is gradually destroyed by rust. ❑ *In the yard wa an old car which had been rusting away for years.*

rustle /'rʌsəl/ (**rustles, rustling, rustled**)

○ **rustle 'up**

1 If you **rustle** something **up**, you provide or obtain it quickly, with very little planning. [INFORMAL]
rustle up something or **rustle something up** ❑ *He managed to rustle up a couple of blankets.* ❑ *He had no trouble rustling up 35 friends and colleagues to invite to the party.*
2 If you **rustle up** a meal, you cook it quickly, using whatever food you have available at the time.
rustle up something or **rustle something up** ❑ *I'll rustle something up.* ❑ *We could rustle up an omelette.*

Ss

saddle /'sædəl/ (saddles, saddling, saddled)

○ saddle 'up

If you **saddle up** or **saddle up** a horse, you put a saddle on a horse.

saddle up ❑ I saddled up and rode off.

saddle up something or **saddle something up** ❑ He ordered the men to saddle up their horses and be ready to ride.

○ 'saddle with

If you **are saddled with** something or someone that you do not want, or if someone **saddles** you **with** them, you have to deal with them. = **land with, lumber with**

be saddled with something ❑ I don't want to be saddled with a kid at my age. ❑ He had been saddled with the unpleasant task of telling John the news.

saddle someone with something ❑ You haven't solved the problem, you've just saddled me with it.

saddle yourself with something ❑ The last thing I want is to saddle myself with more debt.

sail /seɪl/ (sails, sailing, sailed)

○ sail 'through

If you **sail through** something or **sail through**, you deal with an experience easily and successfully. = **romp through**

sail through something ❑ Some women just sail through their pregnancies. ❑ At the rehearsal, she had sailed through, knowing every line.

salivate /'sælɪveɪt/ (salivates, salivating, salivated)

○ 'salivate over

If someone **salivates over** something, they look at it or think about it with too much pleasure.

salivate over something ❑ We were all salivating over a shiny red sports car.

sally /'sæli/ (sallies, sallying, sallied)

○ sally 'forth [LITERARY]

If someone **sallies forth**, they go to a place quickly or energetically. ❑ Boldly they sallied forth to meet them.

○ sally 'out [LITERARY]

If someone **sallies out**, they leave a place in order to go somewhere. ❑ She would sally out even on bitterly cold nights to keep her appointments.

salt /sɔːlt/ (salts, salting, salted)

○ salt a'way

If you **salt away** money, you save it or keep it somewhere for the future.
= **stash away**

salt away something or **salt something away** ❑ He was said to have salted away £4 million. ❑ They salt their funds away in numbered Swiss bank accounts.

be salted away ❑ People don't know how much he's got salted away.

sand /sænd/ (sands, sanding, sanded)

○ sand 'down

If you **sand down** a surface, you rub it with rough paper until it is smooth.

sand down something or **sand something down** ❑ Sand down the wood before you start painting it. ❑ It took us ages to sand the doors down.

save /seɪv/ (saves, saving, saved)

✪ save 'up

1 If you **save up**, or **save up** money, you collect money by not spending it, usually in order to buy a particular thing.

save up ❑ [+ to-infinitive] Their relatives all saved up to put the child through school. ❑ I'm saving up until I can afford my own place.

save up something ❑ [+ for] His plan is to save up enough money for a bicycle. ❑ She works at weekends and saves up her wages.

save something up ❑ [+ for] They're saving some money up for a holiday.

2 If you **save** something **up**, you keep it to use or deal with later.

save something up ❑ She saved the chocolate up to eat after everyone had gone.

save up something ❑ I've been saving up this question until last. ❑ She had kept all the children's drawings, saved up in a folder.

savour /'seɪvə/ (**savours, savouring, savoured**)

> **Savour** is also spelled **savor** in American English.

○ **'savour of** [FORMAL]

If something **savours of** a particular quality or thing, usually a bad one, it seems similar to or connected to it. = **smack of**
savour of something ❑ She disliked anything that savoured of the supernatural.

saw /sɔː/ (**saws, sawing, sawed, sawn**)

> The past participle is either **sawed** or **sawn**.

○ **saw 'off**

If you **saw** something **off** or **saw** it **off** something else, you cut a piece from something, using a saw.
saw something off ❑ We sawed the legs off.
saw off something ❑ Jack had sawn off the broken branch.
saw something off something ❑ The lock had been sawn off the door. ● Something that is **sawn-off** has been made shorter by being cut with a saw. [BRITISH] ❑ The robbers used sawn-off shotguns.
NOTE In American English, **sawed-off** means the same as **sawn-off**.

○ **saw 'up**

To **saw** something **up** means to cut it into pieces, using a saw.
saw something up or **saw up something** ❑ We had to saw the chairs up for firewood. ❑ He spent all day sawing up wood.

scale /skeɪl/ (**scales, scaling, scaled**)

○ **scale 'back**

If you **scale** something **back**, you make it smaller or less than before. = **decrease**
scale back something or **scale something back** ❑ UK manufacturers are having to scale back production. ❑ We haven't decided whether to cancel the whole project or just scale it back.

○ **scale 'down**

If something **is scaled down** or if you **scale** it **down**, it is made smaller or less.
be scaled down ❑ It was like any other hospital, only scaled down.
scale down something or **scale something down** ❑ It would be wise to scale down our expectations. ❑ France reconsidered its military presence in the country, scaling it down.

○ **scale 'up**

If you **scale** something **up**, you make it larger or more than before. = **increase**
scale up something or **scale something up** ❑ The company has been scaling up production to prepare for clinical trials. ❑ [+ to] I scaled the image up to 1200 x 800 pixels.

scare /skeə/ (**scares, scaring, scared**)

○ **scare a'way**

■ To **scare** animals or people **away** means to frighten them so that they go away. = **scare off**
scare someone/something away or **scare away someone/something** ❑ The smallest movement would scare the fish away. ❑ You can hang shiny material in your garden to scare away birds. ❑ The children had been scared away by a man waving a stick.

■ To **scare** people **away** means to make them decide not to do something because they are worried or nervous.
scare someone away or **scare away someone** ❑ This kind of sensational reporting scares customers away. ❑ The cover of a book should be designed to attract readers, not scare them away.
NOTE **Discourage** is a more formal word for **scare away**.

○ **scare 'off**

■ If you **scare** people or animals **off**, you frighten them so that they go away. = **scare away**
scare someone/something off or **scare off someone/something** ❑ I thought of scaring them off with a few shotgun pellets. ❑ The boys made so much noise that they scared off all the birds.

■ If something **scares** people **off**, it makes them worried or nervous, so that they do not want to do something.
scare someone off or **scare off someone** ❑ Stories about the pills being harmful had scared people off. ❑ He named a price he thought would scare me off.
NOTE **Deter** is a more formal word for **scare off**.

○ **scare 'up** [AMERICAN, INFORMAL]

If you **scare up** something, you manage to find or obtain it.
scare up something or **scare something up** ❑ An all-star game might scare up a bit of interest. ❑ Why don't you see if you can scare up a cup of coffee?

scarf /skɑːf/ (**scarfs, scarfing, scarfed**)

○ **scarf 'down** [AMERICAN, INFORMAL]

If you **scarf** food **down**, you eat it very quickly and greedily.
scarf something down or **scarf down something** ❑ They were scarfing down the burgers.

scatter /'skætə/ (**scatters, scattering, scattered**)

● **scatter a'round** (or **scatter about** [mainly BRITISH])

◼ If you **scatter** things **around** or **scatter** them **around** a place, you throw or drop them over an area in a careless way.
scatter something around or **scatter around something** ❑ The children scatter their food about and make a mess.
scatter something around something ❑ Keep all your documents in one place rather than scattering them around the house.
be scattered around ❑ We saw pots scattered around and the remains of a campfire.
be scattered around something ❑ Food was scattered about the table.
◼ If things or people **are scattered around** an area or **are scattered around**, they are spread over an area in many different places.
be scattered around something ❑ She now has five shops scattered around the town.
be scattered around ❑ My family are scattered around all over the country.

scavenge /'skævɪndʒ/ (**scavenges, scavenging, scavenged**)

● **'scavenge for**

If people or animals **scavenge for** something, they try to find it by searching through waste.
scavenge for something ❑ The children lived on the streets and scavenged for food.

school /sku:l/ (**schools, schooling, schooled**)

● **'school in** [FORMAL]

If someone **is schooled in** something or someone **schools** them **in** something, they are trained or educated to do something or to behave or think in a particular way.
be schooled in something ❑ At that time, girls were schooled in domestic duties.
school someone in something ❑ Her parents had schooled her in classical music.

scoff /skɒf/ (**scoffs, scoffing, scoffed**)

● **'scoff at**

If you **scoff at** something or someone, you speak about them in a way that shows you think they are silly.
scoff at something/someone ❑ At first I scoffed at the idea. ❑ She scoffs at the critics who say that the party needs a new leader.

scoop /sku:p/ (**scoops, scooping, scooped**)

○ **scoop 'out**

If you **scoop** something **out**, you make

a space in something by removing the inside part.
scoop out something or **scoop something out** ❑ He scooped out a deep trench in the earth. ❑ Slice the tops off the tomatoes and scoop the seeds out.

○ **scoop 'up**

If you **scoop** something **up**, you put your hands under it and lift it quickly.
scoop something up or **scoop up something** ❑ Stephanie scooped one of the kittens up. ❑ I watched Patrick scoop up a handful of snow from the window ledge.

scope /skəʊp/ (**scopes, scoping, scoped**)

○ **scope 'out**

If you **scope** something **out**, you find out about it and look at it, especially before you decide to go ahead with a plan.
scope out something or **scope something out** ❑ Angie flew to Canada to scope out some potential filming venues for her movie. ❑ We went to the venue beforehand and scoped it out.

score /skɔ:/ (**scores, scoring, scored**)

○ **score 'off**

◼ If you **score off** someone, you make a clever or insulting reply to something they have said.
score off someone ❑ They spent the whole evening scoring off each other.
◼ If you **score** something **off** or **score** it **off** a list, you draw a line through it to show that it is not wanted or has been dealt with.
= **cross off**
score something off or **score off something** ❑ Score off each number as it is read out. ❑ You'll find it easier if you score them off when you've answered them.
score something off something ❑ I asked him to score my name off the list of players next Saturday.

○ **score 'out**

If you **score** something **out**, you draw a line through it so that people cannot read it or to show that it is not wanted. = **cross out**
score something out or **score out something** ❑ The article was too long, and I had to score a couple of paragraphs out. ❑ The name was scored out.
NOTE **Delete** is a more formal word for **score out**.

scour /skaʊə/ (**scours, scouring, scoured**)

○ **scour a'way**

If water or wind **scours away** land, it gradually removes it. = **erode**
scour away something or **scour something away** ❑ Rainwater had scoured away the hillsides. ❑ Rivers scoured the soft sandstone away.

scout /skaʊt/ (**scouts, scouting, scouted**)

○ **scout a'round** (or **scout round** [mainly BRITISH])

If you **scout around**, you go to different places looking for something. ❑ [+ for] *I spend most of my time scouting round for books.* ❑ [+ to-infinitive] *We'd scout around to see if anyone was in the rooms nearby.*

○ **scout 'out**

If you **scout out** something that you want or need, you search an area for it and find it. = **locate**

scout out something or **scout something out** ❑ *Their mission is to scout out places where helicopters can land.*

○ **scout 'round** → see **scout around**

scrabble /'skræbəl/ (**scrabbles, scrabbling, scrabbled**)

○ **scrabble a'round** (or **scrabble about** [mainly BRITISH])

If you **scrabble around**, you use your hands in order to try to find something that you cannot see. ❑ *We scrabbled about in the grass and leaves and found the packet.* ❑ *Kate scrabbled around, trying to find her glasses.*

○ **'scrabble for**

If you **scrabble for** something that you cannot see, you try to find it by using your hands.

scrabble for something ❑ *He scrabbled for some coins in his desk drawer.*

scramble /'skræmbəl/ (**scrambles, scrambling, scrambled**)

○ **'scramble for**

If people **scramble for** something, they all try to get it.

scramble for something ❑ *Journalists were scrambling for an interview with the couple.*

scrape /skreɪp/ (**scrapes, scraping, scraped**)

○ **scrape a'long**

If you **scrape along**, you have enough money for the things you really need, but not for a very comfortable life. = **get by** ❑ *She was not content just to scrape along in life.* ❑ [+ on] *They'd be able to scrape along on her savings.*

○ **scrape a'way**

If you **scrape** something **away**, you remove it using a sharp object. = **scrape off**

scrape away something or **scrape something away** ❑ *I had to scrape away the dirt with a knife.* ❑ *The paint had been scraped away.*

○ **scrape 'back**

If someone **scrapes back** electronic data, they get it back when it has been stolen.

scrape back something or **scrape something back** ❑ *We will take legal action to scrape back the data.*

○ **scrape 'by**

If you **scrape by**, you have enough money to buy the things that you need to survive, but nothing more. = **get by** ❑ [+ on] *They had to scrape by on forty pounds a week.* ❑ *We scrape by, but we never have much fun.*

○ **scrape 'in**

If you **scrape in**, you only just manage to get a place in a school, university, etc. or to get a job. ❑ *His party scraped in, but without winning an overall majority.* ❑ *My dad wanted me to go to Cambridge and somehow I scraped in.*

○ **scrape 'into**

If you **scrape into** a place or a position, you only just manage to get a place in a school, university, etc. or to get a job.

scrape into something ❑ *He only just scraped into university because of poor A levels.*

○ **scrape 'off**

If you **scrape** something **off** or **scrape** it **off** a surface, you remove it using a sharp object.

scrape something off or **scrape off something** ❑ *Scrape as much wax as possible off with your fingernails.* ❑ *I used a knife to scrape off some of the dirt.*

scrape something off something ❑ *The men had to scrape snow off the railway tracks with shovels.*

○ **scrape 'out**

When you **scrape** something **out**, you remove everything that is left in a container with a tool such as a spoon or knife.

scrape out something or **scrape something out** ❑ *She scraped out her bowl greedily.*

○ **scrape 'through**

If someone or something **scrapes through** something or **scrape through**, they just manage to succeed in a course, an exam or a competition.

scrape through something ❑ *I scraped through school and left as soon as I could.*

scrape through ❑ *I came top in English and just scraped through in maths.* ❑ *Spurs scraped through 2-1 against Arsenal.*

○ **scrape to'gether**

If you **scrape together** money or things that you need, you manage with difficulty to obtain them. = **scrape up**

scrape together something or **scrape something together** ❑ *If we could scrape together a dozen people, we could hire a minibus.*

❏ Schools are trying to scrape funds together from their hard-won budgets.

○ **'scrape up**

1 If you **scrape up** money, you manage with difficulty to get the money you need. = **scrape together, get together**

scrape up something or **scrape something up** ❏ He scraped up the cash to start a restaurant. ❏ They managed to scrape enough money up to send their boys to school.

2 If you **scrape** something **up**, you remove it from the ground, especially using a sharp tool.

scrape up something or **scrape something up** ❏ She scraped up as much of the powder as she could.

scratch /skrætʃ/ (**scratches, scratching, scratched**)

○ **scratch a'round** (or **scratch about** [mainly BRITISH])

1 If you **scratch around** a place or **scratch around**, you try to find something that you cannot see on the ground, using your hands or a sharp tool.

scratch around ❏ They scratched around in the dirt looking for precious stones.

scratch around something ❏ Chickens were scratching around the yard.

2 If you **scratch around**, you try to find or get something when this is difficult, especially because there is not very much of it. ❏ [+ for] I've been scratching around for something interesting to write about. ❏ We were short of players and had to scratch around to get a full team.

○ **scratch 'out**

If you **scratch** something **out**, you draw a line through it with a pen or a sharp tool so that it cannot be seen. = **cross out**

scratch something out or **scratch out something** ❏ He scribbled some lines and then scratched them out again.

screen /skriːn/ (**screens, screening, screened**)

○ **'screen for**

To **screen for** a disease or **screen** someone **for** a disease means to do a test to make sure that they do not have the disease.

screen for something ❏ Screening for diabetes can easily be done in the doctor's surgery.

screen someone for something ❏ I was recently screened for breast cancer.

○ **screen 'off**

If a part of a room **is screened off** or if you **screen** it **off**, it is separated from the rest of the room by something such as a screen or curtain. = **partition off**

be screened off ❏ The room had a sleeping area screened off. ❏ [+ from] Their work stations were screened off from the general office.

screen something off or **screen off something** ❏ [+ from] Torn curtains screened off the sleeping area from the rest of the cabin.

○ **screen 'out**

1 To **screen out** particular people means to identify them and prevent them from entering a place or taking part in something.

screen someone out or **screen out someone** ❏ They try to screen out passengers who might have an infectious illness.

2 To **screen** something **out** means to identify something harmful and get rid of it or keep it separate.

screen someone out or **screen out someone** ❏ The ozone layer screens out most of the sun's UV radiation. ❏ The filter screens out junk mail and moves it to a separate folder.

screw /skruː/ (**screws, screwing, screwed**)

○ **screw 'down**

1 If you **screw** something **down**, you fasten it firmly in position using screws.

screw something down or **screw down something** ❏ Make sure you screw all the cables down firmly. ❏ The cover of the air vent was screwed down.

2 If you **screw** something **down**, you close a lid tightly by turning it.

screw something down or **screw down something** ❏ When the bottles are full, screw the caps down tightly and put them in the refrigerator.

○ **screw 'out of** [BRITISH, INFORMAL]

If you **screw** something **out of** someone, you persuade them to give it to you using force or strong arguments.

screw something out of someone ❏ I managed to screw a bit more money out of him.

○ **screw o'ver** [mainly AMERICAN, INFORMAL]

If someone **screws** you **over**, they trick you or do something that causes problems for you in order to gain an advantage for themselves.

screw someone over or **screw over someone** ❏ We have been contacted by users who have been screwed over by such companies. ❏ It would be better to help those people than screw them over.

○ **screw 'up**

1 If you **screw** something **up**, you bend or twist it firmly so that it is full of small untidy folds. = **scrunch up**

screw up something ❏ She screwed up the piece of newspaper and tossed it into a corner. ❏ My clothes were screwed up in a white plastic bag.

screw something up ❏ He read the note, then hurriedly screwed it up.

2 If you **screw up** your eyes, you close them very tightly.
screw up something ❑ She screwed up her eyes as she faced the sun.
screw something up ❑ Shut your eyes and screw them up tight.

3 If you **screw up** your face, you twist it so that your mouth and nose are closer together, often to show dislike of something.
screw up something ❑ The man screwed up his face in disgust.
screw something up ❑ She screwed her nose up at the bitterness of the coffee.

4 If you **screw up** or if you **screw** something **up**, you make a mistake or cause something to fail or go wrong. [INFORMAL]
screw something up ❑ She could screw things up for us. ❑ What screwed the project up was the rise in fuel prices.
screw up something ❑ He can't come on Wednesday – that screws up all my arrangements.
screw up ❑ The best thing to do is admit you screwed up.

5 If something or someone **screws** someone **up**, they cause them to have serious emotional problems. [INFORMAL]
screw someone up or **screw up someone**
❑ Her childhood screwed her up. ❑ If she carries on like this, she's going to screw up her children.

• Someone who is **screwed-up** has serious emotional problems, usually because of experiences they have had. [INFORMAL]
❑ Soldiers came back from the war really screwed-up.

scribble /ˈskrɪbəl/ (**scribbles, scribbling, scribbled**)

○ **scribble 'down**
If you **scribble** something **down**, you write it quickly or roughly.
scribble down something or **scribble something down** ❑ I attempted to scribble down the names. ❑ He took my name and address, scribbling it down in his notebook.

scrimp /skrɪmp/ (**scrimps, scrimping, scrimped**)

○ **'scrimp on**
If you **scrimp on** something, you spend as little money as possible on it.
scrimp on something ❑ Scrimping on safety measures can be a false economy. ❑ It might be tempting to scrimp on sunglasses, but the more you spend, the greater the protection for your eyes.

scroll /skrəʊl/ (**scrolls, scrolling, scrolled**)

○ **scroll 'down**
If you **scroll down**, you make the information on a computer screen move

down. ❑ If you scroll down a bit, you will be able to see the picture.

○ **scroll 'up**
If you **scroll up**, you make the information on a computer screen move up. ❑ Scroll up to the top of the document.

scrounge /skraʊndʒ/ (**scrounges, scrounging, scrounged**)

○ **scrounge 'up** [AMERICAN, INFORMAL]
If you **scrounge** something **up**, you get someone to give or lend it to you.
scrounge up something or **scrounge something up** ❑ Golf and fishing can be arranged if you can scrounge up your own equipment.

scrub /skrʌb/ (**scrubs, scrubbing, scrubbed**)

○ **scrub 'off**
If you **scrub** something **off** or **scrub** it **off** something, you remove it by rubbing hard.
scrub something off or **scrub off something**
❑ He tried without success to scrub the stain off.
❑ Here's a brush for scrubbing off the dirt.
scrub something off something ❑ I scrubbed the dried mud off my skirt.

○ **scrub 'out**
If you **scrub** a place **out**, you clean it very thoroughly, usually with water and something such as a brush or a rough cloth.
= **clean out**
scrub something out or **scrub out something**
❑ We need to scrub the bath out. ❑ She agreed to scrub out the hall in return for lessons.

scrunch /skrʌntʃ/ (**scrunches, scrunching, scrunched**)

○ **scrunch 'up**
1 If you **scrunch** something **up**, you bend or twist it so that it no longer has its natural shape and has many small folds.
scrunch something up or **scrunch up something** ❑ She started to read the letter, then scrunched it up and threw it in the bin. ❑ He got up from the table, scrunching up his napkin.

• A **scrunched-up** object is bent or twisted so it no longer has its natural shape and has many small folds. ❑ I found a scrunched-up ten-pound note in my pocket. ❑ My jacket was all scrunched up from someone sitting on it.

2 If you **scrunch up**, or if you **scrunch** your body or part of your body **up**, you fold or twist your body or part of your body into a small space.
scrunch up ❑ She turned her back and scrunched up into an awkward position.
be scrunched up ❑ I lay scrunched up for hours on a tiny bed.
scrunch something up or **scrunch up**

something ❏ *He has to scrunch up his legs uncomfortably in the plane.*

al /si:l/ (**seals, sealing, sealed**)

seal 'in

To **seal** a smell or liquid means to prevent it from getting out of a food.

seal in something or **seal something in**
❏ *The coffee is freeze-dried to seal in all the flavour.*
❏ *Frying the meat in hot oil first seals the juices in.*

seal 'off

◼ If you **seal off** a place, you prevent people from getting into it or out of it. = **cordon off**
seal off something ❏ *Police had already sealed off one of the entrances.*
seal something off ❏ *They sealed the main road off.* ❏ *The whole area has been sealed off because of the risk of an explosion.*

◼ If someone **is sealed off** from something, or if they **seal** themselves **off**, they remain separate from it and do not take part in it.
= **cut off**
be sealed off ❏ [+ from] *He lives as a recluse, sealed off from the rest of the world.*
seal yourself off ❏ [+ from] *They have sealed themselves off from modern technological development.*

seal 'up

If you **seal** something **up**, you close it so that nothing can get in or out. = **close up**
seal up something or **seal something up**
❏ *They were already sealing up the exits.*
❏ *The windows on the west side were sealed up.*

arch /sɜːtʃ/ (**searches, searching, searched**)

search a'round

If you **search around**, you look in different places for something.
search around ❏ *It is worth searching around to find the best voucher codes for the items you wish to buy.* ❏ [+ for] *I've been searching around for the best way to record conversations.*

search 'out

If you **search** something or someone **out**, you look for them until you find them.
= **hunt out, unearth**
search out something/someone or **search something/someone out** ❏ *I have been searching out old photographs.* ❏ *He sent a company of soldiers to search them out.*

search 'up

If you **search** something **up**, you look for information online using a search engine.
search up something ❏ *If you search up her name, you'll see that she has a Wikipedia page.*
search something up ❏ *I searched him up online and got in touch.*

secede /sɪˈsiːd/ (**secedes, seceding, seceded**)

○ **se'cede from** [FORMAL]

If a region or group **secedes from** the country or larger group to which it belongs, it becomes a separate country or stops being a member of the larger group.
secede from something ❏ *Singapore seceded from the Federation of Malaysia and became an independent sovereign state.*

section /ˈsekʃən/ (**sections, sectioning, sectioned**)

○ **section 'off**

If an area **is sectioned off** or if you **section** it **off**, it is separated from the surrounding area.
be sectioned off ❏ [+ from] *The kitchen is sectioned off from the rest of the room by a half wall.* ❏ *Could part of the hall be sectioned off to create a work space?*
section something off or **section off something** ❏ *We sectioned off some space at the end of the yard.*

see /siː/ (**sees, seeing, saw, seen**)

○ **'see about**

If you **see about** something, you deal with it or arrange for it to be done.
see about something ❏ *He went to the station to see about Thomas's ticket.* ❏ *Let's deal with the main problem first, and see about the rest later.*
● If you say **we'll see about that**, you mean that you are not willing to do or decide something at the present time. ❏ *He wants to borrow my car, but we'll see about that.*

○ **see a'round**

◼ If you **see** someone or something **around**, you notice them more than once in different places.
see someone/something around ❏ *I've seen him around, but I don't really know him.* ❏ *You see some very expensive cars around in this part of town.*

◼ If you say that you will **see** someone **around**, you mean that you are likely to see them again without making an arrangement to do so.
see someone around ❏ *Bye then, Bob – I'll see you around.*

◼ → see **see round**

○ **'see as**

If you **see** someone or something **as** a particular thing, you believe that they are that thing or have that quality.
see someone/something as something
❏ *He saw her as the perfect woman.* ❏ *The committee saw higher education as completely separate to schools.*

see yourself as something ❏ *He no longer saw himself as a contender in the election.*

NOTE **Consider** is a more formal word for **see as**.

○ **'see in**

> In meaning 2, the stress is on **'in**.

1 If you **see** something **in** someone or something, you believe that they have a particular quality or characteristic.

see something in someone/something
❏ *I saw a gentleness in him that I had never seen before.* ❏ *No one understood what she saw in Dave.*

2 If you **see** someone **in**, you go with them to the door of a building or room as they enter it.

see someone in *or* **see in someone** ❏ *I was seen in by an assistant.*

○ **see 'into**

If you **see** someone **into** a place, you go with them and make sure that they go in there.

see someone into something ❏ *He saw me into a taxi.* ❏ *Hattie left after seeing me safely into the apartment.*

○ **see 'off**

1 When you **see** someone **off**, you go with them to a place that they are leaving from, and say goodbye. **= wave off**

see someone off *or* **see off someone** ❏ *She saw him off on the school bus.* ❏ *I went to Heathrow Airport to see them off.*

2 To **see** someone or something **off** means to force them to leave a place.

see someone off *or* **see off someone** ❏ *Some children had come into the yard, but he saw them off.* ❏ *She had seen off an intruder with a shotgun.*

3 If you **see off** someone or something, you succeed in defeating them. [BRITISH]

see off someone/something *or* **see someone/something off** ❏ *Burgess used his fast pace to see off the opposition.* ❏ *The company at this point had seen off most of its competitors.*

○ **see 'out**

1 If you **see** someone **out**, you go with them to the door of a building or room as they leave.

see someone out *or* **see out someone**
❏ *Don't bother to see me out. I know the way.*
❏ *[+ of] Security guards saw him out of the building.*

2 If you **see out** a period of time, you continue with what you are doing until that period is over. **= stick out**

see out something *or* **see something out**
❏ *He has decided to see out one last term in his teaching job.* ❏ *I have a four-year contract and I plan to see it out.*

3 If something or someone **sees** something **out**, they last or survive until the end of a particular period. **= last out**

see out something *or* **see something out**
❏ *The doctor felt that she probably wouldn't see out the night.* ❏ *I bought some food yesterday to see the week out.*

4 If something **sees** you **out**, it lasts for a long as you remain alive or continue doin something.

see someone out ❏ *My predecessor held the jo for 10 years – I reckon five will see me out.*
❏ *Hopefully this latest heart bypass will see him out.*

○ **see 'over**

1 If you **see over** a place, you go there to look at the different parts of it. **= look rou**

see over something ❏ *We've seen over two houses today, but I didn't like either of them.*

2 An **overseer** is someone who watches work being done to make sure that it is done properly.

○ **see 'round** (or **see around**) [BRITISH]

If you **see round** or **see round** a place, you visit it and look at the different parts of it.
= look round

see round something ❏ *I'm going to see roun house this afternoon.*

see round ❏ *Would you like to see round?*

○ **see 'through**

1 If you can **see through** something or **se** someone or something **through** it, you are able to see things that are on the other sid of something by looking through it.

see through something ❏ *He couldn't see through the clouds of white dust.*

see something/someone through something ❏ *I could see a shape through the canvas.* ❏ *She saw him through the kitchen window.* ● **See-through** clothes are made o thin cloth, so that you can see a person's body or underclothes through them.
❏ *She was wearing a T-shirt under a see-through blouse.*

2 If you **see through** someone or something, you realize what someone's hidden intentions are.

see through someone/something ❏ *Only Marsha saw through him from the beginning.*
❏ *Her excuses were weak but he did not see throu them.*

3 If something **sees** you **through** a period of time or **sees** you **through**, it is enough t last until the end of that period.

see someone through something ❏ *They ha been busy gathering enough fuel to see them through the winter.*

see someone through ❑ *I only have 50 dollars to see me through until my next paycheck.*

4 If someone **sees** you **through** something, they support you during a difficult time. **= get through**

see someone through something ❑ *He was a great friend and saw me through all the hard times.*

5 If you **see** something **through**, you continue to do it until it is successfully completed. **= stick out**

see something through or **see through something** ❑ *There is great satisfaction in planning a job and seeing it through.* ❑ *[+ to] I just wanted to see the campaign through before I left.*

○ **'see to**

If you **see to** something or someone, you do what needs to be done to deal with them.

see to something/someone ❑ *Don't worry, I'll see to all the arrangements.* ❑ *A man was there to see to our luggage.* ❑ *Is this customer being seen to?*

seek /siːk/ (**seeks, seeking, sought**)

○ **seek 'out** [FORMAL]

If you **seek out** someone or something, you try to find them.

seek out someone/something or **see someone/something out** ❑ *Her eyes scanned the room, seeking out David.* ❑ *I sought her out after school in order to ask her advice.*

seize /siːz/ (**seizes, seizing, seized**)

○ **'seize on** (or **seize upon**)

If you **seize on** something, you immediately notice it and often try to use it to your advantage.

seize on something ❑ *She seized on his mistake as an excuse for getting rid of him.* ❑ *He seized on my suggestion with great enthusiasm.*

○ **seize 'up**

If a part of your body or a machine **seizes up**, it suddenly stops moving or working. ❑ *I bent down and my back seized up.* ❑ *The engine just seized up, and we couldn't get it started again.*

○ **'seize upon → see seize on**

select /sɪˈlekt/ (**selects, selecting, selected**)

○ **select 'out**

1 To **select out** something means to identify something or someone you do not want and avoid it being chosen.

select out something/someone or **select something/someone out** ❑ *If there were any jurors the lawyers did not want on the jury, they could select them out.*

be selected out ❑ *Harmful genes would be selected out if they served no useful function.*

2 If you **select** things **out**, you choose the things you want from a group.

select out something or **select something out** ❑ *Ferguson selected out the team members he wanted for the match.* ❑ *[+ for] A few people were selected out for special treatment.*

sell /sel/ (**sells, selling, sold**)

○ **'sell for**

If something **sells for** a particular price or someone **sells** it **for** a particular price, that is the price that someone pays for it.

sell for something ❑ *The painting sold for $50,000.*

sell something for something ❑ *He started a company that was eventually sold for $125 million.* ❑ *The online store sells them for £7.99.*

○ **sell 'off**

If you **sell** something **off**, you sell it to get rid of it, usually for a low price.

sell something off ❑ *They plan to break up the company and sell it off.* ❑ *[+ to] The government intends to sell these historic buildings off to the highest bidder.*

sell off something ❑ *We are selling off all our old stock at half price.* ❑ *[+ to] The land had been sold off to developers.* ● A **sell-off** is the sale of a business as a way of raising money. ❑ *He opposed the sell-off of British companies to foreign owners.*

SELL OFF + noun
sell off **assets**
sell off **land**
sell off **property**
sell off **stock**
sell off **a business**
❑ *They were forced to sell off most of their assets.* ❑ *We sold off our business.*

○ **sell 'on**

In meaning 2, the stress is on **'sell**.

1 If you **sell** something **on**, you sell it to someone else soon after buying it, usually in order to make a profit.

sell something on or **sell on something** ❑ *Mr Farrier bought cars at auctions and sold them on.* ❑ *[+ to] The weapons had been bought by a businessman and then sold on to government departments.*

2 If you **are sold on** something or if someone **sells** you **on** it, you have been persuaded to accept it or be enthusiastic about it. [INFORMAL]

be sold on something ❑ *I'm not really sold on the idea of boarding school.* ❑ *He was totally sold on the ethic of free enterprise.*

sell someone on something ❑ *He tried to sell me on the idea of having a movie made about my life.*

✪ sell 'out

1 If something **sells out**, or if a shop **sells out** of it, it has all been sold.

sell out ❑ [+ of] *Shops almost immediately sold out of the product.* ❑ *The bread always seems to sell out before I get there.*

be sold out ❑ [+ of] *I'm sorry, we're sold out of lemons.* ❑ *The toy was so popular, every store in town was sold out.*

2 If a performance **sells out** or **is sold out**, all the tickets have been sold.

be sold out ❑ *The first performance was sold out and the play became a tremendous hit.* ❑ *Most of the dates on his tour are already sold out.*

sell out ❑ *Glastonbury festival sold out within hours.* ● If a performance is a **sell-out**, it is very successful because all the tickets are sold. ❑ *The show was a sell-out.* ❑ *He performed in front of sell-out crowds all over the country.*

3 If you **sell out** or **sell** something **out**, you sell your property or business. [AMERICAN]

sell out ❑ *I hear she's going to sell out and move to the city.*

sell out something ❑ *We are selling out our interests in the olive oil business.*

sell something out ❑ [+ to] *I had a share in the shop, but when I married I sold it out to my brother.*

4 If someone **sells out** or **sells out** their principles, they accept money or other benefits for doing something that is against their principles.

sell out ❑ *Some of his fans thought that by making such a commercial film he had completely sold out.* ❑ [+ to] *He sold out to the Establishment and went to work in a bank.*

sell out something ❑ *He was accused of selling out his ideals for the sake of political expediency.*

● A **sell-out** is behaviour in which someone does something against their principles in order to gain an advantage. [INFORMAL] ❑ *Taking a job like that is a complete sell-out.*

● A **sell-out** is someone who does something against their principles in order to gain an advantage. [INFORMAL] ❑ *They saw him as a sell-out who had turned his back on socialism.*

5 If you **sell** someone **out**, you betray them in order to gain an advantage.

sell out someone ❑ *Some people would sell out their country rather than take a stand.* ❑ *They sold out their friends to avoid going to jail.* ❑ [+ to] *He sold out his co-workers to the secret services.*

sell someone out ❑ *I hated myself for selling him out – he was always a good employer.*

○ sell 'up [BRITISH]

If you **sell up**, you sell your property or your business. ❑ *The owners have sold up and gone.*

send /send/ (sends, sending, sent)

○ send a'head

If you **send** something or someone **ahead**, you arrange for them to go somewhere before you.

send something/someone ahead or **send ahead something/someone** ❑ *He had sent h baggage ahead.* ❑ *A messenger had been sent ahead to announce their arrival.*

NOTE **Forward** is a more formal word for **send ahead**.

✪ send a'way

1 If you **send** someone **away**, you tell ther to go away from you.

send someone away ❑ *A servant came in with tea, but she sent him away.* ❑ *She sent her friends away, saying she had a headache.*

send away someone ❑ *The children came in, wanting to watch TV, and were sent away.*

2 If you **send** someone or something **away** you arrange for them to be taken to anothe place to do a particular thing.

send someone/something away ❑ [+ to] *They sent all their children away to boarding school.* ❑ *He was only eight when they sent him away.*

be sent away ❑ [+ to] *Her mother was ill and sh was sent away to her aunt's.* ❑ [+ for] *The sample were sent away for analysis.*

send away someone/something ❑ *He sent away his watch to be repaired.*

○ send a'way for

If you **send away for** something, you write to an organization and ask them to send it to you. = **send off**

send away for something ❑ *She sent away for a free sample.* ❑ *If the job looks interesting, send away for more details.*

✪ send 'back

If you **send** something **back**, you return it to the place that it came from because you do not want it.

send something back ❑ *I sent her a gift, but sh sent it back unopened.*

send back something ❑ *She sent back her breakfast tray untouched.*

○ send 'down

1 If a student **is sent down**, he or she is made to leave a university or college. [BRITISH]

be sent down ❑ *He was sent down from Trinity College for failing his first year exams.*

2 If someone **is sent down** or if a judge **sends** them **down**, they are sent to prison. [BRITISH, INFORMAL]

be sent down ❑ [+ for] *His brother had been sen down for robbery.*

send someone down or **send down someone**
❑ The judge found him guilty and sent him down.
NOTE Jail is a more formal word for
send down.

'send for

1 If you **send for** someone, you ask them to
come and see you by sending a message.
send for someone ❑ I think we should send for
the doctor. ❑ Did you send for me, sir?
2 If you **send for** something, you ask for it
to be brought or delivered to you by sending
a message.
send for something ❑ You can send for a copy
by writing to this address. ❑ The doctor sent for
hot water and towels.

send 'forth [LITERARY]

If you **send** someone **forth**, you arrange or
tell them to go somewhere for you.
send someone forth or **send forth someone**
❑ I'm sending you forth on your voyage of discovery.

send 'in

1 If you **send** something **in**, you send a
message or document to an organization.
= submit
send in something ❑ I was expected to send in
a written report every two months. ❑ Harry sent in
his resignation.
send something in ❑ [+ to] If you have any
money-saving ideas, send them in to the magazine.
2 To **send** people **in** means to send them to
a place in order to deal with a dangerous or
difficult situation.
send someone in or **send in someone**
❑ The government threatened to send the troops in.
❑ They had to send in a team of divers to bring up
the ship.
be sent in ❑ Bailiffs had been sent in to evict the
camp.
3 If you **send** someone **in**, you tell them to
go into a room where someone is waiting to
see them.
send someone in or **send in someone**
❑ 'Mr Clarke is here to see you.' – 'Send him in.'
❑ [+ to] When you've finished talking to her, please
send her in to me.

send 'off

1 If you **send** something **off**, you send it
somewhere by post, email, or text message.
send off something ❑ [+ to] I sent off letters of
enquiry to all the big firms.
send something off ❑ It's a good idea to re-read
your emails before you send them off.
2 If you **send off** for something, you send a
message to someone asking them to send it
to you. **= send away** ❑ [+ for] I've sent off for
some books from a website.
3 If you **send** someone **off**, you ask or tell

them to go somewhere else. **= send away**
send someone off ❑ I sent Georgie off with
strict instructions not to come back till later.
❑ [+ to] She sent him off to her sister's so we could
talk in private.
be sent off ❑ [+ to-infinitive] I was sent off to
fetch tea for the guests. ❑ [+ to] She was terrified
of being sent off to a nursing home.
4 If a player **is sent off** or if someone **sends**
them **off**, they are made to leave the field
during a sports game as a punishment for
seriously breaking the rules.
be sent off ❑ Henry was sent off after
deliberately kicking a defender. ❑ [+ for] You could
be sent off for arguing with the referee.
send someone off or **send off someone**
❑ Referee! Send him off!
5 A **send-off** is an occasion when people
come together to say goodbye to someone.
[INFORMAL] ❑ They gave us a great send-off.

send 'on

If you **send on** something, you send a
message or package to someone else after
you have received it.
send on something or **send something on**
❑ If I leave you my new address, will you send my
mail on? ❑ [+ to] If she sends me the details I'll send
them on to you.
be sent on ❑ [+ to] The patient's files had been
sent on to us.
NOTE Forward is a more formal word for
send on.

send 'out

1 If you **send** something **out**, you send
copies of something to a lot of people.
send out something ❑ [+ to] The company sent
out questionnaires to 34,000 doctors.
send something out ❑ [+ to] The school sends
regular newsletters to parents.
2 If you **send** someone **out**, you send them
to a place in order to do something there.
send out someone ❑ We called the heating
company and they sent out an engineer.
send someone out ❑ [+ to] If your car breaks
down, we will send a mechanic out to you within an
hour. ❑ [+ to-infinitive] He sent people out to
spread the word on the streets.
3 To **send out** a sound or a light means to
produce it. **= give out**
send out something ❑ The searchlight sends
out a flashing beam.
send something out ❑ The alarm sends distress
signals out to anyone nearby.
NOTE Emit is a more formal word for **send
out**.
4 If you **send out** particular **signals**, you show
by your behaviour what you think or feel.

❑ *She was sending out very strong signals that she was bored.* ❑ *I think he liked me. He was sending out all the right signals.*

5 When a plant **sends out** roots or shoots, they grow from it. **= produce**
send out something or **send something out** ❑ *If you cut the plant back, it should send out new side shoots.*

○ **send 'out for**
If you **send out for** something, you call or send a message and ask for it to be delivered to you.
send out for something ❑ *Let's send out for a pizza and watch The Late Show.*

○ **send 'up**
1 If you **send** someone **up**, you copy them in a way that makes them look silly. **= take off** [BRITISH, INFORMAL]
send someone up or **send up someone**
❑ *Stop sending me up!* ❑ *He used to send up his teachers to make his friends laugh.* ● A **send-up** is a piece of writing or acting in which someone or something is imitated in order to make them look silly. [BRITISH, INFORMAL]
❑ *I love his send-ups of politicians.*
2 If someone **is sent up**, they are found guilty and sent to prison. **= send down** [AMERICAN, INFORMAL]
be sent up ❑ *He got sent up and served his time.* ❑ [+ for] *What were you sent up for?*

sensitize /ˈsensɪtaɪz/ (**sensitizes, sensitizing, sensitized**)

○ **'sensitize to** [FORMAL]
To **sensitize** people **to** a particular problem or situation means to make them aware of it.
sensitize someone to something ❑ *A recycling program will help sensitize the public to environmental issues.*

separate /ˈsepəreɪt/ (**separates, separating, separated**)

○ **separate 'into**
1 To **separate** something **into** something means to divide it so that it is in smaller parts or groups.
separate something into something
❑ *Simon separated the stones into three piles, then weighed each pile.*
2 If a group of people or things **separates into** smaller groups, it divides into them.
separate into something ❑ *Let's separate into smaller groups.*

○ **separate 'off**
If you **separate** something **off**, you remove it from a group or do not think of it as part of a group.

separate something off or **separate off something** ❑ [+ from] *Is there any scientific basis for separating off gorillas from other animals?* ❑ *They reformed the school system, separating off primary schools.*
be separated off ❑ [+ from] *She was in a private room, separated off from the rest of the floor.*

○ **separate 'out**
1 If you **separate out** things or people, you divide them into smaller groups.
separate something/someone out or **separate out something/something** ❑ *Most schools separate out their pupils into classes according to age.* ❑ [+ into] *We gave him some toys and watched him separate them out into two piles.*
2 If a mixture **separates out**, it divides into the different substances from which it was made. ❑ *This substance is added to prevent the cheese from separating out.*

serve /sɜːv/ (**serves, serving, served**)

◉ **'serve as** (or **serve for**)
If one thing **serves as** another thing, or if it **serves** someone **as** that thing, it is used instead of that other thing. **= do for**
serve as something ❑ *There was a long, grey building that served as a cafeteria.* ❑ *A linen basket had to serve for the baby's cot.*
serve someone as something ❑ *The streets and parks serve these young people as social centres.*

○ **'serve on**
1 If you **serve on** a formal or official group, you are a member of it.
serve on something ❑ *He served on the organizing committee for five years.* ❑ *Have you ever served on a jury?*
2 If you **serve** a legal document **on** someone, you deliver it to them.
serve something on someone ❑ *The council served a summons on us yesterday.*

○ **serve 'out**
1 If you **serve out** food, you put it onto plates for people. **= serve up, dish up**
serve out something or **serve something out** ❑ *Clare and I served out slices of cold meat.* ❑ *We cook the school lunches and serve them out.*
2 If someone **serves out** a period of time, they spend all of an agreed period doing a job, or all of an agreed period in prison.
serve out something or **serve something out** ❑ *The governor refused to resign and insisted he would serve out his term.* ❑ *He served out the remainder of his sentence in solitary confinement.*

◉ **serve 'up**
1 If you **serve up** food, you put it onto plates for people. **= dish up**
serve up something ❑ *They serve up far more food than we could possibly eat.*

serve something up ❑ *She served the cake up on a glass plate.* ❑ *When the stew was ready, he served it up in large bowls.*

2 If entertainment **is served up** or if someone **serves** it **up**, it is presented to people.

be served up ❑ *The amount of music served up at the festival is incredible.* ❑ *Most of what is served up on television is rubbish.*

serve up something or **serve something up** ❑ *The state TV and radio channels serve up a diet of propaganda.*

○ **'serve upon → see serve on**

○ **'serve with**

To **serve** someone **with** a legal document means to officially give it to them.

serve someone with something ❑ *Immigration officers tried to serve her with a deportation order.*

set /set/ (**sets, setting**)

> The form **set** is used in the present tense and is the past tense and past participle of the verb.

○ **set a'bout**

1 If you **set about** doing something, you start to do it in an energetic or determined way.

set about something ❑ *The next morning they set about cleaning the house.* ❑ *I set about finding a flat area of ground on which to pitch my tent.*

2 If one person **sets about** another, they start to attack them violently. [LITERARY]

set about someone ❑ *They set about him, repeatedly kicking him as he lay on the ground.*

○ **'set against**

1 If one thing **is set against** another, or if you **set** one thing **against** another, you compare it with the other thing in order to understand it more clearly. = **balance against**

be set against something ❑ *This slight improvement has to be set against an increase in crime.*

set something against something ❑ *If you set the film against more realistic dramas, it begins to seem ridiculous.*

2 If you **set** an amount of money **against** another amount, or if it can **be set against** it, you are allowed to subtract it from that amount. = **set off against**

set something against something ❑ *This counts as income, and you can set it against your tax allowance.*

be set against something ❑ *These tax credits can be set against tax liability.*

3 To **set** one person **against** another means

to make them become enemies or rivals.

set someone against someone ❑ *The last thing I wanted to do was to set her against me.* ❑ *Civil war sets friend against friend and neighbour against neighbour.*

4 If you **are set against** something, you have firmly decided that you do not want it or like it.

be set against something ❑ *He wanted to go into the army, but his mother was set against it.* ❑ *They were dead set against her marrying me.*

5 If something or someone **is set against** a background, or if you **set** them **against** it, they are placed in front of something so they can be clearly seen.

be set against something ❑ *The box contained a large diamond set against black velvet.*

set something/someone against something ❑ *The painter had set her against the light so it shone on her hair.*

6 If a book or film **is set against** a particular background, the story happens in a particular time or place.

be set against something ❑ *The book is a historical romance set against the background of the French Revolution.*

set something against something ❑ *She has taken a traditional love story but set it against an exotic backdrop.*

○ **set a'part**

1 If something **is set apart** for a particular purpose or if someone **sets** it **apart**, it is kept only for that purpose.

be set apart ❑ [+ for] *One day of the week should be set apart for relaxation.* ❑ *People could read quietly in a small room set apart at the end of the corridor.*

set something apart or **set apart something** ❑ [+ for] *He set these men apart for special duties.*

2 If something **sets** someone or something **apart**, it makes them different from other people or things in a way that is easy to notice.

set someone/something apart ❑ *His priest's clothes set him apart.* ❑ [+ from] *These attributes set humans apart from other primates.* ❑ *What sets it apart from other, similar small towns is the huge cathedral in the centre.*

○ **set a'side**

1 If you **set** something **aside**, you keep it for a particular purpose. = **put aside**

set aside something ❑ *Set aside a fixed amount every month towards your pension.*

set something aside ❑ *I try to set some money aside in case of emergencies.* ❑ [+ for] *There is another room, but we have set it aside for meetings.*

be set aside ❏ [+ for] *Some time should be set aside for preparation.*

2 If you **set aside** a belief, principle, or feeling, you decide not to be influenced by it. **= put aside**

set aside something ❏ *He called on them to set aside party dogma and unite to lead the nation towards recovery.*

set something aside ❏ *I still had doubts, but I tried to set them aside.*

3 If a judge or court **sets aside** a decision, they state that it has no legal force. **= overturn**

set aside something or **set something aside** ❏ *He believes that the courts have the right to set aside acts of Congress.*

4 If you **set** something **aside**, you put it down or somewhere else for a short period while you deal with something else. **= put aside, lay aside**

set something aside or **set aside something** ❏ *Paint the first coat, then set it aside to dry.* ❏ *He set aside his book and listened to what she had to say.*

○ **set 'back**

1 If something **sets** someone or something **back**, it causes a delay. **= hold up**

set someone/something back ❏ *This mistake could set the project back months.* ❏ *The unusually cold spring had set them back with the painting.*

set back something/someone ❏ *Funding difficulties set back his plans.* • A **setback** is an event that delays progress or makes someone or something less likely to succeed. ❏ *The defeat of this proposal in parliament is a serious setback for the government.* ❏ *She recovered from the initial setback.*

2 If a building **is set back**, it is some distance away from the road.

be set back ❏ [+ from] *The cottages were set back from the road and almost hidden behind high hedges.*

3 If something **sets** you **back** a certain amount of money, it costs you that much. [INFORMAL]

set someone back something ❏ *The legal costs of the case set him back around £10,000.*

○ **set 'down**

1 If you **set** something **down**, you put it on a surface or on the ground. **= put down**

set something down ❏ [+ on] *He poured two cups and set them down on the table.*

set down something ❏ *He set down his knife and fork and stared at her.* **= put down**

2 If you **set** something **down**, you write it down in order to keep a record.

set down something ❏ *They were asked to set down a summary of their views.*

set something down ❏ *When my thoughts get confused I find it helpful to set them down.*

3 If something **is set down** or if someone **sets** it **down**, it is officially recorded as being a law or rule. **= lay down**

be set down ❏ *The council would be unable to reach its recycling targets as set down by the government.*

set down something ❏ *The legislation sets down minimum wages for workers.*

set something down ❏ *You need to agree some ground rules and set them down.*

4 If a bus or train **sets** you **down**, it stops and lets you get out. **= put down**

set someone down or **set down someone** ❏ *The bus stops on request to set down passengers*

5 If a plane or helicopter **sets down**, it lands. ❏ *The pilot looked for a safe place to set down.*

○ **set 'down as**

If you **set** someone **down as** something, you decide that they are a particular kind of person, although you might be wrong.

set someone down as something ❏ *Some people have set him down as foolish, but I disagree.* ❏ *People who like to be alone are often set down as eccentrics.*

○ **set 'forth**

1 If you **set forth** something, you explain it clearly in writing or speech. [FORMAL]

set forth something or **set something forth** ❏ *Our proposals are set forth in Chapter 5.*

NOTE **Expound** is a more formal word for **set forth**.

2 If you **set forth**, you start a journey. **= set out, set off** [LITERARY] ❏ *The next morning they set forth on the trail.*

○ **set 'in**

If something unpleasant **sets in**, it begins and seems likely to continue. ❏ *By the time he got back, panic had set in.* ❏ *They had to find shelter before the cold weather set in.*

○ **'set in** (or **set 'in**)

If something **is set in** a surface, it is fixed into a hollow part or hole in the surface of something.

be set in something ❏ *The handle of the sword had a large green stone set in bronze.* ❏ *He dropped the keys down a large drain set into the pavement.*

• If an object is **inset** with something, a decoration or material has been fixed into its surface. ❏ *The plates were made of gold and silver inset with gems.*

○ **set 'off**

1 When you **set off**, you start a journey. **= set out** ❏ *What time do we need to set off* tomorrow? ❑ She set off down the road. ❑ [+ on] He set off on another of his expeditions. ❑ [+ for] We decided to set off for the airport.

2 If something **sets** something **off**, it causes a process or series of events to start happening. = **trigger off**

set off something ❑ The speech set off a chain of events that almost ended in war. ❑ A suspicious vehicle parked outside a police station set off a security alert.

set something off ❑ There was a lot of debate about what actually set the riots off.

3 If someone or something **sets off** an alarm, they cause it to make a loud sound.

set off something ❑ The burglars fled when they set off an alarm.

set something off ❑ I touched the alarm switch by mistake and set it off.

4 If you **set off** a bomb or firework, you cause it to explode.

set off something or **set something off** ❑ Happy crowds cheered and set off fireworks.

5 If something **sets** someone **off**, it makes them start doing something.

set someone off ❑ [+ on] This question set him off on one of his long stories. ❑ Marcus looked ill; just the mention of sea-sickness had set him off.

6 If one thing **sets** another thing **off**, it makes the other thing look more attractive or more noticeable. = **show off**

set something off or **set off something** ❑ The different colours seem to set each other off. ❑ She wore a black dress that set off her pale skin.

NOTE Enhance is a more formal word for **set off**.

○ **set 'off against**

If you **set** one amount **off against** another, or if one amount **is set off against** another, it is taken away from the other amount. = **set against**

be set off against something ❑ The loss on one deal can be set off against the taxable profits on another.

set off something against something or **set something off against something** ❑ Companies are allowed to set off charitable gifts against tax.

○ **'set on**

1 If someone **sets** animals or people **on** you, they cause them to attack you.

set someone/something on someone ❑ Let's get out of here before they set the dogs on us. ❑ She set her guards on him.

2 The **onset** of an unpleasant situation or event is its beginning. ❑ They prepared themselves for the onset of war. ❑ The onset of the illness was very sudden.

○ **'set on** (or **set upon**)

To **set on** someone means to suddenly physically attack them.

set on someone ❑ A rival gang set on them. ❑ He was set upon by a group of men wearing masks.

○ **set 'out**

1 When you **set out**, you start a journey. = **set off** ❑ We set out along the beach. ❑ Shortly after seven they set out on bicycles. ❑ [+ for] The next day we set out for home. ● The **outset** of a process or period of time is its beginning. ❑ You should explain this to him at the outset. ❑ The police had been involved from the outset.

2 If you **set out** to do something, you intend and begin to do it. ❑ [+ to-infinitive] They had failed in what they had set out to do. ❑ He had set out to establish his own business.

3 If you **set** something **out**, you explain facts or ideas clearly in writing or in speech.

set out something or **set something out** ❑ Darwin set out his theory in detail in 'The Origin of Species'. ❑ His conclusions were set out in his article.

SET OUT + noun

set out **a framework**
set out **guidelines**
set out **a vision**
set out **criteria**
set out **principles**
set out **objectives**
set out **recommendations**
set out **a strategy**
❑ We have set out clear guidelines for you to follow. ❑ The report sets out some recommendations for change.

---

4 If you **set** things **out**, you put them somewhere carefully. = **lay out**

set out something or **set something out** ❑ She had set out plates and a jug of water. ❑ A chess board had been set out on the table. ❑ [+ to-infinitive] I took off my boots and set them out to dry.

○ **set 'to**

1 If you **set to**, you start working or doing something in an energetic way. ❑ The nurses set to, scrubbing the room. ❑ When the steak arrived he picked up his knife and fork and set to.

2 If two people **set to**, they begin arguing or fighting. [OLD-FASHIONED] ❑ For a minute, it looked as if they would set to, but things calmed down. ● A **set-to** is a fight or violent argument. [INFORMAL] ❑ That night we had a real set-to.

○ **set 'up**

1 If you **set** something **up**, you place or build a structure somewhere.

set up something ❏ *Police set up road blocks on routes going out of town.* ❏ *We want to set up a monument in memory of the dead men.*

set something up ❏ *I'll set the table and chairs up so we can have tea in the garden.*

2 If you **set** something **up**, you make the necessary arrangements for it to start.

set up something ❏ *The government had decided to set up an investigation.*

set something up ❏ *She set a meeting up for me with the head of the company.* ❏ *If you want to open a new account, give us a call and we'll set it up.*

> ### SET UP + noun
>
> set up **a business**
> set up **a company**
> set up **a committee**
> set up **a commission**
> set up **an inquiry**
> set up **a meeting**
>
> ❏ *He has plans to set up his own business.*
> ❏ *The government has set up a commission to investigate the affair.*
> ● A **set-up** is a particular system or way of organizing something. ❏ *I've only been working here a couple of days and I don't know the set-up.*

3 If you **set up** a piece of machinery or equipment or **set up**, you put things together or arrange them so that it is ready to use.

set up something ❏ *I set up the computer so that she could work from home.*

set something up ❏ *An engineer came to the office to set the phones up for us.*

set up ❏ *I got on the stage and began setting up.*

4 If you **set up** or **set up** a business, you start a business.

set up ❏ *The firm is run by a former designer who set up on his own.* ❏ [+ as] *Anyone can set up as a contractor.*

set up something ❏ *I set up my company in 2017.*

set something up ❏ *They set the company up to provide computer services to private individuals.*

set yourself up ❏ *He's set himself up in business.* ❏ [+ as] *I decided to set myself up as a piano teacher.* ● A **set-up** is an organization. [INFORMAL] ❏ *Our business is a small set-up, with one full-time and two part-time employees.*

5 If you **set up home**, you establish your home somewhere. ❏ *They married, and set up home in York.*

6 If you **set up shop**, you start a business. ❏ *She set up shop as a web designer.*

7 If something **sets** you **up**, it puts you in a good condition or position.

set someone up ❏ [+ for] *This contract would set him up for life.* ❏ *They had a big breakfast to set them up for the day.*

8 If something **sets up** a process, it causes it to begin and continue.

set up something or **set something up** ❏ *The mixture of acid and alkali sets up a reaction.* ❏ *Physical appearances can set up prejudices in our minds.*

9 If someone **sets** you **up** or if you **are set up**, someone makes people think that you have done something wrong when you have not. **= frame** [INFORMAL]

set someone up ❏ *He was paid to set the Mayor up.*

be set up ❏ *The man insisted he was innocent and that he had been set up.* ● A **set-up** is a situation in which someone makes it seem as if an innocent person has committed a crime. [INFORMAL] ❏ *The whole thing was just a set-up, organised by his enemies.*

10 If you **set** one person **up** with another, or if you **set** them **up**, you arrange for people to spend time together in a romantic way.

set someone up or **set up someone** ❏ *Jeremy and Claire are both single – why don't we set them up?* ❏ [+ with] *She's always trying to set up her friends with her brother's friends.* ❏ *He offered to set me up on a date.*

○ **'set upon →** see **set on**

settle /'setəl/ (**settles, settling, settled**)
○ **settle 'down**

1 If you **settle down** to something, you start doing it, with the intention of doing it for some time. ❏ [+ to-infinitive] *He had settled down to watch a sports programme.* ❏ [+ to] *After a cup of coffee I settled down to my work.* ❏ [+ for] *At eight o'clock he settles down for supper.*

2 If people **settle down** or if you **settle** them **down**, they become calm or quiet. **= calm down**

settle down ❏ *Settle down, children. You're making too much noise.* ❏ *After a few angry exchanges the meeting settled down again.*

settle someone down ❏ *It took the teacher several minutes to settle the class down.*

3 If something **settles down**, it becomes calmer or stops changing. ❏ *His stomach had settled down enough for him to eat a sandwich.* ❏ *When things settle down a bit you'll have to come and visit us.*

4 If someone **settles down**, they start living in one place and intend to stay there for a long time. ❏ *Your parents want you to get a job and settle down.* ❏ [+ with] *I hope he'll find a nice girl to settle down with.*

5 If you **settle down** for the night, you lie down and get ready to sleep. ❑ [+ for] *They put up their tents and settled down for the night.* ❑ [+ to] *At last the children settled down to sleep.*

○ **'settle for**
If you **settle for** something, you choose or accept it even though it is not what you really want.
settle for something ❑ *Don't settle for second best.* ❑ *If there was no steak he would settle for a hamburger.*

○ **settle 'in**
If you **settle in** or you **are settled in**, you become used to a new place or new job.
settle in ❑ *When I moved here it took me months to settle in.* ❑ [+ to] *How is he settling in to his new school?*
be settled in ❑ *My colleagues were very helpful while I was getting settled in.*

○ **settle 'into**
If you **settle into** something, you become used to it or start doing it in a regular way that seems likely to continue.
settle into something ❑ *Some babies are slow to settle into a routine.* ❑ *Have you settled into village life yet?*

○ **'settle on** (or **settle upon**)
1 If you **settle on** something, you decide to have it or use it. = **decide on**
settle on something ❑ *She tried on several outfits before settling on a black skirt and jacket.* ❑ *Have you settled on a name for the baby yet?*
2 If something **settles on** a place or person, it lands on them and stays there.
settle on something/someone ❑ *Her gaze moved around the room before settling on me.* ❑ *Snow had settled on the ground.*
3 If money **is settled on** someone, it is left to them in a will. [FORMAL]
be settled on someone ❑ *Some money was settled on him when his father died.*

○ **settle 'up**
If you **settle up**, you pay someone what you owe them. = **square up** ❑ [+ with] *I will settle up with him as soon as I get paid.* ❑ *I went to the hotel reception to settle up.*

○ **'settle upon** → see **settle on**

sew /səʊ/ (**sews, sewing, sewed, sewn**)
○ **sew 'back** (or **sew back on**)
When a surgeon **sews back** someone's hand, arm, ear, etc., they fix it back in its correct place by sewing.
sew back something or **sew something back** ❑ *A team of surgeons attempted to sew back her arm.* ❑ *He needed 50 stitches to sew his ear back on.*

○ **sew 'on**
If you **sew** something **on** or **sew** it **on** something, you attach it to something else by sewing it.
sew on something or **sew something on** ❑ *I had to sew on a button that was coming loose.*
sew something on something ❑ *She sewed a name tag on his coat.*

○ **sew 'up**
1 If you **sew up** something, you join it together by sewing it.
sew up something or **sew something up** ❑ *She found a needle and thread to sew up the torn lining.* ❑ *A doctor was sewing up the cut over his eye.*
2 If you **sew up** something or if it **is sewn up**, you have arranged everything so that you cannot fail or get a bad result. [INFORMAL]
sew up something or **sew something up** ❑ *The ruling party seem to have sewed up this year's elections.*
be sewn up ❑ *The contracts should be sewn up by tonight.*

sex /seks/ (**sexes, sexing, sexed**)
○ **sex 'up** [INFORMAL]
If you **sex** something **up**, you make it more exciting.
sex something up or **sex up something** ❑ *The journalist admitted he had sexed up his reports of the incident.* ❑ *They have been brought in to sex up classical music.*

shack /ʃæk/ (**shacks, shacking, shacked**)
○ **shack 'up** [INFORMAL]
When people **shack up**, they start living together as lovers. ❑ [+ with] *He wants to shack up with me.* ❑ [+ together] *After a year, we decided to shack up together.*

shade /ʃeɪd/ (**shades, shading, shaded**)
○ **shade 'in**
If you **shade** something **in**, you fill an area on a page with a darker colour. = **colour in**
shade in something or **shade something in** ❑ *She was finishing her drawing, shading in the background.* ❑ *Areas on the map with the highest population density are shaded in.*

○ **shade 'into**
If one thing **shades into** another, you cannot clearly see or tell where one thing ends and the other begins. = **merge into, blend into**
shade into something ❑ *The painting has reds shading into pinks.* ❑ *Memory sometimes shades into imagination.*

shake /ʃeɪk/ (shakes, shaking, shook, shaken)

○ **shake 'down**

■ If someone **shakes** you **down**, they use threats or force to get money from you. [AMERICAN, INFORMAL]
shake down someone or **shake someone down** ❑ Tourists were being shaken down by local gangs.

■ If something **shakes down**, it happens in a particular way. = **work out** [INFORMAL] ❑ We'll need to wait and see how it shakes down.

■ If a group of people **shake down**, they become used to a new situation or to being or working together. [BRITISH, INFORMAL] ❑ The team has not yet shaken down.

○ **shake 'off**

■ If you **shake off** an illness, unpleasant feeling or bad habit, you manage to get rid of it.
shake off something ❑ It's not easy to shake off bad habits learned at a young age. ❑ A brisk walk is a good way to shake off tiredness.
shake something off ❑ I've had a cough for two weeks – I can't seem to shake it off.

■ If you **shake** someone **off**, you manage to get away from someone who is following you.
shake off someone ❑ It had taken Frank several hours to shake off the police.
shake someone off ❑ He's been following me around all day. I can't shake him off.

■ If you **shake** someone **off**, you move your arm or body quickly so that they are no longer touching you.
shake off someone or **shake someone off** ❑ He grabbed my arm. I shook him off. ❑ She shook off his restraining hand.

○ **shake 'out**

■ If you **shake** something **out**, you shake it to make it flat or get rid of dirt or water.
shake out something or **shake something out** ❑ She took a tablecloth, shook it out, and spread it on the table.

■ To **shake** something **out** means to change it and get rid of things that stop it from succeeding.
shake out something or **shake something out** ❑ They pledged to shake out British industry, to make it more efficient.

○ **shake 'up**

■ If something **shakes** you **up**, it makes you feel very shocked and upset.
shake someone up or **shake up someone** ❑ Did that lightning shake you up? ❑ The final scene really shook up the audience. ● If you are **shaken up**, you feel very shocked or upset by something. ❑ The accident left me a bit

shaken up, but unharmed. ❑ He looked really shaken up after seeing her.

■ If you **shake** something **up**, you shake a container, often in order to mix the contents. = **mix up**
shake something up or **shake up something** ❑ Here are the raffle tickets; shake them up well before you pick one. ❑ Don't shake up the bottle.

■ If you **shake** something **up**, you make big changes in it in order to improve it.
shake something up or **shake up something** ❑ The management aims to shake up the company. ❑ I think we should shake things up a bit, get some new people in. ● A **shake-up** is a major change in something such as an organization. ❑ Many people wanted a shake-up of the two-party system. ❑ I felt my life needed a shake-up.

shame /ʃeɪm/ (shames, shaming, shamed)

○ **'shame into**

If you **shame** someone **into** doing something, you force them to do it by making them feel ashamed.
shame someone into something ❑ She shamed me into helping with the cleaning. ❑ Father was shamed into a confession.

shape /ʃeɪp/ (shapes, shaping, shaped)

○ **shape 'up**

■ If someone or something **is shaping up** in a particular way, they are developing or progressing in that way. ❑ [+ to-infinitive] This event is shaping up to be a very special day for the school. ❑ This summer was shaping up very differently to the last one.

■ If someone or something **shapes up** or **is shaping up**, they are doing well in a particular situation or activity.
shape up ❑ [+ as] I did have a few worries about how Harry and I would shape up as parents.
be shaping up ❑ I hear the new recruits are shaping up very well. ❑ Let's try her as team leader and see how she shapes up.

■ If you **shape up**, you become fit and healthy or prepared for something. ❑ [+ for] We were shaping up for a big new campaign. ❑ According to his doctor, he'll be dead within a year if he doesn't shape up.

■ If you tell someone to **shape up**, you are telling them work harder or behave better. [INFORMAL] ❑ 'Shape up. Set an example,' he said briskly. ❑ She told them to shape up and do something useful.

share /ʃeə/ (shares, sharing, shared)

○ **'share in**

If you **share in** something, you are one of a number of people who achieve or accept it.

share in something ❑ *The company is offering you the chance to share in its success.* ❑ *Everybody shares in the household chores.*

share 'out

If you **share** something **out**, you divide it into parts and give some to each person in a group.

share out something or **share something out** ❑ [+ among] *Housework and childcare is shared out among all the residents.* ❑ *Elizabeth cut the cake, then shared it out.* • If there is a **share-out** of something, several people are given equal or fair parts of it. ❑ *Workers will be involved in a share-out of the profits.*

sharpen /'ʃɑːpən/ (**sharpens, sharpening, sharpened**)

sharpen 'up

1 If you **sharpen up** a knife or other tool, you make it sharper.

sharpen up something or **sharpen something up** ❑ *First the chef sharpens up his knives.* ❑ *My tools were blunt so I had to sharpen them up.*

2 If something **sharpens up** or if you **sharpen** it **up**, it becomes better or more active.

sharpen up ❑ *The campaign against the new law was sharpening up.*

sharpen up something or **sharpen something up** ❑ *These games can sharpen up your mental ability.*

shave /ʃeɪv/ (**shaves, shaving, shaved**)

shave 'off

1 If someone **shaves off** their hair or beard, they remove it by shaving.

shave off something or **shave something off** ❑ *He had shaved off his beard.* ❑ *He used to have a moustache, but he shaved it off.*

2 If you **shave off** a thin piece of something, you cut it off.

shave off something or **shave something off** ❑ [+ from] *You'll need to shave off a small amount from the bottom of the door.*

3 If you **shave** an amount **off** something, you reduce it by that amount.

shave something off something ❑ *The company shaved $20 million off its production costs.* ❑ *He shaved three seconds off his previous best time for that distance.*

shear /ʃɪə/ (**shears, shearing, sheared, shorn**)

> The past participle can be either **sheared** or **shorn**.

shear 'off

If part of something **shears off**, it suddenly breaks off or is cut off. ❑ *The aeroplane's wing sheared off.*

sheathe /ʃiːð/ (**sheathes, sheathing, sheathed**)

'sheathe in [LITERARY]

If something **is sheathed in** something, it is covered in something which fits it closely.

be sheathed in something ❑ *Her long legs were sheathed in black tights.* ❑ *The structure had been sheathed in glass.*

shell /ʃel/ (**shells, shelling, shelled**)

shell 'out [INFORMAL]

If you **shell out** for something or **shell out** money, you spend money on something, usually a large amount. = **fork out**

shell out something ❑ [+ for] *I'm not willing to shell out a hundred dollars for a pair of sneakers.* ❑ [+ on] *I shelled out sixty quid on that meal.*

shell out ❑ [+ for] *Parents are willing to shell out for products they think will help their child's development.*

shin /ʃɪn/ (**shins, shinning, shinned**)

'shin down

If you **shin down** something, you climb quickly down it using both hands and legs to grip it.

shin down something ❑ *She shinned down the drainpipe to the lawn.*

'shin up

If you **shin up** something, you climb quickly up it using both hands and legs to grip it.

shin up something ❑ *I shinned up a lamp post to get a better view of the procession.*

shine /ʃaɪn/ (**shines, shining, shone**)

shine 'out

If something **shines out**, it shines brightly so it can be seen easily. ❑ *Lights shone out, coming from the road.*

shine 'through (or shine out)

If a good quality **shines through** or **shines through** something, it is easy to see or notice.

shine through ❑ *Even when she was tired and upset, her warm good nature shone through.* ❑ *Kathleen had some spiritual quality that seemed to shine out.*

shine through something ❑ *His confidence shines through everything he says and does.*

ship /ʃɪp/ (**ships, shipping, shipped**)

ship 'in

1 If goods **are shipped in** or someone **ships** them **in**, they are brought into a place, especially by boat.

be shipped in ❑ [+ from] *The rice is shipped in from Thailand.*

ship something in or **ship in something**
❑ [+ from] *To fill the order we had to ship goods in from Kansas City.*

2 If people or things **are shipped in**, they are brought to a place. [INFORMAL]
be shipped in ❑ *A group of students had been shipped in to fill the empty seats.* ❑ *More chairs had to be shipped in from another office.*

○ **ship 'off**

If people or things **are shipped off** or if someone **ships** them **off**, they are taken somewhere, especially when they do not want to go.
be shipped off ❑ [+ to] *Refugees are just put on a bus and shipped off to wherever the government wants.* ❑ [+ to-infinitive] *Young men were being shipped off to fight in the war.*

ship someone/something off or **ship off someone/something** ❑ *They load the sheep onto trucks and ship them off.*

○ **ship 'out**

1 If goods **are shipped out** or if someone **ships** them **out**, they are taken somewhere, especially by boat.
be shipped out ❑ [+ from] *The building materials will have to be shipped out from England.* ❑ *His crop is shipped out by rail.*

ship someone/something out or **ship out someone/something** ❑ *We had to ship all the furniture out to the new house.*

2 If people or things **are shipped out**, they are taken to a place.
be shipped out ❑ *They shipped her out to work in a remote clinic.*

3 If people **ship out**, they leave a place.
❑ *They told everybody that they had had enough, that they were shipping out.*

shock /ʃɒk/ (**shocks, shocking, shocked**)

○ **'shock into**

If you **are shocked into** doing something or something **shocks** you **into** it, you are so shocked or surprised that you do it.
be shocked into something ❑ *The assembly was shocked into silence.*

shock someone into something ❑ *They try to shock people into giving up smoking.*

shoehorn /ˈʃuːhɔːn/ (**shoehorns, shoehorning, shoehorned**)

○ **'shoehorn into**

To **shoehorn** something or someone **into** something means to fit them into something that is only just big enough or only just long enough.
shoehorn something/someone into

something ❑ *Their cars are shoehorned into tin spaces.* ❑ *Five games have been shoehorned into the next two days.*

shoo /ʃuː/ (**shoos, shooing, shooed**)

○ **shoo a'way**

If you **shoo** a person or an animal **away**, you wave your arms or hands at them to make them go away.
shoo away someone/something or **shoo someone/something away** ❑ *She shooed away the pigeons that gathered around her.* ❑ *They shooed her away as if she were a dog.*

shoot /ʃuːt/ (**shoots, shooting, shot**)

○ **shoot a'way**

If something **is shot away**, a bullet or explosion destroys it. = **blow away, blow o**
be shot away ❑ *One of the ship's masts had bee shot away.*

○ **shoot 'back**

If someone **shoots back** an answer, they reply quickly and often angrily.
shoot back something ❑ *'It did not succeed,' Kelly said. 'That's for sure,' Hamilton shot back.*

○ **shoot 'down**

1 If someone **shoots** something or someone **down**, they make them fall to the ground by hitting them with a bullet or missile. = **bring down**
shoot down something/someone or **shoot something/someone down** ❑ *The enemy claimed to have shot down 22 of our planes.* ❑ *Armed police chased him and shot him down.*

2 If you **shoot** someone or something **down**, you say that their ideas are silly and refuse to consider them.
shoot down something/someone or **shoot something/someone down** ❑ *My suggestion was immediately shot down by everyone else at the meeting.*

○ **'shoot for** [INFORMAL]

If you **shoot for** something, you try to achieve it. = **aim for**
shoot for something ❑ *I intend to win. You hav to shoot for the top.* ❑ *These kids should be shooting for the highest grades.*

○ **shoot 'off**

1 If someone or something **shoots off**, the leave quickly. ❑ *We saw the bus shoot off at a terrific speed.* ❑ *Bob went shooting off in the othe direction.*

2 If you say you are going to **shoot off**, you mean that you are going to leave a place. [BRITISH, INFORMAL] ❑ *I have to shoot off now because I'm late.*

3 If something **is shot off** or someone **shoots** it **off**, it is destroyed or removed by

a bullet or explosion. = **blow off, blow away**
be shot off ❑ *One poor man had his foot shot off.*
shoot something off or **shoot off something**
❑ *He took a step back and shot the lock off.*

○ **shoot 'out**

1 If someone **shoots out**, they leave a place
very quickly. ❑ [+ *of*] *He just shot out of the room
before I could say anything.* ❑ *Someone shot out in
front of my car and I had to slam on the brakes.*
2 If something **shoots out**, it moves
suddenly so that it is sticking out. ❑ *His arm
shot out to point at her.* ❑ *The frog's tongue shot
out to catch a fly.*
3 A **shoot-out** is a fight in which people
shoot at each other with guns. ❑ *He was
wounded during a shoot-out with British troops.*

○ **'shoot through**

1 If something or someone **shoots through**
a barrier or doorway, they suddenly move
through it.
shoot through something ❑ *He shot through
the door and bolted upstairs.*
2 If a feeling **shoots through** you, you
experience it suddenly and strongly.
shoot through someone ❑ *Fear shot through
me.* ❑ *The jolting movement sent pain shooting
through him.*

○ **shoot 'through with**

1 If something **is shot through** with
something, it contains a lot of it in
different parts of it.
be shot through with something ❑ *Her hair
was brown, shot through with reddish highlights.*
❑ *His writing is shot through with humour.*
2 If you **are shot through with** something,
you feel it strongly through your whole body.
be shot through with something ❑ *My body
was shot through with pain.*

○ **shoot 'up**

1 If the amount or number of something
shoots up, it grows or increases very
quickly. ❑ *Their rent shot up and they struggled
to pay it.* ❑ [+ *to*] *The temperature shot up to 43
degrees.*
2 If part of someone's body **shoots up**, they
suddenly raise it. ❑ *His eyebrows shot up in
surprise.* ❑ *When I asked the question, several
hands in the audience shot up.*
3 If someone **shoots up**, they grow taller
very quickly. ❑ *Your children have really shot up
since the last time I saw them.*
4 If things **shoot up**, they suddenly appear.
❑ *With so many new hotels shooting up, the price
of land has risen.*
5 If someone **shoots up** a place, they cause
a lot of damage in it by shooting a gun
repeatedly.

shoot up something or **shoot something up**
❑ *Armed robbers shot up the place.*
6 If someone **shoots up**, they inject illegal
drugs into themselves. [INFORMAL] ❑ *He died
after shooting up with contaminated drugs.*

shop /ʃɒp/ (**shops, shopping, shopped**)

○ **shop a'round**

1 If you **shop around**, you compare the
price of something in different places
before you buy it. ❑ *You can save a lot of money
if you're willing to shop around online.*
2 If you **shop around** for something, you
compare what you can get from different
places before you decide what is best for you.
shop around ❑ [+ *for*] *Under the new system,
patients can shop around for their treatment.*
❑ *Different banks offer different services so it pays
to shop around.*

shore /ʃɔː/ (**shores, shoring, shored**)

○ **shore 'up**

1 If you **shore** something **up**, you
strengthen something that is weak or
likely to fail.
shore up something or **shore something up**
❑ *The government wants to shore up public
confidence in the system.* ❑ *More money is needed
to shore the company up.*
2 If you **shore** a structure **up**, you put
something next to it or under it to support
it and stop it from falling down. = **prop up**
shore up something or **shore something up**
❑ *The villagers shored up their sagging huts.*
❑ *The tunnels have not been properly shored up.*

shortlist /'ʃɔːtlɪst/ (**shortlists, shortlisting,
shortlisted**)

○ **'shortlist for** [mainly BRITISH]

If someone or something **is shortlisted for**
a job or a prize, or if someone **shortlists**
them **for** it, their name is on a list of people
who may be chosen for it, which has been
made from a longer list.
be shortlisted for something ❑ *He was
shortlisted for the Nobel Prize for literature.*
shortlist someone for something ❑ *The
company has now shortlisted five candidates for
the post.*

shoulder /'ʃəʊldə/ (**shoulders,
shouldering, shouldered**)

○ **shoulder a'side**

If you **shoulder** someone **aside**, you push
past them using your shoulder.
shoulder someone aside or **shoulder aside
someone** ❑ *The police officers rushed past him,
shouldering him aside.* ❑ *He shouldered aside
several people to see what was happening.*

shout /ʃaʊt/ (shouts, shouting, shouted)

○ **shout 'down**

If people **shout** someone **down**, they prevent the person from being heard by shouting. = **hoot down, howl down**
shout someone down or **shout down someone** ❑ The crowd shouted the speaker down. ❑ He stood up to protest, but he was shouted down.

○ **shout 'out**

If you **shout out** or **shout** something **out**, you suddenly shout something. = **call out**
shout out ❑ I just had time to shout out and warn them not to cross the road.
shout out something or **shout something out** ❑ Her friends shouted out encouragement. ❑ Kate applauded and shouted out, 'Bravo!'

shove /ʃʌv/ (shoves, shoving, shoved)

○ **shove 'off**

1 If you tell someone to **shove off**, you are telling them rudely to go away. = **buzz off, push off** [BRITISH, INFORMAL] ❑ Shove off, you!
2 If you **shove off**, you start a boat moving away from the land by pushing against the land. ❑ The boatman shoved off, letting the current carry him downstream.

○ **shove 'up** (or **shove over**) [BRITISH, INFORMAL]

If you tell someone to **shove up**, you are telling them fairly rudely to move in order to make more room. = **budge up** ❑ Shove up, let me sit down.

show /ʃəʊ/ (shows, showing, showed, shown)

○ **show a'round** (or **show round** [mainly BRITISH])

1 If you **show** someone **around** a place or **show** them **around**, you take them to different parts of a place and show them its interesting or important features. = **take around**
show someone around something ❑ I was showing a group of visitors around the school. ❑ It was Ivan's job to show him around the city.
show someone around ❑ We'll eat now and then I'll show you round.
2 If you **show** something **around**, you give it to several people to look at.
show something around ❑ I showed my holiday photos around at work.

○ **show 'in**

When you **show** someone **in**, you lead them into a room or building. ≠ **show out**
show someone in or **show in someone** ❑ A man came to the door and showed me in. ❑ Isabel showed in a guest.

○ **show 'off**

1 If you **show off**, you try to impress people by showing them what you can do or telling them what you have done, usually in a way that is annoying. ❑ Stop showing off
❑ The boys were showing off on the diving board.
❑ [+ about] He's always showing off about how important his job is. ● If someone is a **show-off**, they try to impress people by showing what they can do or telling people what they have done, usually in a way that is annoying. [INFORMAL] ❑ She's such a show-off, always dancing and singing in public.
2 If you **show off** something that you own, you show it to a lot of people because you are proud of it.
show off something ❑ She was eager to show off her new car.
show something off ❑ [+ to] He had won a medal and wanted to show it off to us.
3 If something **shows off** another thing, it emphasizes its good qualities. = **set off**
show off something or **show something off** ❑ The white dress showed off her tanned arms beautifully. ❑ Your presentation should show off your skills to their best advantage.
NOTE **Enhance** is a more formal word for **show off**.

○ **show 'out**

When you **show** someone **out**, you go with them to the door as they leave a room or building. ≠ **show in**
show someone out or **show out someone** ❑ Will you show Ms Nester out please? ❑ [+ of] After she had shown him out of the office, she sat down wearily.

○ **show 'round** → see **show around**

○ **show 'through**

1 If something **shows through** something else, it can be seen behind it.
show through something ❑ The dawn light showed through the curtains.
2 If your feelings **show through**, other people can see that you have them, often without you intending them to. ❑ She smiled, but her sadness showed through. ❑ His positive attitude showed through right from the start.

○ **show 'up**

1 If you **show up**, you arrive at a place where people are expecting you. = **turn up** ❑ [+ at] Over a hundred people showed up at the meeting. ❑ I waited for half an hour, but she didn't show up.
2 When something **shows up** or something **shows** it **up**, it can be seen clearly.

show up ❑ [+ against] *Dark colours will not show up against a similar background.* ❑ [+ as] *The injury shows up as a dark area on the X-ray.*
show something up ❑ *A cream carpet will show the dirt up terribly.*
show up something ❑ *The red dye in these tablets shows up areas where the teeth have not been cleaned properly.*
3 If something **shows up** or if someone or something **shows** it **up**, it can be noticed as a result of a test or experiment.
show up ❑ *When we tested the samples for traces of the substance, nothing showed up.* ❑ [+ as] *She had not been pregnant long enough for the test to show up as positive.*
show up something or **show something up** ❑ *Infertility tests showed up a problem.* ❑ *Conventional X-rays don't show them up very well.*
be shown up ❑ *Some of these infections aren't shown up by routine blood tests.* ❑ [+ as] *The painting was examined and shown up as a fake.*
4 If someone **shows** you **up**, they make you feel embarrassed by their behaviour.
show someone up or **show up someone** ❑ *You showed me up in front of the whole school.* ❑ *She's always showing up her parents in public.*

show 'up as
If something or someone **is shown up as** being bad or something **shows** them **up as** bad, people start to realize that they are bad.
be shown up as something ❑ *They have been shown up as being very undemocratic.*
show someone/something up as something ❑ *He tried to discredit them by showing them up as traitors.*

shrink /ʃrɪŋk/ (**shrinks, shrinking, shrank, shrunk**)

shrink a'way
If you **shrink away**, you move away from something you find frightening or very unpleasant. ❑ *The boys shrank away in horror.* ❑ [+ from] *He shrinks away from any physical contact.*

'shrink from
1 If you **shrink from** someone or something, you move away or keep away from them because you do not like them.
shrink from someone/something ❑ *He always shrank from crowds of people.*
2 If you **shrink from** something, you do not want to do it because it is difficult or unpleasant. = **shy away from**
shrink from something ❑ *We must not shrink from our obligations.*

shrivel /ˈʃrɪvəl/ (**shrivels, shrivelling, shrivelled**)

> American English uses the spellings **shriveling** and **shriveled**.

○ **shrivel 'up**
If something **shrivels up** or if something **shrivels** it **up**, it becomes dry and wrinkled. = **wither**
shrivel up ❑ *The fish had shrivelled up a bit.*
shrivel something up or **shrivel up something** ❑ *The sun had shrivelled the tomatoes up.*
be shrivelled up ❑ *I was late for tea, and mine would be shrivelled up in the oven.*

shroud /ʃraʊd/ (**shrouds, shrouding, shrouded**)

○ **'shroud in**
If something **is shrouded in** mystery, uncertainty, or secrecy, people do not know much about it.
be shrouded in something ❑ *For centuries the organization has been shrouded in secrecy and closed to outsiders.*

shrug /ʃrʌg/ (**shrugs, shrugging, shrugged**)
○ **shrug 'off**
If you **shrug** something **off**, you ignore it or treat it as if it is not really important or serious. = **brush off**
shrug something off or **shrug off something** ❑ *Many men tend to shrug this problem off.* ❑ *The Chairman shrugs off any criticism that their business is unethical.*

shuffle /ˈʃʌfəl/ (**shuffles, shuffling, shuffled**)
○ **shuffle a'round**
If you **shuffle around**, you move your feet while standing or you move your bottom while sitting, often because you feel uncomfortable or embarrassed. ❑ *He shuffled around in his chair, clearly embarrassed at the question.*

○ **shuffle 'off**
If you **shuffle** something **off**, you try to avoid talking about it or dealing with it because you find it difficult or embarrassing.
shuffle something off or **shuffle off something** ❑ *He shuffled the question off and changed the topic.* ❑ [+ onto] *The Government should not try to shuffle the responsibility off onto the public.*

shut /ʃʌt/ (**shuts, shutting**)

> The form **shut** is used in the present tense and is the past tense and past participle of the verb.

○ **shut a'way**

1 If you **shut** someone **away** or if they **are shut away**, they have to stay in a place where they cannot meet people or travel around. **= lock away**

shut someone away or **shut away someone** ❑ *I don't believe in shutting the elderly away in care homes.*

be shut away ❑ *People are shut away in their houses all winter and rarely see one other.*

2 If you **shut** yourself **away**, you stay in one place for a long time and avoid meeting people.

shut yourself away ❑ *He became an intensely private man, shutting himself away in his small apartment.* ❑ *I shut myself away in the library to work.*

3 If you **shut** something **away**, you try not to think about it or to admit that it exists.

shut something away or **shut away something** ❑ *We shut away some aspects of ourselves that we do not want to confront.* ❑ *I didn't want the memory of her to be shut away.*

○ **shut 'down**

1 If someone **shuts down** a factory or business or if it **shuts down**, it closes and stops working. **= close down**

shut down something ❑ *They shut down the water processing plants, and told residents to buy bottled water.*

shut something down ❑ *The company would be forced to shut the whole factory down.* ❑ *Inspectors said the restaurant was dirty and shut it down.*

shut down ❑ *More than 50 businesses in the town have shut down this year.* • A **shutdown** is the closing of a factory or business. ❑ *1,000 workers lost their jobs in factory shutdowns.*

2 If a machine or an engine **shuts down** or if it **is shut down**, it stops working for a short time. **= shut off**

shut down ❑ *His computer overheated and shut down.*

shut down something ❑ *There is an emergency mechanism for shutting down the system.*

shut something down ❑ *One of the plane's engines had been shut down after showing a fault.*

3 If you **shut** something or someone **down**, you completely stop something from happening or stop someone from doing something.

shut something/someone down or **shut down something/someone** ❑ *One of their attacking players began a run but the defence shut it down.* ❑ *The authorities are working to try to shut down these email scams.*

○ **shut 'in**

1 If you **shut** a person or animal **in** or **shut** them **in** something, you put them in a room or place and close the door so they cannot leave. **= shut up**

shut someone in ❑ *His brother pushed him in a wardrobe and shut him in.* ❑ *The dog was shut in for the night.*

shut someone in something ❑ *She shut her husband in the garage by mistake.*

NOTE **Imprison** and **confine** are more formal words for **shut in**.

2 If you **shut** yourself **in** a room or **shut** yourself **in**, you go in and shut the door so that nobody else can get in.

shut yourself in something ❑ *She shut herself in the bathroom and cried.*

shut yourself in ❑ *I ran out to the shed and shut myself in.*

○ **shut 'off**

1 If you **shut** something **off**, you turn off the supply of something such as power or water. **= turn off**

shut off something or **shut something off** ❑ *I stopped the car and shut off the engine.* ❑ *You need to shut off the water at the mains.*

2 If a machine **shuts off**, it stops operating, often because of a fault. ❑ *If an incorrect key is used, the engine will shut off after a few seconds.*

3 If someone **shuts** the supply of something **off**, they stop sending or giving that thing to people who normally use it. **= cut off**

shut off something or **shut something off** ❑ *They threatened to shut off the supply of oil to the country.* ❑ *The government could reduce our funding or shut it off altogether.*

4 If something **shuts off** a view of something, it prevents it from being seen. **= block out**

shut off something or **shut something off** ❑ *The house was shut off behind high hedges.* ❑ *[+ from] Our table was shut off from the rest of the dining room by screens.*

5 If you **shut** yourself **off**, you avoid talking to other people or getting involved with them.

shut yourself off ❑ *[+ from] He tends to shut himself off from the other patients.*

○ **shut 'out**

1 If you **shut** a person or animal **out**, you prevent them from getting into a place, for example by closing the doors.

shut someone/something out ❑ *Parents use to shut their children out all day to play.* ❑ *She slammed the bedroom door, shutting him out.*

shut out someone/something ❑ *Keep the screen door closed to shut out flies.*

2 To **shut out** sound, light, or a substance means to prevent it from entering or reaching a place.

shut out something ❑ *He put his hands over his ears to shut out the noise.* ❑ *High walls shut out the sunlight.*

shut something out ❑ *The holes are covered to shut the water out.*

3 If you **shut out** a thought or feeling, you try to stop yourself from thinking about it. = block out, blot out

shut out something ❑ *She found it impossible to shut out the pain.*

shut something out ❑ *He decided to shut it out of his mind.* ❑ *If you try to shut memories out, they can disturb you later in life.*

4 If you **shut** someone **out**, you do not allow them to get involved in something.

shut someone out or **shut out someone** ❑ [+ of] *She is very private, to the point of shutting me out of her life.* ❑ *Please don't shut out people who want to help you.*

○ **shut 'up**

1 If you **shut up**, you stop talking. [INFORMAL] ❑ *Everybody shut up as soon as she walked in.* ❑ *I'm going to shut up now and let my colleague explain the rest.*

2 If you tell someone to **shut up**, you are telling them rudely to stop talking or that you do not like what they have said. [INFORMAL] ❑ *'You like him.' – 'Shut up! I do not!'*

3 If someone or something **shuts** you **up**, they make you stop talking. [INFORMAL]

shut someone up ❑ *Let the kids go watch TV. That usually shuts them up.* ❑ *I just said yes to shut her up.*

shut up someone ❑ *That should shut up all the people who said she'd never be successful.*

NOTE **Silence** is a more formal word for **shut up**.

4 If you **shut** someone **up** somewhere, or if they **are shut up** somewhere, they are kept there and cannot leave. = shut in

shut someone up ❑ *He doesn't believe in shutting kids up in the classroom all day.*

shut up someone ❑ *We need to shut up more criminals.*

be shut up ❑ *He was shut up for life as a dangerous criminal.* ❑ *I'm sick of being shut up in an office.*

NOTE **Imprison** and **confine** are more formal words for **shut up**.

shy /ʃaɪ/ (**shies, shying, shied**)

○ **shy a'way from**

If you **shy away from** something, you avoid doing it or dealing with it because it is difficult or unpleasant for you. = shrink from

shy away from something ❑ *We mustn't shy away from the real problems.* ❑ *They shied away from mentioning divorce.*

sick /sɪk/ (**sicks, sicking, sicked**)

○ **sick 'up** [INFORMAL]

If you **sick** food **up** or **sick up**, you vomit. = bring up, throw up

sick something up or **sick up something** ❑ *The baby sicked his milk up all over Karen.*

sick up ❑ *He's sicked up on the carpet.*

side /saɪd/ (**sides, siding, sided**)

○ **'side against**

If people **side against** you, they oppose you in a disagreement or argument. = gang up; ≠ side with

side against someone ❑ *The newspapers have largely sided against the protesters.*

○ **'side with**

If you **side with** someone, you support them in a disagreement or argument. ≠ side against

side with someone ❑ *Louise automatically sided with her sister.*

sidle /ˈsaɪdəl/ (**sidles, sidling, sidled**)

○ **sidle 'up**

If someone **sidles up** to you, they approach you in a cautiously, as if they do not want anyone to notice. ❑ [+ to] *She sidled up to me and whispered in my ear.* ❑ *I sidled up and tapped her on the shoulder.*

sift /sɪft/ (**sifts, sifting, sifted**)

○ **'sift through**

If you **sift through** information or documents, you examine a large amount of them carefully and thoroughly, usually to look for something.

sift through something ❑ *Every day he sifted through all the news reports.* ❑ *This software can sift through huge amounts of data.*

sign /saɪn/ (**signs, signing, signed**)

○ **sign a'way**

If you **sign** something **away**, you sign a legal document stating that you no longer own it or have a right to it.

sign away something or **sign something away** ❑ *They were tricked into signing away their land.*

○ **'sign for**

If you **sign for** something, you sign a document stating that you have received it

sign for something ❑ *When your order is delivered, check the contents before signing for it.* ❑ *Will you sign for this parcel, please?*

✪ **sign 'in**

1 If you **sign in** or if someone **signs** you **in**, you sign your name to show that you have arrived at a place where you intend to stay for a time, such as a hotel. **= book in**

sign in ❏ [+ at] *Please sign in at the reception desk.* ❏ *She signed in under the name Joanna Smith.*

sign yourself in ❏ *He went to a psychiatric hospital and signed himself in.*

sign in someone ❏ *A smiling lady was behind the desk, signing in the new students.*

sign someone in ❏ *We arrived at the hotel and the clerk signed us in.*

NOTE **Register** is a more formal word for **sign in**.

2 If you **sign** someone **in**, you sign your name to say that they are entering a place as your guest or with your permission.

sign someone in or **sign in someone** ❏ *If you're not a member, get someone to sign you in.* ❏ *You have to be a full member to sign in guests.*

○ **sign 'off**

1 If someone **signs** something **off**, they officially approve or agree to it.

sign off something or **sign something off** ❏ *Ministers hope to sign off the £2.7 billion pound rail link next month.* ❏ *The text has to be signed off by a senior supervisor before going to print.*

2 If you **sign off**, you write or say that you are about to finish a message or broadcast. ❏ *It's time for me to go so I'll sign off now. With love from Dad.* ❏ *He signed off for the last time on Friday as host of the BBC's 'This Morning'.*

3 If someone **signs off**, they leave work at the end of the day. ❏ *She finished the piece she was working on, then signed off for the night.* ❏ *He signed off early that evening and went home.*

4 If a doctor **signs** someone **off** or **signs** them **off** work, he or she writes a note to say that they are too ill to work. [BRITISH]

sign someone off ❏ [+ for] *She went to the doctor who signed her off for two weeks.*

sign someone off something ❏ *I've had an operation and been signed off work.*

5 If someone **signs off** or **signs off** government benefits, they stop claiming money from the government as an unemployed person, because they have found a job. [BRITISH]

sign off ❏ *All I want is to get a job and sign off.*

sign off something ❏ *He managed to sell some of his art so he could sign off benefits.*

○ **sign 'off on**

If you **sign off on** something, you officially approve or agree to it.

sign off on something ❏ *We haven't signed off on any deal yet. We are waiting for the right price.* ❏ *No software is released to the customer until the quality control people have signed off on it.*

○ **sign 'on**

1 If you **sign on** or if someone **signs** you **on**, you sign an agreement to do a particular job or course of study. **= sign up**

sign on ❏ [+ for] *This isn't the kind of work I signed on for.* ❏ *MacGregor liked the script and the director was confident that he would sign on.*

sign someone on or **sign on someone** ❏ *The club signed him on and he played for them for five years.* ❏ [+ for] *The college is signing on new students for the Diploma in Management.*

2 If you **sign on**, you type your name or a password into a computer in order to enter a computer system or start using a piece of software. ❏ *The system will allow parents to sign on and see what their child has eaten at school.* ❏ [+ to] *He was having problems signing on to the system.*

3 If you **sign on** or **sign on** government benefits, you go to a government office and state that you are unemployed, so that you can receive money from the government. [BRITISH]

sign on ❏ *Some of these men have been signing o for years.*

sign on something ❏ *He lost his job and had no choice but to sign on the dole.*

○ **sign 'out**

1 If you **sign out**, you sign an official record to show that you are leaving a place such as a hotel or hospital. ❏ *Patients must sign out every time they leave the ward.* ❏ [+ of] *At weekends students were allowed to sign out of the halls until midnight.*

2 If you **sign out**, you type something or press a key to leave a computer system or stop using a piece of software. ❏ *It's very important to sign out when you've finished.* ❏ [+ of] *You have to sign out of the application before you can sign in to another one.*

3 If you **sign** someone **out**, you sign your name to say that they are leaving a place with your permission, or leaving a place that they have entered as your guest.

sign someone out or **sign out someone** ❏ *You' have to find the doctor on duty to sign you out.* ❏ *At the reception desk, he had to be signed out.*

4 If you **sign** something **out**, you sign your name in an official record to say that you have taken or borrowed it.

sign something out or **sign out something** ❏ *People were waiting at the library desk to sign out their books.* ❏ *The car was unavailable – someone had signed it out for the weekend.*

○ **sign 'over**

If you **sign** something **over**, you sign a legal document giving it to someone else.

sign over something or **sign something over**
❏ *I filled in a form signing over ten percent of my income to charity.* ❏ [+ to] *One way of avoiding the tax might be to sign the house over to your son now.*

sign 'up

1 If you **sign up**, you sign an agreement to do a job or course of study, or join an organization. ❏ [+ for] *The following year he signed up for a film that was very different from his usual work.* ❏ [+ to-infinitive] *She signed up to do an MA after graduating from Columbia.* ❏ [+ as] *At the age of 18 he signed up as an apprentice.* ❏ [+ with] *Toby decided to sign up with an online dating agency.*

2 If you **sign** someone **up**, you get them to sign a contract to do a job or join an organization.
sign up someone ❏ *The record label had signed up some exciting new talent.* ❏ [+ to-infinitive] *Richard was signed up to play the lead in the film.*
sign someone up ❏ *The Arsenal manager saw him play and signed him up immediately.*

3 If someone **signs up**, they join the armed forces. ❏ *He went into an army recruiting office to sign up.* ❏ [+ for] *I signed up for military service in July 2010.*

4 If you **sign up**, you agree to do or take part in something. ❏ [+ for] *Anyone who signs up for this challenge knows it's not going to be easy.* ❏ [+ to-infinitive] *When I agreed to go on holiday with you, I didn't sign up to organize everything.*

signal /ˈsɪɡnəl/ (**signals, signalling, signalled**)

> American English uses the spellings **signaling** and **signaled**.

'signal to

If you **signal to** someone, you make a movement or sound to tell them something.
signal to someone ❏ *She signalled to Sharon that she was leaving.* ❏ [+ to-infinitive] *He signalled to the waiter to bring him another drink.*

silt /sɪlt/ (**silts, silting, silted**)

silt 'up

If an area of water **silts up** or is **silted up**, it becomes blocked with very fine earth or sand.
silt up ❏ *The lake gradually silted up.*
be silted up ❏ *The river was so silted up that boats could no longer pass down it.*

simmer /ˈsɪmə/ (**simmers, simmering, simmered**)

simmer 'down [INFORMAL]

If you **simmer down**, you stop being angry or too excited about something. = **calm down, cool down** ❏ *Give him time to simmer down before you ask him.* ❏ *'Simmer down,' I said. 'It's not our problem.'*

sing /sɪŋ/ (**sings, singing, sang, sung**)

sing a'long

If you **sing along**, you sing a piece of music while you are listening to someone else perform it. ❏ [+ with] *My daughter can sing along with all the tunes on the radio.* ❏ [+ to] *We sung along to all those classic Beatles songs.* ❏ *Members of the audience were all singing along.*

sing 'out

1 If you **sing** something **out**, you say it loudly and clearly.
sing out something or **sing something out**
❏ *'Time to go!' Ella sang out.* ❏ *She sang out a greeting as we approached.*

2 If you **sing out**, you sing loudly. ❏ *From the choir, a hundred voices sang out together.*

sing 'up

If you **sing up**, you sing more loudly.
❏ *You boys at the back! Can you sing up?*

single /ˈsɪŋɡəl/ (**singles, singling, singled**)
✪ single 'out

If you **single** someone or something **out**, you choose them from a group for special attention or treatment. = **pick out**
single someone/something out ❏ [+ as] *Did you single any ideas out as being particularly interesting?* ❏ [+ for] *They singled him out for praise.*

single out someone/something ❏ [+ for] *We have singled out a few issues for particular attention.* ❏ [+ as] *Police identified several men, and singled out one as the ringleader.* ❏ *I don't understand why I've been singled out in this way.*

sink /sɪŋk/ (**sinks, sinking, sank, sunk**)

sink 'back

1 If you **sink back**, you allow yourself to lean or fall gently backwards so that you are sitting or lying. ❏ [+ on] *She sank back on her pillows.* ❏ [+ in] *Sonny sank back in the leather armchair.* ❏ *I sank back, feeling weak.*

2 To **sink back** into a state you were in before, especially a bad one, means to return to it. ❏ [+ into] *Without her, he would sink back into his old habits.* ❏ *The next day he sank back into a coma.*

sink 'down

If you **sink down**, you sit or let yourself fall gently from an upright position.
❏ [+ on] *Hagen sank down on the grass, exhausted.* ❏ [+ into] *They sank down into deep leather armchairs.*

○ sink 'in

> In meanings 3, 4, and 5, the stress is on 'sink.

1 If something **sinks in**, it goes deeper into the ground, water, or other substance. ❏ *We threw stones out onto the soft mud and watched them sink in.*

2 If something **sinks in**, you gradually realize or understand it. ❏ *I made my announcement, then waited to let the news sink in.* ❏ *It gradually sank in that he was serious.*

3 If you **are sunk in** a particular state, you are in it and cannot easily get out of it.
be sunk in something ❏ *She remained sunk in silent contemplation.* ❏ *The students all seemed sunk in lethargy.*

4 If you **sink** something sharp **in** something, you cause it to go deeply into it.
sink something in something ❏ *The cat sank her claws in his neck.*
sink in something or **sink something in**
❏ *The animal sinks in its teeth and holds on.*

5 If you **sink** money **in** something, you spend money on it in the hope of making more money. = **sink into**
sink something in something ❏ *I sank all my savings in a business.*

○ sink 'into

> In meaning 4, the stress is on 'sink.

1 If something **sinks into** the ground, water, or other substance, it moves downwards and deeper into it.
sink into something ❏ *Her chair was sinking into the sand.*

2 If you **sink into** something or **sink** yourself **into** it, you sit or lie on it so that your body is completely relaxed and supported.
sink into something ❏ *Floyd sank into a comfortable leather chair.*
sink yourself into something ❏ *She sank herself into the soft pillows.*

3 If you **sink** something sharp **into** something, or if something sharp **sinks into** something, the sharp thing goes deeply into it.
sink something into something ❏ *She sank her teeth into his finger so that he let go.*
sink into something ❏ *The cat's claws sank into his shoulder.*

4 If you **sink into** a particular state, you gradually enter it and cannot easily get out of it.
sink into something ❏ *After she left he sank into a deep depression.* ❏ *The family were sinking further into debt.*

5 If you **sink** money **into** something, you spend money on it in the hope of making more money. = **plough into, sink in**
sink something into something ❏ *He's sunk a lot of money into that theatre group.*

○ 'sink to

If something **sinks to** a lower level or standard, it falls to that level or standard.
sink to something ❏ *Share prices sank to 5.25p* ❏ *The quality of life in the country has sunk to unacceptable levels.*

sip /sɪp/ (sips, sipping, sipped)

○ 'sip at

If you **sip at** something, you repeatedly drink small amounts of a drink.
sip at something ❏ *Sandra sipped at her hot te*

siphon /'saɪfən/ (siphons, siphoning, siphoned)

> **Siphon** is also spelled **syphon**.

○ siphon 'off

1 If you **siphon off** a liquid, you get it out o a container using a tube.
siphon off something or **siphon something off** ❏ *He had siphoned off gas from his neighbour's car.*

2 If you **siphon off** money or other resources from a source or supply, you separate or remove them from the rest, often to use them in a way that was not intended.
siphon something off or **siphon off something** ❏ *They stole investors' money by siphoning it off into their personal accounts.*

sit /sɪt/ (sits, sitting, sat)

○ sit a'round (or sit about, sit round [mainly BRITISH])

If you **sit around** or **sit around** a place, you stay sitting in a place not doing very much
sit around ❏ *We sat around happily in the hotel lounge.* ❏ *The men sat about drinking coffee.*
sit around something ❏ *All I ever did was sit around the house, reading.*

○ sit 'back

1 If you **sit back**, you lean backwards against something. ❏ *Just sit back, relax, and enjoy the movie.* ❏ *She sat back in her chair and opened her book.*

2 If you **sit back**, you deliberately do not become involved in something or take any action. ❏ *We cannot afford just to sit back and wait for the next crisis.* ❏ *Just sit back and let me cook the dinner.*

○ sit 'by

If you **sit by** while something is happening especially something bad, you allow it to happen without doing anything. = **stand by** ❑ *I wasn't going to sit by and let him cheat you again.* ❑ *You can't just sit by and watch a child destroy something.*

sit 'down

1 If you **sit down** or **sit** yourself **down**, you lower your body until you are sitting on something. ≠ **stand up**
sit down ❑ *We were both looking for a place to sit down.* ❑ *He sat down on the edge of the bed.* ❑ *After a while we all sat down to dinner.*
sit yourself down ❑ *She sat herself down beside me.* ● If you have a **sit-down**, you sit down and rest for a short time. ❑ *When we got to the top of the hill we had a sit-down.* ● A **sit-down** meal is a large or formal meal eaten while sitting at a table. ❑ *There won't be time for a sit-down meal before the theatre, so we'll just get a sandwich.* ● A **sit-down** protest or a **sit-down** is a protest in which people sit down in their workplace or a public place and refuse to move. ❑ *They staged sit-down strikes that stopped the traffic.* ❑ *He was involved in civil rights marches, demonstrations, and sit-downs.*
2 If you **sit** someone **down**, you make them sit down or help them to sit down.
sit someone down ❑ *I helped him onto the bus and sat him down on a convenient seat.* ❑ *Dad sat me down and gave me a telling-off.*
3 If you **sit down** and do something, you spend time and effort doing it. ❑ *They are not willing to sit down and negotiate.* ❑ *I sat down and wrote my first book.*

sit 'for

1 If you **sit for** an artist or a picture, you stay still while a picture of you is painted, drawn, or taken.
sit for someone/something ❑ *She had sat for painters like Rossetti.* ❑ *I have sat for my portrait before.*
2 If you **sit for** an examination, you take it by answering questions or doing tests.
sit for something ❑ *Keynes sat for the Civil Service exams but didn't pass.*
3 If you **sit for** someone, you go to their house and look after their children. [INFORMAL]
sit for someone ❑ *I've asked Mum to sit for us next Saturday.*

sit 'in

1 If you **sit in**, you are allowed to be present at a meeting or event but do not take part. ❑ [+ on] *I'd love to have sat in on the meeting.* ❑ *At case conferences, I used to sit in as an observer.*
2 A **sit-in** is a protest in which people sit in a public place and refuse to leave. ❑ *There was a sit-in in the university's administration building.*

sit 'on

1 If you **sit on** an official group such as a committee or the board of a company, you are an official member of it.
sit on something ❑ *She does a lot of charity work and sits on various committees.*
❑ *Representatives of the workers should sit on the boards of directors.*
2 If someone **sits on** something, they avoid taking any action relating to something that they have or something that they should deal with.
sit on something ❑ *They decided to sit on the information for a while and see what happened.*

sit 'out

1 If you **sit out** somewhere, you sit outside rather than inside a building. ❑ *Groups of people were sitting out on the grass during their lunch hour.*
2 If you **sit** something **out**, you wait for an event or period of time to finish before doing anything.
sit out something or **sit something out**
❑ *He planned to just sit out the war without getting involved.* ❑ *The traffic was so bad that we decided to stop, get something to eat, and sit it out.*
3 If you **sit** something **out** or **sit out**, you stop taking part in a dance, game or sport for a short time.
sit something out or **sit out something**
❑ *Thanks, but I think I'll sit this one out.*
sit out ❑ *Tom was tired and decided to sit out.*

sit 'over

In meaning 2, the stress is on **'over**.

1 If you **sit over** a meal or drink, you spend a long time eating or drinking. ❑ *Sitting over breakfast the next morning, they chatted.*
2 If you **sit over** someone, you spend a long time with them watching them carefully.
sit over someone ❑ *I sat over him while he filled in the form.*

sit 'round → see sit around

sit 'through

If you **sit through** something, you stay until it is finished, especially when you are not enjoying it.
sit through something ❑ *The professor sat through the film with growing impatience.*

sit 'up

1 If you **sit up**, you move into an upright sitting position when you have been leaning back or lying down. ❑ *The students all sat up straight when the headteacher walked in.*
● **Sit-ups** are an exercise in which you repeatedly move from lying down on the

floor to a sitting position. ❏ *We did push-ups, sit-ups, and knee bends.*

2 If you **are sitting up**, you are in an upright sitting position.

be sitting up ❏ *He was sitting up in bed and looked much better.* ❏ *You can do these exercises sitting up in a chair.*

3 If you **sit** someone **up**, you move them into a sitting position when they have been leaning back or lying down.

sit someone up ❏ *She sat him up and made him comfortable.*

4 If you **sit up**, you do not go to bed although it is late at night. **= stay up** ❏ *She sat up all night and waited.* ❏ *Ellen would sit up working on her drawings.*

5 If you **sit up**, you suddenly pay attention to what is happening. ❏ *This made the whole audience sit up.* ❏ *We need to do something that will make the world sit up and listen.*

size /saɪz/ (sizes, sizing, sized)

○ **size 'up**

If you **size up** someone or something, you examine them in order to make a judgment about them. **= weigh up**

size up something or **size something up** ❏ *He had sized up the situation very quickly.* ❏ *The teams looked at each other, sizing each other up.*

skate /skeɪt/ (skates, skating, skated)

○ **skate 'over** (or **skate around, skate round** [mainly BRITISH])

If you **skate over** something, you avoid discussing or dealing fully with a difficult subject or problem. **= skirt around**

skate over something ❏ *His autobiography skates over his first marriage and divorce.* ❏ *Her speech skated around the more controversial issues.*

NOTE **Evade** is a more formal word for **skate over**.

sketch /sketʃ/ (sketches, sketching, sketched)

○ **sketch 'in**

1 If you **sketch** something **in**, you add it quickly and roughly to a drawing.

sketch in something or **sketch something in** ❏ *He showed me the photograph, then used a pencil to sketch in a large moustache.* ❏ *If your focus is on flowers in the foreground, sketch them in first.*

2 If you **sketch** something **in**, you give a few details about something, but do not deal with it fully. **= sketch out**

sketch in something or **sketch something in** ❏ *First, I'm going to sketch in a bit of the background to the story.*

NOTE **Outline** is a more formal word for **sketch in**.

○ **sketch 'out**

1 If you **sketch** something **out**, you draw all the main features, but do not include the details.

sketch out something or **sketch something out** ❏ *With a pencil and ruler he sketched out the route.* ❏ *When they have agreed a basic idea for the ad, the artist sketches out a storyboard.*

2 If you **sketch** something **out**, you give a brief, general description of it, not including the details. **= sketch in**

sketch out something or **sketch something out** ❏ *We will just sketch out an outline of the two systems.* ❏ *She sketches the bare bones of the story out first, then begins to fill in details.*

NOTE **Outline** is a more formal word for **sketch in**.

skill /skɪl/ (skills, skilling, skilled)

○ **skill 'up**

If workers **skill up** or if someone **skills** them **up**, they improve their skills or learn new skills.

skill up ❏ *For people wanting to get back to work, now is a good time to skill up.*

skill someone up or **skill up someone** ❏ *One of the main problems for managers trying to skill up their workforce is cost.*

skim /skɪm/ (skims, skimming, skimmed)

○ **skim 'off**

1 If you **skim** something **off** or **skim** it **off** something, you remove a substance which is floating on top of a liquid.

skim off something or **skim something off** ❏ *Skim off the froth, and strain the lemonade into a bottle.* ❏ *They skim the cream off to put in their coffee.*

skim something off something ❏ *Allow the soup to cool, then skim the fat off the top.*

2 If someone **skims** something **off** or **skims** it **off** something, they take the best part of something, or money which belongs to other people, for themselves.

skim off something or **skim something off** ❏ *Rich football clubs can simply skim off all the best players.*

skim something off something ❏ *Politicians are skimming money off our salaries.*

○ **'skim through**

If you **skim through** something, you read it quickly without looking at the details. **= flick through**

skim through something ❏ *She didn't have time to read the report properly, but she skimmed through it.*

skimp /skɪmp/ (**skimps, skimping, skimped**)

○ **'skimp on**

1 If you **skimp on** something, you use or do less of it than is really needed, so that the result is not good.

skimp on something ❑ *You can reduce your food intake without skimping on nutrients.* ❑ *In today's busy world, there is a lot of pressure to skimp on sleep.*

2 If you **skimp on** something, you do not spend enough money on it.

skimp on something ❑ *Companies should not be tempted to skimp on quality.*

skirt /skɜːt/ (**skirts, skirting, skirted**)

○ **skirt a'round** (or **skirt round** [mainly BRITISH])

1 If you **skirt around** something, you go around the edge or the outside of it.

skirt around something ❑ *They skirted around the town centre to avoid the traffic.* ❑ *The path skirts around a large pond.*

2 If you **skirt around** a difficult subject, you avoid discussing or dealing with it.

skirt around something ❑ *He accused the government of trying to skirt round the question of cost.*

skive /skaɪv/ (**skives, skiving, skived**)

○ **skive 'off** [BRITISH, INFORMAL]

If you **skive off** or **skive off** something, you avoid work that you should be doing by staying away from work or school.

skive off ❑ *Bob's not in the office. He's skiving off again.*

skive off something ❑ *He used to skive off school a lot.*

slack /slæk/ (**slacks, slacking, slacked**)

○ **slack 'off**

1 If someone **slacks off**, they do not work as hard as they should. ❑ *Bill won't allow anyone to slack off.*

2 [BRITISH] → see **slacken off**

slacken /'slækən/ (**slackens, slackening, slackened**)

○ **slacken 'off** (or **slack off** [BRITISH])

If something **slackens off**, it becomes slower, less active, or less intense. = **slack off, slow down, ease off** ❑ *What will happen to all this property when the tourist boom slackens off?* ❑ *Economic growth slacked off in the second quarter.*

slag /slæg/ (**slags, slagging, slagged**)

○ **slag 'off** [BRITISH, INFORMAL]

If you **slag** someone or something **off**, you criticize them in an unpleasant way.

slag someone/something off or **slag off someone/something** ❑ *He's always slagging people off behind their backs.* ❑ *People are complaining that we have slagged off their favourite band.*

slam /slæm/ (**slams, slamming, slammed**)

○ **slam 'down**

1 If you **slam** something **down**, you put it down with a lot of force.

slam something down or **slam down something** ❑ *She slammed the money down and shouted 'Take it!'* ❑ [+ on] *He accidentally slammed the lid down on my fingers.*

2 If you **slam** the phone **down**, you end a telephone conversation suddenly, because you are angry.

slam something down or **slam down something** ❑ *When he gave his name she slammed the phone down.* ❑ *'Leave me alone!' I shouted, and slammed down the phone.*

slap /slæp/ (**slaps, slapping, slapped**)

○ **slap a'round**

If someone **slaps** someone **around**, they hit them several times. = **rough up**

slap someone around or **slap around someone** ❑ *Does he think it's acceptable to slap people around?*

○ **slap 'down**

1 If you **slap** something **down**, you put it forcefully onto a surface, making a loud noise.

slap something down or **slap down something** ❑ *She shuffled the cards loudly and slapped them down.* ❑ *She slapped down a plate in front of him.*

2 If you **slap** someone **down**, you disagree with them or criticize them harshly.

slap someone down or **slap down someone** ❑ *He was afraid to be romantic in case she slapped him down.* ❑ *Rather than slapping down young people with new ideas, we ought to encourage them.*

○ **slap 'on**

If you **slap** a substance **on** or **slap** it **on** something, you put it carelessly onto a surface.

slap something on or **slap on something** ❑ *Have you seen the way she slaps make-up on?*

slap something on something ❑ *I think I'll slap a bit of paint on that wall.*

○ **'slap onto**

If you **slap** something **onto** something, you put it carelessly or forcefully onto a surface.

slap something onto something ❑ *He quickly counted out some notes and slapped them onto the counter.*

slather /'slæðə/ (**slathers, slathering, slathered**)

○ '**slather with**

If you **slather** something **with** a substance, you put the substance on it in a thick layer.

slather something with something ❑ *Ella slathered her legs with sun cream.* ❑ *He was eating a piece of toast slathered with butter.*

slave /sleɪv/ (**slaves, slaving, slaved**)

○ **slave a'way**

If you **slave away**, you work hard at something for a long time. = **slog away** ❑ *I'm slaving away, cooking and cleaning, while you do nothing.*

○ '**slave over**

If you **slave over** something, you work hard to do it or make it.

slave over something ❑ *Instead of slaving over housework on my days off, I've been going to the gym.*

● If you say that you **are slaving over a hot stove**, you are humorously saying that you are cooking. ❑ *When you're busy all day you don't want to spend hours slaving over a hot stove.*

sleep /sliːp/ (**sleeps, sleeping, slept**)

○ **sleep a'round** [INFORMAL, RUDE]

If someone **sleeps around**, they have sex with a lot of different people. ❑ *These young people do not sleep around, drink alcohol, or smoke.*

○ **sleep 'in** [BRITISH]

If you **sleep in**, you stay asleep in the morning for longer than you usually do. = **lie in** ❑ *I slept in and missed my bus.* ❑ *She got the chance to sleep in at weekends.*

○ **sleep 'off**

If you **sleep** something **off**, you recover from the effects of something by sleeping.

sleep something off or **sleep off something** ❑ *You've had too much to drink. You should go and sleep it off.*

○ '**sleep on**

If you **sleep on** something, you delay making a decision until the next day.

sleep on something ❑ *Are you sure you don't want to sleep on it? You may have changed your mind by tomorrow.*

○ **sleep 'out**

If you **sleep out**, you sleep outdoors. ❑ *The kids wanted to sleep out in a tent in the garden.* ❑ *It's much too cold to sleep out.*

○ **sleep 'over**

If someone **sleeps over**, they stay at a friend's house for one night.

sleep over ❑ *I missed the last train, so I slept over at Anna's.* ● A **sleepover** is an occasion where a child stays at a friend's house for a night. ❑ *Ella's on a sleepover at Mollie's tonight.*

○ '**sleep through**

If you **sleep through** something, you remain asleep while it is happening.

sleep through something ❑ *The baby slept through everything.* ❑ *How could you sleep through that storm last night?*

○ '**sleep together**

1 If two people **sleep together**, they have sex. ❑ *She thought that her husband and her friend were sleeping together.*

2 If people **sleep together**, they sleep in the same bed or room. ❑ *We only have two bedrooms, so the children have to sleep together.*

❂ '**sleep with**

1 If you **sleep with** someone, you have sex with them.

sleep with someone ❑ *I heard all the gossip about who was sleeping with whom.* ❑ *She doesn't think you should sleep with someone until you're married.*

2 To **sleep with** someone means to sleep in the same bed or room as them.

sleep with someone ❑ *The baby sleeps with his mother.*

slice /slaɪs/ (**slices, slicing, sliced**)

○ **slice 'off**

If you **slice** something **off**, you remove it by cutting it.

slice off something or **slice something off** ❑ *She sliced off another chunk of cheese.*

○ '**slice through** [LITERARY]

If something **slices through** something or someone, it moves through them quickly, like a knife.

slice through something/someone ❑ *The ship sliced through the water.* ❑ *Pain sliced through him.*

○ **slice 'up**

If you **slice** something **up**, you cut it into thin pieces.

slice up something or **slice something up** ❑ *Slice up the salami and arrange it on a plate.* ❑ *She started to slice the bread up and make sandwiches.*

slick /slɪk/ (**slicks, slicking, slicked**)

○ **slick 'back**

If you **slick** your hair **back**, you push it away from your face and put water or oil on it to make it smooth and shiny.

slick something back or **slick back something** ❑ *Clarke straightened his tie and slicked back his hair.*

○ **slick 'down**

If you **slick** your hair **down**, you make it

smooth and shiny by putting something such as water or oil on it. = **smooth down**
slick something down or **slick down something** ❑ *Their hair was neatly combed and slicked down.*

slim /slɪm/ (slims, slimming, slimmed)

○ slim 'down

1 If an organization **slims down** or someone **slims** it **down**, it employs fewer people in order to save money or become more efficient.
slim down ❑ *Many firms have had little choice but to slim down.*
slim down something or **slim something down** ❑ *They will almost certainly have to slim their workforce down.* ❑ *The team was slimmed down to nine full-time staff.*

2 If you **slim down** or **slim** part of your body **down**, you try to make yourself thinner and lighter.
slim down ❑ *Doctors have told Richard to slim down.* ❑ *She had slimmed down, and she looked younger.*
slim down something or **slim something down** ❑ *These treatments claim to slim down thighs.* ❑ *I want to tone my arms and slim them down.*

slip /slɪp/ (slips, slipping, slipped)

✪ slip a'way

1 If you **slip away**, you leave a place without being noticed. = **slip off** ❑ *I hope we can slip away before she notices.* ❑ *I slipped away down a side street.*

2 If something **slips away**, it disappears or passes, especially when you do not want this to happen. ❑ *I woke up, and the dream slipped away.* ❑ *I feel my life is slipping away to no purpose.*

○ slip 'by

1 If time **slips by**, it passes, especially when you do not want this to happen. ❑ *We should not allow the time to slip by without taking any action.* ❑ *The last days of August had slipped by.*

2 If someone or something **slips by** or **slips by** someone, they go past quietly, without being noticed.
slip by ❑ *The canoe slipped by quite slowly.*
slip by something/someone ❑ *I managed to slip by him.*

○ slip 'down

1 If someone or something **slips down** or **slips down** something, they fall down by sliding.
slip down ❑ *She pulled up her sock which had slipped down.*

slip down something ❑ *He must have slipped down the steps.* ❑ *My glasses keep slipping down my nose.*

2 If someone or something **slips down** or **slips down** something, they move to a lower rank or level on a scale.
slip down ❑ *He seems to have slipped down in the public's estimation.*
slip down something ❑ *She wanted to be the most important thing in his life, but feared she had slipped down the ladder.*

3 If something **slips down** or **slips down** your throat, it is pleasant and easy to drink or eat.
slip down ❑ *Ice cream slips down nicely when you have a sore throat.*
slip down something ❑ *The wine was slipping down their throats all too easily.*

✪ slip 'in

1 If you **slip** something **in** or **slip** it **in** something, you put it somewhere quietly or smoothly, especially without anyone noticing.
slip in something ❑ *He shook my hand and slipped in a twenty pound note.*
slip something in ❑ *She managed to open the drawer and slip something in.*
slip something in something ❑ *The device is so small, you can slip it in your handbag without anyone noticing.*

2 If you **slip** something **in**, you mention it in a way that seems casual while talking about something else.
slip in something ❑ *She managed to slip in the fact that she was at Oxford University.*
slip something in ❑ *Could you ask him about the money – just slip it in somehow?*

3 If you **slip in** or **slip in** a place, you go into a place quietly without being noticed.
slip in ❑ *Somebody must have slipped in unnoticed and taken it.*
slip in something ❑ *He slipped in the back door and went straight upstairs to bed.*

✪ slip 'into

1 If you **slip into** a place, you go into it quietly, without being noticed.
slip into something ❑ *She slipped into the room while he was speaking and sat at the back.*

2 If you **slip** something **into** a place, you put it there quietly or smoothly.
slip something into something ❑ *The man picked the letter up and slipped it into his pocket.*

3 If you **slip** something **into** a conversation, you mention it in a way that seems casual while talking about something else.
slip something into something ❑ *He slipped into the conversation that his father was very wealthy.*

4 If you **slip into** something, you quickly put on a piece of clothing, usually a comfortable one.
slip into something ❑ *I slipped into my pyjamas.*
5 If you **slip into** a situation or state, you begin to be in it, often without intending to.
slip into something ❑ *The country was slipping into recession.* ❑ *We frequently slip into the habit of telling lies.*

○ **slip 'off**
1 If you **slip off**, you leave a place quietly, without being noticed. **= slip away** ❑ *I was hoping to slip off early that day.*
2 To **slip off** or **slip off** something means to fall off by slipping.
slip off ❑ *His sunglasses were slipping off.*
slip off something ❑ *My foot slipped off the pedal.* ❑ *A truck had slipped off the road.*
3 If you **slip** something **off**, you take clothing off quickly and easily.
slip off something or **slip something off**
❑ *She sat on the grass and slipped off her shoes.* ❑ *He slipped off his jacket and dropped it on the bed.*

○ **slip 'on**
If you **slip** something **on**, you put clothing on quickly and easily.
slip on something or **slip something on**
❑ *He slipped on his shoes and went out.* ❑ *Just let me slip my jacket on and I'll come with you.*

✪ **slip 'out**
1 If you **slip out**, you leave a place for a short time, usually without being noticed.
❑ [+ to-infinitive] *I slipped out to phone the police.* ❑ [+ for] *I just slipped out for a breath of fresh air.* ❑ [+ of] *She had slipped out of her seat and escaped.*
2 If something **slips out**, you tell it to someone without intending to. ❑ *I'm sorry, I was just talking to him and your name slipped out.* ❑ *I didn't mean to say anything. It slipped out.*

○ **slip 'out of**
If you **slip out of** something, you take off clothing quickly and easily.
slip out of something ❑ *She slipped out of her working clothes.*

○ **'slip through**
1 If you **slip through** something, you move quietly through it, usually without being noticed.
slip through something ❑ *He slipped through an open window and was gone.*
2 If something or someone **slips through** a system or **slips through**, the system allows something to happen that it should have prevented.

slip through something ❑ *How did these criminals slip through the security checks?* ❑ *Too many young people slip through the net and end up without a proper education.*
slip through ❑ *If you don't pay close attention, mistakes will slip through.*
● If something or someone **slips through** your **fingers** or **hands**, they escape or are lost. ❑ *He had allowed an amazing opportunity to slip through his fingers.*

○ **'slip to**
1 If you **slip** something **to** someone, you give it to them secretly.
slip something to someone ❑ *Eva slipped a £20 note to the woman.*
2 If something **slips to** a lower level or standard, it falls to that level or standard.
slip to something ❑ *Shares slipped to 117p.* ❑ *The club had slipped to the bottom of Division Four.*

○ **slip 'up** [INFORMAL]
If you **slip up**, you make a mistake. ❑ *We must have slipped up somewhere.* ❑ *She's slipped up in her calculations.* ● A **slip-up** is a careless mistake. [INFORMAL] ❑ *We can't afford any slip-ups.* ❑ *There's been a slip-up somewhere.*

slog /slɒg/ (**slogs, slogging, slogged**)
○ **slog a'way**
If you **slog away**, you work hard at something for a long time. **= slave away, beaver away** ❑ [+ at] *The kids are slogging away at their revision.* ❑ *He's been slogging away all morning clearing the yard.*

○ **'slog through**
1 If you **slog through** something, you move through it with a lot of difficulty and effort. **= plough through**
slog through something ❑ *They had to slog through twenty feet of snow to get there.*
2 If you **slog through** something, you do something that takes a long time and a lot of effort. **= plough through**
slog through something ❑ *We still have four more games to slog through before the end of the season.*

slop /slɒp/ (**slops, slopping, slopped**)
○ **slop a'round** (or **slop about** [mainly BRITISH])
1 If you **slop around** or **slop around** a place, you spend time in a place being lazy and doing nothing. **= slouch around**
slop around ❑ *If you want to slop around reading the paper all day, you can.*
slop around something ❑ *She spent the whole day slopping around the house in her slippers.*
2 If liquid **slops around** or **slops around** a

place, it moves around inside a container.
slop around ❑ *The fuel in the can slopped around as he walked.*

slop around something ❑ *Water was slopping around the bottom of the boat.*

slop 'out [BRITISH]
To **slop out** means to empty buckets that prisoners use as toilets. ❑ *Prisoners have to slop out first thing in the morning.*

slop 'over
If a liquid **slops over** or **slops over** something, it spills over the edge of a container.
slop over ❑ *Some of the milk slopped over onto the grass.*

slop over something ❑ *Water from the basin slopped over her feet, soaking her shoes.*

slope /sləʊp/ (slopes, sloping, sloped)
slope 'into [INFORMAL]
If someone **slopes into** a place, they go into it quickly and quietly so that no one notices them.
slope into somewhere ❑ *They sloped into their hotel at 6am.*

slope 'off [INFORMAL]
If you **slope off**, you go away quickly and quietly, especially in order to avoid something. ❑ *He must have sloped off home early today.*

slope 'out of [INFORMAL]
If someone **slopes out of** a place, they leave it quickly and quietly, especially in order to avoid something.
slope out of somewhere ❑ *Richard sloped out of the room.*

slosh /slɒʃ/ (sloshes, sloshing, sloshed)
slosh a'round
1 If a liquid **sloshes around** or **sloshes around** somewhere, it moves around in different directions.
slosh around ❑ *Water was sloshing around in the canoe.*

slosh around something ❑ *The water sloshed around the bridge.*

2 If you **slosh** a liquid **around** or **slosh** it **around** something, you make it move around in different directions.
slosh something around ❑ *She poured a glass of milk and sloshed it around.*

slosh something around something ❑ *He took a mouthful of water and sloshed it around his mouth.*

3 If money **is sloshing around** or **sloshing around** a place, there is a lot of it available or people are spending a lot. [INFORMAL]
be sloshing around ❑ *There is plenty of poverty*

in the country but there is also a lot of money sloshing around.

be sloshing around somewhere ❑ *The oil wealth sloshing around the region has drawn people from many places.*

slot /slɒt/ (slots, slotting, slotted)
slot 'in
1 If someone or something **slots in**, or if you **slot** them **in**, a time or place is found for them in a system, an organization or an activity.
slot in ❑ *With her fashionable hair and clothes, she slotted in perfectly.*

slot someone/something in or **slot in someone/something** ❑ *She managed to slot in an interview with the President.*

slot someone/something in something ❑ *Can you slot another meeting in your schedule?*
2 If something **slots in**, or if you **slot** it **in**, it fits into a narrow space.
slot in ❑ *The metal parts slot in here.*

slot something in or **slot in something** ❑ *Tamsin slotted in a fresh filter, measured coffee into it, and switched on the machine.*

slot something in something ❑ *The monastery is basically a rectangle slotted in a gap in the hillside.*

slot 'into
1 If someone or something **slots into** something, or if you **slot** them **into** it, a time or place is found for them in a system, an organization or an activity.
slot someone/something into something ❑ *We can slot a few more sessions into the timetable somewhere.*

slot into something ❑ *It can be difficult for new students to slot into the class.*

● If things **slot into place**, they form a whole that makes sense or that you can understand. ❑ *The different aspects of my job were beginning to slot into place.*
2 If something **slots into** something, or if you **slot** it **into** something, it fits into a narrow space in it.
slot into something ❑ *Your card slots into the machine here.*

slot something into something ❑ *The frame was built separately and then slotted into place.*

slouch /slaʊtʃ/ (slouches, slouching, slouched)
slouch a'round (or slouch about [mainly BRITISH])
If you **slouch around** or **slouch around** a place, you spend time being lazy and not doing anything. = **slop around**
slouch around ❑ *She slouched about in a dressing gown.*

slouch around something ❏ *Are you just going to slouch around the house all day?*

slough /slʌf/ (sloughs, sloughing, sloughed)

○ **slough 'off**

1 If you **slough** something **off**, you get rid of something that you no longer need. [FORMAL]

slough off something or **slough something off** ❏ *He saw the move as an opportunity to slough off unwanted friendships.*

2 If an animal **sloughs off** its outer skin, the skin comes off as part of a natural process.

slough off something or **slough something off** ❏ *The snake regularly sloughs off its skin.*

3 If something such as skin **is sloughed off** or **sloughs off**, it comes away from the body part it is attached to and comes off or out of the body. = **shed**

be sloughed off ❏ *As the dead cells are sloughed off, the skin becomes red and irritated.*

slough off ❏ *He rubbed more grease over the patches where the skin had sloughed off.*

slow /sləʊ/ (slows, slowing, slowed)

✪ **slow 'down** (or **slow up**)

1 If something or someone **slows down**, or if something or someone **slows** them **down**, they start to move or happen more slowly. ≠ **speed up**

slow down ❏ *The van slowed down and then stopped.* ❏ *The driver asked if we needed help as he slowed up.* ❏ [+ to] *He noticed the police car so he slowed down to thirty miles an hour.*

slow something down ❏ *The driver slowed the train down.* ❏ *Concentrate on your breathing, trying to slow it down.* ❏ *The steep hill at the end of the race slowed them up.*

slow down something ❏ *If you slow down the recording, you can see more clearly what happened.*

NOTE **Decelerate** is a more formal word for **slow down**.

2 If something **slows down** or if you **slow** it **down**, it becomes less active or intense.

slow down ❏ *Economic growth has slowed down dramatically.* ❏ *Shopkeepers have complained that business is slowing down.*

slow something down ❏ *It is not possible to reverse the progress of the disease, but you can slow it down.*

slow down something ❏ *These procedures can slow down productivity.* ● A **slowdown** is a reduction in speed or activity. ❏ *There were no signs of an economic slowdown.* ❏ [+ in] *He predicts a slowdown in the rate of expansion of world trade.* ● A **slowdown** is a protest by

workers in which they deliberately work slowly. [AMERICAN] ❏ *There were rent strikes and work slowdowns.*

3 If someone **slows down**, or if something **slows** them **down**, they become less active or energetic. = **relax**

slow down ❏ *You're working too hard. You need to slow down.*

slow someone down or **slow down someone** ❏ *He had arthritis, which was slowing him down a little.*

○ **slow 'up** → see **slow down**

smack /smæk/ (smacks, smacking, smacked)

○ **'smack of**

If something **smacks of** something bad, it seems to be or have that thing. = **savour of**

smack of something ❏ *These secret consultations smacked of a cover-up.*

smart /smɑːt/ (smarts, smarting, smarted)

○ **smart from** (or **smart over**)

If you **are smarting from** criticism or failure, you feel upset about it.

be smarting from something ❏ *The team is still smarting from its 7-0 defeat.* ❏ *He is smarting over criticism of his work.*

smarten /'smɑːtən/ (smartens, smartening, smartened)

○ **smarten 'up**

If you **smarten up** a person or place or if someone **smartens up**, they look neater and tidier. = **spruce up**

smarten up ❏ *We should smarten up a bit before we go out.*

smarten someone/something up or **smarten up someone/something** ❏ *The old cinema has been smartened up.* ❏ *Can't you smarten yourself up a bit?*

smash /smæʃ/ (smashes, smashing, smashed)

○ **smash 'down**

If you **smash** something **down**, you hit it and break it so that it falls onto the ground

smash something down or **smash down something** ❏ *He threatened to smash the door down if I didn't open it.* ❏ *The hurricane smashed down trees and houses.*

○ **smash 'in**

To **smash** something **in** means to hit it very hard so that it breaks, often so that the pieces fall inwards.

smash something in or **smash in something** ❏ *We'll smash the window in.* ❏ *Someone had overturned furniture and smashed in the television*

smash 'up

1 If you **smash** something **up**, you hit it so that it breaks into many pieces and is completely destroyed.
smash something up or **smash up something** ❑ He started smashing up all the furniture. ❑ Vandals came in and smashed the place up.

2 If you **smash up** your car, you badly damage it by crashing it into something. **= wreck**
smash something up or **smash up something** ❑ Six students smashed up a car. ❑ Her car got smashed up in a road accident.

• A **smash-up** is a bad car crash. [INFORMAL] ❑ We saw a terrible smash-up on the way home.

smell /smel/ (smells, smelling, smelled/smelt)

'smell of

1 If something or someone **smells of** a particular thing, they have a smell like that thing.
smell of something ❑ The room was hot and smelt of hospitals. ❑ She smelled of soap and toothpaste.

2 If something **smells of** an unpleasant quality, it seems to have that quality. **= smack of, savour of**
smell of something ❑ Such an action would have smelt of defeat.

smell 'out

1 If you **smell** someone or something **out**, you are able to find them, even when they are hidden or not obvious. **= root out**
smell out something/someone or **smell something/someone out** ❑ She was a reporter who could always smell out a good story.

2 If a person or animal **smells** something **out**, they find it by following its smell.
smell out something or **smell something out** ❑ We'll take the dog – she'll smell those rabbits out.

smoke /sməʊk/ (smokes, smoking, smoked)

smoke 'out

1 If you **smoke out** a person or animal, you force them to come out of a place by filling it with smoke.
smoke out someone/something or **smoke someone/something out** ❑ The man was smoking out a bees' nest.

2 If you **smoke** someone or something **out**, you find them or force them to reveal themselves.
smoke out someone/something or **smoke someone/something out** ❑ We are using modern technology to smoke out tax evaders.

smooth /smuːð/ (smooths, smoothing, smoothed)

smooth 'down

If you **smooth** something **down**, you press it with your hands to make it flat. **= flatten**
smooth down something or **smooth something down** ❑ Gertrude smoothed down her dress. ❑ She smoothed down her short blonde hair.

smooth 'out

1 If you **smooth** something **out**, you press it with your hand or with a tool in order to make it flat. **= flatten**
smooth out something or **smooth something out** ❑ Martha smoothed out the newspaper on the table. ❑ He put a clean sheet on the bed and smoothed the creases out.

2 If something **smooths** something **out** or if it **smooths out**, it becomes flat or even after having had lumps or bumps.
smooth out something or **smooth something out** ❑ These skin creams claim to smooth out wrinkles.
smooth out ❑ The wind dropped and the sea smoothed out.

3 If you **smooth out** a process or situation, it becomes more even and regular and its problems are solved. **= even out**
smooth out something or **smooth something out** ❑ We still need to smooth out a few problems in the system. ❑ I'll see if I can smooth things out with her.

smooth 'over

If you **smooth over** something, you make a problem or difficulty seem less serious and easier to deal with. **= gloss over**
smooth over something ❑ I tried to smooth over the awkwardness of this first meeting.

snag /snæg/ (snags, snagging, snagged)

'snag on

If you **snag** something **on** a sharp or rough object, or if something **snags on** a sharp or rough object, it gets caught on the object and tears or gets damaged.
snag something on something ❑ She snagged her scarf on a rose bush.
snag on something ❑ Annie's hair snagged on her bracelet.

snap /snæp/ (snaps, snapping, snapped)

'snap at

1 If someone **snaps at** you, they speak to you in a sudden angry way.
snap at someone ❑ 'Shut up, Maria!' Phil snapped at her.

2 If an animal such as a dog **snaps at** you, it tries to bite you.

snap at someone/something ❑ *The dog snapped viciously at my hand.*

○ **snap 'out**

If something **snaps out**, it is heard suddenly and loudly. ❑ *The sound snapped out in the night like a pistol shot.*

○ **snap 'out of**

If you **snap out of** a sad mood or a moment of concentration, you suddenly change so you are more cheerful or are paying attention to things around you.

snap out of something ❑ *I snapped out of this gloomy mood the moment a friend called.* ❑ *She suddenly snapped out of her daydream.*

● If you tell someone to **snap out of it**, you want them to stop being sad. ❑ *It's no use just telling a depressed patient to snap out of it.*

✪ **snap 'up**

1 If you **snap** something **up**, you buy it as quickly as possible.

snap something up ❑ *The painting is valued at £8 million, and there are wealthy buyers waiting to snap it up.*

snap up something ❑ *They were snapping up shares in steel companies.*

be snapped up ❑ *These houses are usually snapped up as soon as they go on the market.*

2 If you **snap** something **up**, you take advantage of an opportunity as quickly as possible.

snap something up ❑ *When offered a job in government, he snapped it up.*

snap up something ❑ *I would have expected him to snap up a chance like this.*

snarl /snɑːl/ (**snarls, snarling, snarled**)

○ **snarl 'up**

1 When traffic **snarls up** or **is snarled up**, it cannot move freely because the road is blocked.

be snarled up ❑ *The traffic was snarled up due to an accident on the motorway.*

snarl up ❑ *There were fears that traffic in the city would snarl up completely.*

2 If a process **is snarled up**, or if something **snarls** it **up**, it is prevented it from continuing or working smoothly.

be snarled up ❑ *The whole investigation is snarled up in bureaucracy.*

snarl up something or **snarl something up** ❑ *There are so few hospital beds that even a few extra emergency patients snarl up the system.*

snatch /snætʃ/ (**snatches, snatching, snatched**)

○ **snatch a'way**

If you **snatch** something **away**, you take it

from someone with a sudden forceful movement. = **grab**

snatch away something or **snatch something away** ❑ *He snatched away the letter before she could read it.* ❑ [+ **from**] *She snatched the scissors away from the baby.*

○ **snatch 'up**

If you **snatch** something **up**, you pick it up with a sudden forceful movement. = **grab**

snatch up something or **snatch something up** ❑ *I snatched up the glass just as it began to fall.* ❑ *The phone rang. She snatched it up.*

sneak /sniːk/ (**sneaks, sneaking, sneaked**)

> The form **snuck** is also used in American English for the past tense and past participle.

○ **sneak 'up on**

1 If someone **sneaks up on** you, they try and approach you without being seen or heard. = **creep up on**

sneak up on someone ❑ *She sneaked up on him and shouted 'Surprise!'.*

2 If something **sneaks up on** you, it happens when you are not expecting it. = **creep up on**

sneak up on someone ❑ *It's hard to know exactly when the illness began. It sneaks up on you*

sneer /snɪə/ (**sneers, sneering, sneered**)

○ **'sneer at**

If you **sneer at** someone or something, you talk about them or smile in an unpleasant way that shows you do not respect them.

sneer at someone/something ❑ *He always sneered at my choice of clothes.*

sneeze /sniːz/ (**sneezes, sneezing, sneezed**)

○ **'sneeze at**

If something is **not to be sneezed at**, it is worth having. = **not to be sniffed at** ❑ *Three thousand pounds a month is not to be sneezed at.* ❑ *It was an invitation not to be sneezed at.*

sniff /snɪf/ (**sniffs, sniffing, sniffed**)

○ **sniff a'round** (or **sniff about, sniff round** [mainly BRITISH])

1 If someone **sniffs around** or **sniffs around** a place, they try to find out information, especially information that someone does not want them to know. = **nose around**

sniff around ❑ *We don't want journalists sniffing around.*

sniff around something ❑ *A few days ago some guy was sniffing around the site, asking questions.*

2 To **sniff around** someone means to try to get them, for example as a sexual partner, employee, or client. [INFORMAL]

sniff around someone ❏ *When I went away, I was sure that other men would be sniffing round her.*

'sniff at

If you **sniff at** something, you say or suggest that it is not very good.

sniff at something ❏ *To get respect from those who sniff at our efforts, we have to be the best.*

● If something is **not to be sniffed at**, it is worth having. ❏ *A fee of three per cent was not to be sniffed at.*

sniff 'out

1 If you **sniff** something **out**, you discover it, especially when it is hidden or secret. **= nose out** [INFORMAL]

sniff out something or **sniff something out** ❏ *They sniffed out some lovely little quiet beaches.* ❏ *Good reporters don't get stories just by paying for information – they sniff them out.*

2 When a dog **sniffs** something **out**, it finds it using its sense of smell.

sniff out something or **sniff something out** ❏ *A police dog, trained to sniff out explosives, found evidence of a bomb in the apartment.*

sniff 'round → see **sniff around**

snipe /snaɪp/ (snipes, sniping, sniped)

'snipe at

1 If someone **snipes at** someone or something, they criticize them.

snipe at someone/something ❏ *The two party leaders have continued to snipe at each other through the media.*

2 If someone **snipes at** someone, they shoot at them from a hidden position.

snipe at someone ❏ *Gunmen have repeatedly sniped at U.S. Army positions.*

snitch /snɪtʃ/ (snitches, snitching, snitched)

'snitch on [INFORMAL]

If someone **snitches on** a person, they tell a teacher, parent, etc. about something wrong which that person has done.

snitch on someone ❏ *She felt like a fifth-grader who had snitched on a classmate.*

snow /snəʊ/ (snows, snowing, snowed)

snow 'in (or snow up)

If you **are snowed in**, you are prevented from leaving a place because there is so much snow on the ground.

be snowed in ❏ *We were snowed in for a week and couldn't get to school.* ❏ *We used to get snowed up in the winter.*

snow 'under

If you **are snowed under**, you have more work to deal with than you can manage.

be snowed under ❏ *I'm sorry I haven't answered your e-mail yet – I'm snowed under.* ❏ [+ with] *We are snowed under with orders.*

○ **snow 'up** → see **snow in**

snuff /snʌf/ (snuffs, snuffing, snuffed)

○ **snuff 'out**

1 To **snuff** something **out** means to end it using violence or force. **= crush**

snuff out something or **snuff something out** ❏ *He vowed to snuff out corruption.*

be snuffed out ❏ *Their lives had been snuffed out.*

2 If you **snuff out** a candle or a flame, you put it out by pinching or covering it.

snuff out something or **snuff something out** ❏ *She snuffed out the candle and closed her eyes.*

NOTE **Extinguish** is a formal word for **snuff out**.

snuggle /'snʌgəl/ (snuggles, snuggling, snuggled)

○ **snuggle 'down**

If you **snuggle down**, you move deeper into your bedclothes in order to be warm and comfortable. ❏ *We got sleeping bags out and snuggled down.* ❏ *Snuggle down and go to sleep, now.*

○ **snuggle 'up**

If you **snuggle up**, you settle yourself into a warm, comfortable position close to someone. **= cuddle up** ❏ [+ to] *The child snuggled up to me to listen to the story.*

soak /səʊk/ (soaks, soaking, soaked)

○ **'soak in**

If you **soak** yourself **in** something, you study a subject very intensely.

soak yourself in something ❏ *I soaked myself in the works of Dickens and George Eliot.*

○ **soak 'off**

If you **soak** something **off** or **soak** it **off** a surface, you remove it using water to loosen it.

soak off something or **soak something off** ❏ *Soak off the labels overnight.*

soak something off something ❏ *He's going to soak all the paint off it.*

○ **soak 'through**

If someone or something **is soaked through**, they are completely wet.

be soaked through ❏ *By morning, their gear was soaked through.*

⊙ **soak 'up**

1 If something **soaks up** a liquid, it absorbs it. **= absorb**

soak up something ❏ *The dry soil soaked up a huge volume of water.*

soak something up ❑ Put some towels on the spilt water to soak it up. ❑ The thick paper soaks ink up like a sponge.

2 If you **soak** something **up**, you enjoy experiencing it. [INFORMAL]

soak up something ❑ The first time I went to New York I wandered around in a daze, soaking up the atmosphere. ❑ She listened avidly, soaking up every word.

soak something up ❑ She sat outside in the sunshine soaking it up. ❑ They paused to soak the scene up.

3 If something **soaks up** money or resources, it uses them.

soak up something ❑ Checking all the files is going to soak up a lot of man-hours.

soak something up ❑ Legal costs soaked a lot of the money up.

sob /sɒb/ (**sobs, sobbing, sobbed**)

○ **sob 'out**

If someone **sobs out** something, they try to say it while they are crying.

sob out something or **sob something out** ❑ He sobbed out the story of what had happened.

sober /'səʊbə/ (**sobers, sobering, sobered**)

○ **sober 'up**

If someone **sobers up** or if something **sobers** them **up**, they become less affected by the alcohol they have drunk.

sober up ❑ Police left him in the cells overnight to sober up.

sober someone up or **sober up someone** ❑ Walking in the rain seemed to have sobered him up.

sod /sɒd/ (**sods, sodding, sodded**)

○ **sod 'off** [BRITISH, INFORMAL, RUDE]

Sod off is an offensive way of telling someone to go away. ❑ They told him to sod off.

soften /'sɒfən, AM 'sɔːf-/ (**softens, softening, softened**)

○ **soften 'up**

1 If you **soften** someone **up**, you try to please them because you want them to do something for you. = **butter up**

soften someone up or **soften up someone** ❑ They tried to soften him up with bribes. ❑ He was hoping to soften up the committee before introducing his proposal.

2 To **soften** someone or something **up** means to make them weaker or easier to defeat by attacking or hurting them.

soften up someone/something or **soften someone/something up** ❑ Sleep deprivation is used to soften up prisoners and make them talk. ❑ The air assault was intended to soften the

country up for an invasion.

3 If someone **softens up**, they become more friendly or gentle, and less harsh. ❑ After discussing it with his wife, he softened up slightly. ❑ She has certainly softened up since I lo worked with her.

soldier /'səʊldʒə/ (**soldiers, soldiering, soldiered**)

○ **soldier 'on**

If you **soldier on**, you continue trying to d something even though it is difficult or unpleasant. ❑ It's hard to soldier on without a support.

sop /sɒp/ (**sops, sopping, sopped**)

○ **sop 'up**

To **sop** something **up** means to remove it from a surface by absorbing it.

sop up something or **sop something up** ❑ I sopped up the sauce on my plate with a piece of bread. ❑ If you spill some, use paper napkins t sop it up.

sort /sɔːt/ (**sorts, sorting, sorted**)

✪ **sort 'out**

1 If you **sort** things **out**, you arrange the so that they become organized, tidy, or ready. = **arrange**

sort out something ❑ It took quite a while to sort out all our luggage.

sort something out ❑ Sort them out alphabetically.

be sorted out ❑ Now I've got the spare room sorted out, with some new shelves and cupboards

2 If you **sort** things **out**, you divide them into different categories.

sort out something ❑ The test was intended t sort out the children capable of attempting the papers. ❑ [+ from] It is difficult to sort out fact from fiction.

sort something out ❑ [+ into] He gave me a li of names and I started sorting them out into groups.

3 If you **sort** something **out**, you solve a problem, misunderstanding, or disagreement.

sort something out ❑ They had been arguing, so we left them to sort it out. ❑ I want to sort things out between us.

sort out something ❑ Have you sorted out th mix-up with the dates?

sort itself out ❑ Problems like this often sort themselves out with time.

NOTE **Resolve** is a more formal word for **sort out**.

4 If you **sort** something **out** or **sort** someone **out** with something, you get or provide something for someone.

sort out something ❑ [+ *for*] Can we sort out some food for these people?

sort something/someone out ❑ I said I needed a car, and he promised to sort one out. ❑ Go to any sports shop and they will sort you out.

sort someone out something ❑ I'll sort you out some drinks while you're waiting.

5 If you **sort** yourself **out**, you deal with any problems, tasks or decisions that you have so that you are ready to continue life in a normal way. = **get yourself together**

sort yourself out ❑ If I leave the bedding here, can you sort yourselves out?

6 If you **sort** someone **out**, you punish them forcefully or violently. [BRITISH, INFORMAL]

sort someone out or **sort out someone** ❑ Her dad threatened to go down to his house and sort him out.

sound /saʊnd/ (**sounds, sounding, sounded**)

◗ **sound 'off** [INFORMAL]

If you **sound off**, you express your opinions strongly without being asked. ❑ [+ *about*] He was sounding off about the cost of living. ❑ [+ *on*] She's quite happy to sound off on any subject.

◗ **sound 'out**

1 If you **sound** someone **out**, you try to find out their views.

sound someone out or **sound out someone** ❑ I decided to sound out other members of the department first.

2 When a noise **sounds out**, it can be heard clearly above all the other sounds that are present. ❑ The ambulance's siren sounds out as it drives off.

soup /suːp/ (**soups, souping, souped**)

◗ **soup 'up** [INFORMAL]

1 If you **soup** something **up**, you make it more powerful.

soup up something or **soup something up** ❑ They fit new stereos to their cars and soup up the engines. ● A **souped-up** car has been altered so that it is more powerful. ❑ She drove a Mini with a souped-up engine.

2 If you **soup** something **up**, you improve it or make it more successful.

soup up something or **soup something up** ❑ She saw a way to soup up her faltering career. ● A **souped-up** version of something is an improved or more successful one. ❑ This is a souped-up version of their previous product.

pace /speɪs/ (**spaces, spacing, spaced**)

◗ **space 'out**

1 If you **space** things **out**, you arrange them so that they are not too close together, but have spaces or time between them.

space out something or **space something out** ❑ We began to space out our meetings. ❑ The document is easier to read if you space the columns out.

2 If someone is **spaced out**, they feel strange and cannot think clearly. [INFORMAL] ❑ He had just got off a 12-hour flight, and was feeling a bit spaced out.

spar /spɑː/ (**spars, sparring, sparred**)

○ **'spar with**

1 If you **spar with** someone, you practise fighting with them.

spar with someone ❑ I promised I'd spar with Willie Limond to help him prepare for his fight.

2 If you **spar with** someone, you argue with them but not in an aggressive or serious way.

spar with someone ❑ He has publicly sparred with Jackson on various issues.

spare /speə/ (**spares, sparing, spared**)

○ **'spare for**

If you **spare** time, money etc., **for** a particular purpose, you make it available for that purpose.

spare something for something ❑ She said that she could only spare 35 minutes for our meeting. ❑ We didn't have any money to spare for a holiday.

spark /spɑːk/ (**sparks, sparking, sparked**)

○ **spark 'off**

If one thing **sparks off** another, it causes it to exist or happen.

spark off something or **spark something off** ❑ His letter had sparked off a friendship between them. ❑ There are various rumours going around about what sparked the riots off.

speak /spiːk/ (**speaks, speaking, spoke, spoken**)

✪ **'speak for**

1 If you **speak for** people, you represent them and explain their views.

speak for someone ❑ We believe that we speak for the majority of the British people.

2 If you **speak for** an idea, a proposal, or a set of beliefs, you support it by explaining it and saying what is good about it. = **stand up for**

speak for something ❑ I spoke for going south. ❑ Lord Green stood up to speak for the plan.

3 If you **speak for** yourself, you say what you think, although it may not be what other people think.

speak for yourself ❑ I'm only speaking for myself, not for my colleagues.

• If you say to someone **speak for yourself!**, you mean that what they have just said is not true for you. ❏ *'We're all getting older and fatter.' – 'Speak for yourself!'*

4 If something **speaks for** itself, it is very obvious what it indicates, so it does not need explaining.

speak for itself ❏ *The facts in the case speak for themselves.* ❏ *The results of these experiments speak for themselves.*

5 If someone is **spoken for**, they are married or already have a boyfriend or girlfriend. ❏ *She liked a boy, but he was spoken for.*

6 If something is **spoken for**, it is not available because it is already being used by someone or for something. ❏ *Every minute of her time was spoken for.*

○ **speak 'out**

If you **speak out**, you say clearly and publicly that something or someone is bad or wrong. ❏ [+ against] *She spoke out against her husband at the hearing.* ❏ *If we see injustice, we must speak out.* • If you are **outspoken**, you give your opinions openly and honestly, even if they may shock or offend people. ❏ *She has been one of the government's most outspoken critics.*

❍ **speak 'up**

1 If you **speak up**, you say publicly what you believe. ❏ [+ for] *Never be frightened of speaking up for your beliefs.* ❏ *Why do they not speak up for themselves?* ❏ *If you object to this idea, then speak up.*

2 If you **speak up**, you speak more loudly. ❏ *Could you please speak up? We can't hear you at the back.*

speed /spiːd/ (**speeds, speeding, speeded**)

❍ **speed 'up**

1 If something **speeds up** or if you **speed** it **up**, it moves or travels faster.

speed up ❏ *The driver speeded up as he approached the lights.*

speed up something ❏ *He looked at the time and speeded up his pace.*

speed something up ❏ *Pressing the accelerator speeds the car up.* ❏ *You can do some slower movements, then speed them up a bit.*

NOTE **Accelerate** is a more formal word for **speed up.**

2 If a process **speeds up** or if something **speeds** it **up**, it happens at a faster rate.

speed up something ❏ *You can soak the prawns in warm water to speed up the defrosting process.* ❏ *Applying online can speed up your application.*

speed something up ❏ *The new government is determined to speed reforms up.*

speed up ❏ *Technological change is not slowing down; it is speeding up.*

NOTE **Accelerate** is a more formal word for **speed up.**

spell /spel/ (**spells, spelling, spelled/spelt**)

○ **spell 'out**

1 If you **spell** something **out**, you explain in detail or in a very clear way.

spell out something or **spell something out** ❏ *Isn't it obvious what he wants, or do I need to spell it out?* ❏ *He sometimes had to have things spelled out for him.*

NOTE **Explicate** is a more formal word for **spell out.**

2 If you **spell out** a word, you write or speak each letter in the word one after the other.

spell out something or **spell something out** ❏ *We had to spell out the words we heard.* ❏ *He gave his name to the receptionist and spelled it out.*

spew /spjuː/ (**spews, spewing, spewed**)

○ **spew 'out**

1 If an object **spews** something **out** or if something **spews out** of it, it produces something very quickly.

spew out something or **spew something out** ❏ *A bus passed, spewing out diesel fumes.*

spew out ❏ [+ of] *He stared at the paper spewing out of the fax machine.*

2 If someone **spews** something **out** or if something **spews out** of them, they say a lot of things quickly, especially angry or offensive things.

spew out something or **spew something out** ❏ *I was just talking, spewing out whatever came into my mind.*

spew out ❏ [+ of] *Spiteful, cutting remarks spewed out from his mouth.*

○ **spew 'up** [INFORMAL]

If someone **spews up**, they vomit. = **throw up** ❏ *He spewed up as soon as he got outside.*

spice /spaɪs/ (**spices, spicing, spiced**)

○ **spice 'up**

1 If you **spice** something **up**, you make it more exciting or lively.

spice something up or **spice up something** ❏ *Their relationship had become dull and she wanted to spice it up a bit.* ❏ [+ with] *The journalist tried to spice up the story with a few invented details.*

2 If you **spice** food **up**, you make it taste stronger or more interesting by adding spices.

spice something up or **spice up something** ❏ *If you want to spice things up, add a touch of cayenne pepper.*

pill /spɪl/ (spills, spilling, spilled/spilt)

○ **spill 'out**

1 If liquids or objects **spill out**, they fall out of a container. ❑ [+ of] *Water spilled out of the vase.* ❑ [+ onto] *Petrol spilled out onto the ground.*

2 If people or things **spill out** of a place, large numbers of them come from it in a disorganized way. = **pour out** ❑ [+ of] *People were spilling out of bars, talking loudly.*

3 If light **spills out**, it can be seen coming from inside a place. ❑ [+ from] *Light spilled out across the landing from under the bedroom door.* ❑ *The front door opened and light spilled out into the yard.*

4 If you **spill** something **out** or if it **spills out**, you tell someone or talk about something in a hurried way, often without intending to.

spill out something or **spill something out** ❑ *He will spill out his life story to a total stranger.*
spill out ❑ *The words just spilled out before I could stop them.*

○ **spill 'over**

1 If liquid **spills over** or **spills over** something, it flows or is spilled over the edge of a container.
spill over ❑ *The bucket was full of water, almost spilling over.*
spill over something ❑ *His hand trembled and some coffee spilt over the edge of his cup.*

2 If people or things **spill over** into a place, they move into it because there are too many of them to fit or stay somewhere. ❑ [+ into] *Crowds filled the pavements and spilled over into the road.* ● The **overspill** from a place consists of people or parts of it which do not fit there and so have to go somewhere else. ❑ *The overspill from Heathrow Airport became concentrated on Gatwick.*

3 If something **spills over** into another area of activity, it has an accidental or negative effect on it. ❑ [+ into] *Troubles at work could also spill over into your private life.*

4 If someone's feelings **spill over**, they express them suddenly because they can no longer control them. ❑ [+ into] *Some of these tensions could spill over into violence.*

pin /spɪn/ (spins, spinning, spun)

○ **spin a'round** (or **spin round** [mainly BRITISH])

1 If someone **spins around**, they turn their head or body quickly to face in a different direction. ❑ *She spun around angrily to glare at them.* ❑ *I heard a noise behind me and spun around.*

2 If something or someone **spins around**, they turn quickly around a central point. ❑ *A tyre blew out, and the car spun around and skidded off the track.* ❑ *The dancers started spinning round and round.*

○ **spin 'off**

1 If a part of a business **is spun off**, or if you **spin** it **off**, you separate it from the rest in order to create a new company.
be spun off ❑ *This was a minor division of the company that could easily be spun off.*
spin something off or **spin off something** ❑ *They spun off their media departments to create a separate company.* ● A **spin-off** is something useful that develops unexpectedly as a result of activities which were intended to achieve something else. ❑ *These substances now in common domestic use are spin-offs from the space program.*

2 If you **spin** something **off**, or if something **spins off**, you create something such as a new book, film, or television show using ideas or characters from something that is already successful.
spin something off or **spin off something** ❑ *The toys even spun off their own show.* ❑ [+ into] *The TV series became so popular that Disney spun it off into a movie.*
spin off ❑ [+ from] *A successful concert tour spun off from the show.* ● A **spin-off** is a new book, film, or show that is created using ideas or characters from a book, film, or show that is already successful. ❑ *When the series ended he starred in his own spin-off.*

○ **spin 'out**

If you **spin** something **out**, you make it last as long as possible.
spin out something or **spin something out** ❑ *I tried to spin out the conversation until the others arrived.*

○ **spin 'round** → see spin around

spirit /'spɪrɪt/ (spirits, spiriting, spirited)

○ **spirit a'way** (or **spirit off**)

If someone or something **is spirited away** or if you **spirit** them **away**, they are quickly and secretly taken away.
be spirited away ❑ *At the end of the concert the band is spirited away in a minibus.*
spirit someone/something away or **spirit away someone/something** ❑ *He was alleged to have spirited away hundreds of war criminals to safe havens.*

spit /spɪt/ (spits, spitting, spat)

○ **spit 'out**

1 If you **spit** something **out**, you get rid of it from your mouth by blowing hard.
spit out something or **spit something out**

❑ He spat out a mouthful of water. ❑ She tasted the soup, then spat it out with an expression of disgust.

2 If you **spit out** words, you say them in an angry way.

spit out something or **spit something out**
❑ The man spat out a string of insults. ❑ 'Traitor!' he spat out. ❑ He spat his answer out contemptuously.

3 If you tell someone to **spit it out**, you are encouraging them to say something when they seem to be finding this difficult. [INFORMAL] ❑ Spit it out, Wesley – what are you trying to say?

splash /splæʃ/ (splashes, splashing, splashed)

○ **splash 'down**
When a space vehicle **splashes down**, it lands in the sea at the end of a space flight. ❑ The three astronauts splashed down safely this morning. ● A **splashdown** is the landing of a space vehicle in the sea after a flight.

○ **splash 'out** [BRITISH, INFORMAL]
If you **splash out**, you spend a lot of money on something. ❑ [+ on] We splashed out on a four-star hotel. ❑ I decided to splash out and get some new shoes.

split /splɪt/ (splits, splitting)

The form **split** is used in the present tense and is the past tense and past participle of the verb.

○ **split 'off**
1 If you **split off** a part of something, or if it **splits off**, it becomes separated from the rest. **= break off**
split off something or **split something off**
❑ He split off a big piece of wood using an axe. ❑ [+ from] A busy ring-road splits the suburbs off from the city.
split off ❑ [+ from] A particle splits off from the nucleus of the atom.
2 When people **split off**, they stop being members of a group and form a separate one. **= break away** ❑ [+ from] The far left split off from the rest of the party. ❑ They decided to split off and form their own club.

○ **'split on** [BRITISH, INFORMAL]
If you **split on** someone, you tell a secret about them to other people. **= tell on**
split on someone ❑ If I wanted to tell, I could split on you any time.

◑ **split 'up**
1 If you **split** something **up** or if it **splits up**, it is divided into smaller sections or parts. **= separate**

split something up ❑ [+ into] The children might work better if you split them up into small groups. ❑ We decided to split the task up and each tackle one aspect.
split up something ❑ [+ into] One idea is to split up the session into a series of activities. ❑ Weeks and months are our way of splitting up the year.
split up ❑ [+ into] I think we should split up into working groups.
2 If people **split up** or if something or someone **splits** them **up**, they are separated.
split up ❑ We'll split up and approach the village from different directions.
split someone up ❑ Unemployment splits families up, as people travel to find work. ❑ [+ from] We don't want to split him up from his friends.
split up someone ❑ I had to split up two girls who always talk in class.
be split up ❑ If you are split up for any reason, go to the meeting point by the gate.
3 If two people **split up** or if something **splits** them **up**, they end their relationship or marriage.
split up ❑ I went out with him for a year and then we split up for three months. ❑ [+ with] After he split up with his wife, he went to Arizona.
split someone up ❑ Nothing is ever going to split us up.
split up someone ❑ A tragedy like this can split up even the most devoted couple.

spoil /spɔɪl/ (spoils, spoiling, spoiled/spoilt)

○ **'spoil for**
If you **are spoiling for** something, you want to have an argument or fight and are willing to try and start one.
be spoiling for something ❑ He came into work in a foul mood, spoiling for a fight.

sponge /spʌndʒ/ (sponges, sponging, sponged)

○ **sponge 'down**
If you **sponge** something or someone **down**, you clean them by wiping them with a wet sponge or cloth.
sponge down something/someone or **sponge something/someone down**
❑ Sponge down the work surface with a wet cloth. ❑ You may need to sponge him down with cool water to lower his temperature.

○ **'sponge on** (or **sponge off**) [INFORMAL]
If someone **sponges on** other people, they get money and other things from them without giving anything back.

sponge on someone ❏ She didn't like the way his sister sponged on them. ❏ They believe these people are lazy and sponging off the government.

spoon /spu:n/ (spoons, spooning, spooned)
○ **spoon 'out**
If you **spoon out** food, you serve portions of it using a spoon. = serve out
spoon out something or **spoon something out** ❏ Cut the stuffed pumpkin open and spoon out the filling. ❏ [+ of] He was spooning baked beans out of a pan.

○ **spoon 'up**
If you **spoon up** food, you eat it or pick it up using a spoon.
spoon up something or **spoon something up** ❏ She spooned up the last of her soup. ❏ He spooned the rice up and fed it to the baby.

spout /spaʊt/ (spouts, spouting, spouted)
○ **spout 'out**
If someone **spouts out** something, they say it without really thinking about what they are saying.
spout out something ❏ He spouted out a lot of clichés about business.

sprawl /sprɔ:l/ (sprawls, sprawling, sprawled)
○ **sprawl 'out**
If you **sprawl out** or **are sprawled out**, you sit or lie with your arms or legs spread out in a relaxed way. = stretch out
sprawl out ❏ Steven sprawled out on the couch.
be sprawled out ❏ Thomas was sitting under a tree, his legs sprawled out.

spread /spred/ (spreads, spreading)

The form **spread** is used in the present tense and is the past tense and past participle of the verb.

○ **spread 'out**
1 If something **spreads out** or if you **spread** it **out**, it grows wider or covers a wider area than before.
spread out ❏ Rain is spreading out from the west across the rest of the country.
be spread out ❏ Her long black hair was spread out across the pillow.
spread something out ❏ Spoon a little filling onto each pancake and spread it out evenly.
spread out something ❏ She spread out the ribbon to form a fan shape.
2 If people **spread out**, they move away from each other so that they are further apart. ❏ They spread out, checking all the exits. ❏ The gang spread out across the pavement, completely blocking it.

3 If people or things **are spread out**, they are far apart over a large area.
be spread out ❏ There are several excellent Indian restaurants spread out all over London. ❏ The team should be more spread out on the field.
4 If something **is spread out** or **spreads out**, you can see it covering a large area.
spread out ❏ I turned around at the top of the hill. The farmland spread out below me.
be spread out ❏ The lights of Lisbon were spread out before them.
5 If you **spread** something **out**, you open it or arrange it on a surface. = lay out
spread out something ❏ The surgeon spread out his instruments on the table. ❏ The nets had been spread out to dry.
spread something out ❏ She shuffled the cards and spread them out. ❏ He spread the reports out on the desk.
6 If you **spread out** parts of your body, you stretch and move them so that they are far apart.
spread something out ❏ He spread his arms and legs out to steady himself.
spread out something ❏ She spread out her hands in a gesture of helplessness. ❏ She lifted up a hand and held it there, the fingers spread out.
7 If you **spread** something **out**, it happens over a long time period or with spaces of time in between events, rather than all at one time.
spread something out ❏ You can choose to pay the whole amount at once or spread the payments out.
spread out something ❏ [+ over] They propose to spread out the reforms over a number of years.
be spread out ❏ [+ over] You hardly notice the damage because it is spread out over such a long period of time.

○ **'spread over**
If something **is spread over** a period of time or **spreads over** it, it happens throughout that period, rather than at a single point.
be spread over something ❏ The job losses may not seem so bad when spread over a longer period.
spread something over something ❏ You can spread repayments over 6, 12, or 18 months.
spread over something ❏ They had experience spreading over twenty years.

spring /sprɪŋ/ (springs, springing, sprang, sprung)
○ **spring 'back**
If something **springs back**, it quickly returns to its original position or shape. ❏ After you stretch a muscle, it will spring back into place.

○ **'spring from** (or **spring out of**)

1 If one thing **springs from** another, it is caused by it.

spring from something ❏ *Many psychological problems spring from self-doubt.* ❏ *Her hostility to him sprang out of sheer envy.*

2 If you ask **where** someone or something **has sprung from**, you are surprised to see them. ❏ *Hello, Nick, where did you spring from?* ❏ *So where had all these new towns suddenly sprung from?*

○ **'spring on**

1 If you **spring** something **on** someone, you suddenly say or do something which surprises them.

spring something on someone ❏ *I decided to spring a little surprise on him.* ❏ *Why did you spring it on me at the last minute like that?*

2 If a person or animal **springs on** you, they suddenly attack you. = **leap on**

spring on someone ❏ *They had opened the door of a tiger's cage, and the beast had sprung on me.*

○ **spring 'out of** → see **spring from**

⊕ **spring 'up**

1 If something **springs up**, it suddenly appears or starts to exist. ❏ *Grass will spring up within days of a rainstorm.* ❏ *These friendships spring up and very often don't last.*

2 If you **spring up**, you stand up very quickly. = **jump up** ❏ *He immediately sprang up to volunteer.*

○ **'spring upon** → see **spring on**

sprinkle /'sprɪŋkəl/ (**sprinkles, sprinkling, sprinkled**)

○ **'sprinkle with**

If you **sprinkle** a thing **with** a liquid or powder, you put small amounts of the liquid or powder all over it.

sprinkle something with something ❏ *Sprinkle the meat with salt.* ❏ *At the festival, candles are blessed and sprinkled with holy water.*

sprout /spraʊt/ (**sprouts, sprouting, sprouted**)

○ **sprout 'up**

If things **sprout up**, large numbers of them suddenly appear. = **spring up** ❏ *New buildings were suddenly sprouting up in the town.*

spruce /spruːs/ (**spruces, sprucing, spruced**)

○ **spruce 'up**

1 If you **spruce** yourself **up** or **spruce up**, you make yourself look cleaner and tidier or better dressed.

spruce yourself up ❏ *You need to spruce yourself up if you want her to go out on a date with you.*

spruce up ❏ *She came home from work, spruced up, and went straight out again.*

be spruced up ❏ *The children were all spruced up for the occasion.*

2 If you **spruce** something **up**, you improve its appearance.

spruce something up or **spruce up something** ❏ *If you spruce the house up a bit, it will be easier to sell.*

spur /spɜː/ (**spurs, spurring, spurred**)

○ **spur 'on**

If something **spurs** you **on**, it encourages you.

spur someone on or **spur on someone** ❏ *It was personal ambition that spurred him on.* ❏ *Spurred on by the cheers of the crowd, he crossed the finish line.*

spurt /spɜːt/ (**spurts, spurting, spurted**)

○ **spurt 'out**

If liquid **spurts out**, it comes out quickly and suddenly. ❏ *Blood spurted out from the wound.*

sputter /'spʌtə/ (**sputters, sputtering, sputtered**)

○ **sputter 'out**

1 If something **sputters out**, it gets weaker as it gradually stops existing or finishes. = **die** ❏ *The fire kept threatening to sputter out.* ❏ *The music starts very powerfully, but sputters out at the end.*

2 If someone **sputters out** something, they say it with difficulty, stopping and starting again suddenly.

sputter out something or **sputter something out** ❏ *I sputtered out awkwardly 'Sounds great!'* ❏ *He tried to sputter out a few words of explanation.*

spy /spaɪ/ (**spies, spying, spied**)

○ **'spy on** (or **spy upon**)

1 If you **spy on** someone, you watch them secretly.

spy on someone ❏ *From this balcony, they could spy on people in the garden below.* ❏ *She hid behind a bush to spy on him.*

2 If you **spy on** someone or something, you find out secret information about them and tell it to an enemy.

spy on someone/something ❏ *They asked him to spy on his own country.*

○ **spy 'out**

1 If you **spy out** an area, you look around it in order to get information about it.

spy out something or **spy something out** ❏ *They sent advance scouts to spy out the land.*

2 If you **spy** something **out**, you find it or notice it by looking.

spy out something or **spy something out**
❏ *They spied out some good picnic sites from their boat.*

'spy upon → see **spy on**

quare /skweə/ (**squares, squaring, squared**)

square a'way [AMERICAN]
If you **square** something **away** or get it **squared away**, you deal with it so that the situation is satisfactory.
be squared away ❏ *Once your work is all squared away, you can go.* ❏ *I apologized and tried to get things squared away with them.*
square away something or **square something away** ❏ *Negotiators have already squared away a lot of the agreements.*

square 'off
◼ If you **square** something **off**, you make its edge or corner straight.
square off something or **square something off** ❏ *Cut the bread and square off the slices by removing the crust.*
be squared off ❏ *The rounded corners would have to be squared off with a chisel.*
◼ If people or groups **square off**, they prepare to fight or compete with each other. ❏ [+ with] *Teenage gang members squared off with their rivals on the streets.* ❏ [+ against] *Top brands will square off against each other in our consumer tests.*

square 'up
◼ If you **square up** to someone, you stand facing them in a threatening way. ❏ [+ to] *At one point the two girls squared up to one another.* ❏ *The men were squaring up for a fight.*
NOTE **Confront** is a more formal word for **square up.**
◼ If you **square up** with someone, you pay money that you owe them. = **settle up** [INFORMAL] ❏ *Do you want to square up now or later?* ❏ [+ with] *I've got to square up with the bank before I can pay you.*

square 'up to
If you **square up to** a problem, you accept that you have to deal with it.
square up to something ❏ *You've got to square up to failure and try to carry on.*

quash /skwɒʃ/ (**squashes, squashing, squashed**)

squash 'in
If someone or something **squashes in** or is **squashed in**, they manage to get or be put into a place where there is not much room. = **squeeze in**
squash in ❏ *The crowd squashed in under the shelter.*

be squashed in ❏ *They had a tiny bedroom with a baby's cot squashed in at one side.*

squash 'into
If you **squash into** a place or **are squashed into** it, you manage to get inside it, even though there is not much room. = **squeeze into**
squash into something ❏ *All seven of them squashed into one car.*
be squashed into something ❏ *Too many people were squashed into one apartment.*

squash 'up
If someone **squashes up** or if someone or something **is squashed up**, they are very close together in a small space.
squash up ❏ *Can you squash up a bit?*
be squashed up ❏ *The four children sat squashed up inside the car.* ❏ *Her dress was squashed up in her case.*

squeak /skwiːk/ (**squeaks, squeaking, squeaked**)

'squeak through (or **squeak by**)
To **squeak through** or **squeak through** something means to only just be successful or accepted.
squeak through ❏ *He squeaked through by two votes.* ❏ *The Raiders only squeaked by with a 9-8 win.*
squeak through something ❏ *The tax package just squeaked through the Senate 51-50.*

squeal /skwiːl/ (**squeals, squealing, squealed**)

'squeal on [INFORMAL]
If someone **squeals on** another person, they inform the police or authorities about something wrong they have done.
squeal on someone ❏ *Someone must have squealed on us to the police.* ❏ *These kids would never squeal on their friends.*

squeeze /skwiːz/ (**squeezes, squeezing, squeezed**)

squeeze 'in
◼ If you **squeeze in** or **are squeezed in**, you manage to sit or stand in a place where there is not much room.
squeeze in ❏ *She squeezed in beside me.* ❏ *Can I just squeeze in there?* ❏ *Two could squeeze in if they weren't too large.*
be squeezed in ❏ *The passengers were all squeezed in on the back seat.*
◼ If you **squeeze** something **in**, you manage to fit it into a place where there is not much room.
squeeze in something ❏ *They were always trying to squeeze in more products on the overloaded shelves.*

squeeze something in ❏ If it's a very small piece of luggage, I might be able to squeeze it in.
be squeezed in ❏ A new bathroom had been squeezed in under the stairs.
3 If you **squeeze** something **in**, you manage to find time to do it. = **fit in**
squeeze in something ❏ Can we squeeze in another revision session before the exam?
squeeze something in ❏ I like to go for a run if I can squeeze it in before breakfast.
be squeezed in ❏ Leisure activities have to be squeezed in between school and homework.

○ **squeeze 'into**
1 If you **squeeze into** a place, you manage to get inside it, even though there is not much room. = **squash into**
squeeze into something ❏ Jill squeezed into the seat beside me.
2 If you **squeeze** something **into** a place or container, you manage to fit it into a place where there is not much room.
squeeze something into something
❏ Excitement grew as yet more cameramen squeezed their equipment into the back of the room.
3 If you **squeeze** something **into** a period of time, you do it in that time.
squeeze something into something ❏ We squeezed a lot into this morning's session.

○ **squeeze 'off**
If you **squeeze off** a shot, you fire a bullet from a gun.
squeeze off something ❏ I braced my rifle and squeezed off a shot.

○ **squeeze 'out**
1 If you **squeeze** something **out** of something, you make it come out by pressing very hard.
squeeze something out or **squeeze out something** ❏ Wet the sponge, then squeeze the surplus water out. ❏ [+ of] The breath was being squeezed out of his lungs.
2 If you **squeeze** something **out** of someone, you manage to persuade them to give it to you.
squeeze something out or **squeeze out something** ❏ [+ of] Has he been able to squeeze any more cash out of his parents?
3 If you **squeeze** someone **out**, you prevent them from taking part in an activity or group.
squeeze out someone or **squeeze someone out** ❏ Supermarkets have squeezed out the small producers.
be squeezed out ❏ The independent press have been squeezed out by official media.
NOTE **Exclude** is a more formal word for **squeeze out**.

○ **squeeze 'through**
If you **squeeze through** something or **squeeze through**, you manage to get through a small space.
squeeze through ❏ She opened the gate and squeezed through.
squeeze through something ❏ He escaped by squeezing through the window.

squirrel /'skwɪrəl, AM 'skwɜːrəl/ (**squirrels, squirrelling, squirrelled**)

American English uses the spellings **squirreling** and **squirreled**.

○ **squirrel a'way**
If you **squirrel** something **away**, you put it somewhere secret or safe to use later.
= **stash away, hoard**
squirrel away something or **squirrel something away** ❏ The CEO had managed to squirrel away funds in a Swiss bank account. ❏ He used to pick up interesting objects and squirrel them away all over the house.

stack /stæk/ (**stacks, stacking, stacked**)

○ **stack 'up**
1 If you **stack** things **up**, you arrange them in a tall pile. = **pile up**
stack up something or **stack something up** ❏ Melanie stacked up the plates and carried them to the sink. ❏ He carried in crates of oranges, stacking them up.
be stacked up ❏ The chairs were stacked up in piles at the sides of the hall.
2 If things **stack up** or if they **are stacked up**, there are a large number of them waiting to be dealt with.
stack up ❏ I like to deal with my emails quickly, as they soon stack up.
be stacked up ❏ I feel I've got too many jobs stacked up.
3 If planes **stack up** or **are stacked up**, they fly in circles at different levels above an airport, waiting to land.
stack up ❏ Over the bay he could see the early morning flights beginning to stack up.
be stacked up ❏ We were stacked up for 25 minutes at Heathrow.
4 If you talk about how one person or thing **stacks up** against others, you are talking about how they compare. [INFORMAL]
❏ [+ against] How does our marketing stack up against our rivals'? ❏ We investigated how the two competing theories stack up.
NOTE **Compare** is a more formal word for **stack up**.
5 If something does not **stack up**, it does not make sense or give the results you expect.

not stack up ❏ *There have been a number of explanations, but none of them stack up.* ❏ *We can see now that our forecasts don't stack up.*

staff /stɑːf, stæf/ (**staffs, staffing, staffed**)

○ **staff 'up**

When a firm **staffs up**, it increases the number of people it employs. ❏ *They have a core workforce of 450, but staff up for big contracts.*

stagger /'stægə/ (**staggers, staggering, staggered**)

○ **stagger 'on**

If someone or something **staggers on**, they continue but with a lot of difficulty. ❏ *The existing coalition might yet stagger on.* ❏ *The marriage staggered on for a little while longer.*

stake /steɪk/ (**stakes, staking, staked**)

○ **'stake on** (or **stake upon**)

If you **stake** something valuable **on** something, you risk losing it if something does not work as you thought it would. **stake something on something** ❏ *He has staked his reputation on this claim.* ❏ *I wouldn't like to stake my life on that bridge being safe.*

○ **stake 'out**

1 If you **stake** something **out**, you mark an area of land to show that it belongs to someone or is to be used for a particular purpose. **stake out something** or **stake something out** ❏ *The settlers were staking out territory in the South.* ❏ *They staked out a large plot for a vegetable garden.*

2 If you **stake** something **out**, you announce clearly what your opinion or intention is. **stake out something** or **stake something out** ❏ *The negotiations began with each side staking out their position.*

3 If someone **stakes out** a building, they stay outside it and watch it secretly for some time. **stake out something** or **stake something out** ❏ *The burglars must have staked out the house to see when it was empty.* ● A **stake-out** is a situation in which someone stays hidden near a building in order to watch anyone who enters or leaves it. ❏ *He was arrested after a police stake-out.*

○ **'stake upon** → see **stake on**

stammer /'stæmə/ (**stammers, stammering, stammered**)

○ **stammer 'out**

If you **stammer** something **out**, you say it with difficulty and a lot of hesitation because you are nervous. **stammer out something** or **stammer something out** ❏ *I stammered out some sort of explanation.* ❏ *'I think she's lovely,' Marsha stammered out.*

stamp /stæmp/ (**stamps, stamping, stamped**)

○ **stamp 'down**

If you **stamp** something **down**, you put your feet down hard on it to make it flatter or firmer. **stamp down something** or **stamp something down** ❏ *She buried the money, stamping down the earth over it.* ❏ *He put the cardboard boxes in a heap and stamped them down.*

○ **'stamp on**

1 If you **stamp on** something, you put your foot down on it very hard in order to damage it or hurt it. **stamp on something** ❏ *The boys stamped on beetles and ants.* ❏ *Someone stamped heavily on my foot and muttered, 'Sorry'.*

2 If you **stamp on** something, you act immediately and firmly to stop it. **stamp on something** ❏ *The tone of her voice was designed to stamp on this topic of conversation once and for all.* ❏ *He is determined to stamp on any signs of rebellion.*

3 If you **stamp** a word or symbol **on** something, you mark it firmly with that word or symbol, usually using a stamp. **stamp something on something** ❏ *He stamped the word 'Urgent' on the envelope.* **be stamped on something** ❏ *'Eat before July 14' was stamped on the label.*

○ **stamp on** (or **stamp upon**)

To **stamp** something **on** a person or thing means to have a strong and usually permanent effect on that person or thing. **stamp something on something** ❏ *She quickly stamped her personality on the workplace.* **stamp yourself on something** ❏ *His achievement really stamped itself on the public consciousness.* **be stamped on something** ❏ *The words were indelibly stamped on his memory.*

○ **stamp 'out**

1 If you **stamp** something **out**, you end it or destroy it completely. **stamp out something** or **stamp something out** ❏ *They are determined to stamp out racism.* ❏ *The protests were quickly stamped out.*

NOTE **Eliminate** and **eradicate** are more formal words for **stamp out**.

2 If you **stamp out** something that is

burning, you tread on it with your feet in order to stop it burning.

stamp out something or **stamp something out** ❏ A small fire was going and he stamped it out. NOTE **Extinguish** is a more formal word for **stamp out**.

◪ If something **is stamped out**, it is cut from a substance by a machine or tool. **= punch out**

be stamped out ❏ [+ of] A round hole was stamped out of the centre of the piece of wood.

○ **'stamp upon** → see stamp on

stampede /stæmˈpiːd/ (stampedes, stampeding, stampeded)

○ **stamˈpede into**

If you **stampede** someone **into** something, you make them do it even though they do not want to do it.

stampede someone into something ❏ I had been stampeded into a hasty decision.

stand /stænd/ (stands, standing, stood)

○ **stand aˈround** (or **stand about, stand round** [mainly BRITISH])

If you **stand around** or **stand around** a place, you stand in a place without doing anything in particular.

stand around ❏ They seemed content to stand around chatting. ❏ He stood about for a while, unsure what to do.

stand around something ❏ Passengers stood around the ticket counters waiting for them to open.

○ **stand aˈside**

◼ If you **stand aside**, you move to a position where you will not block other people. ❏ [+ to-infinitive] Gareth stood aside to let him pass.

◼ If someone **stands aside**, they resign from an important job or position. **= stand down** [BRITISH] ❏ The President said he was willing to stand aside if that would stop the violence.

◪ If you **stand aside**, you refuse to become involved in a disagreement or difficult situation. ❏ [+ from] We wish to stand aside from these quarrels. ❏ He always stood aside quite passively during any arguments.

○ **stand ˈback**

◼ If you **stand back**, you move away from something or someone. ❏ Stand back, please, while I light the flame. ❏ [+ from] He stood back from the doorway, allowing her to enter.

◼ If you **stand back**, you avoid being too closely involved in a situation. ❏ I think someone ought to stand back and look critically at this issue.

◪ If a building **stands back**, it is some distance away from a road or other area. **= be set back** ❏ The hospital stands back behind trees. ❏ [+ from] The cottage stands back from the road.

○ **stand beˈtween**

To **stand between** a person and something that might happen or exist means to prevent the thing happening or existing.

stand between someone and someone/something ❏ They would kill anyone who stood between them and their liberty.

○ **stand ˈby**

> In meaning 4, the stress is on **'stand**.

◼ If you **stand by**, you allow something bad to happen without trying to do anything to stop it. **= sit by** ❏ We cannot stand by and watch while our allies are attacked. ● A **bystander** is a person who is present when something happens, but does not take part in it. **= onlooker** ❏ If they fight, innocent bystanders may get hurt.

◼ If you **stand by**, you are ready to provide help or take action if it becomes necessary. ❏ [+ to-infinitive] Government engineers were standing by to provide emergency repairs. ❏ Stand by with lots of water in case a fire breaks out.

● A **stand-by** is something that is ready to be used if it is needed. ❏ If you don't know what to cook, there's always that old stand-by, beans on toast. ● Someone or something that is **on standby** is ready to so something or to be used. ❏ A plane was on standby to fly her home if necessary. ● A **standby** ticket is a cheap ticket that you buy just before a journey or performance. ❏ Call the airline and see if there are any standby tickets.

◪ If you **stand by** someone, you continue to support or help them when they are in trouble. **= stick by**

stand by someone ❏ If they try to make you resign, we'll stand by you.

◪ If you **stand by** something, you continue to believe that it is correct or true. **≠ go back on**

stand by something ❏ We still stand by our earlier decision to dismiss him.

NOTE **Abide by** and **adhere to** are more formal expressions for **stand by**.

○ **stand ˈdown**

◼ If someone **stands down**, they leave an important position or job. **= step down** ❏ Would you be prepared to stand down in favour of a younger candidate? ❏ [+ as] She has made it clear she will never stand down as monarch.

◼ If someone **stands down**, they leave the

witness box in a courtroom. ❑ *The defendant may now stand down.*

'stand for

1 If a letter **stands for** a particular word or name, it is an abbreviation for that word or name.

stand for something ❑ *What does GCSE stand for?* ❑ *EU stands for European Union.*

2 The things that someone **stands for** are the ideas or values that they support or represent.

stand for something ❑ *Our organization has always stood for individual liberty.* ❑ *Everything we stood for had been destroyed.*

3 If someone **stands for** something, they are a candidate in an election.

stand for something ❑ *No-one would stand for election.* ❑ *It is very difficult to stand for local government as an independent.*

4 If you **will not stand for** something, you will not allow it to happen or continue. **= put up with**

not stand for something ❑ *I won't stand for any more of this bad behaviour.* ❑ *His partners will not stand for any delay to the reforms.*

NOTE **Tolerate** is a more formal word for **stand for**.

stand 'in

If you **stand in** for someone, you take their place or do their job when they are ill or not there. ❑ *[+ for] She had to miss a rehearsal so one of the other singers agreed to stand in for her.*

● A **stand-in** is a person who takes someone else's place or does their job when the other person is ill or not there. ❑ *My doctor was on holiday and her stand-in got my name wrong.*

stand 'off

1 If you **stand off**, you stay some distance away from something that is happening and do not get involved. ❑ *The sea was so rough that rescue boats had to stand off.*

2 If you **stand** someone **off**, you stop them from coming close to you or interfering with what you are doing.

stand someone off or **stand off someone** ❑ *She stood off curious intruders by day and by night.*

stand 'out

1 If something **stands out**, it can be seen very clearly. ❑ *The name on the van stood out clearly.* ❑ *Use a different font to make the title stand out.*

2 If something **stands out**, it is much better or more important than other things of the same kind. ❑ *[+ as] Two findings stand out as being particularly significant.* ❑ *[+ from] There was one episode which stood out from the*

rest. ● A **stand-out** is something which is much better or more important than other things of the same kind. ❑ *There are a lot of fairly good songs on the album, but no real stand-outs.* ● A **stand-out** person or object is much better or more important than others. ❑ *Paul was a stand-out performer in that match.* ● Something or someone that is **outstanding** is much better or more important than other things of the same kind. ❑ *She would never be an outstanding actress.*

3 If a debt or a problem is **outstanding**, it has not yet been dealt with or paid. ❑ *There is fifty pounds outstanding, I believe.* ❑ *There is one outstanding problem that needs working on.*

○ stand 'out against

If you **stand out against** something, you remain opposed to it, even though a lot of other people do not agree with you.

stand out against something ❑ *It's not easy for a politician to stand out against popular opinion.*

○ stand 'out for

If you **stand out for** something, you want it and refuse to accept anything else. **= hold out for, stick out for**

stand out for something ❑ *The union decided to stand out for its original claim.*

○ stand 'over

If you **stand over** someone, you stand close to them and watch them, usually to make sure that they do something.

stand over someone ❑ *He wasn't hungry, but she stood over him and made him eat his lunch.* ❑ *He won't do any work unless I'm standing over him.*

○ stand 'round → see stand around

✪ stand 'up

1 If you **stand up**, you change your position so that you are standing rather than sitting or lying. **= get up** ❑ *The pupils stand up when the teacher comes into the room.* ❑ *I put down my glass and stood up.* ● **Stand-up** comedy is comedy in which a comedian stands alone in front of an audience and tells jokes. ❑ *He is an actor and a stand-up comedian.*

● A **stand-up** fight or argument is one in which people fight or argue in an angry, uncontrolled way. ❑ *A slight disagreement developed into a stand-up argument.*

2 If a claim or piece of evidence **stands up**, it is accepted as true. ❑ *The prosecution had no evidence which would stand up in a court of law.* ❑ *These claims just don't stand up.*

3 If you **stand** someone **up**, you fail to keep an arrangement to meet them, especially someone you were beginning a romantic relationship with. [INFORMAL]

stand someone up or **stand up someone**
❏ *I feel really bad about standing you up that day.* ❏ *I think I've been stood up.*

○ **stand 'up for**
If you **stand up for** someone or something, you do or say something to defend them from criticism or attack. = **defend**

stand up for something/someone ❏ *Only one man stood up for me and he was laughed at.* ❏ *Don't be afraid to stand up for your rights.*

stand up for yourself ❏ *His father taught him to stand up for himself.*

○ **stand 'up to**
1 If something or someone **stands up to** something, they remain in a good state or condition despite bad treatment or a lot of use.

stand up to something ❏ *This carpet will stand up to continual use.* ❏ *My mother stood up to the ordeal very well.*

NOTE **Withstand** is a more formal word for **stand up to**.

2 If you **stand up to** someone, especially someone more powerful than you are, you defend yourself against their attacks or demands.

stand up to someone ❏ *The best way to deal with bullies is to stand up to them.*

stare /steə/ (stares, staring, stared)

○ **stare 'down** (or **stare out**)
If you **stare** someone **down**, you stare into their eyes until you make them look away.

stare someone down or **stare down someone** ❏ *He glared at Sue, but she stared him down with hard, angry eyes.* ❏ *He is aggressive in meetings, staring out people who try to question him.*

start /stɑːt/ (starts, starting, started)

○ **start 'back**
1 If you **start back**, you begin returning towards the place where you have come from. ❏ *It's getting late, so we should start back.* ❏ *We started back on the long journey home.*

2 If you **start back**, you suddenly move backwards because something has shocked or surprised you. ❏ *She started back in terror.*

○ **start 'in**
If you **start in** something, you begin to do it or deal with it. ❏ *If you start in early enough, you can do it.*

○ **start 'off**
1 If you **start off**, you begin to move and go somewhere. = **move off, set off** ❏ *The bus started off down the hill.* ❏ *We were due to start off for the coast that morning.*

2 To **start** something **off** means to cause i to begin.

start off something ❏ *We need to understand what starts off the growth of a tumour.*

start something off ❏ *I asked a simple questic to start the interview off.* ❏ *She gets a lot of headaches, and it's usually stress that starts them off.* ● The **starting-off** point for something is the time when it begins. ❏ *This could be the starting-off point for a fairer housing policy.*

3 To **start off** means to begin an activity. ❏ *[+ by] Let's start off by sorting out who is involve*

4 To **start off** means to begin something i a particular state or condition. ❏ *He started off with nothing, and now he's a millionaire.* ❏ *Al rice starts off brown.* ❏ *[+ as] I started off as a bookseller in Bristol.*

5 To **start** someone **off** means to help the to begin doing something.

start someone off ❏ *I will give you a few ideas to start you off.*

6 To **start** someone **off** means to make them begin crying, laughing or talking about something. = **set off**

start someone off ❏ *The mention of their nam would start her off again, crying and shouting.*

○ **'start on**
1 If you **start on** something, you begin doing it or doing something with it.

start on something ❏ *You clean the kitchen while I start on the bathroom.* ❏ *She had eaten al cookies and started on a second packet.*

2 If someone or something **starts** someon **on** an activity, they cause them to begin doing something new.

start someone on something ❏ *We want to start her on music lessons soon.* ❏ *They immediately started the patient on antibiotics.*

3 If someone **starts on** you, they start talking to you in an unpleasant way, especially by criticizing or teasing you. [INFORMAL]

start on someone ❏ *Don't start on me just because you didn't get what you wanted!*

○ **start 'on about** [INFORMAL]
If someone **starts on about** something, they start complaining about it or talking about it in a way that annoys people.

start on about something ❏ *[+ on] As soon a she got in, she started on about the mess.*

○ **start 'out**
1 If you **start out**, you begin to move and go somewhere. = **set off, set out, start off** ❏ *They started out early the next morning.* ❏ *The boat started out towards the island.* ❏ *[+ for] At last we started out for home.*

2 To **start out** means to begin something in a particular way or by doing a particular thing. = **start off**; ≠ **end up** ❑ *He started out in his early twenties with a small shop.* ❑ [+ *as*] *What started out as fun has become a duty.* ❑ *A bruise would start out black and blue, then become purple.*

3 If you **start out** to do something, you intend to do it. = **set out** ❑ [+ *to*-infinitive] *You've done what you started out to do.*

○ **start 'over** [AMERICAN]

If you **start over**, you begin doing something again from the beginning. ❑ *You've done it all wrong. You'll have to start over.*

○ **start 'up**

1 If you **start** something **up**, or if you **start up**, you start a new business or project; if a business **starts up**, it begins. = **set up**

start up something ❑ *She wanted to start up a little country pub.*

start something up ❑ *We wanted our own magazine, and found someone who was willing to start it up and run it for us.* ❑ *Why don't you start a book group up with some friends?*

start up ❑ *Every year many people decide to start up in business.* ❑ *The company started up in 1997.*

● **Start-up** money is used to start a new business or activity. ❑ *The bank may be willing to help you with start-up costs.* ● A **start-up** is a new company. ❑ *Many of the students were planning to join high-tech start-ups.*

2 If you **start up** an engine, machine or motor vehicle, or if it **starts up**, it begins to operate.

start something up ❑ *When we got into the car mum didn't start it up immediately.* ❑ *I started the engine up and the radio came on.*

start up something ❑ *He got out the lawn-mower and started up the motor.*

start up ❑ *There was a car starting up in the background.* ❑ *Does your computer take ages to start up?*

3 If something **starts up** or if you **start** it **up**, it begins to happen or exist.

start up ❑ *The music started up in the ballroom.* ❑ *The rain has started up again.*

start up something ❑ *The book started up a literary controversy.*

start something up ❑ *I don't want to start another argument up.*

4 If you **start up**, you move suddenly into a sitting or standing position because you are worried or surprised. ❑ *Michael was dozing, then started up anxiously and looked at his watch.*

5 An **upstart** is someone who thinks that they are important even though they are

very new in a job or place. ❑ *To his colleagues he was considered an upstart from the provinces.*

starve /stɑːv/ (**starves, starving, starved**)

○ **'starve for**

If you **are starved for** something or **are starving for** it, you want it very much, usually because you do not have enough of it.

be starved for something ❑ *These children are starved for affection.*

be starving for something ❑ *He seemed desperate to be liked, starving for Peggy's approval.*

○ **'starve into**

If someone **starves** someone **into** something or if they **are starved into** something, they are forced to do something by being prevented from getting food.

be starved into something ❑ *These people could never be starved into submission.*

starve someone into something ❑ *They tried to starve the city into surrender.*

○ **'starve of**

If someone or something **is starved of** something, or if you **starve** them **of** it, they are prevented from getting something that they need.

be starved of something ❑ *She realized that he was starved of love.* ❑ *If cells are starved of oxygen, they die.*

starve someone of something ❑ *If we starve him of publicity, he will give up.*

○ **starve 'out**

To **starve** people **out** means to force them to surrender or leave a place by preventing them from getting food.

starve someone out or **starve out someone** ❑ *In a short time the soldiers starved us out.*

stash /stæʃ/ (**stashes, stashing, stashed**)

○ **stash a'way**

1 If you **stash** something **away**, you put it somewhere secret or safe.

stash away something or **stash something away** ❑ *I took the letter and stashed it away with all the others.*

be stashed away ❑ *He had a little money stashed away.*

2 If someone **is stashed away**, they are hiding somewhere secret or safe.

be stashed away ❑ *Mel suspected she had a lover somewhere, stashed away.*

stave /steɪv/ (**staves, staving, staved**)

○ **stave 'off**

If you **stave off** something bad, you manage to avoid it happening.

stave off something or **stave something off** ❑ *The company staved off bankruptcy earlier this year.*

❏ The collapse of the system is inevitable. We can't stave it off for ever.

NOTE Avert is a more formal word for **stave off**.

stay /steɪ/ (stays, staying, stayed)

○ **stay a'head**

To **stay ahead** of someone or something means to remain more successful or at a higher level than them. ❏ [+ of] Their pay is only just staying ahead of inflation. ❏ Successful firms must stay ahead in the technology race.

❍ **stay a'way**

If you **stay away**, you do not go to a place. ❏ These areas are unsafe and we recommend you stay away. ❏ [+ from] He started staying away from school because he was being bullied.

❍ **stay a'way from**

1 If you **stay away from** a person, you try to avoid meeting them or talking to them.
stay away from someone ❏ He told me to stay away from his sister. ❏ Stay away from him – he's dangerous.
2 If you **stay away from** something, you avoid becoming involved with or mentioning it.
stay away from something ❏ He thinks sportspeople should stay away from politics. ❏ I tried to stay away from the subject of money.

○ **stay 'back**

If you **stay back**, you remain in a place and do not move forward or leave. ❏ Someone will have to stay back and look after the children.

○ **stay be'hind**

If you **stay behind**, you remain in a place after other people have gone. ❏ The teacher made me stay behind after school. ❏ [+ to-infinitive] She stayed behind to talk to us.
NOTE Remain is a more formal word for **stay behind**.

○ **stay 'down**

1 If someone **stays down**, they remain underwater. ❏ I was eventually able to stay down for over three and a half minutes.
2 If food **stays down**, you do not vomit after eating it. ❏ If this stays down, she can try a little more at the next meal.

❍ **stay 'in**

If you **stay in**, you remain at home rather than going out. = **stop in**; ≠ **go out** ❏ She had to stay in and do the dishes. ❏ I'm staying in tonight – I've got an early start tomorrow. ❏ We stayed in the whole evening.

○ **stay 'off**

If you **stay off** or **stay off** something, you do not go to work or school, for example because you are ill.

stay off ❏ If I'm not better, I think I'll stay off tomorrow.
stay off something ❏ I think you should stay o[ ] school today.

❍ **stay 'on** [BRITISH]

If you **stay on**, you remain in a place or continue to attend it regularly. ≠ **leave** ❏ [+ at] Pupils have to stay on at school till they are 16. ❏ He had stayed on after work to have a drink.

❍ **stay 'out**

1 If you **stay out**, you remain away from home, especially when you are expected to be there. = **stop out** ❏ We stayed out all night. ❏ Her mother didn't like her to stay out late.
2 If workers **stay out**, they remain on strike. [BRITISH] ❏ The men stayed out for almost a year.

❍ **stay 'out of**

1 If you **stay out of** a place, you do not enter it.
stay out of something ❏ They warned him to stay out of the area. ❏ Please stay out of the kitchen while I'm cleaning it.
2 If you **stay out of** a situation or activity, you do not get involved in it or take part in it. = **keep out of**
stay out of something ❏ When they argue, I usually try to stay out of it. ❏ I hope you can stay out of trouble.

○ **stay 'over**

If you **stay over**, you spend the night at someone's house. ❏ Why don't you stay over and leave early the next morning?

❍ **stay 'up**

If you **stay up**, you go to bed late. = **stop up** ❏ I'll stay up until you get back. ❏ These children stay up far too late.

○ **'stay with**

1 If you **stay with** something, you continue doing it, using it, or talking about it rather than changing to something else.
stay with something ❏ I think I'll stay with my original plan. ❏ Staying with the topic of education, what do you think about university fees?
2 If something **stays with** you, you continue to think about it or remember it for a long time.
stay with someone ❏ Memories of that time have stayed with her ever since. ❏ I enjoyed the film, and it really stayed with me.

steal /stiːl/ (steals, stealing, stole, stolen)

○ **steal a'way** [LITERARY]

If you **steal away**, you leave a place quietly or secretly. ❏ They stole away in the middle of the night.

steal 'over

1 If light **steals over** a place, it gradually starts to shine on it. [LITERARY]

steal over something ❏ *The sun rose and light stole over the ship.*

2 If a feeling or emotion **steals over** you or you heart or mind, you start to feel it.

steal over someone/something ❏ *They wrapped themselves in blankets, and sleep stole over them.*

steal 'up

If you **steal up**, you move quietly until you are near someone or something, usually in order to surprise or attack someone.

= **sneak up, creep up** ❏ *The youth had stolen up silently behind him.*

steal 'up on

If something **steals up on** you, it starts to happen to you gradually, without you realizing.

steal up on someone ❏ *Old age just sort of steals up on you.*

:eam /stiːm/ (steams, steaming, steamed)

steam a'way

1 If something **steams away**, it produces a lot of steam. ❏ *The kettle was steaming away on the stove.*

2 If something **steams away**, it leaves a place quickly, especially using steam power. ❏ [+ from] *The liner steamed away from New York.*

steam 'off

1 If you **steam** something **off** something or **steam** it **off**, you remove it from a surface using steam.

steam something off or **steam off something** ❏ *They clean the jars and steam off the labels.*

steam something off something ❏ *You can steam the stamps off the envelopes.*

2 If you **steam off**, you head quickly in a particular direction in a determined way. [INFORMAL] ❏ *He steamed off down the field with the ball.*

steam 'up

1 If something **steams up** or if something **steams** it **up**, it becomes covered with steam or mist. = **mist up**

steam up ❏ *My glasses steamed up as soon as I walked into the room.*

be steamed up ❏ *The windows always get steamed up when I'm cooking.*

steam up something or **steam something up** ❏ *She wouldn't let me have a bath, saying it steamed up the bathroom.*

2 If someone is **steamed up**, they are very angry or upset about something. = **het up** ❏ *What was she getting so steamed up about?*

steer /stɪə/ (steers, steering, steered)

○ steer a'way from

If you **steer away from** something or **steer** someone or something **away from** it, you avoid talking about it or getting involved with it.

steer away from something ❏ *I like to steer away from serious topics.*

steer someone/something away from something ❏ *Kitty was steering all the conversation away from herself.*

stem /stem/ (stems, stemming, stemmed)

✪ 'stem from

If something **stems from** something, it is caused by that thing.

stem from something ❏ *Attitudes like these stem from ignorance.* ❏ *There are obvious risks which stem from regular alcohol drinking.*

step /step/ (steps, stepping, stepped)

○ step a'side → see step down

○ step a'way

1 If you **step away**, you move away from something.

step away ❏ *The waiter looked surprised, then quickly stepped away.* ❏ [+ from] *Maybe you should step away from the computer and go for a walk.*

2 If you tell someone to **step away** from something, you are humorously saying that they should stop doing what they are doing there.

step away from something ❏ *Put down the mince pies and step away from the chocolates.*

○ step 'back

1 If you **step back**, you think about a problem or situation carefully, without being influenced by personal feelings or old habits. = **stand back** ❏ [+ from] *She was able to step back from the situation which had seemed so hopeless.* ❏ *Step back and look at your life, and think about how you could change it.*

2 If you **step back**, you return to an earlier time or situation. ❏ *As soon as she went home she stepped back into her old life.* ❏ *He would give anything to be able to step back in time.*

✪ step 'down (or step aside)

If you **step down**, you leave an important job or position. = **stand down** ❏ [+ as] *She decided to step aside as vice-presidential candidate.* ❏ *The CEO stepped down last month because of illness.*

○ step 'forward

If someone **steps forward**, they offer to help or to do something for someone. ❏ *He volunteered to lead the team when no-one else stepped forward.* ❏ [+ to-infinitive] *Close* relatives immediately stepped forward to take their place.

○ **step 'in**

If you **step in**, you get involved in a situation and try to help. ❑ *She hoped he might step in and sort everything out for her.* ❑ [+ to-infinitive] *The government sometimes has to step in to protect employees from employers.* NOTE **Intervene** is a more formal word for **step in**.

○ **step 'on**

If a driver **steps on** the accelerator, they make a vehicle go more quickly.
step on something ❑ *She really stepped on the gas when we reached the highway.*
● If you tell someone to **step on it**, you are telling them to drive fast. ❑ *We've only got 35 minutes so step on it.*

○ **step 'out**

1 If someone **steps out**, they leave a place for a short time. ❑ *He's just stepped out for a minute. Can I take a message?* ❑ [+ of] *The teacher had stepped out of the classroom to speak to a parent.*
2 If someone **steps out** of a role or situation, they leave it. ❑ [+ of] *For once he stepped out of his policeman's role.*
3 If someone **steps out**, they appear in public, especially with a boyfriend or girlfriend. [OLD-FASHIONED] ❑ [+ with] *She was said to be stepping out with actor Matt Dillon.*

○ **step 'up**

1 If you **step up** something, you increase its speed, amount, or intensity.
step up something ❑ *The nation was stepping up arms production.* ❑ *You're going too slowly. Step up the pace a little.*
step something up ❑ *The candidate is stepping his campaign up as the election approaches.* ❑ *We stepped it up in the second half and played much better football.*
● If you **step** something **up a gear**, you increase its intensity. ❑ *We need to step our efforts up a gear if we are to make any difference.*
● A **step-up** in something is an increase in speed, amount, or extent. ❑ *We need a step-up in production.* ❑ *There has been a marked step-up in police activity.*
2 If you **step up**, you take responsibility for something or agree to do something. ❑ *We hope people will step up and volunteer to help their community.*
● If you **step up to the plate**, you offer to do something or take responsibility for something when this is needed. ❑ *Nobody was taking charge of the situation, so I stepped up to the plate.*

stick /stɪk/ (sticks, sticking, stuck)

○ **stick a'round** [INFORMAL]

If you **stick around**, you stay in a place and do not leave. = **hang around** ❑ *I'll stick around and keep you company.* ❑ [+ for] *I decided not to stick around for the second half of the game.*

○ **'stick at**

1 If you **stick at** something, you continue trying to do it although it is difficult.
= **keep at, stick to**
stick at something ❑ *He never stuck at one job for long.* ❑ *I know you're tired, but try to stick at it.* NOTE **Persevere** is a more formal word for **stick at**.
2 To **stick at** something means to stop at a particular amount, stage, or point.
stick at something ❑ *He stuck at his offer of twelve thousand.*

○ **stick 'back** [INFORMAL]

If you **stick** something **back**, you put it somewhere again after it has been removed.
stick something back ❑ *He stuck the wallet back in his pocket.*

○ **'stick by**

1 If you **stick by** someone, you continue to help or support them when they are in difficulty. = **stand by**; ≠ **abandon, desert**
stick by someone ❑ *It was her duty to stick by him, whatever happened.* ❑ *He was a good officer who stuck by his men when they got into trouble.*
2 If you **stick by** something, you continue to use it or believe in it and do not change your mind. ≠ **abandon**
stick by something ❑ *We stick by what we have always argued.* ❑ *I stick by the traditional methods which have stood the test of time.*
NOTE **Adhere to** is a more formal expression for **stick by**.

○ **stick 'down**

1 If you **stick** something **down**, you put it somewhere. [INFORMAL]
stick something down ❑ *Just stick all the boxes down here.*
2 If you **stick** something **down**, you seal it or attach it firmly to something else, usually by using glue or tape and then pressing it.
stick something down or **stick down something** ❑ *He stuck down the envelope and wrote Pearson's name on the front.*
3 If you **stick** something **down**, you write or draw it quickly or roughly. [INFORMAL]
stick something down or **stick down something** ❑ *Just stick it down and we'll look at it properly later.* ❑ *I stuck down a few ideas before the meeting.*

stick 'in

In meaning 4, the stress is on **'stick**.

1 If you **stick** something or someone **in** a place, you put them there or cause them to go in there. [INFORMAL]

stick something/someone in something
❏ Don't just stick it in your pocket and forget about it.

2 If you **stick** something **in** something or **stick** it **in**, you push something sharp into a surface; if something **sticks in** something or **sticks in**, it is pushed into a surface.

stick something in something ❏ He stuck a spade in the ground.

stick something in ❏ The nurse prepared the needle and stuck it in.

stick in something ❏ Some of the darts don't stick in the board.

stick in ❏ Push it harder to make it stick in.

3 If you **stick** something **in** or **stick** it **in** something, you attach it somewhere using glue or tape.

stick something in or **stick something in**
❏ I cut out the article, and stuck it in at the back of my diary.

stick something in something ❏ He stuck a poster in his window. ❏ I need to sort those photos out and stick them in albums.

4 If something **sticks in** your mind or memory, you continue to remember it very clearly.

stick in something ❏ This strange conversation stuck in Maria's mind. ❏ Some things stick in your memory for ever.

5 If you **stick** something **in**, you add it quickly to a piece of writing or drawing. ≠ **take out, remove** [INFORMAL]

stick something in or **stick in something** ❏ I drew a house and garden, then stuck a few trees in. ❏ Stick in a few quotations to earn extra marks.

6 If you **get stuck in**, you start a task with energy or enthusiasm. [INFORMAL] ❏ We rolled up our sleeves, got stuck in and made a start.

stick 'on

1 If you **stick** something **on** or **stick** it **on** a surface, you attach it to a surface using glue, tape, or pins.

stick something on or **stick on something**
❏ The hat seems to be stuck on with glue. ❏ We decorated the hat with ribbon and stuck on some artificial flowers.

stick something on something ❏ Stick a numbered label on each case. ❏ She cut out the picture and stuck it on the noticeboard.

• **Stick-on** things have a layer of glue on one side so that they can be attached to surfaces. ❏ We bought some stick-on labels.

• **Stuck-on** things have been attached to a surface with glue. ❏ They wore stuck-on tattoos.

2 If you **stick** something **on**, or **stick** it **on** something, you put it somewhere. [INFORMAL]

stick something on something ❏ Stick another lump of coal on the fire.

stick something on or **stick on something**
❏ I'll just stick on some make-up before we go.

3 If you are **stuck on** an object or an idea, you like it and are not willing to change your mind about it. [INFORMAL] ❏ I don't think we should be too stuck on the idea of redecorating the room.

4 If you are **stuck on** someone, you like them and find them attractive. [mainly AMERICAN, INFORMAL] ❏ He's stuck on his driving instructor.

❍ stick 'out

1 If you **stick** something **out**, you push or stretch it away from you.

stick something out ❏ [+ of] Lally stuck her head out of a window. ❏ Is your tummy really that big, or are you sticking it out?

stick out something ❏ Lynn stuck out her tongue. ❏ He stuck out his hand and said 'Pleased to meet you.'

2 If something **sticks out**, it extends beyond something else. ❏ She put a scarf over her hair, but a few strands still stuck out. ❏ [+ of] There was a little chimney sticking out of the roof. ❏ [+ from] A large rock sticks out from the shore. ❏ She sat down, her legs sticking straight out in front of her.

NOTE **Protrude** is a more formal word for **stick out**.

3 If something or someone **sticks out**, they are very obvious or noticeable, especially because of being very different to things or people around them. ❏ He wore a grey suit, that would not stick out in any workplace.

• If someone or something **sticks out like a sore thumb** or **sticks out a mile**, they are very noticeable, especially when this is a bad thing. = **stand out** ❏ Strangers stick out like a sore thumb in a place like this. ❏ The fact that she did not like him stuck out a mile.

4 If you **stick** something **out**, you continue in a difficult or unpleasant situation, rather than leaving it.

stick something out or **stick out something** ❏ Sometimes I wonder if I can stick this job out much longer. ❏ I stuck it out as long as I could, but in the end I left.

NOTE **Endure** is a more formal word for **stick out**.

○ **stick 'out for**

If you **stick out for** something, you keep demanding it until you get it. = **hold out for**

stick out for something ❏ *He stuck out for twice the usual salary, and got it.*

◐ **'stick to**

1 If something **sticks to** a surface, it becomes accidentally attached to it.

stick to something ❏ *He was sweating, and his clothes stuck to him.* ❏ *The eggs stuck to the pan.*

NOTE **Adhere to** is a more formal word for **stick to**.

2 If you **stick to** something, you continue to do what you have decided or what is expected. = **keep to**

stick to something ❏ *The government intends to stick to its policy.* ❏ *The diet won't work unless you stick to it.*

3 If you **stick to** something or someone, you stay close to them.

stick to something/someone ❏ *It's best to stick to well-lit roads.* ❏ *She stuck to my side all evening.*

4 If you **stick to** a subject, you talk only about it, and not about anything else. = **keep to**

stick to something ❏ *I think we should stick to the point.* ❏ *Don't give your opinions, just stick to the facts.* ❏ *I think writers should stick to what they know.*

5 If you **stick to** something, you do what a rule or principle says you must do.

stick to something ❏ *Everyone must stick to the rules.*

6 If you **stick to** someone, you keep supporting and trusting them. = **stand by, stick by**

stick to someone ❏ *She stuck to her husband through all his troubles.*

◐ **stick to'gether**

1 If you **stick** things **together**, you attach things or parts to each other, especially in order to make one whole object.

stick something together ❏ *Can you stick the cup together again?*

stick together something ❏ *I was working on my speech, sticking together bits of text with sellotape.*

2 If things **stick together** or **are stuck together**, they become attached to each other and are difficult to separate.

stick together ❏ *Shake the pan to loosen any potatoes that have stuck together.*

be stuck together ❏ *Some of the pages were stuck together.*

3 If people **stick together**, they stay with

each other and support each other. ❏ *We stick together when times are hard.* ❏ *Some parents stick together for the sake of their children.*

◐ **stick 'up**

1 If you **stick** something **up**, you attach it to a vertical surface so that it can be seen.

stick up something ❏ *They stick up pictures on the classroom walls.*

stick something up ❏ *Write down things to remember on scraps of paper and stick them up around the house.*

2 If something **sticks up**, it points upward in an upright position. ❏ *He trod on a nail sticking up from a board.* ❏ *His hair stuck up at all angles.*

NOTE **Protrude** and **project** are more formal words for **stick up**.

3 If you **stick** something **up** somewhere, you push it inside there. [INFORMAL]

stick something up something ❏ *The child had stuck a pea up his nose.*

4 If someone **sticks up** a place, they rob it using a gun. = **hold up** [AMERICAN, INFORMAL]

stick up something ❏ *The gang was notorious for sticking up banks.* ● A **stick-up** is a robbery in which the thieves use guns. [AMERICAN] ❏ *There was a stick-up at the liquor store.*

5 If you describe someone as **stuck-up**, you mean that they think they are better than other people. [INFORMAL] ❏ *She's so stuck-up she won't even talk to us.*

○ **stick 'up for**

If you **stick up for** someone or something, you support or defend them when others attack them. = **stand up for**

stick up for someone/something ❏ *My friend stuck up for me, but nobody else did.*

stick up for yourself ❏ *At school you have to be able to stick up for yourself.*

◐ **'stick with**

1 If you **stick with** something, you continue to use it or do it, rather than changing. = **stick at, stick to**

stick with something ❏ *I stuck with a simple diet of rice and vegetables.* ❏ *He never sticks with anything.*

2 If you **stick with** someone, you stay close to them.

stick with someone ❏ *Stick with me and you'll be okay, don't you worry.*

3 If you **are stuck with** someone or something, you have to deal with them or stay with them when you do not want to.

be stuck with someone/something ❏ *I'm tired of being stuck with the baby all day on my own.* ❏ *He has been stuck with a load of goods he* can't sell. ❏ We don't like the situation, but we're stuck with it.

4 If something **sticks with** you, you continue to remember it for a long time.
stick with someone ❏ One memory in particular stuck with him. ❏ I liked his idea, and it stuck with me.

tiffen /'stɪfən/ (**stiffens, stiffening, stiffened**)

▸ **stiffen 'up**

If a part of your body **stiffens up**, or if something **stiffens** it **up**, it becomes difficult to bend or move.
stiffen up ❏ If you are nervous, you tend to stiffen up. ❏ A few hours after the race I could feel my muscles stiffening up.
stiffen up something or **stiffen something up** ❏ These clothes restrict your movement and stiffen up the whole body.

tir /stɜː/ (**stirs, stirring, stirred**)

▸ **'stir from**

If you do not **stir from** a place, you stay in it and do not leave.
stir from something ❏ She had not stirred from the house that evening. ❏ He was unwilling to stir from his chair.

▸ **stir 'in**

If you **stir** a substance **in**, you mix it with another substance, using a tool such as a spoon. = **mix in**
stir something in or **stir in something** ❏ Stir the flour in gradually. ❏ She had stirred in the sugar.

▸ **stir 'into**

If you **stir** one substance **into** another, you mix it with the other substance so that they are blended together. = **mix into**
stir something into something ❏ He stirred some cream into his coffee. ❏ Strain the liquid and stir it into the sauce.

▸ **stir 'up**

1 To **stir** something **up** means to cause trouble or to cause people to have a particular feeling, especially a harmful or unpleasant one.
stir up something ❏ They were stirring up trouble among the workers. ❏ Being back in the hospital stirred up unpleasant memories.
stir something up ❏ She was one of those people who likes stirring things up.
● If someone **stirs it up**, they deliberately cause trouble or cause people to get angry or upset. ❏ He was jealous and tried to stir it up, cause arguments between them.
NOTE **Provoke** and **incite** are more formal words for **stir up**.

2 If something **stirs up** memories, it makes you remember something, usually something bad.
stir up something ❏ Her death stirred up memories of his own sister's death.

3 To **stir** someone **up** means to make them angry or upset.
stir someone up ❏ These incidents stir people up and excite their passions.
stir up someone ❏ They tried to stir up the population, provoke them into action.

4 To **stir up** a substance means to cause it to move around.
stir up something ❏ Gentle winds stirred up the dust. ❏ The mud at the bottom of the river gets stirred up.
stir something up ❏ As you stir the water up, the reflections change.
NOTE **Disturb** is a more formal word for **stir up**.

stitch /stɪtʃ/ (**stitches, stitching, stitched**)

○ **stitch 'up**

1 If someone **stitches up** a wound or the person who has the wound, they use a special needle and thread to join the edges of a wound together. = **sew up**
stitch up something/someone or **stitch something/someone up** ❏ She scraped the dirt out of my wounds and stitched up my finger. ❏ Two patients came in who needed stitching up.
NOTE **Suture** is a more technical word for **stitch up**.

2 If you **stitch up** something that has come apart, you join two parts of something, especially cloth, using a needle and thread. = **sew up**
stitch something up or **stitch up something** ❏ He stitched up his boots, using a sailmaker's needle.

3 To **stitch** someone **up** means to trick them so that they are put in a difficult situation or blamed for something they have not done. [BRITISH, INFORMAL]
stitch someone up or **stitch up someone** ❏ He claimed that a police officer had threatened to stitch him up. ❏ He felt he had been stitched up in court. ● A **stitch-up** is a trick that results in someone being blamed for something they have not done. ❏ The money was found in his apartment, but he claims it was a stitch-up.
NOTE **Frame** is a more formal word for **stitch up**.

4 If you **stitch** something **up**, you agree all the details of a deal or arrangement. [BRITISH, INFORMAL]

stitch up something or **stitch something up**
❏ Shiraz has stitched up major deals all over the world.

NOTE Secure is a more formal word for **stitch up**.

stock /stɒk/ (**stocks, stocking, stocked**)

○ **stock 'up**

1 If you **stock up** with things, you buy a lot of them. ❏ [+ with] Stock up with groceries and canned foods once a fortnight. ❏ [+ on] I stocked up on frozen food.

2 If you **stock** something **up**, you fill a place or container with food or other things.

stock something up or **stock up something**
❏ [+ with] I had to stock the boat up with food.
❏ Customers travel from hundreds of miles away to stock up their freezers.

stoke /stəʊk/ (**stokes, stoking, stoked**)

○ **stoke 'up**

1 If you **stoke up** a fire, you make it burn faster by adding more fuel and poking it with something.

stoke up something or **stoke something up**
❏ He crouched to stoke up the flames. ❏ I stoked the fire up.

2 If you **stoke up** feelings such as anger or enthusiasm, you encourage people to feel them more strongly. = **stir up**

stoke up something or **stoke something up**
❏ He accused politicians of stoking up prejudice.
❏ He stoked up their anger with his insensitive remarks.

stoop /stuːp/ (**stoops, stooping, stooped**)

○ **'stoop to**

If you say that a person **stoops to** something, you are criticizing them because they do something bad to get what they want.

stoop to something ❏ I didn't think he would stoop to cheating. ❏ Do you seriously believe that he would stoop to criminal behaviour?

stop /stɒp/ (**stops, stopping, stopped**)

○ **stop a'way** [BRITISH, INFORMAL]

If you **stop away**, you deliberately do not go to a place. = **stay away** ❏ If the weather is bad, many people will stop away.

○ **stop be'hind** [BRITISH, INFORMAL]

If you **stop behind**, you stay in a place after other people have left. = **stay behind** ❏ Mr. Piggott made the whole class stop behind.

○ **stop 'by**

If you **stop by** a place or **stop by**, you visit a place for a short time. = **drop by**

stop by ❏ I thought I might stop by and say hello.

stop by something ❏ They invited us to stop by the house for coffee.

○ **stop 'in**

1 If you **stop in**, you visit a place for a short time. = **stop by, stop off** ❏ Yesterday, I stopped in to visit a friend of mine. ❏ [+ at] I stopped in at the supermarket on my way home from work.

2 If you **stop in**, you stay at home rather than going out. = **stay in** [BRITISH, INFORMAL] ❏ I stopped in on Friday night because I was tired.

✪ **stop 'off**

If you **stop off** somewhere, you stay there for a short time in the middle of a journey. ❏ On the way home I stopped off in London to attend a conference. ❏ [+ at] I need to stop off at the office and collect some files.

○ **stop 'out** [BRITISH, INFORMAL]

If you **stop out**, you stay out late at night when you are expected to come home. = **stay out** ❏ Billie stopped out all night last Saturday. ● A **stop-out** is someone who stays out late at night when they ought to come home. [BRITISH, INFORMAL] ❏ Where have you been, you little stop-out?

○ **stop 'over**

1 If you **stop over** somewhere, you stay there for one or more nights in between two parts of a journey. = **stop off** ❏ [+ in] I stopped over in Paris on my way here.

● A **stopover** is a short stay in a particular place between parts of a long journey. ❏ It's a twenty-hour flight, with a six-hour stopover in Beijing.

2 If you **stop over**, you visit a place for a short time. = **stop by, come over** ❏ Why don't you stop over sometime?

3 If you **stop over**, you spend a night at someone's house. [BRITISH, INFORMAL] ❏ If you miss the last train home, you can always stop over. ❏ [+ at] My son is stopping over at a friend's tonight.

○ **stop 'up**

1 If you **stop** something **up**, you cover or fill a hole or gap so that nothing can get through. = **block up**

stop up something or **stop something up**
❏ They had to stop up leaks with chewing gum.
❏ The pipes had been stopped up long ago.

2 If you **stop up**, you go to bed much later than usual. = **stay up** [BRITISH, INFORMAL] ❏ I stopped up to watch the match.

store /stɔː/ (**stores, storing, stored**)

○ **store a'way**

If you **store** something **away**, you keep it somewhere until it is needed. = **stow away**

store something away or **store away**

something ❏ *The body takes the energy it needs and stores away the rest.* ❏ *The goods were stored away at the back of the warehouse.*

○ **store 'up**

To **store** something **up** means to keep it until it is needed or can be used. = **save up**
store something up or **store up something**
❏ *Plants store up energy in the summer.* ❏ *She had some spare food stored up for emergencies.*

storm /stɔːm/ (**storms, storming, stormed**)

○ **storm 'in**

If you **storm in**, you enter a place suddenly and loudly, usually because you are angry.
❏ *Peter stormed in, demanding to see the manager.*

○ **storm 'into**

If you **storm into** a place, you enter it suddenly and loudly, usually because you are angry.
storm into something ❏ *Ravinder stormed into his room.* ❏ *A customer came storming into the shop.*

○ **storm 'off**

If you **storm off**, you leave a place suddenly because you are very angry. ❏ *Within minutes, he'd stormed off.* ❏ *In a rage I stormed off to complain.*

○ **storm 'out**

If you **storm out**, you leave a place suddenly because you are very angry. ❏ *He said a few strong words to the owner and stormed out.*
❏ *[+ of] Furious, Marta stormed out of the room.*

stow /stəʊ/ (**stows, stowing, stowed**)

○ **stow a'way**

1 If you **stow** something **away**, you put it carefully in a place until it is needed.
= **store away**
stow something away or **stow away something** ❏ *He accepted the money gratefully and stowed it away in his suitcase.* ❏ *His baggage was safely stowed away in the plane.*
2 If someone **stows away**, they hide in a ship, aeroplane, or other vehicle in order to make the journey secretly. ❏ *He made his escape and stowed away to America.* ● A **stowaway** is a person who hides in a ship, aeroplane, or other vehicle in order to make the journey secretly. ❏ *They found a stowaway on the flight.*

straighten /'streɪtən/ (**straightens, straightening, straightened**)

○ **straighten 'out**

1 If you **straighten** something **out**, or if it **straightens out**, it becomes straight or flat after being twisted, bent, or crumpled.

straighten out something or **straighten something out** ❏ *Sylvia sat down and straightened out her legs.* ❏ *He straightened out the paper.*
straighten out ❏ *When it reaches the valley, the road straightens out.*
2 If you **straighten** something **out**, you succeed in dealing with a problem or a confused situation. = **sort out, straighten up**
straighten out something or **straight something out** ❏ *An apology would straighten things out between you, I'm sure.* ❏ *We need an expert to get the accounts straightened out.*
3 If you **straighten** something **out**, you tidy a place and put things back where they belong.
straighten out something or **straighten something out** ❏ *It took days to straighten out the house after the party.* ❏ *Go and straighten your room out.*
4 If you **straighten** someone **out**, you help them with their problems and stop them from being confused or doing bad things.
straighten someone out or **straighten out someone** ❏ *Geoff had his problems, but I straightened him out.* ❏ *The teacher was just trying to straighten the kid out.*

○ **straighten 'up**

1 When you **straighten up**, you move into an upright position with your back or body straight. ❏ *Once outside the tent, she straightened up slowly.*
2 If you **straighten** something **up**, you succeed in dealing with a confused situation. = **sort out, straighten out**
straighten up something or **straighten something up** ❏ *I think there's been a misunderstanding, and we need to get things straightened up.*

strain /streɪn/ (**strains, straining, strained**)

○ **'strain at**

If you **strain at** something, you pull very hard on something such as a rope or cord.
strain at something ❏ *The men strained at the ropes.* ❏ *The dogs were barking and straining at their leashes.*

○ **strain 'off**

If you **strain** a liquid **off**, you separate it from the solid part of a mixture.
strain something off or **strain off something** ❏ *When the mixture is boiling, strain it off into jars.* ❏ *Strain off the water and allow the rest to dry.*

strap /stræp/ (**straps, strapping, strapped**)

○ **strap 'in**

If you **strap** someone **in**, you fasten them firmly into a seat, using a belt or strap.
= **buckle in**

strap someone in or **strap in someone** ❏ *I put the baby in his high chair and strapped him in.* ❏ *Check to see that the children are strapped in securely.*

strap yourself in ❏ *Charlie sat in his seat and strapped himself in.*

○ **strap 'into**

If you **strap** someone **into** a seat, you fasten them firmly there, using a belt or strap.
= **buckle into**

strap someone into something ❏ *She strapped the twins into their seats.*

strap yourself into something ❏ *He strapped himself into the cockpit.*

○ **strap 'on**

If you **strap** something **on**, you fasten it in position, using a belt or strap.

strap on something or **strap something on** ❏ *Mona hastily strapped on her skis.* ❏ *He strapped his new watch on.*

○ **strap 'up**

If you **strap** something **up**, you put a bandage or support around part of someone's body so they cannot use it.

strap something up or **strap up something** ❏ *They strapped my arm up for me at the hospital.* ❏ *A harness kept his right leg strapped up.*

stress /stres/ (**stresses, stressing, stressed**)

○ **stress 'out** [INFORMAL]

If something **stresses** you **out**, it makes you feel tense and worried.

stress someone out or **stress out someone** ❏ *Planning this wedding is really stressing me out.* ❏ *Bosses are stressing out their employees by expecting them to work long hours.*

● If you are **stressed out**, you feel very tense and worried. [INFORMAL] ❏ *I'm so stressed out I can hardly concentrate.* ❏ *Sport can be a great relaxation for stressed-out office workers.*

stretch /stretʃ/ (**stretches, stretching, stretched**)

○ **stretch a'way**

If an area of land **stretches away**, it extends for some distance. ❏ *The beach stretched away in a gentle curve.* ❏ *The sunny meadow stretches away as far as the eye can see.*

❂ **stretch 'out**

1 If you **stretch out** or **stretch** yourself **out**, you lie flat with your legs and body in a straight line.

stretch out ❏ *I just want to stretch out in my own bed.*

stretch yourself out ❏ *She groaned and stretched herself out on the sofa.*

2 If you **stretch** part of your body **out**, you hold it out straight.

stretch out something or **stretch something out** ❏ *He stretched out his arm and took my hand.* ❏ *She stretched her hand out for the money.*

strike /straɪk/ (**strikes, striking, struck**)

○ **'strike as**

If something or someone **strikes** you **as** being a particular thing or having a particular quality, you think that they are that thing or that they have that quality.

strike someone as something ❏ *He struck me as a very serious but friendly person.* ❏ *The situation suddenly struck her as funny.*

○ **'strike at**

If you **strike at** someone or something, you attack them.

strike at something ❏ *The opposition had struck at the root of Labour's strategy.* ❏ *He saw a chance to strike at his enemy.*

○ **strike 'back**

If you **strike back**, you attempt to harm someone because they have harmed you.
= **hit back** ❏ *If you keep humiliating him, eventually he will strike back.* ❏ [+ against] *She was determined to strike back against her critics.*

○ **strike 'down**

1 If someone **is struck down** or if something or someone **strikes** them **down**, they are badly injured or killed.

be struck down ❏ *President Kennedy was struck down by an assassin's bullet.* ❏ *Struck down by flu, he was unable to take part in the competition.*

strike someone down or **strike down someone** ❏ *Polio struck him down.*

2 To **strike down** a law means to stop it being or becoming law.

strike down something or **strike something down** ❏ *The judge declared the law unconstitutional and struck it down.*

○ **'strike from** [FORMAL]

If you **strike** words **from** a document or an official record, you remove them.

strike something from something ❏ *Her name had been struck from the register.* ❏ *They struck some clauses from the contract.*

○ **strike 'off**

1 If someone such as a doctor or lawyer **is struck off** or **struck off** a list, their name is taken off an official list and they are no longer allowed to work in their profession. [BRITISH]

be struck off ❏ *A dentist who behaved like this would be struck off and not allowed to practise again.*

be struck off something ❏ *He was struck off the medical register for dishonesty.*

2 → see **strike out**

'strike on (or strike upon)

If you **strike on** something, you suddenly and unexpectedly think of a solution or idea. = **hit on**

strike on something ❏ He struck on the idea of writing novels when he was reading to his children.

strike 'out

1 If you **strike out**, you begin to do something different, often because you want to become more independent. ❏ He decided to strike out on his own. ❏ The company was striking out in new directions in technology.

2 If you **strike out**, you try to hit someone or something. = **hit out** ❏ He struck out blindly, trying to get away. ❏ [+ at] She was a whirlwind of fury, striking out at anything in her path.

3 If you **strike out** at someone or something, you criticize or attack them. ❏ [+ at] They are reformers who strike out boldly at what they believe to be wrong. ❏ When we are criticized we often strike out in return.

4 If you **strike out** words in a document, you put a line through them because the information is wrong, for example. = **cross out**

strike out something or **strike something out** ❏ Strike out the questions which do not apply to you. ❏ She read through her essay and struck a few words out here and there.

NOTE **Delete** is a more formal word for **strike out**.

5 In baseball, if a batter **strikes out**, or if a pitcher **strikes** the batter **out**, the batter fails to hit three balls and is out.

strike out ❏ Canseco, suffering from a back injury, struck out.

strike out someone or **strike someone out** ❏ He struck out ten batters, and allowed only two runs.

6 If someone **strikes out**, they fail. [AMERICAN, INFORMAL] ❏ Their lawyer had struck out completely.

strike 'out (or strike off) [LITERARY]

If you **strike out** somewhere, you start to move in a determined way in a particular direction. ❏ He decided to leave the path and strike out across the grass. ❏ We struck off northward through the woods.

strike 'through

If you **strike through** words in a document, you put a line through them because the information is wrong, for example.

strike through something or **strike something through** ❏ If you disagree with part of the contract, simply strike it through and write your initials.

strike 'up

1 If you **strike up** a conversation or friendship, you begin it.

strike up something ❏ Alice and I struck up a friendship immediately. ❏ He's a talkative guy and I soon struck up a conversation with him.

2 If musicians **strike up** or **strike up** something, they begin to play music.

strike up ❏ The band struck up and everyone started dancing.

strike up something ❏ The orchestra struck up the national anthem.

3 If a piece of music **strikes up**, it begins to be played. ❏ 'The Wedding March' strikes up to announce the bride's arrival in church.

'strike upon → see strike on

string /strɪŋ/ (strings, stringing, strung)

string a'long

1 If you **string** someone **along**, you deceive them by encouraging them to believe something that is not true, especially something about your intentions. [INFORMAL]

string someone along or **string along someone** ❏ Gareth's just stringing you along; he won't marry you. ❏ They were making plans for war while stringing along several Western leaders.

2 If things are **strung along** somewhere, or if you **string** them **along** somewhere, they are positioned along the length of something with spaces in between them.

be strung along something ❏ Pretty little cottages are strung along the river.

string something along something ❏ I have strung Christmas lanterns along the mantelpiece.

3 If you **string along**, you go somewhere with someone for a short time. = **tag along** [INFORMAL] ❏ [+ with] Is it OK if I string along with you?

string 'out

1 If things are **strung out**, or if someone **strings** them **out**, they are spread out in a long line.

be strung out ❏ These towns are strung out along dirt roads.

string out something or **string something out** ❏ They were hammering in concrete posts and stringing out wire.

2 If you **string** something **out**, you deliberately make it last for a longer time than necessary.

string something out or **string out something** ❏ They seem to want to string the case out as long as possible. ❏ She managed to string out the assignment for about six months.

3 If someone is **strung out**, they are feeling ill and cannot think normally, especially because of drugs. [INFORMAL] ❑ [+ on] He's strung out on drugs and booze. ❑ I was tired and strung out from everything that had happened.

○ **string to'gether**

If you **string** words or sentences **together**, you add them to each other one at a time, in order to make a longer piece of speech or writing.

string something together or **string together something** ❑ I was dizzy, and I could hardly string two sentences together. ❑ She was finding it difficult to string together her thoughts.

○ **string 'up**

1 If you **string** something **up**, you hang or tie it along a string or cord. = **put up**
string something up or **string up something** ❑ They strung lights up all over the garden. ❑ She strung up a washing line on the balcony.

2 To **string** someone **up** means to kill them by hanging them. [INFORMAL]
string someone up or **string up someone** ❑ 'People like that should be strung up,' she declared.

3 If you are **strung up**, you feel tense and nervous. [INFORMAL] ❑ I was too strung up to eat anything.

strip /strɪp/ (**strips, stripping, stripped**)

○ **strip a'way**

1 If you **strip away** something that is attached to a surface, you remove it completely. = **strip off**
strip away something or **strip something away** ❑ The pale grey wallpaper had been stripped away.

2 To **strip away** something means to remove or get rid of it completely, especially so that you can see what something or someone is really like.
strip away something or **strip something away** ❑ If you strip away the commercialism, there is a beautiful meaning behind the festival. ❑ All his authority had been stripped away.

○ **strip 'down**

1 If you **strip down** or **are stripped down**, you remove all or most of your clothes.
strip down ❑ [+ to] He stripped down to his underpants and dived in.
be stripped down ❑ [+ to] The men were working in the heat, stripped down to trousers and boots.

2 If you **strip down** an engine or a piece of equipment, you take it to pieces, usually in order to clean it or repair it.
strip down something or **strip something down** ❑ She offered to help them strip down the bike. ❑ Can you fix the engine without stripping it down?

○ **'strip of**

1 If someone **is stripped of** something or if someone **strips** them **of** something, especially their rights or powers, those things are taken away from them.
be stripped of something ❑ These people have been stripped of their civil rights.
strip someone of something ❑ They stripped him of his title and academic post.

2 If something **is stripped of** something or if someone **strips** it **of** something, that thing is removed or taken away.
be stripped of something ❑ The ship had to be stripped of its fittings.
strip something of something ❑ Thieves stripped the bodies of all their valuables.

○ **strip 'off**

1 If you **strip off** your clothes or **strip off**, you remove your clothes.
strip off something ❑ Ben stripped off his remaining clothes.
strip off ❑ They stripped off and dived in.

2 If you **strip** something **off**, you completely remove something that is attached to a surface. = **strip away**
strip off something or **strip something off** ❑ They spent two weeks stripping off all the paint. ❑ The bark could easily be stripped off.

○ **strip 'out**

1 If you **strip** a place **out**, you take out everything that is inside it.
strip something out or **strip out something** ❑ The nursery was stripped out and painted white.

2 If you **strip** something **out**, you do not include it in a list, calculation, or piece of writing.
strip something out or **strip out something** ❑ The letter made no sense, as if all the verbs had been stripped out.

struggle /ˈstrʌɡəl/ (**struggles, struggling, struggled**)

○ **struggle 'on**

If you **struggle on**, you manage with great difficulty to continue doing something. = **soldier on** ❑ After he left the business, I struggled on alone.

stub /stʌb/ (**stubs, stubbing, stubbed**)

○ **stub 'out**

If someone **stubs out** a cigarette, they stop it burning by pressing the end against something.
stub out something or **stub something out** ❑ Phillip stubbed out his cigarette and lit another.

NOTE Extinguish is a more formal word for **stub out**.

stuff /stʌf/ (stuffs, stuffing, stuffed)
○ **stuff 'up**
If you **stuff** something **up**, you make a mistake or do it badly.
stuff something up ❑ *You have to get it right – if you stuff it up, you'll have to wait another four years for another opportunity.*
stuff up something ❑ *They'll probably stuff up the negotiations.*

stumble /'stʌmbəl/ (stumbles, stumbling, stumbled)
○ **'stumble across** (or **stumble on, stumble upon**)
If you **stumble across** something or someone, you discover or meet them unexpectedly. = **come across**
stumble across something/someone ❑ *In the course of their search they stumbled across something interesting.* ❑ *Sir Alexander Fleming stumbled on his great discovery of penicillin quite by accident.*

stump /stʌmp/ (stumps, stumping, stumped)
○ **stump 'up** [BRITISH]
If you **stump up** or **stump up** a sum of money, you pay a sum of money, often reluctantly. = **cough up**
stump up *or* **stump up something** ❑ *They hope investors will stump up £50m to help finance the film.*

style /staɪl/ (styles, styling, styled)
○ **style 'out** [INFORMAL]
If you **style out** something, you wear it and look good in it.
style out something *or* **style something out** ❑ *Are you brave enough to style out this new haircut?*
○ **style 'up**
If you **style** someone or something **up**, you make them more fashionable.
style someone/something up *or* **style up someone/something** ❑ *Style up your cakes with these edible decorations.*

subcontract /sʌbkən'trækt/ (subcontracts, subcontracting, subcontracted)
○ **subcon'tract to**
If one company **subcontracts to** another company or **subcontracts** work **to** them, it pays the other company to do part of the work that it has been employed to do.
subcontract to someone ❑ *We would never subcontract to builders who are unfamiliar with our high standards.*
subcontract something to someone ❑ *They are cutting costs by subcontracting work to other local firms.*

subject /səb'dʒekt/ (subjects, subjecting, subjected)
○ **sub'ject to**
If you **subject** someone or something **to** something, you make them experience something unpleasant.
subject someone to something ❑ *Their decision subjected the children to unnecessary hardship.* ❑ *The air bases were subjected to intense air attack.*
subject yourself to something ❑ *I was not willing to subject myself to these humiliating tests.*

subjugate /'sʌbdʒʊgeɪt/ (subjugates, subjugating, subjugated)
○ **'subjugate to** [FORMAL]
To **subjugate** one thing or person **to** another thing or person means to treat them as being less important.
subjugate something/someone to something/someone ❑ *Many mothers subjugate their own needs to those of their children.*

submerge /səb'mɜːdʒ/ (submerges, submerging, submerged)
○ **sub'merge in**
If you **submerge** yourself **in** an activity, you give all your attention to it and do not think about anything else.
submerge yourself in something ❑ *Vicky tried to submerge herself in her work and forget about Paul.* ❑ *He would submerge himself entirely in the music.*

submit /səb'mɪt/ (submits, submitting, submitted)
○ **sub'mit to**
▪ If you **submit to** something, you allow something to be done to you, or you do what someone wants even though you do not want to.
submit to something ❑ *If I submitted to their demands, they would not hurt me.*
▪ If you **submit** a proposal, report, or request **to** someone, you send it to them so that they can consider it or make a decision about it.
submit something to someone ❑ *Several proposals were submitted to the committee.*

subordinate /sə'bɔːdɪneɪt/ (subordinates, subordinating, subordinated)
○ **sub'ordinate to** [FORMAL]
To **subordinate** something **to** another thing means to treat it as less important than the other thing.

subordinate something to something
❏ *We have subordinated our desire for liberty to our desire for security.*

subscribe /səbˈskraɪb/ (subscribes, subscribing, subscribed)

○ **subˈscribe to**

■ If you **subscribe to** an opinion or belief, you have this opinion or belief.
subscribe to something ❏ *Sam did not subscribe to any organized religion.* ❏ *Few people nowadays subscribe to this theory.*

■ If you **subscribe to** something such as a magazine or newspaper, you arrange to receive it regularly, often by paying one sum of money for a long period.
subscribe to something ❏ *She subscribes to the Wall Street Journal online.* ❏ *To receive this channel you must subscribe to a cable TV service.*

substitute /ˈsʌbstɪtjuːt, AM -tuːt/ (substitutes, substituting, substituted)

○ **ˈsubstitute for**

If you **substitute** one thing or person **for** another, or if one thing or person **substitutes for** another, the first thing or person takes the place or performs the function of the second thing or person.
substitute something/someone for something/someone ❏ *Try substituting yoghurt for cream.* ❏ *Peaches can be substituted for plums if you prefer.*
substitute for something/someone ❏ *A two-week course can't substitute for a proper education.* ❏ *He was substituting for the injured William Wales.*

subtract /səbˈtrækt/ (subtracts, subtracting, subtracted)

○ **subˈtract from**

If you **subtract** one number **from** another number, you take the first number away from the second number.
subtract something from something
❏ *If you subtract 2 from 5, you get 3.*

suck /sʌk/ (sucks, sucking, sucked)

○ **suckˈinto**

If you **are sucked into** a bad situation or if someone or something **sucks** you **into** it, you are unable to prevent yourself from becoming involved in it.
be sucked into something ❏ *He didn't want to be sucked into a relationship with her.*
suck someone into something ❏ *He had once again sucked her into a discussion she did not want to have.*

○ **suckˈoff** [RUDE]

To **suck** someone **off** means to lick or suck their genitals to give them sexual pleasure.

○ **suckˈup to** [INFORMAL]

If you **suck up to** someone in a position of authority, you try to please them by flattering them or by doing things for them, especially in order to gain some advantage for yourself.
suck up to someone ❏ *I hate the way he sucks up to the bosses.*

sucker /ˈsʌkə/ (suckers, suckering, suckered)

○ **suckerˈinto** [AMERICAN, INFORMAL]

If you **sucker** someone **into** doing something, you deceive them to make them do it, usually when this is against their own interests. = **trick into**
sucker someone into something ❏ *He had been suckered into parting with nearly all his money.*

sum /sʌm/ (sums, summing, summed)

⊙ **sumˈup**

■ If you **sum** something **up**, you briefly describe its most important aspects.
= **summarize**
sum up something ❏ *Harry summed up the situation well when he said, 'It's a mess.'*
sum something up ❏ *She was searching for the words that would sum it up.*
NOTE **Encapsulate** is a more formal word for **sum up**.

■ If something **sums up** a situation, it represents or suggests its most important and typical features.
sum up something ❏ *One place in particular seems to sum up the horror of that war.*
sum something up ❏ *For me, that incident sums the whole evening up.*
NOTE **Epitomize** is a more formal word for **sum up**.

■ If someone **sums up**, they briefly repeat the main points of a speech or debate as a conclusion. = **summarize** ❏ *At the end of the discussion, he summed up, and added a few points.* ❏ *To sum up: within our society there still exist major inequalities.*

■ When a judge or lawyer **sums up**, he or she makes a speech at the end of a trial reminding the jury of the evidence and the main arguments of the case. ❏ *Summing up, the judge said that this was a very serious offence.* ❏ *Mr Marashi is about to start summing up for the defence.* ● The **summing-up** at the end of a trial is a speech in which the judge reminds the jury of the evidence and the main arguments of the case. ❏ *In his summing-up, the judge again returned to the motive.*

■ If you **sum** someone or something **up**,

you form an opinion or make a judgment of them. = **size up**

sum someone/something up or **sum up someone/something** ❑ He was able to sum us up in a very short time.

sum yourself up ❑ If I had to sum myself up, I'd say I was a relaxed, easy-going person.

• A **summing up** is an opinion or judgment about something or someone. ❑ 'She was all right,' was Lester's summing up.

ummon /'sʌmən/ (**summons, summoning, summoned**)

○ **summon 'up**

1 If you **summon up** something such as strength, courage or enthusiasm, you manage to find enough of it to do something. = **muster up**
summon up something or **summon something up** [+ to-infinitive] She did not seem able to summon up the effort to reply. ❑ He eventually summoned the courage up to ask them if Melanie was there.

2 If you **summon up** support, help, or resources, you persuade people to give you support or help. = **drum up**
summon up something or **summon something up** ❑ He was hoping to summon up support for his measures. ❑ Almost overnight he seems to have summoned up a team of great talent.

3 If you **summon** someone **up**, you order them to come to you. = **call up** [FORMAL]
summon up someone or **summon someone up** ❑ She summoned up the remainder of the family. ❑ We waited to be summoned up.

4 If you **summon** something **up**, you think of or remember a word or fact.
summon up something or **summon something up** ❑ We hope he will be able to summon up the facts. ❑ I summoned the name up from somewhere in my brain.

5 If something **summons** something **up**, it causes you to have a particular thought or feeling. = **conjure up, evoke**
summon up something or **summon something up** ❑ The smell summoned up memories of my childhood.

uperimpose /su:pərɪm'pəʊz/ (**superimposes, superimposing, superimposed**)

• **superim'pose on** (or **superimpose onto**)

If one image **is superimposed on** another or you **superimpose** one image **on** another, one image is put on top of another so that you can see both images.
be superimposed on something ❑ A photo

of his face was superimposed on a picture of a woman's body.

superimpose something on something ❑ You can superimpose the lettering directly onto one of your pictures.

surge /sɜːdʒ/ (**surges, surging, surged**)

○ **surge 'up**

1 If a feeling or memory **surges up**, you suddenly feel it very intensely. = **well up** [LITERARY] ❑ I felt anger surge up inside me. ❑ Memories surge up in her mind.

2 If a sound **surges up**, you suddenly hear it very loudly and powerfully. = **rise up** [LITERARY] ❑ A huge roar of applause surged up from the crowd.

3 An **upsurge** is a sudden and serious increase in something. ❑ [+ of] There has been a massive upsurge of social unrest. ❑ [+ in] There has been an upsurge in the prison population.

surround /sə'raʊnd/ (**surrounds, surrounding, surrounded**)

○ **sur'round with**

If you **surround** yourself **with** particular people or things, you make sure that you have a lot of them near you all the time.
surround yourself with someone/ something ❑ The Prime Minister surrounded himself with talented advisers. ❑ I like to surround myself with beautiful things.

suss /sʌs/ (**susses, sussing, sussed**)

○ **suss 'out** [BRITISH, INFORMAL]

1 If you **suss** someone or something **out**, you discover the truth about them. = **work out**
suss out something/someone or **suss something/someone out** ❑ He talked about how to suss people out by their body language. ❑ She had me sussed out in ten minutes.

2 If you **suss** something **out**, you are able to solve a problem or understand something. = **work out**
suss out something or **suss something out** ❑ We've looked at the map and sussed out the best route. ❑ Don't worry, you'll soon suss it out with a bit of practice.

swab /swɒb/ (**swabs, swabbing, swabbed**)

Swab is also spelled **swob** in American English.

○ **swab 'down**

If you **swab** something **down**, you clean a surface thoroughly with a wet mop or cloth and water. = **wash down**
swab something down or **swab down something** ❑ She swabbed down the table. ❑ The men were ordered to swab the deck down.

○ **swab 'out**

If you **swab** something **out**, you clean a room or container thoroughly with a wet mop or cloth and water. = **wash out**

swab something out or **swab out something** ❑ The men have to swab out their sleeping quarters in the morning. ❑ Swab it out with hot water and a little disinfectant.

swallow /'swɒləʊ/ (**swallows, swallowing, swallowed**)

○ **swallow 'down**

If you **swallow** something **down**, you make it pass from your mouth into your stomach. = **gulp down**

swallow something down or **swallow down something** ❑ She took the medicine, and swallowed it down. ❑ He swallowed down the last lump of bread.

○ **swallow 'up**

❶ If an animal **swallows** something **up**, it takes it into its mouth and causes it to pass into its stomach.

swallow something up or **swallow up something** ❑ It was said that a whale had swallowed him up. ❑ The snake swallows up its prey whole.

❷ If something **is swallowed up** by something else, or if the other thing **swallows** it **up**, it becomes part of it and no longer has a separate identity. = **be absorbed**

be swallowed up ❑ The old centre of the village was being swallowed up by new housing estates.

swallow something up or **swallow up something** ❑ Large corporations drive out small producers by swallowing them up.

❸ If someone or something **is swallowed up**, or if something **swallows** them **up**, they are hidden by something or disappear into something. = **be engulfed**

be swallowed up ❑ He saw her briefly before she was swallowed up in the crowd of passengers.

swallow up something or **swallow something up** ❑ Deep shadow swallowed up the foot of the stairs.

❹ If something **swallows up** money or resources, it uses them. = **use up**

swallow up something or **swallow something up** ❑ Policing the event swallowed up a large percentage of our budget. ❑ Slot machines had swallowed all his cash up.

swap /swɒp/ (**swaps, swapping, swapped**)

Swap is also spelled **swop**.

○ **swap a'round** (or **swap round** [mainly BRITISH])

If you **swap** things **around**, you move them into different places, usually so that each one is in a place where one of the others was before.

swap something around or **swap around something** ❑ I swapped them round when he wasn't looking. ❑ If we swap around the furniture we can make more space in the room.

○ **'swap for**

If you **swap** one thing **for** another thing, you remove the first thing and replace it with the second, or you stop doing the first thing and start doing the second.

swap something for something ❑ Despite the heat, he'd swapped his shorts for a suit and tie. ❑ He has swapped his hectic rock star's lifestyle for that of a country gentleman.

○ **swap 'over**

❶ If you **swap** two things **over** or if they **swap over**, you move them or they move so that each is in the place where the other one was before.

swap something over or **swap over something** ❑ If the other one looks better we can always swap them over. ❑ He secretly swapped over their plates of food.

swap over ❑ As you move your head the images seem to swap over.

❷ If people **swap over**, they exchange positions or activities so that each one is where the other one was before, or doing what the other was doing before. ❑ I drove for the first two hours, then we swapped over.

❸ If you **swap over** to something, you start doing something different. ❑ [+ to] I studied Psychology for a year before swapping over to Philosophy. ❑ When you've done sixteen leg raises swap over and do the other leg.

○ **swap 'round** → see **swap around**

swarm /swɔːm/ (**swarms, swarming, swarmed**)

○ **'swarm with**

If a place **is swarming with** people, animals or insects, there are a lot of them there.

be swarming with something ❑ Within minutes the area was swarming with police officers. ❑ The lake was swarming with fish.

swear /sweə/ (**swears, swearing, swore, sworn**)

○ **'swear by**

If you **swear by** something, you believe that it is the best thing for a particular purpose.

swear by something ❑ Gas is better than electricity for cooking, I always swear by it. ❑ Some swear by vitamin tablets, and others put their trust in eating fresh fruit and vegetables every day.

swear 'in
When someone **is sworn in**, they make a formal promise in a court of law or at an official ceremony before starting an important job.
be sworn in ❑ *The jury has been sworn in at his trial.* ❑ *[+ as] Moore was sworn in as President.*
● A **swearing-in** is an occasion when someone makes a formal promise before starting an official job. ❑ *The swearing-in of a new Assembly took place on 8 May.*

swear 'off [INFORMAL]
If you **swear off** something, you decide not to consume or do it any more. = **give up**
swear off something ❑ *I've sworn off coffee for the time being.*
NOTE **Renounce** is a more formal word for **swear off**.

sweat /swet/ (**sweats, sweating, sweated**)

sweat 'off
1 If you **sweat off** weight, you lose weight by causing yourself to sweat heavily.
sweat off something or **sweat something off** ❑ *He managed to sweat off five pounds before the weigh-in.*
2 If you **sweat off** an illness, you get rid of it by causing yourself to sweat heavily.
sweat off something or **sweat something off** ❑ *Just wrap up warm in bed and try to sweat it off.*

sweat 'out
1 If you **sweat** something **out**, you live through a difficult period of time, waiting for it to end.
sweat something out or **sweat out something** ❑ *The problem was how to sweat out the next six weeks.*
● If someone **sweats it out**, they wait for a bad situation to end because there is nothing else they can do. ❑ *I decided to let him sweat it out for a couple of weeks before giving him my answer.*
2 If you **sweat** something **out**, you get rid of an illness or harmful substance from your body by causing yourself to sweat heavily.
sweat out something or **sweat something out** ❑ *He went running to try and sweat out the virus.* ❑ *Will you go to the doctor, or just go to bed and sweat it out?*

'sweat over
If you **sweat over** something, you work very hard at it.
sweat over something ❑ *They sweated over every scene in that film.* ❑ *I really sweated over my essay and she didn't even mark it.*

sweep /swiːp/ (**sweeps, sweeping, swept**)

sweep a'side
To **sweep** something **aside** means to make it seem unimportant or not to pay any attention to it.
sweep something aside or **sweep aside something** ❑ *His enthusiasm swept aside many obstacles.* ❑ *My suggestion was swept aside.*

sweep a'way
1 To **sweep** something **away** means to destroy or remove it entirely.
sweep away something ❑ *A violent revolution swept away the old regime.* ❑ *Almost the entire manufacturing base has been swept away.*
sweep something away ❑ *Modernization has swept all those old ideas away.*
NOTE **Eradicate** is a more formal word for **sweep away**.
2 If someone or something **is swept away**, or if something **sweeps** them **away**, they are carried off or destroyed by something such as a very strong wave, wind, or current.
be swept away ❑ *The current was so powerful he was in danger of being swept away.*
sweep away something ❑ *A gust of wind swept away his papers.*
sweep something away ❑ *A mudslide had swept their tents away.*
3 If someone **is swept away** or if something or someone **sweeps** them **away**, their emotions are so strong that they cannot behave calmly and sensibly. = **be carried away**
be swept away ❑ *She never allowed herself to be swept away by passion.*
sweep someone away or **sweep away someone** ❑ *He swept her away with a proposal of marriage.*

sweep 'out
1 If you **sweep** something **out**, you remove dirt or dust from it using a brush.
sweep out something or **sweep something out** ❑ *She swept out the grate and laid a new fire.* ❑ *They're in Grandfather's old room. I've swept it out and put some sheets on the beds.*
2 If you **sweep** something **out**, you remove it from a place using a brush.
sweep out something or **sweep something out** ❑ *I had to sweep out the cobwebs in the attic.* ❑ *[+ of] She swept the leaves out of the yard.*

sweep 'up
1 If you **sweep** something **up** or **sweep up**, you collect something such as dirt with a brush in order to get rid of it.
sweep up something ❑ *The girls were sweeping up leaves on the path .*

sweeten

sweep something up ❑ *You should sweep that broken glass up before someone treads on it.*
sweep up ❑ *He offered to sweep up afterwards.*
2 If you **sweep** something **up**, you quickly pick it up with a large movement of your arm.
sweep up something ❑ *She swept up her coat and left.*
sweep something up ❑ *I put the money on the table and he swept it up at once.* ❑ *Mona swept the child up to protect it from the animal.*
3 If you **are swept up** in something, you become very involved in it, often without meaning to. = **be caught up**
be swept up ❑ *[+ in] She became swept up in the general excitement.* ❑ *She was swept up by a passion of creativity.*

sweeten /'swi:tən/ (**sweetens, sweetening, sweetened**)
○ **sweeten 'up**
If you **sweeten** someone **up**, you do something nice for them or give them something, in order to get them to agree to what you want. = **butter up, soften up**
sweeten someone up or **sweeten up someone** ❑ *They sweetened him up by offering him another £5,000 a year.* ❑ *Bribes were used to sweeten up corrupt customs officials.*

swell /swel/ (**swells, swelling, swelled, swollen**)

> The past participle can be either **swelled** or **swollen**.

○ **swell 'up**
1 If a part of your body **swells up**, it becomes larger than normal, usually as a result of an injury or illness. = **puff up**; ≠ **go down** ❑ *A mosquito had bitten her and her whole arm had swollen up.*
2 If a feeling **swells up**, it suddenly becomes much stronger. ❑ *She was overwhelmed by the anger swelling up in her.* ❑ *Seeing them together, the old jealousy swelled up.*
3 If a sound **swells up**, it becomes much louder. ❑ *A glad shout swelled up and died away again.* ❑ *I love the way the guitars swell up in the chorus.*
4 If the sea **swells up**, the waves become larger. [LITERARY] ❑ *People who saw the tsunami described how the sea swelled up.*
○ **'swell with** [LITERARY]
If you **swell with** a feeling, you suddenly have a lot of that feeling.
swell with something ❑ *She swelled with pride when her son received the award.*

swill /swɪl/ (**swills, swilling, swilled**)
○ **swill a'round** (or **swill round** [mainly BRITISH])
1 If a liquid **swills around** in a container, o if you **swill** it **around**, it moves around.
swill around ❑ *There was a lot of water swilling around in the bottom of the boat.*
swill something around ❑ *She swilled the water around in her glass.*
swill something around something ❑ *I swilled the water round my mouth before swallowing it.*
2 If money **is swilling around** or **is swilling around** somewhere, there is a lot of it available. [INFORMAL]
be swilling around ❑ *There is much less money swilling around nowadays.*
be swilling around something ❑ *There is a lo of cash swilling around the football club.*
○ **swill 'down**
1 If you **swill** a drink **down**, you drink quickly or enthusiastically.
swill down something or **swill something down** ❑ *Everyone laughed and swilled down another drink.*
2 If you **swill** food **down**, you drink something at the same time as you are eating. = **wash down**
swill down something or **swill something down** ❑ *[+ with] He swilled down his steak with a glass of red wine.* ❑ *How about a drink to swill it down?*
○ **swill 'out** [mainly BRITISH]
To **swill out** something means to clean it b pouring water over it.
swill out something or **swill something out** ❑ *He finished his coffee and swilled out the mug.* ❑ *She swilled the bucket out.*
○ **swill 'round** → see **swill around**

swim /swɪm/ (**swimming**)
○ **'swim in**
If something **is swimming in** a liquid, it is covered with a lot of it.
be swimming in something ❑ *The meat was swimming in a thick sauce.* ❑ *The chips were swimming in oil.*

swing /swɪŋ/ (**swings, swinging, swung**)
○ **swing a'round** (or **swing round** [mainly BRITISH])
If you **swing around**, you suddenly turn and face in the opposite direction. = **turn around** ❑ *There was a knock on his door. He swung round startled.* ❑ *She swung around to face me, looking furious.*
○ **'swing at**
If you **swing at** someone or something, you

try to hit them with your arm or with something that you are holding.
swing at someone/something ❏ *I picked up the baseball bat and swung at the ball.*

swing 'by
If you **swing by**, or **swing by** a place, you make a short visit to a person or place while you are on your way to another place. ❏ *I'm in the neighborhood. Can I swing by?*
swing by somewhere ❏ *Do you want me to swing by the house and pick you up?*

swing 'round → see swing around

swing 'round to [BRITISH]
If a conversation **swings round to** something, or if you **swing** it **round to** something, you start talking about a particular topic. **= turn to**
swing round to something ❏ *Now the conversation swung round to cooking family meals.*
swing something round to something
❏ *After a time he swung the conversation round to discussing the police.*

wipe /swaɪp/ (**swipes, swiping, swiped**)
'swipe at
If you **swipe at** someone or something, you try to hit them by making a swinging movement with your arm.
swipe at someone/something ❏ *She swiped at Rusty as though he was a fly.*

vitch /swɪtʃ/ (**switches, switching, switched**)
switch a'round (or **switch round** [mainly BRITISH])
1 If you **switch** things **around**, you move them into different places, usually so that each one is in a place where one of the others was before.
switch something around or **switch around something** ❏ *Someone had switched the cups around and we didn't know which was which.*
2 If someone **switches around**, they change to something different or start doing something different. ❏ *Nurses in junior positions are encouraged to switch around and work in different areas.*

switch 'off
1 If you **switch** something **off** or **switch off**, you stop something working by pressing a switch. **= turn off; ≠ switch on**
switch something off ❏ *He switched the radio off.* ❏ *When you've finished working on your computer, please switch it off.*
switch off something ❏ *She went round the house switching off all the lights.*
switch off ❏ *Thousands of viewers switched off in disgust.*

2 If an electrical device **switches off**, it stops working. ❏ *The radiators switch off automatically when it reaches 20 degrees.*
3 If you **switch** a feeling or behaviour **off**, you suddenly stop feeling or behaving in that way. **≠ switch on**
switch off something or **switch something off** ❏ *The soldiers try to switch off their personal feelings and do their job.* ❏ *He seems to be able to switch his charm on and off when he wants to.*
4 If you **switch off**, you stop listening or paying attention. [INFORMAL] ❏ *The lecture was so boring I just switched off.* ❏ *I tend to switch off when she starts talking about her job.*

⚙ **switch 'on**
1 If you **switch** something **on** or **switch on**, you start something working by pressing a switch. **= turn on; ≠ switch off**
switch on something ❏ *He ran up the stairs and switched on the light on the landing.* ❏ *I sat down in front of the TV and switched on the news.*
switch something on ❏ *She had switched the heating on because she felt cold.* ❏ *The oven was cold because I had forgotten to switch it on.*
switch on ❏ *Does your computer take a long time to boot up when you switch on in the morning?*
2 If an electrical device **switches on**, it starts working. ❏ *What time does the heating switch on in the morning?*
3 If you **switch** behaviour **on**, you suddenly start behaving in a particular way, especially when this is not sincere.
≠ switch off
switch on something or **switch something on** ❏ *The girl switched on an automatic smile as he approached.*
4 Someone who is **switched-on** is clever, and aware of what is fashionable and up-to-date. [INFORMAL] ❏ *Kate's got some switched-on mates like Sadie Frost and Jo Wood.*

○ **switch 'over**
1 If you **switch over**, you change from using or doing one thing to using or doing something else. ❏ [+ to] *Airlines and hotels have switched over to online booking.* ❏ *I switched over from History to Politics at the end of my first year.* ● A **switchover** is an occasion when someone changes from using or doing one thing to using or doing something else. ❏ *Viewers were told how to adjust their TV sets for the switchover to digital broadcasting.*
2 If you **switch over**, you start watching a different channel on television. ❏ *My father always switches over during the adverts.* ❏ [+ to] *She switched over to Channel 4.*

○ **switch 'round → see switch around**

○ **'switch to**

To **switch to** something different or **switch** something **to** something different means to change to it.

switch to something ❏ *He started speaking in French and then switched to English.*

switch something to something ❏ *Getting no response, he switched his attention to what she was doing.* ❏ *He had switched his loyalty to another party.*

○ **switch 'up** [INFORMAL]

1 If you **switch** something **up**, you exchange it for something different, usually something better.

switch up something or **switch something up** ❏ *You can switch up your service from silver to gold.*

2 If you **switch** things **up**, you change between different things to avoid getting bored.

switch up something or **switch something up** ❏ *I love switching up my nail colour.* ❏ *I play tennis in summer, but I like to switch things up, so I run, do Pilates and swim.*

swivel /'swɪvəl/ (**swivels, swivelling, swivelled**)

American English uses the spellings **swiveling** and **swiveled**.

○ **swivel a'round** (or **swivel round** [mainly BRITISH])

1 If you **swivel around**, especially when you are sitting, you turn quickly and face in another direction. **= turn around** ❏ *I swivelled right round in my chair.* ❏ *He swivelled around to greet her as she came in.*

2 If you **swivel** something **around**, you turn it quickly.

swivel something around ❏ *Michael slowly swivelled his chair around.*

swob /swɒb/ (**swobs, swobbing, swobbed**)
→ see **swab**

swoop /swuːp/ (**swoops, swooping, swooped**)

○ **swoop 'down**

1 When a bird **swoops down**, it suddenly moves down through the air towards the ground. ❏ *An eagle swooped down on its prey.*

2 If a group of people **swoops down**, they suddenly move towards a person or place

and attack them. ❏ [+ *on*] *Troops swooped down on their headquarters.* ❏ *From time to time raiders would swoop down to steal horses or catt*

○ **'swoop on**

If police or soldiers **swoop on** a place, they go there suddenly and quickly, usually in order to arrest someone or to attack the pla **swoop on something** ❏ *The terror ended whe armed police swooped on the car.* ❏ *Immigration officers swooped on the warehouse and arrested three men.*

swop /swɒp/ (**swops, swopping, swoppe** → see **swap**

swot /swɒt/ (**swots, swotting, swotted**)

○ **swot 'up** [BRITISH, INFORMAL]

If you **swot up** a subject or **swot up**, you tr to learn as much as you can about a subje usually before a test. **= mug up**

swot up something or **swot something up** ❏ *He swotted up American history before meetin the President.* ❏ *They won't be able to answer th questions if they haven't swotted the subject up.* **swot up** ❏ [+ *on*] *I was swotting up on my Engl grammar.*

NOTE **Revise** is a more formal word for **swot up**.

sympathize /'sɪmpəθaɪz/ (**sympathizes sympathizing, sympathized**)

○ **sympathize with**

1 If you **sympathize with** someone who i in a bad situation, you are sorry for them. **sympathize with someone** ❏ *I really sympathize with all those people who have lost their jobs.*

2 If you **sympathize with** someone's feelings you understand them.

sympathize with something ❏ *I can sympathize with your fears and anxieties.* ❏ *He liked Max, and sympathized with his ambitions.*

3 If you **sympathize with** someone or something you approve of them and support them.

sympathize with someone/something ❏ *Most of the people living there sympathized wi the protesters.* ❏ *Conrad sympathized with the Democratic Party in the United States.*

syphon /'saɪfən/ (**syphons, syphoning, syphoned**) → see **siphon**

Tt

ack /tæk/ (**tacks, tacking, tacked**)

tack 'down

If you **tack** something **down**, you fix it to a surface using small nails.

tack something down or **tack down something** ❏ *You should tack that rug down before someone slips on it.* ❏ *Carpets should always be tacked down securely.*

tack 'on

If something **is tacked on** or if you **tack** something **on**, it is added or joined to something already complete, often in a way that seems unsatisfactory. = **tag on**

be tacked on ❏ [+ to] *The second point is tacked on to the end of Regulation 4.*

tack something on or **tack on something** ❏ [+ to] *They've tacked a garage on to the house.*

tack 'up

If you **tack** something **up**, you fasten it to a vertical surface using small nails.

tack up something or **tack something up** ❏ *I saw advertisements tacked up on telegraph poles.*

ag /tæg/ (**tags, tagging, tagged**)

tag a'long

If you **tag along**, you go somewhere with someone, especially when they have not asked you to. ❏ [+ with] *My younger sister always wanted to tag along with us when we went out.* ❏ *Do you mind if I tag along?*

tag 'on

If something **is tagged on** or if you **tag** something **on**, it is added to the end of something that is already complete. = **tack on**

be tagged on ❏ [+ to] *The web address is often just the company name with 'dot com' tagged on to the end.*

tag something on or **tag on something** ❏ *When the series ended we tagged on an extra show by popular demand.*

ail /teɪl/ (**tails, tailing, tailed**)

tail a'way (or **tail off**)

If someone's voice **tails away**, it gradually becomes quieter and then silent. ❏ *As I*

walked in her voice tailed away. ❏ *Conversation tended to tail off when he approached.*

○ tail 'back [BRITISH]

If traffic **tails back**, a long line of it forms, moving very slowly or not at all. ❏ *Traffic tailed back from the roundabout to the motorway junction.* ● A **tailback** is a long line of traffic that is moving very slowly or not at all. ❏ *They hit a tailback of rush hour traffic in the Midland Road.*

○ tail 'off

1 If something **tails off**, it gradually becomes less in amount or value, often before ending completely. ❏ *The rains tail off in September.*

2 → see **tail away**

tailor /'teɪlə/ (**tailors, tailoring, tailored**)

○ 'tailor to

If you **tailor** something **to** someone's needs or a particular purpose, you change it to make it suitable for them.

tailor something to something ❏ *We can tailor the program to the patient's needs.* ❏ *The scripts are tailored to American comedy audiences.*

take /teɪk/ (**takes, taking, took, taken**)

○ take a'back

If you **are taken aback** by something or if something **takes** you **aback**, you are surprised or shocked by it.

be taken aback ❏ *I was a bit taken aback by his sudden change of mind.* ❏ *He was taken aback at how different she looked.*

take someone aback or **take aback someone** ❏ *The sound of her voice took him aback.*

○ take 'after

If you **take after** someone, you are like a member of your family in your appearance, behaviour, or character.

take after someone ❏ *Anna doesn't look like her mother, so she must take after her dad.* ❏ *He's very determined – he takes after his grandmother.*

○ take a'gainst [BRITISH]

If you **take against** someone or something, you start to dislike them, often without a good reason. ≠ **take to**

take against someone/something ❏ *My boss seems to have taken against me for some reason.*

✪ take a'long

If you **take** someone or something **along**, you take them with you when you go somewhere.

take someone/something along ❏ [+ with] *I asked a friend to take me along with him.* ❏ *It's a show for all the family, so take your children along.*
take along someone/something ❏ *I took along a small black bag.*

✪ take a'part

1 If you **take** something **apart**, you separate it into the different parts that it is made from. ≠ **put together**
take something apart ❏ *He liked to take engines apart.*
take apart something ❏ *Most of these machines have to be taken apart to be cleaned.*
NOTE **Dismantle** is a more formal word for **take apart**.
2 If you **take** something **apart**, you analyse it carefully, often in order to show what its weaknesses are.
take apart something ❏ *The last chapter takes apart the official line on the country's foreign policy.*
take something apart ❏ *The professor took my essay apart.*
3 If you **take** someone **apart**, you completely defeat them or show them to be completely wrong or mistaken.
take apart someone or **take someone apart** ❏ *A member of the audience stood up and began to take the speaker apart.* ❏ *He was afraid the reviewers were going to take him apart.*

◯ take a'round (or take round [mainly BRITISH])

If you **take** someone **around** a place or **take** them **around**, you go to a place with them and show them its interesting or important features. = **show around**
take someone around something ❏ *I took my son around my laboratory.* ❏ *He took us around the islands in his small boat.*
take someone around ❏ *We take parties of visitors round on Saturday afternoons.*

◯ take a'side

If you **take** someone **aside**, you separate them from the rest of a group in order to talk to them privately.
take someone aside or **take aside someone** ❏ *He took Daniel aside and told him not to worry.* ❏ *The best thing to do is take aside the boy or girl who is causing trouble.*

✪ take a'way

1 If you **take** something **away**, you remove it from a place and put it somewhere else. ≠ **put back**
take something away ❏ [+ from] *She took her hands away from her eyes and looked.* ❏ *I don't want this. Take it away.*
take away something ❏ *The rug had been taken away for cleaning.* ● A **takeaway** is a shop or restaurant which sells cooked food that you eat somewhere else, for example home. [BRITISH] ❏ *He works at the Chinese takeaway.* ● **Takeaway** food or a **takeaway** is hot cooked food that is sold to be eaten somewhere else. [BRITISH] ❏ *I'm too tired to cook – let's have a takeaway.* ❏ *They were eating takeaway pizzas.*
NOTE In American English, **take-out** means almost the same as **takeaway**.
2 If you **take** something **away**, you remove it from someone and prevent them from having it any more.
take away something ❏ *They took away all my possessions, and sent me down to the cells.* ❏ [+ from] *Even his rights as a citizen had been taken away from him.*
take something away ❏ [+ from] *I took the knife away from him.* ❏ *These men wanted to help them keep their land, not take it away.*
3 If someone **takes** you **away**, you go with them to stay in another place.
take someone away ❏ [+ with] *She had taken the children away with her to her parents' house.* ❏ [+ from] *I want to take you away from all this stress.* ❏ *Some friends have taken her away on holiday.*
4 If someone **takes** you **away**, they force you to go with them.
take someone away ❏ *They had taken her away. They had kidnapped her.* ❏ [+ to] *Two officers took the man away to the cells.*
take away someone ❏ *The police came and took away her husband.* ❏ *She was taken away by an ambulance.*
5 If something **takes** you **away**, it prevents you from being with someone or doing something.
take someone away ❏ *My husband's job took him away a lot.'* ❏ [+ from] *She enjoys her work but it takes her away from her family.*
6 To **take** something **away** means to destroy or get rid of something such as a quality or idea.
take away something ❏ *This would take away the justification for war.* ❏ *Nothing seems to take away his appetite.*
take something away ❏ [+ from] *His jokes took some of the tension away from the situation.* ❏ *Drugs can reduce the pain, but nothing takes it away completely.*

7 If something **takes** your **breath away**, it is so beautiful, exciting, or surprising that you are unable to speak or breathe normally for a moment. ❑ *Her beauty took his breath away.* ❑ *His suggestion was so daring it took my breath away.*

8 If you **take** something **away** from an experience or situation, you learn it as a result.

take something away [+ from] *The main thing I took away from the experience was how important friends are.* ❑ *I suggested some useful ideas for her to take away with her.*

9 If you **take** one number or amount **away** from another, you subtract the first from the second.

take something away or **take away something** ❑ *The children are learning to add numbers up to ten and take them away.* ❑ *If I have 50 and I take away 19, what is left?* ❑ [+ from] *This last amount is taken away from your annual earnings.*

take a'way from

1 If someone **takes** you **away from** your husband, wife, or lover, they cause you to leave your husband, wife, or lover, and have a relationship with them instead.

take someone away from someone ❑ *Nobody could ever take me away from you.* ❑ *She took my boyfriend away from me.*

2 To **take away from** or to **take** something **away** from something means to make it lower in value or quality than it should be or than it was.

take away from something ❑ *She doesn't like all the equipment, which in her view takes away from the sport.*

take something away from something ❑ *The opposition were not very strong, but I don't want to take anything away from the team's performance.*

NOTE **Detract from** is a more formal expression for **take away from**.

take 'back

1 When you **take** something **back**, you take it to the place where you were before or where it was before.

take something back ❑ *Nobody wanted coffee so he took the tray back.* ❑ [+ to] *I filled a plastic bottle with water and took it back to the car.* ❑ *Will you take those books back upstairs please?*

take back something ❑ *They returned home, taking back the money they had earned.*

2 If you **take** something **back**, you return it to the place where you bought it or the person that you borrowed or took it from.

take something back ❑ [+ to] *We're taking the laptop back to the shop because it doesn't work properly.* ❑ *If it doesn't fit, take it back.*

take back something ❑ *Can you take back clothes that you've already worn?*

3 If you **take** something **back**, you agree to accept it again from someone who you gave or sold it to.

take back something ❑ *He refused to take back the engagement ring, saying she should keep it.* ❑ *Shops will not take back damaged goods.*

take something back ❑ *If it doesn't work, the store must take it back.*

4 If you **take** something **back**, you make someone return it to you, usually using force.

take something back ❑ *You should just have taken your money back.* ❑ *They took something from me and I intend to take it back.*

take back something ❑ *They threatened to take back their land.*

5 If you **take** someone **back** to the place where they were or to your home, you go with them there.

take someone back ❑ [+ to] *I'll take you back to your hotel.* ❑ *Someone needs to take the girls back home.* ❑ *A truck picked us up in the morning and took us back at the end of the day.*

6 If you **take** someone **back**, you allow them to return to a relationship or job after they have left it.

take someone back ❑ *She had many affairs, but he always took her back.*

take back someone ❑ *She said she would be willing to take back her husband.*

7 If you **take** something **back**, you admit that something you said or thought was wrong.

take back something ❑ *I'm going to have to take back all those things I thought about you.*

take something back ❑ *I'm sorry. I take it back. You're not mean.*

NOTE **Retract** is a more formal word for **take back**.

8 If you **take** someone **back** to the past, you start discussing or considering what happened then.

take someone back ❑ [+ to] *If I can just take you back to yesterday, can you tell me what happened?* ❑ *We can use the archaeological record to take us back in time.*

9 If something **takes** you **back** or **takes** you **back** a number of years, it makes you think of a time in your past.

take someone back ❑ [+ to] *The smell of hot jam took Tom back to his childhood.* ❑ *Hearing that song really took me back.*

take someone back something ❑ *The show took us back thirty years.*

✪ take 'down

1 If you **take** someone or something **down** or **take** them **down** something, you go with them, or make them go with you, to a lower level, position, or place. ≠ **take up**
take someone/something down ❑ [+ from] *She had taken her washing down from the line.* ❑ [+ to] *The judge ordered the prisoner to be taken down to the cells again.*
take someone/something down something ❑ *Hold his hand and take him down the steps carefully.*

2 If you **take** someone or something **down** to a place, you go with them to a different part of the country, usually one that is further south.
take someone/something down ❑ [+ to] *We took our grandson down to the seaside for a holiday.* ❑ *When you go to London next week, will you take some stuff down for me?*

3 If you **take** something **down**, you reach up and get it from a high place. ≠ **put back**
take down something ❑ *I went over to a shelf and took down a can.*
take something down ❑ *He found the book he wanted and took it down.* ❑ [+ from] *She took a suitcase down from the top of the wardrobe.*

4 If you **take** something **down**, you remove it from a high or vertical place where it has been attached. ≠ **put up**
take down something ❑ *It's always sad when we have to take down the Christmas decorations.*
take something down ❑ *He refused to take the sign down.* ❑ *I unhooked the curtains, took them down, and washed them.*

5 If you **take** something **down**, you separate its parts and remove it or put it away. ≠ **put up**
take down something ❑ *We took the tent down and set out for home.* ❑ *The shed has gone – they must have taken it down.*
take down something ❑ *They have taken down all the play equipment in the park.*
NOTE **Dismantle** is a more formal word for **take down**.

6 If you **take** something **down**, you remove it from a website or from the internet.
take something down ❑ *He said he regretted writing the page and had since taken it down.*
take down something ❑ *He threatened that if they didn't take down the blog he would sue.*

7 If you **take down** information that someone tells you, you write it down.
take down something ❑ *She got a pencil to take down the message.*
take something down ❑ *An official took all our names down.* ❑ *He hadn't taken it down correctly*

and had to ask her to repeat it.

8 If you **take** something **down**, you lower your trousers or underwear without removing them.
take down something *or* **take something down** ❑ *He took down his trousers so the doctor could look at his leg.* ❑ *Her mother had to help her take her tights down.*

9 If you **take** someone **down**, you defeat or kill them, or have them punished.
take someone down *or* **take down someone** ❑ *He threatened to take them all down with him if he was caught.*

10 If someone or something **takes** you **down**, they make you feel less confident or less happy. [INFORMAL]
take someone down ❑ *He stopped drinking, because the booze took him down.*
● If you **take someone down a peg**, you make them feel less confident or proud of themselves, usually because they deserve this. ❑ *She needs to be taken down a peg or two.*
NOTE **Demoralize** is a more formal word for **take down**.

11 If you **take it down**, you start doing something less loudly or intensely. [INFORMAL] ❑ *He thought I was too loud, and asked me to take it down.* ❑ *The team seems to have taken it down a notch this season.*

○ 'take for

If you **take** someone or something **for** someone or something else, you wrongly believe them to be that person or thing.
take someone/something for something ❑ *I took him for a much younger man.* ❑ *He took it for a valuable antique.*
● People say **What do you take me for?** to mean that the person they are speaking to is treating them as if they are an unpleasant or foolish kind of person. ❑ *I wouldn't steal his money – what do you take me for?*

○ take 'forward

1 If you **take** an idea or a plan **forward**, you carry it out.
take something forward ❑ *Thank you. We will take your recommendations forward.*

2 If someone **takes** a business **forward**, they help it to improve in the future, as its leader.
take something forward ❑ *I don't think he's the right person to take the company forward.*

✪ take 'in

1 If you **take** someone or something **in**, you go with them into a room, building, or other place.
take someone/something in ❑ *You can take your drinks in with you to dinner.* ❑ *I drove him to*

the town centre – he said he didn't want to take his car in. ❑ I took him in to meet Miss Gray.

take in someone/something ❑ I'll take in the coffee.

2 If you **take** someone **in**, you allow them to live at your house or in your country.

take someone in ❑ When I had nowhere to go, they took me in. ❑ After the hurricane, neighbours offered to take homeless families in.

take in someone ❑ She lives alone and takes in lodgers to help with the mortgage.

3 If an organization **takes** you **in**, you are allowed to enter it, for example as a member, student, or patient.

take someone in ❑ He told me that unfortunately the clinic couldn't take me in.

take in someone ❑ The Department takes in between 80 and 90 undergraduates a year.

● An organization's **intake** is the group of people who come into it at a particular time. ❑ The school runs an induction programme each September for the new intake.

4 If the police **take** you **in**, they make you go with them to a police station in order to ask you questions or arrest you.

take someone in ❑ If you don't co-operate, we'll have to take you in. ❑ [+ for] A man was taken in for questioning.

5 If you **take** something **in**, you pay attention to it so that you understand, remember, or experience it fully.

take in something ❑ I didn't take in everything that he was saying. ❑ He took in the situation at a glance. ❑ It was all too much to take in.

take something in ❑ Alex had been the perfect pupil, listening and watching and taking it in. ❑ I stood there for a moment, trying to take the scene in.

6 If you **are taken in** by someone or if they **take** you **in**, they deceive or trick you.

be taken in ❑ I gave him the money before I realized I had been taken in. ❑ I wasn't going to be taken in by her smiles.

take someone in or **take in someone** ❑ I confess he completely took me in.

7 To **take** something **in** means to include it.

take in something or **take something in** ❑ The course takes in many aspects of manufacturing and business. ❑ The Bishop's Diocese takes in all the northern regions of Canada. NOTE **Embrace** is a more formal word for **take in**.

8 To **take in** something means to see it or visit it, especially as part of a holiday or when travelling somewhere.

take in something or **take something in** ❑ I might take in a show while I'm in London.

❑ The group plans to take in several museums on their tour of the region.

9 If you **take in** something, you bring it into your house from outside.

take in something or **take something in** ❑ It's going to rain. I should take the washing in.

10 If you **take in** something such as washing or sewing, you earn money by doing a particular type of work at home for people.

take in something ❑ His mother took in ironing for the well-off people in the area. ❑ Jane took in clerical work at home.

11 If you **take** something **in**, you take a machine or vehicle to a place where it can be checked or repaired.

take something in or **take in something** ❑ I had to take the car in this morning.
❑ [+ to-infinitive] We took in the sewing machine to be repaired. ❑ [+ for] I'm taking my bike in for a service.

12 When people or animals **take in** something, it enters their bodies, for example because they breathe it or swallow it.

take in something or **take something in** ❑ Sharks take in water through the mouth.
❑ She sat taking in breaths of fresh air.

● Someone's **intake** of something is the amount that enters their body. ❑ What is the average daily intake of iron in a normal diet? ❑ He needs to reduce his calorie intake. ● An **intake** of breath is an occasion when someone breathes in. ❑ There was a sharp intake of breath when she saw the damage.

13 If you **take** something **in**, you make an item of clothing smaller and tighter.
≠ **let out**

take in something or **take something in** ❑ He lost so much weight that he had to take in all his trousers. ❑ You can have my dress – I'll take it in for you.

14 To **take in** an amount of money means to earn it from selling goods or services.

take in something or **take something in** ❑ The business took in $450,000 in its first year. ❑ The city takes in millions from the public during the tournament.

❍ **take 'into**

1 If you **take** someone or something **into** a place, you go with them there.

take someone/something into something ❑ I took my cup of tea into the sitting room. ❑ I'll take you into town if you like.

2 If you **take** someone **into** an organization, you allow them to enter it, for example as a member, student, or patient.

take someone into something ❑ *My boss offered to take me into the firm as a partner.* ❑ *He was taken into the local psychiatric hospital.*

3 When people or animals **take** something **into** their bodies, it enters them, for example because they breathe it or swallow it.

take something into something ❑ *I tried not to take the dust into my lungs.* ❑ *The fish takes the bait into its mouth.*

4 To **take** someone **into** something means to make them consider or become involved in a particular subject or activity.

take someone into something ❑ *What had taken him into politics in the first place?*

5 To **take** someone or something **into** a state or situation means to cause them to be in it.

take someone/something into something ❑ *The government took the bank into public ownership.* ❑ *Police took him into custody.* ❑ *Her children were taken into care.*

6 If something will **take** someone or something **into** a future time, it will last or continue to be effective until that time.

take someone/something into something ❑ *These policies will take farming into the next decade in a successful state.* ❑ *The project is due to last ten weeks, which takes us into May.*

○ **take 'off**

1 If you **take** something **off** or **take** it **off** something, you remove it or separate it from the place where it was. ≠ **put on**

take something off ❑ *Take the lid off and cook for about ten more minutes.* ❑ *Why are those shoes on the table? Take them off.*

take off something ❑ *He took off the top of the jar.* ❑ *I took off a few flowers that were starting to wilt.*

take something off something ❑ *The congestion charge has taken a lot of traffic off London roads.* ❑ *Take the pan off the heat and leave it to cool down.*

2 If you **take** clothing **off**, you remove it. ≠ **put on**

take off something ❑ *He took his coat off and hung it up.* ❑ *She took off her earrings.*

take something off ❑ *I took my clothes off and got into the bath.* ❑ *She undid her shoes and took them off.*

3 If you **take** something **off** someone, you use force or your authority to get it from them.

take something off someone ❑ *You cannot take things off other people by force.* ❑ *They take money off you by selling you insurance you don't need.*

4 When an aeroplane or bird **takes off**, it leaves the ground and starts flying. ≠ **land** ❑ *A steady stream of aircraft was taking off and landing.* ❑ *We took off on time.* ❑ *The swans took off from the lake.* ● **Takeoff** is the beginning o a flight, when an aircraft leaves the ground. ❑ *Please fasten your seat belts ready for takeoff.*

5 If something **takes off**, it becomes very successful or popular. ❑ *If the product takes off, you could make your money back within a year.* ❑ *His career never really took off.*

6 If you **take off** or **take** yourself **off**, you go away, often unexpectedly.

take off ❑ [+ for] *They took off for a weekend in the country.* ❑ *He took off without telling her where he was going.*

take yourself off ❑ *I thought I would take mysel off on a little trip.*

7 If you **take** someone **off**, you make them go to particular place with you.

take someone off ❑ [+ to] *They took him off to prison.* ❑ *She collapsed and was taken off in an ambulance.*

8 If you **take** someone **off** something, you stop them doing a particular task or being on a particular list.

take someone off something ❑ *The next day, I found Laura had taken me off the invitation list.* ❑ *The bosses ordered him to be taken off the case.*

9 If you **take** time **off**, you spend it doing something different from your normal activities or job.

take something off or **take off something** ❑ [+ from] *I took time off from work to look after my sick mother.* ❑ *I won't be here tomorrow as I'm taking the day off.* ❑ *Your contract entitles you to take off twenty days a year.*

take something off something ❑ *They could not afford to take a day off work.* ❑ *If you take too much time off school your studies will suffer.*

10 If you **take off** something or **take** it **off** a total, you subtract it from a total. ≠ **add on**

take off something or **take something off** ❑ *You don't have to pay VAT, so I'll take that off.* ❑ *Half a point would be taken off for a spelling mistake.*

take something off something ❑ *Calculate your costs and take them off the total.*

11 If you **take** someone **off**, you imitate their appearance or behaviour, usually in order to make people laugh. = **mimic** [BRITISH

take off someone or **take someone off** ❑ *Mike can take off his father to perfection.*

● A **takeoff** is an imitation of someone's appearance or behaviour, done in order to make people laugh. ❑ *He did a very amusing take-off of the headmaster.*

12 If someone **takes** you **off** something, they stop you from being given a particular type of medical treatment. ≠ **put on**

take someone off something ❑ What would happen if we took him off his medication?

13 If a service **is taken off** or if someone **takes** it **off**, it stops operating or is no longer available.

be taken off ❑ The 7.18 London train was taken off for the winter.

take off something or **take something off** ❑ They've taken off the night bus.

NOTE **Be withdrawn** is a more formal expression for **be taken off**.

14 If a play or show **is taken off** or if someone **takes** it **off**, it stops being performed or broadcast.

be taken off ❑ The musical 'My Fair Lady' was taken off at the peak of its success.

take off something or **take something off** ❑ They took the play off after only a short run.

take something off something ❑ That's such a stupid show – they should take it off TV.

▸ **take 'on**

1 If you **take on** a job, task, or responsibility, you accept it and try to do what is required.

take on something ❑ She takes on more work than is good for her.

take something on ❑ It's a big responsibility and it's good of him to take it on.

2 If something **takes on** something, it develops a new quality, appearance, or meaning.

take on something ❑ His voice took on a new note of uncertainty. ❑ The word 'profession' is taking on a new meaning.

NOTE **Assume** is a more formal word for **take on**.

3 If someone **takes** you **on**, they employ you.

take someone on ❑ They took me on because I was a good mathematician. ❑ [+ to] I was keen to take him on to my editorial staff.

take on someone ❑ Employers take on fewer young people.

4 If you **take on** a rival or opponent, you fight or compete against them. = **tackle**

take on someone/something ❑ British industry, he said, was well equipped to take on competition from abroad.

take someone/something on ❑ The Government decided to take the unions on. ❑ If you take him on, you'd better be prepared to lose.

5 If a vehicle **takes on** passengers, goods, or fuel, it allows passengers to get on or goods or fuel to be loaded.

take on something or **take something on** ❑ Buses stopped by request to take on more passengers. ❑ We're only stopping briefly to take on fuel.

6 If you say **'Don't take on'**, you are telling someone that they should not get so angry or upset about something. [OLD-FASHIONED, INFORMAL] ❑ Now don't take on, darling! I'll only be gone for a few days!

7 → see **take upon**

○ **take 'out**

1 If you **take** something **out**, you remove it from a container or from the place where it was. ≠ **put back**

take out something ❑ Emma opened her bag and took out her phone. ❑ [+ from] He took out a photo from his wallet.

take something out ❑ [+ of] Please don't take those reference books out of the classroom. ❑ I felt in my jacket for my address book, and took it out.

• A **takeout** or **take-out** food is hot cooked food that is sold to be eaten somewhere else. [AMERICAN] ❑ He's gone to get Chinese takeout. ❑ We had takeout pizza.

NOTE In British English, **takeaway** means almost the same as **take-out**.

2 To **take** something **out** means to remove it permanently.

take something out ❑ When you edit the film you can take that bit out. ❑ [+ of] This is a process for taking the sulphur out of natural gas. ❑ If you don't like the fireplace you can take it out.

take out something ❑ He had to have two teeth taken out.

3 If you **take** someone **out**, you take them to a place such as a restaurant or cinema with you, and usually pay for them.

take someone out ❑ [+ to] I took Andrea out to dinner one evening. ❑ Why don't you take the children out? ❑ [+ for] He offered to take us out for a drink.

4 If you **take** someone or something **out**, you kill or destroy them. = **wipe out** [INFORMAL]

take out someone/something ❑ He and his brother have taken out 58 enemy soldiers. ❑ Several miles of railway line were taken out by bombs.

take someone/something out ❑ Their orders were to identify the target and take it out.

5 If you **take out** something such as a licence, an insurance policy, or a bank loan, you arrange to get it.

take out something ❑ I want to take out a mortgage. ❑ The former jockey intends to take out a licence to become a trainer.

take something out ❏ How much the policy pays depends on when you took it out.

> **TAKE OUT + noun**
>
> take out **a mortgage**
> take out **a loan**
> take out **insurance**
> take out **a subscription**
> take out **a pension**
> take out **a lease**
>
> ❏ We took out a loan to buy the car. ❏ She took out a lease on a building in the city centre.

6 If you **take** money **out**, you obtain it from your bank account.

take something out ❏ You can take cash out at any ATM.

take out something ❏ What is the best way to take out money when travelling abroad?

NOTE **Withdraw** is a more formal word for **take out**.

7 If you **take** a book **out**, you borrow it from a library.

take something out or **take out something** ❏ Can I take a book out right away? ❏ You can take out up to six titles.

8 If you **take** time **out**, you spend time doing something that is not your work or not what you normally do. = **take off**

take time out ❏ [+ to-infinitive] In the middle of the campaign, he took time out to attend a meeting of local officials. ❏ [+ for] The plumber was taking time out for a cup of tea. ❏ [+ from] She would have to take a day out from her bread baking.

9 If you **take** something **out**, you make an item of clothing larger.

take out something or **take something out** ❏ If they're too tight I'll take out the waistband for you. ❏ I can wear my mother's wedding dress if I take it out a little.

○ **take 'out of**

1 If something **takes** a particular quality **out of** something, it removes it.

take something out of something ❏ Poor visibility can take the fun out of skiing. ❏ There are plenty of websites designed to take the stress out of planning a wedding.

2 If something **takes** a lot **out of** you, it makes you very tired. [INFORMAL]

take something out of someone ❏ I find that meeting people takes so much out of me. ❏ The work an artist can take a lot out of him.

• If something **takes it out of** you, it makes you very tired. ❏ A five-block walk in that heat can take it out of you.

3 If something **takes** you **out of** yourself, it makes you stop thinking about your problems or worrying about a situation.

take you out of yourself ❏ People will adore

this film: it takes you right out of yourself. ❏ She needs a hobby – something to take her out of herself.

○ **take 'out on**

If you **take** something **out on** someone, you make them suffer because you feel angry or upset, even though it is not their fault.

take something out on someone ❏ When Kurt was unhappy, he took it out on his family.

☉ **take 'over**

1 To **take over** a business means to gain control of it by buying it or buying a majority of its shares. = **buy out**

take over something ❏ Some people wanted to take over my father's oil importing business. ❏ The I.P.C. was taken over by the Reed Paper Group.

take something over ❏ He's made a great success of the restaurant since he took it over.

• A **takeover** is the act of gaining control of a company by buying it or buying a majority of its shares. ❏ The company is a likely candidate for takeover. ❏ His firm might be vulnerable to a takeover bid.

2 If people **take over** an area or **take over**, they gain control of an area, usually with the help of an army.

take over ❏ Once again the military had taken over.

take over something ❏ Well-trained and equipped troops could probably take over the country.

take something over ❏ They had preferred to destroy the town rather than take it over. ❏ He wanted to send in the National Guard and take the city over. • A **takeover** is the act of gaining control of an area, usually with the help of an army. ❏ There is a real danger of a military takeover.

3 If people **take over** a building, they enter it and take control of it as a protest.

take over something ❏ Protesters took over the country's Embassy.

take something over ❏ Students stormed the state-run radio station and took it over. ❏ There were strikes, and workers took factories over.

NOTE **Occupy** is a more formal word for **take over**.

• A **takeover** is the act of occupying a building as a form of protest. ❏ The student takeover was just the beginning.

4 If you **take over** a building, you buy it or start living in it or using it.

take something over ❏ She had taken the house over some months before.

take over something ❏ I suggested she take over my flat while I was in California.

5 If you **take** something **over** or **take over**, you start doing or being responsible for something instead of someone else.

take over ❑ [+ as] *Thorn took over as secretary in 2010.* ❑ [+ from] *He felt he had a good chance of taking over from the Prime Minister.* ❑ *The driver was taken ill, and someone else had to take over.*

take over something ❑ *The officer returned to take over the questioning.*

take something over ❑ *She's been brilliant in the role, and whoever takes it over will have a lot to live up to.*

> **TAKE OVER + noun**
>
> take over **responsibility for** something
> take over **duties**
> take over **control of** something
> take over **command of** something
> take over **the leadership of** something
> take over **ownership of** something
> ❑ *I have taken over responsibility for new staff.*
> ❑ *He took over command of the army.*

6 If you **take** trouble, care, or time **over** something, you do it carefully or slowly.

take something over something ❑ *They took time over their meal.* ❑ *He had taken particular pains over the report.*

7 If you **take** something or someone **over**, you carry them or lead them to a particular place or person.

take someone/something over ❑ [+ to] *You wait in the car while I take him over to the house.* ❑ *He took a chair over and sat down next to her.* ❑ [+ to-infinitive] *I'll take her over to see Grandma.*

take over someone/something ❑ [+ to] *The manager told me to take over two bottles of wine to their table.* ❑ *If you're going to Marta's, will you take over this letter?*

take someone over something ❑ *George was ill so I took him over some fruit.*

8 If something **takes** you **over**, it affects you very strongly or takes nearly all of your time.

take someone over ❑ *Just let the music take you over and dance.* ❑ *Once she had the idea, it seemed to take her over completely.*

9 If one thing **takes over** from another, it becomes more important or successful and eventually replaces it. ❑ [+ from] *At first, people thought that electronic publishing would take over from traditional book publishing.* ❑ *The science of medicine took over from the art of healing.* ❑ *By this time, supermarkets were taking over.*

○ **take 'round** → see **take around**

○ **take 'through**
If you **take** someone **through** something, you explain it to them or show them how to do it in detail.

take someone through something ❑ *He took the actors through the scene again.* ❑ *I can take you through the figures if you're not clear.*

○ **'take to**

1 If you **take to** someone or something, you begin to like them. ≠ **take against**

take to someone/something ❑ *The child seemed to take to her immediately.* ❑ *I was taught Geography at school but never took to it.*

2 If you **take to** doing something, you begin to do it regularly.

take to something ❑ *He took to wearing black leather jackets.* ❑ *He had taken to a life of crime.*

3 If you **take to** a place, you go there, usually as a result of a difficult or dangerous situation.

take to something ❑ *I took to my bed with a fever.* ❑ *The local inhabitants took to the streets to defend their property.*

● If you **take to** your **heels**, you run away. ❑ *Panicking, she took to her heels and raced home.*

○ **take 'up**

1 If you **take** someone or something **up** or **take** them **up** something, you go with them, or make them go with you, to a higher level, position, or place. ≠ **take down**

take something/someone up ❑ *I'll take her tea up.* ❑ [+ to] *I can take you up to your room if you're tired.*

take up something ❑ *She took up some clean sheets and changed the beds.*

take something/someone up something ❑ *A guard took them up the hill.*

2 If you **take** someone or something **up** to a place, you go with them to a different part of the country, usually one that is further north.

take someone/something up ❑ [+ to] *His grandparents took him up to Scotland.*

3 If something **takes up** time, space, or effort, it uses it.

take up something ❑ *T-shirts don't take up much space in your suitcase.* ❑ *The baby took up all her energy and attention.*

take something up ❑ *At the moment rehearsing the play is taking a lot of my time up.*

NOTE **Occupy** is a more formal word for **take up**.

4 If you **take up** an activity or job, you start doing it. = **go in for**

take up something ❑ *I thought I'd take up fishing.* ❑ *She decided to take up medicine as a career.*

take something up ❑ *You're good at art. You should take it up professionally.*

5 If you **take up** a point, idea, or issue, you discuss it or deal with it. = **pick up**

take up something ❑ *The committee will take up the question of the government's role in the arts.* ❑ *I'd just like to take up something the last speaker said.*
take something up ❑ *The interviewer took this point up immediately and questioned him on it.* ❑ *[+ with] If you've got a problem, take it up with the manager.*
NOTE **Pursue** is a more formal word for **take up**.

• If you are **quick on the uptake**, you understand an idea or situation quickly. If you are **slow on the uptake**, you are slow to understand. ❑ *She was not very quick on the uptake and didn't realize they were laughing at her.*

6 If you **take up** an offer, challenge, or opportunity, you accept it. ≠ **decline**
take up something ❑ *She wished Jane would take up Derek's offer to decorate the house.* ❑ *If you take up the challenge to exercise more and lose weight, you will certainly benefit.*
take something up ❑ *I won a scholarship to a grammar school but my mother wouldn't let me take it up.* • **Take-up** is the rate at which people apply for or buy something which is being offered to them. ❑ *There was a huge take-up of mobile phone services between 2009 and 2010.*

7 If you **take up** a particular attitude, belief, or way of doing something, you start to have it.
take up something ❑ *They abandoned their traditional ways and took up European ones.*
take something up ❑ *His wife became a vegetarian, then he took it up too.* ❑ *Such styles may later be taken up by the general public.*

• If someone **takes up arms**, they decide to fight using weapons in order to achieve something. ❑ *Young people were willing to take up arms and die for this cause.*
NOTE **Adopt** is a more formal word for **take up**.

8 If you **take up** something, you continue doing it from a point where it was interrupted or stopped.
take up something ❑ *Bella stopped talking, and let Sam take up the story.*
take something up ❑ *She kept abandoning the plan and then taking it up again.*

• If you **take up where** you **left off** or **take up from where** you **left off**, you continue doing something from a point where you had stopped. = **pick up** ❑ *After a short break, she took up where she had left off.*

9 If you **take up** something, you start singing or shouting something with other people.
take up something or **take something up** ❑ *'Long live the King!' someone shouted, and the crowd took up the cry.* ❑ *She began a song and the other women took it up.*

10 If you **take up** an object, you pick it up. = **pick up** [OLD-FASHIONED]
take up something or **take something up** ❑ *When they had finished eating, the men took up their tools again.* ❑ *She took it up, and threw it.*

11 If you **take up** a position, you move to it.
take up something or **take something up** ❑ *Fire trucks had taken up position by the runway.* ❑ *The captain let his men pass, and took up the rear*

12 If something **is taken up** or if someone **takes** it **up**, it is removed from a surface where it has been fixed. = **pull up**
be taken up ❑ *The rails were taken up and used to make weapons.*
take something up or **take up something** ❑ *Then she took the carpet up, and scrubbed the boards underneath.* ❑ *They had to take up the floorboards to repair the pipe.*

13 If you **take up** a piece of clothing, you make it shorter. ≠ **let down**
take something up or **take up something** ❑ *She took all her skirts up when minis were in fashion.* ❑ *I can take up those trousers for you.*

14 If someone **takes** you **up**, they help and support you.
take someone up or **take up someone** ❑ *An agent took her up and encouraged her to audition for roles.* ❑ *As a young writer he had been taken up by an influential society couple.*
NOTE **Patronize** is a more formal word for **take up**.

15 To **take up** a substance means to absorb it.
take up something or **take something up** ❑ *Red blood cells take up oxygen.* • A person's or machine's **uptake** of something is the amount of it that they use. = **intake** ❑ *An athlete has a maximum oxygen uptake of four litres per minute.* ❑ *Some foods may interfere with the body's uptake of nutrients.*

16 If you **take up** a collection, you collect money for a charity or cause.
take something up ❑ *He took up a collection and sent the money to Ethiopia.*

○ '**take upon** (or **take on**)
If you **take** something **upon** yourself, you decide to do it or deal with it yourself.
take something upon yourself ❑ *Mrs Cook took matters upon herself.*

• If you **take it upon** yourself **to** do something, you decide to do it without asking for permission or approval.
❑ *Mrs Kaur took it upon herself to turn round and say 'Be quiet!'* ❑ *I couldn't take it on myself to provide you with that information.*

take 'up on

1 If you **take** someone **up on** an offer they have made, you accept their offer.

take someone up on something ❑ *They took her up on her offer to babysit.* ❑ *It was an absurd suggestion, and no one took him up on it.*

2 If you **take** someone **up on** something, you ask them to explain or justify what they have said or done. **= pick up on**

take someone up on something ❑ *I would like to take Tony up on something that he said.*

take 'up with

1 If you **take up with** someone, you begin to spend a lot of time with them.

take up with someone ❑ *He's taken up with a new group of friends.* ❑ *After his divorce he took up with a woman called Natasha.*

2 If you **are taken up with** something, you are busy doing it, talking about it, or thinking about it.

be taken up with something ❑ *She was too taken up with her own feelings to pay attention to his.* ❑ *I've been very taken up with the baby.*

talk /tɔːk/ (talks, talking, talked)

talk a'round (or talk round [mainly BRITISH])

If people **talk around** a subject, they discuss it in a general way without dealing with the main points.

talk around something ❑ *I feel we've just talked around the point.*

'talk at

If you **talk at** someone, you talk to them without letting them speak.

talk at someone ❑ *Don't just talk at them – give them a chance to ask questions and express their views.*

talk a'way

If you **talk away**, you talk continuously for a period of time. ❑ *You were talking away like a little kid.* ❑ *She wandered around the garden talking away to herself.*

talk 'back

If someone, especially a child, **talks back**, they answer someone in authority in a rude way. **= answer back** ❑ [+ to] *Don't talk back to your mother like that!* ❑ *The teacher punished him for talking back.*

talk 'down

1 If someone **talks** you **down**, they talk longer or louder than you so that you have to stop talking.

talk someone down or **talk down someone** ❑ *I objected to the proposal, but they talked me down.* ❑ *He made another weak protest and was talked down.*

2 To **talk down** a pilot means to give them instructions over the radio so that they can land an aircraft.

talk someone down or **talk down someone** ❑ *He was on the radio to the helicopter pilot, talking him down.*

3 To **talk** someone **down** means to calm them by talking to them when they are very upset or angry. [INFORMAL]

talk someone down or **talk down someone** ❑ *He wanted to go out and get involved, but his wife talked him down.*

4 If someone **talks down** something, they make it seem less interesting, valuable, or likely. **≠ talk up**

talk down something or **talk something down** ❑ *The government tried to talk down the prospect of an early agreement.* ❑ *Her achievements are huge, but she tends to talk them down.*

5 To **talk** someone or something **down** means to persuade someone to accept less money than they originally asked for. [BRITISH]

talk someone/something down or **talk down someone/something** ❑ *We talked them down and struck a deal.* ❑ *The management is trying to talk down wages.*

talk someone down something ❑ *When he makes you an offer, you send me in and I'll talk him down another thousand.*

○ talk 'down to

If someone **talks down to** you, they talk to you as if they are more important or more intelligent than you.

talk down to someone ❑ *Adolescents hate it when their parents talk down to them.* ❑ *I think some of the employees felt they were being talked down to.*

NOTE **Patronize** is a more formal word for **talk down to**.

○ talk 'into

1 If you **talk** someone **into** doing something, you persuade them to do it. **≠ talk out of**

talk someone into something ❑ *She talked me into taking a week's holiday.* ❑ *He talked the rebel leaders into ending the uprising.* ❑ *I didn't want to go, but he talked me into it.*

2 If you **talk** yourself **into** a particular situation or state, you get yourself into it by talking.

talk yourself into something ❑ *He has talked himself into a position where he will have to resign.* ❑ *We can talk ourselves into any job.*

○ talk 'out

1 If people **talk** something **out**, they discuss it thoroughly.

talk out something or **talk something out**
❏ They began talking things out between themselves.

2 If you **talk** yourself **out**, you talk so much that you have nothing more to say.
talk yourself out ❏ He said little, simply letting me talk myself out.'

○ **talk 'out of**
1 If you **talk** someone **out of** doing something, you persuade them not to do it.
≠ **talk into**
talk someone out of something ❏ He tried to talk me out of buying such a big car. ❏ Fortunately, she talked her husband out of his plan.

2 If you **talk** yourself **out of** something, you get yourself out of a situation or state by talking.
talk yourself out of something ❏ I tried to talk myself out of trouble.

○ **talk 'over**
If you **talk** something **over**, you discuss it with someone.
talk something over ❏ [+ with] She said she would talk it over with her husband and let me know. ❏ There's plenty of opportunity for you to talk your problems over.
talk over something ❏ We all met in Pat's room, to talk over what we had seen.

○ **talk 'round** [BRITISH]
1 If you **talk** someone **round**, you persuade them to agree with you or to do what you want them to do.
talk someone round ❏ He didn't really want to go to France, but I managed to talk him round.
2 → see **talk around**

○ **talk 'through**
1 If people **talk** something **through**, they discuss a problem or plan thoroughly until something has been agreed or resolved.
= **talk over**
talk through something ❏ We had already talked through many problematic areas and wanted to move on. ❏ [+ with] I talked through the options with Jennifer.
talk something through ❏ [+ with] We often find that people like to talk it through with someone before they decide. ❏ Can we talk the arrangements through one last time?
2 If you **talk** someone **through** something, you explain something to them.
talk someone through something ❏ While the ambulance is on its way we can talk the caller through what to do. ❏ Your coach will talk you through the training session.

○ **talk 'to**
1 If you **talk to** someone, you have a conversation with them.

talk to someone ❏ I just wanted to talk to you. ❏ [+ about] I talked to my students about applying to university. ❏ I find her so easy to talk to.
2 If you give someone a **talking-to**, you speak to them seriously or angrily about something they have done wrong. ❏ She took the boys outside and gave them a talking-to.
3 If you **talk to** a subject, you talk about that subject, especially in a formal situation such as a business meeting.
[FORMAL]
talk to something ❏ Next we will be looking at the strategic review and Andrew will be talking to that.

○ **talk 'up**
1 If someone **talks up** something, they make it seem more interesting, valuable, or likely. ≠ **talk down**
talk up something or **talk something up** ❏ Politicians accuse the media of talking up the possibility of a riot. ❏ I thought there was a chance we would do well, though I didn't want to talk it up.
2 To **talk** someone or something **up** means to persuade someone to pay more money than they originally offered or wanted to.
≠ **talk down** [BRITISH]
talk someone/something up ❏ Allan kept talking the price up. ❏ [+ to] The saleswoman managed to talk him up to £150.

○ **'talk with** [mainly AMERICAN]
If you **talk with** someone, you have a conversation with them.
talk with someone ❏ [+ about] I'd like to talk with you about your husband. ❏ I spent an hour talking with a new student called Kathleen.

tally /'tæli/ (tallies, tallying, tallied)
○ **'tally with**
If one number or statement **tallies with** another, they agree with each other or are exactly the same.
tally with something ❏ His estimate of three hundred tallies with that of another survey. ❏ This description didn't seem to tally with what we saw.

tamp /tæmp/ (tamps, tamping, tamped)
○ **tamp 'down**
If you **tamp** something **down**, you press it down so that it becomes more solid.
tamp something down or **tamp down something** ❏ It will probably be necessary to tamp the clay down. ❏ One man shovelled earth into the hole, the other tamped it down.

tamper /'tæmpə/ (tampers, tampering, tampered)
○ **'tamper with**
If you **tamper with** something, you touch it or try to change it when you should not.
= **interfere with**

tamper with something ❑ *Someone had tampered with the company's records.* ❑ *He claimed that his briefcase had been tampered with on the flight.*

tangle /'tæŋgəl/ (tangles, tangling, tangled)

○ tangle 'up

1 If something **is tangled up** or if you **tangle** it **up**, it is twisted in an untidy way which is difficult to separate.

be tangled up ❑ *Use a light cord rather than a string which gets tangled up.*

tangle something up or **tangle up something** ❑ *He tangled up the cables so we couldn't tell which was which..*

2 If someone or something **is tangled up** in wires or ropes, they are caught or trapped in them so that it is difficult to free them.

be tangled up ❑ [+ in] *His kite was tangled up in a tree.*

3 If you **are tangled up** in a complicated or unpleasant situation, you are involved in it and cannot escape from it.

be tangled up ❑ [+ in] *He got tangled up in a scandal.* ❑ *They were tangled up in a legal battle.*

4 If things **are tangled up**, they are connected in a confused way, and it is difficult to separate them.

be tangled up ❑ [+ in] *The issue got tangled up in arguments about the environment.* ❑ [+ with] *His feelings about the case were tangled up with his desire for revenge.*

○ 'tangle with [INFORMAL]

If you **tangle with** someone, you get involved in a fight or disagreement with them. = **mess with**

tangle with someone ❑ *I wouldn't tangle with him if I were you.*

tap /tæp/ (taps, tapping, tapped)

○ 'tap for [INFORMAL]

If you **tap** someone **for** something, especially money, you persuade them to give it to you.

tap someone for something ❑ *I'll tap my Dad for a loan.* ❑ *He sensed they were trying to tap him for information.*

○ tap 'in

1 If you **tap** something **in**, you force something sharp into a surface by hitting it with quick, light blows.

tap in something or **tap something in** ❑ *He tapped the drawing pins in gently with a book.*

2 If you **tap** something **in**, you type letters or numbers by pressing keys or buttons. = **key in**

tap in something or **tap something in** ❑ *Simply put your card into the machine and tap in*

your personal number. ❑ *You have to tap a code in before you can get access to the information.*

○ tap 'into

1 If you **tap into** something, you use it as a source of something that you need.

tap into something ❑ *An actor taps into their own emotions and experiences when playing a part.* ❑ *Find out if there is any local expertise you could tap into to help with your project.*

2 If you **tap into** a phone or phone call, you use a device to secretly listen to someone's conversations.

tap into something ❑ *He tapped into a secret CIA phone line.*

○ tap 'out

To **tap out** a sound means to produce it by hitting a surface lightly and repeatedly.

tap out something or **tap something out** ❑ *He tapped out the rhythm with his fingers on the table.*

tape /teɪp/ (tapes, taping, taped)

○ tape 'up

If you **tape** something **up**, you fasten tape around it.

tape something up or **tape up something** ❑ *She put the money into an envelope and taped it up securely.* ❑ *They taped up the windows to keep the dust out.*

taper /'teɪpə/ (tapers, tapering, tapered)

○ taper 'off

If something **tapers off** or if you **taper** it **off**, it gradually becomes less until it stops completely.

taper off ❑ *His voice tapered off as he ran out of things to say.*

taper something off or **taper off something** ❑ *I trained hard for a month, then tapered it off in the week before the race.*

tart /tɑːt/ (tarts, tarting, tarted)

○ tart 'up [BRITISH, INFORMAL]

1 If you **tart** yourself **up**, you try to make yourself look especially attractive. = **doll up**

tart yourself up ❑ *I didn't know whether to tart myself up or just go in my normal clothes.*

2 If someone **tarts up** something, they try to improve its appearance.

tart up something or **tart something up** ❑ *They tarted up the place with new furniture, carpets, and curtains.* ❑ *Just buy a cake and tart it up with some cream and chocolate curls.*

task /tɑːsk, tæsk/ (tasks, tasking, tasked)

○ 'task with

If you **are tasked with** a particular activity or piece of work, someone in authority asks you to do it.

be **tasked with** something ❑ *The minister was tasked with checking that British aid money was being spent wisely.*

taste /teɪst/ (tastes, tasting, tasted)

○ **'taste of**

If something **tastes of** something, it has that particular flavour, which you notice when you eat or drink it.

taste of something ❑ *I drank a cup of tea that tasted of diesel.* ❑ *This lipstick tastes of cherries.*

tax /tæks/ (taxes, taxing, taxed)

○ **'tax with** [FORMAL]

If you **tax** someone **with** something, you ask them to explain or justify something bad that you think is their fault.

tax someone with something ❑ *A colleague taxed him with this change of view.* ❑ *Critics have taxed the actor with the violence in his movies.*

team /tiːm/ (teams, teaming, teamed)

○ **team 'up**

If two or more people or organizations **team up**, they join together in order to do something. ❑ [+ with] *In 1996 NBC teamed up with Microsoft to launch the news channel MSNBC.* ❑ [+ to-infinitive] *The two musicians have teamed up to produce a really great album.*

tear /teə/ (tears, tearing, tore, torn)

○ **tear a'part**

■ To **tear** something **apart** means to pull it into pieces violently.

tear something apart or **tear apart something** ❑ *A lion could tear a goat apart in seconds.* ❑ *The force of the blast tore apart buildings.*

■ If someone **tears** a place **apart**, they search it very thoroughly, causing a lot of damage.

tear something apart or **tear apart something** ❑ *They tore the place apart but found nothing.* ❑ *Someone had torn his room apart looking for the money.*

■ If something **tears** a group or organization **apart**, it creates arguments which cause it serious damage.

tear something apart or **tear apart something** ❑ *He claimed that the controversy was tearing the Church apart.* ❑ *Communities have been torn apart by these crimes.*

■ If something **tears** you **apart**, it makes you feel extremely unhappy.

tear someone apart or **tear apart someone** ❑ *It tears me apart to be away from you.* ❑ *The child's illness is tearing his mother apart.*

■ If someone **tears** something **apart**, they criticize it severely. = **pull apart, take apart**

tear something apart or **tear apart**

something ❑ *He tore the theory apart.* ❑ *His arguments are torn apart in her latest book.*

○ **'tear at**

To **tear at** something means to try violently to pull it into pieces.

tear at something ❑ *He took the meat and began to tear at it.*

○ **tear a'way**

■ If you **tear** someone **away**, you force them to leave a place or stop doing an activity.

tear someone away ❑ [+ from] *It seemed a shame to tear Laura away from the party.* ❑ *If I can just tear you away for a minute, I'd like a quick word.*

tear yourself away ❑ [+ from] *The conversation was so entertaining that I couldn't tear myself away.*

■ To **tear** something **away** means to pull it violently away from something or someone.

tear something away or **tear away**

something ❑ *She tore the blanket away to see what was underneath.* ❑ [+ from] *They tore away the meat from the chicken bones with their teeth.*

■ A **tearaway** is a young person who behaves in a wild and uncontrolled way. [BRITISH] ❑ *Colin was a tearaway in his youth.*

○ **tear 'down**

If you **tear down** something such as a building or a tree, you destroy it completely. = **pull down**

tear down something or **tear something**

down ❑ *It is often cheaper to tear down the buildings than to repair them.* ❑ *We have to stop tearing the rainforests down.*

NOTE **Demolish** is a more formal word for **tear down**.

○ **tear 'into**

■ If you **tear into** someone or something, you criticize them very strongly. = **lay into**

tear into someone/something ❑ *Furious, she tore into George, demanding to know what he was doing.* ❑ *He really tore into my paper at the seminar.*

■ If someone or something **tears into** something, they begin to attack, eat, or bite it with a lot of force.

tear into something ❑ *He tore into the roast pork hungrily.* ❑ *The dog leapt and tore into the stranger's leg.* ❑ *Bullets tore into the trees.*

○ **tear 'off**

■ If you **tear off** your clothes, you take them off quickly and violently.

tear off something or **tear something off** ❑ *I opened the window and tore off my shirt.* ❑ *She tore her sandals off and jumped in.*

2 If you **tear** something **off** or **tear** it **off** something, you remove it from the thing it is attached to by pulling it violently.

tear off something or **tear something off**
❑ She tore off a leaf and looked at it.

tear something off something ❑ He tore the metal tab off his beer can.

3 If you **tear off** somewhere, you go there very quickly. [INFORMAL] ❑ He tore off home. ❑ I watched them tearing off into the distance. ❑ He jumped into the car and tore off like a race driver.

tear 'out

If you **tear** something **out**, you separate it from something it is attached to with your hands, using force.

tear out something or **tear something out**
❑ I write the list in my book and tear out the top copy. ❑ [+ of] She tore several sheets of paper out of the back of the book.

tear 'up

1 If you **tear** something **up**, you pull it into a lot of small pieces with your hands.
= rip up

tear up something ❑ He tore up the cheque, saying 'You don't owe me anything.'

tear something up ❑ We tore a large sheet up to make bandages. ❑ She folded the letter, intending to tear it up.

2 If something **is torn up** or if someone or something **tears** it **up**, it is violently removed.

be torn up ❑ Thousands of trees have been torn up in recent years. ❑ Parks were being torn up in favour of factories.

tear up something or **tear something up**
❑ They tore up paving stones and threw them at the police. ❑ If anything is hidden under the floorboards, we will tear them up.

:ase /tiːz/ (**teases, teasing, teased**)

tease 'out

1 If you **tease** something **out**, you separate or remove it very carefully from something.

tease something out or **tease out something** ❑ He removed a splinter from her foot, using tweezers to gently tease it out. ❑ She teased out the tangles in his curly hair.

NOTE **Extract** is a more formal word for **tease out**.

2 If you **tease out** information or a solution, you succeed in obtaining it even though this is difficult.

tease out something or **tease something out** ❑ They try to tease out the answers without appearing to ask. ❑ [+ of] We studied the letter carefully, trying to tease the meaning out of the text.

tee /tiː/ (**tees, teeing, teed**)

○ **tee 'off**

1 When a golfer **tees off**, he or she hits the first shot at the start of a round of golf.
❑ Hit a few practice shots before you tee off.

2 If someone or something **tees** you **off**, they make you angry or annoyed.
[AMERICAN, INFORMAL]

tee someone off or **tee off someone**
❑ Something the boy said to him teed him off.

NOTE **Annoy** is a more formal word for **tee off**.

○ **tee 'up**

1 To **tee up** a ball or **tee up** means to place a golf ball on a tee (=small object that is stuck in the ground to support the ball) so that it is ready to hit.

tee up something or **tee something up**
❑ I asked Ben to tee up a ball and hit it onto the green. ❑ One of the men teed it up and got a hole in one!

tee up ❑ On June 17 Europe's leading golfers will tee up in the Open.

2 If you **tee up** something, especially a ball, you put it into the right position so you can hit or kick it in the direction that you want.

tee up something or **tee something up**
❑ The striker had plenty of time to tee up the ball and score.

3 If you **tee up** a situation, you set it up, organize it, or plan it.

tee up something ❑ The company is teeing up ambitious expansion plans.

teem /tiːm/ (**teems, teeming, teemed**)

○ **'teem down**

If it **is teeming down**, it is raining very heavily. = pour

be teeming down ❑ It was teeming down and we all got soaked.

○ **'teem with**

If you say that a place **is teeming with** people or animals, you mean that it is crowded and the people and animals are moving around a lot.

be teeming with something ❑ For most of the year, the area is teeming with tourists.

tell /tel/ (**tells, telling, told**)

○ **tell a'gainst** [BRITISH]

If something **tells against** a person or plan, it makes them less likely to succeed.
= count against

tell against someone/something ❑ His extraordinary calm told against him when the case came to court.

○ **tell a'part**

If you can **tell** people or things **apart**, you can identify them because you can recognize the differences between them.
tell someone/something apart or **tell apart someone/something** ❏ *It is impossible to tell the suitcases apart.* ❏ [+ from] *The twins are so alike that only their mother can tell them apart.*

○ **'tell from**

If you can **tell** one person or thing **from** another, you can identify them because you can recognize the differences between them.
tell someone/something from someone/something ❏ *Their shaved heads and pale skin made it hard to tell one from the other.*

◐ **tell 'off**

If you **tell** someone **off**, you speak to them angrily because they have done something wrong.
tell someone off ❏ [+ for] *The headmistress told the girls off for wearing the wrong colour blouse.* ❏ *I broke a plate, and my mum told me off.*
tell off someone ❏ *He would tell off anyone who parked outside his house.* ❏ [+ for] *I was told off for talking in class.*
NOTE **Reprimand** is a formal word for **tell off**.

● If you give someone a **telling-off**, you speak to them angrily because they have done something wrong. = **ticking-off**
❏ *She gave him a real telling-off for lying.*

○ **'tell on**

1 If you **tell on** someone, you inform someone in authority about something they have done wrong. = **grass on** [INFORMAL]
tell on someone ❏ *Stop copying my work or I'll tell on you.*
2 If something **tells on** someone, they begin to show that it is too difficult for them to cope with.
tell on someone ❏ *After six months in the job, the pressure was beginning to tell on him.* ❏ *The strain of too many matches is telling on many of the players.*

tend /tend/ (**tends, tending, tended**)

○ **'tend to**

If you **tend to** someone or something, you take care of them. = **attend to**
tend to someone/something ❏ *Excuse me, I have to tend to the other guests.* ❏ *In his spare time he tends to the family business.*

○ **'tend towards**

1 If something or someone **tends towards** a quality, they usually show it.

tend towards something ❏ *Both of them ten towards optimism, and love new ideas.* ❏ *The flavours of these coffees tend towards acidity.*
2 If something or someone **tends toward** something, they are likely to make a particular decision or develop in a particular way.
tend towards something ❏ *They are trying t control a universe that tends towards chaos.*

tense /tens/ (**tenses, tensing, tensed**)

○ **tense 'up**

If you or the muscles in your body **tense u** your muscles become stiff, usually becaus you are afraid or are preparing to move. = **tighten up** ❏ *Try to relax while you're speaki and don't tense up.* ❏ *He heard a noise downstai and his muscles tensed up.* ● If you are **tensed up**, you feel nervous and worried and cannot relax properly. = **worked up** ❏ *Rela You're too tensed up.* ❏ *I was all tensed up for another argument.*

test /test/ (**test, testing, tested**)

○ **'test for**

If you **are tested for** a particular medical condition, or if a doctor **tests for** the condition, you are examined in order to find out whether you have that condition.
be tested for something ❏ *My doctor wants me to be tested for diabetes.*
test someone for something ❏ *A series of doctors tested her for multiple sclerosis.*
test for something ❏ *We had to think much harder about what it could be and decided to test for measles.*

○ **test 'out**

If you **test** something **out**, you try using i or doing it to see if it works correctly.
test something out or **test out something** ❏ *When buying a bed, test it out thoroughly befo you buy it.*

testify /'testɪfaɪ/ (**testifies, testifying, testified**)

○ **'testify to** [FORMAL]

If one thing **testifies to** another, it suppor the belief that the second thing is true.
testify to something ❏ *Recent excavations testify to the presence of inhabitants on the hill during that period.*

tether /'teðə/ (**tethers, tethering, tethered**)

○ **'tether to**

If you **tether** an animal or object **to** something, you attach it there with a rop or chain so that it cannot move very far.

tether something to something ❑ *The officer dismounted, tethering his horse to a tree.*

haw /θɔ:/ (thaws, thawing, thawed)

thaw 'out

1 If you **thaw out** frozen food, or if it **thaws out**, you take it out of the freezer for some time so that it is no longer frozen. = **defrost**
thaw out ❑ *There was a joint thawing out on the kitchen table.*
thaw something out or **thaw out something** ❑ *You can freeze the raw pastry to cook later, but thaw it out first.* ❑ *Make sure the chicken is properly thawed out before you cook it.*
2 If you **thaw out**, you get warm after you have got very cold outside. ❑ *It's lovely to thaw out in front of the fire with a mug of hot tea.*

hin /θɪn/ (thins, thinning, thinned)

thin 'down

If you **thin down** a liquid, you add water or another liquid to make it weaker and less thick.
thin down something or **thin something down** ❑ *Thin down the mayonnaise with the cream.* ❑ *The paint has been thinned down too much.*

thin 'out

If something **thins out** or if you **thin** it **out**, a place becomes less crowded as some things or people move away or are removed.
thin out ❑ *Higher up the slope the trees thin out.* ❑ *In the evening, the crowds of tourists start to thin out.*
thin out something or **thin something out** ❑ *When the seedlings are larger, thin them out.*

hink /θɪŋk/ (thinks, thinking, thought)

think a'head

If you **think ahead**, you make plans or arrangements for the future. = **plan ahead**
❑ *We need to analyse the situation and think ahead.* ❑ [+ to] *The company is already thinking ahead to the next decade.*

think 'back

If you **think back**, you make an effort to remember things that happened in the past. = **look back** ❑ [+ to] *Think back to your lessons at school.* ❑ [+ over] *It gives you an opportunity to think back over the year.* ❑ *Thinking back, I often regret not staying to talk with him.*

'think of

1 If you can **think of** something or someone, you know them and can therefore suggest them to other people.
think of something ❑ *I can think of at least two examples of his incompetence.* ❑ *Can you think of anyone who could help us?*
2 If you **think of** an idea, you create it.

think of something ❑ *I began to think of new methods.* ❑ *This was an idea which, so far as he knew, had never been thought of before.*
3 If you **think of** doing something, you consider the possibility of doing it.
think of something ❑ *We began to think of moving house.* ❑ *I'm thinking of buying him a present.* ❑ *Have you ever thought of adoption?*
4 If you **think of** someone, you show consideration for them and pay attention to their needs.
think of someone ❑ *I'm only thinking of you.* ❑ *You never think of anyone but yourself.*

○ **think 'out**

If you **think** something **out**, you prepare it in detail before doing anything. = **work out**
think out something or **think something out** ❑ *She needed time to think out a strategy to deal with him.* ❑ *You ought to think it out before you start writing.*

❂ **think 'over**

If you **think** something **over**, you consider it carefully before making a decision.
think over something ❑ *I wanted to think over one or two business problems.*
think something over ❑ *I offered her the job and she said she'd think it over.*

❂ **think 'through**

If you **think** something **through**, you consider a situation and its possible consequences carefully.
think something through ❑ *They don't seem to have really thought this through.*
think through something ❑ *You sometimes need time to think through a difficulty.*

❂ **think 'up**

If you **think** something **up**, you create a new idea. = **devise**
think up something ❑ *I kept thinking up ways I could get a better job.*
think something up ❑ *Did you think this up all by yourself?*

thirst /θɜ:st/ (thirsts, thirsting, thirsted)

○ **'thirst for** [LITERARY]

If you **thirst for** something, you want it very much.
thirst for something ❑ *The story is so exciting it makes you thirst for the next episode.*

thrash /θræʃ/ (thrashes, thrashing, thrashed)

○ **thrash a'round** (or **thrash about** [mainly BRITISH])

If a person or their arms or legs **thrash around** or if a person **thrashes** their arms or legs **around**, they move in a wild or violent way.

thrash around ❑ *Her limbs were thrashing around desperately.*

thrash something around ❑ *He slept badly, thrashing his legs around under the blankets.*

○ **thrash 'out**

1 If people **thrash** something **out**, they make a plan or agreement together after a lot of discussion. **= hammer out**

thrash out something or **thrash something out** ❑ *For hours the negotiators thrashed it out behind closed doors.* ❑ *The details of the deal still have to be thrashed out.*

2 If you **thrash** something **out**, you discuss a problem in detail until you find a solution.

thrash out something or **thrash something out** ❑ *Try and thrash out these questions between the three of you.* ❑ *The whole family needs to sit down and thrash it out once and for all.*

throttle /ˈθrɒtəl/ (**throttles, throttling, throttled**)

○ **throttle 'back** (or **throttle down**)

If you **throttle** something **back**, or if you **throttle back**, you make a vehicle or aircraft go slower by reducing the pressure on the accelerator.

throttle something back or **throttle back something** ❑ *I throttled the motor right back.* ❑ *He quickly throttled back the engine.*

throttle back ❑ *He throttled down, and the boat settled into a slow drift.*

throw /θrəʊ/ (**throws, throwing, threw, thrown**)

○ **throw a'round** (or **throw about, throw round** [mainly BRITISH])

1 If you **throw** your arm or arms **around** someone, you embrace them or hug them suddenly.

throw something around someone/ something ❑ *She threw her arms around his neck and kissed him passionately.* ❑ *He threw his arms round his brother and began to cry.*

2 If you **throw** yourself **around** or **throw** your body **around**, you move your body suddenly and in different directions.

throw yourself around ❑ *The child threw himself around wildly in a tantrum.*

throw something around ❑ *The animal was throwing its head about.*

3 If you **throw** things **around** or **throw** them **around** a place, you throw them in different directions.

throw something around ❑ *He got into a rage and started throwing things around.*

throw something around something ❑ *The boy began to throw bread about the dining room.*

4 If people **throw** something **around**, they throw it from one person to the other.

throw something around ❑ *I saw him throwing a ball around with some other boys.*

5 If you **throw** money **around**, you spend freely and in large amounts.

throw something around ❑ *I can't afford to throw money around like that.*

6 If someone **throws** a word **around**, they mention it frequently or without thinking about it enough.

throw something around or **throw around something** ❑ *Occasionally, he throws fancy words around.*

7 If you **throw** ideas **around**, you discuss them in a casual way.

throw something around or **throw around something** ❑ *We threw a few ideas around in rehearsals.* ❑ *These weren't serious theories, just idle thoughts that they threw around.*

8 If you **throw** an object **around** something, you place it so that it surrounds the other thing.

throw something around something ❑ *They threw a rope around a tree.* ❑ *She had thrown a scarf round her neck.*

9 If someone **throws** a barrier **around** a place, they create it there so that people cannot enter or leave.

throw something around something ❑ *A police cordon has been thrown around the crime scene.*

○ **throw a'side**

1 If you **throw** something **aside**, you move it quickly to one side so that it no longer blocks or covers something.

throw something aside or **throw aside something** ❑ *She threw the bedclothes aside and jumped out of bed.* ❑ *He threw aside the cover to see what was underneath.*

2 If you **throw** an attitude, principle, or idea **aside**, you suddenly stop having it or believing it.

throw aside something or **throw something aside** ❑ *The time had come to throw aside caution.* ❑ *All divisions between the parties had been thrown aside.*

❍ **'throw at**

1 If you **throw** an object **at** someone or something, you try to hit them with the object by throwing it.

throw something at someone/something ❑ *Rioters threw stones at police officers and passing cars.*

2 If you **throw** a look, remark, or question **at** someone, you quickly look at them, speak to them, or ask them a question.

throw something at someone ❑ *She threw nervous glances at him every now and again.* ❑ *They were throwing questions at me, confusing me.* ❑ *The men threw insults at each other.*

3 To **throw** something **at** someone means to attack or challenge them with it.

throw something at someone ❑ *They threw all their forces at the enemy.* ❑ *They could throw the law at me if they chose.*

4 If you **throw** money **at** a difficult situation or problem, you try to solve a problem by spending money rather than by thinking of other solutions.

throw something at something ❑ *The Prime Minister said we cannot simply throw money at the inner cities.*

5 If you **throw** yourself **at** someone or something, you run or jump quickly towards them.

throw yourself at someone/something ❑ *He threw himself at the moving car and managed to leap inside.*

6 If you **throw** yourself **at** someone, you show in a very obvious way that you are attracted to them and want to have a relationship with them.

throw yourself at someone ❑ *He thought if he was a rock star girls would throw themselves at him.*

throw a'way

1 If you **throw** something **away**, you get rid of it because you no longer want or need it. ≠ **keep**

throw something away ❑ *You should throw those old shoes away.* ❑ *I can make soup with the leftover chicken, so don't throw it away.*

throw away something ❑ *Throw away medicine when it passes its use-by date.* ❑ *Millions of tonnes of refuse are thrown away in the UK.*

NOTE **Discard** is a more formal word for **throw away**.

● A **throw-away** product is intended to be used only once or only for a short time. = **disposable** ❑ *The bag was just a cheap throwaway thing.* ❑ *I got one of those throw-away cameras.*

2 If you **throw** something **away**, you throw it so that it moves quickly away from you.

throw something away ❑ *She read a few paragraphs of the book, then threw it away angrily.*

throw away something ❑ *They were munching apples as they walked along and throwing away the cores.*

3 If someone **throws away** something valuable that they have, they waste it rather than using it sensibly.

throw something away ❑ *He is evidently prepared to throw his money away.* ❑ *It's such*

a great opportunity – why throw it away?

throw away something ❑ *They threw away their advantage.* ❑ *She would never throw away her career for a man.*

4 A **throwaway** remark is one which seems very casual and not important, although it may actually be important. ❑ *He added, almost as a throwaway remark, 'The job's yours if you want it.'*

● **throw 'back**

1 If you **throw** something **back**, you put or drop it carelessly in the place where it was before.

throw something back ❑ *If the fish are too small the fishermen throw them back.*

throw back something ❑ *He started to eat the grapes, throwing back any squashed ones.*

2 If you **throw** someone **back** somewhere, you force them go back to a place where they were before.

throw someone back ❑ *They recaptured him and threw him back in jail.* ❑ *He was thrown back onto the street by his landlord.*

3 If you **throw back** a covering, you quickly pull it away so that it is no longer covering something else.

throw back something ❑ *She threw back the covers and jumped out of bed.* ❑ *He threw back the curtains.*

throw something back ❑ *She threw her hood back to reveal her face.* ❑ *The door was suddenly thrown back and a man stood there.*

4 If you **throw back** your head or another part of your body, you move it backwards suddenly.

throw something back ❑ *She threw her head back and laughed.*

throw back something ❑ *I threw back my head and yelled 'Help!'.*

throw yourself back ❑ *Valentino threw himself back in his chair and roared with laughter.*

5 If you **throw back** a drink, you drink it quickly. = **knock back, put back**

throw back something *or* **throw something back** ❑ *He grabbed his drink and threw it back.*

6 If something **throws back** light or sound, it reflects it.

throw back something *or* **throw something back** ❑ *The disturbed water threw back a blurred image of them both.* ❑ *Candles flickered, their light thrown back by mirrors all around the room.*

7 To **throw** someone **back** to an earlier time means to cause them to remember it or return to it, especially when they do not want to.

throw someone back *or* **throw back someone** ❑ [+ to] *The government is throwing us* back to the 1930s, to a time of depression and deprivation. ● If something is a **throwback** to something that existed a long time ago, especially something that you disapprove of, it reminds you of it. ❑ *His attitudes were a throwback to the old colonial days.*

8 If you **throw back** something, you reply quickly and angrily to someone.

throw back something or **throw something back** ❑ *'You're not so great yourself,' she threw back.* ❑ *He left, throwing an insult back over his shoulder.*

9 If you **throw** something **back** at someone, you use something they said or done to hurt them, in a way that is unkind or ungrateful.

throw something back or **throw back something** ❑ [+ at] *I knew he would throw my words back at me and blame me.* ❑ *I made a big effort with you and you threw it back.*

● If you **throw** something **back in** someone's **face**, you reject something they have done for you or use it to hurt them, in a very unkind way. ❑ *To spend your life trying to please someone and then have it thrown back in your face is terrible.*

○ **throw 'back on**

If you **are thrown back on** someone or something, you have to rely on them because other things have failed or are not available.

be thrown back on something/someone ❑ *Without a TV or phone she was completely thrown back on her own resources.*

○ **throw 'down**

1 If you **throw** something **down**, you drop it with some force so that it falls quickly.

throw down something ❑ *He threw down his napkin and left the room.* ❑ [+ on] *She threw down her keys on the table.*

throw something down ❑ [+ on] *He threw the gun down on the floor.*

2 If you **throw** yourself **down**, you let yourself fall or move quickly towards the ground.

throw yourself down ❑ *She threw herself down on her knees and prayed.* ❑ *He threw himself down beside me on the bed.*

3 If people **throw down** their **arms** or **weapons**, they surrender or stop fighting. ❑ *The soldiers threw down their arms and joined the protest.*

4 If you **throw** something **down**, you eat or drink it very quickly.

throw down something or **throw something down** ❑ *He threw down the rest of his coffee and stood up.* ❑ *Don't just throw your food down like that.*

5 If you **throw down a challenge** or **throw down the gauntlet**, you challenge someon to try to compete with you or overcome a problem. ❑ *We are throwing down a challenge t our readers to come up with a new title for the magazine.* ❑ *The company has really thrown dow the gauntlet with this innovative new product.*

○ **throw 'in**

In meaning 2, the stress is on '**throw**.

1 If you **throw** something **in** or **throw** it **in** something, you casually put or drop it into something such as a container or mixture

throw in something ❑ *Add a teaspoonful of salt, and throw in the rice.*

throw something in ❑ *I like to throw a few spices in as well.* ❑ *'Have you got room for my bag in your car?' – 'Sure, throw it in.'*

throw something in something ❑ *I threw it a drawer and forgot about it.* ❑ *They threw the fis in the river, and went home.*

2 If someone **throws** a person **in** a place such as a prison, they force them to enter i and stay there.

throw someone in something ❑ *The cop threatened to throw all of us in jail.*

3 If you **throw** something **in**, you add a word or statement in a casual or unexpected way. = **toss in**

throw in something ❑ *I introduced myself as John P. Taylor – I threw in the 'P' just for fun.*

throw something in ❑ *Her father is the headteacher. Just thought I'd throw that in.* ❑ *He couldn't resist throwing a few comments in.*

4 If you **throw in** an extra item when you are selling something or arranging something, you add or include it to make a deal more attractive to someone.

throw in something ❑ *She bought the dress after I threw in a matching scarf.*

throw something in ❑ *We liked the carpets an curtains and they agreed to throw them in.*

5 If something **is thrown in**, it is included in a mixture or situation.

be thrown in ❑ *The film has songs, stories, and few jokes thrown in.* ❑ *I'm part Spanish, part Scottish, with a little bit of French thrown in.*

6 If you **throw** something **in**, you give it u or stop doing it. [INFORMAL]

throw in something or **throw something in** ❑ *She had thrown in her job and gone back to her home town.* ❑ *I feel like throwing it all in.*

● If you **throw in the towel**, you give up trying to do something because you feel you cannot succeed. ❑ *He finally threw in the towel and dropped the case.*

7 To **throw** people **in** means to send them to fight or compete.

throw in something/someone or **throw something/someone in** ❑ He threw in all his best troops, but to no avail.

⊞ If a player **throws in** the ball or **throws in**, he or she throws the ball onto the pitch from the side after it has been kicked out.

throw in something or **throw something in** ❑ He threw in a long ball that went straight to the forward.

throw in ❑ He threw in quickly. ● A **throw-in** is an occasion in a football match when a player throws the ball onto the pitch from the side after it has been kicked out. ❑ A quick throw-in gave the State players a chance to score.

○ **throw 'into**

1 If you **throw** an object **into** something such as a container or mixture, you casually put or drop it there.

throw something into something ❑ I quickly threw a few things into a suitcase. ❑ I picked up the toys and threw them into a cupboard.

2 If someone **throws** a person **into** a place such as a prison, they force them to enter it and stay there.

throw someone into something ❑ They arrested him and threw them into prison.

3 If you **throw** yourself **into** a place, you move or let yourself fall there quickly.

throw yourself into something ❑ She threw herself into his arms. ❑ I threw myself into the road shouting 'Stop!'

4 To **throw** someone or something **into** a state means to cause them suddenly to be in that state.

throw someone/something into something ❑ He turned out the light, throwing the room into darkness. ❑ Her voice threw me into a rage.

5 If you **throw** yourself **into** something, you begin a task or activity with a lot of effort and energy.

throw yourself into something ❑ To take her mind off her troubles, she threw herself into her work. ❑ Everyone threw themselves energetically into clearing up.

6 If you **throw** energy or resources **into** something, you use a lot of energy or resources to try and make it succeed.

throw something into something ❑ She threw all of her energies into her career.

○ **throw 'off**

1 If you **throw off** clothes or a cover, you quickly remove them.

throw off something or **throw something off** ❑ Laverne threw off her jacket. ❑ He was hot, and had thrown his blankets off.

2 If you **throw off** something that is limiting your freedom, you make yourself free from it.

throw off something or **throw something off** ❑ She urged her people to throw off their chains. ❑ We need to throw these old superstitions off.

3 If you **throw off** an illness, you recover from it quickly.

throw off something or **throw something off** ❑ When he gets a cold he usually throws it off very quickly.

4 If you **throw** someone **off**, you manage to escape from someone who is following or chasing you.

throw someone off or **throw off someone** ❑ Agents were set to tail him, but he always threw them off. ❑ He threw off his pursuers by jumping on a bicycle.

5 To **throw** someone or something **off** means to cause them to make a mistake or to fail.

throw someone/something off or **throw off someone/something** ❑ There was an ambiguity in the question that threw me off. ❑ A faulty gauge can throw your calculations off.

6 To **throw** someone **off** something means to cause them to depart from what they were intending or planning to do.

throw someone off something ❑ These problems have thrown the project off schedule.

● If you **throw someone off the scent, track,** or **trail,** you deliberately deceive or confuse them so that they cannot achieve what they intended. ❑ They told a story to throw the police off the scent. ❑ I put on an Italian accent to throw her off the trail.

7 If something **throws off** heat, light, or another form of energy, it releases it.

throw off something or **throw something off** ❑ The furnace threw off a lot of heat. ❑ Light thrown off by the water flashed on their boat.

NOTE **Emit** is a formal word for **throw off.**

○ **throw 'on**

If you **throw on** clothes, you put them on quickly and carelessly.

throw on something or **throw something on** ❑ He threw on his jeans and went downstairs. ❑ I threw a jacket on over my dress.

○ **'throw on** (or **throw upon**)

1 If you **throw** yourself **on** someone or something, you run towards them and let yourself fall on them, embrace them, or attack them.

throw yourself on something/someone ❑ She threw herself on the bed and sobbed ❑ Joseph threw himself on his father, kissing his face.

2 If something **throws** light or shadow **on** someone or something, it causes them to be covered in it. [LITERARY]

throw something on something ❑ *The flames threw a red light on her face.* ❑ *A large beech tree threw its shadow upon the grass.*

3 To **throw light on** something means to help people to understand it or solve it. ❑ *He questioned them in an attempt to throw light on the situation.* ❑ *The diaries throw a new light upon certain incidents.*

4 To **throw** doubt or suspicion **on** someone or something means to cause people to doubt them or suspect them.

throw something on someone/something ❑ *A re-examination of the evidence has thrown doubts on this view.* ❑ *He tried to throw suspicion on the two youths.*

○ **throw 'onto** (or **throw on to**)

If you **throw** something or someone **onto** something, you cause them to fall with force on top of it.

throw something/someone onto something ❑ *She threw her books violently onto the floor.*

throw yourself onto something ❑ *She threw herself onto the sofa.*

✪ **throw 'out**

1 If you **throw out** something, you throw it so that it moves quickly away from you.

throw something out ❑ *They threw the net out and could not pull it back in.* ❑ *[+ of] He looked again at the papers and threw them out of the window.*

throw out something ❑ *She threw out handfuls of corn for the chickens.*

2 If you **throw out** something you no longer want, you get rid of it. = **throw away**

throw out something ❑ *People used to throw out their rubbish on to the street.* ❑ *I can remember my parents throwing out their old furniture.*

throw something out ❑ *There's a bit of rice left – should I throw it out and wash the pot?* ❑ *Don't throw your old clothes out – give them to charity.*

3 If you **throw** something **out**, you reject it because you find it unacceptable.

throw out something ❑ *For every painting he finished, he threw out a hundred sketches.* ❑ *They must not be tempted to throw out the principles of democracy.*

throw something out ❑ *The Grand Jury threw the Bill out.*

4 If you **throw** someone **out**, you force them to leave a place or job.

throw out someone ❑ *They'll throw out their MP if he doesn't vote for it.* ❑ *[+ of] He was nearly thrown out of college.*

throw someone out ❑ *She threw her husband out after an argument.* ❑ *[+ of] They can throw you out of the country if you don't have a visa.*

5 If a judge **throws out** a case, he or she rejects it and the trial does not take place.

throw out something or **throw something out** ❑ *The defense wants the district judge to throw out the case.*

6 If you **throw out** ideas or suggestions, you mention them for people to consider.

throw out something or **throw something out** ❑ *I'll just throw out a few ideas for titles and you tell me if you like them.* ❑ *Actors worked from suggestions thrown out to them from the audience.*

7 If something **throws out** smoke, light, or heat, it produces and releases it.

throw out something or **throw something out** ❑ *The factory chimney throws out huge plumes of black smoke.*

NOTE **Emit** is a formal word for **throw out**.

8 If you **throw out** a hand, arm, or leg, you move it suddenly away from your body.

throw out something or **throw something out** ❑ *Bond stumbled and threw out his hand for support.* ❑ *She threw her arms out in welcome.*

○ **throw 'over**

1 If you **throw** one thing **over** another or **throw** it **over**, you throw it so that it moves above another thing from one side to the other.

throw something over something ❑ *I threw my briefcase over the wall.*

throw something over ❑ *The children had thrown the ball over into the neighbour's garden.*

2 If you **throw** something **over** something you casually place it on top of the other thing so that it covers it or lies across it.

throw something over something ❑ *You could throw a blanket over that old sofa.* ❑ *He took off his coat and threw it over a chair.*

3 If you **throw** something **over**, you pass it to someone casually, often by throwing it.

throw over something or **throw something over** ❑ *He threw over a newspaper.* ❑ *[+ to] He threw some cans of cola over to us.*

throw someone over something ❑ *Will you throw me over the remote control, please?*

4 If you **throw over** a boyfriend or girlfriend, you end your relationship with them. = **chuck** [OLD-FASHIONED]

throw someone over or **throw over someone** ❑ *Eventually she threw him over for someone else.*

○ **throw 'overboard**

1 If you **throw** something or someone **overboard**, you throw them over the side of a ship into the water.

throw something/someone overboard or **throw overboard something/someone** ❑ *When no-one was looking she threw the box* overboard. ❏ They threatened to throw him overboard.

2 If you **throw** an idea or plan **overboard**, you reject it completely, often when you had accepted it before.

throw something overboard or **throw overboard something** ❏ They had thrown their neutrality overboard in the crisis. ❏ You had to throw overboard everything you thought you knew.

○ **throw 'round** ➜ see **throw around**

○ **throw to'gether**

1 If you **throw** something **together**, you make it or put together its parts quickly and not very carefully.

throw together something or **throw something together** ❏ I'll just throw together something for dinner. ❏ She looked as if she had thrown her outfit together in a hurry.

2 If people **are thrown together** or if something **throws** them **together**, a situation or chance event causes them to meet.

be thrown together ❏ They were thrown together in Paris in the 1930s.

throw someone together or **throw together someone** ❏ Ten years later, circumstances threw them together once again.

○ **throw 'up**

1 If something **throws up** something, it causes small particles such as dust or stones to rise into the air.

throw up something ❏ A passing car threw up a cloud of white dust.

throw something up ❏ The fire threw sparks up into our faces.

2 If you **throw** something **up**, you throw it upwards into the air.

throw something up ❏ Adam threw the ball up and they started to play. ❏ [+ in] She tore the paper into little pieces and threw them up in the air.

throw up something ❏ Howard threw up a coin. ❏ They were trying to throw up a rope onto the bridge.

3 If you **throw up** part of your body, you raise it suddenly.

throw something up or **throw up something** ❏ Mrs Pringle threw her hands up in astonishment. ❏ He threw up an arm to protect himself.

4 If someone **throws up** a building or structure, they build or make it very quickly.

throw up something or **throw something up** ❏ They had managed to throw up a basic shelter. ❏ 'These modern buildings, they just throw them up,' he said.

5 To **throw up** something means to produce or create a particular type of thing. [BRITISH]

throw up something or **throw something up** ❏ The new equipment threw up major problems over safety. ❏ Your research has thrown up some fascinating questions, hasn't it?

6 If you **throw** something **up**, you suddenly leave or stop doing something. = **chuck in**

throw up something or **throw something up** ❏ Why would she throw up a good job like that?

7 If someone **throws up** or **throws** something **up**, they vomit. [INFORMAL]

throw up ❏ I felt like I was going to throw up.

throw something up or **throw up something** ❏ She drank the milk, then threw it up immediately.

○ **'throw upon** ➜ see **throw on**

thrust /θrʌst/ (**thrusts, thrusting**)

> The form **thrust** is used in the present tense and is the past tense and past participle of the verb.

○ **'thrust on** (or **thrust upon**)

To **thrust** something **on** someone means to force them to have it, deal with it, or experience it.

thrust something on someone ❏ They suddenly thrust a change of plan on us. ❏ An enormous responsibility had been thrust upon me.

○ **thrust 'up** [LITERARY]

If something **thrusts up** somewhere, it is higher than the surrounding things and can be clearly seen. ❏ The peak is an imposing rock needle thrusting up at least 250 feet.

thumb /θʌm/ (**thumbs, thumbing, thumbed**)

○ **thumb 'through**

If you **thumb through** a book or other written material, you read it quickly, turning over the pages without looking at them carefully.

thumb through something ❏ I thumbed through a magazine while I waited.

thump /θʌmp/ (**thumps, thumping, thumped**)

○ **thump 'out**

If you **thump out** music, especially on the piano, or if it **thumps out**, you play it very loudly.

thump out something or **thump something out** ❏ The band thumped out a rousing tune. ❏ She used to thump old songs out on the piano.

thump out ❏ Music was thumping out from a party across the street.

tick /tɪk/ (**ticks, ticking, ticked**)

○ **tick a'way**

1 If time **ticks away**, it passes, especially when you are waiting for something to happen. ❏ *Time was ticking away and he just couldn't think of the answer.* ❏ *The minutes ticked away towards noon.*

2 If something **ticks away**, it makes a continual ticking noise. ❏ *I could hear my watch ticking away.*

○ **tick 'by**

If time **ticks by**, it passes, especially when you are waiting for something to happen. ❏ *The minutes ticked by. Then he announced his decision.*

○ **tick 'down**

If time **ticks down**, it passes, usually before something important happens or ends. ❏ *As the final minutes of the game ticked down, both sides desperately tried to score a winning goal.* ❏ [+ to] *The clock is ticking down to the deadline for an agreement to be reached.*

○ **tick 'off**

1 If you **tick** things **off**, you write a tick or other mark next to items on a list, to show that they have been dealt with. [BRITISH]
tick off something or **tick something off**
❏ *The teacher ticks off the names as she calls them out.* ❏ *Tick them off as each job is finished.*

2 If you **tick** things **off**, you say them one by one, usually touching your fingers with another finger at the same time. [BRITISH]
tick something off or **tick off something**
❏ *'Who's coming?' She ticked them off. 'Grandma, Grandpa, Uncle Bob...'* ❏ *She named all the colours of the rainbow, ticking them off on her fingers.*

3 If you **tick** someone **off**, you speak crossly to them because they have done something wrong. = **tell off** [BRITISH, INFORMAL]
tick someone off or **tick off someone** ❏ [+ for] *David had ticked her off for getting her sums wrong.* ❏ *Why tick off the children when the parents are just as rude?*

NOTE **Scold** is a more formal word for **tick off**.

• If you give someone a **ticking-off**, you speak crossly to them because they have done something wrong. = **telling-off** [BRITISH, INFORMAL] ❏ *He got a ticking-off for coming in late.*

4 If something **ticks** you **off**, it annoys you. [AMERICAN, INFORMAL] ❏ *I just think it's rude and it's ticking me off.* ❏ *He managed to tick off everyone in the room.* • If you are **ticked off**, you are annoyed. ❏ *She's really ticked off at him for forgetting her birthday.*

5 If a clock **ticks off** time, or if time **ticks off**, time passes, especially before something important happens or ends.
tick off something ❏ *The clock ticked off the minutes to the meeting.*
tick off ❏ *The final seconds of the game ticked off.*

○ **tick 'on** → see **tick away**

○ **tick 'over**

1 If an engine or device **ticks over**, it operates steadily or slowly, just enough so that it does not stop. [BRITISH] ❏ *She kept the car engine ticking over while she sat and waited.*

NOTE **Idle** is a more technical word for **tick over**.

2 If something **is ticking over**, it continues to work or exist, but not at a very high or intense level. [BRITISH]
be ticking over ❏ *Eat moderate amounts so that your digestive system is ticking over, but not overburdened.*

○ **tick 'up**

If something **ticks up**, it rises by a small amount. ❏ *Hepworth shares ticked up 3p to 200 yesterday.*

tide /taɪd/ (**tides, tiding, tided**)

○ **tide 'over**

If something **tides** someone **over**, it is enough to help them get through a difficult period of time.
tide someone over ❏ *I only want to borrow a few dollars to tide me over till Monday.* ❏ *We'll be eating very late, so have a snack to tide you over.*
tide someone over something ❏ *These grain stores helped tide the world over the shortages.*

tidy /'taɪdi/ (**tidies, tidying, tidied**)

○ **tidy a'way**

If you **tidy** something **away**, you put it back in the place where it is stored after using it.
tidy something away or **tidy away something** ❏ *It's time to tidy your toys away now.* ❏ *I tidied away everything on my desk before I went home.*

○ **tidy 'out**

If you **tidy** something **out**, you make a room or container look tidy by getting rid of things you do not want and putting the other things back neatly.
tidy out something or **tidy something out** ❏ *I'm going to tidy out the loft this weekend.* ❏ *I can't find anything in this drawer – we need to tidy it out.*

◑ **tidy 'up**

1 If you **tidy** something **up** or **tidy up**, you make a place look tidy by putting all the things back in their proper places.
tidy something up ❏ *He went back to the studio and tidied it up.*
tidy up something ❏ *Mum asked me to tidy up my room.*
tidy up ❏ *Eva was tidying up after lunch.* ❏ *If you're going to play games in here, please tidy up when you've finished.*

2 If you **tidy** someone **up**, you quickly make them look cleaner or smarter.

tidy someone up or **tidy up someone** ❑ *She tidied the children up and sent them downstairs to meet the guests.*

tidy yourself up ❑ *I tidied myself up before we landed.*

3 If you **tidy** something **up**, you deal with any small parts of it that are not ready or not satisfactory.

tidy something up or **tidy up something** ❑ *I had a week to tidy up the last-minute details of my trip.*

tie /taɪ/ (**ties, tying, tied**)

○ **tie 'back**

If you **tie** something **back**, you fasten it so that it does not hang straight down.

tie something back or **tie back something** ❑ *She brushed her hair and tied it back.* ❑ *There are velvet ropes for tying back the curtains.*

○ **tie 'down**

1 If you **tie** someone or something **down**, you tie them to the ground or in a low position.

tie something/someone down or **tie down something/someone** ❑ *He was tying down the flap of his tent.* ❑ *One of the prison guards tied him down.*

2 A person or thing that **ties** someone **down** prevents them from being free to do what they want.

tie someone down or **tie down someone** ❑ *She doesn't want children because she says they tie you down.* ❑ [+ to] *I was unable to tie down my colleagues to a specific date.*

tie yourself down ❑ *He didn't want to tie himself down by signing a contract.*

3 To **tie down** troops means to force them to stay in one place. [TECHNICAL]

tie down someone or **tie someone down** ❑ *Successful armed resistance tied down large numbers of troops.*

○ **tie 'in with**

If one thing **ties in with** another, it is closely connected to it, fits in with it, or agrees with it.

tie in with something ❑ *The film ties in with what we've been studying in our History lessons.* ❑ *His beliefs didn't seem to tie in at all with reality.*

○ **tie 'up**

1 If you **tie** something **up**, you put string or rope around it to hold it in place.

tie something up ❑ *She tied the parcel up securely.* ❑ [+ with] *The trousers were too big and he had to tie them up with string.*

tie up something ❑ [+ with] *They tied up the tent flap with some nylon rope.* ❑ [+ in] *Clara came in, carrying some packages tied up in brown paper.*

2 If you **tie** a person or an animal **up**, you fasten ropes or chains around them so that they cannot escape.

tie someone/something up ❑ *I tied my goat up during the day.* ❑ [+ to] *They tied him up to a fence.*

tie up someone/something ❑ *The dog was tied up in the yard.*

3 If you **tie up** laces, you fasten them in a bow. = **do up**

tie up something or **tie something up** ❑ *He saw the man bend down and tie up his shoelace.*

4 When a boat **ties up** or someone **ties** it **up**, it is attached to something with a rope or chain.

tie up ❑ *The ships made for port and tied up.*

tie something up or **tie up something** ❑ *The boat was tied up in the marina.*

NOTE **Moor** is a more formal word for **tie up**.

5 If you **tie** something **up**, you use it and if it **is tied up**, it is being used, so that it is not available for other people or purposes.

tie up something or **tie something up** ❑ *This problem has tied too much management time up already.*

be tied up ❑ [+ in] *Most of his money is tied up in property.*

6 If you are **tied up** or if something **ties** you **up**, you are busy, and not free to do anything else.

be tied up ❑ *I'm tied up right now, can you call me back later?* ❑ [+ with] *Her accountant was tied up with other work.*

tie someone up or **tie up someone** ❑ *The technology just seems to tie people up in more paperwork.*

7 If you **tie up** an issue or problem, you deal with it in a definite way.

tie something up or **tie up something** ❑ *He hoped to tie up the issue through diplomacy.* ❑ *She's got a very smart lawyer who will tie it all up for her.*

● If you **tie up loose ends**, you deal with any remaining small problems so that an issue is completely resolved. ❑ *We've still got a few loose ends to tie up with the contract.*

8 If something **ties up** with something else or **is tied up** with it, it is closely linked with it.

be tied up ❑ [+ with] *Her feelings about it were tied up with her childhood experiences.*

tie up ❑ [+ with] *The theory does seem to tie up with our observations.*

tighten /ˈtaɪtən/ (**tightens, tightening, tightened**)

○ **tighten 'up**

1 If you **tighten** something **up**, you move

something so that it is more firmly in place or holds something more firmly. ≠ **loosen**

tighten up something or **tighten something up** ❑ He tightened up a piece of loose wire. ❑ You'd better tighten those screws up.

2 If a muscle **tightens up** or if you **tighten** it **up**, it becomes tense and stiff rather than being relaxed.

tighten up something or **tighten something up** ❑ These exercises are to tighten up the abdominal muscles.

tighten up ❑ His muscles tightened up as if he was preparing to flee.

3 If you **tighten** something **up** or **tighten up**, you make a rule or system stricter or more effective.

tighten up something or **tighten something up** ❑ There have been demands to tighten up the law. ❑ The conditions for standing as a candidate have now been tightened up.

tighten up ❑ Security has been lax and we need to tighten up. ❑ [+ on] There were calls to tighten up on immigration.

4 If someone **tightens up**, they become less relaxed or friendly. ≠ **loosen up** ❑ People often tighten up in the presence of authority.

time /taɪm/ (**times, timing, timed**)
○ **time 'out**

If a system or a web page **times out**, it stops working because it has not been used for a period of time. ❑ I got a message that my online banking session had timed out.

tingle /'tɪŋgəl/ (**tingles, tingling, tingled**)
○ **'tingle with**

If you **tingle with** a feeling such as excitement, you feel it very strongly.

tingle with something ❑ She tingled with excitement.

tinker /'tɪŋkə/ (**tinkers, tinkering, tinkered**)
○ **tinker a'round** (or **tinker about** [mainly BRITISH])

If you **tinker around**, you make small changes or improvements to something, or try doing different things with it. ❑ [+ with] He likes tinkering around with old cars. ❑ The government should stop tinkering around with education.

○ **'tinker with**

If you **tinker with** something, you make small changes or improvements to it.

tinker with something ❑ I don't think they should tinker with the genetic structure of food. ❑ I kept tinkering with the text trying to make it better.

tip /tɪp/ (**tips, tipping, tipped**)
○ **tip 'off**

If you **tip** someone **off**, you tell them about

something secret that has happened or is going to happen.

tip someone off or **tip off someone** ❑ They tipped the police off. ❑ Someone inside the organization must have tipped off the terrorists. ❑ The press had been tipped off about her arrival at the hotel. ● A **tip-off** is a warning or piece of secret information that you give to someone. ❑ The building was evacuated as the result of a tip-off.

○ **tip 'over**

If you **tip** something **over** or if it **tips over**, it falls or turns onto its side or upside down = **overturn**

tip over something or **tip something over** ❑ He got up quickly, tipping over the chair. ❑ She tipped the pan over and a dozen fish fell out.

tip over ❑ The boat transporting them had tipped over.

○ **tip 'up**

If you **tip up** a container such as a bucket or glass, you make it lean to one side so that its contents begin to pour out of it. = **tilt**

tip up something or **tip something up** ❑ She tipped up the glass to swallow the last drop.

tire /taɪə/ (**tires, tiring, tired**)
○ **'tire of**

If you **tire of** something, you become bored with it and are no longer interested in it.

tire of something ❑ The children soon tired of the game and wandered off. ❑ He stopped talking when he tired of my questions.

○ **tire 'out**

If something **tires** you **out**, it makes you very tired. = **wear out**

tire someone out or **tire out someone** ❑ Even climbing up the stairs would tire him out.

tire yourself out ❑ He would walk back in the evening, in order to tire himself out and be able to sleep. ● If you are **tired out**, you are exhausted. ❑ By the he got there he was tired out. ❑ We have some advice for tired-out parents.

toady /'təʊdi/ (**toadies, toadying, toadied**)
○ **'toady to**

If someone **toadies to** an important or powerful person, they say nice things to them or try to please them in the hope of getting some advantage from them, in a way that other people find unpleasant.

toady to someone ❑ They came backstage afterward, cooing and toadying to him.

tog /tɒg/ (**togs, togging, togged**)
○ **tog 'out** [INFORMAL]

If you **tog** yourself **out** or **are togged out**, you are dressed in special clothing. = **rig out**

tog yourself out ❏ [+ in] *The kids had togged themselves out in their best clothes.*

be togged out ❏ [+ in] *He was togged out in baggy pants and carrying a skateboard.*

tog 'up [INFORMAL]
If you **are togged up**, you are dressed in special clothing.

be togged up ❏ [+ in] *He was togged up in running gear.*

toil /tɔɪl/ (**toils, toiling, toiled**)

toil a'way
If you **toil away**, you work hard at something for a long time. = **slave away**
❏ *Miners spend their lives toiling away in the dark.*
❏ *We've been toiling away all morning making lunch for 30 people.*

tone /təʊn/ (**tones, toning, toned**)

tone 'down
1 If you **tone** something **down**, you make it less strong, severe, or offensive. = **moderate**
tone down something or **tone something down** ❏ *He advised me to tone down my article.*
❏ *You're too aggressive. You should tone it down or nobody will listen to you.*
2 If you **tone down** a colour or a flavour, you make it less bright or strong.
tone down something or **tone something down** ❏ *He was asked to tone down the spices and garlic in his recipes.* ❏ *She added a little grey to the paint to tone it down.*

tone 'in
If something **tones in** with something else, it looks good with it because their colours are similar. = **match** ❏ [+ with] *That carpet doesn't really tone in with the curtains.* ❏ *She had a blue dress, and a coat which toned in nicely.*

tone 'up
If something **tones up** muscles, it makes them firm and strong.
tone up something or **tone something up** ❏ *This exercise should help to tone up the stomach muscles.* ❏ *Your arms will look slimmer if you tone them up.*

'tone with [mainly BRITISH]
If one thing **tones with** another, the two things look nice together because their colours are similar in quality or brightness.
tone with something ❏ *Her handbag toned with her blue dress.*

tool /tuːl/ (**tools, tooling, tooled**)

tool 'up
1 If a person or organization **tools up** or **is tooled up**, they have the machines or equipment they need ready to do or produce something.

be tooled up ❏ *The automotive plant is tooled up and ready to go into operation.*

tool up ❏ *The costs of tooling up to produce the new model were $50 million.*
2 If someone **is tooled up** or **tools up**, they carry a weapon or weapons. [INFORMAL]
be tooled up ❏ *They were going to get tooled up and rob a bank.*
tool up ❏ *They wanted him to tool up and join the fighting.*

top /tɒp/ (**tops, topping, topped**)

top 'off
If you **top** something **off**, you do something to complete it in a satisfactory way. = **round off**
top off something or **top something off** ❏ [+ with] *He ate a plate of steak and eggs and then topped it off with ice cream.*

top 'up
1 If you **top up** a container or a drink, you add more liquid to it, usually when it has been partly emptied.
top up something ❏ *Philip topped up his coffee.*
top something up ❏ *Shall I top your glass up?*
❏ [+ with] *The bath had gone cold, so she topped it up with more hot water.* • A **top-up** is another serving of a drink in the same glass or cup. [BRITISH] ❏ *They offer coffee with free top-ups.*
2 If you **top** something **up**, you add something to it in order to make it larger or more complete.
top up something ❏ *You can use part-time work to top up your income.*
top something up ❏ *In the winter months, she tops her tan up with visits to the tanning salon.*
❏ *The body does not store vitamin D, so you need to keep topping it up.*
3 If you **top up** or **top up** your mobile phone, you make more money available to be spent on calls.
top up ❏ *I usually top up online.*
top up something or **top something up** ❏ *You can top up your phone at the ATM.*

topple /tɒpəl/ (**topples, toppling, toppled**)

topple 'over
If something **topples over**, it becomes unsteady and falls. = **keel over** ❏ *The stack of books looked as though it might topple over.*

toss /tɒs, AM tɔːs/ (**tosses, tossing, tossed**)

toss a'round (or **toss about** [mainly BRITISH])
1 To **toss** something **around** means to move or shake it violently.
toss something around or **toss around something** ❏ *The pianist had long black hair, and she tossed it around as she played.* ❏ *The boat was being tossed around by the stormy sea.*

2 If you **toss** words or ideas **around**, you mention or suggest them in a casual way.

toss around something or **toss something around** ❑ We tossed a few ideas around. ❑ Various possible names for the club were tossed around.

○ **toss a'way**

1 If you **toss** something **away**, you throw it or put it down in a careless way, because you do not want it.

toss away something or **toss something away** ❑ She tossed away her cigarette. ❑ She ate half the ice cream then tossed the rest away.

2 If you **toss** something valuable **away**, you carelessly reject or waste it.

toss away something or **toss something away** ❑ She had tossed away their years of friendship by one thoughtless act. ❑ They had a winning chance and they tossed it away.

○ **toss 'back**

If you **toss back** your head or hair, you move your head back sharply.

toss something back or **toss back something** ❑ He tossed his head back. ❑ She tossed back her long blonde hair.

○ **toss 'back** (or **toss down**)

If you **toss back** a drink, you drink it quickly.

toss back something or **toss something back** ❑ He tossed back another glass of wine. ❑ When the drink came, he tossed it down in one gulp.

○ **toss 'in**

If you **toss** something **in**, you casually say or write something in the middle of a conversation or piece of writing. = **toss out**

toss in something or **toss something in** ❑ I tossed in his name to see how they reacted. ❑ You get extra marks if you toss a few quotes in.

○ **toss 'off**

1 → see **toss back**

2 If you **toss** something **off**, you quickly write something such as a letter or article. = **dash off**

toss off something or **toss something off** ❑ I tossed off a letter to my parents. ❑ A song like that is not a simple little jingle that can be tossed off in an hour.

3 To **toss off** or to **toss** someone **off** means to masturbate yourself or another person. = **jack off, jerk off** [INFORMAL, RUDE]

○ **toss 'out**

1 If you **toss** something **out**, you casually mention or suggest something. = **toss in**

toss out something or **toss something out** ❑ I tossed a few suggestions out to see how they'd react.

2 If you **toss** something **out**, you throw it

away because you do not want it any more [INFORMAL]

toss out something or **toss something out** ❑ I need to toss out some of those old clothes. ❑ Don't toss that out, I can use it.

○ **toss 'up**

If you **toss up**, you make a decision about something by throwing a coin into the air and guessing which side of the coin will be on top when it falls. ❑ [+ to-infinitive] We tossed up to decide who should pay the bill.

● A **toss-up** is a situation in which either of two results seems equally likely. ❑ It was a toss-up who would get there first.

tot /tɒt/ (**tots, totting, totted**)

○ **tot 'up**

To **tot up** numbers means to add them together in order to find the total.

tot up something or **tot something up** ❑ I'll just tot up what you owe me. ❑ We totted all the figures up.

touch /tʌtʃ/ (**touches, touching, touched**)

○ **touch 'down**

When an aircraft **touches down**, it lands. ≠ **take off** ❑ He watched the plane as it touched down. ❑ We touched down at Heathrow.

● A **touchdown** is the landing of an aircraft ❑ The pilot took great care to make a smooth touchdown.

○ **touch 'off**

If something **touches off** a bad situation or series of events, it causes it to start happening. = **spark off**

touch off something or **touch something off** ❑ The police action touched off another night of rioting.

❍ **'touch on**

If you **touch on** something, you mention it or write briefly about it.

touch on something ❑ I've touched on a couple of topics already. ❑ They had touched on the possibility of increasing the budget.

○ **touch 'up**

1 If you **touch** something **up**, you improve its appearance, especially by covering up small marks with paint or another substance.

touch something up or **touch up something** ❑ He touched the car up a bit and sold it. ❑ My lipstick needs touching up. ● A **touched-up** image or object has been improved by having small marks covered. ❑ The cover featured a touched-up photograph of the actor.

2 To **touch** someone **up** means to touch them in a sexual way without their permission. = **feel up** [INFORMAL, RUDE]

touch someone up or **touch up someone**
❑ *Someone tried to touch her up on the bus.*

ᵇ**'touch upon** → see **touch on**

ᵇough /tʌf/ (**toughs, toughing, toughed**)
ᵇ **tough 'out**
If you **tough** something **out**, you do not give in or show any weakness in a difficult situation.
tough something out or **tough out something** ❑ *I think it was very brave of him to tough it out.* ❑ *The minister seemed determined to tough out the crisis.*

ᵇoughen /tʌfən/ (**toughens, toughening, toughened**)
ᵇ **toughen 'up**
1 If you **toughen up**, or if something **toughens** you **up**, you become physically or mentally stronger and less sensitive.
toughen up ❑ *He told me that I would have to toughen up to survive as a police officer.*
toughen someone up or **toughen up someone** ❑ *A month working on a construction site will toughen him up.*
2 If you **toughen** something **up**, you make it stricter or more severe.
toughen up something or **toughen something up** ❑ *The bill toughened up the conditions for acquiring French nationality.*
❑ *He called for the law to be toughened up.*

ᵇout /taʊt/ (**touts, touting, touted**)
ᵇ **tout a'round** (or **tout round** [mainly BRITISH])
1 If you **tout around** for something, you try to obtain it by asking a lot of different people. ❑ [+ for] *He spends a lot of time touting around for old furniture.* ❑ *I've been touting around trying to find work as a tutor.*
2 If you **tout** something **around** or **tout** it **around** a place, you try to sell it or make people interested in it by telling different people about it.
tout something around ❑ *He touted his book around for two years before finding a publisher.*
tout something around something
❑ *His movie script had been touted around various production companies.*

ᵇ **tout 'round** → see **tout around**

ᵇOW /təʊ/ (**tows, towing, towed**)
ᵇ **tow a'way**
If a vehicle **is towed away** or if someone **tows** it **away**, it is removed by being attached to another vehicle and pulled along.
be towed away ❑ *The car broke down and we had to have it towed away.* ❑ *He found his van had been towed away by the police.*

tow something away or **tow away something** ❑ *They'll tow you away if you park there.* ❑ *Police were preparing to tow away an abandoned vehicle.*

tower /taʊə/ (**towers, towering, towered**)
○ **tower a'bove** (or **tower over**)
1 If someone or something **towers above** another person or thing, they are much taller than them.
tower above someone/something ❑ *John towered above the rest of the class.* ❑ *The sides of the great ship towered over them.*
2 If someone or something **towers above** another person or thing, they are much better than them.
tower above someone/something ❑ *Their songs tower above anything produced by any bands today.* ❑ *One company towers above all the others in the scope of its operations.*

toy /tɔɪ/ (**toys, toying, toyed**)
○ **'toy with**
1 If you **toy with** an idea, you consider it casually, without making any decisions about it.
toy with something ❑ *I've been toying with the idea of setting up my own business.* ❑ *She toyed with the possibility of leaving.*
2 If you **toy with** an object, you keep moving it about with your fingers. = **play with**
toy with something ❑ *He picked up a pencil and toyed with it idly.*
3 If you **toy with** food, you touch or move it but eat very little or none at all.
toy with something ❑ *She had no appetite, and toyed with the bread and cheese.*
4 If you **toy with** someone, you pretend to like or be attracted to them when you are not really interested in a serious relationship with them.
toy with someone ❑ *He realised with despair that she was toying with him.*

trace /treɪs/ (**traces, tracing, traced**)
○ **trace 'out**
If you **trace** something **out**, you write it or mark it clearly and carefully.
trace out something or **trace something out** ❑ *She traced out A, B, C in the dust with a stick.*

track /træk/ (**tracks, tracking, tracked**)
○ **track 'down**
If you **track down** someone or something, you find them after searching for some time. = **hunt down**
track down something/someone ❑ *He went to several different shops trying to track down the right type of paint.*

track something/someone down ❑ *Many years later a journalist succeeded in tracking them down.*

trade /'treɪd/ (trades, trading, traded)

○ **trade 'in**

If you **trade** something **in**, you give something such as an old car or machine to a dealer in exchange for a new one at a reduced price.

trade in something or **trade something in** ❑ [+ *for*] *Is it worth repairing, or shall I trade it in for a new one?* ❑ *You could trade in the piano, or sell it.* ● A **trade-in** is a deal in which someone exchanges an old car, machine, or piece of equipment for a new one at a reduced price.

○ **trade 'off**

> In meaning 2, the stress is on **'trade**.

1 If you **trade** one thing **off** against another, you exchange all or part of it for the other thing.

trade off something or **trade something off** ❑ [+ *against*] *It may be possible to trade off manpower costs against computer costs.* ❑ [+ *for*] *An accused person may be able to trade off information for a reduced sentence.* ● A **trade-off** is a compromise between two things, or an exchange of all or part of one thing for another. ❑ *The headline indicates that there was a trade-off at the summit.* ❑ *There is a trade-off between inflation and unemployment.*

2 If someone **trades off** something, they use it for their own advantage, often in an unfair way. [BRITISH]

trade off something ❑ *For too long he has been able to trade off his good looks.*

○ **trade 'on**

If someone **trades on** something, they use it to gain an advantage for themselves, often in an unfair way. **= exploit**

trade on something ❑ *We need to take action against people who trade on the hopes of the desperately ill.* ❑ *He was able to trade on the unpopularity of the two main parties.*

○ **trade 'up**

If you **trade up**, you replace something you own with something newer or more expensive. ❑ [+ *to*] *Mobile phone users are mostly trading up to smartphones.* ❑ *In a good economic climate, homeowners may feel ready to trade up.*

traffic /'træfɪk/ (traffics, trafficking, trafficked)

○ **'traffic in**

Someone who **traffics in** drugs or stolen goods buys and sells them even though it i illegal to do so.

traffic in something ❑ *The president said that anyone who traffics in illegal drugs should be brought to justice.*

trail /'treɪl/ (trails, trailing, trailed)

○ **trail a'way** (or **trail off**)

If someone's voice **trails away** or if they **trail away**, they gradually become silent. ❑ *He didn't finish what he was saying. His voice trailed away.* ❑ *'The problem is…' He trailed off.*

train /'treɪn/ (trains, training, trained)

○ **'train for**

If a person or animal **trains for** a physical activity such as a race or if someone **trains** them **for** it, they prepare for it by doing physical exercises.

train for something ❑ *Neil trained for the London Marathon a couple of years ago.*

train someone/something for something ❑ *He has been training the horse for the Grand National.*

○ **'train on**

If you **train** something **on** someone or something, you aim it at them and keep it pointing towards them.

train something on something/someone ❑ *She trained her binoculars on the car in the distance.* ❑ *One gun was trained on the guard.*

○ **train 'out of**

If you **train** a person or an animal **out of** something, you train them to change their behaviour.

train someone/something out of something ❑ *You need to train yourself out of this self-destructive pattern.* ❑ *Cats can be trained out of scratching on the bedroom door.*

○ **train 'up** [BRITISH]

If you **train** someone **up**, you teach them the skills they need to be able to do something.

train up someone or **train someone up** ❑ *We need to train up large numbers of new teachers.* ❑ *They rented a shop, hired some staff, and trained them up.*

○ **'train upon → see train on**

trample /'træmpəl/ (tramples, trampling, trampled)

○ **'trample on**

1 If you **trample on** something or someone, you walk on them heavily so that they are damaged or hurt.

trample on something/someone ❑ *They ran across the gardens and trampled on the plants.* ❑ *People were trampled on in the rush for the exits.* **2** If someone **tramples on** a person or their feelings or rights, they behave in a very unfair or cruel way towards them.

trample on something/someone ❑ *He trampled on her feelings and took her for granted.*

'trample upon → see **trample on**

ansform /trænsˈfɔːm/ (**transforms, transforming, transformed**)

trans'form into

To **transform** something or someone **into** something else means to change or convert them into that thing.

transform something/someone into something ❑ *Your body transforms food into energy.* ❑ *He transformed the 300-acre grounds into England's first nature sanctuary.*

ansition /trænˈzɪʃən/ (**transitions, transitioning, transitioned**)

tran'sition from

If someone or something **transitions from** one state or activity to another, they move gradually from one to the other.

transition from something ❑ *[+ to] We hope to transition from dependence on fossil fuels to a greater use of green energy.*

tran'sition to

If someone or something **transitions to** another state or activity, they move gradually to it.

transition to something ❑ *They will need support as they transition to democracy.*

anslate /trænzˈleɪt/ (**translates, translating, translated**)

trans'late as

◼ If a name, a word, or an expression **translates as** something in a different language, that is what it means in that language.

translate as something ❑ *His family's Cantonese nickname for him translates as Never Sits Still.*
◼ If a remark, or an action **translates as** something, that is what it really means; if you **translate** a remark or action **as** something, that is what you think it means.

translate as something ❑ *When you talk to these women, you find that 'I love him' often translates as 'He's better than nothing'.*

translate something as something ❑ *I translated his actions as a desire for attention.*

trans'late into

◼ If you **translate** something that someone has said or written **into** another language, you say or write it in the second language.

translate something into something ❑ *Several of his books have been translated into English.*

◼ If one thing **translates into** or **is translated into** another, the second happens or is done as a result of the first.

translate into something ❑ *Reforming the economy requires harsh measures that would translate into job losses.*

be translated into something ❑ *Your decision must be translated into specific, concrete actions.*

transmute /trænzˈmjuːt/ (**transmutes, transmuting, transmuted**)

○ **trans'mute into** [FORMAL]

If something **transmutes into** a different form or if someone or something **transmutes** it **into** a different form, it is changed into that form.

transmute into something ❑ *She ceased to think, as anger transmuted into passion.*

transmute something into something ❑ *Scientists transmuted matter into pure energy and exploded the first atomic bomb.*

be transmuted into something ❑ *Anger is often transmuted into fear or panic.*

transpose /trænsˈpəʊz/ (**transposes, transposing, transposed**)

○ **trans'pose from**

If you **transpose** something **from** one place or situation to another, you move it there.

transpose something from something ❑ *[+ to] Genetic engineers transpose bits of DNA from one organism to the next.* ❑ *The director transposes the action from 16th Century France to post-Civil War America.*

trap /træp/ (**traps, trapping, trapped**)

○ **trap 'into**

If you **trap** someone **into** something, you make them say or do something by tricking them. = **trick into**

trap someone into something ❑ *The journalist tried to trap her into an admission about her past.* ❑ *The student was finally trapped into making a mistake.*

trash /træʃ/ (**trashes, trashing, trashed**)

○ **trash 'out** [AMERICAN, INFORMAL]

If someone **trashes out** a building for which the owners can no longer pay the money they owe the bank, they clear it out and make it secure.

trash out something or **trash something out** ❑ *I once trashed out a home that was 235 cubic yards.* • A **trash-out** is an occasion when a building is cleaned out and secured, when the owners could not pay the money they owed the bank for it. ❑ *Statistics like this have translated to between 75 and 100 trash-outs a week.*

trawl /trɔːl/ (**trawls, trawling, trawled**)

○ **'trawl through**

If you **trawl through** a large number of similar things, you search through them looking for something that you want or something that is suitable for a particular purpose.

trawl through something ❑ *A team of officers is trawling through the records of thousands of criminals.*

treat /triːt/ (**treats, treating, treated**)

○ **'treat to**

If you **treat** someone **to** something special which they will enjoy, you buy it for them or allow them to have it.

treat someone to something ❑ *She was always treating him to ice cream.*

treat yourself to something ❑ *Tomorrow I'll treat myself to a day's gardening.*

○ **'treat with**

If something **is treated with** a particular substance, the substance is put onto or into it in order to clean it, to protect it, or to give it special properties.

be treated with something ❑ *About 70% of the cocoa is treated with insecticide.* ❑ *Each print is treated with varnish to give an aged look.*

trespass /'trespəs/ (**trespasses, trespassing, trespassed**)

○ **'trespass on** [FORMAL]

If you **trespass on** something, you ask someone to do something for you or give you something when this is unfair.

trespass on something ❑ *You are so busy, I hate to trespass on your time.*

trick /trɪk/ (**tricks, tricking, tricked**)

○ **trick 'into**

If you **trick** someone **into** something, you make them do something by not telling them the truth.

trick someone into something ❑ *She has been tricked into marriage.* ❑ *She tricked me into thinking it was gold.*

○ **trick 'out**

If someone or something **is tricked out** or if someone **tricks** them **out** in a particular way, they are made to look that way.

be tricked out ❑ [+ as] *The little boy was tricked out as a king in a crown and purple robe.* ❑ *The display cases are all tricked out to look like gold.*

trick someone/something out or **trick out someone/something** ❑ *They turn their bikes into extensions of themselves by tricking them out with fancy paint, lights, and mirrors.*

trickle /'trɪkəl/ (**trickles, trickling, trickle**

○ **trickle 'down**

If money, benefits or knowledge **trickles down**, it is passed on gradually from the people at the top of a system. ❑ [+ to] *They argue that wealth will trickle down to the rest of* community. ❑ [+ from] *These technical terms gradually trickle down from experts and become understood by the general public.* ● A **trickle-down** effect is a situation in which something is passed on gradually from th people at the top of a system. ❑ *Investment had a trickle-down effect on supplier firms.*

trifle /'traɪfəl/ (**trifles, trifling, trifled**)

○ **'trifle with**

If you **trifle with** someone or something, you treat them in a way that is not seriou: or that does not show respect.

trifle with someone/something ❑ *Mitchel was not someone to be trifled with.* ❑ *One shoul not trifle with such a powerful organization.*

trigger /'trɪgə/ (**triggers, triggering, triggered**)

○ **trigger 'off**

If something **triggers off** an event or reaction, it causes it to happen. = spark of set off

trigger off something or **trigger somethin off** ❑ *The report triggered off a parliamentary debate.* ❑ *He has a violent temper and anything can trigger it off.*

trim /trɪm/ (**trims, trimming, trimmed**)

○ **trim a'way**

If you **trim away** a part of something, you cut it off, because it is not needed.

trim away something or **trim something away** ❑ *Trim away the excess carpet.* ❑ [+ from First she trims the fat away from the chicken.*

○ **trim 'off**

If you **trim off** parts of something, you cut them off, because they are not needed.

trim off something or **trim something off** ❑ *Slice the meat and trim off the fat.* ❑ *I threade the cord through the hole, then trimmed the ends c*

trip /trɪp/ (**trips, tripping, tripped**)

◐ **trip 'over**

1 If you **trip over** something or **trip over**, you knock your foot against something a: fall or nearly fall.

trip over something ❑ *He stuck out his foot, and I tripped over it, but recovered.* ❑ *People cou: trip over toys left lying around.*

trip over ❑ *He tripped over and came down wit a crash.*

2 If you **trip over** something you are

saying, you hesitate or make mistakes because you are nervous.

trip over something ❑ *Flora spoke a few lines, tripping over her words.*

trip 'up

1 If someone or something **trips** you **up** or if you **trip up**, you fall or nearly fall because something catches your feet when you are walking.

trip someone up or **trip up someone** ❑ *The road was full of holes and rocks which could trip you up.* ❑ *He was accused of deliberately tripping up an opponent.*

trip up ❑ *We walked cautiously to avoid tripping up.*

2 To **trip** someone **up** means to confuse them so that they make a mistake or say something they did not intend to; if you **trip up**, you make a mistake. = **catch out**

trip someone up or **trip up someone** ❑ *The judges' questions tripped him up.*

trip up ❑ *They asked her a lot of questions, waiting for her to trip up.*

roll /trɒl, trəʊl/ (trolls, trolling, trolled)

'troll through [mainly BRITISH, INFORMAL]

If you **troll through** papers or files, you look through them in a fairly casual way.

troll through something ❑ *Trolling through the files revealed a photograph of me drinking coffee in the office.*

rot /trɒt/ (trots, trotting, trotted)

trot 'off

If someone, especially a small child, **trots off**, they go somewhere quickly. ❑ *He watched his little girl trotting off to school in her new blazer.*

trot 'out

If you **trot** something **out**, you repeat or say it without really meaning or thinking about it, especially because you have been told to.

trot out something or **trot something out** ❑ *They were politicians who could be guaranteed to trot out the party line.* ❑ *We heard the usual excuses trotted out by the man in charge.*

ruckle /'trʌkəl/ (truckles, truckling, truckled)

'truckle to [OLD-FASHIONED]

If you **truckle to** someone or something, you do what someone tells or wants you to do, especially because they are more powerful than you.

truckle to someone/something ❑ *He did what he believed to be right, and never truckled to popular opinion.*

truss /trʌs/ (trusses, trussing, trussed)

○ truss 'up

If a person or animal **is trussed up** or if someone **trusses** them **up**, they are tied very tightly so that they cannot move.

be trussed up ❑ *A man was found trussed up in the back of the van.* ❑ *The bulls were trussed up with ropes.*

truss up someone or **truss someone/ something up** ❑ *The robbers had trussed up the bank manager and made off with the cash.*

trust /trʌst/ (trusts, trusting, trusted)

○ 'trust in

If you **trust in** someone or something, you believe in them completely.

trust in someone/something ❑ *She trusted in God.*

○ 'trust to

If you **trust to** someone or something, you rely on them.

trust to someone/something ❑ *The people discovered that it is no good trusting to politicians.* ❑ *He would just have to trust to luck.*

try /traɪ/ (tries, trying, tried)

✪ 'try for

If you **try for** something, you make an effort to get it or achieve it.

try for something ❑ *The school advised me to try for Oxford University.* ❑ *They are trying for a baby.*

✪ try 'on

1 If you **try on** a piece of clothing, you put it on to see if it fits you or if it looks nice.

try something on ❑ *I don't buy clothes online because I like to try them on first.* ❑ *Try these shoes on and see how they feel.*

try on something ❑ *She tried on several dresses but couldn't find any she liked.*

2 If someone **tries it on**, they attempt to trick you or annoy you. [BRITISH, INFORMAL] ❑ *She is probably trying it on to see how far she can go with you.* ❑ *I'm in a bad mood today, so don't try it on.*

3 If someone **tries it on** with another person, they attempt to touch them in a sexual way or persuade them to have sex. [INFORMAL, RUDE] ❑ *[+ with] He tried it on with her and she told her husband.* ❑ *If we were alone together he might try it on.*

✪ try 'out

1 If you **try** something **out**, you test it or use it for the first time in order to find out how useful or effective it is.

try out something ❑ *The company is trying out a new idea to help working parents.* ❑ *Going to the park gave him a chance to try out his new bike.*

try something out ❏ *I'm trying a new recipe out on my family.* ● A **try-out** is an occasion when something is tested or used for the first time, to find out how useful or effective it is. ❏ *I don't know if it's going to work. It's only a try-out.*

2 If you **try** someone **out**, you ask them to compete or perform a test, so that you can see if they are suitable for a job or role.

try out someone ❏ *Just try me out for a week and you'll see I can do the job.*

try someone out ❏ *You can try her out in the sales team.* ● A **try-out** is an occasion when someone such as an athlete competes or performs a test, in an attempt to be chosen for a team or role. ❏ *He had a try-out with a professional team.*

○ **try 'out for** [mainly AMERICAN]
If you **try out for** something, you compete or perform a test in an attempt to be chosen for a particular team or role.

try out for something ❏ *He should have tried out for the school football team.* ❏ *Brando tried out for the role of Don.*

tuck /tʌk/ (**tucks, tucking, tucked**)

○ **tuck a'way**

1 If you **tuck** something **away**, you store it in a safe place that is not easy to find. **= stash away**

tuck something away or **tuck away something** ❏ *She folded the letter and tucked it away in her purse.* ❏ *She had a bit of money tucked away.*

2 If something or someone **is tucked away**, they are in a quiet place where very few people go. **= be hidden away**

be tucked away ❏ *The restaurant is tucked away behind the cathedral.* ❏ *He is tucked away in a tiny office at the top of the building.*

○ **tuck 'in**

1 If you **tuck** something **in**, you push the end of it into something or under something, so that it is held in position.

tuck something in ❏ *He tucked a knife in under his belt.* ❏ *She put a sheet on the bed and tucked it in tightly.*

tuck in something ❏ *The teacher told him to tuck in his shirt.*

2 If something **tucks in** or **is tucked in** somewhere, it is positioned close to another thing and behind it or under it, or between two things.

tuck in somewhere ❏ *A ship could tuck in behind the island and be sheltered from the open sea.*

be tucked in somewhere ❏ *The chairs were all neatly tucked in around the well-scrubbed table.*

3 If you **tuck in**, you eat with a lot of pleasure. **= dig in** [BRITISH, INFORMAL]
❏ *There's plenty of food, so tuck in!* ❏ *Mary put a plate of eggs and bacon in front of him and he tucked in appreciatively.*

4 If you **tuck** a part of your body **in**, you us your muscles to keep it inwards.

tuck something in or **tuck in something** ❏ *Tuck your elbows in and sit up straight.* ❏ *She tucked in her stomach as she walked past them.*

○ **tuck 'in** (or **tuck up**)
If you **tuck** someone **in**, you make them comfortable and warm in bed by making sure they are covered well.

tuck someone in ❏ *I'll go and tuck the children in.* ❏ *She gave me some medicine and tucked me up in bed.*

tuck in someone ❏ *Laura was upstairs, tuckin in the child.*

○ **tuck 'into**

1 If you **tuck** something **into** something, you press or push it into a narrow space.

tuck something into something ❏ *She tucke Paul's shirt into his shorts.* ❏ *Madeline crumpled the note and tucked it into her purse.*

2 If you **tuck into** food, you eat it with a lo of pleasure. [BRITISH, INFORMAL]

tuck into something ❏ *They were tucking into huge plates of fish and chips.*

○ **tuck 'up**

1 → see **tuck in**

2 If you **tuck** your legs or your feet **up**, you lift them so that you are sitting on them o sitting with them off the floor.

tuck something up or **tuck up something** ❏ [+ under] *Ellen tucked her feet up under her blac skirt.* ❏ *She was sitting on the sofa with her legs tucked up.*

tug /tʌg/ (**tugs, tugging, tugged**)

○ **'tug at**
If you **tug at** something, you give it a quick strong pull. **= yank**

tug at something ❏ *He tugged at the handle, and it came off in his hand.* ❏ *She was tugging at the horse's reins, trying to make it stop.*

tumble /'tʌmbəl/ (**tumbles, tumbling, tumbled**)

○ **tumble 'down**
If someone or something **tumbles down** or **tumbles down** something, they fall down.

tumble down ❏ *Rocks tumbled down and crashed into the valley below.*

tumble down something ❏ *He tumbled down the steps but was not hurt.* ● A **tumbledown** building is in such a bad condition that it i partly falling down or has holes in it. ❏ *The came across a deserted, tumbledown cottage.*

▸ **tumble 'into** [mainly BRITISH]
If someone **tumbles into** a situation or place, they get into it without being fully in control of themselves or knowing what they are doing.
tumble into something ❑ *Many mothers and children tumble into poverty after divorce.*

▸ **tumble 'over**
If someone or something **tumbles over** or **tumbles over** something, they fall.
tumble over ❑ *She tumbled over and hit her head on the concrete.*
tumble over something ❑ *The barrier is designed to stop cars tumbling over the steep drop.*

▸ **'tumble to** [BRITISH, INFORMAL]
If you **tumble to** something, you suddenly understand it or realize what is happening.
tumble to something ❑ *I soon tumbled to the fact that I was wasting my time.*

une /tjuːn, AM tuːn/ (**tunes, tuning, tuned**)
tune 'in
If you **tune in**, you set the controls of your radio or television so that you can listen to or watch a particular programme. ❑ *Tune in next week to hear how English is taught in China.* ❑ *Millions of people tuned in to see the World Cup final.*

1 If you **tune into** something or **are tuned into** it, you set the controls on your radio or television so that you can listen to or watch a particular channel or programme.
tune into something ❑ *She tuned into the late news.*
be tuned into something ❑ *I've been tuned into the BBC World Service all day.* ❑ *The TV was on, tuned into a kids' channel.*
2 If you **tune into** something, especially how someone feels, you become aware of it or able to understand it.
tune into something ❑ *Children can easily tune into their parents' moods and know when something is wrong.*

▸ **tune 'out**
If you **tune out** or **tune** something **out**, you stop listening or paying attention to a sound.
tune out ❑ *When he starts talking about work, I just tune out.*
tune out something or **tune something out** ❑ *If there's a constant background noise you learn to tune it out.*

▸ **'tune to**
If your radio or television **is tuned to** a particular broadcasting station, you are listening to or watching the programmes

being broadcast by that station.
be tuned to something ❑ *A small colour television was tuned to an afternoon soap opera.*

○ **tune 'up**
1 If you **tune up** or **tune up** a musical instrument, you adjust a musical instrument so that it produces the right notes.
tune up ❑ *The orchestra was tuning up for the concert.*
tune up something or **tune something up** ❑ *He tuned up his cello.* ❑ *She took out her guitar and began tuning it up.*
2 If you **tune up** the engine of a car, you adjust it so that it goes faster or more efficiently.
tune up something or **tune something up** ❑ *The engine needs tuning up.* ❑ *The mechanic's job is to tune it up.*

turf /tɜːf/ (**turfs, turfing, turfed**)
○ **turf 'out** [BRITISH, INFORMAL]
1 If you **turf** someone **out**, you force them to leave a place. = **kick out, chuck out**
turf someone out or **turf out someone** ❑ *He went to his girlfriend's house, but her parents turfed him out.* ❑ *[+ of] You can't just turf people out of their homes.*
2 If you **turf out** unwanted things, you get rid of them.
turf something out or **turf out something** ❑ *You should turf all this out.* ❑ *I turfed out a lot of stuff last week.*

turn /tɜːn/ (**turns, turning, turned**)
○ **turn a'bout**
1 If something or someone **turns about** or if you **turn** them **about**, they move so that they are facing in a different direction. = **turn around** [BRITISH, OLD-FASHIONED]
turn about ❑ *He turned about and tiptoed away.*
turn something/someone about ❑ *They turned the ship about and started to sail towards the island.* ● **About-turn** is a command to turn around and march in the opposite direction. ❑ *Right about-turn! Quick march!*
2 A **turnabout** is a complete change in opinion or attitude. ❑ *I wanted to know what had caused the turnabout.*
3 An **about-turn** is an unexpected and complete change in opinion or attitude. ❑ *He then did an about-turn and agreed to play.* ❑ *One of the reasons for the about-turn was the increasing expense.*

○ **turn a'gainst**
1 If someone **turns against** you or if someone or something **turns** them **against** you, they start to dislike you or disapprove of you.

turn against someone ❑ He was worried that his co-workers might suddenly turn against him. ❑ Public opinion turned against the government.
turn someone against someone ❑ You turn everyone against me.

2 If something **turns against** you, things start to happen in a way that harms or disadvantages you.
turn against someone ❑ Events turned against them and they were unsuccessful. ❑ He realized that the situation was turning against the rebels.

3 If something **is turned against** someone or if someone **turns** it **against** them, it is used to attack or harm them.
be turned against someone ❑ Her fury was all turned against herself.
turn something against someone ❑ They turned their weapons against their own people.

○ **turn a'round** (or **turn round** [mainly BRITISH])

1 If someone or something **turns around**, or if you **turn** them **around**, they move so that they are facing in the opposite direction.
turn something/someone around ❑ He had to turn the car around and go back. ❑ She turned me round to face her.
turn around ❑ After driving for two miles in the snow we decided to turn around.

2 If something such as a plan, project, or business that is failing **turns around** or if you **turn** it **around**, it starts to become successful or profitable.
turn around ❑ If the economy turns around prices will go up.
turn something around ❑ The project is not going well, but I'm confident I can turn it around.
turn around something ❑ He believes he can turn around last year's losses and make a profit.

3 If someone or something **turns** your life **around** or if it **turns around**, it changes completely, usually becoming better.
turn something around ❑ An opportunity like this could turn your entire career around. or turn around something ❑ The organization helps former gang members turn around their lives.
turn around ❑ My life turned around when I met Tom. ●A **turnaround** is a sudden improvement or change, usually so that something is the opposite of what it was before. = **turnround** ❑ His attitude underwent a complete turnaround. ❑ This was a dramatic turnaround in the company's policy.

4 If you **turn** a process or piece of work **around**, you complete it.
turn something around ❑ Is it possible to turn so much work around in 24 hours? ❑ From first

receiving the application it takes them about ten days to turn it around.
turn around something ❑ People are amazed at how fast we can turn around orders. ❑ Some jobs can be turned around in as little as a day.
●A **turnaround** is the time it takes for a process or piece of work to be completed. ❑ We mark and return exam scripts within 14 days which is an extremely fast turnaround.

5 If you **turn** something **around**, you change the way in which it is expressed or considered.
turn around something ❑ You can turn around the sentence and create a whole new meaning.
turn something around ❑ When I asked him about his experience he turned the question around and asked me about mine.

6 If someone **turns around and** does something, they do something surprising, sudden, or unfair. ❑ One day he turned around and announced he was leaving. ❑ You can't just turn round and blame me for everything.

○ **turn a'side** [LITERARY]
If you **turn aside**, you turn or move to one side, away from someone or something. ❑ He turned aside to wipe his nose.

○ **turn a'side from** [LITERARY]
If you **turn aside from** something, you avoid or stop doing something and do something else instead.
turn aside from something ❑ He tried to persuade the Church to turn aside from social issues.

○ **turn a'way**
1 If you **turn away**, you turn or move in a direction away from someone or something. ❑ I had to turn away to avoid letting him see my smile. ❑ [+ from] They turned away from the coast and headed inland.

2 If you **turn** something **away**, you move it so that it is no longer facing in the direction of something or someone.
turn something away ❑ [+ from] She turned her chair away from the window. ❑ When she saw me, she turned her face away.

3 If you **turn** someone **away**, you refuse to allow them to enter a place, or refuse to help them.
turn someone away ❑ We won't turn anybody away just because they can't afford to pay.
turn away someone ❑ The college has been forced to turn away 300 prospective students. ❑ He tried to cross the border, but was turned away.

4 If you **turn away**, you refuse to help or get involved with something. ❑ [+ from] We can't just turn away from these people who need our help.

turn a'way from

If you **turn away from** something, or if something **turns** you **away from** it, you stop doing it, wanting it, or being interested in it.

turn away from something ❑ *She had turned away from her parents' religion.*

turn someone away from something ❑ *We are trying to turn people away from processed food.*

turn 'back

1 If you **turn back** or **are turned back**, you stop a journey and return towards the place you started from.

turn back ❑ *It was getting dark, so we turned back.*

be turned back ❑ *A lot of the cars had been turned back at the border.*

turn back someone ❑ *The police were turning back thousands of people who were trying to get into the city.*

turn someone back ❑ *They tried to leave using the stairs but smoke turned them back.*

2 If you **turn back**, you change your plans and decide not to do something. ❑ *Once we have taken this step it will be difficult to turn back.* ❑ *It's too late to turn back now.*

● If you say **there is no turning back**, you mean that it is not possible to change your plans and decide not to do something. ❑ *She had made her decision and from that point there was no turning back.*

3 If you **turn** something **back**, you fold one part of it over so that it is covering the other part.

turn back something or **turn something back** ❑ *He turned back the blankets so I could sit up.* ❑ *Cover the dish with pastry and turn the edges back.*

turn 'down

1 If you **turn** something or someone **down**, you refuse a request or offer. = **reject**

turn down something/someone ❑ *I turned down an invitation for Saturday.* ❑ *She applied for a job in a restaurant, but was turned down.*

turn something/someone down ❑ *He asked me to help and I couldn't really turn him down.* ❑ *She had several proposals of marriage but turned them all down.*

2 If you **turn** something **down**, you adjust the controls of a device so that it produces less sound or heat. ≠ **turn up**

turn something down ❑ *Turn the sound down.* ❑ *It's a bit hot in here – can you turn the heating down?*

turn down something ❑ *She turned down the gas fire.* ❑ *The volume on the TV was turned down so I didn't know what they were saying.*

3 If the rate or level of something **turns**

down, it decreases. [BRITISH] ❑ *The divorce rate turned down in the 1950s.* ● A **downturn** is a decrease in the rate, level, or success of something. ≠ **upturn** ❑ *The government seemed unable to reverse the economic downturn.* ❑ *There had been a downturn in applications to the university.*

4 If you **turn down** something, you fold it so that one part of it is covering the other part.

turn down something or **turn something down** ❑ *The housekeeper cleaned the room and turned down the bedcovers.* ❑ *Some of the cards were turned down at the edges.*

turn 'in

1 If something **turns in**, it points or moves inwards towards the middle of something. ❑ *The car slowed down as it passed the end of the drive, but did not turn in.* ❑ *His feet turn in slightly.*

2 If you **turn in**, you go to bed. [INFORMAL] ❑ *Before turning in for the night he asked for an early morning call.* ❑ *I'm tired. I think I'll turn in.* NOTE **Retire** is a more formal word for **turn in**.

3 If you **turn** someone **in**, who is suspected of a crime, you take or report them to the police.

turn someone in or **turn in someone** ❑ *Can you trust him? Do you think he might turn you in?* ❑ *They had been turned in by one of their own sons.*

turn yourself in ❑ *He was an escaped prisoner who turned himself in.*

4 If you **turn** something **in**, you give it to someone in authority.

turn in something or **turn something in** ❑ *They agreed to turn in their guns.*

5 If you **turn in** work, you give it to the person who asked you to do it. = **hand in**, **give in**

turn in something or **turn something in** ❑ *Some of the students began to turn in superb work.* ❑ *Don't forget to write your name on your report before you turn it in.*

6 If you **turn** something **in**, you return it to the place or person you borrowed it from. = **return** [AMERICAN]

turn in something or **turn something in** ❑ *A letter arrived telling her to turn in her library books.*

turn 'into

If someone or something **turns into** another thing, or if something **turns** them **into** it, they change and become that other thing.

turn into something ❑ *Maggots turn into flies, and caterpillars turn into butterflies.* ❑ *This situation is turning into a nightmare.*

turn someone/something into something

❑ His experiences turned him into a much kinder person. ❑ The novel had been turned into a television series.

○ **turn 'off**

1 If you **turn off** a device or machine, you make it stop working using its controls; if it **turns off**, it stops working. = **switch off**; ≠ **turn on**

turn something off ❑ Turn the lights off when you leave the room. ❑ I turned on the shower and then couldn't turn it off.

turn off something ❑ George came in and turned off the radio.

turn off ❑ The heating turns off automatically at night. ❑ The tap won't turn off.

2 If you **turn off** something or **turn off**, you leave a road or path and start going along a different one.

turn off something ❑ They turned off the main road. ❑ The bus turns off the High Street and goes down War Lane.

turn off ❑ Why don't we turn off and walk across the fields? ❑ This is where I turn off. • A **turn-off** is a road which leads away from another road. [BRITISH] ❑ Slow down, or you'll miss the turn-off.

3 If something **turns** you **off** or if you **turn off**, you stop being excited or interested. [INFORMAL]

turn someone off or **turn off someone** ❑ Had I turned her off by not being daring enough? ❑ Customers are turned off by this sort of advertising.

turn off ❑ The lecture was so boring that I just turned off. • Something that is a **turn-off** causes you to lose interest or enthusiasm. [INFORMAL] ❑ All this legal jargon is a total turn-off for us.

4 If something or someone **turns** you **off**, you do not find them sexually attractive. ≠ **turn on** [INFORMAL]

turn someone off or **turn off someone** ❑ Aggressive men turn me off completely. • Something that is a **turn-off** stops you feeling sexually attracted. ≠ **turn-on** [INFORMAL] ❑ A dirty, scruffy appearance is a real turn-off.

○ **turn 'on**

In meanings 4-7, the stress is on **'turn**.

1 If you **turn** a device or machine **on**, you make it start working using its controls; if it **turns on**, it starts working. = **switch on**; ≠ **turn off**

turn something on ❑ Shall I turn the lights on? ❑ I have a radio, but I seldom turn it on.

turn on something ❑ She turned on the shower.

❑ I was freezing, even though the heating was turned on.

turn on ❑ You can set a timer so that the oven turns on while you're out. ❑ The tap won't turn on.

2 If someone or something **turns** you **on**, they make you interested or excited, especially sexually. [INFORMAL]

turn someone on or **turn on someone** ❑ He didn't really turn me on. ❑ Some people are turned on by the smell and feel of leather. • A **turn-on** is something or someone that makes you interested or excited, especially sexually. ≠ **turn-off** [INFORMAL] ❑ I find long hair a real turn-on.

3 If you **turn on** something, you deliberately start behaving or feeling in a particular way. = **switch on**

turn on something or **turn something on** ❑ He really knew how to turn on the charm.

4 If a person or animal **turns on** you, they suddenly attack you or show anger towards you. = **round on**

turn on someone ❑ She turned on the men. 'How can you treat your daughters like this!'. ❑ A dog like that could turn on you at any time.

5 If something **turns on** a particular thing it depends on that thing. = **hinge on**

turn on something ❑ His future will turn on whether or not he can convince enough voters. ❑ The whole issue turns on the question of finances.

6 If something **turns on** a subject, it is concerned with that subject.

turn on something ❑ My thoughts turned on the things I had seen that day. ❑ The conversation turned on the question of money.

7 If you **turn** something **on** someone or something, you aim it at them or keep it pointing at them. = **train on**

turn something on someone ❑ The guard turned a flashlight on Karen. ❑ Firefighters turned their hoses on the flames.

○ **turn 'on to**

To **turn** someone **on to** something means to make them become interested in it or excited by it.

turn someone on to something ❑ Watching the Masters on television turned him on to golf. ❑ His parents were keen to turn him on to literature.

○ **turn 'out**

1 If something **turns out** a particular way, it happens in that way. = **work out** ❑ Nothing ever turned out right. ❑ [+ to-infinitive] It turned out to be a really great evening. ❑ It all depends how things turn out.

2 If something or someone **turns out** to be

a particular thing, they are discovered to be that thing. ❑ [+ to-infinitive] Mrs Moffat had turned out to be the perfect hostess.

● If **it turns out** that something is the case, it is discovered to be the case. ❑ It turned out that the message had been intercepted. ❑ As it turned out, he was a friend of my father's.

3 If you **turn** something **out**, you stop a device from giving out light or heat. = **turn off**; ≠ **turn on**

turn something out ❑ She didn't bother to turn the light out when she went out of the room.

turn out something ❑ He forgot to turn out the gas hob in the kitchen.

4 If you **turn** someone **out**, you force them to leave a place. = **turf out, kick out, chuck out**

turn someone out or **turn out someone** ❑ [+ of] He threatened to turn them out of the house.

5 If you **turn out** a container or its contents **out**, you empty it completely.

turn out something or **turn something out** ❑ She ordered him to turn out his pockets. ❑ [+ onto] She opened her purse and turned out the contents onto the table.

6 If a person or organization **turns out** something, it produces it in large quantities. = **churn out**

turn out something or **turn something out** ❑ Universities were turning out thousands of business graduates. ❑ It is difficult to read her novels as quickly as she turns them out.

7 If people **turn out**, they go and take part in or watch something. = **turn up** ❑ [+ to-infinitive] 50,000 people turned out to watch the airshow. ❑ It all depends how many people turn out. ● The **turnout** at an event is the number of people who go to it or take part in it. ❑ Voter turnout was much lower than expected. ❑ We had a really good turnout for the party.

8 If you say **it's turned out nice** or **fine**, you mean that the weather is pleasant. [BRITISH] ❑ It's turned out nice again.

9 The way that someone **is turned out** is the way that they are dressed.

be turned out ❑ They were attractive-looking girls, well turned out and smart. ● Someone's **turnout** is the way they are dressed. ❑ Claude approved of Daniel's turnout.

turn 'over

1 If something or someone **turns over** or if you **turn** them **over**, they move so that they are facing in a different direction or so that the bottom becomes the top.

turn over ❑ She turned over and went to sleep.

❑ The car spun off the track and turned over several times.

turn something over ❑ He turned the box over to read the ingredients. ❑ When the pancake is set, turn it over and cook the other side.

turn over something ❑ She turned over the last card.

2 If you **turn over** or **turn** a page **over**, you move a page so that what was on the back of it is now on the front.

turn over ❑ When you have finished the questions on page 1, turn over. ❑ [+ to] If you turn over to the next page, you will see a diagram.

turn something over ❑ I turned it over and glanced at the signature.

turn over something ❑ Don't turn over the exam paper until your teacher tells you to.

3 If you **turn over** someone suspected of a crime, you take them to the police or authorities. = **turn in**

turn someone over ❑ If she'd suspected him, she'd have turned the man over right away. ❑ [+ to] If you turn me over to the police I'll tell them nothing.

turn over someone ❑ They expected her to turn over her own son.

4 If you **turn** something **over**, you give it to someone or make them responsible for it. = **hand over**

turn over something ❑ [+ to] They have turned over control of the school to parents.

turn something over ❑ [+ to] I turned the cheque over to the Treasurer.

5 If you **turn** something **over** to a different use, you change its use.

turn something over ❑ [+ to] The automobile industry had to turn their production facilities over to weapons manufacturing.

turn over something ❑ [+ to] I turned over part of the shop to antiques.

6 If you **turn over**, you change from watching one television programme to watching another. = **switch over** ❑ We turned over to see what was on the other side.

7 If people or things **turn over**, they leave a place or are sent or taken to a different place. ❑ In a grocery store, milk turns over more rapidly than canned goods. ❑ In a difficult school like this, teachers turn over quickly. ● The **turnover** of people in an organization is the rate at which people leave and are replaced by others. ❑ The group has an extremely high turnover of members.

8 If a company **turns over** an amount of money, that is the money it receives in a year.

turn over something ❑ They turned over more than £4 million last year. ● The **turnover** of a company is the value of the goods or services that it sells during a particular period. ❑ *Annual turnover is about £9,000 million.*

9 If you **turn** something **over**, you think carefully about it. **= chew over, mull over**

turn something over ❑ *I had thought about the problem all day, turning it over in my mind.*

turn over something ❑ *We ate in silence, turning over these thoughts in our minds.*

NOTE **Consider** is a more general word for **turn over**.

10 If an engine **turns over**, it continues running steadily at a low speed. **= tick over** ❑ *The car engines turn over, ready for the race.*

11 If someone **turns** a place **over**, they search it thoroughly, causing a lot of mess or damage. **= do over** [INFORMAL]

turn over something *or* **turn something over** ❑ *The secret police turned over his place a few days ago.* ❑ *They turned the room over – it looked as if a tornado had hit it.*

12 A **turnover** is a small piece of pastry that has been filled with fruit or jam, folded over, and baked. ❑ *She bought an apple turnover.*

○ **turn 'round** [BRITISH]
1 → see **turn around**

2 If you **turn round** something that is failing, you change it so that it becomes successful and profitable.

turn round something *or* **turn something round** ❑ *It's foolish to pretend that you could turn round the economy in a week.* ❑ *The engineering group is fighting to turn its business round.*

● A **turnround** is an improvement or change in something, especially so that it becomes the opposite of what it was before. **= turnaround** ❑ *There has been a turnround in public opinion.*

○ **'turn to**
1 If you **turn to** someone, you turn so that you are looking at them.

turn to someone ❑ *He turned to me and said 'Will you come?'*

2 If you **turn to** someone, you ask them for help or advice.

turn to someone ❑ *If they feel they've been wronged, they'll turn to a solicitor.* ❑ *I have no other friend to turn to.*

3 If something **turns to** another thing, or if something **turns** it **to** it, it changes and becomes that other thing.

turn to something ❑ *My relief at seeing him safe soon turned to anger.* ❑ *The buildings crumble, and eventually turn to dust.*

turn something to something ❑ *The rain had turned the campsite to mud.* ❑ *Everyone stood totally still, as if turned to stone.*

4 If you **turn to** something or someone, you start to discuss a new topic or ask a new person to speak, for example as part of a television report.

turn to something ❑ *Let us turn to a completely different country, Japan.* ❑ *We turn to our economic correspondent now, for more on the current crisis.*

5 If you **turn** your mind or attention **to** something, you start to think about or pay attention to something different.

turn something to something ❑ *He finished the letter, then turned his thoughts to the day's events.* ❑ *They are now turning their attention to preparing for next year's Olympics.*

6 If you **turn to** something, you find a particular page or part of a book or newspaper that you want to read.

turn to something ❑ *Please open your books and turn to Chapter 5.* ❑ *I turned to page 3 to find the rest of the story.*

7 If you **turn to** a particular activity, you start doing it.

turn to something ❑ *These communities are now turning to recycling in large numbers.* ❑ *The Superpowers turned to the task of cutting their nuclear weapons.*

8 If you **turn to** something, you start doing it or using it because you are in a very difficult situation.

turn to something ❑ *Sometimes a depressed person may turn to drink or drugs.* ❑ *What makes these youngsters turn to a life of crime?*

○ **turn 'up**
1 If someone **turns up**, they arrive somewhere where they are expected. **= show up** ❑ *He turned up at rehearsal the next day looking awful.* ❑ *I waited for an hour, but he didn't turn up.*

2 If you **turn up**, you arrive somewhere without being expected or without making a definite arrangement. ❑ *Do I need to book tickets or can we just turn up?* ❑ *A huge crowd turned up and we didn't have space for everyone.*

3 If something **turns up** or if someone **turns** it **up**, it is found, discovered, or noticed.

turn up ❑ *You must be willing to take a job as soon as one turns up.*

turn up something ❑ *Scientists have turned up no useful information on how to treat the disease.*

turn something up ❑ *If I turn anything up, I'll let you know.*

4 When you **turn** something **up**, you increase the amount of sound or heat being produced by a device, by adjusting the controls. **≠ turn down**

turn something up ❑ *Turn the volume up – I can*

hear it. ❏ *If the radiator isn't warm enough, you can turn it up.*

turn up something ❏ *Turn up the heat and let the mixture boil for 10 minutes.* ❏ *The TV was turned up very loud.*

5 If you **turn** something **up**, you shorten a piece of clothing by folding up the bottom edge. ≠ **let down**

turn something up ❏ *Will you turn my jeans up for me, mum?*

turn up something ❏ *She turned up her old dresses for her younger sister.* • **Turn-ups** are the ends of someone's trouser legs which have been folded upwards so that they show on the outside. ❏ *He was wearing a pair of grey flannel trousers, with turn-ups.*

6 If you **turn** something **up**, you move it so that it is pointing in an upward direction.

turn up something or **turn something up** ❏ *She turned up her collar before facing the bad weather.* ❏ *She turned up the palm of one hand in a gesture of resignation.*

7 An **upturn** is an occasion when something such as an economy starts to improve. ≠ **downturn** ❏ *We believe an upturn will come in world trade.* ❏ *There has been an upturn in demand.*

○ **'turn upon** → see **turn on**

tussle /ˈtʌsəl/ (**tussles, tussling, tussled**)
○ **'tussle with**

1 If one person **tussles with** another, they get hold of each other and struggle or fight.

tussle with someone ❏ *They ended up ripping down the fence and tussling with the security staff.*

2 If one person **tussles with** another for something, they complete with each other to try to get it.

tussle with someone ❏ [+ for] *Pezzo tussled with Orvosova for fourth place.*

3 If someone **tussles with** a difficult problem or issue, they try hard to solve it.

tussle with something ❏ *He is tussling with the problem of what to do about inflation.*

twin /twɪn/ (**twins, twinning, twinned**)
○ **'twin with** [BRITISH]

When a place or organization in one country **is twinned with** a place or organization in another country, a special relationship is formally established between them.

be twinned with something ❏ *The town is twinned with Kasel in Germany.*

twitter /ˈtwɪtə/ (**twitters, twittering, twittered**)
○ **'twitter about**

If someone **twitters about** something, they speak about silly or unimportant things, usually rather fast or in a high-pitched voice.

twitter about something ❏ *They twittered about their boring college and their boring friends.*

type /taɪp/ (**types, typing, typed**)
○ **type a'way**

If you **type away**, you type quickly and for a long time. ❏ *Gerald was typing away in his office.*

○ **type 'in**

If you **type** something **in**, you enter it using a keyboard. = **key in**

type in something or **type something in** ❏ *First type in your password.* ❏ *She's typed the wrong name in.*

○ **type 'into**

If you **type** something **into** something, you enter information using a keyboard.

type something into something ❏ *We type all the details into the database.* ❏ *Your responses will be typed into the system.*

○ **type 'out**

If you **type** something **out**, you write it using a keyboard.

type out something or **type something out** ❏ *The secretary typed out the whole document again.* ❏ *I read my essay out to Dave, who typed it out.*

○ **type 'up**

If you **type** something **up**, you produce a completed version of it using a keyboard.

type up something or **type something up** ❏ *I'll go and type up these notes.* ❏ *We agreed on a plan, she typed it up, then we both read it.*

Uu

urge /ɜːdʒ/ (urges, urging, urged)

○ **urge 'on**

If something or someone **urges** someone **on**, they encourage them to do something. **= egg on**

urge someone on or **urge on someone** ❑ *The President, urged on by his vice-president, has decided to attend the talks.* ❑ *[+ to] Envy is a natural response, and can urge us on to greater things.* NOTE **Encourage** is a more formal word for **urge on**.

○ **'urge on** (or **urge upon**)

If you **urge** something **on** someone, you try to persuade them to accept it.

urge something on someone ❑ *He tried to urge the idea on his companions.* ❑ *Mr Profumo accepted the wording urged upon him by his colleagues.*

use /juːz/ (uses, using, used)

⊙ **use 'up**

If you **use up** a supply of something, you finish it so that none of it is left.

use up something ❑ *She did use up a tremendous amount of energy.* ❑ *He used up all the coins he had.*

use something up ❑ *Put the leftovers in a bowl and use them up the next day.* ❑ *Who's used all the milk up?*

usher /ˈʌʃə/ (ushers, ushering, ushered)

○ **usher 'in** [FORMAL]

If one thing **ushers in** another thing, it is the start of it.

usher in something ❑ *The French Revolution ushered in a new age.*

Vv

vacillate /ˈvæsɪleɪt/ (**vacillates, vacillating, vacillated**)

○ **'vacillate between** [FORMAL]

If you **vacillate between** two feelings, ideas, or plans you keep changing from one feeling, idea or plan to the other.

vacillate between something ❑ She vacillated between hope and fear. ❑ Voters vacillate between their desire for change and their doubts about the alternative.

vamp /væmp/ (**vamps, vamping, vamped**)

○ **vamp 'up**

1 If you **vamp** something **up**, you make it more attractive and exciting by adding things to it.

vamp something up or **vamp up something** ❑ You can vamp up a simple dress with high heels and some jewellery. ❑ The company is trying to vamp up its image.

2 If someone **vamps it up**, they dress and behave in a deliberately sexually attractive way. ❑ The video was full of supermodels vamping it up.

varnish /ˈvɑːnɪʃ/ (**varnishes, varnishing, varnished**)

○ **varnish 'over**

If you **varnish over** an unpleasant fact, you try to hide it or pretend that it is not true.
= **gloss over, paper over**

varnish over something ❑ He tried to varnish over the problems by saying the players had been tired.

vault /vɔːlt/ (**vaults, vaulting, vaulted**)

○ **'vault over**

If you **vault over** something, you jump quickly over it, especially by putting a hand on top of it to help you balance while you jump.

vault over something ❑ Ned vaulted over a fallen tree. ❑ Colin walked back to the wall and vaulted over it.

veer /vɪə/ (**veers, veering, veered**)

○ **veer 'off**

If something or someone that is moving in a particular direction **veers off**, they suddenly change direction. ❑ He decided to veer off towards the shore. ❑ As the boat veered off from the white water, they saw a rainbow in the sky.

veg /vedʒ/ (**vegges, vegging, vegged**)

○ **veg 'out** [INFORMAL]

If you **veg out**, you spend time relaxing and not doing much. ❑ In the evenings, we just veg out in front of the TV.

venture /ˈventʃə/ (**ventures, venturing, ventured**)

○ **venture 'forth** [LITERARY]

If you **venture forth**, you go somewhere, especially somewhere that might be dangerous. = **sally forth** ❑ I did indeed venture forth again that night.

verge /vɜːdʒ/ (**verges, verging, verged**)

○ **'verge on** (or **verge upon**)

If one thing **verges on** another, it is very similar to it or has similar qualities.
= **border on**

verge on something ❑ I had a feeling of distrust verging on panic. ❑ His question verged on rudeness.

vest /vest/ (**vests, vesting, vested**)

○ **'vest in** [FORMAL]

If power or responsibility **is vested in** someone or something, or if someone **vests** it **in** them, it is given to them.

be vested in someone/something ❑ Supreme authority was vested in the Church Council.

vest something in someone/something ❑ The constitution had vested power in the National Assembly rather than in the president.

vie /vaɪ/ (**vies, vying, vied**)

○ **'vie for**

If people or things **vie for** something, they compete to get it.

vie for something ❑ They sat one on each side of him, vying for his attention.

○ **'vie with**

If one thing or person **vies with** another, they compete with them to get something or do something.

vie with someone/something
❑ [+ to-infinitive] *The banks vied with each other to offer higher savings interest rates.*
❑ [+ for] *Hundreds of books vied with one another for space.*

visit /ˈvɪzɪt/ (visits, visiting, visited)

○ **'visit upon** (or **visit on**) [FORMAL]
If something unpleasant **is visited upon** someone, it happens to them and if someone or something **visits** something unpleasant **upon** someone, they make it happen to them.
be visited upon someone ❑ *I felt that some dreadful punishment had been visited upon me.*
visit something upon someone ❑ *Victor was determined to visit revenge upon his oppressors.*

○ **'visit with** [AMERICAN]
If you **visit with** someone, you go and see them and spend time with them.
visit with someone ❑ *He had not visited with George since 1996.*

voice (voices, voicing, voiced)

○ **voice 'up**
If an actor **voices up** something that someone else originally said, they say what that person said, pretending to be them.
voice up something or **voice something up**
❑ *Her testimony has been voiced up by an actor.*

vote /vəʊt/ (votes, voting, voted)

○ **vote 'down**
If you **vote** something or someone **down**, of if they **are voted down**, they are defeated in a vote.
be voted down ❑ *My proposal was voted down.*
❑ *This particular group got voted down.*
vote someone/something down or **vote down someone/something** ❑ *The committee advised Parliament to vote down the measure.*

○ **vote 'in**
When people **vote in** a person or group of people, they give them enough votes in an election for them to hold a position of power. **= elect**
vote someone in or **vote in someone** ❑ *Ther are already enough pensioners to vote a governmen in or out.* ❑ *So they voted him in, did they?*

○ **vote 'out**
When people **vote out** a person or group of people, they do not give them enough vote in an election to allow them to continue holding a position of power.
vote someone out or **vote out someone**
❑ *He was voted out in 1983.* ❑ [+ of] *They voted Councillor Hitchcock out of her seat.*

○ **vote 'through**
If people **vote** a law or proposal **through**, o if they **are voted through**, a majority of people accept them in an election.
vote something through or **vote through something** ❑ *The committee voted the motion through by a large majority.*
be voted through ❑ *The new measures were voted through, but only by a small margin.*

vouch /vaʊtʃ/ (vouches, vouching, vouched)

○ **'vouch for**
1 If you say that you can or will **vouch for** someone, you mean that you are sure that they have a good character or are good at something.
vouch for someone ❑ *Don Tomassino vouched for you personally.* ❑ *He said you'd vouch for him.*
2 If you say that you can **vouch for** something, you mean that you know from your own personal experience or knowledge that it is true or correct.
vouch for something ❑ *I can vouch for the accuracy of my information.* ❑ *She was down ther all right. I'll vouch for that.*

Ww

wade /weɪd/ (wades, wading, waded)

◯ **wade 'in**

If someone **wades in**, they start doing or saying something in a forceful way, often without thinking about it enough first, or in a way that annoys other people. ❑ *We can't just wade in and tell people how they should be living their lives.* ❑ *Some boys started fighting, and of course, Tom waded in to stop them.*

◯ **wade 'into**

If someone **wades into** an activity or situation, they become involved in it in a forceful way, often without thinking about it enough first, or in a way that annoys other people.
wade into something ❑ *A few journalists waded into the debate.* ❑ *He has never been afraid to wade into battle with anyone who criticizes him.*

◯ **wade 'through**

If you **wade through** a lot of written material, you spend a lot of time and effort reading it or dealing with it. **= plough through**
wade through something ❑ *I had to start wading through the mass of paperwork.*

wait /weɪt/ (waits, waiting, waited)

◯ **wait a'round** (or **wait about** [mainly BRITISH])

If you **wait around**, you spend time in a place doing nothing while you wait to do something or wait for something to happen. ❑ *Two detectives were waiting around to question the old man.* ❑ *We spent most of the morning waiting about in the clinic.*

◯ **wait be'hind**

If you **wait behind**, you stay in a place after everyone else has left. ❑ *She asked me to wait behind after school.*

◯ **'wait for**

1 When you **wait for** something or someone, you stay in a place or do not do much until something happens or until someone or something arrives.
wait for someone/something ❑ *Phil was waiting for them in the lobby of the hotel.*

❑ *I walked to the corner and waited for the bus.*
2 If something **is waiting for** you, it is ready for you to use, have, or do.
be waiting for someone ❑ *There is a package waiting for you in reception.* ❑ *There'll be a car waiting for you.*

◯ **wait 'in** [BRITISH]

If you **wait in**, you stay at home and do not go out, for example because someone is coming to see you. **= stay in** ❑ *I waited in all afternoon.* ❑ *[+ for] 'I'll wait in for it.' – 'No need for that.'*

◯ **'wait on** [AMERICAN]

If you **wait on** someone, you wait somewhere until they have finished what they are doing and can talk to you or go with you.
wait on someone ❑ *I've got some good news. That's why I waited on you out here.*

◯ **'wait on** (or **wait upon**)

1 If someone **waits on** you in a restaurant or at a formal party, they serve you food and drink.
wait on someone ❑ *They were sitting around a dinner table, being waited on.* ❑ *'Help yourself,' I said. 'I'm not waiting on you.'*
2 If you **wait on** someone, you take care of all their needs and do anything that they ask you to do.
wait on someone ❑ *I found it a remarkable experience to be waited upon by eight servants.*
3 If you **wait on** an event, you wait until it happens before doing or deciding something.
wait on something ❑ *The company is prepared to delay the deal and wait on events.* ❑ *He imagined the future of a world waiting upon their decision.*

◯ **wait 'out**

If you **wait out** a period of time or an event, especially a difficult one, you wait for it to pass. **= sit out**
wait out something or **wait something out** ❑ *They built themselves a small shelter and waited out the night.* ❑ *Anne persuaded her to sit and wait it out.*

wait 'up

1 If you **wait up**, you do not go to bed, because you are waiting for someone else to come home. ❑ *I can't make it home until late. Tell her not to wait up.* ❑ [+ for] *He was waiting up for me when I got in last night.*

2 If you tell someone to **wait up**, you want them to wait until you reach them or finish what you are doing. [AMERICAN, INFORMAL] ❑ *Wait up – I'm coming.*

NOTE In British English, **hang on** means almost the same as **wait up**.

'wait upon → see wait on

wake /weɪk/ (wakes, waking, woke, woken)

American English also uses the form **waked** for the past tense and past participle of the verb.

wake 'up

1 When you **wake up**, or when someone or something **wakes** you **up**, you become conscious again after being asleep.
wake up ❑ *Her baby kept waking up at night and crying.* ❑ *Ralph, wake up!*
wake someone up ❑ *I'll wake Bethany up.* ❑ *I won't wake him up yet.*
wake up someone ❑ *There was enough noise to wake up everyone in the house.* ● A **wake-up** call is a telephone call that you ask someone to make to you so that it wakes you up, for example because you do not have an alarm clock. ❑ *I booked a wake-up call for six thirty.*

2 If you **wake up** or if something **wakes** you **up**, you become more active or interested in something.
wake someone up ❑ *The threat of losing his business really woke Donald up.*
wake up someone ❑ *His reports on the state of the planet really woke up the whole world.*
wake up ❑ *They'll soon wake up if someone gets hurt.* ● If you say that something is a **wake-up** call to a person or group of people, you mean that it will make them notice something and start to take action. ❑ *The Ambassador said he hoped the statement would serve as a wake-up call to the government.*

wake 'up to

If you **wake up to** a problem or a dangerous situation, you become aware of it.
wake up to something ❑ *The West began to wake up to the danger it faced.*

NOTE **Realize** is a more formal word for **wake up to**.

walk /wɔːk/ (walks, walking, walked)

walk a'way

If someone **walks away**, they leave a difficult or unpleasant situation rather than trying to deal with it. ❑ [+ from] *'You can't walk away from this, Frank,' Patterson said.* ❑ *The fact that he had no family made it easier for him just to walk away.*

walk a'way with → see walk off with

walk 'in on

If you **walk in on** someone or something, you enter a room and see them, often when something secret or wrong is happening.
walk in on someone/something ❑ *He walked in on a terrible argument.*

walk 'into

1 If you **walk into** an unpleasant or dangerous situation, you become involved in it unexpectedly, sometimes because you are careless.
walk into something ❑ *He had walked into a trap.* ❑ *How did you walk into a situation like this?*

2 If you **walk into** a job, you manage to get it very easily.
walk into something ❑ *He just walked into the job without even an interview.*

walk 'off

1 If you **walk off**, you leave a place because you are angry or upset. ❑ *He turned then, and walked off without further word.*

2 If you **walk off** an unpleasant feeling, you go for a walk in order to stop having the feeling.
walk off something ❑ *He went out to walk off his anger in the night air.* ❑ *She managed to walk off her headache.*

walk 'off with [INFORMAL]

If someone **walks off with** something, they take it when it is not theirs or they do not deserve it. = go off with
walk off with something ❑ *Not realizing what she was doing, she had walked off with his keys.* ❑ *He left her and walked off with half her money.*

walk 'off with (or walk away with) [INFORMAL]

If you **walk off with** a prize or title, you win it or achieve it very easily.
walk off with something ❑ *One reader will walk off with the £35,000 first prize.* ❑ *She will walk away with the title.*

walk 'on

If you **walk on** in a play, you have a very small part in it, often one in which you do not speak. ❑ *She desperately wants a part in the play, whether she has a leading role or is only walking on.* ● A **walk-on** part is a very minor part in a play. ❑ *My sister had a walk-on part.*

walk 'out

1 If you **walk out**, you leave a place or a performance as a way of showing that you are angry or that you do not like something. ❑ [+ of] Haig walked out of the conference. ❑ Many of the audience walked out through sheer boredom. • A **walk-out** is a protest in which you leave a place or performance to show your dislike or anger. ❑ The students had called for a walk-out.

2 If workers **walk out**, they suddenly stop working and leave the place where they work as a protest. ❑ The firefighters voted to walk out in support. ❑ When 160 men walked out in August, union officials were taken aback. • A **walk-out** by workers is when they suddenly stop working and leave the place where they work as a protest. ❑ A new offer finally ended the 43-day walk-out.

3 If you **walk out**, you leave the person or people you live with and do not come back. ❑ His father walked out when he was a baby.

walk 'out on

1 If you **walk out on** someone with whom you have a close relationship, you leave them suddenly and often end the relationship.

walk out on someone ❑ His girlfriend walked out on him.

2 If you **walk out on** someone, you leave the place where you have been with them, often in a rude or angry way.

walk out on someone ❑ They had walked out on me after the scene at Inge's flat. ❑ If I try to discipline him, he just walks out on me without listening.

walk 'over

1 If someone **walks over** you, they treat you very badly, especially by telling you what to do all the time. = **trample on** [INFORMAL]

walk over someone ❑ They must not allow officials to walk all over them. ❑ My father would not allow himself to be walked over.

2 A **walkover** is a success or victory that is achieved without much effort. ❑ The election was a walkover for Democratic candidates.

all /wɔːl/ (walls, walling, walled)

wall 'in

If someone or something **is walled in**, they are surrounded or enclosed by a wall or barrier. **be walled in** ❑ The yard was small, walled in by bricks with broken bottles on top.

wall 'off

If part of a place **is walled off**, it is separated from the rest of the place by a wall or barrier.

be walled off ❑ [+ from] The side alley was walled off from the back garden.

○ wall 'up

1 If a space **is walled up**, it is filled with bricks.

be walled up ❑ The entrances were walled up in the nineteenth century.

2 If someone **walls up** a person or animal, they put them in a place and prevent them from leaving by blocking every exit with a wall.

wall up something/someone or **wall something/someone up** ❑ Creon punishes Antigone by walling her up alive in a tomb.

wallow /'wɒləʊ/ (wallows, wallowing, wallowed)

○ 'wallow in

1 If you **wallow in** a negative emotion, you allow yourself to continue feeling it in order to get pity or because you enjoy it. **wallow in something** ❑ He spent the entire week wallowing in self-pity.

2 If a person or animal **wallows in** water or mud, they lie in it and enjoy it. **wallow in something** ❑ A hippopotamus was wallowing in the mud. ❑ He wallowed in a lovely warm bath.

waltz /wɔːlts/ (waltzes, waltzing, waltzed)

○ waltz 'off with [INFORMAL]

1 If someone **waltzes off with** something, they take it although it is not theirs or they do not deserve it.

waltz off with something ❑ Their chief executive made a complete mess of the company and then waltzed off with a £10 million pension.

2 If you **waltz off with** a prize or award, you win it easily.

waltz off with something ❑ She swept the board, waltzing off with three gold medals.

want /wɒnt/ (wants, wanting, wanted)

○ 'want for [FORMAL]

If you do not **want for** something, you have as much of it as you want or need. **want for something** ❑ As long as Alan was here, he would not want for hot food.

○ want 'in [INFORMAL]

If someone **wants in** they want to be involved or have a share in a plan, a business or an activity. ≠ **want out** ❑ They've heard about the deal and they all want in. ❑ [+ on] The Swiss wanted in on whatever deal Patterson was trying to put together.

○ want 'out [INFORMAL]

1 If you **want out**, you no longer want to be involved in a plan, a business, or an activity.

≠ **want in** ❏ *I want out. I want to sell up.* ❏ *[+ of] If you want out of the deal, just say so, and I'll understand.*

2 If you **want out** of a place, you want to leave it. ❏ *He knew he was in the hospital and really wanted out.* ❏ *[+ of] I want out of here right now.*

ward /wɔːd/ (wards, warding, warded)

○ **ward 'off**

1 To **ward off** something unpleasant or dangerous means to prevent it from affecting you or harming you.
ward off something or **ward something off**
❏ *They had sufficient food and clothing to ward off hunger and ill-health.* ❏ *We have modern military equipment to ward off further attacks.*

2 If you **ward** someone **off**, you prevent them going somewhere or doing something.
ward someone off or **ward off someone**
❏ *'I'm sorry the room's such a mess,' Elaine said, warding him off.*

warm /wɔːm/ (warms, warming, warmed)

○ **warm 'down**

If you **warm down** after doing exercise, you do some gentle movements before stopping the exercise completely. ❏ *Remember to warm up beforehand and warm down afterwards to avoid stiffness.*

○ **'warm to** (or **warm towards**)

1 If you **warm to** someone, you start to like them more.
warm to someone ❏ *I warmed to him during the course of the meal.* ❏ *Tom found himself warming towards Vic.*

2 If you **warm to** an idea or task, you become more enthusiastic about it.
warm to something ❏ *Harry was warming to his theme, and didn't notice her angry reaction.*

○ **warm 'up**

1 If you **warm up** cold food, you heat it until it is ready to be eaten. **= heat up**
warm something up ❏ *I put some bread into the oven to warm it up.* ❏ *You can warm the food up when you get back.*
warm up something ❏ *Start warming up the soup now.*

2 If the weather, the day, or part of the earth **warms up**, it gradually gets hotter. ❏ *The weather was warming up.* ❏ *Nobody is sure how fast the earth will warm up as gases build up in the atmosphere.*

3 If you **warm up** or if something **warms** you **up**, you start to feel warm again after you have been cold. **= thaw out**
warm up ❏ *She began to warm up.* ❏ *Come in and warm up by the stove.*

warm someone up or **warm up someone**
❏ *A nice bowl of hot soup – that should warm you up!*

4 If you **warm up** just before exercise or another physical activity, you prepare yourself for it, usually by practising or doing some exercises. **= limber up** ❏ *They jogged around the track to warm up.* ❏ *I had a drink while the singers were warming up.*

● A **warm-up** is preparation which you do just before exercise or another physical activity. ❏ *During the warm-up exercises, I was still shaking.*

5 If a situation, event, or activity **warms up**, or if you **warm** it **up**, it becomes more active, interesting or exciting. **= hot up**
warm up ❏ *The campaign against the minister began to warm up.* ❏ *Business will be warming u soon.*

warm something up or **warm up somethin**
❏ *The publication of these photos certainly warmed things up a bit.*

6 When a machine, engine, or electrical device **warms up**, or when you **warm** it **up** it starts working and becomes ready for us
warm up ❏ *It sounded like the engines of jet planes warming up on a distant runway.*
warm up something or **warm something u**
❏ *He gave final instructions to Richie as he warm up the engines.*

7 If someone **warms up** an audience, or i the audience **warms up**, they are prepare for the main show or speaker by being tol jokes, so that they are in a good mood.
warm up something or **warm something u**
❏ *They would always come out and warm up the audience.*
warm up ❏ *The crowd began to warm up.*

warn /wɔːn/ (warns, warning, warned)

○ **warn a'way**

If you **warn** a person or vehicle **away**, you tell them to leave a place because it is dangerous for them to be there.
warn someone/something away or **warn away someone/something** ❏ *[+ from] They tried to warn aircraft away from the firing zone.* ❏ *They were warning us away, waving wildly and shouting.*

○ **warn 'off**

If you **warn** someone **off** or **warn** someone **off** something, you tell them to go away o not to do something because of possible danger or punishment.
warn someone off or **warn off someone**
❏ *She made urgent signs to warn him off.* ❏ *Dog were kept to warn off intruders.*
warn someone off something ❏ *You are*

probably already warned off coffee, alcohol and smoking.

wash /wɒʃ/ (**washes, washing, washed**)

wash a'way

1 If water such as rain, floods, or waves **washes away** something, it carries it away with it. **= sweep away**

wash away something or **wash something away** ❏ The dam collapsed, washing away twenty-five villages. ❏ There was a bridge, but the big flood washed it away. ● A **washaway** is a hollow area caused by the earth being washed away by rain or floods. [AUSTRALIAN] ❏ I camped in a washaway near the ruin of a cottage.

2 To **wash away** smells, tastes, or other qualities of an object or substance means to remove them, usually using water.

wash something away or **wash away something** ❏ Soaps wash away the natural odors of the human body. ❏ He swallowed the medicine, then washed the taste away with water.

3 To **wash away** a problem, feeling, or situation means to cause it to end or to be forgotten.

wash away something or **wash something away** ❏ We will never be able to wash away the shame. ❏ It's no use trying to wash your troubles away.

wash 'down

1 If you **wash down** food, you drink something after eating it or while eating it.

wash down something or **wash something down** ❏ [+ with] She was washing each mouthful down with coffee. ❏ Lunch was chips, washed down with milk shakes.

2 If you **wash down** an object or surface, you wash all of it.

wash down something or **wash something down** ❏ I swept the kitchen and washed down the walls. ❏ He washed the windshield down.

3 If rocks or soil **are washed down** or **are washed down** a place by rain or floods, they are carried by the water to another place.

be washed down ❏ Stones and mud were washed down by the floods.

be washed down something ❏ A row of stone kept the soil from being washed down the steep hills in heavy rain.

wash 'off

1 If you **wash** dirt or other unwanted things **off** or **wash** them **off** something, you remove them from the surface of something using water.

wash off something or **wash something off** ❏ Take them home and wash off the mud and sand. ❏ She washed the blood off.

wash something off something ❏ Wash all the dirt off the sides.

wash off ❏ Once the paint dries, it will not wash off.

2 If you **wash** someone **off**, you remove dirt or another substance from their body, using water.

wash someone off or **wash off someone** ❏ Let Sally wash you off. ❏ Wash yourself off and put these clothes on.

✪ wash 'out

1 If you **wash out** clothes or things made of cloth, you clean them using water.

wash out something ❏ She was washing out her baby's nappies.

wash something out ❏ Go down to the stream and wash your shirt out. ❏ I only had one shirt, so I had to wash it out every evening.

2 If you **wash out** a container, you clean the inside of it with water. **= rinse out**

wash out something ❏ I washed out the coffee things.

wash something out ❏ Wash the bucket out well and fill it with clear water. ❏ Make sure the bottle is empty, then wash it out.

3 If you **wash out** dirt or other substances, or if they **wash out**, they are removed using water.

wash something out or **wash out something** ❏ [+ of] Wash the sand out of the buckets in shallow water. ❏ This process is good because it washes out some of the germs.

wash out ❏ The ink, surprisingly, washed out easily.

4 If you **wash out** a feeling or thought, you cause it to end or to be forgotten.

wash out something or **wash something out** ❏ [+ of] I ought to try to forget it, wash it out of my mind.

5 If someone is or looks **washed-out**, they are or look very tired and lacking in energy. **= run down** [INFORMAL] ❏ I returned to Chamonix, washed-out and depressed.

6 If a colour or a light **washes** you or your face **out**, it makes you look pale and unhealthy.

wash someone/something out or **wash out someone/something** ❏ I never wear black – it really washes me out. ❏ Did you notice how the lights washed her face out?

7 A **washed-out** colour is pale and dull. ❏ She had eyes of washed-out grey. ❏ The room had curtains of washed-out blue.

8 If a game, event, or activity **is washed out**, it is prevented from taking place by rain.

be washed out ❏ *The first day of play was washed out after only 90 minutes.* ● If an event is a **washout**, it is stopped by rain. ❏ *Sadly, the game was a washout.*

9 If an attempt, event, or project is a **washout**, it is a total failure. [INFORMAL] ❏ *No-one came – the whole thing was a washout.*

10 If someone or something **is washed out** from a place by rain or floods, they are carried away by them.

be washed out ❏ *A layer of compost will prevent the seed from being washed out.*

○ wash 'over

1 If something that happens or that someone does or says **washes over** you, you do not notice it or it does not affect you in any way.

wash over someone ❏ *Todd let the words wash over him.* ❏ *Events wash over you and are easily forgotten.*

2 If a feeling or an emotion **washes over** you, you suddenly feel it strongly.

wash over someone ❏ *She was not prepared for the wave of nausea that washed over her.*

○ wash 'up

1 If you **wash up** or **wash up** plates, pans, etc., you clean the things you have used to cook and eat a meal.

wash up ❏ *He insisted on helping me wash up.*

wash up something ❏ *We cleared the table and washed up the dishes.*

wash something up ❏ *Tim carried the plates to the kitchen and washed them up.* ❏ *Did you wash the frying pan up?* ● If you do the **washing-up**, you clean the things that have been used to cook and eat a meal. [BRITISH] ❏ *There was enough water to do all the washing-up.* ❏ *Clean the sink with hot water and washing-up liquid.*

2 If you **wash up**, you clean yourself, especially your hands and face. [AMERICAN] ❏ *He went to the bathroom to wash up and comb his hair.*

3 If someone or something **is washed up** on a piece of land, or **washes up** there, they are carried by the water of a river or the sea and left there.

be washed up ❏ *Their boat was washed up ten miles to the south.* ❏ *Pieces of wood have been washed up on the shores.*

wash up ❏ *Pyle's body washed up under the bridge at Dakao.*

4 If you say that someone is **washed up**, you mean that they are at the end of their career and are no longer successful. [INFORMAL] ❏ *She plays a washed up child star in his latest movie.*

waste /weɪst/ (**wastes, wasting, wasted**)

○ waste a'way

1 If a person or a part of their body **wastes away**, they become extremely thin or weak, usually because of illness. ❏ *I don't want you t waste away.* ❏ *Gradually, her limbs wasted away*

2 If something **wastes away**, it becomes smaller or weaker until it eventually disappears. ❏ *Our planners have allowed rural communities to waste away.*

watch /wɒtʃ/ (**watches, watching, watched**)

○ 'watch for

If you **watch for** something, you wait and look carefully for it because it might be important or unpleasant.

watch for something ❏ *The child was always watching for their reactions.* ❏ *You have to watch for signs of the disease.*

○ watch 'out

If you tell someone to **watch out**, you are warning them to be careful because something unpleasant might happen to them. = **look out** ❏ *If you don't watch out, he might stick a knife into you.* ❏ *You behave yourse or you'd better watch out.*

○ watch 'out for

1 If you **watch out for** something, you try to notice it when it appears or happens because it may cause problems or danger.

watch out for something ❏ *Watch out for the warning signs of depression like insomnia.*

2 If you **watch out for** someone or something, you make sure that you do not allow them to harm you.

watch out for someone/something

❏ *Watch out for that cat – it has very sharp claws.* ❏ *Watch out for holes in the road – you don't want a burst tyre.*

3 If you **watch out for** something or someone, you try to see them because they will probably be interesting or good to see.

watch out for something/someone ❏ *This a good place to watch out for wild animals.* ❏ *Watch out for her latest movie.*

4 If you **watch out for** someone or something, you try to make sure that they are safe or not harmed. = **look out for**

watch out for someone/something ❏ *In th kind of situation, mates have to watch out for eac other.* ❏ *Have a good trip, and watch out for yoursel*

○ watch 'over

If you **watch over** someone or something, you take care of them because you are responsible for them. = **guard**

watch over someone/something ❏ *The women took turns to watch over the children.*

water /'wɔːtə/ (waters, watering, watered)

○ **water 'down**

1 If you **water down** a plan, an idea, an opinion or a statement, or if it **is watered down**, it is made less forceful or less extreme.

water something down or **water down something** ❑ He watered down his views a bit for the TV show. ❑ The government defended their bill against all attempts to water it down.

be watered down ❑ These statements were watered down in the final text because of objections within the Cabinet.

2 If you **water down** drink or another liquid, you add water to it to make it weaker.

water down something or **water something down** ❑ They accused him of watering down the beer.

NOTE **Dilute** is a more formal word for **water down**.

wave /weɪv/ (waves, waving, waved)

○ **wave a'side**

If you **wave** an idea, someone's opinion, or a problem **aside**, you show that you do not want to consider it because you do not think it is important enough. = **brush aside**

wave something aside or **wave aside something** ❑ The Chief waved his objection aside. ❑ Miss Jackson waved aside these little difficulties.

NOTE **Dismiss** is a more formal word for **wave aside**.

○ **wave a'way**

If you **wave** someone or something **away**, you signal with your hand that you do not want them near you at the moment.

wave someone/something away or **wave away someone/something** ❑ She waved him away when he ventured near her desk.

○ **wave 'down**

1 If you **wave down** a vehicle or its driver, you stand by the road or in the road and signal with your hands for the driver to stop. = **flag down**

wave down something/someone or **wave something/someone down** ❑ He waved down a passing army truck. ❑ A police officer waved them down and told them to get off the main road.

2 If you **wave down** people's reactions to you, you signal to them that you do not want to be interrupted.

wave down something or **wave something down** ❑ The Prime Minister waved down the applause. ❑ He waved down my protest.

○ **wave 'off**

1 If you **wave** someone **off**, you wave to them as they leave somewhere. = **see off**

wave someone off or **wave off someone** ❑ They went to wave their boys off on the army trains. ❑ Finally, she waved off the last of the guests.

2 If you **wave** someone or something **off**, you wave your arms as a signal that you want them to go away. = **ward off, fend off**

wave someone/something off or **wave off someone/something** ❑ They suggested a walk, but he waved them off, saying he was too tired.

○ **wave 'on**

If someone in authority **waves** a vehicle or its driver **on**, they signal with their hands for them to continue going forwards.

wave something/someone on or **wave on something/someone** ❑ Police officers were everywhere, waving traffic on and sometimes making people stop.

○ **wave 'through**

If someone in authority **waves** a vehicle or a person **through** or **waves** them **through** a place, they allow them to enter a place.

wave something/someone through or **wave through something/someone** ❑ There were several officials waving vehicles through.

wave something/someone through something ❑ They waved us through the gate.

wean /wiːn/ (weans, weaning, weaned)

○ **wean 'off**

If you **wean** someone or yourself **off** a habit or something harmful, you gradually stop them or yourself doing it or wanting it.

wean someone off something ❑ Politicians want dramatic measures to wean young people off junk food. ❑ Children should be weaned off television.

wean yourself off something ❑ We need to encourage people to wean themselves off their cars.

wear /weə/ (wears, wearing, wore, worn)

○ **wear a'way**

1 If you **wear** something **away** or if it **wears away**, it becomes thin and eventually disappears because it is used a lot or rubbed a lot. = **wear down**

wear away ❑ The softer rock wears away first, and a step is formed.

wear something away or **wear away something** ❑ Much of the grass on the pathway had been worn away by walkers. ❑ Waves had worn the rock away.

2 If something **wears away** emotions or characteristics, it gradually weakens them until they are no longer noticeable.

wear away something or **wear something away** ❏ Time and absence wear away pain and grief.

▊ If a period of time **wears away**, it passes slowly. = **wear on** [LITERARY] ❏ The shadows slowly lengthened again as the afternoon wore away.

○ **wear a'way at**

▊ If something **wears away at** another thing, it rubs it and causes it to become thinner.

wear away at something ❏ The rivers are constantly wearing away at their banks.

▊ If someone or something **wears away at** another thing, they cause it to become weaker.

wear away at something ❏ All these lies wear away at the trust in our relationship.

○ **wear 'down**

▊ If someone or something **wears down** a person or their strength, opposition, etc., they weaken them over a long period of time.

wear down someone/something or **wear someone/something down** ❏ These night calls are wearing me down. ❏ He fought hard and relentlessly, slowly wearing his opponent down.

▊ If you **wear** something **down** or if it **wears down**, the surface of it becomes thinner because it is being rubbed.

wear down ❏ As the teeth wear down, new ones start growing.

wear down something or **wear something down** ❏ Large numbers of visitors have worn down the top of the mountain. ❏ The stairs were worn down like the doorstep.

⊙ **wear 'off**

When a feeling or the effect of something **wears off**, it disappears slowly. ❏ By the next afternoon the shock had worn off. ❏ The effect of the aspirin had worn off and her toothache had come back. ❏ The pain soon wears off.

○ **wear 'on**

If time **wears on**, it seems to pass very slowly. ❏ As the night wore on, the absence of electricity made matters worse. ❏ As Monday wore on they discussed Helen's absence.

⊙ **wear 'out**

▊ When something **wears out** or when you **wear** it **out**, it is used so much that it becomes weak or broken and unable to be used any more.

wear out ❏ Sooner or later the soles of your favourite shoes are going to wear out.

wear out something ❏ He did not want them walking up and down the stairs and wearing out the stair carpet.

wear something out ❏ Horses used for long-distance riding tend to wear their shoes out quicker. ● Something that is **worn out** has become so old, damaged, or thin that it cannot be used any more. ❏ We sat on his worn-out sofa.

▊ If something **wears** you **out**, it makes you become so tired that you cannot continue what you were doing. = **exhaust**

wear someone out ❏ Visitors wear us out more than the children do. ❏ There is no point in wearing yourself out.

wear out someone ❏ They wore out their parents by constantly inviting friends to stay.

● Someone who is **worn out** is extremely tired. ❏ She certainly had looked worn out when he came home.

▊ If someone **wears out** their **welcome**, or if their **welcome wears out**, they stay too long with someone, so that person wants them to leave. ❏ We don't want to wear out our welcome.

○ **wear 'through**

If something such as a piece of clothing **wears through** or **is worn through**, it develops a hole where the material has become weak and thin.

wear through ❏ The knees of his trousers have worn through.

be worn through ❏ The carpet in the hall was worn through in places.

weary /ˈwɪəri/ (**wearies, wearying, wearies**

○ **'weary of** [FORMAL]

If you **weary of** something or someone, you become bored with them and lose interest in them. = **tire of**

weary of something/someone ❏ He eventually wearied of the discussion. ❏ By this time, they had begun to weary of their king.

weed /wiːd/ (**weeds, weeding, weeded**)

○ **weed 'out**

If you **weed out** things or people that are not wanted in a group, you get rid of them

weed out something/someone or **weed something/someone out** ❏ Natural selection has weeded out the weakest animals. ❏ [+ of] Bad teachers should be weeded out of the profession.

weigh /weɪ/ (**weighs, weighing, weighed**)

○ **weigh a'gainst**

▊ If you **weigh** one thing **against** another, you consider which of them is more important in order to decide what you should do. = **balance against, set against**

weigh something against something ❏ You must weigh the benefits against the potential dangers.

2 If a fact or situation **weighs against** something or someone, it makes them less likely to happen or be successful.
weigh against something/someone ❏ *Stronger consumer demand weighs against any further cut in interest rates.*

○ **weigh 'down**

1 If something or someone **is weighed down** or if something or someone **weighs** them **down**, something heavy makes it difficult for them to move.
be weighed down ❏ *[+ with] She was weighed down with parcels.* ❏ *Her clothes lay neatly folded on a chair, weighed down by a pile of books.*
weigh something/someone down or **weigh down something/someone** ❏ *They used chains to weigh the body down.* ❏ *The sand in his shoes weighed him down.*

2 If you **are weighed down** by a difficulty or problem or if it **weighs** you **down**, it causes you to worry a lot.
be weighed down ❏ *[+ with] I was weighed down with problems.*
weigh someone down or **weigh down someone** ❏ *The stress of all the responsibility was beginning to weigh her down.*

○ **weigh 'in**

1 If you **weigh in**, you begin to take part in a discussion or a task rather forcefully.
= come in ❏ *[+ with] The Queen Mother weighed in with some advice.* ❏ *When the time came to lay the concrete, we all weighed in.*

2 When the competitors at an event **weigh in**, they are weighed to check their weight shortly before or after the event. ❏ *[+ at] Weighing in at 200 pounds, he's a little overweight.*
● When there is a **weigh-in** at an event, each competitor is weighed to check their weight shortly before or after the event. ❏ *Angry words were exchanged at the weigh-in this morning.*

○ **'weigh on** (or **weigh upon**)

If a problem **weighs on** you or your conscience, soul, etc., it makes you worry.
weigh on someone/something ❏ *To keep silent about such a situation would weigh heavily upon our consciences.*

○ **weigh 'out**

If you **weigh** something **out**, you measure a certain weight of it in order to make sure that you have the correct amount.
weigh something out or **weigh out something** ❏ *He weighed out a pound of tomatoes.* ❏ *Collect and weigh out all the ingredients before starting.*

○ **weigh 'up**

1 If you **weigh** things **up**, you consider

their importance in relation to each other in order to help you make a decision.
weigh up something ❏ *I weighed up the advantages and disadvantages.*
weigh something up ❏ *Having weighed everything up, he decided it was the right thing to do.*

> **WEIGH UP + *noun***
>
> weigh up **options**
> weigh up **the possibilities**
> weigh up **the risks**
> weigh up **the alternatives**
> weigh up **the benefits**
> ❏ *We have to weigh up all the available options.* ❏ *They are weighing up the benefits of joining the organization.*

2 If you **weigh** someone **up**, you try to find out what they are like and form an opinion of them by watching them and listening to them. **= size up** [BRITISH]
weigh someone up ❏ *He was weighing me up, trying to decide if my interest was genuine.*
weigh up someone ❏ *He weighed up the man opposite him.*

○ **'weigh upon →** see **weigh on**

weight /weɪt/ (**weights, weighting, weighted**)

○ **weight 'down**

If you **weight** something **down**, you add something heavy to it to prevent it moving easily.
weight something down or **weight down something** ❏ *We covered the ground with a plastic sheet weighted down with large stones.*

weird (**weirds, weirding, weirded**)

○ **weird 'out** [INFORMAL]

If someone **is weirded out** by something, that thing frightens them because they think it is strange.
be weirded out ❏ *They didn't seem at all weirded out by the freaky stuff surrounding them.*

well /wel/ (**wells, welling, welled**)

○ **well 'up**

1 If a quantity of liquid **wells up**, it comes to the surface suddenly. ❏ *Tears welled up in his eyes and he brushed them aside.*

2 If an emotion **wells up**, it suddenly affects you quite strongly. **= rise up**
❏ *[+ inside] Happiness welled up inside me.*
❏ *[+ in] All his fury against Zoe welled up in him.*

wheel /wiːl/ (**wheels, wheeling, wheeled**)

○ **wheel a'round** (or **wheel round** [mainly BRITISH])

If you **wheel around**, you turn around suddenly. ❏ *I wheeled around and glared at him.* ❏ *He wheeled round with delight.*

wheel 'out [BRITISH]

If you **wheel** someone or something **out**, you present them or use them, often when you have presented or used them many times before.

wheel someone/something out or **wheel out someone/something** ❑ The American ambassador was wheeled out to express his concern. ❑ All the usual arguments were wheeled out.

wheel 'round → see wheel around

while /waɪl/ (whiles, whiling, whiled)

while a'way

If you **while away** the time in a particular way, you do that thing while you wait for time to pass.

while away something or **while something away** ❑ How about whiling away the time by telling me a story? ❑ We listened to music to help us while the hours away.

whip /wɪp/ (whips, whipping, whipped)

whip 'out [INFORMAL]

If you **whip** something **out**, you produce it from a place very quickly and suddenly.

whip something out or **whip out something** ❑ Quickly, she whipped a knife out and cut herself free.

whip 'up

1 If someone or something **whips up** an emotion, they cause people to feel that emotion. = stir up

whip up something or **whip something up** ❑ The reporters whipped up sympathy with stories of pensioners suffering from the cold. ❑ The hatred is whipped up by the continual flow of rumors.

2 If someone or something **whips** people **up**, they cause them to become excited or angry.

whip up someone or **whip someone up** ❑ [+ into] The television interview whipped up half the American people into a frenzy of rage. ❑ Having whipped up its supporters to this extent, the party can't afford to slow down now.

3 If someone **whips up** support, they try to make people support someone or something.

whip up something or **whip someone up** ❑ The rebels tried to whip up support by claiming that the government had lied.

4 If the wind **whips up** dust or waves, it makes dust or waves rise up suddenly from the surface of something.

whip up something or **whip something up** ❑ A gale can whip up waves measuring 20 to 25m from top to bottom. ❑ A cool breeze whipped up a swirl of dust.

5 If a wind **whips up**, it starts to blow strongly. ❑ An icy wind had whipped up within the last hour.

6 If you **whip up** a substance such as cream or egg, you stir it very fast until it becomes thick and full of small bubbles of air.

whip up something or **whip something up** ❑ I got him to grate the cheese whilst I whipped up eggs for three omelettes.

7 If you **whip up** food or a meal, you make it quickly. [INFORMAL]

whip up something or **whip something up** ❑ I could whip up a salad, if you like.

8 If someone **whips up** a horse or other animal, they encourage it to move faster by hitting it with a whip.

whip up something or **whip something up** ❑ The man on the box whipped up his horses and the van moved out of the yard.

whisk /wɪsk/ (whisks, whisking, whisked)

whisk a'way

If you **whisk** someone or something **away**, you remove them from a place very quickly.

whisk someone/something away or **whisk away someone/something** ❑ The royal couple were whisked away from a brief welcome at the airport. ❑ She whisked away my plate as soon as I'd finished.

whittle /'wɪtəl/ (whittles, whittling, whittled)

whittle a'way

To **whittle** something **away** means to gradually make it smaller or less effective over a period of time.

whittle something away or **whittle away something** ❑ This legislation may whittle away our liberties. ❑ Their 9-12 lead was gradually whittled away in the final quarter of the game.

whittle a'way at

To **whittle away at** something means to gradually make it smaller or less effective over a period of time.

whittle away at something ❑ This constant hunting whittles away at the numbers of fish. ❑ They whittle away at your self-respect until there is nothing left.

whittle 'down

1 To **whittle down** the number of people or things means to make that number smaller.

whittle down something or **whittle something down** ❑ [+ to] He started with a list of five names, which he'd whittled down to two by the afternoon. ❑ Gradually we whittled down the list of songs.

2 To **whittle** something **down** means to gradually make it smaller or less effective over a period of time.

whittle down something or **whittle something down** ❏ *The opposition party was slowly whittling down their majority.*

whoop /wuːp, AM huːp/ (**whoops, whooping, whooped**)

◌ **whoop 'up** [INFORMAL]
If you **whoop it up**, you do things that are enjoyable and exciting. = **live it up** ❏ *He and Janet were whooping it up in France.*

wig /wɪɡ/ (**wigs, wigging, wigged**)

◌ **wig 'out** [BRITISH, INFORMAL]
If someone **wigs out**, they behave in a crazy or very excited way. = **freak out** ❏ *He didn't wig out. He was visibly shaking but he didn't go crazy.* ● A **wig-out** is an occasion when people behave in a crazy or very excited way. [BRITISH, INFORMAL] ❏ *Most of the audience seemed determined to have a wig-out.* ● Someone who is **wigged-out** is behaving in a crazy way. [BRITISH, INFORMAL] ❏ *Toward the end of that time he got pretty depressed and wigged-out.*

will /wɪl/ (**wills, willing, willed**)

◌ **'will to**
If you **will** something **to** someone, you say in a legal document that they should have it when you die.
will something to someone ❏ *He had willed the money to his son.* ❏ *The house was willed to her by her mother.*

wimp /wɪmp/ (**wimps, wimping, wimped**)

◌ **wimp 'out** [INFORMAL]
If you **wimp out**, you decide not to do something because you are afraid or not strong enough. = **chicken out** ❏ *If you decide to wimp out you can catch a ride in the van.* ❏ [+ of] *They wimped out of doing anything that might be even slightly risky.*

win /wɪn/ (**wins, winning, won**)

◗ **win 'back**
If you **win back** something that you have lost or a person you used to have a relationship with, you get them back through your own efforts.
win back something/someone ❏ *He brought them gifts, hoping to win back their good will.* ❏ *Management have won back power from the unions.*
win something/someone back ❏ *She took the seat last year, but the Conservatives are determined to win it back.*
NOTE **Regain** is a more formal word for **win back**.

◌ **win 'out**
If something or someone **wins out**, they succeed or defeat others after a struggle.

❏ *In the end, her good nature won out, and she stepped forward to meet the party.* ❏ [+ against] *The next three months he spent in a military hospital, where he won out against his doctors who wanted to saw off his leg.* ❏ [+ over] *If she did not arrive soon, hunger was likely to win out over curiosity.*

✪ **win 'over** (or **win round** [mainly BRITISH])
If you **win** someone **over**, you persuade them to support or agree with you or you make them like you.
win over someone ❏ [+ to] *Benn had succeeded in winning over those in authority to the workers' cause.* ❏ *I was completely won over by the courtesy and decency of the people.*
win someone over ❏ *His directness and obvious honesty were winning people over.* ❏ *Gentle persuasion soon won him round.*

○ **win 'through**
1 If someone or something **wins through**, they succeed after experiencing difficulties. ❏ *Liverpool won through with a dazzling performance.*
2 If you **win through** a stage of a competition, you defeat your opponents in that stage.
win through something ❏ *Two Birmingham companies have won through the first two rounds of the National Management Game.*

○ **win 'through to**
If you **win through to** a particular stage of a competition, you achieve it by defeating your opponents. = **get through to**
win through to something ❏ *He has won through to the finals of Young Chef of the Year.*

wind /waɪnd/ (**winds, winding, winded, wound**)

○ **wind 'back** [OLD-FASHIONED]
When you **wind back** the tape in a cassette player or the film in a camera, you make it move back towards its starting position.
wind back something or **wind something back** ❏ *The tape will have to be wound back.*
NOTE **Rewind** is a more formal word for **wind back**.

✪ **wind 'down**
1 When you **wind down** the window of a car, you open it by moving it downwards, usually using a switch. ≠ **wind up**
wind down something ❏ *Philip stopped at a red light and wound down his window.*
wind something down ❏ *Can you wind your window down, please?*
2 If a mechanical device such as a clock **winds down**, it gradually works more slowly and eventually stops completely.

= run down ❑ *If the watch has wound down, you can wind it yourself.*

3 When you **wind down** after doing something that has made you feel tired or tense, you gradually relax. **= unwind** [INFORMAL] ❑ *We went to the local pub to wind down.*

4 If a business or organization **winds down** or if someone **winds** it **down**, the amount of work that it does is gradually reduced before it is closed down completely. **= wind up**

wind down ❑ *He had to provide a financial report for a client whose business was winding down.*

wind something down or **wind down something** ❑ *Unfortunately, we had to wind down the Liverpool office.* ❑ *The board had no choice other than to wind the organization down.*

5 If an event **winds down**, it gradually ends. ❑ *The conference was winding down, with most people starting to pack up.* ❑ *The party started winding down and I suggested going on to a bar.*

O **wind 'forward** (or **wind on**) [OLD-FASHIONED]

If you **wind forward** the tape in a cassette player or the film in a camera, you make it move forward to a new position.

wind something forward or **wind forward something** ❑ *Just wind it forward until you can see the number 'one' in the little window.*

O **wind 'up**

1 If you **wind up** a long piece of something, you wrap it round itself to reduce its length and form it into a ball or roll.

wind up something ❑ *Lift the rod, lower it and wind up the line.*

wind something up ❑ *Wind the string up into a ball.*

2 When you **wind up** a mechanical device such as a watch, you turn a part on it round and round in order to make it operate.

wind up something ❑ *Frank wound up the old gramophone.*

wind something up ❑ *I wound the music box up and placed it on the table.* ● A **wind-up** device or mechanism is one that is operated by clockwork. ❑ *He gave me a wind-up racing car.*

3 When you **wind up** the window of a car, you close it by making it move upwards, usually by using a switch. **≠ wind down**

wind up something ❑ *Wind up that window, I'm getting a draught here.*

wind something up ❑ *He saw the man approaching, and wound his window up.*

4 When you **wind up** an activity or event, or when an activity or event **winds up**, it ends.

wind up something or **wind something up** ❑ *By the time we wound up the conversation, it was nine o'clock.*

wind up ❑ *The proceedings wind up at midnight with a final dance.*

5 When someone **winds up** a business or other organization, they close it down completely.

wind up something or **wind something up** ❑ *The company was wound up in 1971.*

● The **winding-up** of a business or other organization is its official closure. ❑ *He left the country after the compulsory winding-up of his firm.*

6 If you **wind up** in a particular place or situation, you are in it as the end result of a series of events or processes. **= finish up, end up**

wind up somewhere ❑ *We wound up at the Szanghi restaurant.*

wind up doing something ❑ *If I stay here long enough, I'll wind up marrying him.*

wind up ❑ [+ in] *He knew he was going to wind up in a fight.*

7 If you **wind** someone **up**, you deliberately say or do things to annoy them. [BRITISH, INFORMAL]

wind someone up or **wind up someone** ❑ *He's always winding his sister up.* ❑ *Gareth's remarks had wound him up to full pitch.*

8 If you **wind** someone **up**, you say untrue things in order to trick them. [BRITISH, INFORMAL]

wind someone up or **wind up someone** ❑ *You're joking. Come on, you're winding me up.*

● A **wind-up** is a trick that is played on someone to make them believe something that is not true. [BRITISH, INFORMAL] ❑ *Is this a wind-up, or what?*

wink /wɪŋk/ (**winks, winking, winked**)

O **'wink at**

1 If you **wink at** someone, you close and open one eye very quickly, usually as a signal that something is a joke or a secret.

wink at someone ❑ *He winked at Ricardo to show he was joking.* ❑ *'Is that drink for me?' he asked, winking at her.*

2 If you **wink at** something bad or illegal, you pretend that you have not noticed it or that you do not know about it.

wink at something ❑ *For years governments have winked at the brutality of this dictator.*

winkle /'wɪŋkəl/ (**winkles, winkling, winkled**)

O **winkle 'out** [BRITISH, INFORMAL]

1 If you **winkle out** information, you get it

often when someone does not intend to give it to you. = **worm out**

winkle out something or **winkle something out** ❑ *The security services will go to any lengths to winkle out information.* ❑ *[+ of] The detective was trying to winkle information out of her.*

2 If you **winkle** someone **out**, you make them leave a place, often when they do not want to. = **flush out**

winkle someone out or **winkle out someone** ❑ *He somehow managed to winkle Picard out of his room.*

winnow /'wɪnəʊ/ (winnows, winnowing, winnowed)

○ **winnow 'out**

If you **winnow out** part of a group of things or people, you get rid of the part that is not useful or keep only the part that is useful. **winnow out something/someone** ❑ *They set tests to winnow out the least able candidates.*

wipe /waɪp/ (wipes, wiping, wiped)

○ **wipe a'way**

If you **wipe away** a substance from something, you remove it using a cloth, a piece of soft paper or your hand. **wipe something away** or **wipe away something** ❑ *She wiped her tears away, still laughing.*

○ **wipe 'down**

If you **wipe** something **down**, you clean it with a cloth or piece of soft paper. **wipe something down** or **wipe down something** ❑ *The walls will have to be wiped down.* ❑ *Make sure you wipe down all the work surfaces.*

○ **wipe 'off**

1 If you **wipe off** a substance or **wipe** it **off** something, you remove it using a cloth, a piece of soft paper, or your hand.

wipe something off or **wipe off something** ❑ *I need a tissue to wipe off the sand.*

wipe something off something ❑ *I wiped a trickle of sweat off my eyebrow.*

2 If something **wipes** an amount **off** the value of something, it reduces the value by that amount.

wipe something off something ❑ *The latest price fall wiped £20 million off the stock market value of the company.*

3 If you **wipe off** a debt or money that is owed to you, you accept that the money will not be repaid. = **write off**

wipe off something or **wipe something off** ❑ *Twelve million pounds was simply wiped off by the Government.*

○ **wipe 'out**

1 If you **wipe out** something, you rub the

inside of it with a cloth or piece of soft paper to clean it.

wipe out something ❑ *You can wipe out the frying pan with kitchen paper.*

wipe something out ❑ *Wipe the bucket out when you've finished.*

2 To **wipe** someone or something **out** means to destroy or get rid of them completely. **wipe out someone/something** ❑ *A series of epidemics wiped out the local population.* ❑ *Uncle Alan was determined to wipe out the memory of his unhappy childhood.*

wipe someone/something out ❑ *A bomb could fall on the house and wipe us both out.* NOTE **Eradicate** is a more formal word for **wipe out**.

3 If something **wipes** you **out**, it makes you extremely tired. [INFORMAL]

wipe someone out or **wipe out someone** ❑ *The simple act of taking a shower wiped me out for hours.*

○ **wipe 'up**

If you **wipe up** a substance, you remove it using a cloth or piece of soft paper. **wipe something up** or **wipe up something** ❑ *He began to wipe up the mess.*

wire /waɪə/ (wires, wiring, wired)

○ **wire 'up**

If you **wire** something **up**, you connect it to something else with electrical wires so that electricity or electrical signals can pass between them.

wire something up or **wire up something** ❑ *[+ to] He was wired up to a heart monitor.* ❑ *He wired up the robot arm so that it would respond directly to an electronic signal.*

wise /waɪz/ (wises, wising, wised)

○ **wise 'up** [INFORMAL]

If someone **wises up**, they realize the truth about a situation. ❑ *[+ to] If companies cheat their customers, people will wise up to the fact pretty quickly.*

wish /wɪʃ/ (wishes, wishing, wished)

○ **wish a'way**

If you **wish** something **away**, you hope to get rid of it although you do not do anything practical to remove it. **wish something away** or **wish away something** ❑ *These errors can't just be wished away.* ❑ *Wishing them away won't get rid of your problems.*

○ **'wish on** (or **wish upon**)

If you **wish** something **on** someone else, you hope very much that it will happen to them. **wish something on someone** ❑ *The one thing I would not wish on my worst enemy is eternal life.*

withdraw /wɪð'drɔː/ (**withdraws, withdrawing, withdrew, withdrawn**)

○ **with'draw from**

1 If you **withdraw** something **from** a place, you remove it or take it away. [FORMAL]
withdraw something from something
❑ *Cassandra withdrew her hand from Roger's.*
❑ *Whitlock slowly withdrew the keys from his pocket.*

2 If you **withdraw** money **from** a bank account, you take it out of that account.
withdraw something from something
❑ *They withdrew 100 dollars from a bank account after checking out of their hotel.*

3 If you **withdraw from** something, you stop taking part in it.
withdraw from something ❑ *The African National Congress threatened to withdraw from the talks.* ❑ *He withdrew from the competition for health reasons.*

○ **with'draw to** [FORMAL]

If you **withdraw to** another room, you go there.
withdraw to somewhere ❑ *I withdrew to my study and made a list of things to do.*

wither /'wɪðə/ (**withers, withering, withered**)

○ **wither a'way**

If something **withers away**, it becomes smaller or weaker until it eventually disappears. ❑ *His view is that it is the Church, not the state, that will in time wither away.*
❑ *Instead of withering away, their job done, the Greens have transformed themselves into a fairly conventional party.*

witter /'wɪtə/ (**witters, wittering, wittered**)

○ **'witter about** (or **witter on about**)

[BRITISH, INFORMAL]

If someone **witters about** something, they talk a lot about something that is silly and boring.
witter about something ❑ *He should go and do something instead of wittering about his problems.*
❑ *He wittered on about how awful he felt.*

wolf /wʊlf/ (**wolfs, wolfing, wolfed**)

○ **wolf 'down**

If you **wolf** food **down**, you eat it all very quickly and greedily. = **gobble down**
wolf something down or **wolf down something** ❑ *I wolfed down an enormous meal.*
❑ *He wolfed the food down, bones and all.*

wonder /'wʌndə/ (**wonders, wondering, wondered**)

○ **'wonder about**

If you **wonder about** something or someone, you think about them, either because you want to know more about them, or because you are worried or suspicious about them.
wonder about something/someone ❑ *He wondered about her relationship with Maguire.*
❑ *She started to wonder about the future.*

○ **'wonder at**

If you **wonder at** something, you are surprised by it and admire it. = **marvel at**
wonder at something ❑ *One can only wonder at children's strength when this kind of thing happens.*

work /wɜːk/ (**works, working, worked**)

○ **'work at** → see **work on**

○ **work a'way**

If you **work away**, you continue working hard for a long time. ❑ *[+ at] Scientists were working away at perfecting the drug.* ❑ *I was able to keep warm as I worked away in the snow.*

○ **work 'in**

1 If you **work** a substance **in**, you rub or mix it gradually and carefully into a mixture or a surface.
work something in or **work in something**
❑ *Sprinkle dry salt on the butter and work it in thoroughly.*

2 If you are doing or saying something and you **work** something else **in**, you manage to include it. = **squeeze in**
work something in or **work in something**
❑ *During his speech, he managed to work in several remarks about the Prime Minister.* ❑ *I'll try and work it in some time during the day.*

3 A **work-in** is a form of protest in which workers occupy buildings and take over the running of a factory or business to protest about plans to close it.

○ **work 'into**

If you **work** a substance **into** a mixture or surface, you rub it in or mix it in gradually and carefully.
work something into something ❑ *Most of her morning was taken up with working creams into her skin and preparing her make-up.*

○ **work 'off**

In meaning 4, the stress is on **'work**.

1 If you **work off** a feeling you do not want you get rid of it by doing something energetic.
work something off or **work off something**
❑ *We should all be able to work off our stress physically.* ❑ *He liked to work off his extra energy by climbing mountains.*

2 If you **work off** something you have eaten, you do something energetic so that it does not make you fat.
work something off or **work off something**

❑ We will need to do a lot of exercise to work off the extra calories.

3 If someone **works off** a debt, they repay it by working to earn money or working without pay for the person who lent them the money.

work off something or **work something off**
❑ He agreed to go without pay until he had worked off the family debt.

4 If a piece of equipment **works off** a particular source of power, this is the source of power that it uses to make it function.

work off something ❑ There is a special wire cutter which works off a battery. ❑ The fridge works off gas.

'work on

1 If you **work on** an idea or a fact you think is true, you rely on it being true or correct when you develop your own ideas or plans.

work on something ❑ British officials are working on the assumption that the captured men are alive. ❑ Evolution theory works on the idea that the fittest survive and produce fit babies.

2 If you **work on** someone, you spend time trying to influence them or persuade them to do something.

work on someone ❑ I want to drive across America. My wife's not keen, but I'm working on her. ❑ He's working on Julian to let us use the house.

'work on (or work at)

If you **work on** something, you spend time and effort trying to improve it.

work on something ❑ He has been working on his game all season. ❑ She works hard at keeping herself fit.

work 'out

1 If you **work out** the answer to a mathematical problem, you calculate it.

work something out ❑ I've worked it out, and it's 3,171.875 tons.

work out something ❑ The weekly rate is worked out by dividing by 52. ❑ Calculate how much you owe each person, then work out how much you can afford to pay each of them.

2 If something **works out** at a particular amount, it is found to be that amount after all the calculations have been made.

❑ The cost of the fuel worked out about a hundred pounds in the end. ❑ [+ at] At the moment her fuel bills work out at £30 a week.

3 If you **work out** a solution or a plan, you think about it carefully and find a solution or decide what to do.

work out something ❑ We should try to work out the best ways to help these young people.

❑ I stopped and sat down to work out where I would go next.

work something out ❑ I've been trying to find a solution and I think I've finally worked it out.

> **WORK OUT + noun**
> work out **a compromise**
> work out **a solution**
> work out **a deal**
> work out **an agreement**
> work out **the details of** something
> ❑ There was disagreement over the money, but eventually they worked out a compromise.
> ❑ We worked out an arrangement to cover the holiday period.

4 If you manage to **work out** something that seems strange, you think about it and manage to understand it. = **figure out**

work out something ❑ At first, he couldn't work out why the room was so familiar. ❑ I'm trying to work out what's wrong.

work something out ❑ I'm not sure what's missing but I'm sure I'll work it out.

5 If you say that you **cannot work** someone **out**, you mean that you cannot understand them. [INFORMAL]

not work someone out ❑ I just can't work you out – you never seem to enjoy anything.

NOTE **Suss out** is a more informal expression for **work out**.

6 If a situation **works out** in a particular way, it happens or progresses in that way. = **turn out** ❑ I asked him how he was, and how his job was working out. ❑ It's funny how life worked out.

7 If a situation, arrangement, or plan **works out**, it is successful. ❑ The business didn't really work out. ❑ He's moody because things aren't working out at home.

8 If you **work out**, you do physical exercises in order to make your body healthy and strong. ❑ She worked out in a ballet class three hours a week. ● A **workout** is a period of physical exercise or training. ❑ They go to the gym for a workout every Wednesday.

9 If a process or a problem **works** itself **out**, it reaches a conclusion or satisfactory end. = **resolve**

work itself out ❑ They will not be paid until the whole process has worked itself out. ❑ By then, we hope the crisis will have worked itself out.

10 If you **work out** a period of time in a job, you continue to work at your job until you have completed that period of time.

work out something or **work something out**
❑ He worked out his military service in an office.
❑ She was asked to leave immediately, rather than working her notice out.

11 If a mine **is worked out**, all the coal or metal has been removed from it. **= be exhausted**

be worked out ❑ *As more and more coal seams were worked out, the danger of pit closures increased.*

○ **work 'over** [INFORMAL]

If someone **works** you **over**, they attack you.

work someone over ❑ *They worked him over till he was barely conscious.*

○ **work 'through**

If you **work through** a problem or difficulty, you deal with it carefully and thoroughly until you find a satisfactory solution.

work through something or **work something through** ❑ *At these meetings, managers work through a series of issues with key employees.* ❑ *The teacher sets the experiment or project and the students work it through.*

○ **'work towards**

If you **work towards** something, you try very hard to achieve it or make it happen.

work towards something ❑ *My mother was working towards her master's degree in education.* ❑ *They called for the government to work towards greater democracy.*

✪ **work 'up**

11 If you **work** yourself **up**, you gradually make yourself very upset, angry or excited about something.

work yourself up ❑ [+ into] *By this time I had worked myself up into a fury and was determined not to let the matter drop.* ❑ *Paul had worked himself up and took a deep breath to calm himself.*

● Someone who is **worked up** is very upset, angry or excited. ❑ *Tell me why you are so worked up over that article.*

2 If someone **works up** a feeling, the energy to do something, or an appetite, they gradually develop it and increase it until they have what they need.

work up something ❑ *She went for a run to work up an appetite.* ❑ *I can hardly work up enough energy.*

work something up ❑ *It took me a long time to work the courage up to ask her out.*

3 If you **work** yourself **up** to do something, you try to make yourself have the enthusiasm or confidence to do it.

work yourself up ❑ [+ to-infinitive] *It took me four days to work myself up to go and tell my boss the truth.* ❑ *The team were working themselves up for the match.*

4 When you are doing something regularly, if you **work up** to a particular amount or level, you gradually increase or improve what you are doing until you reach that amount or level. **= build up** ❑ [+ to] *Repeat movements 1, 2 and 3 four times at first, and gradually work up to about six repetitions.*

5 If you **work up** something, you spend time and effort on it to make it complete or successful.

work up something or **work something up** ❑ [+ into] *One day I may work this idea up into a story.* ❑ *He hope that one day he would be able to work up a sound business.*

worm /wɜːm/ (worms, worming, wormed)

○ **worm 'out of**

If you **worm** information **out of** someone, you gradually find it out from them although they do not want to tell you.

worm something out of someone ❑ *He might worm the story out of her by emotional pressure.* ❑ *The truth had been wormed out of him by his lawyers.*

worry /'wʌri, AM 'wɜːri/ (worries, worrying, worried)

○ **'worry at**

11 If you **worry at** a problem or an idea, you think about it continually in order to find way of solving it or understanding it.

worry at something ❑ *Back at home I used to think a lot, worry at the problems.*

2 When a dog or other animal **worries at** something, it holds it in its teeth, continually shaking it and moving it about.

worry at something ❑ *Their dog was worrying at a bone.*

wrangle /'ræŋɡəl/ (wrangles, wrangling, wrangled)

○ **'wrangle with**

To **wrangle with** someone means to argue with them for a long time about something complicated.

wrangle with someone ❑ *After wrangling with unions, the company agreed to avoid compulsory redundancies as part of its plan.* ❑ [+ over] *They are wrangling with their insurance company over a claim.*

wrap /ræp/ (wraps, wrapping, wrapped)

✪ **wrap 'up**

11 When you **wrap** something **up**, you fold piece of paper, cloth, or other material round it so that it is completely covered. **= do up**

wrap something up ❑ *He had bought a teapot and was waiting for them to wrap it up.* ❑ *We wrapped the glasses up in tissue paper.*

wrap up something ❑ *He had wrapped up a parcel of his papers and a few books.* ❑ *My hair is wrapped up in a towel because I've just washed it.*

2 If you **wrap up**, you put warm clothes on; if you **wrap** someone, especially a child, **up**, you put warm clothes on them.
wrap up ❑ Wrap up well. It's cold outside. ❑ Wrap up warm and relax by going to bed or resting in your chair.
wrap someone up or **wrap up someone** ❑ The children came to school wrapped up in coats and scarves.
3 If you **wrap up** a job, agreement, or activity, you complete or end it in a satisfactory way. **= wind up**
wrap something up or **wrap up something** ❑ The whole deal was wrapped up within a few days. ❑ He was wrapping up a five-week tour abroad with a three-day stopover in Paris.
4 If you tell someone to **wrap up**, you are telling them in a rude way to stop talking. [BRITISH, INFORMAL, OLD-FASHIONED] ❑ Oh, wrap up, Colin, we've heard enough of your moaning.

○ **wrap 'up in**
If someone **is wrapped up in** a particular person or thing, they spend nearly all their time thinking about that person or thing and so have little time for anything else.
be wrapped up in something/someone ❑ They are completely wrapped up in the baby. ❑ He was wrapped up in his work, leaving little time for his family.

wreathe /riːð/ (wreathed)
○ **'wreathe in** [LITERARY]
If something **is wreathed in** something, it is surrounded by it or covered in it.
be wreathed in something ❑ The ship was wreathed in smoke. ❑ We arrived at a house wreathed in ivy.

wrest /rest/ (wrests, wresting, wrested)
○ **'wrest from** [LITERARY]
1 To **wrest** something, especially power or control **from** someone else means to take it from them even though it is difficult.
wrest something from someone ❑ Britain is determined to wrest the title from the Australians this year. ❑ He believes the control of the state could be wrested from the Democrats at the next election.
2 If you **wrest** something **from** someone who is holding it or their hand, you take it from them by pulling or twisting it violently.
wrest something from someone/something ❑ He managed to wrest the knife from Kuhn's grasp.

wrestle /'resəl/ (wrestles, wrestling, wrestled)
○ **'wrestle with**
1 If you **wrestle with** a problem or a

difficult situation, you try to deal with it or find a solution to it.
wrestle with something ❑ For decades, mathematicians have wrestled with this problem. ❑ At that time, he was wrestling with his doubts about religion.
2 If someone **wrestles with** something large, heavy, or difficult to control, they have difficulty holding it or controlling it.
wrestle with something ❑ She wondered if she should go and help the man wrestling with the map. ❑ For a few seconds she wrestled with the steering-wheel.

wriggle /'rɪgəl/ (wriggles, wriggling, wriggled)
○ **wriggle 'out of**
If you **wriggle out of** something, you manage to avoid doing it, often in a way that is unfair. **= get out of**
wriggle out of something ❑ I can't manage to wriggle out of the trip. ❑ They use top lawyers and accountants to wriggle out of paying taxes.

wring /rɪŋ/ (wrings, wringing, wrung)
○ **wring 'out**
1 If you **wring out** a wet cloth or a wet piece of clothing, you squeeze the liquid out of it by twisting it strongly.
wring out something or **wring something out** ❑ She was wringing out a bikini in the shower. ❑ Don't wring it out; pat it dry with a towel.
2 If you **wring** something **out** of someone, you force them to give it to you or tell you about it, although they do not want to.
wring something out or **wring out something** ❑ [+ of] I was trying to wring the costs for this work out of the Legal Aid fund. ❑ They were obviously trying to wring out information from him.

write /raɪt/ (writes, writing, wrote, written)
○ **write a'way** (or **write off**)
If you **write away** to a company or organization, you send them a letter, asking them to send you something. **= send off, send away** ❑ You just write away giving your name and address and enclosing three tokens. ❑ [+ to] Why don't you write off to Sussex University and ask for their prospectus?

● **write 'back**
If you **write back** or **write** a letter **back**, you reply to a letter that someone sent you.
write back ❑ [+ to] Christopher wrote to my father, and my father wrote back to him refusing to lend him the money.
write something back ❑ You could write a letter back saying that you don't want to go.

○ **write 'down**

When you **write** something **down**, you record it on a piece of paper using a pen or pencil. = **put down**

write something down ❑ *The magistrate had to write all the evidence down.* ❑ *When they give me the date and the flight number, I always write it down so I'll remember.*

write down something ❑ *Write down any four digit number.*

○ **write 'in**

1 If you **write in**, you send a letter to an organization. ❑ [+ with] *We are offering a half-price holiday to the first person to write in with the correct explanation.*

2 If you **write in** a piece of information on a form or document, you add the information by writing it in the correct place.

write something in or **write in something** ❑ *He arranged the meeting for Tuesday and wrote it in on the kitchen calendar.*

3 If someone **writes in** a new part to a document or a piece of writing, they add it.

write in something or **write something in** ❑ *He had assumed that a special part was being written in for him.* ❑ *The new contract has the same clause written in.*

4 In the United States, if someone who is voting in an election **writes in** a person whose name is not on the list of candidates, they write that person's name on the voting paper and vote for him or her. [AMERICAN]

write in someone or **write someone in** ❑ *I think I'll write in Pat Wilson.* ❑ *I'm going to write him in on my ballot next year.*

○ **write 'into**

If something **is written into** a document or piece of writing, it is included in it.

be written into something ❑ *The new arrangements have been written into the agreement.*

○ **write 'off**

1 → see **write away**

2 If you **write** someone or something **off**, you decide that they are not worth thinking about because they are not important, interesting, useful or likely to be successful.

write off someone/something ❑ *Don't write off philosophy without even trying it.* ❑ [+ as] *It's too soon to write off the whole consultation process as a failure.*

write someone/something off ❑ [+ as] *It's all too easy to write children like these off as lost causes.*

NOTE **Dismiss** is a more formal word for **write off**.

3 If someone **writes off** a vehicle or other machine, they damage it so badly that it is not worth repairing. [BRITISH]

write something off ❑ *She had crashed the car twice, writing it off completely on the second occasion.*

write off something ❑ *The impact must surely have written off the engine.* ● If a vehicle is a **write-off** after an accident, it is so badly damaged that it is not worth repairing it. [BRITISH] ❑ *The Watsons' car was a write-off so they decided to abandon the trip.*

4 If someone **writes off** a debt or an amount of money that has been spent on a project, they accept that they are never going to get the money back.

write something off or **write off something** ❑ *We are encouraging governments to write off most of these countries' debts.* ● A **write-off** is an official declaration that a debt is not going to be repaid. ❑ *The only state assistance was a write-off of 64 million pounds.*

WRITE OFF + *noun*
write off **a debt**
write off **a loan**
write off **a sum**
write off **an investment**
write off **a cost**
❑ *We will have to write off at least part of the debt.* ❑ *They wrote off the cost of development.*

5 If you **write off** a plan or project, you accept that it is not going to be successful and do not continue with it.

write something off or **write off something** ❑ *The costs were much higher than expected. So we decided to write the project off.*

○ **write 'out**

1 When you **write out** something such as a report, a list, or a word, you write it on paper.

write something out ❑ *When you have done your reports, type them or write them out very clearly.*

write out something ❑ *The editor wrote out a list of places I must visit.* ❑ *His name was Mayhew, it was written out in enormous red letters.*

2 When someone **writes out** an official document, they write all the necessary information on it.

write out something ❑ *I went directly to my office to write out the death certificate.* ❑ *You simply need to write out a cheque and give it to the cashier.*

write something out ❑ *He wrote a receipt out and gave it to me.*

NOTE In American English, **write up** means almost the same as **write out**.

3 If a character in a drama series on television or radio **is written out**, the story is changed so that the character is no longer part of the series.

be written out ❑ [+ of] Shannon was quickly written out of the script. ❑ She is written out of the story early on.

'write to

To **write to** part of a computer or a disk or **write** something **to** it means to record information on it.

write to something ❑ The drives can read and write to existing 100Mb disks.

write something to something ❑ The text and images can be written to your hard drive.

write 'up

1 When you **write up** something that has been done or said, you record it on paper, usually using notes that you have made.

write up something ❑ He usually spent his evenings writing up his work. ❑ Anything I was told, I had to write up in my reports.

write something up ❑ I'll write my notes up and send them to you all. ● A **write-up** is an article in a newspaper or magazine, in which someone describes and gives their opinion of something such as a play, a new product, or a place they have visited. ❑ Somebody told me you got a terrific write-up in the 'Guardian'.

2 If you **write** something **up**, you write it on a wall, board or notice.

write something up or **write up something** ❑ Yes, write it up on the board. ❑ His name was written up everywhere I looked.

3 When someone **writes up** an official document, they write all the necessary information on it. = **write out** [AMERICAN]

write up something or **write something up** ❑ She wrote up the receipt, tore it out, and gave it to me.

X /eks/ (**x's, x'ing, x'd**)

○ **x 'out** [INFORMAL]
If you **x out** someone or something, you
stop thinking about them. = **blot out**
x someone/something out *or* **x out**
someone/something ❑ *When I thought
of Morgan, I simply x'd her out.*

Yy

earn /jɜːn/ (**yearns, yearning, yearned**)
'yearn for [FORMAL]

If you **yearn for** something, you want it very much. = **long for**

yearn for something ❑ *He often yearned for life in a country town again.* ❑ *He yearned for academic recognition.*

ell /jel/ (**yells, yelling, yelled**)
yell 'out

If you **yell out** or if you **yell** something **out**, you shout loudly, for example because you are excited, angry, or in pain. = **shout out**
yell out ❑ *She suddenly yelled out and collapsed.*
yell out something *or* **yell something out**
❑ *The older boys yelled out insults.* ❑ *I yelled out, 'Come down!'.*

ield /jiːld/ (**yields, yielding, yielded**)
'yield to

◼ If you **yield to** someone or something, you stop trying to say no to them or stop trying not to let them influence your actions. [FORMAL]
yield to something/someone ❑ *She was yielding to public pressure.* ❑ *I knew that he would yield to temptation.*

◼ If one thing **yields to** another thing, it is replaced by this other thing. [FORMAL]
yield to something ❑ *Her disappointment yielded to anger: Peter should have briefed her properly before they'd come in.* ❑ *After a while, the forest yielded to open land.*

○ **yield 'up**

◼ If something **yields up** something else, it allows that thing to be seen or known about. = **disclose** [FORMAL]
yield up something *or* **yield something up**
❑ *He is working on methods of making the brain yield up its secrets.* ❑ *The engine room didn't yield up any surprises.*

◼ If someone **yields up** something, they let someone else have it, especially when they do not want to.
yield up something *or* **yield something up**
❑ *He yielded up the castle to Llewelyn.*

yoke /jəʊk/ (**yokes, yoking, yoked**)
○ **yoke to'gether**

If someone or something **yokes** things or people **together**, they connect them or think of them in the same way.
yoke someone/something together *or* **yoke together someone/something** ❑ *After the war, two very different cultures were yoked together.*

Zz

zero /ˈzɪərəʊ/ (**zeros/zeroes, zeroing, zeroed**)

○ **zero ˈin on**

1 If something, especially a weapon, **zeros in on** a target, it is directed very accurately towards it.

zero in on something ❏ *The missile then zeros in on the target.* ❏ *They have guns so powerful they could zero in on Omaha Beach.*

2 If you **zero in on** a subject or a particular aspect of something, you concentrate all your attention on it.

zero in on something ❏ *I want to talk generally before I zero in on any one speciality.* ❏ *The headlines zeroed in on the major news stories.*

3 If you **zero in on** something, you notice it immediately.

zero in on something ❏ *Patients often seem to zero in on the therapist's own problems.*

zhoosh /ʒuːʃ/ (**zhooshes, zhooshing, zhooshed**) → see **zhuzh**

zhuzh /ʒuːʒ/ (**zhuzhes, zhuzhing, zhuzhed**)

○ **zhuzh ˈup**

1 If you **zhuzh** something **up**, you make it more interesting or exciting by adding something to it.

zhuzh up something or **zhuzh something up** ❏ *Zhuzh up your cocktails with pomegranate tonic and pink grapefruit.* ❏ *In the evening, zhuzh it up with jewellery and heels.*

2 If you **zhuzh** food **up**, you mix it in a blender.

zhuzh something up or **zhuzh up something** ❏ *Zhuzh up the yoghurt with a little lime juice.*

zip /zɪp/ (**zips, zipping, zipped**)

✪ **zip ˈup**

1 When you **zip up** something such as a piece of clothing, you fasten it using a zip. = **do up**

zip up something ❏ *She zipped up the dress with difficulty.*

zip something up ❏ *He zipped his jeans up.* ❏ *Put your jacket on and zip it up.* ● A **zip-up** piece of clothing is one which fastens with a zip. ❏ *He wore a zip-up jacket.*

2 If you **zip** someone **up**, you fasten the zip on their clothes for them.

zip someone up ❏ *Could you zip me up at the back, please?*

3 If you **zip up** a computer document or a group of documents, you make them take up less space so that they can be sent or stored more easily.

zip up something or **zip something up** ❏ *I'll zip up the files and email them to you.*

zone /zəʊn/ (**zones, zoning, zoned**)

○ **zone ˈout** [INFORMAL]

If you **zone out**, you stop paying attention to what is going on around you. ❏ *He just zoned out for most of the meeting.*

zoom /zuːm/ (**zooms, zooming, zoomed**)

○ **zoom ˈin**

If a photographer or camera **zooms in**, they make an image seem closer. ❏ [+ on] *He zoomed in on the driver's face.*

○ **zoom ˈoff** [INFORMAL]

If you **zoom off**, you go somewhere in a hurry. ❏ [+ to] *In the summer, we all zoom off to Felixstowe on our bikes.* ❏ *He zoomed off to the USA.*

○ **zoom ˈout**

If a photographer or camera **zooms out**, they make an image seem further away. ❏ *Zoom out now, and get the overall effect.*

EXERCISES

Exercises

The exercises on pages 2 to 15 will help you to increase your knowledge of phrasal verbs in some important areas of everyday life.

The exercises on pages 16 to 29 will improve your awareness of phrasal verbs that are often used in certain ways and those that have related nouns and adjectives.

Relationships

The phrasal verbs on these pages relate to the theme of **relationships**, for example, starting to love someone and ending a relationship.

1 Complete the sentences with these particles.

for	on	up	apart	out

1 We were good friends at school but as we grew older, we **drifted** ....

2 When he met Agnes, he **fell** .... her instantly.

3 My colleagues are great – everyone **gets** .... really well together.

4 I didn't know Alex had a girlfriend. How long has he been **going** .... with Kate?

5 Sadly, after 26 years of marriage, they **split** ....

2 Match the definitions with phrasal verbs from exercise 1.

1 to be very attracted to someone and start to love them
    fall for

2 to end a romantic relationship ....

3 to become less close over a period of time until a relationship ends ....

4 to have a romantic or sexual relationship with someone
....

5 to like someone and have a friendly relationship with them
....

3 Replace the underlined words with these phrasal verbs. Use the correct form of the verb.

> look up to   take against   fall out   get together   make up

1 The former partners <u>argued and stopped being friends</u> over money.
....

2 She has always <u>respected and admired</u> her older brother.
....

3 Sara and Anna had an argument and were very angry with each other, but they've <u>become friends again</u> now.
....

4 Carolina <u>disliked him when she met</u> him because he said something unkind about her best friend.
....

5 Peter and Emma <u>started a romantic relationship</u> at Dan's party.
....

Travel and tourism

The phrasal verbs on these pages relate to the theme of **travel and tourism** and include verbs that relate to leaving a place and starting a journey.

1 **Complete the sentences with the correct verb (a, b or c).**

1 Her plane .... **in** at three o'clock this afternoon.
   a) puts   b) gets   c) sets

2 Our plane .... **off** two hours late due to bad weather.
   a) took   b) made   c) went

3 I had already .... **out** of the hotel when the fire started.
   a) booked   b) checked   c) left

4 I really want to .... **away** somewhere nice and hot for a few days.
   a) take   b) put   c) get

5 We'll have to .... **off** just after breakfast to get to the airport on time.
   a) let   b) set   c) put

6 Lisa flew back from Venice on Sunday but I .... **on** for a few days.
   a) stayed   b) remained   c) rested

2 Match the sentence halves.

1 I found a nice hotel on the internet and

2 Adam has just arrived at the hotel, and he's

3 What time

4 If you're staying in Sydney, you

5 A huge group of tourists suddenly

6 I know she gets back on the 24th, but I'm not sure what date

a **checking in**.

b should **look up** a cousin of mine who lives there.

c **descended on** the old church.

d she **flies out**.

e **booked** myself **in**.

f are they **heading off** tomorrow morning?

Food and drink

The phrasal verbs on these pages all relate to the theme of **food and drink**. They refer to actions such as eating only a little, and eating or drinking quickly.

1 <u>Underline</u> the correct verb in each sentence.

1 The food is ready so shall I *dish / spoon / fork* it out?

2 He was told by his doctor to *put / take / cut* down his alcohol intake.

3 He *wolfed / dogged / horsed* the sandwich down in no time.

4 You've nearly finished your drink, Beth. Can I *brim / top / edge* up your glass?

5 She *pulled / cut / picked* at her food, scarcely eating anything.

6 The girls were happily *tucking / taking / tugging* into huge pizzas.

2 Match these phrasal verbs with their definitions.

1 eat in

2 dig in

3 nibble at

4 knock back

5 gobble down

6 eat out

a to eat all your food very quickly

b to drink an alcoholic drink very quickly

c to eat food slowly, taking small bites, because you are not hungry

d to eat in a restaurant

e to help yourself to some food

f to eat at home

EXERCISES

3 Complete the sentences with phrasal verbs from exercise 2. Use the correct form of the verb.

1 Do you .... a lot in London? I bet there are some fabulous restaurants.

2 The food is on the table. Please ...., everyone, before it gets cold!

3 I've never seen anyone .... a glass of wine so quickly!

4 I don't feel like going to a restaurant tonight. Perhaps we could just ....?

5 Sam must have been so hungry – he .... his food in about five minutes!

6 Polly ate very little. She .... a salad and sipped a glass of water.

Speaking

The phrasal verbs on these pages are all about **speaking** and the things that people do when they speak, such as persuading people, discussing subjects, and telling secrets.

1 (Circle) the correct definition of these phrasal verbs.

1 If you **confide in** someone, you:
   a tell them a lie.
   b tell them about a private matter.
   c speak confidently to them on a subject that you know a lot about.

2 If you **put** something **to** someone, you:
   a tell them about an idea and ask them to consider it.
   b speak angrily to them about something bad that they have done.
   c tell them proudly about something good that you have done.

3 If you **sound off**, you:
   a suddenly stop speaking.
   b express your opinions strongly, often without being asked.
   c describe the most important points of something.

4 If you **run** something **by** someone, you:
   a tell them something so quickly that they do not understand you.
   b decide not to tell them about something.
   c tell them about an idea to find out what they think about it.

5 If you **keep on**, you:
   a continue to talk about something in a boring or annoying way.
   b refuse to talk about something.
   c talk to someone in a way that shows you think you are very important.

6 If you **hold back**, you:
   a express strong opinions about a subject.
   b speak a lot about something.
   c say little about a subject, even though you know something about it.

2 Re-order the sentences, **adding punctuation where necessary.**

EXERCISES

1 didn't **hold back** / she certainly / when we discussed the issue

....

2 to get my hair cut / **keeps on** at me / my mum

....

3 for a product / I have an idea / **run by** you / that I'd like to

....

4 she trusted / to **confide in** him / Sam enough

....

5 that she'd like / has an idea / to **put to** me / Isabel says she

....

6 that annoyed him / **sounding off** / Oliver was / about something

....

Feelings

The phrasal verbs on these pages all relate to **feelings**, both positive and negative. They cover ideas such as getting angry, becoming sad and becoming happier again.

1 Complete the sentences with these particles.

| down | up | down | around | over |

1 Antonio's death was such a terrible shock and I don't think she ever **got** .... it.

2 After a while, the cold and the damp **gets** you ....

3 Ever since the relationship ended, she just **mopes** .... the house all day.

4 It really **winds** me .... when Rob says those stupid things!

5 Come on now, Charlie, stop crying and **calm** ....!

2 Now match the phrasal verbs in exercise 1 with the definitions.

1 to make someone feel unhappy ....*get down*..........

2 to make someone angry ....

3 to recover from a difficult experience ....

4 to become less upset or angry ....

5 to wander around a place, feeling unhappy and doing nothing in particular ....

3 Replace the underlined words with these phrasal verbs. Use the correct form of the verb.

> lash out   pull (yourself) together   hang over
> freak out   get to

1 He took some time alone to <u>start to control his feelings and behave calmly</u>.

....

2 The stress was starting to <u>upset and annoy</u> her.

....

3 If you are angry with someone, try not to <u>suddenly criticize them angrily</u>.

....

4 She has her exams next month and I think that's <u>making her worry at the moment</u>.

....

5 When she saw how high up we were, she <u>suddenly became very scared</u>.

....

Socializing and leisure time

The phrasal verbs on these pages all relate to **socializing and leisure time**. They refer to things people do in their spare time, such as spending time with people and relaxing.

1 (Circle) the correct phrasal verb to complete the sentences.

1 We hadn't seen each other for ages, so it was nice to
.... **up** over lunch.
a) pick   b) take   c) catch

2 At the weekends we like to .... **back** and do very little.
a) kick   b) knock   c) chill

3 Shall we .... **out** that new club on Market Square tonight?
a) see   b) check   c) put

4 Like most teenagers, he just wants to .... **out** with his friends at the weekend.
a) hang   b) fall   c) take

5 Sara was at a party, and didn't .... **in** till four o'clock in the morning.
a) arrive   b) get   c) rest

6 Let's .... **in** next Wednesday for lunch, then, shall we?
a) diary   b) pen   c) pencil

EXERCISES

Match the sentence halves.

1 I thought it would be nice to **get together** for

2 On Wednesday I **called round**

3 I'm quite tired so I really don't want to **stay out**

4 I just want to **chill out**

5 We **stayed up** chatting till

6 I **met up** with Guy in

a to her apartment but she wasn't there.

b and do nothing for a couple of days.

c three o'clock in the morning.

d a drink sometime.

e a restaurant in the town centre.

f late tonight.

Money and spending

The phrasal verbs on these pages all relate to **money and spending**. They include verbs that are used for talking about spending a lot, receiving a lot of money, and using money for a particular purpose.

1 <u>Underline</u> the correct verb to make a phrasal verb in each sentence.

1 He owes a lot of money – he's *totalled / majored / maxed* out all his credit cards.

2 She's just *splashed / thrown / jumped* out on a brand-new sports ca

3 Both companies have done really well out of the deal – they are *taking / gathering / raking* in the money.

4 That meal cost far too much. I think they *ripped / tore / hit* us off because we were tourists.

5 The government has had to *take / slice / cut* back on public spendin,

6 Alicia had a lot of money but she *frittered / littered / wittered* it all away on clothes and make-up.

2 Match these phrasal verbs (1–6) with their definitions (a–f).

1 earmark for ....*b*....

2 get together ....

3 fork out ....

4 invest in ....

5 come into ....

6 sponge off ....

a   to pay a lot of money for something

b   to decide that something should be used for a particular purpose

c   to get money when someone dies

d   to succeed in getting all the money that you need in order to pay for something

e   to take advantage of someone by getting money from them and not giving anything back to them

f   to use your money in a way that you hope will increase its value, for example by buying shares or property

Complete the sentences with phrasal verbs from exercise 2. Use the correct form of the verb.

1   We'd like a holiday if we could just .... the money ....

2   I've just .... £300 for a new bike for her.

3   How much does the company .... pensions?

4   My father .... a lot of money .... his company.

5   Camilla .... a lot of money when her parents died.

6   He never worked. He preferred to live at home and .... his parents.

Phrasal verbs with two particles

The phrasal verbs in this section are made up of three words: they consist of a verb and **two particles**.

1 Match the three-word phrasal verbs with the definitions (a–e).

1 I'm really **looking forward to** seeing Peter. .....*c*.....

2 I don't feel well. I think I'm **going down with** a cold. ....

3 I'll tell Jim when I finally **get around to** calling him. ....

4 Liz has **come up with** an interesting idea. ....

5 He hates cleaning his bedroom and he'll do anything to **get out of** it. ....

a to catch or develop an illness, usually one that is not serious

b to think of a plan or idea and suggest it

c to feel excited about something that is going to happen and expect to enjoy it

d to avoid doing something

e to do something after a long delay, often because you are busy

2 (Circle) the correct meaning (a, b or c) of the three-word phrasal verbs in bold.

1 If you **get up to** something, you:
  a finally do something after waiting a long while.
  b do something that someone else does not approve of.
  c achieve something impressive.

2 If you **get away with** something, you:
  a are not criticized or punished for something bad that you have done.
  b fail to make progress with something.
  c are more successful than other people at a particular thing.

3 If you **stick up for** someone or something, you:
  a attack them physically.
  b support or defend them.
  c say bad things about them.

4 If you **go through with** something, you:
  a make a suggestion, usually in a meeting.
  b fail at what you were trying to achieve.
  c do what you must do in order to achieve it, although it is difficult or unpleasant.

5 If you **talk** someone **out of** doing something, you:
  a persuade them to do it.
  b persuade them not to do it.
  c make them miss an appointment by talking to them for too long.

3 Rewrite the sentences replacing the <u>underlined</u> words with these phrasal verbs. Use the correct form of the verb.

| face up to | come in for | talk down to | come out with |
| put up with | make off with |

1 I don't like the way that the teachers <u>speak to me as if they are more important or cleverer than</u> me.

    ....

2 Someone <u>stole and took away</u> all the money we had earned.

    ....

3 She treats Paul so badly – I don't know how he <u>tolerates</u> her.

    ....

4 I think we just have to <u>accept and deal with</u> the fact that this project isn't going to succeed.

    ....

5 The police have <u>received</u> a good deal of criticism over the matter.

    ....

6 Helen <u>says unexpectedly</u> some funny things sometimes.

    ....

4 Match the sentence halves.

1 I'm so tired. I really need to **catch up on**

2 I don't mind what I do – I'm very happy to **fit in with**

3 Last time we tried to do this we failed because we **came up against**

4 Right, that's enough chat. We have to **get down to**

5 Molly is growing so fast, she's **grown out of**

6 Don't let people walk all over you. You've got to **stand up for**

7 I hope this movie **lives up to**

8 Last month Irina's boyfriend **walked out on**

a all her trousers.

b her.

c some sleep.

d your expectations.

e your plans.

f your rights!

g so much opposition.

h business!

Phrasal verbs in the passive

Some phrasal verbs are often used in the **passive**. In this dictionary, phrasal verbs that are used in this way are shown with the passive structure appearing in bold in the definition. It also appears in a passive phrase that comes before a typical example.

If you **are clued up**, you know about something and understand it.
be clued up ❑ [+ on] *I'm not so clued up on the names of today's pop icons.*

All the phrasal verbs on these pages are often used in the passive form.

1 **Match the phrasal verbs (1–8) with their definitions (a–h).**

1 be cut off ......*C*....

2 be done up ....

3 be frowned upon ....

4 be saddled with ....

5 be sent off ....

6 be snowed under ....

7 be struck down ....

8 be washed up ....

a to be disapproved of

b to have to deal with something difficult or unpleasant

c to be separated from other people and places

d to be badly injured or killed

e to be carried by the water of a river or the sea and left on a piece of land

f to be wrapped in a material or paper and made to look attractive

g to have more work to deal with than you can manage

h to be made to leave the field during a sports game as a punishment for seriously breaking the rules

2 Complete the sentences with phrasal verbs from exercise 1. Use the passive form.

1 In my family, the expression of any emotion was ....

2 She's only 17. She doesn't want to be .... all that responsibility.

3 He handed me a box, nicely .... in pink tissue paper.

4 The village was .... by the snow.

5 Her body was .... ten miles along the coast.

6 Aged only 25, he was .... by a stray bullet.

7 He was .... for arguing with the referee.

8 I've been so .... at work, I haven't had time to call her.

Phrasal verbs in the progressive form

Some phrasal verbs are often used in the **progressive** form. In this dictionary, phrasal verbs that are used in this way are shown in a phrase that comes before a typical example.

> **3** If you ask someone what they **are getting at**, you are asking them what they mean, usually because they have expressed an opinion in a way that is not direct.
> = **drive at** [INFORMAL]
> **be getting at** ❑ *What are you getting at? Have I done something wrong here?*

All the phrasal verbs on these pages are often used in the progressive form.

1 **Match the phrasal verbs (1–6) with their definitions (a–f).**

1 be asking for .....*C*.....

2 be crying out for ....

3 be coming on ....

4 be coming up ....

5 be getting on ....

6 be swarming with ....

a to be going to happen soon

b to be old

c to be behaving in a way that makes it more likely that bad things will happen

d to have a lot of people, animals, or insects in an area

e to need something very much

f to be developing or progressing well

2 Complete the sentences with phrasal verbs from exercise 1.
Use the continuous form.

1 Driving a car as old as that is just .... trouble!

2 Michael must be .... now. Is he in his eighties?

3 I've never seen the town centre so full – it was
.... tourists.

4 The project is .... nicely. It should be finished
by the end of next month.

5 The garden is in a terrible state – it's .... some
attention.

6 The holidays are .... Do you have any plans?

Nouns related to phrasal verbs

A lot of phrasal verbs have related nouns. These nouns are written as a single word, sometimes with a hyphen. These pages contain a selection of nouns formed from phrasal verbs.

1 Sentences 1–6 all contain a phrasal verb. Match each sentence (1–6) with a sentence (a–f) that contains the related noun.

1 I must clear out those drawers – they're full of rubbish. ....*f*......

2 Our car broke down on the way to the concert. ....

3 We should all get together and go out for a drink. ....

4 The government promised to clamp down on street crime. ....

5 He threatened to tell her story to a newspaper unless she paid him off. ....

6 She checked in for a flight to Madrid. ....

a Please go to check-in.

b A payoff to a dishonest official got him out of trouble.

c Unfortunately, we had a breakdown on the motorway.

d We welcome the government's clampdown on street crime.

e We're having a little get-together to celebrate Mark's birthday.

f I'm having a big clear-out and getting rid of all my old books.

EXERCISES

2 Match the nouns (1–6) with the definitions (a–f).

1 a breakdown ....*C*....

2 a payoff ....

3 a clear-out ....

4 check-in ....

5 a get-together ....

6 a clampdown ....

a sudden restriction on an activity by a government or other authority

b an occasion when people meet in order to spend time with each other

c an occasion when a car stops working while you are travelling in it

d an occasion when you throw away all the things that you do not want

e the place at an airport where you show your ticket before getting on a plane

f a payment that someone makes to an official so that the official does not cause trouble for them

Adjectives related to phrasal verbs

Some phrasal verbs have related adjectives. These adjectives are usually written as a single word with a hyphen. These pages contain a selection of adjectives formed from phrasal verbs.

1 Match the adjectives (1–6) with their definitions (a–f).

1 drawn-out ....*b*....

2 throw-away ....

3 stand-out ....

4 follow-up ....

5 see-through ....

6 pared-down ....

a much better or more important than other people or things of the same kind

b taking a long time

c intended to be used only once or only for a short time

d done as a continuation or second part of something done previously

e made of thin cloth that you can see through

f smaller or simpler because parts have been removed

EXERCISES

2 Sentences 1–6 all contain a phrasal verb. Match each sentence (1–6) with a sentence (a–f) that contains the related adjective.

1 The article has been pared down from 800 to 500 words. ....*a*.....

2 The window was so dirty that I couldn't see through it. ....

3 It had been a long session and no-one wanted to draw it out any longer. ....

4 The course is followed up by personal visits from a social worker. ....

5 One performer stood out from the others. ....

6 The jacket was so badly ripped I had to throw it away. ....

a This is very much a pared-down version of the first proposal.

b Pete was the stand-out player of the match.

c Meetings were long, drawn-out affairs.

d This shirt is see-through, so I have to wear a T-shirt under it.

e Three months later, I had a follow-up appointment at the hospital.

f I bought one of those throw-away cameras.

Phrasal verbs used with 'it'

Some phrasal verbs are always used with the word *it*. Together, the phrasal verb and *it* have a particular meaning. Phrasal verbs that are used in this way are shown in bold in the definition, like this:

> **3** If you **hold it together**, you manage in a difficult situation without becoming so upset or worried that you cannot continue. [INFORMAL] ❑ *He only just managed to hold it together during their conversation.*

EXERCISES

1 Match the sentences (1–7) with their definitions (a–g).

1 I know I made a mistake, and I regret it. Don't **rub it in**! .....*e*.....

2 If I can **get it together**, I plan to take the kids camping this weekend. ....

3 You're making good progress – **keep it up**! ....

4 They haven't spoken to each other for a week. I hope they **patch it up** soon. ....

5 The evening was a great success – Dan and Lucy **hit it off** immediately. ....

6 You're going to apply for the manager's job? Hey, **go for it**! ....

7 She wasn't really upset – she was just **trying it on** to get your attention. ....

a to like a person and become friends as soon as you meet

b to become friends again after an argument

c to attempt to trick someone

d to succeed in organizing something

e to remind someone about something that makes them feel upset or embarrassed

f to continue to work hard or to achieve high standards

g used to encourage someone to attempt to do something difficult

Match the sentence halves.

1 Anthony and Dad hit it off

2 Look, you know I'm embarrassed about it, so stop

3 If he can get it together,

4 She's doing so well with her studies – I just hope she can

5 You were such good friends before that argument. Why don't you

6 If you want to train for a marathon,

7 Kids often try it on with a new teacher. The teacher should

a he wants to spend a year working abroad.

b go for it!

c try and patch it up?

d be firm with them and show that they're in charge.

e immediately.

f rubbing it in!

g keep it up.

Answer key

Themes

Exercise 1
1 apart
2 for
3 on
4 out
5 up

Exercise 2
1 fall for
2 split up
3 drift apart
4 go out
5 get on

Exercise 3
1 The former partners fell out over money.
2 She has always looked up to her older brother.
3 Sara and Anna had an argument and were very angry with each other, but they've made up now.
4 Carolina took against him because he said something unkind about her best friend.
5 Peter and Emma got together at Dan's party.

Travel and tourism

Exercise 1
1 b
2 a
3 b
4 c
5 b
6 a

Exercise 2
1 e
2 a
3 f
4 b
5 c
6 d

Food and drink

Exercise 1
1 dish
2 cut
3 wolfed
4 top
5 picked
6 tucking

Exercise 2
1 f
2 e
3 c
4 b
5 a
6 d

Exercise 3
1 eat out
2 dig in
3 knock back
4 eat in
5 gobbled down
6 nibbled at

Speaking

Exercise 1
1 b
2 a
3 b
4 c
5 a
6 c

Exercise 2
1 She certainly didn't hold back when we discussed the issue.
2 My mum keeps on at me to get my hair cut.
3 I have an idea for a product that I' like to run by you.
4 She trusted Sam enough to confid in him.
5 Isabel says she has an idea that she'd like to put to me.
6 Oliver was sounding off about something that annoyed him.

Feelings

Exercise 1

	over	4	up
	down	5	down
	around		

Exercise 2

	get down	4	calm down
	wind up	5	mope around
	get over		

Exercise 3

He took some time alone to pull himself together.

The stress was starting to get to her.

If you are angry with someone, try not to lash out.

She has her exams next month and I think that's hanging over her.

When she saw how high up we were, she freaked out.

Socializing and leisure time

Exercise 1

	c	4	a
	a	5	b
	b	6	c

Exercise 2

	d	4	b
	a	5	c
	f	6	e

Money and spending

Exercise 1

	maxed	4	ripped
	splashed	5	cut
	raking	6	frittered

Exercise 2

1	b	4	f
2	d	5	c
3	a	6	e

Exercise 3

1	get [the money] together	4	invested [a lot of money] in
2	forked out	5	came into
3	earmark for	6	sponge off

Phrasal verbs with two particles

Exercise 1

1	c	4	b
2	a	5	d
3	e		

Exercise 2

1	b	4	c
2	a	5	b
3	b		

Exercise 3

1 I don't like the way that the teachers talk down to me.
2 Someone made off with all the money we had earned.
3 She treats Paul so badly – I don't know how he puts up with her.
4 I think we just have to face up to the fact that this project isn't going to succeed.
5 The police have come in for a good deal of criticism over the matter.
6 Helen comes out with some funny things sometimes.

Exercise 4

1	c	5	a
2	e	6	f
3	g	7	d
4	h	8	b

Phrasal verbs in the passive

Exercise 1

1	c	5	h
2	f	6	g
3	a	7	d
4	b	8	e

Exercise 2

1	frowned upon	5	washed up
2	saddled with	6	struck down
3	done up	7	sent off
4	cut off	8	snowed under

Phrasal verbs in the progressive form

Exercise 1

1	c	4	a
2	e	5	b
3	f	6	d

Exercise 2

1	asking for	4	coming on
2	getting on	5	crying out for
3	swarming with	6	coming up

Nouns related to phrasal verbs

Exercise 1

1	f	4	d
2	c	5	b
3	e	6	a

Exercise 2

1	c	4	e
2	f	5	b
3	d	6	a

Adjectives related to phrasal verbs

Exercise 1

1	b	4	d
2	c	5	e
3	a	6	f

Exercise 2

1	a	4	e
2	d	5	b
3	c	6	f

Phrasal verbs used with 'it'

Exercise 1

1	e	5	a
2	d	6	g
3	f	7	c
4	b		

Exercise 2

1	e	5	c
2	f	6	b
3	a	7	d
4	g		

SUPPLEMENTS

New phrasal verbs: where do they come from?

New words are created all the time. Occasionally, we see a completely new word appear, apparently from nowhere; more often, though, new words come about because people adapt existing ones, using them in a slightly different way. We see new phrasal verbs in all sorts of areas, but especially in the worlds of technology, business, media and social media. They are formed in various ways: for example, people might use a new particle with an existing verb, or they might combine a noun with a particle to create a new phrasal verb.

This section categorizes by topic some of the new phrasal verbs we have included in the dictionary and tells you about the trends and patterns we have found by analysing the Collins Corpus. We have also included information about the meaning of the particle. For more on particles and their meanings, see the Particles index on page 491.

Technology

As technology changes, new words continually come into the language. For phrasal verbs, this is more about ways of using technology, rather than about the computers and devices themselves:

1 **grey out** (meaning of particle: *removing*)
When something such as text or a button on a computer screen **is greyed out**, it is grey rather than black. This indicates that you can't click on it because that option is not available. **Grey out** is mostly used in the passive.

> *Unfortunately, I couldn't click on the link because it was greyed out.*

2 **pop up** (meaning of particle: *happening unexpectedly*)
When you use the internet, messages and adverts sometimes **pop up**, appearing on the screen in front of the window you're looking at.

> *A message popped up telling me I had a thousand new notifications.*
>
> *I never buy stuff from the adverts that pop up in my timeline.*

Phrasal verbs are often transformed into nouns or adjectives. We found lots of examples of this with **pop up**.

> *Avoid opening suspicious texts or clicking on pop-up windows.* (adjective)
>
> *Most websites have a pop-up asking you to accept cookies.* (noun)

3 **power down** (meaning of particle: *ending, closing, stopping*)
Instead of talking about switching off a computer or other device, people are increasingly using the phrasal verb **power down**.

I powered down my laptop and put it in its case.

Halfway through the day, the battery suddenly powered down.

People also use the phrasal verb **power off** with the same meaning.

I'm picking up my phone too much. I'll power it off and go and read a book.

Their phones were powering off when they still had 40% of battery life.

4 **search up** (meaning of particle: *discovering*)
This newly popular phrasal verb seems to have come about as a result of people combining the verb **search** with the preposition *up* to mean looking something up. It is used for talking about searching for information on the internet.

I searched up his name but didn't find anything interesting.

Try searching up 'how to unblock a sink' on YouTube.

Other technology-related phrasal verbs that have made their way into English are:

boot up	*I'm just booting up my laptop.*
	That's the sound of my computer booting up.
bring up	*Call centre staff can bring up your entire banking history.*
	[+ on] *When a customer comes in, we can bring their account up on screen and deal with any queries.*
call up	*He was able to call up the information he needed.*
	This data can be called up at the press of a button.
click on	*You can request tickets by clicking on the link below.*
	Click on the icon to open the program.
come up	*We're waiting for your account details to come up.*
default to	*The system will then default to its own settings.*
flash up	*A strange message just flashed up on my screen.*
go down	*The whole system went down just after lunch.*
hook up	*Why don't you hook your laptop up to an external monitor?*
key in/into	*Employees confirm their identity by keying a PIN into a keypad.*
log in/into	*I can't log into my email for some reason.*
log out/off	*Don't forget to log off at the end of your session.*
	[+ of] *If you're having problems, try logging out of the system and logging back in again.*
mouse over	*You can mouse over any word to see its definition.*
page down	*Page down until you get to the section on health.*
page up	*I paged up to the previous section.*
power up	*The computer takes a while to power up.*
print off	*When making any booking online, print off confirmation of your reservation.*

print out	*You need to print out your combined ticket and boarding pass.*
roll over	*When you need more information about a setting, roll over the text to the left.*
scroll down	*If you scroll down a bit, you'll be able to see the picture.*
scroll up	*Scroll up to the top of the document.*
shut down	*His computer overheated and shut down.*
sign out	*Remember to sign out when you've finished.* *[+ of] You have to sign out of your account before you can sign in to another one.*
start up	*Does your computer take long to start up?*
type into	*We type all the details into the database.*
zip up	*I'll zip up the files and email them to you.*

Business

New phrasal verbs are appearing all the time in the world of business. For example, people might thank you for **reaching out to** them, or information might be described as **cascading down** because people pass it on. You might **loop** someone **in** when discussing a subject, or you might talk about a client **pushing back on** an offer you have made.

1 **cascade down** (meaning of particle: *higher to lower position*)
This phrasal verb is used for talking about how information is passed from person to person from higher to lower levels in an organization.

> *We have monthly departmental meetings to ensure information cascades down to everyone.*

Occasionally it is used transitively, that is, with a direct object.

> *We talked about techniques for cascading down objectives through an organization.*

2 **loop in** (meaning of particle: *including*)
If you **loop** someone **in**, you keep them informed on new developments, especially by copying them in on email messages.

> *Sorry, I missed that meeting. Can someone loop me in?*
>
> *Always loop your boss in so they're aware of the issue.*

3 **manage up** (meaning of particle: *movement to a higher position*)
Manage up is used for talking about forming successful relationships with people above you in a company hierarchy; it sometimes suggests that you are determined to get what you want, even if that means annoying people.

> *She has, in her own words, managed up, seizing the opportunity for greater integration with the club.*

We also found some instances of the phrasal verb **manage down**.

> *Does your manager spend more time managing up, or managing down?*

4 **push back** (meaning of particle: *controlling, suppressing*)
This phrasal verb has two main meanings.

(i) The first meaning is 'resist'. People in business often say that a client **is pushing back** when that client is not accepting an offer or plan.

Florida became the first state to push back, declaring that it would not allow drilling in its waters.

Sometimes this phrasal verb is followed by the preposition *against*.

Wolff pushed back hard against Carr's suggestion.

(ii) The second meaning is 'postpone' or 'move to a later date'.

There are fears that the decision could be pushed back again.

Push back can also be used with a direct object relating to a deadline or date, and is sometimes followed by a preposition such as *by* or *from ... to*.

The start time will be pushed back by a further ten minutes.

The companies pushed back the deadline from the 1st to the 17th October.

5 **reach out** (meaning of particle: *supporting and helping*)
This phrasal verb has already been around for a long time, but we have noticed a slight change in use. It is still used in many contexts to talk about offering people help, advice or comfort, but it has also taken on a broader sense – that of making contact with someone, especially by email.

Hi James, thanks for reaching out. Please find attached the information you require.

6 **roll over** (meaning of particle: *changing and transferring*)
Roll over is used in business to talk about taking your budget that was allocated for a particular year and using it in the next year.

Any unused allowance is lost for ever; it cannot be rolled over into the next tax year.

7 **scope out** (meaning of particle: *searching and finding*)
People in business have been increasingly using this phrasal verb to talk about finding out about something before deciding to go ahead with a plan.

The company has scoped out investment opportunities in Cuba.

8 **pop up** (meaning of particle: *happening and creating*)
When a business **pops up**, it appears suddenly in a town or a music festival, and then closes again after a few days or weeks. This is a practice that has become popular over recent years.

A number of exhibitions will be popping up to celebrate the 250th anniversary of the circus.

Phrasal verbs are often recycled as nouns or adjectives. In this case, we find multiple instances of **pop-up** as an adjective and a few examples of **pop-up** as a noun.

She is opening a pop-up art gallery, which will be open for the duration of the book festival. (adjective)

There will be live music from local bands and street food pop-ups. (noun)

Other business-related phrasal verbs that have made their way into English are:

break into	*Breaking into a new market is challenging.*
buy into	*We've been trying to buy into the publishing industry for years.*
buy out	*He sold off the shops to buy out his partner.*
clean up	*People who buy shares now will clean up when the price rises.*
drum up	*Bezos is in charge of drumming up new business.*
farm out	*Many European businesses farmed out clerical jobs to London agencies.*
go in with	*They invited Jarvis to go in with them but he declined.*
go under	*The smaller businesses could well go under during a recession.*
hive off	*The agency hived off its media department.*
move into	*Could the firm diversify, move into new markets?*
open up	*A new supermarket is opening up down the road from here.*
parachute into	*As a consultant, she parachutes into corporations and helps provide strategic thinking.*
	He was parachuted into the company to try to rescue its failing clothing business.
pick up	*Sales have picked up in recent months.*
pitch for	*Most architects have to pitch for jobs.*
plough back	*Profits are ploughed back into the business in order to expand or create more jobs.*
put out of	*Technological developments may put them completely out of business.*
sell off	*We are selling off all our old stock at half price.*
set up	*I set up my company in 2018.*
shut down	*The company would be forced to shut the whole factory down.*
slow down	*Economic growth has slowed down dramatically.*
start up	*Every year many people decide to start up in business.*
	She wanted to start up a little country pub.
take over	*The I.P.C. was taken over by Reed Paper Group.*
turn around	*The project is not going well, but I'm confident I can turn it around.*
wind down	*He had to provide a financial report for a client whose business was winding down.*
	Unfortunately, we had to wind down the Liverpool office.
wind up	*The company was wound up in 1971.*

Media

The media (for example, TV, radio, magazines and websites) are a great source of new language, and that includes phrasal verbs. One trend we've noticed from our corpus analysis is how frequently new phrasal verbs use the particles *down* and *up*, for example, **dial down/up, double down, tee up** and **lock down**.

1 **dial down** (meaning of particle: *decreasing, lowering, reducing*)

Reporters on the news, for example, often talk about people **dialling down** things like *the rhetoric, the pressure, the drama* or *their expectations*. They mean that people are, or should be, reducing the intensity of these things, especially when they are considered to be harmful or out of control.

> *He told her to dial down the rhetoric when she said that she would rather die than leave the Party.*

> *All sides need to dial down the vitriol.*

On the other hand, if people **dial up** their behaviour, they increase its intensity. This phrasal verb is used with words like *commitment, appetite, emotion, glamour* and *charm*.

> *We must all dial up the commitment to investment and wealth creation.*

> *When we want to dial up the glamour, we combine velvet with copper lighting and marble tabletops.*

2 **double down (on)** (meaning of particle: *fastening, fixing*)

This phrasal verb originates in the world of gambling. It has now taken on the meaning of strengthening your commitment to something.

> *At every stage of his career, the president has doubled down on his European convictions.*

> *The company promised to double down on its green energy plans.*

3 **tee up** (meaning of particle: *preparing*)

Tee up is now often used to talk about setting up a situation, especially for someone to benefit from or in order to prepare them for something. It comes from the world of golf, where players prepare themselves for a shot by lining themselves up with the ball, which is balanced on a small peg called a *tee*.

You can talk about something being *teed up* or you might say that a company or an event *tees up* a new development.

> *His political career is now teed up. He can make it or break it.*

> *The company is teeing up ambitious expansion plans.*

You can also say that an event or experience **tees** someone **up for** something they are about to do.

> *He had a preparation race last month, and that should have teed him up for today.*

> *That experience teed him up for his current post.*

4 **lock down** (meaning of particle: *fastening and fixing*)

Reports from places where a serious incident has taken place often say that the area has been **locked down**. This means that the police are not allowing people to leave. This phrasal verb is often used in the passive.

> *Pupils in the latest attack were confined to their classrooms as the school was locked down.*

> *Officers found his home empty and the town was locked down for several hours.*

Phrasal verbs are often transformed into nouns or adjectives. In our analysis, we found multiple instances of the noun **lockdown**. It refers to a situation in which people aren't allowed to leave a place because of a serious incident that has taken place there.

There was a lockdown at our school yesterday because someone was shooting a rifle in the neighbourhood.

A detention centre was in lockdown last night after a detainee was feared to have Ebola.

Another use of the phrasal verb **lock down** is to talk about finalizing an agreement.

Arrangements have been agreed and locked down until the end of 2025.

Lock down can also be used for talking about limiting (using technological methods) the number of people who can see content on a computer network.

Lock down your privacy settings on social media before you travel.

My Facebook account is completely locked down and it's just for friends and family.

Social media

Social media plays a hugely important part in the creation of new words and phrases, and that includes plenty of phrasal verbs. They often start as slang or informal usages before moving into mainstream. Here are some of the new phrasal verbs that we found being used on social media channels.

1 **hate on** (meaning of particle: *attacking*)
Instances of **hate on** in our social media corpus seem to suggest more than just hating someone. They also include the sense of actually expressing that negative feeling, especially publicly, on social media.

When people hate on you, it's because you've got something they want.

Everyone's hating on each other and there isn't any need for it.

2 **hit up**
This phrasal verb is commonly used by social media users to talk about contacting someone through their social media account.

David is really cool and hits me up all the time to ask how I'm doing.

She hit me up on Instagram asking when the album's coming out.

3 **get down with**
There are lots of varied uses of this phrasal verb on social media, but it mostly seems to be about enjoying, being happy with or agreeing with someone or something. It often seems to be used with *can* or *can't*.

This is movie advice I can get down with!

Her first album was the only one I could ever get down with.

If someone such as a politician is trying to **get down with the kids**, they are trying to relate to someone who is younger than them, or from a different social group. This expression is usually used in a critical or humorous way.

However good-looking you are, if you're over 40, don't try to get down with the kids on the clothing front.

4 **jog on** (meaning of particle: *movement*)

Our corpus analysis revealed this emerging phrasal verb as a new way of telling people to 'go away', especially in the context of someone or their opinions not being wanted. If you use this, you are telling the person that they should just move on and stop bothering you. It is slightly rude, but not as offensive as some other ways of expressing the same idea.

> *Rylan asked me for a loan the other day! I told him to jog on.*

> *I hope she tells him to jog on when he tries flirting with her again in the office.*

5 **pimp up** (meaning of particle: *increasing and improving*)

Social media influencers have provided us with a whole new language for talking about how we decorate our houses, our cars and ourselves. The phrasal verb **pimp up** refers to adding extra decoration or features to a car or an item of clothing in order to make it more individual, often in a way that people consider extreme or in bad taste. It's often used in the passive.

> *British automotive fashion house Kahn is famous for pimping up Range Rovers and Rolls Royces.*

> *She wore a pair of jeans pimped up with jet beads.*

We also found evidence of the variant phrasal verb **pimp out**.

> *I got the car pimped out with black rims and tinted windows.*

6 **switch up** (meaning of particle: *disrupting*)

Another phrasal verb, which is new to British English, but which has been used in American English for some time now, is **switch up**. Influencers and fashion gurus advise us to **switch up** our nail colour, our hair styles and our colour schemes. They might also advise us to **switch it up** or **switch things up**, meaning 'have a change of routine'.

> *I love switching up my nail colour as I'm easily bored.*

> *I play a lot of tennis in summer, but I like to switch things up, so I run, do Pilates, jump rope and swim.*

7 **zhuzh up** (meaning of particle: *improving*)

Finally, you might be advised by a vlogger to **zhuzh up** your house or your wardrobe, meaning to make it more interesting, exciting or stylish. This verb is pronounced /ʒʊːʒ ʌp/, and you might see it spelt in other ways, such as 'zhoosh up' or 'zhush up'.

> *A gold belt will instantly zhuzh up a black dress.*

> *Get a stylist to zhuzh up your interiors.*

Particles index

The Particles index is a guide to the way in which particles are used in English phrasal verbs.

Some particles occur in a large number of different phrasal verbs. The commonest particles are **up**, **out**, **off**, **in**, **on**, and **down**. **Up** and **out**, in particular, are extremely common.

This index covers the 13 most common particles used in phrasal verbs. The different meanings of each particle are explained, and typical examples of phrasal verbs that contain that particle, with that sense, are given. These phrasal verbs each have their own definition. At the end of each section, there is a list of phrasal verbs which share the meaning of the particle.

Some of the meanings of the particles are 'literal': that is, they are the main meanings of the particle. These literal meanings usually relate to physical position or direction of movement. We do not give lists of combinations which have these purely literal meanings.

Many phrasal verbs have more than one sense. Often the particle has the same meaning in all these senses, but sometimes it has different meanings. In these cases, we include the phrasal verb in more than one list, but we add a sense number to avoid confusion.

The meanings of English phrasal verbs are not always obvious. Yet the particles index shows very clearly how phrasal verbs fit into the broad patterns. When a new combination occurs, it also fits into these patterns. The particles index will help you to deal with these new combinations, and phrasal verbs as a whole will become a more manageable part of the vocabulary of English.

about ADVERB, PREPOSITION

About is mainly used for talking about movement in many directions or in circles. **About** is used mainly in British English.

1 Movement
About is used for talking about movement in many different directions, often without a purpose.

drift about: If someone **drifts about**, they live their life with no clear plans or purpose, doing one thing and then another.

get about: If you can **get about** after you have been ill or when you are old, you are able to move around without much difficulty.

scatter something about: If you **scatter** things **about**, you throw or drop them over an area in a careless way.

2 Inactivity and aimlessness

About is used for talking about doing things without any particular purpose.

lounge about: If you **lounge about**, you spend time in a relaxed and lazy way, not doing any work.

mope about: If you **mope about**, you spend time in a place doing nothing and feeling unhappy.

faff about	fiddle about	fool about	hang about 2
kick about	lark about	laze about	lie about
lounge about	mess about	mope about	muck about 1
play about	sit about	stand about	wait about

3 Encirclement

About is used for talking about putting one thing around another to form a circle around it.

throw something about something: If you **throw** your arm or arms **about** someone, you embrace them or hug them suddenly.

4 Turning

About is used to talk about turning to face another direction.

face about: If you **face about**, you turn so that you are looking in the opposite direction.

turn about: If something or someone **turns about**, they move so that they are facing in a different direction.

5 Action

About is used to talk about events happening or people doing something.

bring about something: To **bring about** something means to cause it to happen.

come about: When you say how something **comes about**, you explain how it happens.

bring about	come about	go about 1, 2	set about 1

6 Introduction of subject

About is used with verbs to mean 'concerning a particular subject'.

hear about something/someone: If you **hear about** something or someone, you get news or information about them.

know about something: If you **know about** a subject, you have studied it and understand part or all of it.

around ADVERB, PREPOSITION

Around is mainly used for talking about movement in many directions or in circles. In British English, **about** or **round** is sometimes used instead of **around**, but in American English **around** is usually used.

1 Movement

Around is used for talking about movement in many different directions, often without a purpose.

pass something around: If you **pass** things **around**, you give them from one person to another in a group.

push something around: When you **push** something **around**, you move it from one position to another without lifting it away from the surface that it is on.

run around: If you **run around**, you run in different directions within a particular area.

2 Inactivity and aimlessness

Around is used for talking about doing things without any particular purpose.

be kicking around: If you say that something **is kicking around**, you mean that it is there and unwanted or forgotten.

hang around: If you **hang around**, you stay in the same place doing nothing, usually because you are waiting.

mess around: If you **mess around**, you do unimportant or silly things rather than what you should be doing.

fiddle around	fool around	hang around 1, 2	kick around
lie around	lounge around	mess around 1	mope around
muck around	play around 2	sit around	stand around
stick around	wait around		

3 Turning

Around is used to talk about turning to face another direction.

look around: If you **look around**, you turn to look behind you.

turn around: If someone or something **turns around**, they move so that they are facing in the opposite direction.

look around 1	pull around	spin around	swing around
swivel around	turn around 1	wheel around	

4 Surrounding

Around is used to talk about surrounding or forming a circle around someone or something.

gather around: If people **gather around**, they come together in a group, sometimes surrounding a person or thing.

throw something around something: If you **throw** your arm or arms **around** someone, you embrace them or hug them suddenly.

5 Avoidance

Around is used to talk about avoiding a subject or a physical object.

skirt around something: If you **skirt around** a difficult subject, you avoid discussing or dealing with it.

get around 2	go around 6	skirt around	talk around

6 Focusing

Around is used to talk about concentrating on a particular subject or point.

centre around something: If one thing **centres around** another thing, the second thing is the main point or part of the first.

revolve around something: If a discussion **revolves around** a particular subject, it is mainly about that subject.

away ADVERB

Away is used mainly for talking about movement in a direction farther from you, or about removing, storing, or getting rid of things.

1 Movement

Away is used to show movement in a direction farther from you or from the place where you are.

look away: If you **look away**, you turn your eyes away from something or someone.

run away: If you **run away**, you leave a place or person by running.

break away 2	chase away	come away 1, 3	fall away 2
get away 1, 2	go away 1, 2	look away	move away
pull away 1, 2	run away 1	send away 1	stretch away

2 Withdrawing and non-involvement

Away is used to talk about avoiding an activity or stopping taking part in an activity.

break away: When you **break away**, you stop being part of a group, usually because of a disagreement.

keep away: If you **keep away**, you avoid something or someone or do not go near them.

turn away from something: If you **turn away from** something, you stop doing it, wanting it, or being interested in it.

back away 2	break away 1, 4	get away from	grow away from
keep away	move away from	run away 2, 3	scare away 2
shy away from	stay away	stay away from	steal away
steer away from	turn away from	walk away	whisk away

3 Removing, transferring, and separating

Away is used to show that something is taken from the place where it was or the person who had it, or that it separates from the thing it was attached to.

break away: If a part of something **breaks away**, it separates and moves away.

be called away: If you **are called away**, you are asked to stop doing something in order to go somewhere else.

take something away from someone: If you **take** something **away**, you remove it from a place and put it somewhere else.

PARTICLES INDEX

break away 3	call away	come away 2	fall away 1
get away 3	give away 1, 2, 5	move away 2	pull away 3, 4
sign away	snatch away	take away 1–4, 8	take away from 1
tear away 2	throw away 2	tow away	turn away 1, 2

4 Storing, hiding, and isolating

Away is used to talk about things being put in a safe place or stored or hidden somewhere.

clear something away: When you **clear** things **away**, you put the things that you have been using in the place where they belong.

lock something away: If you **lock** something **away**, you put it in a place which you lock.

pack something away: If you **pack** something **away**, you put it in the bag, suitcase or box where it is usually kept.

bury away	clear away	file away	give away 4
hide away	lock away	pack away 1	put away 1, 3, 4
salt away	shut away 1, 2	squirrel away	stash away
store away	stow away	tidy away	tuck away

5 Getting rid of things and destroying things

Away is used to show that something is removed or destroyed.

drive something/someone away: To **drive** a person or animal **away** means to behave in a way that forces them to leave.

strip something away: To **strip away** something means to remove or get rid of it completely, especially so that you can see what something or someone is really like.

throw something away: If you **throw** something **away**, you get rid of it because you no longer want or need it.

blow away 1–3, 5	brush away	cast away 1	do away with
drive away	explain away	frighten away	scare away
scrape away	strip away	sweep away 1, 2	take away 5
tear away 1	throw away 1, 3	wash away	while away
wipe away			

6 Disappearing

Away is used to show that something gradually disappears or is gradually destroyed.

die away: If a sound or emotion **dies away**, it gradually becomes less loud or weaker and finally disappears.

fade away: If something **fades away**, it slowly ends or disappears.

waste away: If a person or a part of their body **wastes away**, they become extremely thin or weak, usually because of illness.

chip away at	die away	drop away	eat away
eat away at	fade away	fall away 3–5	fritter away
go away 3	melt away	slip away 2	tail away
trail away	waste away	wear away	whittle away

7 Continuous activity

Away is used to show that an activity or a process continues throughout a period of time.

plug away: If you **plug away**, you keep working hard at something even though it is difficult or boring.

work away: If you **work away**, you continue working hard for a long time.

bang away	beaver away	chip away at	grind away
hammer away at	jabber away	plod away	plug away
pump away 1	slave away	slog away	steam away 1
talk away	toil away	work away	

back ADVERB

Back is mainly used to show people or things returning to where they were before or to talk about a time in the past.

1 Returning and movement backwards

Back is used to talk about someone or something returning to a place they were in before.

come back: When someone or something **comes back**, they return.

look back: If you **look back**, you turn to see what is behind you.

start back: If you **start back**, you begin returning towards the place where you have come from.

come back 1	double back	get back 1	go back 1
head back	lie back	look back 1	pull back 2
push back 2	put back 2	sink back 1	sit back 1
spring back	stand back 1	start back 1	turn back 1, 3

2 Position

Back is used to show a position that is away from the place where you are or the place you are talking about.

fall back: If you **fall back**, you suddenly move backwards away from someone or something because they have upset or frightened you.

stand back: If you **stand back**, you move away from something or someone.

tie something back: If you **tie** something **back**, you fasten it so that it does not hang straight down.

beat back	call back 4	draw back	drop back
fall back 1, 2	get back 4	hang back	hold back 4
pull back 1, 3, 4	set back 2	stand back 2, 3	stay back
step back 1	tail back	throw back 4	tie back

3 Time

Back is used for talking about things that happened in the past.

carry someone back: If something **carries** you **back**, it reminds you of something that happened in the past.

think back: If you **think back**, you make an effort to remember things that happened to you in the past.

bring back	carry back	cast back	come back 6
date back	flash back	go back 2–4	hark back to
look back 2	take back 8, 9	think back	throw back 7

4 Returning or retrieving something

Back is used to talk about returning something to a place where it was before or a person who had it before.

give something back: If you **give** something **back**, you return it to the person who gave it to you or who it belongs to.

pay something back: If you **pay** money **back** to someone, you give them money that you borrowed from them.

send something back: If you **send** something **back**, you return it to the place that it came from because you do not want it.

claw back	die back	get back 2, 3	give back
go back 7, 8	hand back	pay back 1	plough back
put back 1, 3, 6	put back into	send back	take back 1–5, 7
throw back 1–3, 6	win back	wind back	

5 Repeating or returning to an action

Back is used to talk about returning to or repeating an action or about doing something to someone that they have just done to you.

answer back: If someone, especially a child, **answers back**, they speak rudely to you when you have spoken to them.

get back into something: If you **get back into** an activity that you were doing before, you start doing it or being involved in it again.

answer back	call back 1–3	fall back on	fight back 1
get back at	get back into	go back 5, 6	go back over
go back to	hit back	pay back 2	read back
report back	talk back	throw back 8, 9	write back

6 Controlling or suppressing

Back is used to talk about controlling something, especially emotions, or preventing something from developing.

choke back something: If you **choke back** something you are saying, you stop yourself from saying it.

fight back something: If you **fight back** a feeling or emotion, you try very hard not to let it affect you.

set something back: If something **sets** someone or something **back**, it causes a delay.

bite back 1	choke back	cut back	cut back on
fight back 2	force back	hold back	keep back 2–8
knock back 4	push back 1	put back 4, 5	rein back
roll back	scale back	set back 1	

7 Drinking

Back is used to talk about drinking something quickly.
knock something back: If you **knock back** an alcoholic drink, you drink it quickly.

| knock back 1 | put back 7 | throw back 5 | toss back |

down ADVERB, PREPOSITION

Down is used mainly to talk about moving from a higher to a lower position or for talking about decreasing the level or amount of something.

1 Higher to lower position

Down is used to show movement from a higher position or place to a lower one.
come down: When someone or something **comes down**, they move from a higher position to a lower one.
pour down: When it **pours down**, it rains very heavily.
talk down: To **talk down** a pilot means to give them instructions over the radio so that they can land an aircraft.

cast down 3	come down 1–3, 10, 13	get down 1–4	go down 1, 3, 6
move down 1, 2	pour down	pull down 1	rain down
reach down	roll down	run down 1, 2	set down 4, 5
splash down	take down 1–4	talk down 2	touch down

2 Movement: people

Down is used to talk about movement from an upright or standing position to a lying or sitting position, or a position with the knees bent.
kneel down: When you **kneel down**, you sit with your legs bent underneath you and your weight on your knees.
lie down: When you **lie down**, you move into a horizontal position, usually in order to rest or sleep.
sit down: If you **sit down**, you lower your body until you are sitting on something.

bend down	bow down 1	crouch down	get down 5
go down 23	hunker down 1	keep down 3	kneel down
lie down	plonk down 2	put down 5, 11	reach down
sink down	sit down 1, 2	throw down 2	

PARTICLES INDEX

③ Movement: things

Down is used to talk about putting things on a surface.

lay something down: If you **lay** something **down**, you put it down on a surface.

set something down: If you **set** something **down**, you put it on a surface or on the ground.

bang down	lay down 1, 2	plonk down 1	plop down
plump down 2	put down 1, 2	set down 1	slam down
slap down 1	stick down 1	throw down 1	

④ Decreasing, lowering, and reducing

Down is used to talk about a decrease in the size, amount, degree or standard of something.

break something down: To **break down** information or a task means to separate it into smaller parts in order to understand it or deal with it more easily.

cool down: If something or someone **cools down**, they become cooler until they reach a satisfactory or comfortable temperature.

go down: If the cost, level or amount of something **goes down**, it becomes lower or less than it was before.

turn down: If the rate or level of something **turns down**, it decreases.

beat down 3	break down 3, 4	bring down 2	come down 8, 9, 15
cool down	count down	cut down 1, 2	cut down on
drive down	go down 7–9, 11	melt down	move down 4, 5
narrow down	play down	quieten down	slow down
turn down 2, 3	water down		

⑤ Fastening and fixing

Down is used to talk about fastening or fixing something to the ground or to a surface.

nail something down: If someone has **nailed** something **down**, it is fastened firmly in place with nails.

weight something down: If you **weight** something **down**, you add something heavy to it to prevent it moving easily.

batten down	bed down 3	lash down 1	lay down 6, 7
nail down 1–3	pin down 1, 2	put down 3	screw down
stamp down	stick down 2	tie down 1, 2	weight down

⑥ Collapsing, attacking, and destroying

Down is used to talk about things being damaged or destroyed, often in a way that makes them fall to the ground.

blow down: If something **blows down**, the wind makes it fall to the ground.

gun someone down: To **gun** someone **down** means to shoot them when they are not in a position to defend themselves.

tear down: If you **tear down** something such as a building or a tree, you destroy it completely.

blow down	burn down	chop down	cut down 3
fall down 1–3	go down 2, 15, 16	gun down	kick down
knock down 1–3	pull down 2	run down 7, 11	shoot down 1
slip down 1	tear down	tumble down	

7 Defeating and suppressing

Down is used to talk about defeating or controlling people.

back down: If you **back down**, you start to accept someone else's opinion or demand, even though you do not want to.

crack down: To **crack down** is to start to be much stricter with people who are not obeying rules or laws, punishing them more severely.

keep someone/something down: If someone or something **keeps** a person, group or country **down**, they stop them from being powerful or successful.

shout someone down: If people **shout** someone **down**, they prevent the person from being heard by shouting.

back down	break down 5	bring down 1, 5	clamp down
climb down	come down on	crack down	drag down
face down	grind down 1	keep down 1, 5	put down 9, 10
shoot down 2	shout down	slap down 2	wear down 1

8 Completing or failing

Down is used to talk about things ending or being completed, and often of failing.

break down: When a machine or a vehicle **breaks down**, it stops working.

break down 1, 2	chase down	close down	fall down 4, 5
hunt down	lay down 8, 10, 11	load down	run down 8
send down	settle down 4	shut down 1, 2	stand down
step down	track down	wave down 1	wind down 4

9 Eating and drinking

Down is used to talk about food and drink going into your stomach and staying there when you eat or drink something.

bolt down something: If you **bolt down** food, you eat it very quickly.

keep something down: If you **keep** food or drink **down**, you are able to keep it in your stomach and not vomit after you have eaten or drunk something.

bolt down	chow down	drink down	get down 7
go down 3	gobble down	gulp down	hold down 6
keep down 6	slip down 3	stay down 2	swallow down
swill down	throw down 4	toss down	wash down 1
wolf down			

10 Writing and recording

Down is used to talk about writing and recording things.

note down something: If you **note down** something, you write it down so you can remember it later.

take down something: If you **take down** information that someone tells you, you write it down.

copy down	get down 8	go down 20	jot down
mark down 1	mark down as	note down	put down 7, 8, 12, 13
put down as	scribble down	set down 2, 3	set down as
stick down 3	take down 7	write down	

11 Cleaning and flattening

Down is used to talk about cleaning or brushing things, or making surfaces smooth.

smooth something down: If you **smooth** something **down**, you press it with your hands to make it flat.

wash something down: If you **wash down** an object or surface, you wash all of it.

brush down	clean down	damp down 4	dampen down 3
dust down 1	hose down	rub down	sand down
slick down	smooth down	sponge down	swab down
wash down 2	wear down 2	wipe down	

12 Work and activities

Down is used to talk about starting to work at something.

buckle down: If you **buckle down**, you start working seriously at something.

buckle down	get down to	knuckle down	settle down 1
sit down 3			

in ADVERB, PREPOSITION

In is mainly used for talking about movement from the outside to the inside.

1 Movement, entering, and arriving

In is used for talking about entering a place or arriving there.

book in: When you **book in**, you announce that you have arrived at a hotel and sign your name in a book.

breeze in: If someone **breezes in**, they enter a place in a happy and relaxed way.

let someone in: If you **let** someone **in**, you allow them to come into a place, usually by opening a door.

pull in: When a train **pulls in**, it arrives at a station and stops.

PARTICLES INDEX

ask in	book in	breeze in	check in
come in 1–5,7,11,16,19	draw in 1,2	drop in	flood in
get in 1–3,8	go in 1–4,6,7	pop in	pour in
pull in 1,2	show in	sign in	squeeze in
swear in			

2 Inserting, penetrating, and absorbing

In is used to talk about putting one thing into another or about getting into something, often going through a barrier of some kind.

come in: When light, sound, air, or rain **comes in**, it gets through a barrier or hole and reaches the place where you are.

hammer something in: If you **hammer** something **in**, you force it into place using a hammer.

come in 6	draw in 3	go in 5,8	hammer in
let in 3	plough in	plug in	pump in
put in 1–4,6	ram in	set in	slip in 1
stick in 1–5	take in 5,12,14	throw in 1–3	

3 Collapsing and damaging, surrendering and ending

In is used to talk about things being damaged or destroyed, often so that they fall inwards, or to talk about being defeated or stopping doing something.

cave in: When a roof, ceiling or other structure **caves in**, it collapses inwards.

give in: If you **give in**, you finally agree to do what someone wants you to do after they have used force or threats.

kick something in: If you **kick in** something such as a door or window, you kick it violently with your foot so that it breaks into pieces.

bash in	break in 1	cave in	chuck in
do in 1,2	fall in 1	give in 1,2	kick in 1
pack in 3,4,6,7	smash in		

4 Mixing and including

In is used to talk about two things being combined or included or belonging together.

fit in with someone/something: If someone or something **fits in with** a person or a situation, they are suitable and convenient for it or make themselves suitable and convenient for it.

squeeze something in: If you **squeeze** something **in**, you manage to find time to do it.

stir something in: If you **stir** a substance **in**, you mix it with another substance, using a tool such as a spoon.

add in	build in	chip in 1	dig in 1
fit in	fit in with	include in	merge in
mix in 1	rub in 1	sketch in 1	squeeze in 3
stir in	tie in with	trade in	work in 1–3

PARTICLES INDEX

5 Gathering, collecting, and fetching

In is used to talk about gathering or collecting things.

get something in: If you **get** something **in**, you bring something inside that is outside, to protect it from the weather.

hand something in: If you **hand in** a piece of work, you give it to someone so that they can read it or deal with it.

rake in something: If someone **rakes in** money, they are earning a lot of money fairly easily.

bring in 2	buy in	call in 4	come in 8, 18
gather in	get in 5, 6	give in 3	hand in
lay in	pull in 3–5	put in 9	rake in
run in 2	send in 1	take in 4, 9, 10	turn in 3–6

6 Filling

In is used to talk about filling a shape or a hole with something.

fill something in: If you **fill in** a hole, you put a substance into it so that the surface becomes level.

block in 2	brick in	colour in	fill in 1–3
ink in 1	pencil in	shade in	

7 Remaining somewhere

In is used to talk about remaining in a particular place or remaining at home.

eat in: When you **eat in**, you have a meal at home rather than going out to a restaurant.

keep someone in: If a parent or teacher **keeps** children **in**, they make them stay indoors or they make them stay late at school, usually as a punishment.

dig in 2	eat in	keep in 1, 3	lie in 1
live in 1	sleep in	stay in	stop in 2
take in 2	wait in		

8 Restricting and preventing

In is used to talk about keeping someone or something in a place and not allowing them to leave.

be hemmed in: If a place **is hemmed in** by things, it has them on all sides.

block someone in: If you **block** someone **in**, you park your car so close to their car that they cannot drive away.

lock someone in: If you **lock** someone **in**, you put them somewhere and lock the door so that they cannot get out.

block in 1	box in	close in 1, 2	crowd in on
fence in	hedge in	hem in	hold in
keep in 1, 3	lock in	rein in	seal in
shut in	snow in	strap in	wall in

9   Being involved and active

In is used to talk about being or becoming involved in an activity or having a relationship with someone.

count someone in: If you **count** someone **in**, you include them in a particular activity.

keep in with someone: If you **keep in with** someone, you stay friendly with them because you want something from them.

muscle in: If you **muscle in**, you force your way into a situation or an activity where you are not welcome.

settle in: If you **settle in**, you become used to a new place or new job.

barge in	break in on	butt in	count in
dabble in	engage in	fall in with	get in on
go in for	join in	keep in with	muscle in
push in	settle in	sit in	step in

10   Beginning

In is used to show that an activity begins.

lead in: If you **lead in** with a particular subject or statement, you start speaking or writing by mentioning it.

set in: If something unpleasant **sets in**, it begins and seems likely to continue.

bring in 1	come in 9, 10, 14, 17, 20	creep in	dig in 4
fade in	kick in 2	lead in	phase in
set in	tuck in 3	usher in	

11   Focusing: actions, attitudes, and qualities

In is used in verbs that are used before nouns to do with actions and opinions.

believe in something: If you **believe in** God or things such as fairies or miracles, you are sure that they really exist or happen.

revel in something: If you **revel in** a situation or experience, you enjoy it very much.

believe in 1–3	confide in	couch in	delight in
glory in	indulge in	luxuriate in	repose in
reside in	result in	revel in	see in 1
wallow in			

into PREPOSITION

Into is mainly used to express the idea of entering something.

1   Movement, entering, and arrival

Into is used to express the idea of entering a place.

crowd into something: If a group of people or things **crowd into** a place, they are all pushed or squeezed into a small place.

see someone into something: If you **see** someone **into** a place, you go with them and make sure that they go in there.

2 Inserting, penetrating, and placing

Into is used to talk about putting one thing inside another or about getting inside something.

bore into something: If someone's eyes **bore into** you, they are staring hard at you.

plug something into something: If you **plug** a piece of electrical equipment **into** something, you connect it to the thing, for example by using a plug.

strap someone into something: If you **strap** someone **into** a seat, you fasten them firmly there, using a belt or strap.

bore into	build into 1	dig into	dip into
dive into 1	drill into	drum into	go into 11
let into 4	plug into	pour into 2	put into
ram into 3	sink into 3	strap into	throw into

3 Mixing and inclusion

Into is used to talk about two things being combined or included.

blend into something: If something **blends into** something in the background, it looks or sounds so similar to it that it is difficult to see or hear it separately.

melt into something: If one thing **melts into** another, it is hard to see where one thing ends and the other starts.

blend into	bring into 2	dissolve into	fall into 1
fit into	fold into	marry into	melt into 1, 2
merge into	mix into	phase into	put into
shade into	sink into 5	stir into	work into

4 Changing

Into is used to describe the process of changing from one form or situation to another.

burst into something: If something **bursts into** flames, it suddenly starts to burn.

turn into something: If someone or something **turns into** another thing, they change and become that other thing.

break into 2	burst into 1–3	fall into 2	fly into
get into 4	go into 7	lapse into	make into
melt into 3	put into 7	roll into 1	sink into 4
slip into 5	throw into 4	turn into	

5 Involvement and activities

Into is used to express the idea of starting to be involved in an activity or finding information about something.

barge into something: If you **barge into** a conversation, you rudely interrupt the person who is speaking.

delve into something: If you **delve into** something, you try in a determined way to discover more information about it.

enter into something: If you **enter into** an agreement or arrangement, you formally agree to it.

PARTICLES INDEX

break into 3	delve into	dive into 2	enter into 1, 2
fling into	get into 3	go into 6	head into 2
inquire into	look into	move into 3	plunge into 2
rush into	take into 5	throw into 5	walk into 1

6 Persuasion and forcing

Into is used to talk about persuading or forcing people to do things.

force someone into something: If you **force** someone **into** doing something, you make them do it, although they do not want to.

trick someone into something: If you **trick** someone **into** something, you make them do something by not telling them the truth.

bluff into	coax into	drag into	draw into
force into	frighten into	goad into	press into
pull into 2	push into 1	shame into	shock into
starve into	sucker into	talk into	trap into
trick into			

7 Contact, colliding, meeting, and attacking

Into is used to talk about hitting against something or fighting or attacking someone or something.

barge into someone/something: If you **barge into** someone or something, you bump against them rather roughly while you are walking.

lay into someone: If someone **lays into** another person, they start to hit or kick them violently.

bang into	barge into 3	bump into	go into 14
lam into	lash into	lay into	pitch into 2
plough into 1	ram into	rip into	run into 3, 5
tear into			

8 Consumption and using

Into is used to talk about using or consuming part of something.

dip into something: If you **dip into** a sum of money or your pocket, you spend some money which you had intended to keep.

eat into something: If something **eats into** resources such as money, land, or time, it gradually uses more of them than was expected or intended.

| break into 5 | cut into | dip into | eat into |
| lay into 3 | tuck into 2 | | |

off ADVERB, PREPOSITION

Off is mainly used for talking about movement away from something or separating from something.

1 Departure

Off is used to talk about leaving a place.
dash off: If you **dash off**, you leave somewhere quickly.
set off: When you **set off**, you start a journey.
wave someone off: If you **wave** someone **off**, you wave to them as they leave somewhere.

bundle off	buzz off	cart off	clear off
dash off 1	give off 1	go off with	head off 1
let off 4–7	lift off	make off	move off
pack off	pop off 1, 2	run off 1–4, 6	send off
set off 1	start off 1	wave off	write off 1

2 Removing and disposing

Off is used to talk about removing or getting rid of something.
cross something off: If you **cross off** one or more words on a list, you draw a line through them to show that they are no longer on the list.
marry someone off: If you **marry** someone **off**, you find a suitable person for them to marry.
peel something off something: If you **peel** the outer layer **off** something, you remove it.
take something off: If you **take** something **off**, you remove it or separate it from the place where it was.

burn off	cast off 1–3	chop off	come off 2
cross off	lop off 1	marry off	peel off 1–3
rub off 1	sell off	slip off 2, 3	strip off
take off 1–3, 8	tear off 1, 2	throw off 1, 2	wash off

3 Obstructing and separating

Off is used to talk about using a barrier to separate one part of something from another part.
be screened off: If a part of a room **is screened off**, it is separated from the rest of the room by something such as a screen or curtain.
block off something: When you **block off** a road or the entrance to a building, you put something across it and cover it completely so that nothing can pass through it.

block off	close off	cordon off	curtain off
cut off 2	divide off	fence off	head off 2
mark off 1	partition off	rope off	rule off
screen off	seal off	separate off	shut off 4

◢ Rejecting

Off is used to talk about not wanting to have or be with something or someone or not wanting to do something.

brush someone off: If you **brush** someone **off**, you avoid them or avoid speaking to them, because you want to end your relationship with them.

put something off: If you **put off** something, you delay it or arrange to do it at a later time than planned.

shrug something off: If you **shrug** something **off**, you ignore it or treat it as if it is not really important or serious.

brush off	fend off 2	keep off 3, 4	laugh off
lay off 1, 3	pass off 2	put off 1	shake off
shrug off	shuffle off	shut off 5	swear off
wipe off 3	write off 2, 3		

◢ Preventing and protecting

Off is used to talk about making someone or something unpleasant go away or preventing something from happening.

drive off something/someone: If you **drive off** someone or something that is attacking or threatening you, you force them to go away.

stave something off: If you **stave off** something bad, you manage to avoid it happening.

beat off	buy off	chase off	drive off 1
fend off 1	fight off	get off 9	head off 3
hold off 1, 2	keep off 1, 2	pay off 2	put off 3, 4
scare off	stand off 2	stave off	throw off 4
ward off	warn off		

◢ Beginning

Off is used to talk about something starting, or causing something to start.

kick something off: When you **kick off** an event or discussion, you start it.

trigger off: If something **triggers off** an event or reaction, it causes it to happen.

cop off with	get off with	kick off 2, 3	lead off 2, 3
set off 2, 5	spark off	start off 2–4	tee off 1
touch off	trigger off		

◢ Stopping and cancelling

Off is used to talk about stopping something or something ending.

call something off: If you **call off** an event or an arrangement that has been planned, you cancel it.

knock off: When you **knock off**, you finish work at the end of the day or before a break.

switch something off: If you **switch** something **off**, you stop it working by pressing a switch.

break off 2–4	call off	come off 5, 7	cut off 3–5
knock off 3, 12	lay off 2	leave off 3, 4	let off 1
log off	rain off	ring off	shut off 1–3
sign off 2-5	switch off	trail off	turn off 1, 3, 4

8 Decreasing

Off is used to show that something is getting less or being reduced.

cool off: If someone or something that is too hot **cools off**, they become cooler.

tail off: If someone's voice **tails off**, it gradually becomes quieter and then silent.

wear off: When a feeling or the effect of something **wears off**, it disappears slowly.

cool off	die off	drop off 3	dry off
ease off	fall off 2	knock off 2	level off 1, 3
slacken off	sleep off	tail off	take off 10
taper off	walk off 2	wear off	work off 1, 2

9 Finishing and completing

Off is used to talk about finishing or completing something.

carry something off: If you **carry off** something that is difficult to do, you succeed in doing it.

pay something off: If you **pay off** a debt or bill, you pay all the money that you owe.

polish something off: If you **polish off** food or a drink, you eat or drink all of it.

bring off	carry off	come off 3, 4	dash off 2
finish off 1–3	go off 6	knock off 6	pass off 1
pay off 1	polish off	print off	rattle off
reel off	round off 1	sign off 1	toss off 2
work off 3	write off 4		

10 Consuming

Off is used to talk about people or machines using something to make them work or to keep them alive.

feed off something: If an idea, feeling, system or process **feeds off** something, it continues to exist or grow because of that thing, often in a way that is unfair.

work off something: If a piece of equipment **works off** a particular source of power, this is the source of power that it uses to make it function.

dine off	feed off	live off 2	run off 8
sponge off	work off 4		

11 Falling asleep

Off is used to talk about falling asleep.

drop off: If you **drop off**, you start to sleep.

doze off	drift off	drop off 2	get off 16
go off 11	nod off		

🔢 Displaying

Off is used to talk about displaying things or making them look attractive.

set something off: If one thing **sets** another thing **off**, it makes the other thing look more attractive or more noticeable.

show something off: If something **shows off** another thing, it emphasizes its good qualities.

finish off 4	mouth off	set off 6	show off
sound off			

🔢 Deceiving

Off is used with phrasal verbs to do with deceiving or tricking someone.

palm something off: If someone **palms** something **off**, they give or sell it to someone in order to get rid of it.

rip someone off: If someone **rips** you **off**, they cheat you by charging you too much money for something.

fob off	goof off	mug off	palm off
pass off as	play off against	rip off	skive off
throw off 4			

🔢 Exploding and firing

Off is used to talk about things such as guns and bombs firing or exploding.

go off: If a gun **goes off**, it is fired and if a bomb **goes off**, it explodes.

fire off 1	go off 2	let off 3	loose off
set off 4			

on ADVERB, PREPOSITION

On is mainly used to show a position where one thing is above another, touching it or supported by it. **Upon** is sometimes used instead of **on**, and is more formal.

🔢 Movement and position

On is used to talk about movement, for instance into a vehicle or building or onto a surface or object.

call on someone: If you **call on** someone, you visit them for a short time.

get on something: If you **get on** a bus, train or plane, you get into the bus, train or plane.

stamp on something: If you **stamp on** something, you put your foot down on it very hard in order to damage it or hurt it.

call on 1	come on 2, 3	come on to 1	descend on 1
fall on 4	get on 1, 2	go on 19	look on
pile on 1	put on 1	put on to 2	sit on 2
stamp on 1	take on 5	throw on 1	trample on 1
wait on	walk on		

2 Holding, attaching, and adding

On is used to talk about holding, attaching or adding things.

hold on: If you **hold on**, you hold something firmly, especially to stop yourself from falling.
put something on something: If you **put** one thing **on** another, you attach or fix it to the other thing.
sew something on: If you **sew** something **on**, you attach it to something else by sewing it.
strap something on: If you **strap** something **on**, you fasten it in position, using a belt or strap.

add on	hang on 1, 3	have on 1	help on with
hold on 1, 3	hold on to 1–4	latch on to 1, 3	pile on 2
pull on 1, 2	put on 2–4, 7, 14, 21, 23	put on to 1	sew on
slip on	stick on 1, 2	strap on	tack on

3 Continuing

On is used to talk about an activity, journey or movement continuing.

carry on: If you **carry on**, you continue doing an activity.
drag on: If an event or process **drags on**, it takes longer than seems necessary.
ramble on: If someone **rambles on**, they talk or write for a long time in a confused way.

bang on	carry on 1–3	drag on	get on 5, 9
go on 1–11	hold on 2	keep on	linger on
press on	rabbit on	ramble on	roll on 1
run on 1–4	soldier on	struggle on	wear on

4 Progressing and encouraging

On is used to talk about things progressing and developing or people encouraging progress.

bring on someone: To **bring on** someone means to improve their ability to do something.
egg someone on: If you **egg** someone **on**, you encourage them to do something foolish, dangerous or wrong.
urge someone on: If something or someone **urges** someone **on**, they encourage them to do something.

bring on 2	cheer on	come on 1, 10	crack on
draw on 1	egg on	get on 7, 8, 13	get on for
go on 12, 21	goad on	lead on	lead on to 1
move on 3, 5	spur on	urge on 1	

5 Beginning and operating

On is used to talk about things starting or happening or operating machines or equipment.

bring on something: Something that **brings on** an illness or pain causes it to occur.
embark on something: If you **embark on** an activity, you start doing it.
switch something on: If you **switch** something **on**, you start it working by pressing a switch.

bring on 1	catch on	come on 4, 6–10	embark on
enter on	get on 6	get on to 1, 4	go on 16
have on 2	jam on	latch on to 2	log on
put on 8–11	set on 2	start on 1, 2	switch on 1–3
turn on 1–3			

6 Focusing: effects, actions, and feelings

On is used to talk about actions or situations that affect someone or something or someone's feelings about something or someone.

cheat on someone: If you **cheat on** your sexual partner, you secretly have a sexual experience or relationship with someone else.

prevail on someone: If you **prevail on** someone to do something, you persuade them to do something that they did not want to do.

weigh on someone/something: If a problem **weighs on** you or your conscience, soul, etc., it makes you worry.

cheat on	dote on	foist on	force on
frown on	inform on	lavish on	lean on 1
prevail on	rebound on	skimp on	spring on 1
spy on	weigh on	wish on	

7 Attacking

On is used to talk about attacking or criticizing someone.

round on someone: If you **round on** someone, you suddenly criticize or attack them.

turn on: If a person or animal **turns on** you, they suddenly attack you or show anger towards you.

beat on	dump on	fall on 5	jump on
pick on 1	pounce on 1, 2	prey on	round on
set on	spring on 2	start on 3	trample on 2
turn on 4			

8 Closeness, interference, and connections

On is used to talk about things that are close to something or interfere with something.

border on something: A country that **borders on** another country is next to that country and shares a border with it.

intrude on something: If someone **intrudes on** a situation that involves another person, they upset the other person by being present or becoming involved.

bear on	border on	close on	encroach on
fasten on to	impinge on	impose on	impress on 2
infringe on	intrude on	prey on 3	verge on

9 Discovering

On is used to talk about discovering or finding things or facts, information, etc.

hit on something: If you **hit on** an idea, you think of it.

stumble on something/someone: If you **stumble on** something or someone, you discover or meet them unexpectedly.

chance on	come on 6	happen on	hit on 1
light on 1	strike on	stumble on	

10 Subjects and topics

On is used for talking about talking or thinking about subjects.

dwell on something: If you **dwell on** something unpleasant, you think or speak about it a lot.

pronounce on something: If you **pronounce on** something, you give an opinion or judgment about it.

remark on something: If you **remark on** something, you say or write something that shows you have noticed it.

brood on	centre on	chew on	decide on
dwell on	elaborate on	enlarge on	expand on
fix on	insist on	pronounce on	reflect on 1
remark on	settle on 1	sleep on	touch on

11 Depending and expecting

On is used to talk about depending on something or expecting something to happen or exist.

count on something: If you **count on** something, you expect it to happen and include it in your plans.

hinge on something: If one thing **hinges on** another, it depends completely on the other thing.

bank on	bargain on	bet on 2	call on 2
count on	depend on	figure on	gamble on
hinge on 1	lean on 2	pin on 2	plan on
reckon on	rely on	turn on 5	work on 1

12 Using

On is used to talk about things that use something or have something as their basis.

base something on something: If you **base** one thing **on** another thing, it takes its general form, subject or ideas from that other thing.

draw on something: If you **draw on** something, you make use of it in order to do something.

act on	base on	build on	draw on
model on	pattern on	trade on	

13 Consuming

On is used to talk about people eating something or machines using something to make them work.

live on something: If you **live on** something, it is the only kind of food you eat.
run on something: If a machine or piece of equipment **runs on** a particular type of power, it uses it in order to work.

batten on	dine on	feed on	live on 2
run on 5	sponge on		

out ADVERB

Out is mainly used for talking about movement from the inside of a closed space or container to the outside of it.

1 Leaving

Out is used to talk about movement from the inside of a closed space or container to the outside of it or to talk about starting a journey.

break out: If someone **breaks out**, they escape from a place where they are a prisoner.
come out: When someone **comes out** of their house or room, or a place where they were hidden, they leave it or appear from it.
set out: When you **set out**, you start a journey.

back out 2	break out 1, 3	check out 1, 6	clear out 1
come out 1, 4	get out 1, 11	let out 1, 2	move out 2, 3
run out 1	see out 1	set out 1	ship out
show out	start out 1, 2	storm out	want out 2

2 Removing, excluding, and preventing

Out is used to talk about removing or getting rid of people or things, or forcing people to leave a place.

breathe out: When you **breathe out**, you make the air in your lungs come out through your nose or mouth.
cut out something: If you **cut out** part of something, you remove it by cutting it.
throw out: If you **throw out** something you no longer want, you get rid of it.
wash something out: If you **wash out** dirt or other substances, you remove them using water.

airbrush out	block out 1–4	breathe out	cross out
cut out 1, 2, 4, 6, 7	drown out	filter out 1, 2	grey out
hound out	keep out	leave out 1	let out 3, 8
push out 1, 2	shut out	strike out 4	tear out
throw out 1–5	wash out 3	weed out	

3 Searching, finding, and obtaining

Out is used to talk about searching for and finding things or information.

dig something out: If you **dig** something **out**, you find it and get it out after it has been hidden or stored for a long time.

find out something: If you **find out** something, you learn something that you did not already know.

worm something out: If you **worm** information **out** of someone, you gradually find it out from them although they do not want to tell you.

dig out 1, 2	ferret out	figure out	find out
fish out 1	get out of 3	hunt out	pick out 1
prise out	puzzle out	search out	scope out
seek out	sniff out	suss out	winkle out
work out 1, 3–5	worm out of		

4 Appearing

Out is used to talk about things appearing, often when they have been hidden before.

hatch out: If an egg or a baby bird or other animal **hatches out**, they come out of the egg by breaking the shell.

pop out: If someone or something that you could not see **pops out**, they suddenly appear.

stand out: If something **stands out**, it can be seen very clearly.

break out 5	bring out 2, 3	burst out 3	come out in
get out 10	hatch out	jump out at	jut out
leap out	leap out at	let out 5	mark out 2
poke out	pop out 1	stand out 1, 2	stick out 3

5 Locations outside and away from home

Out is used to talk about being away from somewhere, especially away from home, or doing things that are different from your usual activities.

ask someone out: If you **ask** someone **out**, you invite them to go somewhere with you.

branch out: If you **branch out**, you do something different from your normal activities or work.

eat out: When you **eat out**, you have a meal at a restaurant instead of at home.

ask out	branch out	break out 3	camp out
dine out	eat out 1	get out 5	go out 2, 3, 4
invite out	move out 1	sleep out	stay out 1, 2
step out 3	stop out	strike out 1	take out 3, 8

6 Producing and creating

Out is used to talk about producing sounds, smells, light, heat, etc. or to talk about making things.

blare out: When noise or music **blares out**, loud noise or music is produced.

churn something out: To **churn** things **out** means to produce them in large numbers very quickly.

yell something out: If you **yell** something **out**, you shout loudly, for example because you are excited, angry or in pain.

bark out	beat out 1	blare out	blurt out
churn out	crash out 1	knock out 5	let out 4
shine out	shout out	speak out	tap out
throw out 6, 7	thump out	trot out	yell out

7 Increasing size, shape, or extent

Out is used to talk about people or things becoming bigger in size or amount or actions and events lasting longer.

fill out: If a thin person **fills out**, they become fatter.

pad something out: If you **pad out** a piece of writing or a speech with unnecessary words or pieces of information, you include them in order to make it longer.

string something out: If you **string** something **out**, you deliberately make it last for a longer time than necessary.

belly out	broaden out	bulk out	drag out
draw out 2, 3, 6	fan out	fill out 2	flesh out
let out 7	open out	pad out	plump out
shoot out 2	spread out 1–4, 6	stick out 1, 2	stretch out
string out 1, 2			

8 Thoroughness and completeness

Out is used to describe actions that are done thoroughly or completely.

clean something out: If you **clean** something **out**, you clean it very thoroughly and remove anything that should not be there.

fit someone/something out: If you **fit** someone or something **out**, you provide them with equipment and other things that they need.

hammer something out: If you **hammer out** something such as an agreement, you achieve it after a long or difficult discussion.

argue out	brush out	carry out	clean out
clear out 2	do out	dry out	hammer out
hear out	map out	plan out	rig out
rinse out	talk out 1	thaw out	write out 1, 2

9 Duration and resisting

Out is used to show that people or things continue with something until it is completed, even if it is difficult to do so.

hold out: If you **hold out**, you manage to continue or survive despite an attack or very difficult situation.

last out: If something or someone **lasts out**, they manage to stay alive or continue to function.

brave out	brazen out	hold out 3, 6	hold out on
last out	ride out	see out 2, 3	sit out 2, 3
stand out for	stare out	stick out 4	stick out for
sweat out 1	tough out	wait out	win out

10 Ending or disappearing

Out is used to talk about activities ending, often because all of something has been used or because people are unable or unwilling to continue.

back out: If you **back out**, you decide not to do something you previously agreed to do.
peter out: If something **peters out**, it gradually stops completely.
sell out: If something **sells out**, it has all been sold.

bow out	burn out	chicken out	die out
drop out	fizzle out	give out 2, 3	peter out
phase out	pull out 4, 5	run out 3–6	sputter out 1
stamp out 1, 2	tire out	wear out	

11 Arranging, dividing, selecting, and distributing

Out is used to talk about arranging things in groups, choosing things, or giving things to several people.

give out something: If you **give out** a large number of things, you give them to a lot of people.
single someone/something out: If you **single** someone or something **out**, you choose them from a group for special attention or treatment.
sort something out: If you **sort** things **out**, you arrange them so that they become organized, tidy or ready.

count out 1	deal out 2	dole out	give out 1
hand out 1	lay out 1, 3, 6	measure out	parcel out
pick out 2	ration out	separate out	serve out 1
single out	sort out 1, 2	tease out	weigh out

12 Paying attention and awareness

Out is used to talk about paying attention, often because of the possibility of danger.

look out: You say **look out** to warn someone about something that you have noticed, especially danger.

| listen out for | look out 1 | look out for | mind out |
| point out | watch out | watch out for | |

13 Supporting and helping

Out is used to talk about helping or supporting someone.

bring someone out: To **bring** someone **out** means to encourage them to be less shy or quiet.
help someone out: If you **help** someone **out**, you do something to help someone.

bail out 1, 2	bear out	bring out 4	call out 2
draw out 5	get out 4	hand out 2	help out
put out 12	reach out to 1	straighten out 4	take out of 3

14 Attacking, criticizing, and protesting

Out is used to talk about attacking or criticizing someone or protesting against something.

hit out: If you **hit out**, you attack or criticize someone strongly.

take out on: If you **take** something **out on** someone, you make them suffer because you feel angry or upset, even though it is not their fault.

call out 4	chew out	cry out against	deal out 1
dish out 3	fight out	hit out	kick out against
knock out 4	lash out 1, 2	mete out	punch out 4, 5
shoot out 3	sort out 6	take out on	

over ADVERB, PREPOSITION

Over is used mainly to talk about movement across a surface or a position above something.

1 Movement and position

Over is used to talk about movement across a surface or a position above something, or to talk about moving or going towards a place.

ask someone over: If you **ask** someone **over**, you invite them to come and visit you.

bend over: If you **bend over**, you move the top part of your body downwards and forwards.

cross over: When you **cross over**, you go across to the other side of something, especially a road or border.

pass over: When something **passes over**, it moves above someone or something without stopping.

ask over	bend over	bring over	call over
come over 1–3	cross over 1	go over 1–3	invite over
lean over	move over 1, 2	pass over 3	put over 2
run over 1	sit over 2	stand over	throw over 1, 3
tower over			

2 Overflowing and overwhelming feelings

Over is used to talk about something spilling from a container or someone having strong emotions.

boil over: When a liquid that is being heated **boils over**, it rises and flows over the edge of its container.

enthuse over something: If you **enthuse over** something, you talk about it in a way that shows that you are excited and pleased about it.

boil over	bowl over 2	brim over	bubble over with
come over 6, 7	drool over	enthuse over	fall over 2
flow over	fuss over	get over 3	moon over
run over 3	slop over	spill over	take over 8

3 Falling

Over is used to talk about something falling or being pushed to the ground.
blow over: If something **blows over**, the wind makes the thing fall to the ground.
topple over: If something **topples over**, it becomes unsteady and falls.

blow over 3	bowl over 1	fall over 1	go over 6
heel over	keel over	kick over 1	knock over
push over 1	run over 2	tip over	topple over
trip over 1	tumble over		

4 Covering and hiding

Over is used to talk about covering or hiding things, and for avoiding or hiding unpleasant situations.
cover something over: To **cover** something **over** means to cover it completely with something else.
gloss over something: If you **gloss over** a problem or a mistake, you ignore it or deal with it quickly in order to make it seem unimportant.
ice over: When something **ices over**, it becomes covered with a layer of ice.

cloud over	cover over	film over	freeze over
frost over	glaze over	gloss over	heal over
ice over	paint over	paper over	pass over 2
pave over	skate over	smooth over	varnish over

5 Considering and communicating

Over is used to talk about thinking about or looking at something in a thorough way, or to talk about giving people information and making sure they understand.
mull something over: If you **mull** something **over**, you think about it for a long time.
pore over something: If you **pore over** something, you read or look at it very carefully for a long time.
put something over: When you **put** an idea **over**, you succeed in describing or explaining it to someone.

brood over	come over 5, 8, 9	get over 4	go over 4, 7
look over	mull over	pick over	pore over
put over 3	puzzle over	rake over	read over
run over 4	talk over	think over	turn over 9

6 Changing and transferring

Over is used to talk about changing one thing for another, or changing the ownership of something to another person.

sign something over: If you **sign** something **over**, you sign a legal document giving it to someone else.

swap something over: If you **swap** two things **over**, you move them or they move so that each is in the place where the other one was before.

carry over	change over	come over 4	cross over 2
do over 2	go over to	hand over	hand over to
make over	move over 3, 4	sign over	swap over
switch over	take over 1–5, 9	turn over 4–7	win over

7 Ending and recovering

Over is used to talk about something unpleasant being finished, usually in a satisfactory way.

blow over: If an argument or problem **blows over**, it ends and people forget about it.

get over something: If you **get over** a problem or difficulty, you find a way of dealing with it.

blow over 1, 2	get over 1, 2	get over with	give over
throw over 4	tide over		

through ADVERB, PREPOSITION

Through is mainly used to talk about movement from one side of something to the other or to talk about getting to the end of a task or a period of time.

1 Movement

Through is used to talk about passing from one side of something to the other.

poke through: If something **pokes through**, a small part of it starts to appear, although the rest is still covered.

see through something: If you can **see through** something, you are able to see things that are on the other side of something by looking through it.

2 Completion and thoroughness

Through is used to talk about completing a task, process or activity, finishing an experience, or surviving a bad experience.

get through something: If you **get through** a task, you succeed in finishing it.

go through something: If someone **goes through** something such as a series of actions or movements, they perform it.

pull through: When someone who is very ill **pulls through**, they do not die.

sail through something: If you **sail through** something, you deal with an experience easily and successfully.

carry through 1	come through 5	follow through 1	get through 1
go through 9	muddle through	pull through 2	push through 3
rattle through	run through 3	rush through	sail through
scrape through	see through 5	sit through	think through
win through			

3 Reading or looking

Through is used to talk about turning the pages of a book and reading it, or picking up a series of things and looking at them.

flick through something: If you **flick through** pages or papers, you turn them over quickly and look at them quickly.

rifle through something: If you **rifle through** sheets of paper or the pages of a book, you look at them briefly, turning the pages quickly.

flick through	go through 7	leaf through	look through 2
pick through	read through	riffle through	rifle through
sift through	skim through	thumb through	wade through

4 Communication

Through is used to talk about communicating with someone, especially by telephone.

get through: If you **get through**, you succeed in contacting someone on the telephone.

put someone/something through: If you **put through** a phone call or the person making the call, you connect them with the person they want to speak to.

| come through 3 | get through 3 | phone through | put through 7 |

5 Obviousness and visibility

Through is used to talk about things that are obvious or visible.

shine through: If a good quality **shines through**, it is easy to see or notice.

show through: If your feelings **show through**, other people can see that you have them, often without you intending them to.

| break through 3 | come through 6 | see through 2 | shine through |
| show through 2 | | | |

up ADVERB, PREPOSITION

Up is mainly used to talk about movement from a lower position to a higher one or about increasing amounts or levels of something.

1 Movement and position

Up is used to talk about movement from a lower position to a higher one.

help someone up: If you **help** someone **up**, you help them to get into a standing position.

pick up someone/something: If you **pick** something or someone **up**, you lift them up from a surface.

bubble up	come up 1, 2, 4, 5, 14	dig up 1	get up 1–5
go up 1, 2, 4, 5, 9	help up	jump up	pick up 1, 4
reach up	rise up 1, 2	sit up 1–3	spoon up
spring up 2	stand up 1	throw up 1–3	tip up

2　Increasing and improving

Up is used to talk about increasing the quality or degree of something.
beef something up: If you **beef** something **up**, you add to it, making it bigger, stronger or more interesting.
be looking up: If a situation **is looking up**, it is improving.
speed up: If something **speeds up**, it moves or travels faster.

beef up	brighten up	brush up on	build up 1–5
dial up	heat up 1, 3	jazz up	liven up
look up 4	perk up 1–3	pick up 21–24	scale up
shoot up 1	speed up	step up 1	stoke up
touch up 1			

3　Preparing and beginning

Up is used to talk about preparing things or about things starting
open up: If a new shop or business **opens up**, it starts to do business.
rustle up something: If you **rustle up** a meal, you cook it quickly, using whatever food you have available at the time.
train up: If you **train** someone **up**, you teach them the skills they need to be able to do something.

build up to	draw up 1	gear up	heat up 3
knock up	limber up	make up 3, 7	open up 2, 3, 12
power up	rustle up	saddle up	set up 3–6, 8
tool up 1	train up	warm up 1, 4, 6, 7	whip up 6, 7

4　Fastening and restricting

Up is used to talk about fastening or blocking things or limiting their movement.
bandage something up: If you **bandage up** a wound or part of someone's body, you wrap a bandage around it.
block up something: If you **block up** something, you close it up completely so that nothing can get through it.
do something up: If you **do** something **up**, you fasten it.
lock someone up: To **lock** someone **up** means to put them in prison or a place where they cannot escape.

bandage up	block up	brick up	buckle up
clog up	coop up	do up 1–3, 5	lock up 1, 2, 4
plug up	seal up	stitch up 1	strap up
string up 1	tie up 1–6	tighten up 1	wrap up 1, 2
zip up			

5 Approaching

Up is used to talk about things or people moving or being moved closer together.

catch up: If you **catch up**, you reach someone who is in front of you by walking faster than they are walking.

creep up on someone: If you **creep up on** someone, you move slowly closer to them without being seen by them.

line up: If people or things **line up**, they form a row or line.

catch up 1, 2	come up 3, 12	come up against	creep up on 1, 2
cuddle up	draw up 3	keep up 1, 4–11	keep up with
line up 1, 2	loom up	queue up 1	run up against
sidle up	sneak up on	snuggle up	steal up

6 Disrupting and damaging

Up is used to talk about something that has been spoiled or damaged or something that is not working correctly.

be playing up: If a machine **is playing up**, it is not working properly.

blow up: If something **blows up**, it is destroyed by an explosion.

mess something up: If you **mess** something **up**, you spoil it or do it badly.

muddle something up: If you **muddle** things **up**, you cause them to become mixed up or in the wrong order.

act up	bash up	blow up 1, 2	botch up
crack up 1	foul up	jumble up	mess up
mix up 1, 2	muck up	muddle up	pack up 3, 4
play up 2–4	slip up	smash up	trip up

7 Completing and finishing

Up is used to talk about actions that have been completed or done very thoroughly, and to talk about consuming or using all of something.

eat up something: If people or animals **eat up** food, they eat all the food that they have been given or all that is available.

hang up: If you **hang up**, you end a phone call.

tear up: If you **tear** something **up**, you pull it into a lot of small pieces with your hands.

wind up something: When you **wind up** an activity or event, you end it.

buy up	clean up 1–4	clear up 1–4	drink up
eat up 1, 2, 5	end up	grind up	hang up 3
heal up	mop up	rip up 1	soak up 1, 3
sum up 1, 3, 4	swallow up 1, 4	tear up 1	tidy up 1, 3
wind up 4–6			

8 Rejecting and surrendering

Up is used to talk about giving things away, or showing that you do not want them.

pass up something: If you **pass up** an opportunity, you do not take advantage of it.

pay up: When you **pay up**, you give someone the money that you owe them, although you do not want to.

bring up 4	cast up	chuck up 2	cough up
deliver up	give up 4–6	give up to	pass up
pay up	sell up	settle up	stand up 3
stump up	throw up 7	wash up 4	

9 Happening and creating

Up is used to talk about things happening or being created.

crop up: If something **crops up**, it happens or appears, sometimes unexpectedly.

turn up: If someone **turns up**, they arrive somewhere where they are expected.

bring up 2	call up 4	come up 6–11, 18	come up with 1
conjure up	cook up 1, 2	crop up	dream up
make up 2	open up 6, 9	pop up 1	show up 3
spring up 1	summon up 4	think up	throw up 5
turn up 3			

10 Collecting and togetherness

Up is used to talk about people or things being collected together, and sometimes being put in a container or becoming part of a group.

bag something up: If you **bag up** something, you put it into a bag or bags.

gather something up: If you **gather up** a number of things, you bring them together into a group.

heap something up: If you **heap** things **up**, you put them on top of each other in a large pile.

join up: If one person **joins up** with another person, they decide to go somewhere together.

bag up	box up	collect up	gang up
gather up 1	heap up	hit up	join up
link up	meet up	mix up 3	pair up
round up 1, 2	sign up 1	stack up 1	store up
team up	tie up 8		

11 Revealing and discovering

Up is used to talk about information being found or told.

dig up something: If you **dig up** information that is not generally known, you discover it after searching.

own up: If you **own up**, you admit that you have done something wrong.

catch up 3	chase up 2	dig up 3, 4	dredge up
fess up	hunt up	look up 2	own up
pick up 16–18	rake up 1	scrape up 1	search up
show up 2, 4	show up as	throw up 5	weigh up 2
yield up 1			

12 Separating

Up is used to talk about things or people moving away from other things or people or being separated from them.

break up: When something **breaks up**, it becomes divided into smaller parts.
divide something up: If you **divide** something **up**, you separate it into completely separate groups or parts.

break up 1–3	bust up 3	carve up 1	chop up
cut up 1	divide up	divvy up	give up 7
hide up	hole up	lay up 4	lie up
parcel up 2	saw up	slice up	split up

Single-word equivalents

In English, it is quite common for a phrasal verb to have a single-word equivalent.

The single-word verb is often more formal than its phrasal-verb equivalent, but this is not always the case. For example, the list below contains the single-word verb *quit*, but *quit* is, in fact, a rather informal word. Similarly, the phrasal verb *refer to* is often found in written English and rather formal contexts.

In the following list, we have labelled some verbs as *formal* or *informal*, where this is an important part of their usage. However, even if there is no label, you should keep in mind that in most cases, the single-word verb is a little more formal than its phrasal-verb equivalent.

This list will help you if you know a single-word verb, and you are looking for an equivalent phrasal verb.

If you know a phrasal verb, and you want to find a single-word verb with a similar meaning, you can find help by looking at the definitions, synonyms highlighted in bold (indicated by =) and language information notes at individual entries in the main part of this dictionary.

Single word		Phrasal verb
absorb *These fibres absorb moisture from the body.*	→	**soak up** *Press the bread down, so that it soaks up some of the juice.*
accelerate *She accelerated along the straight road.*	→	**speed up** *He jogged for a mile or so and then speeded up.*
accept *I was happy to accept their offer of accommodation.*	→	**take up** *He was always ready to take up a new opportunity.*
accumulate *I have accumulated a lot of papers over the years.*	→	**build up** *They have built up a wonderful art collection.*
address *These issues are addressed in Chapter 7.*	→	**deal with** *I'll deal with the problem when I get back.*
admire *I have always admired his writing.*	→	**look up to** *He always looked up to his father.*
	→	**marvel at** *The jewels are now in the British Museum for all to marvel at.*
annoy *All this extra work really annoys me.*	→	**get to** *Their disrespectful attitude really gets to me.*
approach *He approached the girl and offered her some food.*	→	**come up to** *She came up to me at a party and introduced herself.*

Single word		Phrasal verb
arrange *I'm trying to arrange a trip to Paris for my parents.*	→	**fix up** *I'd like to fix up a meeting next week.* **sort out** *Could you sort out a hotel for us, please?*
arrive *They did not arrive until the afternoon.*	→	**come in** *Her train came in at 10.*
	→	**turn up** *We never know what time he's going to turn up.*
attack *He used the article to attack his critics.*	→	**set on** *He was set on by a gang of men.*
	→	**turn on** *Even his friends turned on him, accusing him of lying.*
avoid *I tried to avoid doing any work.*	→	**get out of** (informal) *She'd do anything to get out of the washing up.*
begin *The next course begins in June.*	→	**go ahead** *If I'm not there, you can go ahead without me.*
	→	**set in** *The cold weather has set in now.*
block *Fallen leaves have blocked the drains.*	→	**jam up** *The paper tore and jammed up the printer.*
break *My pen has broken.*	→	**fall apart** *These shoes are falling apart.*
break *He used a stone to break the window.*	→	**smash up** *Vandals smashed up the furniture.*
calculate *We have calculated how much we owe the bank.*	→	**figure out** *Can you figure out how much profit we are likely to make?*
	→	**work out** *She worked out that the building was over 300 years old.*
cancel *Next week's meeting has been cancelled.*	→	**call off** *She called off the wedding a week before it was due to take place.*
capitulate (formal) *We will never capitulate to their demands.*	→	**cave in** (informal) *I nagged her so much that in the end she caved in.*
cause *His behaviour has caused so many problems.*	→	**bring about** *They hope to bring about change in the region.*
	→	**set off** *The announcement set off protests in several cities.*

Single word		Phrasal verb
chase We chased them down the street.	→	**run after** They ran after us, shouting insults.
cheat These people will try to cheat you if you're not careful.	→	**rip off** (informal) I think the shopkeeper ripped me off.
choose I chose a silver necklace.	→	**opt for** We opted for a trip to Stratford.
	→	**settle on** He settled on black for the jacket.
close He had to close the factory.	→	**shut down** They shut down the business in 2003.
cohabit (formal) If you are cohabiting, you may not have the same legal rights.	→	**live together** We lived together for four years before we got married.
collapse Many buildings collapsed in the earthquake.	→	**fall down** Our tent fell down in the middle of the night.
communicate (formal) They had good ideas, but they failed to communicate them clearly.	→	**get across** I think we managed to get across our point of view.
	→	**put across** He used the speech to put across a message of hope.
complete We hope to complete the building work by Christmas.	→	**finish off** I finished off my essay last night.
	→	**see through** I intend to stay in my job long enough to see this project through.
comprise (formal) The crowd comprised several hundred students and some lecturers.	→	**make up** The committee is made up of local people.
conceal She tried to conceal her crime.	→	**cover up** He invented new stories to cover up the original lies.
confess He confessed that he had lied.	→	**own up** She owned up to taking the money.
connect Water is coming through at the point where the two pipes connect.	→	**join up** The roads join up just south of the city.
consider I hope you will consider my proposal seriously.	→	**think over** I need some time to think this over.
	→	**weigh up** We are still weighing up our options.

Single word		Phrasal verb
consult (formal) *You may consult your text book if you need to.*	→	**refer to** *I have several books on biology that I often refer to.*
consume (formal) *Most of us consume too much salt.*	→	**eat up** *Make sure you eat up all your dinner.*
contact *When she first contacted me, Frances was upset.*	→	**reach out** *I'm reaching out to you to see if you're available to work on our next project.*
continue *I cannot continue with this project.*	→	**carry on** *After a brief rest, we carried on walking.*
	→	**go on** *There was so much noise, she could not go on with her speech.*
criticize *She was criticized in the media for her poor fashion sense.*	→	**call out** *They were quick to call him out for his racist comments.*
	→	**do down** (informal) *He took every opportunity to do down his rival.*
	→	**get at** (informal) *She's always getting at the children.*
deceive *He deceived his employers about his qualifications.*	→	**take in** *She said she was a doctor, and we were all taken in.*
decelerate (formal) *He saw the barrier and decelerated sharply.*	→	**slow down** *Slow down as you approach the junction.*
decrease *Crime has decreased in this area.*	→	**come down** *Temperatures are likely to come down next week.*
	→	**dial down** *All sides need to dial down the criticism of each other.*
	→	**go down** *The price of oil has gone down.*
defeat *He was defeated in the championship final.*	→	**face down** *She went on TV and faced down her critics.*
	→	**put down** *Government forces have put down a rebellion in the north.*
defend *She defended her son against criticism from the newspapers.*	→	**stand up for** *His colleagues stood up for him when he was accused of dishonesty.*

Single word		Phrasal verb
delay *Bad weather forced us to delay the climb.*	→	**put off** *The meeting was put off until a later date.*
	→	**set back** *These problems have set the project back by several months.*
delete *Delete any information that does not apply to you.*	→	**cross out** *She crossed out the word 'expensive'.*
	→	**strike through** *Strike through anything in the contract that you disagree with.*
demand *They demanded a meeting with the minister.*	→	**call for** *Protestors are calling for a limit on directors' salaries.*
demolish *The building was demolished in the 1990s.*	→	**knock down** *They knocked down the cinema to build apartments.*
descend (formal) *Slowly they descended the stairs.*	→	**come down** *They came down the mountain just before sunset.*
despise (formal) *They are tired of politics and they despise politicians.*	→	**look down on** *They tend to look down on people from the villages.*
destroy *The fire destroyed large areas of woodland.*	→	**smash up** *They smashed up all our furniture.*
	→	**wipe out** *The disease has wiped out whole communities.*
deter (formal) *These laws do nothing to deter criminals.*	→	**scare off** *The dogs are there to scare off intruders.*
die *She died last week.*	→	**pass away** *His wife recently passed away.*
dilute *Dilute the mixture with water.*	→	**water down** *They watered down the juice for the younger children.*
disappear *All her money worries disappeared overnight.*	→	**go away** *Your problems won't just go away if you ignore them.*
	→	**melt away** *My feelings of anxiety gradually melted away.*
discard (formal) *Wash the spinach and discard any tough stalks.*	→	**throw away** *He opened the letter and threw away the envelope.*

Single word		Phrasal verb
discover *I discovered that we were related.*	→	**find out** *Where can I find out about accommodation?*
discuss *We had a meeting to discuss Bob's proposal.*	→	**talk over** *They've offered me the job, but I need to talk it over with my family.*
disintegrate *The packaging completely disintegrated in the rain.*	→	**fall apart** *I've only had these shoes a week and they're falling apart already.*
dismantle *(formal)* *I helped him dismantle the book case.*	→	**take apart** *You can take the engine apart to clean it.*
eat *Who has eaten all the cake?*	→	**polish off** *She polished off a huge bowl of pasta.*
eliminate *(formal)* *We are trying to eliminate the threat of disease.*	→	**cut out** *He has lost weight by cutting out snacks.*
	→	**do away with** *This new treatment does away with the need for surgery.*
emerge *(formal)* *They emerged from their room looking pale and tired.*	→	**come out** *He came out of the house an hour later.*
emit *(formal)* *These materials emit radiation.*	→	**give off** *It gave off a terrible smell.*
encounter *(formal)* *I first encountered him at a conference in Paris.*	→	**come across** *I came across this book in the library.*
encourage *My teacher encouraged me to apply to university.*	→	**egg on** *(informal)* *He began to hit the boy, egged on by his mates.*
	→	**spur on** *She was spurred on by ambition.*
endure *(formal)* *They had to endure terrible living conditions.*	→	**stick out** *(informal)* *He stuck the job out for a month and then left.*
enjoy *I enjoy trying new foods.*	→	**delight in** *She seems to delight in shocking people.*
	→	**lap up** *(informal)* *He lapped up all the attention.*
enlist *He decided to enlist in the army.*	→	**join up** *Most of the young men had joined up.*
enter *(formal)* *You may enter the theatre now.*	→	**come in** *Please come in to the meeting room.*
	→	**go in** *Can we go in yet?*

Single word		Phrasal verb
erase (formal) *Some words at the bottom of the page had been erased.*	→	**rub out** *You can rub out the pencil marks later.*
escape *He escaped from jail.*	→	**break out** *The four men broke out under cover of darkness.*
	→	**get away** *I got away from home by taking a job on a ship.*
establish (formal) *The society was established in 1986.*	→	**set up** *The government set up a committee to investigate the issue.*
examine *A journalist was allowed to examine the documents.*	→	**look at** *You need to get a doctor to look at that leg.*
excuse *Being upset does not excuse this kind of behaviour.*	→	**explain away** *She tried to explain away the mistake by saying she had been tired.*
exhale *Take a deep breath, then exhale through your nose.*	→	**breathe out** *Breathe out as you bend forward.*
exhaust *All the travelling has exhausted him.*	→	**wear out** *I've been looking after the children, and they've worn me out.*
expel (formal) *His army was expelled from the area.*	→	**drive out** *They drove out foreign invaders.*
experience *They have experienced a lot of problems.*	→	**go through** *After everything we've been through, we need a rest.*
	→	**run into** *The project has run into difficulties.*
explain *That explains why he was so late.*	→	**account for** *He can't account for the missing money.*
	→	**spell out** *You need to spell out the consequences of their behaviour to them.*
explode *A bomb exploded near where we were standing.*	→	**blow up** *A spark caused the whole building to blow up.*
extinguish (formal) *They battled all day to extinguish the fire.*	→	**put out** *They used water from the river to put out the fire.*
extract (formal) *The dentist had to extract the tooth.*	→	**pull out** *She pulled out a notebook from her pocket.*

Single word		Phrasal verb
fade *The sound of their laughter faded into the distance.*	→	**die away** *The heat of the sun was beginning to die away.*
fail *Their business venture failed.*	→	**break down** *Talks between the two sides have broken down.*
	→	**fall through** *Their plans fell through.*
faint *I always faint at the sight of blood.*	→	**pass out** *She passed out from lack of oxygen.*
fasten *(formal)* *Make sure you fasten your seat belt.*	→	**do up** *I did up my coat.*
fill *The crowd filled the hall.*	→	**take up** *All these books take up a lot of room.*
find *I found a key on the floor.*	→	**come across** *I came across this book in the library.*
	→	**track down** *I eventually managed to track down the owner of the house.*
finish *We finished all the food.*	→	**use up** *They used up the remaining oil.*
follow *Her talk was followed by a coffee break.*	→	**come after** *The job in London came after my trip to Germany.*
gather *He gathered all his supporters.*	→	**round up** *They tried to round up the animals.*
guard *A soldier was sent to guard him.*	→	**watch over** *A nurse watched over her in the night.*
handle *I handle all the customer queries.*	→	**deal with** *I know how to deal with difficult staff.*
hide *She tried to hide her mistakes.*	→	**cover up** *The president tried to cover up the affair.*
ignore *She ignored all our advice.*	→	**brush aside** *He brushed aside their concerns.*
illuminate *(formal)* *The castle is illuminated at night.*	→	**light up** *The garden was lit up by coloured lights.*
imply *She seemed to be implying that he was not telling the truth.*	→	**hint at** *His writing hints at links with criminals.*
imprison *They were imprisoned in the castle.*	→	**lock up** *They are criminals and they should be locked up.*

Single word		Phrasal verb
improve *I hired a tutor to improve my maths.*	→	**brush up** *I need to brush up my French before the trip.*
improve *When I moved to London, my life improved considerably.*	→	**look up** *Things are beginning to look up for Emma now.*
incorporate *(formal)* *We have tried to incorporate plenty of time for study.*	→	**build in** *They have built in plenty of legal safeguards.*
increase *The level of unemployment has increased.*	→	**dial up** *This sort of talk just dials up the anger.*
	→	**go up** *Prices have gone up rapidly.*
	→	**mount up** *His debts were mounting up.*
increase *I decided to increase my working hours.*	→	**step up** *The factory has stepped up production to meet the increased demand.*
indicate *(formal)* *He indicated the fire exit.*	→	**point out** *She pointed out a small window at the top of the stairs.*
inflate *The tyres must be fully inflated.*	→	**blow up** *We blew up the balloons.*
inhale *Inhale deeply through both nostrils.*	→	**breathe in** *Breathe in and then hold your breath for a few seconds.*
interrupt *I didn't want to interrupt the lesson.*	→	**break in** *'That's a lie!' Shona broke in angrily.*
	→	**butt in** *(informal)* *I wish he wouldn't keep butting in.*
intervene *(formal)* *The government intervened to strengthen the economy.*	→	**step in** *She stepped in to run the company.*
introduce *They plan to introduce new legislation.*	→	**bring in** *They brought in a new law banning smoking in public places.*
invent *She invented a family in Canada.*	→	**make up** *He made up an excuse for being late.*
investigate *Police are investigating the robbery.*	→	**look into** *She promised to look into our concerns.*
leave *We left just before sunrise.*	→	**head off** *(informal)* *I'm going to head off now. Bye all!*
	→	**set off** *They set off after breakfast.*

Single word		Phrasal verb
lift *He lifted the bundle of wood onto his shoulder.*	→	**pick up** *I picked up the baby.*
maintain *I don't think he'll maintain this level of enthusiasm for long.*	→	**keep up** *We kept up the pace of work all day.*
manage *I can only just manage on the money I earn.*	→	**get by** *He gets by on what he earns from selling vegetables.*
meet *We usually meet about once a month.*	→	**get together** *We got together to celebrate Hannah's engagement.*
mention *Did anyone mention the subject of diet?*	→	**bring up** *I didn't want to bring up his family life.*
	→	**touch on** *We touched on a few legal issues.*
mix *Mix the flour and the sugar.*	→	**add together** *She added together the raisins and the sugar.*
moderate *(formal)* *The new treatment did moderate the effects of the disease.*	→	**tone down** *He toned down the language for the TV.*
murder *She was murdered by a stranger.*	→	**bump off** *(informal)* *He paid someone to bump off his business rival.*
notice *Did you notice how often he said the word 'success'?*	→	**pick up on** *She picked up on our embarrassment.*
obstruct *(formal)* *Fallen trees were obstructing the roads.*	→	**block up** *Leaves had blocked up the drains.*
omit *(formal)* *I decided to omit the section on Proust.*	→	**leave out** *He left out any reference to his time in Paris.*
oppress *(formal)* *These people were oppressed for centuries.*	→	**keep down** *It's just an attempt to keep women down.*
participate *(formal)* *When the dancing started, he refused to participate.*	→	**join in** *We all joined in the singing.*
pass *I often passed him in the street.*	→	**go by** *Three other buses went by before ours arrived.*
patronize *I try to talk to the children without patronizing them.*	→	**talk down to** *He never talks down to his patients.*

Single word		Phrasal verb
persevere (formal) *The diet is difficult, but I'm determined to persevere with it.*	→	**soldier on** *Despite the rain, we soldiered on to the end of the walk.*
persuade *I hope I can persuade him to come with us.*	→	**talk into** *She talked me into giving her the money.*
	→	**talk round** *Mum says we can't go to the party, but I'll try and talk her round.*
postpone (formal) *The meeting was postponed.*	→	**put off** *I decided to put off my holiday for another month.*
pressurize *They pressurized us to sign the document.*	→	**lean on** *Government ministers denied that they leant on the police.*
pretend *I pretended to be interested in what she was saying.*	→	**make out** *He tried to make out he hadn't seen us.*
prevent (formal) *Loud music prevented conversation.*	→	**rule out** *His illness ruled out a trip to the USA.*
	→	**ward off** *Regular exercise helps to ward off colds.*
proceed (formal) *We decided to proceed with legal action.*	→	**go ahead** *The building work is planned to go ahead in June.*
produce *They have produced a low-fat version of the biscuits.*	→	**bring out** *They brought out a new album last month.*
prolong (formal) *We did not want to prolong their suffering.*	→	**drag out** *There's no point in dragging out the talks.*
protrude (formal) *We could see a piece of wood protruding above the water.*	→	**jut out** *A large rock juts out into the sea.*
	→	**stick out** *She was so thin, her ribs were sticking out.*
prove *The photograph proved that she had met him.*	→	**bear out** *The facts seem to bear out his story.*
provoke *His comments provoked outrage.*	→	**stir up** *The speech was designed to stir up resentment.*
quit (informal) *I quit smoking last year.*	→	**give up** *I've had to give up sport.*

SINGLE-WORD EQUIVALENTS

Single word		Phrasal verb
raise *They raised their family in Africa.*	→	**bring up** *The children were brought up on a farm.*
realize *I didn't realize he was your brother.*	→	**cotton on** (informal) *They've been teasing him all this time, and he's only just cottoned on.*
recover *He had flu very badly, and it took a long time for him to recover.*	→	**bounce back** *She seems to have bounced back after her operation.*
reduce *I used ice to reduce the swelling.*	→	**bring down** *A good harvest should bring down the cost of wheat.*
refuse *He refused their offer of help.*	→	**turn down** *She turned down several job offers.*
regain (formal) *She struggled to regain control of the party.*	→	**win back** *He is hoping to win back support from farm workers.*
relax *I listen to music in order to relax.*	→	**chill out** (informal) *We spent the weekend chilling out at home.*
relinquish (formal) *He was not prepared to relinquish power.*	→	**give up** *She gave up her position as head of the organization.*
remove *We hope to remove some of the barriers to education.*	→	**strip away** *All their rights were stripped away.*
	→	**take away** *They took away our freedom.*
renovate *They are renovating an old cottage.*	→	**do up** *We did up the shed and made it into a summer room.*
repair *I need to get my boots repaired.*	→	**patch up** *We patched up the roof with pieces of metal.*
repay *Eventually we managed to repay the loan.*	→	**pay back** *I'll pay you back next week.*
replace *He replaced the vase carefully on the shelf.*	→	**put back** *Please can you put the books back when you've finished with them?*
represent *For the Irish, he represents a time of great cruelty.*	→	**stand for** *Our party stands for respect and decency.*
reprimand (formal) *They were forced to reprimand some of their staff.*	→	**tell off** *She told me off for reading her emails.*

Single word		Phrasal verb
request (formal) *He telephoned to request a meeting with the manager.*	→	**ask for** *I asked for a drink.*
require (formal) *This is a sport that requires both strength and speed.*	→	**call for** *The situation calls for a lot of patience.*
rescue *She rescued me from a very difficult situation.*	→	**bail out** *When he got into debt, his father bailed him out.*
resemble (formal) *He resembles his brother in every way.*	→	**take after** *She takes after her aunt.*
reserve *We reserved some of the money for emergencies.*	→	**keep back** *Keep back some of the fruit to decorate the cake.*
resign *She resigned from her post.*	→	**stand down** *He decided to stand down as chairman.*
retaliate (formal) *If you hurt them, they are likely to retaliate.*	→	**fight back** *Their rivals fought back desperately.*
retreat (formal) *The army was forced to retreat.*	→	**back away** *She backed away from the dogs.*
return (formal) *I need to return this book to Moira.*	→	**give back** *He hasn't given back my umbrella yet.*
	→	**take back** *I took back the plates I had borrowed from her.*
return *They hope to return to Zimbabwe soon.*	→	**come back** *Tom hasn't come back from work yet.*
	→	**go back** *I went back to my old school to give a talk.*
revolve *The whole restaurant revolves very slowly so you can admire the view.*	→	**go round** *The wheels go round when you pedal.*
ridicule (formal) *Everyone ridiculed his ideas at the time.*	→	**laugh at** *I'm worried that people will laugh at me.*
rise *Prices are rising all the time.*	→	**go up** *I hope the temperature won't go up any more.*
see *I could see a boat on the horizon.*	→	**make out** *We could just make out a figure near the gate.*
select *They selected a rug from the catalogue.*	→	**pick out** *She picked out two children to read their poems.*
separate *His parents separated soon after he was born.*	→	**split up** *My girlfriend and I split up last month.*

SINGLE-WORD EQUIVALENTS

Single word		Phrasal verb
serve *Joanna served the soup.*	→	**dish up** *He dished up a beef pie.*
solve *These clues helped us solve the mystery.*	→	**sort out** *They need time to sort out their problems.*
specify *You need to specify your exact requirements.*	→	**pin down** *Video evidence helped them pin down the exact time of the crime.*
spoil *Simon's illness spoiled our holiday.*	→	**mess up** *The delays messed up all our arrangements.*
squander (formal) *She squandered her opportunity for a fantastic career.*	→	**fritter away** *He frittered away all his money on designer clothes.*
start *Our weekend started badly, when one of the children had an accident.*	→	**kick off** (informal) *The meeting kicked off with a presentation about recycling.*
steal *She stole a shirt from the shop.*	→	**make off with** (informal) *Thieves made off with his bike.*
strengthen *We really need to strengthen our security measures.*	→	**beef up** (informal) *The company wanted to beef up its sales force.*
submit (formal) *I submitted an application for the job.*	→	**send in** *Please send in ideas for the show.*
subside (formal) *We waited for the excitement to subside.*	→	**die down** *Gradually, the noise began to die down.*
subtract *You need to subtract your tax from that figure.*	→	**take away** *This figure is taken away from the total.*
succeed *If you try hard enough, I'm sure you will succeed.*	→	**win out** *The best team won out in the end.*
	→	**win through** *Eventually their army won through.*
suggest *We suggested several ideas.*	→	**put forward** *He put forward a proposal to sell the land.*
summarize *He asked me to summarize my research.*	→	**sum up** *She summed up the situation with the word 'terrible'.*
support *My family supported me during my ordeal.*	→	**back up** *I'm happy to back you up if there's any trouble.*
	→	**hold up** *The shelter was held up by four large branches.*

Single word		Phrasal verb
suppress (formal) *I did my best to suppress my annoyance.*	→	**block out** *She tried to block out memories of the war.*
	→	**fight down** *He had to fight down his panic.*
surprise *It surprised me to see him there.*	→	**take aback** *I was rather taken aback when I realised he was her brother.*
surrender *We will never surrender.*	→	**give in** *Eventually, she gave in to their demands.*
survive *She was lucky to survive the accident.*	→	**come through** *They came through the experience unharmed.*
	→	**pull through** *She's seriously ill, and may not pull through.*
terminate (formal) *We decided to terminate the contract.*	→	**break off** *They have broken off talks with the management.*
test *I'm going to test my ideas in the laboratory.*	→	**try out** *She tried out her teaching methods on a small group of children.*
tolerate (formal) *We will not tolerate this kind of behaviour.*	→	**put up with** *She puts up with a lot of pain.*
transmit (formal) *The disease is transmitted by human contact.*	→	**pass on** *They passed on diseases such as measles.*
trust *I know that I can trust Helen.*	→	**depend on** *I have to be able to depend on my staff.*
understand *At first, it was difficult to understand what he was telling us.*	→	**take in** *It's impossible to take in so much information at once.*
unite *They united to defeat their common enemy.*	→	**band together** *We banded together to set up a very basic hospital.*
wait *I had to wait over an hour to see the doctor.*	→	**hang around** (informal) *She hung around outside while her friend was in her piano lesson.*
watch *She took the money when nobody was watching.*	→	**look on** *They kicked and punched each other while a crowd looked on.*
withhold (formal) *They accused him of withholding important information.*	→	**keep back** *She kept back some of the money to pay for food.*

SINGLE-WORD EQUIVALENTS